THE CATHOLIC CHURCH IN SPAIN, 1875–1998

WILLIAM J. CALLAHAN

The Catholic University of America Press
Washington, D.C.

The paper used in this publication meets the minimum requirements of
American National Standards for Information Science—Permanence of Paper
for Printed Materials, ANSI Z39.48-1984.
Library of Congress Cataloging-in-Publication Data
Callahan, William James, 1937–
The Catholic Church in Spain, 1875–1998 / William J. Callahan.
p. cm.
Includes bibliographical references and index.
1. Catholic Church—Spain—History—19th century. 2. Spain—Church
history—19th century. 3. Catholic Church—Spain—History—20th century.
4. Spain—Church history—20th century.
I. Title.
BX1585.C213 2000
282'.46'09034—dc21
99-37180
ISBN 978-0-8132-0961-6 (cloth: alk. paper)
ISBN 978-0-8132-1981-3 (pbk: alk. paper)

THE CATHOLIC CHURCH IN SPAIN, 1875–1998

For Solita and Juan Marichal

CONTENTS

MAPS AND TABLES

Maps

Tables

PREFACE AND ACKNOWLEDGMENTS

Few institutions have been more closely linked to Spanish social and political life than the Catholic Church. The Church remained the established Church of the State until 1978 save for the period of the Second Republic (1931–1939). The constitution of 1978 ended the centuries-old ties between the civil and ecclesiastical orders, but even in the democratic Spain of the post-Franco era, the Church secured important advantages from the country's new democracy.

The role of the Church in modern Spain has generated controversy that continues to this day, although with less stridency because of the impact of the Second Vatican Council and the political changes introduced following General Francisco Franco's death in 1975. Until these changes occurred, critics perceived the Church as a powerful institution intent upon forcing a rigid, vaguely theocratic ideology on the country.

But this view of a highly organized, monolithic institution efficiently going about the work of converting the country into a bastion of Catholicism disguised a far more complex situation. Clerical visions of a resurrected Catholic Spain, a modern version of the glorious Catholic Spain of the sixteenth century, proved impossible to realize both because of external circumstances emerging from changing political, social, and economic developments and because of the Church's often disorganized and ineffective approach to its religious mission.

The growing volume of work by Spanish and non-Spanish scholars, to whom I owe a great debt, has made it possible to draw a more complete picture of the complexities of the modern Spanish Church than was possible just a few years ago. I am especially indebted to Adrian Shubert and José Nemesio Martínez, who read the manuscript and offered helpful suggestions. I also wish to thank William Christian, Jocelyn Hillgarth, and John Habron, who read portions of the manuscript, and Antonio Cazorla Sánchez, who provided me with valuable bibliographical information. I am grateful to the editors of the *Catholic Historical Review*,

Journal of Church and State, *Church History*, and the *Revista Canadiense de Estudios Hispánicos* for permission to use materials contained in my articles published in their journals. The support provided by the Victoria University Research Fund has helped make publication of this book possible. Finally, I wish to acknowledge the constant encouragement that I received while writing this book from Solita and Juan Marichal, Diana Harney, and Trinidad Aboitiz.

W. J. C.

ABBREVIATIONS

AN/AP	Acción Nacional/Acción Popular
ACNP	Asociación Católica Nacional de Propagandistas
ASP	Acción Social Popular
AVB	Arxiu Vidal i Barraquer
CEAS	Comisión Episcopal del Apostolado Seglar
CEDA	Confederación Española de Derechas Autónomas
CEE	Conferencia Episcopal Española
CCP	Comunidades Cristianas Populares
CNCA	Confederación Nacional Católico-Agraria
CNT	Confederación Nacional del Trabajo
CONCAPA	Confederación Católica de Padres de Familia y Padres de Alumnos
CpS	Cristianos por Socialismo
CSIC	Consejo Superior de Investigaciones Científicas
ETA	Euskadi ta Askatasuna
FERE	Federación Española de Religiosos de Enseñanza
FET	Falange Española Tradicionalista y de la JONS
FNSOCL	Federación Nacional de Sindicatos Obreros Libres
GDC	Grupo de Democracia Cristiana
HOAC	Hermandades Obreras de Acción Católica
JC	Juventud Católica
JOC	Juventud Obrera Católica
PCE	Partido Comunista de España
PP	Partido Popular
PNV	Partido Nacionalista Vasco

PSOE	Partido Socialista Obrero Español
PSP	Partido Social Popular
SCFE	Sindicato Católico de los Ferroviarios Españoles
STV	Solidaridad de Trabajadores Vascos
UCD	Unión del Centro Democrático
UGT	Unión General de Trabajadores
UP	Unión Patriótica

Map 1: Dioceses, 1875–1950

THE CATHOLIC CHURCH IN SPAIN, 1875–1998

CHAPTER I

A CHURCH TRANSFORMED

The Church and Liberalism, 1808–1868

On May 20, 1939, the day following the military parade marking the still fresh triumph of Nationalist Spain over the Second Republic, Francisco Franco mounted the steps of the royal church of Santa Bárbara in Madrid bearing in his hands the "sword of victory" for presentation to the Cardinal Archbishop of Toledo, Isidro Gomá y Tomás. The primate of the Spanish Church accepted the gift that he announced would be placed in the cathedral of his diocesan seat as "eloquent testimony of the faith of our Catholic people so worthily represented by their *Caudillo* in this culminating and transcendental moment of our nation's [history]."[1]

That the Spanish Church contributed significantly to the victory of the Nationalist cause is beyond dispute. Through pastoral letters, sermons, radio broadcasts, sophisticated argument, and simple propaganda, the clergy with few exceptions saw the struggle as a "duel to the death between the Church and the revolution" in which "the cross and the sword again come together and form a single weapon ready to realize the most brilliant triumphs."[2] That the Church, stung by the anticlerical legislation of the Second Republic between 1931 and 1933 and terrified of the future after the Popular Front electoral victory in February 1936, looked to the military rebellion for salvation is understandable. It is less clear why the Church embraced the Nationalist cause with a crusading militancy last seen over a century earlier during the conflict between the absolutist King Fernando VII (1814–1833) and the emerging forces of Spanish liberalism.

The immediate causes of ecclesiastical support for the military rising of 1936 are to be found in the political history of the twentieth century. A more distant but

1. Quoted in Anastasio Granados, *El Cardenal Gomá, Primado de España* (Madrid, 1969), p. 220.
2. Eugenio Fernández Almuzara, *Evangelio de la Nueva España* (Valladolid, 1937), pp. 12, 79.

no less fundamental cause can be traced to the ambiguous relationship of the nineteenth-century Church to the political institutions and society created by Spanish liberalism. The great Church of the eighteenth century—the creation of centuries of institutional development, the possessor of immense wealth, an ally of absolute monarchy through a tangled web of mutual cooperation and self-interest, mirror of the extreme inequalities of a noble-dominated hierarchical society—collapsed before the assault of new political forces intent on restraining the unlimited exercise of royal power and ending the privileges of the kingdom's traditional social elites.[3] Circumstances allowed the liberal revolution to take hold before the failure of absolute monarchy against the Napoleonic intervention of 1807–1813. Between 1810 and 1813, the liberal Cortes of Cádiz, the nation's first modern parliamentary assembly, laid the foundations of an episodic but ultimately successful constitutional revolution. Fernando VII's restoration to absolute power in 1814 temporarily interrupted the process of change, but the liberal revolution of 1820 again challenged the exercise of unrestrained royal authority.

In 1823, the king recovered the unfettered power he so dearly cherished, retaining it until his death in 1833. But his determination to secure the throne for his young daughter, Isabel, born in 1830 to the monarch and his new wife, María Cristina, opened the door to liberalism's triumph over absolute monarchy. Supporters of the king's brother, Carlos, the monarch's heir until the birth of Isabel, refused to accept her accession and rose in revolt after Fernando's death. Following a brief but unsuccessful attempt to carry on a modified version of absolute monarchy, the queen regent turned to Spanish liberals, who appeared as the only political force capable of saving Isabel's throne before the Carlist rebellion. When a former deputy of the Cortes of Cádiz, Francisco Martínez de la Rosa, became prime minister in January 1834, liberalism began its dominance of the nation's political life, which would endure in one form or another until the coup d'état of General Miguel Primo de Rivera in 1923.

The consolidation of liberal institutions after 1834 was not easily accomplished.[4] Carlism, committed to the restoration of absolute monarchy, posed a serious threat to the new regime until its defeat in 1840 and remained a nagging danger thereafter. But the greatest weakness confronting the nascent liberal State lay in the severe internal divisions among its supporters. Liberals agreed on the necessity of imposing constitutional restraints on royal power but disagreed on the exact political configuration of their new order. The more conservative and prosperous landowners, merchants, and lawyers eventually formed the Moderate party,

3. For general descriptions of the organization and resources of the eighteenth-century Church, see Antonio Domínguez Ortiz, *La sociedad española en el siglo XVIII* (Madrid, 1955), pp. 133–66; *Sociedad y Estado en el siglo XVIII español* (Madrid, 1976), pp. 359–82; William J. Callahan, *Church, Politics and Society in Spain, 1750–1874* (Cambridge, Mass., 1984), pp. 1–52.

4. The vicissitudes of nineteenth-century liberal Spain have been ably discussed by Raymond Carr, *Spain, 1808–1939* (Oxford, 1966).

which favored a strong executive power and a narrow electoral franchise. This oligarchic liberalism was opposed by a more radical group drawn from the middle and lower ranks of the urban bourgeoisie, who eventually gathered in the Progressive party, which demanded a broader franchise and more flexible economic policies.[5] Conflict between the opposing camps of liberalism dominated the country's political history from the mid-1830s to the revolution of 1868.

The failure of Spanish liberalism to devise a mechanism allowing for the peaceful transfer of power from government to opposition constituted the gravest weakness of the new regime. Instability became a fact of political life during the three decades following the end of absolutism. Military intervention and the urban riot, rather than parliamentary procedures, produced changes in government. The struggle between the liberal parties tilted first towards the Progressives between 1836 and 1843 and then towards the Moderates, who imposed their vision of a highly centralized State administered by a restricted elite for much of the period between 1844 and 1868.

Liberalism's triumph also brought in its wake changes that ended a traditional, hierarchical society identified with absolute monarchy. The new society created by liberalism was as conservative as the one it replaced, but it eliminated legal discrimination in favor of the nobility characteristic of the old social order. It destroyed the corporate autonomy once enjoyed by craft guilds, municipalities, and other social groups in favor of an unbridled emphasis on the individual within the social organization. The economic changes introduced by liberalism also produced significant social change. The sale of Church and municipal common lands between 1835 and 1860 created a class of bourgeois landowners whose ruthless economic exploitation of tenant farmers and day laborers aggravated the already difficult circumstances of much of the rural population.[6] Industrial and commercial development, whether in the form of textiles in Catalonia or banking in Madrid, encouraged by the unabashed capitalism promoted by successive liberal governments, produced a new class of rich whose social ambitions knew few limits. The liberal elite of bankers, financiers, industrialists, generals, and prosperous landowners was open to anyone in possession of money or power. But for those unequipped to engage in the give-and-take of this freewheeling society, life became more difficult. Deprived of the threadbare survival provided by access to municipal common lands, the landless day laborers of the south saw their already miser-

5. The Progressives did not endorse a democratic program resting on universal suffrage until the 1860s. Until then they advocated a larger suffrage than that imposed by the Moderates during their periods of rule with a view to giving the vote to the urban classes from whom they drew support.

6. The sale of Church and municipal lands has generated an abundant literature surveyed by Vicente Cárcel Ortí, "El liberalismo en poder, 1833–1868," in Vicente Cárcel Ortí et al., *Historia de la Iglesia en la España contemporánea, 1808–1975* (Madrid, 1979), pp. 137–38. Three general surveys of the disentailment are Francisco Simón Segura, *La desamortización española del siglo XIX* (Madrid, 1973); F. Tomás y Valiente, *El marco político de la desamortización en España* (Madrid, 1974); Germán Rueda, *La desamortización de Mendizábal y Espartero en España* (Madrid, 1986).

able situation deteriorate still further, while in regions of peasant land ownership, agriculturalists fell victim to the exploitation of usurers in a society lacking mechanisms to provide credit to the struggling farmer. Workers in the handful of manufacturing towns scattered through the kingdom were scarcely better off, as an uneven and episodic industrial revolution began to develop during the 1840s and 1850s.

Liberalism's challenge to absolute monarchy and to the social institutions associated with it provoked conflict with the Church from the time of the Cortes of Cádiz.[7] Clerical unease with the legislation of the Cortes developed into open hostility following the suppression of the Inquisition in January 1813, thus beginning a long conflict between liberalism and an institution determined to retain social and economic privileges acquired over centuries through the alliance of Throne and Altar.[8] By 1840 the Church had lost the battle. Sympathy for the Carlist cause was widespread among the clergy during the 1830s, as ecclesiastics dreamed of a final apocalyptic victory that would restore absolutism and save the Church from liberal reform. The military defeat of Carlism at the end of the decade destroyed this illusion. With its financial resources depleted and its moral fervor exhausted by decades of conflict, the Church had no choice but to come to terms with the new political order.

The issue dividing the Church from liberalism was never the question of whether the kingdom should or should not be officially Catholic. Every constitution, from the conservative text of 1812 to the democratic charter of 1869, affirmed the State's confessionality.[9] No liberal government between 1834 and 1873 ever seriously considered disestablishment. Successive ministries, whether in Moderate

7. Among the important works for the history of the Church under liberalism between 1808 and 1873 are Emilio La Parra López, *El primer liberalismo español y la Iglesia: las Cortes de Cádiz* (Alicante, 1985); José Manuel Cuenca Toribio, *D. Pedro de Inguanzo, 1764–1836: último prelado del antiguo régimen* (Pamplona, 1965); *La Iglesia española ante la revolución liberal* (Madrid, 1971); *Iglesia y burguesía en la España liberal* (Jaén, 1979); *Estudios sobre la Iglesia andaluza moderna y contemporánea* (Córdoba, 1980); *Sociedad y clero en la España del XIX* (Córdoba, 1980); *Estudios sobre el catolicismo español contemporáneo* (Córdoba, 1990); Manuel Revuelta González, *Política religiosa de los liberales del siglo XIX: trienio constitucional* (Madrid, 1973); *La exclaustración, 1833–1843* (Madrid, 1976); Luis Alonso Tejada, *Ocaso de la Inquisición en los últimos años del reinado de Fernando VII* (Valencia, 1978); Vicente Cárcel Ortí, *Política eclesial de los gobiernos liberales españoles, 1830–1840* (Pamplona, 1975); *Iglesia y revolución en España, 1868–1874* (Pamplona, 1979); Jesús Longares Alonso, *Política y religión en Barcelona, 1833–1843* (Madrid, 1976); *La ideología religiosa del liberalismo español, 1808–1843* (Córdoba, 1979); José Antonio Portero, *Púlpito e ideología en la España del siglo XIX* (Zaragoza, 1978); Santiago Petschen, *Iglesia-Estado: las Constituyentes de 1869* (Madrid, 1974); Francisco Martí Gilabert, *La cuestión religiosa en la revolución de 1868–1874* (Madrid, 1989); and *Iglesia y Estado en el reinado de Isabel II* (Pamplona, 1996).

8. For a description of clerical opposition to the reforms of the Cortes of Cádiz, see Isidoro de Villapadierna, "El episcopado español y las Cortes de Cádiz," *Hispania Sacra* (1955), vol. 8, pp. 275–335; Francisco Martí Gilabert, *La abolición de la Inquisición en España* (Pamplona, 1975).

9. The language of constitutional texts varied. Thus the constitution of 1837 stated that the "nation is obliged to maintain the cult and the ministers of the Catholic religion which Spaniards profess." The more conservative constitution of 1845 went further, declaring that the "religion of the Spanish nation is the Catholic, Apostolic [and] Roman." Quoted in Juan María Laboa, *Iglesia y religión en las constituciones españolas* (Madrid, 1981), pp. 28–29.

or Progressive hands, continued to hold tenaciously to the historic regalist privileges of the old monarchy that provided the State with extensive control over ecclesiastical finances and patronage.

Liberal policies towards the Church varied from one government to another according to the views of the party in power. But beneath the inconsistencies ran the common thread that the Church must renounce the pervasive influence it had enjoyed under absolute monarchy before the demands of a political elite that, whatever its internal contradictions, was determined to form society and government according to its own designs. Liberalism in all its guises rejected the vaguely theocratic ideology of the eighteenth-century monarchy, with its mingling of the sacred and the secular. It resented the enormous landed wealth possessed by ecclesiastical institutions. It regarded the Church's pretension to control intellectual life as an obstacle to cultural and scientific progress. What liberalism expected of the Church was that it should confine itself to a purely spiritual and vaguely philanthropic role in which religion would be "pure, peaceful and perfect," a natural complement to a secular elite in control of its own destiny.[10]

There was never any prospect that the Church would voluntarily renounce its traditional claims to wealth and influence, although a minority of priests cooperated with liberal governments.[11] In the end, liberalism forced changes on the Church that transformed its place within Spanish society. The most significant of these changes was the sale of ecclesiastical property between 1835 and 1860. The immense revenues of bishops, cathedral chapters, religious orders, and charitable institutions had made the Church the kingdom's single most powerful economic institution by the late eighteenth century.[12] Although ecclesiastical wealth declined after 1808 as the result of war and economic upheaval, it remained impressive on the eve of disentailment. The very extent of Church property made it a natural object of liberal scrutiny from the time of the Cortes of Cádiz. On theoretical grounds, liberals opposed the collective ownership of land by the "dead hands" of corporate institutions such as the Church. The forced sale of ecclesiastical landholdings offered the double appeal of rescuing the chronically hard-pressed finances of successive liberal governments and allowing the regime to build a base of support

10. Longares Alonso, *Política y religión en Barcelona*, p. 182.

11. For the role of priests who cooperated with liberalism's attempt to reform the Church, see Callahan, *Church, Politics and Society*, pp. 93–94, 119–21, 163–64, 171–72, 216–17, 258–59; "Un clero liberal, 1868–1871," in *La voluntad de humanismo: homenaje a Juan Marichal*, ed. B. Ciplijauskaitė and C. Maurer (Barcelona, 1990), pp. 45–56.

12. Gonzalo Anes, *Las crisis agrarias en la España moderna* (Madrid, 1970), p. 292. The Ensenada cadastral survey of 1749, although it applied only to the twenty-two provinces of Castile, showed that ecclesiastical institutions received nearly one-fourth of the region's agricultural income without taking into account the generous funds derived from the tithe, loans, and the ownership of nearly 3 million head of grazing stock. On average, Church corporations possessed approximately 15 percent of the land in the provinces surveyed, with higher percentages, 20 percent or higher, being recorded south of the Guadarrama Mountains. These figures are based on Antonio Matilla Tascón, *La única contribución y el catastro de Ensenada* (Madrid, 1947), pp. 535–43.

among prospective purchasers.[13] Although a partial disentailment was carried out during the liberal revolution of 1820–1823, it fell to Prime Minister Juan Álvarez Mendizábal to initiate in 1835–1836 the economic revolution that over the next quarter-century demolished the financial base that had sustained the Spanish Church for centuries. Mendizábal ordered the suppression of the male religious orders (with a handful of exceptions) and the sale of their property at public auction, with the proceeds to be used to reduce the national debt. Similar legislation in 1841 subjected the property of the diocesan clergy to the same fate, although political changes in 1843 delayed the final assault until 1855. By 1860, the bulk of the Church's vast holdings had been sold.

The liberal State did not intend to leave the Church to its own economic devices. Every liberal government undertook to support the diocesan clergy, although a workable system took years to develop.[14] The clergy did not regard an official subsidy as fair compensation for the sale of Church property, "the sacking of the patrimony of Jesus Christ."[15] Government support diminished in periods of political upheaval, while even in prosperous years the ecclesiastical belief was that the funds provided amounted to far less than the Church deserved.

The sale of ecclesiastical property deprived the mid-nineteenth-century Church of the immense resources that once allowed it to engage in an ample round of social and economic activities. Eighteenth-century bishops built bridges, established manufactures, financed schools, and indulged in other secular benefactions, while living in considerable comfort.[16] After the sale of Church lands, bishops could no longer afford the seigneurial extravagances and public-spirited generosity of their predecessors.

Nor could the Church sustain the numerous charities that had given it a unique social role in the hierarchical society of the past. Ecclesiastical poor relief ranged from the soup distributed at monastery gates to the more organized work of a mul-

13. The liberal State's motives were made abundantly clear in the disamortizing decree of October 11, 1835. The kingdom's monasteries were judged "useless and unnecessary"; their vast property holdings were regarded as "prejudicial" to the economic welfare of the nation. It was imperative, therefore, "to place them in general circulation to increase the resources of the State and open new sources of wealth." A later decree of February 19, 1836, noted the political benefits expected to flow from the enforced sale, which would create "a copious family of proprietors . . . whose existence will rest principally on the complete triumph of our actual institutions." Quoted in Simón Segura, *La desamortización*, p. 85.

14. The 1851 concordat with the papacy established funding arrangements between Church and State that would endure except for brief periods until 1931. The diplomatic negotiations over the concordat's financial terms are discussed in detail by Cuenca Toribio, *Iglesia y burguesía en la España liberal*, pp. 117–32. Until 1851, liberal governments adopted several different schemes to support the diocesan clergy. José Ramón González Armendia, *Dotación del Estado a la Iglesia española (siglos XIX–XX)* (Salamanca, 1990), pp. 38–78.

15. *La Revista Católica* (1842), p. 126.

16. Cardinal Lorenzana, Archbishop of Toledo between 1772 and 1797, for example, attempted to revive the decaying silk industry of his diocesan seat and built a large charity hospital from the proceeds of his extensive revenues, the largest of any bishop of the eighteenth-century Church, while at the same time indulging in his expensive taste for the purchase of rare books. Joseph Townsend, *A Journey through Spain in the years 1786 and 1787* (3 vols., London, 1791), vol. 3, p. 56.

titude of charitable associations. Although these efforts were uncoordinated, resting as they did on the initiative of individual institutions, they provided a measure of protection to a population exposed to the periodic crises characteristic of an agrarian society unable to raise food production to a level sufficient to meet the needs of an expanding population. The sale of Church property, including that of charitable organizations functioning under religious auspices, dealt a fatal blow to the operation of the traditional poor relief system. The inability of the Church to provide assistance to the poor comparable to that of the eighteenth century may well have contributed to its weakening influence over the urban population, a fact made painfully evident during the violent anticlerical riots that swept Madrid and Barcelona in 1834 and 1835.[17]

The suppression of the male regular clergy ordered by Mendizábal also diminished the Church's internal vitality. Although the regulars numbered only 30,906 in 1835, a substantial decrease from the approximately 50,000 reported in the censuses of the late eighteenth century, the religious orders still furnished the Church with its vanguard of popular evangelizers, preachers, and educators.[18] Their sudden disappearance left the spiritual and educational direction of the faithful in the hands of a diocesan clergy ill prepared for the task. The nearly universal suppression of the regulars accelerated a demographic decline among the clergy, which by 1840 had fallen well below eighteenth-century levels.

Clerical attempts to resist liberal reforms, whether through support for Carlism or simple foot-dragging, proved ineffective. In the end, the internal divisions of liberal politics saved the Church from further erosion of its position. By 1843, the hostility of the Moderate party to the rule of General Baldomero Espartero, who was identified with the Progressives, led to a revolution that initiated a long period of conservative rule, allowing the Church to regroup its disorganized and dispirited forces within the new political society created by liberalism.[19]

For the Moderates, intent on excluding their political opponents from power and yet determined to preserve for their supporters the gains made from the destruction of the hierarchical social order (including the sale of ecclesiastical property), an accommodation with the Church seemed tactically sound. A mutually acceptable arrangement promised to undercut the appeal of Carlism in the northern

17. Pablo García Colmenares, "Transformaciones urbanísticas e industriales," in *La desamortización en la Península Ibérica*, ed. Germán Rueda (Madrid, 1993), pp. 210–11. The sale of the property of charitable institutions began as early as 1798. Richard Herr estimates that 15 percent of ecclesiastical property in Castile, composed largely of the holdings of hospitals, orphanages, and charitable associations, was auctioned off between 1798 and 1808. *Rural Change and Royal Finances in Spain at the End of the Old Regime* (Berkeley, 1989), pp. 132–33. The fullest and most recent discussion of the riots of 1834 and 1835 is Revuelta González, *La exclaustración*, chapters 4 and 5.

18. Juan Sáez Marín, *Datos sobre la Iglesia española contemporánea, 1768–1868* (Madrid, 1975), p. 200.

19. Carlos Marichal has studied the conflicts within liberalism during the conflictive decade that followed its final triumph in 1834 in *Spain, 1834–1843* (London, 1977).

countryside, where it continued to enjoy popular support, and to win the backing of an institution fearful of another round of reform should the Progressives return to power. For the Church, a settlement with the conservative liberalism represented by the Moderates became indispensable. By 1846, twenty-nine of the kingdom's sixty dioceses lacked bishops, while the chronic financial difficulties besetting every government after 1834 left the diocesan clergy without a dependable source of income.

The working out of an accommodation between the Church and the Moderates took longer than the clergy expected, following the overthrow of Espartero in 1843. In 1851, the papacy and the Moderate government agreed upon the terms of a concordat that would govern civil-ecclesiastical relations until 1931.[20] The settlement between Rome and Madrid was a practical arrangement designed to regularize the situation of the Church within the liberal political system. Pope Pius IX (1846–1878) accepted the sale of Church property carried out until that time, confirmed the traditional patronage rights of the Spanish Crown over episcopal appointments, and endorsed the principle of diocesan and parish reorganization. In turn, the government accepted responsibility for supporting the diocesan clergy, recognized the right of the bishops to act independently in the exercise of their pastoral functions, and consented to a limited reestablishment of the male religious orders in an ambiguous clause soon to arouse controversy. Article 1 of the concordat affirmed that Catholicism "to the exclusion of any other cult continues being the only religion of the Spanish nation" and, as such, was to enjoy "all the rights and prerogatives" corresponding to it "according to the law of God and the sacred canons." Article 2 declared that education at all levels must conform to "the purity of the faith's doctrine."[21]

To contemporaries, the concordat appeared to be exactly what it was, a pragmatic arrangement accepted by both sides to further their respective interests. The Moderates saw the agreement as a means of consolidating their rule, although they were uneasy about the accusation of a sellout levied against them by the Progressives. Catholic opinion recognized that regularization of the Church's position was desirable, but it was far from enthusiastic about some of the concordat's terms.[22] The pro-clerical press noted that the rotund affirmations of Articles 1 and 2 carried no specific recommendations for their implementation, while the parish clergy ex-

20. For the background to the concordat, see the solidly researched articles of Nancy Rosenblatt, "The Spanish Moderados and the Church," *Catholic Historical Review* (1971), vol. 57, no. 3, pp. 401–20; "Church and State in Spain," *Catholic Historical Review* (1976), vol. 62, no. 4, pp. 589–603; "The Concordat of 1851 and Its Relation to Moderate Liberalism in Spain," *Iberian Studies* (1978), no. 1, pp. 30–39.

21. Quoted in Federico Suárez, "Génesis del concordato de 1851," *Ius Canonicum* (1963), vol. 3, pp. 233–34.

22. The newspaper *El Católico* remarked in its edition of May 13, 1851, "It should not be regarded as strange that there should be lively fears that . . . what appears favorable to the Church in this concordat will not be fulfilled . . . and even that which is favorable to the Church will be turned to its disadvantage."

pressed dismay at the low salaries established for priests engaged in parochial work. Moreover, the government's insistence on retaining its historic regalist rights over episcopal appointments showed its determination to preserve control over the crucial area of ecclesiastical patronage.

The 1851 settlement remained the cornerstone of civil-ecclesiastical relations until the proclamation of the Second Republic save for three brief challenges to its existence. As a result of the concordat, the Church secured the financial support it required after the sale of its property and the condition of legal normality necessary for institutional recuperation. But the Moderates got the better of the bargain. The papacy recognized the legitimacy of the liberal State and made a substantial concession by accepting the sale of Church property. The Moderates also realized their objective of winning the support of the kingdom's ecclesiastical elite against the dangers of radical political revolution and Carlism, despite the ongoing commitment of the lower clergy in some regions to the pretender's cause. The price paid by the regime for the concordat was modest. The government's acceptance of its financial obligations towards the Church merely reaffirmed the intent of virtually every liberal ministry since 1834.

The concordat provided the basis for an orderly relationship between the Church and the liberal State, albeit in its most conservative version. But it did not resolve the dilemma posed by the existence of an established Church committed to philosophical ideals and a practical program that came into frequent conflict with some of liberalism's basic principles. The concordat opened a new period in civil-ecclesiastical relations. But it would not be an "era of peace." From the beginning, the concordat became a "symbol of contradiction and polemic" in the turbulent world of liberal politics.[23] Although the Moderates were willing to placate the Church, within limits, as one of the many interest groups supporting the regime, they had no intention of restoring the enormous privileges once enjoyed by the institution. Nor were they prepared to renounce the government's historic regalist rights over ecclesiastical affairs.

The Church accepted Isabel II as queen within a liberal parliamentary system, however narrow its political base. The clergy demanded as much from the Moderates as it had expected from Fernando VII in the fields of religious dissent, education, and the control of public morality. As a result, tension inevitably developed between the government and the Church over specific policies, even in periods of Moderate rule. Between 1851 and 1868, the Church's persistent efforts to impose its view of education and morality on successive ministries experienced varying degrees of success. In 1866, the installation of a semi-dictatorial government under General Ramón Narváez, supported by a small clique of extremist Moderates

23. Manuel Revuelta González, "La confesionalidad del Estado en España," in *Iglesia, sociedad y Estado en España, Francia e Italia (ss. XVIII al XX)*, ed. Emilio La Parra López and Jesús Pradells (Alicante, 1991), p. 383.

and an increasingly unpopular queen, led to significant concessions to the Church. But clerical euphoria was short-lived. Intense opposition to the government on a broad front finally coalesced into a revolutionary movement that in 1868 drove Isabel II from the throne and destroyed the Moderate State.

An Internal Transformation

For the Church, the impact of the extended liberal revolution meant more than the loss of economic power and direct political influence. The long conflict with liberalism transformed institutional attitudes and practices that made the mid-nineteenth-century Church a different institution from its eighteenth-century predecessor. Nowhere was the change more evident than in a shift of episcopal loyalty from the Crown to the papacy. The Bourbon monarchs of the eighteenth century, particularly Carlos III (1759–1788) and Carlos IV (1788–1808), successfully constructed what might be termed a royal Church.[24] The Crown used its patronage rights to appoint bishops who could be relied upon to cooperate with the civil authorities on a wide range of issues, and for all practical purposes it controlled the Church's temporal administration. Some prelates, notably Bishop Carvajal y Lancaster during the 1760s, resented the extent of royal dominance, but the vast majority of the hierarchy viewed the omnipresent intervention of the Crown in ecclesiastical affairs as a positive development.[25]

The papacy's influence over the Spanish Church declined progressively during the eighteenth century. But the liberal reforms first manifested at the Cortes of Cádiz began a long process of internal adjustment that saw the bishops abandon regalism in favor of a deep emotional loyalty to the pope, who appeared as the Church's only protector in the face of liberal ecclesiastical reform. The conversion became complete between 1840 and 1843, when the government of General Espartero attempted to impose a revolutionary reorganization of the Spanish Church that would have reduced the role of the pope to the purely ceremonial.[26]

The spontaneous reaction of the clergy undermined the government's plans

24. The concordat of 1753 vastly increased the patronage rights of the Crown over ecclesiastical benefices. Isidoro Martín, "En el segundo centenario del concordato español de 1753," *Revista Española de Derecho Canónico* (1953), vol. 8, pp. 754–55. The powerful and persistent offensive of the eighteenth-century Bourbons on behalf of the Crown's regalist rights over every aspect of ecclesiastical affairs except in the realm of doctrine has been studied by Teófanes Egido, "El regalismo," *Iglesia, sociedad y Estado en España, Francia e Italia*, pp. 193–217.

25. For an analysis of clerical opposition to the increasing role of the Crown in ecclesiastical affairs, see C. C. Noel, "Opposition to Enlightened Reform in Spain, 1765–1775," *Societas* (1973), vol. 3, no. 1, pp. 21–43.

26. In May 1841, the government proposed a radical plan of reorganization that called for a redrawing of an ecclesiastical map that had remained unchanged for centuries. Toledo, the traditional seat of the primate of the Church, was to be reduced to the status of a simple diocese, while Madrid and Barcelona were to be given archdiocesan status. Seventeen thinly populated dioceses faced suppression,

for the creation of a national Church bound to Rome only by the loosest ties. The battle cry "Rome is our end! Rome is our hope!" swept through clerical ranks.[27] Through a campaign of civil resistance supported by Pope Gregory XVI (1831–1846), the clergy frustrated the government's intentions until the revolution of 1843 reduced the scheme to a dead letter. By 1843, the papacy had won a degree of influence over the clergy inconceivable fifty years earlier. Long reduced to a secondary role in questions affecting the Spanish Church, the pope now emerged to defend its interests in negotiations with the liberal State. The Moderates' willingness to conclude a new concordat in 1851, replacing the strongly regalist agreement of 1753, acknowledged ultramontanism's final triumph among bishops and priests.

Years of conflict with liberalism also affected the intellectual vitality of an institution that had once participated fully in the kingdom's cultural life. The active clerical culture of the eighteenth century, closely tied to the Spanish Enlightenment and the reforming initiatives of royal absolutism, gradually disappeared as the clergy retreated into a narrow intellectual exclusivism hostile to intellectual and scientific initiatives judged incompatible with its theocratic vision of human existence.[28] The desertion of candidates for the priesthood from the universities, where the clerical elite had been educated for centuries, to diocesan seminaries symbolized the change. The Church must begin sacerdotal education, said a seminary rector at mid-century, "by separating the young from the corruption of the world."[29] The Church viewed with deep unease the proliferation of newspapers, theaters, and other cultural institutions of the secular society promoted by liberalism. In 1841, the clergy of Santiago de Compostela attacked the construction of a theater in the town as "most prejudicial to the decorum of religion which the Spanish profess."[30] Clerics also saw the capitalist evolution of Spain under liberalism as a triumph of selfish materialism over spiritual values. Educated in the scholastic tradition, with its emphasis on the just price and the mutual social responsibilities incumbent on all social classes, churchmen lamented the emergence of a society

---

although thirteen new dioceses located in larger towns were to be created. The State also proposed to eliminate more than three thousand canonries and chaplaincies and to reduce the number of parishes from nineteen thousand to fifteen thousand. A later proposal submitted to parliament in January 1842 imposed such limitations on relations between the pope and the bishops that it reduced the former's role to the purely ceremonial. Callahan, *Church, Politics and Society,* pp. 167–68.

27. *La Cruz* (1842), p. 98.

28. A general study of the vitality of eighteenth-century clerical culture, albeit one that developed within an essentially conservative framework, is Émile Appolis, *Les jansénistes espagnols* (Bordeaux, 1966). Aspects of the question are also discussed by Richard Herr, *The Eighteenth-Century Revolution in Spain* (Princeton, 1958), and Jean Sarrailh, *L'Espagne éclairée de la seconde moitié du XVIIIe siècle* (Paris, 1954).

29. Quoted in José Manuel Cuenca Toribio, *Notas para el estudio de los seminarios españoles en el pontificado de Pío IX* (Valencia, 1973), p. 67.

30. *El Católico* (1841), no. 307, p. 7.

"occupied with industrial progress, mercantile circulation, the hunger for gold, the thirst for pleasure, ostentatious luxury, dissipation, scientific and literary vanity, political delirium and refined egoism."[31] Obsessed with the danger of "libertinism," the wanton expression of individual tastes and pleasures, the Church regarded the social and intellectual world created by liberalism as a form of "rebellion against God and human society."[32]

The prolonged conflict with liberalism also forced the Church to learn the rules of a new political game. The proliferation of newspapers, political clubs, and other institutions associated with the functioning of a parliamentary system meant that the Church could no longer rely on the time-honored formula of securing its objectives through the influence of an all-powerful sovereign. By the early 1840s, the Church began to learn the lessons of liberal politics. For the first time, a moderately effective Catholic press appeared that sought to influence public opinion in a modern way rather than through the pompous tracts of earlier times. Although unsuccessful, an 1841 proposal to create a Catholic Association of 1 million members to defend ecclesiastical interests in ongoing battles with the Espartero government showed that the Church finally recognized the necessity of building an organization capable of mobilizing opinion to influence official policy.

Decades of conflict with liberalism also left a legacy of anticlericalism that carried into the twentieth century. Hostility against the clergy and ecclesiastical institutions was not a fixed, unchanging phenomenon appearing in the same form over distinct historical periods. Historians of eighteenth-century Spain might well claim that the existence of an extensive satirical literature ridiculing the foibles of the clergy showed the presence of anticlerical sentiment before the rise of liberalism. But such examples prior to the nineteenth century were either purely literary exercises available to a restricted readership or, in the case of occasional violence directed against the clergy, too isolated and episodic to be significant. Close ties between civil and ecclesiastical authorities protected the Church from attack in a prerevolutionary age.

During the first three decades of the nineteenth century, the collapse of the consensus sustaining Throne and Altar exposed the Church for the first time to a new form of anticlericalism. The process began with ecclesiastical opposition to the Cortes of Cádiz. Clerical support for the restoration of absolute monarchy in 1813–1814 and later, between 1814 and 1820, for the royal dictatorship created by Fernando VII upon his return from exile in France, made the issue of the Church, its privileges, and political influence a source of public controversy. For liberals, the Church appeared an obstacle to their constitutional revolution—hence the distinctly more hostile character of legislation on ecclesiastical matters during the

31. Jaume Balmes, "La religión en Barcelona," April 1, 1843, in *La Sociedad* (4th ed., Barcelona, 1873), p. 153.

32. *El Católico* (1841), no. 159, pp. 537–39.

revolutionary period 1820–1823 compared with that of the Cortes of Cádiz.[33] The identification of the Church with absolutism between 1814 and 1820 laid the foundation for a political anticlericalism expressed in parliament and the press throughout the liberal period.

Anticlericalism in the early nineteenth century also developed a new social dimension. The attempt of ecclesiastical institutions after 1814 to reestablish their claims to tithes, seigneurial dues, and other financial rights in a time of economic crisis caused deep resentment in the countryside among peasants who worked the lands of wealthy monasteries and led frequently to violence against monks.[34] In the towns, the crisis of clerical finances that had deepened during the war against Napoleon prevented the Church from dispensing assistance at the eighteenth-century level. Moreover, the politicization of the urban masses accompanying the development of liberalism carried with it an ingrained hostility towards the clergy virtually unknown during the preceding century.[35]

The changes imposed by liberalism on the Church after 1834 destroyed any prospect of returning to the privileged ecclesiastical world of the eighteenth century. Liberalism forced the Church to adapt, however reluctantly, to new political, social, and economic circumstances. But the question of its relationship to the civil order and its response to dramatic social changes remained a source of controversy. The concordat of 1851 never won the support of the Progressive party, while a small band of Republicans rejected outright the idea of an established Church. The determination of the politicians opposing the Moderates to overturn the concordat, and the ecclesiastical leadership's resolve to make the agreement serve its interests through the application of lobbying tactics that clerics and their supporters had learned from liberal politics, meant that the issue of the Church remained unsettled and divisive. The unqualified support of the hierarchy for the increasingly discredited Moderate government of Narváez, and continuing enthusiasm for

33. The suppression of the Inquisition and the Jesuits by the liberal Cortes that had come to power as a result of the revolution of 1820 aroused clerical hostility, but it was the controversial *ley de monacales*, ordering a rationalization of the regular clergy, that provoked widespread anger in the Church. Under the legislation, far more extreme than anything done at the Cortes of Cádiz, 801 monasteries and friaries were closed and their property sold.

34. In 1813, for example, the municipal government of Ripoll protested to the Cortes against the return of the Benedictines to their monastery near the town, abandoned during the struggle against the French. The population especially objected to the monks' intention to resume collecting the tithe that had gone unpaid for years. This hostility against the regulars took a more violent form in 1822–1823 as the armed struggle between the liberal government and absolutist supporters entered a decisive phase. Thus the residents of the Catalan town of Poblet invaded the locality's wealthy monastery, burned the choir and organ, and carried off everything of value. Cayetano Barraquer y Roviralta, *Los religiosos en Cataluña durante la primera mitad del siglo XIX* (4 vols., Barcelona, 1915–1917), vol. 1, p. 54; Callahan, *Church, Politics and Society*, p. 126.

35. The period of liberal rule between 1820 and 1823 was of critical importance for creating a new kind of urban politics in which the city masses were used by the various liberal factions to achieve their goals. The work of Alberto Gil Novales, *Las sociedades patrióticas, 1820–1823* (2 vols., Madrid, 1975), is fundamental for the study of this phenomenon in its early stages.

Carlism among the lower clergy, exposed the Church to new dangers when the monarchy of Isabel II and the Moderate State collapsed in 1868.

From Revolution to Republic, 1868–1873

Early in 1868, Queen Isabel II received the Golden Rose, a decoration awarded by Pope Pius IX to recognize the sovereign's contribution to Catholicism. The papal award was hailed as a tribute to "the glory of the government [and] the Spanish nation."[36] But the splendor of the occasion in the royal palace and the self-congratulatory rhetoric accompanying it contrasted with the increasing difficulties of the authoritarian Moderate government in power since 1866, as it drifted towards the crisis that would soon bring it to an inglorious end. The regime rested on a narrow political base composed of the most conservative Moderates, some military men, and the queen herself, whose growing unpopularity intensified her desire to save her throne at any cost. Further, the government of General Narváez embarked on a campaign of harassment against a varied political opposition made up of Progressives and some Moderates hostile to the government's dictatorial methods. Many had cooperated in a coalition government, the Liberal Union, that governed the country between 1858 and 1863. For differing reasons, Republicans and Carlists joined the opposition hoping to turn the regime's crisis to political advantage. The death of the prime minister in the spring of 1868, the unpopularity of the queen, and, finally, the beginning of a severe economic crisis created the circumstances that allowed a disparate opposition and discontented army and navy officers to launch a military rising in September 1868, accompanied by popular revolt.

The "Glorious Revolution" followed the well-worn path of revolutionary upheaval in liberal Spain. Discontented generals and urban radicals came together, as they had in 1840 and 1854, to oust a Moderate government that refused to recognize the existence of a parliamentary opposition with a legitimate right to power as a result of the normal workings of the political process. But the 1868 revolution was more than a repetition of the traditional conflict between the two great parties of liberal Spain. The contribution of local revolutionary juntas to the success of the September rising moved the provisional government, led by Generals Francisco Serrano and Juan Prim, representing supporters of the former Liberal Union and the Progressives respectively, to accept a sweeping democratic program including universal suffrage as well as freedom of association and the press.

The question of the State's constitutional form was left aside for the moment save for the determination that a Bourbon would not sit on the throne in the event of a decision to continue a monarchy. From the beginning, the new regime suffered

36. *La Cruz* (1868), p. 147.

from severe internal conflicts that eventually caused its collapse. Tension among the partners in the governmental coalition constantly threatened its stability. The forceful leadership of Prim provided a measure of unity, but the general's assassination in December 1870, immediately before the arrival of the new king, Amadeo of Savoy (who had been offered the throne after intense political debate), encouraged divisions among the coalition parties. The regime also encountered opposition from the Carlists, infuriated by the government's secularizing and democratic policies, and from Republicans, outraged by the decision to reestablish the monarchy, albeit a constitutional one, in the person of Amadeo of Savoy.

The hierarchy made no secret of its preference for the dictatorial ministry of Narváez. The alliance between the Church and the most conservative Moderates was troubled by issues such as the publication in Spain of Pius IX's indictment of liberalism, the *Syllabus of Errors* (1864), which even Narváez refused to sanction, and by clerical demands for active Spanish intervention in Italy to defend the Papal States.[37] Despite these strains, relations between the bishops and the government were close enough between 1866 and 1868 to allow the Church to expand its role in public education. The ecclesiastical authorities acquired significant control over the appointment of new teachers and school curricula. Further, the personal devoutness of the queen, encouraged by the royal confessor Antonio Claret, gave the Church leverage in negotiations involving episcopal appointments and the authorization of religious orders. The Narváez government also treated the Church generously by increasing the budgetary allocation for clerical salaries and the maintenance of churches well above the amount stipulated in the 1851 concordat.[38]

The ecclesiastical leadership's willingness to identify itself with the Isabelline monarchy and the Narváez ministry proved counterproductive. With the outbreak of revolution, the issue of the Church again moved to the center of intense public debate.[39] The provisional government acted quickly against the male religious orders that Narváez had allowed in restricted numbers. The new regime announced its intention to punish the Church for its ties to the discredited Moderate government through an attack on the regular clergy. Religious communities, a decree asserted, "formed an integral and principal part of the shameful and oppressive regime which the nation has just overthrown with so much glory." It was "necessary and urgent" to eliminate them "to consolidate . . . the revolution and con-

37. José Manuel Cuenca Toribio and S. Miranda García, "Notas sobre el pontificado burgalés de Fernando de la Puente y Primo de Rivera (1858–1867)," in José Andrés-Gallego et al., *Estudios históricos sobre la Iglesia española contemporánea* (El Escorial, 1979), pp. 294–96. Jesús Pabón has examined the impact on Spanish politics of the Roman question in *España y la cuestión romana* (Madrid, 1972).

38. In 1851 the State assigned 153 million reales to the clerical budget, a figure that rose to 180 million on the eve of the revolution of 1868. "Datos estadísticos relativos al personal y a la dotación del clero y del culto," *La Cruz* (1870), pp. 400–402.

39. The role of the Church during the revolutionary period has been studied by Cárcel Ortí, *Iglesia y revolución en España, 1868–1874*, and Martí Gilabert, *La cuestión religiosa en la revolución de 1868–1874*.

struct new institutions."[40] The government also sought to restrict clerical influence over education to counter "the unbridled and blind reaction against spontaneous manifestations of human understanding" that in its view had taken place prior to the revolution.[41]

Government legislation directed against the orders provoked a strong reaction among clergy and laity. As early as December 1868 an alliance of ecclesiastics and laymen, drawn largely from the Carlists and the extreme Right of the Moderate party, the group known as "neo-Catholics," formed the Association of Catholics of Spain to contest the first parliamentary elections held following the revolution.[42] Formed with papal approval, the Association declared its intention "to propagate and defend the doctrines, institutions and social influence of the Church, particularly its liberty and the Catholic unity of Spain . . . through peaceful means and under the protection of the law."[43]

The Association was not formally linked to either of the groups from which it drew its members, in deference to the pope's desire for political neutrality and in recognition of the potential damage that the divisive issue of the Carlist pretender might cause in the organization. But internal dissension developed, which contributed, along with inadequate financing and confusion over the conduct of the campaign, to a dismal showing in the elections of January 1869. For the first time within a relatively free electoral process, however, a modern political alliance was forged between the Church and conservative forces committed to defending its interests.

Smarting from the overwhelming electoral defeat of its defenders, the Church then faced a dose of bitter medicine. The provisional government announced its intention to introduce religious liberty for the first time in the country's history. The proposal represented "a protest against the theocratic spirit introduced with

40. "Decreto del Gobierno Provisional," October 12, 1868, *La Cruz* (1868), p. 347. Religious houses opened since 1837 without formal government authorization were ordered closed. The government also ordered a 50 percent reduction in the number of convents of nuns save for those belonging to orders engaged in charitable work.

41. "Manifiesto del Gobierno Provisional a la nación," October 25, 1868, in ibid., pp. 357–58.

42. The origin of the term "neo-Catholic" is not entirely clear. Critics of the Church's role in Spanish society used it as a blanket term of condemnation against those whom they perceived as political and religious reactionaries. The work of Begoña Urigüen, however, has established that "neo-Catholicism" was a specific movement, although never a political party. It emerged from the right wing of the Moderates during the 1850s and owed its ideological inspiration to Donoso Cortés, the mid-century Spanish political thinker. Reflecting Cortés's fear that liberalism carried within it the germs of popular radicalism and social revolution that eventually would overthrow the existing social order, "neo-Catholics" saw the existence of a strong centralized government controlled by a restricted elite as necessary to prevent such an occurrence. They also believed that religion and the Church were essential to the survival of a conservative social order. Despite the movement's origins in the Moderate party, little survived of its liberalism by the time of the revolution of 1868. Its leading figure during this period was a former Moderate minister, Cándido Nocedal, who refused an official position under the Narváez government because he believed that it was not doing enough to contain the forces of revolution. Begoña Urigüen, *Orígenes y evolución de la derecha española: el neo-catolicismo* (Madrid, 1986), pp. 22–23, 258.

43. Quoted in *La Cruz* (1868), p. 504.

such insidious persistence in the essence of our institutions by the previous regime."[44] Although Spanish Protestantism had failed to recruit a significant number of converts since proselytizing efforts began during the late 1830s, the Church saw the prospect of religious toleration as a terrible evil certain to destroy Catholicism and endanger society—hence the determined campaign to block parliamentary approval of the new constitution's article to this effect. Although nearly 3 million signatures were gathered by clergy and laity for a massive petition opposing religious liberty, the support of former Liberal Unionists, Progressives, Republicans, and others made the result a foregone conclusion. In parliament, Emilio Castelar, a Republican leader and the most celebrated political orator of the day, delivered an eloquent and emotional speech on behalf of religious liberty that evoked tumultuous applause from the deputies.[45] Less than a month later, the appropriate constitutional text was approved by an overwhelming majority.

Establishment of religious toleration led to a marked deterioration in civil-ecclesiastical relations. Catholic newspapers announced the parliamentary vote on pages bordered in black, while the bishops ordered services of atonement in the churches. The situation grew steadily worse from the Church's perspective. Legislation authorizing civil marriage (1870) was denounced by the clergy as nothing more than official approval of "public concubinage." Many bishops and priests refused outright to take the oath to the 1869 constitution demanded by the government. Only 24 of the 189 parish priests in the Almería diocese, for example, were willing to swear loyalty to the constitution.[46]

Relations between the Church and successive ministries of the constitutional monarchy continued to worsen until the regime's disintegration in February 1873. In the summer of 1871, after the collapse of the governmental coalition dominated by Liberal Unionists and Progressives, power drifted uncertainly to the leaders of the Progressive parliamentary factions, Manuel Ruiz Zorilla and Práxedes Sagasta. Both adopted harsher policies towards the Church because of the support given by some clergy to a second great Carlist rebellion that broke out during 1872. In March, the government imposed a jurisdictional relic of the eighteenth-century monarchy by requiring official permission (*exequatur*) before any papal bull or brief could be published in Spain.

The internal divisions of the coalition, the personal unpopularity of the new king, and the failure to break the Carlist rebellion, as well as the Cuban rising for independence that began in 1868, combined to make the constitutional monarchy unworkable. During 1872, ministry followed ministry as factionalization made stable government impossible. In February 1873, Amadeo of Savoy, recognizing that his position was untenable among politicians and the public, announced his

44. "Manifiesto del Gobierno Provisional a la nación," ibid., pp. 357–58.
45. Carmen Llorca, *Emilio Castelar: precursor de la democracia cristiana* (Madrid, 1966), p. 142.
46. *La Cruz* (1869), pp. 706–10, 141.

decision to abdicate. He did so on February 11, leaving parliament with the responsibility for deciding upon any changes in the State's constitutional organization. The deputies, having attempted one constitutional experiment and lacking enthusiasm for a Bourbon restoration, turned to a republic as the only solution to their political dilemma.

The First Republic entered through a political backdoor rather than over the barricades. For this reason, its proclamation aroused little violent opposition save among the Carlists, who viewed the Republic as a continuation of the constitutional monarchy they so despised. The appearance of the Republic did not evoke a strong clerical reaction. Even the new regime's commitment to the separation of Church and State led to only ritualistic protests. "How can anyone speak of separation," asked a Catholic journal, in reference to the secularizing legislation implemented since 1868, "when it is already an accomplished fact?"[47]

Despite conflicts between the ecclesiastical authorities and the government, the issue of the Church was less central to Republican concerns than to the constitutional monarchy that inherited the strongly regalist view of civil-ecclesiastical relations characteristic of every ministry, absolutist and liberal, since the eighteenth century. Republicans had a simple solution at hand, the separation of Church and State. They also had sufficient troubles of their own without becoming unduly preoccupied with the ecclesiastical question. Severe dissension over the Republic's organization, whether it should be unitary or federal, endangered the regime's stability from the moment of its appearance. The outbreak of local risings during the summer of 1873 designed to establish city states (cantons) virtually independent of the central government and a succession of Carlist military victories made survival more important than resolving the problem of the Church.

Church and Republic shared an uneasy ground of common self-interest before the cantonalist movement and the social agitation that began to sweep through the southern countryside. The central government viewed the former as a threat to its authority, while the Church saw it as nothing less than a latter-day version of irreligious Jacobinism resulting from anticlerical measures taken by the cantons of Cádiz, Sanlúcar de Barrameda, Málaga, Jerez, and Córdoba. The Republican authorities, fearing that Carlist propagandists would exploit the situation to their advantage, expressed their regrets on more than one occasion for the extreme actions taken against the Church by some cantons.[48] The Republic and the Church were no less hostile to social unrest in the southern countryside, particularly in Extremadura and Andalucía. The seizure and redistribution of land in some areas of

47. *El Consultor de los Párrocos*, February 20, 1873.

48. During the height of the cantonalist rising in Málaga, for example, when the bishop was forced to vacate his palace, the minister of grace and justice expressed his regrets: "The government of the Republic is completely divorced from the measures taken by the municipality. It understands and laments the trouble to which you have been put." Minister of grace and justice to Bishop Pérez Fernández, July 7, 1873, *La Cruz* (1873), p. 242.

the south by its landless and impoverished population seemed to herald the day of revolution feared by Republican politicians and clergymen alike. The vigorous measures taken by the government to crush social unrest were welcomed by the Church.

The Republic did not abandon its commitment to the separation of Church and State. A draft constitution provided for a break in the historic pattern of civil-ecclesiastical relations. The bishops attacked separation as a scheme "to erect persecution of the Church into a system of government."[49] In fact, the proposed changes were less drastic than those adopted by the Second Republic between 1931 and 1933. The draft constitution of 1873 recognized the right of the Church to conduct its affairs "with complete independence" and to own property subject only to the general laws of the nation.[50] The government also promised to continue paying pensions to nuns as stipulated in the 1851 concordat, to honor contracts already made for the repair of churches, and to guarantee that all buildings used for religious purposes would continue to be so employed.

The much-heralded separation of Church and State never took place, as the regime desperately sought to survive before cantonalist revolt, the Carlist rebellion, and the Cuban rising for independence. In September 1873, the accession to the presidency of Emilio Castelar eased clerical apprehensions. Castelar's defense of religious liberty in 1869 did not endear him to Catholic opinion, but he was the least anticlerical of the Republic's four presidents, while his determination to break the cantonalist movement and crush social agitation calmed churchmen fearful of social and political revolution. Castelar also attempted to broaden the popular base on which the Republic rested by making limited concessions to the Church. To the irritation of Carlists and others, the president conducted successful negotiations with the papacy to fill numerous vacancies in the hierarchy.

Castelar's attempt to create a republic acceptable to institutions and social classes fearful of revolution foundered on divisions within Republican ranks as well as on the government's inability to defeat the Carlists and the Cuban rebels. When a political crisis forced the president's resignation on January 3, 1874, a miniature coup d'état executed by the captain-general of Madrid ended the Republic for all practical purposes. Following the coup, a government of national union emerged that rested on the supporters of the constitutional monarchy produced by the 1868 revolution. Two failed constitutional experiments now opened the way to a Bourbon restoration in the person of Isabel II's son, Alfonso.

49. *El Consultor de los Párrocos*, July 31, 1873.
50. *La Semana Católica* (1873), pp. 510–11.

CHAPTER II

THE CHURCH AND THE RESTORATION, 1874–1901

A New Compromise, 1874–1881

Neither monarchical nor republican, the regime installed by the military intervention of January 1874 was a constitutional hybrid resting on little but the manipulating abilities of its principal figure, General Francisco Serrano, "Chief of the Executive Power." Supporters of a Bourbon restoration had been conspiring against the governments in power since 1868. In 1870, they laid the foundation of their campaign by persuading an unpopular Isabel II to renounce her dynastic rights in favor of her son, Alfonso.[1] As the regime introduced by the 1868 revolution gave way to an ineffectual republic, momentum for a restoration intensified among politicians and generals sympathetic to the cause of the young pretender.

The campaign's principal strategist was one of the most astute tacticians in the history of Spanish parliamentary government, Antonio Cánovas del Castillo (1828–1897). A former schoolteacher from Málaga, Cánovas had come to Madrid like many provincials before him to make a career in the turbulent world of mid-nineteenth-century liberal politics. Moved by his analysis of the problems of Moderate governments prior to 1868, Cánovas concluded that stability could be achieved only by a constitutional monarchy resting on as broad a base as possible and a strong government capable of restraining military interventionism as well as political and social radicalism.[2] Emerging from the middle-of-the-road group of

1. Melchor Fernández Almagro, *Historia política de la España contemporánea* (Alianza Editorial edition, 3 vols., Madrid, 1968), vol. 1, pp. 231–32.

2. It has been argued that Cánovas sought to create a new version of the Liberal Union through the reconciliation of "*reasonable* Moderates" with "*cautious* Progressives . . . 'to restore the harmony of the

Moderates, Cánovas had little sympathy for the democratic policies pursued by the alliance of some Liberal Unionists and Progressives between 1868 and 1872. But his commitment to parliamentary government and his distaste for the dictatorial methods employed by Narváez separated him from the right wing of the Moderate party. After being named leader of the Bourbon cause by Alfonso in 1873, Cánovas began to weave together the complex political threads necessary to unify the liberal factions.

Cánovas was not averse to allowing military officers a role in the political maneuvering of 1873 and 1874.[3] Although he did not wish to see the generals become the political arbiters of the nation, as they often had been in the past, a military rising begun by General Arsenio Martínez Campos on his own initiative at Sagunto on December 29, 1874, toppled Serrano and gave Cánovas the opportunity for which he had long planned. Lacking political ambitions of his own, Martínez Campos deferred to Cánovas, who formed a provisional government in the name of Alfonso XII (1875–1885) two days after the success at Sagunto.

Cánovas remained head of the government for the next six years except for two brief periods. By the time he yielded power to the opposition leader, Práxedes Sagasta (1825–1903) in 1881, he had designed the constitutional and political framework of a liberal State that endured until its overthrow in 1923. Cánovas's objectives were straightforward: first, to avoid the recourse to military intervention and popular violence characteristic of liberal politics since 1834; second, to create a political system based on a more disciplined party structure that would allow for the development of an opposition loyal to the dynasty and capable of assuming power in due course; and third, to fashion a regime secure against revolutionary assault.

Serious difficulties confronted Cánovas as he began to lay the foundations of yet another version of liberal constitutional monarchy. Continuation of the Carlist and Cuban revolts threatened the regime with the same fate visited upon the monarchy of Amadeo of Savoy and the Republic. But in several respects Cánovas assumed the direction of the government in favorable circumstances. The strongest opponents of a Bourbon restoration—Carlists, Progressives, and Republicans—were beset by internal divisions. The Progressives had broken into two camps; one, under the leadership of Ruiz Zorilla, drifted towards republicanism, while the other, under Sagasta, moved towards an accommodation with the new political order. The intransigent Moderates, who once supported General Narváez, learned nothing between 1868 and 1874. Known as "Historics," they demanded a revived version of the regime overthrown by the "Glorious Revolution." They rejected the democratic constitution of 1869 and wished to settle the political score with those re-

liberal family'" that had eluded liberalism since it triumphed over absolute monarchy. Esperanza Yllán Calderón, *Cánovas del Castillo: entre la historia y la política* (Madrid, 1985), p. 204.

3. Ibid., p. 212.

sponsible for it. They preferred Isabel II to her son and were hostile to Cánovas, whom they suspected of being willing to compromise with the liberal opponents of the Isabelline monarchy. Early in 1875, the "Historics" began a strident campaign through their well-financed press to force Cánovas to conform to their ideas. Central to that campaign was the issue of religious liberty. The "Historics" pressed relentlessly for abrogation of the toleration introduced by the 1869 constitution and immediate acceptance of the 1851 concordat, with its unequivocal commitment to the State's confessionality.[4] The Catholic opposition to Cánovas realized all too well that the prime minister needed an accommodation with the Church to undercut the appeal of Carlism.[5]

The "Historics" won the support of key allies within the hierarchy as they began their lobbying campaign. Although many bishops welcomed Alfonso as king with apparent enthusiasm through messages of congratulations and services of thanksgiving, initial euphoria soon yielded to a more hardheaded assessment of events. In early 1875, an alliance of certain bishops, notably Antolín Monescillo of Jaén, with the "Historics" and the intransigent papal nuncio, Giovanni Simeoni, demanded a return to the religious monopoly enjoyed by the Church prior to September 1868.[6] What the Church expected from Cánovas, declared *La España Católica,* the Madrid newspaper of the "Historics," was that "all the laws, all the dispositions, all the acts of the government should be moved by a Catholic spirit."[7] Bishop Monescillo went further in a public letter to the king threatening the withdrawal of Catholic support unless the monarch took immediate action to heed the Church's demands.[8]

The vociferous campaign conducted by the "Historics" and some members of the hierarchy posed a danger to the stability of the Alfonsine monarchy during the first year and a half of its existence. Although the prime minister was a practicing Catholic and believed that religion imbued Spanish society with a moral content it could not acquire from any other source, he was also a realist who recognized that the religious unanimity of earlier times had long since broken down.[9] Cánovas recognized that he could not afford to alienate supporters of the 1869 constitution,

4. In January 1875, the papal chargé d'affaires reported to the Vatican that Cánovas did not wish to recognize the concordat as it stood but wanted the original agreement revised. The prime minister indicated that he was not willing to deal with the concordat if this meant alienating the political parties supporting the new regime. Cristóbal Robles Muñoz, *Insurrección o legalidad: los católicos y la Restauración* (Madrid, 1988), p. 97.

5. José Varela Ortega, *Los amigos políticos: elecciones y caciquismo en la Restauración, 1875–1900* (Madrid, 1977), p. 94.

6. When Simeoni presented his credentials to Alfonso XII, he gave the king a letter from Pius IX in which the pope demanded recognition of the 1851 concordat "in its full vigor" because "Spain cannot have in its midst any other cult than the Catholic." Quoted in María F. Núñez Muñoz, *La Iglesia y la Restauración, 1875–1881* (Santa Cruz de Tenerife, 1976), p. 56.

7. *La España Católica,* January 5, 1875.

8. "Exposición dirigida a S. M. por el obispo de Jaén," *La España Católica,* February 26, 1875.

9. José María García Escudero, *Vista a la derecha* (Madrid, 1988), pp. 32–33.

whose acceptance of the restored monarchy was necessary for its survival. Pressure from the German Empire and the United Kingdom on behalf of religious freedom for Spain's minuscule Protestant minority also influenced the prime minister to seek a solution that would not preclude diplomatic recognition of the new regime.[10] Rejecting the narrow sectarianism of Carlists and "Historics," he elaborated a delicate balancing strategy to resolve the contentious issue of religious liberty.

During the first year of the new government, Cánovas appeased the Church by restoring ecclesiastical finances to pre-1868 levels.[11] The government also abrogated a 1873 law allowing former members of the religious orders to marry, and it reestablished prerevolutionary legislation making canonical marriage the only legal form of matrimony for Catholics.[12] Further, the minister responsible for education, the marqués de Orovio, abolished academic freedom in the universities and dismissed professors, including well-known figures such as Gumersindo de Azcárate, Nicolás Salmerón, and Francisco Giner de los Ríos, whose views were judged hostile to religion. Orovio, who was sympathetic to the cause of the "Historics," acted without consulting Cánovas.[13] But the measures against academic freedom and the expulsion of leading intellectuals from their chairs were welcomed unreservedly by churchmen and their lay supporters.

These concessions failed to distract the pro-clerical alliance from its primary objective, the immediate restoration of the Church's religious monopoly. The prime minister successfully avoided the issue during the few weeks separating the installation of the new regime and the arrival of Alfonso XII on the grounds that such an important question could not be resolved without the king's presence. When the young sovereign arrived in mid-January 1875, he faced a barrage of aggressive petitions from the partisans of "Catholic Unity." Cánovas used his enormous influence over Alfonso to defer any decision until the issue was referred to a constituent parliament scheduled to assemble in early 1876.

As defenders of clerical interests realized that the question of religious liberty would be decided by an assembly chosen by the government through electoral manipulation, they redoubled their attacks on Cánovas. The "Historics" complained of censorship imposed on the Catholic press for expressing its opinion on the issue while "filthy Protestant sheets vomited insults against the Catholic religion."[14]

10. Robles Muñoz, *Insurrección o legalidad*, p. 103.

11. The appropriation for the Church fell drastically between 1868 and 1873 from 47 million pesetas in 1867 to 3 million in 1873. During the first year of the regime it rose to 39 million. J. María Palomares Ibáñez, "La recuperación económica de la Iglesia española, 1845–1931," in *Iglesia, sociedad y Estado en España, Francia e Italia (ss. XVIII al XX)*, ed. Emilio Parra López and Jesús Pradells (Alicante, 1991), p. 160.

12. Robles Muñoz, *Insurrección o legalidad*, p. 93.

13. Varela Ortega, *Los amigos políticos*, pp. 103–6.

14. *La España Católica*, June 2, 1875. The newspaper was suspended twice by the government in 1875. The Carlist *El Siglo Futuro* also suffered suspension, as did the diocesan bulletin of the bishop of Jaén.

The prime minister, declared *La España Católica*, was following a policy that "has alienated the sympathies of the conservative party, while bringing upon himself the universal antipathy of Catholics" for his ambiguity on the question of religious liberty.[15]

With a characteristic mixture of legalism and crass political opportunism, Cánovas decreed that the elections for the constituent parliament should be conducted on the basis of universal suffrage as established in the 1869 constitution, although everyone understood that the results would be rigged to provide the prime minister with a suitable majority. Despite this, the Church and its supporters made an effort to influence the outcome. Cardinal Barrio of Valencia warned the faithful against electing deputies favoring religious liberty, "a most lamentable liberty which cannot less offend God than cause evil." The bishops of the ecclesiastical province of Tarragona declared unequivocally, "No Catholic can vote for this liberty of perdition, nor can he send to the Cortes anyone who is disposed to establish it in Spain."[16] These interventions, as well as the energetic offensive of the Catholic press, intensified bitterness against Cánovas, but they did not affect the election results; the prime minister received his desired majority.

Having successfully moved resolution of a potentially damaging issue to parliament, Cánovas then attempted a compromise capable of satisfying liberal politicians and the Church to a greater or lesser degree. The prime minister also had to keep in mind the problem of maintaining good relations with the papacy, which objected strenuously to anything less than the complete restoration of the Church's religious monopoly.[17] Reports that the government did not intend to restore the pre-1868 state of affairs as far as religious liberty was concerned caused the nuncio to threaten to leave the country as early as the spring of 1875.[18] Well before parliament met in February 1876, the government appointed a select committee of thirty-nine political notables, including a substantial representation of supporters of the 1869 constitution, to draft a constitutional article dealing with religious liberty. Cánovas used his authority and his well-honed political skills to guide the discussions in the direction he wished. The compromise was embodied in Article 11 of the constitution of 1876:

15. *La España Católica*, June 3, 1875.

16. "Resolución del cardenal arzobispo de Valencia a la consulta hecha por el clero de su diócesis sobre la unidad católica," January 10, 1876, *La Cruz* (1876), p. 46; "Contestación a una consulta sobre las elecciones próximas," January 10, 1876, ibid., p. 123.

17. The instructions given to Simeoni stressed that the nuncio "will insist" on complete implementation of Article 1 of the 1851 concordat and "will oppose especially the public exercise of dissident cults, and any act of the Government which tends to recognize legally the liberty of cults." Quoted in *Instrucciones secretas a los nuncios de España en el siglo XIX, 1847–1907*, ed. F. Díaz de Cerio and M. F. Núñez Muñoz (Rome, 1989), p. 173.

18. Robles Muñoz, *Insurrección o legalidad*, p. 107. The complex diplomatic game played between the government and the Vatican is discussed in detail in pp. 101–20, and in Núñez Muñoz, *La Iglesia y la Restauración*, pp. 55–77.

> The Catholic, Apostolic, Roman religion is that of the State. The nation assumes the obligation to maintain the cult and its ministers.
>
> No one shall be disturbed in Spanish territory for his religious beliefs nor for the exercise of his own religion except for the respect due to Christian morality.
>
> However, ceremonies or public manifestations other than those of the religion of the State will not be permitted.[19]

The prime minister hoped that Article 11 would appease Catholic opinion through its explicit recognition of Catholicism as the official religion of the State and its commitment to restrict the practice of other confessions to the narrow area of private observance. But he also hoped that the second clause, allowing individuals to hold personal religious beliefs without fear of official persecution, would assuage supporters of full toleration in some measure.

The terms of Article 11 were known to the public before parliamentary debate began. The hierarchy undertook a determined campaign to persuade deputies to reject it outright on the grounds that even the restricted religious toleration proposed represented a conspiracy "to de-Catholicize the Spanish people."[20] The bishops of the ecclesiastical province of Granada wrote directly to Alfonso XII urging him to act unilaterally to restore the Church's religious monopoly. If the king did not do so, the prelates implied, he would be acting "contrary to the law of God, the teachings of the Catholic Church and the Roman Pontiff, its visible head."[21] In March, Pius IX entered the battle publicly with the appearance in a Madrid newspaper of a statement from the papal secretary of state opposing Article 11.[22] As a result, the Catholic press redoubled its attacks on the proposed constitutional text. Within parliament the debate occupied fifty days, although the outcome was certain. A young deputy, Alejandro Pidal y Mon, led the unsuccessful effort of the few "Historics" sitting in the chamber to defeat the government's proposal.[23]

Cánovas succeeded in winning his political gamble. Article 11 satisfied the majority of former Moderates and Liberal Unionists and left the "Historics" isolated. Pius IX, after formally protesting "against every innovation offensive to the sacred rights of the Church, every violation of the concordat and against all the conse-

19. Quoted in Earl R. Beck, *A Time of Triumph and Sorrow: Spanish Politics during the Reign of Alfonso XII, 1874–1885* (Carbondale, 1979), pp. 53–54.

20. "Exposiciones del episcopado: del metropolitano y sufragáneos de Toledo," January 22, 1876, *La Cruz* (1876), p. 166.

21. *La Cruz* (1876), p. 183.

22. Giovanni Barberini, "El artículo 11 de la constitución de 1876," *Anthologica Annua* (1961), vol. 9, p. 310. The papacy's strategy on Article 11 was more nuanced than that of the nuncio. Cardinal Antonelli, the papal secretary of state, was willing to accept *de facto* toleration in the sense of not demanding some form of legal persecution against religious dissenters but only if "Catholic unity" was formally recognized by the government and there was no *de jure* recognition of other confessions. Rafael María Sanz de Diego, "La actitud de Roma ante el artículo 11 de la constitución de 1876," *Hispania Sacra* (1975), vol. 28, pp. 188–89.

23. The vote was taken on May 12, 1876; 222 members of the congress of deputies voted in favor of the constitutional text. Radicals and Republicans voted against, as did the forty deputies representing the "Historics." Robles Muñoz, *Insurrección o legalidad*, p. 122.

quences which can flow from the ill-fated principle of liberty or tolerance for heterodox cults," grudgingly accepted what had been done.[24] The pope did so on the understanding that Article 11 would be strictly enforced and that the Spanish government would introduce legislation enhancing the Church's role in education. Some bishops proved less accommodating. Cardinal Moreno of Toledo was so angered by Article 11 and the requirement that the clergy take an oath of loyalty to the new constitution, thus implying endorsement of the limited toleration it provided, that he urged the Vatican to break off diplomatic relations.[25] Supporters of the 1869 constitution were also unhappy with the limits placed on religious freedom. Although some rejected Article 11, many accepted it as the best that could be managed given the political circumstances.

After defusing the explosive issue of religious liberty, the prime minister sought an accommodation with the diverse groups committed to the constitution of 1869. The development of a new party under the direction of Práxedes Sagasta facilitated acceptance of the Alfonsine monarchy by opponents of a Bourbon restoration. The formation in December 1878 of what eventually was known as the Liberal party provided the loyal opposition that Cánovas believed necessary for the regime's survival. The prime minister had little sympathy for the reformist program of the Liberals, but he recognized that the opposition would have to govern in due course to avoid a return to the pattern of popular violence and military intervention characteristic of liberal politics since 1834. Early in 1881, Cánovas paid the political price he believed necessary to achieve stability by resigning as prime minister in favor of Sagasta.

The political system of the Restoration represented a brilliant achievement of pragmatic politics. The regime rested on a broad coalition of forces drawn from the diverse factions of Spanish liberalism gathered into two parties, the Liberal-Conservative of Cánovas and the Liberal of Sagasta. Both were loyal to the reigning dynasty, hence the term "dynastic" often used to describe them. Although Cánovas's version of a liberal constitutional monarchy provided a measure of stability during the Restoration's first two decades, the regime carried within it the seeds of its own destruction. Government and opposition alternated in power, but not through a normal parliamentary process. Elections were held, but the results were managed from the Ministry of the Interior (Gobernación) to produce whatever majority seemed desirable to the two chieftains of the dynastic parties.

This political system permitted enough flexibility to allow for important reforms, such as trial by jury and universal suffrage, introduced by Sagasta during his long ministry (1885–1890). But the dishonesty of the electoral process and the artificiality of the dynastic parties limited the practical effect of these changes. The so-

24. Quoted in ibid., p. 147.
25. Ibid., p. 131.

cial base on which the parties rested made it impossible for the regime to expand its appeal to include industrial workers and much of the rural population. Cánovas devised a system depending on a broader clientele than that dominating the Isabelline monarchy during its last days. The regime drew support from estate owners in the south, the urban professional classes, prosperous wheat farmers in Old Castile, and the financial, commercial, and industrial interests of Madrid, Barcelona, and Bilbao. That Cánovas relied upon these elites to buttress the regime during its early history was understandable given the political turbulence that preceded it. But over the long term the Restoration failed to develop the flexibility necessary to accommodate the demands of social classes excluded from the circles of power.

The role of the Church as the established Church of a liberal State created ambiguities and conflicts that persisted throughout the Restoration. Cánovas's policy of limited concessions to the Church achieved the goal of reducing the ability of Carlists to attack the regime for its ecclesiastical policy. A pragmatically disposed hierarchy accepted with reservations a deal that provided the Church with constitutional recognition, government financial support, episcopal representation in the senate, and other concessions.[26]

The *modus vivendi* between the new regime and the clerical leadership did nothing to diminish the visceral hostility of clerical and lay opinion towards liberalism as a political philosophy and towards its most recent institutional embodiment in the Restoration.[27] The regime did not face a serious threat from the Carlists, demoralized by military defeat (1876) and internal squabbling, or from the "Historics," who were isolated politically. The significance of the drumbeat of harsh criticism directed against the Restoration during its formative stage from the pages of the Catholic newspapers, such as the Carlist *El Siglo Futuro* and *La España Católica* of the "Historics," lay in the strong ideological legacy of opposition towards political and religious pluralism that persisted for generations among Spanish Catholics.

26. The first ecclesiastical senators, nine in number, were elected in April 1877. Some bishops saw their presence in the upper chamber as a clever trick by the regime to acquire political legitimacy among Spanish Catholics. The archbishop of Valladolid believed that the participation of the clerical senators gave political support to "a system which is not destined to do any good for either the Church or the country." Quoted in Robles Muñoz, *Insurrección o legalidad*, p. 169. The small number of bishops committed openly to Carlism found other ways to express their displeasure with the Restoration. In 1878, for example, the bishop of Osma refused to authorize a *Te Deum* in his cathedral upon Alfonso XII's marriage. *La Cruz* (1878), p. 513.

27. The origins of Spanish Catholicism's deep hostility towards liberalism and more radical movements arose in part from years of conflict between liberal governments and the Church. But it also developed from broader intellectual currents within European Catholicism, particularly those associated with French Catholic thinkers such as De Maistre, Bonald, and others. Pius IX's synthesis of prevailing antiliberal ideas, the *Syllabus of Errors* (1864), gave Catholic antiliberalism a coherent justification backed by papal prestige. In Spain, the *Syllabus* became the intellectual foundation of all forms of Catholic antiliberalism, although some were more extreme than others. Marta M. Campomar Fornieles, *La cuestión religiosa en la Restauración: historia de los heterodoxos españoles* (Santander, 1984), pp. 20–23, 27–36.

Cánovas's intention of winning the Church's support while neutralizing controversy over its place within the State and society rested on a glaring contradiction, namely, the existence of a legally privileged Church within a liberal political system rejected outright by many Catholics and tolerated by others only as a practical necessity. The Restoration's ecclesiastical settlement failed to calm the apprehensions of Liberals and Republicans who viewed the privileges given to the Church as craven concessions certain to be abused.

The real power of the Church was less formidable than its critics supposed. Cánovas remained faithful to the regalist tradition of government control over ecclesiastical finances and patronage that had formed part of the liberal inheritance since the Cortes of Cádiz. The prime minister did not shrink from censoring the pro-clerical press during the conflicts of 1875 and 1876. He moved vigorously against the Carlist organizers of an 1877 pilgrimage to Rome that became an anti-regime demonstration.[28] Despite concessions to the Church, Cánovas denied it the complete independence from State control demanded vociferously by the clergy and the Catholic press. The government's retention of regalist rights ensured that the historic tensions affecting civil-ecclesiastical relations would continue.

Conflicts appeared before the ink on the 1876 constitution had dried. During the summer, the Catholic press complained that the government was failing to implement Article 11 by allowing Protestant churches to post signs on their doors announcing religious services. A second furor developed when the sub-governor of the island of Mahón, where Protestants had established a church and three schools, forbade any advertisement of religious services; he even prohibited singing within the church on the grounds that it could be heard outside its walls and therefore constituted a "public manifestation" under the terms of Article 11. This action took Cánovas by surprise, but the clamor raised by the clergy and the Catholic press forced him to issue an order containing highly restrictive guidelines on the interpretation of the phrase "public manifestations."[29] The Mahón controversy was the first in a long series of incidents involving the rights of Spanish Protestants as defined in Article 11. The hierarchy maintained constant pressure on successive governments to enforce the article's terms as rigidly as possible, thereby creating the circumstances for periodic conflict with the civil authorities.

If Protestantism was a red flag certain to provoke a strong clerical reaction, the

28. The pilgrimage was the idea of Cándido Nocedal, a former Moderate minister, who directed Carlist political forces in Spain, and his son Ramón. It was intended to embarrass the Cánovas government and affirm in spectacular fashion the commitment of Spanish Catholics to the Carlist cause. Some eight thousand pilgrims journeyed to Rome, where the refusal of Ramón Nocedal to call upon the Spanish ambassador to the kingdom of Italy (which, of course, Carlists rejected), provoked Cánovas to summon Nocedal home. The pilgrims were harassed by the customs authorities on their return. Domingo Benavides Gómez, *Democracia y cristianismo en la España de la Restauración, 1875–1931* (Madrid, 1978), pp. 31–34; *La Cruz* (1876), pp. 606, 617.

29. Beck, *A Time of Triumph and Sorrow*, p. 59; "Presidente del Consejo de Ministros: Circular," October 23, 1876; *El Consultor de los Párrocos* (1876), no. 47, pp. 379–81.

role of the Church in education was another. Cánovas attempted to strike a balance between the clergy's demand for a pervasive role in all aspects of education and the liberal State's determination to retain authority over schools and universities.[30] The Church believed that Article 2 of the concordat, with its stipulation that teaching must conform to the "purity of the faith's doctrine," meant that the clergy should possess significant control over curriculum and the appointment of teachers. The bishops demanded that "the government should recognize its obligation to defend religious and moral truth since Catholicism is the official religion of the State."[31]

In 1878, the prime minister presented the text of a proposed education law. It reaffirmed the concordat's article allowing the bishops to carry out inspections of public primary and secondary schools to guarantee that teaching "touching upon dogma and morals" conformed "to the doctrine of the Roman, Apostolic and Catholic religion."[32] Publication of the draft legislation provoked a whirlwind of controversy despite its apparent deference to the Church. Bishops complained that the proposed law reaffirmed the State's supremacy over the school system in an area of activity where the Church demanded complete autonomy: "The authority of the government . . . exclusively directs . . . and supervises education: the authority . . . of the Church directs nothing."[33] Although the proposed law declared that sanctions would be imposed on teachers failing to respect Catholic doctrine and morality in the classroom, the hierarchy believed that this provision did not go far enough. The bishops also objected to the legislation's failure to make specific mention of the Church's right to establish its own schools. And, for good measure, they protested against the clauses establishing obligatory primary education as a violation of parents' rights to decide whether their children should attend school or not.[34]

Between 1876 and 1881, Cánovas followed a policy of limited concessions to the Church. But he had no intention of giving it a blank check. After the dismissal of university professors in 1875, the prime minister resisted relentless pressure for the imposition of a narrow clerical imprint on the country's intellectual life. Government authorization of the Institución Libre de Enseñanza, founded in 1876 by Francisco Giner de los Ríos, led to harsh criticism from the clergy. A primary and secondary school with a modern curriculum neutral on religion, the Institución Libre was attacked as nothing less than "a revolutionary club" that would lead "to the ruin of Catholicism."[35] In 1878, the government also resisted clerical efforts to

30. A full discussion of the debate over education in the early Restoration can be found in Yvonne Turin, *La educación y la escuela en España de 1874 a 1902,* trans. J. Hernández (Madrid, 1967).

31. "Discurso del Señor Obispo de Salamanca," October 27, 1881, *La Cruz* (1881), p. 603.

32. Ibid. (1878), p. 577.

33. "Exposición que El Excmo. e Ilmo. Señor Arzobispo de Granada con los dignos sufragáneos . . . ha dirigido al Congreso," ibid., p. 507.

34. Robles Muñoz, *Insurrección o legalidad,* pp. 181–83.

35. *El Consultor de los Párrocos* (1876), no. 26, p. 207.

amend a proposed press law forbidding direct attacks on religion to include indirect criticism as well.[36]

Tensions inherent in civil-ecclesiastical relations as a result of the continuation of the regalist tradition became more acute during periods of Liberal party rule. As the ideological heirs of the Progressives, Liberals viewed the Church's privileges with suspicion and resented clerical pretensions to control the nation's intellectual life. After becoming prime minister in 1881, Sagasta reestablished academic freedom for university professors and restored to their chairs the professors dismissed in 1875. These measures, said the bishop of Calahorra, "injured the rights of the Catholic Church, the unique depository of revelation, master of the truth, outside of which there is no salvation," while a group of laymen wrote directly to the king stressing the necessity of "protecting the Church from any attack on the part of the official teaching establishment."[37] Further controversy developed over the government's project for a new law code that would permit civil marriages for "unbelievers" on the grounds that the State could not employ coercive measures against Catholics who no longer observed their religion. The hierarchy launched a general attack against the proposal, the bishop of Barcelona declaring that civil marriage was nothing more than "a form of public concubinage."[38]

These conflicts took on a sharper edge than they had had under the Cánovas government, but Sagasta's attitude towards the Church did not differ dramatically from his predecessor's. Upon taking office for the first time, the prime minister emphasized that he did not intend to introduce radical changes in the government's ecclesiastical policy.[39] When all is said and done, Cánovas and Sagasta saw the settlement worked out during the regime's first decade as a pragmatic arrangement directed towards reconciling the Church with the monarchy and the liberal State. Both recognized the need for equilibrium between the clergy's demand that government legislation should reinforce the regime's Catholic character with the limited pluralism inherent in the liberal political system. The balance between these two objectives was never steady during the 1880s and 1890s, but it was sufficient to prevent the issue of the Church and its privileges from disrupting the Restoration's stability.[40] Despite the hostility of much of Catholic opinion to the regime and frequent civil-ecclesiastical conflicts, the bishops, by and large, did not press their

36. *La Cruz* (1878), p. 573.

37. "La circular última sobre instrucción pública del Señor Obispo de Calahorra," March 10, 1881; "Exposición de la Unión Católica contra la última circular del ministro de Fomento," March 6, 1881, *La Cruz* (1881), pp. 333–34, 330–32.

38. *La Cruz* (1881), p. 689.

39. Robles Muñoz, *Insurrección o legalidad,* p. 279.

40. Upon his return to power in 1883, for example, Cánovas found himself embroiled in a strident controversy with certain bishops, notably Bishops Sancha of Ávila and Casas Souto of Plasencia, who had raised strong objections to the lecture of Professor Miguel Morayta inaugurating the academic year of 1884–1885 in the Universidad Central (Madrid). Morayta's defense of academic freedom in the presence of a government minister, the former "Historic" Alejandro Pidal y Mon, led to clerical denunciations,

complaints too far, recognizing the practical advantages enjoyed by the Church as a result of its official status. Further, the succession of Pope Leo XIII (1878–1903) to the papacy reinforced the Alfonsine monarchy. The pontiff discreetly recognized its legitimacy by stressing the necessity of political independence on the part of the Spanish Church, an independence that implied dissociation from Carlism.[41]

Division and Disarray, 1881–1885

The divisions of Catholic opinion over the liberal State's legitimacy gave the politicians of the dynastic parties a breathing space that reduced the danger of an effective political challenge from vociferous defenders of clerical interests. Conflict among Catholics accepting or rejecting the Restoration undermined all efforts to forge unity among the faithful. Spanish Catholicism was no stranger to internecine struggles, but during the early Restoration these divisions took on a sharper edge, to the point of "endless insubordinations, irreverences, rebellions . . . including hostility and aversion towards the Holy See and the Spanish hierarchy."[42] Politicians and supporters of the dynastic parties, most of whom were practicing Catholics, saw no contradiction between Catholicism and the liberal political system. Carlists and a heterogeneous group, remnants of the "neo-Catholics" and the "Historics," either rejected the regime outright or believed it seriously deformed because it was too permissive on a range of issues, particularly religious liberty and education.

They agreed on little else. Carlists insisted on the installation of the pretender as king, the creation of some form of a corporatist State, and reestablishment of the constitutional autonomy of the kingdom's historic regions destroyed by liberal administrative reorganization.[43] Supporters of the Isabelline monarchy during its last days saw this program as archaic and doomed to failure. They yearned to return to

street demonstrations, and bitter parliamentary debate in which supporters of the Church demanded Morayta's dismissal. The prime minister refused to take action and lodged a formal protest with the Vatican over the violent rhetoric of Bishop Casas Souto. Cánovas was also the object of strong criticism for his decision in 1893 to permit the construction of a Protestant chapel on Beneficencia Street in Madrid. Sagasta faced similar protests in 1896 when he reappointed Odón de Buen, whose works had been condemned by the papacy, to the chair of natural history in the University of Barcelona. José Andrés-Gallego, *La política religiosa en España, 1889–1913* (Madrid, 1975), pp. 22–24; "Construcción de una capilla protestante," *La Cruz* (1893), pp. 30–49; "Reposición de un catedrático hereje condenado por León XIII en una cátedra de Barcelona," *La Cruz* (1896), p. 409.

41. Robles Muñoz, *Insurrección o legalidad*, p. 263.

42. Vicente Cárcel Ortí, *León XIII y los católicos españoles* (Pamplona, 1988), p. 22.

43. Carlism was far from unified. Carlists were divided about the wisdom of the rising that began in 1872 and ended in failure in 1876. Moreover, the tendency of the pretender's delegate in Spain between 1879 and 1885, Cándido Nocedal, to emphasize Carlism as a movement primarily concerned with the defense of Catholicism rather than one committed to the installation of the Carlist dynasty, created internal difficulties. Moderate Carlists resented the intransigence and authoritarian style of Nocedal's leadership of the party. Following his death in 1885, the differences between Don Carlos, the Carlist pretender, and Nocedal's followers, now led by his son Ramón, produced a total break. In 1889, Nocedal es-

the authoritarian, centralized State identified with Narváez between 1866 and 1868, believing that only a strong government could prevent revolution and strengthen Catholicism as the nation's established religion.

The aggravation of Catholic political divisions during the early Restoration developed from several causes. Although the regime's politicians worried constantly about the danger of Carlist rebellion, the movement's military defeat in 1876 shifted attention away from armed struggle to the arena of public opinion within a system that, for all its deficiencies, allowed a relatively free press and, within limits, the expression of political dissent. Even as its military fortunes declined, and despite its archaic, romantic vision of the Catholic Spain of the past, Carlism produced in Cándido and Ramón Nocedal, father and son, two masters of modern political propaganda. Skilled polemicists and journalists, they aspired to make their newspaper, *El Siglo Futuro,* the "active organizer of the Catholic masses," an objective never before achieved in the history of the confessional press.[44] Their ideas, derived primarily from Donoso Cortés, drew a terrifying picture of Christian civilization threatened by an "apocalyptic" catastrophe at the hands of diverse "revolutionary" forces, including liberalism, socialism, republicanism, and anarchism. The Nocedals maintained that no compromise was possible between Christianity and the new social and political movements of the time. Because religion alone guaranteed civilization's survival, the State's interests must be subordinated to those of the Church.[45]

The Nocedals largely attained their goal. *El Siglo Futuro* became the daily of

tablished the Partido Integrista Español, which remained intransigently Carlist in ideology, that is, deeply hostile to liberalism and the liberal State but free of dynastic entanglements. Javier Real Cuesta, *El Carlismo Vasco* (Madrid, 1985), pp. 21–22, 108–13; Solange Hibbs-Lissorgues, *Iglesia, prensa y sociedad en España, 1868–1904* (Alicante, 1995), pp. 127–28. The battle between Nocedal and supporters of the pretender during the 1880s, which led to the formation of the Integrist party, is described in Hibbs-Lissorgues, pp. 319–44, and María Obieta Villalonga, *Los integristas guipuzcoanos, 1888–1898* (Zarauz, 1996), pp. 37–92. Ramón Nocedal defined his new organization as "a political party which wishes to bring to the government of Spain the Catholic principles of our ancestors." Quoted in Obieta Villalonga, *Los integristas guipuzcoanos,* p. 311.

44. Campomar Fornieles, *La cuestión religiosa en la Restauración,* p. 56. Despite the often precarious financial situation of *El Siglo Futuro,* the newspaper became a "prestigious integrist publication with sufficient weight . . . to orient the great religious manifestations of the Restoration." Hibbs-Lissorgues, *Iglesia, prensa y sociedad en España,* pp. 119–20.

45. Alfonso Botti, *Cielo y dinero: el nacionalcatolicismo en España, 1881–1975* (Madrid, 1992), p. 34. The Integrist party saw politics as nothing less than "the act of applying on a grand scale the principles and rules of Religion to human societies." Quoted in Obieta Villalonga, *Los integristas guipuzcoanos,* p. 281. The idea of an inextricable link between Catholicism and the nation received a brilliant intellectual justification during this period in the work of Marcelino Menéndez y Pelayo (1856–1912), *Historia de los heterodoxos españoles* (3 vols., Madrid, 1880–1881). The author shared the widespread view among Spanish Catholics that the most glorious epoch in the country's history corresponded to the dominance of Catholicism until eighteenth-century bureaucrats and thinkers began to undermine Church and religion, a process continued by liberalism. Although Carlists welcomed the ideological ammunition provided by Menéndez Pelayo, they were less enthusiastic about his discreet criticism of the thought of Donoso Cortés. Menéndez Pelayo was uncomfortable with the aggressive propagandistic use of his work by "neo-Catholics" and Carlists, although he was unwilling to challenge them directly. Campomar Fornieles, *La cuestión religiosa en la Restauración,* pp. 75–80.

choice for the lower clergy soon after its foundation in 1874.[46] In provincial cities, a network of Carlist newspapers followed the Nocedal line. What was significant about *El Siglo Futuro* was less that it outstripped the influence of the Catholic press, urging some form of accommodation with the Restoration, than that it functioned autonomously beyond the control of either the papacy or the hierarchy. The Nocedals directed the deep antiliberalism of clergy and laity into a powerful source of opposition to the regime.

The Nocedals' growing influence occurred at a crucial moment in the Catholic Church's history. The succession of Leo XII to the papacy in 1878 brought to the papal throne a more pragmatic figure than Pius IX had been. Although the new pontiff did not disavow the *Syllabus of Errors,* he developed a more flexible response to the political evolution of European governments, which was most successfully realized through an accommodation with the French Third Republic during the 1890s. The pope attached priority to ending the chronic political and dynastic divisions prevailing among Spanish Catholics, although, to judge from the detailed reports submitted by papal nuncios in Madrid, he was aware of the formidable obstacles to achieving this goal without alienating clergy and laity committed to Carlism.

The dream of uniting Spanish Catholics to defend the interests of the Church, rather than their respective dynastic and political causes, was not new. The formation in 1869 of the Association of Catholics to combat revolutionary legislation represented the first serious attempt to forge a united front including Carlists and supporters of Isabel II. But, poorly organized, the Association failed dismally to elect pro-clerical deputies to parliament. The Carlist rebellion that began in 1872 ended this attempt at uniting Catholics in an effective organization free of dynastic entanglements.

As Cánovas consolidated the new regime, several laymen once prominent in the Association of Catholics, including the former "Historic" Alejandro Pidal y Mon and the moderate Carlists León Carbonero y Sol, editor of *La Cruz,* and the conde de Orgaz, advanced a proposal for the formation of a broadly based Unión Católica "to defend religious interests attacked by revolution."[47] They argued that the nation's "bulwark of faith" was threatened not only by antireligious forces but also "by the lack of unity among Catholics." The Unión's advocates attempted to appease divided Catholic opinion by declaring that the new organization would be nonpolitical and would regard the *Syllabus of Errors* as its "credo and norm of con-

46. Bishop Casañas y Pagés of Urgel informed the papal nuncio, for example, that "nearly all the clergy of Catalonia" subscribed to *El Siglo Futuro.* Bishop Salvador Casañas y Pagés to the papal nuncio, Mariano Rampolla, February 25, 1883, *Instrucciones secretas a los nuncios de España,* p. 278.

47. "Circular de los representantes de la Unión Católica en Madrid a los Señores Obispos," January 14, 1881, *La Cruz* (1881), p. 187. The proposal was a direct imitation of a similar association formed in the French Third Republic at the initiative of Bishop Freppel of Angers. Cárcel Ortí, *León XIII y los católicos españoles,* p. 25.

duct."[48] This program embodied many of the Church's objections to the Restoration's liberal underpinnings. The new organization sought "to reconquer Catholic unity . . . ; to ensure that teaching would be Christian . . . ; that the clergy would live with decency and independence . . . ; that the religious orders would be able to spread without hindrance . . . ; [and] that licentious practices of impiety and blasphemy would be repressed."[49]

Supporters of the proposal, aware of the hostility of Cándido and Ramón Nocedal towards any organization not specifically committed to their dynastic cause and political program, sought the approval of leading members of the hierarchy. The response was mixed. Archbishop Monzón of Granada feared that the project failed to take into account the deep divisions prevailing among Catholics. He warned that the Unión Católica ran the risk of stimulating more intense discord among clergy and laity.[50] Cardinal Moreno of Toledo, primate of the Spanish Church, although sympathetic, insisted that the proposed organization should be purely religious in character and should function under episcopal direction.[51]

This restrictive interpretation disappointed Pidal, who hoped that the Unión Católica would develop into a Catholic political party similar to the Center party in Germany. But the Unión's advocates had to accept the more limited association proposed by Moreno, who issued the document of foundation in January 1881.[52] Although the papal nuncio, aware of the minefields of Spanish Catholicism, initially viewed the proposal with caution, Leo XIII approved the new organization in May 1881.[53] The creation of a nonpolitical association authorized by the pope and supported by much of the hierarchy to defend the Church's interests on the basis of an openly antiliberal ideology would seem to have offered a program that Catholic opinion could accept, whatever its dynastic loyalties.

Instead, formation of the Unión Católica provoked furious controversy. Although Pidal y Mon and his moderate Carlist supporters stressed the association's political neutrality and its determination to oppose government policies judged

48. "Circular de los representantes de la Unión Católica," p. 187.

49. Ibid., p. 188.

50. Quoted in Campomar Fornieles, *La cuestión religiosa en la Restauración*, p. 65. Even Bishop José María Urquinaona of Barcelona, who had been severely criticized by intransigent Carlists, believed that the proposed Unión Católica would aggravate dissension within his diocese, where the battle between the two camps had become exceptionally virulent. He reluctantly accepted the Unión's establishment but argued that it must be politically neutral if it was to stand any chance of succeeding. Even moderate Catholic priests and laity in Catalonia opposed to the intransigence of the Nocedal line entertained doubts about the creation of a Catholic political party in the form of the Unión Católica. They believed that such a party would serve "to increase existing divisions" among Catholics. Hibbs-Lissorgues, *Iglesia, prensa y sociedad en España*, pp. 150–51, 216.

51. Campomar Fornieles, *La cuestión religiosa en la Restauración*, pp. 68–69.

52. "Bases constitutivas de la Unión Católica," January 19, 1881, *La Cruz* (1881), pp. 234–36. The first organizational meeting of the new association was held in the cardinal's Madrid residence on February 14. A majority of the bishops expressed their support, although six had clear reservations about the project. *La Unión Católica: datos para su historia* (Madrid, 1881), p. 14.

53. Cárcel Ortí, *León XIII y los católicos españoles*, pp. 27–28.

unacceptable by the Church, they intended it to function within the legally established order. For Cándido and Ramón Nocedal, the Unión Católica's nonpolitical character signified neutrality on the dynastic question and implied acceptance of the liberal State. As the direct representative of the Carlist pretender, Cándido Nocedal directed the movement on the basis of a simple principle, that every Spanish Catholic must be a Carlist. Carlism and Catholicism were inextricably linked; one could not exist without the other. "If there is some good Catholic who is not a Carlist, he is either unconcerned with or does not understand politics," declared one bishop in his assessment of the movement's influence.[54] For the Nocedals and their supporters, no compromise was possible either on the dynastic question or on the issue of accepting the regime as the nation's legitimate government.

From the pages of *El Siglo Futuro,* the Nocedals savagely attacked Pidal and the Unión Católica. The Unión was described as nothing less than a betrayal of Catholicism by weak-kneed opportunists prepared to sell out to the liberal State. Foundation of the Unión ignited a propagandistic civil war between those believing that the Church must come to terms in some measure with political reality and those maintaining that it could defeat its principal enemy, liberalism, only by intransigent opposition to the regime through Carlism.

As the battle raged during 1881 and 1882, the Nocedals subjected the Unión Católica and its advocates to further barrages of violent rhetoric. In provincial cities, the local Carlist press followed their example and surged to the attack.[55] Pidal and his supporters exercised little influence over Catholic opinion outside Madrid and could not match their opponents' extensive propaganda network, based on *El Siglo Futuro* and provincial Carlist newspapers.[56] Emotions spread beyond the press to involve the clergy. Bishop Salvador Casañas of Urgel, a Carlist sympathizer, criticized his episcopal colleagues in Barcelona and Tarragona for publicly opposing Carlist conduct during the controversy. According to the bishop, hundreds of Carlists attending Mass with general communion in the Barcelona cathedral were so disgusted by the local prelate's sermon to this effect that they abandoned the church in the middle of the service to receive the sacrament elsewhere. The situation had so deteriorated, claimed the prelate of Urgel, that "an abyss" had opened between the bishop of Barcelona and his clergy. In Tarragona, where many priests sympathized with Carlism, the archbishop closed the seminary because it had become a "center of ignoble and almost criminal in-

54. Casañas to Rampolla, February 25, 1883, in *Instrucciones secretas a los nuncios de España,* p. 279.

55. In Santander, for example, the local organ of the anti-Unión faction, *La Verdad,* scarcely let a day pass "without making the Unión the object of criticism . . . ," Julio de la Cueva Merino, *Clericales y anticlericales: el conflicto entre confesionalidad y secularización en Cantabria, 1875–1923* (Santander, 1994), pp. 85–86. The civil war that engulfed the Catholic press over the Unión Católica is described in Hibbs-Lissorgues, *Iglesia, prensa y sociedad en España,* pp. 143–74.

56. Benavides Gómez, *Democracia y cristianismo,* p. 89. In Santander, for example, supporters of the Unión were poorly organized and lacked a newspaper to advocate their views. Cueva Merino, *Clericales y anticlericales,* p. 86.

trigues," meaning that the students and faculty sympathized with the anti-Unión faction. In Salamanca, Bishop Martínez Izquierdo was ostracized by the city's "Catholic cream," many of whom stirred the waters of controversy with local Jesuits, avid followers of the *El Siglo Futuro* line.[57]

Even Leo XIII's 1882 encyclical *Cum Multa*, appealing for calm and unity, failed to quiet the controversy.[58] The intensity of the debate over the Unión Católica destroyed any possibility that it could function effectively. Papal and episcopal support failed to overcome the traditional identification of Catholic opinion with Carlism. In 1883, the nuncio, Mariano Rampolla, sent a diplomatic but firm letter to the bishops urging them to curb the politicization of the clergy, Catholic organizations, and the confessional press.[59] Although Carlists, the Nocedals, and *El Siglo Futuro* were not mentioned by name, the letter left little doubt that they were the principal culprits behind the disruption and divisions of Spanish Catholicism.[60]

By 1884 the short and controversial history of the Unión came to an end, as Pidal, despairing of its future, entered the government of Cánovas. Even the Unión's disintegration failed to bring peace, as another divisive controversy broke out with the 1884 publication of a slim volume, *Is Liberalism a Sin?*, by a leading religious propagandist, fervent Carlist, and collaborator of the Nocedals, the Catalan priest Félix Sardá y Salvany. He used many of the hackneyed philosophical arguments found in clerical attacks on liberalism, particularly criticizing its exaltation of individualism and rationalism. But Sardá's book was primarily a thinly disguised assault on Pidal and the liberal State designed by Cánovas. Sardá criticized liberalism as "a complex of false ideas" and declared that to be a liberal is "more sinful than to be a blasphemer, thief, adulterer or murderer." The most repugnant thing of all

57. Casañas to Rampolla, February 25, 1883, p. 275; "Disolución y clausura del seminario conciliar de Tarragona," *La Cruz* (1883), pp. 48–49; *Memorias del P. Luis Martín, General de la Compañía de Jesús, 1846–1906*, ed. J. R. Eguillor, M. Revuelta González, and R. M. Sanz de Diego (2 vols., Rome, 1988), vol. 1, p. 553. The identification of many Jesuits with the Nocedals' position remained a constant preoccupation of Father Martín even before he became head of the order's province of Castile in 1887. The regular clergy massively supported the antiliberal line. Cárcel Ortí, *León XIII y los católicos españoles*, p. 57.

58. Benavides Gómez, *Democracia y cristianismo*, p. 85. In Valencia, for example, *Cum Multa* had virtually no effect. In fact, the papal intervention intensified the battle between supporters and opponents of the Unión Católica. Vicente Cárcel Ortí, *Historia de la Iglesia de Valencia* (2 vols., Valencia, 1987), vol. 2, p. 655. The papal nuncio admitted the same: "Notwithstanding the counsels given by His Holiness, [the conflicts] are still continuing in some parts of Spain scandalizing the faithful." Quoted in Hibbs-Lissorgues, *Iglesia, prensa y sociedad en España*, p. 207. In 1882 another battle divided bishops and clergy over a proposal of Cándido Nocedal for a pilgrimage to Rome in reparation for the forced removal of the pope from the Quirinal Palace by the kingdom of Italy. Arguing that the pilgrimage must be "purely and exclusively Catholic," the organizers announced that supporters of an accommodation with the Restoration, whom they derisively labeled *mestizos*, would not be allowed to participate. Quoted in Campomar Fornieles, *La cuestión religiosa en la Restauración*, p. 70.

59. The text of the nuncio's letter of April 30, 1883, is reproduced in Cárcel Ortí, *León XIII y los católicos españoles*, pp. 58–64.

60. On the Catholic press, for example, the nuncio declared that it could not "in any way" seek "to deceive the faithful with false displays of orthodoxy," a clear allusion to the tactics of Carlist publications. Quoted in ibid., p. 61. Rampolla's letter represented "a serious warning to the Carlist party" in the view of Robles Muñoz, *Insurrección o legalidad*, p. 387.

was the belief that "liberalism and Catholicism were in any way compatible." Rather, they were "irreconcilable and hostile" to one another.[61] The book quickly went through eight editions (it would enjoy a similar popularity in Franco's Spain), and provoked another round of polemic.

By 1885, the nuncio's frustration with the Nocedals' often brilliant evasive tactics before the papacy's attempt to unify Spanish Catholics reached the breaking point, when the Carlist press began to attack Leo XIII. When *El Siglo Futuro* argued that the bishops were not obliged to follow the nuncio's direction, Rampolla took action. The Vatican condemned the newspaper's stand as the papacy began to abandon the caution with which it dealt with the divisive issue of Carlism, although the lower clergy remained loyal to the Nocedals.[62] Despite their propagandistic genius, they miscalculated. The bishops' loyalty to the Holy See and their adverse reaction to attacks on Leo XIII with few exceptions effectively alienated them from Carlism. Although the Nocedals won the battle against the Unión Católica, they began to lose the war through their intemperate journalistic assaults on the papacy. The death of Cándido Nocedal in 1885 and the decision of his son to break with Carlism and establish his Integrist party in 1889 also contributed to the further fragmentation of Catholic antiliberalism, although it remained on the scene to agitate clergy and laity for decades to come.[63]

The Search for Political Unity, 1886–1897

The intense conflicts of the early and mid-1880s revealed again that the old dream of uniting Spanish Catholics in an effective organization, political or otherwise, was as far from reality as ever. But this was not a dream to be abandoned easily. During the mid-1890s the idea was taken up by Cardinal Antonio María Cascajares of Valladolid, an ex-military man turned priest, who believed that the moment was opportune for the creation of a Catholic political party, inspired in part by Leo XIII's 1894 exhortation urging Spanish Catholics to resolve their differences. The pontiff explicitly praised Queen Regent María Cristina (1885–1902) for

61. Félix Sardá y Salvany, *¿El liberalismo es pecado?* (2d ed., Barcelona, 1884), pp. 14, 20, 26. The book became "the bible of integrism" and a "practical guide about how to combat liberalism." Hibbs-Lissorgues, *Iglesia, prensa y sociedad en España*, pp. 263, 269. The best treatment of this work, its publication history and ideas, inspired by Donoso Cortés, is by Hibbs-Lissorgues, pp. 261–72. Sardá y Salvany (1844–1916) was a well-known author of popular religious tracts and editor of the *Revista Popular* of Barcelona, which had long supported the Nocedal line and vigorously opposed the Unión Católica. For further details of his biography, see José Ricart Torrents, *Así era el Doctor Sardá y Salvany* (Barcelona, 1966).

62. Robles Muñoz, *Insurrección o legalidad*, pp. 388–89.

63. About thirty Carlist publications and a substantial number of Carlists abandoned the movement to join Nocedal's Integrists. Andrés-Gallego, *La política religiosa*, p. 30. Divisions among the Jesuits between supporters of the new Integrist party and followers of Carlism caused fierce dissension at the order's provincial congregation held at Loyola in 1889. The "fire of battle" between the two camps raged through several sessions. *Memorias del P. Luis Martín*, vol. 1, p. 901.

her "piety and devotion to the Church."[64] Cascajares was not alone in perceiving the similarities of the governing parties and criticizing them for neglecting the country's social and economic problems in favor of their narrow political interests. He believed that the time had come for the foundation of a conservative Catholic party "to Christianize legislation through loyal and sincere acceptance of the monarchy of Alfonso XIII."[65] Although the cardinal schemed for years to bring about the creation of such a party, he was no more successful than advocates of the Unión Católica had been. As long as the dynastic parties controlled elections through the exercise of corruption and manipulation, there was no possibility that a new party could break their political monopoly. Moreover, neither Carlists nor their new ideological cousins, the Integrists of Ramón Nocedal, would accept a party committed to acceptance of the liberal constitutional monarchy.

The failure to create a Catholic party, or even an effective nonpolitical organization capable of uniting Catholics, deprived the Church of leverage in its dealings with governments of the Restoration.[66] Nor did the institution have at its disposal other means of bringing direct pressure on the regime. The Catholic press could match neither the circulation nor the influence of its liberal counterparts. In 1887, an edition of Madrid's *El Liberal* contained more pages each day than the city's several Catholic newspapers combined, while no Catholic paper equaled the circulation (fifty to one hundred thousand copies) of journals such as *El Imparcial*.[67] The real weakness of the Catholic press lay in the chronic bickering and mutual exchange of insults between newspapers loyal to the ruling dynasty and those opposed to it. The result, according to one disgusted critic, served only to intensify "the inflamed struggle of factions" among Catholics.[68] Given the sterile polemics filling the pages of Catholic newspapers, it was scarcely surprising that the liberal press, "whose machines vomited forth an untold number of copies," became "the daily food of many . . . who carry the sign of the cross on their brows, without realizing that the most formidable enemy of that same cross is the newspapers that they are reading."[69] To counter the influence of the liberal press, bishops often forbade the faithful to read it, although without much effect, to judge by the frequency of such prohibitions.

64. Quoted in Andrés-Gallego, *La política religiosa*, p. 62.

65. Quoted in ibid., p. 65. For a full discussion of the cardinal's project, see ibid., pp. 61–66.

66. The failure of the Unión Católica did not dissuade some bishops from attempting to organize Catholics through the formation of new associations that fell directly under episcopal control in an effort to avoid dissension on the dynastic issue. The first Catholic Congress in 1889 was an early example of the new formula of an apolitical organization operating under the immediate supervision of the hierarchy.

67. *La Unión Católica*, June 16, 1887. It has been estimated that the circulation of the Catholic press, including periodicals, was 279,765 copies of a total national circulation of 1,610,600 for all publications. Palomares Ibáñez, "La recuperación económica de la Iglesia española," p. 169.

68. José Polo Benito, *Del periodismo católico* (Madrid, 1908), p. 23.

69. *La Cruz* (1907), p. 311.

Given the extent and intensity of the political divisions among Catholics, the Church had no choice but to accept the Restoration's ecclesiastical settlement with its contradictory mingling of privilege and regalist restraints. The hierarchy compensated for the failure to create a united front by solidifying its links with Catholic notables from the aristocracy and middle classes who accepted the liberal constitutional monarchy. During the 1880s and 1890s, before the era of modern mass politics reared its head in Spain, the clerical leadership relied upon these notables in periodic campaigns to influence government policy.[70] None was more prominent than Claudio López Bru, marqués de Comillas (1853–1925). Heir to a large fortune based on mining, banking, shipping, and colonial investments, the marqués's personal loyalty to the reigning dynasty made him an ideal figure to defend the Church's interests through his connections with the regime's political oligarchy.[71]

The hierarchy also became adept at cultivating the support of the influential. According to a 1890 report of the nunciature to the Vatican, a number of bishops were well connected to the Restoration's ruling elites. Cascajares, then bishop of Calahorra, was on good terms with the royal family. Bishop Martínez Vigil of Oviedo maintained close relations with the influential Pidal brothers, both prominent Conservative politicians, while Archbishop Moreno of Granada had ties to the "heads of the actual regime and with other high military and civil personages in Madrid." Similarly, Bishop Bryan y Livermore of Cartagena was related to Francisco Silvela, Cánovas's successor as leader of the Conservative party.[72] Even on relatively minor concerns, the ecclesiastical authorities used their social connections to advance the Church's interests. In 1893 they sought the help of a group of women, including "grandees of Spain, powerful because of their wealth," and others "united by family ties to influential men in all political parties," in a campaign to force closure of a Protestant chapel in Madrid.[73] Although the effort failed, the women gained easy access to Prime Minister Sagasta, who heard them out in spite of the Liberal party's dislike of the restricted religious toleration established by the constitution.

Sagasta's willingness to receive the delegation provides a small testimony to the

70. Despite frequent statements by the bishops that the Church was apolitical, it functioned within the Restoration as a "pressure group" or lobby of a distinctly modern kind. Fernando García de Cortázar, "La nueva historia de la Iglesia contemporánea de España," in *Historiografía española contemporánea: X Coloquio del Centro de Investigaciones Hispánicas de la Universidad de Pau: balance y resumen*, ed. Manuel Tuñón de Lara, (Madrid, 1980), p. 208.

71. Although some members of the hierarchy believed that Comillas was "the person called providentially" to play a key role in the formation of a Catholic party along the lines suggested by Cascajares, the marqués believed that such an initiative was ill advised given the fate of the Unión Católica. He also doubted that a new party would be successful. Andrés-Gallego, *La política religiosa*, p. 67. The standard biography of Comillas is Constantino Bayle, *El segundo marqués de Comillas, Don Claudio López Bru* (Madrid, 1928).

72. Antonio Vico, "Informe sobre el episcopado y los cabildos de España," December 31, 1890, in Cárcel Ortí, *León XIII y los católicos españoles*, pp. 213, 236, 242, 246.

73. *La Cruz* (1893), p. 38.

success of Cánovas's ecclesiastical policy that sought to remove the issue of the Church and its privileges from the realm of divisive public controversy. The issue was by no means neutralized, but the *modus vivendi* between the liberal State and the Church worked well enough during the late 1880s and early 1890s to prevent a full-blown crisis. There were examples of genuine compromise between the civil and ecclesiastical authorities even in periods of Liberal party rule. In 1893–1894, the Sagasta government proposed a reform of secondary education that called for the introduction of new subjects in the social and natural sciences. These curricular changes were criticized immediately by the hierarchy as "positivistic and egoistical." But quiet negotiations between the government and the bishops holding seats in the senate produced a compromise providing for the creation of new positions in "Religion and Morality" along with the other new subjects.[74] For the first time since 1868, the teaching of religion was allowed in public secondary schools, a concession to the Church that Cánovas had never dared make.[75]

But the tensions inherent in the existence of a privileged established Church within the liberal political system never disappeared. The ambiguities and contradictions of the Church's position during the early Restoration were illustrated by the observations of the moderate Catholic press upon the assassination of Cánovas in August 1897. That the prime minister was a practicing Catholic who had restored many of the privileges enjoyed by the Church prior to 1868 could not be denied. The regime's hostility towards social and political radicalism, a desirable objective in the eyes of Catholic opinion, deserved recognition. Cánovas earned praise for his "civic virtues and affection for the country." But these positive achievements were vitiated by his political education "in the liberal school," which caused him to open "the frontiers . . . of the nation to all the liberties of perdition," which served "as a powerful arm to de-Catholicize a people who before had been devout and believing."[76]

The Church and the Disaster of 1898

The assassination of Cánovas occurred in the midst of the first serious crisis faced by the Restoration since the political battles of 1875–1876. The regime sub-

74. Turin, *La educación y la escuela en España*, p. 312.

75. Manuel de Puelles Benítez, "Secularización y enseñanza en España," in *España entre dos siglos, 1875–1931: continuidad y cambio*, ed. José Luis García Delgado (Madrid, 1991), pp. 201–2. Religion classes were not obligatory, however.

76. *La Cruz* (1897), p. 197. This assessment of Cánovas was also held by the nunciature in Madrid. In a 1896 report to the Vatican, Cánovas was described as a "master of doctrinaire liberalism . . . so much in vogue in Europe." Far from proclaiming "the restoration of religious principles," Cánovas "adopted the system of transactions, and sustained errors and the spirit of the [liberal] school, which have caused so many convulsions not only in the religious and moral order, but also in the political and social." Alejandro Bavona, "Informe sobre la acción católica en el orden público," December 1896, in Cárcel Ortí, *León XIII y los católicos españoles*, p. 901.

dued the first Cuban rising for independence (1868–1878), but the question of the island's future remained unresolved. Partisans of the colonial status quo struggled with a number of groups favoring some form of autonomy for Cuba. Political infighting between and within the dynastic parties, the pressure of the military, and a jingoistic press prevented the achievement of a settlement that might have avoided or at least postponed another rebellion against Spanish rule.[77]

The failure to resolve the Cuban problem left the country exposed to a more dangerous situation when the second independence rising began in 1895. Spain was ill prepared to undertake another long and costly colonial conflict, particularly in view of possible American intervention. Neither Cánovas nor Sagasta wanted war, but the Restoration's aging chieftains lacked the decisiveness of purpose that alone could have avoided disaster. The rapid and catastrophic military defeat suffered at the hands of the United States in 1898 not only stripped away the remnants of a great empire in the New World, it also exposed the glaring weaknesses of the liberal political system.

The disaster of 1898 revealed that the opportunistic politics so skillfully practiced by the leaders of the dynastic parties were inadequate to deal with a crisis of serious proportions. Government finances stood on the verge of collapse. The power-sharing consensus between the dynastic parties, so central to the Restoration's stability, was threatened for the first time by divergences over Cuban policy. The Liberals moved gradually to accept substantial autonomy for the island, while the Liberal-Conservatives insisted that concessions could not be made until a military victory was achieved. The catastrophe of 1898 did not threaten the survival of the regime, but it threw its internal contradictions into sharp relief.

The reaction of the Church to the Cuban revolt and the American war marked a significant stage in its attitude towards the Restoration. Clerics had long promoted a Catholic patriotism that identified the nation's past imperial glories with religion. Although on occasion this moved the Church to support the government's foreign policy, as in 1859 when a military expedition was sent to Indo-China, more often than not the clergy viewed the liberal State suspiciously as a representative of patriotic values. The liberal regime was perceived as a "rationalist State" based on the principle that "modern nations are governed . . . with independence of divine and ecclesiastical laws, as if God had nothing to do with . . . government."[78] Clerics saw the liberal State as a devouring monster intent upon exerting control over every aspect of the nation's social, economic, and cultural life. Such a regime could not meet the definition of patriotism as defined by the Church, that is, one committed to advancing the cause of religion. In 1890, Bishop Sancha of Madrid

77. For a detailed analysis of the Cuban question, see Raymond Carr, *Spain, 1808–1939* (Oxford, 1966), pp. 379–88.

78. Salvador Casañas y Pagés, "Exhortación pastoral que sobre la guerra empeñada con los Estados Unidos dirige a sus diocesanos," April 23, 1898, *La Cruz* (1898), p. 476.

warned against confusing the interests of the *patria* with those of the "rationalist State." He expressed the widespread objections of many bishops to the introduction of universal military service by the government because it extended State power into an area where it did not belong. The formation of mass armies through conscription was not patriotic but an example of materialism and rationalism "characteristic of pagan civilization."[79]

These reservations about the role of the military and the regime's concept of patriotism receded upon the outbreak of the Cuban rebellion. The Church backed the war effort unreservedly. In 1896, Bishop Martínez Vigil of Oviedo asserted that patriotism demanded that everyone should support the government, "whatever it might be." Cardinal Cascajares of Valladolid issued a pastoral letter urging that national "discord" be set aside in favor of national unity. "We offer our treasury and our blood to the public powers so that they will feel strength from the energetic backing of the entire nation."[80] Bishops provided similar moral support when the United States entered the conflict. Cardinal Casañas published an extensive theological and philosophical tract affirming the justice of the Spanish cause against the Americans. He saw the conflict as a struggle between the principles of good and evil, between "the Catholic idea and sentiment embodied in the heart of the Spanish" and "that people separated from God and . . . governed by masonic and Protestant sects." The cardinal left no doubt of his belief that divine providence stood on Spain's side. "The Catholic bishops will follow the Spanish squadrons . . . in spirit accompanied by the clergy blessing them in the name of the Lord and pleading for the triumph of their arms," while the American ships would sail "alone and abandoned to the mercy of storms, hearing, perhaps, some diabolical imprecation from certain masonic centers."[81] Bishops everywhere supported public subscriptions designed to raise funds for the war effort. Cardinal Cascajares organized a committee to seek donations for a hospital to care for wounded veterans, while Bishop Martínez Vigil assumed the presidency of a committee of Asturian notables who undertook to recruit a battalion of one thousand men.[82]

The hierarchy's enthusiastic support of the war effort intensified the religiously inspired patriotism that had formed part of the Church's modern tradition since the

79. Quoted in *Crónica del Segundo Congreso Católico Nacional Español celebrado en Zaragoza*, ed. León Carbonero y Sol (Madrid, 1890), p. 48.

80. *El Movimiento Católico*, March 3, 1896; "Pastoral . . . del Cardenal Arzobispo de Valladolid . . . sobre la actual guerra de Cuba," *La Cruz* (1896), p. 334.

81. Casañas y Pagés, "Exhortación pastoral," p. 478. There were many other examples of clerical support for the war effort. The bishop of Coria ordered prayers said in all the churches of his diocese "for the rapid triumph of Spanish arms over the rebels of Cuba." Patriotic fervor even spread to local parishes, as in the village of Blancas (Zaragoza) during the winter of 1896, where the local parish priest organized a rogatory procession that wound its way through the village's narrow lanes in the midst of a snowstorm. *El Movimiento Católico*, January 3, 1896; *La Cruz* (1896), p. 340. Sebastian Balfour has also noted that "The Church played an important role in stirring up jingoist sentiments." *The End of the Spanish Empire, 1898–1923* (Oxford, 1997), p. 98.

82. *La Cruz* (1896), p. 338.

war of resistance against Napoleon at the beginning of the century. It also contributed to diminishing clerical suspicions of the military as agents of the liberal State, thereby laying the foundations for later sympathy between the army and the Church that would have significant political repercussions. Clerical support for the Cuban and American wars allowed the *modus vivendi* between the civil and ecclesiastical authorities to function as smoothly as possible, given the inherent tension characteristic of Church-State relations under the Restoration.

The events of 1898 marked an important turning point in the history of the country. They stimulated general debate about the causes of the catastrophe that involved the Church in different ways. The Church itself was perceived by some critics as one of many national institutions whose lack of vitality contributed to the pervasive atrophy seen as ultimately responsible for the disaster. Although the bishops backed the military effort that ended in diplomatic and military humiliation as vigorously as any group within Spanish society, their collective memory proved remarkably short. In the aftermath of the catastrophe, they quickly shifted gears to raise doubts about the Restoration's inadequacies, which, if not entirely dormant over the preceding decade, had receded given the relatively good relations existing between the civil and ecclesiastical authorities.[83]

The disaster of 1898 did not create the sense of national crisis that swept the country after the war's end. Angel Ganivet's *Idearium español,* published in 1897, called attention to the country's decline and argued that Spain was suffering from a deep malaise affecting the very being of the nation. At a more pragmatic level, the Aragonese lawyer Joaquín Costa campaigned during the 1890s for a program of economic, fiscal, and educational reform needed to modernize a society left adrift by the opportunism of the governing parties. The defeat of 1898 gave these earlier concerns an urgency that led quickly to widespread demands for national reform or regeneration, as it was called, from intellectuals, industrialists, businessmen, newspaper editors, and some politicians.

Given the disparate nature of the groups demanding the country's modernization, regenerationism did not form a coherent movement. But regenerationists shared common ground in their criticism of the governing parties for failing to introduce the reforms required to resolve fundamental social and economic problems. Even as staid a body as the Chamber of Commerce of Upper Aragón denounced widespread government corruption, administrative abuses, and the overblown size of the military establishment.[84]

The subject of the national crisis and its causes was taken up by some ecclesi-

83. Fernando García de Cortázar, "La Iglesia en la crisis del Estado español, 1898–1923," in *VIII Coloquio de Pau: la crisis del Estado español, 1898–1936,* ed. Manuel Tuñón de Lara et al. (Madrid, 1978), p. 349.

84. Joseph Harrison, "The Regenerationist Movement in Spain after the Disaster of 1898," *European Studies Review* (1979), vol. 9, pp. 9–11.

astics with all the enthusiasm of secular regenerationists. The Restoration's difficulties and inadequacies provided an opportunity for prominent members of the hierarchy to raise fundamental questions about the liberal regime. Cardinal Cascajares criticized the Liberal and Conservative parties for being more interested in "truces of reciprocal convenience that allow them the periodic distribution . . . of personal advantages." These opportunistic politics left "our finances ruined, our industry in agony, our agriculture extinguished," and caused the people to lose "confidence in those who governed them."[85] Bishop Sánchez de Castro of Santander attacked the practices of electoral dishonesty employed by the governing parties, while Bishop Tomás Cámara of Salamanca singled out the regime's lack of foresight in colonial policy as the cause of the Cuban disaster.[86] No less than their secular counterparts, bishops called for a movement of national reform: "Reason dictates it and common sense proclaims it," declared Sánchez de Castro.

The views of secular and ecclesiastical regenerationists coincided in blaming the ruling parties for the crisis. But for the most part they parted company in their explanations of its causes. Some clerics, notably Cardinal Cascajares, who still nourished faint hopes for the creation of a Catholic political party, came close to the secular regenerationists by emphasizing the need for new social and economic policies. The pragmatism of secular commentators, who attributed the regime's troubles to a failure of energy and will on the part of the governing class, found few echoes, however, among bishops and priests. Many interpreted the disaster of 1898 from a theological perspective, with strong overtones of prophetism. An ecclesiastical journal declared that "although many dozens of reformers . . . have come forth . . . to express in newspapers the plans they believe necessary to regenerate the nation," they have missed the fundamental cause of the catastrophe, "immorality and the lack of religion [that] have hurled Spain into an abyss of calamities." Sánchez de Castro, citing the lament of Jeremiah over an unrepentant Jerusalem, affirmed that God used the "perfidy and power" of the United States "to punish our inequities. . . . We ourselves . . . are the moral cause of our ruin; our faults have called ruin down upon us."[87]

For the bishop, the causes of moral, religious, and national ruin were easily established. They came from "the bitter fruits of the lamentable tree of so-called liberty. Our men of government have gloried in their liberalism, in their possession of liberty of thought, liberty of conscience, liberty of cults, liberty of publication and

85. "Males que afligen a España y su remedio: pastoral del Emmo. Sr. Cardenal Cascajares," February 20, 1898, *La Cruz* (1898), pp. 194, 199.

86. "Causas de nuestras desdichas: pastoral del Obispo de Santander," February 2, 1899, *La Cruz* (1899), p. 296; "Importantísima comunicación del Obispo de Salamanca al Sr. Moret, Ministro de Ultramar," May 8, 1898, *La Cruz* (1898), pp. 455–60.

87. "La regeneración de España," *La Voz Católica de Madrid,* May 1, 1899; "Causas de nuestras dedichas," p. 300. This moralizing interpretation of the results of the war was common among the bishops who emphasized that only the moral reform of individuals would open the door to national regeneration. García de Cortázar, "La Iglesia en la crisis del Estado español, 1898–1923," p. 350.

liberty of association." "Official Spain deceived the Spanish people" and led the nation "to the horrible depths of its greatest ruin." Such intemperate words were by no means uncommon. "The men who govern us," asserted Cardinal Casañas, "have wished the nation of Mary to make common cause with apostate nations directed by masonry and Protestantism."[88]

For those clergymen who saw themselves as modern prophets, the nation had but one course to follow if it wished to return to its past glory: "We must abjure our errors; we must follow the footsteps of our fathers and continue the chain of our ancient, glorious traditions" opposed to "the liberties of perdition" introduced by liberalism.[89] On the specific question of how this objective would be realized, ecclesiastical prophets were less certain. Few had anything definite to propose other than to hurl anathemas at liberalism as a political philosophy and to call for the creation of a regime based on religion. Sánchez de Castro suggested that Spain needed "a government or a man uncontaminated by liberalism, a man . . . of generous heart and a strong arm who comes as minister of the Lord to uproot and to destroy, to raze to the ground, to build and to plant."[90] Such heady rhetoric may have appealed to Carlists and Integrists, with their visceral hostility towards the liberal State, but there was virtually no possibility that the political messiah of the bishop's dreams would materialize.

Not all churchmen took the prophetic line. In a widely publicized pastoral letter of 1898, Cardinal Cascajares avoided the harsh rhetoric of Sánchez de Castro and Casañas. He wrote respectfully of Cánovas and Sagasta and opposed Carlism or Integrism as alternatives to the existing system. By this time, the cardinal recognized that his dream of a Catholic political party loyal to the ruling dynasty was fading because of the divisions of Catholic opinion. Cascajares had little to suggest other than to call upon Spaniards to trust in God to use "the mysterious means of divine providence" to save the nation.[91] This spiritual invocation was disingenuous. Having seen his scheme for a Catholic party come to nothing, the cardinal was now deeply involved in machinations designed to orient the Conservative party in a distinctly more pro-clerical direction than Cánovas would have tolerated.[92]

In the national debate following the events of 1898, some regenerationists saw the Church as part of the problem. Damián Isern, former parliamentary deputy and member of the Royal Academy of Political and Moral Sciences, took the clergy to

88. "Causas de nuestras dedichas," pp. 300, 308; "Exhortación pastoral," pp. 484–85.

89. "Exhortación pastoral," pp. 484–85.

90. "Causas de nuestras desdichas," p. 314.

91. "Males que afligen a España," p. 203.

92. Andrés-Gallego has brought to light the cardinal's intricate political scheming during the mid-1890s. In 1896, Cascajares developed an elaborate plan to oust Cánovas, form a Catholic political party, and reach a compromise between the reigning dynasty and the Carlist pretender. *La política religiosa*, pp. 73–80. After the war, the cardinal changed direction. He hoped to see Sagasta ousted from power and Silvela removed from the direction of the Conservatives in favor of the vague regenerationist schemes of General Polavieja. García de Cortázar, "La Iglesia en la crisis del Estado español," p. 351.

task for failing to keep pace with the demands of modern society. As a result, he argued, clerics contributed directly to the cultural impoverishment of the nation that was one of the fundamental causes of the national crisis. Ricardo Macías Picavea, a former schoolteacher and Republican, believed that the Church was caught in the same malaise as the country as a whole: "Religion, Church and clergy walk among us with the same prostration, unconsciousness and contortion as the entire society."[93]

Macías Picavea's perception of the place of the Church within Spanish society was perceptive. Unmoved by the trivial anticlericalism prevalent in some circles, he recognized the "historic-social legitimacy" of religion and believed that the Church could make a contribution to the "moralization" of society. The Church failed to perform a valuable social function because it had made itself into a kind of political party pursuing obsessive causes that hindered effective pastoral work in the face of growing signs of religious alienation. Its persistent and aggressive demands for the restoration of its religious monopoly were "impossible" because of the internal dissension this would produce within the country and because it isolated Spain from "the civilizing movement of Europe." Like Isern, he lamented the cultural decadence of the clergy, whose hostility to modern thought and science contributed "to the intellectual depression of the middle classes." Until the Church recognized that its role was primarily religious and pastoral, he maintained, it would remain a source of division and contention within Spanish society.[94]

Towards New Battles

It was not regenerationist criticism that again converted the Church into a subject of intense public controversy, but the course of political events following the death of Cánovas and the 1898 disaster. Cánovas's disappearance from the scene and Sagasta's age and fragility stimulated factionalism within the governing parties previously held in check by the manipulative skill of the political leadership. Within the Conservative party, Francisco Silvela, whose highly moralistic view of politics led him to oppose the opportunism of Cánovas, emerged as the key figure.[95] Sagasta continued as leader of the Liberals, but restless elements within the party, revolving around a former academic and journalist, José Canalejas (1854–1912), began to press for new directions in party policy. By the spring of 1899, Sagasta, called to office by Queen Regent María Cristina in 1898 to negotiate peace with the United States, saw his majority in parliament so reduced by in-

93. Damián Isern, *Del desastre nacional y sus causas* (Madrid, 1900), pp. 86–87; Ricardo Macías Picavea, *El problema nacional: hechos, causas, remedios* (Madrid, 1899), p. 241.

94. Macías Picavea, *El problema nacional*, pp. 238, 229–31.

95. Carr, *Spain, 1808–1939*, p. 477.

fighting within his own party that he resigned. After attempts to reconstitute the Liberal majority failed, the regent called Silvela to form a government.

Francisco Silvela served as president of the Council of Ministers for nineteen months (March 1899–December 1900). He assumed power with a reputation for high ethical standards. He believed that the time had come to end the electoral corruption and administrative abuses ingrained in the political system. Early in his tenure of office he exhorted his ministers to "a work of radical reform, of a true revolution from above" that would involved "profound modifications in . . . our political, administrative and social existence."[96]

These lofty sentiments suggested that Silvela intended to abandon the Restoration's politics-as-usual approach. To attain his goal, the prime minister attempted to create a Conservative Union based on representation of the country's conservative forces rather than on narrow party factions. The cabinet included Manuel Durán y Bas, a prominent Barcelona politician appointed to placate Catalan regionalists, and General Camilo Polavieja, popular hero of the war against the Philippine rebels. The new ministry took office with a program calling for honesty in government, limited decentralization, particularly at the provincial and municipal levels, fiscal austerity, the reform and modernization of the military establishment, moderate social reform, and an emphasis on economic development.

Silvela's attempts to make the political system responsive to national needs foundered on their own contradictions and the dissension that quickly appeared among the ministers and the parliamentary factions supporting them. Despite the prime minister's commitment to electoral honesty, the government, fearing the strength of the Liberals and a reviving republicanism, managed the elections of April 1899 to return a Conservative majority.[97] A series of ministerial conflicts followed this inauspicious beginning. The demands of General Polavieja, minister of war, for increased funds to modernize the military establishment were rejected by the minister of finance, leading to the former's resignation from the cabinet. The government also imposed new taxes on small businesses that aroused furious opposition, especially in Catalonia, where the economy was still reeling from the loss of colonial markets. The departure of Durán y Bas demolished Silvela's tentative effort to accommodate Catalan regionalist sentiment. By the autumn of 1899, the Conservative Union dissolved for all practical purposes, although Silvela continued in office.

The Silvela ministry marked another modest shift of attitude towards the regime among the bishops. Carlism and Integrism remained on the scene and continued to attract the support of the lower clergy. But it was increasingly evident that neither posed a serious threat to the dynastic parties controlling the Restoration.

96. Quoted in Fernández Almagro, *Historia política de la España contemporánea*, vol. 3, p. 221.
97. Ibid., p. 222.

The dream of forming a Catholic party lingered still but with little prospect that it would become a reality. In these circumstances, the Silvela government appeared a promising alternative to the hierarchy despite continuing reservations about the liberal political system. Silvela enjoyed a reputation for devout Catholicism. His opposition to Cánovas, who always remained attached to a strongly regalist view of civil-ecclesiastical relations, offered the hope that the new government could be persuaded to make substantial concessions. Shortly before taking office, Silvela praised the policies promoted by the papacy, while the Conservative party program for 1898 stressed the necessity of "Catholic defense."[98]

The Church's expectations were expressed in a letter of the bishops sent to the prime minister in September 1899. The hierarchy asked the new ministry, "being the government of a Catholic nation," to demonstrate the fact through its "public acts." The bishops submitted a long shopping list, including demands for the strict interpretation of Article 11, abolition of "imprudent liberty of the press," the introduction of legislation to give the bishops significant control over education, the dismissal of university and secondary school teachers "who departed from Catholic doctrine," and a substantial increase in clerical salaries.[99]

There was little prospect that Silvela could meet these demands, as he recognized in his reply. His language was conciliatory, but he made clear that because of the government's financial difficulties, an increase in the budgetary appropriation for the clergy was out of the question. Silvela expressed sympathy with the other demands, but he informed the bishops that government initiative was limited by the constitution. The nation's fundamental law limited official action "in many aspects of the life of the State."[100]

In fact, Silvela's ecclesiastical policy did not differ in its essentials from that of Cánovas and Sagasta. It was not so much what the Conservative government did for the Church, which was little, but how the Liberal and Republican opposition viewed the Conservative Union that led to the first widespread anticlerical disturbances in the Restoration's history. The formation of the Union appeared as a dangerous new political force threatening to monopolize power for a long period, overturn civil liberties, and embark on a policy of wholesale concessions to the Church.[101] The veteran Republican leader, Emilio Castelar, issued a scathing in-

98. Andrés-Gallego, *La política religiosa*, p. 145.

99. "Exposición al Señor Presidente del Consejo de Ministros," September 4, 1899, *La Cruz* (1899), pp. 283–89.

100. "Contestación del Presidente del Consejo de Ministros," September 28, 1899, in ibid., p. 290. Although favorable to the Church, Silvela by no means abandoned regalism completely. He believed it necessary to reduce the number of regular clergy and to conduct negotiations with the Vatican to this effect. He also remained opposed to providing any form of subsidy to the religious orders. Cristóbal Robles Muñoz, "Frente a la supremacía del Estado: la Santa Sede y los católicos en la crisis de la Restauración, 1898–1910," *Anthologica Annua* (1989), vol. 36, pp. 330–35.

101. There were other points of division between the dynastic parties. The Silvela government's 1899 proposal for a new education law that would reduce the presence of the sciences in the curriculum

dictment accusing Silvela of intending to abolish trial by jury, universal suffrage, and secular education, while allowing the Vatican to dictate government policy.[102]

There was nothing new about such charges. But they now took on a sharper edge because some prominent Liberals, concerned with the apparent strength of the Conservative Union, began to seek the means of undermining it politically. The spark came from an unexpected source through an article published in a Madrid newspaper in January 1899 by a former Conservative politician of dubious reputation, Romero Robledo, who had broken with Cánovas and Silvela. Romero Robledo argued that the Conservative party was moving in a direction threatening to destroy the liberal consensus that lay at the foundation of the Restoration's stability. Liberal unity had to be reestablished "to raise the country from the abyss into which it has fallen." He later identified regionalism and ultramontanism as the specific dangers from which the nation needed salvation. These articles evoked a chorus of approval from some Liberal newspapers and party leaders. In June 1899, José Canalejas caused a political stir by expounding the need for a new party program opposed to the reactionary character of the Conservative Union that was based on "clericalism," "militarism," "regionalism," and unbridled "capitalism." By "clericalism," Canalejas meant specifically the remarkable growth of the religious orders that had occurred since the late 1870s and their ever-increasing role in education.[103]

An ailing, elderly Sagasta was reluctant to raise an issue that would lead in his judgment to severe political divisions dangerous to the Restoration's stability.[104] But gradually he began to yield to the pressure of party reformers, although he did so with misgivings. The decision of the Liberal party to move the question of the Church to the center of political debate undermined the partial neutralization of the clerical issue that Cánovas saw as necessary to prevent the recurrence of deep and lasting divisions within the disparate forces of Spanish liberalism.

The shift in Liberal strategy revived anticlericalism as a major divisive force between the dynastic parties. The Liberal party now embraced a program certain to galvanize its supporters and provoke a counterreaction among Conservatives and the Church's defenders in general. The expression of different forms of anticlerical-

---

in favor of the humanities and require students entering secondary school to be examined in the catechism provoked both Liberals and Republicans, who attacked the legislation in no uncertain terms. Andrés-Gallego, *La política religiosa*, p. 152.

102. Ibid., p. 146. Castelar had established an accommodation with Sagasta during the 1880s and early 1890s, but after his withdrawal from active politics in 1894, he returned to the more aggressive republicanism that he advanced during the 1860s and early 1870s. Ibid., p. 145.

103. Quoted in ibid., pp. 144–45, 156–57.

104. Sagasta did not share Canalejas's view that the Liberal party needed to take a "belligerent" attitude on the clerical question. He believed it sufficient for government to use the tools provided by the 1851 concordat and the regalist powers of the State. Cristóbal Robles Muñoz, "Frente a la supremacía del Estado: la Santa Sede y los católicos en la crisis de la Restauración," *Anthologica Annua* (1987), vol. 34, p. 233.

ism had by no means disappeared during the early Restoration. Disturbances occurred from time to time, as in Seville in 1882 during a religious procession, when cries of "Death to the Jesuits! Death to the clergy!" were heard before Catholic participants and their opponents engaged in a pitched street battle with umbrellas and sticks.[105] Intellectuals opposed the clergy's persistent attempts to control cultural life; Republicans remained committed to the separation of the civil and ecclesiastical powers. Since the regime more or less respected freedom of the press, a strident yellow journalism appeared to devote its attention to exclusively anticlerical ends. *El Motín*, *Las Dominicales del Libre Pensamiento*, *El Resumen*, and *Tintinnabulum* were newspapers specializing in extreme and sensational accusations against the clergy. In 1882, for example, *El Motín* published articles about a priest accused of raping five girls, a Barcelona convent alleged to be selling medicine designed to induce abortions, a nun in Igualada said to have forced a burning iron on the hand of a pupil, and the Capuchin friars of Manresa, who were charged with irregular financial dealings.[106] Anticlericalism remained alive and well during the 1880s and early 1890s, but the partial neutralization of the clerical question desired by Cánovas functioned well enough to avoid widespread anticlerical disturbances.

As had been the case in earlier periods, anticlericalism did not form a coherent movement beyond the vague objective of resisting clerical influence. There were "anticlericals for every taste."[107] The expression of anticlericalism took many forms, literary, intellectual, journalistic, political, populist, and social.[108] Even within organized political groups, such as the Republican parties, there were dif-

105. José A. de Sobrino, *El Venerable Spínola: perfil y espíritu* (Madrid, 1984), pp. 51–52.

106. *El Motín*, July 23, September 3, October 8, 1882.

107. Julio Caro Baroja, *Introducción a una historia contemporánea del anticlericalismo español* (Madrid, 1980), p. 220.

108. Manuel Revuelta González has analyzed anticlericalism at the turn of the century in terms of two broad categories. The first revolves around the attitude of Spaniards towards religion. There was an "irreligious anticlericalism," identified with figures such as Blasco Ibáñez, Lerroux, and others, who saw religion as a body of "superstitions opposed to human progress." There was also an anticlericalism "compatible with respect for religion," which embraced diverse groups. Some, such as the prominent intellectual Gumersindo de Azcárate, promoted a deistic view of religion and advocated religious freedom based on the idea that all religions were equally valid. Many progressive writers, such as Galdós, "esteemed fundamental Christian values, especially charity," and took the Church to task for failing to live up to its lofty moral purpose. There was also a "Catholic anticlericalism" identified with segments of the Liberal party, especially José Canalejas, who believed that the role of the Church had to be redefined within a modern society. Finally, there was a "clerical anticlericalism" promoted by former priests "who sought the internal purification of the Church." The second category rests on functional norms, a political anticlericalism associated with Canalejas and with republicanism, with its commitment to the separation of Church and State; an ideological anticlericalism, manifested by the professors and intellectuals of the Institución Libre de Enseñanza, who objected on philosophical grounds to clerical obscurantism as a barrier to civilization and progress, especially in education. Finally, there was the "social anticlericalism" of Socialists and various anarchist groups who resented the identification of the Church with a capitalist society. Manuel Revuelta González, "La recuperación eclesiástica y el rechazo anticlerical en el cambio del siglo," in *España entre dos siglos*, pp. 217–31. José Manuel Cuenca Toribio has stressed the importance in anticlericalism of a collective psychology characterized by "an antagonism . . . towards the clergy which did not always obey rational elements." "Un posible punto de partida para el análisis de una

ferences between those who wished "to secularize the State, but not society," and those who wished to go further.[109] Anticlerical currents had ebbed and flowed throughout the history of liberal Spain. After the turn of the century, they moved towards new heights for several reasons. After the disaster of 1898, the diverse currents of regenerationist thought often interpreted the Church's role in society as one of the causes of Spanish decadence.[110] A strong and broadly based reaction developed against "clericalism," the ascendancy of an institution with a deeply antiliberal policy that to critics appeared increasingly aggressive in its efforts to force its values on an entire society.[111] Anticlericalism also became more intensely politicized after 1900, as exemplified in the program of the new Radical Republican party and the Liberal party's move towards a more activist policy with respect to the Church.[112] Studies of conflicts between Catholics and diverse anticlerical groups in cities as diverse as Santander, Valencia, and Málaga have shown that after the turn of the century, the struggle over the Church's influence became central to Restoration politics at the local level.[113] Further, Andrés-Gallego has established that the geographical distribution of anticlerical demonstrations underwent a significant change between 1900 and 1910. An older regional pattern of manifestations concentrated in Catalonia, Valencia, and Andalucía, with pockets in the Ebro Valley, Badajoz, Madrid, Valladolid, León, and Oviedo, expanded to become national in scope, although the focus and intensity of anticlericalism varied within and among regions.[114] "The religious question was converted into a national problem."[115]

---

cuestión clave de la historia española contemporánea: el anticlericalismo," in *Masonería, política y sociedad*, ed. J. A. Ferrer Benimeli (2 vols., Castellón [Zaragoza], 1989), vol. 2, p. 712.

109. Quoted in Cueva Merino, *Clericales y anticlericales*, p. 133.

110. Revuelta González, "La recuperación eclesiástica y el rechazo anticlerical," p. 216.

111. Joan Connelly Ullman, "The Warp and Woof of Parliamentary Politics in Spain, 1808–1939: Anticlericalism versus 'Neo-Catholicism,'" *European Studies Review* (1983), vol. 13, pp. 155–61.

112. Julio de la Cueva Merino makes the persuasive case that after 1900 Republicans employed a "populist discourse" based on "the manicheist division between the good people and the wicked representatives of clericalism . . . ; the mythification and simplification of the latter in order to arouse the lowest passions of the former; the obsession with blaming all the evils of the country on a clerical conspiracy aimed at taking hold of Spain by means of its previous moral and material ruin; and the orientation of the people's wrath towards clericalism as the only, or main, enemy." "The Stick and the Candle: Clericals and Anticlericals in Northern Spain, 1898–1913," *European History Quarterly* (1996), vol. 26, no. 2, p. 260.

113. The theme of anticlericalism is central to the work of Cueva Merino, *Clericales y anticlericales;* Ramiro Reig, *Blasquistas y clericales: la lucha por la ciudad en la Valencia de 1900* (Valencia, 1986); Elías de Mateo Avilés, *Piedades e impiedades de los malagueños en el siglo XIX: una aproximación a la religiosidad española contemporánea* (Málaga, 1987).

114. José Andrés-Gallego, "Sobre las formas de pensar y de ser: la Iglesia," in *Historia general de España y América* (19 vols., Madrid, 1985–1992), vol. 16, pt. 1, pp. 301–2. Cuenca Toribio has noted the differences, for example, between Galicia, where a centuries-old rural anticlericalism continued into the modern period, and the industrial areas of the Cantabrian coast, where it developed in the nineteenth century under the impact of economic development. The character of anticlericalism depended in part on the institutional development of ecclesiastical institutions, which varied from one region to another. Cuenca Toribio, "Un posible punto de partida para el análisis de una cuestión clave de la historia española contemporánea: El anticlericalismo," pp. 713–14.

115. Revuelta González, "La recuperación eclesiástica y el rechazo anticlerical," p. 213.

The crisis produced by the events of 1898 was the general cause of the wave of political and popular anticlericalism that swept the country during the summer of 1899. The immediate cause was a debate about the role of the religious orders in the collapse of Spanish rule in the Philippine Islands. The question ignited fierce controversy that soon spread beyond parliamentary halls and the press. Critics of the regulars alleged that the oppressive economic and political influence the religious orders once enjoyed in the islands undermined the possibility of reform that might have saved the colony for Spain. The regular clergy's defenders replied in kind, alleging that the attack upon them represented an international masonic conspiracy "to annihilate the Catholic religion."[116]

The controversy was soon transformed into a debate on the role of the religious orders within Spain itself. Spanish liberalism was identified historically with hostility towards the regular clergy. The widespread support of the religious orders for absolutism between 1810 and 1813 and 1820 and 1823, as well as the enthusiasm of some monks and friars for the Carlist cause during the civil war of the 1830s, left a score that liberals were determined to settle after their victory over absolute monarchy. The suppression of most of the male orders and the sale of their property in 1835 and 1836 struck the decisive blow. The Moderate party, during its domination of Spanish politics after 1843, was willing to allow a selective reintroduction of male religious as the price paid for the 1851 concordat, but even the Moderates were reluctant to permit a massive restoration of the regular clergy. In 1860 the national census reported the existence of only sixty-two establishments for male religious, with less than two thousand residents.[117]

Clerical pressure for the large-scale return of the male regulars became intense during the Restoration's early years. Cánovas again produced a balancing formula designed to satisfy the Church without provoking the Liberal opposition unduly. The government followed a policy of allowing the male religious orders to establish their foundations more or less freely but made clear that it would assume no financial responsibility for them. Cánovas may have expected that financial constraints would limit the number of new religious houses. If he did so, he was mistaken, for the male regulars experienced a period of remarkable demographic growth between the late 1870s and 1900.[118]

The rapid growth of the regular clergy sooner or later would have provoked a reaction on the part of Liberals restive with the terms of the Restoration's ecclesiastical settlement. Sagasta recognized this in 1887 by yielding to demands in the party for a Law of Associations requiring the religious orders to register with the civil authorities. But the legislation lacked the teeth necessary to limit further

116. *La Cruz* (1899), p. 319; Andrés-Gallego, *La política religiosa*, p. 143.

117. *Censo de la población de España, 1860* (Madrid, 1863).

118. The number of male religious rose from the 1,683 reported in the 1860 census to 10,745 by 1901.

growth. Continued expansion, as well as the regulars' expanding role in education, ensured that the question would arise again.

Hostility towards the religious orders lay behind the anticlerical agitation of 1899. It rapidly developed into a general protest against the apparently pro-clerical policy of the Silvela government. The motives of those opposing the regulars were diverse, ranging from the precise political objectives of Liberal reformers, such as Canalejas, who believed that expansion violated the terms of the 1851 concordat, to the more flamboyant propagandistic intentions of Republican politicians and publicists. The novelist Vicente Blasco Ibáñez, for example, strongly Republican in sympathy, subjected the orders to savage criticism that questioned their very right to exist. The anticlerical movement also owed something to growing exasperation with the Silvela government's tax policy, which produced widespread strikes and disturbances. Opposition to the religious orders, particularly to the Jesuits, who were regarded as avid supporters of the Silvela-Polavieja alliance, soon led to widespread street demonstrations.[119] In Seville, the army was called out to disperse agitators threatening to set the Jesuit college ablaze, and in Valencia an unruly crowd attempted to attack the Jesuit residence, while in Zaragoza demonstrators invaded the national shrine of the Virgin of the Pillar and attempted to make off with the sword left by General Polavieja in holy tribute upon his return from the Philippines.[120]

Further tension developed over an apparently innocuous practice promoted by the Church, the installation of plaques dedicated to the Sacred Heart on the exterior walls of private houses. As the cult of the Sacred Heart developed in Spain following its introduction in the eighteenth century, it took on political overtones that had little to do with religious devotion. During the nineteenth century, the cult became a symbol of opposition to liberalism. In the civil wars of the 1830s and 1870s, Carlist troops sometimes entered battle with a badge to the Sacred Heart pinned to their uniforms. The controversial plaques of 1899 were of recent origin, but they continued the identification of the Sacred Heart with the antiliberal tradition. In

119. Polavieja, widely admired in Catholic circles as "the Christian general," was a man of obscure political ambitions. His appeal arose from the possession of one of the few unsullied military reputations to survive in a time of defeat; he also appeared as a neutral political figure uncontaminated by the corruption of the political system, while his support for limited autonomy for Catalonia attracted the support of its foremost advocates, the region's conservative Catholic bourgeoisie. Although the general may have toyed with the idea of casting himself in the role of national savior through the installation of a dictatorship, he had enough common sense to pursue the less dangerous course of entering into an alliance with Silvela, an association that prominent clerics, such as Cardinal Cascajares, supported enthusiastically.

120. Andrés-Gallego, *La política religiosa*, p. 165. In fact, Jesuits were divided between a majority still loyal to Carlism and Integrism and a small minority who embraced a "possibilist" approach to working within the existing political system. Robles Muñoz, "Frente a la supremacía del Estado," *Anthologica Annua* (1987), vol. 37, pp. 212–13. By this time, hostility towards the Jesuits as responsible for all the evils suffered by the country had become commonplace among anticlericals. Elías de Mateo Avilés, *El anticlericalismo en Málaga, 1874–1923* (Málaga, 1990), p. 62.

fact, their creator was dismissed from a government post for refusing "to compromise with . . . liberal policy."[121]

The plaques became the symbol around which defenders and opponents of the Church struggled during that agitated summer of 1899. The decision of municipal authorities in Castellón to remove them from the walls of houses led to widespread protests from the local clergy and the faithful. As protesters wearing badges to the Sacred Heart moved through the streets of the city, they clashed with anticlericals amidst the hurling of sticks and stones. The Castellón disturbances led to demands for vigorous government action by the bishops and the Catholic press. The bishop of Tortosa called upon the Silvela government to repress "these abuses and assaults against religion . . . with a strong hand." If it did not do so, he threatened, "the blood of the disturbers of public order will stain the streets."[122] The disorders in Castellón and other cities embarrassed the Silvela government. Although it defended the right of Catholics to use the plaques, it also urged prudence on the ecclesiastical authorities.[123]

Despite anticlerical agitation and the response of the Church's defenders, the government retained control of the country, although there were moments when it feared that events might get out of hand. By the end of 1899, it was clear that the protective shield that had more or less protected the Church from widespread and open anticlerical onslaughts was disappearing.[124] The aggressive reaction of the Church's defenders and opponents showed that the gloves were off in the controversy over the Church, its relationship to the State, and its place within Spanish society.

The events of the summer of 1899 began a period in which the so-called clerical question became a central topic of public debate. Controversy continued through the end of the Silvela ministry in December 1900 and through that of his successor, General Azcárraga. The new Conservative government faced renewed controversy over the religious orders brought on by the possibility of a massive influx of French religious, in view of the legislation against the regulars being discussed during January 1901 by the French Chamber of Deputies.

As if this were not enough, another strident and emotional public debate began at the end of the month with the presentation in the Teatro Español of Madrid of the play *Electra,* written by the celebrated novelist Benito Pérez Galdós. The play revolved around a young woman forced into a convent through the machinations

121. Alberto Risco, *El Padre Francisco de Paula Tarín* (Madrid, 1921), p. 413.

122. "Pastoral del Ilmo. Sr. Obispo de Tortosa," *La Cruz* (1899), p. 108.

123. The hierarchy generally cooperated with the civil authorities to ease tension, although the bishop of Tortosa continued to urge the faithful to install the plaques. Andrés-Gallego, *La política religiosa,* p. 165.

124. These years intensified anticlerical reactions and produced violence that was "absolutely unknown until the turn of the century." Mateo Avilés, *El anticlericalismo en Málaga,* p. 73.

of a character symbolizing clerical reaction and obscurantism. An anticlerical work by one of the country's most famous authors would have generated controversy in itself. The fact that a legal case on the topic of the play was being conducted at the same time added a dash of realism to the highly charged emotions that surfaced from the moment of the first performance.[125] The crowd shouted "Down with reaction!" "Down with the Jesuits!" at various points in the performance. So intense was the audience's emotional state that when the actor playing the sinister clerical role appeared to take his bows, he was greeted with shouts of "Kill him! Kill him!"[126] In Málaga, a crowd moved through the streets carrying a portrait of Galdós while shouting *vivas* to *Electra* and "Death to the clergy!"[127]

Like the plaques to the Sacred Heart, *Electra* became a symbol around which violent controversy raged. The Catholic press saw the play as "an arm of combat . . . against religion, against the religious orders."[128] Throughout the country bishops issued pastoral letters forbidding the faithful to attend performances. The archbishop of Burgos saw the play as a grand conspiracy designed to visit "vengeance and extermination" on the Church, a sign of a "black wave of revolution" about to descend on the nation.[129] In a number of cities, the play's supporters held demonstrations deemed so threatening that the government imposed martial law on February 14.[130]

The uproar surrounding *Electra* coincided with a political crisis. Silvela's departure from office in December 1900 arose from the failure of his ambitious plans for national reform and from the chronic divisions of the Conservative party. The caretaker administration of General Azcárraga gave the Conservatives a breathing space in which to attempt to reconstitute a workable government. When these efforts failed, the regent called Sagasta to form a Liberal ministry in March 1901.

As the elderly Liberal chieftain took office for the last time, he faced a very different situation from the one that had greeted him in 1881, when he first became president of the Council of Ministers. This was especially true in the case of the Church. The Liberal-Conservative consensus on ecclesiastical policy protecting the Church through the mid-1890s was disintegrating. The problem of the Church could no longer be handled within the traditional wheeling and dealing of the ear-

125. The case of Adelaida de Ubao, being argued before the Supreme Court, was, however, somewhat different. The girl had entered a convent on her own initiative without her mother's permission. The case arose from the mother's attempt to force her daughter to return home. The symbolism of this legal battle can be appreciated through the fact that the opposing lawyers in the case were Nicolás Salmerón, former president of the First Republic, representing the mother, and Antonio Maura, a future Conservative prime minister, representing the daughter. Andrés-Gallego, *La política religiosa*, p. 192.

126. *La Cruz* (1901), p. 402.

127. Mateo Avilés, *El anticlericalismo en Málaga*, p. 76.

128. *La Cruz* (1901), p. 396.

129. "Circular del Sr. Arzobispo de Burgos contra las manifestaciones anticlericales," April 4, 1901, in ibid., p. 413.

130. Andrés-Gallego, *La política religiosa*, p. 192.

lier period. Influential Liberals demanded a harder line on the religious orders, while Republicans began to appreciate the propaganda value of anticlericalism as an issue capable of attracting popular support. At the same time, the Church and its supporters were determined to defend themselves as aggressively as possible both politically, by drawing closer to the Conservative party, and organizationally, through the creation of Catholic associations committed to defend "religion and the nation" by resisting "the abominable propagation of dissolving ideas put forth by our enemies."[131] As the Restoration entered a new phase in its history, it was certain to confront continuing, divisive, and passionate controversy over the place of the Church within Spanish society.

131. *La Cruz* (1901), p. 48.

CHAPTER III

POLITICS AND THE CHURCH, 1901–1912

The Restoration in Crisis

The twelve years separating Sagasta's return to power and the assassination of Prime Minister José Canalejas in 1912 saw the debate over "clericalism" reach new levels of intensity. Controversy over the Church's legal privileges and the dramatic expansion of the religious orders occurred as the system designed by Cánovas faced a series of challenges. Electoral manipulation by successive governments functioned less efficiently in urban areas, thereby opening the door to greater parliamentary representation by the opposition parties.[1] The emergence in Catalonia of a strong autonomist movement deprived the dynastic parties of the national political monopoly they had enjoyed since the regime's foundation. The question of how a highly centralized State should deal with Catalan aspirations produced new tensions in an already strained political system. A revived republican movement began to subject the regime to withering criticism in parliament, the press, and, in some cases, through agitation on the streets. Cánovas and Sagasta had worked effectively to neutralize the fragmented republican groups surviving the First Republic's collapse. Although the regime tolerated this reformist republicanism, it now confronted a new breed of Republican politician who wished to have nothing

1. This trend developed from several causes. It reflected in part the decision of successive governments to introduce a limited degree of fairness into the electoral process. In 1903, for example, the Conservative minister of the interior (Gobernación), Antonio Maura, allowed the general elections of that year to take place without resorting, according to a republican politician, to the "bad electoral arts" associated with the dynastic parties. Quoted in Cristóbal Robles Muñoz, *Antonio Maura, un político liberal* (Madrid, 1995), pp. 138–39, note 153. It also became more difficult for the government to rig elections in urban areas. Javier Tusell, "The Functioning of the Cacique System in Andalusia, 1890–1931," in *Politics and Society in Twentieth-Century Spain*, ed. Stanley Payne (New York, 1976), p. 8.

to do with the compromises of the established order.[2] With the election to parliament in 1901 of Alejandro Lerroux (1864–1949) and the subsequent formation of the Radical Republican party, notice was served on the politicians of the dynastic parties that the traditional behind-the-scenes resolution of the regime's difficulties through networks of patronage and the mutual exchange of favors would no longer escape public scrutiny.[3] Lerroux, a master of demagogic oratory, an unscrupulous manipulator of the press, and a superb political organizer, inflamed republicanism with an intensity that it had previously lacked. In Valencia, an aggressive populist republican party founded in 1899 by the novelist Vicente Blasco Ibáñez experienced considerable success at the municipal level during the century's first decade.[4] The limited pluralism of the political system allowed it to tolerate the older version of republicanism with its lofty view of the republic as the embodiment of civic virtue. For the dynastic parties, the new republicanism appeared to threaten the survival of the political system.

There was no immediate danger that the movement towards populist radicalism would lead to revolution. But the bold tactics and violent rhetoric of Lerroux and Blasco Ibáñez confirmed a long-held obsession of the regime's politicians. Cánovas sought to eliminate the popular violence that had accompanied all the significant political upheavals of liberal Spain between 1834 and 1873. He believed that violence in the streets not only contributed to the chronic instability of the liberal system but that it also threatened to introduce revolutionary social and political changes. The agitated history of the democratic monarchy and the First Republic reinforced the apprehensions of the Restoration's elite before the danger of the "revolution."

This did not refer, as it would later, to a revolution identified with specific forms of radicalism, but to a variety of disrupting forces thought capable of emerging at any moment to sweep away the established political and social order. Manifestations of revolutionary violence during the Restoration, however diverse their origins and motivation, kept alive fear of a violent assault on the State and society. The history of anarchism, after its introduction into Spain following the revolution of 1868, deepened this fear. During the first three decades of the Restoration, anarchism established itself as a mass movement only in the south, particularly in An-

2. Raymond Carr, *Spain, 1808–1939* (Oxford, 1966), pp. 533–35.

3. Lerroux later recalled the significance of the 1901 elections in breaking the monopoly of the dynastic parties: "These elections were of the greatest importance. The bosses of the monarchical parties lost Barcelona forever. The regionalists entered Spanish public life for the first time as an organized party. The republicanism of Barcelona was revived. The workers of the city were being awakened and soon would enter politics in a massive way." Quoted in Octavio Ruiz Manjón, *El Partido Republicano Radical, 1908–1936* (Madrid, 1976), p. 33. For an excellent study of the career of Lerroux, see José Álvarez Junco, *El emperador del Paralelo: Lerroux y la demagogia populista* (Madrid, 1990).

4. The party of Blasco recruited a largely young and dynamic clientele and contained few representatives of the older nineteenth-century republican parties. Ramiro Reig, *Blasquistas y clericales: la lucha por la ciudad en la Valencia de 1900* (Valencia, 1986), p. 229.

dalucía, among the region's landless agricultural laborers and in its early stages among urban artisans. Occasional outbreaks of violence, such as the invasion of Jerez de la Frontera in 1892 by a peasant force armed with sickles and sticks, were brutally suppressed by the authorities. Despite government repression, the rural anarchism of the south survived to reappear during the great wave of strikes and disturbances that swept Córdoba province in 1903 and 1904.

Between 1890 and 1910, the acts of individual anarchists, who were entirely separate from the rural anarchists of the south, provided a more visible and frightening example of revolutionary violence. The deadly bomb hurled in the Liceo theater of Barcelona in 1893, the assassination of Cánovas in 1897, the wounding of Prime Minister Maura in 1904 during the royal visit to Barcelona, the attempted murder of King Alfonso XIII and Queen Victoria Eugenia on their wedding day in 1906, and a series of terrorist attacks in Barcelona between 1904 and 1910 gave immediacy to the chronic fear of revolution felt by defenders of the established order.[5]

During the first decade of the century the regime also faced economic problems that contributed to social unrest. A poor harvest in Castile in 1902 and an even more damaging agricultural depression between 1904 and 1906 hindered economic recovery following the disastrous war with the United States. The loss of the empire brought near ruin to industrial Catalonia, heavily dependent on colonial markets. Factory closures, wage reductions, and the widespread dismissal of workers set off a wave of strikes in the region during 1903.[6] The hard line taken by employers led to worker support first for Lerroux and his Radical Republicans and then, beginning in 1910, for a new anarcho-syndicalist trade union, the Confederación Nacional del Trabajo (CNT). The Socialist union, the Unión General de Trabajadores (UGT), founded in 1888, saw its membership grow from fifteen thousand in 1900 to nearly eighty thousand by 1911, while the movement's political party, the Partido Socialista Obrero Español (PSOE), elected its first deputy to parliament in 1910 in the person of its leader, Pablo Iglesias. The modest growth of socialism and the movement of Catalan industrial workers towards anarcho-syndicalism posed no threat to the regime. But their development signaled a fundamental change in the organization of the working class that boded ill for a regime that had failed to come to grips with the social problems produced by economic dislocation.

By the first decade of the century, the regime's politicians could no longer move as easily within the narrow political and social circumference drawn by Cánovas. The internal problems of the dynastic parties also made the task of adapting to new realities difficult. The fragile unity imposed by Sagasta on the Liberal party disin-

5. Joaquín Romero Maura provides a detailed discussion of anarchist terrorism during the first decade of the century. "Terrorism in Barcelona and Its Impact on Spanish Politics, 1904–1909," *Past and Present*, no. 41 (1968), pp. 130–83.

6. Joseph Harrison, *An Economic History of Modern Spain* (New York, 1978), pp. 76–81.

tegrated in the years following his death. One faction gathered around an elderly former minister of the democratic monarchy, Eugenio Montero Ríos, and looked back to the principles of mid-nineteenth-century liberalism as embodied in the Progressive party. Another formed around the figure of Segismundo Moret, who embodied the opportunism of Sagasta but with a keener sense of changing political realities. A more openly reformist group supported José Canalejas, who formed his own party in 1907.

For a time the Conservatives appeared less troubled by internal fragmentation. When an exhausted and disillusioned Silvela decided to abandon the party leadership, there was a measure of agreement on his eventual successor, Antonio Maura, who became prime minister briefly in 1904. But Maura's second tenure as head of the government (1907–1909) loosed the same divisive forces already present among Liberals. Another ingredient in the boiling political pot of the era (between 1902 and 1907 there were fourteen separate governments), was the attitude of King Alfonso XIII. Having reached the age of majority in 1902, the monarch soon showed a disposition to meddle in political affairs, albeit within the limits of his constitutional responsibilities.

The battle over the religious orders was fought within a framework of political factionalism within the dynastic parties, an aggressive populist republicanism, and growing social unrest. At one level, the debate took on a purely juridical character revolving around the government's historic regalist claims, now fully identified in the minds of reformers with the exercise of the State's sovereign powers.[7] The papacy, in turn, relied on the 1851 concordat to defend the regular clergy against unilateral government restrictions as a violation of diplomatic agreements between Madrid and the Vatican. The concordat stipulated that three masculine orders were entitled to a protected status similar to that enjoyed by the secular clergy. It specifically recognized two orders, the Vincentians and the Oratorians, for this privileged protection.

The civil and ecclesiastical authorities could never agree on an order to fill the third place. The majority of the male and female regulars occupied a different juridical situation. Beginning in the late 1870s, governments approved the foundation of new monasteries, friaries, and convents through ordinary but not always uniform administrative procedures. Proposals for a new religious establishment required the approval of the Ministry of Justice and the civil governor of the province where it was to be located. If the new foundation imposed no financial burden on the public treasury, approval was easily forthcoming. Sagasta's Law of Associations

7. An advocate of government restrictions on the growth of the religious orders argued that regalism formed an essential part of the State's sovereign rights. "Any measure that violates this right of sovereignty cannot be recognized in Spain," he argued in a clear reference to the Vatican's attempt to defend the regular clergy against unilateral government action. Luis Morote, *Los frailes en España* (Madrid, 1904), p. 187.

(1887), requiring the registration of all civil and religious organizations, did not affect the expansion of the orders, since most ignored the legislation.[8]

The Church regarded the nearly automatic approval of requests for authorization as an administrative precedent that could not be reversed through ex post facto legislation. Reformers concerned with the massive expansion of the orders saw nothing unreasonable in government action designed to limit their growth, since the concordat failed to mention the vast majority of religious communities.

At another level, the debate about the religious orders was intensely political. It acted as a lightening rod attracting different views about the role of the orders within Spanish society and, by extension, the Church's privileges within the regime. At the same time, the hyperbolic, sometimes violent anticlerical rhetoric of populist republicanism ensured that the question of the regulars and the Church's legal status would remain central to public debate. The pattern of anticlerical violence established in 1899 continued in sporadic fashion through the century's first decade. The stoning of religious buildings, especially those belonging to the regular clergy, the disruption of religious processions by anticlericals, and occasional street battles between them and the Church's defenders never coalesced into an organized movement. Nor did the civil authorities allow disturbances to spread. But these incidents showed that in urban areas hostility towards the Church among some sectors of the population stood ready to take violent form.[9]

For clergy and laity, the events of the decade appeared ominous. Sporadic violence against priests and religious and the strident anticlerical rhetoric of populist republicanism deepened fears of a full-scale assault on the Church. Liberal party proposals to control the growth of the religious orders, establish full religious liberty, and revise the 1851 concordat appeared to threaten the Restoration's ecclesiastical settlement and open the door to a fully secularized State.

Few clergy and laity disagreed that the Church needed to meet the perceived threat to its interests with an organized and vigorous response, but achieving this goal proved elusive. The idea of forming a new version of the Unión Católica to defend the Church resurfaced in various forms, only to founder on the rancorous divisions between Catholics willing to accept the constitutional monarchy and Carlists and Integrists who remained steadfast in their opposition to a political system tainted by liberalism. But some bishops, clergy, and laity began to assess the

8. Before a royal order of April 1902 required strict fulfillment of the registration procedures demanded by the 1887 law, only 372 religious houses of the more than two thousand in existence had seen fit to register. *Antonio Maura: treinta y cinco años de vida pública*, ed. J. Ruiz-Castillo, (2 vols., Madrid, 1917), vol. 1, p. 182, note 1.

9. The Jesuits, long an object of hostility by anticlericals of various stripes, suffered particularly between 1901 and 1909. In 1902, for example, the Jesuit college of Zaragoza was surrounded by a crowd that stoned it and fired shots in the air. A few months later, a mob shouting "Death to the Jesuits!" stoned the order's residence in Seville. For a description of physical attacks on the Jesuits during this period, see Manuel Revuelta González, *La Compañía de Jesús en la España contemporánea* (2 vols., Madrid, 1984, 1991), vol. 2, pp. 742–50.

problem of how the Church could defend itself within the regime from a more realistic perspective. Despite the vituperative opposition of resolute opponents of a compromise with the regime, support for the Conservative party as the best vehicle for defending the Church's interests developed by 1907 among a significant body of bishops, priests, and laypeople. Although there was no prospect of creating a confessional political party uniting all Catholics, for the first time in the Restoration's history the Church's supporters began to mobilize their constituency at the local level through the formation of Catholic political and social associations that to a limited degree overcame the chronic dynastic and ideological divisions of Spanish Catholicism. These essays in modern organizational activity failed to give the Church and its supporters a decisive role within the Restoration system. But for the first time the Church was able to use the so-called Catholic masses in a more focused way to defend its interests.

The First Battles, 1901–1905

Sagasta took office in March 1901 aware that he had to appease Liberal hardliners. In late March, the minister of public instruction, the conde de Romanones, reaffirmed the academic freedom of university professors and removed religion as an obligatory subject in public secondary schools. These measures provoked a strong clerical reaction. The bishop of Santander saw them as a step on the road to a revolutionary upheaval that would bring about "the extermination of the Church of Christ, the redistribution of the property of the bourgeoisie," and the installation of "an atheist republican regime."[10] In fact, Sagasta considered a more ambitious policy of ecclesiastical reform with some reluctance. He expressed his apprehensions about the dangers inherent in the revival of controversy over the Church in a speech to the Liberal deputies delivered in early May.[11]

Having arranged for a suitable majority in the May 1901 elections, Sagasta presented his views on the religious orders through the speech from the throne on June 11. Mindful of the pressure from within his own party for vigorous action, the prime minister announced his intention to resolve the controversy over the orders once and for all "within the existing laws." The government also declared that it would reduce the *culto y clero* budget and would seek to re-negotiate the terms of the 1851 concordat with the Vatican.[12]

The program advanced on June 11 was little more than a vague statement of intentions. It failed to provide the specifics of government policy and for a good reason. Sagasta believed that changes in ecclesiastical policy were required "to calm political agitation . . . in the interests of peace and order," but he hoped to accom-

10. "Pastoral del Obispo de Santander," September 8, 1901, *La Cruz* (1901), p. 314.
11. José Andrés-Gallego, *La política religiosa en España, 1889–1913* (Madrid, 1975), p. 203.
12. Ibid.

plish this goal on the basis of amicable negotiations with the Holy See.[13] But neither the Liberal party nor the cabinet could agree on the details of reform. Canalejas insisted that the orders not enumerated in the concordat should be compelled to meet all the terms of the 1887 Law of Associations and that the State should defend its regalist privileges aggressively. Sagasta disagreed with Canalejas's view that the government should act belligerently.[14] Others within the party believed that official authorization of the religious orders since the late 1870s, even by Liberal governments, had set a juridical precedent which could not be legally reversed.[15] Many also entertained doubts about imposing limits on the right of free association.

Sagasta, seeking a balance among the contending factions, undertook a revision of the 1887 Law of Associations. He named a supporter of Canalejas, Alfonso González, to the ministry (Gobernación) responsible for drafting the decree of revision. The new law (September 19, 1901), ordered that all organizations required to register under the 1887 legislation should do so with the civil governors of their respective provinces within six months. The revised law also set special terms for foreigners wishing to establish organizations in Spain, a clause directed specifically against a possible influx of religious from the anticlerical measures then being taken in France. With his usual caution, Sagasta saw to it that the religious orders were not specifically mentioned in the text, although everyone understood that it was directed against them.[16]

The purpose of the revised law of associations was to assert the right of the State to control the expansion and development of the regular clergy. The legislation contained nothing new or radical but represented a moderate application of regalist principles long associated with Spanish liberalism. The Liberal party's anticlericalism after 1900 was "moderate . . . and pragmatic, limited to modest objectives" designed to fend off secularizing pressures from the Left while not provoking the Church too much.[17] Even Jesuit administrators recognized that a general law of associations was preferable to the more damaging alternative of a law specifically directed against the regular clergy.[18] But the law's passage produced a strong reaction among the bishops, many of whom urged the regular clergy not to register.

13. Quoted in Cristóbal Robles Muñoz, "Frente a la supremacía del Estado: la Santa Sede y los católicos en la crisis de la Restauración," *Anthologica Annua* (1987), vol. 34, p. 230. The minister of justice in the Sagasta government, a close friend of Bishop Guisasola of Jaén, informed the papal nuncio that the government wished to be "respectful" with the Church and reach an agreement that "would protect priests, while maintaining them within the sacred limits of their mission." Quoted in ibid.

14. Robles Muñoz, "Frente a la supremacía del Estado," *Anthologica Annua* (1987), vol. 34, p. 233.

15. Although the Jesuits formed a redoubt of antiliberalism, especially during the first two decades of the Restoration, neither Liberal nor Conservative governments attempted to restrict the foundation of new establishments by the order. Revuelta González, *La Compañía de Jesús en la España contemporánea*, vol. 2, p. 43.

16. Andrés-Gallego, *La política religiosa*, pp. 204–9.

17. Julio de la Cueva Merino, *Clericales y anticlericales: el conflicto entre confesionalidad y secularización en Cantabria, 1875–1923* (Santander, 1994) p. 218.

18. Revuelta González, *La Compañía de Jesús*, vol. 2, p. 80.

Sagasta's effort to solve the question of the orders came to little in the end. The prime minister's usual caution emerged triumphant when the government entered into secret negotiations with the Vatican to see if it would accept the revised law in one form or another. The resulting *modus vivendi* of April 1902 watered down the original legislation on an important point. Although still insisting that all religious communities were protected by the concordat, the papacy accepted the idea that those not authorized by the government should be required to register on condition that registration could not be refused. In practical terms, the Church won a significant concession, for the act of registration, now virtually automatic, itself signified authorization.

News of the agreement reached the press in the form of a letter to the bishops from the papal nuncio, who informed them that registration, and therefore authorization, could not be denied to the religious orders. A storm of protest broke within the Liberal party among advocates of ecclesiastical reform who believed that the government had given away what it had announced with so much fanfare months earlier. Although Canalejas was a member of the cabinet that concluded the *modus vivendi*, his dissatisfaction with it caused him to break with Sagasta and abandon the government.[19] The cabinet also discussed a much vaunted proposal for a revision of the 1851 concordat, although there was no possibility that the Vatican would agree to the substantial administrative reorganization of the Church that the government desired and even less to the proposed reduction in the *culto y clero* budget.[20]

With his party divided on the question of ecclesiastical reform, Sagasta lost a vote of confidence on a minor issue in December 1902. The failure of his policy on the orders left segments of the Liberal party determined to raise the issue of reform again, a papacy suspicious of the State's intentions, and a Church ready to galvanize itself for a vigorous defense of its position.

Following the regime's customary practice of alternating power between the dynastic parties in moments of major or minor crisis, Alfonso XIII called upon Francisco Silvela to form a Conservative government. Silvela took office for a second time with a weariness that contrasted with the enthusiasm with which he had embarked on his first ministry in 1899. There was no pretense of forming a grand conservative coalition to bring about national regeneration. Although Silvela re-

19. Andrés-Gallego, *La política religiosa*, pp. 222–28. The revised law, even with the *modus vivendi*, at least secured the registration of the vast majority of religious communities. Some 2,611 registered under the law; only 354 refused to do so.

20. The "Teverga Project," named after its author, the marqués de Teverga, the minister of justice, called for a substantial reduction in the *culto y clero* budget through the suppression of fourteen dioceses, the closure of most of the country's so-called "collegiate" churches, and a reduction in the number of parishes by eliminating those possessing less than five to six hundred members. Ibid., p. 244. The marqués, who was a personal friend of Bishop Guisasola of Jaén, hoped that the Vatican would be willing to consider his proposal. Robles Muñoz, "Frente a la supremacía del Estado," *Anthologica Annua* (1987) vol. 34, p. 230.

mained head of the government for only six months, he too attempted to resolve the conflict over the religious orders by negotiating an agreement (*decreto concordado*) with the Vatican. Like Sagasta, Silvela attempted to reconcile the demands of the Church for a blank check, as far as the expansion of the regular clergy was concerned, and the pressure of progressive opinion for strict controls over future growth. The government was prepared to recognize the legality of the existing orders and to exempt them from conforming to the law of associations, although they were expected to sign a special register in the Ministry of Justice. In return, the cabinet insisted that no financial assistance should be provided to any religious community, that no new foundations should be established without the permission of the State, and that monasteries and convents with less than twelve members should be closed. In effect, the government accepted the expansion of the orders that had already taken place, in exchange for controls over future growth. Silvela's solution to the problem proved no more successful than Sagasta's, however, as announcement of the *decreto concordado* provoked a storm of protest from all sectors of the parliamentary opposition, who argued that the blanket legalization contained in the agreement constituted nothing less than a sellout of the State's rights.

The hostile reaction of the Liberal party to the *decreto concordado* showed that the issue of the religious orders was becoming a source of major division between the dynastic parties. The tacit understandings of the past between Sagasta and Cánovas on the clerical question gave way to confrontation. This became evident in 1904 during the brief ministry of Antonio Maura (1853–1925). A native of Mallorca, the fifty-year-old Maura was a former Liberal who joined the Conservatives because of his disgust with the opportunism of Sagasta and the appeal of the lofty regenerationist principles of Silvela. Maura's political program did not differ in its essentials from that of Silvela.[21] Both believed in the necessity of a vast movement of national revival, in honest rather than manipulative politics, and in administrative reform, particularly in the direction of decentralization. Discouraged by the failure of his efforts, Silvela abandoned the struggle. Maura was made of tougher fiber. Called the "eaglet" by his Mallorcan friends, he was an individual of scrupulous personal conduct who was convinced of the rightness of his ideas.[22]

Maura abandoned the prudent regalism that even Silvela had shown in his ecclesiastical policy in favor of a more pro-clerical stance certain to provoke a hostile Liberal reaction. Signs of the change appeared with the appointment of a controversial figure, the Dominican friar Bernardino Nozaleda, to the archbishopric of Valencia. Although the Vatican was unenthusiastic about Nozaleda and attempted to stop his appointment, the government insisted on proceeding, although there is

21. Carr, *Spain, 1808–1939*, p. 481.
22. Rafael Pérez Delgado, *Antonio Maura* (Madrid, 1974), p. 511.

evidence that the appointment did not originate with Maura but with the minister of justice, Sánchez de Toca, who may have wished to discredit the prime minister in the Conservative party's internal struggles. But once the appointment was made and a whirlwind of controversy loosed, Maura stood firm.[23]

The appointment was impolitic, to put it mildly. Even Silvela had refused to appoint the controversial Dominican to a Spanish bishopric. Nozaleda's notoriety arose from his alleged conduct as archbishop of Manila at the time of the American victory, when he elected to remain at his post, thereby, according to his opponents, betraying Spain. His appointment to Valencia also revived the controversy over the role of the religious orders in the Philippines. To make matters worse, the nomination of Nozaleda to the most republican and anticlerical city in the country invited trouble that was not long in appearing. Blasco Ibáñez launched a full-scale propaganda offensive against the Dominican friar, bluntly declaring that only "cannons and bayonets" would allow him to take up his post.[24] Liberals attacked the appointment. Republicans saw it as a provocation. The Church and its supporters rallied to Maura, who insisted that the nomination stand.[25] The bishop of Santander told the prime minister that he was offering prayers on his behalf so that the "ship of State" would not sink into "the abyss of irreligion," while the parish priest of the village of Torralba de los Sisones declared more crudely, "It is time these Republicans were shut up."[26] Maura's stubbornness in the Nozaleda affair was a tactical error. It provoked an ugly anticlerical reaction at a time when moderation was needed, even if in the short term the support Maura received from the bishops, the clergy, and their lay supporters promised a political advantage.

Until the appearance of Maura, the Conservative party had more or less adhered to Cánovas's policy of seeking to prevent the issue of the Church from disrupting the political balance between the dynastic parties essential for the regime's stability. Far from moving the question to the margins, Maura brought it to the center. In a parliamentary address on July 11, 1903, he set forth his position without ambiguity. Although denying that he had ever "mingled Catholicism with questions of public law," he declared that during "all my life I have believed that the State commits a great error . . . when it uses its power . . . to contradict religious sentiment, which in Spain is equivalent to Catholicism."[27] The latter, he argued, is "an

23. Santiago Petschen, "Año 1904: primer gobierno Maura: el arzobispo Nozaleda es rechazado en Valencia," *Historia Internacional* (1976), no. 10, p. 40. Vicente Cárcel Ortí, *Historia de la Iglesia de Valencia* (2 vols., Valencia, 1987), vol. 2, p. 699.

24. Quoted in Reig, *Blasquistas y clericales*, p. 291.

25. Maura's position has been defended by Robles Muñoz, who has argued that the appointment was a reasonable solution to the problem of providing for the Spanish bishops returning to Spain after the end of the Spanish-American War. Robles Muñoz, *Antonio Maura*, p. 154.

26. Quoted in Santiago Petschen, "Maura y los obispos se ganan a las derechas," *Historia Internacional* (1976), no. 15, pp. 60–62.

27. This and the other quotations in this paragraph are drawn from *Antonio Maura: treinta y cinco años de vida pública*, vol. 1, pp. 205–6.

immense force . . . perhaps the most powerful political force in Spanish society." Once it had been guilty of "sinister manifestations" in the use of power; now it was necessary "to pour it into democratic molds . . . in order to take action against the forces of the Left." For Maura, the Church provided "the primary foundation of the conservative classes and the defense of order."

There is no reason to doubt Maura's sincerity in seeking to convert the Church and its supporters into active participants within the liberal political system, although it was far from certain that any effort to dislodge the historic antiliberalism of clergy and laity would succeed.[28] By encouraging Catholics to defend the social order through support of the Conservative party, Maura promoted a degree of political involvement on the part of the Church that was new in the history of the Restoration and certain to provoke a hostile reaction among Liberals and Republicans. Both rejected the Conservative party's change in direction. Liberals feared that Maura intended to alter the traditional rules of the political game by appealing to a constituency historically identified with opposition to political and cultural pluralism. Republicans saw the attempt to attract Catholics to the Conservative cause as the first stage in the construction of a vaguely authoritarian, proclerical regime.

Maura attempted to resolve the problem of the religious orders by resurrecting Silvela's *decreto concordado*. Negotiations with the Vatican produced a version of the earlier agreement in a *convenio* signed by both parties in June 1904. Liberals attacked it in parliament and the press. They accused Maura of compromising the State's independence by yielding to the Vatican.[29] Lerroux and Blasco Ibáñez launched a campaign against the legislation deemed so violent by the government that it laid charges against them for violating the press laws. Passionate public debate was accompanied by street clashes between opponents and supporters of the *convenio*. In some respects, Maura's initiative was no more extreme than Silvela's. But again he acted injudiciously, for he must have realized that a proposal already rejected once by the Liberal party would not win its consent on its second appearance. Maura left office having failed to resolve the impasse over the religious orders or quiet agitated public opinion. Controversy over the orders simmered into the summer of 1905, when the king called upon the elderly Liberal leader Eugenio Montero Ríos to form a government. The fight over the regular clergy now entered its most blistering phase.

28. The case for Maura's attempt to show that liberalism and Catholicism were not incompatible has been most fully developed by Robles Muñoz, *Antonio Maura*.

29. Montero Ríos accused the Conservative party of lacking "patriotic sentiments" for refusing to defend the supremacy of the civil power against "ultramontanism." Quoted in Robles Muñoz, "Frente a la supremacía del Estado," *Anthologica Annua* (1989), vol. 36, p. 361.

The Liberals and the Church, 1906–1907

The attempt of Montero Ríos to resolve the problem of the regular clergy rested on a political philosophy formed thirty years earlier during his service as a minister of the democratic monarchy. The prime minister remained attached to a strongly regalist view of civil-ecclesiastical relations and to what he regarded as an essential tenet of liberalism, the right of all citizens to come together freely in associations. He attempted to reconcile these principles by confirming the privileged juridical status of the two religious orders mentioned in the concordat and by subjecting the remainder to the ordinary process of the law, on the assumption that these communities would be allowed to exist as legitimate organizations of citizens.[30] This program fell short of what Liberal reformers expected. As a result of the prime minister's resignation over the extraordinary events of the *Cu-Cut!* affair, power passed to a leading contender for the political mantle of Sagasta, Segismundo Moret, who proposed an ambitious program of ecclesiastical reform.[31]

Moret did not view the so-called clerical question with the same intensity that Canalejas did, but he was a shrewd politician who realized that the Liberal party required an issue capable of disarming a resurgent republicanism. The prime minister had at hand the example of the Waldeck-Rousseau legislation in France, which showed that political advantage could be secured from measures against the religious orders. Moret also realized that a substantial body of opinion within the Liberal party now favored a bolder initiative. A member of the new generation of Liberal politicians, the conde de Romanones put the issue simply: "The Liberal program [based on] the great principles of universal suffrage and jury trial was exhausted . . . : it was necessary to give it new substance through an anticlerical policy."[32]

In May 1906, Moret presented the government's program. It included proposals for the introduction of religious liberty, a new law of associations, the secularization of cemeteries, and a revision of legislation on civil marriage. To accomplish these changes, Moret believed that parliament should be dissolved and new elections held to give the government a clear mandate to proceed. The opposition of

30. Ibid., p. 382.

31. On November 24, 1905, a group of army officers burned the premises of the satirical magazine *Cu-Cut!* in Barcelona. The magazine had boasted of the recent electoral victories of regionalist candidates. Some within the Liberal party were strongly opposed to the autonomist movement and were sympathetic to the officers' action. The prime minister, however, believed that "the first duty of the Government was to defend the civil power to the last extremity" and therefore opposed army pressure for a new law expanding the jurisdiction of the military over press offenses "against the Nation and the Army" moved by the events in Barcelona. Although Montero Ríos received the support of the cabinet, it is likely that the attitude of Alfonso XIII caused him to resign. Conde de Romanones, *Notas de una vida, 1868–1912* (2 vols., Madrid, n.d.), vol. 2, pp. 135, 137–39.

32. Ibid., pp. 180–81.

many of the party's leaders to a dissolution forced the prime minister to resign without having implemented his program.[33]

It fell to an elderly veteran of the ancient battles of liberalism, General López Domínguez, to preside over the government that would introduce the most far-reaching legislation on the Church since the days of the democratic monarchy. The proposal in its details came from the minister of the interior (Gobernación), Bernarbé Dávila, but its inspiration was José Canalejas, who enjoyed the confidence of the cabinet, although he was not a member. In a letter to the prime minister in August 1906, Canalejas outlined his program. Its terms were not new. Some had been announced earlier by Moret. Others owed a debt to the French legislation of Waldeck-Rousseau. Canalejas presented his recommendations with a discussion of the historical origins of the clerical question and an astute analysis of the political danger to reforming liberalism from a growing republican movement, should the government and the Liberal party fail to act. If both did not move decisively, Canalejas argued, they would appear open to the charge of deserting "the democratic flag . . . to retain power and ingratiate ourselves with the throne and conservative elements."[34] Canalejas called for a new law of associations similar to the original version of the legislation passed in 1902; he asked for increased government support of public education and stricter controls over Church schools. Like Moret, he urged a reform of legislation governing civil marriage and appealed for the introduction of complete religious liberty.

The cabinet plunged into the battle. It ordered private schools operating without formal government authorization to seek official approval immediately or face closure—a measure aimed directly at the schools of the religious orders. As minister of justice, the conde de Romanones commanded that no declaration of religious affiliation could be exacted from those wishing to be married in a civil ceremony. Finally, in October, the government presented its proposal for a new law of associations.

There was little prospect that the draft legislation would be passed because of serious differences within Liberal ranks and the opposition of King Alfonso XIII. Moret and Montero Ríos believed the proposed law was a "chimera," while even the conde de Romanones saw it as too extreme.[35] But announcement of the legislative project and other proposals, such as the liberalization of marriage legislation, provoked a strong reaction among bishops, clergy, and the Church's lay de-

33. Andrés-Gallego, *La política religiosa*, pp. 282–83.

34. Quoted in ibid., pp. 288–89.

35. Robles Muñoz, "Frente a la supremacía del Estado," *Anthologica Annua* (1989), vol. 36, p. 410. The king objected strongly to the proposed law of associations and attempted to prevent it from being presented in parliament. When the cabinet threatened to resign over the issue, Alfonso XIII signed the appropriate documents allowing the measure to be introduced. He also believed that it would not secure legislative approval.

fenders. The bishop of Tuy set the tone for the clerical riposte in a controversial letter to his clergy attacking civil marriage as concubinage. The minister's order on civil marriage, declared the bishop, was "for many the equivalent of formal apostasy" because it encouraged Catholics to despise divine and ecclesiastical laws on matrimony.[36] The suggestion that Romanones had committed the sin of apostasy led the minister to lay charges against the prelate in the Supreme Court. But the bishop of Tuy did not stand alone. Throughout the country, bishops, cathedral chapters, and ordinary parish priests expressed their support for his stance.[37] In León, the clergy launched a campaign against newspapers supporting the government, while the bishop of Guadix attributed government policy to a masonic plot designed to destroy the Church.[38]

In the past the ecclesiastical establishment had occasionally ventured from the supposedly neutral corner where Cánovas had placed it to castigate the government. But the campaign of the hierarchy against Liberal ecclesiastical policy in 1906 went beyond previous interventions. A deluge of complaints and criticism in the Catholic press was followed by a series of massive public meetings, particularly in the north. To the cries of "Down with this subversive project! Long live the Virgin of Begoña!" sixty thousand protesters demonstrated against the government in Vizcaya, while in Guipúzcoa twenty thousand assembled to protest the proposed law of associations.[39] The campaign even reached the august halls of the royal palace. After receiving his cardinal's biretta from the hands of Alfonso XIII, according to custom, Marcelo Spínola, archbishop of Seville, addressed the monarch in language that came close to inviting him to exceed his constitutional responsibilities:

> There are in Spain, Sir, subterranean currents which are seeking to undermine the foundations of the nation; there are tendencies . . . hostile to the only true religion; there are misguided men who wish to bring to Spain the impious currents of a neighboring country, and I implore Your Majesty not to permit the seed of impiety to take root in our country.[40]

The heated atmosphere produced by the government's ecclesiastical policy led to street clashes between defenders of the Church and their opponents. In Vizcaya,

36. "Circular del Exmo. y Rvdmo. Sr. Obispo de Tuy," September 1, 1906, *La Cruz* (1906), p. 298. The political storm raised by the letter did not quiet the bishop, who continued the campaign in a subsequent letter in which he complained of "frequent and habitual omissions, apparently systematic, without respect for the protection . . . of the Religion of the State." These omissions, he claimed, originated "in the very regions of power obliged to protect it." *La Cruz* (1906), pp. 303–4.

37. See, for example, the pastoral letters of the archbishop of Valencia and the bishop of Córdoba in *La Cruz* (1906), pp. 305 ff.

38. Andrés-Gallego, *La política religiosa*, p. 286. The case was resolved when the bishop agreed to write a letter of apology to Romanones in which he declared that he had not intended "to offend Your Excellency either in his person or his high office." *La Cruz* (1906), p. 330.

39. *La Semana Católica* (1907), pp. 21, 71.

40. Ibid., p. 19.

Catholic demonstrators pursued and beat small groups of protesters who attempted to disrupt protest meetings. But in republican and anticlerical Valencia, street demonstrations against Archbishop Guisasola became so widespread that the prelate left the city in fear of violence against his person.[41]

Pastoral letters, protest meetings, and press campaigns did not save the Church from the policies of the López Domínguez government; the chronic divisions of the Liberal party did. Montero Ríos and his followers announced their opposition to the proposed law of associations, while the astute Moret, resentful of his ouster from office, intrigued against the old general in spite of having advanced a similar program scarcely a year earlier. To resolve the political crisis, the king called upon Antonio Maura to form a Conservative government.

Liberalism and the Church

In an era of ministerial instability, Maura accomplished the rare feat of staying in office for two and one-half years. During this time the prime minister received increasing support from clergy and laity, although Carlists and Integrists regarded him suspiciously as a representative of liberal values. A clerical opponent of the constitutional monarchy included Maura with Canalejas, Moret, and Lerroux as exemplars of a corrosive political philosophy hostile to religion.[42] But Maura's stature among Catholics rested on his reputation as a Church member inspired by high ethical standards, his opposition to the Liberal party's ecclesiastical policy, his commitment to defense of the established social order, and his firmness before the anticlerical agitation of 1904. With the prospect of uniting all Catholics in a confessional party as remote as ever, Maura and the Conservatives appeared a promising alternative, although the prime minister remained committed to the liberal political system.[43]

The drift towards Maura developed within the framework of the Church's search for a means of defending its interests in the face of continuing discord between Catholic supporters of the liberal regime and their Carlist and Integrist opponents. Repeated exhortations by Popes Leo XIII and Pius X (1903–1914), urg-

41. The protests followed Guisasola to Alcoy, where he complained of "injurious acts" that prevented him "from freely carrying out our sacred duty." Quoted in ibid., p. 492.

42. Cueva Merino, *Clericales y anticlericales*, p. 231.

43. In 1902, the marqués de Comillas, the country's most influential layman, expressed serious reservations about any attempt to establish a Catholic political party. He believed that such a party would deepen the already powerful antagonisms existing among Catholics and stood little chance of electoral success, a position supported by the papal nuncio. José-Leonardo Ruiz Sánchez, *Política e Iglesia durante la Restauración: la Liga Católica de Sevilla, 1901–1923* (Seville, 1994), p. 231. Maura, declared one of his defenders, remained a "convinced liberal" who favored a "constitutional regime . . . of political liberties" opposed to both a personal monarchy and absolutism. He wanted nothing to do with the "old political regime, already proscribed by all civilized nations," to which some Spanish Catholics wished to return. Benito Mariano Andrade y Uribe, *La Iglesia y la política: católicos y liberales* (Burgos, 1911), pp. 312, 314.

ing Spanish Catholics to set aside dynastic and ideological differences on behalf of the higher good of defending the Church against secularization and anticlericalism, failed to inspire unity. The Vatican and a minority of bishops, particularly Cardinal Sancha of Toledo and Bishop Salvador y Barrera of Madrid, angered Carlists and Integrists by advocating full participation in the nation's political life. "The sectarian and anti-Christian orientation of some parties," declared the cardinal primate in 1907, imposed an "imperious necessity" on the faithful "to abandon the timid and prejudicial withdrawal from [politics] that has prevailed until the present."[44] Sancha had long believed that unyielding hostility towards the liberal State was counterproductive. His pragmatic recognition that Catholics could and should defend the Church by working within the regime made him the object of sustained and savage attacks launched by Ramón Nocedal from the pages of *El Siglo Futuro*.[45]

This obstructionism more or less achieved its goal for a considerable period. Despite constant pressure from the Vatican and the nuncio, most bishops, fearing the abusive reaction of the Integrist press, were afraid to imitate the example of Cardinal Sancha.[46] In 1900, Bishop Menéndez of Tuy believed the situation had reached a point of desperation for the hierarchy. According to his gloomy assessment, Catholics were, in the great majority, enemies of liberal governments and felt no scruple about accusing the bishops of being "excessively compliant" with the civil authorities, to the point that "they rebel against and threaten us." As a result, prelates remained "indecisive and disoriented. . . . Most do nothing, because we do not know what to do."[47]

This situation gradually changed. Despite reservations about the State's liberal foundations, the papacy and the bishops became stronger in their support of the

44. *La Cruz* (1907), p. 395.

45. Sancha maintained contacts with politicians of the dynastic parties. His friendship with some of them "made him sensitive" to their concerns with respect to the Church. Robles Muñoz, "Frente a la supremacía del Estado," *Anthologica Annua* (1989), vol. 36, p. 323. In 1899, Sancha published a pamphlet advocating sincere acceptance of the constitutional monarchy as the best way of defending the Church's interests. Domingo Benavides Gómez, *Democracia y cristianismo en la España de la Restauración, 1875–1931* (Madrid, 1978), p. 169. The Integrist press attacked the cardinal so fiercely that he published a pastoral letter to the faithful of his diocese censuring Nocedal's *El Siglo Futuro* as a "grave obstacle to peace and union" among Catholics. The "pathological state" of the newspaper had produced "confusions, rebellions and disorders" that endangered souls and hindered the Church from warding off attacks against religion. *Carta pastoral sobre la obediencia debida a los prelados* (Toledo, 1899), pp. 3, 28, 40. The controversy expanded when an ardent Integrist, Canon José Roca y Ponsa of Seville cathedral, publicly attacked Sancha's position on the grounds that "in Spain liberalism is the only enemy of the Church." Quoted in Ruiz Sánchez, *Política e Iglesia durante la Restauración*, p. 70.

46. The cardinal did not entertain a high opinion of most of his episcopal colleagues, none of whom publicly supported him in the 1899 controversy with Nocedal and the canon of Seville. In a 1900 letter to the nuncio, Sancha described the bishops as prelates who "look backward and maintain that the present is intrinsically bad and that there is no other remedy for this than the flood or to return to the times of Philip II. What can be expected from this way of thinking?" Quoted in Robles Muñoz, "Frente a la supremacía del Estado," *Anthologica Annua* (1987), vol. 34, p. 221.

47. Quoted in Robles Muñoz, *Antonio Maura*, p. 111.

constitutional monarchy, although this commitment was far from unambiguous.[48] At the same time, some movement took place among once resolute clerical supporters of intransigence, who began to set aside their dynastic and ideological preoccupations, given what they perceived as the more important task of defending the Church against the Liberal party's ecclesiastical policy and republican anticlericalism. The new attitude surfaced dramatically in 1905, when the Jesuit journal *Razón y Fe* published an article by Father Venancio Minteguiaga, who applied to politics ideas developed by Catholic moralists concerning the "lesser evil" ("el mal menor").[49] The question discussed was straightforward. Could a Catholic vote for a candidate of the dynastic parties under any circumstances? If there were no obvious "Catholic" candidates, the author declared, then it was licit to choose the "lesser evil" of voting for the liberal candidate who would best defend or least injure the Church's interests.[50] Minteguiaga left no doubt that this tactic was directed against Socialists and Republicans. Catholics, he declared, must vote for candidates who are "always less hostile to Religion against those . . . who are going to persecute more."[51] The Jesuits of Tortosa applied the principle of the "lesser evil" in November when they voted in municipal elections for candidates of the dynastic parties to deny victory to Republicans.[52]

The declarations of *Razón y Fe* fell like a bombshell on Ramón Nocedal and his followers, since they contradicted the Integrist and Carlist belief that under no circumstances could a Catholic vote for a liberal candidate, however conservative his views. Although in poor health, Nocedal sallied forth in his last great propaganda campaign to prevent Catholics from accepting the constitutional monarchy either directly or indirectly. The battle over the concept of the "lesser evil" was as fierce as the conflict over the Unión Católica during the 1880s.[53] But Pope Pius X rejected the Integrist case, declaring in 1906 that the declarations of *Razón y Fe* contained

48. In 1902, for example, the bishops attending the Catholic Congress in Santiago de Compostela affirmed their fidelity to Alfonso XIII. They suggested that the monarchy was a popular institution in its own right apart from the liberal political system. The king replied graciously but took pains to inform the bishops that he functioned strictly within the limits defined by the constitution. Robles Muñoz, "Frente a la supremacía del Estado," *Anthologica Annua* (1987), vol. 34, pp. 294–95. Although the Vatican often censured the divisive tactics of Carlists and Integrists, it never issued a general condemnation of either movement. In 1910, for example, Cardinal Merry del Val, the papal secretary of state, told Cardinal Aguirre of Toledo that although the papacy did not support the anti-dynastic program of Carlists and Integrists, it found nothing of a doctrinal nature in their policies that deserved condemnation. Robles Muñoz, *Antonio Maura*, p. 315.

49. Despite the Jesuits' earlier sympathy for Integrism, by 1905 "ample sectors of the Company" favored breaking their links to the movement in favor of the Conservative party. Revuelta González, *La Compañía de Jesús*, vol. 2, p. 765.

50. Benavides Gómez, *Democracia y cristianismo*, p. 187.

51. Quoted in Revuelta González, *La Compañía de Jesús*, vol. 2, p. 769.

52. Ibid., p. 773. On their way to the polling station the Tortosa Jesuits were insulted and threatened by angry young Republicans to the point that the Civil Guard was needed to escort the clergy to their destination.

53. Revuelta González has described the bruising propaganda battles among Catholics over "el mal menor." Ibid., pp. 769–77.

nothing objectionable on doctrinal grounds. The pope accepted the argument that Catholics, "considering the circumstances of the times," could vote for candidates who would safeguard the "interests of religion and the country in the exercise of their public charge."

The papal statement represented a public defeat for Nocedal, whose death in 1907 further eroded Integrism's influence over Catholic opinion. The door was now open to support for Antonio Maura. During the 1907 general election campaign, the clergy turned to Maura, although some Integrist and Carlist diehards remained firm in their opposition to the Conservative party. A prominent clerical journalist declared: "It is an absolute necessity . . . that we Catholics support and protect those who from the heights of power have the force and desire to bring about the triumph of Christ's cause."[54] Cardinal Sancha went further and threatened to excommunicate Catholics who voted for candidates favoring the Liberal party's proposed law of associations.[55]

Despite growing admiration for Maura, the swing in his direction among clergy and laity did not represent a sudden conversion of Catholic opinion to liberalism even in its most conservative version. "Now we will unite with the liberal monarchist parties to get rid of the Republicans," declared a Jesuit priest. "When they are out of the way we will unite with the Conservatives to get rid of the Fusionists [Liberals], and finally, we will declare ourselves independent, . . . masters of the field."[56] This crude assessment may not have been shared by more sophisticated clerical observers, but it contained an element of truth. Clerical and lay supporters of Maura saw him in practical terms as the only figure capable of blocking the Liberal party's ecclesiastical plans and holding anticlerical republicanism in check.

The Church did not place all its eggs in the Conservative basket. The idea of political action based exclusively on defense of the Church rather than on dynastic and ideological concerns remained alive. It took the form of local electoral associations, the Catholic Leagues that proliferated during the century's first decade. In 1901, Archbishop Marcelo Spínola of Seville, apprehensive over the Sagasta government's intentions, encouraged the formation of the first league. In the style of the Unión Católica, membership was open to all Catholics who accepted papal condemnation of "modern errors" and were willing to follow episcopal direction. The Seville league's political objective was straightforward: to organize the electorate to vote for "clearly Catholic candidates" irrespective of their dynastic or ideological loyalties.[57] Other leagues were also established in direct response to clerical and lay perceptions of a Church under siege. The Catholic League of Valencia

54. *La Semana Católica* (1907), p. 347.
55. *La Cruz* (1907), p. 395.
56. Quoted in Revuelta González, *La Compañía de Jesús*, vol. 2, p. 773.
57. Quoted in Ruiz Sánchez, *Política e Iglesia durante la Restauración*, pp. 97–98.

was established in 1902 to fight Liberal ecclesiastical legislation at the national level and the populist and aggressively anticlerical republicanism of Blasco Ibáñez at the municipal. A similar association, the Centro Católico Electoral, emerged in Santander in 1907 from the protest movement organized against the proposed law of associations presented by the López Domínguez government.[58] In theory, membership in the leagues was open to all Catholics. In practice, this rarely meant Liberals or Conservatives who remained suspect in the eyes of Integrists and Carlists.[59] But by giving priority to defending the Church within the political system, the leagues shifted emphasis away from the primary objective of Carlists and Integrists—the end of the liberal State. This point was not lost on Ramón Nocedal. Despite his followers' participation in the leagues, the Integrist leader feared that the new associations threatened the traditional Catholic parties. In 1905, he bluntly told Archbishop Spínola that the leagues were "an immense misfortune, a catastrophe, a disaster" that would ruin attempts to unify Catholics politically.[60]

The leagues' success was limited, although some, notably the Catholic League of Valencia, fared better than most. The leagues tended to focus on local issues and battles beyond their vague general purpose of defending the Church's interests. In Valencia, for example, the league fought decisions of a city government under the influence of the followers of Blasco Ibáñez when it eliminated subsidies for certain religious celebrations and attempted to impose a tax on church bells. In general elections, on those occasions when they were conducted with a degree of honesty, league candidates failed to appeal to Catholic voters who supported Maura. In any event, there was little prospect that the leagues could break the near monopoly of the dynastic parties in national politics. The Conservatives viewed the leagues as unwelcome competitors for a Catholic electorate that the party wished to make its own.[61]

The Catholic Leagues contributed to the evolution of Spanish Catholicism in two ways. They helped push Carlism and Integrism to the margins by stressing the necessity of defending the Church as the overriding objective of Catholic political action. They also attempted to mobilize the Catholic electorate in distinctly modern fashion. The Catholic League of Valencia, for example, felt no scruple about

58. Reig, *Blasquistas y clericales*, p. 87; Cueva Merino, *Clericales y anticlericales*, pp. 92–93.

59. Only three Conservative party members signed the Seville league's document of foundation, in contrast to eight Carlists and Integrists. In its early stages, the Centro Católico Electoral of Santander excluded anyone who failed to profess antiliberalism, including members of the Conservative party. Ruiz Sánchez, *Política e Iglesia durante la Restauración*, p. 99; Cueva Merino, *Clericales y anticlericales*, p. 94.

60. Quoted in Benavides Gómez, *Democracia y cristianismo*, p. 186.

61. In 1909, for example, the Conservative press in Seville attacked the separate candidacies presented by the Catholic League in recent municipal elections. The league was blamed for dividing the "Catholic" vote, thereby ensuring victory for "anticlericals, the Church's very enemies." Quoted in Ruiz Sánchez, *Política e Iglesia durante la Restauración*, p. 260. In 1907, the Conservative press of Valencia was more circumspect in its criticism but left no doubt that the party was "reticent and irritated" by the electoral competition of the local league. Reig, *Blasquistas y clericales*, p. 89.

imitating the propaganda and organizational techniques employed so successfully by the republicanism of Blasco Ibáñez.[62] This attempt to create what has been called "ultramontane populism," based on organizing the so-called Catholic masses, did not produce the results its promoters expected. As long as the dynastic parties controlled the political system and Maura appeared an adequate defender of the Church's interests, there was little chance of creating a modern Catholic political party on the basis of the leagues.[63] The possibilities of Catholic populism were further limited by the overwhelming role in league organizations played by local social elites drawn from ranks of the professional classes, landowners, and, in some cases, aristocrats. But for the first time, however limited their success, the leagues showed that the Church's supporters had begun to learn the lessons of mass politics.

The Failure of Maura, 1907–1909

Maura did not owe his 1907 electoral triumph to the Church. The government delivered the vote through the usual means, whatever the prime minister's lofty opinions on the evils of political dishonesty. Yet the elections did mark a significant change in the place of the Church within the Restoration. There was never an explicit alliance between Maura and the ecclesiastical leadership, but the hierarchy moved from a position of relative political neutrality to active support of the Conservative party.[64] Curiously, the Church obtained few important concessions from Maura. The government sought more amicable relations with the Vatican; it used troops to force the return of Archbishop Guisasola to Valencia from where he had fled before anticlerical agitation. The government also abandoned efforts to enact a new law of associations regulating the religious orders. But Maura failed to increase the budget for clerical salaries despite insistent appeals from bishops and priests. He also remained faithful to a historic regalist objective of Spanish liberalism by insisting on a reduction in the number of dioceses. As was the case with Silvela during his first ministry, it was not so much what Maura did for the Church but what his policies signified for the Liberal party and the Republican opposition. Maura's attempt to come to terms with Catalan regionalism, his proposal for harsh antiterrorist laws, and the support that he received from the clergy appeared to the opposition as a sinister portent of a semi-dictatorial regime bent on a pro-clerical and reactionary policy. The politically astute Moret issued an appeal towards the end of 1908 for a Union of the Left to resist the advance of political reaction and clericalism. The Liberal party factions came together to launch a campaign of meetings and propaganda on the basis of a program affirming the supremacy of the

62. Reig, *Blasquistas y clericales*, p. 105.
63. For a fuller discussion of the concept of "ultramontane populism," see ibid., pp. 17–20, 71.
64. Andrés-Gallego, *La política religiosa*, p. 328.

civil power over the ecclesiastical, the necessity of constitutional reform including full religious liberty—a strategy thought capable of undercutting the growing appeal of the Republican parties.

The Union of the Left did not cause Maura's downfall. In 1909, a political crisis developed as a result of the government's decision to send conscripts to bolster the faltering military campaign against Rif tribesmen resisting the establishment of a Spanish protectorate in Morocco. Maura had once opposed an ambitious military policy across the straits. He now yielded to pressure from the army and those with economic interests in the region. The decision to expand operations and employ conscripts drawn from the lower classes through an unfair selection process committed the government to an unpopular war, although the Liberal opposition was by no means adverse to the government's initiative.[65]

Hostility towards the war ran highest in Barcelona, the principal point of embarkation for the new troops being sent to Morocco. The first incidents occurred on July 18, when sullen crowds gathered along the route followed by the first contingents moving towards the port. As the troops and the swelling crowd reached the docks, sullenness gave way to anger, when society ladies distributed religious medals and cigarettes to the unhappy conscripts. To cries of "Throw away your guns!" and "Let the friars go!" soldiers were forced aboard the transport awaiting them. The police dispersed the crowd on shore by firing into the air and arresting troublemakers.[66]

This modest beginning of the antiwar movement scarcely seemed to herald the outbreak of a widespread popular protest that would involve a general strike, the raising of street barricades, sporadic violence, and a wave of church and convent burnings the likes of which had not been seen in the country since the summer of 1835. The causes of the events of the Tragic Week (July 26–August 1, 1909), were many. The ineptness of the civil and military authorities, particularly during the early stages of the conflict, allowed the situation to get out of control. The increasing militancy of the city's working class and the labor union, Solidaridad Obrera, intensified the workers' sense of economic deprivation and general victimization at the hands of the Restoration's social elites. Industrial workers had developed a deep hostility towards the Church as the result of years of effective propaganda by Alejandro Lerroux and his Radical Republican party. Further, anarchist militants, long active in the city, saw the events of the Tragic Week as the spark capable of igniting the great revolutionary upheaval of which they had long dreamed.

All three groups participated in the agitation and incendiarism of the Tragic Week. But the differences separating them made the possibility of a successful as-

65. Joan Connelly Ullman, *The Tragic Week: A Study of Anticlericalism in Spain* (Cambridge, Mass., 1968), pp. 129–31.

66. Ibid., p. 136.

sault on the liberal State remote at best. There was little possibility that a protest in one city and its environs would spread throughout the country. The government and conservative opinion saw the events of the Tragic Week as the result of a conspiracy designed to launch popular revolution. But there was never a concerted plan of action among the principal groups involved in the agitation, as the authorities discovered in their judicial inquiries after the event. There were no systematic attacks on property save for those directed against street cars and church buildings, and there was little loss of life. Punctilious incendiarists even escorted priests and nuns from their residences before setting buildings ablaze.[67] But collective anger focused on the Church. Eighty religious buildings, including twenty-four Church schools, fourteen parish churches, sixteen monasteries and convents, as well as a variety of edifices used for charitable purposes, were put to the torch.[68]

Why the Church was singled out by workers who refrained from attacking employers and their businesses is not entirely clear.[69] Educational and charitable institutions bore the brunt of the assault on ecclesiastical buildings. Church schools appeared an obstacle to working-class demands for a free, secular system of education, while the charitable organizations seemed well-financed attempts to lure the workers away from militant labor organizations. Yet few workers came in contact with the Church's charitable and educational activities. It has been suggested that the assaults of the Tragic Week arose less from specific grievances than from the perception of the Church as a symbolic "protagonist" identified with a political and social system that was frustrating working-class aspirations for profound change.[70] The workers "know," said one labor spokesman, that "every convent is a perpetual conspiracy against every principle of democracy, against all ideas of liberty and all aspirations to progress."[71]

The physical damage inflicted during the Tragic Week was repaired within a year. The political effects on the Restoration were more serious. Heavy-handed repression by the Maura government, especially its decision to accuse a well-known anarchist, Francisco Ferrer, of being the chief of a revolutionary conspiracy, plunged the regime into crisis. Ferrer's execution set off a wave of international protests that evoked an image of the inquisitorial Spain of centuries past. When the legislature reopened in October, Republicans and Liberals joined in a furious attack on the gov-

67. Only three religious were killed during the agitation. Ibid., p. 285.

68. Ullman argues that the Radical Republicans, sometimes openly, sometimes covertly, encouraged the church burnings as a means of diverting popular hostility from a more direct revolutionary purpose so that the party could preserve its dominance in Barcelona. Ibid., pp. 324–25.

69. Joaquín Romero Maura has provided an excellent analysis of the diverse explanations of the reasons behind the assault on the Church. *La rosa de fuego: republicanos y anarquistas: la política de los obreros barceloneses entre el desastre colonial y la Semana Trágica* (Barcelona, Buenos Aires, and Mexico City, 1975), pp. 519–42.

70. Ibid., pp. 536–37.

71. Quoted in Ullman, *The Tragic Week*, p. 327.

ernment. Maura's insensitivity to parliamentary criticism led the Liberals, according to the conde de Romanones, to issue a "cry of war without quarter" against the cabinet. Moret's speech directed to Maura "reached tones of violence never before felt or employed" in the parliamentary history of the Restoration.[72] Whether the Liberals set out to destroy Maura for crude political advantage, as some historians allege, is uncertain.[73] But the differences separating the dynastic parties broadened to create the most serious crisis faced by the regime since its foundation. The decision of the Liberal party to withdraw from parliament forced the issue. Maura went to Alfonso XIII seeking royal endorsement to continue in office. The king decided against Maura and called Moret to form a Liberal government. An enraged Maura announced his "implacable hostility" towards the new cabinet.[74]

In the late summer and autumn of 1909, the Catholic press attempted to explain the causes of the violent assaults against ecclesiastical institutions, while bishops and parish priests deluged Maura with letters and telegrams demanding firm measures to prevent a repetition of what had occurred in Barcelona. The burning of religious buildings was seen as the beginning of the long-feared revolution to overthrow Church, State, and the social order. "The seditious movement in Barcelona," declared the Catholic newspaper *El Universo,* "was entirely revolutionary."[75] What began as a street disturbance, according to another Catholic journal, became a "formidable revolution that was cut short because Divine Providence touched us with its hand."[76] Religion bore the brunt of the attack, said the bishops of Catalonia, because "the men of the revolution know that the Church is the firmest bulwark of society and the nation."[77]

That the Tragic Week arose from a planned conspiracy appeared self-evident to pro-clerical commentators. Blame was assessed, however, in different proportions. For the prominent Catalan Jesuit Ignaci Casanovas, the attack on the Church was the result of "a most cowardly, masonic and anarchist plot."[78] The Capuchin friar Miquel d'Esplugues singled out the Radical Republicans of Lerroux, who, "believing themselves lords of nearly all Catalonia and with sufficient strength in the rest of Spain," launched "the decisive battle against religion, the monarchy and the social order."[79] *El Universo* initially blamed the anarchists but on the following day

72. Romanones, *Notas de una vida,* vol. 2, p. 241.

73. José María García Escudero has argued, with respect to the Liberal assault on Maura, "In no case is it possible to excuse the Liberals' attitude, which was not only politically suicidal, but also morally unspeakable," *Vista a la derecha* (Madrid, 1988), p. 127.

74. Quoted in Andrés-Gallego, *La política religiosa,* p. 364.

75. *El Universo,* August 4, 1909.

76. Miquel d'Esplugues, "Post Nubila . . . ," *Estudios Franciscanos* (1909), no. 33, p. 163.

77. " Nueva protesta de los prelados de la provincia eclesiástica de Tarragona," August 30, 1909, *La Cruz* (1909), p. 312.

78. Ignaci Casanovas, "Nuestro estado social" (1910), in *Estudios Sociales* (Barcelona, 1952), p. 203.

79. d'Esplugues, "Post Nubila . . ." p. 163.

broadened its horizons by alleging that between the Rif tribesmen of Morocco and the Catalan revolutionaries a common link existed, namely, Freemasonry![80]

If Catholic observers differed on exactly who was to blame, they generally agreed that the liberal State's weakness in tolerating political, social, and cultural dissent was ultimately responsible. "The sectarian hatred of fanatical mobs," declared Bishop Sánchez de Castro, developed logically from "the liberties of perdition under the protection of which the most dangerous ideas were propagated."[81] In a letter to Maura, the national committee of the Catholic Action organization traced the troubles directly to "the excessive liberty that has been granted for the propagation of revolutionary ideas in so-called neutral or lay schools, in the newspaper, in the pamphlet and in public meetings."[82]

The prime minister was told in no uncertain terms how he should deal with "ideas subversive of religion and the nation."[83] The bishops of the Toledo ecclesiastical province declared that it was necessary "to attack the evil in its origins; to extirpate it in its roots."[84] The bishops of the Burgos province called upon the government to punish the guilty "with a strong hand, without vacillation or vain fears," a sentiment echoed by the administrator of the Barcelona diocese who called upon the authorities to discharge "all the rigors of the penal law against these fathers of crime who from the columns of the newspapers are incessantly and directly inciting the masses to incendiarism, pillage and assassination."[85]

This reaction was understandable up to a point, but it did not represent a realistic assessment of the Tragic Week. Although the liberal State had failed to resolve serious political and social problems, it did not stand on the verge of collapse before revolutionary assault. The rhetoric of Catholic spokesmen is significant because it reveals how deeply the fear of a sudden and violent revolution had penetrated the mentality of Spanish Catholics. Reaction to the Tragic Week also reinforced the idea of the Church as a bulwark of the social order. The extensive literature in Church publications referred incessantly to the defense of order, authority, the family, and property.

80. *El Universo*, August 6, 1909. There was one exception to the general chorus of Catholic commentators who saw the origins of the Tragic Week in a conspiracy. So-called "social Catholics," convinced that the Church needed to win the support of the working classes, analyzed the Tragic Week in more sophisticated terms. Severino Aznar, a prominent figure in the movement, blamed the incendiarism on "ignorance on the part of the people" who were manipulated to this end by agitators. He also placed responsibility on "the egoism and frivolity of the rich and governing classes" as well as on "the cowardice and disorganization of Catholics." "Lecciones de la revolución," *La Paz Social* (1909), p. 619.

81. "Circular del Señor Obispo de Santander," August 14, 1909, *La Cruz* (1909), p. 238.

82. "De la Junta Central de Acción Católica al Sr. Presidente del Consejo de Ministros," August 6, 1909, *La Cruz* (1909), p. 243.

83. "Representación del los Reverendísimos Prelados de la provincia eclesiástica de Toledo al Excelentísimo Sr. Presidente del Consejo de Ministros," in ibid., p. 309.

84. Ibid.

85. "Exposición de los Revdmos. Prelados de la provincia de Burgos al Sr. Presidente del Consejo de Ministros," August 21, 1909, in ibid., p. 219; "Del Reverendísimo Sr. Obispo de Eudoxia, Vicario Capitular de Barcelona al Sr. Presidente del Consejo de Ministros," August 6, 1909, in ibid., p. 228.

The Church also moved to a stronger identification with the Alfonsine monarchy and the army. The dynastic reservations and studied neutrality of an earlier generation of bishops gave way to vigorous statements of support for the throne.[86] Criticism of the army, which the hierarchy had once viewed with misgivings as an agent of liberalism and devouring centralism, yielded to extravagant praise of the military as saviors of Church and society. "Our brave army," asserted the Catalan bishops, "has raised the Spanish flag in Africa . . . to defend civilization and the cross," while in Spain it opposed "the unbridled revolution that broke out in Barcelona."[87] Praise was not directed towards the liberal State, despite clerical support for Maura. As during the Cuban war, churchmen preferred to speak of the "nation" and "patriotism." If they referred to the regime at all, it was to berate it for laxity in dealing with dissent.

The response of the Church and its defenders to the Tragic Week revealed that Maura was no more successful at resolving the problem of the Church within a constitutional regime than his predecessors had been. The prime minister's goal of integrating Catholics into the liberal system as a means of defending the social order complicated the political situation even more. The Liberal party refused outright to accept such an expanded role for the Church; Republicans saw a conservative alliance as a provocation. At the same time, the events of the Tragic Week promoted serious doubts among some clerics about the regime's ability to protect the Church from revolutionary assault. These sentiments were not widespread, but they began to appear. "The fact is," said the administrator of the Barcelona diocese, "that the sacred interests of the Catholic Religion which the State ought to protect by every means, both repressive and preventive, remained exposed for at least two days to the mercy of the enemies of the Church, the nation and the monarchy."[88]

After the Tragic Week, clergy and laity were even less disposed to accept the limited pluralism associated with the liberal regime. By 1910 the Church had emerged as a powerful interest group committed to the defense of the social order, the monarchy, and the army. Its always ambiguous commitment to the political principles of the liberal State would be further tested by another round of reforming ecclesiastical legislation introduced between 1910 and 1912.

86. The bishop of Sigüenza extravagantly praised Maura's "fervent love for the monarchy" as displayed in his actions before the events of the Tragic Week. *La Cruz* (1909), p. 310.

87. "De los Revdmos. Prelados de la provincia eclesiástica tarraconense," August 21, 1909, in ibid., p. 236. Praise of the army for ending the agitation in Barcelona was to some extent misplaced. Anticlericalism was by no means absent among army officers, hence the indifference of some of them before the church burnings, when prompt action might have saved some buildings from the flames. Ullman, *The Tragic Week*, p. 209.

88. " Del Reverendísimo Sr. Obispo de Eudoxia," pp. 227–28.

Canalejas and the Reform of the Church, 1910–1912

Following the successful Liberal assault on Maura, Moret did not remain in office for long. Harassed by a Conservative opposition aware of his contribution to its fall from power and weakened by doubts within his own party about the wisdom of seeking Republican support through the Union of the Left, in February 1910 Moret yielded to the figure most closely identified with ecclesiastical reform, José Canalejas. That the king chose the leader of a small party who had broken with the Liberals because of their timidity in dealing with the religious orders testified to the political system's increasing fragility. But it was a shrewd choice by Alfonso XIII. Canalejas was committed to the defense of the constitutional monarchy and opposed to an accommodation with the Republican parties. An accomplished politician and parliamentarian, he saw the necessity of reforms to ensure the regime's survival by moving liberalism in a democratic direction.[89]

Until the prime minister's assassination in November 1912, the government pursued a reform program on several fronts. The State intervened to improve conditions for industrial workers through the arbitration of salary disputes and the creation of unemployment and accident insurance plans.[90] It abolished an unpopular sales tax, the *consumos*, in favor of more equitable arrangements. Canalejas also saw the need for agrarian reform that involved the expropriation of *latifundio* lands in southern Spain, where an impoverished rural proletariat lived in misery. The prime minister was well served by a keen political intelligence that allowed him to develop policies through a realistic assessment of national problems. He realized, for example, that an accommodation would have to be made with Catalan autonomist aspirations despite his earlier opposition to regionalism.

Whether the reforms of Canalejas would have transformed the regime in a democratic direction is a matter of discussion. But whatever their practical effects, government initiatives in ecclesiastical matters dominated political debate during 1910 and 1911. Canalejas was aware that a renewed attempt to limit the growth of the religious orders, reduce the number of dioceses and parishes, develop a modern system of public education, and expand the constitutional scope of religious liberty would unleash a whirlwind of criticism and agitation.[91] But he believed that the liberal State's evolution in a more democratic and pluralistic direction depended on its ability to resolve the contradiction of a parliamentary, constitutional form of government with the existence of an established Church determined to impose its rigid and vaguely theocratic ideas on a rapidly changing and increasingly secular society.[92]

89. Salvador Forner Muñoz, *Canalejas y el Partido Liberal Democrático, 1900–1910* (Madrid, 1993), p. 38.

90. Carr, *Spain, 1808–1939*, pp. 492–94.

91. Robles Muñoz, "Frente a la supremacía del Estado," *Anthologica Annua* (1989), vol. 36, p. 486.

92. Shortly after taking office, Canalejas met with the papal nuncio, Antonio Vico. The nuncio reported to the Vatican that the prime minister declared himself a practicing Catholic who wished to re-

For clergy and laity, the government's plans represented "a sectarian campaign that established the solidarity of the ministers of His Most Catholic Majesty with the most disturbing elements of the antireligious, antisocial, and antipatriotic sect," a clear reference to Freemasonry.[93] Few political figures in the Restoration's history endured more vilification by Catholic detractors than Canalejas. The rhetoric directed against the prime minister wildly overshot the mark. Canalejas was a practicing Catholic. He accepted the privileges conceded to the Church in the 1876 constitution and wished to maintain good relations with the Vatican. But he remained committed to a strongly regalist view of civil-ecclesiastical relations. The Church's privileges, he maintained, could not limit the State's legislative authority in those areas of competence that corresponded to it alone.[94]

The government focused on the regular clergy, education, and religious liberty. Canalejas wished to resolve the problem of the religious orders' growth and juridical status through a new law of associations. Draft legislation resembling that of 1906 was presented to parliament in 1911 but remained unpassed at the time of the prime minister's death. But the government instructed civil governors to dissolve religious communities that had failed to register under the terms of the *modus vivendi* of 1902. In late 1910, parliament passed the controversial Padlock Law (*Ley del candado*). It prohibited the establishment of any new religious foundations for two years or until a new law of associations was passed.[95]

Catholic opinion regarded the Padlock Law as an example of intolerable government interference. In fact, the legislation represented a compromise. Canalejas, recognizing that time would be required to overcome opposition to a new law of associations, agreed to the two-year limitation as the best that could be managed under the circumstances. Maura and the Conservative party regarded the law as bad legislation. But they were unwilling to provoke a no-holds-barred parliamentary battle over the issue, fearing that such a conflict combined with massive Catholic street demonstrations against the law could endanger the regime's stability.[96] Although many bishops urged the faithful to participate in protest demonstrations, prelates holding seats in the senate showed a more pragmatic attitude. Bishop Salvador y Barrera of Madrid approached Canalejas and proposed the compromise embodied in the law's final version. This formula was accepted by the eight

main loyal to the Church. But he criticized the intellectual state of the clergy, the aggressive attitude of the bishops, and the clergy's pretension to dominate society. He made clear that he intended to introduce ecclesiastical reforms but that he did not want to go too far. Ibid., pp. 485–86.

93. Antolín López Peláez, *Por la Iglesia española: discursos parlamentarios durante el Gobierno del Señor Canalejas* (Madrid, 1913), p. 77.

94. Forner Muñoz, *Canalejas*, pp. 80–81.

95. Andrés-Gallego, *La política religiosa*, pp. 366 ff.

96. Had Maura ordered Conservatives in parliament to abstain, there would not have been a quorum and the Padlock law would not have passed. Maura's decision to allow the legislation through was severely criticized in the confessional press. Robles Muñoz, "Frente a la supremacía del Estado," *Anthologica Annua* (1990), vol. 37, p. 231; *Antonio Maura*, p. 306.

bishops holding seats in the senate and the cabinet on condition of its acceptance by the Holy See.[97] Despite massive Catholic protests against the Padlock Law, it was only a stopgap measure, a political truce designed to ease tension until the far more controversial law of associations came up for parliamentary debate. In the end, Canaleja lost his gamble. The strong opposition of the Vatican, the king, and the Conservative party and divisions within Liberal ranks kept the proposed new legislation from passage, although in 1912 the Padlock Law was extended for a second two-year term, after which it lapsed for good.

Canalejas's educational reforms were little more than pinpricks to Catholic sensibilities. Parish priests were deprived of the right, often unexercised, to supervise religious and moral education in private schools, while the teaching of religion in State normal schools was made an elective subject. The prime minister drew back from explicit new legislation on religious liberty in favor of an order to government officials instructing them to interpret Article 11 of the constitution as liberally as possible. Canalejas did not advocate either the separation of Church and State or a break with the Vatican, despite the strong tensions that developed between the two during 1910 and 1911.

The reforms of Canalejas imposed only minor limits on the Church's privileges. But the clergy and their lay supporters gave vent to an outburst of extreme rhetoric and threatening public demonstrations. The organizational skills and propaganda techniques that Catholic opinion was now acquiring emerged in full force. Telegrams and letters of protest poured into the prime minister's office. Bishops convoked services of reparation in the churches, while Catholic newspapers protested incessantly against the government. Press attacks against Canalejas reached such a level of intensity that Bishop López Peláez of Jaca felt compelled to apologize publicly to the prime minister in the senate.[98]

Mass meetings were organized throughout the country in 1910 to protest government legislation. The movement became especially virulent in the Basque Provinces, where the influence of Carlism remained strong. The cabinet, fearing that a massive protest planned for Bilbao on the feast of Saint Ignatius would get out of hand, prohibited the meeting, but such measures failed to quiet the intense emotions aroused in the north. Passions were still high when a similar meeting was planned for San Sebastián at the beginning of August. Catholics must attend, declared one parish priest, "to defend Religion to the last drop of their blood."[99] The government banned the meeting, suspended the publication of some Catholic newspapers, and for good measure dispatched two regiments of cavalry and seven hundred Civil Guards to the city. Although the cabinet correctly assumed that political groups opposed to the constitutional monarchy were prepared to use the

97. Robles Muñoz, *Antonio Maura*, p. 300.
98. López Peláez, *Por la Iglesia española*, p. 89.
99. Quoted in Andrés-Gallego, *La política religiosa*, p. 386.

religious issue against the regime, it overreacted. There was little danger that the protest movement could be converted into an assault on the State. Although protests continued through 1911, many bishops began to have second thoughts about the wisdom of conducting a sustained campaign of hostility against the government. As a result, the protest movement began to take on a less extreme character. In 1911, the government took the conciliatory step of allowing the king to attend the services of the international Eucharistic Congress held in Madrid.[100]

By the time of the prime minister's death, controversy over the Church had begun to recede. Canalejas faced a series of difficult problems on other fronts that drew his attention away from ecclesiastical reform. He may also have realized that his efforts had failed to produce results in the face of the effective pressure tactics of the Church and its supporters. At the end of the day, he proved no more successful at resolving the question of the Church's place within the constitutional monarchy than his predecessors had done. This was unfortunate. Canalejas was not an extremist. He was a realist who recognized that unless some modifications were introduced into civil-ecclesiastical relations, the issue of the Church and its privileges would reemerge as a major source of division and controversy. He was perhaps naive in believing that the "principles of Catholicism and liberalism" were "perfectly harmonious and compatible in everything," in view of the deep antiliberalism of clergy and laity that lay beneath their pragmatic acceptance of the regime.[101]

100. Ibid., p. 406. The government made its regalist point on this occasion by refusing to allow the king to attend the inaugural session of the congress.

101. Quoted in Robles Muñóz, "Frente a la supremacía del Estado," *Anthologica Annua* (1990), vol. 37, p. 252, note 412.

CHAPTER IV

CATECHISM, WAR, AND SOCIAL CONFLICT, 1913–1922

Following the assassination of Canalejas, the political system came under increasing pressure. The factionalization of the Conservative and Liberal parties intensified. A protracted colonial war in Morocco and the growing strength of regional movements in Catalonia and the Basque Provinces created ongoing problems for the regime. The effects of the First World War subjected the country's social fabric to further strains. In these circumstances, the Church receded as a focus of controversy before a broader question. Could the Restoration settlement survive social unrest, economic crisis, and political division?

From Old to New Battles, 1913–1916

The post-Canalejas era opened with another struggle between a Liberal ministry and the Church. After tortuous manipulations designed to exclude Maura from power, the conde de Romanones employed the nimble political footwork for which he was celebrated to become prime minister. He remained in office until dislodged by a crisis within Liberal ranks in October 1913. The Church's supporters viewed the ascent of Romanones with suspicion. "No one," declared the influential Catholic newspaper *El Debate,* had been "so prejudicial for the interests of religion" in his official career than "the present President of the Council [of Ministers]."[1] The prime minister's decision to oblige the members of certain religious orders to serve their compulsory military service as ordinary soldiers rather than as chaplains appeared to clergy and laity a sign of the government's sinister intentions.

1. *El Debate,* February 22, 1913.

A rumored plan to end the obligatory teaching of the catechism in public elementary schools generated massive protests reminiscent of the heady campaign against the Padlock Law. In February 1913, *El Debate* declared that the prime minister intended "to suppress the obligatory teaching of the catechism in the schools."[2] This intelligence, incorrect as events would prove it, led the newspaper and its editor, Angel Herrera, an emerging figure of influence within Spanish Catholicism, to spearhead widespread protests against the government. Episcopal denunciations, editorials in the Catholic press, and telegrams to parliamentary deputies poured forth. Protest meetings were held throughout the country, including one for "the Catholic women of Madrid" attended by twenty-four duchesses, thirty-three marquises, and twenty-five viscountesses who, it is reasonable to assume, were not educating their children in public schools.[3] The aristocratic members of the executive committee of an association of Catholic parents founded to defend the Church's role in education declared its intention to build a "dike against the secularization of teaching" and save the young "from the clutches of laicization."[4] As the culmination of the protest campaign, *El Debate* announced plans for a giant rally in the capital.

The campaign against the government was disproportionate to the legislation contained in a royal decree of April 26. It declared that the teaching of Christian doctrine and sacred history would remain obligatory in State primary schools, but that children belonging to a "religion distinct from the Catholic" could be excused from attending religion classes if their parents desired.[5] Republican and Socialist deputies ridiculed the decree as a completely ineffective means of extending liberty of conscience. Its limited terms failed to calm a Catholic opinion aroused to fever pitch by extravagant descriptions of a plot to secularize teaching by the government and "sectarians" possessed of "an infernal desire to de-Christianize Spain."[6]

That the Church and its supporters were carried away on the winds of rhetorical excess did not reflect any particular concern with improving the teaching of religion. This much-vaunted responsibility was fulfilled indifferently at best and neglected completely at worst.[7] The conflict formed another stage in the debate over the extent of the Church's legal privileges in relation to the restricted religious liberty recognized in the 1876 constitution. For the Church, the issue was clear. Spain was constitutionally a Catholic State and the right to liberty of conscience a private

2. Quoted in Teódulo García Regidor, *La polémica sobre la secularización de la enseñanza en España, 1902–1914* (Madrid, 1985), p. 290.

3. *El Debate*, March 3, 1913.

4. *La Enseñanza Católica* (1913), no. 73, pp. 6–7. The executive committee of the Junta Nacional de Padres de Familia was composed, among others, of the vizconde de Val de Erro; the condes de las Almenas, Casal, Retamoso; the duque de la Vega, and the marqués de Castellanos. Ibid., no. 77, p. 7.

5. Quoted in García Regidor, *La polémica sobre la secularización de la enseñanza*, p. 318.

6. *La Enseñanza Católica* (1913), no. 89, p. 1.

7. See chapter XI, pp. 260–61.

and personal concession that should not intrude in any way upon the functioning of public institutions. The catechism decree appeared as the proverbial eye of the needle that would soon open wide the gates to educational secularization.

The Liberal party had long promoted a gradualist policy of interpreting the constitutional clauses on liberty of conscience as generously as possible.[8] The motives of Romanones in advancing the tepid reform of 1913 are not entirely clear, but he did not intend an aggressive anticlerical policy. This would have been out of character, as even *El Debate* admitted. The prime minister declared that although the government intended to enact legislation based on "a spirit of tolerance," it had no intention of confronting "national opinion, which is Catholic."[9] Moreover, the government kept the Vatican informed of its intentions. Unlike inflamed Catholic publicists, the papacy understood the limited scope of the government's action. Fearing that the protest movement might get out of hand, the Vatican restrained its leaders from launching a full-scale propaganda offensive.[10]

The era of flamboyant battles between Liberal governments and the Church ended with the catechism controversy. The 1913 protest showed that the Church was unwilling to admit either a reduction in its legal privileges or any concession, however limited, in the direction of religious toleration. The mild reform advanced by Romanones revealed how little will the Liberal party had for another confrontation with the Church, although Liberal governments won occasional victories in their efforts to modernize education.[11] The conflict revealed again that the Church and its supporters, if unable to thwart all challenges to ecclesiastical privilege, possessed enough influence to block significant change.

The broader question remained of how the Church could realize its vaguely theocratic schemes to re-Christianize the country from an effective power base within the liberal political system. Achieving this goal through a confessional party was still impossible. Liberal ecclesiastical policy between 1910 and 1913 intensi-

8. For a discussion of the arguments of each side in this dispute, see García Regidor, *La polémica sobre la secularización de la enseñanza*, pp. 300–318.

9. Quoted in Juan María Guasch Borrat, *"El Debate" y la crisis de la Restauración, 1910–1923* (Pamplona, 1986), p. 156.

10. *El Debate* declared that Romanones was shrewder than Canalejas because he avoided "publicly insulting Catholics" and did not indulge in anticlerical speech-making, although it saw the prime minister as no less dangerous. *El Debate*, February 22, 1913. Angel Herrera was forced to call off the giant rally on instructions from the bishop of Madrid, who as a member of a government advisory body on education, the Council of Public Instruction, was the hierarchy's representative in dealing with the government on educational matters. As a result of his conversations with the prime minister and advice received from Rome, the bishop considered that there were sufficient reasons "to tranquilize Catholic opinion in Spain." Quoted in García Regidor, *La polémica sobre la secularización de la enseñanza*, p. 293.

11. In 1911, for example, the Canalejas government appointed the historian Rafael Altamira to administer a new Dirección General de Enseñanza Primaria designed to improve primary schools, in part by depriving conservative local school boards, often under clerical influence, of autonomy. Altamira, seen by the Church as an ally of the hated Institución Libre de Enseñanza, was the object of a sustained campaign of journalistic abuse by the Catholic press until his resignation in 1913. García Regidor, *La polémica sobre la secularización de la enseñanza*, pp. 350–54.

fied commitment to Maura, who was seen as a savior, the "heroic remedy," as *El Debate* later described him, capable of protecting clerical interests.[12] Maura's Catholic supporters expected him to reverse Liberal ecclesiastical legislation when he took power and remake the Conservatives into a version of the great Catholic party of which so many had dreamed.

After the events of 1909, Maura continued as head of the Conservative party. He remained unrepentant of his conduct as prime minister, aggrieved over the treatment he had received from Alfonso XIII, but confident that eventually he would be recalled as the dynastic parties followed political custom by alternating in power. Replaying this scenario according to the traditional formula would not be so easily accomplished. The king, whom Maura had indirectly but obviously criticized for refusing to keep him in office, was unenthusiastic. Republicans and Socialists nourished deep resentments against Maura for the Tragic Week and the harsh punishments imposed in its aftermath. Liberals, apprehensive over the possibility of a "bloc of the Right" being formed by the former prime minister, were also hostile, as the cry "Maura—No!" entered the political vocabulary of the day.

Maura's resignation from the Conservative leadership in early 1913 further muddied the political waters. Maura resigned in the early stages of a crisis brought on by divisions within the Liberal party. It was only a question of time until Romanones lost his parliamentary majority before the desertion of a discontented Liberal faction.[13] Maura, believing that the call to office should come to him under the terms of the principle of alternation, resigned his party leadership because, in effect, he wished to change the rules of the game. In his letter of resignation, he argued that the looming political crisis must not lead to "an ordinary change [of power] between Liberals and Conservatives." The old tactics of political wheeling and dealing involving the Crown itself, which in his judgment had led to his forced resignation in 1909, could not be repeated. Maura demanded new rules of the game that would guarantee that any government he formed would be allowed to stay in office until another "fit" party "different from the actual Conservative party" was established to alternate in power.[14] In effect, Maura denied that the Liberal party as then constituted could participate in the political process.[15]

When the long-awaited crisis occurred in the autumn of 1913, Maura, who had rescinded his resignation as party leader after theatrical protestations of loyalty from Conservative stalwarts, made his views known to the king. There was no pos-

12. Quoted in *El pensamiento de "El Debate": un diario católico en la crisis de España, 1911–1936*, ed. José María García Escudero (Madrid, 1983), p. 565.

13. The specific issue in dispute revolved around Romanones's decision to proceed with legislation authorizing a highly limited form of autonomy for Catalonia (*Mancomunidad*), a measure strongly opposed by many Liberals. A contender for the party leadership, Manuel García Prieto, and his supporters also resented the prime minister's failure to call parliament into session for long periods.

14. The letter of resignation is reproduced in José Gutiérrez-Ravé, *Yo fui un joven maurista* (Madrid, 1946), pp. 92, 97.

15. Raymond Carr, *Spain, 1808–1939* (Oxford, 1966), p. 481.

sibility of Maura's demands being accepted; hostility against him was too great. His call for a fundamental revision of the way in which Restoration politics functioned was too obviously directed against the Liberals to be received with anything but opposition on their part. Some Conservative politicians also grew restless with Maura's rigidity, which threatened to keep the party out of power for years. The existence of these discontents allowed for resolution of the crisis within the usual rules of the game. Alfonso XIII called upon a leading Conservative politician, Eduardo Dato, to form a government. He agreed, thereby sending Maura to the wings, where he would remain, except for brief interludes, until his death in 1925.

An observer of Spanish politics might have appreciated the marginalization of Maura in 1913. The majority of Conservative deputies rallied behind Dato.[16] But a minority within the party, led by young activists such as Angel Ossorio y Gallardo, proclaimed their loyalty to Maura and attacked the treachery of Dato for having participated in the "proscription" of the Conservative chief.[17] Thus began the ambiguous movement known as "Maurism," ambiguous because of the delphic stance of the figure it was designed to return to power.[18] On one hand, Maura welcomed the assistance he received from his young supporters, who threw themselves into propaganda activities on his behalf with an energy new to Conservative politics, even to the point of manufacturing cigarette paper embossed with the words "Maura. Sí!" On the other, Maura never made clear whether he intended Maurism to serve as the instrument for recapturing control of the party or to become a distinct political organization, an issue that divided Maurists themselves.[19]

Maura's prospect of returning to power was problematic at best, but his program of conservative regenerationism, with its emphasis on "religious sentiment as the marrow of society," limited decentralization, adherence to the monarchy, the purification of political morality within the liberal system, and protective social legislation for workers, appealed to Catholic activists gathered around Herrera and *El Debate* who saw no future in either Integrism or Carlism.[20] Yet *El Debate* wanted

16. Melchor Fernández Almagro, *Historia del reinado de Don Alfonso XIII* (Barcelona, 1933), p. 237.

17. Angel Ossorio y Gallardo, *La España de mi vida: authobiografía* (Buenos Aires, 1977), p. 58. Ossorio, the former civil governor of Barcelona during the Tragic Week, began to rally support for Maura, especially among Conservative youth associations, in October 1913. A national assembly to support the cause of Maura was held in Bilbao at the end of November. Gutiérrez-Ravé, *Yo fui un joven maurista*, pp. 162–64.

18. For a detailed history of Maurism, see Juan Avilés and Javier Tusell, *La derecha española contemporánea: sus orígenes: el maurismo* (Madrid, 1986). See also Stanley Payne, "Spanish Conservatism, 1834–1923," *Journal of Contemporary History* (1978), vol. 13, pp. 782–83.

19. At a special meeting of Maurist youth in 1922, for example, sharp debate took place on the question of whether it was permissible for a member to join "other political groups," an important issue given the desertion of some to the recently organized Partido Social Popular, a conservative Christian Democratic party promoted by Angel Herrera. Among those joining the new party was Ossorio. Maura responded ambiguously when consulted on the question. He replied that "he had always opposed the creation of new parties similar to those that he had known." Quoted in Gutiérrez-Ravé, *Yo fui un joven maurista*, pp. 257–63.

20. Ossorio y Gallardo, *La España de mi vida*, p. 60.

more from Maura than a minimal program acceptable to Catholic opinion. It hoped to persuade him to assume the leadership of a new coalition of the Right committed to defending Catholic interests and breaking the dominance of the dynastic parties.[21]

It was far from clear what precisely Maura would do for the Church should he return to power. As prime minister between 1907 and 1909, he refused to yield to pressure for a substantial increase in clerical salaries. When he headed a short-lived coalition government in 1918, he proposed increases so modest that his initiative produced a "disconsolate impression" among priests.[22] There was even less prospect that Maura would agree to head a political movement based on the "fusion of independent Catholics, Integrists and Carlists with Maurists" to undermine the monopoly of the dynastic parties.[23] Despite a willingness to make limited concessions to the Church on specific issues, Maura remained attached to the principles of nineteenth-century liberalism and the 1876 constitution. Both rested on a political philosophy rejected by the vast majority of Spanish Catholics, despite their pragmatic acceptance of the regime in power.[24]

But the legacy of Maura and Maurism between 1913 and 1923 was significant in the development of the Spanish Right. The implacable criticism directed by Maurists against the shortcomings of the liberal regime weakened respect for the existing political order.[25] The "proscription" of Maura by the Liberal and Conservative parties appeared to confirm again that the creation of a Catholic-oriented party was impossible within the Restoration. The failure of Maurism eventually sent its adherents in search of alternatives. Many turned up in prominent official positions during the Primo de Rivera dictatorship of the 1920s.

Upon the outbreak of the First World War, the possibility that Maura would resume power was diminished further. The politicians realized that the beginning of the European conflict posed a danger of Spanish involvement that the nation, already involved in an exhausting colonial war, could ill afford. Dato, who early made clear the government's intention to keep Spain neutral, received some political benefit from his decision, at least over the short term. Even Maura and his fol-

21. Guasch Borrat, *"El Debate" y la crisis de la Restauracion*, p. 211. Although there was no possibility of Maura assuming the leadership of such a coalition, *El Debate* campaigned for its creation in 1915, believing that its project was close to realization.

22. "En favor del clero," *Ilustración del Clero* (1918), p. 342.

23. Guasch Borrat, *"El Debate" y la crisis de la Restauración*, p. 182.

24. Despite several attempts to unite the followers of Maura with Carlists and Integrists into a new version of Catholic union within a political framework, there was no possibility that this could be accomplished. In 1915, for example, the Carlist leader Juan Vázquez de Mella gave a speech in which he repudiated the parliamentary system in favor of a corporatist assembly. The young Maurist Antonio Goicoechea rejected this option on the grounds that the parliamentary system was "a living reality," a view that Maura certainly would have shared. Avilés and Tusell, *La derecha española contemporánea*, p. 84. The repeated attempts of *El Debate* to persuade Maura to lead a new union of the Right is discussed by Guasch Borrat, *"El Debate" y la crisis de la Restauración*, pp. 112–13, 119, 178–79.

25. Payne, "Spanish Conservatism," p. 782.

lowers suspended their attacks on the prime minister in the interest of a national consensus on the war.[26]

There was never a possibility that Spain would enter the conflict. This did not prevent passionate debate with strong ideological overtones over the issue of support for either the Allies or the Central Powers. Sympathy for Germany and Austria-Hungary was widespread among the nobility, the clergy, some military officers, and, in political circles, among Maurists and Carlists. Juan Vázquez de Mella, moved by hostility to Britain for having defeated Spain in the sixteenth century, proclaimed Emperor William II of Germany an heir of Philip II and urged intervention on the side of the Central Powers. The Radical Republican leader Lerroux called for Spanish participation on behalf of the Allies, who also enjoyed the sympathy of Romanones and Liberal politicians.

This debate spilled over to the Church. Support for the Central Powers was motivated primarily by clerical hostility towards France as an impious nation in which few attended religious services and where such immorality reigned that "young people of both sexes bathed together . . . like Adam and Eve." The separation of Church and State and the expulsion of the religious orders by the Third Republic confirmed the impression of a nation deserving "exemplary punishment" for its actions. Emperor William II was seen as "the avenging angel of French depravity."[27]

These sentiments were widespread among the clergy. But they were neither universal nor capable of being translated into action. The conduct of Germany in Belgium, for example, threw pro-German clerics into some confusion because Belgium was seen as a model Catholic country. Cardinal Mercier, a figure admired by Spanish Catholics, publicly attacked the oppression to which Belgium was subjected at German hands. Archbishop Antolín López Peláez of Tarragona supported the Allied cause in a 1917 interview with the *New York Herald* in which he praised the "heroic conduct" of Mercier, whom he described as "an illustrious philosopher and patriot." The archbishop declared that the "idea that France is the enemy of our religion" was a serious error and that Spanish Catholics "could neither support nor help the cause of Lutheran Germany in any way."[28]

The debate within the Church led nowhere, although it revealed how far some clerics were prepared to go to punish any government judged guilty of anticleri-

26. Tusell and Avilés, *La derecha española contemporánea*, p. 75.

27. Quoted in Manuel Espadas Burgos, "La Iglesia española y la primera guerra mundial," in Manuel Espadas Burgos et al., *Iglesia, sociedad y política en la España contemporánea* (El Escorial, 1983), pp. 145, 146. Gerald H. Meaker has noted that the "vanguard of pro-German sentiment in Spain was the clergy." "A Civil War of Words: The Ideological Impact of the First World War on Spain, 1914–1918," in *Neutral Europe between War and Revolution, 1917–1923*, ed. Hans A. Schmitt (Charlottesville, 1988), p. 12.

28. Quoted in Espadas Burgos, "La Iglesia española y la primera guerra mundial," pp. 150, 138. Pro-German clerics justified their position by arguing that "the Lutheran Christianity of the German Imperial Household was to be preferred over the militant secularism of the French Republic." German propaganda agents in Spain even spread the bizarre rumor that the emperor was "a secret Catholic who was only waiting for the end of the war to reveal himself." Meaker, "A Civil War of Words," pp. 12–13.

calism. In any event, the critical question for the Church was less the issue of neutrality than the social and economic effects of the war that were evident by 1916. The specter of popular revolution would soon preoccupy clergy and laity to the point of obsession.

The Crisis of 1917

The strains inherent in the Restoration's political settlement were evident as 1916 drew to a close. On the surface, the traditional alternation in power of the Liberal and Conservative parties continued, as Dato (October 1913–December 1915) and Romanones (December 1915–April 1917) survived in office for decent intervals despite the sniping of Maura's followers. But the terms of the political deal between the dynastic parties were becoming seriously undone. Ministries faced a series of intractable problems ranging from the conduct of the military campaign to subdue Morocco to a full-blown economic and social crisis brought on by the effects of the European war on the national economy. Although reforming initiatives were not lacking, the factionalization of the dynastic parties prevented the formation of a consensus to confront the nation's difficulties. Governments fell into the habit of proroguing parliament for long periods rather than risk the danger of a vote of confidence in a divided parliament. Liberals and Conservatives also found their political flanks constantly harassed by the non-dynastic parties, Basque and Catalan regionalists, Socialists and Republicans, all of whom were increasingly disposed to flex their muscle before the regime's weaknesses. As if this were not enough, Alfonso XIII showed himself a worthy grandson of Isabel II through political meddling that compromised the sovereign's historic role as the "moderating" power of the constitutional monarchy.

All these circumstances were present as 1917 opened, and before the year was out they combined to undermine the regime's stability. The "pulverization" of the Liberal and Conservative parties intensified.[29] The conde de Romanones resigned in April because of differences with a Liberal faction led by Manuel García Prieto, who succeeded his rival only to leave office two months later in favor of the Conservative leader, Dato. In November he yielded power to a coalition government headed by the man he had displaced. The instability exposed by the appointment of four separate governments between April and November testified to the confusion of the dynastic parties as they confronted two specific problems. The first revolved around the perennial question of the military's political role. The appearance during 1916 of *Juntas de Defensa* among the middle and lower ranks of the officer corps posed a threat to the supremacy of civilian government.[30] Organizers

29. M. García Venero, *Santiago Alba: monárquico de razón* (Madrid, 1963), p. 141.

30. For a thorough study of the juntas, see Carolyn P. Boyd, *Praetorian Politics in Liberal Spain* (Chapel Hill, 1979).

of the juntas exploited the resentment of officers angry over low pay, promotions awarded on the basis of crude patronage, and proposed reforms by the Liberal government to modernize an antiquated military establishment.

Romanones and the cabinet saw that acceding to the juntas' demands would inhibit the government's authority over the military. Efforts to break the juntas, including the arrest of their leading figures, failed before the ambiguous attitude of the king and some senior officers and the increasing boldness of the *junteros*. By early June 1917, the crisis provoked by the pressure of the juntas culminated when the captain-general of Barcelona approved their demands without reference to the cabinet. The García Prieto government recognized that this action was "the equivalent of a military coup d'état" and resigned, thereby initiating "a political crisis of transcendent importance for the future of the constitutional monarchy."[31]

The response to the undermining of civilian government was politics as usual, despite the situation's gravity. Alfonso XIII, instead of using the Crown's influence to initiate political renovation, called Eduardo Dato to head the government. It moved quickly to grant official legitimacy to the juntas. The Republican parties saw concessions to the military as "a triumphant sedition, the natural fruit of an oligarchic politics that has corrupted everything." In early June, Republicans and Socialists agreed to cooperate "to open the road as soon as possible . . . to the republican regime."[32] Left to itself, the Republican opposition could accomplish little. The spark for a constitutional revolution came from an unexpected source, Francesc Cambó, leader of the Lliga Regionalista, the party representing the conservative Catalan bourgeoisie in its quest for regional autonomy. Cambó saw the political crisis as a golden opportunity to realize Catalan autonomist aspirations. When the king and the government refused to heed his call for a constituent parliament to remake the regime by ending the monopoly of the dynastic parties, Cambó and the Lliga defied the authorities by inviting senators and deputies to a parliamentary assembly to be held in Barcelona on July 19. In the end, only sixty-eight Lliga, Republican, and Socialist parliamentarians appeared on the appointed day. They demanded the convocation of a constituent assembly to deliberate on "the organization of the State and the autonomy of municipalities" and an "immediate solution to the military problem."[33]

The Dato government viewed the Assembly movement as a revolutionary attempt to overturn the established order. It responded by suspending constitutional guarantees, expanding press censorship, and sending the police to dissolve the meeting. On one level, government fears were not misplaced. Adoption of the Assembly's program would have struck at the heart of the wheeling and dealing of Restoration politics. But there was little prospect that the Assembly movement

31. Ibid., p. 66.
32. Quoted in Fernández Almagro, *Historia del reinado de Don Alfonso XIII*, pp. 298–99.
33. Ibid., p. 303.

would succeed. The absence of parliamentarians from the dynastic parties, even those committed to reform, weakened its credibility as a vehicle of national protest. The government also cleverly played on the hostility of much of the country to Catalan autonomist demands as a means of undermining the Assembly's influence.[34] Moreover, the alliance between the conservative Lliga and the Socialists in particular was purely tactical. The Lliga desired a political revolution carried out in the interests of the bourgeoisie; Socialists wanted the eventual establishment of a republic and vast social changes. The government also held powerful cards as it confronted the crisis. The king had no intention of endorsing a movement that could trim the sails of royal influence. Nor was there any possibility that the military would support the Assembly movement through the juntas, although Cambó entered into negotiations with their representatives in Barcelona.[35]

Labor agitation added another ingredient to the general effervescence created by the Assembly movement. Periodic food shortages and escalating inflation intensified working-class resentment against a regime that appeared incapable of resolving the country's economic problems. The strikes of the summer culminated in a general strike begun on August 13. The leaders of the socialist UGT, the Socialist party, and the anarcho-syndicalist CNT had a limited goal: to support the bourgeois revolution embodied in the Assembly movement with a view to establishing a democratic republic. The strategy of uniting opposition groups to apply social and political pressure on the regime made sense. Only a common front stood a chance of succeeding.

The political revolution expected from the general strike never materialized. It failed in part because Cambó and the Lliga, although optimistic at first that the strike would work to the advantage of the Assembly movement, drew back before the mounting wave of violence and government repression and in the end denied any connection to the revolutionary initiative. The middle-class Republican parties were also less than enthusiastic. The general strike itself, called prematurely in response to government provocation, fell easy victim to the severe measures ordered by Dato and applied ruthlessly by the army.[36] Dato paid a high price to ward off political change. Repression during and after the general strike exacted a toll of nearly a hundred dead and two thousand arrests, thereby deepening the antagonism of the unions and the parties of the Left towards the regime. The role of the army as the key agent of suppression increased the government's dependence on the military, which expanded its ability to interfere in the country's political life.

Faced with the unrelenting opposition of the Left and the insistent demands of Liberals for power, Dato had few options. His resignation on October 26 triggered

34. Juan Antonio Lacomba, *La crisis española de 1917* (Madrid, 1970), p. 167.

35. Boyd, *Praetorian Politics*, pp. 79–80.

36. Lacomba, *La crisis española*, pp. 266–71; Boyd, *Praetorian Politics*, pp. 82–85; Fernández Almagro, *Historia del reinado de Don Alfonso XIII*, pp. 304–12.

another crisis. There was no question of resorting to the old formula of calling the Liberals. The party's internal divisions and the veto imposed by the army against a Liberal government created an impasse that showed how impaired the traditional political mechanisms of the Restoration had become. Only one solution remained, the formation of a government of "concentration" containing representatives of the principal Liberal and Conservative factions as well as of the Catalan Lliga. Cambó, fearful of another revolutionary assault from the Left, broke completely with his summer allies to take a position in the cabinet. Although the new government, with García Prieto as prime minister, aroused great hopes upon taking office, its internal divisions were so deep that a long-term solution to the country's political difficulties proved impossible.

The Reaction of the Church

As the events of 1917 unfolded, the Church's voice appeared curiously muted. Clerics and the diverse currents of Catholic opinion realized that the role of the juntas, the Assembly movement, and the general strike "put everything in crisis: the regime, the parties, procedures and many directing principles that were believed secure."[37] In a collective letter the bishops declared that Spain was facing "a tremendous crisis" of a "permanent character."[38] But this statement did not appear until months after the summer threat to the regime had passed. Catholic newspapers and journals commented extensively on the crisis, but save for episodic observations about the possibility of social revolution, they viewed its possible solutions with an air of detachment and uncertainty. Several factors account for this cautious reaction. First, the Church was not directly attacked in the political and social agitation of the summer. "Even those parties that carry in their historic programs the principles of the *lay State,*" declared a clerical journal, "are keeping a certain significant silence on these points."[39] Second, the violence that accompanied the general strike and other labor disturbances was not aimed at the Church, as it had been during the Tragic Week. The strike confirmed apprehensions of an imminent overthrow of the established order. But its rapid failure evoked smug expressions of satisfaction at the triumph of "the forces charged with maintaining order" and the humiliation suffered in particular by the Socialist party and the UGT.[40]

In its political dimensions, the crisis of 1917 was viewed by much of Catholic opinion as a positive development. Carlists saw the regime's difficulties as a sign of

37. *La Ciencia Tomista* (1917), vol. 16, p. 404.

38. "El episcopado a los católicos sobre deberes en las presentes circunstancias," December 15, 1917, in *Documentos colectivos del episcopado español, 1870–1974,* ed. Jesús Iribarren (Madrid, 1974), p. 106.

39. *La Ciencia Tomista* (1918), vol. 17, p. 94.

40. *El Debate,* September 1, 1917; *Revista Católica de Cuestiones Sociales* (1917), p. 182.

imminent collapse that they believed would be followed by the installation of a corporatist monarchy. But the Catholic mainstream had no desire to plunge into political adventurism. A prominent Catholic propagandist warned his readers against the "inexact and sterile idea" that a dictatorship would resolve the country's problems.[41] What Catholic opinion expected to emerge from the crisis was the breaking of the historic monopoly of Liberals and Conservatives, thereby making possible the formation of a great Catholic party. The "centralizing oligarchies," declared *El Debate*, with their "sickly and undisciplined parties," had brought the regime to its present state. The system could not be reformed by a simple change of personalities in government. It required fundamental alterations to political "conduct, [and] objectives." The Dominican journal *La Ciencia Tomista*, generally progressive in its outlook compared to much of the Catholic press, rejected suggestions for the abolition of the party system. But it called for political "renovation" that would end domination by "the parties as closed collectivities and monopolists of . . . power."[42] In their collective letter of December, the bishops implicitly endorsed these sentiments by urging the election of those "privileged by God with the . . . aptitudes necessary to command" and exhorting the faithful to "firm and loyal adherence to the institutions of the country."[43]

It was one thing to believe that "the hour of Catholicism had arrived" to turn the crisis to the Church's advantage.[44] It was another to convert expectations of a fundamental remaking of the Restoration into reality. The rudiments of a great Catholic party did not exist. Although some segments of Catholic opinion, particularly those grouped around *El Debate*, welcomed the crisis as the beginning of the end for the dynastic parties, they quickly had second thoughts, fearing that constitutional reform would benefit the Left rather than the Right.[45] As a result, they continued to place their hopes in Maura, "the best statesman who has ruled Spain in a century." Maura's return to the presidency of the council of ministers in March 1918, at the head of a national union government representing the Liberal and Conservative factions as well as the Catalan Lliga, provoked "a patriotic explosion" among Catholics who expected him to inaugurate "a work of true national reconstitution."[46] These hopes were soon frustrated. Divisions between Liberals and Conservatives brought the government down after seven months in office. Despite hopes that the prolonged crisis of 1917 and early 1918 would bring about changes in the regime to make it more responsive to clerical interests, the historic monop-

41. Eugenio Merino Movilla, *Manual de táctica político-social* (Valladolid, 1917), pp. 246–47.

42. *El Debate*, April 15, June 10, 1917, in *El pensamiento de "El Debate,"* p. 691; *La Ciencia Tomista* (1918), vol. 17, p. 89.

43. "El episcopado a los católicos sobre deberes en las presentes circunstancias," pp. 109–10, 107.

44. *La Ciencia Tomista* (1918), vol. 17, p. 92.

45. Guasch Borrat, *"El Debate" y la crisis de la Restauración*, p. 249.

46. *España y América* (1919), no. 63, p. 219; *El Debate*, March 21, 23, 1918, in *El pensamiento de "El Debate,"* pp. 696–97.

oly of the dynastic parties, however fragmented it had become, was far from being broken, as the results of the general elections of February 1918 revealed.[47]

Political Impasse and Social War, 1918–1922

If the failure of Maura's national union cabinet marked the end of "a great illusion, the last illusion of the constitutional monarchy" for public opinion in general,[48] it produced disenchantment among Catholic activists, particularly those gathered around *El Debate*. They had long promoted the idea that only the monopoly of the dynastic parties stood in the way of the creation of a confessional party resting on the Catholic masses. Although Maura implicitly rejected every overture to assume the leadership of a new Catholic political movement and came to power in 1918 at the head of a coalition with a limited mandate precluding such an initiative, his failure confirmed that the old rules of the game were still in play. The restrained optimism of 1917 and early 1918 that fundamental changes in the regime would give Catholics their political due gave way to resentment. Maura's attempt "to close the disastrous circle of party struggles through the infusion of a new civic education in the national conscience" ended with the triumph of the old political order, "a fount of dissensions and disorders, the true center of gravitation of all illegitimate ambition."[49] Maura's failure further eroded the ambiguous confidence of Catholic opinion in the constitutional regime.

With the collapse of the Maura option, politically committed Catholics were adrift in uncertain waters. In 1919, sympathy for a dictatorship began to appear, according to a popular religious journal that warned, however, against such a course as "always extremely dangerous."[50] Other possibilities were also explored. In July 1919 a manifesto from a newly formed Group of Christian Democracy (GDC) appeared in the Catholic press.[51] The group did not pretend to the status of a political party but saw itself as "a circle of studies" devoted to promoting the

47. The elections were conducted without the usual rigging managed by the Ministry of the Interior. The results, therefore, provided some sense of the relative strength of the parties, although electoral pressures were still prevalent in the countryside. The Liberal and Conservative factions easily won a majority of seats in the congress of deputies, the Maurists only twenty-seven, although they enjoyed some local successes. In Seville, for example, a right-wing coalition embracing Maurists and supporters of Dato ran a campaign in defense of "Religion, the Nation and the Monarchy" and elected the head of the local Catholic League. Fernández Almagro, *Historia del reinado de Don Alfonso XIII*, p. 324; Avilés and Tusell, *La derecha española contemporánea*, pp. 138–39.

48. Carr, *Spain, 1808–1939*, p. 507.

49. *España y América* (1919), no. 63, pp. 220–21.

50. Ibid. (1919), no. 62, p. 467. *El Debate*, for example, appealed for the installation of a "civil dictatorship" to be headed by Maura for a temporary period. Guasch Borrat, *"El Debate" y la crisis de la Restauración*, p. 343.

51. The idea of forming the group originated with Severino Aznar, a Catholic social activist who had long argued that the Church's social initiatives, especially with respect to industrial workers, were sadly lacking. Oscar Alzaga Villaamil, *La primera democracia cristiana en España* (Barcelona, 1973), p. 59.

views of Catholic activists who believed that the Church's efforts to attract the working class were deficient.[52] The GDC's program consisted of a contradictory mix of Catholic social principles embracing defense of religion, family, and private property, with appeals for vigorous action to improve the economic circumstances of workers through the creation of strong and independent Catholic trade unions. Although some members of the GDC were democratic in their sympathies, the majority adhered to the old Carlist and scarcely democratic idea of the need to organize Spanish society along corporatist lines.[53]

There was little possibility that the Christian Democratic Group would ever become more than a discussion circle. As one member recognized, Christian Democrats formed "a group of Catholic Don Quixotes" tilting against the windmills of indifference and even hostility.[54] Opponents of the GDC subjected it to relentless attacks and denounced its views to Rome, while in 1921 the country's archbishops rapped its knuckles for being too independent of the hierarchy and too committed to a less confessional approach to the organization of the working class.[55] The attitude of *El Debate* was more generous, at least on the surface. The newspaper praised Christian Democrats as "most prestigious and learned men" and their work as "a very noble undertaking," but it took pains to emphasize that Catholic intellectuals who were "less radical" did not share their ideas.[56]

Efforts to establish a working relationship between *El Debate* and the GDC came to nothing, and for good reason. Herrera and his colleagues had ambitious plans of their own. Finally recognizing that Maura would not fulfill their political dreams, they called for the creation of "great popular Catholic or Christian Democratic party" similar to the Center party of Germany and the Catholic parties of Belgium and Holland.[57] The foundation in 1919 of the Partito Popolare Italiano through the efforts of Father Luigi Sturzo provided Herrera and his followers with an even more attractive political model. "We could, if we imitate the Catholics of Italy," said *El Debate*, "not only influence or collaborate in government, but even govern ourselves."[58] During the following three years, *El Debate* campaigned for

52. Among the signers of the manifesto were prominent advocates of independent Catholic trade unions free of employer influence, such as Canon Maximiliano Arboleya of Oviedo and the Dominican friars Bruno Ibeas and José Gafo, who had clashed frequently with more conservative advocates of Catholic social action.

53. Javier Tusell, *Historia de la democracia cristiana en España* (2 vols., Madrid, 1974), vol. 1, pp. 101–2.

54. Bruno Ibeas, "El grupo 'Democracia Cristiana,'" *España y América* (1919), no. 63, p. 190.

55. Ibid., p. 102; Frances Lannon, *Privilege, Persecution and Prophecy: The Catholic Church in Spain, 1875–1975* (Oxford, 1987), p. 162. For a detailed account of the struggle in Rome, see Domingo Benavides Gómez, *Democracia y cristianismo en la España de la Restauración, 1875–1931* (Madrid, 1978), pp. 343–55; "Conclusiones de los Revmos. Metropolitanos españoles acerca de la acción social católica y sobre el Grupo de la Democracia Cristiana," March 10, 1921, in *Actas de las conferencias de metropolitanos españoles, 1921–1965*, ed. Vicente Cárcel Ortí (Madrid, 1994), pp. 148–55.

56. *El Debate*, August 7, 1919, in *El pensamiento de "El Debate,"* p. 613.

57. *El Debate*, February 18, 1919, in ibid., p. 608.

58. Quoted in Guasch Borrat, *"El Debate" y la crisis de la Restauración*, p. 384.

the establishment of a party founded on two principles.[59] First, the new party must be committed to the "fulfillment of existing laws favorable to the Church." Second, it must rest on a broad alliance of the main political groups within Spanish Catholicism.[60] Achieving this elusive goal delayed the party's foundation until late 1922, when an assembly of leading figures representing the main currents of Catholic opinion met in Madrid.[61]

The program of the Partido Social Popular (PSP) represented another stage in the political modernization of Spanish Catholicism. Proponents of the PSP intended to defend the Church's interests, but they had a more ambitious goal: to create "a genuine organization of the Right" that would challenge the dominance of the dynastic parties.[62] The party's objectives as stated in the founding assembly reflected the differing and sometimes contradictory interests of its constituencies. From Maurists came the demand for fundamental changes in the operation of the parliamentary system through the introduction of proportional representation and administrative decentralization in favor of the regions. From the Carlists sprang a constitutional proposal for corporate representation in the senate. From the more advanced social activists the party took plans for an income tax and the possible expropriation of land in a limited agrarian reform. The program also called for a reduction in the size of the armed forces.[63]

Compared to earlier efforts to forge Catholic political unity, the PSP represented a giant step forward. Its program was modern in that it offered a comprehensive set of proposals for dealing with national problems. Whether the party would have developed into a great Catholic party resting on the support of the so-called Catholic masses is another question. The overthrow of the constitutional regime in September 1923 destroyed the PSP before it could develop an effective party organization. Moreover, the old problem of internal division had by no means disappeared. Influential Maurists, including Maura himself, who naturally objected to the formation of a party that threatened to attract his supporters, opposed the PSP's establishment.[64] Endorsement of the new party was not forthcoming from the eld-

59. According to one of the early supporters of a new party, Herrera preferred to work from "behind the curtain" on behalf of a Spanish version of the PPI. A more active role was taken by members of the Christian Democratic Group from Zaragoza. In 1922, the Zaragoza group produced a "Program of Social Policy" that became the focus of extensive discussions preceding the formal establishment of the new party. Alzaga Villaamil, *La primera democracia cristiana*, pp. 133–41.

60. *El Debate*, October 11, 1921, October 10, 1913, in *El pensamiento de "El Debate,"* pp. 610–11.

61. They included representatives of the Christian Democratic Group, such as Severino Aznar, Fathers Ibeas and Gafo, and delegates from Catholic labor unions and from the ranks of the Asociación Católica Nacional de Propagandistas (ACNP). Maurists and Carlists were also represented in the founding assembly. Tusell, *Historia de la democracia cristiana*, vol. 1, p. 110. A complete listing of the membership of the founding board of directors and regional associations of the party is given in Alzaga, *La primera democracia cristiana*, pp. 201–7.

62. *El Debate*, December 21, 1922, in *El pensamiento de "El Debate,"* p. 617.

63. Tusell, *Historia de la democracia cristiana*, vol. 1, p. 111.

64. As always, Maura's opposition was indirectly expressed. Thanks to the efforts of Ossorio y Gallardo, Maura did not "excommunicate" those of his followers who joined the new party. Alzaga Villaamil,

erly former Carlist chieftain, Vázquez de Mella.[65] Further, the PSP's commitment to some form of decentralization could not disguise the hostility of sectors of Catholic opinion to concessions to the regions that would make Spain "a mosaic of nations" instead of the "glorious Spain of the Catholic Kings."[66] Nor is it clear that aspects of the PSP's social policy would have endured the sustained scrutiny of conservative Catholics.

The significance of the PSP lay less in what it accomplished than in the alternative model it offered of a mass party designed to appeal to the various Catholic constituencies of the Right. In program and incipient organization, the PSP was a modern party committed to achieving power through the mechanisms of mass politics. But its goal of organizing a "new" Right put Spanish Catholicism on a risky path. Its organizers stressed that the party would function "without involving the Church in political questions."[67] Much store was set by the debates of 1922 on the aconfessional character of the PSP. Although the prolix discussions on this point formed another chapter in the long battle over the necessity of an explicit confessional identification for any party committed to defending Catholic interests, the selection of a neutral party name meant little in practical terms. In its program, the PSP made an unequivocal "affirmation of the Catholic religion as [the] religion of the State."[68] There was no indication that the party's constituent groups had forgotten their respective histories of pro-clericalism.[69]

Prospects for the new party were dim because of the chronic divisions among Spanish Catholics and the surprising resiliency of the regime itself. The fragmented dynastic parties staggered on, to the astonishment of much of Catholic opinion. During 1918 and 1919, six separate ministries ruled, although by the autumn of 1919 a fragile and uneasy period of Conservative government began that would endure until 1922.

The social agitation wracking the country after the war had many causes. A dramatic increase in the cost of living angered industrial workers already resentful over sporadic government repression and the profits run up by manufacturers during the European conflict. Workers began to enlist en masse in the UGT and the

---

La primera democracia cristiana, pp. 168–69. But the decision of Ossorio, one of the first advocates of Maurism, to join the PSP was a serious blow to the movement he had once endorsed.

65. Juan Vázquez de Mella had broken with the pretender, Don Jaime de Borbón, in 1919, as a result of discrepancies over Carlist policy towards the belligerents during the European war. He continued to enjoy great prestige, however, among the party's followers, hence the repeated efforts to secure his support for the PSP. Román Oyarzun, *Historia del Carlismo* (Madrid, 1969), pp. 492–95; Alzaga Villaamil, *La primera democracia cristiana*, pp. 150–51.

66. S. M. Rodríguez Merino, "Crónicas científico-sociales," *La Ciencia Tomista* (1919), vol. 20, p. 212.

67. *El Debate*, December 21, 1922, in *El pensamiento de "El Debate,"* p. 615.

68. Alzaga Villaamil, *La primera democracia cristiana*, p. 219.

69. Oscar Alzaga Villaamil has argued the contrary view. He maintains that the PSP paid little attention in its organizing discussions to the role of the Church within the State and that it took a more flexible view of Article 11 of the 1876 constitution. Ibid., pp. 218–22.

CNT. Faced with economic recession as European markets collapsed after November 1918, employers adopted a hard line towards working-class demands. A revived rural anarchism swept through the south beginning in 1918.[70] Finally, there loomed the specter of the Bolshevik Revolution.

The strike wave of 1919 evoked different responses from governments. Official policy oscillated between fierce repression and timid reconciliation. During a short-lived ministry in 1919, Maura sent the army to crush agrarian unrest in the province of Córdoba, while Romanones, during a brief tenure as prime minister in the same year, was on his way to resolving a key strike in La Canadiense, the Anglo-Canadian hydroelectric company of Barcelona, through a policy of concessions to workers. On balance, repression won over moderation. Governments were unable either to resist the intense pressure of employers or to exert control over their own agents. In Barcelona, attempts by the central government to moderate the excesses of the captain-general, Miláns del Bosch, who had arrested or deported fifteen thousand workers and employed provocateurs to engage in armed street warfare with militant trade unionists, ended in failure. In 1920, Dato, once again prime minister, abandoned an initial policy of conciliation in favor of a hard line. General Martínez Anido, appointed to serve simultaneously as captain-general and civil governor of Barcelona, outdid Miláns del Bosch in brutality. This policy provoked a violent response, as mutual assassinations were carried out by radical militants and agents in the pay of the State. Among the victims were leading trade union leaders and Dato himself.[71]

In the eyes of many clergy and laity, the vicious circle of economic crisis, strikes, violence, repression, and terrorism brought the country "to the threshold of the revolution." For some, "the assassinations of employers in Catalonia and the criminal destruction of property in Andalucía" signified the long-anticipated and "feared class struggle." Had not Barcelona reached "the apotheosis of barbarism and 'Bolshevism'" with the assassinations that periodically swept through the city?[72] The principal organs of Catholic opinion expressed little surprise at the course of events. They had been announced "from these pages for years and years," declared one social Catholic journal with grim satisfaction.[73] Although virtually all Catholic commentators recognized the importance of these social conflicts, they interpreted the situation in different ways. The hierarchy took the high ground. Pastoral letters urged implementation of the principles of social Catholicism as the only possible means of restoring class harmony.[74] Cardinal Reig, aware of the

70. Joseph Harrison, *An Economic History of Modern Spain* (New York, 1978), pp. 100–101, 121.

71. Ibid., p. 121; Boyd, *Praetorian Politics*, pp. 130–40.

72. *Revista Católica de Cuestiones Sociales* (1919), pp. 175, 173, 49.

73. Ibid., p. 241.

74. Josefina Cuesta Bustillo, "Una perspectiva ante la crisis de 1917–1920: hubo respuesta católica," in Manuel Tuñón de Lara et al., *VIII Coloquio de Pau: la crisis del Estado español, 1898–1936* (Madrid, 1978), pp. 382–89.

depths of the crisis as bishop of Barcelona, demanded just salaries and reasonable rents for workers, while the bishop of Plasencia called for adoption of a "program of Christian democracy" emphasizing the "strict rendering of justice" to meet working-class demands. This did not imply concessions to Socialists or anarcho-syndicalists, however, whose ideas were reproved as "odious and impious."[75]

Such sentiments could not be translated into action because of the acute nature of social conflict, but they showed some appreciation of its complex causes. Yet beneath this modern veneer a moral explanation for society's ills remained. The bishop of Tortosa believed that Spanish society was morally degenerate and victimized by "the world" in the form of those "new redemptors of humanity" with their "promises of fraternity"; "the flesh . . . the sensual appetite . . . so inflamed in our time," and "the devil," who had become "master of the world . . . because of the wickedness of men," were to blame. The bishop eschewed any appeal to the Catholic social conscience in favor of a simple formula, "sermons, the Eucharist and prayer," as the solution to society's ills.[76] Even Cardinal Reig, more cognizant of the economic roots of social conflict, saw moral regeneration as the key to social peace, for Spain was being consumed "by forbidden vices and pleasures" that prevented the fulfillment of "the sacred duties of justice and charity."[77]

If the bishops chose to take the high road of social Catholic theory and moral exhortation, others moved with obsessive determination to defend society against the threat of revolutionary attack. Defense of the social order predominated over all other concerns. In the early stages of the social conflict, some questioned the effectiveness of pure repression, the policy of relying exclusively on "the stick and the Civil Guard," as *El Debate* expressed it.[78] As the vicious circle of violence, repression, and terrorism widened, these niceties yielded to the straightforward objective of crushing social dissent at all costs. *El Debate* lashed the short-lived Conservative ministry headed by Sánchez de Toca in 1919 for attempting a policy of reconciliation as "worthy of vituperation" for its weakness in confronting violence in Catalonia. Even the usually moderate *La Ciencia Tomista* declared, "One cannot answer crime with gentleness or persuasion."[79] By 1921, support for a policy of outright repression was widespread, even among moderate social Catholics. Father Tomás Sánchez Perancho, for example, who had long supported efforts to es-

75. Enrique Reig y Casanova, "Deberes sociales del momento presente," *Revista Católica de Cuestiones Sociales* (1918), pp. 84–86; quoted in A. de Mirabal, "Crónica social española," in ibid. (1919), pp. 46, 47.

76. Similarly, the archbishop of Granada, alarmed by the increasing number of assassinations in the country, sent a letter to be read in all parish churches calling for "less tolerance with children, less reading of immoral novels by the young, more religious education and more practice of Christian doctrine" as the only way to resolve the situation. *Revista Eclesiástica* (1919), p. 196.

77. Quoted in ibid. (1919), p. 293; Reig y Casanova, "Deberes sociales del momento presente," in ibid. (1918), p. 88.

78. *El Debate*, July 7, 1919, in *El pensamiento de "El Debate,"* p. 625.

79. *El Debate*, December 2, 1919, in ibid., p. 701; *La Ciencia Tomista* (1919), vol. 20, p. 231.

tablish independent Catholic labor unions, endorsed "the great work" of General Martínez Anido for taking action against "the barbarous bullying" of the Barcelona syndicates.[80]

Catholic reaction to social conflict produced unfortunate consequences. It deepened to obsession that historic preoccupation with the danger of social revolution present in Spanish Catholicism since the mid-nineteenth century. The conditions necessary for a successful revolution were not present in view of the implacable attitude of the army. But exaggerated fears of a society verging on collapse strengthened old and apocalyptic forebodings. The country's social conflicts were seen as nothing less than a life-or-death struggle between Christian civilization and revolutionary hordes bent on its destruction. "Everything is at risk," declared a Jesuit journal. "Either one struggles for God or for Satan." "Two great societies are appearing . . . in this struggle, which is about the life or death of contemporary society," declared another clerical journalist. One is "the society of the children of God . . . a Christian, Catholic society, faithful to Holy Mother the Church"; the other is a "revolutionary society, the servant of a malignant spirit, moved by its true originator and chief, Satan."[81] These sentiments were far from universal among Spanish Catholics, but they would resound loudly during the Civil War of the 1930s.

Reaction to social strife also produced an ambiguous political response. The Church traditionally looked to the State to protect it from revolutionary assault, as during the Tragic Week. Despite the reproaches directed against the liberal regime by all sectors of Catholic opinion, there lay behind the cutting rhetoric an implicit recognition that the government alone could save "religion, nation, family and the right of private property . . . those great bulwarks of Christian civilization," hence the repeated exhortations to the authorities to use "a strong hand" to repress "anarchy and disorder."[82] Proposals to remake the Restoration, however exhaustively discussed, took second place to the objective of preserving the existing social system. "Every sacrifice, every expense, every effort" must be made "to contain the rushing avalanche" that threatens the "supreme good [embodied] in the social order."[83] Even *El Debate* exhorted a figure whom it despised, the conde de Romanones, to assume dictatorial powers to counter labor agitation in Barcelona.[84] As long as the liberal regime continued in power, the Church and its supporters required its protection, and they knew it. Until a Catholic party could be formed, *El*

80. *La Ciencia Tomista* (1921), vol. 24, pp. 277–78.

81. "El catolicismo contemporáneo," *Sal Terrae* (1921), p. 39; E. A. Villeloa Rodríguez, "Inevitable disyuntiva," *Revista Eclesiástica* (1920), p. 92.

82. *España y América* (1920), no. 63, p. 386; *España y América* (1919), no. 62, p. 464. Similarly, *El Debate* strongly supported the repressive policy followed by Generals Miláns del Bosch and Martínez Anido and the ministries that supported their efforts. *El Debate*, January 9, 1920, February 10, 1921, in *El pensamiento de "El Debate,"* pp. 675–76, 677.

83. *Revista Católica de Cuestiones Sociales* (1919), pp. 370–71.

84. Guasch Borrat, *"El Debate" y la crisis de la Restauración*, p. 317.

Debate argued in 1920, it will be necessary "to carry out a Catholic policy . . . of collaboration with the regime."[85]

Even as the clergy and the activist laity praised some Conservative ministries for taking a hard line against social dissent, they began to express doubts about the long-term ability of the regime to protect traditional social institutions. These reservations had surfaced in the aftermath of the Tragic Week and they now emerged in full strength. The efforts of Romanones in 1917 and Sánchez de Toca in 1919 to pursue a conciliatory policy to deal with social unrest were seen not as individual ministerial aberrations but as a sign of fundamental weakness in the regime itself. The pro-Comillas *Revista Católica de Cuestiones Sociales* saw the "pardons, insults and amnesties" promoted by Romanones as "the bitter fruit" of the "fatal politics of Spanish liberalism." Even Conservative governments offered little real consolation for the future. A "series of countless interim governments . . . favored involuntarily and unconsciously those conflicts" that have inspired "a great lack of confidence in the prestige . . . vested in the [public] authorities," declared a popular Catholic journal. In a country so "completely orphaned of government . . . one could scarcely see that coercive force [necessary] to compel all citizens to fulfill their duties."[86]

The inability of Liberal, Conservative, or coalition governments to crush social unrest between 1917 and 1922 stripped away the vestiges of confidence that the Church and much of Catholic opinion had placed in the Restoration. They had no effective alternative to replace it, but disenchantment was complete by the time of the regime's fall. The relationship of the Church and its partisans to the liberal State was always ambiguous. As the Restoration staggered towards its demise, little ambiguity remained, although the Church had defended its privileged situation within liberal Spain with surprising ease.

During the last phase of its history, the Restoration suffered a further blow with the catastrophic defeat and annihilation of a Spanish army operating in eastern Morocco on July 21, 1921. The effects of the disaster at Annual on the Church were twofold. First, it strengthened the commitment to the army of the bishops who had long viewed the Moroccan venture favorably.[87] Prelates collected funds for medical relief and issued pastoral letters "anointed with patriotism" that called upon "clergy and people to undertake courageously whatever sacrifices should be necessary so that the name of Spain is not dishonored and take vengeance for the injury suffered by our flag."[88] These less than pacific sentiments were connected to a second significant effect. The "tremendous lesson" of Annual confirmed the long-

85. Quoted in ibid., p. 356.

86. *Revista Católica de Cuestiones Sociales* (1919), p. 173; *España y América* (1920), no. 63, p. 387.

87. See, for example, the praise lavished on the army by Archbishop López Peláez of Tarragona in "La colonización de Marruecos," *Revista Católica de Cuestiones Sociales* (1917), pp. 133–39.

88. "Nuestros pecados y nuestros deberes," *Revista Eclesiástica* (1921), p. 193; *Sal Terrae* (1921), p. 793.

held view that the liberal system had provoked divine wrath by leading Spain on the road to immorality and at last had received punishment. What was needed, said Bishop González García of Málaga, was "national repentance" and "patriotic amendment" to save the nation from "unbridled and corrupt customs."[89] The bishops refrained from specific attacks on the regime, but their reaction to the Moroccan disaster was another sign of their disenchantment with the existing political order.

By 1922, the foundations of the understanding between the Church and the liberal State constructed by Cánovas rested on shaky ground. The Church and its lay supporters were more aggressive, better organized, and restive with their failure to force their vision of politics and society on an increasingly secular and pluralistic society. Although the Church had not done badly during the Restoration, it was clear that the *modus vivendi* between liberalism and the Church, a pragmatic arrangement useful for different reasons to the parties involved, had outlived its usefulness for the Church and its critics. The relationship between the civil and ecclesiastical worlds during the Restoration was ambiguous and contradictory. But in some measure it succeeded in limiting clerical ambitions to influence every aspect of political and social life. This restraint was about to disappear.

89. "Nuestros pecados y nuestros deberes," p. 195.

CHAPTER V

THE STRUGGLE TO ADAPT, 1880–1920

Between 1880 and 1920, the Spanish Church struggled to adapt to conditions imposed by liberalism in the political sphere and a developing capitalism in the economic. At the turn of the century, the redoubtable Carlist bishop of Plasencia still believed that Spain could be saved from "the fatal cloud of liberalism" only by returning to the pristine religious values of the past.[1] But gradually and fitfully some clergy and laity realized that traditional responses to changing circumstances were insufficient. They looked to models developed in France, Belgium, Germany, and Italy, where clerical and lay activists had long sought new approaches to deal with the religious effects of urbanization and industrialization. Discussion of the "social question" reached extensive proportions during these four decades, particularly following the publication of Pope Leo XIII's encyclical *Rerum Novarum* (1891). Clergy and laity encouraged a variety of organizational initiatives directed towards adapting the Church to the demands of the modern world.

The Congress Movement and Catholic Action

The collapse of the Unión Católica did not diminish the urgency felt by the papacy and some members of the hierarchy to find a nonpolitical formula capable of uniting Catholics in defense of clerical interests. By the end of the 1880s, advocates of a renewed effort to achieve unity looked to the example of the Catholic Congress, an institution already functioning successfully elsewhere in Catholic Europe. It says something about the Spanish Church's organizational lethargy that it convoked a congress for the first time in 1889. Similar assemblies "of Catholics in general public conference" had been held in Germany during the 1850s and 1860s,

1. Pedro Casas y Souto, *Carta pastoral sobre la situación de España* (Madrid, 1899), p. 14.

while Belgium had its first in 1863.[2] The Catholic congresses organized in Italy during the 1870s (Opera dei Congressi) provided the immediate model of a public and apolitical forum for the discussion of issues deemed vital for the Church. The congress idea found its first institutional expression in Spain when the bishop of Tortosa convoked a diocesan Assembly of Catholic Associations in 1887. Delegates discussed a variety of issues, including the temporal power of the papacy, the Church's role in education, the necessity of promoting popular piety and works of charity, and the need for church-sponsored associations for workers.[3] The Tortosa meeting's success encouraged other bishops, particularly C. M. Sancha of Madrid, to press for the organization of similar assemblies at the national level.

The congress idea was attractive. The convocation of a broadly based assembly attended by bishops, priests, and lay activists to discuss questions vital to the Church offered the prospect of a highly visible and nonpolitical forum capable of calling the attention of the public and the politicians to the Church's demands. The objectives of the congresses, as defined by Sancha, were "to defend the interests of Religion, the rights of the Church and the papacy, to spread Christian education and instruction, to promote works of charity, and to agree upon the means of bringing about the moral restoration of society."[4] Such a program should have appealed in theory to all the Church's supporters, whatever their dynastic or ideological loyalties. The regulations drafted for the first congress, held at Madrid in 1889, banned the introduction of politics into the proceedings. The bishops also declared their intention to keep a tight organizational rein on the congresses as a means of avoiding dissension. The hopes placed in the congress as a new, apolitical vehicle for rallying Catholic opinion seemed justified by the order and decorum prevailing at the Madrid meeting. But events at the Zaragoza congress in the following year showed that only the refusal of the Integrists to attend the first assembly had brought peace to the deliberations.

In 1890, the Integrists abandoned their abstentionist tactics and infiltrated the church where the meeting was being held. The organizing committee did its best to prevent disruption by removing the Integrist leader, Ramón Nocedal, from the list of speakers. But another emotional orator, the Integrist propagandist Father Sardá y Salvany, remained on the program, perhaps because his topic, a defense of the temporal power of the papacy, appeared safe enough. After attacking the king of Italy as a "usurper," Sardá launched a rhetorical assault on liberalism in which

2. Martin Spahn, "Catholic Congresses," in *The Catholic Encyclopedia*, ed. Charles G. Herbermann (16 vols., New York, 1907–1914), vol. 4, pp. 242–43. The idea of holding a congress in Spain was first discussed in 1884 by Archbishop Bienvenido Monzón of Granada and Bishop C. M. Sancha of Ávila, who were influenced by the success of similar bodies elsewhere in Europe. Rafael M. Sanz de Diego, "La vertiente social de los Congresos Católicos Españoles, 1889–1902," *Revista de Fomento Social* (1977), no. 128, p. 178.

3. José Andrés-Gallego, *La política religiosa en España, 1889–1913* (Madrid, 1975), p. 34.

4. Quoted in ibid., p. 35.

the allusion to Spain was clear. No compromise was possible between "truth and error," as he criticized the "unseemly confraternity that is preached to us by some," an obvious reference to clergy and laity who believed that the Church should reach an accommodation with the liberal State. As the delegates sat in stunned silence, Sardá's supporters shouted their approval, thus causing the civil and military authorities, present as guests of honor, to abandon the meeting to protest what they saw as a flagrant attack on the regime's legitimacy.[5] Dissension at Zaragoza appeared to undermine the effectiveness of the congress movement scarcely a year after its foundation. But in later meetings—Seville (1892), Tarragona (1894), Burgos (1899), and Santiago (1902)—opponents of an accommodation with the regime chose not to repeat their disruptive tactics. Still, the success of the congresses in uniting Catholics around a nonpolitical program based on defense of clerical interests was limited. Meetings provided a forum for discussion on a range of questions, thereby contributing to a clearer awareness of issues among Spanish Catholics. This was particularly true of the evolution of ideas on the social question that moved from being considered within the traditional framework of charity at the first meeting to more realistic assessments at later gatherings.[6] In other areas, the congresses broke little new ground. Every meeting devoted attention to the problem of winning back the allegiance of those who had abandoned the faith and raising barriers against "the currents of impiety" thought to be engulfing the nation. But recommendations to remedy the situation rarely went beyond exhortations to promote devotion to the Stations of the Cross and the Eucharist.[7]

The congresses also devoted attention to the Church's role in education. Here too they added nothing new to an established position. Delegates defended the Church's rights in public instruction as stated in the 1851 concordat and lamented the government's failure to implement them. They rarely commented on the quality of education other than to demand the compulsory teaching of the catechism and religious activities in public schools. But they were moved to indignation by the appearance of "neutral, lay and atheistic schools."[8]

The congresses recorded impressive attendance. More than five thousand participated in the Burgos meeting of 1899. But these massive gatherings served primarily as sounding boards. They were too large to develop into an effective organization over the long term, although an executive committee, the Junta Central de los Congresos Católicos, was responsible for maintaining continuity between

5. Quoted in ibid., p. 38; Domingo Benavides Gómez, *Democracia y cristianismo en la España de la Restauración, 1875–1931* (Madrid, 1978), pp. 148–49. These disruptive tactics proved counterproductive. Following the congress, thirty bishops issued a set of "practical rules" declaring that it was a "praiseworthy undertaking" for Catholics to participate in political life.

6. Feliciano Montero García, *El primer catolicismo social y la "Rerum Novarum" en España, 1889–1902* (Madrid, 1983), pp. 130–59.

7. *Crónica del Segundo Congreso Católico Nacional Español celebrado en Zaragoza*, ed. León Carbonero y Sol (Madrid, 1890), pp. 280–81.

8. Ibid., pp. 282–84.

meetings. The size of the congresses and the excessive number of topics presented for discussion prevented the elaboration of a coherent program. Delegates to the Tarragona meeting complained that they could not focus on important questions because of "the multiplicity of themes" brought before them.[9] They also expressed doubts about the influence of the congress, noting "the lack of knowledge of its recommendations on the part of the people, and especially on the part of the Catholic associations . . . of all Spain."[10]

The hope that politicians in Madrid would pay some attention to congress recommendations was optimistic in the extreme, although copies were dutifully forwarded to the prime minister and the queen regent. After the Zaragoza outburst of 1890, organizers avoided a repetition of direct attacks on the constitutional monarchy and liberal governments. But the apolitical character of the congresses was more nominal than real. A fine mist of antiliberalism and opposition to official policies permeated the proceedings. There ran through the discussions an undercurrent of resentment against the liberal State for failing to heed clerical demands on education, censorship, and the control of public morality. Moreover, there was little reason for liberal politicians to pay much attention to a movement clearly devoid of any political influence. The dynastic and ideological divisions separating Catholics into warring camps was still obvious in the congresses in spite of the thin veneer of unity projected to the public. The presence, for example, of the marqués de Comillas as continuing president of the Junta Central de los Congresos Católicos remained a sore point for Integrists and Carlists, who resented his support for the reigning dynasty.

The congress movement succeeded neither in bringing unity to divided Catholic opinion nor in developing an effective organization capable of sustained initiatives. Its significance lay less in effectiveness than in the organizational formula employed. The appeal of the Burgos congress for the creation of parish, diocesan, and national committees and a single Catholic newspaper to represent their views traced a program of action that would be gradually adopted over the following decade. The Burgos congress also anticipated the development of Catholic electoral involvement after the turn of the century by calling upon the faithful to participate fully in public life and to elect candidates committed to defending the Church's interests.[11] The model of an association pragmatically accepting the regime in power but opposed to many of its policies and operating under episcopal direction later formed the basis for the most influential organization of twentieth-century Spanish Catholicism, Catholic Action (Acción Católica).

During the century's first decade, the hierarchy continued to search for a unify-

9. "Conclusiones aprobadas por el Cuarto Congreso Cátolico Nacional Español celebrado en Tarragona," *La Cruz* (1895), p. 250.

10. Ibid., p. 276.

11. Feliciano Montero García, *El movimiento católico en España* (Madrid, 1993), pp. 20–22.

ing institution capable of transcending Catholic divisions. The gradual decline of Carlism and Integrism favored the emergence of the kind of association promoted by the clerical leadership. The death of the pretender, Don Carlos, in 1909 deprived Carlism of a figure admired by the rank and file as the heroic embodiment of their cause. By 1911, the movement's parliamentary leader, Vázquez de Mella, fell back on the fantasy of imagining that the army, disgusted with the politicians and Alfonso XIII, would install the new pretender, Don Jaime, through a coup d'état. The death of Ramón Nocedal in 1907 dealt a blow to Integrism, already bruised by confrontations with the hierarchy and the papacy. Because Carlists and Integrists had always resisted any suggestion of compromise with the liberal State, previous efforts to join members of both groups with the regime's supporters foundered even at the level of supposedly neutral Catholic associations.

Catholic Action's origins can be traced to several sources, including a skeletal structure of diocesan commissions and the national committee (Junta Central de los Congresos Católicos) created by the congress movement.[12] Although the Junta failed to provide continuity in the years between congress meetings, it survived largely because of the largess of its president, the marqués de Comillas, who endowed it with an organ of opinion in the form of the Madrid newspaper *El Universo*.[13] Another organizational impulse came from the Catholic leagues founded during the first decade of the century by local bishops to fight Liberal ecclesiastical legislation. Concerned with this threat to clerical interests, a group of bishops led by Cardinal Sancha of Toledo met in Madrid during the spring of 1903 to consider means of organizing Catholic forces more effectively. The prelates urged the establishment of Catholic leagues in dioceses where they did not exist. They reformed the national committee of the congresses and assigned it responsibility for the overall direction of what was intended to be "a solid, numerous and social organization of Catholics that would be a well-disciplined force, placed at the disposition of prelates to defend religion against the enemies who are combatting it."[14]

The hopes placed in this early manifestation of Catholic Action were not realized. Carlists and Integrists suspected the reformed national committee because the marqués de Comillas continued as president. In fact, neither group was represented on the executive until 1909, and then only briefly.[15] The Junta proved no more successful than its predecessor at providing centralized direction over the disparate Catholic associations falling under its mandate, although a network of Catholic leagues, Workers' Circles, and agrarian associations continued to de-

12. José Andrés-Gallego, "Génesis de la Acción Católica española, 1868–1926," *Ius Canonicum* (1973), vol. 12, p. 398.

13. Constantino Bayle, *El segundo marqués de Comillas Don Claudio López Bru* (Madrid, 1928), pp. 190–95.

14. "Carta del Exmo. Sr. Cardenal Arzobispo de Toledo al Reverendísimo Señor Obispo de Madrid-Alcalá sobre la Acción Católica," *La Cruz* (1906), p. 333.

15. Bayle, *El segundo marqués de Comillas*, p. 238.

velop. By 1910, circumstances favored another attempt to organize lay activists and Catholic associations. This effort was linked directly to the Catholic reaction to the Tragic Week and the legislation of the Canalejas government, as old divisions began to recede before what were seen as the grave dangers of anticlerical legislation and the growth of radicalism. "The sad reality" of Spanish life, declared a clerical journal, was represented "by the triumph of all the forces of the Left . . . in our major cities; the victory of the apologists of the revolution of July and of the Republicans, enemies of the Church. . . . Demagogy advances; radicalism is more powerful, more insatiable and bolder." What was the response of Spanish Catholics to this threat? "Deplorable divisions, rancors, pessimisms, apathy, paralysis, inertia, and systematic withdrawal."[16]

At the urging of Pope Pius X, the new archbishop of Toledo, Cardinal Aguirre, privately assisted by the marqués de Comillas, drafted a comprehensive plan for "Social and Catholic Action in Spain." The cardinal reaffirmed the responsibilities of Catholics in the political life of the nation and announced a new organizational structure for Catholic Action, based on a national executive committee responsible to himself as pontifical director, and a system of diocesan and parish commissions at the regional and local levels. Aguirre's reform failed to convert Catholic Action into the "well-disciplined" force envisaged years before. Historians have criticized the effectiveness of the organization during this period with some justification.[17] Yet Catholic Action's emergence during the first two decades of the twentieth century marked the beginning of an "ultramontane populism" transcending the historic divisions of Spanish Catholicism in favor of a movement based on defense of the Church's interests and a conservative program that eventually constituted the ideological foundation of a new Catholic Right intent upon promoting a militant mass organization.[18] Between 1903 and 1910, for example, the activities of the Valencian Catholic League, a direct offshoot of Catholic Action, displayed at least some characteristics of the modern political party at the local level. Although the leagues' leading figures, drawn from the local aristocracy and bourgeoisie, represented the traditional Catholic elites of the city, they took the battle directly to the camp of the local Republican party through a sophisticated or-

16. "Reglas de Acción Católica," *Revista Eclesiástica* (1910), p. 3.

17. Frances Lannon, *Privilege, Persecution and Prophecy: The Catholic Church in Spain, 1875–1975* (Oxford, 1987), p. 149.

18. The Vatican urged the hierarchy to organize Catholic Action on the tripartite model employed in Italy, where were were three separate but coordinated associations, a Popular Union to defend religious interests through efficient propaganda methods, a Social-Economic Union to deal with social problems, and a Political Union to elect candidates who would defend the Church's interests. The papal nuncio promoted the idea among the bishops and carried out a survey of clerical and lay notables to ascertain their views on the question. There was general sympathy for the first two organizations proposed but little for the third. Many respondents believed that the political divisions of Spanish Catholics were still too great to allow for the creation of an electoral union. Cardinal Aguirre's reorganization in 1910 made no attempt to form a political association on the Italian model. Montero García, *El movimiento católico*, pp. 32–36.

ganization employing parish priests, Catholic intellectuals, women's groups, and youth associations, all committed to win the masses through direct political combat. According to a Catholic newspaper, the battle did not revolve around "spilling the blood or depriving our adversaries of life. . . . It is concerned only with struggling through legal and peaceful arms, the arms of political suffrage [needed] to conquer our enemies and to oust them from the positions that they occupy." The time had come for Catholics to abandon their "lamentations and cowardices. Soon you will see that when Catholics say 'to the street' what can be accomplished: Catholic Centers, committees, electoral reform, Catholic political propaganda, whatever serves to carry the voice of truth everywhere."[19]

Another attempt to organize the Catholic masses through an elitist mechanism was the Asociación Católica Nacional de Jóvenes Propagandistas (ACNJP), established in 1909.[20] Its founder, the prominent Jesuit educator Father Angel Ayala, encouraged by the papal nuncio, believed that the Church required new methods to defend itself from political and social radicalism. The Church must form an elite whose organizing and propaganda skills could match those employed with such effect by the parties of the Left.[21] The *propagandistas* emerged from a devotional association identified with the Jesuits, the Congregación de San Luis Gonzaga. Ayala secured his first recruits from *luises* whom he directed in Madrid. They were young, university-educated men drawn from the conservative Catholic middle class of the capital. Ayala saw in them the oratorical skills and organizing talents necessary for the elite of which he dreamed. Given the "lack of orientation of the majority of Spanish Catholics," the *propagandistas* were to be "an association of authentically Catholic young men . . . who will throw themselves with decision, disinterest and personal sacrifice into propagating these [Catholic] doctrines using all modern . . . means of communication."[22] Although the first members were only seventeen in number, they represented a new force in Spanish Catholicism. They were energetic; they were more sophisticated in their analysis of contemporary problems, albeit with a conservative mentality, than earlier lay defenders of the Church. They were unsullied by the dynastic quarreling of their elders.

The heart and soul of the ACNJP from its beginning was a twenty-three-year-old lawyer, Angel Herrera Oria (1886–1968). Born into a devout Santander family, Herrera received his legal training at the Jesuit law faculty of Deusto before winning a coveted place in an exclusive body of government lawyers (*abogados del Estado*) in 1907. He possessed the qualities that Ayala believed essential. Intellectually gifted, devout, possessed of organizing ability, firm in his convictions but with

19. Quoted in Ramiro Reig, *Blasquistas y clericales: la lucha por la ciudad en la Valencia de 1900* (Valencia, 1986), pp. 71, 156.

20. "Jóvenes" was later dropped from the organization's name. By 1920 it was known as the ACNP.

21. Nicolás González Ruiz and Isidoro Martín Martínez, *Seglares en la historia del catolicismo español* (Madrid, 1968), pp. 29–33.

22. Quoted in Francisco Cervera, *Angel Ayala* (Madrid, 1975), p. 139.

a dose of pragmatism, Herrera would provide the ACNJP with the impetus that carried it through twenty-five critical years in modern Spanish history. He was also totally consumed by his work, one of his few pleasures being a Sunday excursion to the mountains overlooking the palace-monastery of El Escorial to listen to poetry while contemplating that monumental symbol of Spain's Catholic past.[23]

The *propagandistas* fought their first battles in the campaign against the reforms of Canalejas. Imitating the example of the Radical Republican party that developed the mass political meeting into an effective means of conveying its message, Herrera and several colleagues began to hold similar gatherings throughout Andalucía in December 1910. The use of the *mitín* in place of the bombastic mass demonstration, designed to impress by sheer force of numbers rather than by what actually was said, appeared a daring innovation. On their rounds through Puerta de Santa María, Jerez, Cádiz, Huelva, and Seville, the *propagandistas* scarcely knew what to expect. Would partisans of the Church attend meetings that they associated with the parties of the Left?[24] Would the meetings provoke hostile acts in a region with a strong anticlerical tradition? The beginnings were not auspicious. In one town, the accidental explosion of a photographer's chemicals sent a frightened audience towards the exits until the speakers calmed the excited crowd by shouting, "Long live Christ the King!" What Herrera and his associates told their audiences was not particularly novel. They stressed the threat of Liberal legislation on education, civil marriage, and the religious orders. But they preached their message with a sense of crowd psychology and political effect that was entirely new compared with the heavy-handed and extravagant rhetoric that usually characterized the Church's propaganda efforts. After the end of Canalejas's reforming initiatives, the ACNJP threw its energies into propaganda campaigns designed to promote the foundation of Catholic agrarian syndicates, a cause to which Herrera was deeply committed.

Of the early initiatives of the ACJNP, none was more significant than the acquisition in 1911 of the newspaper *El Debate*. There was no dearth of Catholic newspapers, but most, such the *Gaceta del Norte* of Bilbao, were identified with Carlism or, in the case of *El Siglo Futuro*, Integrism. The Madrid daily *El Universo* once pretended to the role of being the organ of national Catholic opinion. But it was not a commercial success and never succeeded in allaying the suspicions of those who resented the ties of its patron, the marqués de Comillas, to the monarchy. Herrera realized his dream when the financial backing of the publishers of the *Gaceta del*

23. Javier Tusell, *Historia de la democracia cristiana en España*, (2 vols., Madrid, 1974), vol. 1, p. 56. There is no adequate biography covering Herrera's entire career. José María García Escudero, however, has published a collection of his publications and writings that provides abundant information about his political and social views. *El pensamiento de Angel Herrera: antología política y social* (Madrid, 1987).

24. After the first such meeting ever held in Alcalá de Henares, a commentator remarked, "Until then no other meetings had been known except those held . . . by Republicans and Socialists." "Las obras católico-sociales de Alcalá," *Revista de Ciencias Eclesiásticas* (1915), p. 354.

Norte permitted the purchase of the failing *El Debate*.[25] Under Herrera's astute direction, its modest circulation of 4,500 soon tripled.[26] Herrera proved an effective editor. He wanted *El Debate* to be informative on a broad range of issues, not just those concerned with ecclesiastical questions. He intended to keep the newspaper out of the dynastic mudslinging characteristic of Catholic journalism until this time. In this, he was generally successful. Within a few years of its acquisition, *El Debate* emerged as the most influential editorial voice of Spanish Catholicism, the unofficial organ of the hierarchy, and one of Madrid's larger newspapers.[27] Its success did not mean that Spanish Catholics now spoke with unanimity. But for the first time the Church had at its disposal a modern national daily enjoying the support of the hierarchy and, as time passed, much of Catholic opinion.

During its first decade, *El Debate* attempted to synthesize the ideas of the various currents of Catholic opinion with a view to establishing a basis for some form of united political action. The newspaper consistently displayed the historic antipathy of Spanish Catholics towards liberalism as a political philosophy embodying the proverbial "liberties of perdition."[28] From Catholic regenerationism it derived its hostility towards the liberal State for blocking the creation of an authentic party of the Right representing the Catholic masses. The political system was "absurd" because it was "a game" that made inevitable "the progress of the Left and impossible the demands of the Right."[29] From Carlism the newspaper drew its views on the necessity of concessions to regional movements and a reform of the electoral franchise based on the corporate representation of social classes.[30] From social Catholicism it took its strong commitment to the organization of industrial workers and agriculturalists within Catholic syndicalist associations.

The implementation of such a program was another matter. Herrera and *El Debate* did not follow a consistent political line. This reflected the normal reaction to events characteristic of any journal of opinion. But it also rested on a pragmatic or *posibilista* approach to the resolution of national problems. *El Debate* initially supported, for example, the formation of a united Catholic front distinct from the dy-

25. *El Debate* received the enthusiastic support of Bishops López Peláez of Jaca and Salvador y Barrera of Madrid, who wanted a newspaper free of dynastic squabbling that would reflect the principles of Catholic Action. Juan Maria Guasch Borrat, *"El Debate" y la crisis de la Restauración*, p. 45.

26. Herrera did not intend to become the newspaper's editor. Under pressure from Father Ayala, the publisher of the *Gaceta del Norte*, and the papal nuncio, however, he agreed to accept the position. Ibid., p. 99. Angel Herrera, "La fundación de *El Debate*," *Boletín de la Asociación Católica de Propagandistas*, November 15, 1951, reproduced in *El pensamiento de Angel Herrera*, ed. García Escudero, p. 286.

27. By 1918, *El Debate* had a circulation of 40,000 to 45,000, far superior to the other Catholic newspapers in the capital, *El Siglo Futuro* (4,000–6,000), or *El Universo* (8,000–10,000), but well below the 80,000–100,000 of the monarchist *ABC* and the 85,000–90,000 of *El Liberal*. By 1920, *El Debate*'s circulation reached 70,000. Guasch Borrat, *"El Debate" y la crisis de la Restauración*, pp. 200, 303.

28. Guasch Borrat, *"El Debate" y la crisis de la Restauración*, p. 133.

29. *El pensamiento de "El Debate": Un diario católico en la crisis de España, 1911–1936*, ed. José María García Escudero (Madrid, 1983), pp. 573, 574.

30. Guasch Borrat, *"El Debate" y la crisis de la Restauración*, p. 231.

nastic parties "to take to the Cortes a robust and numerous Catholic minority."[31] It early abandoned this commitment to a Catholic political bloc in favor of a union of the Right that it hoped Antonio Maura would lead. Although always retaining admiration for the former prime minister, by 1920 the newspaper, recognizing that Maura had no intention of abandoning his commitment to the liberal political system, returned to its earlier position by promoting the formation of a Catholic party. The pragmatism that *El Debate* displayed in its attitude towards Maura did not carry over to its treatment of other politicians. It described the Radical Republican leader Lerroux as a "national calamity," while it labeled the Socialist chief Pablo Iglesias "the rancid." The leadership of the Liberal party fared no better. The newspaper often singled out the conde de Romanones for attack and savaged the party itself as nothing more than "a putrified cadaver."[32]

The emergence of Catholic Action, the ACNJP, and *El Debate* during the century's first two decades shows that the Church began to adapt its tactics to modern conditions. But when all is said and done, these initiatives failed to produce the results that their promoters expected. The creation of new organizations and the use of modern propaganda methods allowed Catholics to be mobilized more effectively than in the past, but they failed to move Catholic opinion in new directions. These new organizational initiatives, largely controlled by middle-class activists, remained prisoners of the conservative assumptions that had long been the stock-in-trade of Spanish Catholicism. By adapting to the demands of an increasingly politicized society, the Church modernized its methods but lost none of its determination to defend its privileged situation. It became a more powerful lobby, more pragmatic and politically sensitive than ever before, but its ideological inflexibility within a slowly modernizing society created a dangerous mix, the results of which would be felt during the 1930s.

Social Catholicism: The Workers' Circles

Industrialization and urbanization presented nineteenth-century European Catholicism with new and unfamiliar pastoral challenges. With an organization and mentality oriented towards rural populations, the Church struggled to respond to signs of religious alienation among industrial workers. Clerical and lay activists in France, Belgium, and Germany began to develop institutional responses to the "social question." These concerns penetrated the Spanish Church later and with less force than elsewhere.[33] Despite the advance of manufacturing during the second half of the nineteenth century, the country's economy continued to depend heavily on agriculture. As late as 1900, two-thirds of the active labor

31. Quoted in ibid., p. 123.
32. Quoted in *El pensamiento de "El Debate,"* pp. 601, 604, 563.
33. Montero García, *El primer catolicismo social*, p. 16.

force still worked on the land.[34] The agrarian character of the economy and the concentration of industrial activity in a few regions contributed to the general indifference with which bishops, the clergy, and concerned laity regarded the social question until the appearance of Pope Leo XIII's encyclical *Rerum Novarum* in 1891.

Earlier Catholic social commentators had not entirely neglected the effects of social and economic change. As early as the 1840s, Jaume Balmes, the most influential Catholic intellectual of his generation, observed the first conflicts between employers and workers in Barcelona as a development "most alarming to the eyes of every thinking man."[35] To a greater extent than their contemporaries, Catholic social thinkers perceived the destructive effects of industrialization on a traditional agrarian-artisan economy. Inspired by a scholastic intellectual tradition emphasizing the mutual obligations imposed on all social classes for the common good, they saw the individualism and material extravagance produced by the new economy as a shocking abandonment of long accepted social values: "Mathematics, the natural sciences, discoveries, machines, the invention of steam and its application to every kind of industry serve only to enrich entrepreneurs to the prejudice of the working classes, to encourage tyrannical egoism, . . . to form a feudalized aristocracy enemy of the poor."[36]

Hostility towards an economy operating on the basis of the autonomy of the individual and the free play of economic forces corresponded with opposition to the political principles of liberalism itself. As a result, the strongest opponents of the new economic order at mid-century were Carlists who formed a "Noah's ark" floating on the destructive flood of economic liberalism, the waters of which "covered all the peoples of Europe, including Spain."[37] But neither Carlists nor other Catholic critics of liberal economic policy offered practical solutions beyond criticizing abuses, calling for the creation of mutual aid associations among workers, and invoking the charitable instincts of the rich.

The first attempt to come to grips with the social question following the Revolution of 1868 occurred in 1872, when a young Jesuit, Pablo Pastells, founded a Workers' Circle in Alcoy, a city with a long history of troubled labor relations where two thousand workmen belonged to the local federation of the First International. The Alcoy Círculo de Obreros was derivative in both objectives and organization. It followed the model of the French Cercle d'Ouvriers Catholiques promoted by Count Albert de Mun, as did later circles established during the 1870s at Las Palmas and in the diocese of Córdoba by Bishop Ceferino González, one of the few

34. Joseph Harrison, *An Economic History of Modern Spain* (New York, 1978), p. 69.

35. Quoted in Casimir Martí, "Datos sobre la sensibilidad social de la Iglesia durante los primeros 30 años del movimiento obrero en España," in Melquiades Andrés et al., *Aproximación a la historia social de la Iglesia española contemporánea* (El Escorial, 1978), p. 128.

36. Antolín Monescillo, *Manual de seminarista* (Madrid, 1848), p. 19.

37. Severino Aznar, *Estudios religiosos-sociales* (Madrid, 1949), p. 158.

prelates of the time who attached importance to organizing workers under Catholic auspices.[38]

The early circles lived a precarious existence. They did not arise, as in France, from the coordinated efforts of social activists supported by the hierarchy and the clergy[39] but developed from sporadic initiatives undertaken by a few bishops and priests rather than by workers.[40] The circles operated, moreover, with an essentially negative objective, to halt the advance of radical social movements. The Alcoy Circle left no doubt of its purpose: "We ask of God . . . to preserve us from socialist and communist contagion, . . . and to stimulate Catholic workers in other cities to follow our example and to cut off the head of the hydra."[41] The circles' organization also reflected prevailing Catholic theory on the necessity of harmonious relations among all social classes. As a result, they took the form of "mixed" associations composed of employers and workers.

The uneven history of the circles changed with the appearance of one of the dominant figures in Spanish social Catholicism between 1890 and 1912, the Jesuit Father Antonio Vicent (1837–1912). A native of Castellón, where his family occupied a prominent social position, Vicent studied law and briefly worked in the legal office of a well-known Carlist politician, A. Aparisi Guijarro, before entering the Society of Jesus in 1861.[42] Forced into exile as a result of the Revolution of 1868, he spent several years in France, where he became familiar with the Workers' Circles organized by Albert de Mun. Upon his return to Spain, he was assigned to teach biology in the Jesuit college of Valencia, where he resided during the remainder of his life. During the 1880s, Vicent's teaching responsibilities limited his activities in the social field, although he participated in the establishment of circles in Castellón and Roquetas and strongly urged their creation on a broad scale to the

38. José Andrés-Gallego, *Pensamiento y acción social de la Iglesia en España* (Madrid, 1984), pp. 178–90. Bishop González founded the first circle in 1877. He appears to have been inspired to take action as a result of his knowledge of such initiatives elsewhere, especially in France. There is no evidence of a connection between the bishop and the great promoter of Workers' Circles a decade later, Father Antonio Vicent. Luis Palacios Bañuelos, *Círculos de obreros y sindicatos agrarios en Córdoba, 1877–1923* (2d ed., Córdoba, 1985), pp. 22–23.

39. Benjamin Martin, *The Agony of Modernization: Labor and Industrialization in Spain* (Ithaca, 1990), p. 151.

40. One of the few organizations to emerge because of worker initiative was the Patronato de la Juventud Obrera, founded in Valencia by a carpenter, Gregorio Gea y Miquel, in 1883. Although not a Workers' Circle, it engaged in some of the activities common to the circles. The organization was limited in its objectives, which were largely confined to providing social and educational opportunities for young workers. Amparo Sánchez Andrés, "El Patronato de la Juventud Obrera de Valencia," *Saitabi* (1969), vol. 19, p. 187.

41. Quoted in Andrés-Gallego, *Pensamiento y acción social*, p. 181. The preacher at the inauguration of the Córdoba circles in 1877 also left no doubt that one of the new organization's principal objectives was to combat socialism, which he described as a "wild beast in the forest" waiting to pounce on its prey. Quoted in Palacios Bañuelos, *Círculos de obreros*, p. 37.

42. The Vicent family owned a sandal factory in the town, which was managed by the Jesuit's brother Joaquín, who married the daughter of a local landowner. The family was linked to the the city's political boss (*cacique*) through marriage. Samuel Garrido, *Los trabajadores de las derechas* (Segorbe, Castellón de la Plana, 1986), pp. 33–44.

1887 Tortosa Diocesan Assembly.[43] In 1889, he received permission from his superiors to devote his time to the social apostolate and began twenty years of energetic activity as the Church's foremost promoter of Workers' Circles.[44]

The circles promoted by Vicent served four purposes: the religious, "to form honest and solidly Christian workers"; the educational, "to spread among workers religious, moral and technological knowledge"; the economic, to promote the foundation of mutual aid societies and other means of assistance; and the recreational. Membership was divided into two categories, workers (*numerarios*) and non-workers (*protectores*), each of which elected representatives to a common board of directors.[45] As a result of the energetic promotion of Vicent and the enthusiasm for social action created by *Rerum Novarum*, the circles began to spread between 1890 and 1895. Although accurate statistics are difficult to establish, it appears that by the early twentieth century some 257 circles or similar associations with 180,000 members had been formed.[46]

The circles' success varied from one place to another. The circle in Burgos developed a network of mutual assistance institutions, including a savings bank, a pension insurance scheme, and several cooperatives. Many circles arranged conferences and gave night classes on a variety of utilitarian topics. But there is little evidence that the circles as a whole provided their members with effective economic protection. A survey of 1900 showed that only 32 of 150 circles examined had established savings banks and that only 9 had created cooperatives. Circles were unevenly distributed geographically, with the heaviest concentration found in Valencia and nearby districts, the areas close to Vicent's base of operations.[47] Circles were also established in respectable numbers in Madrid, Old Castile, and along the northern coast, but did less well in Andalucía, Catalonia, New Castile, and Aragón.[48]

43. Casimir Martí et al., "El sindicalismo católico en España," in *Historia del movimiento obrero cristiano,* ed. S. H. Scholl (Barcelona, 1964), p. 211.

44. Montserrat Llorens, "El P. Antonio Vicent, S. I. (1837–1912): notas sobre el desarrollo de la acción social católica en España," *Estudios de Historia Moderna* (1954), vol. 4, pp. 395–99; Andrés-Gallego, *Pensamiento y acción social,* p. 191.

45. Andrés-Gallego, *Pensamiento y acción social,* pp. 165–67; Llorens, "El P. Antonio Vicent," pp. 399–400.

46. The difficulties involved in finding accurate statistics on the circles are discussed by Andrés-Gallego in *Pensamiento y acción social,* pp. 203–11. Garrido suggests that the number of circles and the size of their membership were often exaggerated by organizers to counter the growing strength of socialist and anarchist trade unions. *Los trabajadores de las derechas,* p. 181.

47. Vicent's success in organizing circles in the neighboring dioceses of Segorbe and Tortosa was due not only to "his personal capacity and charisma" but also to the support of a team of propagandists that included "influential members of his own family." The bishop of Segorbe during the 1880s, Francisco de Asís Aguilar, was also a strong supporter of Vicent and the circles. As early as 1881, the bishop issued regulations for their organization and governance. Garrido, *Los trabajdores de las derechas,* pp. 262–63; "Reglamento del Círculo de Obreros Católicos de Segorbe," September 21, 1881, in *Relaciones sobre el estado de las diócesis valencianas,* ed. María Milagros Cárcel Ortí (3 vols., Valencia, 1989), vol. 3, pp. 1757–61.

48. Andrés-Gallego, *Pensamiento y acción social,* pp. 173–74, 199–203.

Historical assessment of the circles and their underlying principles has been severe, even among those recognizing the contribution of Vicent to the beginnings of social Catholicism in Spain. Vicent himself, towards the end of his career, believed that his efforts had ended in failure.[49] In his own time and later, critics argued that the circles were incapable of effectively organizing workers under Catholic auspices. Inspired by the scholastic tradition, with its emphasis on harmony among social classes, and by his historical perception of a golden age in the relations between capital and labor under the guild system, Vicent insisted that the circles should be "mixed" organizations of employers and employees.[50] In neither purpose nor organization did the circles approach the emerging labor union or syndicate organized by workers on their own initiative. The role of employers in the circles exposed them to the charge that they were little more than capitalist tools preventing the radicalization of the working class. "Employers have come to believe that they have found the secret [in the circles] of suppressing strikes and the workers," declared a disenchanted member to Vicent.[51] The composition of the board of directors of many circles was scarcely calculated to inspire confidence among workers. A Madrid board in 1895 included two noblemen, a general, an admiral, and a Conservative politician.[52] The Madrid circles also received financial support from the Bank of Spain, the government tobacco monopoly, the shipping company of the marqués de Comillas, and the Northern Railroad Company.[53]

The circles suffered from other weaknesses. They were strictly confessional, as Vicent insisted, to the point of requiring members to meet in a body at least once a year to receive communion. Members of a Valladolid circle during the 1880s were required to be "Apostolic, Roman Catholics of irreproachable conduct."[54] Economic concerns were secondary in importance to religious objectives.[55] Although the emphasis on fulfilling religious obligations reflected a desire to "reconquer" the de-Christianized masses widespread among the clergy of the time, it was an exclusivistic tactic incapable of appealing to workers who had already abandoned reli-

49. Florentino del Valle, *El P. Antonio Vicent, S. J. y la acción social católica española* (Madrid, 1947), p. 256.

50. For the importance of the guild in Vicent's thought, see Llorens, "El P. Antonio Vicent," pp. 402–4.

51. Quoted in Valle, *El P. Antonio Vicent, S. J.*, p. 261.

52. Andrés-Gallego, *Pensamiento y acción social*, p. 164. Martin has argued with justification, "Implicit in the organizational structuring of the circles was the idea that workers were either incapable or untrustworthy of assuming leadership responsibilities." *The Agony of Modernization*, p. 152.

53. *El Obrero Católico* (1895), nos. 1–4, p. 3.

54. Quoted in Elena Maza Zorilla, "Asociacionismo confesional en Valladolid: la Asociación Católica de Escuelas y Círculo de Obreros, 1881–1914," in *Investigaciones históricas: época moderna y contemporánea*, ed. C. J. Hernando Sánchez (Valladolid, 1988), p. 181.

55. José Andrés-Gallego and Antón M. Pazos, "Cien años (y algo más) de catolicismo social en España," in *Un siglo de catolicismo social en Europa, 1891–1991*, ed. Antón M. Pazos (Pamplona, 1993), p. 55.

gious practice. The prominent role played by priests as official councillors reinforced the image of the circles as clerically dominated associations isolated from the real world of labor relations.[56] The circles were also troubled by organizational problems. It proved difficult to recruit competent members capable of assuming positions of responsibility.[57] Nor did the circles succeed in breaking through the reticence with which some priests regarded initiatives departing from traditional pastoral responsibilities. Vicent once complained that "priests and clerics are the worst enemies of the Workers' Circles." His most important work, *Socialismo y Anarquismo* (1893), a conservative gloss on *Rerum Novarum*, provoked serious criticism from Jesuit censors because it advocated the mild reform of profit-sharing in industrial enterprises.[58]

Vicent inherited the Carlist-Integrist interpretation of the social question, which took the liberal economic system to task for its abuses but emphasized the need to resolve labor conflicts on the basis of mutual cooperation and assistance among social classes on the model of institutions believed to have existed in the distant past. Such a vision failed to respond to the harsh reality created by the development of intense class antagonisms in late nineteenth- and early twentieth-century Spain. Moreover, Vicent, like many before and after him, saw the social question in negative terms. The Church must take action not to deal primarily with the economic plight of workers but to save them from socialism, "absurd and unjust in itself, [which] dissolves the family and carries disturbance into the very body of society."[59]

Despite later attempts to create a popularly based trade union movement, the circles of Vicent remained, in terms of numbers, the Spanish Church's most successful effort to develop a response to the social and religious problems created by industrialization and urbanization. That so timid an initiative imprinted itself on the character of social Catholicism for years to come was the result of the practical application of the principles enunciated in 1891 by Leo XIII in *Rerum Novarum*. Many of the ideas advanced in the encyclical—its criticism of socialism, its defense of private property, and its affirmation of the necessity of harmony among social classes—corresponded to opinions already generally accepted by Spanish Catholics concerned with the social question, although *Rerum Novarum* unsettled those opposed to State intervention on any grounds. Both the Integrists and even the ex-followers of the ill-fated Unión Católica expressed reservations about the

56. Andrés-Gallego, *Pensamiento y acción social*, pp. 167–69.

57. On one occasion, Vicent received a desperate appeal for help from the newly elected president of a circle who declared that he lacked the ability to provide leadership and direction. He pleaded with Vicent, "Please come and help us." Quoted in Valle, *El P. Antonio Vicent, S. J.*, p. 261.

58. Ibid., p. 263; Rafael María Sanz de Diego, "El P. Vicent: 25 años de catolicismo social en España, 1886–1912," *Hispania Sacra* (1981), vol. 33, no. 67, pp. 31–32.

59. Quoted in Valle, *El P. Antonio Vicent, S. J.*, p. 135.

encyclical's endorsement of government legislation to protect workers, although Carlists took a more moderate line on the issue.[60]

Rerum Novarum, in any event, laid down general guidelines. Its application was left to bishops and concerned laymen in their respective countries. *Rerum Novarum* stimulated intense discussion in Spain following its publication, although not all bishops saw the encyclical as having pressing importance.[61] The bishop of Segovia delayed publishing it on the grounds that "neither workers nor factories, nor, by the mercy of God, the errors combatted by the encyclical, abound in the city."[62] But the Catholic Congresses, many bishops, and a variety of lay commentators, particularly through the *Revista Católica de Cuestiones Sociales,* founded in 1895, exhorted the faithful to social action. The discussions stimulated by *Rerum Novarum* between 1891 and 1900 gave the social question new importance, but the debate took the form of academic and theoretical discourses produced by clergymen, university professors, lawyers, and journalists drawn in the majority from the middle classes.[63]

Catholic Trade Unions

Recent research has shown that the development of social Catholicism after 1900 was more complex in its intellectual and regional sources than was once supposed.[64] Catholic social action as embodied in the circles and, later, trade unions appeared to offer the hope that clerical and lay activists could transcend historic political and dynastic differences in a cooperative effort to achieve the larger goal of re-Christianizing workers before they were absorbed by revolutionary movements. "Social reform and Christian reconquest . . . of a lost people" led astray by liberalism and socialism formed the cornerstone of Catholic social action.[65] But if there was agreement about the objective, there was none about how to achieve it. By the early twentieth century, several organizational currents emerged.[66] One was

60. Montero García, *El primer catolicismo social,* p. 121.

61. Gabinete de Documentación del Ministerio de Trabajo, "La repercusión de la encíclica 'Rerum Novarum,'" *Revista de Trabajo* (1966), no. 16, pp. 257–60; Montero García, *El primer catolicismo social,* chapters 4, 5.

62. Quoted in Montero García, *El primer catolicismo social,* p. 166.

63. Among the university professors prominent in social Catholicism in Zaragoza, for example, were Armando Castroviejo, holder of a chair in political economy, Inocencio Jiménez, professor of penal law, and Salvador Minguijón, professor of the history of law. This pattern was repeated elsewhere in the country. Andrés-Gallego, *Pensamiento y acción social,* pp. 372–73.

64. For an excellent interpretation of the recent literature on the topic, see Feliciano Montero García, "Catolicismo social en España. Una revisión histórica," *Historia Social* (1988), no. 2, pp. 157–64. See also Josefina Cuesta Bustillo, "Estudios sobre el catolicismo social español, 1915–1930: un estado de la cuestión," *Studia Historica* (1984), vol. 2, no. 4, pp. 193–244.

65. Feliciano Montero García, "Los católicos españoles y los orígenes de la política social," *Studia Historica* (1984), vol. 2, no. 4, p. 58.

66. The complex intellectual sources of the different approaches to Catholic social action among industrial workers have been studied by Salvador Carrasco Calvo, "Pensamiento social y acción sindical

identified with Vicent, the marqués de Comillas, and a group of Castilian Jesuits, of whom Father Sisinio Nevares was the most important. They stressed the importance of class harmony in labor relations and the necessity of confessional identification for Catholic unions and gave employers significant leverage in the operation of Catholic Workers' Circles and syndicates falling under their influence. Another revolved around a group of Dominican friars inspired by a neo-Thomist vision of an integrated, modernized society governed by Catholic principles. Its principal figures, Fathers Pedro Gerard and José Gafo, were as deeply conservative as any Catholic labor organizers in their commitment to the restoration of a fully Christian society, but they believed that realizing this objective among industrial workers required the development of a more realistic approach than that of the Vicent-Comillas-Nevares school. As a result, they promoted Catholic unions entirely free of employer influence and de-emphasized confessionality in their operations. They also blended into their neo-Thomist view of society an eclectic mix of social Darwinism and revolutionary syndicalism derived from the French anarcho-syndicalist thinker Georges Sorel.[67] Other currents also swirled. In Barcelona, the Jesuit Gabriel Palau showed more flexibility than his Castilian counterparts by organizing Catholic trade unions designed to function free of employer influence. Other advocates of independent Catholic unions, notably Canon Maximiliano Arboleya and Severino Aznar, also argued their case, though they lacked the institutional base of the others.

Advocates of Catholic social action faced the central question of what precise institutional form workers' organizations should take. *Rerum Novarum* provided for the creation of "pure" workers' syndicates in contrast to the mixed associations popular until this time. Until 1906 Vicent and the marqués de Comillas remained deeply attached to the older model. In the second edition of *Socialismo y anarquismo* (1895), Vicent regarded the syndicate composed only of workers as an obstacle to the achievement of social peace.[68] Hostility towards the "pure" syndicate was translated into institutional form through the Workers' Circles and the first attempt to provide a national organization of Catholic social action, the Consejo Nacional de las Corporaciones Católico-Obreras, founded at Valencia in 1893 at the initiative of Vicent, the marqués de Comillas, and the archbishop of the diocese, C. M. Sancha. Given its membership of civil and ecclesiastical notables, the Consejo wished to have nothing to do with syndicates made up entirely of workers.

en el catolicismo innovador español," *Escritos de Vedat* (1984), vol. 14, pp. 209–52. He has also called attention to important theoretical differences between Castilian social Catholicism inspired by Donoso Cortés, with his vision of a totally Christian society and the Catalan, which looked back to Jaume Balmes, who approached the economic and social changes affecting mid-nineteenth century Spain from a more eclectic perspective. "El paso del 'Catolicismo social catalán' al pluralismo de los católicos en Cataluña," *Perspectiva Social* (1985), no. 21, pp. 111–32.

67. Carrasco Calvo, "Pensamiento social y acción sindical," pp. 230–32.

68. Llorens, "El P. Antonio Vicent," p. 433.

The Consejo Nacional also undertook with enormous fanfare the organization of a workers' pilgrimage to Rome in 1894. The organizers again imitated a foreign model, the French pilgrimage promoted by León Harmel and Albert de Mun in 1889. From his apparently inexhaustible fortune where Catholic causes were concerned, the marqués de Comillas provided six ships and bargain fares for the pilgrims, who had to run a barrage of stones and catcalls from demonstrators in Valencia, a city with a long anticlerical and republican tradition, which foolishly or naively had been chosen as the port of embarkation. The Consejo Nacional proved considerably less adept at translating the organizational skills invested in the pilgrimage into broader fields of action. It was singularly unsuccessful in imposing any significant degree of unity over the disparate diocesan and local organizations theoretically under its mandate.[69]

The influence exercised by the marqués de Comillas over Catholic social action in its formative phase limited its capacity to adapt to changing circumstances. That the marqués, with a fortune derived from shipping, mining, and finance, should have favored the mixed syndicate was not surprising given his role as one of the country's leading capitalists.[70] Both in his own time and later, critics held him responsible for the failure of social Catholicism to build a flourishing Catholic trade union movement. The marqués owed his influence within the Spanish Church between 1890 and his death in 1925 to several circumstances. He was a successful businessman known for his hard work and organizational skills. His rejection of Carlism and Integrism and his acceptance of the reigning dynasty gave him entry into ruling circles of the Restoration, although he was identified with neither major party. Respected by the bishops and with friends in the Vatican, he quickly established a reputation as the most influential layman of his generation, to the point that his opinion was invariably solicited by the leadership of the Spanish Church.

The marqués's views on the social question were similar to those of Father Vicent, with whom he maintained close and friendly relations.[71] Although both later accepted the necessity of creating "pure" labor syndicates, Comillas never departed from the principles elaborated by social Catholicism during the mid-1890s, with its emphasis on the mutual obligations of all social classes. Comillas's wealth and standing within the Church allowed him to impose his views on the institutions of social Catholicism. In 1895, for example, he financed the most influential social Catholic journal, the *Revista Católica de Cuestiones Sociales,* which in its first issue appealed "to capitalists and employers" to embrace "Catholic and social ideas" as "the only wall capable of containing the eruption of the ideas of utopian socialism

69. Valle, *El P. Antonio Vicent, S. J.*, pp. 159–64; Bayle, *El segundo marqués de Comillas*, p. 211; Benavides Gómez, *Democracia y cristianismo*, pp. 219–22; Andrés-Gallego, *Pensamiento y acción social*, p. 372.

70. Alfonso Botti, *Cielo y dinero: el nacionalcatolicismo en España, 1881–1975* (Madrid, 1992), pp. 46–48.

71. Ibid., pp. 14–16.

and fierce anarchism."[72] The *Revista* and another association founded by Comillas during the same period, the Asociación General para el Estudio y Defensa de la Clase Obrera, a social Catholic "think tank," were dominated by aristocrats, professors, and intellectuals who supported the marqués's narrow interpretation of the social problem, although, in fairness, it should be noted that both supported government legislation designed to afford some measure of protection to industrial workers.[73]

Criticism of the mixed association as fundamental for resolving conflicts between capital and labor surfaced in the early 1890s in France among reform-minded Catholic activists, the precursors of Christian Democracy. The reformers demanded the "effective participation of the worker" in syndicalist organizations on the basis of parallel associations of workers and employers, with disputes to be resolved through compulsory arbitration. They also urged political reform based on the concept of "organic" democracy at the national level, through the representation of such "professional" associations in legislative bodies. These ideas appeared in Spain through a series of articles published by the *Revista Católica de Cuestiones Sociales* in 1898.[74]

The ideas promoted by the advocates of Christian Democracy were neither radical nor representative of a complete rupture with the organizational model adopted by Vicent and his followers. The reformers remained attached to the idea of maintaining harmony among all classes, while their demands for some form of corporate legislative representation arose from their thinly veiled hostility towards the liberal State. In many respects, their ideas represented an evolution of Catholic social thought rather than a revolutionary break. They criticized the Workers' Circles on the grounds that they simply had outlived their usefulness.

Early advocates of a syndicalist organization committed to the interests of workers encountered tenacious opposition from the first generation of Catholic social activists. Maximiliano Arboleya, canon of Oviedo cathedral and a critic of the inertia of social Catholicism after the turn of the century, was attacked as a "dangerous liberal" and a man holding "pernicious ideas."[75] Although Arboleya

72. "Nuestros Propósitos," *Revista Católica de Cuestiones Sociales* (1895), no. 1, p. 4.

73. Andrés-Gallego, *Pensamiento y acción social*, p. 60. Catholic opinion was divided with respect to government intervention to protect workers. The Integrists were not enthusiastic, less on grounds of principle than out of opposition to the liberal regime. A series of protective labor laws passed during the Silvela ministry between 1899 and 1900 attracted considerable Catholic support. The Santiago Catholic Congress of 1902 passed a resolution urging the government to improve the "moral and material condition of workers by all possible means." Quoted in Montero García, "Los católicos españoles y los orígenes de la política social," p. 47.

74. Andrés-Gallego, *Pensamiento y acción social*, pp. 282–85.

75. Quoted in Domingo Benavides Gómez, *El fracaso social del catolicismo español, Arboleya-Martínez, 1870–1951* (Barcelona, 1973), pp. 32–33. Arboleya (1870–1951) was born in the mining town of Polo de Laviana in Asturias, where much of his activity would be concentrated. A graduate of the Spanish College in Rome in 1893 and holder of an ecclesiastical doctorate, he began his career as a professor of theology until winning a canonry in the Oviedo cathedral chapter in 1898. Thanks to the influence of

was moved by the same antisocialist sentiments as his opponents, his early support for labor unions formed exclusively by workers and his rejection of Carlism and Integrism made him *persona non grata* among large sectors of Catholic opinion. Arboleya attempted to promote his views through a variety of publications, notably the newspaper *El Carbayón* that he began publishing at Oviedo in 1901. The results of his efforts to turn social Catholicism in a new direction were disappointing. An attempt in 1903 to convert the Oviedo Workers' Circle into an organizing center for worker-controlled unions failed because of the hostility of traditional social Catholics.[76]

Arboleya was not alone in his criticism of the circles. Another propagandist for a change of direction, the university professor and sociologist Severino Aznar, attacked the dominant role in the circles of "dukes, counts, generals, bankers, ex-ministers, [and] friars." He asked, "What increases in salary have they [the circles] secured? How many have intervened to reduce the hours of work or to improve working conditions? How many strikes have they organized?"[77] Despite the eloquence with which advocates of new initiatives argued their case, there was no possibility that their views would be noticed until the leading figures of social Catholicism were prepared to listen.

By 1906, Father Vicent, troubled by the growing success of the socialist Unión General de Trajabadores (UGT), began to see the light. "Where have the workers gone?" he inquired of a member of a circle in Pontevedra. "Father, all of them have gone off with the Socialists," came the reply.[78] In 1906, Vicent gave a series of lectures in Barcelona in which he proposed the organization of "pure" labor unions drawing upon the circles' membership. He did not entirely abandon his old ideas because he also promoted the creation of employers' syndicates that were to be connected to the new unions through an institution known as the "mixed jury" as a means of resolving disputes between the two groups.[79]

Vicent's change of heart did not represent a radical break with the past. In 1907, the Consejo Nacional de las Corporaciones Católico-Obreras, still dominated by

---

his uncle, who remained bishop of the diocese until his death in 1904, Arboleya was entrusted with a variety of responsibilities, including a significant role in promoting social action. The succession of a new bishop who was totally uninterested in the social question saw a decline in Arboleya's official influence in the diocese. He remained, however, an important propagandist on behalf of a more realistic approach to the social problem.

76. Ibid., p. 42.

77. Quoted in Andrés-Gallego, *Pensamiento y acción social*, p. 281. Severino Aznar (1870–1960) was a law graduate of the University of Madrid. Early in his career he was influenced by Father Vicent, with whom he remained on friendly terms, although his ideas on the social question went well beyond those of the Valencian Jesuit. Aznar's contribution to social Catholicism was primarily as a theoretician, publicist, and propagandist. He published extensively on the social question in a long series of books and articles.

78. Quoted in Benavides Gómez, *Democracia y cristianismo*, p. 251.

79. Llorens, "El P. Antonio Vicent," p. 434.

Comillas and his followers, endorsed the new concept. The crucial question at this stage was not so much acceptance of the principle of the "pure" labor syndicate, but how it would be applied. There was no overall strategy on the part of Catholic social activists. The new trade unions emerged from uncoordinated initiatives that undermined the possibility of success. In Madrid, the circles functioning under the aegis of Comillas's Asociación General para el Estudio y Defensa de la Clasa Obrera began to organize Catholic unions. But critics noted that their effectiveness was limited by their "excessively cautious spirit" and their "subordination" to employers.[80]

A more ambitious effort was undertaken in Barcelona, the center of working-class radicalism in the country, through the efforts of the local bishop, Cardinal Casañas, and the Jesuit Gabriel Palau, who displaced Vicent as the leading figure in Catalan social Catholicism.[81] Palau promoted the formation of "pure" syndicates (Uniones Profesionales) within the larger institutional framework of the Acción Social Popular (ASP) that began to function in 1908 on the model of the German Catholic Volksverein. The ASP has been described as "a public relations and consulting firm whose clients could be virtually any Catholic organization or individual."[82] It was designed to promote social initiatives at a general level through a variety of propaganda activities, including the journal *Revista Social*, and through professional advice rendered to Catholic associations engaged in social action.

Palau recognized that the Uniones Profesionales ran the risk of rejection on the

80. Andrés-Gallego, *Pensamiento y acción social*, p. 306. In some cases, circles became trade unions by simply changing their names, as in the case of the San Vicente Ferrer circle in Valencia. Martí et al., "El sindicalismo católico en España," p. 213.

81. The removal of Vicent by his Jesuit superiors from a key role in organizing the new syndicates in favor of Palau was not accidental, although the reasons are not entirely clear. Thereafter, relations between the two Jesuits remained cool. Sanz de Diego, "El P. Vicent," p. 349. Gabriel Palau (1863–1939) was the most important figure in Catalan social Catholicism between 1907 and 1916, although there was nothing in his earlier career as a Jesuit to foreshadow his later involvement in social action. Alfonso Álvarez Bolado and José J. Alemany Briz, "Gabriel Palau, S. J. y la Acción Social Popular," *Miscelánea Comillas* (1980), vol. 38, no. 72, pp. 126–27.

82. Colin M. Winston, *Workers and the Right in Spain, 1900–1936* (Princeton, 1985), p. 40. The ASP defined itself as "an institution of general character, with a strictly personal organization which has as its purpose to promote by all legitimate means Catholic social action, especially among the most numerous classes." Quoted in José M. Llovera, *Tratado elemental de sociología cristiana* (Barcelona, 1909), p. 403. It was the most successful Catholic organization established in Spain up until that time, as membership grew from 15,200 in 1912 to 27,352 in 1915, on the eve of its disintegration. Its most impressive achievement was in the field of propaganda, where Palau was at his best, at least if the volume of publication is any guide. During its short history it distributed more 7 million individual pieces of published material. Tusell, *Historia de la democracia cristiana en España*, vol. 1, pp. 64–65. The ASP's modest success paled before that of its model, the Volksverein für das katholische Deutschland, founded in 1890. The ASP's base was narrowly regional rather than national like that of its German counterpart, and its membership was insignificant compared with the 850,000 belonging to the Volksverein in 1914, not to speak of the 90 million books and pamphlets it had distributed throughout Germany by 1914. Konrad Repgen, "150 años de catolicismo social en Alemania," in *Un siglo de catolicismo social en Europa*, pp. 232–33.

grounds that they responded "to the intervention and interests of the employer class."[83] To allay this apprehension, the new syndicates were to function with some independence, although they were linked to the ASP through its Labor Office. In practice, the unions promoted by Palau were closely identified with the ASP, an organization dominated by the conservative Catholic bourgeoisie of the region.[84] Although Palau developed a more sophisticated view of the social question than did some of his contemporaries, having once warned that workers would never develop "a sense of their personal and social value . . . if they are perpetually subject to tutelage and protection," he was unable to avoid the weaknesses of the Workers' Circles. The Uniones Profesionales also emphasized religious practice among members in a region where alienation from the Church reached massive proportions. Moreover, the important role played by ecclesiastical advisers in the unions made them appear as clerically dominated institutions to suspicious workers, who found further grounds for mistrust in the tactic of using the membership of the already discredited circles as the basis for the new Catholic unions.[85] Further, the antisocialist rhetoric employed by advocates of these unions, and their unwillingness to take any action that might provoke employers, deprived them of credibility.

The success of Palau's Uniones Profesionales was minimal. At their height, membership stood between six and seven thousand, of whom perhaps five thousand were manual workers in a region with more than two hundred thousand employed in the manufacturing trades.[86] "Pure" syndicates also appeared elsewhere, often as a result of independent local initiatives promoted by the clergy. The first union in Madrid began to function in 1907 and others soon followed. The syndicates of the capital emerged from the Workers' Circles and fell under the influence of the generals, aristocrats, and politicians who dominated the latter's board of directors. The marqués de Comillas, through a close associate, Carlos Martín Álvarez, kept the new unions under close supervision.[87] It is difficult to establish precisely the total membership of Catholic labor syndicates, although a figure of fifteen to twenty thousand between 1910 and 1913 seems reasonable.[88] By 1910 the UGT had already enlisted more than twice this number.

The limited success achieved by Catholic unions might have formed the basis for further development had they been able to break free of the accusation that they were "yellow syndicates" (*sindicatos amarillos*), that is, institutions serving the in-

83. Winston, *Workers and the Right*, p. 43.

84. Salvador Carrasco Calvo argues that the ASP did not maintain "with clarity . . . its preferences for pure syndical activity." "Control social y religión: el caso del catolicismo social innovador," in *Historia ideológica del control social*, ed. R. Bergalli and E. E. Mari (Barcelona, 1989), p. 40.

85. Winston, *Workers and the Right*, pp. 44–47.

86. Ibid., p. 51.

87. Benavides Gómez, *Democracia y cristianismo*, p. 256.

88. Ibid., p. 313.

terests of employers rather than workers. Such a direction proved impossible because of the influence of the Consejo Nacional, dominated by the marqués de Comillas and his followers.[89] They finally accepted the idea of "pure" unions, but within limits so narrow that they prevented them from evolving into syndicates capable of functioning beyond the paternalistic framework characteristic of Spanish social Catholicism since its origins.

The history of the most important of the new syndicates, the Sindicato Católico de los Ferroviarios Españoles (SCFE), founded among the railroad workers of Valladolid (1913), has exposed the ambiguous character of the Catholic labor movement. The union owed its origins to a group of Jesuits closely linked to the marqués de Comillas, of whom the key figure was Father Sisinio Nevares.[90] After arriving in the city in 1912, Nevares began to seek support for the creation of a union among its three thousand railroad workers, many already organized by the UGT.[91] The outbreak of a bitter strike launched by its Unión Ferroviaria in the same year made the establishment of a more compliant syndicate an attractive proposition for conservative social Catholics. Supported by Comillas, who suggested a possible director for the new union, Agustín Ruiz, and by the officers of the Northern Railroad Company, Nevares took an active role in drafting the syndicate's statutes. Catholic unionism had advanced to the point that the statutes accepted the legitimacy of strikes, these being possible, however, only after an exhaustive arbitration process and acceptance by two-thirds of its individual sections.[92]

Within two years of its foundation, the SCFE achieved some success in Valladolid and in other railroad centers of central and northern Spain. In 1915, its director claimed a membership of approximately five thousand. The union found a

89. Even the limited syndicalist activity of the ASP fell victim to the suspicions of the pro-Comillas faction. "A subtle operation" launched by the marqués de Comillas secured him a place on the ASP's board of directors, thereby initiating a "decisive change in direction" in the organization. Moreover, in 1914 Palau lost the support of the new bishop of Barcelona, Reig, who was uninterested in the organization of labor unions and preferred more general "cultural and formative" initiatives to resolve the social question. Palau abandoned the ASP under these pressures in 1916, to spend the next sixteen years as a professor in the Buenos Aires seminary. Carrasco, "Control social y religión," pp. 40–42.

90. Sisinio Nevares (1878–1946) began his career as a professor of history in the Jesuit university of Deusto. During the first decade of the century he became involved in social Catholicism, particularly in the movement that flourished after 1906 to found agrarian syndicates in the region around Valladolid, where he resided. It has been estimated that between 1912 and 1925 he helped found one thousand rural syndicates, cooperatives, and credit banks. The story of his indefatigable activities on behalf of Catholic social action has emerged in the publication of his personal archive. *Iglesia y sociedad en la España del siglo XX: catolicismo social*, ed. Quintín Aldea Vaquero, Joaquín García Granda, and Jesús Martín Tejedor (4 vols., Madrid and Valladolid, 1987–1991).

91. The effort to organize the railroad workers emerged from the activities of a group of Jesuits, including Nevares, who met at Burgos in January 1913 to plan a coordinated campaign of social action. "Conclusiones . . . en la reunión celebrada por indicación del R. P. Provincial en el Colegio de la Merced de Burgos durante los días 4, 5 y 6 de enero de 1913," in ibid., vol. 1, pp. 300–304.

92. Juan José Castillo, *El sindicalismo amarillo en España* (Madrid, 1977), pp. 104–7; Benavides Gómez, *Democracia y cristianismo*, pp. 263–64.

comfortable home for its offices in the Casa Social, an impressive building in Valladolid constructed by Nevares as a regional center for Catholic social work.[93] The Casa's propaganda activities received a generous annual subsidy of 60,000 pesetas from the marqués de Comillas.[94] This limited success was achieved in the face of intense opposition from the UGT. The SCFE hoped to profit from "the grave reverse" suffered by the UGT as a result of the failure of the 1912 strike and saw its own formation as "a reaction against these atavistic principles of *resistance* and struggle."[95] Hostility towards the Socialist union became standard fare in ongoing propaganda battles. In 1917, the secretary of the Madrid branch of Sindicato Nacional de Ferroviarios Católicos stressed again the necessity of harmony between capital and labor. He warned that any effort to the contrary was nothing less than a "criminal attempt that Catholic syndicalists must oppose energetically."[96]

The contradictions inherent in the Catholic union movement became evident during the intense labor agitation of 1916 and 1917. Catholic railway unions opposed the strike called by the UGT in July 1916, as they did the more ambitious general strike in December of the same year. A renewed attempt at a general strike in August 1917 was also rejected by the Catholic syndicates, who did their best to frustrate it, winning in the process the enthusiastic praise of the Catholic press and even of the government, which bestowed the Order of Isabel la Católica on the president of the Valladolid union, Agustín Ruiz. The ceremony was held in the Casa Social, which had denounced the strike as "false, unjust, [and] anti-patriotic" and its leaders as "the most immoral [and] egotistical of men."[97]

The conduct of the Catholic railway syndicates in 1916 and 1917 represented the triumph of the conservative Comillas-Jesuit line over those arguing for unions entirely free of employer influence. In Asturias, Canon Arboleya's efforts to found independent unions beyond the reach of employers were attacked by the Casa Social as "distant" from Catholic tendencies.[98] But the heaviest fire was directed against the attempt of the fiery Dominican Pedro Gerard to found *sindicatos libres* unencumbered by the confessional baggage and the association with employers

93. The inauguration of the Casa Social in 1915 was attended by ten thousand people, including the leading figures of Spanish social Catholicism, among them Gabriel Palau and Angel Herrera. For newspaper descriptions of the event, see *Iglesia y sociedad . . . catolicismo social*, vol. 1, pp. 359–67.

94. Nevares to his Jesuit superior, José Barrachina, February 12, 1920, in ibid., vol. 2, p. 687.

95. Quoted in Castillo, *El sindicalismo amarillo*, p. 105.

96. *El Debate*, January 2, 1917.

97. *Revista Católica de Cuestiones Sociales* (1917), pp. 182–83. For a more detailed discussion of the role of the Catholic railway union in the general strike attempts of 1916–1917, see Castillo, *El sindicalismo amarillo*, pp. 111–28.

98. Quoted in Benavides Gómez, *El fracaso social del catolicismo español*, p. 69. Alarmed by the growing strength after 1910 of the UGT in Asturias, particularly in coal mining districts, Arboleya promoted the establishment of *sindicatos independientes* beginning in 1911. In the following year Arboleya grouped a small number of such syndicates into the Federación de Sindicatos Independientes. This attempt to found "pure" unions, however, failed to take hold in the mining zones because of the hostility of the marqués de Comillas, who did everything he could to frustrate Arboleya's plans. Benavides Gómez, *El fracaso social del catolicismo español*, pp. 281–88. Adrian Shubert, "Entre Arboleya y Comillas: el fracaso del

characteristic of most Catholic unions.[99] Active between 1911 and 1919, Gerard shared the same hostility towards socialism as his fellow social Catholics, but he felt deeply the injustice to which the Spanish working class was exposed. "Slaves are better fed," he once remarked, "because they produce more."[100]

Gerard attacked the emphasis on religious practice and the obsession with maintaining harmony between capital and labor characteristic of Catholic attempts to organize labor. The Workers' Circles he judged useless: "It was believed that the Circles . . . would satisfy workers' aspirations. This was our error." His criticism of Catholic unions pretending to be "pure" was no less harsh. "If you create a mixed syndicate, it will fail, sooner or later." Although Gerard insisted upon the Catholic character of his free unions, he reproached both the circles and the later syndicates for making religious practice "almost their unique purpose."[101] The history of Spanish social Catholicism, he concluded, "has not produced until now any benefits worth mentioning."[102]

For Gerard, there was only one possible course of action, to establish "true societies of resistance," syndicates that would function free of employers' influence and could use every legitimate means, including the strike, to realize their just demands.[103] Gerard first advanced his ideas in 1911 while living in Jerez de la Frontera, where he founded the first Sociedad Católica de Resistencia. In 1912, he achieved national prominence for a speech delivered at a Catholic conference on social questions, the Semana Social, which met at Pamplona.[104] The Dominican friar demanded a complete change in the direction of social Catholicism. He told the delegates that workers saw the Church as identified with employers and their injustices. He declared that the time had come for social Catholics to recognize that socialist unions had succeeded because they secured real economic

---

sindicalismo católico en Asturias," in G. Jackson et al., *Octubre 1934: cincuenta años para la reflexión* (Madrid, 1985), p. 246.

99. Pedro Gerard (1871–1919) entered the Dominicans in 1886. After ordination in 1895, he took a degree in science and served as a professor in various houses of the order. In 1910 he came in contact with Father Georges C. Rutten, a Belgian Dominican who advocated a more energetic and advanced approach to organizing workers. Gerard began his attempt to implement the ideas he had derived from Rutten in 1911. Matías García, "El Padre Gerard," *La Ciencia Tomista* (1919), vol. 19, p. 182. Rutten, who founded the National Confederation of Free and Christian Syndicates in 1912, believed that unless the economic plight of workers was improved through effective trade unions, Catholic social action stood little chance of succeeding and halting the advance of socialism. Emmanuel Gerard, "El catolicismo social en Bélgica," in *Un siglo de catolicismo social en Europa*, p. 169.

100. Quoted in P. S. Perancho, "El obrero, el socialismo y los sindicatos libres: ideas sociológicas del Padre Gerard," *La Ciencia Tomista* (1921), vol. 23, p. 189.

101. Quoted in ibid., pp. 195, 196, 197.

102. Quoted in Andrés-Gallego, *Pensamiento y acción social*, p. 320.

103. Ibid.; Perancho, "El obrero, el socialismo y los sindicatos libres," pp. 196–97.

104. The Semana Social was another import. The Spanish version imitated similar conferences held in Germany and France during the 1890s. The first meeting in Spain was held in 1906, with subsequent gatherings in 1908, 1909, 1910, and 1912. For a discussion of their work, see Andrés-Gallego, *Pensamiento y acción social*, pp. 356–57; Rafael González Moralejo, "Las Semanas Sociales de España," *Revista de Trabajo* (1966), no. 16, pp. 219–39.

benefits for the worker and had given him the means of "developing his personality."[105]

Gerard's appeal was scarcely revolutionary, but his words, as well as the foundation of *sindicatos libres* embracing ten thousand workers in various cities, provoked a storm of controversy.[106] Publications under the influence of Comillas and Nevares attacked Gerard for advocating the class struggle. No shrinking violet, the Dominican replied by accusing his opponents of being supporters of "yellow unions." The sordid struggle dogged Gerard until his death. "The Calvary is daily, incessant," characterized by "how many jealousies, how many calumnies, how many persecutions!" he once remarked bitterly. His adversaries "appeared blind. They do not see, they do not comprehend that salvation lies in syndicalism."[107] Rancorous divisions prevented the formation of a national Catholic union until 1919, when the Confederación Nacional de Obreros Católicos was established. A concerted effort by Cardinal Aguirre to create a national federation of Catholic workers in 1912 through the Comillas-dominated Consejo Nacional de las Corporaciones Católico-Obreras was rejected by Gabriel Palau, while a 1915 proposal from Nevares's Casa Social in Valladolid to establish a Unión General de Trabajadores Católicos de España collapsed before the suspicions of more advanced social Catholics. Similarly, Gerard's 1913 plan for a national Catholic labor federation fell victim to Jesuit opposition, to the Dominican's intense irritation.[108]

With the succession of Victoriano Guisasola to the primatial see of Toledo in 1914, new initiatives seemed possible. More than any bishop of his generation, Guisasola understood the gravity of the problem facing the Church. His pastoral letter of 1916, *Justicia y caridad*, was the most progressive episcopal document of its kind in the history of Spanish social Catholicism up until that time, although he dis-

105. Quoted in Benavides Gómez, *Democracia y cristianismo*, p. 277. Salvador Carrasco has pointed out, however, that Gerard's Jerez initiative responded to an approach by the city sherry entrepreneurs, alarmed over radical agitation among their workers. After consulting with Father Rutten, he drafted regulations for the new organization, which he presented to employers in the house of Patricio Garvey, one of the city's leading wine merchants. Gerard insisted, however, that his new Casa del Trabajo should display the "most absolute independence from employers." Salvador Carrasco Calvo, "Teoría y práctica del sindicalismo católico libre y profesional, 1911–1936," in *La crisis de la Restauración: España, entre la primera guerra mundial y la Segunda República*, ed. José Luis García Delgado (Madrid, 1986), p. 317.

106. Gerard's syndical organization estimated a membership of ten thousand. Carrasco believes that the Sindicatos Católicos Libres formed "an entity more apparent than real" between 1913 and 1918, although they experienced limited success in organizing unions in the Basque Provinces, Navarra, Palencia, Zaragoza, and Santander. "Teoría y práctica del sindicalismo católico," pp. 322–23.

107. Quoted in Benavides Gómez, *Democracia y cristianismo*, pp. 279–80; Perancho, "El obrero, el socialismo y los sindicatos libres," pp. 198–99. The year 1916 saw the battle between Gerard and his syndicates, with their more conservative opponents within the Catholic labor movement, reach new levels of intensity. Carrasco, "Teoría y práctica del sindicalismo católico," p. 324. Similar attacks were made on a young Dominican associate of Gerard, José Gafo (1881–1936), who took up the cause of the *sindicatos libres* after 1916 as Gerard was forced to reduce active work under the pressure of his superiors. Gafo founded a center of free syndicates in Madrid in 1914 and propagandized on their behalf through the pages of the Dominican journal *La Ciencia Tomista*.

108. In a statement appearing in *El Debate* (June 13, 1912), Palau supported the idea in principle but expressed serious doubts about attempting to realize the project at the moment. He also made clear

played traditional Catholic hostility towards socialism and the liberal State. The former was inspired by "hatred," the latter by a "secular, rational and atheistic" ethic "unjust to the family, the Church, [and] to the individual dignity of man."[109] He defended the right of private property, although he noted that this was not unlimited, an opinion that not all social Catholics would have shared. But Guisasola also attacked "the abuse of capital that is called *capitalism* and which the Church condemns and reproves with the greatest severity." He defended the rights of workers to come together in syndicates as "the best means of securing immediately improvements in the material and moral interests of the worker." The cardinal primate expressed his opposition to "any revolutionary spirit" in such organizations, but he argued that they could "resist every unjust oppression by all legal means."[110]

Guisasola endorsed the idea of independent Catholic unions free of employer influence. Despite the essentially conservative nature of *Justicia y caridad*, its publication alarmed the marqués de Comillas, who called on the cardinal to warn him of the dangerous consequences that could result from his pastoral letter. By this time, the marqués had lost any realistic sense of the changes that had taken place in the Spanish labor movement. His views in 1916 were essentially unchanged from those of the 1890s. He informed Canon Arboleya, "it is most convenient" for the workers that their associations should be as "employer-oriented as possible."[111]

Discouraged by the cool reception given his pastoral letter by the supporters of Comillas, Guisasola had little heart for undertaking a renewed attempt to unify the badly divided Catholic syndicalist movement. But in 1918 he heeded Arboleya's warning that disaster loomed if the pretensions of the Comillas faction went unchecked. Despite the resistance of the marqués, the cardinal persuaded the nearly moribund Consejo Nacional de las Corporaciones Católico-Obreras to convoke an assembly of the leading figures of social Catholicism to propose a course of action. After some skirmishing between the factions represented, the delegates agreed to the convocation of a workers' congress to establish a national organization.[112]

The Comillas faction, using its control of the Consejo Nacional and its superior organization, easily arranged a sympathetic majority among the 192 delegates representing sixty thousand workers in Catholic labor unions. Meanwhile, Father Gerard, who had organized a Federación Nacional de Sindicatos Obreros Católicos

---

that he had no intention of allowing the Consejo Nacional a role in the affairs of the ASP. His statement is reproduced in Aldea Vaquero et al., *Iglesia y sociedad . . . catolicismo social*, vol. 1, pp. 245–47. The provisional statutes of the UGTCE are reproduced at p. 392. Relations between Gerard and Palau were also difficult. The Catalan Jesuit expressed his resentment in 1913 about the possible creation of Gerard's "free" syndicates in Barcelona. Carrasco, "Teoría y práctica del sindicalismo católico," p. 321.

109. Victoriano Guisasola, *Justicia y caridad en la organización cristiana del trabajo* (Madrid, 1916), p. 9.

110. Ibid., pp. 34, 37, 40, 42, 44.

111. Benavides Gómez, *Democracia y cristianismo*, p. 307; quoted in Benavides Gómez, *El fracaso social del catolicismo español*, pp. 84–85.

112. Benavides Gómez, *Democracia y cristianismo*, pp. 308–310.

Libres in 1916, declared that there was no need of a new national organization since the FNSOCL already served this purpose. Although he was eventually persuaded that delegates from the *sindicatos libres* should participate, the congress opened in an atmosphere of tension. Attacks were launched on the independent syndicates organized in Asturias by Arboleya as not truly Catholic. The delegates representing Gerard's union abandoned the meeting after an exchange of insults and recriminations with their opponents.[113] It appeared that the congress would dissolve in anarchy.[114]

That anything was saved from the debacle was due to the influence of Guisasola, Aznar, and Arboleya. The congress managed to agree on a theoretical program that reflected their views. The delegates approved "pure" syndicates as the only institution capable of representing workers' interests, rejected "yellow" unions, and endorsed circumstantial alliances with non-Catholic syndicates. But the victory proved hollow. The new national organization rested in the hands of the Comillas faction, which had no intention of applying in practice the principles endorsed by the congress. Supporters of a new direction for the Catholic labor movement, including Guisasola, were disillusioned. The embittered *sindicatos libres* of Gerard saw the new Confederación Nacional de Obreros Cátolicos as a front for the Comillas-Jesuit faction.[115]

Despite the foundation of a national Catholic labor syndicate in 1919, social Catholicism failed in its thirty-year effort to organize workers on a massive basis under Catholic auspices. During the preceding decade, the UGT and the CNT made spectacular gains. By 1919, nearly 1 million workers were enlisted in their ranks, compared to the approximately sixty thousand grouped in Catholic unions. With the new national syndicate firmly under the control of Comillas and his supporters, there was little possibility of significant further expansion. "Pure" unions formed according to the model of Gerard and Arboleya were unable to contest the triumph of their more conservative opponents.[116] The former's *sindicatos libres* either lost membership or disappeared into other labor organizations only tangentially related to social Catholicism, while the latter's *sindicatos independientes* in Asturias were already declining.[117] Isolated unions inspired by Catholic social prin-

113. Nevares received a description of the proceedings, which accused the supporters of Gerard of obstructionist tactics. Ildefonso Arroyo to Nevares, April 30, 1919, in Aldea Vaquero et al., *Iglesia y sociedad . . . catolicismo social*, vol. 2, p. 661.

114. Juan N. García Nieto, *El sindicalismo cristiano en España* (Bilbao, 1960), p. 138; Benavides Gómez, *Democracia y cristianismo*, pp. 311–14.

115. Benavides Gómez, *Democracia y cristianismo*, pp. 316–17.

116. The bitter debate did not come to an end. In a speech given at the Princesa theater in Madrid in 1921, the Dominican friar Bruno Ibeas complained, "Catholic employers, even more so than those who are not [Catholic], are waging a bloody war against Catholic syndicalism." *La Ciencia Tomista* (1921), vol. 23, p. 255.

117. Membership in Gerard's free syndicates declined significantly between 1919 and 1923. Their organization in Jerez de la Frontera collapsed entirely, while some "free" Bilbao unions went over to the new national federation. Carrasco, "Teoría y práctica del sindicalismo católico," p. 327.

ciples and operating independently of employer influence, such as the Solidaridad de Trabajadores Vascos (STV) founded at Bilbao in 1911, survived, but largely because of specific local circumstances. The STV was as firmly antisocialist as other Catholic unions, but its identification with Basque nationalism, it independence from Catholic "yellow unions," and its determination to struggle against "the rapacity of employers" provided the inner strength to survive as an effective labor organization in the region.[118]

The failure of social Catholicism's efforts to organize Spanish workers between 1880 and 1920 had many causes. Ongoing battles over the confessional character of Catholic labor unions created a confusing and contradictory situation that undermined whatever appeal they might have had for industrial workers, although it should be noted in fairness that even in Germany and Belgium, where effective Catholic labor organizations developed, social Catholicism was wracked by intense and sometimes bitter controversy over the question.[119] Internal factionalism played a role, as did the lack of positive theory of social action corresponding to socioeconomic reality. The dominance of the marqués de Comillas and his followers prevented the development of more effective organizing strategies. The forced dissolution of the ASP in 1916 occurred primarily because of the opposition of Comillas and Nevares to Palau's timid attempt to free the movement's unions from employer control.[120] Yet even the more conservative social action of Nevares encountered powerful opposition among his fellow Jesuits.[121] Nor would adoption of the syndicalist model supported by Gerard, Arboleya, and others necessarily have brought success. Unions free of employer influence developed more realistic goals and organization, but they suffered from many of the same weaknesses characteristic of conservative Catholic syndicates. Neither arose from the ranks of workers themselves but from the initiatives of clerical and middle-class lay activists. Fur-

118. Joaquín Perea, *El modelo de Iglesia subyacente en la pastoral del clero vasco, 1918–1936* (4 vols., Bilbao, 1991), vol. 3, pp. 1496–1512.

119. During the early years of the century, Father Rutten and his strong supporter, Cardinal Mercier of Malines, became the "object of severe criticism on the part of integrist Catholics of the day." After 1900, several German bishops campaigned actively against the participation of Catholics in the labor unions promoted by the Volksverein because they admitted Protestant workers and called themselves "Christian" rather than "Catholic." Gerard, "El catolicismo social en Bélgica," in *Un siglo de catolicismo social*, p. 169; Repgen, "150 años de catolicismo social en Alemania," pp. 236–37.

120. The reasons for the dissolution of the ASP in 1916 are not entirely clear. It has been suggested that it was ordered by the bishop of Barcelona, Cardinal Reig, in conjunction with the marqués de Comillas and Father Nevares. The attempt of the ASP to commit Catholic unionists to strike action in 1914 caused the city's Catholic elite to lose confidence in Palau, who was also suspected of being sympathetic to separatism. Carrasco Calvo, "El paso del 'catolicismo social catalán' al pluralismo," p. 120. Correspondence recently uncovered in the archives of the Society of Jesus in Rome has shown that there was strong Jesuit opposition to Palau, who was accused of being too independent of the order. Álvarez Bolado and Alemany Briz, "Gabriel Palau, S. J. y la Acción Social Popular," pp. 139–42.

121. Nevares complained that he had heard "hostile and deprecatory judgments towards Catholic social works" among Spanish Jesuits, including superiors who argued that such activities "are not for us" but should be left to the diocesan clergy. Nevares to José Barrachina, February 12, 1920, in Aldea Vaquero et al., *Iglesia y sociedad . . . catolicismo social*, vol. 2, p. 682.

ther, membership in the Workers' Circles, the "mixed" syndicates, and even the "pure" unions of Arboleya and Gerard drew heavily on artisan or semi-artisan trades, with few exceptions.[122]

Interpretations of social Catholic attempts to organize the industrial working class have stressed failure as its essential characteristic, an idea encouraged by many of the participants in the bruising internal struggles of the early twentieth century and by later historians concerned with Spanish Catholicism's inability to develop a mass labor movement and a Christian Democratic party. Recent scholarship has provided a more nuanced view by stressing the movement's diverse intellectual sources and by placing it within the broader framework of the Church's efforts to create a Christian society through a variety of religious and organizational initiatives.[123] But when all is said and done, Catholic social action among workers contributed little to reaching the objective of re-Christianizing Spanish society.

122. Gerard's first Sociedad de Resistencia in Jerez was dominated by carpenters, locksmiths, employees in retail trade, etc., while the largest of Palau's Uniones Profesionales was composed of white-collar workers. Andrés-Gallego, *Pensamiento y acción social*, p. 317; Winston, *Workers and the Right*, p. 51.

123. Montero García, "Catolicismo social en España," pp. 157–61.

CHAPTER VI

THE STRUGGLE TO ADAPT (II)

The Agrarian Movement

The indifferent results of attempts to organize industrial workers were offset by the success of social Catholicism in the countryside. Between 1900 and 1920, the number of rural credit unions, cooperatives, and agrarian syndicates formed under Catholic auspices expanded from a minuscule base to include several thousand organizations.[1] Before the turn of the century, social Catholics gave some attention to the agricultural sector. Worsening agrarian conditions during the 1890s, produced by the end of a Franco-Spanish commercial treaty in 1892, the destructive effects of the phylloxera in wine-producing districts, and the loss of the Cuban flour market in 1898 produced a crisis in Spanish agriculture that attracted their interest. In 1894, the Tarragona Congress called for improved leasing arrangements for those renting land and a savings scheme to allow renters to purchase their holdings. In the flood of regenerationist sentiment provoked by the disaster of 1898, the 1899 Burgos Congress promoted the foundation of Guilds of Agriculturalists, an idea supported by Father Vicent, and the establishment of rural credit institutions.[2]

During the 1890s, social action in the countryside lagged behind efforts to or-

1. The Confederación Nacional Católico-Agraria claimed that five thousand agrarian syndicates with six hundred thousand members were in existence by 1920. These figures are too optimistic given that official government surveys of 1917 and 1924 set a far lower total for the number of syndicates and their membership, whether Catholic or not. For a discussion of the statistical problem, see Juan José Castillo, *Propietarios muy pobres: sobre la subordinación política del pequeño campesino* (Madrid, 1979), pp. 111–27.

2. José Andrés-Gallego, *Pensamiento y acción social de la Iglesia en España* (Madrid, 1984), pp. 61–62; Monserrat Llorens, "El P. Vicent, S. I. (1870–1912): notas sobre el desarrollo de la acción social católica en España," *Estudios de Historia Moderna* (1954), vol. 4, p. 420; Joseph Harrison, *An Economic History of Modern Spain* (New York, 1978) pp. 33–35.

ganize industrial workers. After the turn of the century, social Catholics focused more attention on rural initiatives. The shift in emphasis reflected broad national concern with the agricultural crisis and the necessity of modernizing a backward rural economy. It also arose from the belief of Catholic activists that the rural population offered superior organizing possibilities. "The peasant masses," remarked Severino Aznar, are "less exposed to [radical] syndicalist preaching" and therefore "constitute perhaps our best base of operations."[3] Social Catholics also admired the success of Catholic rural organizations elsewhere in Europe. In 1896, Father Vicent visited Switzerland to examine the operations of a local agricultural credit institution and endorsed the establishment of similar bodies in Spain. Activists were impressed with Catholic agricultural syndicates organized under French legislation of 1884. The French example received extensive discussion in Spanish social Catholic circles beginning in the late 1890s. The possibility of establishing comparable organizations in Spain attracted wide support at the Catholic Congress of 1902, which urged enactment of similar legislation by parliament.[4]

The First Stage

The organizational surge that swept through social Catholicism as it attempted to organize the countryside produced a variety of institutions, rural credit unions, agrarian syndicates, grain storing associations, and cooperatives. Three principles underlay this institutional expansion. First, the organization of Catholic agricultural associations adhered to the model of the "mixed" association so dear to the founders of Spanish social Catholicism. The fundamental purpose of the Catholic agrarian movement, according to Father Nevares, was to bring about "the union of [social] classes." The interests of agricultural workers and small proprietors were to receive priority, but Nevares left no doubt that the movement would "receive, help and defend" owners of large properties who joined its ranks. Second, the institutions of rural social Catholicism were strictly confessional. Father Vicent early expressed his opposition to admitting members who were not "Catholic." All Catholic rural associations, moreover, were subject to episcopal authority. "The *Catholicism* of any social undertaking," declared a social Catholic journal, "is born from its submission to the authority and hierarchy of the Church."[5]

Third, social Catholicism's rural program attempted to better the lot of peasants and agricultural workers through improvements based on modern technology,

3. Severino Aznar, *Problemas sociales de la actualidad* (Barcelona, 1914), p. 49. Similarly, the bishop of Salamanca declared: "The villages of my diocese, with one exception, are ignorant even of the names of socialism and anarchism." Quoted in Florentino del Valle, *El P. Antonio Vicent, S.J. y la acción social católica española* (Madrid, 1947) p. 279.

4. Andrés-Gallego, *Pensamiento y acción social*, pp. 88, 243–44.

5. Quoted in Castillo, *Propietarios muy pobres*, pp. 71, 256–57, and Andrés-Gallego, *Pensamiento y acción social*, p. 89.

credit institutions, and marketing mechanisms. It rejected the idea of any agrarian reform threatening private property. To be sure, Catholic social theorists, moved by *Rerum Novarum*, debated the evils inherent in the unrestrained use of property as an offense against natural law.[6] But these finely drawn discussions never received practical application. That social Catholicism defended private property was scarcely surprising given its basic assumptions. But its rejection of agrarian reform involving land redistribution rested on more than an atavistic defense of property rights. Spanish social Catholicism formed its ideas on the agrarian question at a time when the issue of land reform had become a topic of intense public discussion. The ideas of Henry George entered the country during the 1890s, while Joaquín Costa's *Colectivismo agrario en España* (1898) raised the possibility of fundamental changes in the distribution of property as a remedy to the nation's agrarian ills. Reacting against these ideas, Catholic apologists sought an alternative model that promised improvements in the material condition of the rural population without disturbing private property. They found their apostle of conservative modernization in an Italian social Catholic theorist, S. Solari, who argued that it was possible to achieve this objective through technological and agricultural improvements that would increase production. The ideas of Solari and his disciples began to spread, beginning in 1903 with the publication of the Biblioteca Agraria Solariana in Seville by the Salesian Order. Thereafter, they provided the theoretical underpinning for a multitude of Catholic agrarian initiatives.[7]

Social Catholicism's success in the countryside was remarkable given the differences of land-tenure arrangements and agricultural production within the country. Spain lacked the base of medium-sized farmers, who in the normal course of events would have been most attracted to a program combining agricultural modernization with the defense of private property. Only in Catalonia, Navarra, and Alava did such farmers exist in considerable numbers. Elsewhere in central and northern Spain, the fragmentation of property produced a varied class of small landowners and tenant farmers who struggled to make ends meet on holdings barely sufficient to sustain family economies. Even in these regions there were extreme differences, for example, between Galicia, with its excessively small plots, complicated leases, and subsistence agriculture, and neighboring areas along the northern coast, from Asturias to the Basque Provinces, where more favorable land-tenure arrangements and a more diverse agricultural base produced a relatively stable and minimally adequate peasant economy. There were also regions of small holdings, such as the fertile Mediterranean plain around Valencia, where small

6. For a brief discussion of some of the historical and philosophical arguments used by some theorists to justify "the social function of property," see A. Valle, "El P. Narciso Noguer, 1858–1935," *Razón y Fe* (1935), p. 95.

7. Josefina Cuesta Bustillo, *Sindicalismo católico agrario en España, 1917–1919* (Madrid, 1978), pp. 58–64.

landholders succeeded in developing a prosperous citrus agriculture. The agrarian map of Spain was also characterized by a fundamental division between the central and northern regions of fragmented property and the southern provinces in Extremadura and Andalucía, where large estates employing masses of impoverished day workers predominated.[8] Further, the economic interests of rural Spain varied substantially from one region to another. The concerns of the cereal grain producers of central Spain, assaulted first by the intrusion of North American wheat into European markets and later by government price regulation, differed from those of Catalan wine growers and Mediterranean citrus farmers intent upon expanding export markets, and from those of Vizcayan milk producers who wished to promote the greater commercialization of their product within Spain.

Despite these obstacles, social Catholicism experienced its first rural successes in areas of northern Spain and the Mediterranean coast just after the turn of the century, through the institution of the rural credit union. Largely self-financed through the modest contributions of their members, credit unions took several distinct forms, but many adopted a German Catholic organizational model (Cajas Rurales del Sistema Raiffeisen).[9] Although the *cajas* spread slowly at first, they began to increase after their successful introduction in Navarra in 1902. Between 1906 and 1912, the number in the province rose from 20 to 155, providing credit to 436 villages. *Cajas* were also established in significant numbers during this period in Valencia because of the efforts of Father Vicent, and in Murcia, Zaragoza, and Cuenca. They appeared in smaller numbers in Galicia, Old Castile, and Extremadura, but scarcely penetrated Andalucía, where day laborers comprised a majority of the agricultural population.[10]

Expansion of the *cajas* provided social Catholicism with its first real success despite an uneven pattern of regional distribution. The reasons for this success are clear. The *cajas*, operating in a straightforward way, provided credit for the purchase of seeds and agricultural equipment in communities of small landowners and tenant farmers who previously lacked access to capital except through the proverbial village usurer. The latter, a sinister figure depicted in countless literary works as the scourge of the countryside, a "slimy beast in its lair," charged helpless clients outrageous interest rates that reached as high as 120 percent.[11] The popu-

8. Harrison, *An Economic History of Modern Spain*, pp. 5–10; Edward Malefakis, *Agrarian Reform and Peasant Revolution in Spain: Origins of the Civil War* (New Haven and London, 1970), pp. 11–34.

9. There is a detailed discussion of the Raiffeisen credit unions in Andrés-Gallego, *Pensamiento y acción social*, pp. 89–128. See also the voluminous study of Narciso Noguer, *Las cajas rurales en España y en el extranjero* (Madrid, 1912). The *cajas* operated on fairly simple principles. Initial capital was raised either through borrowing from another credit institution or from private donations, frequently the small contributions of the members. Prospective borrowers were vetted by the directors before receiving loans at moderate interest rates.

10. Andrés-Gallego, *Pensamiento y acción social*, pp. 96–104.

11. Noguer, *Las cajas rurales*, p. 519. The *cajas* charged an average rate of 5 percent.

larity of the *cajas* arose, in part, from their effort to meet obvious local needs. But the success of individual *cajas* varied from one locality to another. That of Olite (Navarra), founded by Father Victoriano Flamarique, tripled its lending between 1904 and 1910, while establishing cooperatives for the purchase of fertilizers, the milling and sale of grain, and the production of electricity. But other *cajas* in the same region led "an anemic life," according to a report of 1911.[12]

What was significant about the *cajas* was less their limited success in alleviating the chronic shortage of credit than the organizational impulse behind their creation. Unlike the Catholic labor movement, a hothouse plant cultivated in large measure by clerical social activists, the *cajas* arose from diverse sources that, if not entirely from the grass roots, corresponded more closely to local concerns. Although the Consejo Nacional de las Corporaciones Católico-Obreras began in 1903 to promote the creation of rural credit institutions, and clerical advocates of the *cajas* such as the Jesuit Narciso Noguer were tireless in urging their establishment, organizing initiatives usually depended on local activists. In Zamora, the intense propaganda efforts of Luis Chaves Arias, a district landowner well connected to European social Catholic circles, stimulated the first serious effort to establish *cajas rurales* in Spain.[13] In Murcia, the initiative came from Francisco Rivas Moreno, an official of the Ministry of Finance; in Navarra, it was a parish priest, Victoriano Flamarique, who was moved to action after reading the publications of Chaves, while in Plasencia, Father José Polo Benito, professor of sociology in the diocesan seminary and secretary to the bishop, became the principal promoter of *cajas* in the region. These propagandists for Catholic rural credit unions were keenly aware of the necessity of adapting the *cajas* to specific local conditions.[14]

The success of the *cajas* at the village level also depended on the support of parish priests. The *cura* of Los Santos (Extremadura), Ezequiel Santana, moved "by the powerful evils of usury" in his country parish, established a *caja rural*, as did parish priests in hundreds of small villages such as Ruguilla (Guadalajara) and Ambrona (Soria).[15] Although the role of parish priests in the organization and administration of *cajas* generated some local resentment, local priests provided the crucial link between the propaganda of regional social activists and village communities that made the creation of *cajas* possible. This is not to say that all parochial clerics were carried away with enthusiasm. Repeated exhortations by

12. Ibid., p. 508; Andrés-Gallego, *Pensamiento y acción social*, p. 103.

13. Luis Chaves Arias (1863–1917) became interested in finding a means of ending the practice of usury in his region in 1901. He studied the operations of the Cajas Raiffeisen and became their strong promoter. He also maintained contacts with Catholic social activists throughout Europe.

14. Andrés-Gallego, *Pensamiento y acción social*, pp. 90–92, 99. See the work of José Polo Benito, *El problema social del campo de Extremadura* (Salamanca, 1919), for an example of a perceptive analysis of local agrarian and social conditions.

15. "El Cura de Los Santos," *Revista Católica de Cuestiones Sociales* (1917), p. 319; Noguer, *Las cajas rurales*, p. 510.

bishops and clerical publicists for priests to become involved in social action suggest that many clergy remained indifferent.[16]

The Agrarian Syndicates

Cajas rurales continued to be founded during the first two decades of the century, but after 1906 they subsided in importance with the spread of Catholic agrarian syndicates. Although credit unions such as that in Olite sometimes established cooperatives, the majority limited themselves to the limited financial purpose for which they were founded. Between 1900 and 1905, reformers of various stripes, including Liberal and Conservative politicians, campaigned for legislation to authorize the creation of agrarian syndicates as legally sanctioned bodies capable of engaging in a broad range of activities to improve agriculture. In 1906, parliament passed a law to this effect, based largely on a text prepared by the Instituto de Reformas Sociales.[17] Social Catholics, who were represented in the Instituto, claimed credit for the 1906 law, although in fact the legislation received broad support from the country's so-called *fuerzas vivas*.[18]

The law authorized the formation of syndicates by anyone engaged in agriculture: landowners, tenant farmers, and day workers who could form either separate or joint associations as they desired. The legislation established specific objectives for the syndicates. They were to promote the acquisition of farm machinery, fertilizers, seeds, and the like by their members. They were permitted to engage in the sale and export of agricultural products, purchase untilled lands to place them in cultivation, and take whatever measures were necessary to combat the natural "plagues of the countryside." The law also assigned the syndicates a significant lobbying role by recognizing their right to promote the "defense of common agricultural interests."[19]

The 1906 law opened a new and expansive phase in Catholic rural organizations. The legislation permitted any group of agriculturists to form syndicates, but social Catholics with the organizational experience of the *cajas rurales* behind them quickly seized the initiative. The formation of mixed syndicates comprising landowners, tenant farmers, and agricultural laborers also fitted into the long-held assumptions of social Catholicism. Economic conditions characterized by a worsening ratio of agricultural to industrial prices during the first decade of the century created circumstances favorable to the spread of an institution committed to the

16. See, for example, the tracts to this effect of Andrés Manjón, *El problema social y de la acción del clero* (Madrid, 1908), and Victoriano Guisasola, *La acción social del clero* (Valencia, 1910).

17. Founded in 1903, the Institute of Social Reform was a consultative body advising the government in the field of social legislation.

18. Andrés-Gallego, *Pensamiento y acción social*, p. 244; Domingo Benavides Gómez, *Democracia y cristianismo en la España de la Restauración, 1875–1931* (Madrid, 1978), p. 298.

19. Quoted in Andrés-Gallego, *Pensamiento y acción social*, p. 245.

defense of farming interests.[20] Between 1906 and 1912, the Catholic agrarian movement followed a decentralized pattern similar to that of the *cajas*. Social activists prepared the ground through propaganda campaigns such as the one carried out by Luis Chaves Arias in Extremadura during the spring of 1907. The parish clergy again provided the organizational impetus at the village level. Ezequiel Santana, for example, after first establishing a *caja*, founded a syndicate for the purchase of seeds and fertilizers and the sale of agricultural products so that "the economic regeneration of his village might be complete."[21]

The grassroots character of the movement in this early phase contributed to expansion in approximately the same areas where the *cajas rurales* were successful. By 1909, 450 syndicates were operating, with Navarra (53), Zaragoza (48), and Valencia (29) having the largest numbers. Syndicates were distributed in an arc running from Valencia northwest to Cuenca, Teruel, Zaragoza, Soria, Burgos, and Santander and then south to Salamanca, Ciudad Rodrigo, and Coria. Syndicates were also found in limited numbers in Galicia, Asturias, and Gerona. As with the *cajas*, the syndicates failed to penetrate the *latifundio* lands of Andalucía, Extremadura, and La Mancha. Nor did they make a significant impact in certain regions where small landowners and peasant farmers were numerous, such as Ávila, Segovia, Valladolid, and León.[22]

A second wave of expansion occurred between 1912 and 1916, as the syndicates moved from a structure based on disconnected local organizations to an intermediate model resting on regional federations with links to one another. The first federations appeared in 1908 (Ciudad Rodrigo and Santander); by 1916 they numbered eighteen. Although primarily concerned with providing more abundant sources of credit to the local syndicates, the regional federations also provided the Catholic agrarian movement with the organizational muscle it had previously lacked. Thus strengthened, Catholic agrarianism expanded into areas of central and northern Spain, such as Valladolid, Astorga, and León, where it had earlier failed to penetrate. Overall, the number of syndicates expanded from the 450 in 1909 to 1,100 by 1916.[23]

20. Castillo, *Propietarios muy pobres*, p. 45.

21. "El cura de Los Santos," p. 320; Andrés-Gallego, *Pensamiento y acción social*, p. 267. Similarly, at Villalón in the region of the Tierra de Campos, the establishment of the first syndicate was due to the initiative of the parish priest, Father Fulgencio Sánchez, who later became known as "the soul . . . of agrarian syndicates" for his efforts to spread them throughout the district. Mateo Martínez, *Tierra de Campos: cooperativismo y sindicalismo agrario* (Valladolid, 1982), p. 54.

22. Andrés-Gallego, *Pensamiento y acción social*, p. 264. The failure to establish syndicates in regions where they might have been expected to prosper may have arisen because the link between the propaganda of activists and the parish clergy was not forged as it had been elsewhere. During this first phase of the syndicates' history, they also failed to penetrate the Basque Provinces, but for a different reason. The existence there of associations performing similar functions had been promoted by provincial governments since the 1890s, thereby undercutting the appeal of the Catholic syndicates.

23. Benavides Gómez, *Democracia y cristianismo*, p. 300. In 1909, Valladolid had only two syndicates. By 1916 ninety-eight were in existence.

Other circumstances contributed to expansion. Catholic social activists had long extolled the advantages of agrarian syndicates, but their propaganda efforts were sometimes disorganized and fragmented. This situation began to change in 1912, when leading activists attending the Semana Social meeting at Pamplona accorded priority to the organization of the countryside, as did two national assemblies convoked by the usually lethargic Consejo Nacional de las Corporaciones Católico-Obreras in the same year. In 1913, the always energetic Angel Herrera used his position as editor of *El Debate* to assemble a high-powered group of social Catholics, including Father Nevares and Severino Aznar, to consider means of strengthening Catholic initiatives in the countryside. All these groups strongly promoted the expansion of agrarian syndicates.[24] Through *El Debate,* Herrera campaigned vigorously in 1913–1914 on behalf of the syndicates, while teams of young activists belonging to the ACNP traversed the provinces of León, Zamora, Valladolid, Segovia, and Palencia "with a true flood of agrarian social action meetings."[25]

The economic effects of the First World War encouraged the spread of Catholic agrarianism. Steadily rising agricultural prices provided the syndicates with increased capital to finance technological improvements designed to increase production and enlarge markets. But the war also brought problems to the countryside, as a rise in industrial prices outstripped the increase of agricultural prices. In the grain-producing regions of Castile-León, for example, government price controls on wheat created a deep malaise among farmers, who looked to the local and regional syndicates to lobby for the imposition of controls on all articles of consumption.[26] The war, of course, affected regional economies differently, but in almost every case it enhanced the role of the syndicates as lobbies defending agricultural interests. The Federation of La Rioja, for instance, was less concerned with price controls than with obstacles to the expansion of its wine markets raised by high railway freight rates, against which it campaigned vigorously.[27]

Between 1917 and 1920, the Catholic agrarian movement entered its third and final stage of expansion. Through the support of Cardinal Guisasola, syndicates were established in Toledo in sufficient numbers to establish a federation in 1917, the first significant penetration of a region where large estates were common. Catholic agrarianism gained a stronger foothold in Galicia, Catalonia, and Salamanca.[28] In 1919, it attempted to crack the hardest nut of all, Andalucía. The par-

24. Ibid., p. 299.

25. Nicolás González Ruiz and Isidoro Martín Martínez, *Seglares en la historia del catolicismo español* (Madrid, 1968), p. 66.

26. Harrison, *An Economic History of Modern Spain*, p. 89. The Federation of Astorga demanded in 1918 that price controls be imposed "on all articles just as agricultural products have been controlled." Quoted in Cuesta Bustillo, *Sindicalismo católico agrario*, pp. 129–30, note 16.

27. Cuesta Bustillo, *Sindicalismo católico agrario,* p. 109.

28. The number of Catholic agrarian syndicates in Galicia increased from 72 in 1909 to 486 by 1920. Alberte Martínez López, *O cooperativismo católico no proceso de modernización da agricultura galega,*

ticular socioeconomic conditions of the region, with fewer small property owners and tenants than in the north and a vast population of poor day laborers, raised serious obstacles to expansion. Catholic agrarian syndicates were able to adapt to the situation, within limits, by organizing their activities to benefit day workers. The first syndicates in Jaén concentrated their efforts on renting land to agricultural laborers. Catholic propagandists also encouraged wealthy proprietors to donate land to the dispossessed. They held up the example of the marqués de Riscal, who provided a thousand hectares from his estate near Guadalupe for distribution by the local Catholic syndicate. Few landowners imitated his example. In the end, the campaign to organize syndicates in the region failed to meet expectations. The relatively few syndicates in the region lacked the financial resources to do what was necessary to win over the region's rural population, namely, the purchase and distribution of land to those desperate to have it.[29]

Despite limited success in the south, by 1920 the Catholic agrarian movement claimed that it had expanded from eighteen regional federations in 1916 to fifty-nine and that the number of local syndicates had increased from eleven hundred to five thousand.[30] Although these figures were exaggerated, there is no question that Catholic syndicates prospered in this final expansionary surge as a result of the refinement of organizing techniques first developed in the *cajas rurales*. Propagandists at the national level kept up a barrage of publicity urging the formation of syndicates, while region after region received the visits of organizers who traversed dusty country roads to bring the message to remote villages. Father Nevares, for example, often abandoned the Casa Social in Valladolid to engage in organizing campaigns. In the summer of 1918, he appeared in Galicia and founded syndicates in Tuy, Ribadavia, Filgueira, Tomiño, Goyán, El Rosal, Panjón, Bayona, Ramallosa, and Oya, before moving on to do the same in the villages around Santiago.[31]

The creation in 1917 of the Confederación Nacional Católico-Agraria (CNCA) for the first time provided the Catholic agrarian movement with a national organization. Although its foundation strengthened Catholic agrarianism, it also began to move it in an imprecise but noticeable political direction characterized by virulent hostility towards socialism and anarchism and an unwavering commitment to defense of the established social order. These elements were present in the earlier phases of the movement's history but with less ideological fervor than now became the case. Conditions in Spain beginning in 1917 contributed to the development

1900–1943 (Vigo, 1989), p. 65. In the province of Salamanca, only 57 syndicates had been founded until 1916; between 1917 and 1920, 200 were established. Mary Vincent, *Catholicism in the Second Spanish Republic: Religion and Politics in Salamanca, 1931–1936* (Oxford, 1996), p. 129, table 5.1.

29. Cuesta Bustillo, *Sindicalismo católico agrario*, pp. 198, 263, 269, 273. Granada had only 35 syndicates; Seville, 23; Almería, 31; Jaén, 21; and Málaga, 26.

30. Castillo, *Propietarios muy pobres*, p. 115.

31. Cuesta Bustillo, *Sindicalismo católico agrario*, p. 242. Martínez López regards the "enormous propaganda activity" of Nevares and his associate, Antonio Monedero, during the second half of 1918 as crucial to the expansion of Catholic syndicates in Galicia. *O cooperativismo católico*, p. 69.

of an aggressive mood in the Catholic agrarian movement. The unsuccessful Socialist revolutionary general strike in 1917, the impact of the Bolshevik Revolution, the dire effects of the end of the war on the Spanish economy and the resulting wave of strikes in 1919, the spread of anarchism through the southern countryside in the same year, and the chronic political instability of the Restoration constitutional system all contributed to growing fears of impending revolution among Catholic leaders, both lay and clerical. What was taking place, declared a prominent social Catholic organizer, was a "gigantic battle" in which "either the Church kills the revolution, or the revolution kills the Church."[32] The disturbing events of the period gave new urgency to social Catholic activists' attempts to organize the countryside. There was no alternative, declared Father Nevares: "either social Catholicism or Bolshevism."[33] These sentiments penetrated deeply into the ranks of the parish priests who played so crucial a role in the Catholic agrarian syndicates. For the parish priest of Espinaredo (Oviedo), an avid promoter of syndicates in his district, "The devil was the first socialist in the world," and he urged his flock "to condemn, abhor and detest" so dangerous a movement.[34]

It would be premature to suggest that Catholic agrarianism developed a militant counterrevolutionary ideology between 1917 and 1920. Syndicates continued to spend much of their energy on agricultural improvement and lobbying, but the balance of priorities between conservative modernization and ideology began to shift. The establishment of the CNCA encouraged this trend. Although Cardinal Guisasola attempted to create a national agrarian federation more responsive to the currents of opinion among social Catholic activists, he lost the battle. After a struggle as rancorous as the one over the organization of industrial workers, control of the CNCA came to rest in the hands of a fervent associate of the omnipresent Father Nevares, Antonio Monedero (1872–1940).[35]

That a wealthy landowner became the first president of the CNCA testifies to the inner contradictions of Catholic agrarianism. Although some critics contend that the role of Monedero and other large proprietors in the regional federations transformed Catholic agrarianism's focus on the concerns of small landowners and tenant farmers into a defense of property rights, the situation was more complex.[36] Not all regional federations were dominated by large estate owners holding key offices. In the federation of Valladolid, for example, they were weakly represented. But in Salamanca, landowners predominated in the local CNCA.[37] Monedero's ca-

32. Luis Irurzún Muru, *El catolicismo social y el socialismo al desnudo* (Tafalla, 1918), p. 13.

33. Quoted in Martínez, *Tierra de Campos*, p. 155.

34. Juan Guerra Díaz, *El amigo del católico campesino o sea cartas entre un cura de aldea y un feligrés* (Valladolid, 1919), pp. 270, 272. Journals published for the parish clergy during the period 1917–1919 repeatedly warned of the dangers posed by "Bolshevism." See, for example, "El párroco y la cuestión social," *Revista Eclesiástica* (1919), pp. 281–85, 373–75.

35. Benavides Gómez, *Democracia y cristianismo*, p. 301.

36. See, for example, the criticism of Castillo, *Propietarios muy pobres*, pp. 32–33, 64.

37. Vincent, *Catholicism in the Second Spanish Republic*, pp. 126–27.

reer reveals an ambiguous combination of a sincere commitment to improving the lot of small proprietors and tenant farmers and an unwillingness to break free of the archaic norms fixed by the first generation of social Catholics during the 1890s.

Converted to social activism by Father Vicent in 1910, Monedero became a tireless propagandist for and organizer of local syndicates, first in his native Palencia and later in other regions, before becoming the first president of the interregional federation of Old Castile and León in 1914. His views on the social question were by no means reactionary. He rejected, for instance, the opinion of conservative social Catholic theorists that property rights were unlimited according to the principles of natural law. He was also aware of the danger to Catholic agrarianism posed by the influence of large proprietors. He waged an ongoing struggle to limit their influence, maintaining that the movement "must be for and of the people."[38] But Monedero remained a prisoner of the early principles of Spanish social Catholicism enunciated by Father Vicent and later refined by Father Nevares.[39] Insistence on the confessional character of the agrarian movement and hostility to "pure" syndicates that excluded large property owners destroyed the possibility of attracting the day laborers of Extremadura, Andalucía, and La Mancha. Adherence to the historic tenets of social Catholicism effectively blocked further expansion once regions of small owners and tenant farmers had been organized. By the early 1920s, the syndicates' expansionary phase was over.

The combination of inflexibility inspired by social Catholic tradition and the ideological virulence of the period 1917–1920 produced a potentially dangerous political mixture. By the early 1920s, Catholic agrarianism was fixed in a stagnating mold in which the modernizing impulses so crucial to its early history receded before the determination to thwart assault on the traditional agrarian structure. It is ironic that just as Catholic agrarianism entered its most expansive period and developed a mature organizational structure, it produced no new ideas and fell back on the historic refuge of Spanish Catholics in times of trial, a defensive mentality that left little room for innovative solutions to the economic concerns of farmers. Catholic agrarian syndicates would play an important role in right-wing politics during the Second Republic. What began as an experiment in agricultural modernization, albeit of a limited kind, ended in the whirlwind of reactionary politics.

Between 1900 and 1920, the proliferation of Catholic associations of all types provided the Church with something it lacked, the ability to mobilize supporters within a modern political and social system, however tattered the first and conflictive the second. The associational surge that swept through Spanish Catholi-

38. Quoted in Cuesta Bustillo, *Sindicalismo católico agrario*, p. 291.

39. Nevares, influenced by the German Jesuit H. Pesch, elaborated a theory of "solidarismo" based on the idea that social Catholicism offered an alternative to both the individualism of traditional liberal social and economic theory and the collectivism of socialism. Its core, however, remained the avoidance of any suggestion of a class struggle. Martínez, *Tierra de Campos*, p. 155.

cism was part of a broader process of modernization affecting the country as a whole. Despite the disappointing results of efforts to organize the industrial working class, the organizational achievement of clerical and lay activists was considerable. But critics have argued, with some justification, that the new mobilizing capabilities produced by Catholic Action, labor, and agrarian syndicates were manipulated by upper- and middle-class elites to defend the existing social and economic order. Ricardo Lucchini suggests that the effect of industrialization, particularly when it occurred late and within a relatively backward economy, as in early twentieth-century Italy, "pushes into action those classes which were previously passive in political life" in a process of "negative democratization." Instead of promoting solidarity on a national scale, the process enhanced the defensiveness and sense of separateness of those feeling threatened by changing economic circumstances.[40]

The associational expansion of Spanish Catholicism, particularly through the agrarian syndicates, conforms to this pattern of mass participation and mobilization for defensive objectives. Whether the syndicates would have developed in a more positive direction is uncertain. The ideological intensity communicated to social Catholicism between 1917 and 1920 left entrenched attitudes that could not be easily dislodged. Moreover, the end of the constitutional monarchy in 1923 at the hands of General Miguel Primo de Rivera cut off channels of development that might have been possible under a pluralistic political regime. The organizations of social Catholicism reached the critical years of the early 1930s with a frozen ideology incapable of adapting to new political and social realities.

40. Ricardo Lucchini, *Sociologie du fascisme* (Fribourg, 1976), pp. 169–70, 184–85.

CHAPTER VII

THE DICTATORSHIP, 1923–1930

From Restoration to Dictatorship, 1922–1923

On September 13, 1923, the constitutional regime ended with the coup d'état carried out by General Miguel Primo de Rivera. The flamboyant general and his collaborators chose an opportune time to strike the final blow against a liberal State confronted with problems on all sides. The factionalization of the dynastic parties continued to plague the Conservative governments in power until December 1922 and the Liberal ministry of Manuel García Prieto that followed. The new Liberal government promoted reforms based on the supremacy of the civil power, the introduction of proportional representation, reorganization of the senate, ambitious social legislation, and resolution of the difficult Moroccan problem. According to the conde de Romanones, the cabinet wished to strengthen the monarchy through "a complete program" resting on the "foundations of ample democracy."[1]

Whether the last government of the constitutional monarchy represented a final opportunity to recast the regime in a democratic direction or provided another example of failed reform is a matter of debate.[2] But it is clear that the question of the army's relationship to the civil power became even more complicated follow-

1. Quoted in M. Teresa González Calbet, "La destrucción del sistema político de la Restauración: el golpe de septiembre de 1923," in *La crisis de la Restauración: España, entre la primera guerra mundial y la Segunda República*, ed. José Luis García Delgado (Madrid, 1986), p. 103.

2. González Calbet maintains that the García Prieto ministry represented another example of politics as usual and was not serious about implementing its reforming program. *La dictadura de Primo de Rivera: el Directorio Militar* (Madrid, 1987), p. 99. An opposite interpretation has been developed by Shlomo Ben-Ami, who argues that the "parliamentary system was showing signs of becoming genuine, thus turning parliamentary politics into a real threat to the monarchy's previously undisputed position." *Fascism from Above: The Dictatorship of Primo de Rivera in Spain, 1923–1930* (Oxford, 1983), p. 19.

ing the disaster at Annual.[3] The issue of "responsibilities" for the debacle could not be avoided. In 1922, a Conservative ministry ordered an investigation but limited its scope to military responsibilities alone. The Conservatives' attempt to avoid inquiry into the role played by their own government in the disaster aroused resentment among officers who believed that they were being singled out for criticism and punishment while the politicians escaped censure. The García Prieto ministry wanted to avoid going too deeply into the responsibilities question, but political circumstances forced it do so.[4] In July 1923, a parliamentary committee of inquiry was appointed and instructed to report to the legislature when it resumed sitting in October.

The prospect of another round of criticism and perhaps worse provoked more anger among the military, who had other grievances arising from the government's failure to agree upon a forceful military policy in Morocco. By early summer, a coterie of high ranking officers began to discuss plans for moving against the constitutional regime. The situation in the country appeared to favor a bold move. An intensification of violence, especially in Catalonia, again raised fears of revolution. The Catalan upper classes were so terrified of the prospect that Cambó and the Lliga did not disguise their desire for a strong government to put the working class in its place.[5]

The success or failure of the military conspiracy depended on the response of Alfonso XIII. The king's prestige was strong enough among army officers and other critics of the parliamentary system to make his support necessary for an attempt to destroy it. The monarch faced a political dilemma. The terms of the deal between the Liberal and Conservative parties, however undone it had come, threatened to disappear completely if parliament returned indictments against former Conservative ministers in the "responsibilities" question when the legislature began its autumn sitting. This would have destroyed the tattered remnants of the political consensus of the Restoration and might have led to fundamental constitutional changes reducing the king's powers. If the Liberal majority failed to vote indictments, and this was possible, Republicans and Socialists would have redoubled attacks on the regime. The king was aware of the possibility of a military coup, which, if successful, might well trim the sails of royal political influence.[6] There was no easy solution for the monarch.[7] During the summer of 1923 he considered

3. For a full discussion of this question, see Carolyn Boyd, *Praetorian Politics in Liberal Spain* (Chapel Hill, 1979), pp. 209–46.

4. The question of who was to blame for Annual became the subject of intense public controversy during 1922 and 1923. In December 1922, demonstrations were held throughout the country demanding an investigation into the role of the king, the army, and the politicians in the disaster. González Calbet, *La dictadura de Primo de Rivera*, pp. 27–31.

5. Ben-Ami, *Fascism from Above*, pp. 36–44.

6. Boyd, *Praetorian Politics*, pp. 257–58, 263–64.

7. González Calbet, in a revisionist interpretation of Alfonso XIII's decision, argues that the breakdown of the liberal system was so complete by 1923 that a temporary dictatorship was the "only possible

assuming dictatorial powers on a temporary basis but yielded to those, including Antonio Maura, who advised against such a course. The events of September 13 forced the issue. Seeing that there was no significant opposition to the military rising, the king took the fateful decision to abandon the 1876 constitution and entrust the government to Primo de Rivera.

The Church and its lay supporters viewed the developing crisis from the wings. Increasing social strife and violence, including the gunning down of Cardinal Soldevila of Zaragoza, confirmed long-held fears of impending revolution and the incapacity of the liberal State to prevent it. The Church also nourished specific grievances against the García Prieto government. The cabinet intended to introduce measures affecting ecclesiastical interests. The proposed changes fell within the Liberal party's tradition of seeking gradual change in the relationship between Church and State. The government's plan to place the "artistic patrimony" of the nation, including art objects possessed by religious establishments, under official control aroused clerical opposition. A proposal to eliminate the clause in Article 11 of the constitution forbidding public manifestations of religions other than the Catholic provoked another bout of tension between the civil and religious authorities. The bishops rushed to defend "the rights of which we are in full possession." They accused the García Prieto ministry of attempting to revise the concordat of 1851 unilaterally and declared their intention to use all legal means to frustrate the proposed change to the constitution.[8] A Liberal government again yielded to ecclesiastical pressure by withdrawing the proposal.[9]

Resentment against the Liberals for their ecclesiastical policy was a secondary consideration behind the enthusiasm with which bishops and Catholic opinion welcomed the dictatorship. Earlier warnings, even from *El Debate,* about the dangers of a dictatorial solution to the nation's problems had receded by September 1923.[10] The bishops issued pastoral letters supporting the new regime as "the work of Divine Providence." The hierarchy ordered that religious services be held throughout the country "to assist and enlighten" its "Christian governors" moved

solution to the crisis." *La dictadura de Primo de Rivera,* p. 115. She maintains that sentiment was widespread even among politicians of the dynastic parties for a transitional dictatorship of military officers and civilians to institute reforms before returning the country to political normality. The king's mistake, in her judgment, was not that he opted for a dictatorship but that he entrusted all power to a single individual.

8. "El episcopado al gobierno de Su Majestad," 1923, in Jesús Iribarren, *Documentos colectivos del episcopado español, 1870–1974* (Madrid, 1974), pp. 116–17.

9. González Calbet, "La destrucción del sistema político de la Restauración," p. 106. The *Revista Católica de Cuestiones Sociales* (1923) boasted that not only had the bishops forced the government "to desist from the undertaking that it so boldly had initiated," they also made it abandon its "policy of hostility towards the Church." P. 234.

10. In a 1921 editorial, the newspaper warned that a military dictatorship would be a "disastrous and gross error" on the grounds that officers lacked the education and preparation required to direct a complex modern society. *El Debate,* January 1, 1921, in *El pensamiento de "El Debate": un diario católico en la crisis de España, 1911–1936,* ed. José María García Escudero (Madrid, 1983), p. 714.

by the "holy fire of Nation and Religion."[11] Telegrams of support for Primo de Rivera poured into Madrid from parish priests and Catholic associations, while the organs of Catholic opinion wasted little time in urging support for the regime as a "duty of patriotism."[12]

The Expectations of the Church

What did the Church and its supporters expect at the beginning of the dictatorship? Primo de Rivera's manifesto of September 13 vaguely referred to the necessity of purifying morals and promised stern measures against social violence, both seen as desirable objectives by clergy and laity. But it contained no specific promises for the Church.[13] Yet the bishops welcomed the regime in almost messianic terms. The country was "at the dawn of resurrection"; it was embarking on "a great undertaking"; it had entered "a completely new era" that would bring about "the true regeneration of Spain." The dictatorship represented the "beginning of the return of the God of Spain and of Spain to God."[14] Insofar as the bishops were specific in their panegyrics, they voiced, first, the expectation that the new regime would move "to restore a political-social order that rests on God and his divine laws."[15] Second, they affirmed support for "our Catholic monarch" with protestations of loyalty that would have raised an eyebrow in the early days of the Restoration for the intense monarchist sentiments they contained.[16]

Lay and clerical commentators discussing the dictatorship's arrival on the scene stressed certain themes. They expressed satisfaction that the professional politicians had finally gotten what they deserved.[17] Even Canon Arboleya, who had fought a running battle for years on behalf of independent Catholic syndicates, remained a prisoner of the historic antiliberalism and corporatist obsessions of Span-

11. "Ante el nuevo régimen de España: la voz del episcopado," *Sal Terrae* (1923), p. 941; *Revista Eclesiástica* (1923), p. 631. These religious services were requested by Primo de Rivera, who approached the archbishop of Toledo directly. The prelate, moved "by the greatest delicacy and circumspection," showed some restraint upon receiving this request by communicating it to his fellow bishops through a private letter rather than through an official communication.

12. Ben-Ami, *Fascism from Above*, p. 85; *El Debate*, September 14, 1923. The Confederación Nacional de Sindicatos Católicos expressed its support on September 15 in an official communication to Primo de Rivera, as did the Federación de Estudiantes Católicos of Santander in a telegram sent on September 19. *El Debate*, September 16, 19, 1923.

13. The manifesto is reproduced in Federico Bravo Morata, *El golpe de Estado de Primo de Rivera* (Madrid, 1973), pp. 83–90.

14. "Ante el nuevo régimen de España: la voz del episcopado," pp. 940, 942.

15. Ibid., p. 943.

16. Ibid.

17. *El Debate*, in its issue of September 14, 1923, declared that blame for the failure of the Restoration rested squarely on "professional politicians, on the parties of the *turno*." One of the dictatorship's attractions was that it promised "to free us from the professional politicians" (September 14, 1923). Similarly, José María Gil Robles, active in the PSP during 1923, recalled that its hostility to professional politicians was so strong that "it would have been difficult for us to have adopted an initially hostile or even cautiously reserved attitude towards the dictatorship." *La fe a través de mi vida* (Bilbao, 1975), p. 88.

ish Catholicism. Although he later developed reservations about the dictatorship, he welcomed its establishment because it ended "the individualistic regime of liberalism," with its reliance on "ridiculous and absurd universal suffrage."[18] It is likely, as Arboleya suggested, that the majority of Spanish Catholics saw the dictatorship as a permanent solution to all their problems, but from the regime's beginnings Catholic activists saw it as transitional, a prelude to a new constitutional order in which either a great Catholic party or a grand coalition of the Right would emerge.[19]

Before such an outcome was possible, the regime had to complete the task of national purification or *saneamiento*, to use the expression used in the Catholic press. Clergy and laity expected the government to achieve peace in Morocco, end violent social unrest, and repress immorality. But the key to *saneamiento* was political, to eliminate groups and movements that had blocked the creation of a society inspired by Catholic principles. For *El Debate*, the "campaign of moral *saneamiento*" it promoted on September 14 was linked directly to the need for "severe repression of all syndicalist, antimilitarist or separatist propaganda." The Confederación Nacional de Sindicatos Católicos demanded that "the monopoly which Socialists, Communists and other politicians have exercised with such prejudice for the working class should be ended forever."[20]

The hierarchy expected the new regime to provide specific benefits to the Church. In October 1923, the bishops of the Toledo ecclesiastical province wrote to Primo de Rivera requesting that "the religious character" of education be intensified to make the public school "a true hearth of religiosity and patriotism."[21] The bishops also asked for increased State funding to improve the salaries of parish priests and finance repairs to church fabrics.

Primo de Rivera obliged the Church by indulging in extravagant displays of religious sentiment, although his penchant for gambling, drinking, and womanizing scarcely lived up to the moral ideals being promoted by the clergy. Representing the king in 1924 at the annual national dedication ceremony to Saint James in Santiago de Compostela, the dictator declared, "Holy Apostle, Patron of Spain, I come to prostrate myself before your tomb in the name of my King, the people and the Army. . . . Grant me, the most humble of Spaniards, the inspiration . . . to serve

18. Maximiliano Arboleya Martínez, *Sermón perdido: los católicos de "Acción" bajo la dictadura española* (Madrid, 1930), pp. 18–19, 22.

19. Ibid., p. 23. *El Debate* (September 19, 1923) declared within a week of the establishment of the dictatorship that it would be "transitory, because it is the will of the army and the directory that constitutional normality be reestablished as soon as possible" (September 19, 1923), in *El pensamiento de "El Debate,"* p. 723. The newspaper saw the dictatorship as an opportunity to create "a great party of the Right" to replace political organizations eliminated by the regime. González Calbet, *La dictadura de Primo de Rivera*, p. 131. Gil Robles also claimed that in 1924 he had declared his belief that any dictatorship was "a system of force, and, necessarily, must be transitory." *La fe a través de mi vida*, p. 90.

20. *El Debate*, September 14, 16, 1923.

21. *Revista Católica de Cuestiones Sociales* (1923), pp. 283–85.

Spain and the forgiveness of my sins."[22] These essays in bombastic rhetoric sounded sweetly in clerical ears. But specific clerical demands beyond the objective of strengthening a conservative social order must be interpreted in the light of the Church's privileged legal and constitutional situation under the Restoration. The Church expected Primo de Rivera to refrain from any sallies in the direction of religious liberty and any attempt to restrict the growth of the religious orders; it hoped for massive increases in the *culto y clero* budget; it looked to the government to enforce Catholic standards of morality and enhance the Church's influence in education. None of these expectations was new. Some were partially realized under Conservative governments of the Restoration. Insofar as the hierarchy had a program, it was an expanded version of the Restoration ecclesiastical settlement rather than a sweeping theocratic revolution.

The relationship of the Church to the dictatorship was far from straightforward. There has been a tendency to see the Church as expanding its power and privileges under a regime influenced by Catholic values. One historian has interpreted the position of Catholicism during the dictatorship as a "clear anticipation of National-Catholicism under Francoism."[23] There are some grounds for such a comparison. The necessity of organizing the so-called Catholic masses having disappeared with the birth of the dictatorship, Catholic elites formed in agrarian syndicates, Maurism, and the PSP entered the service of the new regime and its ill-conceived single party, the Unión Patriótica (UP), established in 1924.[24] The UP's ideology, with its emphasis on "monarchy, religion and authority" and its commitment to social order, showed the influence of conservative Catholic thought.[25] The State bureaucracy was inundated by Catholic activists ranging from ministers such as José Calvo Sotelo, Eduardo Aunós, and Eduardo Callejo to mayors and civil governors, all forming, according to a clerical journal, a body of "eminent collaborators" who were making "invaluable and immense" contributions to the new regime.[26]

This was undoubtedly heartening for an institution that believed that Catholicism had been kept from influencing public policy for fifty years. But did the

22. *La Ciencia Tomista* (1924), vol. 30, pp. 272–73.

23. Ben-Ami, *Fascism from Above*, p. 102.

24. The antecedent of the UP, the Unión Patriótica Castellana, was organized by social Catholic activists. Herrera and *El Debate* actively promoted it in late 1923 and early 1924 among the leaders and the rank and file of the Catholic agrarian movement. It was especially successful among supporters of the Nevares/Casa Social faction in Valladolid. Herrera undoubtedly hoped that the UPC would allow Spanish Catholics to steal a march over other political groups by creating a party capable of assuming power when the "transitional" dictatorship came to an end. Ben-Ami, *Fascism from Above*, p. 127. The Asociación Católica Nacional de Propagandistas played a key role in promoting the UP in 1924. José Manuel Ordovas, *Historia de la Asociación Católica Nacional de Propagandistas: de la dictadura a la Segunda República, 1923–1936* (Pamplona, 1993), p. 136. The PSP did not formally vote to dissolve itself, but its local sections gradually ceased to function during the course of 1924. Gil Robles, *La fe a través de mi vida*, p. 91.

25. Ben-Ami, *Fascism from Above*, p. 182.

26. *Unión y Caridad* (1928), no. 154, p. 5.

Church substantially enlarge the privileges acquired and sustained during the Restoration? The regime respected the Church's official status. There were no attempts to restrict the growth of the religious orders. The authorities, urged on by the clergy, the Catholic press, and groups like the Royal and Pontifical Association against Blasphemy, waged periodic campaigns against immorality. The regime had scarcely begun to function when the authorities undertook to improve the moral conduct of Spaniards. The governor of Barcelona imposed fines on young people who failed to observe "proper modesty" in movie theaters; his counterpart in Cartagena instructed bars to close at 10:00 P.M., while the police chief of Zaragoza offered a cash prize to the officer who laid the largest number of charges against blasphemers in a three-month period.[27] The duty of the police, declared the director-general of security, was to combat crime and "dry up reservoirs of immorality . . . to prevent anything that contributed to the relaxation of customs."[28]

The dictatorship's moralizing campaigns did not represent a new initiative by a government inspired by Catholic principles. The civil authorities had indulged in bouts of moral crusading since the Restoration's earliest days, albeit in more sporadic form than during the 1920s.[29] Moreover, an unbridgeable gap existed between what the dictatorship wished to do or was capable of doing to restrain "immorality" and what the Church expected. The regime used the tools of censorship and police action to give teeth to its moralizing efforts. But these weapons were not applied with the single-minded efficiency that would characterize the Spain of General Franco.

Much that the Church disapproved of appeared in print, on the stage, and on movie screens. When the operetta *The Count of Luxembourg* was presented at the Gayarre theater in Madrid in 1927 after being attacked as immoral by the local bishop, the producer mounted the stage and announced that all his actors were Catholics. He asked the audience whether there was anything immoral in the operetta, a question that evoked a thunderous "No!" in response. In the face of this act of "protest and rebellion" against "what the prelate had ordered," the ecclesiastical authorities could only express frustration.[30] Despite the regime's moralizing campaigns, its officials were not prepared to impose by force rigid standards of Catholic morality on a regular basis. Their conduct was not so different from that of some governments under the Restoration, something that the Church gradually began to perceive. In 1928, the archbishops wrote to Primo de Rivera with a thinly disguised indictment of the government for failing to use its powers to break "the

27. *La Semana Católica de Salamanca* (1923), no. 40, pp. 559, 572, 617.

28. Manuel S. Cuesta, "La lucha social contra pornografía," *Revista Católica de Cuestiones Sociales* (1924), p. 244.

29. Even under the Liberal ministry of García Prieto on the eve of the dictatorship, the civil governor of Salamanca issued "severe orders to proceed against individuals who blaspheme." *La Semana Católica de Salamanca* (1923), no. 5, p. 71.

30. *Revista Católica de Cuestiones Sociales* (1927), p. 124.

wave of foul pornography" they believed was sweeping the nation.[31] During the same period, complaints were also made about the indifference of the civil authorities to enforcing the law against blasphemy, which they regarded as "a dead letter."[32]

Nowhere did the Church expect more and get less than in the area of ecclesiastical finances. Clerical literature referred incessantly to the need for significant increases in the *culto y clero* budget to compensate for decades of stingy treatment at the hands of Liberal and Conservative governments. The clergy of Segovia declared that in return for "its support and cooperation," it expected that "the [Military] Directory would appreciate its labor and sacrifices and . . . would attend without vacillation to the improvement of its present [economic] situation."[33] These hopes were quickly disappointed. The dictatorship continued the same restrictive financial policy towards ecclesiastical expenditures as its predecessors. Between 1925 and 1928, the national budget increased by approximately 21 percent, while the *culto y clero* appropriation grew by only 2.65 percent.[34] The national meeting of the League for the Defense of the Clergy wrote to Primo de Rivera in 1926 requesting an increase of 30 million pesetas in the budget for clerical salaries. By 1928 the government had provided 8 million.[35] Since the regime engaged in an expansionary financial policy involving heavy borrowing beyond the normal budget, its fiscal treatment of the Church was in some respects even more parsimonious than that of the ministries of the Restoration.

The realization that the authorities intended a financial policy of business as usual produced disenchantment among parish priests who had long felt economically victimized by successive governments. The president of the National League for the Defense of the Clergy minced no words in 1928 when he complained that the "cult and the clergy of a Catholic nation" existed "in a state of slavery [and] poverty."[36] Even the bishops wrote harshly of the regime's failure in a 1928 letter to Primo de Rivera in which they implied that the government was not meeting the State's historic commitment to support the Church in compensation for the loss of ecclesiastical property during the nineteenth century. This sally was not appreciated in official circles. The regime's newspaper, *La Nación*, complained that publication of the episcopal protest in diocesan bulletins was ill advised and would bring "no good to either Church or State."[37]

31. "Sobre la represión de la inmoralidad," October 17, 1928, in ibid., p. 357.

32. Ibid. (1927), p. 246.

33. "Escrito que el clero de la diócesis de Segovia dirige al Excmo. Señor Jefe del Gobierno, Presidente del Directorio Militar," February 12, 1925, *Unión y Caridad* (1925), no. 118, p. 16.

34. "Los haberes del clero," letter of the archbishops to the president of the Council of Ministers, October 17, 1928, in *Revista Católica de Cuestiones Sociales* (1928), p. 356.

35. *Unión y Caridad* (1926), no. 137, p. 9; *La Ciencia Tomista* (1929), vol. 39, p. 124.

36. Federico Santamaría Peña, "Dos magnos peligros para la sociedad española," *Unión y Caridad* (1928), no. 154, p. 7.

37. Quoted in "La situación del clero secular," *La Ciencia Tomista* (1929), vol. 39, p. 123.

The Church's expectations for the conversion of the educational system into a redoubt of religion appeared closer to realization. A decree of February 1924 ordered the dismissal of teachers advocating "such doctrines as are opposed to the unity of the *patria* and are offensive towards religion."[38] Under the influence of the devout minister of public instruction, Eduardo Callejo, teachers were fired, and normal schools established by educational reformers under Liberal governments were restrained from teaching modern pedagogical techniques.[39] The regime also authorized the reestablishment of theological faculties in State universities. In 1928, the government agreed to allow students in the Jesuit and Augustinian colleges of Deusto and El Escorial to receive university degrees, thereby breaching a historic achievement of nineteenth-century liberalism, the absolute monopoly of the State over higher education. This decision, made personally by Primo de Rivera over the objections of some of his advisers, led to widespread protests from students in the State universities and prominent intellectuals.[40]

From a clerical perspective, these achievements did not lead to the conversion of the public educational system into a religious stronghold. The Catholic press naturally hailed the dismissal of teachers judged hostile to religion, but the regime lacked both the means and the will to engage in a ruthless, systematic purge. As late as 1928, educators, some in positions of authority—like the primary school inspector for Granada, who was accused of "notorious irreligiosity"—were being discovered by the Ministry of Education.[41] There was also considerable resistance from within the regime to a plan of Callejo to make religion an obligatory subject in State secondary schools on the grounds that it would be seen as a provocation by the opposition. This foot-dragging disgusted Catholic activists, who launched a propaganda campaign to force the government to take action.[42] Even the controversial university degree issue was a question more of symbol than of substance. The university colleges of Deusto and El Escorial were minuscule in size and had limited curricula compared to the public universities.

38. Quoted in Ben-Ami, *Fascism from Above*, p. 104.

39. At a meeting in December 1923, the country's archbishops lamented the "pernicious influence" of three institutions identified with the educational reforms of Liberal governments, the Escuela Superior del Magisterio, the Museo Pedagógico, and the Junta de Ampliación de Estudios, "bodies that were born and live under the shadow of the Institución Libre de Enseñanza," an institution the Church regarded as a promoter of secularization in teaching. "Acta de la conferencia de metropolitanos españoles celebrada el día 12 de diciembre de 1923," in *Actas de las conferencias de metropolitanos españoles, 1912–1965*, ed. Vicente Cárcel Ortí (Madrid, 1994), p. 179.

40. Ben-Ami, *Fascism from Above*, pp. 104–5; *La Ciencia Tomista* (1928), p. 248; Frances Lannon, *Privilege, Persecution and Prophecy: The Catholic Church in Spain, 1875–1975* (Oxford, 1987), pp. 175–76; James H. Rial, *Revolution from Above* (Fairfax, London, and Toronto, 1986), p. 220.

41. *Revista Católica de Cuestiones Sociales* (1928), p. 60.

42. Nicolás González Ruiz and Isidoro Martín Martínez, *Seglares en la historia del catolicismo español* (Madrid, 1968), p. 139. The archbishops demanded the obligatory teaching of religion in secondary schools at their first meeting following the establishment of the dictatorship. "Acta de la conferencia de metropolitanos . . . el día 12 de diciembre de 1923," p. 180. They were still waiting for it to happen in 1928.

The regime's educational policy was more ambiguous than the veneer of Catholicism suggested. Although willing to make concessions to the Church, the dictatorship embarked on a program of school building and instructional modernization emphasizing scientific and technical training, particularly at the secondary school level.[43] Between the government's program of educational improvements and the Church's desire for a curriculum suffused with Catholic principles, there existed a contradiction. The episodic movement of the school system towards mass education and the development of modern curricula that had begun under Liberal governments after 1900 continued.

When all is said and done, the specific concessions made to the Church by the dictatorship were minimal. Despite the Catholic rhetoric of the regime and its forays into moralizing crusades, the regime continued the pattern of civil-ecclesiastical relations established under the Restoration. Whether through luck or shrewdness, Primo de Rivera paid a small price for the support he received from clergy and laity.

Conflicts and Disappointments

Civil-ecclesiastical relations during the dictatorship were far from untroubled. The regime's hostility towards Catalan autonomist aspirations spilled over to the Church. Although Primo de Rivera came to power supported by conservative Catalan regionalists, he quickly adopted a policy that reflected the army's opposition to anything that appeared to threaten "Spain, One, Great, and Indivisible." The general abolished the *Mancomunidad,* the limited association of the four Catalan provinces authorized in 1914, took measures to eliminate the teaching of Catalan in the schools, and harassed professional bodies using the language in their proceedings.[44]

This implacable hostility to regionalism led to conflict with the Church in Catalonia. Historically identified with the Catalan cultural renaissance and later with the conservative regionalism of the Lliga Regionalista, the Catalan Church struck a deal of sorts with the liberal State. Between 1878 and 1923, nine of the nineteen bishops heading the region's dioceses were native Catalans, while a majority of the remainder, born in Valencia or Mallorca, spoke the language.[45] The region's hierarchy and clergy promoted the use of Catalan as a necessary pastoral tool in sermons,

43. Rial, *Revolution from Above,* pp. 215–18. Between 1923 and 1930 the number of State primary schools expanded from 27,080 to 33,446. For the hierarchy, the "support given by Primo de Rivera to State schools was a threat that required neutralization." Fernando García de Cortázar, "La nueva historia de la Iglesia contemporánea de España," in *Historiografía española contemporánea: X Coloquio del Centro de Investigaciones de la Universidad de Pau: balance y resumen,* ed. Manuel Tuñón de Lara, p. 223.

44. Ben-Ami, *Fascism from Above,* pp. 195–96.

45. José Manuel Cuenca Toribio, *Sociología de una élite de poder de España e Hispanoamérica contemporáneas: la jerarquía eclesiástica, 1789–1965* (Córdoba, 1976), pp. 222–23. The appointment of Antolín López Peláez, a non-Catalan, to the archbishopric of Tarragona in 1913 provoked widespread protests in

religious propaganda, and the teaching of the catechism. The bishops maintained that their support of the language was moved exclusively by pastoral motives. But prominent clerics played a significant role in the regional political movement from its beginnings. Canon Jaume Collell (1846–1932) was one of the founders of *La Veu de Catalunya,* the principal organ of the Lliga. Over several decades he used its pages, sometimes employing heady rhetoric, to promote the cause of political autonomy.[46] Support of regionalism by some clerics did not sit well with Restoration governments, but it failed to undermine the *modus vivendi* between State and Church in Catalonia.[47]

Primo de Rivera regarded the Catalan clergy as separatist and intervened personally to secure the appointment of non-Catalans to head the region's dioceses. Because the government intended to combat separatism, he informed Cardinal Reig of Toledo in 1926, it preferred to appoint to Catalonia bishops "proceeding from other regions" who would not compromise the "unity of Spain."[48] This policy produced conflict with the Vatican, although a compromise of sorts was worked out behind the scenes by Cardinal Reig, who presented the Church's case to the king and the general. Both denied that there was an official policy of excluding Catalans from episcopal appointments. As long as a Catalan priest was "worthy" and had no separatist ideas, declared Primo de Rivera, he could be appointed. In practice, it was difficult for native Catalans to overcome the obsessions of a government that saw "the dangers of Catalanism on all sides." It even refused to approve the appointment to the bishopric of Vich of the conservative and scarcely separatist archdeacon of Tarragona, Isidro Gomá y Tomás.[49]

The authorities took action against priests for allegedly encouraging autonomist aspirations. In 1924, the Capuchins of L'Ajuda were accused of allowing a banned Catalan youth group to meet in their church, while a Jesuit priest was harassed on the grounds that he had told his congregation not to display the Spanish

---

the region. Cánovas "openly favored a collaborationist policy with the Catalan bourgeoisie, which was interested in creating a native episcopacy." Fernando García de Cortázar, "Análisis sociológico del episcopado español de la Restauración," *Revista Internacional de Sociología* (1976), vol. 34, p. 65.

46. In 1900, Collell wrote a controversial article lamenting "the martyrdom of honor and patience of a people which sees itself insulted, frustrated and treated as an idiot by the parliamentary politicians and their proconsuls." Quoted in Antonio Pérez de Olaguer, *El canónigo Collell* (Barcelona, 1933), p. 192.

47. In 1909, for example, the Spanish ambassador to the Vatican complained to the papal secretary of state about articles published by Collell "in which the representative of the government is insulted." In reference to Collell and Bishop Morgades of Barcelona, an ardent supporter of the use of Catalan in religious instruction, the ambassador declared, "I do not believe that the bishop and the canon are fulfilling their duty to respect . . . the constituted powers, nor are they working as ministers of a religion of peace." Quoted in Fernando García de Cortázar, "La Iglesia en la crisis del Estado español, 1898–1923, in Manuel Tuñon de Lara et al., *VIII Coloquio de Pau: le crisis del Estado español, 1898–1936*" (Madrid, 1978), p. 347.

48. Quoted in Vicente Cárcel Ortí, "Iglesia y Estado durante la dictadura de Primo de Rivera, 1923–1930," *Revista Española de Derecho Canónico* (1988), vol. 45, no. 124, pp. 234–35.

49. Ibid., p. 235. The negotiations conducted by Cardinal Reig at the request of the papal secretary of state, Cadinal Gasparri, are described in ibid., pp. 230–35. Gomá was appointed to the non-Catalan diocese of Tarazona in 1927.

flag from their balconies during a eucharistic procession.[50] Before such incidents, the Catalan clergy found a determined protector in the archbishop of Tarragona, Cardinal Vidal i Barraquer, who quickly became *persona non grata* to the regime. Primo de Rivera personally encouraged a campaign against the cardinal despite the prelate's expressed loyalty to the monarchy and his support of the government's efforts at moral *saneamiento*. But the conservatism of Vidal i Barraquer also involved an interpretation of civil-ecclesiastical relations that imposed distinct limits on the extent of official interference in Church affairs that he would tolerate.[51] The cardinal's defense of priests accused by the regime caused him to be unjustly regarded as a separatist. Primo de Rivera attempted to get the prelate out of the way by persuading him to accept a transfer to the archbishopric of either Zaragoza or Burgos.[52]

During the mid-1920s, the Vatican resisted the regime's policy on episcopal appointments in Catalonia, albeit from behind the scenes. In 1928 it shifted gears in spectacular fashion. Primo de Rivera extracted a series of extraordinary decrees from papal congregations that constituted a frontal assault on the use of Catalan by the Church. To the stupefaction of the region's bishops, the clergy stood accused of preaching separatism from the pulpit, denying absolution to penitents who confessed in Castilian, and forcing the children of Castilian speakers to learn the catechism in Catalan. The Vatican also ordered the expulsion of separatist students from seminaries and even saw the widespread use of the Gothic instead of the Roman chasuble in Catalonia as a sign of support for the autonomist cause. Vidal i Barraquer vigorously defended the clergy in his correspondence with Rome. He denied that the Church in Catalonia had ever waged "a revolutionary campaign against Spain" and reasserted its "traditional right to teach the catechism and to preach the divine word in the regional language." He also expressed his resentment at the regime's attempt to manipulate the Catalan clergy into "its Hispanicizing or de-Catalanizing work."[53]

The confrontation between the Catalan Church and the dictatorship developed into an acrimonious debate among the principal organs of conservative opinion. The attitude of Spanish Catholicism to regional movements was ambiguous. Carlism's emphasis on decentralization as a necessary remedy to the devouring centralism of the liberal State had become a general article of faith for many Catholics. In diluted form it found its way into Maurism and social Catholicism,

50. Ramón Muntanyola, *Vidal y Barraquer: el cardenal de la paz* (Barcelona, 1974), pp. 123–25, 131–32.

51. Ibid., p. 118.

52. The dictatorship was more successful in the case of the bishop of Barcelona, Josep Miralles, whose opposition to the regime's anti-Catalan policy with respect to the Church led the authorities to pressure the Vatican to secure his transfer to the less important diocese of Mallorca in 1930. Josep Massot i Muntaner, "El bisbe Josep Miralles davant la dictadura, la república y la guerra civil," in Albert Manent i Segimon et al., *Contribució a la història de l'Església catalana* (Montserrat, 1983), pp. 290–95.

53. Quoted in Muntanyola, *Vidal y Barraquer*, pp. 171–74, 178.

particularly among the supporters of *El Debate*. But there lingered a romantic vision of the unity of Catholic Spain that evoked the memory of the kingdom's distant golden age. The monarchist daily, *ABC*, promoted this view in a series of articles in 1928 reproaching the bishops of Catalonia for insisting on the use of Catalan in catechetical instruction, thereby displaying "an unnecessary hostility to the State and an unjust detriment to the national interest." The newspaper's assertion that control of the obligatory teaching of the catechism in public schools rested with the civil authorities ("in the schools it is the State that commands exclusively"), touched the raw nerves of clergy and laity, whatever their differences. They had complained for years about Liberal governments for advancing a similar claim.[54] The Catholic press, including newspapers of differing political views, such as the Integrist *El Siglo Futuro* and *El Debate*, rallied to the defense of the Catalan Church. The latter had long opposed restrictions on the Catalan language and was growing disenchanted with the regime. It quoted chapter and verse from the bishops to defend "the uninterrupted tradition of the Church in Catalonia" to use Catalan in its pastoral work. The newspaper also took a swipe at the government: "It is deplorable that political interests are being presented as religious interests."[55]

The Church in Catalonia benefited from the support of bishops and laity resentful of the intrusions of the civil power. The Church in the Basque Provinces was less fortunate. The regime was equally hostile to Basque nationalism and mistrustful of local clergy who used the Basque language in religious services. As early as December 1923, the authorities imposed a heavy fine of 500 pesetas on the parish priest of Miravalles, Father Juan de Zuluaga, for preaching in Basque. The military governor of Vizcaya summoned the offending cleric and ordered him to stop giving sermons to adults in the Basque language on the grounds that most of them knew Castilian. In response, Father Zuluaga suggested that the authority to issue such an order rested with his bishop. The officer replied, "There is no bishop who is worth anything. I order you not to preach in Basque."[56] There was no Vidal i Barraquer to rise to the Basque clergy's defense. The bishops of Vitoria during the dictatorship, Zacarías Martínez and Mateo Múgica, tried to avoid public confrontations with the authorities over the language question, preferring to work behind the scenes to allow the selective use of Basque.[57]

The reasons for this contradictory state of affairs lay, first, in the historic differ-

54. Quoted in ibid., pp. 154–55.

55. *El Debate*, February 12, 1928, in *El pensamiento de "El Debate,"* p. 747.

56. Quoted in Joaquín Perea, *El modelo de Iglesia subyacente en la pastoral del clero vasco, 1918–1936*, (4 vols., Bilbao, 1991), vol. 2, p. 721; E. A. Talde et al., *Historia general de la guerra civil en Euskadi* (6 vols., San Sebastián and Bilbao, 1979–1981), vol. 5, p. 92.

57. Bishop Múgica, for example, insisted that in areas where the population spoke Basque exclusively, the language should be used by the clergy in preaching and catechetical instruction. He did not hold the same for areas where the population was bilingual. In any case, he believed that the Church must proceed quietly and avoid "collisions" with the civil authorities. Perea, *El modelo de Iglesia subyacente*, vol. 2, pp. 673–74.

ences between Catalonia and the Basque Provinces. The latter acquired their one and only bishopric, Vitoria, in 1861, in contrast to the centuries-old clerical superstructure of Catalonia. Second, the identification of the Catalan bourgeoisie with the late-nineteenth-century cultural renaissance of the region had no equivalent among the upper and middle classes of the Basque Provinces, who were assimilated into the Restoration's social elites. Conflict over the use of Basque by the Church arose not only because of the attitude of the authorities; it also reflected the opposition of Castilian speakers among the faithful.[58] Third, modern Basque nationalism in the form of the Partido Nacional Vasco (PNV) established by Sabino de Arana developed later and more fitfully than the regional movement in Catalonia. As late as 1923, for example, *El Debate* maintained that Basque nationalism was of no particular importance.[59]

Throughout the nineteenth century, the Basques were regarded as a threat to the stability of the liberal State because of their support for Carlism. Restoration governments inherited these concerns and took pains to ensure that the bishops of Vitoria were non-Basques who would keep the clergy in line.[60] As the political ideas of Arana, based on a combination of intransigent Catholicism and visceral hostility to the central government, supplanted Carlism between 1910 and 1920 among the lower clergy, the bishops of the diocese, Cadena y Eleta (1905–1913), Melo y Alcalde (1913–1917), and Eijo y Garay (1917–1922), natives of Navarra, Burgos, and Galicia respectively, did not disguise their hostility to the nationalist movement.[61] Cadena y Eleta prohibited the use of Basque baptismal names on the grounds that "the Church of Spain has its official language, which is Castilian."[62]

A combination of pastoral and nationalist concerns motivated some clergy in Catalonia and the Basque Provinces. But the coincidence of interest between bishops and priests that was present in one, at least at the pastoral level, was largely missing in the other. Bishop Zacarías Martínez, head of the diocese between 1922

58. Between 1918 and 1920, for example, Catholics in the town of Durango, where much of the population spoke Castilian, clashed over the use of Basque in an annual celebration of the Virgin Mary held during the month of May. The battle had political overtones. Carlists insisted on the use of Castilian, while supporters of the Basque nationalist party, the PNV, demanded that Basque be employed because "it is the best guardian of religion and good customs." Quoted in ibid., p. 713.

59. *El Debate*, November 2, 1923, in *El pensamiento de "El Debate,"* p. 595.

60. Fernando García de Cortázar, "La Iglesia vasca", in *Estudios de historia contemporánea del País Vasco: del carlismo al nacionalismo, 1870–1936*, ed. J. C. Jiménez Aberasturi (San Sebastián, 1982), pp. 231–32; Cuenca Toribio, *Sociología de una élite de poder*, p. 227.

61. Cuenca Toribio, *Sociología de una élite de poder*, pp. 230–42. Arana developed a coherent and modern theory of Basque nationality, something that was lacking in Carlism. He repeatedly stressed that Catholicism was essential to the survival of the Basques as a separate people. He argued that they had to be saved from the moral corruption loosed upon them by liberalism, which was identified in turn with central governments in Madrid. To save a people, therefore, on the verge of moral and religious extinction, required the creation of a separate political identity for which an intransigent Catholicism was absolutely necessary. Javier Corcuera Atienza, *Orígenes, ideología y organización del nacionalismo vasco, 1876–1904* (Madrid, 1979), p. 321.

62. Quoted in Ignacio Villota Elejalde, *La Iglesia en la sociedad española y vasca contemporáneas* (Bilbao, 1985), p. 175.

and 1928, a trained biologist and professor of natural sciences, was sophisticated enough to permit some of his priests to engage in the academic study of Basque language and folklore, but he was less than vigorous in defending his clergy before official persecution.[63] When Father Teodoro Labiduria was about to preach in Basque at Lequeitio, he received orders from the bishop to repeat his homilies in Castilian. After the priest asked the congregation to forgive his grammatical faults in the latter, as "it was not his language," he was summoned to the offices of the civil governor, severely reprimanded, and ordered to make a formal apology. In contrast to the conduct of Vidal i Barraquer, the bishop refused his help and expressed support for the action taken by the authorities.[64] The appointment in 1928 of the region's first Basque-speaking bishop, Mateo Múgica, did not materially change the situation. While more attentive than his predecessors had been to the needs of his priests, and later celebrated for his defense of the Basque clergy against the accusations of the Franco regime, Múgica was strongly conservative and monarchist and no friend of Basque nationalism as he began his tenure.[65] But the dictatorship's actions against alleged manifestations of Basque nationalism within the Church proved no more successful than they had in Catalonia.

The role of the Church under the dictatorship must also be considered in relation to the question that had obsessed Catholic opinion since the days of Cánovas. Could Spanish Catholicism break through its perceived marginalization in national life to find a political formula that would provide a permanent institutional means of exercising influence over public affairs? In one sense, the regime obliged by destroying the dynastic parties that Catholic activists had long seen as the main obstacle to the realization of their ambitions. Yet in another, the dictatorship was as successful as the Restoration had been in preventing the development of an effective political Catholicism, however many of the faithful occupied official posts and held membership in the Unión Patriótica.

As the regime moved from the Military Directory (September 1923–December 1924) to a civilian technocratic government, it began to seek institutional means of assuring its permanence. The co-opted National Assembly of 1927 undertook the thorny task of drafting a new constitution to achieve this goal. Although gov-

63. Talde et al., *Historia general de la guerra civil en Euskadi*, vol. 5, pp. 92–93. For the scholarly work on Basque themes encouraged by Martínez, see Frances Lannon, "A Basque Challenge to the Pre-Civil War Spanish Church," *European Studies Review* (1979), vol. 9, no. 1, pp. 37–38.

64. Quoted in Talde et al., *Historia de la guerra civil en Euskadi*, vol. 5, p. 93.

65. Villota Elejalde, *La Iglesia en la sociedad española y vasca contemporáneas*, p. 178; Francisco Rodríguez de Coro, *Colonización política del catolicismo* (San Sebastián, 1979), p. 31. Múgica was first suggested for the bishopric of Vitoria in 1923. Opponents of the appointment argued against it on the grounds that he was sympathetic to the Basque nationalist cause. Múgica replied with an affirmation of his love for Spain and his fidelity to the monarchy. Criticism resurfaced in 1928 when he finally received the Vitoria appointment, which was not especially welcomed by the local clergy because of the prelate's reputation as a harsh disciplinarian. Fernando García de Cortázar, "Mateo Múgica, la Iglesia y la guerra civil en el País Vasco," *Letras de Deusto* (1986), vol. 16, no. 35, pp. 8, 11.

ernment officials and representatives of the UP dominated the assembly, a few deputies, including some Socialists, ready to criticize the regime, received seats. The draft constitution proposed a hybrid between a traditional parliamentary system and corporate representation.[66] But by this time the political difficulties facing Primo de Rivera were so great that there was no prospect of implementing the constitution. If the regime was unable to find the institutional vehicle for its survival, there was even less possibility that Spanish Catholicism could attain the enduring political presence it had long desired in public affairs, other than to hope that Primo de Rivera would hold power forever.

The dictatorship also failed to realize another expectation of Catholic activists in 1923: that it would assure the final triumph of social Catholicism by eliminating its socialist and anarchist rivals. The regime ended the violence that had wracked the country for years. It suppressed the anarcho-syndicalist CNT in its Catalan strongholds. Primo de Rivera believed that he could domesticate the socialist labor movement. As a result, he allowed the UGT a limited role within a government inspired reorganization of labor.[67] Eduardo Aunós, the minister of labor, inspired by a mix of ideas derived from social Catholicism and Italian fascism, produced a grand corporatist scheme in 1926 designed to transform relations between capital and labor.[68] Operating on the basis of "joint committees of workers and employers from the local and professional level to the regional and national," the regime provided a mechanism, the *comité paritario*, in which employers and workers enjoyed equal representation in the settlement of labor disputes.[69] With characteristic idiosyncrasy, the government permitted the free election of workers' delegates, thereby furnishing the UGT with a golden opportunity to expand and consolidate its position.

With the CNT out of the picture, the UGT used its superior organizing abilities to muscle out the factionalized Catholic labor movement for control over worker representation on the *comités paritarios*, save in Navarra and a few other localities.[70] Since Catholic activists perceived socialism as the single greatest threat to the Church against which "the battle would soon be joined," disenchantment with the regime's labor policy surfaced within days of the official decree establishing the

66. The constitutional draft proposed that half of the deputies in the new parliament should be elected by universal suffrage and the other half by specific professions or classes through special electoral colleges. Melchor Fernández Almagro, *Historia del reinado de Don Alfonso XIII* (Barcelona, 1933), p. 531.

67. Ben-Ami, *Fascism from Above*, pp. 283–85.

68. A former Conservative senator during the Restoration, Aunós was an admirer of the medieval guild system and of a prominent figure in French Catholic social thought of the nineteenth century, the Marquis de La Tour du Pin, whose works he translated into Spanish. Miguel Angel Perfecto García, "Corporativismo y catolicismo social en la dictadura de Primo de Rivera," *Studia Historica* (1984), vol. 2, no. 4, pp. 124–25.

69. Quoted in Ben-Ami, *Fascism from Above*, p. 293.

70. Casimir Marti et al., "El sindicalismo católico en España," in *Historia del movimiento obrero cristiano*, ed. S. H. Scholl (Barcelona, 1964), p. 226.

corporatist system.[71] Despite its initial support of the government's initiative, *El Debate* complained of "a grave defect" in the law, noting that "minorities [i.e., Catholic unions] remained without possible representation in each and every one of the organizations that compose the Corporations." In the following year it returned to the topic, alleging that "the Socialists are seeking to monopolize workers' representation in the national corporations, and, the sad thing is, they have every possibility of achieving it."[72] Far from fulfilling Catholic expectations by destroying the socialist enemy, the dictatorship proceeded to do the opposite, while generating resentment among Catholic social activists.[73]

The period of the dictatorship also frustrated the grand schemes for united political and social action sought by the hierarchy and lay activists for generations. Efforts to form a strong Catholic party collapsed with the desertion of activists from Maurism and the PSP to the service of the dictatorship. As early as 1924–1925, Angel Herrera and *El Debate* saw the unwillingness or inability of the regime to permit a transition to some form of political normality as an obstacle to the creation of a coalition of the Catholic Right. Despite its initial enthusiasm for the regime, the newspaper began to perceive the development of the Unión Patriótica as harmful to the realization of this aspiration. Herrera also objected to the regime's proposed constitution. It was "absurd," he argued, to attempt to introduce a corporatist political organization in Spain on the Italian fascist model.[74] Towards the dictatorship's end, *El Debate* expressed apprehension about the political future of Spanish Catholicism, arguing that the regime had deepened "the division of conservative forces" in the country.[75]

Others judged the regime more harshly. Angel Ossorio, veteran of Maurism and the PSP, expressed reservations about the "messianism" of the regime, while Jerónimo García Gallego, canon of Burgo de Osma, echoed the universal sentiment of Spanish Catholics that the dictatorship was a necessary expedient to resolve certain pressing problems. But in a controversial book published in 1927, he went beyond *El Debate*, which he reproached for its timidity and ambiguity in dealing with the dictatorship. He called for an immediate end to the regime, arguing that it damaged the monarchy and opened the way to an uncertain political future: "It is necessary to democratize the monarchy, if we do not wish it to fall, and this needs to be done soon, quickly, . . . because revolutions, like cerebral hemorrhages, give no

71. José María Taboada, *Los caballeros del ideal* (Madrid, 1928), p. 47.

72. *El Debate*, November 28, 1926, October 2, 1927, in *El pensamiento de "El Debate,"* pp. 738, 739.

73. The *Revista Católica de Cuestiones Sociales* objected violently to the creation of the *comités paritarios* on the grounds that they were "pro-soviet" institutions. Canon Arboleya believed that the committees might have been good for Spanish Catholics but that they had lost the opportunity because of government policy. As a result, "the Socialists have taken over nearly all the *comités paritarios.*" Arboleya-Martínez, *Sermón perdido*, pp. 82–83, 165.

74. Quoted in Ordovas, *Historia de la Asociación Católica Nacional de Propagandistas*, p. 122.

75. Javier Tusell, *Historia de la democracia cristiana en España* (2 vols., Madrid, 1974), vol. 1, pp. 122–23; *El Debate*, January 28, 1931, in *El Pensamiento de "El Debate,"* p. 775.

warning. . . . The dictatorship must end; we must get out of the tunnel where we find ourselves; . . . national reconciliation must be sought."[76] Canon Arboleya took a stance closer to that of *El Debate*. He argued that the Church had lost a splendid opportunity, given that "the dictatorial government has treated the Church with every consideration," to launch a successful campaign to wrest the workers from the grips of socialism.[77]

Arboleya's perception of dictatorship as a time of lost opportunity was unrealistic. The underlying organizational strength and vitality of both anarchosyndicalism and socialism were such that they could not be dislodged as popular mass movements. Nor was a fragmented Catholic labor movement capable of challenging the competition. Cardinals Reig and Segura of Toledo followed a conservative policy designed to keep a tight rein on Catholic labor syndicates. Both prelates insisted on the strict confessionality of Catholic unions and opposed the efforts of the Group of Christian Democracy to promote the formation of an independent Catholic labor movement.[78]

More serious was the decline of the Catholic agrarian movement, the most successful of the Church's social initiatives. Between 1919 and 1929 the number of Catholic agricultural syndicates fell from 4,451 to 2,276, while membership declined from approximately half a million to two hundred thousand.[79] Several causes lay behind the decline. The general prosperity of the 1920s, until the crisis at its end, eased the economic concerns that were essential to the growth of the agrarian movement in the first place. The government, for example, favored the interests of cereal cultivators, who figured prominently in the ranks of Catholic agrarianism. Further, the regime enlisted the services of prominent members of the Confederación Nacional Católico-Agraria and satisfied its constituency by doing nothing to threaten the existing structure of private property. Although by the late 1920s Catholic observers were lamenting "the great crises" that had brought the CNCA "to the edge of death," the organization did not collapse in spite of its difficulties.[80] It retained its infrastructure of regional and local federations that

76. Oscar Alzaga Villaamil, *La primera democracia cristiana en España* (Barcelona, 1973), p. 285; Jerónimo García Gallego, *Miscelánea política y religiosa* (Madrid, 1927), pp. 311–13. Ossorio and a small nucleus of former members of the PSP eventually broke with the dictatorship and attempted to build support for a Christian Democratic party on the Italian model of Luigi Sturzo. Tusell, *Historia de la democracia cristiana*, vol. 1, pp. 126–27.

77. Arboleya-Martínez, *Sermón perdido*, p. 110.

78. Enrique Reig y Casanova, *Carta pastoral: la Acción Católica en España* (Madrid, 1924), p. 11; Lannon, *Privilege, Persecution and Prophecy*, p. 172; Domingo Benavides Gómez, *El fracaso social del catolicismo español, Arboleya-Martínez, 1875–1951* (Barcelona, 1973), p. 394. In 1926, Cardinal Reig issued revised guidelines for the organization of Catholic Action. In fact, the new regulations were drafted by Father Nevares, still an uncompromising supporter of confessionality in Catholic labor syndicates. Feliciano Montero García, *El movimiento católico en España* (Madrid, 1993), pp. 58–59.

79. Juan José Castillo, *Propietarios muy pobres: sobre la subordinación política del pequeño campesino* (Madrid, 1979), pp. 275–76.

80. *La Ciencia Tomista* (1929), vol. 40, p. 106.

would provide an effective base for resistance to the policies of the Second Republic.

If Catholic activists entertained reservations about the corporatist organization of labor, they were united in their opposition to a 1928 proposal from the Ministry of Labor to apply the same model to agriculture. They objected to the scheme on two grounds. First, they began to fear "the increasing role of the State, even a theoretically Catholic one, over social groups."[81] Second, they believed that the corporatist organization of the countryside would endanger their control over the CNCA. The association's supporters and Catholic commentators on social questions waged a determined and successful campaign to prevent the ministry's proposal from becoming law.[82]

Under the uninspired direction of Cardinals Reig and Segura, the broader Catholic Action movement appeared caught in similar difficulties. With the possibility of forming a mass Catholic political party as remote as ever, there was renewed emphasis on the development of elites to wait in the wings for an opportunity to organize the Catholic masses when circumstances allowed. As Herrera's preoccupation with the political future grew, he redoubled efforts to recruit new members for the ACNP, which saw membership expand from 145 to 300 between 1923 and 1929.[83] Herrera and the ACNP also pressed for the establishment of a youth association within Catholic Action. In 1924, the Juventud Católica (JC) was founded in Madrid. By 1928 the association had twelve thousand members organized in 171 parish centers.[84] The JC recruited more broadly than the ACNP, but the new organization served a similar purpose as a "creator of elites." Supporters of the JC denied that it was inspired by political motives. The opposite was true. Herrera saw the organization as fundamental for resolving the "political problems of Spain" in the future.[85] The JC was intended as "the forge of virile characters, . . . making men who could impose themselves as organizers, and who would know how to lead the multitudes."[86] Members of the JC during the 1920s, among them José María Gil Robles and Alberto Martín Artajo, would emerge as influential figures in right-wing politics during the Second Republic.

81. Perfecto García, "Corporativismo y catolicismo social en la dictadura de Primo de Rivera," p. 141.

82. Ibid., pp. 141–46.

83. González Ruiz and Martín Martínez, *Seglares en la historia del catolcismo español*, pp. 127, 141.

84. Ibid., p. 141. Discussions about establishing a youth group similar to those existing elsewhere in the Catholic world began in 1924 among representatives of Spanish Catholic associations for young people on the eve of an international congress of Catholic youth to be held in Madrid. Meeting in March 1924, the delegates approved the creation of a new association based on parish organizations and established a national secretariat to which Angel Herrera belonged. In 1927 the Juventud Católica held its first national congress, which marked its "organizational and propagandistic consolidation." Feliciano Montero García, "Juventud y política: los movimientos juveniles de inspiración católica en España, 1920–1970," *Studia Historica* (1987), vol. 5, no. 4, p. 109.

85. Quoted in Ordovas, *Historia de la Asociación Católica Nacional de Propagandistas*, vol. 1, p. 91.

86. José María Taboada, *La Acción Católica en España* (Barcelona, 1934), p. 71.

The renewed emphasis on the formation of elites implicitly recognized that the political ambitions of Catholic activists were being frustrated by the dictatorship, hence the return to an older organizational model. There were clergy and laity who saw no reason for disenchantment with the dictatorship. But on balance, neither the Church nor lay activists had much cause for satisfaction. The specific demands of the Church were either partially or superficially met by the regime. Sometimes they were not met at all. Primo de Rivera failed to clear the field of the movements that activists blamed for the failure of their organizing efforts among the workers, while his program of educational modernization aroused clerical apprehension.[87] He made the creation of a Catholic political party impossible. In exchange for these dubious benefits, the Church identified itself with a regime unable to ensure its survival. Not for the first time, the Church and many of its supporters had rushed along a dead-end street. They would pay a heavy price for having done so. When the regime collapsed in 1930 under the weight of accumulated problems, the Church, like the monarchy, stood exposed before a precarious future.

87. Fernando García de Cortázar, "La nueva historia de la Iglesia contemporánea en España," p. 223.

CHAPTER VIII

THE ESTABLISHED CHURCH, 1875–1930

Forty years have passed since Gerald Brenan published his pioneering study on the origins of the Civil War. He described the early-twentieth-century Spanish Church as a powerful institution determined to retain and enlarge its privileges: "The Church, though losing every year its influence with the poor, was gaining steadily in riches and political power."[1] There is no question that the Church formed an influential lobby under the Restoration and the Primo de Rivera dictatorship. It appeared to critics as a single-minded, monolithic institution orchestrating a campaign to impose its vision of politics and social organization on society as a whole. But the reality was more complex. The foundation of the Church's influence rested in part on its status as the established Church of the State. But until 1931, the Church's official position reflected that combination of privilege and regalist control characteristic of civil-ecclesiastical relations since the 1830s. Controversy over ecclesiastical privilege arose not because the Church was capable of forcing a theocratic revolution on the country. This would have been impossible even under Primo de Rivera. Conflict developed from the ambiguities inherent in the legal status of an institution neither too powerful nor too weak.

The Established Church

The civil authorities recognized the constitutionally enshrined position of Catholicism in many ways. As representatives of the established Church, bishops attended official ceremonies. They received government decorations that were proudly displayed on ecclesiastical dress in photographs of the day. The archbishop of Toledo possessed an array of distinctions: "Primate, Cardinal, Patriarch of the

1. Gerald Brenan, *The Spanish Labyrinth* (Cambridge, 1943), p. 47.

Western Indies, Great Chancellor of Castile, Principal Chaplain of His Majesty, . . . Grand Chancellor, Principal Minister and Knight of the Order of Charles III, holder of the Grand Cross of Isabel II."[2] Few aspects of civic life escaped manifestations of the ceremonial ties binding Church and State. Sovereigns constantly showed their attachment to the Church, whether in the form of the elaborate rituals of the royal chapel or through patronage of Catholic causes. In 1922, for example, the king and queen accepted the honorary presidency of an organization dear to the bishops, the Pontifical and Royal Catholic Association for the Repression of Blasphemy. Recognition of Catholicism worked its way through the civil and military administration, as in 1913, when the commanding general of the Civil Guard issued an order dedicating this paramilitary force to the Virgin of the Pillar, one of the country's most venerated religious patrons.[3]

This honorific shower confirmed the Church's official status. It cost governments little, of course, to distribute honors with a generous hand. More important were the specific constitutional and legal advantages possessed by the Church as a result of its ties to the civil order. The 1851 concordat and the 1876 constitution governed relations between Church and State. Although Primo de Rivera suspended the constitution upon taking power, he continued to observe its ecclesiastical articles for all practical purposes. The clergy believed that the concordat and the confessional clauses of the constitution required the civil authorities to give substance to their terms through legislation and administrative action. For bishops and priests, the concordat's language establishing Catholicism as "the only religion of the Spanish nation" was absolutely clear.[4] The Church maintained that its privileges and the commitment to enlarge them were embodied in the concordat and the constitution. But the language of these documents was sufficiently general to allow for serious differences of interpretation.

These texts provided three significant privileges: the recognition of Catholicism as the religion of the State, the affirmation that education must conform at all levels to the "purity of the faith's doctrines," and a commitment to pay the salaries of the diocesan clergy. Bishops and priests believed that the State had assumed an unequivocal obligation to fulfill these stipulations. But controversy over Article 11 of the 1876 constitution as well as later disputes, such as clerical attempts to stop construction of an Anglican chapel in Madrid during the 1890s, show that ecclesiastical ambitions directed towards establishing a religious monopoly went beyond what the politicians were willing to accept. The Church prevented the introduction of religious liberty, but it could not impose its restrictive interpretation of Article 11 on successive governments. No government, whether Liberal or Conservative, was prepared to launch a sustained campaign of harassment against the

2. *Revista Eclesiástica* (1920), p. 5.
3. *El Debate,* February 21, 1913; *La Semana Católica* (1923), no. 16, p. 489.
4. Federico Suárez, "Génesis del concordato de 1851," *Ius Canonicum* (1963), vol. 3, pp. 233–34.

Protestant churches. As time passed, the clergy turned increasingly to the courts to enforce constitutional restraints on religious dissenters. In 1913, for example, the parish priest of Figueras went to law because the local Anglican chapel left its doors ajar while slides were being projected, thus, in his view, violating the constitutional prohibition against "public" manifestations by confessions other than the Catholic. He "rushed to denounce the fact to the local court, since the authorities had not taken any initiative in a matter which formed part of their duties."[5]

Throughout the Restoration, bishops and priests never relaxed pressure on the politicians to accept their definition of the extent and nature of the Church's privileges. Clerics also discovered that the courts offered a more effective means of enforcing their claims than did the political process. The judiciary enjoyed limited independence within the civil administration. Judges were conservative in their views, especially at the level of courts of first instance located in small communities, where justices formed part of local elites. The clergy used the courts in different ways. They were employed to harass Spaniards refusing to accord Catholicism the public deference to which the Church believed it was entitled. In 1901, for instance, a parish priest in Ubeda laid charges against an individual "for having refused to doff his hat in the street before the Blessed Sacrament" as it was carried to a dying man. Although the defense attorney argued that prosecution was unjustified because of the guarantee of liberty of conscience contained in Article 11, the judge decided that an offense had been committed against "the cult and beliefs of the nation and the religion of the State."[6] The sentence imposed, eight days in jail, a fine, and payment of all costs, was by no means trivial.

The Church resorted to the courts to enforce the legal requirement of canonical marriage on all Catholics. Civil marriage, although permitted between 1869 and 1873, was limited by the Cánovas government only to those who were obviously non-Catholic, that is, those who had not been baptized in the Catholic Church. Although Liberal governments eventually ameliorated this restrictive legislation, the Church fought any liberalization.[7] Moreover, the clergy defended its position aggressively in the courts. In 1905, the bishop of Madrid arrived in a village of his

5. *El Debate*, March 25, 1913. In a similar case, the parish priest of Monistrol de Montserrat, long vexed by the activities of a Protestant church in the town, laid a charge against its pastor under the terms of Article 11 for having refused to doff his hat as a Catholic procession passed through the streets, thereby offending publicly the religion of the State. Ibid., January 30, 1913.

6. "Sentencia condenatoria del juzgado municipal de Ubeda por ofensa a los sentimientos religiosos," *Revista Eclesiástica* (1901), pp. 487–88. For other cases with similar results, see *La Cruz* (1902), pp. 591–92; *Revista Eclesiástica* (1913), pp. 179–81.

7. An order of the Ministry of Grace and Justice (February 19, 1875) established that canonical marriage was the only valid form of matrimony for Catholics. During his long ministry, 1885–1890, Sagasta attempted a modest change, to recognize the validity of civil marriages by Spaniards living abroad. The papal nuncio and the bishops objected strongly to the proposal, fearing that such a measure was a small step towards allowing Catholics in Spain to marry in civil ceremonies only. The controversy is discussed by Cristóbal Robles Muñoz, *Insurrección o legalidad: los católicos y la Restauración* (Madrid, 1988), pp. 194–209.

diocese to hear from an angry parish priest that a couple, both baptized Catholics, had just married in a civil ceremony performed by an accommodating municipal official. The bishop mounted the pulpit of the local church and denounced the marriage as a violation of the civil code. The matter was not allowed to rest there. The offending official was dragged into court, sentenced to two months in jail, the loss of his job, and the payment of all costs.[8]

Conflicts over cemeteries made their way into the courts with monotonous frequency. The Church claimed that cemeteries were ecclesiastical property over which it had administrative control, meaning in practical terms that it fell to the parish priest to decide who would or would not be buried in consecrated ground. Between 1868 and 1873 the secularization of cemeteries by the government produced endless conflicts between the clergy and local authorities. Cánovas yielded to ecclesiastical pressure and recognized the clergy's exclusive right to determine who was eligible for burial in local cemeteries. The Church denied interment to "public sinners," those who refused extreme unction, or had renounced Catholicism, or were Protestants or freethinkers.[9]

The absence of Protestant or civil cemeteries except in larger cities and towns meant that those dying beyond the pale of Catholicism suffered the public humiliation of burial outside the cemetery walls, often in unkempt grounds. Despite government orders and judicial decisions upholding the Church's jurisdiction over cemeteries, disputes of all kinds continued, particularly after a campaign during the mid-1880s to construct new and more hygienic cemeteries financed by municipalities.[10] Local authorities in villages and small towns, where burial in any other place than the town cemetery reflected adversely on a family's honor and reputation, often clashed with the clergy over the interment of individuals judged to have died outside the bosom of the Church. In 1897, the parish priest of Calonge (Gerona) ordered the removal from the local cemetery of the body of Carmen Huertas after having ascertained that she had been "separated" from the Church at the time of her death. An acrimonious controversy ensued when the mayor and town council insisted that the corpse stay where it was. The parish priest resorted to the courts and won his case, although the affair became so notorious that it was finally resolved by royal order.[11] These "wars of the dead" involving litigation and administrative conflict, as well as the unseemly removal of bodies from one ceme-

8. "Sentencia de la Audiencia de Madrid," *La Cruz* (1909), pp. 77–80.

9. Robles Muñoz, *Insurrección o legalidad*, p. 211.

10. An ecclesiastical journal complained, "Some subordinate civil authorities, contaminated by this spirit of secularization and without sufficient culture to limit their malice, have given rise to an interminable series of conflicts, denying explicitly this [ecclesiastical] jurisdiction." *Revista Eclesiástica* (1899), pp. 286–87.

11. Ibid., p. 288. José Jiménez Lozano, *Los cementerios civiles y la heterodoxia española* (Madrid, 1978), p. 225.

tery to another, show how far the Church was disposed to go to defend its legal privileges.[12]

The clergy also used the courts to protect its status and reputation. The exact juridical situation of the clergy was unclear during the early Restoration. Cánovas refused to restore the special legal arrangements (*fuero eclesiástico*) prevailing before the 1868 revolution that allowed priests to be tried by separate ecclesiastical tribunals. Nor does it appear that the government regarded diocesan priests as civil servants, although they received their salaries and appointments from the State and served ex-officio on local draft, jury selection, and school boards.[13] But by the turn of the century, diocesan priests managed to secure judicial recognition of their status as "public functionaries constituted in authority."[14] An 1895 decision by the Supreme Court ruled that the clergy "formed a specific class of the State" and could appeal for redress of alleged "injuries" to the courts.[15]

The clergy took advantage of the opening provided by the courts. In 1895, the Madrid appeals court sentenced a journalist of the anticlerical newspaper, *El Motín,* to four years in jail for having written a scurrilous article against a Salamanca parish priest. Thereafter, clerics resorted to the courts against their detractors with increasing frequency. As anticlerical sentiment mounted after 1900, these efforts intensified. By the time of the Canalejas government, and with the memory of the Tragic Week still fresh, ecclesiastical journals demanded an end to the "ignoble campaign of derision, defamation and calumny" directed against the clergy. In 1911, a National League for the Defense of the Clergy was established to provide financial and legal assistance to priests who believed themselves victims of a "slanderous press." Only by resorting to the courts, the League declared, could the clergy secure "the severe sanction indicated by the penal code against these infamous aggressions and honor and the human conscience." The League began to publish a journal, *Unión y Caridad,* which reported with satisfaction the successful prosecutions carried out with its support.[16]

Use of the courts to defend clerical privileges produced unfortunate consequences. Although the cases brought by the clergy were often successful, taken as a whole they were incapable of imprinting political and administrative institutions with that exclusive commitment to Catholicism demanded by the Church. The aggressiveness with which cases involving marriage, cemeteries, and the press

12. For other examples up to 1900 see Jiménez Lozano, *Los cementerios civiles*, pp. 225–28.

13. Unlike civil servants, diocesan priests, for example, were not eligible for government pensions upon retirement.

14. Antolín López Peláez, *El derecho español en sus relaciones con la Iglesia* (Madrid, 1902), p. 293.

15. This important decision was reported with considerable satisfaction by *La Cruz* (1896), p. 139.

16. R. Vilariño, "Unión y Caridad," *Sal Terrae* (1912), p. 1094; "Liga Nacional de Defensa del Clero," *Revista Eclesiástica* (1911), p. 193; Daniel García Hughes, "La Liga Nacional de Defensa del Clero," *Revista Eclesiástica* (1911), p. 342.

were pursued intensified anticlericalism at the local level, where the vast majority of charges were brought. By engaging in such tactics, the clergy appeared an institutional bully trampling upon those getting in its way.

The ambiguities of civil-ecclesiastical relations under the Restoration were also evident in education. The clergy demanded that the Church should have a primary, indeed dominant, role in all schools. The Catholic Congress of 1889 declared that "the indisputable right to direct and supervise teaching in all public and private establishments belongs to the Church." This right was "supreme and exclusive" with respect to religious and moral instruction, indirect in the case of other subjects, for only in this way could there be an effective guarantee that nothing would be taught "contrary to the Catholic dogma and morality, as is recognized in the Concordat of 1851 and can be deduced from the existing constitution of the kingdom."[17]

The Church secured substantial educational concessions, although Liberal governments after 1900 came into frequent conflict with the clergy over school reform. The Church enjoyed the right to establish schools wherever and whenever it pleased.[18] Cánovas's decision to allow the massive reentry of the religious orders beginning in the late 1870s provided the teachers needed to staff new Church schools, while a law of 1838 requiring obligatory instruction in the catechism in public primary schools remained on the books.[19] But the Church was far from content. The bishops and the papal nuncio raised a storm of opposition to the Canovas government's attempt to introduce a new law on public instruction between 1876 and 1878 on the grounds that the proposed legislation was "rationalist" in spirit, affirmed the absolute supremacy of the State over education, and failed to offer sufficient guarantees to compel teachers to inculcate their students with Catholic values.[20]

The intense debates provoked by the proposed legislation became endemic to Restoration politics. Although the Conservatives were more disposed to make concessions, they had no intention of abandoning control over education to the clergy. Beginning with the tenure of the conde de Romanones as minister of public instruction in 1901, Liberal governments embarked on a policy of modernization and secularization of the public school system.[21] After the turn of the century, clerics also began to realize with horror that the right of private citizens to establish

17. Quoted in Manuel de Puelles Benítez, *Educación e ideología en la España contemporánea* (Barcelona, 1980), p. 299.

18. A royal order of 1885 authorized the establishment of schools by individuals with the government reserving only a general right of supervision. This measure was highly favorable to the creation of Church schools by the religious orders and concerned Catholic laity. Robles Muñoz, *Insurrección o legalidad*, p. 193.

19. A royal order of 1879 removed the prohibition on teaching by the religious orders imposed by the revolutionary government in 1868. Ibid., p. 188.

20. Ibid., p. 181.

21. Romanones instituted a reform of secondary school teaching that included emphasis on technical education rather than the classics, reestablishment of complete academic freedom in secondary

schools, established early in the history of the Restoration and welcomed by the Church, was now being used to create so-called "neutral" or lay schools.[22] The Primo de Rivera dictatorship provided the Church with some satisfaction as far as education was concerned, but its policies fell far short of converting the school system into the bastion of Catholicism demanded by the clergy.

The financial benefits secured under the terms of the 1851 concordat represented a tacit recognition by the liberal State that it owed compensation to the clergy for the sale of ecclesiastical property. Clerics regarded this obligation as a sacred and absolute commitment rendered in exchange for the despoliation of Church lands. But successive ministries of the Restoration, even those of Cánovas and Maura, took a hard fiscal line towards clerical demands for substantial increases in the *culto y clero* budget. In fact, the appropriation declined from 43,515,556 pesetas during the budget year of 1875–1876 to 41,231,388 by 1908, and of this only 33,000,000 was actually paid to the clergy. According to Bishop Reig of Barcelona, the amount appropriated in 1908 was only marginally greater than that provided for 1851, although the government budget had tripled during this time. The ecclesiastical budget increased to 61,000,000 by 1924–1925, but considering the massive inflation that swept the country during the First World War, the increase fell short of keeping pace with the rise in prices.[23]

The persistent unwillingness of Catholic governments to increase the *culto y clero* budget generated deep clerical resentment, particularly since priests receiving their salaries from the treasury during the Restoration were obliged to swear an oath of loyalty to a constitution about which many held reservations. The Church believed that under the Restoration and the dictatorship the State was failing to live up to the moral and legal undertaking that it had made in 1851.[24] The result of this "systematic conduct" on the part of governments was "to deprive the Church of influence, to humiliate it in the eyes of the people, and to make difficult the exercise

---

schools and universities, and an order that private schools, including those of the Church, should be subject to regular government inspection. These measures provoked cries of outrage by the Church and its supporters. Teódulo García Regidor, *La polémica sobre la secularización de la enseñanza en España, 1902–1914* (Mardid, 1985), pp. 120–32.

22. These schools were not numerous, but their appearance, especially in Barcelona and to a lesser extent in Madrid, provoked intense clerical hostility. The authorities saw the "neutral" schools organized by the anarchist leader Francisco Ferrer as being one of the causes of the events of the Tragic Week. Joan Connelly Ullman, *The Tragic Week: A Study of Anticlericalism in Spain* (Cambridge, Mass., 1968), p. 320. For the history of these schools, see García Regidor, *La secularización de la ensenañza,* pp. 185–256.

23. Q. Aldea Vaquero, "Patrimonio eclesiástico," *Diccionario de historia eclesiástica de España,* ed. Q. Aldea Vaquero et al. (4 vols., Madrid, 1972–1975), vol. 3, p. 1895; Enrique Reig, *Presente y porvenir económico de la Iglesia en España* (Madrid, 1908), pp. 27–29. The clergy never received the actual sum voted in the annual appropriation. Priests, like civil servants, were subject to a substantial tax on their salaries (*descuento*), hence the reduction noted by Reig for 1908 from 41 million to 33 million.

24. This position was summed up by Father Darío del Valle in an article of 1918: "The Spanish State has the obligation to provide priests with the means to live decently . . . because it has formally agreed to do so in the Concordat . . . because the funds of the nation were destined [in part] to compensate for [the sale of the] property of the Church." "La situación económica del clero," *Revista Eclesiástica* (1918), p. 439.

of its divine mission among men."[25] Only "an inhuman regime as cruel as that of the . . . Spanish State" would subject the clergy to such financial hardship, complained one priest in 1918.[26] Until 1923 there was little prospect that ministries would increase clerical salaries significantly. The conservative fiscal policies and chronic financial difficulties of Restoration governments prevented any large-scale financial concessions to the Church. Even the more expansive fiscal course pursued during the dictatorship led to only limited increases in the ecclesiastical appropriation.

The Church possessed other official privileges. Some were minor: bishops enjoyed franking privileges for their official correspondence, while priests could enter railway platforms without paying for the customary ticket. Others were more substantial. The country's nine archbishops and the patriarch of the Indies held seats ex-officio in the senate until 1923, as did nine other bishops elected by a select group of clergy in the ecclesiastical provinces. The bishop of Madrid represented the Church ex-officio on the Council of Public Instruction that advised the government on educational policy, and one cleric had the right to be selected for membership on similar provincial bodies. The Church also enjoyed certain tax exemptions. Churches, rectories, and the residences of the religious orders were exempt, but the clergy was forced to pay a much disliked sales tax, the *consumos,* until its abolition in 1910. Priests and seminarians, however, were not exempt from compulsory military service.[27]

The legal status of the Church under the Restoration and even under the dictatorship rested on contradictions that derived primarily from the compromises on many fronts concluded by Cánovas to assure the political stability of the constitutional regime. Cánovas was no theocrat and had no desire to see a return to the excessive clerical influence over politics of the years immediately preceding the 1868 revolution. Recognizing the need to diminish the appeal of Carlism and aware of the benefits to an essentially conservative regime that might accrue from clerical support, he embarked on an ecclesiastical policy based on the concession of limited privileges. Yet the regime remained liberal in its basic political principles. It recognized, albeit within a constricted framework, the secular and pluralistic nature of Spanish society.

This formula was successful over the short term. Over the long, it provoked deep conflict. The Church remained dissatisfied and resentful that the regime, even under Conservative governments, refused to expand its privileges significantly, hence the aggressiveness with which it sought to get its way through politics or the

25. Ibid., p. 436.

26. J. P. Rodrigo, "El aumento de la dotación del clero," *Revista Eclesiástica* (1918), p. 294.

27. López Peláez, *El derecho español,* pp. 41–43, 150–51, 155, 185, 247. Priests called to military service were usually assigned posts in which they would encounter "less danger" to virtue than in the "common and ordinary life of the barracks." Sabino Olalla, *El servicio militar de los eclesiásticos* (Burgos, 1916), p. 16.

courts. Moreover, the Church remained intransigent before efforts to modify the privileges that it already possessed. It succeeded in blocking any substantial alteration of its privileges under the Restoration and saw them modestly enlarged under the dictatorship. But it paid a price, namely, the growing opposition after 1900 of Liberals, Republicans, Socialists, Anarchists, and intellectuals. In the end, Cánovas's clever balancing act proved a failure. Between the vaguely theocratic demands of the Church for the creation of a totally confessional State and those of an increasingly secular and pluralistic society, there could be no real compromise.

Ecclesiastical Organization: The Bishops

Critics of the Church can be excused for believing that they faced a highly centralized institution capable of carrying out a well-defined program of action. The lobbying and public rhetoric of clergy and laity seemed to show that the Church knew exactly how to attain its objectives. The reality was otherwise. The Church could do little to remove the fount of dissension created by the divided political loyalties of the faithful. But at the level of policy and organization, the Church labored under deficiencies that worked against realizing its goal of re-Catholicizing Spanish society.

Ecclesiastical administration followed the hierarchical model based on diocesan bishops characteristic of the Catholic Church as a whole. The country's sixty-three dioceses were divided into nine provinces, each headed by an archbishop.[28] This apparently rational division disguised a sprawling diocesan organization that owed more to historical circumstance than to planning. The diocesan structure had remained virtually unchanged for centuries despite changing demographic patterns. Only three new dioceses were created, for example, after 1850: Vitoria (1861), Tenerife (1877), and Madrid (1885). That the Spanish capital secured diocesan status only in 1885 and that Barcelona, despite its large population, remained a suffragan diocese to the metropolitan see of Tarragona, says something about the institutional inertia prevailing within the Church.[29]

Towns such as Sigüenza and Osma, once communities of importance but now reduced to insignificance, retained bishops, while the nearby urban centers of Soria and Guadalajara lacked them. Nineteenth-century liberal reformers advanced

28. The metropolitan sees were Toledo, Seville, Santiago, Tarragona, Valencia, Valladolid, Burgos, Zaragoza, and Granada.

29. Until 1885 Madrid remained part of the archbishopric of Toledo. The cardinal primate maintained a residence in the capital, however, where he spent much of his time. The population growth experienced by the city led to pressure to establish a diocese there. But neither Cánovas nor the archbishop of the time, Cardinal Moreno, were enthusiastic about the project. The government did not wish to provide the funds needed for a new diocese and believed it politically advantageous to have the archbishop of Toledo reside in Madrid for extended periods. Cardinal Moreno naturally objected to losing the most populous city of his archdiocese. María F. Núñez Muñoz, *La Iglesia y la Restauración, 1875–1881* (Santa Cruz de Tenerife, 1976), p. 187.

several projects for a more rational diocesan organization. They appeared close to achieving their goal when the 1851 concordat provided for diocesan amalgamation, Barbastro with Huesca, Ceuta with Cádiz, Solsona with Vich, for example. But reform was carried out only to the extent that smaller dioceses were administered by neighboring bishops. The foot-dragging of local ecclesiastical and political interests frustrated attempts to rationalize the diocesan structure. Neither the papacy, the bishops, nor the government had the will to suppress dioceses in the face of vigorous local opposition. During the early 1890s, for example, an attempt to move the diocesan seat of La Rioja from the town of Calahorra to the largest city, Logroño, provoked serious disturbances, including a riot in which the civil governor barely escaped with his life. The government was forced to send four battalions of soldiers to maintain order in Calahorra. In 1902 a proposal to suppress the small diocese of Tortosa produced such impassioned protests in the form of popular demonstrations that the civil and ecclesiastical authorities abandoned the project.[30]

The Church also failed to develop effective means of episcopal consultation. Individual bishops were responsible to the pope and, to a lesser degree, the papal nuncio. The archbishop of Toledo, primate of the Spanish Church, enjoyed a limited preeminence within the hierarchy, as did the prelates (metropolitans) heading the ecclesiastical provinces. Critics saw public expressions of episcopal opinion as a sign of a centralized institution at work. The reality was different. The bishops lacked a collective organ of consultation until 1923, when the Committee of Metropolitans was established.[31] The hierarchy's inability to develop a body where common concerns were discussed was not entirely its fault. The absolute monarchy of the eighteenth century had no desire to see the bishops come together as a group. Liberal governments inherited these regalist preoccupations even to the point of discouraging the convocation of diocesan synods until 1886.[32] When negotiations were needed, liberal governments preferred to deal with the archbishop of Toledo, the papal nuncio, and the Vatican.

By the 1890s, meetings of the bishops of ecclesiastical provinces occurred and the archbishop of Toledo corresponded with his colleagues when controversial is-

30. "Carta del arz. de Valladolid, Antonio María Cascajares y Azara, al nuncio S. Cretoni," July 6, 1895, in *Instrucciones secretas a los nuncios de España en el siglo XIX, 1847–1907,* ed. F. Díaz de Cerio and M. F. Núñez Muñoz (Rome, 1989), p. 323; *La Cruz* (1902), p. 570. Cascajares criticized the delaying tactics of Sagasta, who, he alleged, followed his "standard practice . . . of dragging out the translation, in the hope that someone else would do it, so that he would remain on good terms with both Logroño and Calahorra."

31. Cárcel Ortí provides an excellent survey of repeated attempts to establish a collective organ of episcopal consultation during the Restoration. "Organización y magisterio del episcopado español contemporáneo, 1812–1966," in *Actas de las conferencias de metropolitanos españoles, 1921–1965,* ed. Vicente Cárcel Ortí (Madrid, 1994), pp. 13–29.

32. "Presentación de las instucciones dadas a Monseñor Angelo di Pietro, arzobispo de Nacianzo, nuncio apostólico en España, 1887–1893," in *Instrucciones secretas a los nuncios de España,* p. 287.

sues required discussion.[33] But there was no collective institution capable of marshaling episcopal opinion. The bishops met together only twice during the Restoration, once in Madrid following the funeral of Alfonso XII in 1885, and again in 1907 after years of Vatican prodding. Cardinal Sancha of Toledo promoted the 1907 meeting, although earlier he doubted the wisdom of convoking the bishops as a body.[34] The assembly discussed the threat to clerical interests presented by the Liberal government then in power but was prohibited by papal instruction from discussing many key issues affecting civil-ecclesiastical relations. The success of the 1907 meeting was limited. Nineteen bishops did not attend at all, while the practical results of the deliberations were mixed.[35] In any event, the gathering was an isolated example of episcopal consultation. It is also striking that between 1870 and 1896 the bishops failed to address a single common representation to the government. After 1900 this situation changed, as the Church confronted what it saw as an anticlerical assault by Liberal ministries. Even these collective protests arose more from an ad hoc reaction to events than from an ongoing process of consultation. After years of interminable discussion, the hierarchy finally succeeded in forming the Committee of Metropolitans to meet twice a year to consider issues of general concern. But this body was far from being representative of the hierarchy. It was composed only of the nine archbishops heading the ecclesiastical provinces.[36]

The presence of bishops in the senate of the constitutional monarchy afforded the hierarchy with a limited opportunity to coordinate policy with respect to legislation. At first some prelates doubted the wisdom of allowing bishops to accept seats in the upper house, two of the three ecclesiastical senators appointed by Cánovas in 1876 having been less vigorous in their opposition to Article 11 than the papal nuncio wished. The archbishops of Valladolid, Zaragoza, Granada, and Burgos expressed their intention to refuse the seats offered them on the grounds that accepting senate appointments would signify political support for "a system which is not destined to do [any] good for the Church and the nation."[37] These fears vanished by 1877, with the introduction of an electoral formula confining the selection process to the clergy alone. Thereafter, bishops regularly took their seats. Their participation helped focus episcopal opinion on specific issues but in an essentially reactive way, namely, by halting or altering proposed legislation

33. In 1878, for example, Cardinal Moreno dispatched a circular letter to his fellow metropolitans informing them of the state of the effort to alter the government's proposed law on public instruction. Robles Muñoz, *Insurrección o legalidad*, p. 179.

34. Not all bishops favored calling the meeting, especially Cardinal Martín de Herrera of Santiago de Compostela. Cárcel Ortí, "Organización y magisterio," p. 25.

35. Ibid., pp. 23–28.

36. *Documentos colectivos del episcopado español, 1870–1974*, ed. Jesús Iribarren (Madrid, 1974), pp. 19, 31.

37. Núñez Muñoz, *La Iglesia y la Restauración*, pp. 237–39; quoted in Robles Muñoz, *Insurrección o legalidad*, pp. 168–69.

judged damaging to the Church's interests. Moreover, the ecclesiastical senators did not represent the clergy as a whole. For the ecclesiastical senators who were elected, as distinct from those holding office ex-officio, eligibility was limited to priests who possessed either an income of 20,000 pesetas or paid 4,000 a year in taxes, thereby depriving the vast majority of the clergy of the opportunity to stand for election.[38]

The bishops formed the dominant group within the Church's organization. Although other groups and individuals, the religious orders, prominent laymen, and a variety of Catholic organizations contributed to ecclesiastical life under the Restoration and dictatorship, the bishops stood at its center. No initiative could be taken, no policy adopted, no course of action pursued, without their approval.

The prelates presiding over the dioceses of the Spanish Church between 1875 and 1930 faced challenges as difficult as those of their predecessors. The rise of anarchism and socialism, the increasing secularization of society, abundant signs of religious alienation, and growing hostility towards the clergy among segments of the population all created a situation demanding exceptional qualities of leadership. Unfortunately, the procedures used to appoint members of the hierarchy were ill designed to achieve this goal. Under the right of royal patronage, reaffirmed in the 1851 concordat and observed by successive liberal ministries and the dictatorship, bishops were nominated by the Crown for papal confirmation. In practical terms this meant the government, although Alfonso XIII often intervened on behalf of specific candidates. The civil authorities rarely imposed their nominees through fiat, relying instead on an intricate round of consultations involving the Ministry of Grace and Justice, the papal nuncio, and influential members of the hierarchy.[39]

Governments used the right of patronage to appoint candidates who were either sympathetic to official policies or at least disposed not to rock the boat. Cánovas was no exception. When he took power, he found a hierarchy far below strength as a result of deaths and resignations since the beginning of the 1868 revolution and the resulting impasse with the pope over the confirmation of new bishops. Between 1875 and 1879, the prime minister set a record of sorts by filling thirty-one episcopal vacancies. Cánovas was governed by a simple principle as he selected bishops. He wished to appoint prelates loyal to the reigning dynasty. He insisted that Bishop Caixal of Urgel, who had supported the Carlist cause during the rebellion of the mid-1870s, should not return to his diocese upon the conclusion of hostilities. He also saw to it that Cardinal Moreno of Valladolid, known for his dynastic loyalty, was promoted to the primatial see of Toledo. He secured the appointment of Bishop Herrero of Cuenca, a devoted supporter of Alfonso XII, to the diocese of

38. López Peláez, *El derecho español*, pp. 41–43.

39. The process has been described by José Manuel Cuenca Toribio, *Sociología de una élite de poder de España e Hispanoamérica: la jerarquía eclesiástica, 1789–1965* (Córdoba, 1976), pp. 262–71.

Vitoria, where Carlist sentiment remained strong among the parish clergy.[40] The appointment of Sánchez Carrascosa to the diocese of Ávila led the nuncio to complain "of the continuing insistence of Señor Cánovas . . . who demands absolutely that the ecclesiastic involved should be elevated to the episcopal dignity for having been the first to praise the accession of Alfonso XII to the throne of Saint Ferdinand from the pulpit."[41]

The papacy disliked the political motivation behind certain episcopal appointments. But the best it could do was to engage in wheeling and dealing with the civil authorities, hoping to secure the nomination of some candidates it wanted while accepting others it did not. In 1884, for example, the Holy See agreed to a "transaction" with the government to secure the appointment to Santander of Vicente Sánchez de Castro, whose candidacy for an episcopal post had previously been rejected by the authorities because of his Carlist sympathies. In turn, the Vatican had to accept the nomination to Oviedo of Ramón Martínez y Vigil, who was supported by Alfonso XII and the prominent Conservative politicians, the Pidal brothers.[42] The majority of appointments made during this period arose from the mutual agreement of the government and the nuncio. As the regime was consolidated, disputes between the government and papacy became less frequent. By the early twentieth century,

> Cooperation between the Holy See and the Monarchy, channeled through the nunciature and the Ministry of State, Grace and Justice, moved for extended periods along stable tracks. The mutual desire of both for agreement meant that the candidates selected were not men of strong personality, but were rather accommodating and bureaucratic, enemies by temperament or conviction of posing inconvenient or difficult situations.[43]

From time to time, controversy erupted, as in 1899 when the minister of grace and justice, the Catalan Durán i Bas, pushed the nomination of a well-known figure in the cultural renaissance of Catalonia, Torras i Bages, for the diocese of Vich. Parliamentary critics supported by some newspapers in Madrid accused the prospec-

40. Núñez Muñoz, *La Iglesia y la Restauración*, pp. 142–44, 94, 110.

41. Quoted in ibid., pp. 107–8. An anonymous memorial sent to the papal nuncio in 1880 made the same point. It argued that every effort should be made to reduce royal patronage over episcopal appointments to hinder the government from "using the powerful means, which the exercise of the Real Patronato provides, to increase the number of its supporters." "Sobre cumplimiento del Concordato de 1851," May 8, 1880, in *Instrucciones secretas a los nuncios de España*, p. 251. Sagasta shared Cánovas's view that no candidates should be appointed whose fidelity to the regime was doubtful or whose familes were prominent in Carlism. Fernando García de Cortázar, "Análisis sociológico del episcopado español de la Restauración," *Revista Internacional de Sociología* (1976), vol. 34, p. 66.

42. Antonio Vico, "Informe sobre el episcopado y los cabildos de España," 1890, in Vicente Cárcel Ortí, *León XIII y los católicos españoles* (Pamplona, 1988), p. 222. According to the report prepared by Vico, secretary of the nunciature, the appointment of Martínez y Vigil was "the work of the Pidal brothers, his intimate friends." An "undertaking with the Pidals to support the candidacy of Father Vigil for Oviedo . . . led the Holy Father to accept this appointment." Ibid., p. 236.

43. Cuenca Toribio, *Sociología de una élite de poder*, p. 255.

tive bishop of being a Catalan separatist who had declared that "in his diocese Castilian would not be spoken." The charge was nonsense, although it reflected rising hostility in some circles to demands for Catalan autonomy. In any event, the Conservative government in power refused to withdraw the appointment.[44]

By and large, the Restoration succeeded in its goal of neutralizing the hierarchy as a possible source of opposition, despite frequent episcopal sallies in defense of clerical interests on specific issues.[45] Carlists and Integrists deplored this situation as a matter of course. The bishops of the Restoration and dictatorship, said one, were "deaf and dumb dogs who do not have the strength to bark."[46] This was an extreme judgment. The bishops barked frequently. How deeply they bit is another question.

The hierarchy may not have achieved distinction for its imagination, dynamism, or intellectual creativity. But in contrast to the situation prevailing before the triumph of liberalism, it was relatively open in terms of social recruitment. Virtually every social class was represented in the hierarchy's ranks, which included members of the nobility (Marcelo Spínola, archbishop of Seville, 1895–1906); of the working class (Victoriano Guisasola, archbishop of Toledo, 1914–1920, whose father was a worker in the royal armaments factory of Asturias); of the various sectors of the middle class (Pedro Segura, archbishop of Toledo, 1927–1931, the son of rural school teachers in the province of Burgos, and Isidro Gomá y Tomás, bishop of Tarazona, 1927–1933, whose family owned a paper manufacture in Catalonia). But the hierarchy was dominated by prelates from lower-middle-class and peasant backgrounds.[47] The bishops were also drawn from across the country as a whole, a pattern of recruitment contrasting sharply with that of the army's officer corps. Every region was represented within episcopal ranks. The Catholic north provided a significant number of prelates. Both Navarra and the Basque Provinces furnished, respectively, 5.2 percent and 5.7 percent of the bishops, a proportion substantially higher than their share of the national population. Catalonia furnished more recruits to the hierarchy, 12.1 percent, than any other region save the Catholic heartland of Old Castile, which provided 17.8 percent.[48]

The organizational benefits derived from this flexible and national pattern of recruitment were diminished by the internal criteria used to judge the suitability of candidates. The criteria were more varied than those prevailing before the liberal revolutions of the nineteenth century, but in many respects they continued a his-

44. Joaquim Camps i Arboix, *Durán i Bas* (Barcelona, 1961), pp. 161–63.

45. García de Cortázar, "Análisis sociológico del episcopado español de la Restauración," p. 64.

46. Quoted in Juan de Iturralde, *El catolicismo y la cruzada de Franco* (3 vols., Vienne and Toulouse, 1960–1965), vol. 1, p. 316.

47. Cuenca Toribio, *Sociología de una élite de poder,* pp. 213–17; Javier Fernández Conde, "Pensamiento político social del Cardenal Guisasola (1852–1920)," *Studium Ovetense* (1974), vol. 2, p. 143; Anastasio Granados, *El Cardenal Gomá, Primado de España* (Madrid, 1969), p. 9; García de Cortázar, "Análisis sociológico del episcopado español de la Restauración," p. 69.

48. Cuenca Toribio, *Sociología de una élite de poder,* p. 226.

toric pattern of limiting the pool of candidates to a select group within the clergy. In an age when the majority of diocesan priests emerged from the seminary with only a secondary school diploma, access to the hierarchy depended in part on educational qualifications that most priests could not acquire. Fully 65.2 percent of the bishops held doctorates, generally in theology or canon law, while a further 8.9 percent held lower university degrees in these subjects.[49]

Episcopal career patterns conformed to a less rigid model than in earlier times. But the analysis of careers carried out by Cuenca Toribio shows that service as a cathedral canon or diocesan administrator counted more heavily than pastoral work, although parish priests reached the hierarchy more frequently than in the past. Of the 314 bishops who served between 1878 and 1938, only 37 possessed a background primarily in parish work.[50] A common career model saw priests with the requisite educational qualifications begin their careers with teaching appointments in seminary faculties, the "great springboard to the episcopacy."[51] Julián de Diego, archbishop of Santiago (1925–1927), received a professorial appointment even before ordination at the tender age of nineteen, while Remigo Gandásegui, archbishop of Valladolid (1920–1937), began his ascent at twenty-eight as a professor in the Zaragoza seminary.[52]

Thereafter, there were two roads a priest could follow—membership in a cathedral chapter or service in diocesan administration—although the two were not mutually exclusive. Fully two-thirds of the careers analyzed by Cuenca Toribio fell into these categories. Cathedral canons provided the largest single source of episcopal candidates. Priests lacking advanced studies stood little chance of gaining entry, since admission to a chapter rested primarily on a series of examinations (*oposiciones*) in ecclesiastical subjects. Individual careers varied, of course, but the ascent of two prominent bishops, Enrique Reig y Casanova and Pedro Segura, was not unusual among prelates of the time.

Reig entered the priesthood following the death of his wife and children in the cholera epidemic of 1885. He possessed a doctorate in law from the Universidad Central in Madrid. After a rapid course of study in the seminary of Almería, he was ordained in 1886 at the age of twenty-seven and immediately received an appointment as a professor in the institution where he had been a student. Already marked as a rising star, he was summoned in 1887 by the bishop of Mallorca to serve in the diocesan administration, which he came to head in 1889 with his appointment as vicar general. After performing brilliantly in the *oposiciones* of 1891, he entered the chapter of the cathedral while continuing to hold diverse administrative posts

49. Ibid. It was claimed in 1918 that "nearly all bishops hold doctorates." "Cargos de los prelados españoles al ser promovidos," *Revista Eclesiástica* (1918), p. 313.

50. Cuenca Toribio, *Sociología de una élite de poder*, p. 248.

51. García de Cortázar, "Análisis sociológico del episcopado español de la Restauración," p. 73.

52. *Revista Católica de Cuestiones Sociales* (1927), p. 71; *Revista Eclesiástica* (1920), p. 242.

within the diocese. In 1901, Cardinal Sancha called him to Toledo to assume the post of vicar general of the primatial see. Promotion to the ranks of the hierarchy was now assured. In 1914, he was named bishop of Barcelona, in 1917 archbishop of Valencia, and in 1920 archbishop of Toledo and primate of Spain.[53]

The career of Segura was more spectacular. He was fortunate enough to receive a scholarship to attend the seminary of Comillas, established in 1892 by the Jesuits with the financial support of the marqués de Comillas to train poor youths for the priesthood. Housed in a massive neo-Gothic building perched on a cliff overlooking the Cantabrian sea, the seminary soon outstripped its modest beginnings to become a pontifical university in 1904. Along with the Roman seminaries, the Gregorian and the Angelicum, and the Spanish College in Rome, the Comillas seminary attracted the country's most promising ecclesiastical students, who were drawn by its reputation for producing well-educated priests trained "in the most exquisite urbanity."[54] After ordination in 1906, Segura remained in the seminary for two years to take doctorates in theology and canon law. After a brief period as a rural parish priest, he received a professorial appointment in the Burgos seminary in 1909 and for good measure received a third doctorate in 1911. During the following year, he crossed the ecclesiastical Rubicon by winning a canonry in Valladolid at the age of thirty-two. In 1915, he was named secretary to the diocesan administration, and in 1916, because of the patronage of Cardinal Cos, to the post of auxiliary bishop of Valladolid.

Impetuous to the point of arrogance, the young prelate endeared himself to neither his fellow bishops nor the papal nuncio, who proposed to get him out of the way by having him named in 1920 to the Extremaduran diocese of Coria, the poorest and least prestigious see of the Spanish Church. The minister of grace and justice, an experienced and wily politician, remarked, after thorny discussions over the appointment with a dubious Segura, that "this gentleman is either a fool or a saint."[55] In the end, Segura accepted the appointment. Despite his later reputation as a stubborn monarchist during the early years of the Republic and an eccentric critic of General Franco, this was Segura's finest hour. He threw himself energetically into the task of administering his small diocese with its impoverished population. He became particularly concerned with the state of utter misery prevailing in the district of Las Hurdes, where 90 percent of the inhabitants were illiterate and struggled to eke out a living from a harsh land. He campaigned tirelessly for new schools and roads, tax reductions for the peasantry, improvements in public health, the introduction of electricity and telephone service, as well as for a program of re-

53. "El Cardenal Reig," *Revista Católica de Cuestiones Sociales* (1927), pp. 135–49; "El Cardenal Reig y Casanova," *Revista Eclesiástica* (1927), pp. 246–52.

54. Ramón Garriga, *El Cardenal Segura y el Nacional- Catolicismo* (Barcelona, 1977), p. 51.

55. Quoted in ibid., p. 71.

forestation.[56] When Alfonso XIII visited the region in 1922, he was enormously impressed by the activity of the "apostle of Las Hurdes," as Segura had come to be known. Thereafter, the king used his influence to promote the young bishop's career. He was responsible for Segura's appointment to the archbishopric of Burgos in 1926 and, defying all precedent, to the primatial see of Toledo in 1927.[57] At the age of forty Segura attained the greatest prize within the Spanish Church, a post usually reserved for elderly prelates nearing the end of their careers. No one before or since rose so rapidly through the hierarchy. Yet all the ingredients for a successful *cursus honorum* were present—higher academic degrees, contacts with influential ecclesiastics developed at Comillas, early entrance into diocesan administration and admission to a canonry, the support of powerful clerical patrons, and, last but by no means least, the influence of royal patronage exercised in an immediate and personal way by the king.

Segura's career, although not entirely typical, testifies to the divide that separated bishops from the diocesan clergy. Despite the diverse social origins of the bishops, the Spanish Church translated into the modern period the division between a privileged ecclesiastical elite and the great mass of the clergy characteristic of its organization during the eighteenth century. Differences in wealth and status between the higher and lower clergy were less dramatic than in earlier periods because of nineteenth-century liberal reforms, although they were still substantial.[58] The Church itself, recognizing the morale problems created by the prevailing system of recruitment, attempted with indifferent success to devise a more flexible system of appointment to canonries.[59] But the fact remains that an elite of cathedral canons and diocesan administrators continued to enjoy higher incomes, better career opportunities, and greater prestige than ordinary parish priests.

On paper, the educational background of the bishops would appear to have endowed them with the intellectual tools necessary to function successfully within the cultural life of the country. But taken as a whole, the hierarchy was scarcely distinguished for its intellectual vitality. There were some exceptions, such as Ceferino González (1831–1894), successively bishop of Málaga and Córdoba and

56. Letter of Segura to Alfonso XIII, June 24, 1922, reproduced in *Sal Terrae* (1922), pp. 796–99.

57. Garriga, *El Cardenal Segura*, pp. 77–81, 106–8.

58. In 1900, for example, the bishop of Barcelona received an annual salary of 27,500 pesetas from the government. The highest-paid parish priests of the diocese, and there were only nine in this category, received 2,000. Aldea Vaquero, "Patrimonio Eclesiástico," vol. 3, p. 1906.

59. Several royal decrees of the 1890s attempted to make appointments to canonries more accessible to parish priests. *Revista Eclesiástica* (1899), pp. 121–22. An effort was also undertaken in 1924 to create a more modern system of finding suitable candidates for bishoprics. The dictatorship authorized the establishment of a Junta Delegada del Real Patronato Eclesiástico, composed of the archbishop of Toledo, one archbishop, and two bishops to draw up a list of candidates for submission to the government. Given the naked attempt of Primo de Rivera to force non-Catalans on the dioceses of Catalonia, this initiative seems to have been effectively ignored. *Ilustración del Clero* (1924), p. 98.

archbishop of Seville and Toledo, who still managed to write scholarly works that contributed to the revival of the philosophy of Saint Thomas Aquinas. Zacarías Martínez, bishop of Huesca (1918–1922) and Vitoria (1922–1928) and archbishop of Santiago (1928–1933), acquired a respectable academic reputation as a biologist.[60] But most bishops held a narrower vision of their responsibilities. The biographer of one prelate put it succinctly: "The prelate believed that he was the superintendent whom the Church Our Mother placed at the head of a diocese to govern and sanctify it." The good bishop should explain doctrine to the faithful by word and pen, but above all he was to ensure that "what [the Church] has legislated should be observed . . . by all his lay and clerical subjects."[61]

In the narrow sense, it appears that a vast majority of the hierarchy fulfilled its obligations, although at the beginning of the Restoration, the papal secretary of state, Cardinal Simeoni, expressed serious reservations about the less than vigorous activity of some bishops.[62] In 1890, the nunciature sent a report to the Vatican providing information on the strengths and weaknesses of individual bishops. In an extraordinarily frank assessment, the nunciature singled out some bishops for praise, such as Sancha of Madrid, who was esteemed for his talent and energy. But Archbishop Moreno Mazón of Granada was censured as a poor administrator, especially in financial matters. The nunciature found a hierarchy in need of improvement, although on balance its assessment was more optimistic than it had been fifteen years earlier. The report cited the most prevalent episcopal faults as unseemly haste in carrying out diocesan pastoral visits, poor financial administration, excessive severity with the lower clergy, and a disposition to avoid conflict with the civil authorities lest promotion to a more important diocese be denied.[63] An ecclesiastical critic of the 1920s believed that some unqualified candidates received bishoprics because of "nepotism, caprice or external pressure," but it appears that as the appointment process became more stable and regular after the early Restoration, it more or less avoided the nomination of prelates who were lazy or indifferent to their administrative responsibilities.[64] The career of Vicente Sánchez de Castro, bishop of Santander (1884–1920), provides an example. The prelate saw himself as "a vigilant pastor of orthodoxy, [functioning] with great authority, rectitude and constant work." He visited the parishes of his diocese regularly, reorganized the local seminary, attempted to improve the quality of the parochial clergy through a variety of initiatives, promoted the establishment of a

60. Franco Díaz de Cerio, *Un cardenal filósofo de la historia Fr. Zeferino González, O. P. (1831–1894)* (Rome, 1969), p. 81; P. B. Martínez, "El Ilmo. y Revmo. P. Zacarías Martínez, obispo de Huesca," *España y América* (1919), no. 6, pp. 102–13.

61. Quoted in José Manuel Cuenca Toribio, *Sociología del episcopado español e hispanoamericano, 1789–1985* (Madrid, 1986), p. 288.

62. "Istruzioni per Monsignore Giacomo Cattani, Arcivescovo d'Ancira, Nunzio Apostolico in Madrid," 1877, in *Instrucciones secretas a los nuncios de España*, p. 204.

63. Vico, "Informe sobre el episcopado," pp. 290, 240–41, 202.

64. "Las provisiones de gracia de la Corona de España," *Revista Eclesiástica* (1927), p. 291.

diocesan newspaper, encouraged the foundation of Sunday schools, and lent his support to the foundation of devotional associations.[65]

Administrative conscientiousness carried a price. Bishops ruled their dioceses with absolute authority. There was nothing new about this, but the development of centralized diocesan bureaucracies during the late nineteenth and early twentieth centuries served to isolate the bishop from his clergy. The prelate appointed during the Restoration and dictatorship, recalled Cardinal Tarancón, "never forgot that he was a bishop and that he had to maintain a certain distance from those with whom he was dealing."[66] It would be premature to suggest that bishops and priests, who shared common views on many issues, existed in separate ecclesiastical worlds. But although priests were accustomed to a rigid hierarchical structure, they sometimes expressed their frustration with it. Some complained of "the notable differences [in salary] between canons, bishops and parish priests." Others noted the painfully slow procedures with which "curias and diocesan palaces" dealt with matters sent to them for resolution by the parochial clergy.[67]

Few priests dared go beyond discreet criticism of the hierarchy. One of the few who did was the parish priest of Treceño, Leopoldo Arias Prieto, in a controversial article of 1915 that managed to escape the vigilant eye of the editor of a journal widely circulated among the parochial clergy. A frequent commentator on pastoral questions, Arias Prieto was responding to a spate of publications exhorting parish priests to rouse themselves from lethargy and inaction. He believed that the question had been wrongly put. It should have been, "What can the bishop do?" He reproached the bishops for charging impoverished parish priests for the expenses of their pastoral visits; he urged them to receive their priests graciously and provide financial assistance to the poorest clerics. He asked them to administer the sacrament of confirmation more often and to be more diligent in filling parish vacancies.[68] Such unaccustomed criticism led to a quick disavowal by the journal's editors, who declared that they had been unaware that the article contained "concepts harmful to the authority of the Most Reverend Prelates."[69]

Well educated, assiduous in administration, and possessed of supreme authority in their dioceses, the bishops had the means to provide dynamic leadership, but they rarely did so. The process of selection placed a premium on administrative ability and the prudent skills of the ecclesiastical politician. Moreover, the training of many prelates in the seminaries of Rome and Comillas instilled a conservative mentality hostile to innovation. Few prominent Spanish priests, for example, stud-

65. Santiago Díez Llama, *La situación socio-religiosa de Santander y el Obispo Sánchez de Castro, 1884–1920* (Santander, 1971), pp. 103, 52, 62, 65, 69.

66. Vicente Enrique y Tarancón, *Recuerdos de juventud* (Barcelona, 1984), p. 206.

67. Father Aizpún, "¿Hemos fracasado?," *Revista Eclesiástica* (1936), p. 363; Leopoldo Arias Prieto, "La crisis religiosa," ibid. (1914), p. 441.

68. "Excelente poder del sacerdote en sociedad," *Revista Eclesiástica* (1915), pp. 528, 535.

69. *Revista Eclesiástica* (1916), p. 49.

ied in the theological and philosophical faculties of the University of Louvain, arguably the most advanced center of Catholic ecclesiastical learning on the continent.[70] During the Restoration and to a degree under the dictatorship, the Spanish Church functioned with a hierarchy lacking the organizational cohesion, the sense of realism and, above all, the dynamism necessary to confront challenges of unaccustomed intensity.

70. Cuenca Toribio, *Sociología del episcopado español*, p. 281.

CHAPTER IX

THE SECULAR AND REGULAR CLERGY, 1875–1930

The bishops formed the first rank of an ecclesiastical society organized along hierarchical lines. Although religious apologists liked to describe the clergy as soldiers engaged in a life or death conflict with sundry forces of evil, the military analogy should not be taken too far. Bishops enjoyed theoretical powers superior to those of any general, but they presided over a clerical army that was far from effectively organized. The troops dispatched to the spiritual trenches formed a variegated mass differentiated by social origin, regional disparities, and uneven levels of training.

Clerical Demography

Few issues aroused anticlerical passions more than the increase in the number of priests and religious. Naturally, the Church viewed expansion as a source of pride and a sign of institutional vigor. During the Restoration, the ecclesiastical population grew significantly, following a drastic slippage from eighteenth-century levels as a result of nineteenth-century liberal reforms. Between 1797 and 1860, the number of priests and nuns fell from 148,409 to 63,267.[1] Although the suppression of male religious orders during the 1830s accounted for much of the loss, the diocesan clergy also experienced a decline in strength of approximately one-third.

Despite the controversy over the religious orders' growth during the Restora-

1. "Demografía eclesiástica," in *Diccionario de historia eclesiástica*, ed. Q. Aldea Vaquero et al. (4 vols., Madrid, 1972–1975), vol. 2, p. 733; *Censo de la población de España, 1860* (Madrid, 1863), p. 758.

*Table 1. Priests and Religious, 1860–1954**

	1860	1888	1900	1910	1923	1927	1930	1934	1954
Clergy	44,448	34,183	45,545	—	—	44,221	—	—	29,560
Secular Clergy	42,765	31,436	33,403	—	—	32,002	—	—	22,087
Regular Clergy	1,683	2,747	12,142	13,539	17,210	12,219	—	—	7,493
Nuns	18,819	[1]17,686	42,296	46,357	54,605	—	—	—	72,783
Seminarians	—	18,237	—	11,329	—	—	12,831	7,401	—

1. Does not include the Sisters of Charity

*Sources: *Censo de la poblacion de España, 1860* (Madrid, 1863), 758; *Reseña geográfica y estadística de España* 93-103. "Fomento de vocaciones eclesiásticas," *Revista Eclesiástica* (1913), 385; *Estadística de las comunidades religiosas existentes en España en 17 de abril de 1923* (Madrid, 1923), xxiii; *Anuario estadístico de España, 1927* (Madrid, 1929), 601-5; E. Vargas Zúñiga, "El problema religioso de España," *Razón y Fe* (1935), no 465, 152; Severino Aznar, *La revolución española y las vocaciones eclesiásticas* (Madrid, 1949), 43; J. M. Vazquez, *Realidades socio-religiosas de España* (Madrid, 1967), 73.

tion and the dictatorship, there are less reliable figures for the period than exist for the eighteenth century. Statistics based on census reports were published by the government and by ecclesiastical institutions. Both relied on the same source, the information provided by bishops, parish priests, and the superiors of the religious orders. The gathering of data was not very professional in the best of circumstances and slovenly in the worst. A government survey of 1888 thus reported the existence of dozens of monasteries and convents, which according to the information received were apparently empty! As late as 1923, the official statistical office complained that the data received from the religious orders were confusing and inaccurate.[2]

The figures in Table 1 should be taken for what they are, a grouping of separate compilations made at different times and often on the basis of information that was unreliable and inconsistent. They provide only a rough estimate of long-term trends in clerical demography. The figures for 1860 and 1927, to which limited credit can be given, suggest that the number of priests, secular and regular, was approximately the same at the end of this period as at the beginning. The diocesan clergy appears to have suffered severe losses between 1860 and the late 1880s, a decline blamed on the disruption of recruitment caused by the revolution of 1868 and its aftermath.[3] Thereafter, the seculars maintained their strength within a range of thirty-one to thirty-three thousand, although there were signs of slippage during the later Restoration. The number of newly ordained priests in Navarra, for example, declined by more than 50 percent between 1910 and 1919.[4]

2. *Reseña geográfica y estadística de España* (Madrid, 1888), p. 95; Dirección General de Estadística, *Estadística de las comunidades religiosas existentes en España en 1 de abril de 1923* (Madrid, 1923), p. ix.

3. By 1878 many bishops were lamenting "the diminution of the secular clergy," which in their judgment would soon leave many parishes without priests. *La Cruz* (1878), p. 243.

4. In approximate terms these figures are similiar to those of Joan Connelly Ullman, who estimates the number of secular priests at 33,403 in 1900, 34,920 in 1910, 29,669 in 1920, and 32,446 in 1930–1931. "The Warp and Woof of Parliamentary Politics in Spain, 1808–1939: Anticlericalism versus 'National Catholicism,'" *European Studies Review* (1983), vol. 13, no. 2, appendix 2, p. 17; Antón M. Pazos, *El clero navarro, 1900–1936* (Pamplona, 1990), p. 119.

*Table 2. Parishes and Religious Houses, 1888–1927**

	1888	*1901*	*1910*	*1923*	*1927*
Parishes	19,869	—	20,604	—	20,250
Religious houses (male)	161	529	—	896	970
Religious houses (female)	1,027	2,586	—	3,594	3,728
Total, religious houses	1,188	3,115	—	4,470	4,698

**Sources: Reseña geográfica y estadística* (1888), 101; "Estadística oficial civil de asociaciones religiosas en España," *La Cruz* (1902), 56; "Seminaristas españoles," *Revista Eclesiástica* (1915), 337; *Estadística de las comunidades religiosas . . . en 1 de abril de 1923*, 97; *Anuario estadístico . . .*, 1927, 601.

This relative demographic stability was due to several causes. First, the number of parishes, where the majority of seculars found employment, increased only marginally between 1888 and 1927 (see Table 2). A massive expansion of parishes, particularly in the country's growing cities, would have required a corresponding increase in the budget for the parochial clergy that no government was prepared to undertake. Second, nineteenth-century liberal reforms eliminated for the most part the cornucopia of non-pastoral benefices that had once allowed thousands of secular priests to live comfortably.[5] By the end of the nineteenth century, secular priests had little opportunity to find employment outside of the ecclesiastical list of the *culto y clero* budget.

Following the suppression of the male orders, the diocesan clergy possessed an overwhelming demographic dominance within clerical ranks. But a significant readjustment began when Cánovas began to authorize the establishment of new religious communities during the late 1870s. In doing so, he broke with a historic policy of Spanish liberalism. The Church was suitably grateful for this initiative:

> The present government deserves greater thanks than any previous one. . . . The criteria which the Ministry of Grace and Justice appears to have adopted consists of considering indefinitely the authorization of convents, . . . and to approve those that are founded without any kind of subvention by the State, as long as the local authorities make a favorable recommendation. . . . Spanish piety is still sufficient to meet the costs necessary for the foundation of religious communities.[6]

The generosity, if not the piety, of the country's wealthy Catholic elite proved sufficient. In Barcelona during the 1880s, prominent laypeople, including the marqués de Comillas and Dorotea de Chopitea, whose family was linked to the city's leading commercial and banking houses, spent lavishly to construct the impressive vocational school and workshops placed under the direction of the Salesians of Don Bosco. Similarly, the Jesuits' Toledo province owed its novitiate and astronomical observatory in Granada, its secondary school at Chamartín in Madrid, its

5. According to the 1787 census, 22,776 secular priests held benefices. After only six years of liberal rule, only 6,013 enjoyed such a privilege. Juan Sáez Marín, *Datos sobre la Iglesia española, 1768–1868* (Madrid, 1975), pp. 295, 329.

6. *La Cruz* (1878), pp. 241–42.

celebrated church on the calle de Zorilla in Madrid, and other buildings to the bountiful generosity of rich benefactors, one of whom made "a holocaust of her property" for the order's benefit.[7] Overall, the number of new foundations by the religious orders nearly tripled between 1888 and 1901 (see Table 2).

Demographic expansion was equally spectacular. By the turn of the century, the population of male religious, insignificant in 1860, passed 10,000. Membership in the Jesuits' Toledo province, for example, increased from 230 in 1881 to 564 by 1900.[8] No group experienced more impressive growth than the orders of nuns. Even during the eighteenth-century years of the alliance between Throne and Altar, membership in the female orders rarely exceeded 25,000. Liberal reformers of the mid-nineteenth century dealt less harshly with nuns than their male counterparts. As a result, the female orders survived demographically better than either the secular or regular clergy, although by 1860 membership fell to a historic low of approximately 18,000. By 1900 it rose to more than 42,000 (see Table 1).

The reasons for the dramatic growth of the orders of women, which occurred throughout the nineteenth-century Catholic world, are clear. Expansion took place primarily among orders employed in schools, hospitals, orphanages, and other charitable institutions. In Spain, the female orders devoted themselves historically to prayer and contemplation within cloistered convents. During the eighteenth and early nineteenth centuries, few participated in either education or charitable work, with the exception of the Sisters of Charity. By the later nineteenth century, the balance shifted to religious engaged in active work, when the Church recognized the importance of education and saw in expanded charitable activities a means of extending its influence.

The pace of demographic growth appears to have slowed after 1900, although it was by no means insignificant among female religious. There is contradictory evidence for the male orders. Some sources suggest a marked increase, others relative demographic stability, during the first three decades of the century.[9] Despite this statistical uncertainty, the fact remains that by the early twentieth century the number of priests and religious reached levels unknown since the days of absolute monarchy, although the clerical proportion of the national population in 1900 (0.41 percent) was well below that of the eighteenth century (1.5 percent). From

7. Ramón Alberdi, *Una ciudad para un santo: los orígenes de la obra salesiana en Barcelona* (Barcelona, 1966), p. 52; Manuel Cadenas and Enrique del Portillo, *La provincia de Toledo de la Compañía de Jesús, 1880–1914* (Madrid, 1916), pp. 16, 38, 48, 58, 77. Similarly, the duque de Denia left an impressive legacy of 600,000 pesetas and a house in Madrid to a religious order engaged in charitable work. *La Cruz* (1904), p. 467.

8. Cadenas and Portillo, *La provincia de Toledo*, p. 8.

9. The official statistical survey of 1923 set the number of male religious at 17,210, that of 1927 at 12,219. It is unlikely that the orders would have lost five thousand members during these four years. The latter figure seems closer to the truth. The calculations of Joan Connelly Ullman establish the number of male regulars at 11,436 in 1925, 10,270 in 1928. Ullman, "The Warp and Woof of Parliamentary Politics," appendix 1, p. 174.

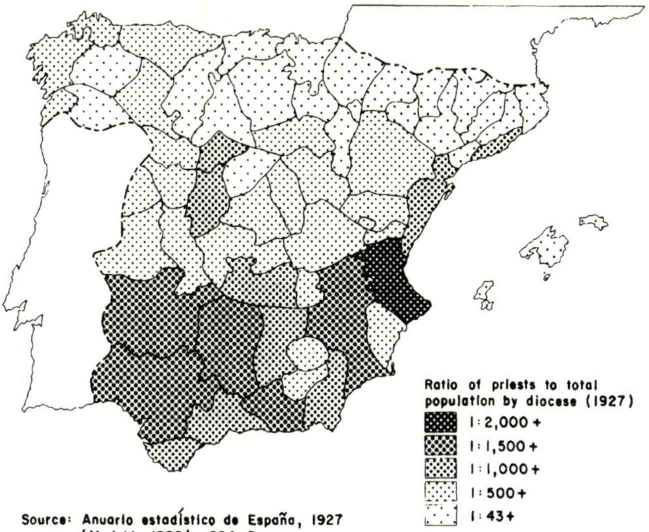

Source: Anuario estadístico de España, 1927 (Madrid, 1929), 604–5.

Map 2

a comparative perspective, the late nineteenth-century expansion of the Spanish religious orders (54,438 members in 1900) shows that the regular clergy increased its personnel more successfully than did the Austro-Hungarian Church, and as well as did the French.[10]

Whether the Church required so many workers in the religious vineyard is a moot point. Its defenders, yearning for the impressive clerical establishment of a past golden age, believed that it did, while critics saw the number of clergy and religious as excessive. But if the conventional modern formula of one priest for every thousand people is taken as a desirable norm, the Spanish Church had little cause for complaint. The 1927 survey ranked sixty dioceses according to a ratio of priests to population. Although differences from region to region were sometimes significant, ranging from 1:43 in Lérida to 1:2,501 in Valencia, forty-three dioceses possessed ratios at or below 1:1,000. Only seven dioceses exceeded the norm to a significant degree (see Map 2).

According to this standard, the geographical distribution of clergy is revealing. The most favorable ratios were found without exception in northern Spain, in an arc running from Gerona through rural Catalonia to the Pyrennean districts of

10. The personnel of the Spanish religious orders, 54,438, in a population of nearly 19 million (1900) contrasted favorably with the 33,988 in Austria-Hungary with a population of 49 million. But the demographic expansion of the Spanish clergy compared favorably with the success of the French Church, with 159,628 priests and religious in a population of 39 million (1901). The number of priests, secular and regular, and religious stood at 87,841 in Spain at the turn of the century. By contrast, the number of priests and religious in Italy was 100,000 in a population of 33 million. *The Catholic Encyclopedia*, ed. Charles G. Herbermann (16 vols., New York, 1907–1914), vol. 2, p. 137; vol. 6, pp. 166, 180; vol. 7, p. 224; vol. 14, pp. 171, 174.

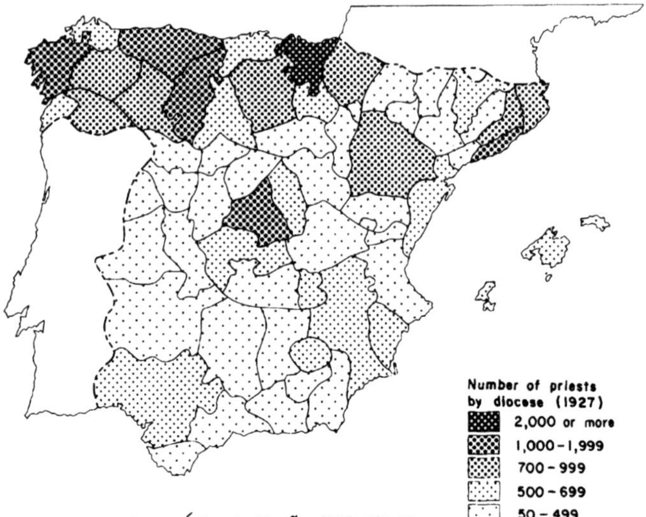

Source: Anuario estadístico de España, 1927, 602-3.

Map 3

Aragón and thence through Navarra, the Basque Provinces, and parts of Old Castile–León to Lugo and Orense in Galicia. The remaining dioceses of central and northern Spain did reasonably well, save for the adjoining sees of Ávila and Valladolid. The dioceses of the Mediterranean littoral, south of Barcelona to Valencia, were less well off. Valencia, an expanding industrial city, possessed the worst ratio of priests to population in the entire country. In Andalucía, Extremadura, and La Mancha, where an impoverished rural population worked the great estate lands, the proportion of clergy to people was uniformly low. The distribution of clergy in absolute numbers confirms this picture (see Map 3). The dioceses with the heaviest concentrations of priests—Vitoria, Barcelona, Madrid, León, and Santiago, in that order—were located in central and northern Spain, as were all the sees in the next category, Orense, Lugo, Astorga, Burgos, Pamplona, Vich, and Gerona. No diocese of the Levante, the Mediterranean coast embracing the bishoprics of Tortosa, Valencia and Orihuela, Andalucía, La Mancha, Extremadura, and New Castile, had priests in comparable numbers.

This imbalanced regional distribution of personnel also characterized the religious orders. The regulars enjoyed a free hand in deciding where to establish their foundations because they did not depend on government financing. That they gravitated towards important urban areas, notably Vitoria, Madrid, Barcelona, Valencia, and Seville (see Map 4) was scarcely surprising. In the cities, the orders could tap the generosity of wealthy benefactors and engage in the educational and social activities that furnished many with a livelihood. The regulars avoided the small and poor rural dioceses of Old Castile, León, Aragón, and Catalonia. Over-

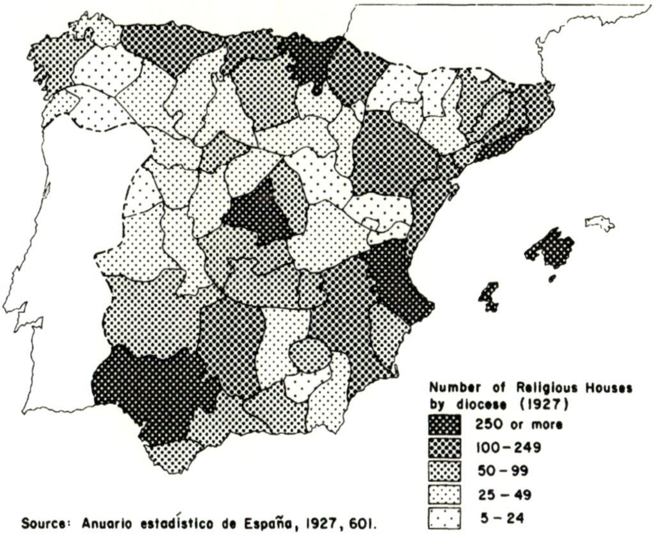

Map 4

all, in 1923, 60 percent of their foundations were concentrated in fifteen provinces containing important population centers; the remaining 40 percent were distributed among the remaining thirty-four provinces.

Two causes account for the uneven geographic distribution of priests and religious. First, the concentration of the diocesan clergy in central and northern dioceses reflected historic settlement patterns based on the dominance of the small rural village. Average parochial populations in the area were uniformly low, often numbering a few hundred parishioners, in contrast to southern parishes, where it was not unusual for a single parish administered by one or two priests to contain several thousand persons (see Map 5).[11] Second, the decision of the religious orders to establish foundations in a particular place did not arise from rational planning but from uncoordinated initiatives undertaken by religious superiors, local bishops, and pious benefactors.

The demographic surge of the clerical population and its uneven geographic distribution created problems. The expansion of the religious orders during the 1880s and 1890s helped revive the historic anticlericalism, based in large measure on hostility towards the regulars, associated with segments of Spanish liberalism since the 1830s. There was also an internal price to pay. Rapid expansion of the or-

11. Father Ramón Sarabia, a Redemptorist priest who worked extensively in southern Spain during the early years of the century, blamed the pastoral difficulties encountered by the Church in the region on the prevalence of excessively large and poorly staffed parishes. He found a common pattern of towns of fifteen to twenty thousand residents served by a single parish priest with one or two assistants. Ramón Sarabia, *Experiencias misionales: testamento misionero del P. Ramón Sarabia*, ed. Pedro R. Santidrián (Madrid, 1959), p. 88.

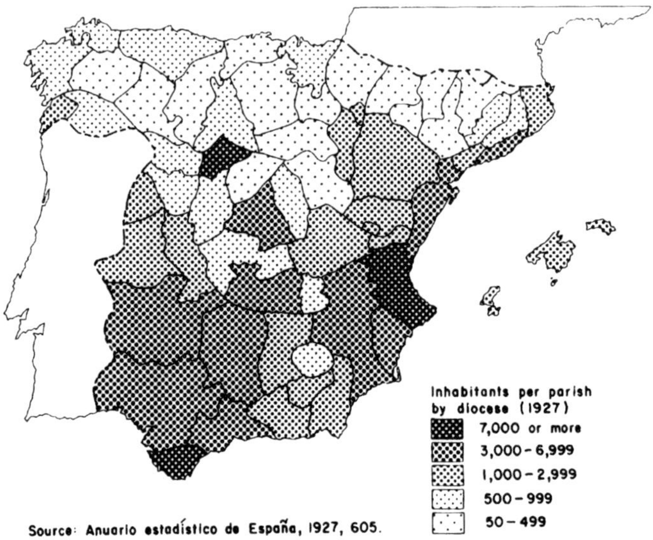

Map 5

ders moved the demographic balance of the clerical population away from diocesan priests in favor of the male and female regulars. Immense financial resources were poured into the construction of the thousands of convents and monasteries necessary to house a growing population of religious in a time when the majority of parish priests eked out a bare living and sometimes possessed insufficient resources even to maintain churches in good repair. The demographic expansion of the orders re-created in modern form the imbalance between a well-endowed regular clergy and a relatively poor parochial clergy characteristic of the Church under the absolute monarchy of the eighteenth and early nineteenth centuries.

The Church could do little to alter the unequal geographic distribution of the parish clergy created by historic settlement patterns, although appeals for a parochial reorganization to redirect personnel to areas of need appeared with some frequency.[12] There were two Spains, as far as the distribution of clergy was concerned. A line drawn from the diocese of Coria near the Portuguese border to Tortosa on the Mediterranean coast demarcated a clear division between regions that were well or poorly staffed with parish priests. In the south, for example, where the rural clergy was thin on the ground, the Church faced a pastoral crisis of staggering proportions as the twentieth century began. Although the causes of the mas-

12. During the 1920s, for example, the controversial canonist Jaime Torrubiano suggested that the suppression of twenty small dioceses would free the funds necessary to pay the salaries of an additional 2,720 parish priests. Víctor M. Arbeloa, "Sobre la Iglesia española en los años veinte," *Aquella España católica* (Salamanca, 1975), pp. 117–18. Similarly, Father Leopoldo Arias, a frequent commentator on pastoral questions, noted in 1914 that the maintenance of the historic parochial organization made little sense because of "the changes introduced by industrial development." "La crisis religiosa," *Revista Eclesiástica* (1914), p. 441.

sive religious indifference of the southern agricultural masses were complex, they developed in part from the weak presence of the parish clergy in the countryside.

The demographic imbalance of clergy between north and south had its roots in the past. The massive expansion of urban populations was of more recent origin, but it created pastoral problems of equal gravity. Between 1900 and 1920, for example, the population of Madrid expanded from 539,835 to 750,896 and that of Barcelona from 533,000 to 710,335, posing an immense organizational challenge to the Church.[13] In fact, both Madrid and Barcelona enjoyed a workable ratio of priests to population. In absolute numbers, only the Basque Provinces possessed more priests.[14] But the abundance of priests in the country's two largest cities disguised severe inequalities in the distribution of clergy. Parishes located in the city center of Madrid were well served but those situated in jerry-built suburbs populated by immigrants from the countryside seeking employment were inadequately staffed. The parish of Santa Bárbara, located near the fashionable Castellana Avenue, possessed a staff of sixteen priests to serve a parochial population of 16,000, while a working-class parish in Puente de Vallecas had only five priests for a population of 80,000.[15] The root of the problem lay in the Church's inability to expand its parochial infrastructure. Despite the massive increase in population that took place between 1900 and 1920, the number of parishes in Madrid, for example, remained fixed at thirty. Madrid and Barcelona, indeed, possessed average parochial populations that were among the largest in Europe by the second decade of the century (see Table 3). By the end of the 1920s, Madrid contained five gigantic and unmanageable parishes, each with more than 50,000 residents.[16]

Diocesan authorities appreciated the gravity of the problems created by explosive urban growth. But in the face of the indifference of successive governments unwilling to finance a massive parochial expansion, and the juridical obstacles existing within the Church itself, little could be done.[17] The resources of the male religious orders might have been employed to remedy the situation, but although the regulars provided some pastoral assistance, they preferred choice locations in city

13. The rate of expansion was considerably lower in other large cities. The population of Valencia expanded from 213,550 to 233,348, that of Seville from 148,315 to 158,217 during this period. *Revista Católica de Cuestiones Sociales* (1928), p. 186.

14. For Madrid, the ratio was 1:1,625 in 1927, for Barcelona, 1:1,125. In absolute numbers, the diocese of Vitoria contained 2,015 priests, Madrid, 1,607, Barcelona, 1,102. *Anuario estadístico de España, 1927* (Madrid, 1929), pp. 604–5.

15. Francisco Peiró, *El problema religioso-social en España* (2d ed., Madrid, 1936), p. 29.

16. *Almanaque popular de cultura religiosa* (Madrid, 1931), pp. 88–89. The imbalance between well-staffed parishes in urban cores and new working-class suburbs also developed in smaller cities. In Salamanca, for example, only one new parish was created between 1900 and 1936, leaving recently settled districts like Garrido with "neither churches nor priests." Mary Vincent, *Catholicism in the Second Spanish Republic: Religion and Politics in Salamanca, 1931–1936* (Oxford, 1996), p. 13.

17. A reorganization of the parochial structure required the cooperation of sitting parish priests, many of whom opposed changes that threatened to diminish the size and resources of their parishes. Hilario Herranz Establés, *El párroco y la parroquia en los tiempos presentes* (Barcelona, 1923), p. 75.

*Table 3. Parochial Populations in European Cities, 1900–1917**

	Number of Parishes	*Parishioners per Parish*
Barcelona	32	18,800
Berlin	31	10,427
Brussels	34	14,446
Cologne	41	8,520
Madrid	30	20,830
Milan	44	11,700
Rome	60	8,256
Turin	42	8,250
Vienna	68	21,200

**Source:* E. Swoboda, tr. J. Moragués, *La cura de almas en las grandes ciudades* (Barcelona, 1921), 173.

centers close to their prosperous clienteles rather than work in impoverished working-class districts, leading one parish priest to complain, "In the churches of the religious orders . . . the sons of the people are rarely seen praying. These churches are well attended, but the faithful seen entering and leaving them belong in the great majority to the upper classes."[18] Moreover, bishops lacked the authority to send the regulars as auxiliaries to parishes needing more priests.

The Spanish Church of the early twentieth century possessed an abundance of clergy by any reasonable standard. But this numerical advantage was in large measure offset by the geographic and functional distribution of personnel. The Church's critics saw the demographic expansion of the clergy as another sign of a monolithic institution going efficiently about its work. In fact, it represented an uncoordinated expansion that exacerbated historic personnel difficulties and created new ones in the process.

Parish Priests: The Professional Framework

The dry bones of clerical demography reveal the existence of pastoral difficulties arising from the number and distribution of ecclesiastical personnel. They say little about the complex reality behind the slogging infantry of the Spanish clerical army, the approximately thirty thousand priests who staffed the country's twenty thousand parishes. Existing in a myriad of distinct geographic, social, and economic conditions, the parish clergy does not lend itself easily to generalization. Between the rural *curas* of the observant agricultural villages of Navarra, the Basque Provinces, Old Castile, and León, and their counterparts working in the religiously nonobservant parishes of the southern countryside, there was a world of differ-

18. José de los Perales y Gutiérrez, *El problema religioso en España* (Madrid, 1909), p. 196.

ence. The gap separating rural priests in any region from their urban fellows was equally large. Poorly paid in their remote villages, priests of country parishes were cut off from the advantages available to their colleagues in the city. Even within urban areas, differences in working conditions varied substantially from one parish to another.

The Church upheld, of course, a uniform ideal of priestly conduct. In the seminary and through clerical publications, especially in the form of manuals written for the parochial clergy's guidance, priests heard a constant drumbeat of advice and instruction.[19] The exemplary priest was expected to show "meekness" of character and "to be a perfect model of submission and docility" towards his superiors. He was to avoid careerist ambition and the quest for personal riches. To fulfill his primary function as a "father and spiritual pastor," he was urged to know his parishioners, visit the sick, and offer counsel to all who sought it.[20]

The good priest should maintain a distance from those he served and at all costs avoid situations that might lead to scandal. He should conduct himself with appropriate "gravity" and display what the manuals referred to as sacerdotal "urbanity," which was manifested by "tranquil, serious, [and] modest" deportment. He was to avoid certain "impertinent habits of language," such as using the familiar *tú* in place of the formal *usted* except when addressing the young. Gambling, public drinking, attendance at the theater, and bullfighting were all considered incompatible with priestly conduct. Even "to laugh uproariously" was considered improper. The responsible priest should always wear a cassock because "dress fixes *the position and relationships* existing among social classes" and assured him of the deference to which he was entitled. Since his parochial residence had "glass walls" as far as his parishioners were concerned, he must be especially scrupulous in his dealings with women, particularly those employed as housekeepers in his residence, to avoid any hint of scandal.[21]

The ideal of the meek priest, submissive to authority and indifferent to worldly concerns, who was deeply committed to his religious mission while standing apart from his parishioners because of his status, disguised a rather different reality. It was impossible for parish priests, wherever they were posted, to confine themselves to a simple and disinterested pastoral role. The parish priest enjoyed quasi-official status, a fact made evident on the very day that he took up his charge through the obligatory reading in his new church of the decree of appointment

19. Among the more widely circulated manuals were Eduardo Genovés Olmo, *Práctica parroquial* (Valencia, 1914); Jerónimo Seisdados Sanz, *El sacerdote y el párroco* (Barcelona, 1918); José Vilaplana Jové, *Teología pastoral y práctica parroquial* (Pamplona, 1918); and Manuel Pérez Arnal, *Compendio de la urbanidad sacerdotal* (Valencia, 1921).

20. Pérez Arnal, *Compendio de la urbanidad*, p. 18; Vilaplana Jové, *Teología pastoral*, 53–54, 57; Seisdados Sanz, *El sacerdote y el párroco*, p. 94.

21. Pérez Arnal, *Compendio de la urbanidad*, pp. 11, 18, 92; Vilaplana Jové, *Teología pastoral*, pp. 56–57, 63–64; Cardinal Victoriano Guisasola, "Sobre el porte exterior del sacerdote," *Revista Eclesiástica* (1915), p. 436.

from the Ministry of Grace and Justice. In rural villages and small country towns, the parish priest served as a local notable who participated in public affairs. In communities with less than ten thousand inhabitants, the parish priest was entitled, ex-officio, to a position on the school board, the jury selection panel, and the local census board when it met at ten-year intervals. In towns where they existed, the parish priest sat on committees dealing with the protection of minors and social assistance for those incarcerated in State prisons.[22]

Whether he sympathized or not with the political system of the Restoration and the dictatorship, the parish priest shared, however modestly, in the exercise of governmental authority at the local level. He inevitably came in contact with the intermingled social and political elites of his town. He was expected to visit "the civil, military and judicial authorities" as well as "well-off and influential persons," and to treat them "with the etiquette required by their lineage, titles or social position."[23] It proved impossible for parish priests to stand above the political struggles besetting liberal Spain. Since the days of the Cortes of Cádiz, the parochial clergy had participated in the battle against liberalism. Some continued to do so under the Restoration through their attachment to Carlism and Integrism; others supported the new regional nationalism in the Basque Provinces and Catalonia, while still others plunged directly into politics by endorsing the Conservative party after the turn of the century and later by supporting the Primo de Rivera dictatorship. The rise of social Catholicism moved the parish clergy into the front lines of the struggle against social radicalism. A primary objective of the responsible *cura,* according to one parish priest, was "to destroy the evil effects of . . . impious, dissolving and antisocial doctrines."[24]

Priests were also drawn into local politics, particularly during the Restoration, which functioned politically through networks of patronage, bribery, and influence peddling at every administrative level. Political bosses (*caciques*) representing the Liberal or Conservative parties dominated local politics. The infighting produced by this system, as well as the general antiliberalism of many parish priests, meant that they were often caught up in bruising struggles with what one clerical journal called this "odious *caciquismo.*" The parish priest who dared challenge the control of a local boss ran the risk of being exposed to "a thousand calumnies," according to a commentator on pastoral questions who saw the role of the

22. Genovés Olmos, *Práctica parroquial,* pp. 703, 675–93. In Aragón, according to the special regional law code (*fuero*), parish priests enjoyed the legal right to receive the wills of the dying when a public notary could not be present for this purpose. *Crónica del Sínodo Diocesano celebrado en Jaca los días 23, 24 y 25 de agosto de 1899* (Madrid, 1899), p. 145.

23. Vilaplana Jové, *Teología pastoral,* p. 55.

24. Juan Guerra Díaz, *Manual del católico campesino o sea correspondencia entre un cura de aldea y un feligrés en que se dan armas a los débiles para defender sus creencias contra los errores y calumnia de los impíos* (Valladolid, 1919), p. 225.

*Table 4. Distribution of Parish Appointments, 1920**

Category of Parishes	*Number of appts.*
Término	1,258
Ascenso	4,127
Entrada	8,194
Rurales	3,400

**Source: Ilustracion del Clero* (1920), 136–7. Does not include parishes without incumbents.

cacique as a major obstacle to the work of the parochial clergy.[25] The matters at issue in these local battles were rarely discussed, but in some cases, such as Galicia, conflict developed from the opposition of *caciques* to the efforts of parish priests to encourage the Catholic agrarian movement, which threatened to diminish the influence of local political bosses.[26]

The official status of the parochial clergy created other difficulties. Pastoral reformers concerned with the state of parish life often lamented the tendency of the population to regard the priest as "a public functionary" exercising civil responsibilities.[27] Although not civil servants in the strict legal sense, parish priests depended on the government for both salaries and the organizational structure of their careers. The details negotiated in the 1851 concordat established employment categories similar to those used for government employees. The ecclesiastical list of the *culto y clero* budget for 1920, for example, contained twenty-two separate salary classifications for the diocesan clergy. Five corresponded to parish appointments that were graded in order of importance (see Table 4).

Substantial differences of income separated one group from another. Parish priests of *término* parishes, which paid the highest salaries, were invariably located in cities. The *curas* of such parishes received from three to four times more than the clergy of country parishes (*rurales*). In fact, only about a fifth of all parish appointments (*término*) and (*ascenso*) carried an income that could be considered adequate by any reasonable standard.[28] The vast majority of parish priests were destined to spend their lives in genteel poverty.[29]

25. Leopoldo Arias Prieto, "La organización religioso-social del clero español," *Revista Eclesiástica* (1914), p. 533; "Estado general de las parroquias," *La Parroquia* (1894), no. 6, pp. 163–64.

26. Alberte Martínez López, *O cooperativismo católico no proceso de modernización da agricultura galega, 1900–1943* (Vigo, 1989), pp. 239–43.

27. "El cura de Los Santos," *Revista Católica de Cuestiones Sociales* (1917), p. 312.

28. By 1920 a daily wage of 10 pesetas a day or 2,200 a year was seen as necessary for the maintenance of a minimally adequate standard of living for an industrial worker. Of the 24,417 diocesan priests on the government's salary list for this year, more than 90 percent received less than this amount. *Ilustración del Clero* (1920), p. 136.

29. A recent work on the finances of the parish clergy in Granada notes that the relative stagnation of the *culto y clero* budget as as well as the declining acquisitive value of the peseta between 1851 and

Given these employment conditions, it is understandable that few topics received more discussion in clerical literature than the way in which the selection of parish priests was carried out. Parochial appointments were made through a system of competitive examinations (*oposiciones*) organized by the local bishop, who received from the examining board a list of the three candidates (*terna*) achieving the best results. Although the prelate indicated his choice upon sending the list to the Ministry of Grace and Justice, the final decision rested with the civil authorities in Madrid.[30] In theory, this was a system designed to eliminate favoritism. The use of examinations had become widespread among Spanish dioceses during the eighteenth century, a reasonable objective in a time when standards of clerical education left much to be desired. But what appeared equitable on paper did not translate easily into practice in a society pervaded by patronage relationships.

Priests were warned repeatedly by commentators on pastoral matters to avoid cultivating the powerful in their quest for advancement.[31] "Some of our young priests," said one, "understand that the road of ascent in what is called the ecclesiastical career . . . is not through study or works of zeal and piety . . . but through introducing themselves into social life, currying favor with influential persons."[32] Bishops were inundated by requests from friends and relatives and even politicians to favor the interests of individual candidates:

> We find deputies, senators, ministers and political bosses . . . who have dedicated . . . months . . . to sending letters to the bishops, asking for protection for persons whom they do not even know. This is the sad reality. But we see things even more shocking. New parish priests who have never served as assistants; others who have obtained *ascenso* parishes without having served in the *rurales* and *entrada* parishes. Is this just? Is this fair?[33]

These complaints had some justification, although there is insufficient evidence to assess the full extent of the problem. The bishops themselves were not above favoring the careers of individual priests by short-circuiting the examination system. In 1901, for example, the bishop of Lugo appointed Father Avelino González to the parish of San Pedro. Although a seminary professor, he finished well down on the

---

1885 led to "a progressive impoverishment of the clergy, above all the rural." María Luisa García Valverde, *Los problemas económicos de la Iglesia en el siglo XIX: el clero parroquial de Granada, 1840–1900* (Granada, 1983), pp. 182–83.

30. Genovés Olmo, *Práctica parroquial*, p. 702; Federico Santamaría Peña, *Provisión de las parroquias en concurso y fuera de él* (Madrid, 1920), p. 16.

31. Seisdados Sanz, *El sacerdote y el párroco*, p. 94; Herranz Establés, *El párroco y la parroquia*, p. 118.

32. Eduardo Jiménez Negrón, "Malos causados por el desconocimiento y falta de apreciación de los servicios prestados a las almas cristianas por los sacerdotes apostólicos," *Revista Eclesiástica* (1912), p. 159.

33. J. Serres, "El escalafón en la provisión de cargos parroquiales," *Revista Eclesiástica* (1911), pp. 207–8. Another critic complained of individuals who "for their own selfish motives bother the bishops with their recommendations. . . . How many intrusions have come from people who have nothing to do with religious matters, many of whom detest them!" Miguel Cortacero y Velasco, *Cuestiones eclesiásticas* (Madrid, 1915), p. 18.

list of examinees, but the bishop placed him first anyway, over the complaints of the other candidates. Similarly, a well-to-do young cleric, Father Victoriano Aparicio, sought his first appointment as a parish priest in 1877 even before ordination and secured it through the good offices of the local bishop. Thereafter, in a career that extended until his death in 1894, he moved from one choice appointment to another because of his ecclesiastical connections.[34]

In fact, the examination system did not work as it should have. When a sufficient number of parish vacancies occurred, bishops were required to give notice to their priests of the positions available and to convoke examinations within a reasonable time. Frequently, they ignored this obligation. Clerical journals complained of long delays that in some dioceses saw the gap between convocations reach ten or even twenty years.[35] Episcopal neglect of the *concursos de curatos* did not mean that parishes were left without clergy. Bishops were able to evade the restriction on their freedom to appoint by naming temporary incumbents (*ecónomos*) who often served for years, thereby provoking the resentment of parish priests seeking to improve their career prospects.[36]

Even when the system functioned properly, it embodied a principle that did little to encourage a commitment to pastoral work. Examinations were purely academic in content; no credit was given for pastoral experience. According to some critics, the recently ordained priest, still fresh from his studies, stood a better chance to succeed in the *oposiciones* than did the experienced *cura*, long away from academic pursuits. It sometimes happened that priests with twenty or thirty years' experience had to suffer the humiliation of having their failure to obtain a place on the *terna* become known to all and sundry.[37] Few experts on pastoral matters doubted that the selection process was ill designed to favor the appointment of "outstanding and hard-working apostolic priests."[38]

These professional concerns and chronic resentment over the poor salaries paid by the government, as well as over inequitable levels of remuneration within clerical ranks, produced what one pastoral reformer called the "malaise felt by the clergy, an indefinable malaise, but terrible."[39] The point was not lost on parish priests that 15 percent of the *culto y clero* budget was spent on the salaries of the 3

34. *Sacerdote según el Corazón de Dios: Don Avelino González López, cura párroco de San Pedro de Lugo, 1871–1924* (Vitoria, 1964), pp. 17–19; Federico Roldán, *El vicario de Écija* (Seville, 1920), p. 28.

35. Arias Prieto, "La crisis religiosa," p. 440. In 1901, Bishop López Mendoza of Pamplona ordered a *concurso* after discovering that a number of parish vacancies in the diocese had not been filled in twenty years. Pazos, *El clero Navarro*, p. 130.

36. According to one severe critic of this practice, "the mere fact of ordination" allowed bishops to appoint temporary incumbents to "preferential places" even if they had little experience or knowledge, thereby provoking "mistrust and later backbiting and jealousy" among parish priests who saw their chances of promotion frustrated. Cortacero y Velasco, *Cuestiones eclesiásticas*, p. 68.

37. Ibid., p. 19.

38. Herranz Establés, *El párroco y la parroquia*, p. 122.

39. Quoted in Jaime Torrubiano Ripoll, *Política religiosa de la democracia española* (Madrid, 1933), p. 23. Complaints about salaries appeared regularly in the clerical press. See, for example, *El Defensor de*

percent of the diocesan clergy who made up the clerical elite of bishops and cathedral canons.[40] Few priests would have dared criticize members of the hierarchy on this score, but some threw an occasional rhetorical rock against the capitular clergy. A cathedral chapter, declared one critic, was not "the most suitable place to develop . . . intense sentiments of apostolic zeal."[41] The gap separating canons from parish priests finally emerged into the open in 1926 at a national clerical meeting, when the capitular clergy expressed their collective "disgust" at a government proposal to award a salary increase only to the "neediest" priests, namely, those serving in the countryside.[42]

Parish priests attempted to do something about their pay and occupational concerns by founding the National League for the Defense of the Clergy in 1911. Although founded in part as a defense against anticlerical assaults, the League owed its existence to a growing awareness among the clergy of the success of organizing initiatives in the "army, judiciary, professoriate, and workers' groups."[43] This version of clerical syndicalism was not particularly successful, although more than eleven thousand priests had signed up by 1919. Governments remained as parsimonious as ever, while there was never the slightest indication that the bishops intended to heed calls for reform in the appointment and examination process.[44] A small minority of priests became so disenchanted with the meager results achieved that they launched a campaign in 1917 to establish a new organization similar to the controversial *Juntas de Defensa*, formed by disgruntled military officers to lobby the government for improved salaries and working conditions. This initiative was doomed to failure. Even priests sympathetic to the need for reform drew back from the challenge to authority that it implied.[45]

To what degree the occupational condition of the parish clergy affected its ability to carry out effective pastoral work is a difficult, perhaps impossible, question to

los Párrocos (1898), Christmas supplement; "Un efecto de la precaria situación económica del clero," *Revista Eclesiástica* (1910), pp. 289–98; *Unión y Caridad* (1928), pp. 8–9.

40. Canons were less well paid than bishops, but on average at the turn of the century, they received 3,500 to 4,000 pesetas a year, well above the 2,000 received by senior parish priests of *término* parishes. "Patrimonio eclesiástico: presupuesto del ministerio de Gracia y Justicia. Año 1900," *Diccionario de historia eclesiástica*, vol. 3, p. 1925.

41. Herranz Establés, *El párroco y la parroquia*, p. 117.

42. *Unión y Caridad* (1926), p. 15.

43. "Liga Nacional de Defensa del Clero," *Revista Eclesiástica* (1911), p. 194. Admiration and envy were expressed with respect to the salary and professional benefits secured by groups who organized themselves effectively, while the parish clergy "remained stationary in its intolerable situation." Arias Prieto, "La organización religioso-social del clero español," p. 530.

44. Clerics calling for the reform of appointment procedures focused on the need for introducing a well-known Spanish social mechanism, the *escalafón*, a system based on promotion through seniority. It was widely used among military officers, schoolteachers, and government employees. J. Serres, "El escalafón en la provisión de cargos parroquiales," p. 98. Father Herranz Establés, an experienced parish priest, supported a reform along these lines on the grounds that "it would serve to reward true merit and service by eliminating surprises and the element of chance connected to the *oposición* especially for priests in the advancing years of life." *El párroco y la parroquia*, p. 122.

45. "Las aspiraciones del clero," *Revista Eclesiástica* (1917), pp. 98–99.

answer. It can scarcely have encouraged parish priests to devote their energies entirely to religious work. The parish clergy keenly felt its financial victimization at the hands of successive governments and the indifference of the hierarchy to its professional concerns, at times to the point of obsession. This was a far from content clerical army. Moreover, the clergy's sense of grievance, exacerbated by the perception of decades of accumulated wrongs at the hands of a Catholic State, provided the worst of preparations when the Second Republic eliminated government financial support for the Church, thereby threatening parish priests with the loss of a threadbare living but one to which they believed that they had an absolute right.

Parish Priests: The Pastoral Framework

That the parochial clergy was preoccupied with salaries and terms of employment was natural enough; it was not very different in this from other occupational groups within Spanish society. Although parish priests carried out official functions, for the Church they remained, first and foremost, pastors responsible for promoting the eternal salvation of the faithful. This general expectation represented something more than a vague ideal applicable to parish priests in every age and generation. The pastoral framework of the parochial clergy in the late nineteenth and early twentieth centuries differed substantially from that of earlier periods.

In contrast to the eighteenth century, when only a third of secular priests engaged in pastoral work, the vast majority of the diocesan clergy worked in parishes as a result of the first phase of liberal ecclesiastical reform. Further, the suppression of the male regulars during the 1830s enhanced the importance of parish priests, a process that was only partially reversed with the demographic resurgence of the orders. As a result of the centralization of ecclesiastical finances through the *culto y clero* budget and the development of diocesan bureaucracies, parish priests lost, however, much of the autonomy they had enjoyed under the elaborate benefice system characteristic of parochial appointments during the eighteenth century.

Other changes transformed the parochial clergy's pastoral role. In the eighteenth century, when religious dissent was totally absent and religious values permeated society through the social controls developed over centuries of alliance between Throne and Altar, the parish priest faced a straightforward task. It consisted primarily of conducting religious services. This simple pastoral world began to tremble even before the beginnings of the liberal revolution; it collapsed entirely after its triumph. As the Church contemplated the new society created by liberalism, it believed itself surrounded by secularization, destructive economic change, moral decadence, and dangerous political philosophies. With the disappearance of the male regulars, the shock troops on whom it had always relied in moments of crisis, the Church had no choice but to turn to parochial clergy as the first line of defense. Parish priests were no longer seen as passive dispensers of religious serv-

*Table 5. Social Origins of Seminarians in the Ecclesiastical Provinces, 1934**

	Agriculture	Industry/Commerce	[1]Middle Classes	[2]Wealthy Classes	Nobility
Burgos	66.67	17.93	13.46	1.79	.15
Granada	45.32	32.77	19.48	2.43	.00
Santiago	76.57	16.41	6.91	.11	.00
Seville	40.21	36.71	19.41	3.32	.35
Tarragona	54.38	37.56	7.25	.81	.10
Toledo	55.39	20.79	21.97	1.85	.00
Valencia	55.83	30.52	11.32	1.97	.36
Valladolid	69.38	18.43	9.00	3.19	.00
Zaragoza	70.06	14.51	15.12	.31	.00

1. Includes teachers, members of families in the liberal professions, government employees
2. Family incomes of more than 40,000 *pesetas* a year

**Source*: Aznar, *La revolución española y las vocaciones eclesiásticas*, Table 43.

ices but as the Church's primary local agents charged with implementing a religious ideology designed to combat the "corrupting" forces that appeared to threaten Catholicism's survival.

The parish priest was expected, of course, to fulfill the traditional pastoral functions of his office. But these were now considerably expanded. The Church had always viewed human society and its works as dangers to religion and morality, but this concern became obsessive when the clergy confronted the social and economic changes accompanying liberalism. The role of the *cura* as the supreme moral censor of his parish took on a new importance in these circumstances. A nineteenth-century manual for the guidance of parish priests thus exalted the ideal of the *cura vigilante*. Living within a morally depraved society, the parish priest must move "continually through all the parish . . . examining everything well, houses, taverns, shops, schools, dance halls, etc., attempting to ascertain what is being said in such places, what is being done or not done, sure in the conviction that he will find abuses to correct and scandals to reprove."[46]

Meeting these expanded responsibilities was no easy task, given the parish clergy's social composition. Under the Restoration and the dictatorship, the majority of parish priests came from the countryside. An analysis of the origins of seminarians in 1934 testifies to the persistence of this recruitment pattern (see Table 5). With the exception of two ecclesiastical provinces, Seville and Granada, students from rural districts outnumbered urban recruits. In Navarra during the early twentieth century, 53.9 percent of priests came from agricultural families and were often the sons of prosperous peasants. In the Ciudad Rodrigo diocese, more than 80 percent of seminarians were drawn from the countryside, although in the neighboring see of Salamanca about half of the students came from the nonagri-

46. Juan Planas, *Arte pastoral o método para gobernar bien una parroquia* (2d ed., 3 vols., Barcelona, 1860), vol. 1, pp. 54, 163–67.

cultural sector.[47] In contrast, the Church found it difficult to attract candidates for the priesthood from industrial centers. During the 1920s, the city of Valencia produced scarcely any, while in the Basque Provinces, with a solidly religious countryside, Bilbao provided only 3.5 percent of seminary students by 1930 even though it contained 17 percent of the population.[48] In some respects, the predominantly rural background of the parochial clergy proved a benefit. Priests familiar with rural conditions were well placed to serve as local promoters of cooperatives, credit unions, and agrarian syndicates in regions where the institutions of social Catholicism took root. But this background was less useful for priests posted to oversized and socially complex urban parishes.

The rural origins of many candidates for the priesthood demanded by its very nature an effective system of education and pastoral training. Students from the countryside, who often left their villages at around the age of twelve to enroll in a minor seminary, arrived with uneven levels of education, personal culture, and hygiene, hence, presumably, the exhortations in some clerical manuals urging the priest to wash his feet at least once a week in winter, twice a week in summer, and to change his underwear weekly.[49] On paper, the Spanish Church maintained an impressive number of minor and major seminaries. Although the best-qualified students might hope for a place either at the Pontifical University of Comillas or the Spanish college in Rome, the vast majority of candidates for the priesthood attended diocesan seminaries.

To generalize about the nature and quality of seminary instruction is as difficult in this case as with almost any other ecclesiastical institution. Seminaries conformed to a common organizational model within the Catholic world. Students pursued an introductory program in Latin and humanities before proceeding to several years of instruction devoted largely to scholastic philosophy and theology, although in Spain they received only a secondary school diploma upon completion of their studies. Seminaries, although funded by the State, were not authorized to grant university degrees. Beyond this, the quality of education varied widely. There were too many small diocesan seminaries to observe a respectable standard of instruction. During the academic year of 1926–1927, for example, the major seminary of the tiny diocese of Menorca contained just twenty-eight students. Many of these seminaries lacked adequate libraries and scientific laboratories, which led to the cultural impoverishment of the students and to "weariness and disillusionment" among professors, according to one clerical critic.[50]

47. Pazos, *El clero navarro*, pp. 225, 233; Vincent, *Catholicism in the Second Spanish Republic*, pp. 23–24.

48. Vicente Cárcel Ortí, *Tercera época del seminario conciliar de Valencia* (Castellón de la Plana, 1970), p. 29; Frances Lannon, "A Basque Challenge to the Pre–Civil War Spanish Church," *European Studies Review* (1979), vol. 9, no. 1, p. 31.

49. Pérez Arnal, *Compendio de la urbanidad*, pp. 8–9.

50. A. Tabera, "La crisis de los seminarios," *Ilustración del Clero* (1936), p. 17.

But intellectual vitality, even within the confines of a narrow ecclesiastical curriculum, was not conspicuous in larger institutions either. Within the Church, few subjects attracted a greater barrage of criticism than the quality of a seminary education. Critics complained of an excessive reliance on the memorization of texts and on the abysmal level of instruction in the sciences and other secular subjects, which was seen as "notably inferior" to that provided in the universities. Others lamented the lack of artistic education, thereby encouraging "countless involuntary crimes" against the beauty of churches throughout the country.[51] A Madrid parish priest who entered the local seminary in 1913 recalled the poor quality of Latin instruction. Students reached classes in philosophy, given in Latin, where they were able "to understand the texts only . . . with the greatest difficulty."[52]

Despite frequent appeals for reform from a host of ecclesiastical critics, little could be achieved without the cooperation of the bishops, who enjoyed absolute supervisory authority over diocesan seminaries. Some prelates took their obligation to improve priestly education seriously. Archbishop Salvador y Barrera of Valencia, for example, undertook a thorough reform of his diocesan seminary's curriculum in 1917 by introducing the study of archeology, art, history, psychology, biology, and agriculture, while Bishop Martínez allowed the teaching of Basque ethnology, prehistory, geology, language, and literature in the Vitoria seminary. After the turn of the century, the seminary of Pamplona developed a well-qualified academic staff, the majority with doctorates, who received advanced training in Rome, Salamanca, Comillas, and other centers of ecclesiastical learning.[53] Between 1892, when the nunciature described a series of serious academic, disciplinary, and religious problems requiring urgent attention, and 1930, the overall quality of seminary education improved as the result of episcopal intervention and pressure from Pope Pius XI (1922–1939), who attached priority to improving the clergy's preparation throughout the Catholic world.[54] Despite these changes, the quality of seminary education remained uneven across the country as a whole.[55]

51. Maximiliano Arboleya-Martínez, "Cartas a un seminarista," *Revista Eclesiástica* (1901), p. 170; Father Aizpún, "¿Hemos fracasado?," ibid. (1936), p. 367; Cortacero y Velasco, *Cuestiones eclesiásticas*, pp. 78, 80–81.

52. Kodasver (pseud.), *Medio siglo de vida diocesana matritense, 1913–1963* (Madrid, 1967), p. 24.

53. Tabera, "La crisis de los seminarios," p. 20; Cárcel Ortí, *Tercera época del seminario conciliar*, p. 29; Lannon, "A Basque Challenge to the Pre–Civil War Spanish Church," pp. 36–37; Pazos, *El clero navarro*, pp. 305–7.

54. The nunciature criticized, among many things, the academic qualifications and commitment of seminary professors, the tendency to admit every student who applied for admission upon presentation of a baptismal certificate and a letter from the local parish priest, and the lack of discipline, particularly among "external" students who did not live within the seminary. Antonio Vico, "Informe sobre el estado de los seminarios en España," December 31, 1891, in Vicente Cárcel Ortí, *León XIII y los católicos españoles* (Pamplona, 1988), pp. 515–24, 528–29. For the attempt of Pius XI to reform seminary education and its impact on Spain, see José González Novalín et al., *Estudios, seminarios y pastoral en un siglo de la historia de la Iglesia en España, 1892–1992* (Rome, 1992), pp. 96–99.

55. By the early 1930s, "Spanish seminaries, globally considered, made a positive and fruitful effort at reform." But a survey carried out in 1933 and 1934 revealed that there were "still serious deficiencies,

Candidates for the priesthood were being prepared for life in the pastoral trenches, in the isolated villages of rural Spain, in middling towns and large cities, and at a time of enormous social and economic change. But they received a traditional education, steeped in the argumentative logic of scholastic philosophy and conservative theological principles. Even in ecclesiastical subjects, they were left unaware of new currents of biblical criticism and philosophy. There were, of course, exceptions. Father Emilio Román Torío, a distinguished scholar and member of the papacy's commission to encourage biblical study, taught the scriptures in the Pamplona seminary. It says something about the conservative nature of the Spanish clergy's intellectual life that he was unjustly accused of "modernism" in his interpretation of the sacred texts.[56]

If seminarians received instruction about the powerful forces of social radicalism that they were expected to combat, it was negative and hostile in character. "Naturalism, rationalism, liberalism, socialism, communism, materialism, realism" were all lumped together as the fatal inheritance of Protestantism and the revolutions that had periodically wracked Europe since 1789.[57] Here too there were exceptions. Father Antonio Yoldi, professor of sociology in Pamplona after the turn of the century and an ardent promoter of social Catholicism, accused some local merchants of being "thieves" and advocated the expropriation of superfluous property, to the anger of the city's commercial interests, who subjected him to a torrent of criticism.[58]

As throughout the Catholic world, seminary life was highly controlled, dominated by "the formal rigidity and inflexibility of the regulations," recalled Cardinal Tarancón of his student days in the Tortosa seminary.[59] Except for summer vacations, seminarians remained isolated from the world. Even the reading of newspapers was forbidden by the draconian rules prevailing in seminaries. This isolation represented the triumph of a mid-nineteenth-century revolution in Spanish clerical education. Large numbers of candidates for the priesthood had once attended universities, but confronted with the secularization of higher education carried out by liberalism and by what the hierarchy perceived as the corruption of the society

---

both in the selection of students and the preparation and competence of professors and superiors, as well as in the relaxation of customs and discipline." Luis Rubio Morán, "Cien años de seminarios en España," *Estudios, seminarios, y pastoral*, p. 103.

56. Pazos, *El clero navarro*, pp. 437–41. The so-called modernist heresy was condemned by Pope Pius X in 1907. Catholic modernism focused on a more critical approach to the study of the scriptures and on rejection of traditional scholasticism. Given the overwhelming intellectual conservatism of the Spanish clergy, the kind of modernism condemned by the pope scarcely existed in Spain. The best discussion of modernism in Spain is Alfredo Botti, *La Spagna e la crisi modernista: cultura, società civile e religiosa tra otto e novecento* (Brescia, 1987).

57. Frances Lannon, *Privilege, Persecution and Prophecy: The Catholic Church in Spain, 1875–1975* (Oxford, 1987), pp. 94–95. The statement of Father Mateo Múgica to the seminarians of the Vitoria seminary in 1898 is quoted in Lannon, "A Basque Challenge to the Pre–Civil War Spanish Church," p. 34.

58. Pazos, *El clero navarro*, pp. 442–50.

59. Vicente Enrique y Tarancón, *Recuerdos de juventud* (Barcelona, 1984), pp. 17, 18.

associated with it, the Church chose to withdraw future priests from any threat of ideological contamination. In one sense, this approach worked well, for it imprinted on generations of priests a fundamental conservatism, hostile to liberalism, democracy, and other "dangerous" political and social movements.[60]

Given the conditions under which parish priests were expected to work among the religiously indifferent masses of the cities and the southern countryside or among the still observant rural inhabitants of northern villages, one would have expected seminarians to have received adequate pastoral training. A chorus of critics within the Church believed not only that this was inadequate but also that it was deficient in preparing future priests "for an apostolate in the modern world." Father Gabriel Palau, prominent in social Catholicism and known for his trenchant criticism of the Spanish Church's weaknesses, complained that seminary professors taught their students as if Spain was still "a Catholic country . . . in the best of times." Another critic noted both the mediocrity of the traditional academic program in seminaries and its unsuitability for priests who were to spend their lives in rural and urban parishes and not on "theological scholarship." With his long years of experience as a parish priest, Father Herranz Establés summed up the question with his usual frankness: "Pastoral work, something of enormous transcendence, is treated as secondary, and, as a result, priests leave [the seminary] devoid of training and unprepared for the cure of souls at the most rudimentary level. This is the truth."[61]

How realistic were these assessments of inadequate pastoral education? There is no doubt that they had some justification. To judge from the frequency of complaints, seminarians received little if any training in preaching techniques, to the degree that one experienced parish priest believed that new priests experienced difficulty in giving even the simplest sermon or homily. Many resorted to the time-honored custom of lifting their discourses from printed collections of sermons, a device that often left simple rural congregations confounded before "the pompous language" employed. Another cleric with years of pastoral experience in southern Spain believed that neglect of preaching had reached such an extreme in the region that some parish priests avoided giving many sermons on the grounds that it was too exhausting for their parishioners to hear the same sermon over again![62] Oth-

60. Not all students resided within the seminary. The Spanish Church continued the practice of allowing some seminarians, known as "externals," to live nearby in pensions or with local families. Bishops and seminary administrations disliked these arrangements. Fearing that the "externals" were more likely to be contaminated by the secular world, they worked mightily to limit contacts between them and residential seminarians to a minimum. A majority of Pamplona's seminarians at the beginning of the century were "externals," although their number gradually began to diminish. Pazos, *El clero navarro*, pp. 273–75.

61. "Nuestro programa," *Revista del Clero Español* (1914), p. 19; Gabriel Palau, *Diario íntimo de un cura español* (Buenos Aires, 1932), p. 103; Father Aizpún, "¿Hemos fracasado?," pp. 367–68; Herranz Establés, *El párroco y la parroquia*, p. 148.

62. Gregorio Martínez Monedero, "Deficiencias en la formación social del sacerdote," *Revista Eclesiástica* (1916), p. 434; Manuel González García, *Lo que puede un cura hoy* (Seville, 1910), p. 69. As late

ers were even more critical. In 1917, the bishop of Córdoba lamented that "months, even years" passed in some parishes of his diocese without any catechetical instruction being given to children by the local *cura*. In another scathing indictment, the leading journal published for the parish clergy during this period censured "the majority of the Spanish clergy" for "the terrible, inexplicable and terrifying fact" that it "abandons or undertakes coldly and incompletely its principal duties of preaching and catechesis."[63] These harsh judgments came not from the pens of the Church's anticlerical opponents but from clergymen themselves. They testify to the existence of serious pastoral deficiencies, but how widespread they were is virtually impossible to establish given the absence of adequate studies of the parochial clergy.

There were specific cases of priests failing to live up to their pastoral obligations. The Jesuit preacher Francisco Tarín recalled the example of the parish priest of Algodonales, whom he encountered on his missionary travels through southern Spain during the 1890s. The *cura* was "a good person, but more devoted to hunting than his parish. . . . After finishing Mass he rushed to the fields, rifle on his shoulder, and there he had to be sought should someone fall sick." Similarly, a Madrid parish priest recalled that between 1915 and 1920 there was still to be found in the rural districts of the diocese "the easy-going, hearty *cura*" addicted to the pleasures of the table and "poor in priestly sensibility, closed to all pastoral initiatives." The capital itself contained priests who seemed relics of earlier times. Some had come from outside the diocese to seek preferment, while others enjoyed sufficient means to live comfortably on their own. The typical priest of this kind was "idle, fond of strolling about the city, an attender of *tertulias*, a friend of good wine and a good table." There were the priests noted by Father Herranz Establés who devoted themselves "to affairs of a commercial order."[64] There remained the historic phenomenon of what the Church labeled clerical concubinage. How widespread this was among the clergy living in isolated villages is difficult to establish. Father Juan Villada, a parish priest in rural Burgos during the 1880s, suffered excommunication for publicly avowing that he had been living with his housekeeper for twenty-six years, defending the idea of a married clergy, and alleging that many priests serving in the countryside existed in similar situations. In 1890, the nuncio complained that the "primary sore" of the clergy in Santiago de Compostela were priests who kept mistresses, *mantenidas*, whose sons often attended the local sem-

as 1913, students in the Madrid seminary received virtually no instruction in preaching, while collections of sermons were still being widely used in the Vitoria diocese, according to one critic, although the educational level of the clergy there was relatively high. Kodsasver, *Medio siglo de vida diocesana*, p. 34; *Revista Eclesiástica* (1918), pp. 116–17.

63. "Los párrocos que se necesitan," *Revista Eclesiática* (1917), p. 60; ibid. (1912), p. 159.

64. Quoted in Pedro María Ayala, *Vida documentada del Siervo de Dios P. Francisco de Paula Tarín de la Compañia de Jesús* (Seville, 1951), p. 587; Kodasver, *Medio siglo de vida diocesana*, p. 57; Herranz Establés, *El párroco y la parroquia*, p. 112.

inary.[65] That there were such examples should not surprise. They had formed part of the social history of the Spanish clergy for centuries despite repeated ecclesiastical censure. No doubt the prospect of a post that offered a measure of education, social status, and a fixed income attracted candidates who saw a clerical career as a job like any other.

The attitude of local populations towards parish priests depended on any number of variables. Regional differences, as well as those between village and city, were certainly important. During the 1880s, the parish priest of Ramón Sarabia's hometown of Polo de Lena (Asturias) performed his duties perfunctorily. They rarely went beyond conducting services and giving the infrequent sermon. Yet the *cura* remained a highly respected local figure, in contrast to conditions observed in the southern district of Huelva around 1910, where parish priests met not so much hostility as indifference.[66] In expanding industrial cities, conditions were scarcely better. Father Herranz Establés recalled "this dark valley of mistrust" that greeted him when he took up his duties as parish priest of the working-class parish of San Sebastián (Madrid) in 1911. He passed days alone in his rectory "without even the devil calling at his door, because no one ever came, not even by mistake."[67]

The degree to which a parish priest fulfilled his expanded role of an apostle of the Church's recast ideology and a rigorous *cura vigilante* also could affect popular attitudes. Father Juan Guerra Díaz, parish priest of Espinaredo (Oviedo) in 1917, operating on the premise that "the times are evil . . . more evil than has ever been seen," believed that within his parish he must above all else "seek the means of excluding the wolves who are trying to devour his sheep and to find a way to defend Religion against the attacks of its enemies." He must attack blasphemy and immorality in its roots and do everything within his power "to halt the flood of errors, heresies and impieties" that in his judgment were to be found even in his small town. Parish priests who acted vigorously, he maintained, would inevitably be exposed to the charge "that they are self-seeking, that they ask money for everything, that they preach morality when they are immoral."[68] Guerra Díaz was not put off by the prospect of unpopularity created by his pastoral denunciations. Other parish priests were less sanguine about the effect of pastoral action that could expose the priest, in the judgment of one authority on parochial matters, "to the dangers of isolation." One parish priest saw this reality in the darkest terms: "The night, with its deep darkness, the cold, the snow, . . . the suffocating heat of the summer, the contempt of the *caciques* of the village, the taunts of the ignorant,

65. Juan Villada, *El matrimonio del clero* (Valladolid, 1896), pp. 21, 24; Vico, "Informe sobre el episcopado y los cabildos de España," December 31, 1890, in Cárcel Ortí, *Leon XIII y los católicos españoles*, p. 229.

66. Pedro R. Santidrián, *El Padre Sarabia excribe su historia, 1875–1958: medio siglo de misiones en España* (Madrid, 1963), pp. 31–32.

67. Herranz Establés, *El párroco y la parroquia*, p. 47.

68. Guerra Díaz, *Manual del católico campesino*, pp. 8, 209–10.

the insults of the incorrigible, . . . all this crushes, surrounds, scourges, . . . tortures and exhausts him."[69]

There can be no doubt that deficiencies and problems existed among parish priests that created unfortunate pastoral and political difficulties for the Spanish Church. But it would be unfair to tar all parish priests with the same brush. Individual cases of improper conduct or inattentiveness to pastoral duties were perhaps more common during this period than in some other countries of the Catholic world, but there is no evidence that the great mass of the parochial clergy was tainted by personal immorality, corruption, or general neglect of its pastoral duties in the narrow sense. In the religiously observant areas of northern Spain, such as Navarra, a respected and well-educated parochial clergy, especially in the countryside, identified fully with parishioners with whom parish priests shared common social origins and concerns.[70]

The failure of the Spanish Church lay in its inability to realize one of the objectives of Catholicism since the Council of Trent, namely, the achievement of consistent pastoral quality among its priests. Within Spain there were significant differences between southern areas, where parish priests often lived in a desert of religious indifference, and the firmly Catholic peasant districts of the north. Father Manuel González García, deeply familiar with conditions in the rural parishes of the province of Huelva, has left one of the few detailed accounts of the difficulties faced by parish priests in the region around 1910. The *cura* entered his church to find it "nearly always empty." Life for the priests of these parishes became "veritable repetitions of Calvary," not one "of three hours, but of many hours, days and years, a Calvary on which one does not die to be resurrected on the third day but lives to suffer more." It says something about the extent of clerical demoralization in the area that González García felt compelled to urge priests to keep their churches clean and to maintain a regular schedule of services. It was precisely in these southern parishes a few years later that Ramón Sarabia observed many parish priests "wounded by life's struggles" listlessly carrying out their duties.[71]

Yet even in the south, the picture was not uniformly bleak. Father Ezequiel Fernández Santana, who became parish priest of Los Santos (Extremadura) in 1909, found a parish of impoverished and illiterate day laborers who were in his judgment effectively de-Christianized. Although he was moved by the antisocialism characteristic of the early-twentieth-century clergy, he possessed impressive intellectual and organizational gifts. True to the principles of social Catholicism with which he was familiar, he conceived the role of the parish priest in broad terms. He believed that the parish priest must do more than provide religious services; he should devote himself to promoting the creation of "a new people, Christian, in-

69. "¿Qué es un párroco?," *La Parroquia* (1895), no. 34, p. 974.
70. Pazos, *El clero navarro*, p. 67.
71. González García, *Lo que puede un cura hoy*, pp. 10–12; Sarabia, *Experiencias misionales*, p. 87.

structed, cultured, conscientious, capable of knowing and expanding their rights and duties" through a vigorous program of social and educational action. Santana founded free schools, a savings bank, a credit union, an agrarian syndicate, an experimental agricultural station, a modest pension scheme for the elderly, and a library. He appears to have enjoyed considerable success. Within ten years, his network of social and educational institutions was flourishing, and he had succeeded in cutting the town's illiteracy rate in half.[72] Fernández Santana's achievement made him a hero to the social Catholic world of his day. But socioeconomic conditions in the southern estate lands did not favor widespread imitation of his example. The pressure of powerful landlords and the orientation of social Catholicism towards the interest of the northern peasantry made the kind of broad pastoral program found in Los Santos difficult to imitate.

Ecclesiastical reformers often questioned the unbalanced distribution of clergy, by which they meant the concentration of priests in the numerous parishes of the rural north. But in a pastoral sense this distribution produced some benefits. In villages where the population possessed a strong communal identity and enjoyed reasonable access to the land, the program of social Catholicism experienced considerable success, thanks in no small measure to the commitment of parish priests, many of whom threw themselves energetically into efforts to found credit unions and agrarian syndicates. Although the practical achievement of connecting religion to social concerns was impressive in some regions, it should be remembered that it took place in areas where the Church had successfully maintained its religious influence. It may have reinforced existing allegiances, but it did not attract new adherents. Moreover, it took place within a changing economy in which the number of those employed in agriculture was declining progressively as a proportion of the national population.

In the cities, the record of the parish clergy is more difficult to establish. A leading historian of the Church in Catalonia has called attention to "a revitalization of the clergy" in the region during the early years of the century.[73] The Catalan clergy, well educated by Spanish standards and supported by a wealthy Catholic elite prolific in its generosity towards religious causes, appears to have been diligent in its pastoral mission by embracing the movement of liturgical reform promoted by Pope Pius X, organizing extensive catechetical campaigns, particularly following the Tragic Week, and establishing a flourishing press committed to religious propaganda, although these efforts failed to dent the massive religious indifference of the region's industrial working class.

In Madrid, Father Herranz Establés experienced some success in his parish on the city's outskirts. Taking up his charge in 1911 after years as a seminary profes-

72. Ezequiel Fernández Santana, *Nuestra escuela* (Los Santos, 1919), pp. 39, 40–61.
73. Josep Massot i Muntaner, *L'Església catalana al segle XX* (Barcelona, 1975), p. 24.

sor, he found a parish with a population of sixteen thousand living in ramshackle and congested housing along a maze of tortuous, unpaved, and ill-lit streets. There were few schools and no social services worth the name. The population was comprised of uneducated immigrants in search of whatever livelihood they could secure. They were "people carried along as in a flood, atomized socially," indifferent to religion because the "struggle for life absorbs them." Like Fernández Santana, Herranz Establés approached his task with the comprehensive view of social Catholicism and, it should be said, with the same antisocialist emphasis. Rejecting charitable efforts as a means of reaching his religiously distant parishioners because these were seen as "odious to the people and will murder any attempt at regeneration," he embarked upon an ambitious program that saw the creation of free parochial schools, occupational associations, and a network of social assistance organizations.[74]

Herranz Establés has left one of the few detailed descriptions of urban parish life for the period. From his experience, he derived a clear idea of the inadequacies of the Spanish Church's response to what he saw as a monumental pastoral crisis among urban working-class parishes. The bishops were criticized for not seeking to establish more and smaller parishes in these districts; cathedral canons were chastised for languishing in their comfortable posts and ignoring the Church's pastoral problems; the wealthy Catholic elite was taken to task for its lack of generosity towards such parishes and for regarding their *curas* as Bolsheviks; recently ordained priests were criticized for being unwilling to serve among the poor. The Spanish Church, he maintained, had got its priorities wrong by failing to accord preeminence to serving "the humble, the dispossessed." Throughout his account there runs the theme that the priests of working-class parishes were "left together nearly alone and without direction in the line of battle."[75] Time was running out for the Church, he argued, if it did not soon take vigorous action to remedy the situation.

There is no evidence that any such action at the parochial level was ever taken or, indeed, that Herranz Establés had many imitators in the country's cities.[76] Perhaps more typical was the example of José Pascual Bono y Boix, parish priest at Vinaroz during the 1920s, who is recalled by Cardinal Tarancón as "a model priest of that era." A man of piety who lived modestly and dispensed charity with a liberal hand to the poor, Bono y Boix fulfilled his pastoral obligations conscientiously.

74. Herranz Establés, *El párroco y la parroquia*, pp. 205, 315, 275, 284–85, 365–68.

75. Ibid., pp. 344–46.

76. One of the few was the curate of the Madrid parish of Chamberí, José María Roquero y Vera, who won the praise of Catholic social activists such as Severino Aznar for his vigorous program of social action between 1904 and 1912. Roquero organized night schools that taught grammar, accounting, drafting, and geometry and promoted the foundation of a savings bank, a dowry fund for poor girls, and a school for apprentices, as well as establishing a parish library. He was also a tireless promoter of devotional associations and Sunday schools and often spent eight hours a day in the confessional. Federico Santamaria Peña, *El apóstol social: D. José María Roquero y Vera* (Madrid, 1912), pp. 19, 212–13, 243, 249.

Yet he conceived them within a narrow religious framework built around liturgical services and devotional activities of various kinds. He always maintained a certain distance from his congregation and had a clear though highly traditional idea of the role of the priest:

> He conceived the sacerdotal ministry as a *power* that carried the obligation of imposing itself to avoid sin and make the people good, even if this had to be done by force. . . . Everyone respected, even admired mosén Bono. But few had true affection for him. . . . Were not the priests of that time ashamed to appear affable, . . . to give any sign of *human weakness* in order not to lose the authority that accompanied their office and to maintain intact the *priestly dignity and seriousness* of which we heard so much in our years in the seminary.[77]

These individual profiles throw some light on the state of the parish clergy during the Restoration and the dictatorship of the 1920s. They illustrate a diversity of pastoral responses; indeed, they show the lack of any coherent program of action even in the strict religious sense. They manifest, too, the pastoral difficulties and problems that arose from the absence of any real consistency in the training and preparation of parish priests. To blame the parochial clergy alone for this situation would be unjust. To a considerable degree, these weaknesses arose primarily from disorganization at the top rather than at the bottom of the Church's hierarchical structure. In this as in so much else, the monolithic facade the Spanish Church projected to itself and to society as a whole disguised serious institutional weakness.

77. Enrique y Tarancón, *Recuerdos de juventud*, pp. 72–73.

CHAPTER X

THE RELIGIOUS ORDERS, 1875–1930

The religious orders' explosive growth and vigorous activism reflected an internal dynamism unmatched by either the hierarchy or the diocesan clergy.[1] The regulars also formed a luxuriant society within the ecclesiastical world. From the medieval period came monastic orders, such as the Benedictines, and the mendicant friars, Dominicans, Franciscans, and Carmelites, and later the formidable order of the Catholic Reformation, the Society of Jesus. From the seventeenth and eighteenth centuries came the Sisters of Charity and the Redemptorists; from the nineteenth the Claretians and a host of new orders of nuns, with Catalonia alone generating twenty new female congregations during this time.[2] A visitor to a major city might have believed from the colorful parade of monks, friars, and nuns dressed in the distinctive habits of their orders that Spain had returned to the golden religious age so often evoked by nostalgic clerical apologists.

But there was little archaic or picturesque about the orders' role in modern Spain. Their defenders recalled centuries of tradition as they gloried in the massive expansion taking place before their eyes. In fact, this sudden growth represented an entirely new phenomenon rooted in political and social conditions during the Restoration. The dissolution of the male orders during the 1830s and the marginal existence of the female contemplative orders through the mid-nineteenth century

1. In 1892, Antonio Vico, secretary of the nunciature, prepared a report for the Vatican on the state of the regular clergy. Unlike similar and mildly critical assessments of the hierarchy and diocesan clergy, the report praised the religious orders for their "spirit, discipline, [and] zeal." "Informe sobre el estado de las órdenes religiosas en España," December 1892, in Vicente Cárcel Ortí, *León XIII y los católicos españoles* (Pamplona, 1988), p. 664.

2. Ana Yetano, *La enseñanza religiosa en la España de la Restauración, 1900–1920* (Barcelona, 1988), pp. 190–94.

signified for all practical purposes an effective break in the institutional history of the Spanish regulars.[3]

The Regulars and the Bourgeoisie

Cánovas's decision to allow the free establishment of new religious communities provided the legal mechanism necessary for expansion; it did not provide the means. These emerged from a new identification of interest between a Church frightened by the secular political revolution that began in 1868 and a wealthy Catholic bourgeoisie alarmed by the prospect of social revolution. Although it is by no means clear, as is sometimes claimed, that the events of 1868–1873 caused the rich and powerful to rediscover religion in a personal sense, revolutionary upheaval moved them to perceive its value more strongly than before as a bulwark of the social order. In turn, the Church proved more than willing to adapt to the reality of bourgeois society by accepting, however ambiguously, the political system of the Restoration and by stressing the values of discipline, competition, hard work, savings, and order so dear to those who had succeeded within the individualistic society created by liberalism.[4]

The orders, religiously committed and increasingly devoted to active work rather than contemplation, appeared to offer a convenient institutional base for the religious reconquest of the urban masses. Moreover, the regulars' zeal and organizing talents promised the quick results deemed necessary to avoid revolution. But it would be incorrect to see this new holy alliance between the Church, the regulars, and the bourgeoisie as the result of some kind of formal or even informal arrangement over the country as a whole. The relationship between the orders and the bourgeoisie was intensely local in character. In Bilbao, with its growing working-class population, the great industrial and commercial families, the Ibarra, Careaga, and Urquijo, rushed to support a number of institutions staffed by the orders, notably the Jesuit university college established at Deusto in 1886. Barcelona, where the obsession with revolution ran deepest among the Catholic bourgeoisie, became "a favorite city" with the regulars thanks to the generous support of wealthy industrialist patrons. By the early twentieth century, ninety-five separate orders were operating within its confines. Valencia, long a stronghold of anticlericalism and republicanism, saw prominent aristocrats, including the marqués de Bellet and the condesa de Alcudia, and rich manufacturers support the foundation of a Jesuit college as soon as the government lifted restrictions on the regulars.[5] The

3. This was implicitly recognized by the nunciature's report of 1892, which referred to the "rebirth" of the male orders. "Informe sobre el estado de las órdenes religiosas," p. 664.

4. Yetano, *La enseñanza religiosa*, p. 13.

5. Frances Lannon, *Privilege, Persecution and Prophecy: The Catholic Church in Spain, 1875–1975* (Oxford, 1987), pp. 68–69; Yetano, *La enseñanza religiosa*, p. 189; Gary Wray McDonough, *Good Fami-*

presence in Madrid of a conservative aristocracy and Catholic bourgeoisie ensured that the capital's religious orders would be generously assisted, a situation that prevailed to a degree in Seville as well.

But the alliance between the orders and the wealthy was by no means universal. At Andújar in Andalucía during a missionary campaign in 1889, the Jesuit Father Francisco Tarín complained, "We expect little from the rich," who lived "distanced from the Church." At Linares, he accused local mine owners of being "sectarians who mock the Church."[6] It was scarcely surprising that Tarín found no support for his evangelizing among the elite of the economically stagnant cities of Andalucía. The alliance between the regulars and the bourgeoisie flourished in larger urban centers gripped to a greater or lesser degree by the dislocating changes associated with developing capitalism. Nor did all orders benefit from the bountiful generosity of the well-to-do. Nuns living in cloistered communities devoted to prayer and contemplation often eked out a bare living because benefactors preferred to donate to religious communities engaged in "the many works of zeal and social action, so necessary for the era in which we live" than to "those convents separated from the world that in other times received the donations of the faithful."[7]

The expansion of the regulars and their work in education and charity became subjects of intense, acrimonious controversy during the Restoration. The orders' promoters praised them as disinterested organizations divorced from politics and committed to beneficial enterprises. They represented, said one lyrical description, "a celestial monument in the midst of the egoisms of the world, a prodigy of love in the midst of contemporary hatreds, a miracle of sacrifice in an era of comfort, positivism and pleasures."[8] The reality was more complex. Although some orders avoided direct involvement in politics, others, notably the Jesuits, were less circumspect, especially in their support of Carlism and Integrism during the first three decades of the Restoration. Father Tarín, strongly Carlist in sympathy, left no doubt of his convictions as he preached throughout southern Spain between 1889 and 1911, declaiming "strongly from the pulpit against liberal policy" and giving sermons that were "like a battering ram against the dark sect [Freemasonry] and false liberties."[9] The regulars have been correctly described as being "to the right of the Spanish Church" and forming "a redoubt of integrism," by which is meant a fundamental opposition to the secular and, such as it was, pluralistic society created by liberalism.[10] The missionary preacher, Father Ramón Sarabia, recalled that

lies of Barcelona: A Social History of Power in the Industrial Era (Princeton, 1986), p. 123; Ramiro Reig, *Blasquistas y clericales: la lucha por la ciudad en la Valencia de 1900* (Valencia, 1986), pp. 98–99.

6. Quoted in Pedro María de Ayala, *Vida documentada del Siervo de Dios P. Francisco de Paula Tarín de la Compañía de Jesús* (Seville, 1951), pp. 292–93, 320.

7. *La Semana Católica* (1929), vol. 48, no. 25, p. 801.

8. "Servicios que prestan al pueblo de Madrid el clero secular y regular," *La Cruz* (1901), p. 453.

9. Ayala, *Vida documentada*, pp. 765, 511.

10. Yetano, *La enseñanza religiosa*, p. 81.

he received an indifferent education at the Redemptorist seminary in Astorga during the 1890s but that students received constant encouragement to read deeply in the works of de Maistre, Chateaubriand, Veuillot, Donoso Cortés, and other Catholic thinkers opposed to liberalism.[11]

The disconnection between the regulars and the social, political, and economic world in which they carried on their activities arose in part from their internal organization. Each order maintained novitiates, seminaries, and colleges for the training of personnel. Members spent their entire lives within an ecclesiastical society sealed against outside influences. The orders preferred, moreover, to attract young candidates who could be easily cast into a specific mold. The first year of training, the novitiate, served to break associations with the past and establish an exclusive identification with the religious community. At Ramón Sarabia's novitiate, candidates followed an austere, rigid, and "at times, inhuman regimen" involving a series of "mortifications," including, on one occasion, a methodical counting of thousands of bricks in the courtyard—all designed to test the students' acceptance of discipline and commitment to the order.[12]

Recruitment practices strengthened the orders' hermetic character. The regulars engaged in teaching employed their schools to attract candidates, but the orders of nuns relied more on the countryside as a source of new members. In Catalonia, for example, they depended on the cooperation of rural parish priests to fill their ranks. Originating in "the most traditional and static areas of Catalonia" and formed within the rigid training system of their orders, these nuns spent their lives in the region's industrial cities wracked periodically by social conflict and deep ideological divisions.[13] This background reinforced the already prevalent idea that the orders formed an integral part of a Church under siege but committed to carrying out a great spiritual reconquest in the midst of hostile conditions.

The pattern of recruitment among the male orders differed from that of their female counterparts. The male regulars recruited more successfully in the cities, although some orders depended on the countryside for new members.[14] During the 1920s, the Marist brothers dispatched a recruiter each summer to trudge through the isolated villages of Castile in search of promising applicants.[15] The success of the male orders in urban recruitment was due to several circumstances. Demographically, there were significantly fewer male religious than female, while many

11. Pedro R. Santidrián, *El Padre Sarabia escribe su historia, 1875–1958: medio siglo de misiones en España* (Madrid, 1963), p. 71.

12. Quoted in ibid., pp. 62, 66.

13. Yetano, *La enseñanza religiosa*, pp. 115–16.

14. One of the few studies of recruitment among the regulars, carried out in 1947, showed that they secured two-thirds of their new members from urban areas. There are no reliable figures for the period prior to 1930, although given the continuity of recruitment patterns for both the secular and regular clergy in the modern period, there is no reason to think that it had changed by the later date. Severino Aznar, *La revolución española y las vocaciones eclesiásticas* (Madrid, 1949), p. 233.

15. Lannon, *Privilege, Persecution and Prophecy*, p. 66.

of the masculine orders offered the prospect of ordination and the higher status that accompanied it. Further, a hierarchy of prestige existed among the orders. Some orders of nuns, notably the Company of Mary, the Ursulines, and the Society of the Sacred Heart, formed an aristocracy of sorts among the female congregations. They recruited carefully from the ranks of the socially acceptable, accorded some attention to the educational preparation of their members, and, above all, served a prosperous clientele through their schools. These orders fully embodied the alliance between the regulars and the Catholic bourgeoisie characteristic of the Restoration. But they formed a small minority among female religious. The majority of nuns could not aspire to the social distinction bestowed by membership in one of the elite orders. With few exceptions, the female orders engaged in education functioned with little concern for the intellectual development of either teachers or students. Girls were educated primarily to be Catholic wives and mothers.[16] As a result, the schools they attended generally lacked the social distinction attached to those administered by the masculine orders. About a third of the female congregations engaged primarily in charitable activities. Spain's largest order, the Sisters of Charity, with nearly eight thousand members in 1923, worked in hospitals, asylums, and orphanages.[17] In a society in which historic prejudices against manual labor remained strong, the charitable orders were unlikely to secure many recruits from the ranks of the wealthy and socially privileged.

The male regulars followed a different pattern. Spain's largest masculine order, the Society of Jesus (2,268 members in 1923) recruited selectively, provided its members with rigorous academic training, and enjoyed enormous prestige within Catholic lay and ecclesiastical circles. The Jesuits established elite schools in major cities and made no bones about who would be educated there. Admission, according to a Jesuit chronicler, was "necessarily limited to a small number of pupils, the sons of well-off families."[18] The Jesuits did not entirely neglect the less privileged, however. In Madrid, they erected a vocational school next to their classical college. But primarily they educated the sons of the aristocracy and the well-to-do bourgeoisie. A list of the graduates of their school in Valencia between 1878 and 1895 is full of the names of prominent families.[19] The Jesuits derived prestige from their role in education and the perception that they formed a rigorous and highly selective clerical elite. They therefore never lacked recruits, many drawn from the graduates of their own schools. The Jesuits' great rivals as educators of the bour-

16. Yetano, *La enseñanza religiosa*, p. 113; Mary Vincent, *Catholicism in the Second Spanish Republic: Religion and Politics in Salamanca, 1931–1936* (Oxford, 1996), p. 48. There were examples of girls' schools with high academic standards, such as the College of the Immaculate Conception in Salamanca run by the Jesuitinas. Ibid., p. 49.

17. Dirección General de Estadística, *Estadística de las comunidades religiosas existentes en España en 1 de abril de 1923* (Madrid, 1923), pp. xvii–xviii.

18. Manuel Cardenas and Enrique del Portillo, *La provincia de Toledo de la Companía de Jesús, 1880–1914* (Madrid, 1916), p. 112.

19. Reig, *Blasquistas y clericales*, p. 99.

geoisie, the Piarists (1,399 members), were also numbered among the largest male orders. The superior academic quality of their schools undoubtedly helped the order to replenish its ranks successfully.

The dramatic expansion of the orders during the Restoration would have provoked controversy in itself given the historic legacy of hostility towards the regulars associated with liberalism. But the debate of the 1830s that led to the suppression of the male orders revolved around a specific issue, namely, the immense property holdings, particularly in the form of agricultural land, held by religious communities. The issue of the regulars' wealth surfaced again under the Restoration and dictatorship, although in somewhat different form. "The religious orders are, in general, very rich," claimed the canonist Jaime Torrubiano, long a thorn in the side of the hierarchy during the 1920s. He alleged that the Jesuits controlled the Madrid electric and streetcar companies as well as the Urquijo Bank, through the device of the limited liability company. Such accusations were not new. Rumors about the immense riches of the regulars had been in general circulation, for example, in Catalonia prior to the Tragic Week. The Jesuits were reputed to control the shipping line of the marqués de Comillas, while the Marists of Barcelona were charged with establishing businesses to compete with local enterprises.[20]

Whether or not the religious orders acquired immense riches is a question unlikely to be resolved because of the lack of reliable information. Although critics alleged that much clerical wealth was hidden from public view through the techniques of modern finance, there is no convincing evidence that, taken as a whole, the orders possessed vast investment holdings. What they had was property, largely urban real estate used for their churches and educational and charitable institutions. While these holdings were substantial, they could not compare to the vast rural properties held by the regulars prior to the disentailment of the 1830s. The orders showed that they were accomplished fund-raisers; of that there can be no doubt. But it is likely that the capital raised from these efforts was poured into the construction of the thousands of new buildings required by expansion rather than salted away in secret investment accounts.

In any event, controversy over the presumed riches of the orders was secondary

20. Víctor M. Arbeloa, "Sobre la Iglesia española en los años veinte," *Pastoral Misionera* (1973), no. 7, p. 562; Joan Connelly Ullman, *The Tragic Week: A Study of Anticlericalism in Spain* (Cambridge, Mass., 1968), p. 109; Stanley Payne, *Spanish Catholicism* (Madison, 1984), p. 109. García de Cortázar has argued that the increase in wealth among some religious orders was "very rapid" during the Restoration. He argues that certain male orders became at adept at using capitalist methods, although he provides little hard information. "La Iglesia en la crisis del Estado español, 1898–1923," in Manuel Tuñón de Lara et al., *VIII Coloquio de Pau: la crisis del Estado español, 1898–1936* (Madrid, 1978), pp. 360–61. Despite the belief of critics of the Jesuits in their vast wealth, Alfredo Vernoy has noted that during the 1920s the order's provinces of León, Aragón, and Castile ran substantial annual deficits to the point that they were forced to mortgage property to finance their activities. *Los bienes de los jesuitas: Disolución e incautación de la Compañía de Jesús durante la Segunda República* (Madrid, 1995), pp. 41–43.

*Table 6. Distribution of the Activities of the Religious Orders, 1923**

	Orders of Men	*Orders of Women*
Contemplative Life	9.38	24.93
Pastoral Work	22.32	—
Missions	7.25	—
Charity	3.57	29.61
Teaching	56.59	35.14
Other	.89	10.32

*Source: *Estadística de las comunidades religiosas . . . en 1 de abril de 1923*, XX.

to a more fundamental debate about their broader role within Spanish society. According to the government survey of 1923, two fields of activity predominated among the regulars, teaching and charitable work (see Table 6). More than half of the male communities were engaged in teaching and one-third in pastoral work, while relatively few devoted themselves to a traditional monastic life. The proportion of contemplative orders was significantly higher among female religious, but education and charity absorbed the energies of two-thirds of the female congregations.

The Orders and Education

The role of the regulars in teaching must be considered within the framework of Spanish education as a whole. Spain lagged behind its more advanced European neighbors in creating an effective public school system. By the turn of the century, thirty-two thousand public schools served a population of approximately 19 million, but nearly fifteen thousand villages lacked even the rudimentary primary schools composing the majority of existing educational institutions. During the nineteenth century, neither the Church nor successive liberal governments concerned themselves unduly with mass education. The suppression of the male orders in the 1830s and the continued dominance of contemplative communities among female religious meant that the Church lacked the personnel for anything more than a token educational effort. Liberals reformed secondary and university education, confined to a small elite of students, but did little to improve the appalling conditions of primary schools.

This situation slowly began to change. The Church perceived that education could be a useful tool in its struggle against secularization, while governments, particularly under Liberal ministries, began to expand and modernize the public school system, an objective that took on added importance following the national soul-searching provoked by the disastrous war with the United States. But the politicians were not carried away by their new enthusiasm for educational reform. As late as 1920, the budget for the Ministry of Public Instruction fell woefully behind that provided to the military.[21]

Public schools were not religiously neutral. A law of 1838 still in force required students in public elementary schools to receive religious instruction from either teachers or the local parish priest. The Church always insisted on its legal rights in public education, but it increasingly saw its efforts there as ineffective. Religious teaching in primary schools, complained one ecclesiastical critic, had been reduced "to unintelligible droning . . . and the routine and unconscious recitation of questions and answers."[22]

The Church concentrated its energies instead on establishing strictly Catholic schools as a means of creating "a new Christian people." Accurate statistics on the number of such schools are virtually impossible to find, although one clerical expert estimated that five thousand existed by 1910.[23] Considerable pride was expressed at this achievement. But despite the number of Catholic schools, the Church's aggressive educational expansion did not result from any sort of planning either at the national or diocesan levels. From an organizational point of view, there was no Catholic educational system. Bishops, parish priests, religious orders, and wealthy benefactors founded schools as the spirit and the resources available moved them. In large measure, the geographic distribution of Catholic schools reflected the uncoordinated decisions of the religious orders. Provinces with large urban populations, where the orders preferred to settle, did well. In 1910, Barcelona possessed 796 Catholic schools and Madrid 246, but Teruel had only 12 and Cuenca 14.[24]

Isolated figures like Father Fernández Santana of Los Santos called for the creation of parochial schools that "ought to be neither for the rich nor the poor alone, because in a parish these distinctions should not exist." But the idea of establishing an integrated and free system of education occurred to few within the Spanish Church, and for a specific reason.[25] Catholic schools came into being to educate specific clienteles determined on the basis of social class. Elite institutions like the Jesuit secondary schools in Madrid, Barcelona, and Valencia served the wealthy Catholic bourgeoisie. The Piarists drew on a less privileged body of students, mainly from families of means but without the social standing of those who attended Jesuit schools.[26] To their credit, the Piarists leavened the social mass of their

21. The budget of 1920 provided 434,522,539 pesetas for the Ministry of War, 152,547,837 for the Ministry of Public Instruction. *Ilustración del Clero* (1920), pp. 136–37.

22. Manuel González García, *Lo que puede un cura hoy* (Seville, 1910), p. 142.

23. José Polo Benito, *De la España católica: las crónicas de un año de acción* (Madrid, 1917), p. 244.

24. Ibid.

25. Ezequiel Fernández Santana, *Nuestra escuela* (Los Santos, 1919), p. 39.

26. In Valencia, for example, the Piarist college was located in the popular district of Hospital and drew its students from the "pequeña burguesía." Reig, *Blasquistas y clericales*, p. 98.

student body by admitting a considerable number of scholarship pupils.[27] The location and grandeur of the elite schools testified to their prominence within the Catholic educational world. They often occupied choice urban properties surrounded by ample grounds. The Jesuit college of San Ignacio at Sarriá, for example, was located on a splendid site filled with ponds and gardens at the foot of the Tibidabo hill. There the order constructed a vast collegiate building between 1915 and 1927 in the neo-Gothic style so dear to Spanish ecclesiastical architects of the time.[28]

Physical location and impressive buildings left no one in doubt of the prestige and importance of schools at the top of the Catholic educational world. Most Catholic schools did not fall into this category. Below the elite institutions there existed a bewildering variety of educational establishments. Large cities invariably contained vocational schools. The Jesuits maintained one alongside their classical college in central Madrid; the Salesians built one in Barcelona; the de la Salle Brothers constructed one in Bilbao with the support of wealthy industrialists. These schools possessed the facilities and teaching staffs necessary to provide effective training to students expected to work in the middling positions of offices and factories, as Catholicism and capitalism came together in cooperative alliance.

The instruction provided in Catholic schools varied according to the social class of the pupils. Prestigious schools furnished strictly academic training designed to prepare students for university entrance, but with the larger purpose of producing an influential elite committed to advancing the cause of Catholicism within politics and society. A participant at the silver anniversary celebrations of the college of San José in Valencia expressed his pride and satisfaction as he contemplated the successful alumni attending the festivities. "There one saw . . . a parliamentary deputy seeking out an artillery captain, a mayor or city councilman being sought by a banker."[29] Schools for the less fortunate had no such lofty purpose. Those operated for the sons and daughters of mining families near Bilbao by the de la Salle brothers and the Daughters of the Cross provided a limited education intended to prepare boys for work in the mines and girls for domestic service. The girls' school established by Father Herranz Establés provided instruction in typing and a variety of domestic tasks designed to free the students from the twin dangers of the "factory" (i.e., socialism) and "dances" (i.e., moral corruption).[30]

27. Of the 2,535 students enrolled in their Barcelona colleges in 1912, 736 attended on full scholarships. Yetano, *La enseñanza religiosa*, p. 254.

28. Ibid., pp. 231–32. Most of the new school buildings of the Jesuits impressed with "their monumental entrances and stairways, the great student chapel, reception hall, dormitories, great dining hall and kitchen, physics laboratories, museum of natural history, classrooms and study halls, library and a section dedicated to the life . . . of the numerous Jesuit community." Manuel Revuelta González, *La Compañía de Jesús en la España contemporánea* (2 vols., Madrid, 1984–1991), vol. 1, p. 722.

29. Quoted in Reig, *Blasquistas y clericales*, p. 102.

30. Lannon, *Privilege, Persecution and Prophecy*, p. 71; Herranz Establés, *El párroco y la parroquia en los tiempos presentes* (Barcelona, 1923), pp. 284–85.

Clerical apologists defended Catholic schools on the grounds that many provided a free education to poor students. A dearth of reliable information makes it impossible to ascertain how many students attended Catholic schools. By the early 1930s, when the matter took on some urgency because of proposed republican legislation on the role of the religious orders in teaching, estimates ranged from 350,000 to 600,000.[31] An earlier (1917) estimate of students receiving a free education in Catholic schools sets a figure of 134,000, or less than 1 percent of the primary school population of the time and clearly a distinct minority of the enrollment in such schools, whatever the total number of pupils attending them.[32]

The majority of students in Catholic schools attended educational institutions specifically designed for "the poor." These sometimes took the form of parish schools, such as those established by Father Herranz Establés in Carabanchel Bajo. Although the number of parochial schools is uncertain, there were relatively few, as it was left entirely to the parish priest to raise the necessary funds.[33] Herranz Establés, envious of the Church's systematic financing of parish schools in the United States, had no alternative but to follow the uncertain route of soliciting donations from wealthy benefactors.[34] The absence of any sort of organizational or financial planning on behalf of parish schools by diocesan authorities, as well as the marked class orientation of Catholic education, prevented the establishment of an effective parochial school system on the American model. Other schools for the poor were founded helter-skelter by pious associations. In Barcelona, for example, the Saint Vincent de Paul Society and Catholic women financed a series of schools of uneven quality. Some of the city's religious orders also maintained a dual system of education by administering free schools in poorer districts. The nuns of the Society of the Sacred Heart operated an exclusive school for girls; they also established a non-fee-paying school for the poor. No one could have been left in any doubt about the relative prestige of the two institutions. On special occasions, students from the former, attired in expensive blue uniforms decorated with sashes, visited the

31. In 1933, *El Debate* claimed an enrollment of 601,950. Mariano Granados questions this figure as too high and the estimate of the Republican government, 350,937, as too low. He sets a figure of 500,000. *El Debate*, February 26, 1933; Mariano Granados, *La cuestión religiosa en España* (Mexico City, 1959), p. 41. Figures for earlier in the century are no more reliable. In 1910, the conde de Romanones estimated the enrollment in the primary schools of the orders at 106,144, a figure that Teódulo García Regidor has raised to 140,000, although even this appears too low. *La polémica sobre la secularización de la enseñanza en España, 1902–1914* (Madrid, 1985), p. 81.

32. Polo Benito, *De la España católica*, p. 244.

33. In the early years of the century only 20 of 158 Catholic schools operated for the poor in Barcelona were parish schools. Yetano, *La enseñanza religiosa*, pp. 362–66.

34. Herranz Establés, *El párroco y la parroquia*, p. 272. There were occasional exceptions. In Valencia, the diocesan authorities established in 1903 a Junta de Escuelas Parroquiales to raise funds for parochial schools. Sufficient funds were obtained to establish four new parochial schools. Cándido Ruiz Rodrigo, *Catolicismo social y educación: la formación del proletariado en Valencia, 1891–1917* (Valencia, 1982), pp. 196–99.

school for the poor, where students dressed in plain white cotton dresses awaited them respectfully.[35]

Few generalizations can be made about the overall quality of these popular schools, although critics like Father Herranz Establés believed that the absence of any organizational framework and the inadequate financial resources invested in them offered "unpromising perspectives for the future."[36] It is unlikely that the educational level of the schools for the poor reached beyond mediocrity, although their existence in a society where illiteracy constituted a national scandal may have provided some benefit to their students. In fairness, it should be noted that Catholic education for the masses was not a complete desert. An obscure diocesan priest from Granada, Andrés Manjón, moved by the desperate poverty and ignorance prevailing among the children living on the outskirts of the city, founded the first of his "Avemaría" schools in 1888. These schools were free and functioned with distinctly modern pedagogical techniques based on the idea that education must recognize the full potential of the child in all its aspects, academic, moral, and physical. Manjón accorded religion an important place in the curriculum, but he did not create a school designed primarily to wrest children away from the clutches of liberalism and socialism, although his personal views were deeply conservative.[37]

Manjón and his schools attracted widespread favorable comment within the Spanish Catholic world. His schools might have provided an organizational and pedagogical model for a proper Catholic school system open to all students irrespective of social class. Although some two hundred "Avemaría" schools were founded by the time of his death in 1923, there was never an organized attempt by the ecclesiastical authorities to promote their establishment. Here, as in so much else within the Spanish Church, initiatives were purely local, depending in most cases on the commitment of individual parish priests. At Los Santos, for example, Fernández Santana, with his customary awareness of the latest developments within Spanish Catholicism, established his parish schools on the "Avemaría" model, seeking the first teachers from Father Manjón.[38] But there was little prospect that these schools could break the dominance of the religious orders over education or move a chaotic array of Catholic schools in a more coherent direction.

Catholic schools may not have formed an integrated system with respect to pedagogy and organization, but they shared a common emphasis on "Piety and Let-

35. Yetana, *La enseñanza religiosa,* p. 131. The pattern of separate schools for middle-class and poor students administered by the same order prevailed elsewhere. In Salamanca, for example, the Salesians ran an elite college, Our Lady Help of Christians, to prepare students for university entrance and another, Saint Benedict, for poor students. "The gulf between the poor school and the college was not designed to be bridged." Vincent, *Catholicism in the Second Spanish Republic,* p. 43.

36. Herranz Establés, *El párroco y la parroquia,* p. 287.

37. Manuel de Puelles Benítez, *Educación e ideología en la España contemporánea* (Barcelona, 1980), p. 301.

38. Fernández Santana, *Nuestra escuela,* p. 40.

ters," to use the official motto of the Piarists (the first term, naturally, took precedence). The ultimate purpose of education was to form individuals with a view to promoting their eternal salvation. One would not expect it to have been otherwise. Students received instruction in Catholic doctrine and morality. Even the poorest schools followed an internal regime that accorded acts of piety a prominent place. In elite residential colleges, social life revolved around festivities linked to the Church's liturgical year. At the Jesuit college in Sarriá, feast days were celebrated with enormous pomp and circumstance. Religious services were held in a chapel filled with flowers, illuminated by candles, and adorned with banners. On such occasions, a literary presentation of some kind took place in an elaborately decorated hall, as the students discoursed on the significance of the religious figure whose virtues were being celebrated.[39]

Teaching in Catholic schools passed beyond a purely spiritual education to embrace a religious ideology fundamentally at variance with the incipient pluralism and tepid secularization introduced by the liberal political system. A catastrophic view of the modern world and its evils pervaded the mentality of the Spanish Church during this period; its schools were no exception, hence the frequent references to the necessity of a religious restoration or reconquest in literature extolling the virtues of Catholic education. A means, namely, the school, had to be found to keep youth "immune from the fetid atmosphere that it is not possible to conquer for the moment," declared Herranz Establés in one of his rare rhetorical flights.[40]

The social duality of Catholic education and its often proclaimed intention to reconquer a corrupt society in the name of a religious ideology constituted one of the root causes of the hostility directed against the orders. In a strictly technical sense, the quality of Catholic education was probably no better or worse than that of the public system. By the standards of the day, the regulars' elite schools provided an excellent education even in scientific subjects, contrary to the view of some of their more extreme critics. But this was never really the issue between the Church and secular reformers, who believed that Spain required a modern, public, free, well-financed, open, and innovative system of education that was also religiously neutral.[41] To achieve an educational revolution of this kind appeared impossible to reformers, given the role of the Church and the orders in teaching. In turn, the regulars and their defenders regarded the prospect of such an educational transformation as an abomination that threatened to destroy their fervent hopes for religious reconquest. For all the modernity of his pedagogical techniques, Andrés Manjón expressed views on the question that most Catholics would have

39. Yetano, *La enseñanza religiosa*, pp. 242–43.

40. Herranz Establés, *El párroco y la parroquia*, p. 291.

41. For a discussion of the views of advocates of a secular reform of education, see García Regidor, *La polémica sobre la secularización*, pp. 240–52.

shared. Religiously neutral schools, he maintained, could only be "nurseries of snakes, seedbeds of crimes, nest of serpents . . . dens of perversion for minors designed to convert them into instruments of a permanent, radical and universal revolution."[42] Between these distinct ideologies there could be no compromise, only an ongoing educational civil war. The Church never relented in its defense of the religious orders and their schools, although the social inequities of Catholic education evoked some clerical criticism.[43]

Was this massive investment of capital and personnel justified even within the framework of ecclesiastical objectives narrowly conceived? Did it achieve that spiritual reconquest of Spanish society so ardently preached by advocates of Catholic education? How successful any system of education can be in forming the values of its students for a lifetime is a much debated question. In the case of Spain, not a few prominent anticlerical figures emerged from the Catholic elite schools, among them Manuel Azaña, later prime minister and president of the Second Republic, a former pupil of the Augustinians, and the sons of the middling bourgeoisie families in Valencia, graduates of the Piarist college, who later played a prominent role in the local republican and anticlerical party of Blasco Ibáñez. But on balance, the elite schools more or less fulfilled their purpose of retaining for the Church the allegiance of the conservative bourgeoisie. Indeed, the modernizing apparatus developed by Spanish Catholicism during the first two decades of the century could not have functioned without the support of the activist elites formed in prestigious Catholic schools.

Success at the top of the social ladder was accompanied by failure at the bottom. The effort to establish popular schools in the industrial cities was disorganized, poorly financed, and in most cases so divorced from social reality as to make impossible the realization of their fundamental objective, "to Christianize the environment of the worker."[44] Some individual schools appear to have functioned well but only in settings, as in Los Santos or Carabanchel Bajo, where the school formed an integral part of a broader social program involving the establishment of syndicates, credit unions, medical clinics, and other institutions designed to bring concrete benefits to workers. But such initiatives required organization, a sophisticated interpretation of the causes of working-class alienation from the Church, and a sufficient and ongoing financial commitment, things rarely found among the promoters of Catholic popular education. The assaults on religious schools in the working-class districts of Barcelona during the Tragic Week reveal how inadequate and counterproductive the Church's educational efforts had become. Partisans of

42. Quoted in ibid., p. 234.

43. One parish priest posed the question in 1909, "Has not the hour arrived to establish the clean and sunny school where poor children can be instructed alongside the sumptous college where the children of the aristocracy are educated?" José de los Perales Gutiérrez, *El problema religioso en España* (Madrid, 1909), p. 196.

44. Herranz Establés, *El párroco y la parroquia*, p. 290.

the religious orders and their schools resorted to the historic practice of blaming assorted scapegoats rather than undertake a serious rethinking of educational policy.

The Orders and Social Assistance

The reason cited more than any other by defenders of the religious orders to justify their existence was their charitable work. How anyone could criticize, much less physically attack, institutions helping the impoverished seemed inexplicable. Without question, the religious orders, particularly the female congregations, contributed to relieving the misery of victims of liberalism's economic policies. But the regulars' involvement was more than an exercise in religiously inspired idealism. Advocates of the orders often evoked a centuries-old charitable tradition to defend their expanding activities in hospitals, orphanages, asylums, old age homes, and other institutions. In fact, the charity practiced under the absolute monarchy of the eighteenth and early nineteenth centuries and the institutional social assistance dispensed by the regulars under the Restoration and the dictatorship had little in common. Catholic moralists of the Restoration referred to the necessity of charity, but they meant something rather different from what their Old Regime predecessors had in mind.

Charity had once been seen as an obligation imposed on every individual for the salvation of his or her soul. The impoverished were "the poor of Christ" and possessed an absolute right to charity. They formed an active, essential element in the quest for salvation for donors. For this reason, eighteenth-century clerical moralists stressed the formidable obstacles, the proverbial "eye of the needle," in the path of the rich man or woman seeking salvation.[45] The self-confident values of liberal bourgeois society left little room for such disquieting spiritual prospects. Far from being seen as a necessity for the saving of one's soul, the poor were now regarded as the passive beneficiaries of the assistance provided by the religiously secure. Charity became a mixture of pity and paternalism. The poor man, declared Father Sardá y Salvany, "is always like a child in the great Christian family."[46]

Eighteenth-century charity emphasized the individual act of giving, not primarily to institutions but directly to the poor themselves. A bishop of Oviedo, when asked whether his generous and indiscriminate almsgiving was not doing harm by encouraging idleness, replied, "Most undoubtedly, . . . but then it is the part of the

45. William J. Callahan, "The Problem of Confinement: An Aspect of Poor Relief in Eighteenth-Century Spain," *Hispanic American Historical Review* (1971), vol. 51, no. 1, pp. 2–3.

46. Quoted in Elías de Mateo Avilés, *Paternalismo burgués y beneficencia religiosa en la Málaga de la segunda mitad del siglo XIX* (Málaga, 1985), p. 19. The clergy no longer regarded wealth as "inimicable to sanctity" in turn-of-the-century Barcelona, as they praised the pious generosity of the marqués de Comillas and Dorotea de Chopitea. "God wished to reward his love for work," declared a priest in praise of the marqués. McDonough, *Good Families of Barcelona*, pp. 129–30.

magistrate to clear the streets of beggars, it is my duty to give alms to all who ask."[47] By the late nineteenth century, such sentiments would have horrified the clergy and the Catholic bourgeoisie. When, for example, Málaga was inundated with beggars seeking help in the midst of an economic crisis, Bishop Spínola rallied a group of businessmen and the city government to establish "a center of reclusion" to house mendicants gathered from the streets in a site so isolated that it had once housed a leper hospital.[48]

Religious orders contributed to the distribution of charitable assistance during the Old Regime but did so in a different way from their nineteenth and early-twentieth-century successors. Some orders, especially the Brothers of Saint John of God and the Sisters of Charity, worked directly with the poor, but they were exceptions. Few regulars entered into immediate contact with the impoverished through work in hospitals, orphanages, and the like. The majority of nuns lived in cloistered communities isolated from the world, while the larger masculine orders engaged primarily in evangelizing and educational activities. Insofar as the religious orders participated in charitable work, they did so through the distribution of alms to the poor gathered at monastery and convent gates.

In any event, the old structure of charity collapsed under the pressure of liberal disamortizing legislation, which stripped the regular and secular clergy of the financial resources once employed to help the poor. The liberal State assumed full jurisdiction over public health and poor relief. Early liberal legislation in 1838 had replaced the traditional mechanisms of assistance with a system based on aid to the poor in their homes. By mid-century, it was evident that this approach had failed. The civil authorities gradually began to return to more institutional forms of poor relief through the creation of public hospitals, orphanages, asylums, and old age homes. It was one thing to reestablish such institutions, another to find qualified personnel to staff them. Initially, many of these new institutions, such as the home for the elderly established by the governor of Málaga in 1846, used salaried employees. But administrative and financial difficulties forced the authorities to seek the help of the religious orders, in this case the Sisters of Charity, who received payment for their services.[49]

The charitable alliance of the regulars and the liberal State developed further during the last years of the Isabelline monarchy. But the relatively small number of religious committed to active work, and the reluctance of the Moderates in power to allow a massive reintroduction of the regulars, limited progress that was cut short in any event by the 1868 revolution. Three circumstances favored expansion under the Restoration: first, the explosive demographic surge of female orders pre-

47. Quoted in Joseph Townsend, *A Journey through Spain in the Years 1786 and 1787* (2d ed., 3 vols., London, 1792), vol. 2, p. 9.

48. Mateo Avilés, *Paternalismo burgués y beneficencia religiosa*, pp. 79–80.

49. Ibid., pp. 56–57.

pared to assist the impoverished; second, the newfound interest of government, particularly at the municipal and provincial levels, in resolving what it saw as the socially dangerous problem of pauperism; and third, the shift in liberal poor relief policy from social assistance as the exclusive preserve "of the public powers impervious to any supplementary collaboration" to "a close cooperation between the public and private sectors."[50] The religious orders alone were in a position to profit from this policy change. They possessed the personnel necessary to staff an expanding number of public assistance institutions. By the end of the century, few cities lacked them.[51] The Sisters of Charity employed their increasing numbers in the hospitals, orphanages, and asylums maintained by city or provincial governments. In Barcelona, they staffed the Provincial Maternity House and the Provincial House of Charity, the latter an impressive establishment containing nearly seventeen hundred residents in 1899.[52]

There is no reason to doubt the personal and professional commitment of the religious who worked in these institutions. But they identified themselves with a poor relief system that could not work to their benefit over the long run. Employment in the public assistance institutions created by the liberal State meant participation in a system that was badly underfunded. In the early twentieth century, the central government spent less than 3 million pesetas a year on poor relief. Municipal and provincial authorities expended more, approximately 45 million, to maintain charitable institutions.[53] This level of funding was completely inadequate to deal with the problem, even within the limited context in which it was viewed by the authorities, particularly when one considers that the total sum spent by official bodies for this purpose was only marginally greater than the amount provided to thirty thousand diocesan priests in the *culto y clero* budget.

Without adequate financial resources, many charitable institutions ran on the cheap, hence the common practice of putting residents to work to raise income through the sale of whatever they produced. The San Bartolomé asylum in Málaga employed its young inmates at printing, cabinet-making, carpentry, shoemaking, and other artisan trades under the direction of the Brothers of Saint John of God, who administered the institution until 1890. Chronic financial difficulties led the administration to subject the residents to intolerable pressure, even to the point of abuse. As often happened in such cases, news of "the hunger, the excessive work

50. Elena Maza Zorilla, *Pobreza y asistencia social en España, siglos XVI al XX* (Valladolid, 1987), p. 193.

51. Jesús María Palomares Ibáñez notes that during the second half of the nineteenth century, of 180 provincial and 426 municipal charitable institutions, 422 were staffed by the religious orders. "La Iglesia española y la asistencia social en el siglo XIX," in José Andrés-Gallego et al., *Estudios históricos sobre la Iglesia española contemporánea* (El Escorial, 1979), p. 139.

52. Lannon, *Privilege, Persecution and Prophecy,* p. 74.

53. Ramón Ruiz Amado, "Spain," in *The Catholic Encyclopedia,* ed. Charles G. Herbermann (16 vols., New York, 1907–1914), vol. 14, p. 190.

and the lack of hygiene" existing within the institution led to harsh criticism by the local liberal press.[54]

By cooperating with the liberal State's poor relief policy, the religious orders accepted its underlying purpose, the removal of mendicants, the sick, abandoned children, orphans, and the elderly from the streets and public view. Eighteenth-century clerics had vociferously opposed the attempts of absolute monarchy to confine the poor in workhouses that they regarded as little more than prisons. The charitable institutions of the Restoration were not quite prisons, but they were designed to confine the poor within four walls and subject them to a strict disciplinary regimen. In Málaga, girls who eked out a pathetic living by selling cigar and cigarette butts could gain admittance to a charitable residence only after promising "to obey the Sisters of Charity" administering the institution. Anyone who left the building "even once" without permission was refused readmission, while girls who proved "incorrigible" were subject to immediate expulsion.[55] Institutional confinement represented official policy, but it could scarcely have been popular among the urban poor, who nevertheless had little choice in the matter. They had hated it in the eighteenth century. There is no reason to think that they grew to love it in the nineteenth and the twentieth.

A poorly funded system of institutionalized assistance provided no solution to the problem of widespread misery created by economic conditions. The hundreds of unemployed agricultural laborers driven into Málaga by a terrible drought in 1907 could be given food; they could not be given what they desperately needed and wanted—land. Well-financed and equipped charitable institutions might have provided a short-term palliative to pauperism. But the charitable enterprises of the religious orders did not exist in isolation. They were tied to the failure of governments to develop the rudiments of an effective social security system. It is one of the supreme ironies of the relationship between the Church and liberalism that in this respect, at least, the regulars, who questioned the political system of the Restoration, should have identified so completely with its poor relief policy.

In addition to public charitable institutions, others were established and financed directly by the Church. The revival of private charity after the upheavals of the revolutionary period owed a debt to Cánovas, who issued a decree in 1875 reorganizing public assistance with a view "to arousing charity" among private individuals and organizations.[56] A later decree of 1899, though reaffirming the government's right of supervision over all charitable corporations, created the legal framework designed to encourage private initiatives. This policy resulted in a massive expansion of charitable foundations; more than nine thousand were inscribed

54. Mateo Avilés, *Paternalismo burgués y beneficencia religiosa*, p. 72.

55. Ibid., p. 78.

56. Maza Zorilla, *Pobreza y asistencia social*, p. 189.

on government registers just after the turn of the century.[57] In Málaga alone, the favorable legal climate led to the foundation of the Asilo de San Bartolomé, established by members of the diocesan clergy, for mendicant children, the Asilo de Nuestra Señora de las Mercedes, which housed children orphaned by the frequent earthquakes in the region, and the Asilo de Nuestra Señora de los Angeles, founded by Bishop Spínola "to help the needy and extinguish mendicity," and there were many others.[58]

These private institutions, usually staffed by the religious orders, depended for their financial survival on the support of wealthy Catholic families—at Málaga, the great distilling and wine house of Larios, at Bilbao, the Villalongas, prominent in the Altos Hornos foundries.[59] The private charitable enterprises operating under religious auspices showed again the alliance between the Church and the Catholic bourgeoisie characteristic of late-nineteenth- and early-twentieth-century Spain. But many of these foundations were even less effective than their public counterparts. The episodic support provided by the rich and the use of raffles, lotteries, and other ingenious fund-raising devices provided insufficient funding for the maintenance of a workable infrastructure of Catholic charitable institutions, which, like schools, were founded helter-skelter on the basis of individual initiatives. There was no coordinated system of Catholic charity, just as there was no coherent organization of schools.

The charitable explosion of the Restoration encouraged by the liberal State in both public and private versions provided the religious orders, particularly the female congregations, with a critical institutional mechanism for expansion. But a price had to be paid for identifying Catholic charity with the interests of a bourgeois government and a society more concerned with public assistance as "a protecting shield of the urban social order" than with resolving the fundamental causes of poverty.[60] No amount of abnegation and idealism on the part of individual members of the religious orders could save them from being exposed to the indictment directed against the regime for failing to come to grips with the social and economic causes of poverty.

Criticism on other grounds was also directed against the religious orders engaged in charity. In urban working-class areas, the sale of products made either by religious or their charges was seen as direct and unfair competition by local residents, particularly women seeking to supplement their meager incomes through piecework of various kinds.[61] There may also have been deeper causes of popular resentment against the orders, causes rooted in the social assumptions governing

57. Ruiz Amado, "Spain," p. 190.

58. Mateo Avilés, *Paternalismo burgués y beneficencia religiosa*, pp. 68–79, 80.

59. Ibid., p. 84; Lannon, *Privilege, Persecution and Prophecy*, p. 72.

60. Pedro Carasa Soto, *Historia de la beneficencia en Castilla y León: poder y pobreza en la sociedad castellana* (Valladolid, 1991), p. 15.

61. Ullman, *The Tragic Week*, p. 38.

Spanish society. With a few exceptions, the male congregations did not engage in charitable work. According to the official survey of 1923, only 3.57 percent of their activities fell into this category. The charity of the religious orders was carried out overwhelmingly by nuns. To what degree the female character of charitable work affected popular attitudes is difficult to establish. Within a society that assigned women a constricted place as wives and mothers, the role of women as the dispensers of charity to the poor in a relationship of complete dependence may have done little to enhance their popularity among the working classes.[62]

The Cultural and Pastoral Contribution

In addition to teaching, the male regulars engaged in varied activities. Some orders possessed the intellectual and material resources to form a cultural vanguard within Spanish Catholicism. The Jesuits, through their journal *Razón y Fe,* the Augustinians through *Ciudad de Dios* and *España y América,* and the Franciscans through the *Revista de Estudios Franciscanos,* provided a certain leaven to Catholic culture. Although the Jesuits were intellectually conservative, the Dominicans, Augustinians, and Franciscans produced a small group of philosophers, theologians, and biblical scholars who broke with prevailing ideas of the Church as an isolated cultural bastion at war with modern civilization.[63] The Dominicans Matías García, Alonso Getino, and Juan González Arintero stirred controversy in Spanish Catholic circles by displaying an openness to modern thought rare among the clergy of the time. The Augustinian Pedro Martínez y Vélez advocated the study of the sacred scriptures in line with new and rigorous standards of biblical criticism, while his fellow religious Graciano Martínez, an admirer of progressive German Catholic theologians condemned by the Vatican, took the unheard-of stance of advocating cooperation between Catholics and Protestants to defend religion against the rising tide of religious skepticism. The Franciscan Miquel d'Esplugues promoted dialogue within the Church on theological and philosophical questions in view of the "new necessities which are emerging continuously in the constant evolution of contemporary understanding."[64] The Capuchin friar Rupert de Manresa also advocated opening "new roads" to purify the faith and create "a school of true disinterest and elevate the spirit, free of prejudices, to the pure love of divine things."[65] The ideas expressed by these religious reformers won them few friends.

62. Frances Lannon has stressed an important positive result of the female orders' role in charitable and educational work: "In a society that give women stiflingly few opportunities for professional training or responsibility beyond their own family, the religious orders, despite their discipline and sexual and social restrictions could, paradoxically, offer liberating scope." *Privilege, Persecution and Prophecy,* p. 63.

63. The intellectual reformism of certain Dominicans, Franciscans, and Augustinians is brilliantly discussed by Alfonso Botti, *La Spagna e la crisi modernista: cultura, società civile e religiosa tra otto e novecento* (Brescia, 1987), pp. 123–52.

64. Quoted in ibid., p. 142.

65. Quoted in ibid., p. 151.

They were subject to constant and at times vitriolic criticism by theological conservatives, who unjustly accused them of the modernist heresy. That reformers were able to express their views publicly shows that renovating currents were not entirely lacking in the early-twentieth-century Spanish Church. But in general, clerical intellectual life displayed little innovation or dynamism, a reflection of a traditional ecclesiastical culture that led one perceptive French observer to remark in 1930, "No sign makes [us] hope for that brilliant renaissance of letters and Christian studies which we have seen in other Catholic countries."[66]

After education, the primary area of activity for the male orders fell into the category of pastoral work (see Table 6). This involved either activities similar to those of the parish clergy through the maintenance of churches or the evangelizing campaigns of domestic missions. The pastoral presence of the regulars reflected the overall distribution of religious characteristic of the orders as a whole. Few foundations of a primarily pastoral character were found in the rural provinces, leading one critic to complain that the regulars left the countryside "abandoned to the greatest spiritual isolation."[67] The heavily agricultural provinces of Teruel, Soria, Orense, Pontevedra, Ciudad Real, and Zamora lacked even a single foundation of religious devoted to pastoral work, according to the 1923 survey.[68]

The conventional pastoral activity of the orders took place in their urban churches, invariably located in or near town centers. These churches often became fashionable places of devotion for the well-to-do. In 1883, the Redemptorists of Madrid grew resentful of the time devoted to a group of aristocratic ladies who made their "spiritual toilette" in the order's new church in the capital. In Barcelona during the early years of the century, "a great part of the bourgeoisie and plutocracy" of the city flocked to the Capuchin church on the Diagonal to hear the sermons of Rupert de Manresa, who was himself well connected to the Catalan social elite.[69]

The male orders successfully attracted prosperous congregations in part because of their identification with specific devotions. The Jesuits encouraged the cult of the Sacred Heart; the Capuchins, the Stations of the Cross, and, in Madrid, devotion to Jesus the Nazarene; the Redemptorists promoted devotion to Our Lady of Perpetual Help, to cite a few examples. The devotional appeal of orders' churches as well as their location in city centers did not endear them to the diocesan clergy. The regulars established their churches where they wished without reference to the existing parochial structure, which was strongest in urban cores.

Parish priests resented the religious competition of the orders, which they

66. "Où va l'Espagne?" *Les Dossiers de l'Action Populaire* (1930), no. 234, p. 6.

67. Jaime Torrubiano Ripoll, *Política religiosa de la democracia española* (Madrid, 1933), p. 134.

68. *Estadística de las comunidades religiosas . . . en 1923*, p. 101.

69. Dionisio' de Felipe, *Fundación de los Redentoristas en España* (Madrid, 1965), p. 223; Josep Massot i Muntaner, *Aproximació a la història religiosa de la Catalunya contemporánea* (Barcelona, 1973), pp. 76–77.

blamed for luring their parishioners away and contributing "to the decadence of parish services occasioned by the opening of new churches by the regulars." As a result, declared one parish priest with some asperity, "There are many who know nothing of religion because they have abandoned the instruction given by their parish priest; today the enthusiasm for novelties in other churches which we will call aristocratic has meant that many have developed a languid faith." The parochial clergy was irritated by what it regarded as the indifference of the orders to the primacy of its pastoral function. Proposals by the regulars to establish new churches within existing parishes often provoked the open hostility of parish priests, who created "every kind of difficulty in the way of the exercise of works of zeal" by the orders.[70]

The regulars' pastoral contribution through their urban churches was minimal and did not develop within a cooperative relationship between them and parish priests. But the male orders dominated one of the most important religious efforts of the Church, the periodic evangelizing campaigns of domestic missions in town and country. Missions had formed part of the Church's tradition in Spain since the Council of Trent, but declined after the 1830s following the suppression of the male regulars. Their reintroduction in the late 1870s saw an intensification of missionary activity. One of the orders devoting special attention to missions, the Redemptorists, returned to Spain only in 1879, but by 1881 they were preaching twenty-four missions and by 1882, thirty-five. Under the Restoration and the dictatorship, levels of activity varied substantially from one period to another. The Redemptorist house of El Espino (Burgos), for example, saw a spectacular increase in the missions preached by its members between 1895 and 1910 during the first great organizational surge of modern Spanish Catholicism, with seventy being preached in 1905 alone. Thereafter, thirty-five to forty missions were given each year on average, save for a short-lived expansion under the dictatorship. Overall, the order's missionary record between 1879 and the eve of the Republic shows that the Church expanded its domestic missionary campaigns to levels unknown since the eighteenth century. The Redemptorists calculated that they had preached 6,776 missions and related services over this fifty-year period.[71]

Many orders engaged in domestic missionary activity. The Jesuits, Redemptorists, and Capuchins were the most active. Missions were highly organized enterprises revolving around a variety of religious activities held over several days. Priests destined for missionary work were carefully chosen and trained. The Redemptorists, for example, required a second novitiate after ordination to prepare

70. Marcelino González, "El párroco y los institutos religiosos," *Sal Terrae* (1917), pp. 603, 599; Narciso Viñas Dausá, *Agenda parroquial y de sus feligresías de 1922* (Madrid, 1922), p. 45.

71. Felipe, *Fundación de los Redentoristas*, p. 191. Tirso Cepedal, "El Espino, misionero," *Espino* (1957), special number, p. 62; Raimundo Tellería, *Un instituto misionero: la Congregación del Santísimo Redentor en el segundo centenario de su fundación, 1732–1932* (Madrid, 1932), p. 436.

priests for these evangelizing campaigns. Priests selected for work in missions often spent their lives in this specialized activity. The Redemptorist Father Ramón Sarabia gave his first mission in 1902, his last during the 1950s, a lifetime of missionary work in which he preached in more than four hundred cities, towns, and villages.[72] The Jesuit Father Francisco Tarín worked the southern mission fields incessantly between 1889 and 1911.

The qualities required of a missionary were many. He had to be a good preacher, capable of holding the attention of his congregation over several days of sermons. He needed to possess enormous physical stamina given the hardships of constant travel, since missionary schedules were often punishing. In 1907 alone, Francisco Tarín preached thirty-two missions and heard twenty thousand confessions as he made his rounds through the towns and villages of southern Spain, and his example was by no means unusual.[73]

The reception a missionary could expect varied from one region to another. Ramón Sarabia delighted in the enthusiastic response that greeted his missions in the observant rural district of La Montaña of Santander during 1909–1910, an area where a "traditional and honest Christianity" was still lived. But even in the north there were villages, such as Torrecilla de Cameros, where his efforts were met with indifference.[74] In 1880, the Redemptorists encountered hostility among the populace of La Seca (Valladolid) so severe that guards had to accompany them to their residence after the conclusion of the evening service.[75] Conditions in the religiously indifferent south were even less favorable; in many cases they were downright hostile to missionary activity. The procession led by Tarín through the streets of one village was greeted by "a rainstorm of stones like the peaches of Aragón," while at a mission in another, the sermon he was preaching in the town square was disrupted by local anticlericals who released a pack of barking dogs into the midst of the congregation. Such events rarely discouraged missionaries, however, who saw themselves as the shock troops of the Spanish Church. Tarín, as tough as any missionary of his time, knew how to take the battle into the enemy camp. When his sermon at Almodóvar del Campo was interrupted by a man shouting, "Why doesn't he shut up!" and creating pandemonium among those in attendance, he immediately began singing a hymn set to the music of the royal anthem. As its last notes died out, he shouted, "War, war against Lucifer!"—a cry taken up by the congregation in a "nearly threatening tone" that reduced the miscreant to silence.[76]

72. Santidrián, *El Padre Sarabia*, pp. 84–91.

73. Alberto Risco, *El Padre Franscisco de Paula Tarín* (Madrid, 1921), p. 375. See also the missionary schedule reproduced in Cardenas and Portillo, *La provincia de Toledo*, p. 254.

74. Santidrián, *El Padre Sarabia*, pp. 141, 97.

75. "Ante un centenario frustrado: Nava del Rey (1879–1970)," *Boletín de la Provincia Española: publicación privada para uso exclusivo de las comunidades de Padres Redentoristas* (December 1979), no. 109, p. 142.

76. Ayala, *Vida documentada*, pp. 372, 422, 455.

The missionaries of this period were aggressive, indefatigable, uncompromising. They crisscrossed all of Spain, visiting cities, towns, and the smallest villages. Their fire-and-brimstone sermons were calculated to arouse a deep emotional response among their hearers. Preachers like Tarín and Sarabia were masters of the missionary art. The religious impact of the missions will be discussed more extensively in the following chapter. But it can be said here that there are real questions about the pastoral effectiveness of missions, not to speak of the inevitable reactions of those who resented the deeply antiliberal sentiments frequently expressed by missionaries. The Redemptorists blamed the hostility they encountered in La Seca on the spread of "Protestant and liberal doctrines" among the local population. At another mission in the province of Burgos in 1900, the missionaries invited the residents to decorate their balconies for the procession held on such occasions. One did so by displaying copies of the newspaper *El Liberal,* behind which he lurked, rifle in hand, ready to fire on the priest should he protest against this act of defiance.[77] Similarly, Francisco Tarín delighted in attacking Freemasonry, the liberal regime, and Protestantism. Indeed, in one extreme sally at Sierra de Gata in the province of Cáceres, where Protestant missionaries were distributing books, he collected hundreds of copies and burned them at high noon in the town square. He then cast the ashes to the winds.[78]

The massive expansion of the religious orders under the Restoration, so often evoked as the most visible sign of a great Catholic revival, proved a mixed blessing. The chaotic nature of the orders' growth meant that even in terms of clerical objectives, much of the effort was dissipated through the inefficient use of personnel. Moreover, the role of the regulars in education, charity, and pastoral work was at least partially counterproductive, for it generated an entirely new set of conflicts and controversies within Spanish society.

77. "Ante un centenario frustrado," p. 142; Cepedal, *El Espino, misionero,* p. 65.

78. Ayala, *Vida documentada,* p. 763.

CHAPTER XI

SPANISH CATHOLICISM, 1875–1930

Father Ramón Sarabia, who crossed the length and breadth of Spain on missionary campaigns between 1902 and 1936, wrote a slim volume on the eve of the Civil War with the provocative title, *Spain . . . Is It Catholic?*[1] Sarabia viewed the state of Spanish Catholicism in his time with pessimism, repeating a motif that, since the first conflicts with liberalism, had existed alongside the more visible triumphalist rhetoric of the "rose legend" that "Spain is Catholic; in Spain everyone is Catholic; Spain is the most Catholic nation in the world."[2] These opposing interpretations arose from a perception widespread among ecclesiastics, namely, that the country would be Catholic or not. There was and could be no middle ground. This highly simplified view, whether in its pessimistic or optimistic version, led to the conclusion that the Church faced a decisive and perhaps final battle for the allegiance of Spaniards.

For the historian seeking to generalize about the condition of Spanish Catholicism, such straightforward assumptions provide little help before an array of ambiguous and often contradictory evidence. On one hand, the centuries-old religious monopoly of Catholicism was never successfully challenged by the appearance of Protestant churches during the nineteenth and early twentieth centuries. As late as 1932, it was claimed that 99.8 percent of the population was nominally

1. Ramón Sarabia, *¿España . . . es católica? Charlas de un misionero* (Madrid, 1939). Although first published towards the close of the Civil War, the book was written in 1936 prior to its outbreak.

2. José Gafo, "La situación religiosa de España," *La Ciencia Tomista* (1927), vol. 35, pp. 186–87. It should be noted that Father Gafo did not agree with this roseate view of Spanish Catholicism. The bishops of the late nineteenth century interpreted the condition of Spanish Catholicism as gloomily as Sarabia did half a century later. According to Bishop Guisasola of Jaén, for example, "true Christian life has suffered a terrible descent in our time." Quoted in Fernando García de Cortázar, "La Iglesia española de la Restauración: definición de objetivos y práctica religiosa," *Letras de Deusto* (1978), vol. 10, no. 16, p. 9.

Catholic.[3] The few shreds of statistical evidence available for the early twentieth century suggest that most parents had their children baptized within two weeks of birth, as the Church desired.[4] Clerical commentators expressed satisfaction with high levels of religious practice in northern areas, notably Galicia, Santander, Navarra, and Old Castile, which constituted a "model of faith and morality."[5] Even in regions where religious observance was low, such as rural Andalucía, the families of agricultural workers kept small statues of the Virgin at home and insisted on baptism for their children.[6] The customs of popular religion, often only tangentially related to the formal liturgy, continued in the region, where pilgrimages, processions, and shrines were identified with local cultures.

On the other hand, the clergy saw clear signs of religious alienation or de-Christianization, as the Church labeled it. Formal observance in the southern countryside attracted only a small minority of the population. "The churches of Andalucía and Extremadura," declared one priest gloomily, "are usually empty in their vast majority, the streets leading to them covered over by grass." Ecclesiastics were also aware of the massive religious absenteeism in the cities, where there were "great nuclei of workers who not only do not practice a religious life, but also hate it."[7]

A Map of Religious Observance

Whether participation in the Church's liturgical life indicates religious commitment, or whether nonparticipation provides concrete evidence of de-Christianization, is by no means certain. Scholars concerned with the question have argued that the very term "de-Christianization" is ambiguous because it suggests a decline from the practices of an idealized society thought to have existed in the past, that "happy epoch" recalled by a bishop of Jaca when Spaniards lived deeply pious and religious lives.[8]

This vision did not correspond to the complex realities of the past even when applied to the era of the alliance between Throne and Altar. Jean Delumeau has argued that Christianization on the eve of the great upheavals that occurred in Europe towards the end of the eighteenth century was "far from being complete."[9] In

3. E. Vargas Zúñiga, "El problema religioso de España," *Razón y Fe* (1935), no. 465, p. 296.

4. Rogelio Duocastella et al., *Sociología religiosa y pastoral de la diócesis de Cartagena (Murcia)* (Barcelona, 1971), chapter 19, p. 1; *Religiosidad y subdesarrollo: estudio sociológico sobre Tierra de Campos* (Madrid and Barcelona, 1971), chapter 6, p. 14.

5. José de los Perales y Gutiérrez, *El problema religioso en España* (Madrid, 1909), p. 92.

6. Jerome Mintz, *The Anarchists of Casas Viejas* (Chicago, 1982), p. 43. A visitor to the southern countryside early in the century noted that virtually all children received baptism in the districts through which he traveled. Rafael Shaw, *Spain from Within* (London, 1910), p. 48.

7. Perales y Gutiérrez, *El problema religioso*, pp. 99, 101.

8. *Crónica del Sínodo Diócesano celebrado en Jaca los días 23, 24 y 25 de agosto de 1899* (Madrid, 1899), p. 19.

9. Jean Delumeau, *Le catholicisme entre Luther et Voltaire* (Paris, 1971), p. 323. See also "Discussion du rapport de M. Rémond sur la déchristianisation au XIXe siècle," *Cahier d'Histoire* (1964), vol. 9, pp. 89–119.

Spain as elsewhere in Catholic Europe following the Council of Trent, the Church made progress, inculcating a basic knowledge of doctrine among the population, at least in some regions. A study of evangelizing efforts in New Castile between 1540 and 1650 has shown that the Church enjoyed some success in spreading its message and securing a commitment to observance in town and country.[10] But even before the alliance between the Church and absolute monarchy came to an end, there were signs in large cities, where the vigilance of the civil and ecclesiastical authorities was less effective, that some individuals evaded their religious obligations. In the Madrid of the 1780s, residents wishing to escape from the compulsory Easter communion obligation could easily do so by purchasing the certificates of compliance demanded by the clergy from the city's prostitutes, who did a brisk trade selling them to the public.[11]

High levels of religious observance during the seventeenth and eighteenth centuries represented in part a manifestation of the power of the established Church backed by the authority of the Crown, rather than an enduring commitment of faith on the part of all those attending services—what Delumeau has called a religious "civilization of habit."[12] The impact of political revolutions and capitalist economic change during the nineteenth century subjected this once stable religious world to severe strains.

The triumph of liberalism meant the disappearance of the Inquisition, for centuries the kingdom's implacable guardian of orthodoxy, and the end of sustained official persecution of religious dissenters, although episodic harassment continued. The quickening pace of urban growth after 1850 made it difficult for the Church to impose religious observance on city populations. The Catalan priest Josep Gatell, recalling Barcelona at mid-century, believed that it was still "a Christian town" in which "our churches were filled with men in their workers' shirts." But "the day arrived when this people, who until then appeared Catholic, abandoned religious practices little by little." The decline in observance was also noted by the city's bishop in 1859: "Who can doubt that people from all parts of the world, of all religions . . . flow to the great centers of manufacturing and commerce, and communicate . . . their religious indifference?" Of his own diocese, he remarked, "The faith has grown languid, . . . religious sentiment has grown weak."[13] Churchmen interpreted these developments as the effect of diverse "corrupting"

10. Jean Dedieu, "'Christianisation' en Nouvelle Castille: catéchisme, communion et confirmation dans l'archevêché de Tolede, 1540–1650," *Mélanges de la Casa de Velázquez* (1979), vol. 15, p. 277; Sara T. Nalle, *God in La Mancha: Religious Reform and the People of Cuenca, 1500–1650* (Baltimore, 1992), pp. 126–33.

11. Joseph Townsend, *A Journey through Spain in the years 1786 and 1787* (3 vols., London, 1791), vol. 2, p. 149.

12. Delumeau, *Le catholicisme entre Luther et Voltaire*, p. 308.

13. Quoted in Josep Benet and Casimir Martí, *Barcelona a mitjan segle XIX: el moviment obrer durant el Bienni Progressista, 1854–1856* (2 vols., Barcelona, 1976), vol. 1, pp. 203–6; *La Revista Católica* (1858), pp. 393, 397.

forces, namely, liberalism, secularization, and dislocating economic changes. But it is by no means certain that the decline in observance noted in some cities around the middle of the nineteenth century meant that many who once possessed a deep religious faith now abandoned it under the influence of what ecclesiastics saw as a conspiracy against religion. It may have represented a simpler development, the collapse of the old religious "civilization of habit" formerly given force by the mechanisms of social control employed by Throne and Altar.

The Church saw attendance at Sunday Mass, the fulfillment of the Easter communion obligation, and participation in other religious services as the touchstones that determined the presence or absence of faith. But, as Delumeau has cautioned, external conformity with the clergy's demands for regular church attendance does not necessarily signify the existence or absence of belief. Faith and the individual beliefs on which it rests are highly personal, matters of individual conscience ultimately unknowable. Community pressure and patterns of sociability, particularly in rural societies, as well as other causes can influence patterns of religious practice either favorably or unfavorably.[14]

Within these limitations, the study of observance provides one means among many to assess the ability of the Church to maintain the allegiance of the population, whatever the state of individual motivations. The school of French social historians and historical sociologists influenced by Gabriel Le Bras and Fernand Boulard has illuminated aspects of Catholicism in France through the analysis of religious observance based on statistical analysis of attendance at Sunday Mass and the like. Students of the Spanish Church are less fortunate, given the lack of reliable data for the period before the Civil War. Until further research is carried out, the material available—fragmentary statistics and the observations of clerics deeply concerned with de-Christianization—permits only tentative conclusions.

There is reasonable evidence that the regional character of Spanish Catholicism was already in place by the mid-nineteenth century. A map based on seminary recruitment in 1854 already shows an unmistakable division between north and south. With the exception of Valencia, dioceses with the largest number of seminarians were concentrated in Old Castile, León, and Navarra and, to a lesser extent, in rural Catalonia. The sees with the worst recruiting records were located in Extremadura, Andalucía, and La Mancha.[15] This picture is confirmed by the results of the vast petition campaign organized in 1869 to protest the introduction of religious liberty. Despite government hostility, nearly 3 million persons signed the document of protest. The geographic distribution of signatures is revealing. With the exception of Alicante, the provinces south of the Guadarrama mountains fur-

14. Delumeau, *Le catholicisme entre Luther et Voltaire*, pp. 325–26; Susan Tax Freeman, "Faith and Fashion in Spanish Religion: Notes on the Observation of Observance," *Peasant Studies* (1978), vol. 7, no. 2, pp. 101–22, provides a social anthropologist's view of the question.

15. J. Vicens Vives et al., *Historia de España y América* (5 vols., Barcelona, 1961), vol. 5, p. 150.

nished fewer signatures than did their northern counterparts. At the bottom of the list stood Albacete and Málaga, at the top, Ávila, Salamanca, Valladolid, Burgos, Lugo, La Coruña, Orense, Santander, the Basque Provinces, Aragón, Teruel, and Castellón.[16]

The results of the campaign provide a general view of regional responsiveness to a coordinated and distinctly modern campaign organized by the Church and its supporters. They do not furnish information on levels of support within individual provinces, nor do they suggest either the causes or the chronology behind the regional divisions of Spanish Catholicism. The poor showing of the southern provinces, as well as anticlerical incidents in the region following the revolution of 1868, indicate that the Church was on the defensive. By the end of the nineteenth century, the clergy saw the religious situation of the south as catastrophic. The bishop of Málaga concluded, after a pastoral visit to the village of Villanueva del Rosario in 1886, that "indifference and even apostasy had spread among the unfortunate inhabitants," many of whom refused to be married in the Church. Similarly, Father Francisco de Tarín has left an account that constitutes nothing less than an atlas of de-Christianization. He found Linares "a focus of corruption and perversion"; Torredonjimeno (Jaén), "a town dominated by religious indifference"; Loja, "a center of impiety, spiritualism and Freemasonry"; El Coronil (Seville), "a town which finds itself in a sad state of indifference"; and Las Cabezas de San Juan, a place whose people had "frozen hearts, colder even than marble."[17]

Clerical perceptions had not changed appreciably when Ramón Sarabia began a six-year period of missionary activity in the south in 1912. Sarabia began his evangelizing career in 1902 in La Rioja. He spent much of the following decade preaching in the cities, towns, and villages of Asturias, Old Castile, and Santander. Although he believed that the practice of religion was far from ideal in what he saw as the Catholic heartland of the nation, he was staggered by the conditions he encountered when he moved southward. In February 1913 he began a mission at Azuaga (Extremadura). Of its population of eighteen thousand, ten men and two hundred women attended Sunday Mass regularly; of these, no more than two dozen fulfilled the Easter communion obligation. At Llerena, with a population of nine thousand composed largely of impoverished day workers employed on the estates of the district, he found that only eight hundred attended Sunday Mass. In his view, the religious condition of Andalucía, Extremadura, and La Mancha was as

16. The following sample illustrates the regional disparity in responses. The figure in parentheses represents the total population of the province according to the census of 1860: Ávila, 37,169 (168,773); Guipúzcoa, 77,513 (162,547); Santander, 73,333 (219,996); Madrid, 34,085 (489,332); Cádiz, 39,565 (401,700); Huelva, 15,636 (176,226); Albacete, 10,542 (206,099); Seville, 59,625 (473,920); Jaén, 39,807 (362,466). This information is drawn from a summary of the petition results in *La Cruz* (1869), p. 495.

17. *Boletín Oficial Eclesiástico del Obispado de Málaga* (Málaga, 1887), pp. 42–47; quoted in Pedro María de Ayala, *Vida documentada del Siervo de Dios P. Francisco Paula Tarín de la Compañía de Jesús* (Seville, 1951), pp. 308, 468, 520, 576, 579–80, 780.

disastrous as ever on the eve of the Civil War. "You must live day after day in these overgrown villages of fifteen or twenty thousand souls to feel the coldness of these hearts, which for all practical purposes live without any kind of religion."[18]

Sarabia saw the characteristics of southern Catholicism in a level of observance that fell as low as 5 percent in many localities, in the massive abstention of men from participation in religious activities, and in the widespread ignorance of the minimal doctrinal knowledge contained in the catechism. He once claimed that 80 percent of the population of Extremadura did not know the words of basic prayers such as the "Our Father."[19] Other clerical observers echoed Sarabia's laments about the religious condition of the south. A survey of the Easter communion duty in the Córdoba diocese carried out in 1918 showed that of the more than 400,000 persons required to fulfill it, 278,000 did not do so.[20] There is no reason to doubt the observations of Sarabia and other clerics, although they allow for little precision in the study of levels of practice. Was there, for example, a higher level of observance in southern cities compared with the countryside?[21] Were there differences in practice between the *latifundio* areas and the poorer hill districts of the region?

The perception among churchmen that the rural population of the south lived "in nearly complete paganism" reflected their catastrophic fear of Catholic Spain being overtaken by de-Christianization, an apprehension reinforced by the spread of anarchism and socialism in the region during the late nineteenth and early twentieth centuries.[22] But was this perception accurate? How can one reconcile the insistence of the rural population on baptism for its children and the popularity of shrines and local pilgrimages with the picture of utter religious desolation painted by clerical observers? Even Father Perales y Gutiérrez, a strong advocate of the de-Christianization thesis, had to admit that in the provinces of Málaga, Seville, and Granada there were centers of "vital Catholicism."[23]

Research on the question of de-Christianization has called attention to the phenomenon of the "sociology of unbelief" in the form of "secular religions" in which strong residues of a "sacred" past persist in new forms.[24] In a pioneering work on

18. Quoted in Pedro R. Santidrián, *El Padre Sarabia escribe su historia, 1875–1958: medio siglo de misiones en España* (Madrid, 1963), pp. 152, 162, 166; Sarabia, *¿España . . . es católica?*, pp. 188, 37.

19. Sarabia, *¿España . . . es católica?*, p. 196.

20. *Ilustración del Clero* (1918), p. 81.

21. Sociological surveys carried out during the later years of the Franco regime show a higher incidence of practice in the cities of Andalucía compared with the countryside. Whether this pattern existed prior to the widespread application in Spain of sociological methods to the study of religious practice beginning in the 1950s is, however, uncertain. José Cazorla, "Religiosidad y estructura social en Andalucía: la práctica religiosa," *Problemas de estratificación social en España* (Madrid, 1973), p. 183.

22. Perales y Gutiérrez, *El problema religioso*, p. 98. Father Sarabia, for example, attributed, at least in part, the religious indifference of Azuaga to "a half dozen impious Socialists and revolutionaries" who controlled the municipal government. Santidrián, *El Padre Sarabia*, p. 152.

23. Perales y Gutiérrez, *El problema religioso*, p. 98.

24. Fernand Boulard, *Matériaux pour l'histoire religieuse du peuple français XIXe–XXe siècles* (Paris, 1982), p. 36.

the spread of anarchism in Córdoba province during the late nineteenth and early twentieth centuries, Juan Díaz del Moral explained the nearly evangelical intensity of the movement as a secular manifestation of the religious millenarianism that had swept through the southern countryside in periodic waves over the centuries.[25] Although modern scholarship has questioned this religious interpretation, it may still have some validity.[26] It is difficult to see the development of rural anarchism as an entirely new phenomenon disconnected from a traditional community culture in which sacred symbols and the practices of popular religion continued whether or not the population attended church services.

These mixed signals suggest that the black-and-white model of either orthodox Catholic piety or total unbelief developed by the clergy oversimplified a more complex situation. It is more likely, as modern religious sociology has suggested, that a model of religiosity based on a wide spectrum, ranging from complete acceptance of religion as defined by the Church to the other pole of atheism, with innumerable gradations in between, comes closer to reality.

Such an interpretation would have provided scant comfort to the Church, which laid down specific obligations expected of every Catholic. In these terms, the religious condition of the south offered little consolation. But the historic causes of widespread noncompliance with clerical demands for a certain level of observance are by no means clear. The institutional weakness of the southern Church may have been a contributing factor. A parochial infrastructure based on extremely large parishes staffed by priests who were often less than vigorous in their pastoral activities can scarcely have helped the Church to communicate its message effectively. Economic and social conditions in the southern estate lands and the corresponding appeal of radical social doctrines also contributed to the spread of religious indifference. Astute clerical observers were aware of the alienation associated with oppressive social conditions. It was scarcely surprising, said one, that the inhabitants of the countryside were indifferent to religion: "The latifundio exhausts their energies, spends their lives, and drains their blood."[27] Yet the Church had no real alternative to offer the impoverished southern rural masses.

There also may have been historical causes rooted in the distant past to account for low levels of observance in the south. Delumeau has maintained that one cannot refer to de-Christianization without establishing the extent of Christianization

25. Juan Díaz del Moral, *Historia de las agitaciones campesinas andaluzas* (2d ed., Madrid, 1967).

26. Temma Kaplan has argued against Díaz del Moral's interpretation on the grounds that it is both simplistic and mechanistic. She argues that far from being millenarian, southern anarchism was a highly rational response to oppressive social and economic conditions. *Anarchists of Andalusia, 1868–1903* (Princeton, 1977), pp. 208–10. Martha Grace Duncan has maintained, however, that this revisionist approach shows "a bias against millenarianism, reflecting an assumption that the religious and the secular, the emotional and the rational, are mutually exclusive." "Spanish Anarchism Refracted: Theme and Image in the Millenarian and Revisionist Literature," *Journal of Contemporary History* (1988), vol. 23, no. 3, p. 343.

27. Perales y Gutiérrez, *El problema religioso*, p. 98.

in the first place. Or, as Father Sarabia put the question with respect to the rural population of the south, "What has been done to win these souls over the years, over the centuries? Nothing or next to nothing."[28] Unfortunately, little is known about the success or failure of the Church to impose its definition of religious belief and practice over the centuries. One can only hazard the hypothesis that southern Spain may have been less successfully evangelized than the highly observant regions of the north.

Even here the historian must proceed with caution. The situation in New Castile, where the Church enjoyed some success in its Christianizing efforts during the sixteenth and seventeenth centuries, appeared effectively de-Christianized to Father Sarabia, who conducted missions in the region between 1909 and 1912. He found the village of Mora de Toledo to have lived "in religious indifference for many years, many centuries." Few towns disturbed him more than Alcalá de Henares. Only three hundred of its twelve thousand inhabitants attended Sunday Mass regularly. The mission was not a success, although in a curious footnote to history, one young man participating in the services was Manuel Azaña, a future president of the Second Republic.[29] Sarabia's observations of low levels of practice in the region by the early twentieth century are undoubtedly accurate. But it is not clear why a decline in observance occurred or when it began.

The clergy derived satisfaction from the high levels of religious practice seen in the peasant regions of northern Spain, where the existence of strong village communities enjoying access to land, if not always in ideal conditions, provided the social glue that was generally absent in the south. The Church, moreover, was closer to the population as a result of the dense infrastructure of rural parishes centered on the small village. In these regions of "traditional and honest Christianity," the population continued to attend religious services in large numbers. Father Sarabia was delighted, for example, with the missions that he preached during the autumn of 1903 in the villages of Burgos, Palencia, and Santander, where "the authentic Christian spirit is lived." On a later campaign in La Montaña de Santander, he marveled at the devotion of the country people who traveled daily to the local parish church for the services. "It was an admirable spectacle to see how they came from all points in the parish . . . how the enthusiasm kept growing; entire villages arrived in the morning, lunched in the meadows and returned home in the evening."[30]

Even Sarabia perceived that the simple dichotomy of a religious north and a de-Christianized south disguised a more complex situation. He noted that observance in some of the provincial capitals of the Catholic heartland—Burgos, Salamanca, and Ávila—was significantly lower than in the countryside. He realized too that

28. Quoted in Santidrián, *El Padre Sarabia*, p. 162.
29. Ibid., pp. 136–37, 148.
30. Ibid., pp. 141, 138.

practice was declining to low levels in towns affected by economic development. During his first mission campaign in 1903 in the small towns and villages of the Asturian mountains, where coal mining had developed over the preceding decades, he found the towns of Soto de Agués, Ladines, and Oviñana still observant, while in others, such as the mining center of Sama de Langreo, "there were not a few enemies of the mission." He received a better reception in the nearby town of La Felguera, where many miners and their families attended the services. On the eve of the Civil War, he recalled nostalgically that "in those times many miners, sons of Asturias, still conserved the faith with fervor and in its entirety," a situation that had changed dramatically for the worse, he believed, by 1936.[31]

Sarabia concluded, as did many commentators on pastoral questions, that "those living in great industrial centers live without religion."[32] In terms of formal religious practice, he was correct. The advance of urbanization and industrialization created conditions that did not encourage observance among those uprooted from rural villages and small towns. The community pressures that in some regions encouraged regular church attendance were absent in the city. Poorly educated and impoverished in a new and unforgiving social milieu, the new immigrants consumed their energies in a brutal struggle for survival. They were, said Father Herranz Establés of the inhabitants of his Madrid parish, "people . . . atomized socially, without any structure, social, civil or religious. . . . The struggle for life absorbs them; their singular and precarious condition isolates them; they scarcely know one another."[33] He was not surprised that they were religiously indifferent. "If you ask many of these people if there is a God, with a shrug of the shoulders they say that they have heard nothing of this." Even Ramón Sarabia was at a loss for words when he asked a fifteen-year-old worker in the mines near Almería if he had ever heard of Jesus Christ. "Jesus Christ," the youth replied. "Look, Father, I do not know this gentleman. I have never seen him in these mines."[34]

Clerical opinion had long viewed the impact of the city on religious practice with unease, but it was aware that urban expansion created an entirely new set of pastoral problems. There is little statistical evidence to indicate how rapidly observance in the cities declined, but the little available suggests that the process be-

31. Ibid., pp. 101–5; Sarabia, *¿España . . . es católica?*, pp. 330, 337. Adrian Shubert, in a study on the mining society of Asturias before 1914, has shown that during the late nineteenth and early twentieth centuries, miners had not yet formed an industrial proletariat. Many were "obreros mixtos" who continued working the land while employed in the mines. "The Social Origins of Labour Militancy in Asturias: 1860–1914," *European Studies Review* (1982), vol. 12, pp. 167–85. This mixed economy gave the agriculturalist-miner a fragile independence and may have allowed for the preservation of traditional values such as those observed by Ramón Sarabia early in the century. The later radicalization of the workers, as they became totally dependent on the mines, may account for his pessimistic assessment on the eve of the Civil War.

32. Sarabia, *¿España . . . es católica?*, p. 337.

33. Hilario Herranz Establés, *El párroco y la parroquia en los tiempos presentes* (Barcelona, 1923), pp. 318–19.

34. Ibid.; Sarabia, *¿España . . . es católica?*, p. 188.

gan early. Already by the late 1850s, a Barcelona parish priest noted that only one-third of his parishioners were fulfilling the Easter communion obligation. During this period of expansion in the city's textile industry, the ecclesiastical authorities became increasingly concerned with signs of declining religiosity. Barcelona was filled, claimed Bishop Costa y Borrás in 1857, with "Spaniards and foreigners of every language with diverse customs whose presence carries errors and prejudices against religion." Similarly, in Logroño, which experienced modest economic development during the later nineteenth century, the percentage of individuals failing the religious test of the obligatory Easter communion rose from 6.68 percent in 1860 to 57.8 percent in 1890, with the greatest loss occurring after 1872.[35]

The clergy saw the religious condition of the country's two largest cities in the bleakest light. For Father Herranz Establés, familiar with the circumstances existing in the capital's working-class suburbs, the situation had reached a point of desperation by the early twentieth century. It had not improved appreciably on the eve of the Civil War, according to the Jesuit Francisco Peiró. He noted that only 7 percent of the eighty thousand inhabitants of the Madrid parish of San Ramón (Vallecas) attended Sunday Mass; only 6 percent fulfilled the Easter duty; and 20 percent chose to be married in civil rather than religious ceremonies. Of those married in the Church, 40 percent did not know the words of the "Our Father." For Peiró, it was in Madrid, Barcelona, Seville, and Bilbao that "great contingents of the population living in complete paganism are to be found."[36]

To what extent low levels of observance among the urban lower classes represented complete religious alienation is difficult to establish, given the inadequate state of research on the question. But fragmentary evidence suggests that it may have been far deeper than was the case in the southern countryside. Less than half of the dying in the parish of San José in the Catalan industrial town of Mataró received the last rites in 1900, a proportion that fell even lower by the eve of the Civil War, when only one-third did so. In Málaga between 1900 and 1920, the proportion of the dying receiving the last sacraments moved between 20 percent and 30 percent, in contrast to the 90 percent who received them in the Old Castilian region of the Tierra de Campos. The statistics gathered by Father Peiró for the parish of San Ramón also show that 25 percent of its children were unbaptized.[37] Given the transcendent importance attached by the clergy to the last rites and baptism,

35. Casimir Martí, *L'Església de Barcelona, 1850–1857* (2 vols., Barcelona, 1984), vol. 2, p. 336; M. Sáez de Ocariz y Ruiz de Azúa, "El cumplimiento pascual en la ciudad de Logroño a lo largo del siglo XIX," *Berceo* (1965), no. 76, pp. 275–79.

36. Herranz Establés, *El párroco y la parroquia*, p. 275; Francisco Peiró, *El problema religioso-social en España* (2d ed., Madrid, 1936), p. 14.

37. Rogelio Duocastella, *Mataró 1955: estudio de sociología religiosa sobre una ciudad industrial española* (Barcelona, 1961), p. 290; Duocastella et al., *El fenómeno religioso y sus condicionamientos socioculturales: estudio socio-religioso de la diócesis de Málaga* (Málaga, 1972), p. 172; Duocastella et al., *Religiosidad y subdesarrollo . . . Tierra de Campos*, chapter 6, p. 21.

the Church clearly faced more than a simple crisis of nonobservance among urban working-class populations.

This may help explain the attraction that socialism and anarcho-syndicalism exercised over the urban working class. There was little likelihood that the religious component of the traditional popular culture of the small rural community could have survived among the uprooted living in the new urban poverty associated with capitalist economic change. Socialism and anarcho-syndicalism represented alternate ideologies that displaced Catholicism. But they represented something entirely new, owing little to a popular culture suffused with religion. This disconnection between the beliefs and practices of the Church and a secular, working-class culture in process of formation may partially account for signs of religious alienation and the sometimes violent hostility directed against the Church by urban workers.

Further research into levels of observance will reveal a more complex pattern than has been described above. But in general terms the outline is clear; high levels of practice in the regions dominated by small peasant holdings and a strong community sense in which religion played an essential part; low levels in the southern countryside and among the urban lower classes. The Church held its own among the conservative bourgeoisie of the cities. Its hold over the urban middle classes imprinted Spanish Catholicism with a distinctive character. Although clerics often extolled the religiosity of those groups that practiced regularly, they did not offer a solid base on which a successful effort at re-Christianization could be launched. The peasant districts of Old Castile, León, Navarra, the Basque Provinces, Santander, Asturias, Galicia, and Aragón, where attendance remained high, had already begun to suffer the dislocating effects of rural depopulation and economic marginalization that could not have created a surge in religious vitality capable of being translated to regions where very different socioeconomic conditions prevailed. The attachment of the urban bourgeoisie to the Church was linked, moreover, to a vague political ideology that regarded religion as a bulwark of the social order. In these circumstances, there was little possibility that the Church could develop a strategy capable of transcending class divisions. Indeed, the opposite proved to be the case.

The Dominance of Ultramontane Piety

There is a tendency to interpret the obligations demanded of the faithful by the Church as a fixed body of custom and practice unchanged over the centuries. But recent scholarship has shown that the forms of institutional Catholic piety changed significantly during the centuries following the Council of Trent.[38] Con-

38. Louis Chatellier, *L'Europe des dévots* (Paris, 1987), pp. 163–64.

fronted with what it regarded as dangerous political philosophies, the rapid progress of secularization, and the social dislocation produced by economic change, the Spanish Church not only struggled to maintain its official privileges; it also adapted its religious strategy to meet challenges deemed as threatening as any in the past. This strategy's components had existed earlier, but during the nineteenth century they came together in a specific configuration that students of modern ecclesiastical history have called ultramontane piety.[39]

It overlapped with an older tradition of popular religion that took the form of a rich and luxuriant variety of pious practices associated with a strong sense of communal identity. Although popular religion owed something to the encouragement of the institutional Church, it was essentially a grassroots movement that sought to give positive meaning to the harsh facts of fragile human existence. Ultramontane piety rested on a profoundly defensive mentality, as the Church universal sought to create throughout the Catholic world a standardized religious culture controlled by the clergy. Above all, it attempted to protect the faithful against the corrosive impact of secular intellectual currents, to form "a people of saints" isolated from the world, in contrast to the earthy realism characteristic of popular religion.[40]

The pastoral letters of the Spanish hierarchy during the Restoration emphasized "the defects and disorders of society."[41] In an address to the diocesan synod of Jaca in 1899, the bishop described in abundant detail contemporary evils that had converted Spain into "an immense theater in which the most repugnant scenes of brazen immorality seek to break . . . the barriers that reason and religion impose." In these depressing conditions, the Church had to follow a single-minded course of erecting "a dike" against the corruption that surrounded it by recalling "the faithful to the saving truths of religion."[42]

The materials composing the dike were many. First and foremost, the Church demanded participation in the external acts of the cult that separated good Catholics from those contaminated by secular evils.[43] The Spanish Church emphasized the "organization for the cult" as its primary responsibility and devoted "practically all its energies to this end."[44] The obligation to attend Sunday Mass was

39. Gérard Cholvy and Yves-Marie Hilaire, *Histoire religieuse de la France contemporaine* (2 vols., Toulouse, 1985), vol. 1, chapter 5; Yves-Marie Hilaire, *Une chrétienté au XIXe siècle? La vie religieuse des populations du diocèse d'Arras, 1840–1914* (2 vols., Villeneuve d'Asoq, 1977), vol. 1, pp. 408–9.

40. Ibid.

41. García de Cortázar, "La Iglesia española de la Restauración," p. 24.

42. *Crónica del Sínodo Diocesano celebrado en Jaca,* pp. 17–18.

43. The synod of Jaca defined the obligations of the faithful in these terms: "to hear a complete Mass on every Sunday and holy day of obligation, . . . to receive communion during the Easter time." Ibid., p. 80.

44. Francisco Carballo and Alfonso Magariños, *La Iglesia en la Galicia contemporánea: análisis histórico y teológico del periodo 1931–1936, II República* (Madrid, 1978), p. 321. Similarly, Cardinal Tarancón recalled that in his early career as a priest during the 1920s, "the most important aspect of pastoral work . . . was the cult." Vicente Enrique y Tarancón, *Recuerdos de juventud* (Barcelona, 1984), p. 80.

so grave, according to the diocesan synod of Jaca, that those failing to assist were guilty of nothing less than "criminal conduct."[45]

After the turn of the century, pastoral commentators influenced by a new movement of liturgical reform promoted by the papacy argued that mere attendance at Sunday Mass was insufficient. The Mass, argued Father José Gafo, must serve as "a necessary exteriorization of faith" based on an inner spiritual life. He questioned whether many attending the sacred liturgy possessed it or were merely participating in "a mimicry without sense even to the point of guilty and monstrous hypocrisy." The conduct of congregations appeared far from edifying to another pastoral critic, who observed that some of the faithful "rushed to prostrate themselves before the statue of Saint Expeditious without paying the slightest attention to what was taking place before the tabernacle," while others said their rosaries or read devotional manuals "without giving attention . . . to the Holy Sacrifice." For ecclesiastical commentators influenced by the liturgical reform encouraged by Pope Pius X, such conduct seemed a manifestation of a "calamitous individualism for Christian life."[46]

Pastoral critics were correct in their assumption that the motives of those attending Mass were diverse, although how accurate they were in their general indictment is impossible to establish. But their harsh judgment was scarcely historical. During the nineteenth century, the Spanish Church developed an approach to the cult that was "profoundly individualist." Saint Antonio Claret, author of the most popular book in the history of Spanish devotional writing, stressed the Mass as a religious service designed for the spiritual improvement of the individual unrelated to the "community of believers."[47]

The Church gloried in the celebration of the cult, from great cathedral to lowly parish, with all the pomp and circumstance allowed by economic circumstances. A visitor to the cathedral of Seville in 1886 marveled at the grandeur of the Christmas midnight Mass, a dazzling "theatrical display" filled with illumination, organ and orchestral music, and magnificently adorned vestments.[48] The limited finan-

45. *Crónica del Sínodo Diocesano celebrado en Jaca*, p. 87.

46. Gafo, "La situación religiosa," p. 376; "La vida parroquial y la sagrada liturgia," *Revista Eclesiástica* (1915), p. 196. This journal published an even more scathing indictment in the previous year: "Most of those present [at Mass] are there to see and be seen; they assist at the Holy Sacrifice with wandering eyes; they bless themselves many times and are bored for the rest of the time, . . . most of them are there for social reasons or because their parents make them go." *Revista Eclesiástica* (1914), p. 145.

47. García de Cortázar, "La Iglesia española de la Restauración," p. 27; Martí, *L'Església de Barcelona*, vol. 2, pp. 359, 360.

48. Henry M. Field, *Old Spain and New Spain* (New York, 1888), pp. 269–71. See the similar comments of Havelock Ellis, who attended a Lenten service in the same cathedral many years later. *The Soul of Spain* (Boston and New York, 1914), p. 367. During the first two decades of the century, the use of orchestras and operatic-style music in services provoked the ire of liturgical reformers who complained of "the deplorable state . . . of the modern Spanish repertory of sacred music." The Church in Catalonia succeeded in introducing Gregorian chant into many parishes of the region after the turn of the century. *Crónica del Segundo Congreso Nacional de Música Sagrada* (Seville, 1909), p. 22.

cial resources assigned to the Church by the government were insufficient to defray the cost of these liturgical extravaganzas. Here too, the support of the urban bourgeoisie proved indispensable. Tomás Heredia, scion of a wealthy commercial and industrial family in Málaga, donated so generously to the cathedral chapter for its liturgical services during the 1880s and 1890s that the grateful canons assigned him a seat in the capitular stalls.[49] Emphasis on the liturgy took precedence over pastoral instruction based on the sermon or homily. Although bishops exalted preaching as a means of "raising sinners from the slime" as they journeyed "on the road to perdition," and demanded that parish priests preach on every Sunday and holy day of obligation, the clergy frequently ignored their admonitions.[50] Ramón Sarabia recalled that during the 1880s in his native town of Polo de Lena (Asturias), the parish priest preached only twice a year. As late as the early 1930s, in a flourishing urban parish of Vinaroz (Castellón), only one sermon was preached among several Sunday Masses.[51]

Another characteristic of ultramontane piety took the form of an offensive in favor of frequent communion. Theological debate had raged for centuries over the desirability and validity of this practice. The papacy repeatedly threw its weight behind advocates of frequent communion against theological rigorists, associated with seventeenth- and eighteenth-century Jansenism, who argued that the sacrament must be approached only in a state of total repentance and, therefore, received infrequently. Pius X ended the debate in (1905) by urging the faithful to receive communion often. The Spanish hierarchy had long endorsed the papal position. The faithful were exhorted by bishops and parish priests to receive the sacrament as frequently as possible. Priests saw the number of communions as further testimony to religious commitment by the population. Indeed, they often kept detailed communion statistics, rather like a sports team recording attendance as an indication of success. In 1912, for instance, the Jesuits reported proudly that 240,000 communions had been distributed in their Madrid church alone.[52]

Clerical pressure for frequent reception of the Eucharist went beyond the historic obligation to receive communion at least once a year. There is evidence that clerical exhortations helped increase the frequency of communion in urban centers.[53] But the Church was less successful in persuading the rural population to follow its counsel even in areas known for high levels of observance. Ramón Sarabia

49. Elías de Mateo Avilés, *Piedades e impiedades de los malagueños en el siglo XIX: una aproximación a la religiosidad española contemporánea* (Málaga, 1987), p. 42.

50. *Constituciones sinodales de la diócesis de Málaga que hizo y ordenó su obispo Excmo. e Ilmo. Señor Dr. D. Juan Muñoz Herrera en el sínodo que celebró el XXVI de diciembre de MCMIX* (Málaga, 1910), p. 107.

51. Santidrián, *El Padre Sarabia escribe su historia*, p. 31; Enrique y Tarancón, *Recuerdos de juventud*, p. 70.

52. Manuel Cadenas and Enrique del Portillo, *La provincia de Toledo de la Compañía de Jesús, 1880–1914* (Madrid, 1916), pp. 144–45.

53. Between 1907 and 1912 the number of communions distributed in the Jesuit church of Madrid increased by over one hundred thousand. Ibid.

recalled that in his native parish few received communion during the early Restoration, except for "two poor women" who were regarded as slightly eccentric for indulging in the practice. The old traditions of rural Spain persisted despite the clergy's determined efforts. As late as 1912, exasperation was expressed over "the ancient and detestable custom" prevailing in certain villages following the end of the Easter season, when "the confessional was carried . . . to the sacristy, there to remain, a useless piece of furniture, until next year."[54]

Frequent communion carried with it the corresponding necessity for periodic confession, an obligation that met with considerable resistance. Alleged abuses of the confessional became the stock-in-trade of an abundant literature highly critical of the Church's influence in Spanish society.[55] The role of the priest as confessor had long been regarded with suspicion by some liberals who saw the confessional as an instrument used by the clergy to promote its political views. Well into the twentieth century, priests regarded political questions as a proper subject for confession. The *Revista Eclesiástica,* a journal published for the guidance of the parochial clergy, always contained a section devoted to answering the queries of its clerical readers. "Has the individual sinned mortally," asked a priest, "who has voted either Liberal or Conservative when there were antiliberal Catholic candidates?" a question posed to the journal in many different variants over the years.[56] To what extent the use of the confessional as a mechanism of political influence alienated some from participating in what the Church regarded as an essential sacramental rite cannot be determined. But neither can its effect be discounted.

Resistance to confession ran deep for other reasons. In the southern estate lands, the vast majority of the inhabitants refused to confess, a circumstance attributed variously to their aversion to losing the few shreds of privacy that remained to them in a closed rural community and to the suspicions directed against parish priests as a result of hearing the confessions of women.[57] Nor was opposition to confession confined to the south. "I? Confess to a priest?" said one young northern fisherman. "Never! I confess to God and my mother, and I want no priest to come between me and God."[58]

The Church's preoccupation with conformity to its demands for observance in

54. Remigo Vilariño, "La comunión frecuente," *Sal Terrae* (1912), pp. 148–49. As late as the early 1960s, villagers in the Old Castilian town of Valdemora received communion only once a year. Susan Tax Freeman, *Neighbors: The Social Contract in a Castilian Hamlet* (Chicago, 1970), p. 97.

55. Stephen Haliczer, *Sexuality in the Confessional: A Sacrament Profaned* (New York and Oxford, 1996), pp. 183–203.

56. "Casos y consultas," *Revista Eclesiástica* (1911), p. 313. In the same year, another reader asked whether Prime Minister Canalejas had not incurred excommunication because of the religious policies of his government. Ibid., p. 413.

57. Mintz, *The Anarchists of Casas Viejas,* p. 69. In a study of the town of Monteros (Andalucía), the social anthropologist Stanley Brandes has argued that in the view of the male population, "priests themselves are considered to be highly sexual beings who use their powerful position to exploit women sexually." *Metaphors of Masculinity: Sex and Status in Andalusian Folklore* (Philadelphia, 1980), p. 184.

58. Shaw, *Spain from Within,* p. 43.

the form of attendance at Sunday Mass, frequent communion, and confession represented a significant expansion of what it expected of those wishing to be regarded as Catholics in good standing. The diocesan synod of Jaca made this clear by requiring that all desiring to confess should be examined at least once a year in Christian doctrine. Priests were forbidden to hear the confession of anyone who could not produce a certificate testifying to successful completion of the exam.[59] This was a strategy designed for those already practicing their faith, and for those living in rural communities who had to live with the threat of not receiving burial in the village cemetery should they die "without being reconciled with the Catholic Church."[60] Even at that, it was not an entirely successful strategy, given the lack of attention accorded to the spiritual dimension of observance, which led to the development of a religion of practice but not of belief, according to one student of religiosity.[61]

Some positive initiatives were undertaken, especially in Catalonia. Clerics prominent in the rediscovery of the literary and artistic glories of the Catalan past, notably Bishop Torras i Bages and Canon Jaume Collell, wished to see the emergence of a deeply conservative and Catholic Catalonia. They argued the sensible point that the Church must rely on the language of the people if it hoped to communicate its message successfully. In his celebrated work, *La tradició catalana* (1892), Torras i Bages stressed the necessity of preaching in Catalan, for "the most numerous class and the one most deserving of attention in our evangelical ministry is the people, and it is certain that it does not understand Castilian or comprehends it poorly."[62] Efforts to introduce Catalan in sermons and homilies were not universally welcomed. In 1900, Bishop Morgades of Barcelona felt compelled to issue a pastoral letter defending the use of Catalan against those "who direct recriminations against the inhabitants of non-Castilian speaking regions." But the Church successfully introduced Catalan into services where canon law permitted and undertook ambitious propaganda efforts in the language.

In general, the Church produced a formula of observance with a strong dose of social compulsion that appealed primarily to the Catholic bourgeoisie of the cities. Even the essential rites of baptism, marriage, and burial were dispensed in accordance with social and financial status. In the diocese of Málaga towards the end of the nineteenth century, there were six categories of baptismal ceremonies. Those willing to pay the substantial fee of 120 pesetas received an elaborate service conducted by a priest attired in full liturgical dress, the ceremony taking place in a richly adorned chapel illuminated by eighty-six candles, with an organist and choir

59. *Crónica del Sínodo Diocesano*, p. 88.

60. Ibid., p. 87.

61. García de Cortázar, "La Iglesia española de la Restauración," p. 34.

62. J. Torras i Bages, *La tradició catalana* (1892), in *Obres completes* (Barcelona, 1948), pp. 22–23; J. Morgades i Gili, "Predicación de la palabra divina y enseñanza del catecismo en lengua catalana," *La Cruz* (1900), p. 103.

intoning the *Magnificat*. The faithful who could afford only a payment of 4.50 pesetas had to settle for a priest wearing a surplice and stole, two candles, and no music.[63] By giving explicit recognition to social class in certain rites and by expanding the religious qualifications imposed on the faithful beyond the historic norms that had existed for centuries, the clergy left few bridges to the substantial groups within the population that had abandoned formal practice.

Moreover, the Church expected more from the faithful than a minimal knowledge of doctrine and participation in religious services. Secular critics often took the Church to task for developing an all-encompassing ideology, labeled "clericalism," which passed well beyond religious concerns. There is some justification behind this charge. Every Catholic was obliged, according to the diocesan synod of Orense in 1908, to "reject and condemn" a series of dangers to the faith, including Protestantism, rationalism, Freemasonry, and socialism. Liberalism stood condemned above all. It was "the principal error of modern times," and the "true Catholic" could not accept it "under pain of eternal condemnation."[64]

The nature of the guidance given to the faithful, as set forth in the published proceedings of diocesan synods held during the Restoration, was almost entirely negative in intent. The clergy were less concerned with stressing the positive aspects of their message than with calling attention to the means of "containing impiety and error."[65] The faithful were warned to avoid reading books condemned by the Church under pain of sin. They must examine their libraries and "resolutely throw out prohibited books." They were told it was sinful to attend non-Catholic schools, "the pestilential germ of religious indifference." To ensure that religion remained inviolate, they were urged to join pious associations from which, however, an ample number were excluded, including those who had not made their first communion or who were ignorant of "the rudiments of the faith."[66] The Church developed, then, into an increasingly exclusivistic institution at a time when competing secular ideologies began to exercise a powerful appeal for large segments of the population. Operating with an inflexible mentality, its ability to reach out to those whom it was seeking to re-Christianize was seriously compromised as a result.

The synods also devoted considerable attention to the regulation of sexual morality. The Church, to be sure, had always attached importance to marriage and the family. It is revealing that eighteenth-century manuals of Christian morality, although condemning adultery and sexual vices, discussed matrimony and family

63. Mateo Avilés, *Piedades e impiedades de los malagueños*, p. 157.

64. *Constituciones sinodales promulgadas por el Excmo. e Ilmo. Señor Dr. D. Eustaquio Ilundain y Esteban* (Orense, 1908), pp. 15, 17.

65. *Constitucionales sinodales . . . de Málaga*, p. 107.

66. Ibid., p. 110; *Constituciones sinodales* (Orense), p. 25; *Crónica del Sínodo Diocesano*, p. 70.

life in positive terms.[67] The triumph of liberalism and the emergence of a more secularized society during the nineteenth century caused the clergy to change its emphasis. The positive aspects of earlier works yielded to an obsessive conviction that vigorous action had to be taken to dam "the flood of slimy lust" sweeping the nation as a result of the disappearance of traditional instruments of moral control. "The liberty of modern customs and the impunity which libertines enjoy," said the Orense synod, "have so multiplied the dangers and occasions of foul sin" that "today more than ever" the Church must warn the faithful against "every kind of pornography, [theatrical] spectacles, songs, . . . dangerous reading and modern dances."[68]

In its resolutions dealing with "the Christian people," the synod considered sexual questions entirely within the context of a threat to morality, to be resolved through punishment and severe admonitions. Public adulterers and those living in concubinage were to be denied the sacraments. Priests were told to keep "their flocks away from certain places of perdition, where the most solid and fervent virtues could be drowned." Parents in country districts were warned to keep their daughters home at night and never to permit them to remain alone with their future spouses. Women were exhorted to follow "the practice of Christian modesty" in dress.[69]

The clerical assumption that Spain was awash in a cesspool of moral depravity scarcely conformed to reality in a society in which much of the population lived in the countryside, where traditional values persisted whether people went to church or not, and in which many city dwellers consumed their energies in a desperate struggle for survival. The assumption flowed inevitably from the Church's perception, developed progressively over the nineteenth century, that it no longer had at its disposal the instruments of control once available to it in the nostalgic days of the alliance between Throne and Altar. The Church never abandoned efforts to pressure the State into accepting a return to a morality of compulsion. But with its new emphasis on external conformity through increased religious practice and an ideology closed to the political, social, and economic currents transforming Spanish society, the Church increasingly turned to building a religious institution that was a fortress isolated from large segments of the population.

67. See, for example, the discussion of marriage and the dangers to it in Antonio Arbiol, *La familia regulada con doctrina de la sagrada escritura y santos padres de la Iglesia* (Barcelona, 1746), libro 1, chapters 12–13.

68. *Constituciones sinodales* (Orense), p. 192.

69. Ibid., pp. 193–200.

Missions, Catechism, and Devotionalism

This admonitory view of religion should be communicated to the faithful, according to the synods of the Restoration, with all the fire and brimstone the clergy could muster. The Málaga synod warned preachers against playing down the torments of hell and purgatory. In fact, priests were urged to stress them as a means of calling attention "to the great horror which sin deserves, since God punishes it with penalties of such magnitude."[70]

The most spectacular expression of this pastoral approach took the form of an expanding round of domestic missions. The mission served primarily "to stir the religious sensibility of the hearers and to arouse in them a sentiment of guilt which would carry them to the reception of the sacraments."[71] To achieve this objective, preachers chosen for their oratorical and organizing talents prepared the ground carefully. With the cooperation of the parish priest and, usually, of accommodating municipal officials, abundant publicity preceded a mission so that "the entire locality, the good as well as the bad, heard that the mission was about to take place." The missionary organized religious services for maximum psychological effect "in acts and scenes which in themselves deliver strong blows against the rebellious sinner."[72]

A mission generally lasted for one or two weeks. Masses and sermons were held daily in conjunction with other activities, the nocturnal adoration of the Eucharist, an early morning rosary procession through the darkened streets of the town, catechism classes, and finally the culminating moment in which all who had attended the mission services received communion. Each of these activities contributed to the creation of an atmosphere of religious immersion through the organization of the parish and its environs into "a sacred territory" from which worldly concerns were excluded.[73]

The success of a mission rested on the ability of preachers to arouse intense emotions. With a keen sense of crowd psychology, the missionary attempted to arouse "the holy fear of God" among his hearers, particularly in the customary sermon on the last judgment. Ramón Sarabia recalled a sermon on the subject so effective that the entire church rose en masse at its close pleading for mercy, only to hear the preacher say, "There is neither pardon nor mercy for you sinners." Some in the congregation fell stunned to the floor, while others banged their heads repeatedly against the wall in despair. The missionary then changed his tone of voice from one of implacable judgment to one of gently mercy. Raising the crucifix high

70. *Constitucionales sinodales . . . de Málaga*, p. 108.

71. García de Cortázar, "La Iglesia española de la Restauración," p. 25.

72. Pedro María de Ayala, *Vida documentada del Siervo de Dios P. Francisco Paula Tarín de la Compañía de Jesús* (Seville, 1951), p. 262.

73. William Christian, *Moving Crucifixes in Modern Spain* (Princeton, 1992), p. 29.

in his hands, he told his hearers, "Here is mercy!" A relieved congregation left the church filled "with the fear of God."[74]

The fire-and-brimstone quality of missions persisted into the twentieth century. But missions gradually became more sophisticated. There were substantial differences, for example, between the preaching of Francisco Tarín during the last decade of the nineteenth century and that of Ramón Sarabia during the early decades of the twentieth. Tarín's messianic preaching, moved by his view of the preacher as a modern prophet surrounded by wickedness and immorality, yielded to a more comprehensive "apostolate of the masses." Ramón Sarabia recognized that Spanish society was changing and that the fiery preaching of an earlier generation of missionaries was no longer sufficient. Missions, he believed, could no longer depend solely on the work of the preacher as prophet but must be carefully coordinated with a variety of ongoing pastoral activities, particularly in the field of religious education.[75]

In the pastoral sphere, the mission was the most aggressive evangelizing instrument employed by the Church. But it was an institution designed primarily for the rural parish, where the clergy could create an atmosphere of religious immersion capable of sweeping an entire population on a wave of revivalism. The objectives of a mission—"that everyone should confess, that those who have lived for many years separated from the Church should approach the sacraments, that those living in illicit relationships should marry or separate, that enemies should be reconciled, that occasions of sin should be suppressed"—were easier to realize in the countryside given the intense emotions aroused by successful missions preached in relatively homogeneous rural communities.[76] But Ramón Sarabia recognized that "missions do not transform totally the religious life of the great cities," where competing secular currents made the residents "drunk with pride" and hence resistant to the missionary's appeals.[77] Conditions of urban life made it impossible

74. Ramón Sarabia, *Experiencias misionales: testamento misionero del P. Ramón Sarabia*, ed. Pedro R. Santidrián (Madrid, 1959), p. 158. There were many different variants of this technique. William Christian has noted that the two Capuchin friars giving a mission at Limpias in 1919 "seemed to perform separate socio-emotional roles, a little like the bad-cop, good-cop routine. One of them preached frightening sermons about hell and damnation, and the other emphasized God's goodness and mercy." *Moving Crucifixes*, pp. 32–33.

75. Santidrián, *El Padre Sarabia*, p. 372. Similarly, the Capuchin missionaries in Limpias organized a series of catechism lessons for children and youths as well as lectures. Christian, *Moving Crucifixes*, p. 30.

76. "Ante un centenario frustrado: Nava del Rey (1879–1970)," *Boletín de la Provincia Española: publicación privada para uso exclusivo de las comunidades de Padres Redentoristas* (December 1979), no. 109, pp. 144–45. Missionaries dutifully recorded their successes. The Redemptorists, for example, noted, "certain rich people who have not gone to confession in twenty years have confessed . . ." (La Coruña, 1896); "numerous reconciliations and very edifying since many sought pardon [from their enemies] in the street" (Riego del Camino, 1885); "the missionaries were much consoled by the Daughters of Mary for abstaining from [attending] any dance" (Villalcampo, 1886).

77. Ramón Sarabia, *La España de hoy y la España de mañana* (Madrid, 1952), p. 361; *Experiencias misionales*, p. 184.

for the clergy to create the mood of intense religious emotion that they judged essential for success. There were examples of large-scale urban missions. In 1917, Cardinal Reig engaged one hundred priests to preach eighty-three missions in Barcelona, although there is no evidence that this ambitious campaign overcame the religious indifference of the city's working class.[78]

The missions of the late nineteenth and twentieth centuries were successful where one would have expected them to be, in the northern peasant districts of "honest Christianity" so fondly evoked by Ramón Sarabia. Missions conducted in the south had "a much weaker penetration than those in the north." Even the usually redoubtable Francisco Tarín admitted more than once, "Everything is lost. All the zeal of a saint would be dashed to pieces" before the indifference of southern populations.[79]

The Church saw religious education as fundamental to curbing the spread of irreligion among Spaniards. "It is of absolute necessity" for the Church to do everything within its power to educate the young in the doctrine and morality of the faith, declared the bishop of Lugo to a national catechetical congress held at Valladolid in 1913.[80] The delegates in attendance labored under few illusions as they contemplated the state of religious education in their time. They discovered to their dismay that twenty-three dioceses were still using the ancient, though updated, text of Gaspar Astete (1599), while another seventeen employed a similar work of Jerónimo Ripalda (1618) as their official catechism.[81] A parish priest lamented the spread of an "enervating pessimism" among his colleagues, who, he believed, frequently abandoned their catechetical responsibilities. Even when instruction was given, it followed a tradition of rote learning. "I never heard any explanation of the catechism either in the school or the church," recalled Ramón Sarabia of his boyhood. "Everything was reduced to knowing the questions by memory and reciting the *Astete* like parrots."[82]

The Church undertook a reform of religious instruction as a result of the exhortations of the 1913 congress. Parish priests were urged to abandon memorization of questions and answers in favor of a modern pedagogy relying on simple texts, slides, and a dialogue with students.[83] For all practical purposes, the Church

78. "El Cardenal Reig," *Revista Católica de Cuestiones Sociales* (1917), vol. 33, p. 142.

79. Quoted in Santidrián, *El Padre Sarabia* (Madrid, 1921), p. 148; quoted in Alberto Risco, *El Padre Francisco de Paula Tarín* (Madrid, 1921), p. 423.

80. *Crónica oficial del Primer Congreso Catequístico Nacional Español* (2 vols., Valladolid, 1913), vol. 1, p. 129.

81. Ibid., p. 329.

82. Ibid., p. 395; Santidrián, *El Padre Sarabia,* p. 32. An expert on religious education complained that many youths about to perform their obligatory military service arrived without even a basic knowledge of the catechism, so much so that many had not yet made their first communion. Germán Prado, "Alientos del catequista," *Revista Eclesiástica* (1920), p. 129.

83. The prominent Catholic educator Andrés Manjón played a prominent role in the reform of religious education, applying the progressive methods he had developed in his "Avemaría" schools. His addresses to the Valladolid congress repeatedly stressed the necessity of teaching through a "conversa-

attached less and less importance to the teaching of the catechism in public elementary schools, where it remained a compulsory subject until 1931. At the height of the dictatorship, an authority on religious education complained, "The teaching of the catechism is simply not being done. In the vast majority of schools it is routine; in the others they do not even talk about it."[84]

The Church concentrated its efforts on catechetical instruction conducted by voluntary associations of priests and laypeople. Some were older foundations, such as the Escuelas Dominicales, established in the mid-nineteenth century and widespread early in the twentieth, which provided religious education to poor girls of urban parishes. Others were of more recent origin. The events of the Tragic Week, for example, led the clergy of Barcelona to form the Association of Ecclesiastics for the Popular Apostolate. By 1916, nearly fourteen thousand students were being taught by its members.[85] The relative success of this association and others like it, as well as the adoption of modern pedagogical techniques, did not produce the results expected. Despite repeated exhortations by bishops and concerned clergy on the importance of catechetical instruction, the fact of the matter was that the Church proved no more adept at building an effective and comprehensive system of religious education than it had in organizing a Catholic school system. Catechetical efforts were disorganized, depending as always on a multitude of uncoordinated individual or group initiatives.

If the reform of catechetical instruction produced uneven results, the intense development of devotionalism during the nineteenth and early twentieth centuries created a flourishing religious subculture within the Spanish Church, representing, perhaps, the greatest triumph of ultramontane piety. Although devotions revolving around the Virgin and individual saints were as old as Christianity itself, they developed within a specific context in the modern Church. Originating in seventeenth- and eighteenth-century France and Italy, the new devotionalism shared certain characteristics. It was identified with the religious orders that avidly promoted specific cults. The Jesuits encouraged devotion to the Sacred Heart of Jesus while the Capuchin friars emphasized the Stations of the Cross, to give two examples among many. The expansion of the religious orders after 1875 naturally propelled the devotionalist wave to new heights.

The proliferation of devotions represented in the first instance a form of piety created and directed by a clergy uneasy about uncontrolled manifestations of religious expression. The Spanish Church became more tolerant of the rich variety of pious practices associated with popular religion than it had been during the eigh-

---

tional" method. *Crónica oficial del Primer Congreso Catequístico*, vol. 1, pp. 173–78; "Don Andrés Manjón," *La Enseñanza Católica* (1926), no. 375, p. 1.

84. Manuel S. Cuesta, "La enseñanza del catecismo," *Revista Católica de Cuestiones Sociales* (1927), p. 342.

85. José Polo Benito, *De la España católica: las crónicas de un año de acción* (Madrid, 1917), p. 24.

teenth century, when bishops frequently sought to purify religious ceremonies through the eradication of "superstition," although old suspicions did not entirely disappear. In 1899, the diocesan synod of Jaca devoted considerable attention to the question of "devotions that ought to be preserved and abuses that must be eliminated."[86]

The new devotionalism also transcended national boundaries. By the later nineteenth century, devotions to numerous cults originating elsewhere were well established. The Nocturnal Adoration of the Eucharist was introduced from France in 1877. The French devotion to Our Lady of the Miraculous Medal, associated with the Vincentians and the Sisters of Charity, Spain's largest religious order, made its appearance at mid-century and soon acquired widespread popularity, as did services in honor of Our Lady of Perpetual Help, introduced by the Redemptorists during the 1880s. An array of new devotions to the Virgin, building upon an older Marian tradition, proliferated, such as the practice of the three daily "Hail Marys" identified with the Capuchins and the custom, of Italian origin, of dedicating the month of May to the Virgin.[87]

Modern devotionalism differed in emphasis from the corporate piety that predominated in the country's religious life prior to the nineteenth century. The new devotions stressed affective emotion, individual acts of piety, and a simplicity of form that contrasted with the elaborate external rituals organized on the basis of the *cofradías* and *hermandades,* pious associations representing the distinct social classes of a traditional hierarchical society. Although *cofradías* survived into the nineteenth and twentieth centuries, they were increasingly displaced by the new devotionalism, which exercised a broad appeal because of its simplicity and, not least, because of an individualist character that fitted neatly into the social values created by liberalism.

The new devotionalism also contrasted with the old in another respect. The popular piety of the Old Regime was overwhelmingly local in character, intimately connected to the collective life of the rural village and the small town. The new was primarily urban, national, and even international. The presence of the religious orders in the cities and their distribution throughout the country facilitated the spread of the new piety, as did the transportation and communications revolution of the nineteenth century that represented "a quantum leap in the accessibility of the sacred."[88] The development of the railroad and the steamship made it possible for thousands of pilgrims to travel to distant shrines and to Rome itself, as pious travel for those with the necessary means became an early example of modern mass tourism, albeit with a religious purpose. Eight thousand journeyed to Rome, for

86. *Crónica del Sínodo Diocesano,* p. 71.
87. Baldomero Jiménez Duque, *La espiritualidad en el siglo XIX español* (Madrid, 1974), pp. 145–49.
88. Christian, *Moving Crucifixes,* p. 14.

example, in 1876, on the celebrated pilgrimage to the Vatican that provoked the anger of the Cánovas government. Mass pilgrimages to the great shrine of Our Lady of Lourdes attracted the Spanish devout after the turn of the century. Between 1925 and 1928, about eighteen thousand pilgrims a year journeyed to southern France. At the same time, inexpensive tracts, magazines, and books were produced in massive numbers by religious publishing houses. In Catalonia alone, an organization established in 1916, the Foment de Pietat Catalana, annually published and distributed thousands of copies of such works through the cities, towns, and villages of the region.[89]

The new piety also displayed a marked Christological and Marian emphasis to the detriment of cults to individual saints, as at Málaga, where the ancient devotion to the city's patrons, Saints Ciriac and Paula, declined after the mid-nineteenth century in favor of the Virgin of Victory.[90] The traditional devotion to Saint James, whom Castilian monarchs had proclaimed patron of their realms centuries earlier, survived because it was seen by both Church and State as a symbol of patriotism affirming modern nationalism and its identification with Catholicism. The annual celebration of the saint's feast day, July 25, saw the sacred and the secular mingle in a manifestation of civic religion. The king or his representative rose in the midst of an elaborate service at the great basilica of Santiago de Compostela to pledge the nation's loyalty to its patron and make a financial offering specifically provided for in the government's budget.

The traditional cult of Our Lady of the Pillar, celebrated in the greatest of the country's Marian shrines at Zaragoza, shared these characteristics. Long identified with patriotic sentiments, it received special encouragement after the turn of the century from the bishops, who saw it as a counterweight to the anticlerical atmosphere of the times. In 1905 they organized a massive pilgrimage that culminated in the coronation of the Virgin with a crown of precious gems. In 1908 the Conservative government of Antonio Maura gave expression to its religious-patriotic sentiments by conceding to Our Lady of the Pillar the full honors of captain-general, the highest military distinction in the realm.[91]

These cults represented an adaptation of traditional devotions into a form of civic religion. An important example of the new Christological piety, devotion to the Sacred Heart of Jesus, began as a purely religious cult. Originating in seventeenth-century France, it made its way into Spain during the 1730s, promoted by the Jesuits. It emphasized Christ's love for men and women and his redemptive role in salvation. Offering a positive message and functioning through simple religious

89. Josep Massot i Muntaner, *L'Església catalana al segle XIX* (Barcelona, 1975), pp. 72–74.

90. Mateo Avilés, *Piedades e impiedades de los malagueños*, p. 87.

91. *La Cruz* (1904), pp. 19–20; *Diccionario de historia eclesiástica de España*, ed. Q. Aldea Vaquero et al. (4 vols., Madrid, 1972–1975), vol. 4, p. 2316.

services, it soon acquired widespread popularity. Although the devotion declined with the expulsion of the Jesuits in 1767, it reappeared in 1815 upon the restoration of the absolutist Fernando VII.

The appeal of the Sacred Heart in the nineteenth and early twentieth centuries lay in its simple, affective message, easy for all to understand. This purely religious emphasis slowly began to merge with another, as the cult shifted towards the Sacred Heart as an object of atonement in reparation for the injuries inflicted on the Church by its enemies. The sometimes violent struggle between Catholics and anticlericals over the placing of plaques dedicated to the Sacred Heart during 1899–1900, testifies to the ever more ideological character of the devotion.

Its growing popularity and the increasingly pro-clerical stance of the Conservative party after 1900 converted it into a religious-patriotic cult rivaling that of Saint James. By 1919, funds had been gathered to erect an imposing monument in the geographical center of the country, the Cerro de los Angeles. Although the political system of the Restoration was staggering under the weight of accumulated problems, King Alfonso XIII, Prime Minister Maura, and an array of notables, "having closed their ears to tenacious campaigns, terrible strikes and revolutionary threats," assembled for the ceremony of consecration. The king referred to the country's "strength and constancy in its love for Religion and the Monarchy" as he commended the nation to the Sacred Heart. The clergy hailed the dedication as an "unforgettable day for Spanish Catholicism." Liberals, Socialists, and others uneasy about the theocratic undertones of the ceremony saw it as either unnecessary or as a provocation.[92]

Devotion to the Sacred Heart was closely linked to renewed emphasis on adoration of the Eucharist and the campaign on behalf of frequent communion. Eucharistic associations multiplied, among them the Archconfraternity of Eucharistic Thursdays, founded in 1907, and the Association of Tres Marías y de los Discípulos de San Juan, established in 1910 by the prominent religious propagandist Father (later Bishop) Manuel González García, an energetic advocate of eucharistic devotion. The "Marías" became enormously popular, enrolling more than 2 million women by 1925. Through a widely circulated magazine, *El Granito de Arena*, González García promoted adoration of the Eucharist with the same purpose as advocates of devotion to the Sacred Heart, to offer reparation for the crimes and injuries inflicted against religion.[93] Adoration of the Eucharist formed an essential aspect of ultramontane piety. It reached its culmination in periodic eucharistic congresses attended by bishops, priests, and laypeople who gathered in the thousands over several days for liturgical services, sermons, and study sessions. Na-

92. *La Ciencia Tomista* (1919), p. 78; "Acto de la Consagración," *Ilustración del Clero* (1919), p. 12; Kodasver [pseud.], *Medio siglo de vida diocesana matritense, 1913–1963* (Madrid, 1967), p. 52.

93. Jiménez Duque, *La espiritualidad en el siglo XIX*, pp. 149–50.

tional eucharistic meetings were held at Valencia (1893), Lugo (1896), and Toledo (1926) and at Madrid (1911) for the most impressive of all, an international congress.[94]

Devotion to the Virgin Mary had ancient roots in Spain, but during the nineteenth century it too developed within the framework of ultramontane piety. It was vigorously promoted by the clergy, who encouraged a variety of individualist devotions. At mid-century, Saint Anthony Claret campaigned for the saying of the rosary, which, according to one authority on religiosity, became "the great Marian devotion" of the modern Spanish Church. The rosary was said in churches even during Mass, in a multitude of separate devotions to the Virgin, and in Catholic schools. Marian associations, particularly the Hijas de María, found in numerous parishes by the end of the century, attracted thousands of pious women to devotions for the Virgin.[95]

Ultramontane piety provided the Church with a workable replacement for the religious forms of the past that had been eclipsed by the triumph of liberalism. That a massive devotional resurgence took place is beyond dispute. In some respects, it achieved its objective of reorganizing and redirecting religious sentiment towards personal acts of piety fully compatible with liberal individualism. Moreover, as Mateo Avilés observed in his study of religiosity in Málaga, the easy availability of inexpensive statues and other holy objects manufactured in massive quantities encouraged an intimate, familial piety in the home that was in accord with the assumptions of a Catholic, bourgeois society.[96]

The long-term impact on religiosity is less clear. There were critics within the Church who viewed the proliferation of devotions with deep unease. Writing in 1914, the Augustinian friar Bruno Ibeas complained that many did little to instill an "intimate sense of moral rectitude" but had become, rather, "a mixture of formulistic and routine devotion . . . with idolatrous traces."[97] As trenchant as ever, Father José Gafo attacked "the plague of false piety" that he believed had taken hold within the Spanish Church. He directed harsh criticism against the clerical promoters of new devotions:

> Since so many souls lacked a deep and strong religious spirit and were unaware of their faith and of that beautiful and austere symbolism embodied in the Catholic liturgy, it was necessary to create *religious preciosity*, or, in other words, a baroque overburdening of . . . the cult and a constant novelty in all that . . . seduces the senses within the churches. Churches have been converted into theaters or nightclubs, . . . people go to the former as to the latter . . . [to be] entertained or satisfied.[98]

94. "Congresos eucarísticos," *Diccionario de historia eclesiástica*, vol. 1, pp. 604–7.
95. Jiménez Duque, *La espiritualidad en el siglo XIX*, pp. 155–56.
96. Mateo Avilés, *Piedades e impiedades de los malagueños*, pp. 58–60.
97. Bruno Ibeas, "Nuestro cristianismo," *España y América* (1914), vol. 12, no. 3, p. 514.
98. Gafo, "La situación religiosa de España," pp. 382, 385.

Gafo was moved by reforming liturgical currents. He forgot that the Church itself encouraged the new devotionalism as a means of reaching the masses when many religious practices associated with the collectively organized piety of earlier times collapsed under the shock of social and political change. Yet he perceived that the sentimentality and the extravagance of the new devotionalism raised an obstacle to the clergy's goal of re-Christianizing Spaniards who had abandoned religious practice. Many had fled "this external and theatrical Catholicism" with some justification, he argued. Was there not a fundamental contradiction between the incredible number of devotions and pious associations and "enormous religious absenteeism in Spain?" The elaborate dressing of statues, the perpetual round of novenas and other devotional services, the reliance on a multitude of external symbols, scapulars, medals, and the like were designed to convert Spanish Catholicism into "a patrimony made up nearly entirely of women."[99]

Gafo was not alone in arguing that the clergy were promoting an "easy apostolate of women" instead of concentrating their energies on seeking effective means of reaching men.[100] This criticism of the feminization of devotion ignored the participation of men especially in the peasant regions of the north, but it came close to the mark in perceiving that a devotionalism based on emotion and a kaleidoscope of pious practices exercised little appeal for the religiously alienated of the cities. In a time when urban workers and the dispossessed of the southern countryside were grasping for a collective remedy to their desperate problems, attendance at a novena or the wearing of a religious medal offered no solution. It was scarcely surprising that pilgrims on their way to visit the "moving crucifix" of Limpias in 1919 were harassed, according to the Catholic press, by "a group of sooty women of the kind who load and unload coal on the docks." The pilgrims attempted to sing hymns as they moved from the railroad station to the church, only to have their voices drowned out by a chorus of "scurrilous songs."[101]

The effect of ultramontane piety and its myriad of devotions and cults on the Church's pastoral aspirations was ambiguous. On the one hand, it allowed the Church to find a new formula capable of appealing to the Catholic bourgeoisie and that part of the rural population in certain regions remaining attached to religious practice. On the other, its identification with a conservative political ideology and highly individualist forms of religious expression reinforced the perception of a devotional world divorced from the social and economic conditions under which much of the population lived.

99. Ibid., pp. 386, 381.

100. *Grito de alarma dirigido a los católicos de nuestros días por el presbitero* N. S. (Valladolid, 1922), pp. 164, 167.

101. Quoted in Christian, *Moving Crucifixes*, p. 102.

Popular Religion

Since the eighteenth century, foreign visitors to the Iberian peninsula had been fascinated and sometimes repelled by the existence of a luxuriant world of popular religious practice. No description can do justice to the variety, complexity, and, occasionally, the extravagance of such customs that have persisted into the twentieth century. Some were practices antedating the introduction of Christianity itself. "In the very remote country districts," observed one early-twentieth-century visitor, "priest and doctor . . . are quite powerless to deal with customs that seem to precede the dawn of civilization."[102] In Galicia, for example, where belief in magic and witchcraft endured among the rural population, the eve of the feast of Saint John continued to provide the occasion for rites designed to ward off evil interventions. A cult of the dead also flourished in the region, where peasants feared the "Holy Company" composed of the souls of the dead who wandered through the night seeking to ensnare the living into their ghostly ranks.[103]

Other practices represented extensions of the formal liturgy, although they often developed an autonomous existence of their own. Throughout the country, Holy Week furnished the occasion for elaborate processions of hooded penitents who conducted statues depicting the last days of Christ through the streets to the somber strains of funeral music. The ceremonies of Holy Week also gave rise to more curious examples of popular religious sentiment, as in the ritualized destruction of effigies of Judas, "shot-gunned and burned all over Spain" on Easter Sunday.[104] Further, few villages lacked a holy patron who was seen as an immediate protector of the community and its members.

The existence of this luxuriant religious world has long been recognized even by a clergy sometimes distressed over its manifestations. A precise definition of "popular" religion is not easy to make, however. Sociologists of religion, pastoral theologians, and social anthropologists have discussed the question, but from distinct disciplinary perspectives that have stimulated abundant discussion but little agreement.[105] Social anthropologists have properly called attention to popular religion as a complex and not necessarily consistent phenomenon that must be studied "like a series of geological strata" formed in distinct periods and transformed over time.[106] Whether a precise definition can ever be established is debatable, given the enormous diversity and complex nature of popular religious customs. But there is no question that these practices shared certain characteristics. First, they were intensely local, closely linked to a specific sacred geography and to ba-

102. Samuel L. Bensusan, *Home Life in Spain* (2d ed., London, 1910), p. 58.

103. Carlos Pascual, *Guía sobrenatural de España* (Madrid, 1976), pp. 26, 33–34.

104. Timothy J. Mitchell, *Violence and Piety in Spanish Folklore* (Philadelphia, 1988), p. 96.

105. See the informative discussion on this question by Bernard Plongeron, "Avant-Propos," in *La religion populaire*, ed. B. Plongeron (2 vols., Paris, 1976), vol. 2, pp. 15–23.

106. William Christian, *Person and God in a Spanish Valley* (New York, 1972), p. 82.

sic human needs, especially in the countryside. William Christian's study of the Nansa Valley (Santander) has shown the importance of this highly localized piety connected to numerous chapels scattered about the district, with individual shrines attracting the devotion of specific clusters of villages. There is nothing comparable to Christian's study for the rest of Spain, although other regions possessed their sacred geographies. Within Córdoba province, for example, there were numerous local shrines to the Virgin at La Fuensanta, Araceli, Pozoblanca, and the Sierra de Cabra, the last particularly favored by the gypsies of the district.

The local shrines, cults, and vows abounding in the countryside were not destined to win the grace necessary to attain salvation of which theologians spoke. Rather, they sought to protect men and women from earthly disasters, bring them good fortune in this life, and secure a personal intercessor for the passage to eternity.[107] They served as a kind of protective talisman, resting on a bargain, an informal contract with God, the Virgin, and individual saints, all of whom were represented in immediate terms by sacred places, statues, and intercessory rites distinct from those of the formal liturgy. The patron, indeed, who failed to live up to his side of the bargain was soon reminded of his obligations. The residents of Peralbillo (Ciudad Real) hurled the image of Saint Mark, the village patron, into a nearby river if he failed to heed their prayers for rain in periods of drought, while the fishermen of Albufera (Valencia) turned the statue of the Infant Jesus, their special protector, towards the wall if he proved unable to maintain the catch at its usual level.[108]

Often local cults originated in a past—sometimes distant, sometimes not—when villagers sought a holy patron to protect them when natural disasters threatened. A celebrated local pilgrimage (*romería*) in the Toledo hill towns of Hontanar and Navahermosa began in 1778 during a period of severe drought. The inhabitants of each village moved in procession imploring it to rain. As the two groups encountered one another at a crossroads, the providential rain began to fall. The residents constructed a shrine to mark the place of the happy event. Thereafter, they commemorated their deliverance with an annual pilgrimage.[109]

Social anthropologists have also stressed the importance of popular religious customs as a powerful social mechanism for establishing distinct communal identities and as a vehicle for the expression of local patterns of sociability. The inhabitants of Baza and Guadix (Granada), for example, had engaged in a pious competition over a disputed Virgin since the late fifteenth century. An icon of the Virgin in Baza, to which the residents of Guadix believed they were entitled, became the object of a ritualized competition called the fiesta of the *Cascamorras*. A volunteer from Guadix attired in an elaborate costume and bearing a banner was dispatched

107. William Christian, *Local Religion in Sixteenth-Century Spain* (Princeton, 1981), pp. 23–33.
108. Mitchell, *Violence and Piety*, p. 31.
109. Ibid., p. 32.

each year to the neighboring town to recover the icon for his home town. Upon entering the Baza municipal limits, he was set upon by crowds of youths. He was "pushed, shoved, cursed, punched and covered with nauseous substances," as he engaged on his hopeless quest, the ordeal ending only when he entered a local church and fell to the ground before a statue of the Virgin of Pity. Even so, having failed in his mission, he had to return to Guadix, where his fellow townsmen greeted him as rudely as had the residents of Baza.[110]

Second, popular religious practices were community undertakings rather than purely ecclesiastical ones. The clergy participated in many, to be sure, but their role was secondary. The priest who dared to interfere with traditional customs ran the risk of arousing intense opposition, as Francisco de Tarín discovered to his cost during a mission at Utrera in 1894. He ordered the removal of a statue of Our Lady of Consolation, patroness of the city, from the shrine outside the city walls where it was always kept, to the mission church, believing that its presence would enhance the devotion of those in attendance. Tarín ascended the pulpit already uneasy at the restlessness of the congregation, which soon began to shout, "The Virgin to her house!" Several rushed forward before the eyes of the astonished priest and carried the statue from the church, accompanied by virtually the entire congregation chanting, "God save you Mary, full of grace. You will not sleep in Utrera but in your own house."[111] A similar event took place a few years later in the town of Guadalupe, when the government had to dispatch a company of the Civil Guard to protect workmen sent to remove several paintings from the local monastery for an exhibition in Madrid. The angry villagers "were well assured that misfortune would follow if they were removed" from the town.[112]

Popular expressions of religiosity flourished in the countryside and small towns, where they had long been identified with local tradition and culture. Social conditions in developing urban areas did not favor the survival of communally oriented customs excepted in a limited way. Moreover, in the cities, the Church emphasized the individualist devotions of ultramontane piety to the detriment of collective expressions of religiosity, over which it exercised little or no control.

Cities continued to organize processions during Holy Week, as they had done for centuries. On the surface, these expressions of popular urban piety appeared to fulfill the didactic and spiritual inspiration that had led to their appearance in

110. Ibid., pp. 112–13. The competitive aspect of local cults to the Virgin was noted by an early-twentieth-century visitor: "The Spaniard who worships one of these regards the others as strangers and will take no account of them. In fact, although his theology teaches him that there is no more than one Virgin, he will be heard to speak very disrespectfully . . . of all Virgins save his own." Bensusan, *Home Life in Spain*, p. 53.

111. Quoted in Ayala, *Vida documentada*, p. 458.

112. Shaw, *Spain from Within*, p. 55.

the fifteenth and sixteenth centuries.[113] Havelock Ellis's description of the processions in Seville at the turn of the century could have been written a century earlier:

These *pasos* take place everywhere and all day long on Good Friday, and to some extent on the two preceding days. The whole city is given over to them, all vehicular traffic is stopped. . . . Every procession consists of a single sacred figure, or a group representing a scene from the Passion, of more than life-size proportions, borne on the heads of some twenty-five invisible men at an extremely slow pace, and accompanied by the members of the *cofradía*, or lay brotherhood, to whom it belongs, dressed in their peculiar costume, which varies in colour in the different brotherhoods, but is essentially a long gown with a stiff, peaked cowl, covering the face, with loopholes for the eyes, while each brother carries a lighted candle.[114]

Visitors to Seville were impressed by these great ceremonies "full of the suggestion of awe and mourning, . . . terrible in their realism, of the Tragedy of Calvary." The processions were viewed "not only with reverence, but with awe, the people falling on their knees with the utmost devotion."[115] That Holy Week processions continued to make a religious impact is certain. Yet, in many respects, the processions differed substantially from their Old Regime predecessors. Their essentially communal character, expressed through the *cofradías*, was considerably diminished. The vital social role that these associations had once played in the life of the pre-industrial city had long since vanished, as urban societies changed under the influence of liberalism and economic change.[116]

Given the regional diversity of Spanish Catholicism, any generalizations about the religious character of Holy Week processions must be advanced with caution. But there is evidence that in some localities, particularly in the south, they became manifestations of a municipal civic religion organized by urban notables who viewed them as sources of local pride and, increasingly, as tourist attractions. During Holy Week at Seville, for example, prices rose appreciably, for "hotel proprietors, restaurant keepers and shop managers will not lightly leave the golden harvest," according to one early twentieth-century observer.[117] The city's *cofradías* seemed closer to social clubs than to associations committed to a religious purpose. In 1926, abuses among Seville's lay confraternities came to the attention of the ecclesiastical authorities, who were distressed to discover that the members

113. The statutes of the confraternity of the True Cross (1588) "explained that by personally reenacting Christ's trial, members were sharing in the pain of redemption." Maureen Flynn, *Sacred Charity: Confraternities and Social Welfare in Spain, 1400–1700* (Ithaca, 1989), p. 131.

114. Ellis, *The Soul of Spain*, pp. 364–65.

115. Bensusan, *Home Life in Spain*, pp. 70–71; Field, *Old Spain and New Spain*, p. 281.

116. In 1841, for example, the government of General Baldomero Espartero ordered the sale of the property of the *cofradías* for the benefit of the public treasury, thereby reducing them to the status of simple, voluntary associations.

117. Bensusan, *Home Life in Spain*, p. 73.

were seeking alms, ostensibly to defray the expenses of processions. In fact, they were spending the donations on a round of dances and banquets.[118]

Similarly, at Málaga the number of participating confraternities declined significantly during the second half of the nineteenth century. Those remaining were taken over by the city's commercial and industrial elite as membership became identified with social status. It was scarcely surprising that the mass of the population came to regard the processions with either indifference or hostility, not least because of the participation of military units and the feared Civil Guard in the line of march. Even so, the processions took place sporadically until the 1920s, when they were revived thanks to the intervention of merchants and shopkeepers seeking a tourist attraction for the city.[119]

Studies carried out by modern social anthropologists have illuminated important characteristics of popular religion. On the whole, they have addressed the question in terms of community needs and aspirations. To assess the role of popular religiosity from the pastoral perspective of the Church raises a number of different and equally difficult issues. Was popular religion a source of strength or weakness? Was it simply a cultural manifestation of a society imprinted with Catholicism for centuries, but one that had little to do with formal belief and observance as the Church defined it? "Can we describe these people as Christians?" asked the anthropologist Carmelo Lisón-Tolosana in his discussion of seventeenth- and eighteenth-century religious customs in the town of Belmonte de los Caballeros.[120]

There is no certain answer to these questions. Historically, the Church itself had been far from certain about the value of some manifestations of popular religiosity. During the eighteenth century, bishops influenced by the reforming ecclesiastical currents of the time viewed certain aspects of popular religion with suspicion and sought to eradicate practices that they judged superstitious. Bishop Felipe Bertrán of Salamanca warned against popular customs that were "so opposed to the simplicity of the Gospel of Jesus Christ" that "they threatened to suffocate the seed of true and healthy doctrine."[121]

During the nineteenth century, a church besieged by liberalism became more tolerant of popular religious practices once viewed as superstitious. In Spain as elsewhere in Catholic Europe, the clergy began to perceive popular religion as an impure vein of religious belief capable of being refined into orthodoxy. The people of Andalucía, remarked a pastoral commentator early in the century, may not have

118. Gafo, "La situación religiosa de España," p. 392.

119. Mateo Avilés, *Piedades e impiedades de los malagueños*, pp. 73–81.

120. Carmelo Lisón-Tolosana, *Belmonte de Los Caballeros: A Sociological Study of a Spanish Town* (Oxford, 1966), p. 278.

121. *Colección de las cartas pastorales y edictos del Exmo. Señor Don Felipe Bertrán* (2 vols., Madrid, 1783), vol. 1, p. 56.

known "the a, b, c's of the catechism," but they "breathe a Christian atmosphere and carry out religious acts."[122]

Whether this assumption was correct is far from certain. There is no indication that the prevalence of processions, shrines, and pilgrimages in rural Andalucía provided a bridge to orthodoxy and observance. It is more likely that popular religious customs reinforced belief and practice in regions where the population conformed to the Church's demands and did not do so where it had long ignored them. Moreover, under the Restoration and the dictatorship, the Church never developed a strategy to exploit the imagined mine of popular religiosity in terms of its pastoral objectives.

It is striking but not surprising that the Church did not do so. The diocesan synods of the Restoration did not condemn popular religious customs often related only tangentially to the formal liturgy, although they censured abuses.[123] Popular religious practices were, after all, a sign, if a shaky one, that Spain remained a Catholic nation. But the synods preferred to exhort the faithful towards orthodox belief and the practices of ultramontane piety, although the line separating popular religion and clerically controlled piety was not always clear. The clergy left no doubt of its preference for the latter.

Even the sensational events of 1919–1923 associated with the "moving crucifix" of Limpias (Santander), so brilliantly analyzed by William Christian, conform to the model of ultramontane piety, despite the highly charged emotions, more characteristic of popular religion, generated among the hundreds of pilgrims who journeyed from near and far to witness it. The short-lived cult owed much to the activities of the clergy, especially Capuchin missionary friars, Bishop Sánchez de Castro of Santander, and Catholic notables, who saw the moving Christ as a sign of divine protection for a Church under siege by liberalism and radical social movements. Although fervent supporters of the Christ of Limpias interpreted its message in different ways, from the catastrophic to the millenarian, in essence it was another example of the politicized ultramontane piety characteristic of the devotional resurgence of the late nineteenth and early twentieth centuries. The rapid decline of the cult, moved in part by opposition from within the Church, suggests that the Christ of Limpias failed to gain the broad clerical approval necessary for it to be accepted as a legitimate devotion within the confines of ultramontane piety.[124] The intense emotions aroused among its supporters and the extraordinary claims

122. Perales y Gutiérrez, *El problema religioso*, p. 98. Gérard Cholvy has noted a similar development in France, where the clergy saw popular religious customs as forming building blocks "for Christianization." "Réalités de la religion populaire dans la France contemporaine," in *La religion populaire*, vol. 2, p. 157.

123. *Crónica del Sínodo Diocesano*, p. 71.

124. The papal nuncio Francesco Ragonesi entertained serious doubts about the Christ of Limpias, as did the Dominican friar Luis Urbano, who expressed his reservations in a book and in the pages of *La Ciencia Tomista*, one of the more intellectual and progressive publications of the Spanish Church. Christian, *Moving Crucifixes*, pp. 77–78.

made on its behalf came uncomfortably close, perhaps, to those aspects of popular religious manifestations about which many Church authorities remained uneasy.

In the end, there is no definitive answer to Ramón Sarabia's question. Spanish Catholicism represented less a highly unified structure of faith and practice than a complex, multilayered body of orthodox belief, regular observance, ultramontane piety, and popular religiosity that defied clerical attempts to create a single religious model applicable to all Spaniards in every region of the country.

CHAPTER XII

THE SECOND REPUBLIC, 1931–1933

Spain began another experiment with republicanism on April 14, 1931. The Second Republic imitated the First (1873–1874) in its determination to separate Church and State. The brief existence of the nineteenth-century Republic kept it from carrying out its intention. In contrast, the Second implemented a policy that disestablished the Church, destroyed its financial and legal privileges, and converted the State into a powerful agent of secularization and cultural change. It was scarcely surprising that dissension developed in view of the contentious history of civil-ecclesiastical relations prevailing since the 1830s. The Republic was neither the first government to attempt ecclesiastical reform nor were its policies towards the Church the most radical. Conflict over what contemporaries called "the religious question" surfaced within days of its proclamation and remained a source of national controversy and divisiveness.

If Spain's modern history proved anything, it showed that any attempt to alter the Church's privileges provoked resistance. In this respect, the Second Republic faced a more formidable institution than did its nineteenth-century predecessor. The expansion of the religious orders, the proliferation and modernization of Catholic associations, particularly in the field of social Catholicism, and the identification of ecclesiastical interests with those of an educated, wealthy bourgeoisie provided the Church with a more resilient foundation for resistance than that available to the clergy struggling against nineteenth-century liberalism.

The fall of Primo de Rivera in January 1930 opened the way to political normalization, as long-suppressed parties hostile to the monarchy and the dictatorship reemerged. The bill for the uncritical support rendered by the clergy to the discredited regime now fell due. Primo de Rivera was gone. Church and monarchy remained to suffer the consequences. Finally, the issue of the Church, its privileges, its role in education, and its cultural influence served as a lightning rod drawing to it the deep and fundamental concerns of Right and Left about the future of Spanish society.

Monarchy or Republic, 1930–1931

On Holy Thursday (April 2, 1931), King Alfonso XIII and Queen Victoria Eugenia performed a traditional rite of the Spanish court. In the presence of the papal nuncio, the royal family, grandees of Spain, and the diplomatic corps, the monarchs knelt to wash the feet of twelve men and women chosen to represent the kingdom's poor.[1] The royal gesture may have symbolized the virtues of humility and Christian charity, but for a country long divided by intense social antagonisms, it meant little. Even so, the Holy Week services at the palace were conducted with full regal and ecclesiastical splendor, a brilliant display of Crown and Church on the eve of the monarchy's collapse.

As these colorful ceremonies were taking place, the king was playing the last political cards of a deck that had begun to shrink following Primo de Rivera's fall from power.[2] Before a resurgent opposition, evident in growing popular support for a republic, the monarch sought a formula that would preserve a measure of his authority, the "moderating power" enshrined in the 1876 constitution. But a return to the pre-1923 constitutional monarchy was out of the question. The issue of the king's responsibility for subverting the constitution he had sworn to uphold moved to the center of political debate in 1930 and early 1931. Moreover, the dictatorship had destroyed the dynastic parties forming the Restoration's political base. By 1930, they were beyond resurrection. Some survivors of the old parties began to drift either towards republicanism or a kind of "republicanized" monarchism in which the king would be reduced to a figurehead within a democratic, liberal system. Whether early acceptance of the second option would have saved the monarchy is debatable, but it offered Alfonso his only chance at survival. The king refused to drink what a veteran Liberal politician called this "elixir of long life for the Monarchy."[3] Instead, Alfonso persisted in efforts to restore the political system that he had rejected in 1923. To test the political waters, the king agreed to the convocation of municipal elections on April 12.

The monarchy's supporters tried vainly to divest April 12 of a plebiscitary character, but opinion throughout the country appreciated its singular importance, although few predicted the rapid unfolding of events. Monarchists carried the countryside; the Republican parties won decisively in the cities. The king now faced a

1. José Gutiérrez-Ravé, *España en 1931* (Madrid, 1932), pp. 82–84.

2. For a detailed account of Spain's political history during this period, see Shlomo Ben-Ami, *The Origins of the Second Republic in Spain* (Oxford, 1978).

3. Quoted in Ramón Garriga, *El Cardenal Segura y el Nacional-Catolicismo* (Barcelona, 1977), p. 139.

simple choice: either resort to the military and the strong possibility of civil war or face the end of his rule. Recognizing that his position was politically untenable and rejecting an appeal to force, Alfonso renounced his powers on April 14, as a provisional government took office in the name of the Second Republic.

The dictatorship's collapse and the prolonged constitutional uncertainty following in its wake produced general apprehension throughout the Church. Although its resentful memory of nineteenth-century wrongs revolved more around liberalism than republicanism, it had not forgotten that the First Republic intended the separation of Church and State. But as long as a republic seemed a distant political option, the Church paid little attention to it. By the early 1930s, the situation had changed dramatically. The growing strength of republican sentiment suggested that the unthinkable was becoming a possibility.

The Church's concern focused on republicanism's commitment to the separation of Church and State and the anticlericalism judged its inseparable companion, although in fact the First Republic was far less extreme in this respect than the liberal governments of the mid-1830s and early 1840s had been. Some clerical apologists saw hostility towards the Church and Catholicism as lying at the very heart of republicanism. The idea of a republic was born "in the shadow of unbelief and modern rationalism." Inevitably, it "would be hostile to Religion."[4]

The corollary was obvious. "In Spain the Monarchy represents tradition, and that tradition is essentially Catholic."[5] These sentiments were widely shared by the clergy in a vague sort of way. Translating them into action was another matter. In fact, the hierarchy as a body never addressed the country's political future between January 1930 and April 1931. The Committee of Metropolitans wrote collectively on various issues during the dictatorship. During 1930 and early 1931, it remained silent before a question passionately engaging a body of Catholic opinion largely monarchist in sympathy.[6] The omission is significant. It suggests that the bishops were either unable to agree on a course of action or, more likely, that they believed that the Church needed to proceed cautiously in a time of political uncertainty. Such a reaction was understandable. The bishops of the Restoration, many still on the scene during the early 1930s, were not known for initiative or dynamism. As critics frequently observed, they owed their positions to the skills of the ecclesiastical politician operating within the give-and-take of the Restoration system. Neither temperament nor experience prepared them for direct action during the monarchy's constitutional crisis.

Not all bishops were so inclined. Prelates owing preferment to Primo de Rivera

4. Hilario Yaben, *¿Monarquía o república?* (Madrid, 1931), pp. 111–12.

5. Ibid.

6. The Committee of Metropolitans did not issue any collective statement between October 16, 1928, and May 9, 1931. *Documentos colectivos del episcopado español, 1870–1974*, ed. Jesús Iribarren (Madrid, 1974), pp. 125, 130.

broke with passivity to express their preference for a monarchical and authoritarian solution to the nation's problems. Zacarías Martínez, appointed archbishop of Santiago in 1927, lamented the fall of the dictator, whom he described as a providential figure sent to save Spain from social revolution.[7] Cardinal Pedro Segura of Toledo, whose antiliberalism surged to new and erratic heights, was the foremost episcopal advocate of the monarchy. He owed his spectacular ascent within the Church to the dictatorship's ecclesiastical patronage and to his personal friendship with Alfonso XIII. Although the cardinal's freewheeling use of the limited powers conceded to him as primate of the Spanish Church generated resentment among his fellow bishops, Segura wasted little time in seeking to move the faithful into political action. In a controversial pastoral letter of 1930, he urged them to organize politically. "Catholics," he warned, "must not abandon the government and administration of the commonwealth to the hands of their enemies."[8] Although he did not say so outright, he meant that they should organize to defend the Church against any threat to its interests either from a republic or from a reconstituted liberal monarchy. The cardinal also employed his considerable skills as a backroom manipulator to exhort Catholic lay associations against a republic and to urge the king, whom he visited weekly, against a democratic solution to the constitutional crisis.[9]

Segura was not alone in these sallies. Only days before the April 12 elections, Bishop Mateo Múgica of Vitoria instructed the faithful of his diocese to vote for monarchist candidates. Among the clergy, a well-known ecclesiastical publicist, Father Hilario Yaben, achieved fame among monarchists and notoriety among Republicans for his propaganda in defense of the Crown.[10] These interventions were imprudent and politically foolish. They rested on the shopworn idea that the so-called Catholic masses were ready and waiting to unite politically to defend the Church's interests, an assumption often made in the past and invariably proven wrong by events. Clerical partisans of Alfonso XIII also entertained impoverished notions about the contours of their idealized Catholic monarchy. In many cases, these came down to little more than warmed-over versions of the dictatorship. Even Yaben, one of the few ecclesiastical apologists for the monarchy to present his political views in detail, could propose nothing more original than a royal government managed by disinterested technocrats.[11]

7. Francisco Carballo and Alfonso Magariños, *La Iglesia en la Galicia contemporánea: análisis histórico y teológico del periodo 1931–1939, II Republica* (Madrid, 1978), p. 116.

8. Quoted in *Documentos colectivos del episcopado español*, p. 35.

9. Ben-Ami, *The Origins of the Second Republic*, pp. 174–76; Garriga, *El Cardenal Segura*, pp. 140–42.

10. Hilario Yaben (1876–1945), canon of Sigüenza cathedral and editor of the Catholic newspaper *El Henares*, published two books in 1931 opposing the establishment of a republic. In addition to *¿Monarquía o república?* he wrote *El problema religioso en España* (Sigüenza, 1931). He also expressed his political views in clerical journals directed at the parish clergy. His 1931 article "Gobiernos de partido y gobiernos de capacidades" described party politics as "disastrous" for Spain. *Revista Eclesiástica* (1931), p. 113.

11. Ibid., p. 123.

Clergy supporting the monarchy also ignored political reality, namely, the extreme disarray of the several monarchist and regional parties that were expected to forge a united front in the Church's defense. No union was possible among Carlists, Integrists, authoritarian monarchists, liberal monarchists, and Catholic regionalists in the Basque Provinces, Catalonia, and Valencia, and the social Catholics gathered around *El Debate*.[12] They agreed on defending the Church but on little else. Although the course advocated by Segura and other clerics led to a political dead end, it proved damaging. The republican opposition, already acerbic in its criticism of ecclesiastical support for the dictatorship, saw clerical defense of the monarchy as yet another sign of intransigence despite the timidity of much of the ecclesiastical establishment. It also drew attention away from a significant change occurring among a minority of Spanish Catholics. José Gafo called attention to the political conversion of prominent laymen to the republican cause, which he saw as a hopeful sign that promised "respect and conciliation" between the Church and a future republic. Gafo realized that in a new regime the clergy would have to renounce "certain historic privileges" but believed that an accommodation between the Church and a republic was entirely possible.[13]

The Search for Compromise, April–September 1931

Following the Republic's proclamation, Gafo's cautious optimism appeared justified. Pope Pius XI slightly delayed recognizing the new regime, but the Vatican had long since learned the lesson of expediency when faced with political reality. The bishops issued pastoral letters that, if less than ringing endorsements of the Republic, at least accepted it as a fact of life.[14] Even Cardinal Segura initially adopted the position of "complete prudence and caution" urged on the hierarchy by Cardinal Vidal i Barraquer.[15] The bishops' attitude was widely shared among the

12. Ben-Ami, *The Origins of the Second Republic*, p. 177.

13. José Gafo, "Crónicas científico-sociales," *La Ciencia Tomista* (1931), vol. 43, p. 106. Gafo mentioned no names, but it is clear from his text that he received firsthand information from Catholic Republicans. "We have certain notice from some of them that they have entered the revolutionary movement on the assumption and word of honor that there will be no attack on the Catholic Church."

14. On May 9, the Committee of Metropolitans issued a collective statement on the change of regime. The archbishops reminded "the faithful of the duties which tie them to the constituted authorities and the obligation incumbent on them to cooperate for the common good and the maintenance of social order." "Metropolitanos españoles a los fieles," in *Documentos colectivos del episcopado español*, p. 131. Diocesan bishops also published similar exhortations for Catholics to respect the new political order. Mary Vincent, *Catholicism in the Second Spanish Republic: Religion and Politics in Salamanca, 1931–1936* (Oxford, 1996), pp. 134–35. Similarly, the Vatican, through the papal nuncio, Federico Tedeschini, urged Spanish Catholics to respect the "constituted powers." In April 1931, the Holy See viewed the change in regime "with serenity" and showed no "anti-republican animosity." Gonzalo Redondo, *Historia de la Iglesia en España, 1931–1939* (2 vols., Madrid, 1993), vol. 1, p. 135.

15. Vidal i Barraquer to Segura, May 1, 1931, in *Arxiu Vidal i Barraquer: Església y Estat durant la Segona República Espanyola, 1931–1936*, ed. M. Batllori and V. M. Arbeloa (4 vols., Montserrat, 1971–1991), vol. 1, parts 1–2, p. 30 (henceforth cited as *AVB*). Privately, Bishop Gomá of Tarazona expressed very dif-

clergy, although a minority of priests viewed the coming of the Republic in more positive terms. A Catalan clerical journal associated with a more pluralistic approach to the role of the Church in the modern world even admitted "the perfect compatibility of Catholicism with a republican form of government."[16]

The official prudence of the papacy and the hierarchy represented a strategy designed, in the words of Vidal i Barraquer, "to gain time, to save everything possible, . . . to seek an interim agreement [with the government] . . . while negotiations for a Concordat are carried on."[17] The cardinal emerged as the Church's principal negotiator following the enforced exile of Cardinal Segura in mid-May. Although reluctantly accepting the Church's recognition of the Republic, Segura had not remained silent for long. In a pastoral letter of May 1, he sharply criticized the authorities for enacting legislation "damaging to the Church." They would do worse, he suggested, if Catholics failed to form a united front against the Republic's secularizing projects. Segura also exceeded his temperamental penchant for indiscretion by praising Alfonso XIII and a monarchy "always respectful of the Church's rights."[18]

Segura's intervention led the government to demand that the papal nuncio get him out of the country. Although he continued his meddling from afar, his removal was significant. Leadership of the hierarchy passed to Vidal i Barraquer, who received special powers from the papacy to negotiate with the Republic on May 17. The archbishop of Tarragona held opinions as conservative as those of Segura. He viewed the country's future as "obscure and dangerous" and feared the possibility of social revolution.[19] Nor was he averse to the restoration of the monarchy. But, unlike the cardinal primate, he was a realist who recognized that the Republic had come to stay and that the Church had better come to terms with it. For this reason, he strongly opposed the conspiratorial activities into which some monarchists had rushed following the Republic's proclamation. Such a course, he maintained, could only lead to "fatal and disastrous repercussions."[20] Vidal i Barraquer's collegial style also encouraged a positive attitude towards negotiations. Unlike Segura, the cardi-

---

ferent sentiments. "We have entered the vortex of the storm," he declared on April 15, as he contemplated "the monstrosity" committed on the previous day. Ibid., p. 19.

16. "La república dels cristians," *La Paraula Cristiana* (May 1931), vol. 7, no. 77, p. 385. Similarly, a Madrid ecclesiastical journal, after criticizing the regalist controls imposed on the Church by the monarchy, praised "the ample liberty and prosperity" enjoyed by the Church under republics elsewhere in the world. "A la raíz del mal," *Vida Eclesiástica* (May 1931), vol. 4, p. 1.

17. Vidal i Barraquer to Eugenio Pacelli, June 27, 1931, *AVB*, vol. 1, parts 1–2, pp. 91–92.

18. "El Cardenal Arzobispo de Toledo al clero y fieles de la archidiócesis," May 1, 1931, in Jesús Requejo San Román, *El Cardenal Segura* (Toledo, 1931), pp. 141, 139. Another incident in mid-May created difficulties between the Church and the Republic. Miguel Maura accused Bishop Múgica of fomenting opposition to the regime through a series of pastoral visits to his diocese. Maura ordered the prelate's expulsion from the country. Víctor Manuel Arbeloa, "La expulsión de Monseñor Mateo Múgica y la captura de documentos al Vicario General de Vitoria, en 1931," *Scriptorium Victoriense* (1971), vol. 18, pp. 157–58, 168–71.

19. Vidal i Barraquer to Pacelli, June 27, 1931, *AVB*, vol. 1, parts 1–2, p. 91.

20. Ibid.

nal relied heavily on the advice of the archbishops forming the Committee of Metropolitans, who shared his cautious approach.[21]

The provisional government rested on a coalition of diverse republican parties. Although its composition was not entirely promising from the Church's point of view, there were reasonable grounds for believing that the cabinet would seek a negotiated settlement with the Church. Two practicing Catholics, Niceto Alcalá-Zamora, a former Liberal cabinet minister under the Restoration, and Miguel Maura, son of the former Conservative party leader, occupied the key posts of president and minister of the interior (Gobernación). As advocates of conservative republicanism, both were committed to a policy of compromise with the Church. Agreement in principle for a negotiated settlement won the support of other ministers, particularly the Socialist minister of justice, Fernando de los Ríos, and the Radical Republican minister of state, Alejandro Lerroux. The members of the government knew their Spanish history well enough to wish to avoid a repeat performance of the divisive confrontations that had bedeviled civil-ecclesiastical relations in the past.

Between April and September 1931, negotiations between the parties followed a roller-coaster course determined by the complexity of the process itself and the intrusion of external events, a wave of incendiarism against church buildings in May, another imprudent sally by the exiled Segura in mid-August, and other incidents.[22] Although on more than one occasion the negotiations threatened to go off the rails, on September 14 they finally resulted in a secret agreement (*acuerdo reservado*), later approved in cabinet by a vote of eleven to one. It proposed according special status to the Church as a special legal association (corporation of public law) and recognized the Church's right to carry on its religious and teaching activities. It also called for a negotiated *modus vivendi* with the Holy See to replace the 1851 concordat, which had lapsed for all practical purposes, and promised respect for the existence and property of the religious orders.[23]

In two respects, the *acuerdo reservado* represented an expanded version of the moderate liberal regalism characteristic of the Restoration. First, it did not take the

21. The archbishops were generally more moderate in their approach, in contrast to some bishops appointed under the dictatorship who viewed the new regime with the deepest suspicion. Vicente Cárcel Ortí, *La persecución religiosa en España durante la Segunda República, 1931–1939* (Madrid, 1990), p. 103. The archbishops publicly defended Segura before the wave of criticism directed against him for the pastoral letter of May 1, but in private they entertained reservations about the primate's intervention. They also resisted Segura's attempt to write on his own the collective letter of the metropolitans published on May 9. Redondo, *Historia de la Iglesia en España*, vol. 1, p. 138. Vidal i Barraquer believed strongly in a policy of "dialogue" in all aspects of his position, whether dealing with the clergy, the laity, or the civil authorities. Josep Benet, "La lluita del Cardenal Vidal i Barraquer coma home d'Església," *Presbyterium* (1970), no. 4, p. 27.

22. The course of the negotiations is described in detail in *AVB*, vol. 1, parts 1–3. There is an excellent summary in José Manuel Cuenca Toribio, *Relaciones Iglesia-Estado en la España contemporánea, 1833–1985* (Madrid, 1985), pp. 18–39.

23. Hilari Raguer, *La espada y la cruz: la Iglesia, 1936–1939* (Barcelona, 1977), pp. 31–39.

form of a unilateral settlement of the religious question, something that the hierarchy and the Vatican had sought to avoid since the radical ecclesiastical reforms imposed by liberalism during the 1830s and early 1840s. Second, the promised status of a corporation of public law assured the Republic of certain regulatory powers over the Church.[24] Neither the government nor the parties supporting it favored the nineteenth-century republican formula, "a free Church in a free State." Spanish politicians were always reluctant to allow the Church to function as an ordinary civil association subject only to the general laws of the nation; with few exceptions, republican politicians proved no different. Even Alcalá-Zamora, the strongest voice in the cabinet arguing for a "friendly, gradual, correct [and] decent separation of Church and State," wished the government to retain the right to enact "braking legislation" over religious matters. He justified his position by appealing to the historic precedent set by eighteenth-century regalists and nineteenth-century liberals. A handful of republican deputies even believed it necessary to maintain official civil-ecclesiastical ties within a regalist framework as a means of controlling the Church. According to one, the government should appoint republican bishops and canons to create a "republican Church" that would serve the regime's interests.[25]

If implemented, the *acuerdo reservado* would have offered the Church as reasonable an arrangement as it could have expected in the circumstances. But the negotiations of the summer and early autumn suffered from a fatal flaw. They were conducted in private without reference to the shifting tides of party politics and public opinion.

From Liberal to Radical Regalism

The failure to carry out a settlement on the basis of the *acuerdo reservado* has been attributed to the resurgence of a revanchist anticlericalism on the part of republican parties determined to punish the Church.[26] During the Franco regime,

24. As a corporation of public law, the Church would have received a special juridical recognition not accorded to other religious confessions in return for government "inspection and control" over its activities. Dolores Gómez Molleda, *La masonería en la crisis española del siglo XX* (Madrid, 1986), p. 339.

25. Niceto Alcalá-Zamora, *Los defectos de la constitución de 1931* (Madrid, 1981), p. 113. Víctor M. Arbeloa, "La separación de la Iglesia y el Estado en la constitución de 1931," *Revista Española de Derecho Canónico* (1978) vol. 34, no. 98, p. 360. The Socialist Indalecio Prieto believed that the concordat of 1851, with its regalist tinges, should continue to be observed "as an effective way for the State to intervene in the life of the Church and, as a result, place it in its service in some form." Redondo, *Historia de la Iglesia en España*, vol. 1, p. 152.

26. Vicente Cárcel Ortí argues that the Republican parties were not "purely secularist, pacifistic and democratic" but took a position that was "offensive and belligerent" towards the Church. *La persecución religiosa*, p. 143. James R. O'Connell also maintains that the Socialist/Republican coalition dominating parliament made a "decision . . . to embark on a 'crusade'" against the Church in 1931. "The Spanish Republic: Further Reflections on Its Anticlerical Policies," *Catholic Historical Review* (1971), vol. 57, no. 2, p. 279.

every effort was made to blame the Republic for launching a deliberate campaign of persecution, often described as masonic in origin.[27] The theory of a single-minded conspiracy hatched in masonic lodges served the propaganda purposes of the Franco dictatorship. Freemasons were prominently represented in the government and parliament.[28] Their largely bourgeois backgrounds and liberal sympathies made them natural advocates of a secular State and society. But their views on the religious question covered a broad range of opinion, from the tolerant to the extreme. In fact, only a minority of masonic deputies favored a hard line with respect to the Church.[29]

This is not to deny that strong anticlerical currents were sweeping through republican opinion during 1931 or that they contributed to the radicalization of the clauses in the new constitution dealing with the Church. But the parties supporting the governing coalition were far from agreed on the specific terms to be applied in the separation of Church and State.[30] In fact, the absence of a "vertebrate program" on the religious question among and within the coalition parties contributed to the drift away from liberal to radical regalism.[31]

Another familiar specter lurked behind the facade of official negotiations and parliamentary politics, the violent expression in the streets of hostility towards the Church. Even before the proclamation of the Republic, the burning of the Jesuit church in Gijón on December 15, 1930, suggested that trouble lay ahead.[32] It burst forth between May 11 and 13 as a wave of incendiarism swept Madrid, Málaga, Alicante, Orihuela, Cádiz, Murcia, Granada, Seville, and Valencia.

27. See, for example, the work of Juan Ordóñez Márquez, *La apostasía de las masas y la persecución religiosa en la provincia de Huelva, 1931–1936* (Madrid, 1968), p. 257. The idea of a masonic conspiracy had long formed part of modern Spanish Catholicism's political baggage. It reemerged with a vengeance after 1931, often in conjunction with anti-Semitic currents. Vincent, *Catholicism in the Second Spanish Republic*, pp. 217–19.

28. The number of Freemasons holding seats in parliament is a matter of discussion. Gómez Molleda estimates 151 in a chamber of 468, Arbeloa, 129. Gómez Molleda, *La masonería*, p. 261; Víctor M. Arbeloa, "La masonería y la legislación de la República," *Revista Española de Derecho Canónico* (1981), vol. 37, no. 108, p. 369.

29. Gómez Molleda calculates that 42.7 percent of masonic deputies voted for the harsh proposal to suppress the religious orders and nationalize their property discussed by parliament in October 1931. *La masonería*, p. 355.

30. Gómez Molleda divides republican opinion on the Church into three categories. First there were the liberal intellectuals gathered in the Acción Republicana party of Manuel Azaña and a looser political grouping, the Agrupación al Servicio de la República, which included prominent professors and writers, among them the historian Gregorio Marañón and the philosopher José Ortega y Gasset, who viewed the religious question primarily in cultural terms. They saw the Church, especially in teaching, as an obstacle to modern cultural development. The Radical Republicans of Alejandro Lerroux and the Radical Socialists of Álvaro de Albornoz, in Molleda's second category, shared this preoccupation, although they placed greater emphasis on the Church as a political institution that had identified itself in the past with monarchy and dictatorship. These sentiments were also common among Socialists, the third group, who attached greater importance, however, to the Church as an ally of capitalist economic interests. *La masonería*, pp. 283–97; Víctor M. Arbeloa, *Socialismo y anti-clericalismo* (Madrid, 1973), pp. 152–53.

31. Cuenca Toribio, *Relaciones Iglesia-Estado*, p. 21.

32. The assault on the Jesuit church followed disturbances and a general strike in the city provoked by the execution of two Republican army officers who had rebelled against the monarchist government

Dozens of religious buildings, including churches, friaries, convents, and schools lay in ruins, although the level of destruction was far higher in Madrid, Málaga, and Alicante than elsewhere. The *quema de conventos* was confined geographically to Madrid, Andalucía, and the Levante region of the Mediterranean coast. There was no loss of life, but the disturbances came as a nasty surprise to Church and government.[33]

The *quema de conventos* generated enormous controversy. The Church reproached the authorities for failing to act decisively at the first sign of trouble, an issue that also caused bitter dissension within the cabinet.[34] In the end, the government called out the army and explicitly condemned the violence.[35] Given the already formidable task of consolidating republican institutions, the ministers had every reason to curb disturbances that might have led to popular revolution and monarchist rebellion if left unchecked.

The incendiarism of May 1931 was local in character. Significant differences separated the burnings in Madrid and Málaga, for example. In the capital, religious buildings bore the brunt of attack, but in Málaga crowds looted and destroyed commercial warehouses as well as the Unión Mercantil and the Chamber of Commerce, symbols of the city's bourgeois economic interests. The disturbances there also showed traces of the primitive anticlericalism last seen on a massive scale during the violent disturbances of 1834–1835 and, to a lesser extent, during the Tragic Week, in contrast to the situation in Madrid, where the attacks were confined to church burnings. In Málaga, rioters sacked the bishop's palace and paraded about

---

in Jaca. A crowd of young men, watched by a crowd of eight thousand, sacked the church, profaned its altars, and set religious objects to the torch. Alfredo Vernoy, *Los bienes de los Jesuitas. Disolución e incautación de la Compañía de Jesús durante la Segunda República* (Madrid, 1995), p. 53.

33. Barcelona, site of a wave of burnings during the Tragic Week of 1909, escaped unscathed on this occasion, largely because Francesc Macía, president of the autonomous government of Catalonia, summoned "extremist leaders" and persuaded them to refrain from violence. Vidal i Barraquer to Pacelli, June 27, 1931, *AVB*, vol. 1, parts 1–2, p. 85. The exact number of buildings involved has never been resolved, although there is no question that the highest level of destruction occurred in Málaga. José M. Sánchez sets a figure of 107 for the entire country; Jackson gives a rough approximation of two dozen. Gafo estimated 63 took place outside of Madrid. If this figure is combined with Gutiérrez-Ravé's list of 11 churches and convents burned in Madrid, a total of 74 emerges. José M. Sánchez, *Reform and Reaction: The Politico-Religious Background of the Spanish Civil War* (Chapel Hill, 1962), p. 95; Gabriel Jackson, *The Spanish Republic and the Civil War, 1931–1939* (Princeton, 1965), p. 33; José Gafo, "Crónicas científico-sociales," *La Ciencia Tomista* (1931), vol. 44, p. 82; Gutiérrez-Ravé, *España en 1931*, p. 154. Jesuit churches, residences, and schools were particular objects of attack. In Granada, for example, a crowd seized the order's church, flew a red flag from its tower, and sang the *Marseillaise*. Fearing further outbreaks of violence, the government ordered Jesuits to abandon their residences. By the end of May, the order's authorities believed that an official dissolution was only matter of time. Vernoy, *Los bienes de los Jesuitas*, pp. 69–72.

34. Vidal i Barraquer to Alcalá-Zamora, May 17, 1931, *AVB*, vol. 1, parts 1–2, pp. 56–58. Controversy within the government developed over the request of Miguel Maura to call out the Civil Guard at the first signs of trouble in Madrid. The resistance of Manuel Azaña, minister of war, to employing a force long regarded as repressive, delayed strong measures for forty-eight hours. Both Maura and Alcalá-Zamora reproached Azaña and the rest of the cabinet for the delay. Miguel Maura, *Así cayó Alfonso XIII* (5th ed., Barcelona, 1968), pp. 250–51; Niceto Alcalá-Zamora, *Memorias* (Barcelona, 1977), p. 186.

35. Gutiérrez-Ravé, *España en 1931*, p. 157; Jackson, *The Spanish Republic*, pp. 32–33.

in episcopal regalia while singing "liturgical hymns"; they opened tombs in churches and convents and carried religious statues through the streets in mock procession before casting them into the flames.[36]

The authorities offered differing and contradictory explanations of the causes of the disturbances and the motivations of the perpetrators. Alcalá-Zamora blamed monarchists for provoking "the explicable and legitimate indignation of the republican people," which left-wing extremists exploited for their own political ends. Vidal i Barraquer took a similar line, arguing that radicals torched churches to see "if the sparks would take" and lead to the "expulsion of the religious orders and social, political and religious revolution." José Gafo offered a sweeping historical explanation, seeing in the riots the explosion of "an oceanic accumulation of vengeful hatreds and rancors."[37] There is little hard evidence to prove the existence of an incendiary conspiracy. Few were actually arrested, although the timing of the burnings in Madrid and the arrest of twenty-three Communists caught in the act in Málaga suggests something more than purely spontaneous demonstrations.[38]

A definitive explanation remains elusive. But there is no question that the burnings were linked to fears of monarchist conspiracy and the still unresolved struggle among supporters of the Republic over its future direction. Events in Madrid were triggered by clashes between republican and monarchist groups on May 10 that plunged the city into a state of acute tension. A massive crowd gathered in the Puerta del Sol at midnight (May 10–11) to hear speeches from various "commissions." Who composed them is uncertain, although it appears that some of their members came from the Ateneo, a prominent literary club known for its strong republican sympathies. Speakers demanded the disarming of the Civil Guard, long seen as an instrument of repression, the dismissal of Maura, accused of allowing the Guard to fire on demonstrators on the previous day, the suppression of publications judged "enemies of the nascent Republic," and the expulsion of the religious orders.[39]

Speeches were one thing, a wave of incendiarism quite another. No direct link has ever been established between the midnight demonstration and the first of the assaults on the Jesuit church in central Madrid at 10:00 A.M. on May 11. Were the incendiarists goaded into action by what they had heard hours before in the Puerta del Sol? Or did they follow a prearranged program of violence, given the chrono-

36. Antonio García Sánchez, *La Segunda República en Málaga: la cuestión religiosa, 1931–1933* (Málaga, 1984), pp. 242–51. Joan Connelly Ullman, *The Tragic Week: A Study of Anticlericalism in Spain* (Cambridge, Mass., 1968), pp. 246–77.

37. Gutiérrez-Ravé, *España en 1931*, pp. 157–59; Vidal i Barraquer to Pacelli, June 27, 1931, *AVB*, vol. 1, parts 1–2, p. 85; José Gafo, "Crónicas científico-sociales," p. 82. Maura offered yet another explanation, blaming "a small group of intellectuals from the Ateneo" for provoking "a rabble of loafers" to violence. *Así cayó Alfonso XIII*, p. 254.

38. Sánchez, *Reform and Reaction*, pp. 93–95; García Sánchez, *La Segunda República en Málaga*, p. 267.

39. Gutiérrez-Ravé, *España en 1931*, pp. 152–53.

logical sequence of the burnings that moved throughout the day in distinct waves?[40] As evening fell, observers outside the city looked towards the terrible beauty of the skyline as "flames mingled with the glowing red of the sun's last rays."[41]

A definitive answer to these questions is not possible given the present state of research. But the *quema de conventos* sent an unmistakable message. In Madrid, the burnings were carried out by a few hundred demonstrators, but thousands watched and applauded them as they went about their work.[42] Significantly, the burnings in the capital paralleled the Tragic Week of 1909 in that the buildings of the religious orders bore the brunt of attack; the capital's parish churches escaped unscathed. It was in the interest of both the government and the hierarchy to interpret these events as the isolated actions of extremists, a temporary obstacle in the way of a negotiated settlement.[43]

Others drew different conclusions. For a Catholic commentator, the disturbances represented a deliberate effort to secure the expulsion of the orders "through roads of fire." A republican observer believed that the *quema de conventos* told national politicians "to secularize the State, declare the laicization of teaching, . . . and extinguish the religious orders." The municipal council of Málaga lamented the actions of the "parasites and malefactors" it judged responsible for the burnings but concluded that they illustrated the necessity of prompt action to separate Church and State, dissolve the orders, and confiscate their property.[44]

40. Demonstrators first attacked the Jesuit church on the calle de Flor in central Madrid. At 11:00 A.M., the nearby Carmelite church in the Plaza de España fell victim; at 1:15 P.M., the Jesuit vocational school nearby was assaulted. There were two distinct waves of burning during the afternoon, one at 3:00 P.M., another at 6:00 P.M. Ibid., pp. 154–55.

41. Eugenio Vegas Latapié, *Memorias políticas: el suicidio de la Monarquía y la Segunda República* (Barcelona, 1983), p. 112.

42. According to a contemporary account of the burning of Madrid's Jesuit church, "the thousands of citizens who surrounded the property, applauded . . . although they did not take an active part in setting the fire." José María de la Chica, *Las luchas políticas: cómo se incendian los conventos de Madrid* (Madrid, 1931), p. 60.

43. On behalf of the hierarchy, Vidal i Barraquer protested the church burnings in a strongly worded letter to Alcalá-Zamora, president of the provisional government. Despite the gravity of events, the bishops remained "fully cognizant of the difficulties in which Governments find themselves according to the circumstances." The cardinal reaffirmed the Church's desire for a "harmonious and intelligent" resolution of civil-ecclesiastical problems. Alcalá-Zamora replied by restating the government's repudiation of the burnings and acknowledging the commitment of the hierarchy to "peace and concord," a circumstance that he believed would work to the advantage of both Church and State. Vidal i Barraquer to Alcalá-Zamora, May 17, 1931; Alcalá-Zamora to Vidal i Barraquer, May 23, 1931, *AVB*, vol. 1, parts 1–2, pp. 56–57, 61. As relations between the Republic and the Church worsened during 1931 and 1932, the papal nuncio suggested in a formal protest note to the government (November 21, 1932) that the church and convent burnings of the preceding year arose because of "permissivity or passivity on the part of the State." Quoted in Concha García Prous, *Relaciones Iglesia-Estado en la Segunda República española* (Córdoba, 1996), p. 48.

44. Luis González Alonso Getino, *Incendios de conventos de España y supresión de misiones y colegios españoles de ultramar* (Madrid, 1932), p. 19; Chica, *Las luchas políticas*, introduction of R. Castrovido; García Sánchez, *La Segunda República en Málaga*, p. 286.

These events showed that powerful extra-parliamentary pressures were building for a radical solution to the religious question, particularly with respect to the orders. The composition of the Republic's first elected Cortes further complicated the search for a compromise settlement between Church and State. The elections of June 28 returned a decisive majority of deputies representing the republican parties of the Left/center and the Socialists.[45] Although serious differences of opinion on the religious question continued to divide parliamentary supporters of the governing coalition, the elections introduced a significant change into the search for an ecclesiastical settlement, one deeply feared by the Church.

Parliament now held responsibility for drafting a constitution for the Republic. The new cabinet, virtually identical in composition to the provisional government with Alcalá-Zamora as prime minister, continued to negotiate in good faith with the Church, but the election of a constituent parliament reduced its freedom of action. In considerable measure, initiative passed from the cabinet to the Cortes, where "the most extreme groups of the Chamber would make a *tabula rasa* of the government's conciliatory attitude."[46] During the summer, a parliamentary committee, chaired by the Socialist Luis Jiménez de Asúa, began work on a draft constitution.[47] Its majority stood considerably to the left of the cabinet on the religious question, favoring a dramatic shift away from liberal to radical regalism in the form of a unilateral ecclesiastical settlement representing what a Socialist newspaper called "the imperial and integral laicization of the State."[48]

In mid-August, the committee presented its final text. It declared, as expected, that the State had no official religion, but it failed to mention the special legal status (corporation of public law) that had figured prominently in negotiations between the government and the Church. Further, it denied the Church financial

45. Various Republican parties and the Socialists won 250 seats, of which the largest number, 120, were held by the latter. The Radical Republicans of Lerroux formed the center of the new parliament with 100 seats. Only 80 seats were won by various right-wing parties committed to defending the Church at all costs: they included the "Agrarians," a loose grouping representing conservative agricultural interests in Castile and Andalucía (25 seats), the strongly Catholic deputies of the Basque nationalist party (PNV) (14 seats) and those of the Lliga Catalana (10 seats). Jackson, *The Spanish Republic*, pp. 41–42. For Vidal i Barraquer's highly pessimistic assessment of the political situation, see Vidal i Barraquer to Pacelli, June 27, August 12, 1931, *AVB*, vol. 1, parts 1–2, pp. 89, 203.

46. Alcalá-Zamora, *Los defectos de la Constitución*, p. 107.

47. In May, Alcalá-Zamora appointed a special committee (Comisión Jurídica Asesora) to prepare a draft constitutional text. Chaired by the liberal Catholic Republican Angel Ossorio y Gallardo, it produced moderate proposals on the religious question. Differences among the ministers about various aspects of the text caused the cabinet to set it aside. There was also strong opposition to it from *El Debate*, which criticized it in several editorials. There was never much likelihood of its being accepted by the parties of the Left, as even Ossorio y Gallardo admitted. Fernando de Meer, *La cuestión religiosa en las Cortes Constituyentes de la II República* (Pamplona, 1975), p. 65; *El Debate*, July 2, 5, 15, 1931, in *El pensamiento de "El Debate": un diario católico en la crisis de España, 1911–1936*, ed. José María García Escudero (Madrid, 1983), pp. 933–35; Angel Ossorio y Gallardo, *La España de mi vida: autobiografía* (Barcelona and Buenos Aires, 1977), pp. 121–22.

48. Quoted in Víctor M. Arbeloa, *La semana trágica de la Iglesia de España, 1931* (Barcelona, 1976), p. 76.

support from national, regional, and local governments. Finally, in its most controversial clause, it recommended the dissolution of the religious orders and the nationalization of their property.[49]

The committee's text aroused deep clerical apprehension. Vidal i Barraquer saw it as preparing "the terrain for an absolutely atheistic and secular constitution," a sign of the "apostasy of the Spanish State."[50] Since the terms of the proposal stood in sharp contradiction to those being discussed in official negotiations between Church and State, the government found itself in a difficult political position, one made all the more sensitive because of the heated emotions aroused by public discussion of the constitutional project. As if this were not enough, Cardinal Segura struck again through a pastoral letter published in an intransigent Catholic newspaper. Segura attacked the proposed text as the result of "a plague of laicism" developed from the "modern liberties" first established by the French Revolution that had become "the intangible patrimony of democracies hostile to the Church."[51]

Segura's outburst provoked indignation among republican deputies, many growing increasingly restless on the religious question, and widespread condemnation on the part of newspapers supporting the government. As Vidal i Barraquer recognized, the cabinet lacked "a disciplined majority" among republican deputies for its compromise policy.[52] In view of the political uproar caused by Segura's letter, the government believed that it could not defend its commitment to the Church in parliament without first securing Segura's resignation from the archbishopric of Toledo. Vidal i Barraquer urged the Holy See to act accordingly, recognizing that without the primate's removal, "obtaining guarantees in the Constitution" would prove impossible.[53] Although Segura resisted Vatican pressure as long as he could, he finally submitted his resignation, which was announced on September 30.

Before the opening on October 8 of full parliamentary debate on the religious clauses of the constitutional draft, the Republic had introduced religious liberty and taken other measures against the Church's historic privileges.[54] Although these initiatives provoked controversy, they paled into insignificance before the intense, emotional discussions, "undoubtedly, the most passionate of the entire Constitu-

49. Meer, *La cuestión religiosa*, pp. 77–78.

50. Vidal i Barraquer to Alcalá-Zamora, August 3, 1931, *AVB*, vol. 1, parts 1–2, p. 178.

51. Pedro Segura, "Sobre el proyecto de Constitución y deberes de los católicos," in *Documentos colectivos del episcopado español*, pp. 137, 146.

52. Vidal i Barraquer to Pacelli, September 10, 1931, *AVB*, vol. 1, part 3, pp. 300–301.

53. Ibid. For a discussion of the political backlash created by Segura, see Arbeloa, *La semana trágica*, pp. 26–28; Raguer, *La espada y la cruz*, pp. 32–36. The reaction against Segura was strengthened by another incident, the seizure in Irún of Father Justo Echeguren, vicar-general of the Vitoria diocese, who had in his possession documents written by Segura providing instructions on how the ecclesiastical authorities should dispose of Church property to avoid its nationalization. The government regarded the instructions as nothing less than advice to commit fiscal fraud.

54. The provisional government decreed full religious liberty and the voluntary character of religious teaching in public schools. Later, provisional legislation secularized cemeteries (July 9, 1931),

tion," that now took place.[55] The clergy, politicians, and their respective constituencies saw the outcome as vital to the future of the country. Whether the cold facts of the situation justified this attitude is debatable given the enormous social and economic problems faced by the Republic on other fronts.

In any event, the key to implementing the *acuerdo reservado* and to resolving the contradiction between cabinet and parliament lay in Article 24 (Article 26 in the constitution when it was approved), the key proposal of the constitutional draft. After Segura's resignation, the ministers agreed to seek modifications aimed at saving the religious orders from extinction. Given the looseness of the republican coalition, the government could not expect a disciplined and unified response in parliament. By late September, opinion on Article 24 formed a seething mass of agitation and disagreement among and within the republican parties.[56] The fluidity of parliamentary politics meant that nothing could be taken for granted as full debate began.

There was nothing new about the fundamental issue at stake. The problem of reconciling the right of free association and liberty of conscience with the powers of the State ran through the discussions, as they had done repeatedly since the triumph of liberalism during the 1830s. Although deputies of all persuasions advanced innumerable cultural, historical, social, and economic arguments in their highly charged exchanges, the question was straightforward.[57] Where would the regalist pendulum stop—at an expanded version of the moderate regalism of the Restoration or at the more radical form implemented by the liberals of the 1830s who suppressed the male orders outright?

The debate was emotional and divisive. Appeals to moderation by several ministers, notably Fernando de los Ríos and Alejandro Lerroux, and by other Republicans mingled with the sharp attacks of the minority of right-wing deputies and the violent diatribes of extreme anticlericals. As the veneer of cabinet solidarity began to crumble in the midst of an increasingly impassioned atmosphere, momentum quickly passed to the deputies, found to a greater or lesser degree in all the republican parties, who demanded passage of the original draft of Article 24.[58] Faithful to their anticlerical tenets, the Radical Socialists remained intransigent. Lerroux, the old anticlerical lion now regarded as the "idol of the sacristies" for his moderation on the religious question, proved unable or unwilling to control the

eliminated chaplains from the armed forces, forbade government officials from attending religious ceremonies, etc. Cárcel Ortí, *La persecución religosa*, pp. 161–62.

55. Gutiérrez-Ravé, *España en 1931*, p. 352.

56. These divisions are discussed in detail by Gómez Molleda, *La masonería*, pp. 325–41.

57. For a detailed treatment of the debates, see Arbeloa, *La semana trágica*, passim.

58. Ibid., p. 106; Gómez Molleda, *La masonería*, pp. 294, 363. Álvaro de Albornoz, the minister of development, deserted his colleagues by siding with the intransigent stand of his Radical Socialists. There were other differences among the ministers. Fernando de los Ríos, for example, suddenly abandoned his earlier commitment to granting the Church special juridical status as a corporation of public law, a shift which was severely criticized by Azaña.

increasing restlessness of extremist Radical Republicans.[59] A powerful current of opposition to any modification of Article 24 gathered force among the Socialists despite the key role played by Fernando de los Ríos in negotiations with the Church. By October 13, divisions on the religious question threatened the fragile unity of the governing coalition.

The possibility of a deal between liberal and radical regalism to resolve the impasse emerged from the Radical Republicans through their parliamentary leader, Rafael Guerra del Río, a veteran of the party's early-twentieth-century anticlerical campaigns and a hard-liner on the religious question.[60] On October 10, "*he set the price of the transaction*" by demanding the suppression of the Jesuits and a future law of associations to determine the status of the remaining orders.[61]

It was far from certain that a majority could be secured to modify Article 24 even at this price. The political skills of Manuel Azaña, minister of war and leader of the liberal bourgeois Acción Republicana party, now proved crucial. In the most famous parliamentary speech delivered during the Republic's history, Azaña produced the specific formula that saved the governing coalition from disintegration: the immediate suppression of the Jesuits, the survival of the other orders at the sufferance of the State, and the regulation of their activities through a future law on religious congregations. Azaña added a new ingredient to the mix by demanding that the orders be prohibited from teaching, although some of his supporters entertained serious doubts about imposing so drastic a limitation on the historic liberal right of association.[62]

59. Gómez Molleda, *La masonería,* pp. 363, 366–67.

60. Radical deputies moved towards a more extreme position as a result of a vote on October 1 granting the franchise to women, a development that they believed would work to the Church's benefit. The measure was supported by an unlikely alliance of the Socialists and right-wing deputies. As a result, many Radicals threatened to take as extreme a position as possible in the upcoming debates on the religious clauses of the constitution. Ibid., pp. 351–52; "Informaciones de Ricardo Gómez Rojí," October 1–2, 1931, *AVB,* vol. 1, part 3, p. 349.

61. Gómez Molleda, *La masonería,* p. 366. The origins of hostility towards the Jesuits are complex. In part, it represented the persistence, even among Republicans, of the regalist opposition to the order first displayed by the reformers of absolute monarchy in the eighteenth century, who saw the Jesuits as an obstacle to the exercise of the State's authority. Nineteenth-century liberals inherited these views and suppressed the Jesuits in 1820, 1836, 1854, and 1868. It is significant that Álvaro de Albornoz, the minister of justice at the time of the order's suppression in 1932, resorted to the eighteenth-century example, arguing that Charles III's pragmatic sanction expelling the Jesuits had never been revoked. The Republic, therefore, was fully justified in extinguishing the order. The Jesuits were also strongly criticized, especially by the Socialists, for their elitist educational system and their activist involvement in the least progressive aspects of social Catholicism. "Manifestacions del ministre de Justicia, Álvaro de Albornoz, a la premsa, sobre el decret de dissolució de la Companyia de Jesús," January 16, 1932; *AVB,* vol. 2, parts 1–2, p. 377; Arbeloa, *La semana trágica,* pp. 212–14. A virulent press campaign against the Jesuits began in early October, when two liberal newspapers demanded the order's dissolution. An editorial in *Crisol* indicted the order because of its record of "political interference, its influence in the bosom of families and, in particular, on the formation of youth, which has given origin to a human character harmful to society." The newspaper called for the order's suppression without compromise. Quoted in Vernoy, *Los bienes de los Jesuitas,* p. 95.

62. The full text is reproduced in *Manuel Azaña: obras completas,* ed. Juan Marichal (4 vols., Mexico City, 1966–1968), vol. 2, pp. 49–58.

Until this time, the minister of war had not been a key player in efforts to deal with the religious question. Azaña and his party favored the creation of a secular State in the style of the French Third Republic and viewed the Church's intellectual and educational role as an obstacle to modern cultural development.[63] But they had opposed an extreme solution to the problem, particularly with respect to the religious orders. In fact, Azaña had voted for the *acuerdo reservado* of September 14. Why did he now seize the initiative? Vidal i Barraquer found his intervention "unexpected and surprising."[64] There is little doubt that Azaña acted for a specific political motive, to allow the government to escape, as he expressed it, "from a very difficult moment of peril."[65] Vidal i Barraquer also correctly assessed the reasons behind the speech. Azaña possessed the "clear vision of parliamentary reality" that allowed him to establish "the link of union among the republican parties" seriously divided on the religious question.[66]

Long celebrated for his mordant rhetoric, Azaña used it to full effect in his speech, particularly in the famous phrase "Spain has ceased to be Catholic," a statement that outraged the Church's supporters, who misinterpreted its meaning.[67] In the heat of the moment, Vidal i Barraquer saw Azaña as an agent of "antireligious conspiracy." The "Agrarian" deputy José María Gil Robles attacked the final constitutional text as "an elaboration of the masonic lodges and a trick of an audacious politician [Azaña]." Even moderate Republicans were aghast at the implications of the Azaña formula. The historian Gregorio Marañón saw the new constitution's religious policy as a "great, enormous error," an example of "arbitrary persecution, which must wound our love for liberty," while the philosopher José Ortega y Gasset pronounced the widely cited aphorism that the religious clauses of the constitution were "exploding cartridges" capable of shattering the Republic's stability.[68]

Passage of the constitution marked an important divide in the history of relations between Church and Republic. The constitution represented the unilateral settlement of the religious question so long feared by the clergy. In December 1931, fifty-nine bishops joined in a "collective reprobation" not only of the constitution

63. Juan Marichal, *La vocación de Manuel Azaña* (Madrid, 1968), p. 119.

64. Vidal i Barraquer to Pacelli, October 16, 1931, *AVB*, vol. 1, part 3, pp. 388–90.

65. "Memorias políticas y de guerra," *Manuel Azaña: obras completas*, vol. 4, p. 179. Alfredo Vernoy also maintains that the decision to suppress the Jesuits saved the government from a "fratricidal war" in its midst. *Los bienes de los Jesuitas*, p. 104.

66. Vidal i Barraquer to Pacelli, October 16, 1931, *AVB*, vol. 1, part 3, pp. 388–90.

67. Azaña was not advocating a campaign to de-Catholicize Spain, as some of his critics alleged. He recognized the existence of "many millions of believing Spanish Catholics" entitled to practice their religion as a matter of conscience. He rejected, however, the identification of Catholicism with the State, a union that in the past had allowed the Church to use the powers of the government "to impel consciences even against their will." *Manuel Azaña: obras completas*, vol. 2, pp. 51, 52; Marichal, *La vocación de Manuel Azaña*, pp. 205–7; Vicente Enrique y Tarancón, *Recuerdos de juventud* (Barcelona, 1984), p. 150.

68. Vidal i Barraquer to Pacelli, October 16, 1931, *AVB*, vol. 1, part 3, p. 396; Gutiérrez-Ravé, *España en 1931*, p. 392; quoted in Arbeloa, *La semana trágica*, pp. 235–37, and in Meer, *La cuestión religiosa*, p. 107.

but also of an entire range of government legislation, particularly that involving education and divorce. Although the prelates urged Catholics to do everything within their power to resist what they saw as a secularizing onslaught representing "an implacable war against the Church," they avoided urging the faithful into illegal acts.[69] The military analogy used by the bishops found ample echo in the pages of the Catholic press. After affirming that "absolutely all [Catholics]" were "against the Constitution," *El Debate* urged them to work "with maximum energy" in a "war" against it, albeit within the framework of legality.[70]

The outbreak of civil war in 1936 has lent a prophetic quality to the predictions of contemporaries who saw looming catastrophe in the 1931 constitution. Did the circumstances justify these pessimistic assessments? Was there an "implacable war" against the Church? The term "persecution," used by the Church's defenders in 1931 and by some historians, is relative, ultimately a question of judgment. The harassment to which the Church was subject between 1931 and 1933 cannot be compared, for example, to the harshness of government policy in Mexico during the same period and certainly not to the brutal actions of totalitarian governments in eastern Europe following the Second World War. The Spanish situation more closely approximated the conflict between the Church and the French Third Republic at the beginning of the century. The separation of Church and State, the suppression of the regular clergy, and the end of official financial support carried out by the Third Republic produced a short-term negative reaction among Catholics similar to that prevailing in Spain during the early 1930s. But over the long term the French Church adapted to its new circumstances.

The Spanish Church lost or was about to lose the privileges that had sustained it during the Restoration and the dictatorship. As a result, it faced a financial crisis of serious proportions and remained subject to regalist controls in certain areas of activity. But the Republic did not engage in the systematic exile of bishops employed on a large scale by some nineteenth-century liberal governments. Although the authorities resorted to temporary suspensions of Catholic newspapers, they did not attempt to destroy the confessional press, some of it violently critical of the regime. Nor did they interfere, on the whole, with the innumerable Catholic devotional, social, and educational associations created by the Church. On the contrary, there is strong evidence of a significant revival of associational activity compared to the institutional languor of the 1920s. Even the constitutional ban on teaching by the orders remained unenforced for the time being because of an acute shortage of teachers, of which the government was all too aware. In fact, the orders were told in no uncertain terms to remain at their posts or face the instant loss of their property!

69. "Episcopado a los fieles," in *Documentos colectivos del episcopado español*, pp. 170, 176, 178.
70. *El Debate*, October 6, 15, 1931, in *El pensamiento de "El Debate,"* p. 940.

The Republic also freed the Church from the burden of government ecclesiastical patronage, something that even the redoubtable Hilario Yaben appreciated. The Republic, he declared, liberated the Church from "true servitude" by renouncing the appointment rights associated with the monarchy.[71] The Catholic law professor Eloy Montero y Gutiérrez saw separation as a positive development that would lead to a process of internal purification and self-examination both necessary and beneficial to the Church.[72] Further, Azaña's formula on the regular clergy, although restrictive and unfair in many respects, promised the legalization of all the orders save the Jesuits. No government of the Restoration, not even the dictatorship, had dared as much.[73] Moreover, as Miguel Maura recognized at the time and as historians have since acknowledged, whatever his motives, Azaña saved the Church from a worse fate, the total suppression of the religious orders.[74]

The Republic imposed no significant limitations on the right of the Church to conduct religious services, although there were widespread incidents between the clergy and republican municipalities. Local anticlericalism had a long history reaching back in its modern form to the 1868 revolution. It now reemerged in spectacular fashion. Given that city and town councils held limited responsibility for the regulation of public order, it was inevitable that they would seek to implement a secularizing program at the local level. Their initiatives ranged from the comic to the oppressive. In La Coruña, the authorities were so determined to keep priests from accompanying funeral processions that they ordered horse-drawn hearses to proceed "at the trot," leaving a puffing clergy far behind.[75] The Ávila city council followed a widespread practice by substituting republican street names for those of the saints. Other municipalities prohibited religious processions through the streets, removed sacred statues from public sites, and imposed special taxes on the ringing of church bells. Although there were a few serious incidents involving violence, by and large municipal anticlericalism did not seriously interfere with the conduct of religious services.

Neither Catholics nor their critics saw it this way, of course. Local anticlericalism assumed a symbolic quality and importance that went far beyond its specific manifestations for both its promoters and the faithful. Conflict reached even the

71. Hilario Yaben, "¿Hacia un concordato?," *Revista Eclesiástica* (1934), p. 130.

72. Eloy Montero y Gutiérrez, *El porvenir de la Iglesia de España* (Madrid, 1933), pp. 2–8.

73. Marianos Granados, *La cuestión religosa en España* (Mexico City, 1959), p. 33.

74. Arbeloa, *La semana trágica*, p. 263. The liberal Catholic historian Hilari Raguer has argued that Azaña's intervention provided the Church "with the most effective help" to save what was possible "in that very critical moment" and to avoid "a great disaster." Even Vicente Cárcel Ortí, who renders a harsh judgment against the religious policy of the Republic, admits that the original draft of Article 24, if passed, would have been "fatal for the Spanish Church." He acknowledges that "the maneuvering of Azaña succeeded in avoiding it." Hilari Raguer, "La Iglesia española en la II República," *Arbor* (1981), vol. 109, nos. 426–427, p. 61; Cárcel Ortí, *La persecución religiosa*, p. 150.

75. *El Debate*, July 16, 1931.

small towns of the countryside, as in Salamanca province, where village populations protested against the removal of crucifixes from local primary schools.[76] These battles paralleled, albeit in chaotic fashion, the struggle between the Republic and the Church taking place at the national level.

Nowhere was this more evident than in the resurgence of the "wars of the dead" following the provisional secularization of cemeteries in July 1931. After decades of using the power to determine who should or should not be buried in consecrated ground, the Church now found the tables turned. Municipalities demolished the highly symbolic wall separating civil from consecrated plots. In Seville, the city council marched in solemn procession to the local cemetery, where the mayor presided over the wall's demolition to cries of "Long live the Republic!" and the tunes of a children's chorus. In regions where Christian burial was seen as an essential aspect of religious and community life, the secularization of cemeteries, combined with the bureaucratic requirement that anyone wishing a religious burial must so indicate through a formal legal document, produced resentment and another round of the "wars of the dead."[77]

Before 1931, the "wars of the dead" had proceeded from the Church's determination to ensure that those judged to have died outside the faith should not be buried in consecrated ground. The republican version took the form of a glorification of secular values through rituals that paralleled those of the Catholic liturgy, with lay hymns, often the *Marseillaise,* and invocations resembling prayers.[78] Despite the emotions aroused by the "wars of the dead," there was no massive desertion to the republican liturgy. The vast majority of funerals continued to be carried out according to traditional religious rites.[79] The significance of these conflicts lies not so much in what was done to the Church, harassing though it was, but in the vehicle they provided for spreading the struggle between Catholics and the Republic to the level of town and village on a scale previously unknown.

Conflict at the local level took different forms, from street battles to the apocalyptic and messianic movement associated with visions and prophecies in the Basque town of Ezquioga beginning in June 1931. Like the Fatima visions of 1916 and 1917 in Portugal, the events at Ezquioga took place within an intense emo-

76. Vincent, *Catholicism in the Second Spanish Republic,* pp. 185–86.

77. José Jiménez Lozano, *Los cementerios civiles y la heterodoxia española* (Madrid, 1978), p. 245. In a village near Ciudad Rodrigo, for example, a woman who had received the last sacraments but was unable to sign the required certificate because of illness was denied a religious burial. Vincent, *Catholicism in the Second Spanish Republic,* p. 188.

78. Jiménez Lozano, *Los cementerios civiles,* p. 250.

79. Montero y Gutiérrez, *El porvenir de la Iglesia,* pp. 147–48. In October 1932, for example, 875 of the 963 burials carried out in Madrid were conducted by the Church. Cárcel Ortí, *La persecución religiosa,* p. 174. In Salamanca, the number of religious burials in 1931–1932 scarcely differed from the period before the proclamation of the Republic. Vincent, *Catholicism in the Second Spanish Republic,* pp. 68–69.

tional atmosphere generated by a powerful reaction in this strongly Catholic rural area against the apparent assault on Church and religion by the Republic.[80] The visionaries of Ezquioga reworked a historic theme of Spanish Catholicism by describing a world threatened by catastrophe and divine punishment for its sins identified with the antireligious Republic. The country was caught "in the midst of a sea of dangers, . . . the hurricane wind tells us that we are two steps away from the most terrible of storms, from which we will hardly be able to emerge without divine help."[81] Seers predicted a terrible time of trial. One declared that the Virgin "has announced a tremendous chastisement of three important cities in Spain, if they do not change their ways." Three cities "will be reduced to ashes in a moment, in an instant, in a flash."[82] Another declared that the "hurricane will ravage the earth," while the "power of Jesus with the sword of Michael will smite the evil and the persecutors of religion. . . . Millions will fall crushed like snowflakes in the burning hole. Afterward, the world will be in peace, the people content and blessed, because prayer will reign."[83]

The sensational events at Ezquioga attracted national attention, as thousands of the devout rushed to the region to hear the prophecies of hundreds of seers. Although the authorities first dismissed the visions and predictions as inconsequential, they later had second thoughts. In 1932, the civil governor attacked them as "reactionary," declaring, "I will not tolerate this kind of politics disguised as religion."[84] This concern was misplaced. Although the visions and prophecies attracted some clerical support, Bishop Múgica of Vitoria remained implacably opposed to the Ezquioga manifestations and took action against priests who promoted them. William Christian's analysis of these events also suggests that the papal nuncio, Federico Tedeschini, saw Ezquioga as an obstacle to the realization of his plans for an accommodation with the Republic and used his influence to curb the movement.[85]

The religious policy of the Republic as set forth in the 1931 constitution and its chaotic implementation at the local level represented a halfway house between the application of historic liberal principles and a determination to keep the Church under tight rein in view of its past support for monarchy and dictatorship. It represented a radical extension of the regalism associated with the Restoration. However unfairly treated in certain areas of activity, the Church was not subjected to an "implacable war" capable of reducing it to impotence. It remained a formidable institution.

80. William Christian, *Visionaries: The Spanish Republic and the Reign of Christ* (Berkeley, Los Angeles, and London, 1996), p. 6.

81. Quoted in ibid., p. 29.

82. Quoted in ibid., p. 355.

83. Quoted in ibid., p. 359.

84. Quoted in ibid., p. 137.

85. Ibid., pp. 151, 154–55.

The Strategy of Defense, 1931–1933

Despite the increasingly militant tone of episcopal rhetoric following the constitution's passage, the clerical leadership retained its sense of political realism. The Committee of Metropolitans remained committed to the search for an accommodation with the regime even as its members drafted the strongly worded collective letter of December 1931. Although realizing that the grounds for establishing a working relationship with the Republic had narrowed, the archbishops wanted to avoid a break in relations. They recognized that modification of the constitution and related religious legislation was out of the question for the moment, given the composition of parliament. Over the long term, they looked to future elections to return a government disposed to modify the constitution. In the meantime, the Church had only one alternative, to deal as best it could with the Republic, with a view to ameliorating the effects of its religious legislation.[86] Above all, the archbishops sought to avoid a replay of Article 26 when debate began on the future law of religious congregations.

Through a round of contacts with government ministers and moderate republican deputies, the metropolitans believed it possible to secure "the progressive mitigation of the current radicalism" existing in parliament.[87] The election of Alcalá-Zamora to the presidency of the Republic offered the hope that the chief of State would use his limited constitutional powers in this direction. The hierarchy viewed Azaña, who had become prime minister in October 1931, with apprehension. But Azaña had no intention of launching a campaign against the Church.[88] Following the constitution's passage, he noted in his diary that "policy towards the Church must [now] be carried on in another *way.*" In a November 1931 meeting with Cardinals Vidal i Barraquer and Ilundain, the prime minister expressed his conviction that the situation of the Church would improve now that the regime's constituent period and the "effervescence and extremism" associated with it had passed.[89]

During the first six months of 1932, the policy of mitigation bore some fruit as the government made a few concessions to the Church. The Ministry of Justice acted to restrain the excesses of municipal governments bent on excluding the clergy entirely from conducting religious services in the now secularized cemeteries. For a time, the cooperation of moderate republican deputies and the prime

86. Metropolitans to Pius XI, December 7, 1931, *AVB*, vol. 2, part 1, pp. 177–78; Vidal i Barraquer to Pacelli, December 7, 1931, ibid., pp. 208–9.

87. Ibid.

88. Both Alcalá-Zamora and Maura resigned from the government following the passage of Article 24 (Article 26 in the final version of the constitution) to protest what they regarded as the government's failure to live up to its negotiated commitment with the Church.

89. *Manuel Azaña: obras completas*, vol. 4, p. 242; "Reseña de la entrevista de los Sres. Cardenales con Sr. Azaña," November 20, 1931; *AVB*, vol. 2, part 1, p. 180. The report was prepared by Cardinal Ilundain.

minister offered the possibility that parish priests would be able to enjoy their official salaries until death or retirement, although the project foundered in the end on the opposition in the cabinet of the strongly anticlerical Radical Socialists. Taken as a whole, the concessions granted the Church were not substantive.

The events of the previous year revealed that the place of the Church within the Republic transcended the narrow field of civil-ecclesiastical negotiations. The cabinet rested on the same parliamentary majority that had passed the constitution's religious clauses. On more than one occasion, Azaña informed the hierarchy that while the government was disposed to seek "a legal formula" that might rescue "what might be saved" for the Church, such an arrangement could not contradict either the intent or the terms of the constitution.[90] The cabinet and parliament remained committed to an ample program of secularization and wasted little time implementing it.

During early 1932, the Jesuits were suppressed and their property nationalized; a final law on the secularization of cemeteries was passed and divorce legalized. The authorities moved rapidly in the field of education by removing religion as a subject taught in public schools and by ordering the removal of crucifixes and other sacred symbols from classrooms. The government also carried out the first stage of eliminating the *culto y clero* appropriation by ordering a substantial reduction for the 1932 fiscal year.

These measures raised a storm of protest among clergy and laity. Mindful of the benefits it hoped to secure through its strategy of mitigation, the hierarchy generally showed restraint in its criticism. Vidal i Barraquer protested against the suppression of the Jesuits as a consecration of legalized violence but reaffirmed his commitment to the policy of moderation, "whatever the actual state of affairs."[91] The Catholic press proved less discreet, waging a sustained campaign of vociferous criticism against the regime that caused the government to suspend publication of some newspapers, including *El Debate*.[92] Despite its links to the hierarchy, the principal organ of Catholic opinion showed few signs of moderation. In an April editorial marking the Republic's first anniversary, it concluded that the government was following a "petty, narrow [policy] inspired by class hatred and official hostility towards the Catholic Church."[93]

The religious legislation of early 1932 also exacerbated local conflicts between defenders and opponents of the Church that had surfaced with a vengeance during the previous year. Attempts to remove crucifixes from public schools provoked protest demonstrations in areas known for high levels of religious observance, as

90. Azaña to Vidal i Barraquer, January 2, 1933, *AVB*, vol. 3, part 3, p. 615.

91. Statement of Vidal i Barraquer, January 25, 1931, reproduced in *El Debate*, March 26, 1932.

92. *El Debate*'s vigorous attacks on the suppression of the Jesuits led the government to suspend its publication between January 19 and March 25, 1932.

93. *El Debate*, April 14, 1932.

did the refusal of some municipal authorities to grant officially required permission for religious processions. As before, these incidents ranged from the slightly ridiculous, as when nurses armed with sticks chased carpenters from a public hospital where they had been sent by local authorities to remove religious symbols, to the serious. To cite a few examples among many, in January there were attempts at church burnings in districts near Valencia; republican extremists fired shots into the Holy Week procession in a village of Toledo province; and in a small town in Cáceres province, enraged Catholics attempted to lynch two individuals who had mocked a procession as it made its way through the streets. At the grassroots level, passions remained as inflamed as ever.[94]

The continuation of these local battles and the general reaction of Catholic opinion to the religious legislation of early 1932, as expressed in the confessional press, scarcely provided the conditions necessary for the kind of limited truce with the regime being sought by the hierarchy. In important respects, the Catholic protest movement shared the same lack of discipline shown by the republican parties on the religious question, and with equally ambiguous results. The Catholic reaction resembled a concentric circle with the policy of the hierarchy and the Vatican at the center. Beyond, there revolved the circle of Catholic politicians and newspapers, who, though accepting the official line in principle, advocated a policy of legal confrontation that did not reflect the caution of the hierarchy. The movements of the two inner circles were far from synchronized, but they followed the same path, more or less, in contrast to an outer circle of Carlists, Integrists, authoritarian monarchists, and antiliberal clergymen who moved uncontrollably in relation to the other two.

But, as the archbishops recognized, the key to their strategy lay in their ability to control and direct Catholics to form an effective political lobby within the regime, while avoiding extreme reactions certain to provoke a harsh reaction on the part of the government and the parties supporting it. In fact, the views of the metropolitans were not so different from those of Azaña. In November 1931, Vidal i Barraquer warned again of the danger posed by an "*integrist extremism*" committed to undermining any accommodation, however limited, with the Republic. The Committee of Metropolitans agreed on the necessity of exercising "vigilance" over the "damaging spirit" of Catholics opposing the hierarchy's "revisionist campaign" on the grounds that it would help "consolidate the Republic."[95]

In the best of circumstances, the bishops' ability to keep a tight rein over Catholic opinion was problematic, despite the Church's hierarchical structure. As in the past, political divisions among Catholics prevented the successful implementation of a policy resting solely on the defense of clerical interests. The bish-

94. Ibid., January 14, 19, and March 27, 30, 1932.

95. Vidal i Barraquer to Pacelli, December 7, 1931, *AVB*, vol. 2, part 1, pp. 176–77.

ops lacked, moreover, the experience and the institutional means of exerting effective control over the editorial policy of the confessional press and the statements of Catholic politicians. The hierarchy neither owned newspapers nor possessed the organizational mechanisms, even in the case of a press more or less disposed to follow its counsels, to ensure that episcopal views on relations with the Republic would receive the kind of unequivocal support it believed necessary. The hierarchy's attempt to come to terms with the regime was held hostage by the far less compromising attitude of the confessional press and Catholic politicians. The circumstances demanded extreme caution and prudence. Father José Gafo urged Catholics "to keep quiet, to show restraint, to fortify themselves inwardly" if they hoped "to conquer . . . the people."[96] This advice went unheeded. The aggressive and sometimes vituperative rhetoric employed by the Catholic press in its reaction to the religious legislation of early 1932 fanned the flames of Catholic frustration and anger, a circumstance scarcely calculated to encourage broad support among the republican parties for a policy of concessions. But as Vidal i Barraquer recognized as early as the spring of 1931, the greatest danger to the Church's effort to safeguard its interests within the new political order lay in the intransigent opposition of a mixed group of Carlists, Integrists, and authoritarian monarchists to the Republic's very existence.

Catholic ultras represented a minority of laypeople and priests, but they possessed the capacity to do enormous damage to efforts to reach a working arrangement with the regime. The hierarchy paid a heavy price for its inability to control even Church publications. The well-known ecclesiastical propagandist Father P. M. Vélez, for example, experienced no difficulty in publishing an ideological attack on the Republic that trotted out a range of arguments commonplace in the ultra ideological arsenal. The Republic's origins could be traced to the French Revolution, "stepmother" to every subsequent revolution and to the "false liberties" introduced by Spanish liberalism. Conciliation between traditional Catholicism and modern liberalism was "impossible."[97] Vélez saw the conflict between Catholicism and the Republic as an epic battle between a "society of God" and a "society of Satan" upon which the future of Christian civilization would depend.[98]

Ideological criticism of the regime was one thing, rebellion against it quite another. Although plotting against the Republic began immediately following its proclamation, the constitution's passage and later legislation on religious matters broadened the appeal of a resort to force. According to José Gafo, "the feverish impassioning of spirits" created as a result gave new impetus to discussions on "the legality or illegality of adherence or submission . . . to the constituted powers; the

96. José Gafo, "Crónicas científico sociales," *La Ciencia Tomista* (1932), vol. 45, p. 141.

97. P. M. Vélez, "La lección divina de la revolución española," *Religión y Cultura* (1933), no. 64, pp. 10–14.

98. Ibid., p. 21.

legality or illegality of resistance to Authority, [and] of the right to rebellion or revolution."[99] During the constitutional debates of the previous autumn, the clerical deputy Canon Antonio Pildain threw the chamber into a furor by arguing that legal, passive, and "active armed resistance" against unjust laws was compatible with Catholic doctrine. Articles on the right of "active resistance to the public power[s]" and "the legality of insurrection" even began to appear in respected clerical journals.[100]

Justifications of the right to armed resistance took the form of speculative discussion derived from sixteenth- and seventeenth-century scholastic philosophy. They generally did not exhort Catholics to support the conspiratorial activity of specific groups on the extreme Right. But along with the drumbeat of intense criticism directed against the government by the confessional press and Catholic politicians, they served to deepen suspicions towards the regime.

Within this framework, disaffected groups on the Right rebelled against the Republic on August 10, 1932. Encouraged by prominent Carlists and authoritarian monarchists, the former head of the Civil Guard, General José Sanjurjo, rose in a revolt easily quelled by the government. Vidal i Barraquer quickly informed the prime minister that the bishops "lamented" the rebellion and that "none of our prelates is capable of supporting or involving themselves in such affairs."[101] Similarly, Catholic newspapers, including *El Debate,* condemned the rising. The Barcelona Catholic daily *El Matí,* closely linked to Vidal i Barraquer, attacked the conspirators as "a disaffected minority disobedient to the Church."[102]

The perennial republican preoccupation with a monarchist revolt linked to the clergy was reinforced by the activities of a handful of priests in Salamanca, among them a clerical ultra of the first order, Canon Aniceto de Castro Albarrán, who was alleged to have facilitated the escape of some conspirators to Portugal.[103] "It is unfortunate," Azaña informed Vidal y Barraquer, that the example of the bishops in condemning the rising had not been followed "by all those under Your Excellency's authority."[104] The alleged participation of Bishop Guitart of Urgel in the conspiracy, along with Cardinal Segura, who was rumored to have been hiding in Andorra, stimulated a series of attacks in the republican press, although the accusations lacked foundation.[105]

99. José Gafo, "Crónicas científico-sociales," *La Ciencia Tomista* (1933), vol. 47, p. 390.

100. Arbeloa, *La semana trágica,* p. 295; see, for example, the article of Hilario Yaben, "La resistencia al poder," *Revista Eclesiástica* (1932), pp. 625–39.

101. Vidal i Barraquer to Azaña, August 15, 1932, *AVB,* vol. 3, part 1, p. 185.

102. *El Debate,* October 10, 1932, in *El pensamiento de "El Debate,"* pp. 956–57; *AVB,* vol. 3, part 1, note 2.

103. *AVB,* vol. 3, part 1, p. 210, note 1. Outside of Salamanca, the authorities accused Canon Andrés Coll y Pérez of Málaga, a vociferous critic of the Republic, of being involved in the conspiracy and exiled him to Spanish West Africa. Ibid., p. 185, note 2.

104. Azaña to Vidal i Barraquer, September 5, 1932, *AVB,* vol. 3, part 1, p. 210.

105. Excerpts on the controversy from the republican press are given in ibid., pp. 200–203.

These events kept alive republican fears about the Church. In the days following August 10, another outbreak of church burnings in Andalucía provided an ominous sign that the popular anticlericalism identifying the Church with conspiracy against the Republic was far from dead. Vidal i Barraquer feared the rebellion's damaging influence on republican opinion, as the cabinet and parliament were about to begin discussion of the long-awaited law dealing with the religious orders.[106] In a strongly worded letter to the cardinal, Angel Ossorio y Gallardo, a former activist in the PSP who had converted to republicanism, expressed similar convictions, arguing that the hierarchy's repudiation of the revolt was insufficient to assure Republicans of the Church's sincerity towards the regime. The bishops, he declared, must act more vigorously to keep all sectors of Catholic opinion under control or face an adverse political reaction. He exhorted the hierarchy to issue a statement ending once and for all the "confusion" of attitudes towards the Republic prevailing among Catholics. The bishops needed to act decisively "to place them fully within the Republic." If they did not do so, he warned, "it is easy to guess how far republican and socialist reaction can go."[107]

Reaction to the Sanjurjo revolt formed an unsettling prelude to the beginning of public debate on the law on the religious orders that began with the appearance of the government's draft text in October 1932. Since the proposed law took the form of enabling legislation of the constitution's religious clauses, it ranged beyond the issue of the regular clergy. The controversy accompanying its passage through parliament resembled the divisive constitutional battle of the autumn of 1931. The Committee of Metropolitans followed its usual strategy of seeking to avoid the worst. The republican parties remained divided on various aspects of the new law, although on this occasion the final version was only slightly more extreme than the government's original draft. True to their anticlerical tenets, the Radical Socialists attempted to alter the proposed law in line with their implacable hostility towards the religious orders. They advocated, unsuccessfully, seizure of the regular clergy's property and a ban on teaching even by individual religious acting in their capacity as private citizens.[108] Catholic deputies followed the well-traveled road of seeking to amend the legislation, while the confessional press directed a constant stream of criticism against it as a vehicle for "stripping [the Church] of its property and rights."[109]

The reaction of clerical and lay opinion to parliamentary approval of the Law on Religious Confessions and Congregations (May 17, 1933) brought the Church closer to an open break with the Republic than at any time since its inception. On May 25, the Committee of Metropolitans issued a long and comprehensive state-

106. Vidal i Barraquer to Alcalá Zamora, August 16, 1932, ibid., p. 187.
107. Ossorio y Gallardo to Vidal i Barraquer, August 23, 1932, ibid., p. 191.
108. Alcalá-Zamora, *Memorias*, p. 19.
109. *El Debate*, October 10, 1932, in *El pensamiento de "El Debate,"* p. 982.

ment of grievances. The archbishops criticized the Republic's failure to recognize the hierarchy's "serene requests and peaceful advice" in favor of a policy violating "the Catholic conscience and confessional rights." They berated it for the unilateral settlement of religious matters, "the breaking of solemn treaties with the Church." The Church found itself subject to a "notoriously unjust" new law that treated it in the "harshest" possible terms.[110] Archbishop Gomá, recently promoted to the archbishopric of Toledo and long unhappy with Vidal i Barraquer's policy of accommodation, saw the law as nothing less than outright persecution and urged the faithful to passive resistance.[111] On June 3, Pius XI issued the encyclical *Dilectissima Nobis*, which compared the situation in Spain to the persecution inflicted on the Church by Mexico and Soviet Russia.[112]

The Law on Religious Confessions and Congregations was the most important piece of religious legislation passed by the Republic. First, it represented as coherent a statement of principles as the regime ever produced on the Church. "The majority of civilized peoples" saw separation of Church and State as "the only system possible in a democratic Republic." This did not mean "the total indifference and abandonment of every social manifestation of religious spirit on the part of the State," which affirmed its commitment to "liberty of conscience and freedom of religion."[113]

Second, along with this affirmation of modern liberal thought ran another underlying theme, the necessity of keeping the Church and the clergy under government control. The Church could not be allowed to function as an ordinary civil association subject to the common law. "Religious freedom and liberty of conscience are, naturally, liberties limited to the purely religious" and "by motives concerning the security of the State and public order."[114] Vidal i Barraquer's prediction of 1931 that the forthcoming law on the religious orders announced in the constitution would take the form of the projected, though unpassed, 1906 Law of Asso-

110. "Metropolitanos españoles a los fieles," May 25, 1933, in *Documentos colectivos del episcopado español*, pp. 190–91, 193. Attempts to persuade President Alcalá-Zamora to veto the legislation came to nothing. Given the overwhelming support for the law in parliament, the president believed that a veto would create a serious political crisis and might lead to a repeat of the "quema de conventos." García Prous, *Relaciones Iglesia-Estado*, p. 168.

111. Anastasio Granados, *El Cardenal Gomá, Primado de España* (Madrid, 1969), pp. 59–60.

112. Pius XI criticized the Republic for adopting a form of Church-State separation that was "hostile to the faith which the immense majority of citizens profess." Separation was even more "burdensome and unjust" because it violated the liberty that the Republic promised to all its citizens. Quoted in Redondo, *Historia de la Iglesia en España*, vol. 1, p. 218. There is evidence that as early as November 1931 Pius XI believed that the policy being followed by Vidal i Barraquer and Cardinal Pacelli, the papal secretary of state, was not sufficiently aggressive. At that time, the pope communicated to the bishops a document dealing with how Spanish Catholics should interpret his papal statements on the situation of the Church in Spain. The "Gravis theologi sententia" urged the hierarchy to warn them of the evils threatening the Church and to take appropriate measures to resist them "passively or actively" using all legal means. There is no indication, however, that the document altered the hierarchy's strategy. "Introducción a la primera parte," *AVB*, vol. 2, part 1, p. 36.

113. "Preámbulo del proyecto del Gobierno," *AVB*, vol. 3, part 3, p. 1025.

114. Ibid., pp. 1026, 1027.

ciations was fulfilled in the legislation of 1933.[115] The Law on Religious Confessions and Congregations saw regalism in full flood. The motives behind it were not so different from those that had inspired nineteenth-century liberalism to maintain controls over the Church as a means of protection against the political threat posed by Carlism. Throughout the 1933 law runs a similar preoccupation with defense of the Republic and the assumption that the Church must be kept from aiding and abetting its enemies.

In practice, what did this mean? The legislation established a contradictory balance between liberal principles and State control.[116] Although the government had renounced any rights to ecclesiastical patronage in 1931, the law now gave it authority to veto Church appointments bestowed on individuals judged "dangerous for the order or security of the State." No limitation was placed on the conduct of services within religious buildings, but the Church was specifically warned against using them for political purposes. It was allowed to conduct its internal administration freely but was obliged to inform the government of any changes in administrative boundaries. In future, the Church would be able to acquire property and investments but, if the authorities so decided, it could be forced to invest its capital in treasury notes. The regular clergy received legal recognition but were subject to a barrage of bureaucratic controls and restrictions limiting their work to exclusively religious activities. A far-reaching provision of the new law echoed the unpassed republican constitution of 1873 and a Liberal government proposal of 1923 by providing that cathedrals, parish churches, rectories, and episcopal palaces should become the property of the nation, although there was no intent to deprive the Church of their use. The legislation delivered the final blow to the teaching of the religious orders by ordering its elimination within a matter of months.

The Law on Religious Confessions and Congregations embodied the fundamental strengths and weaknesses of the Republic's policy towards the Church. The separation of Church and State and the commitment to religious liberty and freedom of conscience, although sullied on occasion by manifestations of crude anticlericalism, were by any standard significant achievements. The Republic did not intend to destroy Catholicism, nor was its legislation even remotely capable of reducing the Church to religious, social, and political impotence. But it erred in abandoning nineteenth-century republicanism's commitment to a "free Church in a free State." The Republic continued in more extreme form the historic regalism long associated with Spanish governments. Although the Church profited from nineteenth-century regalism in some respects, it had always resented its restrictions. The more extreme republican version, laced as it was with strong anticlerical residues, made conflict with the Church inevitable. Having rejected a negoti-

115. Vidal i Barraquer to Pacelli, October 16, 1931, *AVB*, vol. 1, part 3, pp. 398–99.

116. The specific terms cited are drawn from the text of the law reproduced in *AVB*, vol. 3, part 4, pp. 1025–39.

ated settlement with the Church and the papacy, the Republic needed to liberate itself from the ghosts of ancient civil-ecclesiastical battles through the creation of a secular State in which the Church could function free of government tutelage.

Breaking free of the regalist past involved some risk, given the real danger posed by extreme right-wing groups viscerally opposed to the regime. But in and by itself, the Church posed no threat to the Republic. Historically, its involvement in politics in the form of clerical support for various movements opposed to liberalism had led to nothing but failure and severe internal divisions. Insofar as the Church managed to recover some of the ground lost during liberalism's most radical phase (1835–1843), it did so because those in power—the Moderates during the late 1850s and mid-1860s and Cánovas del Castillo in the 1870s—were willing to strike a deal within a regalist framework to prevent the Carlists, in particular, from using defense of the Church as a means of mobilizing Catholics on behalf of their cause.

The Republic faced a similar dilemma but chose to reject a negotiated settlement, while expanding regalist controls as a mechanism for keeping the Church and its supporters in line. Historians agree that this strategy proved counterproductive because it offered a ready-made justification for a range of theoretical and conspiratorial onslaughts.[117] There was no guarantee that implementing the idea of a "free Church in a free State" would have undercut opposition to the Republic. The ideological animosity of Carlists, Integrists, and authoritarian monarchists rested on much more than the single issue of defending the Church. They had resolutely opposed the Restoration despite its concessions to the Church and were even less likely to change their attitudes towards the Republic, whatever its religious policies. Even so, implementing separation of the civil and ecclesiastical powers while allowing the Church to function according to the norms of freedom of association would have been worth the risk. At worst, its political cost would have been no higher than that exacted through the continuation of regalist controls. At best, it would have taken some of the wind from the billowing sails of Catholic criticism of the regime.

The Church would not have easily accepted a straightforward separation depriving it of historic privileges in return for complete institutional autonomy. There was nothing in its background that prepared it to play such a role within a pluralistic society.[118] Although sincere enough, the policy of accommodation pursued by Vidal i Barraquer and the Committee of Metropolitans rested in the end on the acceptance of what had to be endured to safeguard ecclesiastical interests rather than on an appreciation of the benefits that the Church might secure as a result of its separation from the civil power.

117. Raguer, *La espada y la cruz*, p. 42; Sánchez, *Reform and Reaction*, p. 134.
118. M. Fernández Areal, *La política católica española* (Barcelona, 1971), p. 28.

Yet it was possible, if one takes episcopal statements at face value, that having lost the battle to preserve remnants of its old privileges between 1931 and 1933, the Church would have been willing, albeit grudgingly, to accept the concept of "a free Church in a free State." Ecclesiastical critics of the 1933 law focused on a civil rights argument based on the idea that the Republic had violated its commitment to the liberal principle of freedom of association.[119] Ironically, the hierarchy now saw the old republican formula rejected by the nineteenth-century Church as preferable to the combination of no privileges and regalist controls imposed by the Republic.

The Law on Religious Confessions and Congregations by no means crippled the Church. It contained no significant limitations on religious practice.[120] For all the restrictions placed on processions conducted outside of religious buildings, the Spanish Church was not forced into the catacombs. Nor did the imminent removal of the religious orders from teaching mean the end of Catholic education. By the time of the law's passage, the hierarchy had already elaborated detailed plans for the creation of private schools managed by groups of laypeople organized in legal associations (*mutuas*); some were already operating in Madrid and Barcelona.[121]

Objections to the regalist aspects of the 1933 law had ample justification, but the Church could have lived with them, just as its counterpart in France managed to do without suffering institutional collapse following similar legislation passed by the Third Republic earlier in the century. Despite his disillusionment at the government's conduct, Vidal i Barraquer recognized as much following passage of the new law, when he declared that it would be necessary "to lend a certain cooperation" to its implementation "to avoid grave damage to the Church."[122] The cardinal also recognized that the government of Azaña intended to implement the law without "aggravating" its application.[123]

The most serious effect of the law lay not so much in what it did to the Church as in its impact on Catholic opinion. The legislation confirmed the widespread view identifying the Republic with religious persecution. It produced another outpouring of aggressive rhetoric even among Catholics ostensibly supporting the hierarchy's official line. In February, José María Gil Robles attacked the proposed leg-

119. The Committee of Metropolitans argued in their May 25 statement that the law contradicted constitutional guarantees of liberty and conscience and religious practice as well as freedom of association by subjecting the Church to a regime of exception. This represented an attack on "the international rights of man and the citizen" opposed to "fundamental principles of true civilization and modern political culture." *Documentos colectivos del episcopado español*, p. 191.

120. The law confirmed existing government policy requiring permission for services conducted outside churches. In practice, this referred primarily to religious processions.

121. In January 1932, for example, Vidal i Barraquer sent his suffragan bishops a set of model statutes, drawn up with legal advice, for the establishment of *mutuas* by Catholic parents. "Estatuts per a les Mútues dedicades a l'ensenyament," *AVB*, vol. 2, part 3, 606–12.

122. Vidal i Barraquer to Pacelli, July 16, 1933, *AVB*, vol. 3, part 4, p. 918.

123. Vidal i Barraquer to Pacelli, June 23, 1933, *AVB*, p. 867.

islation as a "law of hatred" that Catholics would have to disobey.[124] Further, it stimulated a new wave of intransigence among Catholic ultras "acting directly or indirectly against the directives of the hierarchy" in the interests of "specific political parties."[125] A report on the ultra press prepared for Vidal i Barraquer singled out the Integrists associated with *El Siglo Futuro* and the Carlists for sowing division through repeated attacks on publications supporting the Church's official policy as "anti-Catholic and sinful." The role of some priests and religious in "fomenting divisions and struggles among Catholics" received special censure. The report fell close to the mark when it compared the situation within the Church to the ideological civil war between Carlists and supporters of the Restoration that had wracked Spanish Catholicism during the 1880s.[126]

By the summer of 1933, the religious question remained a source of deep division within the Republic and the Church. Two years of propaganda battles, ideological struggle, and street battles on the part of the Republic, the Church, and their respective supporters aggravated the problem considerably, although the efforts of the hierarchy and republican authorities kept the situation within bounds.

The reasons behind the inability of Republic and Church to reach a reasonable accommodation were many and complex. Some can be traced to the workings of republican politics, others to internal divisions among Spanish Catholics and the cultural divide separating them from Republicans. Still others can be linked to Spain's burdensome legacy of civil-ecclesiastical conflict. The failure to resolve the religious question between 1931 and 1933 added another chapter to that long and unhappy tale. Nor can one forget that the struggle took on an emotional, symbolic character that aroused passions on both sides beyond anything merited by the reality of the situation. The religious question was not insoluble. But its solution required a degree of self-discipline that neither of the parties possessed.

As a result, the Republic found itself in conflict with millions of its citizens and the Church at a time when it faced a host of difficult social and economic problems. It has been argued that the religious legislation between 1931 and 1933 did more damage to the Republic's interests than to the Church by accomplishing something that had eluded generations, the mobilization of Spanish Catholics.[127] Achieving this long-sought goal came at a price, however. The Church had long exercised political influence in modern Spain, but since the Restoration it had done so from the wings as a powerful lobby. Under the Republic, it began to enter the political game as a direct player, a fateful decision that carried with it unforeseen consequences.

124. *El Debate*, February 21, 1933.

125. "Report sobre la premsa integrista," *AVB*, vol. 3, part 4, p. 935.

126. *AVB*, pp. 936–37. Among the specific incidents cited were the publication in *El Siglo Futuro*, official organ of the Integrist party, of a letter from Cardinal Segura endorsing the newspaper's hard line on the religious question.

127. Lannon, *Privilege, Persecution and Prophecy: The Catholic Church in Spain, 1875–1975* (Oxford, 1987), p. 186.

CHAPTER XIII

THE REPUBLIC, 1933–1936

The breakdown of the governing coalition saved the Church from full implementation of the Law on Religious Confessions and Congregations. By September 1933, the Radical Republicans of Lerroux, uneasy over the Socialists' role in the government and emboldened by success in recent municipal elections, moved into opposition. The Socialists were also disillusioned with Azaña because of the slow pace of economic reform and the repression of social disorder, especially in the southern countryside. Socialist militants and some of the leadership believed that the party had secured few benefits from its participation in the parliamentary coalition supporting the cabinet. Although the political crisis was long in the making, it ended with Azaña's fall from power, the dissolution of parliament, and the convocation of general elections for November 19.[1]

The campaign followed an entirely different course from that of 1931. The decision of the Socialists to go it alone rather than cooperate with other republican parties within a voting system favoring broad electoral coalitions proved costly. The PSOE lost half of its seats, while Azaña's Acción Republicana saw its parliamentary ranks severely reduced. In contrast, the disarray of the Right in 1931 gave way to an organized and well-financed campaign revolving around a recently formed Catholic party, the Confederación Española de Derechas Autónomas (CEDA). For the first and only time in Spanish Catholicism's modern history, a confessional party achieved a significant electoral success. The CEDA won 110 seats and became the largest single party in parliament, followed by the Radical Republicans with 100 deputies.

1. Gabriel Jackson, *The Spanish Republic and the Civil War, 1931–1939* (Princeton, 1965), pp. 113–15; Paul Preston, *The Coming of the Spanish Civil War: Reform, Reaction and Revolution in the Second Republic* (London and New York, 1978), pp. 82–91.

The results promised the Church a respite from the secularizing legislation associated with the Azaña government. Even before the elections, Vidal i Barraquer concluded on the basis of information received from Alcalá-Zamora that a new cabinet headed by Lerroux and dominated by the Radical Republicans but dependent on the CEDA for its survival would reopen negotiations with the Vatican for a *modus vivendi*.[2] The president also believed it possible to modify the clauses of the constitution "prejudicial to the Church."[3]

Until the general elections of February 1936, successive Radical ministries, mindful of their dependence on the CEDA, followed a policy of benign neglect with respect to the religious legislation passed between 1931 and 1933. Although the government fulfilled clerical expectations by granting pensions to older parish priests and by failing to enforce many of the terms of the Law on Religious Confessions and Congregations, it was unable to conclude a formal agreement with the Vatican.[4] Nor could it marshal the two-thirds parliamentary majority required to meet another of the Church's aspirations, the modification of the constitution's religious clauses.

The hierarchy and the organs of Catholic opinion supporting its strategy welcomed the election results and the formation of a government committed to ameliorating official policy towards the Church. *El Debate* also saw the elections and the strong showing of the CEDA as a harbinger of a "great Catholic majority" destined to assume power in due course.[5] Vidal i Barraquer was less optimistic. While thankful for the turn of events that had removed the Azaña government, he saw the political situation as still "very dangerous." Within a month of the elections, the cardinal recognized the essential instability of the parliamentary alliance sustaining the cabinet, inspired as it was by "diverse ideologies with respect to Religion, property and regime."[6] Moreover, he was aware that a definitive resolution of the

2. The exclusion of the CEDA from the Lerroux cabinet represented a clear recognition of the fragility of the center/right alliance and the ability of Socialists and other parties of the defeated coalition to create a full-blown political crisis should the party be given seats in cabinet. Raymond Carr, *Spain, 1808–1939* (Oxford, 1966), p. 630.

3. Vidal i Barraquer to Pacelli, November 3, 1933, *Arxiu Vidal i Barraquer: Església y Estat durant la Segona República Espanyola, 1931–1936*, ed. M. Batllori and V. M. Arbeloa (4 vols., Montserrat, 1971–1991) (henceforth cited as *AVB*), vol. 4, part 1, p. 141.

4. Negotiations began in July 1934 and continued through successive Radical ministries. The reasons for their failure were many. The parties of the Left strongly opposed an agreement involving concessions to the Church, as did extremist monarchists who feared any accommodation between the Church and the Republic. In the end, the negotiations foundered because the government, although willing to accede to the Vatican's demands in some areas, insisted that any settlement had to be compatible with the constitution, particularly Article 26. Antonio Marquina Barrio, *La diplomacia vaticana y la España de Franco* (Madrid, 1983), pp. 35–41. There were also serious differences both between the nuncio, Federico Tedeschini, and the papal curia and between Vidal i Barraquer and the archbishop of Toledo, Isidro Gomá y Tomás, about the Church's strategy with respect to the elaboration of a *modus vivendi*. Gonzalo Redondo, *Historia de la Iglesia en España, 1931–1939* (2 vols., Madrid, 1993), vol. 1, pp. 426–33.

5. *El Debate*, November 21, 1933, in *El pensamiento de "El Debate": un diario católico en las crisis de España, 1911–1936*, ed. José María García Escudero (Madrid, 1983), p. 1005.

6. Vidal i Barraquer to Pacelli, December 6, 1933, *AVB*, vol. 4, part 1, p. 822.

religious question within the Republic still had to reckon with the popular strength of the parties of the Left despite their electoral defeat and the intransigence of "extremists of the Right," who remained determined to overturn "even the Constitution" through force.[7]

The cardinal correctly assessed the political difficulties that would beset the coalition that emerged from the November elections. He foresaw the principal cause of its instability, the anomaly of a minority Radical Republican government depending for its survival on an alliance of parties agreed on little more than excluding the opposition from power. Further, the CEDA accepted its exclusion from the cabinet only as a matter of tactical, temporary necessity. As time passed, the party and its leader, José María Gil Robles, pressed demands for a key role in the government as a prelude to the next general elections through which the old dream of a Catholic parliamentary majority would be finally realized.

Whether the emergence of a powerful confessional party supported by the hierarchy served the best interests of the Church within a society divided by intense political and social conflict is questionable. Although under the Restoration and the dictatorship, the Church had dipped its hand into politics more than once, it had observed the hoary and oft-repeated formula that it stood above the partisan fray at least to the extent that it refrained from identifying itself exclusively with a single political party, save for its brief flirtation with Maura and the Conservatives. Under the Republic, it cast this theoretical neutrality aside.

If the CEDA had confined itself to defending the Church's interests narrowly conceived within a republican framework, its role would have been less ambiguous. But the party entertained larger ambitions, namely, to carry out, as Gil Robles expressed it, "a true and deep revolution with the cross in hand."[8] The CEDA's program, although far from coherent on many issues, reflected the conservative preoccupations of social Catholicism, despite frequent expressions of heady rhetoric to the contrary. Its leadership and membership, overwhelmingly monarchist and bourgeois, inevitably evoked the suspicions of the parties of the Left, who questioned its republican credentials. Far from reducing the already acute tensions existing within the Republic over the Church, the emergence of the CEDA added a new element to a potentially explosive political mix.

A Political Catholicism

Since the 1880s, the leadership of the Spanish Church had dreamed of creating a "union of Catholics" committed to defending its interests within a parliamentary

7. Ibid.

8. Quoted in José R. Montero, *La CEDA: el catolicismo social y político de la II República* (2 vols., Madrid, 1977), vol. 1, p. 304.

system, although there was considerable ambiguity about its precise organizational form. Dynastic divisions and the political monopoly exercised by Conservatives and Liberals during the Restoration made the prospect of forming an effective confessional party remote at best. Angel Herrera and the social Catholics under his influence envied the success of Catholic parties in Germany, Belgium, and Italy. They finally succeeded in founding the short-lived Partido Social Popular (PSP) in 1922, the first serious attempt to create a modern party transcending the dynastic infighting of the past and operating within the arena of mass politics. The PSP disappeared after the establishment of the Primo de Rivera dictatorship, but Herrera and his followers, increasingly aware of the impermanence of the regime as the 1920s progressed, believed it imperative for Spanish Catholics to organize a party capable of exercising significant influence upon the return of political normality.

The idea survived among an activist elite, but the political inertia prevailing among Catholics under the dictatorship prevented it from being realized. Similarly, the prolonged constitutional crisis of the monarchy in 1930–1931, which few Catholics expected to end in the establishment of a republic, made the necessity of forming a confessional party seem less pressing. The proclamation of the Republic suddenly exposed the political weakness of Spanish Catholicism. The dynastic parties of the Restoration, which to a greater or lesser degree protected the interests of the Church under the terms of the ecclesiastical settlement devised by Cánovas del Castillo, were dead. A handful of parties specifically committed to defending the Church remained on the scene. But their appeal was limited by either their regional nature or their narrow ideological and dynastic programs.[9] The possibility of creating a new monarchist party to replace the expired dynastic parties was also remote. There was little prospect of attracting Catholics, largely monarchist in sympathy, to the conservative republicanism of Alcalá-Zamora and Maura, an option rejected, in any event, by the influential activists gathered around Angel Herrera and *El Debate*.[10]

The transition from the political disarray of 1931 to the formation of the CEDA in March 1933 and its remarkable success in the November elections is generally

9. Of the regional parties on the scene at the time of the Republic's proclamation, the Partido Nacionalista Vasco and the Derecha Regional Valenciana were the most important. Although the PNV enjoyed the support of many Basque priests and stoutly defended the Church in the battles over the religious question in 1931, its commitment to a high degree of autonomy for the region was viewed with suspicion by clergy and lay activists elsewhere in the country. Only recently founded, the DRV possessed only a small following in Valencia. The strident and resolutely antiliberal Integrist party was, for all practical purposes, an organization without significant popular backing. In any event, its frequent battles with the hierarchy dating back to the 1880s pushed it to the margins of Catholic political activity. Although Carlism, now renamed the Traditionalist Communion, retained considerable support in Navarra, its narrow regional base, dynastic program, and blatant hostility towards the Republic removed it as a possible vehicle for achieving the "union of Catholics."

10. Montero, *La CEDA*, vol. 1, pp. 238–39.

attributed to the galvanizing effects of republican religious legislation on a Catholic opinion aroused at last to political action.[11] Reaction to the Republic's policy towards the Church as well as fear of social revolution provided the glue necessary to cement together the diverse constituencies forming the backbone of the CEDA.

Other circumstances also favored the foundation of the mass party that had eluded the grasp of Spanish Catholics for generations. The constitutional crisis of 1930 and 1931 created a political vacuum on the Right. The disappearance of the dynastic parties and the absence of a practical alternative in the form of a new monarchist party left the field open to the activists associated with Angel Herrera and *El Debate,* who were ready and willing to take advantage of this political disorganization and the opportunities created by the Republic's introduction of a democratic electoral system. Although few Catholics would have appreciated it, the Republic gave them something that neither the Restoration nor the dictatorship had ever done. For the first time in Spanish Catholicism's modern history, advocates of a confessional party were able to implement their ideas freely, liberated from the historic blocks to political action erected by the Restoration and the dictatorship.

Between the proclamation of the Republic and the June 1931 general elections, little could be done to establish an effective political organization. But never one to wait passively upon events, Angel Herrera moved quickly to lay a foundation for the future. His prestige as a longtime defender of the Church, his excellent relations with the hierarchy and the papal nuncio, Archbishop Tedeschini, and the resources he commanded as the editor of the country's largest Catholic newspaper placed him in an ideal position to launch an initiative.[12] Moreover, his monarchist sympathies, combined with a certain pragmatism with respect to the new regime, offered a glimmer of hope to the bishops, who saw the creation of a "union of Catholics" as a necessary complement to efforts to reach a settlement with the Republic. This "two-armed" strategy, as Vidal i Barraquer described it early in the regime's history, was based on formal negotiation with the government, on the one hand, and the political organization of Spanish Catholics along the lines advocated by Herrera, on the other.[13]

On the afternoon of the Republic's proclamation, Herrera met with the editorial board of *El Debate* to discuss possible tactics before the dramatic turn of events.

11. See, for example, the conclusions of Javier Tusell, *Historia de la democracia cristiana en España* (2 vols., Madrid, 1974), vol. 1, p. 164; Frances Lannon, *Privilege, Persecution and Prophecy: The Catholic Church in Spain, 1875–1975* (Oxford, 1987), p. 186.

12. A fervent supporter of the Italian Catholic party, the Partito Popolare Italiano founded by Luigi Sturzo, the nuncio admired Herrera and his project for a similar initiative in Spain. Tedeschini's links to the hierarchy and his influence in the Vatican provided powerful support for Herrera's plans. Montero, *La CEDA,* vol. 1, pp. 136–38.

13. Vidal i Barraquer to Pius XI, December 7, 1931; *AVB,* vol. 2, parts 1–2, p. 211.

From this meeting emerged the idea of organizing Acción Nacional (later called Acción Popular). Herrera was too realistic to believe that he could organize a full-blown party to contest the upcoming elections. At first he envisioned a defensive grouping embracing all Catholics, whatever their political affiliation, in the hope that a sufficient number of deputies could be elected to influence legislation affecting the Church.[14] Although the organization did poorly in the elections, it soon recast itself into a formal political party. Given the monarchist sympathies of its supporters, the AN/AP, as would the CEDA later, adopted the controversial "accidentalist" position adopted by *El Debate* following the Republic's proclamation. According to this scholastic view of the world, the Church was indifferent to specific forms of government, whether monarchical or republican. What mattered was not the "accidental" form of a regime, but its "essential" character, which in practical terms meant its concept of the nature and purposes of human society.

The idea of "accidentalism" was not new. The Church followed a similar line towards the First Republic without provoking controversy. The highly charged political atmosphere of the early 1930s produced a different reaction. Republicans and later critics saw "accidentalism" as a sign of fundamental insincerity of the part of the Church and its supporters, a perception reinforced by the stubborn adherence of the AN/AP and the CEDA to it throughout their respective histories.[15] There is some justification behind this criticism. Despite the philosophical and theological arguments advanced to justify "accidentalism," it represented little more than a tactic designed to throw as wide a political net as possible over a Catholic electorate whose attitude towards the Republic was ambiguous at best.[16] But the willingness of a monarchist hierarchy and laity to accept the Republic, if only as a practical necessity, represented a step forward given Spanish Catholicism's earlier history. In and of itself, "accidentalism" did not raise an insuperable obstacle to an accommodation with the Republic. But in contrast to the situation in 1873, its direct link to a specific political cause converted it into a source of ongoing controversy within the Republic that was missing in its earlier apparition.

More crucial to the political expression of Catholicism as embodied in the AN/AP and the CEDA was the interpretation of the "essential." Both organizations went beyond the limited goal of seeking political influence as a means of allowing the Church to conduct its religious and educational activities within a pluralistic society. Fear of revolution always lurked beneath the surface of Spanish Catholi-

14. For a detailed discussion of the party's foundation, see Montero, *La CEDA*, vol. 1, pp. 120–28.

15. The fullest discussion of this controversial issue is provided in ibid., vol. 2, pp. 39–88.

16. Even before the Republic was installed, Herrera warned members of the Madrid ACNP on February 21 against organizing politically on monarchist or republican lines. "Leave aside the form of government. Do not rush to declare yourselves monarchist or republican. . . . The most important things are Spain and the Church, attacked in their roots by socialism in the service of masonic lodges." If Catholics organized as Monarchists or Republicans, it was "inevitable" that a "civil war" would develop "among us." Quoted in José Manuel Ordovas, *Historia de la Asociación Católica Nacional de Propagandistas: de la dictadura a la Segunda República, 1923–1926* (Pamplona, 1993), pp. 171–72.

cism, to emerge virulently in periods of social tension. The coming of the Republic and the abundant signs of labor and agrarian unrest that followed revived old apprehensions. Acción Nacional's first policy statement made no attempt to disguise its purpose as "an organization of social defense . . . to defend institutions and principles not linked in any essential way to a specific form of government."[17]

As longtime advocates of social Catholicism, Herrera and his supporters were not blind to the deeply rooted antagonisms and economic conflicts existing within Spanish society. Their ideas were not in the stick-in-the-mud tradition of the Comillas-Nevares school, but in the end they came down to the same thing—a defense of the social and economic order before the threat of Marxist revolution embodied, especially, in the Socialist party.[18] Given the overwhelmingly bourgeois membership of the AN/AP, it was not surprising that defense of the Church went hand in hand with defense of a conservative social order, for danger "threatens our altars, . . . our pocketbooks and our families."[19] The perceived enemies of a Christian social order were numerous, but there was little disagreement, even among clerical activists like Arboleya and Gafo, that socialism in the form of the PSOE posed the greatest threat of revolution. Progressive social Catholics appreciated, at least, the complex economic causes of socialist strength; others indulged in excessive and inaccurate denunciations of a party that was in fact seriously divided on questions of strategy. A malicious "socialist" version of the "Ten Commandments" circulated among Catholics. The Socialist was expected "to hate God, . . . profane religious feast days, disdain father and mother, murder without scruple, . . . rob everything that he could," and so on.[20] Socialism and Catholicism were seen as fundamentally incompatible. The clergy were informed that absolution in confession could not be granted to a Catholic "who obstinately wishes to remain in the party" in view of the "intrinsically evil" nature of its program.[21] Hostility towards socialism had been the stock-in-trade of social Catholicism since the late nineteenth century. Under the Republic it rose to new and often hysterical heights.

Defending a Church under attack and a society deemed on the verge of revolutionary upheaval within the framework of a pragmatic, ambiguous acceptance of the Republic constituted a powerful but essentially negative program capable of appealing to diverse Catholic constituencies. There was nothing particularly novel about the AN/AP's ideological formulation, which embodied ideas that had long floated around social Catholicism. But between 1931 and 1933, the party broke

17. Quoted in Luis Miguel Moreno Fernández, *Acción Popular Murciana: la derecha confesional en Murcia durante la II República* (Murcia, 1987), p. 53.

18. Montero, *La CEDA*, vol. 2, p. 119.

19. Quoted in ibid., vol. 1, p. 114.

20. *La Cruzada Católica* (1933), vol. 2, no. 12, p. 8.

21. This response appeared in a section of a journal for the parish clergy devoted to answering questions posed by confessors. In this case, the question was straightforward: "Can I absolve a person affiliated to the Socialist or Radical-Socialist party [who] refuses to separate himself from his respective party?" *Revista Eclesiástica* (1933), pp. 609–10.

new ground in the history of Catholic political activity by creating an effective infrastructure at the national and local levels without which the formation of the CEDA would have been impossible. In Murcia, for example, where the Right stood in total disarray following the Republic's proclamation, the local branch of the AN/AP developed from its scattered remnants to achieve remarkable progress by 1933. On the eve of the CEDA's creation, it had at its disposal a successful newspaper, established thanks to Herrera's efforts in 1931, and a flourishing party structure in thirty-eight towns with a total membership of thirty-five thousand. The Bloque Agrario of Salamanca province, founded in 1931 with similar objectives, successfully mobilized Catholic opinion in the region by appealing to the resentment of the rural population, already well organized in Catholic syndicates, against the Republic's agricultural reforms through effective propaganda campaigns. By 1933, the Bloque's leadership of the countryside was "virtually undisputed."[22]

The organizational surge of the AN/AP, unique in the history of Spanish confessional parties, arose in part from the use of propaganda techniques that skillfully exploited resentment at the Republic's religious legislation and deeply rooted fears of social upheaval. It also owed a debt to the willingness of the Church to identify itself with a political organization that offered the promise of "seeing its defensive theses triumph within the Republic."[23] In their collective statement of May 9, 1931, the bishops reaffirmed the old formula that the Church stood above partisan politics. In practice, they gave firm support to the AN/AP. At the local level, clergymen often took an active role in the organization's activities. In Murcia, two prominent ecclesiastics, Canon Antonio Reverte and Father Rego Machinea, used their considerable influence to encourage the formation of a local branch in 1931.[24]

The Church's response to the AN/AP went beyond providing moral support. Despite repeated episcopal statements affirming the neutrality of the numerous Catholic associations created during the organizational resurgence of the early twentieth century, for all practical purposes the Church placed them at the disposition of the AN/AP. Nothing was more striking about its leadership than the phenomenon of "double militancy," the interlocking relationship between the direction of supposedly neutral Catholic associations and that of the party, at both the national and local levels. Angel Herrera moved easily from his key role as the driving force behind the formation of the AN/AP to the presidency of the governing committee of Catholic Action in 1933. Nor did he see any contradiction in using members of the Asociación Católica Nacional de Propagandistas, which he had served as president since 1909, to organize Acción Nacional in 1931.[25] In Murcia,

22. Moreno Fernández, *Acción Popular Murciana*, p. 116; Mary Vincent, *Catholicism in the Second Spanish Republic: Religion and Politics in Salamanca, 1931–1936* (Oxford, 1996), p. 193.

23. Montero, *La CEDA*, vol. 1, p. 142.

24. Moreno Fernández, *Acción Popular Murciana*, p. 64.

25. Members of the Madrid ACNP met on April 26, 1931, and decided "to throw ourselves resolutely into decisive political action" by establishing Acción Nacional. Quoted in Ordovas, *Historia de la Aso-*

the lay membership of the diocesan committee of Catholic Action was virtually interchangeable with that of the AN/AP and, later, the CEDA.[26]

In theory, Catholic Action was designed to create a lay apostolate capable of contributing to the re-Christianization of the nation through a variety of religious and social initiatives divorced from the political realm. The idea so often sustained by the bishops that politically active members of Catholic associations did so only in their capacity as private citizens would have been difficult to realize in the best of circumstances. In practice, it was little more than a fiction. With some justification, José Gafo warned that the Church ran the risk of being seen as a "*deus ex machina*" lurking behind specific groups if it allowed the movement to become involved "in partisan struggles" as a result of the political activities of its members. Although moved by ulterior political motives, an opponent of "accidentalism" made the same point when he complained of the anomaly of *El Debate* serving simultaneously as the official organ of Catholic Action and of the AN/AP. As a result, the Church was "unfairly compromised" by identifying its interests with "the fate of a party."[27] These assessments of the ambiguous relationship between politics and a religious apostolate came close to the mark. Catholic Action, particularly after Herrera assumed the presidency of its governing body, saw itself as a powerful arm of combat against "the legal aggressions" of the Republic. Its duty was "to maintain the Catholic conscience awake [and] alive, in a state of continuous protest" against "the magnitude of the parricide" carried out by the Republic when it killed the "close solidarity that exists between . . . Church and Spain."[28]

Among the associations tied to Catholic Action, none played a more central role in the formation and development of the AN/AP than the Asociación Católica Nacional de Propagandistas. It has been seen as "*the long hand* of the ecclesiastical power," the "mediating element" between a supposedly neutral Church and ac-

---

ciación Católica Nacional de Propagandistas, 1923–1936, p. 180. Seven of the ten directors of AN, chosen on May 18, belonged to the ACNP. Ibid., p. 181.

26. Moreno Fernández, *Acción Popular Murciana*, pp. 34–35. In Salamanca, the president of the local branch of Acción Popular was involved in various organizations associated with Catholic Action. Mary Vincent, "The Spanish Church and the Popular Front: The Experience of Salamanca Province," in *The French and Spanish Popular Fronts: Comparative Perspectives*, ed. Martin S. Alexander and Helen Graham (Cambridge, 1989), p. 83.

27. "Informe reservado sobre las causas de la actual situación religiosa en España," *AVB*, vol. 4, part 2, p. 455. Recalling his days as a young priest active in Catholic Action, Cardinal Tarancón posed the same question in his memoirs. Was the organization "purely and clearly apostolic?" He concluded that circumstances encouraged "confusion" and converted Catholic Action "practically into a pseudo-political organization which we pretended would be an efficacious instrument of evangelization." Vicente Enrique y Tarancón, *Recuerdos de juventud* (Barcelona, 1984), pp. 129–30. A prominent member of the ACNP in 1931 expressed similar reservations about Herrera's decision to involve the organization in politics. Ordovas, *Historia de la Asociación Católica Nacional de Propagandistas, 1923–1936*, p. 177.

28. *El Debate*, February 1934, extraordinary number. The activities of Catholic Action took place within "an environment of struggle" that endowed them with "a more polemical than apostolic character," according to one historian of the movement. Miguel Benzo Mestre, "Tres etapas de la Acción Católica Española," *Ecclesia* (1964), no. 1,178, p. 185.

tivists committed to the political organization of the Catholic masses.[29] For the first time since its establishment in 1909, the ACNP was able to implement the theory of an elite directing the Catholic population first developed by its founder, Angel Ayala, and sustained for two decades by Angel Herrera. The AN/AP's national organization was dominated by *propagandistas,* among them José María Gil Robles and Carlos Martín Álvarez, who would later occupy key positions in the CEDA.[30] The organization was also closely linked to Catholic Action, especially during the presidency of Herrera, when ACNP members formed three-quarters of its national committee.[31] Although the membership of the ACNP numbered less than six hundred in 1931, it was drawn from the ranks of the university-educated, professors, lawyers, doctors, and economists forming "an elite of elites" within Spanish Catholicism. The talent, energy, and total commitment of the *propagandistas* to Herrera's grand political design more than made up for their small numbers. In Murcia, for example, the determination and organizing abilities of fifteen or sixteen members composing the local ACNP formed the nucleus of the AN/AP in the region.[32]

The political initiatives of the *propagandistas* would have led nowhere without access to the multitude of Catholic associations falling under the Church's institutional umbrella. For all the lamentations about the damage done to the Church by the Republic, a significant organizational expansion took place that contrasted sharply with the institutional languor of the 1920s. Between 1928 and 1932, the youth wing of Catholic Action saw the number of local chapters double from 700 to 1,400, with much of the expansion concentrated in the republican period. Similarly, the Association of Fathers of Families, formed in 1913 to combat the educational legislation of Romanones, possessed only 34 associations outside of Madrid in 1929; by early 1933, there were 154. Under the Republic, its membership rolls increased spectacularly from nine thousand in 1931 to eighty-five thousand by 1934.[33] Although, in common with other groups tied to the Church, the association proclaimed its political neutrality, it made no bones about supporting the CEDA during the 1933 electoral campaign. Similarly, the support of the Confederación Nacional Católica Agraria (CNCA), with its extensive network of thirty-eight regional federations and nearly two thousand local syndicates, provided another important political base. Although ostensibly apolitical, the CNCA was closely linked to the initiatives of Herrera through the same interchangeability of

29. Montero, *La CEDA,* vol. 1, p. 475.

30. Herrera served as president of Acción Nacional through September 1931. He announced his intention to resign because of his responsibilities as head of the ACNP. He also privately expressed his personal distaste for direct involvement in politics. In October, José María Gil Robles was elected president of AN. Ordovas, *Historia de la Asociación Católica Nacional de Propagandistas, 1923–1936,* pp. 220–21.

31. Montero, *La CEDA,* vol. 1, p. 511.

32. Moreno Fernández, *Acción Popular Murciana,* p. 126.

33. *El Debate,* January 1, 1933, February 1934, supplement.

personnel characteristic of other Catholic associations. José María Gil Robles, collaborator in *El Debate*, member of the ACNP, president for a time of Acción Popular, and future leader of the CEDA, had served, for example, as the organization's secretary general during the 1920s.[34]

Between 1931 and 1933, circumstances finally came together to permit political initiatives so long denied to advocates of a Catholic party. They enjoyed the support of the hierarchy and, at long last, reaped the organizational benefits derived from the expansion and modernization of confessional associations over three decades. The disarray of the Right in 1931 left the field open to the energetic initiatives of Herrera and his followers, while the democratic system of the Republic removed historic obstacles to the creation of a political "union of Catholics." The resentment generated by the Republic's religious legislation and fears of social revolution provided the fertile ground for erecting a political infrastructure between 1931 and 1933 from which the CEDA finally emerged.

The "Union of Catholics" and the Church, 1933–1936

The CEDA's formation appeared to realize the old dream of a "union of Catholics" committed to defending the Church within a modern parliamentary system. More than forty political parties and rightist associations were represented at its founding congress (February 28–March 4, 1933), of which Acción Popular and the Derecha Regional Valenciana were the most important.[35] But the divisions of the past were far from dead. Authoritarian monarchists had long opposed the "accidentalism" of the AN/AP, fearing that it would help consolidate republican institutions by avoiding an explicit commitment to restoring the monarchy. As the CEDA was being founded, they established the Renovación Española party with an openly anti-republican program.[36] Carlists gathered in the Traditionalist Commu-

34. Juan José Castillo, *Propietarios muy pobres: sobre la subordinación política del pequeño campesino* (Madrid, 1979), pp. 356–57. Similarly in Salamanca province, the Bloque Agrario was dominated by figures prominent in the CNCA. Vincent, *Catholicism in the Second Spanish Republic*, p. 139.

35. Four hundred delegates representing Catholic parties, Catholic unions, and other groups with a membership of 553,000 attended the meeting, which was held in the headquarters of Acción Popular; the same building housed *El Debate* and the Madrid chapter of the ACNP. Montero, *La CEDA*, vol. 1, pp. 290–91. Founded in March 1930, the DRV was based on a coalition of Catholic parties. Its leader, Luis Lucía, was linked both to the ACNP and Catholic Action during the 1920s. The DRV maintained close relations with Acción Popular between 1931 and 1933. Lucía promoted the foundation of the CEDA, whose organization reflected that of the DRV. Rafael Valls, *La derecha regional valenciana: el catolicismo político valenciano, 1930–1936* (Valencia, 1992), pp. 60, 104, 169.

36. Renovación Española did not spring out of the blue. As early as 1931, antiliberal monarchists established a journal, *Acción Española*, which promoted an anti-republican and authoritarian program. Although monarchists gathered around the publication initially accepted the idea of cooperating with Acción Popular in a broad alliance of rightist parties, they strongly opposed its "accidentalist" policy from the beginning. See, for example, the early attack of Eugenio Vegas Latapié, "Historia de un fracaso: El 'ralliement' de los católicos franceses a la República," *Acción Española* (1931–1932), vol. 1, p. 595. The ideological origins of Renovación Española were diverse. They owed a debt to Spanish antiliberal thinkers of the nineteenth and early twentieth centuries, particularly Jaume Balmes, Marcelino Menén-

nion remained committed to their dynastic loyalties and as hostile as ever towards the Republic and liberal democracy.[37] Two Catholic regionalist parties of pronounced democratic character, the well-established Partido Nacional Vasco and the relatively new Unió Democràtica de Catalunya, also remained outside of the CEDA.[38]

The CEDA's role between November 1933 and the February 1936 elections generated controversy among contemporaries and has produced passionate historical debate since. The parties of the Left, especially the Socialists, saw the "accidentalist" acceptance of the Republic by the party as little more than a fiction, its commitment to revise the constitution as a cover for the introduction of an authoritarian government, and its support for a corporatist reorganization of society as a dangerous sign of fascist tendencies.[39] Further, the hyperbolic rhetoric of the CEDA leader José María Gil Robles, with its frequent invocations of national salvation and the defense of Christian civilization, hardly poured oil on the troubled waters of Spanish politics.

Some historians have seen the CEDA as anti-republican, anti-democratic, and socially reactionary; others have argued that its "accidentalism" represented less an example of insincerity towards the regime than a simple recognition of political reality by a leadership fearful of the divisive impact of unqualified acceptance of the Republic on the party's diverse constituencies.[40] They have maintained that despite the authoritarian tendencies present in some segments of the party, especially its youth wing, the CEDA was essentially "moderate" and committed to defending the

---

dez y Pelayo, Juan Vázquez de Mella, and Donoso Cortés. They were also influenced by the authoritarian monarchism promoted by Charles Maurras and the Action Française movement. Raúl Morodo, *Los orígenes ideológicos del franquismo: Acción Española* (Madrid, 1985), pp. 52–57.

37. In his first manifesto to the Carlist faithful, the pretender, Alfonso Carlos de Borbón-Este, attacked the 1931 constitution as "the ideal of an atheistic Republic born unexpectedly from violence." Because Spaniards formed "the most Catholic people on the earth," he "rejected with all the forces of my soul the liberty of cults established in the Constitution" as "the most hypocritical of tyrannies against the conscience of a believing people, who do not practice any other cult than that of the altar of the Catholic faith, spiritual center of all history." Quoted in Redondo, *Historia de la Iglesia en España,* vol. 1, p. 301.

38. Despite its earlier identification with antiliberalism and uncompromising defense of Catholicism, especially evident in 1931, the PNV evolved in a democratic and more secular direction by 1933. This shift reflected the influence of a new and young leadership, personified by José Antonio Aguirre (1904–1960), who gradually came to see the possibility of realizing the party's objective of autonomy within the Republic, a strategy that provoked the intense hostility of Carlists and Integrists in the region with whom the PNV had earlier cooperated. Founded in 1931, the Unió Democràtica de Catalunya never enjoyed the popular success of the PNV. But despite its ideological debt to Carlism and the conservative Catholic regionalism identified with Bishop Torras i Bages, the party adopted a distinctly modern program based on the model of the Italian Christian Democratic party of Luigi Sturzo. Fernando García de Cortázar, "La Iglesia vasca: del carlismo al nacionalismo, 1870–1936," in *Estudios de historia contemporánea del País Vasco,* ed. J. C. Aberasturi (San Sebastián, 1982), pp. 263–65; Hilari Raguer, *La Unió Democràtica de Catalunya i el seu temps, 1931–1939* (Montserrat, 1976), pp. 80–84.

39. Preston, *The Coming of the Spanish Civil War,* pp. 92–93, 96–100.

40. José R. Montero's massive two-volume history of the CEDA presents a strongly critical analysis of the party, its leadership, and its program. Only Luis Lucía and the Derecha Regional Valenciana escape the author's detailed and devastating critique. Although unwilling to go as far as some historians who have seen the DRV as an example of a Christian Democratic party in the Sturzo tradition, he concedes

legitimate rights of the Church and the reform of society through application of papal teachings on social justice rather than through a Spanish version of fascist corporatism.

In this debate, historians assessing the CEDA's role negatively have proved more convincing. In part, opposing interpretations have arisen because of what has been called "the contradictory political sinuosity" of the party's program beyond the straightforward issue of defense of the Church.[41] Behind the rhetoric of union advanced by CEDA apologists, there stood the reality of an organization deeply divided over key issues. It was less a conventional party functioning with a coherent program than a political "conglomeration" held together by an essentially defensive commitment to protect the Church and a determination to deny power to the parties of the Left.[42]

The CEDA included figures of democratic views, among them Luis Lucía, leader of the Derecha Regional Valenciana, who viewed the Republic in relatively positive terms and appreciated the need for serious social and economic reform.[43] It also contained the openly reactionary. In 1934, the CEDA deputy Ramón Serrano Suñer, later a prominent figure in the Franco regime, called for the creation of a new political order to replace the degeneracy of the parliamentary system.[44] Moreover, the party's repeated affirmations of its commitment to economic reform and class harmony in accord with papal teachings failed to resolve the historic internal conflicts of social Catholicism. The CEDA included representatives of its most liberal wing, notably Manuel Giménez Fernández, who appreciated the necessity of serious agrarian reform. It also embraced resolute defenders of private property linked to the CNCA, who were determined to frustrate changes to the existing economic structure. When push came to shove, they felt no scruples about sabotag-

---

that it was "the most brilliant mirror of the CEDA, illustrating . . . the ideological goodness of social Catholicism at the political level." *La CEDA*, vol. 1, p. 352. The recent work of Rafael Valls suggests, however, that the DRV was much closer to the CEDA model than Montero suggests, although its leader, Lucas Lucía, remained committed to "accidentalism" even after the February 1936 elections, a decision that earned him a death sentence from the Franco regime. *La Derecha Regional Valenciana*, pp. 160–67. Javier Tusell has made the best case for the CEDA. He admits that it was not Christian Democratic in the sense of being composed of "democrats of Christian inspiration" adhering to a "social program" that approximated that of the bourgeois Left. But he argues that although the CEDA was not socially or politically advanced, neither was it "reactionary." *Historia de la democracia cristiana*, vol. 1, pp. 202–3. Richard Robinson has taken a stronger position, declaring that "the policies of the CEDA bore quite close resemblance to the Christian Democratic parties of Western Europe." *The Origins of Franco's Spain: The Right, the Republic and Revolution, 1931–1936* (Pittsburgh, 1970), p. 116.

41. Montero, *La CEDA*, vol. 1, p. 423.

42. In spite of his positive view of the CEDA, Tusell has argued that its "great defect" lay in its character as a defensive "antiparty movement." *Historia de la democracia cristiana*, vol. 1, p. 198.

43. For detailed analysis of the DRV and the role of Lucía, see Tusell, *Historia de la democracia cristiana*, vol. 1, pp. 149–60. Rafael Valls has stressed, however, the ambiguity of Lucía and the DRV on certain questions. Lucía remained committed, for example, to the idea of a confessional state, while in 1934 the party declared in favor of a corporatist organization of society. *La Derecha Regional Valenciana*, pp. 68–69.

44. Lannon, *Privilege, Persecution and Prophecy*, p. 190.

ing Giménez Fernández's agrarian reform projects during his brief tenure as minister of agriculture in 1935.[45]

The CEDA's attitude towards regional autonomy was also ambiguous. Resentment over the centralism of the State and support for a devolution of power had formed part of the political baggage of Spanish Catholicism since the days of nineteenth-century Carlism and found its way into the CEDA program. But neither Gil Robles nor the party's powerful Castilian interests were sympathetic to the idea of a high degree of autonomy within a modern nationalist framework, promoted from within by the Derecha Regional Valenciana and from without by the Partido Nacionalista Vasco and the Unió Democràtica de Catalunya.[46] The party's inability to come to terms with the insistent demands of the strongly Catholic PNV for parliamentary approval of a Basque Statute similar to that granted to Catalonia early in the Republic's history proved especially costly over the long run by alienating a potential ally.

The "union of Catholics" long sought by the ecclesiastical leadership and achieved in some measure through the CEDA proved as unproductive a political option as had earlier examples of clerical support for the Conservative party and the Primo de Rivera dictatorship. Although Gil Robles would later deny that he intended to move the CEDA in an authoritarian direction by executing a civilian coup d'état through the electoral process, the presence within the party of interest groups hostile to the democratic ideals of the Republic and determined to block significant social change encouraged, at best, a high degree of political ambiguity and, at worst, expressions of open counterrevolutionary sentiment.

The emergence of the AN/AP and the CEDA added a new dimension to the religious question. Defense of the Church became inextricably linked to a political party whose motives and intentions were viewed with suspicion by the Republican and Socialist opposition. The historic buffer, however thin and inadequate, that had kept the Church from identifying its interests with those of a specific party was stripped away, leaving the institution exposed to the give-and-take of intense partisan struggles.

The triumph of the center/right parties in the November 1933 elections initially produced a period of moderate government. But after October 1934, Radical Republican ministries pressured by the CEDA attempted to demolish the modest social and economic reforms achieved by the Azaña coalition between 1931 and 1933. The lofty principle of class harmony preached by the CEDA quickly degenerated into outright support of repression involving the suspension of civil liberties, censorship, strikebreaking, and violent police action against labor unions and peasant organizations, in the name of preventing the social revolution that had

45. Montero, *La CEDA*, vol. 1, pp. 201–2; Jackson, *The Spanish Republic*, pp. 169–70; José Calvo and Javier Tusell, *Giménez Fernández: precursor de la democracia española* (Seville, 1990), pp. 89–90.
46. Montero, *La CEDA*, vol. 2, pp. 230–32.

long obsessed social Catholicism. These measures eventually provoked a wave of labor agitation and deepened the fears of the parties of the 1931–1933 coalition that the country was on the verge of a counterrevolution aimed at undermining the Republic's liberal, democratic, and reformist foundations.

Azaña and some Socialist leaders opposed a recourse to violence, but sentiment was already building within the PSOE during late 1933 for a an insurrectionary response to the government's dismantling of earlier social legislation and its use of heavy-handed repression. But to a considerable extent, this took the form of extreme rhetoric designed to bring pressure on the government rather than serious nuts-and-bolts planning for a rising.[47]

For the Socialists and the entire Republican opposition, the key to avoiding the effective dismantling of the Republic lay in the exclusion of the CEDA from the government. The party used its hold over a succession of unstable Radical ministries, however, to provoke a series of political crises designed to secure representation in the cabinet. The CEDA finally got its way in October 1934, when a reluctant Alcalá-Zamora approved the appointment of three of its members to the government. Although the parties of the Azaña coalition condemned the ministerial change without exception, reaction was strongest among the Socialists, who soon launched a general strike and attempted a rising against a government that they now regarded as openly counterrevolutionary.

The authorities easily suppressed the October revolution, save in Asturias, where an alliance of Socialist, Communist, and anarcho-syndicalist workers seized control of the province for approximately two weeks before succumbing to the army. The reasons for the rising's failure elsewhere in the country were many. Although the CEDA and its supporters saw the revolt as the result of a massive and carefully planned conspiracy, the reality was otherwise. Few adequate preparations were made by Socialists over the country as a whole. Confusion reigned among the rank and file over whether the party intended a general strike in the style of 1917 or a real attempt at insurrection. As a result, workers in Madrid rallied to the general strike but refused to rise in rebellion.[48] In Barcelona, where the cooperation of anarcho-syndicalists was indispensable for success, the Confederación Nacional del Trabajo sat on its hands. The regional government of Catalonia, the Generalitat, embroiled in controversy with Madrid over attempts to curb its autonomy, joined the insurrection, although its resistance was easily broken. Neither massive nor coordinated, the rising fell easy victim to government repression. There is evidence

47. Preston, *The Coming of the Spanish Civil War,* pp. 101–2.

48. David Ruiz, *Insurrección defensiva y revolución obrera: el octubre español de 1934* (Barcelona, 1988), pp. 42–44. In the city of Salamanca, the strike enjoyed some success because of the support of transport and metallurgy workers as well as bakers, printers, and hairdressers. The strike movement was broken, however, when the authorities arrested Socialist municipal councillors and trade union leaders. There were also some attempts at church and convent burnings. Vincent, *Catholicism in the Second Spanish Republic,* p. 229.

that Gil Robles was aware of the weakness of the revolutionary initiative and even welcomed it as a means of dealing a crushing blow to working-class political and union organizations.[49]

The October rising marked an important divide in the Republic's history by exacerbating the deep social antagonisms around which the political system revolved. The radical reorganization of society demanded by the revolutionary alliance in Asturias—the seizure of property and sporadic executions of factory managers, priests, and landowners in the region—confirmed the worst fears of rightist politicians. Given the glaring weaknesses of the revolutionary movement, it was evident from the start that the insurrection stood little chance of becoming a Spanish version of the Bolshevik revolution of 1917. The parties sustaining the government, none more so than the CEDA, magnified the danger of the revolutionary threat. Implacable pressure from the CEDA impelled the government into a policy of widespread repression that included arrests in the thousands, summary executions, and a series of show trials against prominent politicians, including Azaña, who had nothing to do with the insurrection.[50]

From the Church's perspective, the October revolution added a disturbing new element to the historic problem of anticlericalism. For the first time since 1835, an attack on the Church involved not only physical attacks on religious buildings but significant loss of life among the clergy. Although the violence was largely confined to Asturias, thirty-four priests and religious were assassinated and more than fifty churches set ablaze, including the cathedral of Oviedo and the diocesan seminary, with its library of twelve thousand volumes. The incendiarism of 1909 and 1931, which avoided loss of life with a few exceptions, yielded to a paroxysm of hostility against the clergy unknown in Spain for a century.

The scenes played out during the two weeks of revolutionary upheaval resembled those that would become common during the early months of the Civil War. Priests of the Passionist order in Mieres received a warning of sorts from voices in the night urging them to abandon their residence before their throats were cut. By day, they were besieged by an angry crowd of women and children shouting, "Let the dogs die!"—a threat that was carried out later as several of their number perished in the midst of "terrible blasphemies against all that is holy." A parish priest of Oviedo was forced to wear a red skirt and endure the insults of his captors before being shot. There were examples of cadavers being profaned and of priests who had managed to escape to the countryside being hunted down and executed.[51]

49. Preston, *The Coming of the Spanish Civil War*, p. 123.

50. Jackson, *The Spanish Republic*, pp. 159–65.

51. *Episodios de la revolución en Asturias: los pasionistas de Mieres y la revolución de octubre de 1934: episodios narrados por los mismos protagonistas* (Santander, 1935), pp. 9–10, 24–25; "In Memoriam: los sacerdotes, víctimas de la revolución," *Revista Eclesiástica* (1934), p. 448.

A horrified Church saw these events as a systematic attempt to eliminate the clergy through blood and fire throughout Asturias, the beginning of an effort "to eradicate all religious belief from the face of Spain."[52] In fact, the high degree of confusion existing among local revolutionary committees seeking to establish control over a turbulent situation produced different reactions from one area to another. Although many priests were arrested, they were treated decently by some disciplined local authorities who had no interest in promoting a bloodbath certain to damage the revolution's objectives.[53] Violence against priests and religious was concentrated in three specific areas—the provincial capital of Oviedo and the mining towns of Mieres and Turón. The assassinations carried out in Oviedo resulted largely from indiscriminate roundups on the part of uncontrolled groups roaming the streets in the name of revolutionary justice. Sacerdotal status alone constituted sufficient cause for arrest. One of the victims was Canon Aurelio Gago, a close associate of one of the most advanced figures within social Catholicism, Maximiliano Arboleya.[54]

The situation in Mieres and Turón was different. These mining towns had a long history of intense conflict between workers and employers. Historians have noted the progressive radicalization of the Asturian working class between 1931 and 1933.[55] Nowhere was it more fully realized than in the harsh physical and social environment of these coal-mining valleys. Violence against the clergy was moved by a specific motive and was far from aimless in direction. In Mieres, where Communists were prominently represented on the local revolutionary committee, the Church was perceived not simply as an ally or symbol of conservative interests (the pattern, more or less, of earlier examples of anticlerical violence), but as a direct agent of counterrevolution and capitalism. A young militant told a priest, "I am a revolutionary worker, fully persuaded of the mission assigned in the world to the proletariat." There are individuals under arrest who are "incompatible" with the revolution. For them, "no salvation is possible."[56] The revolutionary authorities gave special attention to hunting down priests associated with Catholic political organizations, among them a Passionist serving as president of a local branch of Acción Popular.

The reach of the committee extended to the nearby town of Turón, where eight Christian Brothers, teachers in a free school for miners' children, were shot. Here, too, revolutionaries drew a connection between the Church and capitalism/reac-

52. *Episodios de la revolución de Asturias*, p. 10.

53. Ruiz, *Insurrección defensiva*, p. 128.

54. Ibid.; "In Memoriam," pp. 442–44; Domingo Benavides Gómez, "Maximiliano Arboleya y su interpretación de la revolución de octubre," in G. Jackson et al., *Octubre 1934: cincuenta años para la reflexión* (Madrid, 1985), p. 259.

55. For an analysis of this change, see Manuel Pérez Ledesma, "El movimiento obrero antes de octubre: de la moderación a la violencia revolucionaria," in ibid., pp. 209–29.

56. *Episodios en la revolución de Asturias*, p. 219.

tion. During the initial days of the rising, a crowd invaded the Brothers' residence, demanding the arms they believed had been hidden there by "the fascists of Catholic Youth," i.e., Catholic Action. A contemporary Catholic commentator on the events at Turón expressed surprise that "not a few of the former pupils" of the order's nine schools for working-class students in Asturias had joined the insurrection.[57] There was little surprising about it. The order's schools existed under the patronage of industrial firms with a long record of strikebreaking and opposition to independent labor unions. The Hulleras de Turón founded and subsidized the Brothers' school in the locality. It taught the values of social docility deeply resented by the workers but esteemed "by all persons of order."[58]

The violence against the clergy in Mieres and Turón developed in considerable measure from the radicalization of the working class in the district and from the freedom of action enjoyed by the local revolutionary committee in the midst of a movement lacking effective centralized control.[59] Elsewhere in Asturias, its example was not widely imitated. But the assassinations testified to a significant change at the grassroots level. Spanish Marxists, whether Socialist or Communist, had never seen the Church as a primary enemy in the class struggle. It appeared, at worst, as one of many buttresses sustaining capitalist economic interests. Anticlerical violence was regarded as a tactic employed by demagogic bourgeois parties to distract the working class from its real objective, the transformation of the economy and society through revolution.[60] There is nothing to suggest that the Socialist or Communist leadership abandoned this view, at least in theory. But the violence in Mieres and Turón against the clergy suggests that a fundamental change was taking place among the rank and file, who were coming to regard the Church as more than a secondary ally of capitalism and the bourgeoisie.

The clergy reacted to the revolution's failure with a collective sigh of relief, but from different perspectives. Vidal i Barraquer welcomed the suppression of a movement that he believed intended "to develop and implant sovietism." But true to his pastoral principles, he wrote to Alcalá-Zamora appealing for clemency for those condemned to death by the Barcelona military tribunal. Juan Luis y Pérez, bishop of the diocese where the bloodiest scenes had been played out, also called for the pardon of those who had been misled into "rebellion and crime."[61] As a result of long years of struggle with employers and conservative social Catholics, Maximiliano Arboleya knew the conflictive labor history of Asturias as well as anyone

57. *Los mártires de Turón: notas biográficas y reseña del martirio* (Madrid, 1935), pp. 58, 79.

58. Ibid., p. 79.

59. A provincial revolutionary committee existed in Oviedo, but its "writ . . . did not run into the coalfields, where the revolutionary impetus of the miners far exceeded the limited official objectives of the rising." Adrian Shubert, "The Epic Failure: The Asturian Revolution of October 1934," in *Revolution and War in Spain, 1931–1939*, ed. Paul Preston (London and New York, 1984), p. 130.

60. Victor M. Arbeloa, *Socialismo y anti-clericalismo* (Madrid, 1973), pp. 152–53.

61. Vidal i Barraquer to Alcalá-Zamora, October 12, 1934, *AVB*, vol. 4, part 2, p. 578; "Los últimos consejos de un prelado a sus diocesanos," October 20, 1934, *Revista Eclesiástica* (1934), p. 524.

within the Church. He took a hard, clinical line in his interpretation of events. "The ferocious, fanatical and savage hostility" directed against the "established social order" did not come out of the blue. In the midst of a "tremendous catastrophe," "we must ask ourselves if some responsibility touches us." Spanish Catholics, he declared, had repeatedly shown themselves "deaf and even hostile to the recommendations of Leo XIII" on the need for social justice and had finally reaped the whirlwind of their negligence.[62]

Neither the charitable sentiments of Vidal i Barraquer nor Arboleya's critical assessment of the insurrection's causes were widely echoed elsewhere in the Church. Although some historians have maintained that the insurrection's leaders saw their action primarily as a "preventive-defensive" mechanism rather than as an attempt to carry out a great social revolution, the clergy emphasized with some justification the revolutionary intentions of some groups on the Left, although ecclesiastical rhetoric failed to take into account the far from unanimous reaction of left-wing parties and organizations to the revolutionary initiative.[63] The October rising intended, declared a journal for the parish clergy, a revolution "of the Soviet type." Even the usually moderate Dominican journal, *La Ciencia Tomista*, singled out Socialists as "traitors to the Mother Country, in whose breast they plunged daggers directed by the International and poisoned by Jewish hatred." The forces of order were praised for having "extirpated . . . two cancers, Marxism and separatism." The October revolution represented nothing less than a decisive battle between an "antireligious and atheist" Marxist revolution and the principles of Christianity. If the insurrection had triumphed, "Spain would be the new Russia."[64]

If this view of a conflict to the death between the absolutes of good and evil found its way into a mainstream Catholic journal, it resonated even more strongly among the ultra clergy. Neither the CEDA's electoral success nor the repression carried out after the October revolution satisfied the right-wing parties committed to overturning the Republic. On the contrary, between 1934 and 1936, Carlists, Integrists, and the authoritarian monarchists of Renovación Española redoubled their attacks on both limbs of the Church's "two-armed" strategy. The "accidentalist" tactics endorsed by the Church and given expression in the CEDA were subject to a barrage of violent criticism. Herrera was denounced as "a failed apostle" who had caused "profound damage to the fundamental principles which integrate . . . the Spanish soul, always Catholic and monarchist," and the hierarchy for its "vulgar

62. Maximiliano Arboleya-Martinez, "Causas y remedios," *Revista Eclesiástica* (1935), p. 517. Arboleya objected especially to an attempt by Angel Herrera to convert Vicente Madera, who had resisted by force a revolutionary assault in the Asturian town of Aller, into a national hero of social Catholicism. Benavides Gómez, "Arboleya y su interpretación de la revolución de octubre," pp. 264–65.

63. Ruiz, *Insurrección defensiva*, p. 148.

64. "Los ideales de la revolución," *Revista Eclesiástica* (1935), p. 513; V. L. Gómora, "Crónicas científico-sociales," *La Ciencia Tomista* (1934), vol. 50, p. 395; A. Carrión, "Crónicas científico-sociales," ibid. (1935), vol. 51, p. 407.

and leaden" pastorals urging acceptance of the Republic.[65] The republican opposition saw "accidentalism" as insincere; extremists on the Right perceived it as a threat to the realization of their political objectives. For the same reason, they had long opposed the efforts of the papal nuncio and Vidal i Barraquer to negotiate a settlement with the Republic. The prospect that an agreement might be reached with the government in power after November 1933 led them to intensify their campaign to prevent realization of what they saw as a Spanish version of the French *ralliement* of the 1890s.

How many priests sympathized with the extreme Right is difficult to establish. Cardinal Tarancón's recollection of "sacristies . . . converted into centers of conspiracy" in the name of a "*holy war*" against the Republic seems exaggerated.[66] The diocesan clergy more or less followed the Church's official line; members of the religious orders were more restive and less easy to control. But the greatest thorn in the hierarchy's side remained a small number of clerical publicists who continued to express their adamant opposition to a compromise with liberal democracy in any way, shape, or form.

The bishops' attempts to control priests opposed to their strategy had not been particularly successful during the first two years of the Republic. It was even less so between 1933 and 1936, when clerical attacks on the Church's policy towards the Republic escaped the confines of obscure ecclesiastical journals to take the form of detailed critiques and sweeping visions of a resurrected Catholic Spain. Canon Castro Albarrán, who had stirred the muddy waters of conspiracy by deed in 1932, now did so with the pen through an aggressive volume published in 1934, aptly titled *The Right of Rebellion* (*El Derecho a la rebeldía*). Although the author avoided an explicit exhortation to insurrection, the implication was clear. Further, his hostility to the *ralliement* between the French Church and the Third Republic constituted a thinly disguised indictment of the hierarchy's "two-armed" strategy towards the regime.[67] Not surprisingly, the Committee of Metropolitans regarded the book as "imprudent and inopportune" and inspired by a "destructive purpose."[68] The Jesuit Zacarías García Villada ascended to the lofty heights of providentialism in a book published on the eve of the Civil War. Catholic Spain was called to fulfill its historic destiny by saving the nation from the dangers of socialism and the lay State through a conflict perceived in terms of absolutes, between good and evil, between the city of God and the city of Satan. Similar ideas had sur-

65. J. Cortés Cavanillas, *Gil Robles ¿monárquico? Misterios de una política* (Madrid, 1935), pp. 37, 81.

66. Enrique y Tarancón, *Recuerdos de juventud*, p. 131.

67. "Parer de Félix Bilbao, bisbe de Tortosa, sobre *El derecho a la rebeldía* por A. de Castro Albarrán," *AVB*, vol. 4, part 1, p. 257.

68. Vidal i Barraquer to Pacelli, January 15, 1934, *AVB*, vol. 4, part 1, p. 205. The papal nuncio Tedeschini was "deeply offended" by the book because of its opposition to the conciliatory line that he was promoting. The nuncio's pressure forced Castro Albarrán to resign his position at the important seminary of Comillas in September 1934. Redondo, *Historia de la Iglesia en España*, vol. 1, p. 225.

faced often enough within Spanish Catholicism since the first conflicts with liberalism, but García Villada made no bones about identifying Spain's providential mission with the authoritarian monarchist cause.[69]

A respected educator, the Augustinian Teodoro Rodríguez, avoided the explicit partisan sympathies of Castro Albarrán and García Villada, but his 1935 book advocating a fundamental reorganization of the Catholic Right was uncompromising, even chilling, in its view of present and future. Spain was caught in a primitive struggle between "revolutionaries who have turned against the natural order of society and deny the existence of God" and "antirevolutionaries," advocates of "the Christian organization of society." Between them no compromise was possible. "The enemies of Catholicism have declared open war, a war to the death, upon us under the influence of a Jewish-masonic world association." The strategy of Catholics who maintained that "it is necessary to live with everyone and tolerate to be tolerated, through pacts, understandings, and collaborations with the enemy" was nothing less than "a moral and juridical monstrosity." In the future, Catholics must abandon this "confused" attitude in favor of a union based on resolute opposition to "modern liberties," whether freedom of association, freedom of the press, or academic freedom. For Rodríguez, the choice was straightforward, either "revolution or counterrevolution."[70]

By 1935, the balance sheet of the Church's "two-armed" strategy towards the Republic was far from favorable. The religious legislation passed between 1931 and 1933 remained on the books, though it went largely unenforced by the Radical governments in power. After a promising beginning, official negotiations between Madrid and the Vatican for a diplomatic settlement of outstanding issues between Church and State came to a standstill. The political limb of the official strategy had produced a successful confessional party in the CEDA, but the ambiguity of its program and tactics exacerbated differences with the parties of the Left that produced an atmosphere of mutual hostility made worse by the outbreak of the October revolution and the repression following in its wake. Determined to bring down the Republic at all costs, the parties of the extreme Right, aided and abetted by some clergy, were waging sustained guerrilla warfare against the diplomatic and political aspects of the Church's official policy in the name of an antidemocratic program.

The hierarchy and the Vatican devised and supported the "two-armed" strategy to maximize the Church's options as it sought to defend its position within the Re-

69. Morodo, *Los orígenes ideológicos del franquismo*, pp. 144–58.

70. Teodoro Rodríguez, *El problema social y las derechas: nuevas orientaciones* (El Escorial, 1935), pp. 43–44, 100, 102–3, 106, 352–55, 386. A prolific author, Rodríguez (1864–1954) was well known within the Church for his often polemical defense of the Church's rights in education. He also held a series of important positions within his order, including the rectorship of the Universidad de María Cristina in the Escorial.

public. The negotiating option produced few concrete results between 1931 and 1936. In the end, there remained only the political option tying the Church to the fortunes of a single political party, the CEDA.

As Vidal i Barraquer recognized following the November 1933 elections, given the inherent instability of the parliamentary forces sustaining the government, it was only a question of time before general elections would be called. The determination of Gil Robles not only to increase CEDA representation in the cabinet but also to supplant the Radical Republicans as the governing party was the immediate cause of the final crisis. But the realization of these plans depended on the attitude of the president, who held responsibility for ordering a dissolution if in his judgment a stable ministry could not be formed from the existing parliament. Alcalá-Zamora deeply mistrusted Gil Robles, whose commitment to the Republic he judged insincere, and refused to call the CEDA leader to form a government.[71] Instead, the president dissolved parliament on January 7, 1936, and convoked elections for February 16.

The campaign brought to a boil the accumulating passions of Right and Left. The electoral propaganda of the CEDA and its supporters abandoned the studied "accidentalism" of the past in favor of the historic providentialism long associated with apologists for the extreme Right. It was necessary, said *El Debate*, "to conquer the revolution to defend the rights of God and the Church. Marxism and its allies are seeking the ruin of the Catholic man of Spain, the only principle of our unity as a nation and our best historic glory."[72] The millions of leaflets distributed by the CEDA as part of a massive propaganda effort made the point more crudely. One declared luridly that a victory of the Left would lead to "the arming of the rabble; burnings of private houses and banks; distribution of private goods and lands; wild looting and the common ownership of women."[73]

The hierarchy avoided these excesses, though it left little doubt where its sympathies lay, however discreetly expressed. Cardinal Ilundain of Seville, long an associate of Vidal i Barraquer in efforts to reach an accommodation with the Republic, told the faithful of his diocese that they should not only pray for divine assistance in view of "present necessities," they must also do whatever was necessary to prevent the aggravation of "the evils already endured by religion and the Catholic Church." Bishop Félix Bilbao of Tortosa was more direct when he stressed the need for union among Catholics "in defense of the Church and the Nation," while Bishop Antonio García of Tuy instructed the faithful to vote for candidates who

71. Angel Herrera recalled that he advised Gil Robles to make every effort to establish friendly relations with Alcalá-Zamora and avoid at all costs making the president his political adversary. Gil Robles paid no attention to this advice. Angel Herrera, *El pensamiento de Angel Herrera: antología política y social*, ed. José María Escudero (Madrid, 1987), p. 220.

72. *El Debate*, February 2, 1936, extraordinary supplement.

73. Quoted in Preston, *The Coming of the Spanish Civil War*, p. 172.

would work for "the prosperity and peace of Spain in every field and especially the religious."[74]

Although the clergy saw the elections as "a transcendental event" of "enormous gravity," the virulence of the campaign and the CEDA's freewheeling propaganda gave the political process a life of its own that pushed the Church to the political margins, despite its contribution to the party's creation.[75] The "two-armed" strategy had rested on the idea that the hierarchy would be able to direct a "union of Catholics" in accord with a middle-of-the-road policy capable of transcending Catholic divisions without provoking a powerful reaction by the parties of the Left. In the best of times, this would have been difficult to achieve. In the turbulent circumstances of the early 1930s, it proved impossible, for once loosed, the political arm of the CEDA swung largely on its own in the quest for power and in reaction to the specific ideological and social concerns of its members.

In any event, the election results exposed the flaws of the Church's policy. The great electoral victory of the CEDA, the proverbial basket in which the Church had placed all its eggs, did not materialize. The parties of the Left, having learned the hard political lesson of November 1933, formed a broad electoral coalition, the Popular Front, and won a decisive parliamentary majority. Manuel Azaña returned as prime minister and clerical apprehensions grew apace. "We do not know the future that Our Lord God has reserved for the Church of Spain," declared a clerical journal in its assessment of the implications of the Popular Front victory.[76] A decisive shift in government policy was inevitable as the possibility of concluding successful negotiations with the Vatican vanished, and the new government insisted on full implementation of the religious legislation passed between 1931 and 1933. At the same time, a resurgent popular anticlericalism led to a new wave of physical assaults on church buildings and the clergy.

The failure of the Church's policy at both the diplomatic and political levels destroyed the illusions sustaining many clergy until the very eve of the February elections. After investing its energies for five years in its "two-armed" strategy, the hierarchy now found itself adrift, with no clear alternative at hand. Significantly, the Committee of Metropolitans published no sweeping collective statements offering guidance to the faithful as it had done in 1931 and 1933. Although the bishops remained committed to a "union of Catholics," they now gave priority to internal spiritual and moral renewal rather than to political action. Many prelates directed their clergy to stay out of politics and to be "courteous and thoughtful with the civil authorities, showing that you desire peace."[77] Despite his extremely

74. *El Debate*, January 26, February 7, 1936; Francisco Carballo and Alfonso Magariños, *La Iglesia en Galicia contemporánea: análisis histórico y teológico del periodo, 1931–1939, II Republica* (Madrid, 1978), p. 558.

75. "La última lección: comentario electoral," *Razón y Fe* (1936), vol. 36, p. 433.

76. Ibid., p. 451.

77. "Normas de vida para el clero en la hora presente," *Revista Eclesiástica* (1936), p. 92.

conservative views and his conviction that the victory of the Popular Front represented "the revolution triumphant," even Cardinal Gomá of Toledo felt compelled to inform the clergy of his diocese that they must avoid political activities and concentrate their energies on preaching and catechesis. Only in this way could "a Christian restoration" be achieved that would allow the Church to survive a stark reality that could not be ignored: "We are no longer masters of the thought of our people, who look upon us, not only with suspicious caution, but also as enemies of their welfare."[78]

The February elections produced two significant effects on the Church. With the "two-armed" strategy in ruins, the hierarchy retreated from its active, behind-the-scenes involvement with the CEDA and its aggressive response to the Popular Front in favor of an emphasis on spiritual renewal as the only means of securing the Church's position in its new time of trial. Withdrawal from the partisan arena also represented a tacit admission on the part of the clerical leadership that it faced a political situation completely beyond its control. As the Republic entered the conflictive six months preceding the outbreak of Civil War, the Church withdrew to the sidelines. Initiative passed to the fragmented hosts of an intensely politicized Catholicism: Integrists, Carlists, authoritarian monarchists, disaffected members of the CEDA, and others who agreed on little more than their determination to destroy the Republic by whatever means necessary. By July 18, 1936, when the army rose in rebellion against the regime after months of conspiratorial intrigue, nothing was left of the elaborate and ambiguous tactics through which the Church had sought to protect itself over the preceding five years. It had become a prisoner of events, some of its own making.

Change and Renewal

The Church placed confidence in diplomatic negotiations and political activity as the best means of protecting its interests within the Republic. But it could not ignore the need to adapt ecclesiastical administration and finances to the reality created by the separation of Church and State. The clergy saw disestablishment as an ill wind blowing little good. In fact, it forced positive changes on an institution too often gripped by lethargy in the past. Or, as the Committee of Metropolitans informed the faithful in 1931, "God knows how to secure great good from worse evils."[79] Results were mixed, but they suggest that the Church possessed sufficient resiliency to manage its affairs better than prophets of doom had predicted upon the separation of the civil and ecclesiastical powers.

78. Quoted in Anastasio Granados, *El Cardenal Gomá, Primado de España* (Madrid, 1969), pp. 73–75.

79. "Metropolitanos españoles a los fieles," November 21, 1931, in *Documentos colectivos del episcopado español, 1870–1974*, ed. Jesús Iribarren (Madrid, 1974), p. 158.

No problem appeared more pressing than the financial. The 1931 constitution ordered gradual suppression of the *culto y clero* subsidy. The Republic provided a two-year cushion but reduced the 66,234,430 pesetas of the pre-April 14 budget to 42,435,826 for the 1932 fiscal year and to 5,000,000 for 1933. The center/right government in power after November 1933 satisfied clerical demands to the extent that a 1934 law appropriated 16,500,000 to fund pensions for older priests. It did not reestablish the *culto y clero* budget.[80] In one form or another, the Church received government funding on an annual basis between 1931 and 1936, but the reduction in income was massive by any standards.

There is no adequate study of how the Church managed to finance clerical salaries and diocesan administration during the Republic. Ecclesiastical administrators attempted to squeeze as much as possible from sources of income remaining under Church control. In the dioceses of Galicia, the parish clergy raised surplice fees for baptisms, marriages, and funerals and charged for a wide range of other services ranging from conducting novenas to drafting genealogical trees for parishioners. To increase revenues for diocesan needs, bishops imposed a tax on every possible source, including the income derived from renting pews. The hierarchy also moved quickly to increase the amount expected from the faithful under the terms of the historic *bula de la cruzada,* a donation rendered in return for certain indulgences and dispensations. Returns doubled and tripled in some cases, but neither the *bula* nor increased surplice fees ever approximated the amount provided by the old *culto y clero* budget.[81]

As soon as the Republic's fiscal intentions became clear, the hierarchy turned its attention to raising money through special monthly collections and pledge campaigns. Bishops and priests bombarded Catholics with emotional exhortations appealing to duty and conscience. While the laity donated generously to political causes, it sometimes proved less enthusiastic about supporting the clergy. Gifts were "laughably small" in the view of one critic, who regarded the parsimony of

80. These reductions were distributed in different proportions among the clergy. Bishops lost 50 percent of their salaries; the parish clergy, 18 percent. The 1934 law was based on recognition of the traditional bureaucratic principle of "acquired rights," namely, the obligation of the State to continue the salaries of priests originally appointed by the Ministry of Justice, whose status, the Church argued, should be regarded as similar to that of civil servants. "Obligaciones eclesiásticas que subsisten en 1932," *Ilustración del Clero* (1931), p. 304; Hilario Yaben, "El Estado y la situación económica del Clero," *Revista Eclesiástica* (1933), p. 572.

81. Carballo and Magariños, *La Iglesia en la Galicia contemporánea,* pp. 224–26; "Vidal i Barraquer al cardenal Raffaello Carlo Rossi, secretari de la Congregació Consistorial, sobre l'Obra del Culte i del clergat," January 25, 1932, *AVB,* vol. 3, part 1, pp. 132–33; "Introducción a la segunda parte," ibid., part 2, p. 314. The returns from the *bula* were not uniformly favorable. In Seville, for example, they fell well below expectations. How much the Church received beyond the government subsidy before April 14, 1931, is not entirely clear, although the figure of 10 million pesetas suggested by Pilar García i Jordan seems reasonable, although she points out that additional income was derived from various Church properties. Her estimate of 76 million corresponds with the estimate of 80 million advanced by *El Debate* as the minimum amount required to pay clerical salaries and maintain churches. *Els catòlics catalans i la Segona República, 1931–1936* (Barcelona, 1986), p. 122; *El Debate,* January 7, 1933.

the "Catholic bourgeoisie" as scandalous.[82] In 1933, for example, Acción Popular collected half a million pesetas virtually overnight from Madrid supporters lined rows deep to make contributions to the party.[83] The amount collected equaled the sum raised over an entire year by the dioceses of Catalonia under a resource-sharing plan. But in Madrid, parish priests successfully conducted pledge campaigns, although no hard figures are available.[84] In Galicia, where the Church depended on a practicing but poor peasantry, results were disappointing, amounting in the case of the Tuy diocese to no more than 4 percent of the *culto y clero* appropriation. The diocese of Salamanca fared better, raising about a third of the old government grant.[85] Responses varied from region to region, but the constant and worried attention given to financial questions by the Committee of Metropolitans during the period suggests that donations fell far short of the 80 million a year thought necessary to meet ecclesiastical expenses.[86]

Despite the financial crisis, the Church managed to keep parishes staffed and to prevent even a single church from being closed, or so it was claimed.[87] Parish priests appear to have survived on whatever they could secure locally and from sporadic donations produced by diocesan resource-sharing schemes.[88] Complaints surfaced alleging that priests were forced into civilian occupations to supplement their incomes; clergymen were even urged to do so in the Santiago archdiocese. How many followed this counsel is impossible to establish, although there is no convincing evidence that the parochial clergy was unable to remain fully committed to pastoral responsibilities because of financial need.

Fiscal problems also forced the Church to consider a modification of the historic financial autonomy of dioceses. Prior to the Republic, no mechanism existed to redistribute resources among dioceses in accord with pastoral and financial needs. Differences of income among dioceses were once ameliorated to some extent by the flat-rate salaries for parish priests set in the *culto y clero* appropriation.

82. H. R. Romero Flores, *Perfil moral de nuestra hora* (Madrid, 1935), p. 66.

83. Montero, *La CEDA*, vol. 1, p. 798.

84. According to a Madrid parish priest, pledge campaigns in the capital were so successful that it became possible "to make up fully the suppressed salaries of the State's budget." Kodasver [pseud.], *Medio siglo de vida diocesana matritense, 1913–1963* (Madrid, 1967), p. 112.

85. Carballo and Magariños, *La Iglesia en la Galicia contemporánea*, p. 220; Vincent, *Catholicism in the Second Spanish Republic*, p. 35.

86. At its meeting in November 1931, the Committee of Metropolitans devoted considerable attention to ecclesiastical finances, a theme that figured prominently in its sessions until 1936. "Acta de la conferencia de Metropolitanos españoles celebrada los días 18–20 de noviembre de 1931," in *Actas de las conferencias de metropolitanos españoles, 1921–1965*, ed. Vicente Cárcel Ortí (Madrid, 1994), p. 282.

87. Eloy Montero y Gutiérrez, *El porvenir de la Iglesia de España* (Madrid, 1933), p. 147.

88. One of the few detailed studies of ecclesiastical incomes for the republican period, based on parochial records in the diocese of Tuy, has established that the average annual income of parish priests between 1933 and 1935 was 2,193 pesetas or 6.09 pesetas a day, an income that fell somewhere between that of moderately skilled workmen and schoolteachers. Although modest, this exceeded the average daily income of 3 to 5 pesetas a day estimated by Cárcel Ortí as paid to parish priests under the pre–April 14 subsidy. Carballo and Magariños, *La Iglesia en la Galicia contemporánea*, pp. 230–33; Vicente Cárcel Ortí, *La persecución religiosa en España durante la Segunda República, 1931–1939* (Madrid, 1990), p. 84.

Under the Republic, the need for dioceses to raise their own revenues threatened to exacerbate financial disparities between richer and poorer sees.

No one was more aware of the damaging effects of this development than Cardinal Vidal i Barraquer. Although he presided over the Catalan dioceses organized in the ecclesiastical province of Tarragona, the cardinal was a poor financial cousin to the bishop of Barcelona, whose more populous diocese offered greater fund-raising opportunities. In 1931, Vidal i Barraquer proposed an interdiocesan fund (*caja interdiocesana*) to redistribute income to the less fortunate dioceses of the ecclesiastical province. The cardinal also used his influence as president of the Committee of Metropolitans to advocate creation of a financial system designed to share resources through a three-tiered organization of diocesan, interdiocesan, and national funds.[89]

The centralized scheme desired by Vidal i Barraquer never fully materialized, largely because of disagreements among the bishops and with the Vatican over its precise form.[90] Prelates of prosperous dioceses were often less than enthusiastic about sharing resources. Bishop Eijo Garay of Madrid, whose parochial clergy managed to raise funds through pledge campaigns, rejected the idea that the diocese might share its good fortune with others: "Let parish priests elsewhere work as hard as mine have done." Vidal i Barraquer complained to Rome that the dioceses most reluctant to participate in resource sharing were precisely those with "economic means to spare."[91] In the end, a network of diocesan, interdiocesan, and national funds appeared, although, contrary to Vidal i Barraquer's original plan, bishops retained a high degree of financial autonomy.

The amounts raised and redistributed proved disappointing. The diocesan funds of Galicia sputtered along without providing significant relief to poor parishes. The Tarragona interdiocesan fund managed to dispense on average from 400,000 to 500,000 pesetas a year, only about 5 percent of former receipts from the *culto y clero* budget. The Committee of Metropolitans fared no better. In 1934, it collected approximately 250,000 from the dioceses, scarcely enough to make a difference for poor sees.[92] Although results fell far short of expectations, they at least represented the first serious attempt to remedy the historic inequalities of ecclesiastical finances.

The fiscal crisis also encouraged the Church to introduce changes into its inflexible personnel structure with a view to using the secular clergy more effectively.

89. García i Jordan, *Els catòlics catalans*, pp. 124–26.

90. Controversy arose over the extent of fiscal authority to be held by *cajas interdiocesanas*. Some prelates and the Vatican believed that while they were desirable, they should not compromise the financial autonomy of the bishops. Ibid., pp. 126–28.

91. Quoted in Kodasver, *Medio siglo de vida diocesana*, p. 112; Vidal i Barraquer to Pacelli, November 3, 1933, *AVB*, vol. 4, part 1, p. 139.

92. Carballo and Magariños, *La Iglesia en la Galicia contemporánea*, pp. 204–6; García i Jordan, *Els catòlics catalans*, p. 134, Table 5; "Acta de la conferencia de los Excmos. Metropolitanos celebrada en Madrid los días 15, 16, 17 y 18 de noviembre de 1934," *AVB*, vol. 4, part 2, p. 627.

In some respects, the situation resembled that of the mid-nineteenth century, when suppression of the male religious orders forced the Church to assign new importance to the parochial clergy's pastoral function. During the early 1930s, the Church faced two related personnel problems, the beginnings of a demographic decline among diocesan priests and the rigidity of the ecclesiastical appointment system. The first must be kept in perspective. The number of priests, secular and regular, declined in absolute numbers during the republican period from 32,446 in 1931 to 29,902 by 1936, a significant but far from catastrophic loss. Moreover, the country as a whole continued to enjoy a favorable ratio of clergy to people according to the norm of one priest per thousand of population.[93]

But there were disturbing signs for the future. Seminary enrollments that had stood around eleven thousand for two decades fell to seven thousand by 1934, a still impressive number when all is said and done, but the effects of the decline in vocations began to be felt by 1935–1936. In many dioceses, there were insufficient replacements for an aging clergy. By 1935, more than one-half of the parish priests in the Toledo archdiocese were over fifty-five; only five new priests were available to fill thirteen parish vacancies. Circumstances were even worse in Málaga, where three priests were being ordained annually to fill twenty-five positions. Similarly, the Seville archdiocese required at least twenty new priests a year but ordained only ten.[94] The prospect of a clerical demographic crisis moved the hierarchy to pay serious attention to a long ignored question, how to employ the parochial clergy as efficiently as possible for pastoral objectives.

The bureaucratic hardening of the arteries characteristic of the clerical appointment system until 1931 blocked the hierarchy's ability to make effective use of personnel. Cathedral canons and benefice holders could not be compelled to take up parish work, nor could *curas* be easily transferred from one parish to another because of the *concurso* system. They were virtually irremovable, according to canon law, except for grave cause. Before the new economic limitations and the prospect of a clerical demographic crisis, the bishops stressed the need for greater flexibility in the distribution of priests "to meet the needs of the faithful."[95] In 1932, the Committee of Metropolitans requested the Vatican's permission to remove the canonical straitjacket preventing the bishops from transferring priests to meet pastoral necessities; the archbishops also insisted that cathedral chapters,

93. Carballo and Magariños, *La Iglesia en la Galicia contemporánea*, pp. 72–73. A contemporary source, however, estimated the number of priests at 33,587, a figure that falls within the 31,000–33,000 range characteristic of clerical demography since the turn of the century. E. Vargas Zúñiga, "El problema religioso de España," *Razon y Fe* (1935), no. 465, p. 152. Given the decline in vocations, the estimate of Carballo and Magariños is certainly closer to the truth.

94. Severino Aznar, *La revolución española y las vocaciones eclesiásticas* (Madrid, 1949), p. 43; Manuel González García, *El decrecimiento de las vocaciones sacerdotales y sus causas* (Palencia, 1936), pp. 5–6; Francisco Peiró, *El problema religioso-social en España* (2d ed., Madrid, 1936), p. 29.

95. "Acta de la conferencia de los Rdmos. Metropolitanos celebrada en Madrid los días 3, 4, 5 y 6 de noviembre de 1932," *AVB*, vol. 3, part 2, p. 326.

long regarded as isolated from the harsh reality of life in the religious trenches, should maintain only a minimum complement, with the excess to be directed into parochial work.[96] How effectively these measures dealt with the historic imbalances in the clergy's career structure is difficult to assess. But they provided an indication of a long overdue change in institutional attitudes by taking into account something that advocates of parish reform had been demanding for at least two decades, namely, a recognition of the fundamental importance of the parish and its clergy to the Church's religious mission.

This is not to suggest that a revolution in pastoral methods took place. By and large priests continued along a traditional path, emphasizing celebration of the Mass, dispensation of the sacraments, and the conduct of a myriad of devotions associated with ultramontane piety, although greater emphasis was given to the scriptures in preaching.[97] But the loss of State financial support produced a leveling effect among the clergy that diminished distinctions of income and enhanced the importance of those standing at the bottom of the ecclesiastical organization. The practical changes introduced as a result were limited and in many instances inadequate, but they anticipated, albeit imperfectly, a renewed emphasis on pastoral work that would develop following the Second Vatican Council.

Dire predictions of approaching disaster as a result of the disappearance of the *culto y clero* appropriation were not universally shared within the Church. The old ecclesiastical budget, recognized the ever polemical Canon Hilario Yaben, served as a powerful bond that "chained the Church to the State." "The liberty of the Church" secured as a result of the subsidy's suppression was a cheap price to pay even at the cost of the "unjust penury" endured by the clergy.[98] The Committee of Metropolitans also believed that the financial cloud contained a silver lining, namely, that it would stimulate "Catholic consciences" not only to generosity but also towards an "interior renovation of religious idealism."[99]

Spain's religious condition between 1931 and 1936 has received less attention than have relations between the Church and the Republic. Clergy and laity focused on the secularization of public schools, legalization of divorce, the removal of obstacles to civil marriages, and educational restrictions placed on the regular clergy as part of an official campaign "to de-Catholicize the nation."[100] The hierarchy feared that such measures made the faithful vulnerable to efforts to submerge them in a sea of irreligion. The bishops publicly defended the idea that Spaniards re-

96. Ibid.

97. Carballo and Magariños, *La Iglesia en la Galicia contemporánea*, p. 361. For a description of the elaborate world of ultramontante piety in the Salamanca diocese, see Vincent, *Catholicism in the Second Spanish Republic*, pp. 82–108.

98. Hilario Yaben, "¿Hacia un concordato?," *Revista Eclesiástica* (1934), p. 130.

99. "Metropolitanos españoles a los fieles," November 21, 1931, in *Documentos colectivos del episcopado español*, p. 158.

100. *La Semana Católica* (1931), vol. 50, no. 42, p. 351.

tained their loyalty to the faith, that Spain was Catholic.[101] Privately, they were deeply pessimistic. In December 1931, the Committee of Metropolitans informed Pius XI that the coming of the Republic had "revealed disconsolate realities" in the form of low levels of religious observance in the cities. Whatever nostalgia the archbishops may have felt for the era of Primo de Rivera, they acknowledged that the "officialism of religion during the past regime" favored "the external appearance of a Catholic Spain," when in fact "religious sentiment was neither deep nor vital."[102]

The metropolitans' expression of concern quickly spread, as a wave of discussion over the country's "religious crisis" surged from all parts of the Church, irrespective of individual political views. Cardinal Vidal i Barraquer lamented, "Ignorance in religious matters is so great that in many villages the people fulfill their obligations towards the Church because of tradition or to follow the counsels of their parents, that is to say, through human faith, not through conviction or divine faith." These sentiments were not very different from those expressed by his more conservative rival, Archbishop Gomá of Toledo: "The living rock of our old faith" has yielded to a "religion of credulity, sentiment, routine, and thoughtlessness." In the same vein, the ultra apologist Father P. M. Vélez attacked external "appearance and routine" as the dominant characteristics of Spanish piety, while a Carlist cleric scathingly denounced "bloated, comfort-loving [and] smug" middle-class Catholics who "more or less fulfilled the obligation to attend Sunday Mass, but who vegetated in formidable religious ignorance."[103]

The liberal Catholic intellectual José Bergamín, editor of the progressive journal *Cruz y Raya,* saw Spanish Catholicism as plagued by hypocrisy and indifference and in desperate need of renovation. Father Bruno Ibeas, long a trenchant critic of the clergy's cultural backwardness, viewed religion in Spain as "a failure which once contained a beautiful essence, of which there remains only a touch of perfume. We abound in processions, confraternities, novenas, pilgrimages, . . . but we lack life, . . . and religion is above all life." On the eve of the Civil War, a clerical journal put the question simply when it asked, "Have we failed?"[104]

The difficulties affecting the Church were seen by some as a blessing in disguise, a "providential punishment" that ended the "Phariseeism" of the past and opened

101. As the 1931 constitution was being drafted, Vidal i Barraquer maintained, "It cannot be denied that the immense majority [of Spaniards] are baptized, married and buried in accord with the Catholic rite, they live on the sap of the Church and practice religion more or less perfectly." Vidal i Barraquer to Alcalá-Zamora, August 3, 1931, *AVB,* vol. 1, parts 1–2, p. 179.

102. Metropolitans to Pius XI, December 7, 1931, ibid., vol. 2, parts 1–2, p. 207.

103. Vidal i Barraquer to Pacelli, August 18, 1934, *AVB,* vol. 4, part 2, p. 486; quoted in Granados, *El Cardenal Gomá,* p. 59; P. M. Vélez, "La lección divina de la revolución española," *Religión y Cultura* (1933), vol. 22, no. 64, pp. 24–25; Juan de Iturralde, *El catolicismo y la cruzada de Franco* (3 vols., Vienne and Toulouse, 1965), vol. 1, pp. 320–21.

104. Lannon, *Privilege, Persecution and Prophecy,* pp. 182–83; Bruno Ibeas, "*¿Se puede?*," *Religión y Cultura* (1933), vol. 21, no. 61, p. 92; *Revista Eclesiástica* (1936), p. 361.

the way to inner renewal.[105] How revitalization could be accomplished was another matter. Extensive discussion about the "religious crisis" led to widespread appeals for a reinvigorated faith. But although advocates of change suggested a wide range of specific measures, their ideas not only failed to coalesce into a coherent program of renewal, they also focused on possible solutions in substantially different terms. Supporters of innovation were moving away from the nineteenth-century concept of Spanish Catholicism as an isolated, inward-looking moral fortress deeply suspicious of modern cultural and political conditions. The clergy in Catalonia, long exposed to liturgical reform and the currents of European Catholic thought, displayed some initiative, especially through the creation in 1931 of a "moderate and renovating" youth association, the Federació de Joves Cristians, while in Galicia, a small group of priests gathered around the journal *Logos* embraced the thought of contemporary Catholic theologians and philosophers such as Jacques Maritain and Paul Claudel.[106]

Other advocates of renewal came to fundamentally different conclusions. According to Archbishop Gomá, a Church assaulted by external enemies who had opened an "enormous breach of irreligion" and weakened by routinism needed to withdraw within itself to regroup its spiritual forces before it could mount an effective defense of "the city of God in our Spain."[107] Thus strengthened, the Church could proceed to launch the campaign of religious reconquest of which the clergy had dreamed since the late nineteenth century. Circumstances demanded reinforcement of the Church as a spiritual redoubt implacable in its hostility towards the irreligion and immorality identified with the Republic.[108]

Within a hierarchically organized Church, any movement towards renewal depended ultimately on the bishops. Between 1931 and 1936, the Committee of Metropolitans produced a plethora of recommendations "to intensify religious culture," but there was little that was innovative or imaginative about their proposals.[109] In 1932, they exhorted parish priests to devote more attention to their traditional duties of preaching and catechesis. Insofar as the hierarchy attempted

105. Romero Flores, *Perfil moral de nuestra hora*, p. 67.

106. García i Jordan, *Els catòlics catalans*, p. 36; Carballo and Magariños, *La Iglesia en la Galicia contemporánea*, p. 507. Founded in 1931 by the parish priest of Vilafranca de Penedès, Albert Bonet, the FJC had nine thousand members by 1935. It was distinguished from the youth section of Catholic Action in two respects: its commitment to autonomy for Catalonia and its less rigorous confessional preoccupations. It did not insist, for example, on imposing a religious test as a condition for membership. The FJC was open to all young people, "practicing or non-practicing, believers or non-believers," and deliberately chose "Christian" rather than "Catholic" for its official name. Josep Massot i Muntaner, *Aproximació a la historia religiosa de la Catalunya contemporánea* (Barcelona, 1973), pp. 98–100; Lannon, *Privilege, Persecution and Prophecy*, p. 231; Pere Codinachs i Verdaguer, *La Federació de Joves Cristians de Catalunya, 1931–1936* (Barcelona, 1990), p. 93.

107. Quoted in Granados, *El Cardenal Gomá*, p. 41.

108. Carballo and Magariños have called this the "spirituality of the *ghetto*," which became "active and militant" during the Republic. *La Iglesia en la Galicia contemporánea*, p. 302.

109. "Acta de la conferencia de los Rdmos. Metropolitanos celebrada en Madrid los días 3, 4, 5 y 6 de noviembre de 1933," *AVB*, vol. 3, part 2, p. 321.

an initiative, it took the form of reforming Catholic Action with the objective of creating a "secular apostolate" to incorporate the laity into the Church's religious mission.

Within these limits there were successes. Despite periodic reorganizations since its founding earlier in the century, Catholic Action reached 1931 lacking a well-defined purpose and a coherent program. No one, recalled Cardinal Tarancón, an active participant as a young priest in the movement between 1931 and 1933, had "a clear idea" of what it ought to be.[110] Under the prodding of Pius XI, the hierarchy in 1933 abandoned the older model of a multitude of disparate associations gathered under a leaky organizational umbrella in favor of a centralized institution extending downward from a national executive to diocesan and parish committees.[111]

The reorganization appears to have worked, although some bishops were uneasy about the concentration of authority in a national committee headed by Angel Herrera. Cardinal Tarancón concluded that the hierarchy successfully realized the objective of converting the laity into "*active and responsible members of the Church.*"[112] But, as the cardinal recognized, this achievement was directly linked to the strong Catholic reaction, as much political as religious, towards republican legislation dealing with the Church. Catholic Action remained, moreover, within the tradition of the elitist model of organizing the faithful so dear to activists since the turn of the century. It was seen as "the nerve of future action" designed to stimulate "the creation . . . of a Catholic conscience among the masses."[113] Members of the ACNP dominated the national and diocesan committees. Further, the organization's membership of forty-one thousand on the eve of the Civil War did not represent a broad cross-section of the Catholic population. Like so many confessional associations of the time, it rested primarily on the Catholic middle classes of the cities.[114]

The Church also managed to profit from its situation during the Republic to carry out an expansion and improvement of religious education. The elimination of catechetical instruction from public schools was attacked by the clergy and the

110. Vicente Enrique y Tarancón, *Recuerdos de juventud* (Barcelona, 1984), p. 124.

111. The reorganization eliminated the position of pontifical director, held invariably by the archbishop of Toledo, and bestowed executive authority on a national committee and its president. The movement was divided into four clearly delimited sections: men, women, young men, and young women. Although the metropolitans favored a decentralized organizational framework that would not embrace all confessional associations, Pius XI imposed the more centralized and inclusive model of Italian Catholic Action. "Introducción a la tercera parte," *AVB*, vol. 2, part 3, pp. 530–36. The hierarchy encountered some difficulties in its reorganization. It wanted to use the existing Confederación de Padres de Familias as the core of the male section of Catholic Action. After some resistance, it attained its objective in 1935. Feliciano Montero García, *El movimiento católico en España* (Madrid, 1993), p. 72.

112. Enrique y Tarancón, *Recuerdos de juventud*, p. 178.

113. *El Debate*, January 1, 1935, special supplement.

114. *Ecclesia* (1941), no. 9, p. 11; no. 21, p. 11; José María Escudero, "La eficacia del catolicismo español," in Carlos Santamaría et al., *Catolicismo español: aspectos actuales* (Madrid, 1955), p. 113.

confessional press. In fact, the loss of this dubious privilege forced the Church to rely on its own initiative rather than on a system of compulsion that had never worked satisfactorily, according to experts on religious education. Well before 1931, the Church began to shift emphasis away from religion classes in public schools to those given by catechetical associations staffed by clergy and laity. Although these groups, organized in different forms, continued into the Republic, the bishops concentrated their attention on developing an infrastructure based on the parishes. In 1932, the bishop of Alicante ordered the organization of catechetical classes in every parish of the diocese, an example that was widely imitated. In Madrid, a central commission was established to prepare appropriate texts and coordinate the activities of religious education committees recently formed in all the capital's parishes. These and similar initiatives undertaken in dioceses as different as Santiago de Compostela, Salamanca, and Tarragona suggest that only during the Republic did the Church succeed in giving religious education the serious consideration that ecclesiastical reformers had first demanded at the national catechetical congress of 1913.[115]

Neither the limited reforming initiatives of the Church nor the deeply feared effects of republican legislation dramatically altered the country's religious condition. Patterns of alienation, on the one side, and of belief and practice, on the other, had taken generations to develop. The period between 1931 and 1936 formed too brief a period to permit a transformation of entrenched attitudes one way or the other. There was some evidence of change, but within a narrow framework reinforcing existing patterns of belief and nonbelief.

Not all within the Church shared a pessimistic view of the country's religious future. "Since the persecution of 1931 was initiated, the fervor of Spanish Catholics has redoubled in a visible manner," declared one cleric who argued the thesis that a revival was taking place. Others echoed these sentiments. In 1932, *El Debate* maintained that "a renaissance of fervor" was occurring throughout the country. Was there any time in the past, asked another, when churches were fuller, when reception of the sacraments was greater, than under the Republic?[116]

Advocates of the revival thesis did not maintain that religiously alienated urban workers or southern agricultural laborers were embracing religion. They referred to an intensification of commitment and observance among practicing Catholics. No statistics on observance are available to permit verification of these claims, although the persistence with which they were made suggests that they may have had a basis in fact. In any event, some critics saw signs of religious fervor as a tem-

115. *El Debate,* November 20, 1932; Carballo and Magariños, *La Iglesia en la Galicia contemporánea,* pp. 349–59; "Relación de lo realizado en la Archidiócesis de Tarragona referente a la instrucción catequística durante el año 1933–1934," *AVB,* vol. 4, part 2, pp. 439–40; Vincent, *Catholicism in the Second Spanish Republic,* p. 33.

116. Rafael García y García de Castro, *¿El catolicismo en crisis?* (Madrid, 1935), p. 53; *El Debate,* April 3, 1932; Montero y Gutiérrez, *El porvenir de la Iglesia,* p. 147.

porary phenomenon of no great significance. Father Ramón Sarabia shared the view that a revival was taking place, but believed it would not prove "very lasting." Another saw the embracing of religion by urban, middle-class youth as motivated more by aesthetic and political considerations than by spiritual conversion, as "a Catholicism that had little theological about it."[117]

To attempt to interpret the intentions of the thousands participating in church services during the Republic would be presumptuous, but there seems little doubt that a link, whether strong or weak, existed between religious practice and politics. Or, as *El Debate* aptly expressed it, "the splendid manifestations of religious faith" taking place throughout the country were due to the "persecution" inflicted by the Republic, which united "all forces of the Right . . . in defense of the faith."[118]

Services, especially those historically identified with Catholicism as a civic religion, often assumed a double character. They were religious, but they also took the form of massive public testimonies to a faith believed to be under siege by its enemies. In 1933, at Santiago de Compostela during the traditional annual tribute to Saint James, which was identified with a militant Christianity and Spanish nationalism, the faithful heard that "a hurricane of persecution had been unleashed on the country" by the forces of "satanic hatred."[119] At Barcelona in 1935, fourteen thousand people attended the inauguration of a giant statue to the Sacred Heart on the Tibidabo Hill dominating the city. That the religious authorities chose to hold a massive ceremony in an area where hostility towards the Church had a long history testifies to the ambiguous character of the act. The service of dedication to this powerful symbol of antiliberalism within a Spanish context was as much political as religious. Indeed, *El Debate* hailed it as an example of "the triumph of the religious spirit of a fundamentally Catholic people in struggle against the laicizing and de-Christianizing obsession of that demagogic wave that is invading everything."[120]

The crowds who turned out at Tibidabo Hill, as well as those appearing at hundreds of other religious "acts of affirmation," suggests that the Church may have consolidated its hold over the conservative middle classes of the cities. The massive religious alienation of urban workers, so graphically described by Father Peiró before the Civil War, continued unabated during the republican period. There were signs that the problem went from bad to worse, but, on balance, the damage had been done long before the Republic appeared on the scene.[121]

117. Quoted in Pedro R. Santidrián, *El Padre Sarabia escribe su historia, 1875–1958: medio siglo de misiones en España* (Madrid, 1963), p. 253; Romero Flores, *Perfil moral de nuestra hora*, p. 69.

118. *El Debate*, November 17, April 3, 1932.

119. Quoted in Carballo and Magariños, *La Iglesia en la Galicia contemporánea*, p. 337.

120. *El Debate*, February 10, 1935, special supplement.

121. The number of dying receiving the last rites, for example, in the Catalan industrial town of Mataró declined significantly between 1930 and 1934. Rogelio Duocastella, *Mataró 1955: estudio de sociología religiosa sobre una ciudad industrial española* (Barcelona, 1961), p. 291.

The Church developed no clearer idea of how to reach the workers than it had before 1931. Proposals to create an effective national trade union, free of employer influence and beyond the immediate control of the Church, surfaced again only to arouse old dissensions over the issue of confessionality or non-confessionality.[122] After another round of infighting, representatives of existing Catholic unions managed to establish the Confederación Española de Sindicatos Obreros in 1935. Although not formally confessional, the new organization based its program on an "absolute subordination to the principles of Christian morality." Its vigilant defense of private property, commitment to the corporatist reorganization of society, and open hostility towards working-class parties and trade unions, described as "destructive and catastrophic," scarcely constituted a program capable of appealing to the hundreds of thousands already enrolled in the UGT and the CNT.[123]

The pre-1931 religious condition of the countryside changed little during the Republic. Observance in the Catholic peasant regions of the north remained high. In the rural diocese of Tuy, for example, the faithful continued to fulfill the Easter communion obligation in much the same way as before.[124] This pattern probably prevailed elsewhere in the north, although, as always within the Church, regional variations undoubtedly came into play. Redemptorists circulating through the province of Burgos on periodic missionary campaigns concluded that in this area, long identified as highly observant, "levels of religious practice have gone down since the advent of the Republic." In fact, what the missionaries found was not a universal decline, but a checkered pattern of non-practice in villages where socialist agrarian organizations had gained a foothold and of strong practice in those where the people remained "very Christian." As the priests moved from one to the other, they felt, as one expressed it, that they were leaving purgatory for heaven.[125]

From the Church's perspective, the religious state of the southern countryside continued to be catastrophic. A report submitted to Cardinal Vidal i Barraquer in 1932 by concerned laity, including the composer Manuel de Falla, pointed to pas-

122. The Jesuits of the Casa Social of Valladolid defended confessionality as central to the character of the unions with which they were identified. José Gafo led the campaign to persuade the hierarchy to jettison a specific confessional identification in view of the special circumstances created during the Republic. In a strictly technical sense, Gafo won the argument, as many bishops and the Vatican accepted his point of view. Given the program of the new organization that finally emerged in 1935, it is unlikely that its ostensibly non-confessional character made very much difference. "Introducción a la tercera parte," *AVB*, vol. 2, part 3, pp. 536–41.

123. Antonio Elorza, "La Confederación Española de Sindicatos Obreros, 1935–1938," *Revista de Trabajo* (1971), no. 33, p. 158.

124. Carballo and Magariños, *La Iglesia en la Galicia contemporánea*, pp. 322–25.

125. *Boletín de la Obra de la Defensa de la Fe en España* (1935), no. 94, pp. 130, 125. Mary Vincent notes that although in the Salamanca diocese the vast majority of newborns were baptized, some parents delayed the ceremony. Vincent, *Catholicism in the Second Spanish Republic*, p. 65. Religious sociologists have seen delay of baptism as an early sign of de-Christianization, although it is not clear in the Salamanca case whether postponing the ceremony represented a secularizing reaction associated with the arrival of the Republic.

toral deficiencies similar to those described by Manuel González García two decades earlier. It complained that in many southern parishes, priests paid little attention to liturgical decorum as they rushed through the Mass in fifteen minutes, while constantly interrupting the service with short homilies except at the moment of the host's consecration.[126] There is no indication of any change in religious attitudes among the dispossessed of the south. In the Seville archdiocese, where alienation from the Church was already entrenched, Cardinal Ilundain estimated that 80 percent of women and 94 percent of men failed to attend Sunday Mass or fulfill the Easter communion obligation.[127] The situation in Villanueva del Rosario, described by the bishop of Málaga as already disastrous during the 1880s, had scarcely changed by the mid-1930s, when Redemptorist missionaries visited the town. They regarded its population of four thousand as effectively de-Christianized. Not a single man attended Sunday Mass, dozens had never been baptized or married in the Church, while a majority of the dying expired without receiving the last rites.[128] In the past, the Church had failed to devise an effective pastoral strategy for the rural south. It proved no more successful during the Republic in a region where, in any event, acute social tensions, often accompanied by violence, made the prospect of effective action even more remote.

The state of religion on the eve of the Civil War remained essentially unchanged from what it had been in 1910 or 1920. Spanish Catholicism continued to rest on islands of strength among the peasantry of Old Castile, León, Galicia, the Basque Provinces, and Navarra, and among the Catholic middle classes of the cities, who were moved to more active participation in religious activities and confessional organizations. Insofar as a change took place, it took the form of a heightened perception among clergy and laity that Republicans of all stripes were intent upon undermining the remaining bastions of faith.

If the republican period stimulated, on one hand, a wave of self-criticism within the Church, on the other, it strengthened the ancient idea of a sinister conspiracy against religion. The Redemptorist missionaries visiting Villanueva del Rosario entertained no doubts about the causes of religious alienation in the village. It was the exclusive responsibility of "Socialists, renegades and blasphemous Protestants."[129] This simple black-and-white view of the religious crisis from the clerical grass roots ignored de-Christianization's complex origins, but it reinforced the thesis lurking within the Church since the days of its first conflicts with liberalism that the future of Spanish Catholicism would depend on an imminent, decisive battle

126. Manuel de Falla and others to Vidal i Barraquer, July 14, 1932, *AVB*, vol. 3, part 1, p. 44.

127. Frances Lannon, "The Church's Crusade against the Republic," in *Revolution and War in Spain, 1931–1939*, ed. Paul Preston (London, 1984), pp. 51–52; Juan Ordóñez Márquez, *La apostasía de las masa y la persecución religiosa en la provincia de Huelva, 1931–1936* (Madrid, 1968), p. 221.

128. *Boletín de la Obra de la Defensa de la Fe en España* (1935), no. 95, p. 144.

129. Ibid.

between the gathering hosts of good and evil.[130] For the experienced Redemptorist missionary Ramón Sarabia, the outbreak of the Civil War was, therefore, inevitable and in a sense to be welcomed: "In the end the gigantic struggle broke out between believers and those without God. The sword triumphed that God placed in the hands of our *Caudillo*, Franco. And there arose from his hands and from the blood of millions of heroes and martyrs, the new Spain, Catholic Spain."[131]

130. Writing in 1896, Father Francisco Tarín had no doubt that a decisive conflict between Catholic and anti-Catholic Spain was near at hand. Spanish Catholics, he declared, would open their eyes to the danger facing them only "when the flames, the smoke and the dust rising from the ruins of this Catholic society" would force them to take action. Quoted in Pedro María de Ayala, *Vida documentada del Siervo de Dios P. Francisco Paula Tarin de la Compañia de Jesús* (Madrid, 1951), p. 765.

131. Ramón Sarabia, *¿España . . . es católica?* in *Charlas de un misionero* (Madrid, 1939), pp. 288–89.

CHAPTER XIV

THE CIVIL WAR, 1936–1939

On July 17, 1936, Bishop Eijo y Garay of Madrid departed for his native Galicia after receiving advice to leave the capital from someone aware of plans for a military rising on the following day. The bishop lacked knowledge of the conspiracy's nuts and bolts. But he believed that the revolt would follow the course of past interventions by the army, a quick, surgical coup leading to the installation of a conservative government more or less accepted by a population weary of social agitation and political conflict.[1] Events soon disappointed this expectation. By the end of July, the insurrection dominated Navarra, Old Castile, Galicia, and the Balearic Islands. In Andalucía, the army took control of a triangle bounded by Algeciras, Cádiz, and Seville. By early September, the Nationalists swept through Extremadura to join their previously separate areas of conquest. But by mid-month the Republic rallied loyal military forces and popular militia units who halted the Nationalist advance at the outskirts of Madrid. As a result, the Republic continued to control a majority of the population, the country's largest cities, and its industrial centers. Nationalist hopes for a rapid triumph vanished as both sides prepared for a long struggle.

Long a minor player in European history, Spain moved to center stage during the conflictive years preceding the outbreak of the Second World War. For the first time since the Napoleonic invasion of the early nineteenth century, Spanish affairs became entangled in a broader struggle that reflected the political and ideological divisions of Europe. Within and outside of Spain, the causes and purposes of the Civil War produced controversy among contemporaries and initiated scholarly debate that continues to this day.

1. Vicente Enrique y Tarancón, *Recuerdos de juventud* (Barcelona, 1984), pp. 182–83.

The Church's role during the war has provoked no less discussion.[2] Although clergy and laity were rarely absent from earlier manifestations of civil conflict, their emotional and nearly unanimous commitment to the Nationalist cause had few parallels in the country's history. Only the implacable campaign directed against Napoleon during the early nineteenth century could match the crusading zeal attached by the Church of the 1930s to the insurrection against the Second Republic.

Why the Church chose to sanctify the conspiracy is a source of ongoing controversy. Although no single reason can explain its commitment to the rebellion, the clergy expected the war to alter the rules of a game long regarded as prejudicial to its interests. The conflict offered an unexpected opportunity to stack the deck in the Church's favor by creating the conditions necessary for attaining a goal that had eluded generations of clergy, the re-Christianization of the nation. As the Church offered its support to the generals, it had no specific political purpose in mind. At first, the bishops reaffirmed the frayed accidentalist formula of the past as far as the constitutional form of the State was concerned. Whatever the new regime's political configuration, the hierarchy knew what it wanted, namely, a government ready and willing to act aggressively on behalf of a Church anxious to seize the moment to realize old dreams of religious reconquest. But such a policy carried risks because it exposed the Church to the crude give-and-take of Nationalist politics influenced by powerful regalist currents.

The Two Cities

The events of July 18 came as no surprise to bishops and priests long on edge over an endless stream of rumors predicting a military coup. A majority of clergy sympathized with the revolt from its beginning. The priests of Tuy, recalled the future Cardinal Tarancón of his stay in that city during July, "accepted the military rising with joy and supported the army as a duty of conscience."[3] But, as in 1923, the Church watched the conspiracy unfold from the sidelines, although some

2. There is no complete bibliography of the literature dealing with the Church and the war. There are, however, abundant references in Vicente Cárcel Ortí, "La guerra civil," in *Historia de la Iglesia en España*, ed. Ricardo García Villoslada (5 vols., Madrid, 1979–1982), vol. 5, pp. 363–94, and in Gonzalo Redondo, *Historia de la Iglesia en España, 1931–1939* (2 vols., Madrid, 1993), vol. 2, pp. 632–51. See also two bibliographical articles, "La Iglesia en la guerra civil de España: boletín bibliográfico," *Miscelánea Comillas* (1986), vol. 44, pp. 523–55; "L'Església i la guerra civil: bibliografia recent, 1975–1985," *Revista Catalana de Teología* (1986), vol. 11, pp. 119–252. There is a useful bibliography in José M. Sánchez, *The Spanish Civil War as a Religious Tragedy* (Notre Dame, 1987), pp. 213–29, and in the same author's "The Spanish Church and the Second Republic and Civil War," *Catholic Historical Review* (1996), vol. 82, no. 4, pp. 661–68.

3. Enrique y Tarancón, *Recuerdos de juventud*, p. 210. A parish priest in Asturias recalled that when he heard news of the military rising, "My satisfaction was great, . . . we saw the army as the only remedy of salvation." Quoted in Angel Garralda García, *La persecución religiosa del clero en Asturias (1934 y 1936–1937)* (2d ed., 2 vols., Avilés, 1983), vol. 1, p. 409.

priests, especially in Carlist Navarra, cooperated actively with rebel forces from the war's earliest days.[4]

During these weeks, the Church lacked a clear idea of the military's political and ecclesiastical plans. Cardinal Gomá, who had replaced Vidal i Barraquer as president of the Committee of Metropolitans in April, entertained few doubts about the rightness of the insurrection against the Republic he had mistrusted from the day of its proclamation.[5] In his first communication to Pope Pius XI following the war's outbreak, the cardinal primate maintained that the revolt's failure would lead to nothing less than "the installation of a Communist regime" and the perpetration of "greater crimes than in Soviet Russia." Despite his deeply conservative views and desire for a pro-Catholic government, Gomá worried over the Church's place in a regime that had begun without a well-defined program. Given the differences among the rightist groups supporting the rebellion, the cardinal believed that "great problems" would arise when the moment came to decide the future form of the State, its relations with the Church, its economic and social policies, and its attitude towards regional movements.[6]

The cardinal's early apprehension was not misplaced. The military's initial proclamations said nothing about defending Church and religion. The presence on the Junta National of Defense of General Miguel Cabanellas, well known for his republican views, albeit in a conservative sense, and for his identification with Freemasonry, aroused clerical concern, as did the attitude of one of the conspiracy's key figures, General Emilio Mola. The general's statement on July 19—"We believe that the Church ought to be separated from the State for the good of both institutions"—troubled a Church intent on reestablishing official confessionality.[7] Even Francisco Franco, proclaimed head of the government and generalissimo of the armies on September 29, caused consternation when he remarked in a radio ad-

4. José Angel Tello, *Ideología y política: la Iglesia católica española, 1936–1959* (Zaragoza, 1984), p. 55. In Salamanca, the Jesuits were "among the first volunteers to present themselves to the military authorities. They were put to work immediately, attending to prisoners and offering the last sacraments to those condemned to death." The Capuchin and Dominican friars of the city also made donations to the war effort. Mary Vincent, *Catholicism in the Second Spanish Republic: Religion and Politics in Salamanca, 1931–1936* (Oxford, 1996), p. 248.

5. Although Gomá was primate of the Spanish Church as archbishop of Toledo and became a cardinal in December 1935, he was initially unable to displace Vidal i Barraquer from his position, largely because of the reluctance of the nuncio, Archbishop Tedeschini. Gomá lobbied intensely in Rome and eventually achieved his goal. In any event, Vidal i Barraquer's influence diminished after he was forced into exile as a result of the wave of persecution that swept through Catalonia following July 18. The key role of Gomá during the war has been a source of controversy. The cardinal has been defended in two important works, Anastasio Granados, *El Cardenal Gomá, Primado de España* (Madrid, 1969), and María Luisa Rodríguez de Aisa, *El Cardenal Gomá y la guerra de España: aspectos de la gestión pública del primado, 1936–1939* (Madrid, 1981). For a more critical judgment see Hilari Raguer, "El Cardenal Gomá y la guerra de España," *Arbor* (1982), vol. 111, no. 436, pp. 43–82.

6. "Informe acerca del levantamiento cívico-militar de España en julio de 1936," in Rodríguez de Aisa, *El Cardenal Gomá y la guerra de España*, pp. 373, 376, 377.

7. Quoted in Guy Hermet, *Les catholiques dans l'Espagne franquiste* (2 vols., Paris, 1981), vol. 2, p. 41.

dress of October 1, "The State, without being confessional, will seek agreement with the Church, respecting the national tradition and the religious sentiments of the immense majority of Spaniards." This apparent commitment to an aconfessional government, as well as a warning that the regime would not permit clerical interference in "the direction of the specific affairs of the State," deeply upset Cardinal Gomá, who immediately protested to the general.[8] Nor did all the political groups rallying to the military rising in the summer of 1936 accept the idea of restoring the confessional State of the past and its array of ecclesiastical privileges. Supporters of the country's quasi-fascist party, the Falange, desired amicable relations with the Church, but on the basis of a clear separation of the civil and ecclesiastical powers that excluded "intervention and any activity that diminished the dignity of the State or the national integrity."[9]

As a result, the hierarchy moved cautiously during the war's early months.[10] The bishops issued no sweeping collective statements similar to those of 1931 and 1933. Bishops Múgica of Vitoria and Olaechea of Pamplona provided the one exception to this official silence when they published a pastoral letter on August 6 addressed to the faithful of their dioceses. Actually written by Gomá, the statement endorsed the rising by condemning the support given by many Basque Catholics to a Republican government on the verge of recognizing the region's autonomy under the staunchly Catholic Partido Nacionalista Vasco (PNV). Although it occasionally fell into rhetorical excess, the letter differed in tone from later episcopal declarations on the war by expressing sentiments less of belligerence than of injured surprise that the Basques had chosen to break the unity of Catholic ranks by supporting the Republic.[11]

8. Quoted in Antonio Marquina Barrio, *La diplomacia vaticana y la España de Franco* (Madrid, 1983), p. 47. Franco, however, quickly explained that he had not intended to question the desirability of reestablishing a confessional State. The general's brother, Nicolás Franco, later told Gomá that the statement on aconfessionality had been inserted to counteract "the intense propaganda which was promoted in Germany accusing the movement of being . . . in the service of the *curas*." Quoted in José Andrés-Gallego, *¿Fascismo o Estado católico? Ideología, religión y censura en la España de Franco, 1937–1941* (Madrid, 1997), p. 30.

9. Ramón Serrano Suñer, *Entre el silencio y la propaganda, la historia cómo fue. Memorias* (Madrid, 1977), p. 278. Serrano Suñer, Franco's brother-in-law and a key figure in the regime's politics during this period, asserts in his memoirs that the founder of the Falange, José Antonio Primo de Rivera, and other important theoreticians of the movement rejected the confessionality of the State. This principle "was maintained and even exacerbated at the beginning of the war," in part because of Falange opposition to Carlists and authoritarian monarchists who wished to reestablish official confessionality. Quoted in ibid., p. 279.

10. Hermet, *Les catholiques*, vol. 2, p. 44.

11. "Instrucción pastoral de los obispos de Vitoria y Pamplona," August 6, 1936, in Antonio Montero Moreno, *Historia de la persecución religiosa en España, 1936–1939* (Madrid, 1961), pp. 682–86. Gomá had the pastoral broadcast without having received final approval of the text from either Múgica or Olaechea. Rumors circulated in the Basque Provinces that Múgica had not approved the document. Despite imminent difficulties with the Nationalist authorities, who regarded the bishop of Vitoria as a separatist, there is little doubt that Múgica sympathized with the military rising at its beginning. Hermet, *Les catholiques*, vol. 2, pp. 45–46; Juan José Ruíz Rico, *El papel político de la Iglesia católica en la España de Franco, 1936–1971* (Madrid, 1977), p. 39. Canon Alberto de Onaindia, who defended the interests of

By early September, the hierarchy began to abandon its reticence. Although he continued his public silence, Gomá saw the return of crucifixes to schools under Nationalist control, the censorship of textbooks by the authorities, and the generally good relations prevailing between the military and the clergy as hopeful signs that the Church "would enjoy ample liberty and protection" under the new regime.[12] The cardinal also took consolation from the military's participation in religious services proliferating throughout the Nationalist zone. Even Cabanellas and Mola, hardly models of piety, made a point of displaying their religiosity. Mola, indeed, prostrated himself before one of Spain's great symbols of religion and nationalism, the statue of the Virgin of the Pillar in Zaragoza. By this time, as well, the Church's position began to harden as information spread on the extent of the persecution inflicted on priests and religious in Republican Spain. The hierarchy also delayed taking a public stance until the Vatican commented on the Spanish situation. On September 14, Pius XI's remarks condemning the persecution of priests, religious, and laity removed this obstacle, although the pope fell short of specifically endorsing the Nationalist cause.

The hierarchy's abstention from public comment was moved by temporary, tactical considerations. Spanish Catholicism's diverse constituencies felt no such momentary doubts. Thousands of Carlists joined the Traditionalist Communion's militia (*requetés*) under the motto, "Long live Christ the King!" Laymen active in Catholic associations, such as Catholic Action and the Asociación Nacional Católica de Propagandistas, rushed to support the rebellion.[13] The bishops were unlikely to remain behind the rank and file for long.

When the hierarchy presented its views publicly, it offered a sweeping religious justification of the war and the Nationalist cause as well as an unyielding denunciation of the Republic. The ingredients on the bishops' ideological plate formed a stale mixture long present on clerical menus. The idea of a war of absolutes between Christian civilization and the forces of barbarism, the exclusive identification of Spanish nationalism with Catholicism, and the appeals to providentialism tinged with Old Testament prophetism echoed the arguments directed against the French invader by an earlier generation of episcopal militants.

Given the Church's resentment against the laicizing legislation of the Republic, its deeply rooted fear of social revolution, and its horror at the deaths of priests and

---

the Basque Republic abroad during the Civil War, accused Gomá of inspiring the pastoral letter and abusing the attitude of Múgica and Olaechea. *Hombre de paz en la guerra: cápitulos de mi vida* (Buenos Aires, 1973), p. 304. For a discussion of Onaindia's extensive activities on behalf of the Basque Republic, see Herbert R. Southworth, *Guernica! Guernica! A Study of Journalism, Propaganda and History* (Berkeley, Los Angeles, and London, 1977), pp. 137–52.

12. Quoted in Rodríguez de Aisa, *El Cardenal Gomá y la guerra de España*, pp. 26–27.

13. Hermet, *Les catholiques*, vol. 2, pp. 34–36. The local centers of the ACNP were deserted in the months following the war's outbreak as members of military age joined the army. Mercedes Montero, *Historia de la Asociación Católica Nacional de Propagandistas: la construcción del Estado confesional, 1936–1945* (Pamplona, 1993), pp. 38–39.

religious in the Republican zone, it was scarcely surprising that the vast majority of the clergy supported the insurrection. The Church had rallied to Primo de Rivera in 1923 with much less cause. But its decision to cloak its support in crusading zeal added a religious dimension to justifications for the war that, if not entirely new, had rarely been expressed before with such vigor. Moreover, the clergy voluntarily offered a religious interpretation of the conflict that came as a "pleasant surprise" to a military seeking to achieve legitimacy by all possible means.[14]

Further, the clergy offered ideological support long before the Church reached a definitive ecclesiastical settlement with the authorities. Indeed, the Church presented the same blank check to the generals that it had bestowed on Primo de Rivera following the coup d'état of 1923. Although the hierarchy restated the accidentalist formula of the past by refusing to express preference for a specific form of government, it expected the new regime to meet its demands for significant concessions. Even during the early months of the war, there were signs that the authorities, however ostentatious their public affirmations of Catholicism, knew how to drive a hard bargain.

The idea of the Civil War as primarily a religious conflict surfaced soon after July 18.[15] It assumed definitive form upon the publication on September 30 of a lengthy pastoral letter by Bishop Pla y Deniel of Salamanca.[16] The pastoral letter initiated an outpouring of episcopal statements as well as innumerable books, articles, and pamphlets by clerical writers.[17] Although the case justifying the legitimacy of the war ranged from Old Testament evocations comparing the conflict to an "exterminating angel" sent to purge a corrupt people of their sins, to nostalgic appeals for the resurrection of the imperial, Catholic Spain of Ferdinand and Isabella, these arguments represented little more than elaborations of the Bishop of Salamanca's thesis.[18] Pla y Deniel now gave full legitimacy to an idea long cherished

14. Hilari Raguer, *La espada y la cruz: la Iglesia, 1936–1939* (Barcelona, 1977), p. 67.

15. The first use of the term "crusade" by a bishop to describe the conflict appeared on August 23 in a published statement of Bishop Olaechea of Pamplona. The term was also used a few days later by Archbishop Rigoberto Doménech of Zaragoza and Archbishop Tomás Muñiz Pablos of Santiago. Redondo, *Historia de la Iglesia en España*, vol. 2, pp. 72–73.

16. Although on September 15 Cardinal Gomá had publicly expressed his satisfaction at the capture of Toledo by the Nationalists, he was reluctant to publish an official statement of the hierarchy's views. Bishop Pla y Deniel believed that the time had come for such a declaration and received the cardinal primate's encouragement to proceed, although Gomá declared that he could not depart from his attitude of "reserve" until the Vatican assessed the situation in Spain in more definitive fashion. Hermet, *Les catholiques*, vol. 2, p. 46; Rodríguez de Aisa, *El Cardenal Gomá y la guerra de España*, p. 108.

17. For a detailed analysis of the views of the bishops, see Hilari Raguer, "Los obispos españoles y la guerra civil," *Arbor* (1982), vol. 112, nos. 439–440, pp. 295–320.

18. Luciano Pérez Platero, "La intensificación de la vida cristiana," March 14, 1937, *Boletín Oficial del Obispado de Segovia* (1938), p. 94. For the old clerical ultra, Canon de Castro Albarrán, the Nationalist regime represented nothing less than the rebirth of "the Spain of the Catholic Kings." *Guerra santa: el sentido católico del movimiento nacional español* (Burgos, 1938), p. 69. According to one severe critic, many of the clergy's publications on the war formed "an extensive, fanaticized bibliography, [written] with patriotic-religious exaltation and in delirious tones." Feliciano Blázquez, *La traición de los clérigos en la España de Franco* (Madrid, 1991), p. 38.

within some sectors of Spanish Catholicism.[19] The war constituted nothing less than the decisive battle between good and evil so long heralded by generations of clerical apologists.

The bishop entitled his pastoral letter "The Two Cities," in reference to Saint Augustine. "On the soil of Spain two conceptions of life, two sentiments, two forces are today engaged in cruel struggle." One represented the "celestial city of the children of God" exemplified by "soldiers and volunteers who are fighting for God and country," the other, the "earthly city embodied by Communists and anarchists, the sons of Cain" inspired by "hatred of God and everything that carries his stamp." On one side there was Catholic Spain, the "authentic Spain, mother of so many nations, . . . immortal champion of spirituality." On the other stood the laicizing Republic that had declared, "Spain is no longer Catholic." Indebted to "foreign elements," the lay State of the Republic was "no longer Spain."[20]

The Church's fear of social revolution also emerged in full force, although Pla y Deniel shifted his attention away from the Socialists, long perceived as the Church's principal enemy, to the Communists for reasons that are not entirely clear, given the party's relative political weakness during the summer of 1936.[21] The bishop claimed that the war was not being fought over a specific form of government. Its purpose was far greater, nothing less than "a crusade against Communism to save religion, the nation, and the family."[22]

The war's causes were complex and deeply rooted in decades of social and economic conflict. Pla y Deniel's pastoral and the numerous episcopal statements that followed, including the hierarchy's controversial Collective Letter of 1937, reduced an exceptionally complicated situation to a black-and-white struggle between religion and its enemies. Historians have long debated the reasons behind the clergy's early "sacralization" of the conflict.[23] It is clear from this discussion that many reasons lay behind the Church's response. An intellectual legacy of antilib-

19. In his discussion of the pastoral letter, Redondo sees the bishop of Salamanca as the "archetype of the most radical Catholic traditionalist thought." *Historia de la Iglesia en España*, vol. 2, p. 95.

20. Enrique Pla y Deniel, "Las dos ciudades," in Montero Moreno, *Historia de la persecución religiosa*, pp. 688, 689, 704. This distinction between "Spain, . . . traditional and Christian" and "anti-Spain," "treasonous, . . . lay, foreign dominated, unnatural" found its way into much of the clerical literature on the war. For an extravagant restatement of this thesis, see Teodoro Rodríguez, *Así es España y así la anti-España* (Madrid, 1942), pp. 206–7. The case against the Republic was made at greater length in the hierarchy's 1937 Collective Letter to the Catholic bishops of the world. The bishops rejected the Republic's legitimacy on various grounds, arguing that the war constituted nothing less than "an armed plebiscite" between the forces in contention. "Episcopado español a los obispos de todo el mundo," July 1, 1937, in *Documentos colectivos del episcopado español, 1870–1974*, ed. Jesús Iribarren (Madrid, 1974), p. 229.

21. Although Pla y Deniel singled out the Communists as primarily responsible for the assault on the Church, historians agree that the party was not the "motivating force behind the anticlerical fury." Sánchez, *The Spanish Civil War as a Religious Tragedy*, p. 20.

22. Pla y Deniel, "Las dos ciudades," p. 699.

23. See, for example, Tello, *Ideología y política*, pp. 56–61; Hermet, *Les catholiques*, vol. 2, pp. 41–42, and the discussion of Sánchez on the hierarchy's Collective Letter of 1937, *The Spanish Civil War as a Religious Tragedy*, chapter 7. Despite his defense of the Church's role in the Civil War, even Vicente Cárcel Ortí implicitly rejects the reductionist argument employed by the hierarchy by warning against inter-

eralism and a historic fear of social upheaval and clerical resentment against the Republic's ecclesiastical legislation were in place before the war began. The persecution inflicted on priests and religious following July 18 and the attempts at social revolution, largely the work of anarchists, anarcho-syndicalists, and other left-wing extremists, confirmed the clergy's worst apprehensions. The fate of the Church and of religion itself seemed at risk. During the Restoration and the Republic, political reality had restrained the hierarchy from giving full expression to ancient political and social fears. In clerical eyes, the course of events in the Republican zone justified an end to restraint and demanded extraordinary measures. The Church, declared Pla y Deniel, could neither rely on prayer nor tempt God by asking for a miracle to deliver it from its enemies. It must use all "natural means" to rescue the Church "from the evil of those enthroned in power."[24]

For a Church that had long seen itself besieged by governments either indifferent or hostile to its religious interests, as well as by dangerous secularizing currents and radical social movements, the war offered an undreamed of opportunity to reverse decades of religious slippage. Pla y Deniel stressed a theme that appeared repeatedly in clerical statements about the conflict. Its results would be "truly redemptive," for the war would rescue Spaniards from sin and moral laxity.[25] Other clerics extolled the movement towards "spiritual reinvigoration" that would emerge following the triumph of Nationalist arms.[26] For the clergy, the opportunity to implement a vast program of religious reconquest constituted the single most important purpose of the war. The situation created by the conflict, declared Gomá, was "more efficacious than . . . missions with respect to the revival of Christian faith and piety." If de-Christianization had reached "incalculable and frightening proportions" under the Republic, the Church now had within its grasp the possibility, once apparently remote, of taking advantage of "the new national situation to filter the spirit of Jesus Christ Our Lord into the blood of the younger generations."[27] Bishops and priests recognized that such an opportunity might never come their way again. "Our revolution," declared a prominent ecclesiastical pro-

preting the conflict's causes in manichaean terms. *La persecución religiosa en España durante la Segunda República, 1931–1939* (Madrid, 1990), p. 194.

24. Pla y Deniel, "Las dos ciudades," p. 696.

25. Ibid., p. 704.

26. Nicolás Rodríguez Ancieto, *Necesidad de la vigorización espiritual de España* (Salamanca, 1938), p. 4. Another cleric put the question simply: "With the enemy vanquished in war, Spain will conduct a great spiritual combat in peace. . . . All of Spain must see a Christian restoration." Luis Carreras, *Grandeza cristiana de España: notas sobre la persecución religiosa* (Toulouse, 1938), p. 271. In their public statements, the bishops also saw the war as offering the Church an extraordinary opportunity to re-Christianize the nation. Alfonso Álvarez Bolado, *Para ganar la guerra, para ganar la paz: Iglesia y guerra civil* (Madrid, 1995), pp. 75–78.

27. Quoted in Marquina Barrio, *La diplomacia vaticana*, p. 46; Luciano Pérez Platero, "Carta pastoral," September 14, 1936, *Boletín Oficial del Obispado de Segovia* (1936), p. 346; "La intensificación de la vida cristiana," ibid., p. 97. The theme of re-Christianization appeared frequently in the pastoral letters of the bishops during the war. Alfonso Botti, *Cielo y dinero: el nacionalcatolicismo en España, 1881–1975* (Madrid, 1992), p. 93.

pagandist, "can bring about a renaissance of faith." Under no circumstances could the Church afford to lose the "historic opportunity" presented by the insurrection against the Republic.[28]

The clergy were too realistic to expect that the Church alone could carry out the spiritual reconquest of its dreams. The Nationalist cause furnished the vehicle needed to eliminate the forces judged hostile to religion and create the legal framework necessary for priests and religious to re-Christianize the alienated masses.[29] The Church expected the State to support the "movement for a religious restoration with the full weight of its authority."[30] Further, the government's role in promoting spiritual reconquest was not to be limited to supporting the clergy in campaigns of peaceful evangelization. On the contrary, ecclesiastics wished the government to act aggressively on its behalf: "The work of the Church which uses exhortation will not be sufficient. It is necessary that the . . . public power, which threatens with temporal punishments, should be seen behind the preacher who indicates those that are eternal."[31]

If the bishops attached transcendental importance to a war conceived as a battle between moral absolutes, they were also perfectly aware of the possibility of receiving more tangible benefits from the new regime. In his influential pastoral letter, Pla y Deniel presented a shopping list of clerical demands. These included the abrogation of the Republic's ecclesiastical legislation, especially the 1933 Law on Religious Confessions and Congregations, the return of cemeteries to the clergy, a reform of marriage legislation, a new concordat with the Vatican, and above all recognition of the Church's "independence and liberty" in its relations with the civil power.[32] Although these demands represented a warmed-over version of Church privileges that had existed before 1931, they showed that the clergy viewed the war and its consequences with shrewd practicality. In the midst of lofty theological and philosophical discourse, the Church saw an extraordinary opportunity to reverse the very course of Spanish history.

The prism of reductionism served another purpose. The hierarchy knew the fragmented history of Spanish Catholicism in its political dimension well enough to realize that something more than a narrow program based on restoring the Church's privileges was needed to create yet another version of the elusive "unity of Catholics" the clergy had sought for decades. In his first communication to Pius XI, Gomá outlined the differences over the future organization of the State and so-

28. Ignacio Menéndez-Reigada, *Acerca de la guerra santa* (Salamanca, 1937), p. 17.

29. There appeared in clerical literature on the war an ill-disguised satisfaction that "regionalism, socialism, syndicalism and communism . . . exotic diseases carried by the new barbarians," were about to be swept from the field, where ecclesiastics believed they had conspired to de-Christianize the nation. Eugenio Fernández Almuzara, *Evangelio de la Nueva España* (Valladolid, 1937), p. 19.

30. Joaquín Azpiazu, *El Estado católico* (Burgos, 1939), p. 31.

31. P. Crisógono, *Grandeza, ruina y resurgimiento de España* (San Sebastián, 1941), p. 207.

32. Pla y Deniel, "Las dos ciudades," pp. 705–6.

ciety existing among the generals and the three rightist groups most active in support of the insurrection—the Carlist Traditionalist Communion, the authoritarian, monarchist Renovación Española, and Spain's quasi-fascist party, the Falange.[33] Although all affirmed their commitment to Catholicism, Gomá recognized that serious policy differences divided them. In these circumstances, elevating the war to a religious crusade moved defense of religion to a higher moral ground, one designed to provide a measure of ideological integration that would transcend partisan differences.[34] The ultimate religious purpose of the war demanded unity at all costs. "It is a grave responsibility," declared one preacher, "to sow discord and to contribute to disunion. . . . For God and Spain antagonism must be set aside."[35]

The clergy's commitment to transcendence came at a price. By identifying exclusively with the Nationalist cause, the Church denied itself even a limited mediating role in the conflict. If the war was a struggle "without quarter between revolution and counterrevolution," a conflict launched from "the gates of hell" against "the faith and the Church," there was no middle ground, no reason for the Church to use its influence on behalf of a compromise peace.[36]

Despite ecclesiastical rhetoric arguing that the liberty and independence of the Church would be protected under the new regime, the opposite was the case. Having bestowed a blank check on the generals, the Church again became the captive of events into which it had rushed. The repression unleashed by the Nationalists in the areas under their control raised a moral dilemma for a clergy ostensibly committed to the practice of Christian charity.[37] Few priests imitated the example of Father Juan Galán Bermejo, a chaplain in an elite military unit who patted the gun on his belt, declaring, "Here it is; this little pistol which has rid the world of more than a hundred Marxists."[38] From the beginning of the war, the hierarchy knew of indiscriminate reprisals being carried out, especially by the Falange. The bishops called for mercy on occasion but refrained from publicly condemning the execu-

33. Gomá, "Informe acerca del levantamiento," pp. 376–77.

34. Tello, *Ideología y política*, p. 59.

35. Antonio Bahamonde, a former Nationalist propagandist, heard these words in a sermon preached in Badajoz cathedral on August 14, 1937. *Memoirs of a Spanish Nationalist* (London, 1939), p. 63.

36. Teodoro Rodríguez, *Nueva reconquista de España* (Valladolid, 1938), p. 8. León del Amo, *Las dos espadas o la Iglesia y el Estado* (Valladolid, 1938), p. 105; Tello, *Ideología y política*, pp. 64–65. Insofar as there was a serious attempt at mediation, it arose from the initiative of the Vatican during the spring of 1937. Monsignor Giuseppe Pizzardo, secretary of the Commission on Extraordinary Ecclesiastical Affairs, consulted the governments of the United Kingdom, France, and Belgium about the possibility of mediating the conflict. The Nationalist government rejected the proposal out of hand, and it came to nothing. Marquina Barrio, *La diplomacia vaticana*, pp. 62–63.

37. In his balanced assessment of the role of the Church during the Civil War, José M. Sánchez has argued, "The clergy's greatest scandal occurred in their involvement with reprisals against both Republican soldiers and militiamen and against civilians arrested by the purge committees in those areas which the Nationalists had conquered." *The Spanish Civil War as a Religious Tragedy*, p. 111.

38. Quoted in Bahamonde, *Memoirs of a Spanish Nationalist*, p. 67.

tions.[39] Moved by the violence directed against priests and religious in Republican Spain, the clergy saw Nationalist excesses as regrettable but to a degree understandable given the transcendence they attached to the conflict. "Perhaps the Fascists should be reproached for the harshness of [their] reprisals," was all the cardinal primate could say to the pope on August 13.[40]

There were examples of clerical protest against the reprisals in the Nationalist zone. In November 1936, Bishop Marcelino Olaechea of Pamplona made an emotional appeal for compassion and pardon. Let there be "No more blood!" "Not a drop more of the blood of vengeance!" the prelate pleaded.[41] This public appeal for an end to indiscriminate violence against those regarded as enemies of the regime was not welcomed. Olaechea became the object of hostile rumors and threats. Carlist militiamen declared that they would cut off his hair just as they had done to women judged traitors to the Nationalist cause. Similarly, two prison chaplains were shown the door after they dared to protest the execution of innocent victims to the Seville police chief, who told them in no uncertain terms that they had been deceived by Marxists.[42]

The Church also became a prisoner of the powerful antiseparatism of a military determined to root out autonomist sympathies, especially among the Basques.[43] When General Cabanellas discovered priests sympathetic to regional autonomy still teaching in the Vitoria seminary, he is said to have remarked, "And this canaille is still alive? We have killed less guilty priests."[44] Historically, the hierarchy's attitude towards regional movements had been ambiguous at best, downright hostile at worst. Yet Gomá, a Catalan and no friend of separatism, realized that the Church's religious interests could suffer serious damage as a result of an implacable

39. In their 1937 Collective Letter, the hierarchy criticized in the name of Christian justice and charity the "excesses" being committed in the Nationalist zone. However, this condemnation was placed within a broader context, namely, that reprisals in Republican Spain were far worse. "Episcopado español a los obispos de todo el mundo," in *Documentos colectivos del episcopado español*, p. 239.

40. Gomá, "Informe acerca del levantamiento," p. 376.

41. Quoted in Raguer, *La espada y la cruz*, pp. 163, 165; Sánchez, *The Spanish Civil War as a Religious Tragedy*, pp. 112–13. Similarly, on the eve of the fall of Madrid to the Nationalists in 1939, Bishop Eijo y Garay instructed his clergy to oppose any "manifestation of hatred, vengeance, reprisals." Quoted in José Andrés-Gallego, Antón M. Pazos, and Luis de Llera, *Los españoles entre la religión y la política: el franquismo y la democracia* (Madrid, 1996), p. 28.

42. Juan de Iturralde, *El catolicismo y la cruzada de Franco* (3 vols., Vienne and Toulouse, 1965), vol. 2, p. 456; Bahamonde, *Memoirs of a Spanish Nationalist*, p. 59.

43. For discussion of the persecution of Basque clergymen and the controversy over Catholic support in the region for the Republic, see E. A. Talde et al., *Historia general de la guerra civil en Euskadi* (6 vols., San Sebastián and Bilbao, 1978–1981), vol. 5, pp. 33–39, 246–53; Joseba M. Goñi Galarraga, *La Guerra Civil en el País Vasco: una guerra entre católicos* (Vitoria, 1989); Javier Sánchez Erauskin, *Por Dios hacia el imperio: nacionalcatolicismo en las Vascongadas del primer franquismo, 1936–1945* (San Sebastián, 1994); Sánchez, *The Spanish Civil War as a Religious Tragedy*, pp. 70–87; Raguer, *La espada y la cruz*, pp. 198–212; Juan Pablo Fusi and Fernando García de Cortázar, *Política, nacionalidad e Iglesia en el País Vasco* (San Sebastián, 1988), pp. 81–89.

44. Quoted in Inak de Aberrigoyen, *Sept mois et sept jours dans l'Espagne de Franco* (Paris, 1938), pp. 74–75.

persecution of Basque priests and religious.[45] The execution of fourteen Basque clerics by lower-level Nationalist authorities (September–November 1936), the imprisonment of others, and the relentless pressure on ecclesiastical administrators to transfer suspect priests to dioceses elsewhere in the country placed the Church in an untenable position.

The response of Gomá took the form of an avoid-the-worst policy similar to that pursued by the Church before the Republic's laicizing legislation. The anger of the Junta of National Defense focused early on Bishop Múgica, although the prelate had signed the pastoral letter of August 6 and attempted to curry favor with the authorities through the donation of funds, patriotic exhortations, and participation in ceremonies celebrating the Nationalist cause.[46] Although the bishop later condemned the persecution of Basque priests, he strongly supported the rising against the Republic during the summer of 1936.[47] But his refusal in 1932 to yield to rightist pressure to judge voters who favored the Basque autonomy statute being discussed at the time as guilty of mortal sin, and his inability or unwillingness to curb the support of many of his clergy for the Partido Nacionalista Vasco in the February 1936 elections, made him suspect in Nationalist eyes.[48]

The prelate's efforts to ingratiate himself with the new regime failed to save him from the military's obsessive determination to destroy separatism root and branch. The Junta of National Defense demanded that Múgica leave his diocese and made it plain to Gomá that if the bishop did not do so, a decision might be taken that could produce serious difficulties between Church and State. Gomá and other bishops shared the view that Múgica had not done enough to bring priests favoring the PNV into line, but the cardinal primate worked behind the scenes to protect the bishop of Vitoria from the gathering wrath of the generals.[49] Although Gomá criticized the Junta for its excessive harshness, he defended Múgica largely on jurisdictional grounds. The military's demand he saw as "injurious to the rights of the Church."[50] But fearful of the controversy's effect on civil-ecclesiastical relations, Gomá yielded to government pressure, and Múgica was forced to abandon his diocese.

Gomá at least succeeded in finding a face-saving formula that allowed Múgica to leave the country without actually being expelled by the government. Lesser ecclesiastical administrators felt the full weight of official pressure. The vicar-general

45. Gomá thus opposed an extreme proposal, probably made by Archbishop Manuel de Castro Alonso, that Basque nationalists should be excommunicated for supporting the Republic. Redondo, *Historia de la Iglesia en España,* vol. 2, p. 245.

46. Sánchez Erauskin, *Por Dios hacia el imperio,* pp. 137–41. The author regards the efforts of Múgica to win the favor of the generals as "enormously pathetic." Ibid., p. 137.

47. Ibid., pp. 137–41; Ruiz Rico, *El papel político de la Iglesia católica,* p. 39.

48. Goñi Galarraga, *La Guerra Civil en el País Vasco,* pp. 78–79.

49. The bishop of Ciudad Rodrigo, for example, believed that responsibility for the failure to curb "separatist" clergy rested on Múgica's inner circle of ecclesiastical advisers. Ibid., p. 103.

50. Quoted in Rodríguez de Aisa, *El Cardenal Gomá y la guerra de España,* p. 44.

of the Vitoria diocese received a list of suspect priests from the military governor of Guipúzcoa, who ordered him to transfer them immediately to other dioceses because of their identification with "the wicked, anti-Catholic conduct of Basque nationalism." When the vicar-general replied that he required evidence of their misdeeds, his patriotism was questioned and he was told to proceed "without delay to apply a measure which all good sons of this noble country demand."[51] Despite efforts to mitigate the regime's policy towards the Basque clergy, the Church chose to swallow a dose of bitter medicine that even the Republic had not dared administer between 1931 and 1933. The bishop of Palencia put the issue simply, in reference to the military's attitude towards separatism. The Church could not afford to make even the slightest misstep that might "indispose these good Castilians and lead to . . . troubles for everyone."[52]

Controversy over the Basque clergy and support in the region for the Republic also revealed in glaring fashion the failure of the hierarchy's attempt to use the war as a means of creating a new version of Catholic unity.[53] The onslaught against Basque priests sympathetic to regional autonomy came not only from the military; it also emerged within the Church. Bishop Javier Lauzurica, administrator of the Vitoria diocese between 1937 and 1943, was a native Basque and fluent in the language, but he carried out a rigorous purge to eliminate priests sympathetic to the movement for autonomy.[54] Nationalist clerics elsewhere in the country subjected the Basque clergy to a campaign of severe criticism at best, outright vilification at worst.[55] Even within the region, parish priests committed to the insurrection felt no scruples about denouncing to military authorities colleagues favoring autonomy.[56] Clergy supporting the regime imagined that once "the nightmare" of "illicit, monstrous, and scandalous" separatism was swept away, the Basque clergy and

51. Quoted in Pedro de Basaldu, *En España sale el sol* (Buenos Aires, 1946), pp. 191–93. The author, an advocate of Christian Democracy, served as private secretary to José Antonio Aguirre, the Catholic head of the Basque autonomous republic authorized by the Second Republic in October 1936.

52. Quoted in ibid., pp. 195–96.

53. In January 1937, the president of the Basque Republic and leader of the Catholic PNV, José Antonio Aguirre, gave a radio address in which he reproached the hierarchy for its silence and complicity before the persecution of Basque priests by the Nationalists. Deeply wounded by this and other accusations, Gomá defended his conduct in an "open letter" to Aguirre. For the controversy generated by this exchange, see Rodríguez Aisa, *El Cardenal Gomá y la guerra de España*, chapter 6.

54. The clerical purge carried out by Lauzurica and other ecclesiastical administrators was both "without precedents and any parallel in the rest of the peninsula." Sánchez Erauskin, *Por Dios hacia el imperio*, p. 16.

55. In a lengthy tract directed against Basque clerics who supported the Republic, the role of priests sympathetic to autonomy was subject to violent criticism on the grounds that "a part of the Basque clergy was poisoned against Spain." Centro de Infomación Católica Internacional, *El clero y los católicos vasco-separatistas y el Movimiento Nacional* (Madrid, 1940), p. 200.

56. Aberrigoyen, *Sept mois . . . dans l'Espagne de Franco*, p. 71. A clerical civil war of sorts erupted in the Basque Provinces between pro-Nationalist priests and those supporting the autonomous government. Fusi and García de Cortázar, *Política, nacionalidad e Iglesia*, p. 85. Even the modest efforts of the vicar-general of the Vitoria diocese prior to the appointment of Lauzurica to protect the latter as best he could came under attack. He was told by the parish priest of Elorrio, "Many priests have sustained propaganda and authorized this nationalism (the ally of the worst enemies of religion), and, unfortunately,

faithful would contribute to the construction of the "New Spain" to which the rest of the Church was committed.[57] In fact, the sustained clerical campaign against priests in the region sowed the seeds of future division within the Church.

Basques accepting the Republic formed the largest group of Spanish Catholics, who rejected outright the religious justification of the war offered by the hierarchy and clerical apologists. There were others. Although Canon Arboleya did not explicitly support the Republic, he asked why the Church had "to defend itself under the protection of machine guns and bayonets!" With years of experience in the trenches of Catholic labor action, he saw the war's origins rooted in the "abandonment of the masses" by a conservative society with which the Church had identified itself.[58] The Catholic politician Angel Ossorio y Gallardo, long active in efforts to integrate the Church within a democratic Spain, and the prominent lay intellectual José Bergamín supported the Republic, as did some laymen and priests involved in the Unió Democràtica de Catalunya.[59]

Even Cardinal Vidal i Barraquer, while sympathetic to the goals of the military rising, entertained serious reservations about the hierarchy's strategy. Kept in permanent Italian exile by the Nationalist authorities, who regarded him as *persona non grata* for his attempt to secure an accommodation between Church and Republic, the cardinal was able to view events in Spain with some perspective. He refused to sign the most controversial episcopal document of the war, the 1937 Collective Letter of the hierarchy to the bishops of the world.[60] This lengthy statement pushed the ideas advanced early in the conflict by Pla y Deniel to new levels of rhetorical overstatement.

---

you have been one of their most efficacious promoters." Quoted in *El clero y los católicos vasco-separatistas*, p. 200.

57. Rafael García y García de Castro, *La tragedia espiritual de los vascos* (Granada, 1938), pp. 305, 307.

58. Quoted in Domingo Benavides, *El fracaso social del catolicismo español, Arboleya-Martínez, 1870–1951* (Barcelona, 1973), p. 715, and Raguer, *La espada y la cruz*, p. 179.

59. For a fuller discussion of Spanish Catholics who supported the Republic, see Raguer, *La espada y la cruz*, pp. 177–87. Bergamín wrote one of the strongest indictments of the hierarchy's conduct during the Civil War. The bishops must share, he declared, "the terrible responsibility of [shedding] innocent blood in the name of political purity. . . . They placed a priestly mask over the bloody terror of the hangman." *Detrás de la cruz: terrorismo y persecución religiosa en España* (Mexico City, 1941), pp. 12–13.

60. Álvarez Bolado provides a perceptive analysis of the controversy and the stages in the document's preparation. *Para ganar la guerra, para ganar la paz*, pp. 154–65. Cárcel Ortí argues that the bishops had no choice but to publish the Collective Letter in view of the persecution inflicted on the Church in Republican Spain. Cardinal Tarancón, a key figure in moving the Church towards acceptance of democracy during the 1970s, also has defended the bishops on the grounds that they were responding to "popular clamor" and believed that they acted in accord with their pastoral responsibilities. He has also maintained that the letter was not a "blank check" in support of the Nationalist regime. Sánchez contends that the letter served no useful purpose. It failed to influence world opinion and compromised the Church still further, with the Nationalist regime already deeply involved in reprisals "that no Christian—and especially no cleric—should allow." Lannon maintains that the letter committed the Church "to the defence and justification of one side in the war." Redondo asserts that there was little new in the letter, which represented a restatement of long-held clerical views about the country's Catholic character, although these were sharpened by reaction to religious persecution. He suggests, however, that the letter

Vidal refused to sign the collective letter for several reasons. He resented the pressure placed on the hierarchy by General Franco to publish a statement designed to counter foreign propaganda against the Nationalists. "We must not pay too much attention to the insinuations and suggestions of persons outside the hierarchy," he told Cardinal Gomá, the author of the text. They were working in their own interest, just as the Church must see to its own interest, namely, "the glory of God and the good of souls."[61] Vidal was apprehensive that the exclusive identification of the Church with the regime boded ill for the future. The bishops, he maintained, must stand above "all partisanship" if the Church was to fulfill its mission of promoting "peace, charity and concord." The cardinal also feared that publication of an aggressive defense of the Nationalist cause would further endanger long-suffering priests and laity in Republican Spain.[62]

Vidal i Barraquer's resistance to the course Gomá and the bishops had set for the Spanish Church had little effect other than to increase the determination of the Nationalist authorities to keep him out of the country at all costs and, if possible, to remove him as archbishop of Tarragona.[63] Yet the cardinal correctly assessed the problems, both political and pastoral, created for the Church by its partisan identification with the Nationalists. Once again, the Church had chosen to place all its hopes in a regime expected not only to grant significant concessions but also to initiate a new age of religious revivalism. The clergy looked forward to a spiritual transformation of messianic proportions through the alliance of cross and sword. Whether in twentieth-century Europe such a sweeping vision could ever be realized, given the nature of the regime and the religious alienation of large segments of the population, was another matter.

---

achieved its purpose in the light of the favorable responses received from Catholic bishops throughout the world. Álvarez Bolado, although critical of several of its intellectual assumptions, maintains that it abandoned the "Hispanic messianism" characteristic of earlier episcopal declarations on the war and that when all is said and done, "it was probably convenient to write it." He argues that Gomá saw the necessity of explaining the Spanish Church's position to the international Catholic community "more clearly and panoramically than Vidal." Cárcel Ortí, *La persecución religiosa,* p. 280; Vicente Enrique y Tarancón, *Confesiones* (Madrid, 1996), pp. 206–7; Sánchez, *The Spanish Civil War as a Religious Tragedy,* p. 102; Frances Lannon, *Privilege, Persecution and Prophecy: The Catholic Church in Spain, 1875–1975* (Oxford, 1987), p. 204; Redondo, *Historia de la Iglesia en España,* vol. 2, pp. 315–16; Álvarez Bolado, *Para ganar la guerra, para ganar la paz,* pp. 159, 161, 163.

61. Quoted in Ramón Muntanyola, *Vidal i Barraquer: el cardenal de la paz* (Barcelona, 1974), pp. 323, 319. In a meeting with Gomá on May 10, 1937, Franco suggested that the hierarchy should consider publishing a collective statement designed to counter the unfavorable impressions of the regime held by some Catholic bishops elsewhere in the world. In fact, Gomá had already been working on such a document for several months. Redondo, *Historia de la Iglesia en España,* vol. 2, pp. 248–50, 274–76.

62. Quoted in Muntanyola, *Vidal i Barraquer,* p. 324.

63. The determined campaign against the cardinal is described by Marquina Barrio, *La diplomacia vaticana,* pp. 127–41.

Religion and War

The hierarchy's rhetoric gave the impression of a self-confident Church ready to seize the moment to carry out the spiritual reconquest of its dreams. In private, the bishops were less optimistic that a Nationalist triumph would produce the abundant religious benefits so confidently predicted in public. They realized that the Church faced a crisis unlike any other in its history. In Republican Spain, the massive destruction of ecclesiastical buildings, the execution of nearly seven thousand priests and religious, and the collapse of diocesan and parochial administrations sent the Church into the catacombs and posed problems of physical, religious, and organizational reconstruction that left it "enormously traumatized."[64] Even Cardinal Gomá contemplated the situation with foreboding. In October 1936, he told Cardinal Vidal i Barraquer, "We shall end up totally drained, impoverished and with an abyss of hatreds that will endure for generations."[65]

When the cardinal primate expressed this grim prediction, he was aware of the enormity of the losses being suffered by the clergy in the Republican zone, what one historian has called "the greatest clerical bloodletting in the entire history of the Christian Church."[66] By the end of the Civil War, 13 bishops, 4,184 diocesan priests, 2,365 male religious, and 283 nuns had perished as a result of anticlerical violence, especially during the six months following July 18. The extent of the attack on the Church has been well documented.[67] There is no dispute about either its scale or intensity.

Research conducted by writers drawn largely from clerical ranks has established the facts. The causes of the massive assault on the Church are less easily ascertained. Ecclesiastical authors have often seen the burning of churches and the assassination of priests as the result of two causes, first, a long "process of decomposition" in the "religious conscience of Spain" dating back to what were seen as the corrosive, antireligious values of the eighteenth century, and second, a deliberately planned conspiracy designed to eradicate Church and faith from the soil of Spain.[68] For Antonio Montero Moreno, author of the most detailed history of these events, "The burning of convents and hatred of the Church . . . were orchestrated by two forces, . . . Freemasonry and Communism."[69] Gonzalo Redondo's magisterial study

64. Rodríguez de Aisa, *El Cardenal Gomá y la guerra de España*, p. 56.

65. Quoted in ibid., p. 57, note 69.

66. Sánchez, *The Spanish Civil War as a Religious Tragedy*, p. 8.

67. Although rejecting the polemical interpretations of some clerical authors about religious persecution during the war, the progressive Catholic historian Hilari Raguer concluded that a "terrible historical reality" must be recognized: "during various months, it was enough that someone should be identified as a priest, religious or simply as a member of a congregation or apostolic movement to be executed without due process." Raguer, *La espada y la cruz*, p. 147.

68. José María Sanabre Sanromá, *Martirologio de la Iglesia en la diócesis de Barcelona durante la persecución religiosa* (Barcelona, 1943), p. 26.

69. Montero Moreno, *Historia de la persecución religiosa en España*, p. 40. Although this work remains the standard general account of the persecution suffered by the Church, it has been the object of

of the Church during this period attributes the savagery of religious persecution to the violence associated with attempts at radical social revolution and to years of anticlerical propaganda.[70]

Cárcel Ortí, while admitting that no documentary evidence proves that "the Government of the Republic ordered the general persecution of the Church," argues that the "cruelty and determination" with which it was carried out within a matter of months was impossible without the existence of "specific verbal indications" from higher authority.[71] However massive the reprisals directed against the Church, there is little evidence of a carefully organized conspiracy.[72] As in the spring of 1931, the Republican government realized that violence against the clergy only damaged its interests, although it moved quickly to pass severe legislation against the religious orders.[73] Moreover, the bloodiest phase of the anticlerical fury, the three months following July 18, corresponded to the period when the authority of the central government virtually collapsed before the bold seizure of power by local revolutionary committees and tribunals.[74] As the Republic began to reestablish control, albeit slowly and incompletely, violence against the Church diminished, although it never disappeared entirely.[75]

The checkered pattern of attacks on the clergy suggests less a planned assault carried out implacably in every corner of Republican Spain than a series of outbursts dependent on the strength or weakness of the established authorities in both town and country in the face of revolutionary movements and the attitude of local populations towards the clergy. In Catalonia, for example, the region's autonomous

---

criticism, especially for its failure to differentiate between the distinct chronological divisions of anticlerical violence and its uncritical acceptance of the black-and-white interpretation of the Republic. Hilari Raguer, "Antonio Montero, *Historia de la persecución religiosa en España, 1936–1939,*" *Revue d'Histoire Ecclésiastique* (1962), vol. 57, pp. 626–27.

70. Redondo, *Historia de la Iglesia en España,* vol. 2, pp. 25–26.

71. Cárcel Ortí, *La persecución religiosa,* p. 222.

72. Redondo maintains that it is difficult to establish the responsibility of the Republic's government in the anticlerical violence that followed July 18, although he argues that it did little to repress it. *Historia de la Iglesia en España,* vol. 2, p. 26. A report sent to the nunciature from Asturias after the Civil War declared that "the attacks and persecutions of a religious kind, which took place during the period of red domination, did not correspond to a premeditated plan." "Borrador de la relación enviada a la nunciatura sobre los hechos ocurridos durante la guerra civil," in Angel Garralda García, *La persecución del clero en Asturias, 1934 y 1936–1937* (2d ed., 2 vols., Avilés, 1983), vol. 1, p. 492.

73. A decree of July 27, for example, ordered the occupation of all buildings owned by the regular clergy. Whether this and similar measures represented a legitimization of "revolutionary excesses," as Salas Larrazábal has argued, is by no means clear. Ramón Salas Larrazábal, "Situación de la Iglesia en la España republicana durante la Guerra Civil," in Manuel Espadas Burgos et al., *Iglesia, sociedad y política en la España contemporánea* (El Escorial, 1983), p. 190.

74. Gabriel Jackson, *The Spanish Republic and the Civil War, 1931–1939* (Princeton, 1965), pp. 276–77, 287.

75. In the diocese of Barcelona, for example, clerical executions reached a peak of nearly 240 for the month of August 1936. Thereafter, they began a gradual decline to approximately ten a month by January 1937. They remained at this level, with one brief exception, until the end of the war. José María Sanabre Sanromá, *Martirologio de la Iglesia en la diócesis de Barcelona durante la persecución religiosa* (Barcelona, 1943), p. 467.

government, the Generalitat, faced a popular revolution, largely anarchist and strongly anticlerical in character, but retained enough prestige and maneuverability to arrange the exile of prominent clergymen, among them Cardinal Vidal i Barraquer.[76] In general, priests arrested by its police in Barcelona escaped with their lives; the vast majority of those seized by anarchist patrols roaming the city perished before firing squads.[77] In Villafranca del Penedés, a majority of the inhabitants had long ago abandoned religious practice and viewed the Church with hostility. During the October 1934 revolution, for instance, numerous churches in the area were set ablaze. After July 18, twenty-two of the district's priests were killed, the largest number of clerical assassinations in Catalonia outside of Barcelona. In contrast, the peasant region of San Celoni, close to the historically observant diocese of Vich, lost only four of its twenty-three priests because of the intervention of local parishioners. In Asturias, a similar pattern prevailed. In some towns, such as Mieres, the revolutionaries "conducted themselves relatively well," but in villages "a few kilometers away, bloody terror reigned."[78]

Violence against the clergy represented in part the extreme expression of the intense local anticlericalism, which, if ancient in origin, intensified following the Republic's proclamation. The church burnings of May 1931 and the innumerable, rancorous battles over implementation of republican ecclesiastical legislation created a climate of aggressive confrontation that enveloped the entire country from its largest cities to its smallest villages. Although the historic development of anticlericalism, particularly in its local dimension, formed a prelude to the violent events that followed July 18, it should be remembered that between the summer of 1835 and October 1934 attacks on the Church had taken the form of assaults against property rather than persons. Neither the church burnings of the Tragic Week of 1909 nor those of May 1931 involved significant loss of life among the clergy.

The October 1934 rising in Asturias dramatically altered this century-old pattern. For the first time since 1835, an anticlericalism of assassination joined an older tradition of violence against buildings and sacred objects. The identification of the clergy and activist laity with what an increasingly radicalized working class saw as a counterrevolutionary and anti-republican movement played a role in this significant transformation. The Asturian rising differed from earlier anticlerical outbursts by identifying the Church not only as a secondary ally of conservative interests but also as a primary symbol of opposition to economic and social change, one that took concrete form in every town or village possessed of a parish church or other religious and educational institutions.

76. The authorities of the Generalitat succeeded in saving "hundreds of human lives and a good part of the artistic and cultural patrimony of the Church in Catalonia." Josep M. Piñol, *El nacionalcatolicisme a Catalunya i la resistència, 1926–1966* (Barcelona, 1993), p. 55.

77. Sanabre Sanromá, *Matirologio de la Iglesia*, p. 31.

78. Ibid., pp. 89, 82–83; "Borrador de la relación enviada a la nunciatura sobre los hechos ocurridos durante la guerra civil," p. 492.

No single explanation can account for the attack on the Church following July 18. But in the summer and autumn of 1936, intense local hostility against the clergy, raised to new heights in reaction to the military rising and by the sudden surge of revolutionary movements, transformed old forms of anticlericalism into a dangerous threat never before encountered by the Church in such magnitude and intensity. The decentralized nature of the popular movement, expressed through a multitude of revolutionary committees and tribunals operating beyond the control of the central government, provided the vehicle for bringing revolution and local anticlericalism into explosive combination.

Until historians direct their research to this aspect of the assault against Church and clergy, the full story of the anticlerical fury cannot be told. Although no specific group monopolized violence against the Church, the conjunction of inflamed local anticlericalism and decentralized revolution favored the emergence of a fierce hostility against religion and its ministers primarily identified with the anarchists.[79] Complex in its origins and development, Spanish anarchism arrived at the summer of 1936 possessed of a virulent anticlerical tradition more central to its concerns than to those of the Socialist and Communist parties. Since the later nineteenth century, anarchists had shared views on religion and the clergy widespread among anticlericals of differing social and economic backgrounds. The Church appeared as an obscurantist opponent of progress, while religion seemed a powerful soporific preventing change among a population rendered passive by exhortations to Christian resignation.[80]

Anarchist anticlericalism went beyond these widely held ideas in two respects. Anarchism retained a millenarian and moralistic character. Anarchist literature gave prominence to Christ as a supreme moral example of laudable poverty, justice, and defense of the poor betrayed by the Church through its support of the rich and powerful. Church and clergy were bitterly reproached for their treason against the gospels, described as "sacrilegious apostates, who deny their principles and forget the doctrines taught by the heroic master sacrificed on Calvary."[81] This essentially religious message was given a specific revolutionary content in anarchist texts through the identification of the Church with those forces judged hostile to working-class aspirations, "the malign trilogy" of Church, State, and capitalism.[82]

79. According to Jackson, "The main purging in the big cities was done on the initiative of the left-wing elements of the Popular Front. In Madrid, the CNT, the UGT and the Communist party all had their list of suspects." *The Spanish Republic*, p. 284. There is considerable agreement among historians about the role of the anarchists, although other groups were involved in the religious persecution, especially the Partido Obrero de Unificación Marxista (POUM) in Catalonia. Piñol, *El nacionalcatolicisme a Catalunya*, p. 53; Redondo, *Historia de la Iglesia en España*, vol. 2, pp. 28–29.

80. José Álvarez Junco, *La ideología política del anarquismo español, 1868–1910* (2d ed., Madrid, 1991), pp. 204–14.

81. Quoted in ibid., p. 209.

82. Ibid., p. 211.

Anarchist exhortation to a "war against the bourgeoisie of the cassock!" circulated long before the 1930s,[83] but the "verbal aggression" characteristic of anarchist writing became more intense during the first months of the Civil War.[84] Some anarchist leaders of the anarcho-syndicalist Confederación Nacional del Trabajo condemned the widespread violence taking place within the Republican zone, but the decentralized and local character of the popular revolution and the anarchist movement itself gave the initiative to groups of "uncontrollables" who singled out the Church and the clergy as the primary objects of their attacks, although recent research has shown that other left-wing groups were also involved.[85] An anarchist publication of Barcelona put the matter simply and brutally: "Bishops and cardinals must be shot. And ecclesiastical property must be expropriated."[86]

Anarchist groups, particularly the extremist Federación Anarquista Ibérica (FAI), were especially active in the cities, towns, and villages of Catalonia and Aragón.[87] Although laymen identified with the Right also fell victim to reprisals, the clergy were pursued with relentless determination. The residents of one country town were told to reveal the hiding places of any priests and threatened with death if they dared to offer them refuge. An element of caprice occasionally saved those on the verge of execution. In the town of Balaquer, for example, FAI militiamen decided to free three religious from certain death at the last moment: "Since you are young and have lived deceived, we free you from death. We hope that from now on you will be good citizens and conduct yourselves properly."[88] Their older companions suffered the fate visited upon the vast majority of priests falling into anarchist hands. They were taken from the town by truck and machine-gunned on a nearby country road.

The destruction of churches and the assassination of priests and religious were accompanied by a wave of blasphemy and sacrilege. The profanation of tombs in monasteries and convents, mock processions, burlesque Masses, sacramental rites, and the shooting of religious statues repeated throughout the Republican zone

83. Quoted in ibid.

84. Julián Casanova, *Anarquismo y revolución en la sociedad rural aragonesa, 1936–1938* (Madrid, 1985), p. 163.

85. In his study of rural Aragón, Julián Casanova has concluded that "persecution of the clergy was even more obsessive than that unleashed against individuals considered fascist, wealthy landowners or participants in the military rising." Ibid., p. 165. Julio de la Cueva argues that although anarchists may well have predominated in anticlerical violence, they were not alone. He notes that in areas where anarchism was weak, such as New Castile, where the PSOE was the most important political force, similar attacks on the clergy took place. He also argues that the term "uncontrollables" is simplistic because trade union and party members engaged in violence against clerics enjoyed carte blanche for their activities as a result of their status. "Religious Persecution, Anticlerical Tradition and Revolution: On Atrocities against the Clergy during the Spanish Civil War," *Journal of Contemporary History* (1998), vol. 33, no. 3, p. 358.

86. Quoted in Casanova, *Anarquismo y revolución*, p. 165.

87. Albert Manent i Segimon and Josep Raventós i Giralt, *L'Església clandestina a Catalunya durant la guerra civil, 1936–1939* (Montserrat, 1984), pp. 31–34.

88. Quoted in Montero Moreno, *Historia de la persecución religiosa*, p. 214.

during the war's early months testified to the existence of deep emotional hostility to Church and religion. In one village, a mock procession moved through the streets accompanied by a militiawoman dressed in clerical vestments, who offered to hear confessions from the jeering multitude that filled the streets.[89]

Different explanations have been offered for this reversal of religious ritual, but it is unclear why it appeared with such force and universality in 1936.[90] Although these primitive manifestations had appeared before, as during the Málaga *quema de conventos* in 1931 and, episodically, during October 1934, they were generally absent from earlier examples of massive anticlerical violence. The historian must go back to the summer of 1835 to find a precedent even remotely resembling the events of 1936 in this respect. The widespread pattern of religious mockeries that occurred during the war revealed an animus against religion and its external symbols unprecedented in both scale and intensity. In many ways, it represented another aspect of the transformation of the local anticlericalism that lay behind the virulence of the attack on the Church. Earlier manifestations of violence sought to teach the clergy a lesson or realize a political purpose. Those of 1936 sought to eradicate the Church's physical presence, its priests, and its symbols.

Anticlerical violence also swept away the organization of the twenty-eight dioceses within the Republican zone. Their bishops were either dead or had managed to take refuge abroad or in the territory controlled by the generals. All normal ecclesiastical activity came to a halt, as priests struggled to save their lives through every conceivable stratagem. The ravaging of clerical ranks reached catastrophic proportions. The diocese of Tortosa lost 61.9 percent of its priests, Lérida, 65.8 percent, while the tiny see of Barbastro saw its clergy almost completely eliminated.[91] When Cardinal Gomá returned to Toledo, which had lost nearly half of its priests, he encountered the archdiocese "very broken in every respect, the churches abandoned, priests murdered, . . . with a frightening descent of faith and Christian customs." The elderly and ill cardinal primate wondered whether he was capable of the "superhuman effort" needed to continue working "in the arid field of [this] battered Christianity."[92]

89. Ibid., p. 648.

90. José Sánchez maintains that these acts of profanation and blasphemy arose from two motives, a desire to break through the restrictive "shell of tradition" imposed by Catholicism by turning ritual on its head, and a deep "desire to purge fear" by exposing the "dark" side of religious life, manifested particularly through the invasion of monasteries and convents and the opening of the tombs therein. *The Spanish Civil War as a Religious Tragedy,* pp. 42–43. Bruce Lincoln has argued from an anthropological perspective that "the macabre ritual of opening tombs and displaying corpses often developed in primitive millenarian societies in the deliberate flouting of such fundamental taboos as those against incest, cannibalism, and abuse of the dead." In the Spanish case, he argues, the indignities heaped upon the bodies of religious were in part "the spontaneous dramatization of *absolute* liberation from all bonds of the past, even from those of common decency." "Revolutionary Exhumations in Spain, July 1936," *Comparative Studies in Society and History* (1985), vol. 17, no. 2, pp. 251–52.

91. Montero Moreno, *Historia de la persecución religiosa,* pp. 763–64.

92. Quoted in Rodríguez de Aisa, *El Cardenal Gomá y la guerra de España,* p. 330, note 154.

Despite the devastation suffered by the Church in Republican Spain, the practice of the cult did not disappear. In general, priests seeking to say Mass in the countryside faced a more perilous situation than did their colleagues in large urban centers such as Madrid and Barcelona.[93] Here too, regional differences were important. A long tradition of religious observance in the rural diocese of Vich allowed individual priests, traveling by bicycle, to move from place to place saying Mass in private homes. Conditions in the diocese of Tortosa, where anticlerical currents ran deep, were different. There priests ran a far greater risk of exposure and death for engaging in religious activities.[94]

Circumstances in metropolitan centers favored the emergence of a clandestine Church.[95] Their sheer size and urban complexity allowed the appearance of a rudimentary ecclesiastical organization and the development of a network of safe houses and underground communications, including the use of a special telephone argot that permitted a revival of the cult once the bloodiest phase of the anticlerical fury had passed. By the autumn of 1936, a clandestine Church was already functioning in Barcelona and Gerona. By mid-1937, it is estimated that twenty-five hundred priests were living in hiding in Barcelona and that they said more than two thousand Masses daily.[96] Moreover, the authorities increasingly turned a blind eye to their activities and for a time even considered authorizing public religious practice, largely to placate international opinion and to satisfy the insistent demands of the Basque autonomous republic.[97] Although nothing came

93. In his study of the diocese of Barcelona, José Sanabre Sanromá asserted, "The situation of the rural clergy during the first month of the revolution is indescribable; there was no other escape than either death or flight to Barcelona." *Martirologio de la Iglesia*, p. 30.

94. Josep Franquesa i Alberch, *Reports biografies d'en Pere de la Pipa* (Vich, 1972), pp. 84–85; Enrique y Tarancón, *Recuerdos de juventud*, p. 245.

95. The emergence and development of a clandestine Church in the Republican zone has been studied by Montero Moreno, *Historia de la persecución religiosa*, chapter 4. The most detailed account of the underground Church, though limited to Catalonia, is Manent i Segimon and Raventós i Giralt, *L'Església clandestina a Catalunya*. There is a useful summary in Sánchez, *The Spanish Civil War as a Religious Tragedy*, pp. 60–69.

96. Manent i Segimon and Raventós i Giralt, *L'Església clandestina a Catalunya*, pp. 54–55, 73, 114.

97. This initiative was associated with Manuel Irujo, a practicing Catholic and Basque nationalist, who, first as minister without portfolio and later (May 1937–January 1938) as minister of justice in the Republican cabinet, sought to persuade the government, the Vatican, and the highest ecclesiastical authority remaining in Barcelona, the vicar-general Josep Torrent, to approve a public restoration of the cult. Although by the time the project was being discussed the Republican authorities had made some concessions to the Church by authorizing the use of military chaplains in limited cases, by creating a Commission of the Cult, and by inviting Cardinal Vidal i Barraquer to return to Tarragona, there was little prospect of an agreement. The issue became enmeshed in the complex diplomatic game being played by the Vatican, the Nationalists, and the Republic. There were also powerful groups within the regime, notably the anarchists, opposed to any concessions. In any event, Torrent rejected Irujo's overtures on the grounds that the government was unwilling to provide the Church with sufficient guarantees. There are extensive discussions of this question in Raguer, *La espada y la cruz*, pp. 198–212; Manent i Segimon and Raventós i Giralt, *L'Església clandestina a Catalunya*, pp. 154–63, 184–93, 197–206; Salas Larrazábal, "Situación de la Iglesia en la España republicana," pp. 195–210; Redondo, *Historia de la Iglesia en España*, vol. 2, pp. 383–94.

of this attempt, by 1939 the Church, at least in Barcelona, had managed to emerge from the underground to function in a state of "semi-clandestinity."[98]

From the beginning of the war, the hierarchy gave priority to the religious and material reconstruction of dioceses conquered by the Nationalist armies. While the conflict continued, there was no prospect that a financially pressed government would furnish the funds needed to begin the monumental task of rebuilding ruined or destroyed churches. The Church concentrated its energies on reintroducing the cult and finding enough clergy to staff parishes. The bishop of Tortosa dispatched six priests to his diocese, among them Vicente Enrique y Tarancón, to begin the task of pastoral reconstruction. They found churches stripped of altars and sacred ornaments. In larger towns, priests emerged from hiding but, afflicted by the "terrible trauma" of their experience, they were less concerned with pastoral activity than with a determination "to eradicate at its roots the evil weed" that had caused them so much suffering. Although enough clergy were found to staff parishes on a provisional basis, the diocesan authorities had no plan of action other than to secure the resumption of the cult "*as if nothing had happened*" between 1936 and 1939.[99]

The diocesan clergy focused attention on realizing the Church's traditional objective of ensuring that as many as possible performed their religious obligations without worrying too much about the motives of their congregations. Pastoral activities followed the "fixed models" of the past, emphasizing attendance at Mass and the fulfillment of sacramental obligations on the part of the population. Primarily concerned that "all Spaniards *should appear* as members of the Church," priests sought to increase the number of confessions and communions, while augmenting the number of Sunday services, "although the Masses might be . . . boring and although participation was moved nearly exclusively by material considerations."[100]

Little thought was given to devising a pastoral strategy designed to meet a religious challenge unique in the history of the Spanish Church. The bishops knew, of course, that the Church had to do something, in Gomá's words, to achieve a "reconquest of the soul of the people, especially of the working masses whom we are on the verge of losing."[101] Although the cardinal primate addressed the question of religious reconstruction as early as December 1936 and the Committee of Metropolitans considered it at its meetings in 1937 and 1939, the strategy followed by the bishops came down to little more than a repackaging of long-circulating ideas that accorded priority to organizational change rather than to innovative pastoral methods. Gomá called for a reform of seminary education, the elimination of non-

98. Manent i Segimon and Raventós i Giralt, *L'Església clandestina a Catalunya*, p. 238.

99. Enrique y Tarancón, *Recuerdos de juventud*, pp. 249, 250.

100. Ibid., pp. 316, 319–20.

101. Quoted in Rodríguez de Aisa, *El Cardenal Gomá y la guerra de España*, p. 25.

pastoral positions, and benefices among diocesan priests and the reorganization of Catholic Action.[102] These recommendations, as well as those elaborated by the Committee of Metropolitans, saw the solution to the religious crisis at the grass-roots level in traditional terms, as an objective to be achieved by the clergy and Catholic lay elites.

There was little prospect that even this limited program could be implemented while the war continued. Despite the high hopes placed in Catholic Action by the hierarchy, the movement was in no position to play its historic role of an activist elite directing the Catholic masses. Its ranks had been drastically reduced in the Republican zone, while in the Spain of the generals, many of its younger members were lost to military service.[103] The movement itself was viewed with suspicion within the Franco regime for its earlier identification with the "accidentalist" strategy pursued by the hierarchy towards the Republic. Angel Herrera, now a student for the priesthood in Switzerland, encountered a chilly reception during a brief visit to Spain at the end of 1937, when Franco refused to receive him, while the efforts of his supporters to recover control of the Editorial Católica, publisher of *El Debate* before the war, were frustrated by the machinations of Serrano Suñer.[104] Even in areas where Catholic Action continued to function, its impact proved less than impressive. In 1938, an assembly of clergy of the diocese of Mallorca called for the movement to play a key role in "Spanish reconstruction," but its only specific recommendation came down to urging Catholic Action to carry out a campaign of "moralization of the beaches during the coming summer."[105] The ACNP, with many of its members in the army, scarcely functioned during the years of the war.[106]

102. "Acción ministerial y Acción Católica," *Documentación presentada por el cardenal Gomá a la Santa Sede en su viaje a Roma en diciembre de 1936*, in ibid., pp. 394–98.

103. One in four of the members of the Madrid ACNP were assassinated during the war. Overall, one-sixth of the organization's membership perished in the anticlerical violence. Montero, *Historia de la Asociación Católica Nacional de Propagandistas . . . 1936–1945*, p. 30.

104. The attitude of Carlists, Falangists, and authoritarian monarchists of Renovación Española towards the ACNP, for example, was one of "distrust and lack of confidence, due fundamentally to its collaboration with the Republic" during the early 1930s. Montero, *La Asociación Católica Nacional de Propagandistas . . . 1936–1945*, pp. 40, 90–91. In private, Herrera expressed his doubts about the wisdom of a military rising as a solution to the country's problems, although he supported it in public. He expressed similar reservations about the hierarchy's Collective Letter of 1937. Ibid., pp. 28–29, 87. The struggle for control of the Editorial Católica is described in ibid., pp. 73–79. The press of the Falange crudely attacked Herrera and *El Debate* for "obstinately and insistently" recommending acceptance of the Republic during the early 1930s. Pedro Laín Entralgo, a young intellectual of the Falange, provided a more sophisticated and damning indictment of the work of Herrera and Catholic Action before 1936. He argued that Herrera's attempt to achieve the "peaceful re-Catholicization of Spain" through the activities of a "select minority" was an abysmal failure. Quoted in José Andrés-Gallego, "La crítica falangista del catolicismo político," *Hispania Sacra* (1991), vol. 43, no. 87, pp. 106, 110.

105. Josep Massot i Muntaner, *Església i societat a la Mallorca del segle XX* (Barcelona, 1977), pp. 176, 171.

106. "It can be said that the activity of the propagandists was slight, above all when compared with that realized during the republican years." Montero, *La Asociación Católica Nacional de Propagandistas . . . 1936–1945*, p. 106.

If the formidable effort of physical and pastoral rebuilding had scarcely begun in the former Republican zone by 1939, the Church encountered a situation highly favorable to its interests in those areas controlled by the Nationalists at the beginning of the conflict. Ecclesiastical buildings and the clergy escaped destruction, while the Church's identification with the new regime stimulated a resurgence of Catholicism as a civic religion last given unrestrained expression during the Primo de Rivera dictatorship. But it now took on a sharper political edge. Elaborate religious ceremonies testifying to the revived union and common purpose of Church and State were held throughout the war. On August 15, 1936, feast day of the Assumption of the Virgin, Cardinal Ilundain of Seville presided over a solemn Mass attended by military officers and members of the Falange, many carrying pistols and daggers. An altar to the Virgin stood "resplendent with surrounding bayonets" before the congregation. In his sermon, the cardinal avoided a specific political endorsement of the Nationalist cause, although he left little doubt where his sympathies lay. A preacher at a similar ceremony in the cathedral of Badajoz a year later was less restrained. "This is a moving scene," he declared, as he exhorted those present to "Union, complete submission to the chief, to make a Spain like that of Ferdinand and Isabella. The cross and the sword united will give days of glory to our Fatherland, which, once again, is fulfilling its historic mission of saving the world from barbarism."[107]

These political-religious ceremonies were by no means confined to the cities. During the autumn of 1937, in a small village of Segovia province, the inhabitants carried banners and sang hymns and patriotic songs as they formed a procession a kilometer long that made its way to a monument to the Sacred Heart, that great symbol of conservative Catholicism whose statues had been dynamited throughout the Republican zone. The parish priest called for a spiritual revival in "great and heroic Spain" committed to the defense of "God and the tradition of our race." At the ceremony's conclusion, the crowd began to sing in swelling voice a well-known hymn to the Sacred Heart, "You shall reign! You shall reign!"[108]

Ceremonies of this kind say more about politics than about the state of religion in Nationalist Spain. Whether the war produced the spiritual revival expected by the clergy is a more difficult question to answer, given the dearth of statistical evidence on religious observance for the period. Churchmen believed that attendance at Sunday Mass and other services increased dramatically. In his balanced account of his experiences in Galicia and the diocese of Tortosa, Vicente Enrique y Tarancón recalled that in both regions, "everyone—even those who never fulfilled their religious duties before," now did so.[109]

There is no reason to doubt the accuracy of this observation. The reasons be-

107. Bahamonde, *Memoirs of a Spanish Nationalist,* pp. 56, 57, 63.
108. *Boletín Oficial del Obispado de Segovia* (1937), pp. 362–65.
109. Enrique y Tarancón, *Recuerdos de juventud,* p. 252.

hind the resurgence in observance are more difficult to establish. In some respects, it represented a continuation in more militant form of the fervor among some Catholics that appeared after 1931 in reaction to the Republic's ecclesiastical legislation. It also recognized the hard facts of life among those who once avoided attending church. Cardinal Tarancón recalled that in 1939 the residents of Vinaroz, long known for republican and liberal sympathies, felt obliged to assist at services, believing "friendship with the clergy provided the best safe conduct" as the Nationalist authorities began to settle old scores.[110] The parish priest of Rota (Cádiz) told his congregation in no uncertain terms what the Church expected of them: "You don't deceive me. I know you all very well. And I give you this warning—on Sundays, all, all of you to Mass; I take no excuses. . . . Anyone who doesn't come will suffer the consequences."[111]

Whatever its causes, the "religious inflation" taking place in Nationalist Spain fell short of being the spiritual revival of an entire population envisioned by the Church. With his characteristic realism, Cardinal Vidal i Barraquer went to the heart of the matter in 1939. He told the pope that massive "external manifestations of the cult," whether in the form of mass communions, processions, and pious devotions to the Sacred Heart, were less "acts of religious affirmation" than a "political reaction against the persecuting laicism of the past." Not only was its religious impact likely to be "ephemeral," it ran the grave risk of making "religion odious to the indifferent and partisans" of the opposing side in the war. If its "thousands and thousands" of supporters were temporarily subjugated, "they preserve their old ideology within themselves."[112]

In the Nationalist zone, signs of increased religious observance and the benefits derived from the derogation of republican ecclesiastical legislation, as well as the relentless purge of those whom the clergy judged its enemies, strengthened the Church's position. But the politicized character of religious practice and the strong dose of compulsion accompanying it, the failure to elaborate a coherent pastoral strategy, and the difficulties in civil-ecclesiastical relations created by a strongly regalist government left the Church far short of fulfilling its historic aspirations as the war drew to a close.

In one area of activity, the Church attained a long-cherished objective. It not only succeeded in securing abrogation of the Republic's educational legislation, it also won a degree of influence over schools at all levels that went far beyond the situation prevailing before April 1931. The clergy was consumed by a desire to execute an educational coup d'état of unprecedented proportions. Re-

110. Ibid. Tarancón believed, however, that at least some of those who had previously lived "apart from the Church" now accepted "a sincere reconciliation" with it. Ibid., p. 324.

111. Quoted in Bahamonde, *Memoirs of a Spanish Nationalist*, p. 62.

112. Quoted in Muntanyola, *Vidal i Barraquer*, p. 422. The cardinal addressed these remarks to Pius XII in an interview of November 1939.

Christianization and education constituted the Church's "two great obsessions" during the Civil War.[113] Throughout the conflict, the Church demanded that the new regime deliver education into its hands. "Education must be . . . *Catholic,*" declared a prominent clerical writer, "because the truth is only one, and this is taught by the Catholic Church, whose doctrines the majority of Spaniards profess."[114]

The Nationalist government obliged by allowing the Church to develop its private school system free of the restrictions imposed by the Republic and by a relentless campaign to re-Catholicize the public system. "We will organize schools," declared General Mola bluntly, "in which the teachers will teach love of God and country."[115] The Church secured an early and important beachhead through the appointment of Catholics sympathetic to its objectives to the Commission on Culture and Teaching, created in 1936 by the new regime to deal with education. The Commission's president, a longtime member of the ACNP, José María Pemán, and its other members promoted a program of re-Catholicization of State schools in accord with the views of the hierarchy. In an early decree, the Commission announced that the public system "has ceased being lay," as a prelude to a series of orders issued in the autumn of 1937 that made the teaching of religion and sacred history obligatory in both primary and secondary schools.[116]

Other measures, designed to reverse the democratic character of the curriculum prevailing under the Republic, commanded school principals and university rectors to eliminate from their libraries books "opposed to Christian morality" and "the healthy ideals of citizenship and patriotism." The Commission also proceeded to dismantle much of the state secondary school system, long regarded by Catholic opinion as a hotbed of republicanism and radicalism. Fifty-two schools were closed in September and October 1937 alone. Moreover, there was no question of allowing private schools known for their secular curricula and progressive educational methods to survive. The celebrated Institución Libre de Enseñanza was accused of being "a cenacle of apostles of doubt, unbelief, of the defamation of Spain." It was "anti-Catholic, anti-Spanish." "Not a stone of it" would be allowed to stand.[117]

Hostility to the Republic's educational reforms inevitably led to a determined attempt to remove teachers, 75 percent of whom were alleged to have betrayed the nation.[118] As early as August 28, 1936, the regime ordered the beginning of what

113. Juan María Laboa, *Iglesia e intolerancias: la guerra civil: una historia que habla de dos Españas* (Madrid, 1987), p. 121.

114. R. S. de Lamadrid, "La enseñanza religiosa en la Nueva España," *Razón y Fe* (1938), vol. 114, p. 47.

115. Quoted in Alicia Alted Vigil, *Política del nuevo Estado sobre el patrimonio cultural y la educación durante la guerra civil española* (Madrid, 1984), p. 180.

116. Quoted in Gregorio Cámara Villar, *Nacional-catolicismo y escuela: la socialización política del franquismo* (Jaén, 1984), p. 70.

117. Quoted in ibid., pp. 71, 79, 72.

118. Enrique Gervilla Castillo, *La escuela del nacional-catolicismo: ideología y educación religiosa* (Granada, 1990), p. 90.

would later become a systematic purge. Pemán singled out those "who directly or indirectly contributed to sustain or propagate the parties, ideology and institutions of the so-called 'Popular Front.'"[119] Anyone, even those who had merely sympathized with the "poisoners of the popular soul" or who had failed to attend church regularly, fell under the scrutiny of purging committees created at the national and provincial levels.[120] These commissions were not particularly well organized, largely for financial reasons.[121] But the purges achieved their purpose. By November 1937, fifty thousand primary school teachers had been fired, subjected to temporary loss of employment, or punished with diverse administrative sanctions.[122] The Burgos Commission, for example, ordered the dismissal of Valentina López Veganzones, a teacher in the village of Medina de Pomar, because "her religious ideas are disastrous." There was no place in the "New Spain" for "teachers of such abominable political-religious background."[123]

The Commission on Teaching and Culture devoted its energies primarily to destroying the republican school system and eliminating teachers sympathetic to its objectives. It fell to Pedro Sáinz Rodríguez, minister of education (1938–1939) in the first Nationalist cabinet, to lay the foundation for the religiously oriented public schools that would endure throughout the history of the Franco regime. University professor, monarchist, and writer, Sáinz Rodríguez had vociferously defended the religious orders and their schools as a parliamentary deputy between 1931 and 1936. Deeply suspicious of the totalitarian designs of the Falange with respect to education, he saw to it that key posts in his ministry were occupied by Catholics committed to the existence of an extensive network of Church schools and to an educational ideology in public schools based on the identification of Spanish nationalism with Catholicism.[124] "The first sustaining principle of Spanish nationality," declared his director of secondary teaching, "was fused with its Catholic ideology."[125]

Sáinz Rodríguez and his collaborators, perhaps aware of the ineffectiveness of religious instruction in public schools before 1931, were determined to convert education into a powerful tool designed to indoctrinate youth with a conservative, Catholic nationalist ideology. Every aspect of teaching in primary schools, declared

119. Quoted in Camara Villar, *Nacional-catolicismo y escuela*, p. 76.

120. Ibid. Provincial commissions sent a questionnaire to local mayors, parish priests, commanders of the Civil Guard, and some parents. The questions dealt with every aspect of an individual's political and religious conduct. The rate of response was highest among parish priests. Jesús Crespo Redondo, *Purga de maestros en la guerra civil* (Valladolid, 1987), p. 115.

121. For a discussion of the administrative and financial problems of provincial committees, see ibid., pp. 93–98.

122. Cámara Villar, *Nacional-catolicismo y escuela*, p. 76.

123. Quoted in Crespo Redondo, *Purga de maestros*, p. 197.

124. Cámara Villar, *Nacional-catolicismo y escuela*, pp. 89–91. Sáinz Rodríguez corresponded frequently with Cardinal Gomá over educational matters during the period of his ministry. Alted Vigil, *Política del nuevo Estado*, p. 158.

125. Quoted in Cámara Villar, *Nacional-catolicismo y escuela*, p. 82.

a ministry order of 1938, must be employed to convey religious and moral instruction. The purpose of primary education, asserted a later ministerial directive, must serve to inculcate principles "saturated with the religious and patriotic spirit, which constitutes the essence of our National Movement."[126]

A thorough remaking of secondary education in 1938 abandoned the modest attempts to modernize the curriculum made by successive governments since 1900 in favor of a thoroughly classical education. Students were required to study Latin and Spanish literature with a view to developing "the heroic vocation of our youth" based on "the classical and humanistic studies of our sixteenth century which produced that Pleiad of statesmen and warriors . . . of our imperial epoch." The 1938 legislation sought nothing less than a "total transformation of the mentalities of the New Spain" through a curriculum based on religious indoctrination and a course of study designed to revive the glories of a vanished empire. A spokesman for Catholic teachers concluded that the educational legislation of 1938 delivered a "most telling blow against the anti-Spanish and anti-Christian revolution."[127]

The Church's successful reconquest of education arose less from institutional pressure, great as it was, than from the complex political juggling of Franco, as he sought to satisfy the diverse interest groups supporting the regime. If the Falange received satisfaction through a corporatist reorganization that eliminated Catholic university student syndicates, the Church secured recognition of its claims in education. Pre-1936 members of the Falange, strongly in favor of a single public school system in accord with the party's vaguely totalitarian pretensions, were far from pleased with this development. Despite periodic skirmishing over education and some difficulties between the civil and ecclesiastical authorities over certain organizational aspects of the regime's education policy, the issue was never really in doubt. The changes introduced were to "the entire satisfaction of the principles and interests of the Church's hierarchy and to the political and social sectors attached to it."[128]

In practical terms, the circumstances created by the war prevented full realization of this grand design. The financial difficulties of Church and State, as well as the demographic decline of the male orders, which lost approximately one-fifth of their membership during the conflict, meant that significant expansion of private schools administered by the regular clergy had to await better times. Moreover, the 1938 reform of public secondary education, although significant for the future, was applied to a system that had been effectively dismantled by school closings and teacher purges and by a reduced student body as a result of the recruitment of older pupils into military service.

126. Quoted in ibid., pp. 85, 89.

127. Quoted in ibid., pp. 92, 94.

128. Ibid., p. 119. The 1938 legislation on secondary teaching elicited numerous congratulations sent to Sáinz Rodríguez by the bishops. Alted Vigil, *Política del nuevo Estado*, p. 163.

As the war neared its end, the Church had achieved a historic objective through the reconquest of education. On balance, it represented one of the few areas in the "New Spain" being created during the Civil War where the Church succeeded in securing what it saw as an essential mechanism for the re-Christianization of the nation. But despite the identification of Church and State displayed in triumphalist religious ceremonies and public rhetoric following the Nationalist victory, the future was far from certain. The tense state of relations with the government left a hierarchy troubled about the Church's place within the new regime. It was still unclear where the resources would be secured to finance the immense task of physical reconstruction. The destruction of the Republic and the repression of its followers removed an immediate threat to clerical interests. It did nothing to resolve the historically intractable problem of how the Church would realize its objective of re-Christianizing the religiously alienated, who, though subdued, remained on the scene in the millions. The deck of cards that the clergy had long seen as stacked against the Church's interests now inclined in the other direction, but its stability remained in doubt as the Church entered an entirely new phase in its history.

Regalism and Franco's "New Spain"

Early in the war, Cardinal Gomá took comfort from "the consoling piety" displayed by the rebel generals and their troops. No one impressed the primate, in this respect, more than Franco. Even before his first meeting with the general, the cardinal expressed confidence that the pious head of the Nationalist government "will be a great collaborator in the Church's work from the lofty position that he occupies."[129] Although Franco's religiosity was sincere enough, it took the form of that popular, ultramontane piety characteristic of Spanish Catholicism during the late nineteenth and early twentieth centuries. During the course of the war, this straightforward faith took a providentialist leap, as the general came to believe that God had called him to save nation and religion.[130]

Gomá's roseate view of the benefits the Church could expect from the new regime as a result of the personal religiosity of the general and his collaborators ignored a centuries-old lesson of Spanish history. The faith of the country's rulers, however sincerely expressed, rarely meant that the interests of Church and State coincided with perfect harmony. The tumultuous history of civil-ecclesiastical relations during the eighteenth century, when the alliance of Throne and Altar was

129. "Informe acerca del levantamiento . . . en julio de 1936," in Rodríguez de Aisa, *El Cardenal Gomá y la guerra de España*, p. 375; quoted in ibid., p. 33. On a visit to Rome in December 1936, the cardinal primate reported that Franco was a "practicing Catholic, who I am told says the rosary every day . . . and who does not conceive the Spanish State outside of its traditional lines of Catholicism in every respect." Quoted in ibid., p. 71.

130. Javier Tusell, "Los gobernantes españoles y el catolicismo," *XX Siglos* (1990), vol. 1, no. 1, pp. 99–100.

at its height, showed that a common religion could not eliminate discord created by the State's determination to exercise a high degree of control over ecclesiastical affairs.

Franco intended to restore a confessional State. But defining its precise character in the light of the Church's historic demands and the policies of the Vatican proved exceptionally difficult. Despite assurances given by the general to Gomá in December 1936 that the government would provide the Church "with maximum guarantees with respect to its liberty . . . in the exercise of its functions," the regime looked to the regalist past for its model of civil-ecclesiastical relations.[131] Its ecclesiastical policy focused on the restoration of the 1851 concordat, which conceded the Crown ample powers over episcopal nominations. The papacy had long disliked the prerogatives associated with royal patronage and welcomed their disappearance during the Republic. But the Vatican and Gomá seriously underestimated the regalism of Franco and his ministers.[132] The regime's relentless prosecution of its regalist program led to inevitable conflict with a papacy unwilling to restore privileges that it saw as anachronistic.

Conflict over patronage rights was exacerbated by the Vatican's wait-and-see attitude on the question of extending diplomatic recognition to the Nationalist government. Although Pius XI named Gomá as his personal representative to Franco in December 1936, the Vatican delayed full recognition until May 1938.[133] The regime employed every pressure tactic at its disposal to persuade the papacy to move quickly on the diplomatic front. Before what the Spanish authorities saw as Roman foot-dragging, they allowed the officially controlled press on occasion to attack the papal secretary of state, Cardinal Pacelli, under the slogan, "Catholics, yes; Vaticanists, no!"[134] The eventual granting of recognition failed to resolve other outstanding points of conflict between the Vatican and the Nationalist government.

131. "Escrito del cardenal Gomá al cardenal Pacelli, Secretario de Estado, conteniendo los puntos aprobados en su primera entrevista oficial con el general Franco," January 1, 1937, in Rodríguez de Aisa, *El Cardenal Gomá y la guerra de España*, p. 402.

132. Marquina Barrio, *La diplomacia vaticana*, p. 60.

133. The Vatican's chargé d'affaires in Madrid remained until November 4. His departure represented a de facto break in relations with the Republic, although the nunciature did not formally close its doors. Salas Larrazábal, "Situación de la Iglesia en la España republicana durante la Guerra Civil," p. 193. The motives behind the Vatican's reluctance to extend prompt recognition were complex. The ill-disguised expulsion of Bishop Múgica, the execution of Basque priests in the Nationalist zone, the influence in Rome of ecclesiastical moderates like Archbishop Tedeschini, the papacy's determination not to yield on the patronage issue, its desire to avoid endangering the Catholic population of Republican Spain, its apprehensions over the possible totalitarian drift of the regime as well as its fears over involving the Church with one of the two blocs forming among the nations of Europe, were all important considerations. Antonio Marquina Barrio, "El Vaticano y la guerra civil española," in Aldo Albónico et al., *Italia y la guerra civil española* (Madrid, 1986), pp. 92–93; Sánchez, *The Spanish Civil War as a Religious Tragedy*, pp. 124–29. Redondo provides a detailed treatment of relations between the regime and the Holy See. *Historia de la Iglesia en España*, vol. 2, chapters 3, 6.

134. Quoted in Rodríguez de Aisa, *El Cardenal Gomá y la guerra de España*, p. 294.

The question of the government's ecclesiastical patronage rights remained a source of contention. A bruising diplomatic struggle over the issue did not end until a compromise agreement was reached in 1941. The regime insisted that it should enjoy all the powers conceded by the papacy to every government before it save those of the First and Second Republics. Officials arguing the case cited precedents dating as far back as the 1753 concordat, the most sweeping triumph of regalism over the Holy See ever achieved in the long history of Spanish civil-ecclesiastical relations.[135] Franco and his ministers showed a commitment to regalism fully within the tradition of official control of the Church identified with the eighteenth-century Bourbons and nineteenth-century liberal governments.

The attempt to recover the Crown's patronage rights reflected the regime's intention to defend its jurisdictional claims. But its motives were also practical. The government was determined to exclude episcopal candidates who held separatist opinions or views perceived as incompatible with Nationalist values. In 1937, the regime first bared its teeth on the issue. Pius XI, following the precedent of free appointment adopted under the Republic, named a Vincentian priest, Carmelo Ballester, as bishop of León without consulting the Nationalist authorities. Ballester was neither a separatist nor particularly objectionable for his political views, although his friendship with Archbishop Tedeschini, the papal nuncio identified with the Vatican's effort to reach an accommodation with the Republic, aroused hostility in official circles. Ballester possessed estimable personal qualities and administrative talent, besides enjoying the friendship of Cardinal Gomá. But the regime saw the appointment as a provocation. The candidate's long residence in France, and his participation during the 1920s in a stratagem designed to circumvent a decree of Primo de Rivera confining key posts in the religious orders to Spaniards, caused the government to regard him as a "Frenchified bishop" incompatible with its exalted nationalism.[136]

That the government chose to provoke a diplomatic crisis with the Vatican over this innocuous appointment showed how far it was prepared to go to attain its objective of exercising significant control over episcopal nominations. Although Ballester eventually occupied his bishopric, the regime became intransigent on the patronage issue immediately thereafter. In fact, the determination of Franco's "New Spain" to get its way created an impasse with the Vatican that prevented further episcopal appointments from being made until 1942.

Controversy over diplomatic recognition and patronage complicated the task of regularizing the Church's position within Nationalist Spain. The shopping list of clerical demands presented by Bishop Pla y Deniel in September 1936 and private

135. Marquina Barrio, *La diplomacia vaticana*, p. 87.
136. Ibid., pp. 67–73.

communications between Cardinal Gomá and the Vatican show that the Church expected the regime to satisfy its claims as rapidly as possible. The cardinal primate recognized that wartime conditions and uncertainty about the regime's political organization meant that not all questions affecting ecclesiastical matters could be resolved quickly. But he and his episcopal colleagues believed that prompt action was required to allow a Church "traumatized" by the policies of the Republic and the war to begin institutional recovery. The bishops gave priority to derogation of republican legislation affecting the Church and elimination of the secularized educational system established between 1931 and 1936.[137]

To its dismay, the Church received less than full satisfaction, with the exception of concessions in education and the control of public morality. At least in a technical sense, the bulk of the Republic's ecclesiastical legislation remained on the books far longer than the bishops anticipated. The regime did little to meet clerical demands until formation of its first cabinet in 1938, and even then it moved slowly.[138] Repeated attempts to persuade the government to increase its financial support for priests failed during the war years, as the "clergy of the 'Crusade' had to resign itself to indigence."[139] A worried hierarchy expressed its frustration over the government's reluctance to proceed to rapid derogation of the Republic's laws affecting the Church and the government's refusal to help the clergy financially at the 1937 and 1938 meetings of the Committee of Metropolitans. Although the archbishops recognized that the State was not enforcing such legislation, they complained that its continued existence placed the Church in a "legal state totally hostile to and dissonant with . . . the actuation of the Spanish Catholic people."[140]

The motives behind the regime's reticence were diverse. In 1937, Franco explained personally to Gomá that the government was unwilling to abrogate the Republic's divorce law as rapidly as the Church desired, for two reasons. First, the general offered a curious legal argument, namely, that a law of such fundamental importance could be changed only with the same juridical solemnity with which it had been promulgated in the first place. Second, he maintained that the government's need to win foreign support precluded "excessively rapid action" on its part.[141]

Other motives also inspired official policy. The regime felt no scruples about us-

137. Rodríguez de Aisa, *El Cardenal Gomá y la guerra de España*, pp. 56–57.

138. Redondo, *Historia de la Iglesia en España*, vol. 2, p. 75. For example, the regime did not suspend legal petitions for divorce until March 2, 1938, and did not abrogate the 1932 law on civil marriage until March 12 of the same year. Similarly, the 1933 Law on Religious Confessions and Congregations, so disliked by the Church, remained on the books until February 2, 1939. Alfonso Álvarez Bolado, "Guerra civil y universo religioso: Fenomenología de una implicación (IV)," *Miscelánea Comillas* (1990), vol. 48, p. 42; Rodríguez de Aisa, *El Cardenal Gomá*, p. 315.

139. Marquina Barrio, *La diplomacia vaticana*, p. 101.

140. Quoted in Rodríguez de Aisa, *El Cardenal Gomá y la guerra de España*, pp. 184–85.

141. Quoted in ibid., p. 148.

ing its political and financial muscle to pressure the Vatican on the patronage issue. In 1938, the new Nationalist ambassador to the Vatican argued that the cabinet should refrain from further concessions to the Church until negotiations for a future concordat were concluded to the government's satisfaction. The envoy urged it to use financial support of the clergy as a bargaining lever to force the Vatican's hand with respect to ecclesiastical patronage.[142] The regime adopted this strategy and followed a "carrot-and-stick" policy that yielded nothing to the aggressive regalist tactics of many an earlier Spanish government.

Ecclesiastical frustration with the regime's foot-dragging was also connected to clerical perceptions about its ideological foundations. Although Franco never intended to create a totalitarian State on the fascist model, he was shrewd enough to realize that his hold on power depended on his ability to deal with the factious hosts of the Spanish Right. The general had no specific political program in mind other than a desire to consolidate his position. He cleverly built "his peculiar little system" by juggling the contending interests of monarchists, Carlists, and followers of the Falange.[143]

Whatever the Falange's history and nature before the war, it offered the general a convenient mechanism for organizing "an authoritarian anti-leftist regime in an age of fascism."[144] Moreover, Franco's debt to Nazi Germany for military and financial assistance encouraged the regime to adopt fascist trappings. Although Franco manipulated the Falange into the position of the State's only authorized party, he never intended to convert it into a powerful organization capable of dominating the State.[145]

From the war's earliest days, Cardinal Gomá viewed the emergence of the Falange with a mixture of acceptance and suspicion. If, on the one hand, the party appeared committed "to Catholic unity," working towards the "restoration of the Spain of the Catholic Kings," there was, on the other, the danger of a possible "deviation" in an aconfessional or antireligious direction.[146] As time passed and the regime's totalitarian rhetoric resounded more loudly, the hierarchy's apprehensions about the party's role increased. Long concerned with protecting the Church's "liberty and independence" and understandably ignorant of Franco's real intentions,

142. Marquina Barrio, *La diplomacia vaticana*, pp. 90–92.

143. Stanley G. Payne, *Falange: A History of Spanish Fascism* (Stanford, 1961), p. 198.

144. Ibid., p. 200.

145. In 1937, thanks to the machinations of his brother-in-law, the ex–CEDA deputy Ramón Serrano Suñer, Franco secured the unification of the Falange and the Carlist Traditionalist Communion in a single party, the Falange Española Tradicionalista. The organization, however, existed in a condition of "total subordination to a state founded by military men." Stanley G. Payne, *The Franco Regime, 1936–1975* (Madison, 1987), p. 192.

146. Rodríguez de Aisa, *El Cardenal Gomá y la guerra de España*, pp. 28, 33. The British diplomat Bernard Malley recalled an interview with Gomá in which the cardinal declared that "he had perceived the grave danger of Nazi influence through the medium of the Falange Party." "Survey of the Church in Spain and of Its Attitude towards the Regime," ms., December 12, 1951, p. 7. Public Record Office: Foreign Office/371/102059.

the bishops feared the imposition of a fascist system based on the complete and absolute supremacy of the State in all areas of activity. The hierarchy viewed a decree of 1938 creating a single and obligatory student syndicate as a threat to the survival of Catholic organizations and saw another concerned with the regulation of charitable assistance as opposed to the Church's autonomy in a field of activity where it had long been active.[147] Bishops and the publishers of confessional newspapers and magazines, accustomed to freedom of the press since the days of the Restoration, were no less frustrated and resentful before the regime's unbending determination to control the Catholic press through censorship and a barrage of bureaucratic regulations.[148] The bishops' apprehensions about the regime's future course deepened upon the publication in 1937 of Pius XI's encyclical *Mit brennender sorge*, which condemned the principles of Nazism.[149]

Some priests, notably Father Fermín Izurdiaga, an unabashed Falange propagandist, saw no contradiction between the party and clerical objectives.[150] The bishops were less sanguine. Although Gomá repeatedly expressed his reservations about the Falange's role in private, it was the uncontrollable episcopal veteran of opposition to the Republic who first publicly challenged the apparent drift to totalitarianism. After returning to Spain as archbishop of Seville, Pedro Segura be-

147. Álvarez Bolado, "Guerra civil y universo religioso," pp. 46–47.

148. In 1938, for example, the authorities prevented the publication in a popular Jesuit magazine of articles and Vatican documents attacking racism. Andrés-Gallego, *¿Fascismo o Estado católico?*, p. 185. The government offices charged with controlling the press were dominated by pro-Falange figures, notably Dionisio Ridruejo and Pedro Laín Entralgo, whose policies favored the party's newspapers and magazines to the detriment of the Catholic press. The idea that Catholic newspapers should continue to enjoy the freedom they had possessed before the Civil War found little sympathy in official circles. Long a bulwark of the prewar Catholic press, *La Gaceta del Norte* of Bilbao found itself accused of carrying out "*a disturbing work*" by attempting "to conserve its character as a Catholic newspaper, distinguishing itself from other publications." Since the State was officially Catholic and all publications in Nationalist Spain were "equally Catholic; and the press being today an organism in the service of the State," the idea that a newspaper should pretend to the status of an "advanced post in the defense of Catholic doctrine and the interests of the Church can not be tolerated." Quoted in ibid., p. 148. In a series of interviews with Franco and other officials, Cardinal Gomá attempted to change official press policy but without success. This was not good enough for Cardinal Segura, who urged Gomá in a confidential letter of October 27, 1938, to organize a collective protest by the hierarchy. If the bishops did not protest the regime's initial efforts to control the Catholic press, "trampling upon the rights of the Church without our protest, later it will not be possible to contain the avalanche." Quoted in ibid., p. 152. A full account of Church-State conflicts over the press is found in ibid., chapter 4.

149. The encyclical was published on March 14, 1937. By April 16, Cardinal Gomá had obtained a full text from Cardinal Pacelli, the papal secretary of state. In view of official hostility and intense German pressure to prevent its publication in Spain, the cardinal was persuaded by Bishop Pla y Deniel to abandon his intention of securing Franco's permission to publish the text in favor of sending portions of the encyclical to the bishops to use as they saw fit. The full text was not published in diocesan bulletins until January 1938. Luis Suárez Fernández, *Francisco Franco y su tiempo* (8 vols., Madrid, 1984), vol. 2, p. 217, note 11.

150. Izurdiaga, a diocesan priest of Pamplona, was appointed to the Falange's office of propaganda and later served as one of its national councillors. These appointments, made without the required canonical permission of his bishop, irritated the Vatican. Gomá dared not push Franco too far on the matter, but he informed the general that ecclesiastical discipline and the Church's desire to remove the clergy from political activity made it desirable for Izurdiaga to give up his post. This appeal went unheeded. Rodríguez Aisa, *El Cardenal Gomá y la guerra de España*, pp. 186–88.

came convinced that the Falange intended to convert Spain into a thoroughly fascist State. The cardinal remained his own man, a resolute clerical conservative intent on combating excessive civilian interference in ecclesiastical affairs. He had thrown down the gauntlet before the Republic; he was prepared to do the same before the Nationalists. In 1938, the cardinal provoked the regime's anger by prohibiting the saying of Mass at a party manifestation, regarding such a service as nothing less than a "profanation" of its religious character.[151] In the face of this and other incidents, the regime became as determined as the Republican government of 1931 had been to have him removed from his position.[152]

Segura's clashes with government and party officials represented more than the picturesque jousts of an ecclesiastical eccentric. The regime's 1938 decision to proceed with a reorganization of associational activity along corporatist lines threatened the existence of the network of Catholic groups that had come into being under the aegis of social Catholicism.[153] The prospect of losing the organizational gains of decades sent shock waves through the Church. In a pastoral letter of January 1938, Segura criticized the suppression of Catholic associations already underway in Seville. The cardinal was not alone in expressing such sentiments. Eleven bishops published his pastoral letter in their diocesan bulletins, while the archbishop of Santiago defended the right of the Church's associations to exist on the grounds that "the State can never make a good Catholic."[154] Cardinal Gomá was no less disillusioned by the regime's policy. In 1939, he dared to tell Franco that the government was flagrantly annulling "an unquestionable right of the Church" with measures unequaled even "in the harshest times of the Republic."[155]

The cardinal primate's disenchantment deepened after the war's end. The ongoing suppression of Catholic associations and the regime's continuing intransigence on the patronage issue, directly linked to the question of financial support for the clergy, reduced Gomá to near despair. The cardinal's bitter cup filled to the brim when the regime suppressed the Confederación de Estudiantes Católicos in September 1939 in favor of a single syndicate of university students controlled by the

151. Ramón Garriga, *El Cardenal Segura y el Nacional-Catolicismo* (Barcelona, 1977), p. 260.

152. Segura also touched an "exposed nerve" of the regime in 1939, when he lamented the fate of imprisoned Basque priests held in the Carmona jail by complaining directly to the minister of justice. Lannon, *Privilege, Persecution and Prophecy,* p. 217.

153. The regime's corporatist reorganization meant the end of Catholic labor unions, teacher and student organizations and, eventually, of a key institution of social Catholicism, the Confederación Nacional Católico Agraria. A law of 1941 annulled the legislation of 1906 that had made the development of an effective Catholic agrarian movement possible and ordered the organization's integration into a single, vertical syndicate. The attempts of the CNCA's leadership to avoid losing its institutional identity came to nothing. Mateo Martínez, *Tierra de Campos: cooperativismo y syndicalismo agrario* (Valladolid, 1982), p. 204. It should be noted, however, that the regime did not suppress organizations of a narrowly religious character. Catholic Action survived, but its range of action was considerably restricted in comparison with its activities before the war.

154. Quoted in Álvarez Bolado, "Guerra civil y universo religioso," pp. 68–69.

155. Quoted in Marquina Barrio, *La diplomacia vaticana,* p. 205.

Falange, despite the hierarchy's intense lobbying efforts. Gomá's first pastoral letter after the war discreetly criticized the idea of a totalitarian State reigning supreme over all aspects of social activity and irritated official sensibilities by appealing for a "generous and splendid pardon" to end the bitter divisions produced by the conflict.[156] This diplomatically worded defense of the Church's right to autonomy on its own terms caused the regime to take an action that the Republic had never attempted. The Ministry of the Interior (Gobernación) imposed a "total and rigorous" ban on publication of the document. A deeply offended Gomá protested directly to Franco, only to receive a further dressing down. The pastoral letter, said the general, "filled many Spaniards with unease" because of the "doubts that it sowed in various of its passages."[157] Franco recounted the immense benefits the regime had bestowed on the Church, strongly implying that the hierarchy was not suitably grateful for the concessions showered upon it. Although the bishops rallied behind Gomá, many publishing the offending text in their diocesan bulletins, there was little else they could do other than make private protests to the authorities.

Gomá discovered that the regime entertained a very different idea of the "independence and liberty of the Church" from that sustained by the hierarchy and the Vatican. The ecclesiastical leadership welcomed official measures designed to reinforce Catholicism and to eliminate its perceived enemies. But for all practical purposes, the Church wished to return to the privileged situation it had enjoyed prior to 1931, while preserving the significant advantage of free episcopal appointment acquired by the papacy during the Republic and retaining intact the organizational network that had come into being through the initiatives of social Catholicism. The regime's response to the Church's pretension to enjoy the best of all possible worlds was straightforward. It desired a confessional State, but it had no intention of allowing either the hierarchy or the Vatican to interfere "too much" in its schemes for the political and social reorganization of the country.[158]

On balance, the Church saw its fortunes improve under the Nationalists, but, as so often in the past, it found itself dependent upon a regalist government whose view of civil-ecclesiastical relations left little room for the kind of institutional autonomy sought by the clergy for generations. The Church again paid a price for its privileges. The cost to what one historian has appropriately called a "mortgaged Church" proved high.[159] The dissolution of many of its key lay associations before

156. Quoted in Andrés-Gallego, *¿Fascismo o Estado católico?*, p. 200.

157. Quoted in Marquina Barrio, *La diplomacia vaticana*, pp. 205–6. Bernard Malley recalled that the galley sheets prepared by Gomá for publication of his pastoral letter in a Madrid newspaper "were returned to the writer scored in red pencil from beginning to end. A circular telegram was sent to all civil governors instructing them to prevent the circulation of the Pastoral in any form." "Survey of the Church in Spain," ms., p. 7. Andrés-Gallego maintains that censorship of the pastoral letter reflected the growing totalitarian direction of the regime's press and propaganda office by the autumn of 1939. *¿Fascismo o Estado católico?*, p. 202.

158. Marquina Barrio, *La diplomacia vaticana*, p. 60.

159. Raguer, *La espada y la cruz*, p. 245.

the State's vaguely totalitarian schemes of social organization destroyed the modernizing labor of decades. The disappearance of the associational infrastructure responsible for the success of the CEDA contributed to the failure of efforts, years later, to realize the old dream of creating a Catholic political organization in the form of a Christian Democratic party on the Italian model.

During the Civil War, the Nationalists identified religion and government more thoroughly than had any government since the waning days of absolute monarchy over a century earlier. Yet it also took measures, except in education and the control of public morality, designed to accomplish more or less what nineteenth-century liberals and twentieth-century republicans had attempted, to keep the Church on a tight leash by confining it to the realm of purely religious activities.

At its first meeting following the war's end, the Committee of Metropolitans showed that it was perfectly aware of the cost of the mortgage imposed on the Church by the regime. The agenda prepared by Cardinal Gomá expressed a deep sense of injury that many of the Church's claims were still unmet. In return for placing "all its weight in the service of the National Movement," the Church found that its "generosity" towards the regime had evoked "the meanness of the Government in different forms." As a result, the primate continued, "We find ourselves in a difficult moment in the life of the Spanish Church; an invasion of the forces of the civil power threatens us." Gomá hoped that civil-ecclesiastical tensions would not lead to "open persecution of the Church," but he expressed the fear that the regime desired a "gagged" Church designed only to serve the "interests of the State."[160] "The clergy," declared one official opposed to the regime's policy towards the Church, "was in a situation incomparably worse than in the days of Azaña."[161] The triumphalist rhetoric of the Crusade and the clerical optimism of 1936 seemed distant echoes, as the Church confronted the reality of its position in Franco's "New Spain."

160. Quoted in Marquina Barrio, *La diplomacia vaticana*, p. 219.
161. Quoted in ibid., p. 106.

CHAPTER XV

THE CHURCH AND FRANCO'S "NEW SPAIN," 1940–1953

On November 23, 1975, dignitaries of Church and State gathered in the great square before Madrid's royal palace for the funeral of Francisco Franco. Cardinal Marcelo González Martín, archbishop of Toledo, primate of the Spanish Church, and a conservative member of the hierarchy, preached the homily. After recalling the ceremony of May 20, 1939, in which Franco presented his "sword of victory" to Cardinal Gomá, the cardinal paid tribute to "this exceptional man" and expressed gratitude for his "stimulating fidelity" to nation and religion. The ceremonial head of the Spanish Church was not chosen by the new chief of State, King Juan Carlos I, to preach at the solemn service held four days later to celebrate the beginning of his reign. That honor fell to Cardinal Vicente Enrique y Tarancón, archbishop of Madrid, president of the Episcopal Conference and a strong advocate of change in civil-ecclesiastical relations. In the presence of the sovereign and Franco's last council of ministers, Tarancón expressed support for a political transformation that would allow "all citizens to participate freely and actively in the country's life." Within a new society governed by social justice, he continued, the Church would seek no privilege other than the right to preach its religious message.[1]

These homilies reflected different visions of past and future within the Spanish Church. The cardinal primate looked back nostalgically to the union of Church and State forged as a result of the Civil War; the archbishop of Madrid, aware of the

1. Quoted in Feliciano Blázquez, *La traición de los clérigos en la España de Franco* (Madrid, 1991), p. 232; "Homilía del Cardenal Enrique y Tarancón en la misa de San Jerónimo el Real," in *Los obispos ante la nueva etapa política* (Madrid, 1976), pp. 11, 12.

social and economic changes that had transformed the country since 1960, looked forward to a fundamental reassessment of the Church's position upon the introduction of the democratic reforms already being demanded by the political opposition and public opinion.

By 1975, many bishops, priests, and religious accepted the necessity of changes in the Church's privileged situation advocated for more than a decade by Cardinal Tarancón and other ecclesiastical moderates. Although the process of adapting to new realities was long, turbulent, and divisive, that it happened at all represented a remarkable transformation for the triumphant Church that developed as a result of close ties to the dictatorship in the two decades following the end of the Civil War. The political and religious impact of the Second Vatican Council (1962–1965), the resurgence of regional movements supported by the clergy in the Basque Provinces and Catalonia around 1960, the development of militant Catholic workers' associations and the hierarchy's rediscovery of the cause of social justice, the emergence of new episcopal and clerical generations, and the social changes introduced as a result of economic development all contributed to undermining the apparent consensus sustaining close ties between Church and State through the 1940s and 1950s.

National Catholicism

The gains achieved by the Church in the years following the Civil War projected the image of a powerful institution united in purpose and linked to the dictatorship in a relationship of "privilege unequalled since the dark days of Ferdinand VII's despotic rule."[2] It has become a historical commonplace to describe the ties binding the civil and ecclesiastical powers during the Franco era as "National Catholicism."[3] Some scholars dismiss the term as nothing more than a cliché, a simplistic cover incapable of portraying accurately the complexities of the Church's situation under the regime; others believe that the ideas identified with National Catholicism provided the Church with an effective ideological tool to justify its support of Franco and the privileges received in return.[4] There is little doubt that the premises of National Catholicism, which identified religion with Spanish nationalism, rejected liberalism and secularism, and exalted Franco as a providential savior of faith and nation, contributed to buttressing the regime's legitimacy in

2. Abel Plenn, *Wind in the Olive Trees: Spain from Inside* (New York, 1946), p. 87.

3. The origin of the term, National Catholicism, has been a source of controversy. Juan González-Anleo argues that it emerged in fully developed form in a work by José Pemartín entitled *¿Qué es lo nuevo?* first published in 1938. *Catolicismo nacional: nostalgia y crisis* (Madrid, 1975), pp. 101–4.

4. Among those questioning the historical value of the term are Rafael Gómez Pérez, *El franquismo y la Iglesia* (Madrid, 1986), p. 15; Francesco Amoveri, *Stato cattolico e chiesa fascista in Spagna* (Milan, 1973), p. 14. Others, however, see the term as embodying a distinct political-religious set of ideas crucial to the development of the regime's ideology. See, for example, the work of Alfonso Álvarez Bolado, *El experimento del nacional-catolicismo* (Madrid, 1976), chapter 5.

the mind of the public. Although these ideas appealed to the diverse constituencies supporting the dictatorship during its first two decades, they formed neither a coherent political ideology nor a specific program on which the factions of the Right could agree save for their commitment to the person of General Franco.[5]

Nor did they represent anything new in the vocabulary of Spanish Catholicism. Indeed, they had been in circulation for more than a century, although they took on a sharper edge as a result of the reaction of clergy and Catholic authoritarians of various stripes towards the Republic.[6] Insofar as there was anything novel about the romantic image of a triumphant Catholic Spain and its identification with a regime that apparently embodied its values, it lay in the militancy with which it was projected to the Spanish public and the world.

The crusading spirit produced by the Civil War among clergy and laity gave National Catholicism a distinctive if imprecise character. The idea of a Catholic Spain victorious over its enemies and a bastion of Christian civilization ready to embark on a vast campaign of spiritual reconquest in fulfillment of the nation's "universal destiny" reflected the historic preoccupations of Spanish Catholicism honed to razor sharpness by the conflict.[7] Whether such ideas could be sustained permanently, the definitive realization of the old dream of the "unity of Catholics" was doubtful. The history of Spanish Catholicism in the nineteenth and early twentieth centuries was one of internal division beyond the doctrinal realm. The hierarchy's public rhetoric disguised differences always lurking near the surface of Spanish Catholicism. Commitment to a common faith and the principles of National Catholicism proved just as incapable of realizing the Church's historic dream of achieving monolithic unity as had earlier attempts to forge a united front among Catholics. For a time, support for Franco and a regime that apparently had saved Catholicism from disaster threw a cover over these differences, at least in public. But the relative unity imposed by reaction to the Civil War could not and did not last forever. Despite repeated statements by the clergy and apologists extolling the triumph of cross and sword, the fact remains that National Catholicism proved a temporary phenomenon, a vigorous but circumstantial response of the Church and its supporters to the events of the 1930s.[8] In the end, National Catholicism was left behind, an archaic remnant in the midst of profound changes that took place within Spain and the Catholic Church as a whole.

Catholic defenders of the regime evoked a transcendent vision of religion's future that bore little relation to social reality. The "permanent victory" of the Na-

5. Fernando Urbina has called attention to the "little intellectual substance of the ideologues of 'NC,' who failed to develop fully [its] theological and ecclesiological suppositions." "Formas de vida de la Iglesia de España, 1939–1975," in Fernando Urbina et al., *Iglesia y sociedad en España, 1939–1975* (Madrid, 1977), p. 119.

6. Ibid., p. 113.

7. Pedro Cantero, *La hora católica de España* (Madrid, 1942), p. 71.

8. Javier Tusell, *La dictadura de Franco* (Madrid, 1988), p. 183.

tionalists appeared to open "unlimited horizons" certain to lead to the nation's complete re-Christianization.[9] Ecstatic predictions of this kind ignored the immensity of the problem of religious alienation among segments of the population. The abundant historiography on the Church's role under the Franco regime has shown that realization of this grand vision of a new age of religion promoted by a Catholic, authoritarian government became as firmly enmeshed in the tangle of politics and changing circumstances as had earlier attempts to return to the imagined golden age of sixteenth-century Catholicism so often evoked by earlier generations of clerical apologists.

Further, the theory of civil-ecclesiastical relations endorsed by the Church took little account of the practical difficulties involved in defining its arrangements with the regime. Clerics saw Franco's "New Spain" in the light of canon law as a world composed of two "perfect societies." The Church stood supreme in the religious sphere, the State in the temporal. As far as doctrine and ecclesiastical discipline were concerned, the civil authorities were obliged "to submit to the Church, exactly like any individual Catholic." In those "mixed questions" transcending the limits of each institution's independent field of action, Church and State were expected to resolve difficulties within an atmosphere of "perfect harmony."[10]

The concept of "perfect societies," however symmetrical the movement of its spheres in theory, did not correspond to the hard facts of the regime's political life. Franco valued the Church as an institutional bulwark of his power. But the regime was never free either of regalist preoccupations or of the general's concern with balancing the forces of the Right sustaining his power. The Church and lay activists, drawn primarily from the ranks of the Asociación Católica Nacional de Propagandistas and Catholic Action, formed only one of the political "families," "clans," or "coteries" manipulated by Franco to sustain the dictatorship.[11] Despite the privileges secured from the regime, the Church found itself in a situation similar in some respects to its position under the early Restoration. Stripped of the instruments of autonomous action developed over the three decades before 1936, the Church was reduced again to functioning primarily as a lobby, admittedly a powerful one, engaged in behind-the-scenes jockeying as one of the regime's interest groups, along with the military, the Falange, monarchists, and Carlists.

The new order made substantial concessions to the Church in education and the control of public morality. Some terms of the civil-ecclesiastical mortgage fa-

9. Enrique López Galvá, *Futura grandeza de España según notables profecías* (2d ed., La Coruña, 1941), p. 268.

10. Joaquín Azpiazu, *El Estado católico* (Burgos, 1939), p. 54. For a full discussion of the theory of "perfect societies," see José María Belloso, "'Sociedad perfecta' y 'sacramentum salutis,' dos conceptos eclesiológicos, dos imágenes de Iglesia," in *Iglesia y sociedad en España*, pp. 315–33.

11. Sergio Vilar, *La naturaleza del franquismo* (Madrid, 1977), p. 28; Amando de Miguel, *Sociología del franquismo* (5th ed., Madrid, 1975), p. 11; Tusell, *La dictadura de Franco*, pp. 200–202; Guy Hermet, *Les catholiques dans l'Espagne franquiste* (2 vols., Paris, 1981), vol. 1, pp. 334–35.

vored clerical interests; others represented significant losses in important areas where the Church had long been active. The regime denied it the right to organize labor unions, agricultural syndicates, and student associations, while subjecting the Catholic press to rigorous censorship until 1966. Nor, in a single-party State, was there any question of allowing the appearance of a Catholic political party.

In 1967, Angel Herrera, elderly veteran of decades of struggle on behalf of the Church, now cardinal and bishop of Málaga, made his last public statement. To the irritation of the authorities who prohibited its publication, Herrera posed an astonishing question given the confessionality of the State and the prominent role of professed Catholics within it for three decades. Why had Spanish Catholicism "not succeeded in influencing national public life?"[12] The cardinal perceived a "striking contradiction" between the Catholic principles theoretically inspiring the State and their lack of application at a practical level, especially in the realm of social policy. Although always remaining loyal to Franco, Herrera correctly identified one of the glaring weaknesses of the general's Catholic Spain. Despite years of bombastic rhetoric exalting religion as the foundation of State and society, the regime proved as adept as nineteenth-century liberal governments had been at imposing on the Church a compartmentalization of function designed to remove it from certain areas of activity. In return for substantial concessions in a limited sphere, the regime expected the Church to confine itself to the religious domain and to avoid involvement in social, economic, and foreign policy questions except when it suited the government's purposes. Although Franco's personal commitment to Catholicism and its role within the State was sincere, the regime's policy came down to purchasing clerical support in return for acceptance of a more limited institutional role than the Church had played during the Restoration, the Primo de Rivera dictatorship, or the Second Republic.

For more than two decades, the Church willingly accepted the terms of its mortgage with the regime. But from the beginning, an undercurrent of frustration at the restrictions imposed on what was called the "liberty of the Church" lingered among clergy and committed laity. Although bishops and lay activists from Catholic Action remained loyal to Franco during the 1940s and 1950s, they struggled to break through the exclusions imposed by the regime. As circumstances changed during the 1960s, some bishops, priests, and religious began to question not only this attempt to confine the Church to a narrow role in a time of economic change and social upheaval, but also its identification with an authoritarian State.

As a result, relations between Church and State, even at the height of National Catholicism during the 1940s and 1950s, were characterized less by "perfect harmony" than by what one historian has called "conflictive accommodation."[13] Un-

12. Quoted in José Sánchez Jiménez, *El Cardenal Herrera Oria: pensamiento y acción social* (Madrid, 1986), p. 247.

13. Hermet, *Les catholiques*, vol. 1, pp. 15–16.

til the momentous changes of the 1960s, no period was more difficult for the Church than the years between 1940 and 1944, as the regime attempted to strengthen its institutional foundations.

The Church and the Regime, 1940–1944

Cardinal Gomá's apprehensions about the Church's future within the Nationalist State echoed only within the narrow walls of the hierarchy. Beyond, the war's end produced a surge of exultant rhetoric in the name of patriotism, religion, and the triumph of faith and nation over its enemies. "Victory! Victory! Victory!" proclaimed the Jesuit journal *Razón y Fe* in its first postwar issue. "The host reddened by the Kremlin's diabolic light" stood abased by the "clarity of God" and the humiliation inflicted by the "Lord of Armies."[14]

Religious services following the conflict's end gave exuberant expression to the mingled values of religion and nationalism as a "victorious Christianity" flexed its muscle. In June 1939, thousands, many perched on tree limbs and lampposts, viewed the Corpus Christi procession in Madrid. Marchers and onlookers alike intoned hymns, sang the anthems of the Falange, and gave "constant *vivas* to Christ the King, the Spanish army and its unconquerable *Caudillo*." These impressive displays appeared to initiate "an affirmation of faith" of extraordinary proportions under the motto, "One *Caudillo*, one faith, and advance in the name of God and eternal Spain."[15]

Despite the image of religious and political unity projected by these manifestations, civil-ecclesiastical relations were anything but smooth between 1940 and 1942. Although in 1939 the government removed one obstacle by agreeing to support the clergy financially, the impasse between Madrid and the Vatican over episcopal patronage continued. Spanish authorities viewed the election of Pope Pius XII in 1939 unsympathetically because of his support as Vatican secretary of state of the policy of accommodation towards the Republic.[16] The new pontiff soothed the regime with a speech on April 16, 1939, praising Nationalist Spain for sallying forth "in defense of the faith and Christian civilization," but the Vatican moved cautiously on the problem of resolving differences with Madrid.[17] The pope took a somewhat more conciliatory stance towards the protracted negotiations with the government that had begun before his election, although hard-liners in the papal curia opposed any concessions on ecclesiastical patronage.

The Vatican proceeded slowly for other reasons. Aware of the regime's abolition of Catholic labor, agricultural, and student associations and fearful of the emer-

14. "La oración hispánica de la victoria," *Razón y Fe* (1939), vol. 30, no. 400, pp. 5, 6, 7.
15. *Ya*, June 9, 1939, February 7, 1940.
16. Antonio Marquina Barrio, *La diplomacia vaticana y le España de Franco* (Madrid, 1983), p. 158.
17. Quoted in ibid., p. 160.

gence of a totalitarian State under the Falange, renamed the Falange Española Tradicionalista y de la JONS (FET), it resisted yielding too readily to the government's unrelenting pressure for an agreement. Sentiments such as those expressed in 1939 by the influential pro-Falange minister of the interior, Ramón Serrano Suñer, already regarded suspiciously by the Vatican as pro-German and an advocate of a totalitarian political organization for the country, created further apprehension. A "Catholic spirit" inspired "our movement," the minister declared, but "it does not signify political dependence with respect to Rome. We are not disposed to follow the caprices of Rome."[18]

Prolonged and often tense negotiations finally produced a limited diplomatic agreement through a *convenio* (1941) that fell short of the concordat desired by the government.[19] Franco secured one of his regalist objectives as the Vatican accepted a modified version of royal patronage.[20] Historians agree that the papacy got the better of the bargain by securing recognition of the first four clauses of the 1851 concordat that enshrined Catholicism as the religion of the State, and by winning Madrid's commitment not to legislate on so-called "mixed" questions affecting civil-ecclesiastical relations without the prior consent of the Holy See.[21] From a political perspective, the Vatican limited its compromise with the regime by avoiding the total endorsement that a concordat would have implied.[22] The pope and his advisors remained uneasy about Spain's political organization and the government's foreign policy. With characteristic pragmatism, they realized that too close an identification with Franco's Spain could damage the Holy See's diplomatic maneuvering among the European powers, especially after the beginning of the Second World War. The Vatican also knew that international Catholic opinion viewed the Spanish dictatorship with something less than unanimity.

18. Quoted in ibid., p. 165. There is little doubt that Franco wished to construct "a fully institutionalized and certainly partly fascist authoritarian system . . . in Spain." Stanley Payne, *The Franco Regime, 1936–1975* (Madison, 1987), p. 234. The Vatican nourished other grievances. In a note to the Spanish embassy to the Holy See (June 5, 1940), it complained of the censorship of the pastoral letters of Segura and Gomá, the regime's refusal to allow Cardinal Vidal i Barraquer to reoccupy his diocese, censorship of the Catholic press, and the activities of some government officials who "committed offenses against ecclesiastical liberty and independence." Luis Suárez Fernández, *Francisco Franco y su tiempo* (8 vols., Madrid, 1984), vol. 3, pp. 83–84.

19. The *convenio* was negotiated by Serrano Suñer on the part of the Spanish government. Although one of the regime's hard-liners on the patronage issue, more so than Franco, after becoming minister of foreign affairs in 1940, Serrano Suñer eventually moderated his position, largely because of an internal crisis within the regime that threatened his political influence. Payne, *The Franco Regime,* p. 287. Serrano Suñer's dominance aroused deep hostility among the other "families," especially the military, although monarchists also resented his opposition to restoring the monarchy. Ibid., p. 285.

20. The agreement provided that the nuncio and the government should negotiate a list of six suitable candidates for presentation to the pope, who would select three. This list would then be forwarded to Franco for the final selection.

21. José Manuel Cuenca Toribio, *Relaciones Iglesia-Estado en la España contemporánea, 1833–1985* (Madrid, 1985), p. 97; Marquina Barrio, *La diplomacia vaticana,* pp. 290–91. The *convenio,* however, was opposed by some Basque clergy and by Cardinal Vidal i Barraquer, who informed the Vatican that it did not offer the Church sufficient guarantees. Ibid., p. 289.

22. Cuenca Toribio, *Relaciones Iglesia-Estado,* p. 97.

Official propaganda hailed the *convenio* as a brilliant example of Church-State harmony, but the agreement did not immediately smooth the turbulent waters of civil-ecclesiastical relations. In fact, bishops were not appointed to fill episcopal vacancies until November 1942, for two reasons. First, the Vatican objected to the government's insistence that all diocesan prelates should take an oath of loyalty.[23] There was nothing original about this practice, which had been employed by successive governments during the nineteenth and early twentieth centuries. The Vatican disliked the requirement on principle and objected even more to the wording devised by the regime. Months of further negotiations finally produced a formula acceptable to both parties.

Second, Serrano Suñer, counseled by his close friend and chaplain to the FET's youth wing, the Benedictine Justo Pérez de Urbel, delayed the process of making new appointments while a search for candidates sympathetic to the Falange was carried out.[24] Investigations of priests being considered for episcopal appointments carried out in 1942 by provincial representatives of the FET and the national security police found few enthusiastic supporters of the Falange. Indeed, one FET investigator reported that 95 percent of the clergy were "indifferent" in their attitude towards the organization, although the vast majority of the priests investigated were found to be supporters of the regime. But clerics identified with Basque nationalism or sympathy for the Republic received strongly negative assessments. Father Wenceslao Mayora, parish priest of Durango (Guipúzcoa), accused of protecting Basque nationalist clergy, was judged dangerous to the "National Cause." Similarly, Father Salvador Rial, vicar general of the Tarragona archdiocese, who remained at his post during the Civil War, was censured for having "blindly followed the directions of Cardinal Barraquer." Despite his affirmations of loyalty to the regime, Rial was regarded as opposed to the "National Cause" and as a separatist.[25]

Clerical and papal apprehensions about the Falange's designs frustrated this attempt to pack the episcopacy. But the regime secured the appointment of bishops

23. For a discussion of the controversy over the oath, see Marquina Barrio, *La diplomacia vaticana*, pp. 297–305. The hierarchy avoided becoming embroiled in the dispute, although Cardinal Segura, never one to mince words, told the British diplomat, Bernard Malley, "the episcopal oath was nothing but flagrant Gallicanism and a disgraceful humiliation for the Church." Quoted in Michael E. Williams, *St. Alban's College, Valladolid* (London and New York, 1986), p. 225.

24. Marquina Barrio, *La diplomacia vaticana*, pp. 292–93.

25. "Lista de personas propuestas como posibles obispos con informes de la D. G. S. y FET de las JONS," 1942, in *Documentos inéditos para la historia del Generalísimo Franco*, ed. Fundación Nacional Francisco Franco (4 vols., Madrid, 1992–1994), vol. 3, pp. 102–3, 122–23, 141. A few candidates were singled out for their loyalty to regime and party. The vicar general of Jaén, Rafael García y García de Castro, received praise for his "enthusiasm and adherence" with respect to the FET. His relations with its local branch were characterized by "respect and affection." Not surprisingly, García's career advanced well, first to the bishopric of Jaén and later to the archdiocese of Granada. Despite his involvement in the machinations of the authoritarian Right during the Republic, the celebrated clerical ultra, Canon Aniceto de Castro Albarrán, fared less well. He was identified as an "enemy of Germany" who had little sympathy for the Falange. Ibid., pp. 80, 91–92.

who would not rock the proverbial boat, though at neither this or later stages was it capable of creating a completely docile hierarchy. The appointment of Bishop Enrique Pla y Deniel of Salamanca to the primatial see of Toledo in October 1941 provides an example of the perils involved in the selection process from the government's perspective. The regime would have preferred the pro-Falange bishop of Madrid, Leopoldo Eijo y Garay, but the Vatican disliked the bishop's close identification with the FET. Pla y Deniel seemed a reasonable second choice. His pastoral letter of 1936, "The Two Cities," which had elevated the Civil War to the status of a religious crusade, had won him Franco's esteem. Pius XII, irritated over the overtly political character of some of Pla y Deniel's public statements, was less enthusiastic, although, after a round of diplomatic jousting, he agreed to the appointment.[26]

Over time the regime had some cause to regret its decision. It overlooked what Cardinal Gomá and the papal nuncio had seen when they initially suggested his name. Pla y Deniel held strong views about the restrictions imposed on the "liberty of the Church." Diminutive in stature but combative in spirit, he waged an ongoing behind-the-scenes campaign against press censorship of Church publications and the Falange's totalitarian pretensions. In 1945, for example, a draft law on primary education, which promised the Church less than it expected as a result of pressure from the Falange, provoked the cardinal's vigorous response. After berating the minister of education, Pla y Deniel visited Franco and threatened to resign from parliament and attack the proposed legislation in public if it were not altered. The general "argued, evaded, pleaded, and finally yielded."[27] Although never questioning either the regime's legitimacy or the benefits it provided the clergy, the cardinal was aware of the institutional instability of a personal dictatorship and the danger it posed to the long-term interests of the Church, a perception derived, perhaps, from the Primo de Rivera years, when he served as bishop of Ávila.

Having worked as a young priest in Palau's Acción Popular after the turn of the century, Pla y Deniel also refused to accept the Church's exclusion from social action among industrial workers. A 1940 law on syndical unity prohibited independent labor unions and forced workers into a State system of vertical syndicates dominated by the Falange. Although Catholic unions experienced indifferent success before the Civil War, the legislation represented a significant defeat for the Church, which found itself excluded from a field where it had once been active.[28]

26. Marquina Barrio, *La dipomacia vaticana*, pp. 294–95.

27. Emmet John Hughes, *Report from Spain* (New York, 1947), p. 65; Jesús Iribarren, "La Iglesia y el franquismo en la postguerra: 'Ecclesia' y el Cardenal Pla y Deniel," *Revista de Fomento Social* (1977), no. 128, pp. 426–37.

28. After becoming bishop of Salamanca in 1935, Pla y Deniel promoted a social Catholic agenda by encouraging the development of trade unions and other initiatives designed to benefit workers. Mary Vincent, *Catholicism in the Second Spanish Republic: Religion and Politics in Salamanca, 1931–1936* (Oxford, 1996), pp. 123–24. The 1940 law made no reference to religion, although in 1944, the regime tossed a small bone to the Church by authorizing the appointment of "ecclesiastical counsellors" in the official syndicates. The priests receiving these appointments, however, had little influence over the movement.

Pla y Deniel never directly challenged these undemocratic and bureaucratically controlled labor organizations, but he became patron and protector of a specialized branch of Catholic Action, the Hermandades Obreras de Acción Católica (HOAC), founded in 1946 to engage in "apostolic" activities among workers. Disliked by the regime from the beginning as a disguised, incipient Catholic trade union, it found a stout defender in the cardinal primate, who protected the HOAC from periodic official assaults and the criticism of some of his episcopal colleagues until the formation of the Episcopal Conference in 1966. This was not what the regime had in mind when it secured his appointment in 1941.

Resolution of the impasse over episcopal nominations healed one of the sores irritating civil-ecclesiastical relations. Others remained. Pius XII insisted upon the return of Cardinal Vidal i Barraquer to his diocese. But the government frustrated repeated papal initiatives to this effect and even considered putting this "bad Spaniard" on trial in absentia for treason.[29] But no issue appeared more critical to the Vatican, some bishops, and clergy than the regime's political and social organization. For the Church, the creation of a single-party State in 1937 raised the specter of a totalitarian government, a possibility that appeared even more dangerous to the clergy following the outbreak of the Second World War. Father Jesús Iribarren, editor of the journal *Ecclesia*, official organ of Catholic Action and, indirectly, of the hierarchy, recalled the omnipresence of German propaganda during the early 1940s and the obstacles raised by the authorities to publication of Pius XI's 1937 condemnation of Nazism.[30] Iribarren feared the implementation of ideas advanced in the officially controlled press for the creation of "a totalitarian State, hierarchical and imperial, beneath the unlimited authority of Franco." For a Church quietly apprehensive about the FET's objectives, the suggestion that "the Falange is the way, the truth, and the life" stirred deep fears.[31]

Clerical and lay opinion was far from unanimous in its attitude towards either the Falange or Nazi Germany.[32] Bishop Eijo y Garay, described by a British diplo-

---

Hermet, *Les catholiques*, vol. 1, pp. 257–58. The hierarchy was uneasy about the formation of a totalitarian syndical organization as early as 1937, when the Committee of Metropolitans appointed a special commission to examine the question. Rafael Belda, "La Iglesia y el sindicalismo vertical," in *Iglesia y sociedad en España*, p. 216.

29. For the regime's implacable campaign against the cardinal, see Marquina Barrio, *La diplomacia vaticana*, pp. 129–41.

30. Jesús Iribarren, *Papeles y memorias: medio siglo de relaciones Iglesia-Estado en España: 1936–1986* (Madrid, 1992), p. 60.

31. Quoted in ibid., p. 63.

32. The attitude of clergy and laity towards the Falange, totalitarianism, and Nazi Germany has generated considerable controversy. Defenders of the Church have argued that the bishops and the associations of Catholic Action were resolutely opposed to racist theories, and opposed to totalitarianism, whether in its Spanish or foreign forms. Manuel Vigil y Vázquez, *El drama de la Acción Católica y el "Nacional Catolicismo"* (Barcelona, 1990), pp. 17–20, 48; Mercedes Montero, *Historia de la Asociación Católica Nacional de Propagandistas: la construcción del Estado confesional, 1936–1945* (Pamplona, 1993), pp. 109–10; Francisco Verdera, *Conflictos entre la Iglesia y el Estado en España: la revista "Ecclesia" entre 1941 y 1945* (Pamplona, 1995), pp. 47, 69–70, 89–92. Alfonso Lazo has challenged this view and argued

mat as one of "those bishops who have gone out of their way to claim what is little short of divine right for the mandate of General Franco," remained a firm defender of the FET, serving as religious advisor to its youth wing, the Frente de Juventudes, and as a member of the party's Junta Política. The bishop saw the Frente, governed by "pontifical teachings and the doctrine of the Falange," as "the generation that will save the country."[33] The Falange also won limited support among the lower clergy, while young members of Catholic Action felt no scruples about enlisting in the Blue Division sent by Franco to join the German army fighting in Russia to save "Christian civilization."[34]

In general, the lower clergy, especially in the Basque Provinces, Old Castile, Catalonia, and Navarra, viewed the regime's pro-German policy with apprehension, fearful that an Axis victory would move the regime to a system based on Nazi racial theories and the idea of the State's absolute supremacy over family, Church, and education. An English priest who met with members of the Barcelona clergy in 1942 recalled, "I have not yet become acquainted with anyone imbued with racial sympathies, in fact the majority are inclined towards the allies."[35] The British government, aided and abetted by members of the English hierarchy and the rector of the English seminary at Valladolid, Edwin Henson, waged an effective propaganda war among the clerical rank and file designed to convince priests that Nazi Germany represented a neo-paganism incompatible with Christian values.[36]

---

that the response of bishops and laity was far more ambiguous. He argues that despite periodic tension between the Church and the Falange over specific issues, the Catholic press fully supported the movement. Although recognizing that clergy and laity firmly rejected the racialism of Nazi Germany, he notes that the historic cultural anti-Semitism long associated with the Spanish Right received abundant echo in Catholic newspapers and journals of opinion. He also maintains that opposition to Germany, although strong in 1939 after the invasion of Catholic Poland, changed to sometimes enthusiastic support following the invasion of Soviet Russia but shifted again when it became evident that Germany was about to lose the war. Alfonso Lazo, *La Iglesia, la Falange y el fascismo: un estudio sobre la prensa española de posguerra* (Seville, 1995), pp. 53, 117–21, 138, 155–64, 171, 175, 186–87. Lazo's interpretation of the ambiguous attitude of *Ecclesia* towards totalitarianism has been challenged by Verdera, *Conflictos entre la Iglesia y el Estado*, pp. 69–70, note 9.

33. Bernard Malley, "Survey of the Church in Spain and of Its Attitude towards the Regime," ms. December 12, 1951, p. 11. Public Record Office, Foreign Office/371/102059; quoted in Cantero, *La hora católica de España*, p. 30. Eijo y Garay, like the author of this book, who served later as archbishop of Zaragoza, minimized the totalitarian aspects of the Falange in favor of an emphasis on its "Catholic" character, "inspired by a Christian concept of the individual, the State, life and history." Cantero, *La hora católica de España*, pp. 27–28. It is likely that the bishop of Madrid saw a favorable attitude towards the Falange as offering the Church an opportunity to use it as means of achieving an "easier conquest of the masses." Marquina Barrio, *La diplomacia vaticana*, p. 221. For the strategy of pro-Falange clerics, see also Juan José Ruiz Rico, *El papel político de la Iglesia católica en la España de Franco, 1936–1971* (Madrid, 1977), pp. 92–94.

34. Pedro Cantero's 1942 book cited above provides a detailed justification by one clergyman of a close and cooperative relationship between the Church and the Falange. "Los jóvenes de Acción Católica, soldados apóstoles en Rusia," *Ecclesia*, March 22, 1942, p. 14. In Seville, Cardinal Segura clashed with one of the cathedral's canons, whose violent sermons against the United Kingdom and the United States finally led the prelate to order his suspension. Williams, *St. Alban's College*, p. 225.

35. Quoted in Williams, *St. Alban's College*, p. 221.

36. The archbishop of Westminster and other English bishops sent gifts of money and in kind to their colleagues in Spain. Professors at the English college made periodic trips through the country dis-

To what extent were these fears justified? The regime's foreign policy between 1940 and 1942 rested on Franco's calculating conclusion that Germany would win the war and that Spain must be ready to pick up whatever spoils could be secured at its end. When it became evident by the end of 1942 that Germany would not achieve a quick and decisive victory, the general had second thoughts. He jettisoned Serrano Suñer from the Ministry of Foreign Affairs and began moving with equal calculation towards a policy of neutrality, while remaining convinced until 1944 that the Axis powers would triumph.[37]

The question of the Falange, its plans for the political organization of the nation, and its attitude towards the Church is more complex. Following the 1937 unification of rightist groups in the FET, membership ballooned as the organization became a sprawling agglomeration dominated less by pre-1936 militants than by self-serving opportunists. Although Franco, as artifice of the FET, intended to maintain it as one of the "families" of the regime necessary to sustain his political balancing act, he was also determined to trim the sails of activists who wished to convert the party into the country's dominant and exclusive political force. By the end of 1941, the general successfully carried out a policy of "domesticating" the FET so that it posed no real challenge either to his personal power or the balancing formula on which it rested.[38]

More than once, the FET proclaimed its commitment to Catholicism as a fundamental principle of the "New Spain" that had emerged from the Civil War. The bloated membership emerging from the decree of unification ensured the presence within it of conservative Catholics who wished to have no truck with the totalitarian schemes of some militants.[39] Among FET "old shirts" (*camisas viejas*), an undercurrent of anticlericalism persisted that identified the Church with the capitalist oligarchy of early-twentieth-century Spain that they were determined to displace. They did not question the role of Catholicism as the religion of the State, but more than any other group within the regime they wished to confine the Church to a constricted area of purely religious activity. When clergymen worried about the totalitarian scheming of the FET, they were primarily concerned about its effects on the Church's ability to broaden its range of action. Many bishops and priests also identified militant elements of the Falange with Nazism and feared the introduction into Spain of its policies on the family, race, and the supremacy of the State.

In any event, the hierarchy was not in a position to assess with any clarity the complex, behind-the-scenes maneuvering over foreign and domestic policy. Be-

tributing pro-Allied leaflets, especially in seminaries. Even the Germans recognized that British propaganda efforts among the clergy were successful despite the obstacles placed in their way by the Spanish authorities. Ibid., pp. 221–22; Marquina Barrio, *La diplomacia vaticana*, pp. 262–64.

37. For a discussion of the regime's foreign policy during the Second World War, see Payne, *The Franco Regime*, chapters 13, 14.

38. Ibid., pp. 286–94.

39. Ibid., pp. 203–4.

tween August 1940 and October 1941, the key post of archbishop of Toledo, carrying with it leadership of the Committee of Metropolitans, remained vacant, thereby depriving the Church of a means of influencing official policy. The bishops found themselves as much in the dark about the course of the Second World War as were ordinary citizens, forced to rely on a largely pro-German official press. To secure accurate information about the conflict, the editor of *Ecclesia* was forced to dispatch an agent to listen to BBC shortwave broadcasts in the basement of the British embassy.[40] By 1942, Catholic publications, which for a time saw a German victory over communism as desirable, began to abandon their ambiguous stance. Increasingly, they saw a Nazi triumph as an immediate and frightening possibility with dangerous implications for the Church. *Ecclesia* attacked "the pagan concept of the absolute State," while in 1943 the bishops condemned the Spanish translation of Alfred Rosenberg's racialist *Myth of the Twentieth Century*.[41]

Between 1940 and 1944, the immediate influence of the "Catholic family" in the give-and-take of internal political struggles was minimal.[42] Although the lines separating the regime's interest groups were fluid, in general the "Catholic family" represented laymen from the ACNP and Catholic Action who were close to the hierarchy. All ministers were without exception professed Catholics, and one, José Ibáñez Martín, minister of education and closely linked to the ACNP, helped consolidate the Church's earlier gains in an area that it judged vital to its interests. Members of the ACNP and Catholic Action also filled numerous secondary government positions.[43] But the marginalization of former members of the CEDA, including its former head, José María Gil Robles, and the suspicions directed against Angel Herrera and his followers for their policy of accommodation towards the Republic, prevented the most important figures of the political Catholicism of the early 1930s from playing a significant role. Fierce resentment against them on the part of Serrano Suñer, the Falange, and authoritarian monarchists frustrated attempts to revive *El Debate* in 1939.[44]

40. Iribarren, *Papeles y memorias*, p. 76.

41. Lazo, *La Iglesia, la Falange y el fascismo*, pp. 176, 177.

42. Members of the ACNP were ready and willing to participate in the construction of a "powerful and Catholic Spain," but found that their willingness to do so was "inefficacious because of the lack of confidence that the propagandists continued to arouse in the ruling organs of the nation, due to their former collaboration with the Republic." Montero, *Historia de la Asociación Nacional Católica de Propagandistas . . . 1936–1945*, p. 117.

43. A. Sáez Alba, *La Asociación Católica de Propagandistas: reproducción y métodos de la derecha permanente* (Paris, 1974), introduction, pp. xxxiii–xxxvii.

44. The proprietor of *El Debate*, Editorial Católica, managed to publish a single issue in 1939. Although an ex-deputy of the CEDA that owed so much to the newspaper, Serrano Suñer in his new totalitarian guise prevented it from resuming regular publication. For years, *El Debate*'s supporters, especially those grouped around Angel Herrera, tried to persuade the regime to allow its revival. All such efforts failed. The government permitted the EC to publish a secondary newspaper of the chain, *Ya*, but appointed a toadying editor, Juan José Pradera, a friend of Serrano Suñer and an enemy of Herrera, thus preventing the corporate owner from exercising even limited control over its editorial policy. For the struggle over *El Debate*, see Javier Tusell, *Franco y los católicos: la política interior española entre 1945 y*

In these circumstances, the Church and its lay supporters found themselves on the political margins without a decisive voice in the battles being waged within the regime over domestic and foreign affairs, except in the realm of education. As a result, the hierarchy, still uncertain about the kind of State that was being formed between 1940 and 1942, reduced complex struggles over domestic and foreign policy to a straightforward formula of "Serrano-Falange-Nazism" that failed to take into account either the actual balance of forces within the regime or Franco's always enigmatic intentions. This conclusion was understandable given the aggressive tone of the Falange's rhetoric in 1940–1941 in the wake of German military success.[45]

In May 1942, the papal nuncio, Archbishop Gaetano Cicognani, urged the hierarchy to speak out forcefully against the racial and antireligious ideology of Nazi Germany.[46] Although apprehension about the possibility of the emergence of a totalitarian regime was widespread among the bishops, few had the courage to follow this advice.[47] Indeed, published photographs of certain bishops, their arms raised in the Falange salute, disgusted many members of the lower clergy.[48]

Not all bishops proved so passive. Archbishop Pla y Deniel, preferring to work indirectly through *Ecclesia*, used it in 1943 to publish a statement of Cardinal Van Roey of Belgium rejecting outright a claim made frequently in the official press that Germany was fighting for the cause of Christian civilization. But the cardinal primate was careful not to rock the boat too much in his attitude towards the regime's domestic and foreign policy. In fact, the editorial policy of *Ecclesia* was more ambiguous than its defenders have maintained. In 1941, for example, *Ecclesia* lavished praise on members of Catholic Action in the Blue Division and described the German offensive against Soviet Russia as "a new episode of our crusade, . . . the continuation of the work of defending the Cross."[49] One of the few bishops to state

---

1957 (Madrid, 1984), pp. 26–32; *Ya: medio siglo de historia, 1935–1985*, ed. José María Escudero (Madrid, 1984), pp. 4–5.

45. During this period, the Falange dominated the regime's press and propaganda through the press sub-secretary of the Ministry of the Interior, Antonio Tovar, and the FET's director-general of propaganda, Dionisio Ridruejo. Payne, *The Franco Regime*, p. 286.

46. Marquina Barrio, *La diplomacia vaticana*, p. 312, note 564.

47. The British diplomat, Bernard Malley, identified several bishops who were strongly anti-German, Rafael Álvarez de Lara of Guadix, Javier Lauzurica Torralba of Almería, Carmelo Ballester Nieto of Vitoria, and Antonio García y García of Valladolid. Williams, *St. Alban's College*, p. 224.

48. Iribarren, *Papeles y memorias*, p. 64.

49. "Bajo este signo, muchos jóvenes de Acción Católica se alistan en la División Azul," *Ecclesia*, August 1, 1941, p. 9. Similarly, the journal of the youth wing of Catholic Action, *Signo*, did not disguise its sympathy for Germany and its hostility towards the Allies between 1940 and 1942. Hermet, *Les catholiques*, vol. 2, pp. 143–45. On the issue of the relationship between the Church and the FET, Pla y Deniel declared in 1943 that there was no obstacle to young members of Catholic Action belonging to the Frente de Juventudes. "In a Catholic State with a single party," he declared, "there ought to be intimate cooperation between a Catholic State and the Church"; but he took care to add the disingenuous statement that such a cooperative relationship did not imply that the Church was subject "to any political regime." "No hay incompatibilidad entre las juventudes políticas y las de Acción Católica ni entre éstas y otras asociaciones de apostolado," *Ecclesia*, June 19, 1943, p. 11.

his views openly, Fidel García Martínez of Calahorra, issued a 1941 pastoral letter that angered the authorities for its frank denunciation of Nazism. British propaganda agents thought the statement so effective that they printed thousands of copies for distribution throughout the country.[50]

Cardinal Segura periodically infuriated the regime and won the praise of a British diplomat as "the only brave man on the bench of bishops" for repeated public attacks on racism, Nazism, and the Falange.[51] In a pastoral letter of April 2, 1940, the cardinal declared that it was his duty to speak out "against the enemies of the Holy Church" in favor of "religious liberty" within a society in which the press was "totally controlled by the public power." Segura attacked the censorship imposed on Cardinal Gomá's pastoral letter of 1939 and "the cultural interchanges arranged by our public powers with other nations officially distant from the Catholic faith," a clear allusion to Nazi Germany.[52]

These remarks, as well as the prelate's deliberate snub of Franco when he visited Seville during Holy Week 1940, the cardinal's even more audacious homily on the meaning of the word *caudillo,* and his frequent battles with the Seville Falange angered Franco, who was determined to remove him as archbishop.[53] The Falange regarded him as its "*enemy number one,*" a favor the prelate returned by informing the Vatican that "the Falange . . . is the great enemy of the Spanish Church: in it are gathered all the old enemies of the Church: and from this trench . . . in which they see themselves protected by the State they are firing with impunity . . . against our sacrosanct Religion."[54] The government filed a strong protest with the Vatican over Segura's conduct, but Franco abandoned his intention to expel the cardinal, fearing that an unpleasant comparison would be made between such an action and the prelate's expulsion by the Republic in 1931.[55] Segura remained on the scene, ready

50. Marquina Barrio's suggestion that half a million copies of the pastoral letter were printed by the British falls wide of the mark. *La diplomacia vaticana,* p. 312, note 564. Bernard Malley recalled that fifty thousand were printed in London by the Ministry of Information with the bishop's permission. "Survey of the Church in Spain," ms., pp. 10–11. According to the British embassy, the archbishop of Zaragoza published the pastoral letter of the bishop of Calahorra in his diocesan bulletin only to have all copies seized by the police. Williams, *St. Alban's College,* p. 221, note 34.

51. Quoted in Williams, *St. Alban's College,* p. 225.

52. Quoted in Ramón Garriga, *El Cardenal Segura y el Nacional-Catolicismo* (Barcelona, 1977), p. 273. Segura was referring specifically to a cultural agreement (of 1939) between the Spanish and German governments. The agreement provoked deep episcopal concern and a protest to Franco from Cardinal Gomá, but only Segura dared to question it publicly.

53. In one of his famous Saturday homilies or *sabatinas,* Segura shocked the congregation by asserting that the traditional meaning of *caudillo* was "captain of thieves." Ibid., p. 274.

54. Marquina Barrio, *La diplomacia vaticana,* p. 244; quoted in Garriga, *El Cardenal Segura,* p. 273.

55. For the government's campaign against Segura, see Marquina Barrio, *La diplomacia vaticana,* chapter 6. According to Serrano Suñer, the minister of foreign affairs, General Juan Luis Beigbeder, proposed expelling Segura. Franco, although "wounded and indignant" at the cardinal's conduct, refused to take action because "he understood the damage that this very grave mistake would cause him personally and politically." The general believed that it would be "inadvisable" to revive memories of the Republic's expulsion of Segura. Ramón Serrano Suñer, *Entre el silencio y la propagnada: la historia cómo fue. Memorias* (Madrid, 1977), p. 274.

and willing to induce attacks of official acid indigestion, which he did with frequency until the mid-1950s.

Hostility among bishops and priests towards the Falange and the government's foreign policy between 1940 and 1942 must be kept in perspective. A timid hierarchy provided little coherent direction to the undercurrent of dissatisfaction circulating within clerical ranks. The bishops had no intention of placing the gains secured from the regime at risk, nor were they willing to throw down the gauntlet before Catholics present in all the regime's "families," including the ACNP and Catholic Action, who did not view a German victory in the same light as the Vatican did. Occasional public expressions of hostility towards Nazism and totalitarianism by prelates such as Cardinal Segura and Bishop García Martínez and behind-the-scenes maneuvering did not constitute opposition to Franco by any stretch of the imagination.

The hierarchy and the clergy continued to see the general as a savior who had bestowed immense benefits on the Church in the name of a "providential enterprise."[56] Nor did clerical apprehensions about the possible establishment of a totalitarian State signify the presence of support for even moderate political change in a liberal, democratic direction. The premises of National Catholicism remained firmly in place. In a 1941 pastoral letter, "The Triumph of the City of God and the Resurrection of Spain," Pla y Deniel affirmed the necessity of abandoning the "liberalism that has led [Spain] to ruin." Further, the prelate demanded "a rigorous disinfecting . . . of corrupt doctrines" among "the misguided masses."[57] For all the vitriol directed by Segura against the Falange, Franco, and Nazism, the cardinal remained deeply conservative, hostile to modern liberal values.[58]

To what extent clerical attitudes towards the FET and Germany restrained Franco is a difficult question to answer. It is unlikely that alone they would have made much difference. Joined to the opposition of some of the regime's other interest groups to the Falange and the government's pro-Axis policy, it undoubtedly played a role in tilting the balance of forces against a totalitarian organization of the State and towards neutrality in the foreign arena. In the end, Franco's keen manipulative sense of the need to preserve the coalition that sustained his power, and the course of the Second World War itself, proved more decisive. For the Church, the legacy of 1940–1942 took the form of chronic suspicion towards the FET that would endure for decades and lead to future conflicts. It also left in place an undercurrent of resentment that the Church had been denied the liberty of action to which it believed itself entitled.

56. "La Acción Católica y el Jefe del Estado," *Ecclesia*, January 1, 1941, p. 4.

57. Quoted in José Angel Tello, *Ideología y política: la Iglesia católica española, 1936–1959* (Zaragoza, 1984), p. 110.

58. In 1944, for example, Segura published a pastoral letter that showed his characteristic and contradictory conservative philosophy as he attacked both racism and the modern liberal values censured

Between 1940 and 1944, the Church successfully defended the gains in education secured during the Civil War. The departure of Pedro Sáinz Rodríguez from the Ministry of Education in 1939 deprived the Church of a strong anti-Falange friend at court. Dissatisfaction with the law on secondary education (1938) enacted as a result of the minister's initiative by no means disappeared among FET militants. In 1942, a prominent official of the movement employed in the Ministry of Education reaffirmed the Falange's demand for total control of the school system save in the realm of religious and moral instruction. "Our integral conception of the State exacts educational hegemony." Further, he attacked the dominant role of the religious orders in education, this "amorphous mass . . . directed for a specific purpose by elements foreign to state policy." If action were not taken "to inculcate in the new generations the spirit and sense of national-syndicalist norms" through the schools, the future of a State inspired by the Falange's principles would be at risk.[59] In a series of editorials during 1941 and 1942, *Ecclesia*, reflecting the hierarchy's views, rejected outright these demands for a State educational monopoly.[60]

Opposition within the FET to the Church's educational role was not well organized, but it surfaced frequently enough to alarm a hierarchy already uneasy about the movement's Sindicato de Estudiantes Universitarios (SEU) and the recently formed Frente de Juventudes (1940).[61] Clerical apprehension deepened as a draft law on university education devised by Sáinz Rodríguez remained unpassed because of the opposition of the FET and regalist-minded officials to the creation of Church-controlled universities. In fact, the Falange never constituted a serious threat to the Church's hold over education.[62] FET activists dominated the SEU, but its influence over the rank and file of university students did not run deep. According to a government order of 1941, classes in political education in the schools were made obligatory, and the Frente de Juventudes was assigned responsibility to teach them. But the organization lacked the means to carry out effective indoctrination, especially in the private schools of the regular clergy. A former student recalled that the political education dispensed in his school applied nothing more than a "patina" of Falange ideas that the religious order administering the institution did not take seriously.[63]

The appointment of José Ibáñez Martín as minister of education in Franco's sec-

---

by Pope Pius IX in the *Syllabus of Errors*. "Carta pastoral del Cardenal Segura sobre los principales errores modernos," *Ecclesia*, February 19, 1944, p. 7.

59. Quoted in Gregorio Cámara Villar, *Nacional-catolicismo y escuela: la socialización política del franquismo* (Jaén, 1984), pp. 186–87.

60. Manuel de Puelles Benítez, *Educación e ideología en la España contemporánea* (Barcelona, 1980), p. 379.

61. In 1940, for example, the national congress of the SEU demanded the suppression of private schools that refused to submit to the absolute control of the State. The assembly also attacked the 1938 law on secondary education because of the privileges it accorded to the schools of the religious orders. Cámara Villar, *Nacional-catolicismo y escuela*, p. 216.

62. Ibid., p. 193.

63. Ibid., p. 197.

ond cabinet (1939) also ensured that the Church's earlier gains in this area would be preserved. Although a member of the ACNP, the new minister also belonged to the Falange, as did several of his principal collaborators. As a result, he pursued a more conciliatory policy towards the educational pretensions of the FET than had his predecessor. But in its essentials his program did not alter the educational system that had taken shape during the Civil War. The 1938 law on secondary education so disliked by sectors of the Falange remained on the books. The minister pursued a strategy of consolidating the pro-Church educational system already in place, while seeking to avoid "excessive reactions on the part of the Falange."[64]

This policy meant that the Church did not secure everything it wanted. Suspicious of the SEU, it hoped to secure a beachhead in the universities through a new law, similar to that of 1938, regulating secondary education. Ibáñez Martín, aware of the importance attached by the FET to its student movement, abandoned Sáinz Rodríguez's project in favor of a compromise enacted in 1943. The Church pursued two objectives: first, to convert the State universities into bastions of Catholicism while limiting the ability of the SEU to indoctrinate students; second, to achieve the historic objective of creating its own institutions of higher learning. Militants within the FET were no less determined to impose on university life "a total discipline regulated by the SEU and inspired by the Falange."[65] The 1943 law provided something for everyone. It recognized the right of the Church to establish universities, although postponing any action until a concordat was concluded with the Holy See. It also proclaimed the Catholic character of the university and established a special office to organize obligatory classes in religion. But the law also confirmed the monopoly of the SEU and required that university rectors be members of the FET.[66]

The legislation of 1943 resounded with the rhetoric of the Falange, but its enactment did not represent a decisive victory for the party, as the Church secured a modest institutional foothold in universities. Moreover, the law must be considered in relation to other areas affecting higher education where members of the ACNP and Catholic Action had not been idle. The end of the Civil War left numerous professorships vacant before the exile and purge of republican academics. Angel Ayala, the Jesuit founder of the ACNP, had long urged its members to seek positions in education as part of a broader campaign to penetrate "the vital nerves of society . . . from posts of authority."[67] The organization moved quickly to encourage its members to seek university chairs.[68] To fill professorships, Ibáñez Martín turned to the largely bourgeois constituency of these Catholic associations as well as to the members of a little known group, Opus Dei. By the end of 1940, the *propagandistas* achieved significant progress in their campaign for "the con-

64. Ibid., p. 122.
65. Quoted in ibid., p. 225.
66. Ibid., pp. 220–22.
67. Quoted in ibid., p. 160.
68. Montero, *La Asociación Nacional Católica de Propagandistas . . . 1936–1945*, pp. 144–45.

quest of [university] chairs." Although numbering less than six hundred members in 1940, the ACNP formed a conservative Catholic elite bound together by professional, class, and sometimes family connections ideally suited to maneuvering its members into academic positions.[69]

Their success meant that the Falange hope of exercising total control over universities was doomed. Moreover, in 1942 the government approved the creation of autonomous residential colleges (colegios mayores) within universities that allowed the religious orders and, eventually, the ACNP and Opus Dei to play an influential role in higher education. By 1944, colleges established by the Jesuits, Dominicans, Salesians, and other orders were functioning on several campuses. Their appearance raised another barrier to the imposition of ideological uniformity by the SEU.[70]

By 1944, the Church's position within the regime was stronger than it had been in 1940. The *convenio* of 1941 removed some of the difficulties in civil-ecclesiastical relations, while reaffirming Catholicism as the religion of the State. Over time, clerical fears of a totalitarian Spain linked to Nazi Germany proved exaggerated. The Church consolidated its hold over education. Members of the Catholic elite enrolled in the ACNP and Catholic Action flourished as never before within the world of competing interest groups characteristic of the regime, although their direct political influence was limited. Catholic views on morality found ready acceptance among government officials, who embarked on moralizing campaigns similar to those of the Primo de Rivera era.

The less favorable terms of the Church's mortgage with the regime also continued in place. With the exception of *Ecclesia* (from 1945) and diocesan bulletins, the Catholic press remained subject to rigorous censorship. Although the FET's political sails had been trimmed by Franco, it remained on the scene, an object of constant clerical suspicion. The system of officially controlled labor syndicates prevented any form of social action on the part of the Church, although in 1945 early signs appeared of clerical restlessness with the regime's failure to deal effectively with the widespread misery and poverty that prevailed throughout the country.[71] Finally, there loomed over both the regime and the Church the unsettling implications of an Allied victory in the Second World War.

69. Sáez Alba, *La Asociación Católica de Propagandistas*, introduction, pp. xxii, xl–xliv. Members of the ACNP secured 15.6 percent of the 217 chairs in all faculties, with the exception of law, filled between 1940 and 1945. They won 30.6 percent of the available chairs in law faculties. Montero, *La Asociación Nacional Católica de Propagandistas . . . 1936–1945*, p. 225.

70. Cámara Villar, *Nacional-catolicismo y escuela*, pp. 230–31.

71. In 1945, Bishop Antonio de Pildain of the Canaries published a pastoral letter calling for action to remedy the problem of hunger and disease, which had reached a "lamentable" stage in his diocese. Tello, *Ideología y política*, p. 150; Enrique Martínez Lozano, "La Iglesia ante la evolución socieconómica," in *Iglesia y sociedad en España*, p. 180. The pastoral letter won the enthusiastic support of *Ecclesia*, which defended Pildain against the accusation of the Falange press that he was giving "unconscious support to communism." Verdera, *Conflictos entre la Iglesia y el Estado*, pp. 187–89.

Collaboration and Frustration, 1945–1953

In 1944, Franco moved Spain towards full neutrality in view of the course of the Second World War. This decision failed to impress the Allies, who had pressed the general to move in this direction since 1942. As the conflict drew to a close, public opinion in the Western democracies became increasingly hostile to a regime that had cooperated with Nazi Germany. Aware of the need to recast the government's image in dramatically changed international circumstances, Franco acted in the summer of 1945. Although the general had no intention of compromising his power, he implemented measures aimed at creating an institutional structure less dependent on the Falange, one that offered, on the surface at least, some recognition of civil rights.[72]

The Church and the "Catholic family" occupied an important place in this scheme. Through the appointment of prominent Catholic Action member Alberto Martín Artajo as minister of foreign affairs, Franco attempted to enhance the regime's "Catholic image . . . in order to win the support of the Vatican and reduce the hostility of the democracies."[73] For the Church, the opportunity to move from the political margins to a position of greater influence at the Falange's expense proved irresistible. Although Martín Artajo entertained doubts about accepting a cabinet post on the grounds that it would compromise the theoretically apolitical character of Catholic Action, Archbishop Pla y Deniel had no reservations and urged him to enter the government, as did Angel Herrera.[74]

There was nothing new about this strategy of seeking to influence public affairs within a closed, oligarchic system by inserting members of the Catholic elite into official positions. The theories developed by Angel Ayala decades earlier and promoted by Herrera afterward were directed towards this goal. Ecclesiastical confidence in Franco's good intentions also appeared to promise generous rewards in return for "Catholic" collaboration. The Church saw an opportunity to consolidate

72. These changes involved a cabinet reorganization that reduced the FET's influence and an attempt to diminish the totalitarian aspects of the regime in favor of "an authoritarian administration based on law." The showpiece of this external transformation was the *Fuero de los Españoles,* promulgated on July 17, 1945. Its terms promised Spaniards many of the civil rights enjoyed in the Western democracies, but the law contained other provisions that gave the government the power to curtail these liberties as it saw fit. Payne, *The Franco Regime,* pp. 349, 350–51.

73. Ibid., p. 349. Alberto Martín Artajo had a long record of activity, first, as an activist in Catholic student associations, and later, during the 1930s, as secretary-general and vice president of Catholic Action. In 1940, he became president of its national committee, a post he retained until his appointment as minister.

74. Tusell, *Franco y los católicos,* pp. 61–62. After the fall of Serrano Suñer in 1942, the ACNP began to entertain hopes for a larger role in government. During 1943 and 1944, it began "shaping a political solution for the institutional vacuum of Spain" based on opposition to totalitarianism and the excessive powers of government. A paper presented to the organization's circle of studies in 1944 demanded that the State should revoke "measures which injure the liberty, property, the rights of individuals and their legitimate associations." Montero, *La Asociación Nacional Católica de Propagandistas . . . 1936–1945,* pp. 255, 267, 298.

the benefits already secured from the regime and expand the "liberty of the Church" into new areas. The enactment of a law on primary education in 1945 and the removal of censorship from *Ecclesia* in the same year seemed harbingers of even better things to come.[75]

Beyond the goal of obtaining specific advantages, the Church faced the historic problem of Spanish Catholicism in its political dimension. How could it build a united front among Catholics capable of permanently sustaining a State that served its interests? Although militants of Catholic Action never questioned Franco's role, as the war drew to a close, mindful of its political significance for Spain, they began to develop a more flexible approach to the regime's institutional development. In 1944 and 1945, a series of articles in *Ecclesia* and publications of the ACNP suggested that the time had come to move from a personal dictatorship and its arbitrary consequences to a "State of law" governed by traditional juridical principles and institutions stripped of totalitarian trappings. At a more practical level, the hierarchy became "deeply preoccupied about the vital matter of the succession to General Franco in the event of his death or incapacitation."[76]

Now firmly entrenched in the leadership of the Spanish Church, Archbishop Pla y Deniel embraced this cautious new direction in pastoral letters published in *Ecclesia* on May 13 and August 28, 1945.[77] In the first, the primate praised the recently passed law theoretically endowing Spaniards with civil rights (*Fuero de los Españoles*).[78] He also called for enabling legislation to put the law into practice, the end of censorship, and reestablishment of the right of association. On this last point, Pla clearly had the Falange in mind, warning that "every monopoly or the obligatory nature of a single organization would imply the fundamental destruction of the liberty affirmed" in the *Fuero*.[79] In the second, the archbishop appealed for a general amnesty ("Let the prisons be opened") and the termination of judicial prosecutions arising from the Civil War. He reaffirmed his commitment to the "liberty of the Church": a "Church subject to the civil power . . . cannot be the true Church founded by Christ." His words on the country's political future were even

75. Despite strong resistance to the law on the part of the FET, it was enacted because of intense pressure from the hierarchy. At one point, Archbishop Pla y Deniel threatened to resign from the regime's rubber-stamp parliament and publicly attack an early Falange version of the legislation. Cámara Villar, *Nacional-catolicismo y escuela*, p. 249.

76. Tusell, *Franco y los católicos*, pp. 48–49; Malley, "Survey of the Church in Spain," ms., p. 12.

77. A minority of bishops had serious reservations about Pla y Deniel's strategy. Bishop Eijo y Garay feared that the initiative might lead to the restoration of the monarchy in the person of Alfonso XIII's son, the conde de Barcelona, whom he regarded as dangerously liberal. Bishop Blanco Nájera of Orense viewed the Allied victory not as an opportunity to transform the regime but as a device for reintroducing democracy, Freemasonry, and communism into Spain. Hermet, *Les catholiques*, vol. 2, p. 186.

78. There were earlier indications of Pla y Deniel's flexibility. Upon taking office in 1942, for example, he broached a theme that most of his episcopal colleagues avoided by rejecting a policy of vengeance against the Republic's supporters and appealing for "an hour of reconciliation" among all Spaniards. "El servicio de Dios no nos aleja del sacrificio por la Patria," *Ecclesia*, April 4, 1942.

79. Quoted in Iribarren, *Papeles y memorias*, p. 95.

more surprising: "The [civil] war was not undertaken to raise up an autocratic State over a humiliated nation."[80] The time had come, the archbishop maintained, for the regime to undertake a political transformation: "We believe that the end of the World War and international circumstances urgently counsel the total and definitive restructuring of the Spanish State."[81]

Similar views were held by Angel Herrera, who reemerged from the political shadows where he had languished since returning to Spain in 1943.[82] Now an ordained priest and soon to be appointed bishop of Málaga, Herrera continued to exert enormous influence over the elite of Catholic Action. More than any other figure, he inspired the strategy of collaboration with the regime that Martín Artajo attempted to implement.[83] Like the archbishop of Toledo, Herrera believed that the regime needed to recast its institutional foundations to become a "State of law" protecting the dignity of the human person in order to avoid becoming, he later said privately, "a clock mechanism mounted in emptiness."[84] Early in 1945, Herrera spoke directly to Franco, although with little effect, about the necessity of transforming the regime, restoring *El Debate,* and creating a new Catholic social party.

Neither Pla y Deniel's nor Herrera's words could have fallen sweetly on the ears of many of the regime's supporters. The primate was advocating neither a challenge to Franco, whom he repeatedly praised in public statements, nor political change in a liberal, democratic direction. Pla y Deniel called for the end of censorship, but he also advocated a "rigorous press law" to prevent "the dangerous manipulation of [intellectual] explosives" by journalists.[85] The archbishop of Toledo's shift from the crusading militancy of his pastoral letter of 1936 to one of greater flexibility arose in part from his pragmatic assessment of the international situation. It also reflected his judgment that the "liberty of the Church" would be considerably advanced within a State based on stable institutions and legal principles capable of providing the limited pluralism that would permit the clergy to break through the exclusions imposed by the regime during its formative period.[86] Similarly, Herrera's desire for change implied neither rejection of Franco nor endorsement of democracy. He had

80. Quoted in ibid., pp. 95–96.

81. Quoted in ibid., p. 96.

82. Herrera had left Spain in 1936 to study for the priesthood in Fribourg, Switzerland. His activities before the Civil War, as well as his attempt to prevent the execution by the Nationalists of a prominent member of the Unió Democràtica de Catalunya, caused him to be regarded with deep suspicion by the Falange. Advised to keep a low profile by some within the regime, he served as a parish priest in Santander after his return to Spain. Tusell, *Franco y los católicos,* p. 20.

83. Ibid., p. 42.

84. Quoted in ibid. Herrera's views on the need to transform the regime through stable institutions involving respect for moderate civil liberties and permanent institutions capable of surviving into the future are reproduced in *El pensamiento de Angel Herrera: antología política y social,* ed. José María García Escudero (Madrid, 1987), pp. 230–33.

85. Quoted in Iribarren, *Papeles y memorias,* p. 95.

86. Tusell, *Franco y los católicos,* p. 71. Bernard Malley offered a similar interpretation. Bishops, clergy, and activist laity "believe that Spanish experiments with universal suffrage produced nothing but frustration and disaster and that the country needs an authoritarian government, which, while guaranteeing human rights, would prevent the misuse of freedom and protect the nation from subversion and

little sympathy, for example, with the postwar Italian model of a secular State dominated by a Christian Democratic party. Indeed, if change were to come, he maintained, it would occur only if Franco wished it.[87] In the end, Catholic advocates of a political transformation wanted the regime to eliminate the Falange, establish governing institutions that represented public opinion in some ill-defined way, and introduce a form of constricted political and intellectual pluralism.

These ideas represented something new in the regime's internal dialectic, but they did not form a detailed or coherent blueprint for action. Nor were they free of contradiction. The archbishop of Toledo endorsed the *Fuero de los Españoles,* but the civil rights it guaranteed in theory scarcely applied to Spain's tiny Protestant minority, which suffered constant harassment bordering on persecution at the hands of the authorities. Between 1947 and 1954, the hierarchy remained silent in the face of periodic campaigns of violence, arrests, and imprisonment inflicted on religious dissenters.[88]

Insofar as the political ideas of the "Catholic" family embodied a specific program, it was through Alberto Martín Artajo, who early in his tenure of office presented them to Franco, albeit in piecemeal fashion. The minister's plan contained no suggestion for radical change. He argued that the institutions created in the wake of the Civil War were ad hoc arrangements incapable of providing the regime with an effective, permanent foundation. Spain needed to establish, therefore, "a representative regime without diminishing authority" through the use of "traditional Spanish institutions."[89] Martín Artajo explicitly rejected introducing political parties, individual suffrage, and unlimited freedom of the press, although he urged the elimination of censorship. On the political front, he called for reestablishing the monarchy and stripping from the FET the remnants of its authority in the labor syndicates and the field of political indoctrination.[90]

For a time, Martín Artajo believed that Franco would accept this scheme. As al-

---

anarchy. . . . A majority of bishops would appear to look to an eventual restoration of the Monarchy with due safeguards for control of mass organizations of the Left." "Survey of the Church in Spain," ms., p. 12.

87. Tusell, *Franco y los católicos,* p. 290; "El comienzo del colaboracionismo católico con el franquismo," *Iglesia, Estado y sociedad en España, 1930–1982,* ed. Joaquín Ruiz Giménez (Barcelona, 1984), p. 208; Rafael Diaz-Salazar, *Iglesia, dictadura y democracia* (Madrid, 1981), p. 135.

88. Cardinal Segura did not remain silent. In pastoral letters of 1947, 1949, and 1952, he attacked the Protestant danger in Spain with his usual rhetorical excess. Segura did not call for violence against religious dissenters, but there is little doubt that his furious words threw more wood on the fire of hostility against Spanish Protestants. Manuel López Rodríguez, *La España protestante: crónica de una minoría marginada, 1937–1975* (Madrid, 1976), pp. 38–42. Although the government tolerated the episodic persecution of religious dissenters, the instransigence of the hierarchy on the issue irritated the regime because it complicated the task of establishing improved relations with the Western democracies, particularly the United States. The government privately protested to the papal nuncio about Segura's inflammatory 1949 pastoral letter because it was convinced that "it is imperative to maintain Spain isolated from any international controversy such as those that could be created by the violent criticisms of Cardinal Segura against Protestantism." Quoted in Suárez Fernández, *Francisco Franco y su tiempo,* vol. 4, p. 309.

89. Tusell, *Franco y los católicos,* p. 85.

90. Ibid., pp. 85–87.

ways, the general was prepared to pick and choose among the ideas presented to him, but he had no intention of accepting anything that appeared to compromise his power. Representatives of the FET viewed the minister with deep suspicion, while one of the general's close advisors, Luis Carrero Blanco, devout Catholic though he was, opposed introducing changes that passed beyond the purely cosmetic.[91]

The hope of a modest transformation expected by the "Catholic family" with Martín Artajo's entrance into the government proved illusory. Franco had no intention of modifying the regime in accord with "Catholic" aspirations. The FET remained on the scene, even more suspicious of Catholic Action and its clerical supporters. In 1948, for example, an extremist Falange publication attacked the ACNP for its allegedly lukewarm attitude towards Franco and the nation. Playing upon one of the regime's patriotic mottoes, it called members of the Catholic association "imbeciles before God and Country."[92] Repeated initiatives for a press law eliminating censorship failed with regularity. Franco made one institutional concession by agreeing to the reestablishment of the monarchy in 1947 but made no move to find a king to sit upon the throne. It has been persuasively argued that it was the general and not the Church who derived most benefit from the "collaboration" of the "Catholic family."[93] The hierarchy publicly defended the regime during the period of international ostracism, 1946–1950, thereby strengthening the very system it hoped to modify.[94] If anything, the bishops became more vociferous in their support of Franco after 1945 than they had been before.[95] The clergy naturally welcomed the diminished role of the Falange after 1945. Opposition to the FET on the part of the hierarchy and the elite of Catholic Action during this period undoubtedly encouraged Franco, but it is likely that the general would have followed the same policy anyway, in view of international circumstances.

The program advanced by the "Catholic family" in 1945 did nothing to create the "unity of Catholics" that the hierarchy had seen for generations as essential to the Church's interests. Many professed Catholics in the regime's other clans rejected it outright, while a minority of past and present activists in the ACNP and Catholic Action objected to a collaborationist policy that in their judgment compromised the Church further with an authoritarian regime. José María Gil Robles, the former head of the CEDA who had begun his personal journey from a politi-

91. Ibid., pp. 182–83, 99.

92. Quoted in ibid., p. 195.

93. In his fundamental work on the period, Tusell has argued that the program of Martín Artajo failed utterly to produce any significant change in the regime. He has also argued that in considerable measure Franco "deceived" the "Catholic family" in order to reinforce Spain's international situation. Ibid., pp. 209, 444.

94. In November 1946, the American ambassador left Madrid, while on December 16, the General Assembly of the United Nations voted to urge member states to withdraw their envoys from Madrid. An earlier report to the Security Council had labeled the regime as fascist. Payne, *The Franco Regime*, pp. 356, 358.

95. Hermet, *Les catholiques*, vol. 2, pp. 198–200.

cally ambiguous past to a democratic future, told Herrera that Martín Artajo's entrance into the government represented "a grave error" that would cause "the greatest damage to the Church" by identifying it with a despised, dictatorial regime.[96] The "Catholic" alternative promoted by Pla y Deniel, Herrera, and the elite of Catholic Action led the Church into another of the political dead ends it had entered so often in the past. Insofar as it represented anything positive, it showed that some within the Church were thinking about the future, although still imprisoned within the walls of support for Franco. Whether this "possibilist" approach contained the germ that eventually allowed many clergy and laity to consider alternatives to the regime during the 1960s, as has been suggested, is debatable.[97] Sooner or later, the heterogeneous character of Spanish Catholicism with respect to politics and society was bound to escape from the restraints imposed by National Catholicism.

The jockeying associated with the initiative of the "Catholic family" was conducted beyond public view for the most part. It did not dramatically affect relations between the Church and the regime. With the totalitarian option effectively blocked, the Church settled in to enjoy and enlarge the benefits it had received at Franco's hands. Government financial support for the reconstruction of ecclesiastical buildings destroyed during the Civil War and for clerical salaries provided the material security so long desired by the hierarchy. Religious activities of every kind multiplied. Bishops sat in Franco's rubber-stamp parliament and on the Council of State, while priests held membership on numerous official boards and commissions.[98] The Church contemplated the restoration of the religious monopoly it had possessed before 1931 with complete satisfaction. In 1948, the first statement of the Committee of Metropolitans issued since the Collective Letter of 1937 dealt with none of the questions troubling the hierarchy in private. Rather, it defended Catholicism's religious monopoly, denounced the "liberty of cults" as an "error," and attacked foreign criticism of the regime's policy towards Protestantism.[99]

96. Quoted in Tusell, *Franco y los católicos*, p. 75. These differences grew between 1947 and 1951 following the 1947 referendum restablishing the monarchy but providing no sovereign. This measure caused a break in relations between the regime and the conde de Barcelona, whose commitment to a constitutional monarchy had already strained his relations with Franco. Gil Robles led a minority of the ACNP and Catholic Action in supporting the pretender. The former CEDA leader's contacts with exiled opponents of the regime also exacerbated tensions between "collaborationists" and anti-Franco figures from the "Catholic family." Ibid., pp. 166–78.

97. For the "possibilist" case, see Tusell, "El comienzo del colaboracionismo católico con el franquismo," p. 208.

98. Santiago Petschen, citing clerical participation in official bodies, such as the Council of State, the Council of Charity and Social Works, and the Institute of Spanish Culture, concluded, "Practically speaking, the Church was present throughout the [regime's] network of institutions." *La Iglesia en la España de Franco* (Madrid, 1977), p. 29.

99. "Metropolitanos a fieles sobre la propaganda protestante en España," May 28, 1948, in *Documentos colectivos del episcopado español, 1870–1974*, ed. Jesús Iribarren (Madrid, 1974), pp. 243, 244. This statement shows how firmly the hierarchy remained committed to maintaining the Church's religious monopoly and how grateful it was to the regime for imposing severe limitations on Protestant re-

Civil-ecclesiastical waters were calmer after 1945 than before, but they were not entirely free of turbulence. Clerical resentment over the censorship of Church publications simmered on; periodic skirmishing with the FET continued. A few episcopal loose cannons continued to crash upon official sensibilities. Cardinal Segura seized every occasion to show his displeasure with Franco both at a personal level and through formal protests. In 1947, he rejected an official request to urge the faithful of his diocese to vote in the referendum called to approve reestablishing the monarchy. He regarded the initiative as "this disreputable manoeuvre of the Head of State."[100] Bishop García Martínez irritated the authorities again by questioning the ethical and theological justifications for the referendum. Archbishop Olaechea of Valencia and Bishop Rubio Montiel of Burgo de Osma also expressed reservations about the referendum. The latter "made no secret of his opposition to the continuation of a semi-totalitarian regime and on the occasion of the referendum he made it known that he would be absent from his diocese when the polling took place."[101] Bishop Antonio de Pildain, already viewed with hostility by the authorities for his statements of 1944 and 1945 criticizing the regime's social and economic policies, angered them further in 1946 by attacking the State's patronage rights over episcopal appointments as a "decayed and sad anachronism which is unpleasant for the Church, discredits the State, and deprives the clergy of prestige."[102]

Between 1951 and 1953, a more serious conflict occurred over a draft law proposing to alter the 1938 legislation on secondary education. On this occasion, the struggle was not with the Falange, but, ironically, with the minister of education, Joaquín Ruiz Giménez, whose "Catholic" credentials were impeccable.[103] Wishing to impose a measure of educational standardization on a chaotic educational system, the minister and his collaborators proposed to subject the graduates of Church schools to a rigorous examination process and supervise more closely the general quality of education dispensed in private schools. However moderate in content, the proposed reform led to vigorous protests from the bishops and the regular clergy, who regarded the draft law as nothing less than a regalist intrusion. In the end, difficult negotiations involving Cardinal Pla y Deniel, the papal nuncio,

ligious practice. The government's policy was based on a highly restrictive interpretation of Article 11 of the 1876 constitution. The statement, directed in part to answering the criticism especially of French, American, and English Catholics, also served the regime's political interests abroad. Tusell, *Franco y los católicos*, pp. 133–34.

100. Segura made this comment to Bernard Malley. "Survey of the Church in Spain," ms., p. 10.

101. Ibid., pp. 10–11. According to Bernard Malley, Cardinal Pla y Deniel "cautiously approved" the referendum on the grounds that it was necessary for the institutional transformation of the regime.

102. Quoted in Petschen, *La Iglesia en la España de Franco*, p. 17.

103. Like Martín Artajo, Ruiz Giménez had been active in Catholic student associations. He was also a member of the ACNP. Beginning in 1939, he participated in various international Catholic groups, notably Pax Romana. These contacts served him well during his tenure as ambassador to the Holy See (1948–1951) and minister of education (1951–1956).

and the Vatican produced a compromise. Although the legislation did not threaten the gains secured in 1938, the battle over the new law showed that the Church remained vigilant before anything that appeared to compromise its educational predominance.[104]

The pastoral letters of Bishop Pildain on the social question that so irritated the authorities were unusual for the frankness of their language. Few prelates dared to speak so boldly. But from 1945 onwards, other bishops began to rediscover the social gospel, albeit timidly and with little practical effect. The bishops of the ecclesiastical province of Granada issued a pastoral letter in 1945 lamenting the "accumulation of riches in a few hands, [and] the impoverishment of the multitude," while in the following year, the bishop of Astorga echoed an old theme of social Catholicism: "The possessing classes have learned nothing from the revolution."[105] By the early 1950s, the undercurrent of dissatisfaction with the regime's failure to remedy what many clergy saw as a fundamental cause of religious alienation—the unequal distribution of wealth—produced widespread discussion in clerical circles. In 1950, a pastoral letter of Vicente Enrique y Tarancón, young bishop of the diocese of Solsona, attacking social injustice provoked accusations of "red," and "Communist" in the official press.[106] Taking account of the tepid currents of social criticism, the Committee of Metropolitans issued a statement in 1951 criticizing speculation and demanding a decent wage for workers.[107]

Social policy began to reemerge as an important concern of the Church. Although a precursor of later developments, discussion at this stage rarely passed beyond general criticism of bourgeois selfishness and vague appeals urging the faithful to act with a sense of moral responsibility towards the poor.[108] The hierarchy avoided taking the regime to task for its neglect of social justice except in veiled

104. Despite clerical dislike of the new inspection procedures called for in the new law, "It is certain that confessional teaching remained totally guaranteed" in its basic provisions. Puelles Benítez, *Educación e ideología*, p. 388. For a full discussion of the controversy surrounding the law, see Tusell, *Franco y los católicos*, pp. 299–308.

105. Quoted in Ruiz Rico, *El papel político de la Iglesia católica*, pp. 118, 119.

106. The pastoral letter, "El pan nuestro de cada día," was inspired by the failure of the authorities to provide adequate bread rations to the industrial zones of the Solsona diocese. The bishop acted after repeated requests for action from government officials received no response. The indignant tone of the letter and its pointed indictment of speculation offended "politicians, the new rich . . . and the greater part of bishops, priests and practicing Christians, who considered the existing regime as the best Christian political formula." They protested against "the red bishop, as some said, against the little young and imprudent bishop, as others affirmed more charitably." Bishop Tarancón did not receive, however, any formal protests from either the central government or provincial authorities, although he heard that some ministers were "furious" over his intervention. Vicente Enrique y Tarancón, *Confesiones* (Madrid, 1996), pp. 112, 114.

107. Blázquez, *La traición de los clérigos*, p. 114; "Instrucción colectiva sobre deberes de justicia y caridad," June 3, 1951, in *Documentos colectivos del episcopado español*, pp. 361–62.

108. Martínez Lozano, "La Iglesia ante la evolución socioeconómica," pp. 180–81. In their 1951 statement, for example, the archbishops continued to enunciate a fundamental principle of National Catholicism by attacking liberalism for advocating liberties "contrary to the common good and to divine or natural law." "Instrucción colectiva," p. 261.

terms and refrained from calling for fundamental social or economic reform.[109] The bishops' criticism did not signify acceptance of trade unions within a democratic society. Bishop Pildain had no use for the regime's vertical syndicates, but he was equally vociferous in his denunciations of Spanish liberal thought. As late as 1955, even Bishop Tarancón declared that workers had a duty "to cooperate loyally and actively in the syndicate system of the regime."[110]

Of the benefits conferred on the regime by the "Catholic" family, none was more important than the concordat of 1953. Although in 1946 the Vatican negotiated several formal agreements with Madrid over specific issues, it displayed little enthusiasm for negotiating a comprehensive agreement through a concordat. The papacy remained cautious towards a regime whose legitimacy continued to be questioned by the Western democracies but was unwilling to challenge it.[111] The initiative to begin negotiations came not from the Vatican but from the Spanish ambassador to the Holy See between 1948 and 1951, Joaquín Ruiz Giménez, who was supported by another member of the "Catholic family," Minister of Foreign Affairs Martín Artajo.[112]

That it took five years for the negotiations to produce an agreement says a good deal about the complex state of relations between Madrid and the Vatican.[113] That a concordat emerged at the end of years of difficult negotiations is explained in part by changes on the international scene after 1950. The development of the Cold War and the evolving position of the United States towards the regime allowed Spain to begin moving along the road of international respectability, a circumstance duly noted in the Vatican. Moreover, the lobbying efforts of Ruiz Giménez

109. Bishop Tarancón received, for example, not a single letter of support from his fellow bishops for his pastoral letter. Enrique y Tarancón, *Confesiones*, p. 114.

110. Quoted in Díaz-Salazar, *Iglesia, dictadura y democracia*, p. 146.

111. In June 1950, the United States Department of State received a memorandum providing information on a recent interview between Don Juan de Borbón, conde de Barcelona and pretender to the Spanish throne, and Pope Pius XII. Don Juan sought the pontiff's support in a campaign to oust Franco in favor of a constitutional monarchy. "The Holy Father replied that he is against dictatorships in any form, and that he is unhappy with the situation in Spain. He said, however, that Don Juan must realize that it is not the function of the Pope to interfere in the internal political affairs of any country and particularly Spain where the Church flourishes and indeed receives great protection." Memorandum of Conversation, by the Special Assistant (Xanthaky) to the Ambassador in Portugal (McVeagh), June 28, 1950, in *Foreign Relations of the United States, 1950* (vol. 3, *Western Europe*, Washington, 1977), pp. 1567–68.

112. Tusell, *Franco y los católicos*, p. 242. Although Ruiz Giménez had attempted to persuade Pius XII to begin negotiations in 1949, the Vatican did not authorize the first formal contacts until February 1950. When first approached about the possibility of opening negotiations, the pope appeared far from enthusiastic about the prospect. According to the ambassador, the Vatican's caution arose from several considerations, including doubts about the regime's social policy, especially with respect to workers, and the existence within the curia of a "democratic mentality," on the part of French, Swiss, and American clerics. Ibid., pp. 244, 233–34.

113. For the history of the complicated diplomatic and political maneuvering involved in these negotiations, see ibid., pp. 231–82. According to Malley in his 1951 report, "There is little doubt that the Vatican has delayed action . . . in the hope of political evolution in Spain, the establishment of a less impermanent regime, and the removal of some of the objectionable features of General Franco's government to which the Primate of Spain has so clearly pointed." "Survey of the Church in Spain," ms., p. 18.

and the "Catholic family" in Rome stressed the diminishing influence of the Falange to papal officials long concerned with this question. Supporters of a concordat could count on the support of the Vatican's former nuncio to the Republic, Cardinal Tedeschini, now an influential voice in the papal curia. The Vatican's nuncio in Madrid, Archbishop Cicognani, an unabashed admirer of Franco, also promoted the concordat project.

Negotiations proved long and difficult for several reasons. The Vatican was determined to reopen the patronage issue, enlarge the "liberty of the Church" as much as possible, and enshrine the benefits already secured from the regime in a concordat binding on future governments as an international treaty. Although committed to an agreement, the Spanish cabinet was far from united in its response to several of these questions. Ruiz Giménez wished to compromise on the patronage issue; others were unwilling to yield the regalist concession extracted from the Vatican in 1941. Fernando María Castiella, Ruiz Giménez's successor at the Vatican embassy in 1951, took a tougher line on patronage and on another question dear to the papacy and the hierarchy, securing a greater degree of autonomy for Catholic Action similar to that enjoyed by its Italian counterpart.[114] In any event, Franco remained adamantly opposed to the slightest concession on the State's patronage rights. Indeed, he remarked that allowing the papacy to appoint bishops was like permitting the pope to name provincial governors.[115]

After intense diplomatic wheeling and dealing, an agreement was finally reached. Abandoning its hopes on patronage, the Vatican confirmed the provisions of the 1941 *convenio*.[116] The papacy managed to get the role of Catholic Action inserted in the final text, although the terms were more restrictive than either Rome or the hierarchy wished.[117] The Vatican also succeeded in having specific juridical and financial benefits already enjoyed by the Church recognized as treaty obligations. Although members of the "Catholic family" saw the concordat as a document of transcendental importance in the long history of civil-ecclesiastical relations, the agreement broke little new ground.[118] The concordat's significance lay less in its specific terms than in its political effects.

The concordat of 1953 was hailed by all segments of the Spanish press and the government as a triumph for both Church and State, although there were rum-

114. Tusell, *Franco y los catolicos*, pp. 252–53. Like Martín Artajo and Ruiz Giménez, Castiella had been active in Catholic student associations and later served on the staff of *El Debate*. Unlike them, however, he was closer to the Falange, more regalist and less disposed to yield to clerical pressure. Ibid., pp. 250–51.

115. Ibid., p. 247.

116. The Vatican secured, however, one concession on patronage. The Church recovered complete freedom to appoint parish priests. An agreement of 1946 with the papacy had provided that bishops were obliged to submit nominations to the government, which had the right to veto those to which it objected. Petschen, *La Iglesia en la España de Franco*, p. 22; José Giménez y Martínez de Carvajal, "El concordato español de 1953," *Iglesia, Estado y sociedad*, p. 145.

117. Tusell, *Franco y los católicos*, p. 266.

118. Ibid., pp. 273, 280–81.

blings of discontent from some clergymen and followers of the FET.[119] Franco took the unusual step of addressing parliament before the formal vote of ratification. The general seized the opportunity to recall the clergy's support for the rising against the Republic and to point out how many benefits the Church had received as a result. He exalted the cooperation of the "perfect societies" of Church and State. "In a nation eminently Catholic like ours," separation of the civil and ecclesiastical powers, which "liberal systems advocate," was impossible. Church and State must work together, he continued, "to fulfill the destiny assigned by Providence to our people."[120]

In his speech, the general restated the principles of National Catholicism, which appeared to have reached their culminating moment.[121] The Church saw its legal position and privileges as the established Church of the nation guaranteed as never before through a binding international treaty. The concordat also strengthened the Church's position within the regime as one of its key institutional and ideological buttresses.[122] But there was a less favorable side to the concordat from an ecclesiastical point of view. The agreement's terms appeared to strengthen the Church's pretension to greater freedom of action. In fact, the "liberty of the Church" remained as dependent as ever on the general and his ministers. The Catholic press was still subject to censorship, and the Church's tentative initiatives in the field of social action provoked constant official opposition even as the concordat was being ratified. The extravagant rhetoric vented by the hierarchy and the Catholic press over the concordat could not disguise, moreover, the Church's failure to realize its historic aspiration of influencing public policy through the permanent, institutional influence embodied in the "Catholic family's" attempt to transform the regime. This goal was no closer to realization in 1953 than before.

Franco obtained substantial political benefits from the concordat that reinforced the regime's legitimacy at home and abroad. The agreement not only strengthened the Church's support for the existing order, it also represented for the general "a diplomatic success without precedent" soon to be followed by a second international triumph, the accord with the United States of September 1953.[123] The Vatican showed less public enthusiasm for the concordat than did the Spanish hierarchy, but it placed its seal of approval on a regime about which it had long held

119. According to Martín Artajo, Cardinal Segura advised the Vatican that it should not sign an agreement with the government under any circumstances. There were also reservations from the Falange on the grounds that the concordat made too many concessions to the Church. A professor of canon law at Salamanca complained publicly about the continuation of the State's patronage rights. Ibid., pp. 263–64, 274; Iribarren, *Papeles y memorias*, p. 145.

120. "Mensaje del Jefe del Estado a las Cortes Españolas," *Ecclesia*, October 31, 1953, pp. 55, 56.

121. Ruiz Rico, *El papel político de la Iglesia católica*, p. 147; Blázquez, *La traición de los clérigos*, pp. 110–11; Tusell, *Franco y los católicos*, p. 275; Stanley Payne, *Spanish Catholicism* (Madison, 1984), p. 185.

122. Tello, *Ideología y política*, p. 136.

123. Hermet, *Les catholiques*, vol. 2, p. 216; Díaz-Salazar, *Iglesia, dictadura y democracia*, pp. 117–20; Payne, *The Franco Regime*, p. 420.

reservations.[124] The government needed fourteen years to obtain the concordat praised so extravagantly in 1953. From a historical perspective, the agreement's effects were limited. The ideas inspiring it already appeared anachronistic within the world of the Western democracies, while the Catholic Church as a whole called its assumptions into question during the Second Vatican Council, just a decade away. Even within the Spanish Church, the apparent unity that lay behind acceptance of the concordat disguised fissures that would widen during the next fifteen years. The concordat applied a final coat of veneer to National Catholicism, but failed to strengthen it from within.

124. José Bigorda, "El concordato de 1953: expresión jurídica de las relaciones entre la Iglesia y el nuevo Estado," in *Iglesia y sociedad en España*, p. 295.

CHAPTER XVI

THE FACADE OF NATIONAL CATHOLICISM, 1954–1960

Following the concordat's signing, members of the hierarchy praised Franco in providentialist terms reminiscent of the exalted rhetoric of the Civil War. He was "the man elected by God to reaffirm our Catholic unity," the archbishop of Santiago declared effusively.[1] Ecclesiastical honors were showered upon the general. Pope Pius XII, whose reservations about the regime were now considerably tempered, bestowed the rare dignity of membership in the Supreme Order of Christ, while the Pontifical University of Salamanca granted an honorary degree.[2] Clerical and lay supporters of a twentieth-century version of the alliance between Throne and Altar saw the concordat as initiating the final stage of cooperation between the civil and ecclesiastical authorities that would fully realize the long-cherished idea of a society permeated by spiritual values. Spain appeared to the new papal nuncio as a nation "splendidly consolidated in its Catholicism."[3]

This heady rhetoric failed to correspond to the reality of the Church's situation during the 1950s. Fears about the religious alienation of the working class intensified by mid-decade, while the pattern of "conflictive accommodation" governing relations with the regime continued much as before. On the whole, the Church avoided pressing the government for more concessions in favor of a policy de-

1. Quoted in Feliciano Blázquez, *La traición de los clérigos en la España de Franco* (Madrid, 1991), p. 110. The departing papal nuncio, Cardinal Gaetano Cicognani, was no less extravagant. He praised the general for having established political and social institutions "founded on Catholic truth . . . beneath the designs of Providence." "Discurso del Cardenal Cicognani tras la imposición de birretas por el Jefe del Estado," *Ecclesia*, January 24, 1953, p. 7.

2. Javier Tusell, *Franco y los católicos: la política interior española entre 1945 y 1954* (Madrid, 1984), p. 277.

3. Quoted in Blázquez, *La traición de los clérigos*, p. 107.

signed to consolidate gains already made.[4] Mutual self-interest inspired cooperation between Church and State on a number of issues, including a successful campaign in 1955 to remove Cardinal Segura from the archbishopric of Seville.[5]

By the mid-1950s, the political option endorsed by Cardinal Pla y Deniel, Bishop Herrera, and the "Catholic family" foundered once and for all on the rock of Franco's manipulations. Clerical and lay advocates of the regime's institutional transformation also saw their political influence diminish before the ascendancy of Opus Dei, another of the elitist groups produced historically by Spanish Catholicism. Towards the end of the decade, outright Catholic opponents of the regime began to establish clandestine Christian Democratic parties. By 1960, the possibility of achieving the illusory "union of Catholics" pursued for generations by the hierarchy was more remote than ever. The traditional factionalization of Spanish Catholicism in its political dimension returned to the scene, a prelude to the internal struggles that would deeply divide the Church and its supporters during the regime's final decade and a half.

The "Catholic family's" failure to persuade Franco to accept its plans for limited institutional reform contained important implications for the Church. Despite the hierarchy's extravagant praise of Franco, its leading figures, notably Pla y Deniel and Herrera, appreciated the danger to the Church's interests posed by a regime dependent for its survival on the person of the general. But imprisoned within the walls of fidelity to Franco and fearful of democratic alternatives, the clerical leadership sought to realize its objectives within an ambiguous framework of loyalty to the regime and further attempts to expand the "liberty of the Church."

Conflicts Continued

The facade of the civil-ecclesiastical alliance erected during the Civil War remained in place. Through the early 1960s, the bishops continued to praise Franco in public statements and to occupy a prominent place in official ceremonies.[6] In 1959, the hierarchy turned out en masse at the dedication of the vast underground basilica constructed by Franco in the Guadarrama Mountains near Madrid. At-

4. Juan José Ruiz Rico, *El papel católico de la Iglesia católica en la España de Franco, 1936–1971* (Madrid, 1977), p. 150.

5. Segura squandered whatever capital he had left by snubbing Franco during the general's visit to Seville in 1953. His ban on the ACNP in his diocese, a measure directed against Bishop Herrera and the "Catholic family," used up his ecclesiastical credit. Through the efforts of the pro-Franco papal nuncio, Hildebrando Antoniutti, and Martín Artajo, the cardinal was removed from effective power by the appointment of a coadjutor with right of succession in 1955. Defiant to the end, Segura refused to move out of the episcopal palace. Tusell, *Franco y los católicos*, pp. 341–44.

6. For examples of the "moral support" rendered the regime by individual members of the hierarchy, see the numerous examples cited by Rafael Gómez Pérez, *Política y religión en el régimen de Franco* (Barcelona, 1976), pp. 134–42.

tended by the general, the cabinet, Nationalist war veterans, and twenty-five thousand members of the Falange, the ceremony was less religious than political in character.[7] Like the basilica itself, the gathering celebrated the triumph of the Nationalist cause and appeared to confirm the continuing strength of National Catholicism. But by this time, fissures had already spread over its apparently monolithic surface.

The issues dividing Church and State during the 1950s were not substantially different from those of the 1940s. But they became more sharply delineated, an indication not of a challenge to the regime but of the beginnings of a certain distancing from the static idea of National Catholicism still cherished by Franco. The ink on the concordat had scarcely dried when Church and State became embroiled in a controversy that revealed that the regime had no intention of relaxing its rigorous control over the press, Catholic or otherwise. Until 1954, the ongoing campaign of the hierarchy on behalf of a selective liberalization of the restrictive press law of 1938 was conducted largely behind the scenes.[8] In 1954, the editor of *Ecclesia,* Father Jesús Iribarren, disrupted this pattern of discreet lobbying by publishing a critique of official censorship that fell like a bombshell on official circles.[9]

Iribarren's opinions reflected the substance of the views of Pla y Deniel and Herrera, who had lobbied for years to change press legislation.[10] Although *Ecclesia*'s editor acted on his own without consulting the cardinal, the frank nature of his criticism, combined with the reproduction of his article in the foreign press, particularly the *New York Times,* provoked a counterattack from the regime. The minister of information, Gabriel Arias Salgado, an authoritarian obscurantist of the first order, published a series of blistering attacks on Iribarren, while the authorities applied intense pressure on Pla y Deniel to fire him on the spot. "The heavens broke over me," Iribarren later recalled.[11] Accusations rained down upon him from the Falange and the official press that charged him with being a Freemason, a

7. Ibid., p. 60.

8. Differences between Church and State over censorship were occasionally brought to public attention before this date. In 1950, Cardinal Pla y Deniel published a pastoral letter calling for a new press law that would avoid the dangers of either unlimited freedom or total government control. The cardinal appointed a committee of leading Catholic journalists to draft a legislative proposal in the hope that the regime would accept it as the basis for a new press law. The committee presented its draft in 1952 to no effect, despite the support it received from Martín Artajo and other members of the "Catholic family." Guy Hermet, *Les catholiques dans l'Espagne franquiste* (Paris, 1981), vol. 2, p. 208; Tusell, *Franco y los católicos,* pp. 346–47.

9. Iribarren was moved to action through his recent participation in an international Catholic press congress held in Paris. He was embarrassed and troubled by questions from fellow delegates about the "inferiority complex" to which Church publications in Spain were subject because of official censorship. "Reflexiones de un participante: Cuarto Congreso Internacional de la Prensa Católica," in Jesús Iribarren, *Papeles y memorias: medio siglo de relaciones Iglesia-Estado en España, 1936–1986* (Madrid, 1992), p. 154.

10. For a detailed analysis of the twists and turns of this campaign, see Tusell, *Franco y los católicos,* pp. 344–59.

11. Iribarren, *Papeles y memorias,* p. 157.

Basque separatist, a dangerous liberal, an advocate of Christian Democracy, and an unpatriotic Spaniard.

For a time, the regime's aggressive defense of censorship threatened a crisis in civil-ecclesiastical relations.[12] But when push came to shove, the Church retreated. Although Pla y Deniel sympathized in private with the substance of Iribarren's criticism, he was unwilling to allow the confrontation with the regime to get out of hand, in part because he was aware of the opposition of some bishops to Iribarren's initiative.[13] In the end, after a discreet interval, the cardinal accepted the editor's resignation.

The Church managed to win occasional skirmishes during its ongoing campaign for greater press freedom. Between 1947 and 1950, figures linked to Catholic Action succeeded in publishing a journal of modest circulation, *Criterio,* that won few friends among the regime's hard-liners for its condemnation of fascism and praise of European Christian Democracy. But the journal proved timid and defensive in its comments about the political situation in Spain.[14] In 1952, three years of intense lobbying by members of the hierarchy and the "Catholic family" finally persuaded the regime to allow the Editorial Católica to appoint an editor of its own choosing for the Madrid daily, *Ya.* But the larger issue of selective freedom of the press remained a sore point for the bishops, who continued lobbying but with no more success than before. The regime remained intransigent. Aware of the immense benefits derived from its ties to the State, the Church had nowhere to go on the issue and could do little but continue its ineffectual efforts to change official policy.

Another cause of dissension developed from the hierarchy's desire to fulfill its historic dream of establishing a great Catholic university in a higher educational system monopolized by the State, with two exceptions. In 1949 and 1950, *Ecclesia* argued against the State's monopoly over higher education, while influential members of the "Catholic family" used their influence to break through official regalist suspicions and the outright opposition of the Falange to such a project.[15] Although the concordat of 1953 affirmed the Church's rights in this respect, an elaborate plan to create a higher education federation involving the small Jesuit university of Deusto, the Augustinian university college at El Escorial (neither with a full complement of faculties), and several research institutions operated by religious orders came to nothing because of government foot-dragging. The first full Catholic uni-

12. In January 1955, for example, Bishop Herrera publicly disputed with Arias Salgado, who had claimed that the regime's press policy conformed fully to papal teaching, an argument that the bishop rejected out of hand in a pastoral letter to the faithful of his diocese. José Sánchez Jiménez, *El Cardenal Herrera Oria: pensamiento y acción social* (Madrid, 1986), p. 92; Tusell, *Franco y los católicos,* p. 355.

13. The bishop of Lérida, for example, while accepting that the Church enjoyed the right to call attention to "deficiencies" in official policy, believed it prudent to tolerate them rather than endanger the regime's prestige. Ruiz Rico, *El papel político de la Iglesia católica,* p. 155.

14. Tusell, *Franco y los católicos,* pp. 197–99.

15. Ibid., p. 312.

versity recognized by the Franco regime emerged from an entirely different quarter. In 1960, the government recognized the University of Navarra, founded by Opus Dei. The Church was not inclined to look a gift horse in the mouth, and thirty bishops attended the new university's inaugural ceremony.[16] But the dream of creating a distinguished national Catholic university remained unfulfilled during the remainder of the Franco regime and the years that followed.

Conflicts over press legislation and the university question generated chronic tension between the civil and ecclesiastical authorities. But at no point did the hierarchy contemplate abandoning its support for a regime that had bestowed immense benefits on the Church. The struggle with the government over these issues took place within the framework of pressure group lobbying characteristic of the regime's political life. In this respect, the Church did as well as any of the regime's competing clans. It did not secure everything it wanted, but, as so often in the past, it learned how to adjust its tactics to the rules of the game established by the regime in power.

A New Social Catholicism

Over the long term, the evolving social preoccupations of clergy and laity proved a more serious threat to the stability of National Catholicism. The older currents of social Catholicism resurfaced. Although no less fearful of working-class revolution than it had been before the Civil War, the social Catholicism of the 1950s was accompanied by discontent with the regime for pursuing economic policies that, far from eliminating the danger from below, were seen as exacerbating class antagonisms. A modest agricultural and industrial recovery during the 1950s and implementation of an economic stabilization plan in 1959 threw inequalities in wealth into sharp relief, while illegal strikes in 1951, 1956, and 1958 revealed that the era of passivity among workers of the 1940s was over. A 1954 survey of religious attitudes among industrial workers alarmed the clergy because it showed that years of intense evangelizing directed to the conversion of the religiously alienated had not fulfilled expectations. Even worse, from the Church's point of view, the survey showed that sympathy among workers for clandestine trade unions was on the increase because of "the Marxist virus, that still oxidizes their souls."[17] Restlessness among concerned clergy and laity, stirred by the regime's inability to resolve social problems and combined with chronic feelings of resentment at the Church's exclusion from trade union activity, sharpened differences between the civil and ecclesiastical authorities over social policy.

16. Santiago Petschen, *La Iglesia en la España de Franco* (Madrid, 1977), pp. 112–14.

17. "Resumen de las encuestas realizadas por los asesores religiosos de los sindicatos," in José Castaño Colomer, *La JOC en España, 1946–1970* (Salamanca, 1978), p. 37; Ruiz Rico, *El papel político de la Iglesia católica*, pp. 158–59.

The revived social Catholicism promoted by leading members of the hierarchy, notably Pla y Deniel and Herrera, remained deeply conservative. But the awareness that the regime's economic policies were intensifying social inequalities opened the door to criticism of the regime that was discreet and limited at the level of the clerical leadership but direct at the grassroots level, through the appearance of Catholic, "apostolic" associations of workers first authorized by the hierarchy in 1946 as part of Catholic Action. The protective umbrella provided by Catholic Action allowed these organizations to flourish during the 1950s, although few of their clerical supporters in 1946 could have foreseen the role they would play in challenging the principles of National Catholicism.

As the decade progressed, the hierarchy devoted more attention to social problems. The Committee of Metropolitans issued statements in 1956 and 1960, while individual bishops published an increasing number of pastoral letters on the question. The concerns expressed by the bishops indicated a shift away from traditional pastoral methods to one emphasizing improvements in social and economic conditions as crucial for the Church's religious future.[18] This change in direction did not mean that the hierarchy developed a coherent strategy. Although they had long been restless with the monopoly enjoyed by the regime's vertical labor syndicates, the bishops were unwilling to challenge them directly. Even the 1956 and 1960 statements of the archbishops did little more than elaborate the generalities on behalf of fair wages and an equitable distribution of wealth contained in their 1951 declaration on the subject, although the second moved in the direction of emphasizing social justice rather than the tired formula of Christian charity stressed earlier.[19]

The impetus behind an updated version of social Catholicism came less from the hierarchy as a whole than from individual bishops. In 1954, Bishop Pildain again created consternation in official circles by publishing a pastoral letter with the provocative title, "The Existing Syndical System in Spain: Is It in Agreement or Not with the Church's Social Doctrine?" The prelate affirmed in no uncertain terms that it was not, while lambasting the vertical syndicates as "incapable of leading to authentic peace, to an effective collaboration and cooperation among the different classes of society."[20] This rhetorical assault elicited a prompt response from the government in the form of a protest to the Vatican. Although Pildain acted on his own

18. Enrique Martínez Lozano, "La Iglesia ante la evolución socio-económica," in Fernando Urbina et al., *Iglesia y sociedad en España, 1939–1975* (Madrid, 1977), pp. 191–92.

19. Ibid., p. 188; Ruiz Rico, *El papel político de la Iglesia,* pp. 164–65. The 1960 statement thus praised the regime for its economic development plans but lamented the unequal distribution of its benefits. The archbishops avoided any direct criticism of the vertical syndicates, although they appealed timidly for "a certain participation" of workers in the resolution of social and economic problems. "Declaración sobre actitud cristiana ante los problemas morales de la estabilización y el desarrollo económico," January 15, 1960, in *Documentos colectivos del episcopado español, 1870–1974,* ed. Jesús Iribarren (Madrid, 1974), pp. 332, 335. A more positive assessment of the archbishops' statement can be found in Rafael Gómez Pérez, *El franquismo y la Iglesia* (Madrid, 1986), pp. 78–79.

20. Quoted in Rafael Belda, "La Iglesia y el sindicalismo vertical," *Iglesia y sociedad,* p. 225.

and none of his episcopal colleagues would have dared to challenge the regime so directly, his criticism of the official labor monopoly reflected a growing restlessness within the Church with its exclusion from an area that it judged vital to its future.[21]

The key figures in the revived social Catholicism of the 1950s were Cardinal Pla y Deniel and Bishop Herrera. Loyalty to Franco, apprehension about the country's political future without the general, and a commitment to the legacy of social Catholicism, with its deep fear of radical movements, limited their room to maneuver. But both shared the belief that unless something were done to remedy social injustices, the Church might face again the frightening prospect of popular revolution. In private and sometimes in public, Herrera stressed principles that he had first promoted as editor of *El Debate* in 1911, notably the indifference of the rich towards the common good. "The deepest failure of Hispanic Catholicism," he remarked, "is *the deficient formation of a social conscience,* a defect which dates from long ago."[22]

Herrera's critical views on the social irresponsibility of the "directing classes" sharpened after he became bishop of Málaga in 1947. Moved by the appalling conditions prevailing among the rural laborers working the large estates of the region, he publicly attacked the abuses of the *latifundio* system soon after assuming his post. In 1951, he privately defended Catholic workers' associations against official criticism. In 1954, Herrera took on Franco's gray eminence, Luis Carrero Blanco, who had objected to a meeting sponsored by Bishop Morcillo of Bilbao at which speakers timidly questioned the regime's labor monopoly and defended the right to strike on theoretical grounds derived from papal social teaching.[23]

Herrera replied to this frontal assault by defending the Bilbao proceedings and the right of the Church to engage in a social apostolate. He concurred with the opinion expressed at Bilbao with respect to the relationship of the vertical syndicates to papal social teaching. The official labor monopoly, he declared, did not conform "to the ideal drawn by the popes." But Herrera's correspondence with Carrero Blanco suggests that the bishop saw no resolution to the dilemma created by his loyalty to the regime and his view of the Church's social mission: "The po-

21. Tusell has argued that Pildain's letter had little impact in Spain. Belda has suggested, however, that the bishop's intervention was more significant because it broke the "taboo" against discussing the relationship of the vertical syndicates to papal social teaching. Ibid., p. 225.

22. Quoted in Sánchez Jiménez, *El Cardenal Herrera Oria,* pp. 100–101.

23. Organized by Morcillo with the assistance of Herrera's Instituto León XIII, founded in 1952 to heighten awareness of papal social teaching, the controversial "post-mission" of Bilbao revolved around a series of conferences given by clerical experts on social questions. According to Herrera, their purpose was to move the Church towards "a new phase of religious preaching" directed to forming "a national conscience with respect to civic and social duties." Although participants recognized that the right to strike was legitimate according to papal social teaching, they also agreed that governments had the authority to prohibit strikes in view of the specific circumstances prevailing in their respective societies. "Respuesta del obispo de Málaga al escrito de la Presidencia del Gobierno," in ibid., p. 324; Tusell, *Franco y los católicos,* pp. 360–63; Rafael González Moralejo, "La posmisión social de Bilbao," *Ecclesia,* December 19, 1953, p. 13.

sition of the Spanish Church is, in this terrain, difficult. It cannot defend the existing social regime as ideal for a Catholic. On the other hand, it cannot criticize it in a form which damages the prestige and authority of the State; on the contrary, it ought to strengthen the civil authority . . . out of convenience and gratitude."[24]

Herrera's propagandizing activities contributed to developing a greater awareness of social problems among clergy and laity. The role of Pla y Deniel proved more decisive. Less reflective and more practical than the bishop of Málaga, the cardinal primate possessed an acute political sense of how far the authorities could be pressed. He also adhered tenaciously to an idea of the "liberty of the Church" that rejected the compartmentalization of function imposed on the clergy by the regime at its inception. The convictions inspiring the cardinal—that the Church required a new strategy to deal with social problems and that it could not be excluded from an active social apostolate—made him a more determined and effective skirmisher with the regime than Herrera was.[25]

As cardinal primate with responsibility for Catholic Action, Pla y Deniel supported the formation of "apostolic" workers' associations in 1946.[26] Thereafter, he defended them tenaciously until the end of his career in 1966. The appearance during the late 1940s of the Hermandades Obreras de Acción Católica (HOAC) and the Juventud Obrera Católica (JOC) represented a significant innovation in the Church's long and generally unsuccessful efforts to develop an effective working-class base. On paper, these associations had as conservative a purpose as any in the history of social Catholicism: to achieve the re-Christianization of alienated work-

24. "Respuesta del obispo de Málaga," p. 325. The reasons behind Herrera's reluctance to question the rule of Franco were clearly expressed in 1962 upon Franco's visit to the prelate. Herrera told the general, "The services lent to Church and State by Your Excellency are immense." The bishop recalled the "anarchistic days of a Republic which directly attacked the Church, the State, the Army" in the name of an ideology that was "the antithesis of the national tradition," which carried out its "destructive work" to leave Spain "a field of ruins" by 1939. Quoted in Gómez Pérez, *Política y religión*, p. 138.

25. Pla y Deniel had been active as a young priest in Barcelona in the social apostolate. He established an endowed foundation for this purpose in the working-class district of Pueblo Nuevo in 1905 and collaborated later in a journal devoted to social issues. The cardinal once observed that around 1910 he had been influenced by the example of Cardinal Mercier who promoted a number of successful social initiatives in Belgium. It has been argued that the cardinal's views evolved "with respect to those aspect of the [political] system which had more points of contact with nazi-fascist forms, for example, the vertical syndicate." A. Sáinz Pardo, "Pla y Deniel, Enrique," *Diccionario de historia eclesiástica de España*, ed. Q. Aldea Vaquero et al. (4 vols., Madrid, 1972–1975), vol. 3, p. 1985; Tusell, *Franco y los católicos*, p. 211; Casimir Martí, "Datos para un estudio sobre la Iglesia en la sociedad española a partir de 1939," *Pastoral Misionera* (1972), vol. 8, no. 2, p. 183.

26. The objective of creating specialized sections of Catholic Action for specific occupational groups was not new, although political circumstances did not favor its implementation until the cosmetic reforms introduced by Franco beginning in 1945. In 1941, the secretary-general of its central office, Monsignor Zacarías de Vizcarra, advocated the creation of "specialized centers through which each profession can realize apostolic labor in the most efficient way." "El aniversario de las encíclicas sociales fué solemnemente conmemorado en toda España," *Ecclesia*, June 1, 1941, p. 5. Clergy who viewed the Falange in a more positive light objected, however, to involving Catholic Action in a social apostolate. In 1942, Pedro Cantero, later archbishop of Zaragoza, declared, "The Roman Pontiffs insist today more on pure Catholic Action than on Catholic-social action." *La hora católica de España* (Madrid, 1942), p. 74.

ers through religious and educational activities. They departed from old patterns in two respects, however. First, they were organized by Catholic workers themselves and therefore remained free of the taint of employer influence that had bedeviled most Catholic trade unions before the Civil War. Second, they developed a dynamism of their own based on a realistic perception of working-class demands for social justice.

The HOAC and the JOC were allowed to function legally because they fell under the protective umbrella of Catholic Action.[27] The authorities tolerated them grudgingly at best. In fact, they viewed them as incipient trade unions functioning in the disguise of religious and educational organizations, an ecclesiastical version of the proverbial Trojan horse. The Falange and the leadership of the official labor syndicates regarded them with deep suspicion on these grounds. In 1949, the provincial chief of the Falange in Toledo warned against Catholic workers' associations: "The components of these groups hide, beneath the sign of the cross, the ideals of those against whom we rebelled on July 18," while the national organ of the Falange, *Arriba,* blamed the HOAC for instigating an illegal strike in Bilbao during 1951.[28] In 1956, the regime's syndicates launched a full-scale offensive against the Church's social initiatives, contemptuously referred to as "tainted with the smell of wax." The organization of Catholic workers' associations was attacked as a scheme to displace the vertical syndicates and introduce political parties under the cover of an "ecclesiastical apostolate."[29]

Accusations of this kind were repeatedly denied by Pla y Deniel and the leadership of the HOAC and JOC. The purpose of the JOC, its directors asserted in 1958, was not that of a labor union or political party. Rather, it was "to educate young workers before the problems of life with a Christian spirit and to see that the Church advances among working-class youth."[30] Although, strictly speaking, this was true, in fact the HOAC and JOC went beyond narrow religious and educational activities. Harsh critics of the vertical syndicates, they promoted a reformist program that called into question many of the essential features of the regime's social and economic policies. Although neither became a mass organization, it is estimated that combined they exercised influence over from 150,000 to 180,000 workers.[31] A significant aspect of their activity, virtually unheard of in pre–Civil

27. Although in a general way the HOAC looked to the model of Italian Catholic Action, which had organized Catholic labor groups, Pla y Deniel "recognized that the only way in which Catholic workers' associations would prosper in Spain" was through direct dependence on the hierarchy under the "cover" of Catholic Action. Basilisa López García, *Aproximación a la historia de la HOAC, 1946–1981* (Madrid, 1995), p. 30.

28. Quoted in ibid., p. 51, note 59.

29. "Reunión de mandos nacionales y jefes provinciales de la Delegación Nacional de Sindicatos," July 6, 1956, in Sánchez Jiménez, *El Cardenal Herrera Oria,* p. 329.

30. Quoted in Castaños Colomer, *La JOC en España,* p. 66.

31. Hermet, *Les catholiques,* vol. 1, p. 216. It is difficult to establish with any precision the number of members in the HOAC and the JOC. Neither organization maintained accurate records because of fear

War social Catholicism, lay in their willingness to cooperate with underground Communist and Socialist labor unions. By the end of the 1950s, as the plight of workers worsened after the implementation of the 1959 stabilization plan, HOAC and JOC members joined with clandestine labor groups in a series of illegal strikes and generally adopted an increasingly aggressive stance towards the regime. In July 1960, ten thousand members of the JOC attending its first national congress approved a program calling for just salaries, the fair distribution of wealth generated by economic development, an honest, representative trade union system, and freedom of the press.[32]

That the HOAC and the JOC flourished within a conservative and middle-class Catholic Action was remarkable. Although they might have developed clandestinely on their own, it is unlikely that they would have developed so successfully without the protection afforded by Catholic Action and individual bishops. The hierarchy remained conservative politically, but until around 1960 it showed more flexibility in its attitude towards new social initiatives. Even Pablo Gurpide, appointed bishop of Bilbao because of his conservative views, presided over a joint HOAC-JOC meeting in 1959 that led to arrests and heavy fines for its leading participants. Incensed by the heavy-handed police reaction, the bishop offered to pay the fines himself.[33]

As far as the clerical leadership was concerned, the protective role of Pla y Deniel was especially important. The cardinal secured the appointment of Father Albert Bonet to the post of secretary-general of Catholic Action's central office in 1956. Founder in the 1930s of the Catalan Federació de Jovens Cristians (FJC), a distinctly modern youth association on the model developed by a prominent figure in Belgian social Catholicism, Joseph Cardin, Bonet appreciated the necessity of developing a new strategy based on the initiatives of workers themselves.[34] It was not by chance that beginning in 1957 Catholic Action's headquarters provided financial assistance to both the HOAC and the JOC.[35]

---

of police surveillance. Lannon estimates that membership reached twelve thousand in the HOAC, seventy thousand in the JOC by the early 1960s. Frances Lannon, *Privilege, Persecution and Prophecy: The Catholic Church in Spain, 1875–1975* (Oxford, 1997), pp. 232–33. Benjamin Welles estimated the membership of the HOAC in 1960 at six thousand. "Primate of Spain Warns Franco Church-State 'Conflict' Looms," *New York Times*, December 31, 1960. Castaño Colomer believes that the reach of the JOC extended to three hundred thousand. *La JOC en España*, p. 51. In any event, the number either directly involved as members or influenced by both organizations was small in an active working population of more than 3 million.

32. Rafael Díaz-Salazar, *Iglesia, dictadura y democracia* (Madrid, 1981), p. 207.

33. Castaño Colomer, *La JOC en España*, pp. 68–69.

34. Bonet believed that to avoid the taint of "yellow" unions under employer influence, it was necessary to develop specialized sections within Catholic Action composed of members drawn from the group they were seeking to evangelize. This was a strategy of "evangelization by equals," in which primary responsibility fell upon the "worker apostle" working among his peers. Quoted in López García, *Aproximación a la historia de la HOAC*, p. 32.

35. Castaño Colomer, *La JOC en España*, p. 56; Lannon, *Privilege, Persecution and Prophecy*, pp. 231–32.

There is little doubt that the cardinal primate saw Catholic workers' associations as a means of developing an elite capable of leading independent trade unions should the regime evolve institutionally as he hoped. In public, Pla y Deniel defended the HOAC and the JOC generally on the narrow grounds of the rights guaranteed to Catholic Action by the 1953 concordat and those given to all citizens by the *Fuero de los Españoles*. Neither organization, he declared in an extensive statement of 1958, was designed to challenge the official labor syndicates. Each was engaged in an apostolate permitted by the concordat. In steely language, the cardinal reproached the authorities for raising obstacles against the exercise of this legitimate activity. In a later statement, he went further. The work of Catholic Action in all its branches stood "above all politics [and] regime" because it was spiritual in purpose. The Church respected the existing political order, but neither it nor its members were obliged to accept the wisdom of all its laws.[36] This restatement of the old "accidentalist" formula of the early 1930s did not mean that the cardinal questioned the legitimacy of the regime. But it suggested that the interests of Church and State were beginning to diverge significantly on the issue of social justice.

By 1960, some bishops were growing uneasy as the HOAC and JOC became more aggressive in their denunciations of the regime's shortcomings. But Pla y Deniel continued to support them against official harassment. In 1960, he approved the text of a protest letter sent by the HOAC and JOC leadership to the minister responsible for the vertical syndicates, José Solís. The letter criticized the manipulation and dishonesty involved in recent syndical elections.[37] In reply, Solís wrote to the cardinal protesting against an intervention that in his judgment passed far beyond what the concordat allowed Catholic Action. Ever sensitive to infringement of the "liberty of the Church," and aware of years of official harassment directed against the HOAC and the JOC, Pla y Deniel responded by warning Solís of an impending crisis in civil-ecclesiastical relations if the government persisted in denying Catholic Action its legal rights. Although the cardinal argued on legalistic grounds, he explicitly rejected the idea that the "apostolate of Catholic Action . . . must be limited to prayer and the cultivation of piety carried out within church buildings." He also provided a further indication of his drift away from a rigid, frozen National Catholicism by informing Solís: "I believe that Your Excellency is realistic and will see very clearly that one cannot proceed in [the] Spain of 1960, as in 1940. . . . When during the recent World War many believed that those . . . states with a totalitarian regime would be conquerors, the idea that a totalitarian regime was best was defended. Today, neither within Spain nor outside of it . . . would anyone dare say this."[38]

36. Quoted in Castaños Colomer, *La JOC en España*, p. 71.

37. The text of this letter is reproduced in ibid., pp. 77–80.

38. "Extracto de la carta del Cardenal Pla y Deniel a José Solís, Delegado Nacional de Sindicatos," November 15, 1960, in Vicente Cárcel Ortí, *Pablo VI y España: fidelidad, renovación y crisis, 1963–1978*

Pla y Deniel did not challenge the existing political order, but his rejection of the attempt to limit the Church's activity in the social arena and his restatement of the "accidentalist" formula of the 1930s, at least as far as Catholic Action was concerned, were straws in the wind indicating that he was not prepared to accept an unchanging relationship between Church and State embodied in National Catholicism. The cardinal's tenacious defense of the HOAC and the JOC, and, it should be recognized, the internal vitality of these organizations themselves, provided the Church with its first significant success in its long and sometimes ambiguous campaign to escape from the compartmentalization of function imposed by the regime. The success was relative, perhaps more of a standoff than anything else. But when all is said and done, it represented a definite chink in the armor of National Catholicism.

The Church and the Regime's Future

Pla y Deniel also continued the Church's strategy of blocking the persistent attempts of the Falange to increase its influence at the expense of the regime's other clans. Although Franco had long since trimmed its billowing sails, the FET remained on the scene, a resolute opponent of the "Catholic family's" plans for a limited transformation of institutions. There seemed little possibility that the Falange could achieve its broader political objectives. But in 1956 Franco's balancing act suddenly appeared less stable when faced with an intensification of the factional struggles endemic to the regime's political life. Long-simmering hostility on the part of the Falange towards Minister of Education Ruiz Giménez, who had attempted a modest liberalization of universities and intellectual life, burst into the open.[39]

Violent clashes broke out in Madrid between supporters of the regime's university student syndicate (SEU) and young reformists who strongly objected to its monopoly on the country's campuses. The resulting uproar, involving the FET, now known as the National Movement, and even some military officers who saw the disturbances as a threat to the survival of the regime, did not endanger Franco's hold on power. But true to form, the general moved to restore the political balance

(Madrid, 1997), pp. 861, 863. While accepting that the existing syndicates were not opposed "to the social doctrine of the Church," the cardinal declared that he had explained to Franco that "according to many reports coming not only from the Hermandades de Obreras de Acción Católica, but also from workers in general of our diocese, the workers in the Spanish syndicates do not have sufficient authentic representation [in them]." Quoted in ibid., p. 861.

39. The minister's decision to restore some exiled professors to their university chairs provoked strong criticism from hard-liners who saw it as a subterfuge designed to reintroduce faculty of suspect political views. Ruiz Giménez's attendance at the 1955 funeral of Ortega y Gasset, whose work was regarded as intellectually dangerous by many within the regime, also provoked hostility. Tusell, *Franco y los católicos*, pp. 370–71, 376–77.

by dismissing Ruiz Giménez and increasing Falange representation on the cabinet.[40]

The removal of a minister identified with the "Catholic family" represented a defeat for the plans of Pla y Deniel, Herrera, and the lay elite of Catholic Action. The crisis of 1956 emboldened the Falange. It proposed new laws that would have vastly increased the National Movement's political influence.[41] For a hierarchy obsessed with the Falange's totalitarian machinations since the regime's inception, the proposed legislation raised a red flag signaling danger to the Church's interests.

The clerical leadership regarded the Falange's political offensive as so serious that in December 1957 a delegation comprised of Cardinals Pla y Deniel, Arriba y Castro of Tarragona, and Quiroga y Palacios of Santiago took the unusual step of calling upon Franco. There is no record of what the prelates said to the general, but the atmosphere in the meeting was tense. The prelates presented the general with a written statement. It attacked the proposed legislation as an attempt to establish "a true dictatorship of a single party, such as Fascism was in Italy, National Socialism in Germany or Peronism in Argentina."[42] In their criticism of the draft legislation, the cardinals referred specifically to Pius XI's 1937 encyclical condemning Nazism.

The princes of the Church were not moved by democratic sentiments. They explicitly rejected the return of "the liberalism of an inorganic democracy." But they argued forcefully against the Falange's apparently totalitarian scheme that "*would produce a very dangerous division among Spanish citizens.*" The delegation offered as an alternative the now familiar plan of the "Catholic family," based on full implementation of the *Fuero de los Españoles* as a means of creating a regime founded on "true organic representation" and the "rights of the human person which the Church defends."[43]

Franco had no intention of accepting the limited reform advocated by the cardinals. But in a negative sense, the episcopal intervention was effective. After receiving the delegation, the general declared to José Arrese, the minister of the movement aggressively promoting the new legislation, "I have something here that is very disagreeable and very serious."[44] As so often in the past, Franco dealt with

40. Stanley Payne, *The Franco Regime, 1936–1975* (Madison, 1987), pp. 439–44; Tusell, *Franco y los católicos*, pp. 381–84.

41. Through this proposed legislation, "Old-guard Falangists hoped to perpetuate a new political monopoly for the party after Franco's death." Payne, *The Franco Regime*, p. 447.

42. Quoted in Tusell, *Franco y los católicos*, p. 421. Quiroga Palacios informed a leading member of Opus Dei, Laureano López Rodó, that the meeting was tense. Franco listened to the exposition of Pla y Deniel without comment. He then made a "limited defense" of the proposed legislation, arguing that it was not as serious in its implications as the cardinals maintained. Laureano López Rodó, *Memorias* (4 vols., Barcelona, 1990–1993), vol. 1, p. 76.

43. Quoted in Tusell, *Franco y los católicos*, p. 422. Franco urged Arrese to amend the legislation, although the general gave him the "impression that he still supported his ideas, but had his hands tied by military and clerical opposition." Paul Preston, *Franco: A Biography* (London, 1993), p. 662.

44. Quoted in Tusell, *Franco y los católicos*, p. 425.

the conflict of the regime's clans by seeking to reestablish balance. When legislation dealing with the National Movement was finally approved in 1958, the totalitarian teeth to which the Church objected had been prudently extracted.

The disappearance from the cabinet of Martín Artajo in the important ministerial shuffle of 1957 deprived the "Catholic family" of its last voice in the highest circles of government. As its influence declined, a new Catholic faction made a spectacular entry onto the political scene with the appointment of three members of Opus Dei to key positions. The naming of three economic technocrats, Alberto Ullastres to the Ministry of Commerce, Mariano Navarro Rubio to Finance, and Laureano López Rodó to head a new development planning office, occurred primarily because the general, albeit with some hesitation, and his right-hand man, Carrero Blanco, believed that a change of policy was needed in view of an economy beset by inflation, a forest of often contradictory government economic regulations, and a poor record of performance in comparison with Western Europe.

"They have made us ministers," declared Father José María Escrivá de Balaguer, the founder of Opus Dei, wryly, upon receiving news of the appointment of three of its members to high office.[45] Few Catholic organizations in modern Spain have aroused more controversy than the "Work of God," especially after some of its members entered the government. Detractors saw Opus Dei as a "Holy Mafia," an organization obsessed with secrecy and intent upon extending its tentacles into business, education, and politics with a view to remaking the regime through an updated version of Catholic authoritarianism.[46] Defenders rejected such accusations, arguing, as its founder did on repeated occasions, that Opus Dei imposed no political program on its members. If they chose to accept positions in government, business, and education, the organization maintained, they did so as individuals committed to applying Christian principles to their respective occupations. Upon receiving congratulations on the appointment of Ullastres, Escrivá de Balaguer remarked, "It is all the same to me whether he is a minister or a street cleaner, all that interests me is that he should be a saint in his work."[47]

The reality of Opus Dei's role within Franco's Spain was more complex than this simple religious formula suggests. Opus Dei was unique through its status as a secular institute within the Catholic Church by combining aspects of a religious or-

45. Quoted in Alberto Moncada, *El Opus Dei: una interpretación* (Madrid, 1974), p. 35. Luis Carrero Blanco, as head of the prime minister's technical office, played a key role in securing the appointment of members of Opus Dei in the 1957 cabinet realignment. Why he did so is a matter of debate. It has been suggested that he did so because he regarded the organization as "safer" than Catholic Action, which he viewed uneasily because of its social initiatives, and because he saw Opus Dei as a counterweight to the growing, though temporary, influence of the Falange in 1956. Daniel Artigues, *L'Opus Dei en Espagne: son évolution, idéologique et politique, 1928–1957* (Paris, 1968), pp. 162–64.

46. This highly critical thesis has been most fully developed by Jesús Ynfante, *La prodigiosa aventura del Opus Dei: génesis y desarrollo de la Santa Mafia* (Paris, 1970).

47. Quoted in Andrés Vázquez Prado, *El fundador del Opus Dei: Mons. Josémaría Escrivá de Balaguer, 1902–1975* (Madrid, 1983), p. 289.

der with those of a lay apostolate. Members were divided into two basic categories, a nucleus of priests and some unordained who took the traditional vows of an order, and a larger body of laypeople, some married, committed to following the organization's principles in the secular world. Direct engagement with the world in the name of a Christianizing mission distinguished Opus Dei from conventional religious orders.[48] The combination of a religious with a lay apostolate made Opus Dei different within the Catholic Church's organization. But it also represented another version of the elitist strategy that had formed part and parcel of the Spanish Church's program of religious reconquest for generations. The model of Catholic Action, especially that of the Asociación Católica Nacional de Propagandistas, clearly influenced Escrivá de Balaguer during the formative years of Opus Dei during the 1930s. It has also been suggested that he wished to develop a Catholic intellectual vanguard capable of achieving the same degree of influence attained during the first three decades of the century by the secular, liberal Institución Libre de Enseñanza. Although a favorite *bête noire* of the Church, the Institución Libre was also grudgingly admired, not for its reformist principles but because of its success in producing a group of educators, writers, and politicians whose influence far exceeded their modest numbers. Whether Opus Dei constituted "a parody of the Institución," as one progressive Catholic intellectual put it, is arguable.[49] But Escrivá de Balaguer gave priority to the development of a select, highly educated Catholic elite. Even before the foundation of Opus Dei, he remarked that Catholic intellectuals were like "mountain peaks covered with snow; when they melt, the water descends and makes the valleys fruitful."[50]

Despite the similarities between Opus Dei and the ACNP, there were important differences. *Propagandistas* formed an integral part of Catholic Action. As such, they fell directly under the authority of the bishops. Because of its status as a secular institute, Opus Dei enjoyed the same autonomy from direct episcopal control as that possessed by religious orders. This provided the organization with a high degree of institutional autonomy and the freedom of action necessary to gain a foothold among potential recruits who had long formed the clientele of the ACNP and Catholic Action. Further, the emphasis of Opus Dei on the role of the individual as an agent of Christianization in the secular world made the organization less sympathetic to the idea of an elite directing the Catholic masses through a variety of confessional associations identified with Catholic Action and social Catholicism. Escrivá de Balaguer believed that Opus Dei should focus on the spiritual influence of its members as they worked fully in the secular world, rather

48. In 1947, Pope Pius XII authorized the formation of secular institutes as "associations of clerics or laypeople whose members can exercise the profession of practicing evangelical counsels in the world to acquire Christian perfection and exercise the apostolate fully." Quoted in Artigues, *L'Opus Dei en Espagne*, p. 57.

49. Quoted in ibid., p. 53.

50. Quoted in Vázquez de Prada, *El fundador del Opus Dei*, p. 107.

than imitate the organizational strategy pursued for generations by Catholic Action.[51]

Despite these differences, both the ACNP and Opus Dei were unabashedly elitist. Each sought to recruit bright and committed university students and graduates. But as Opus Dei matured during the 1940s and 1950s, it emphasized the recruitment of members drawn not only from the traditional elite that predominated within Catholic Action—lawyers, university professors and government officials—but also from the ranks of modernizing occupations: economists, engineers, and businessmen. Students of Opus Dei have emphasized the importance of a "bourgeoisie of affairs" in the organization, a managerial elite that reflected the emergence in Western Europe of a new breed of technocratic administrators in the wake of accelerated economic development.[52] If advocates of change identified with Catholic Action stressed the need to carry out an institutional transformation of the regime and the resolution of social conflicts through the application of papal social teaching, the members of Opus Dei who rose to positions of influence in 1957 saw a liberalized, capitalist economy and economic development on the Western European model as fundamental for the survival of Catholic Spain.

The economic stabilization and development plans promoted by ministers belonging to Opus Dei beginning in 1959 were not original, but combined with a series of other measures dealing with public finances and the reorganization of a woefully inefficient government bureaucracy, they formed a reasonably coherent package of reforms. The causes of the extraordinary rise in industrial production during the 1960s and early 1970s, as well as the contribution of Opus Dei technocrats to the process, are a source of controversy.[53] It can be said that the members of Opus Dei holding office were clear about their economic objectives. Their political agenda was less focused, beyond a commitment to the restoration of a conservative monarchy and a certain willingness to accept minimal institutional changes designed to placate the European democracies.

Whether this program can be identified with Opus Dei as an organization is a matter of debate. Even historians critical of Opus Dei's role during this period have warned against identifying the activities of the "politicized clan" holding government office with the organization as a whole.[54] Neither Escrivá de Balaguer, who

51. José Andrés-Gallego et al., *Los españoles entre la religión y la política: el franquismo y la democracia* (Madrid, 1996), pp. 101–4.

52. Artigues, *L'Opus Dei en Espagne*, p. 106; Hermet, *Les catholiques*, vol. 1, pp. 240–41; A. Sáez Alba, *La Asociación Católica de Propagandistas: reproducción y métodos de la derecha permanente* (Paris, 1974), pp. lxxxi–lxxxii.

53. Some economists "reject the view that Spain's much acclaimed economic miracle can be attributed to the planning mechanism." Joseph Harrison, *The Spanish Economy in the Twentieth Century* (London and Sydney, 1985), p. 146.

54. Artigues, *L'Opus Dei en Espagne*, pp. 102–3. Hermet has also warned against the tendency to see Opus Dei as "monolithic" with respect to the program advanced by its members in government. *Les catholiques*, vol. 1, p. 245. A former member of the organization noted that the course set by its techno-

moved to Rome in 1946, nor the Spanish leadership of Opus Dei ever endorsed the program of authoritarian modernization, although they may well have sympathized with it.[55] The combination of secrecy surrounding the organization, the role of its members in government and education, and the organization's extensive but not especially well-managed financial dealings projected, however, the image of a powerful, conspiratorial institution intent upon taking control of the State.[56] But the idea that Opus Dei as such was engaged in a single-minded conspiracy to refashion Franco's Spain according to it own designs can no longer be maintained.[57] What can be said is that members of Opus Dei's "politicized clan" formed a powerful lobby within a dictatorial regime and used their influence to recast it in a modern direction within an authoritarian framework.

The development of Opus Dei from the activities of a small group of university students gathered around Escrivá de Balaguer in Madrid during the early 1930s into a well-organized and effective organization did not occur overnight.[58] Its reappearance following the Civil War was scarcely noticed by the public. But in the favorable circumstances for Catholic initiatives prevailing during the early 1940s, its controversial founder exercised a magnetic appeal among his young, university-educated followers that solidified Opus Dei's still minuscule recruiting base. Escrivá de Balaguer possessed two qualities that were indispensable for the organization's later success—dogged determination in the face of obstacles and a genius for developing connections with ecclesiastical and political figures who used their influence to further his plans.

The entry of Opus Dei into the circle of Catholic elitist groups early aroused the

---

cratic ministers received far from unanimous approval among the rank and file. Moncada, *El Opus Dei*, p. 38. López Rodó argues that even members holding government office did not form a coherent group as far as their political views were concerned. *Memorias*, vol. 1, p. 99.

55. Artigues argues that Escrivá de Balaguer's enormously popular spiritual guide, *Camino*, first published in 1934, embodied the historic conservatism prevalent in early-twentieth-century Spanish Catholicism. The book presented "at the same time a typically Spanish Christianity of crusade, in the traditional sense of the term, and an effective Christianity superficially modernized." He also maintains that the authoritarian ideology of the monarchist Acción Española of the 1930s deeply influenced Opus Dei during its formative period. *L'Opus Dei en Espagne*, pp. 76, 34–35. There is little doubt of Escrivá de Balaguer's sympathy for the Franco regime. The 1942 report of the national security police (Dirección General de Seguridad) on possible candidates for episcopal appointments observed that his commitment to the National Movement was complete and his attitude towards the Falange was "sympathetic." "Lista de personas propuestas como posibles obispos con informes de la D. G. S. y FET de las JONS," in *Documentos inéditos para la historia del Generalísimo Franco*, ed. Fundación Nacional Francisco Franco (4 vols., Madrid, 1992–1994), p. 144.

56. The business dealings of Opus Dei, especially in the banking sector, were extensive. The case against the organization for its participation in diverse enterprises is made in abundant detail by Ynfante, *La aventura prodigiosa*, pp. 229–95. With the knowledge of an insider, Alberto Moncada argues, however, that the organization did not manage its business affairs well. They were "badly administered and totally insufficient to meet present expenses and provide for the future." *El Opus Dei*, p. 31.

57. Hermet, *Les catholiques*, vol. 1, p. 245.

58. Although the founder always gave 1928 as the date of foundation, Opus Dei's real institutional life began during the early 1930s in the form of student residences and private academies established in Madrid.

suspicions of the Jesuits, long the driving force behind the ACNP. With some justification, they viewed Opus Dei as poaching on the clientele that had been theirs for decades. In 1941, the success of Opus Dei in recruiting a select company of brilliant university students in Barcelona provoked Jesuit criticism. A well-known preacher of the order attacked members of Marian Congregations, religious associations of young people under Jesuit direction who had also joined Opus Dei, as nothing less than "traitors."[59] The organization believed itself the victim of "an organized and systematic campaign" waged by certain unidentified religious orders. Opus Dei was accused of promoting the role of the laity and thereby endangering vocations to the priesthood. Some priests even attacked the organization from the pulpit.[60] The civil authorities, egged on by the Falange, viewed Opus Dei for a time as a secret organization that bore close watching. In 1941, the government's Tribunal for the Suppression of Freemasonry even investigated Opus Dei as a secret society on the curious grounds that it was allegedly masonic in purpose. The situation grew so threatening that the papal nuncio advised Escrivá de Balaguer to purchase an airplane ticket in preparation for a quick escape from the country, although there is evidence that Franco already held Escrivá de Balaguer in high regard by this time.[61]

These trials were overcome because of the timely intervention of that most conservative of bishops, Eijo y Garay, who provided Opus Dei with protection by defending the organization against the accusations of its critics and recognizing it as a pious association within the Madrid diocese.[62] Papal recognition in 1943 and the Vatican's decision to grant it the status of a secular institute in 1947 further consolidated its position. By this time, controversy had receded sufficiently to allow Opus Dei to concentrate its activities on the recruitment and training of its members. Insofar as it assumed a public role during this period, it did so through efforts to gain a foothold in higher education. Here the organization used its connections to good effect. During the Civil War, a young chemist and member of Opus Dei, José María Albareda, cultivated the friendship of José Ibáñez Martín when both took refuge in the Chilean embassy. After becoming minister of education in 1939, Ibáñez Martín proved well disposed towards the educational ambitions of Opus

59. Artigues, *L'Opus Dei en Espagne*, p. 30.

60. Amadeo de Fuenmayor, Valentín Gómez-Iglesias, and José Luis Illanes, *El itinerario jurídico del Opus Dei* (Pamplona, 1988), p. 90.

61. Vázquez Prada, *El fundador del Opus Dei*, pp. 226–27. To what extent the campaign of 1941 against Opus Dei and its founder was "directed and organized," as the organization later claimed, is difficult to establish. Clerical criticism focused on the fact that Opus Dei was not "approved by the Church." Ibid. In the margins of a 1942 report on Escrivá de Balaguer, whose name had been proposed as a candidate for an episcopal appointment, Franco wrote, "Ibáñez [minister of education] says he is very good." "Lista de personas propuestas como posibles obispos con informes de la D. G. S. y FET de las JONS," p. 144.

62. Vázquez Prada, *El fundador del Opus Dei*, p. 228. A stout defender of Opus Dei, the bishop of Madrid invited Escrivá de Balaguer to submit a formal request for canonical authorization in March 1940. Fuenmayor et al., *El itinerario jurídico del Opus Dei*, p. 90.

Dei. Albareda was named secretary-general of the regime's new national research institution, the Consejo Superior de Investigaciones Científicas (CSIC). Although Opus Dei as such never controlled the CSIC, with its ample budget and patronage opportunities, the presence of Albareda, who stayed in office until 1966, helped it to develop an effective network of connections within the research community.[63]

Through the direct influence exercised by the minister over the examining boards responsible for recommending professorial appointments, Ibáñez Martín also contributed to the success of Opus Dei in securing university chairs for its members. Although it was never as successful as its numerically superior rival, Catholic Action, Opus Dei did well in the "conquest of chairs." By 1956, it is estimated that the organization held 20 percent of professorial appointments.[64] By the early 1950s, it had also opened *colegios mayores* on several campuses, while in 1952 it obtained permission to establish a quasi-university in Pamplona, the Estudios Generales de Navarra, despite rumblings of discontent from the Jesuits, who saw the new institution as competing with their university at Deusto.[65]

The modernizing character of Opus Dei developed especially through the creation in 1958 of the Instituto de Estudios Superiores de la Empresa (IESE) in Barcelona. Spain's first postgraduate business school based on the American model, the IESE provided advanced instruction to a new generation of managers, most already occupying key posts in their firms.[66] Although the Jesuits later jumped on the entrepreneurial bandwagon by establishing similar institutions, Opus Dei first recognized the importance of extending its influence among businessmen destined to play a prominent role within a liberalized, capitalist economic system.

The educational efforts of Opus Dei also extended to secondary schools, among them the Institución Nacional de Enseñanza Media "Ramiro de Maeztu," strategically located in Madrid near the CSIC. Although the number of such schools was limited in comparison with those maintained by the Jesuits, they became "the most exclusive schools in Spain, seizing from the Society of Jesus . . . part of its clientele comprised of the sons of the bourgeoisie."[67] Opus Dei showed less concern with the social apostolate than did Catholic Action, but it made a nod in its direction by

63. Artigues, *L'Opus Dei en Espagne*, pp. 36–40.

64. The most fruitful period for Opus Dei in this campaign was between 1943 and 1947, although as long as Ibáñez Martín remained in office, there were further successes. The appointment of Ruiz Giménez as minister of education in 1951 reduced the opportunities available to Opus Dei. The new minister took prompt action to diminish his office's ability to determine the composition of examination boards. Ibid., pp. 48–49; Ynfante, *La prodigiosa aventura*, pp. 58–59, 67. It is estimated that Opus Dei had 8,000 Spanish members in 1956, Catholic Action, 640,467 in 1958. Gómez Pérez, *Política y religión*, pp. 158, 257.

65. Artigues, *L'Opus Dei en Espagne*, p. 114.

66. By 1965, 796 students had graduated: 305 occupied top level managerial positions, 248 were in middle management, while 243 were beginning their business careers. Ibid., p. 63.

67. Ynfante, *La prodigiosa aventura*, p. 70.

establishing a vocational school in Madrid that taught fifteen hundred working-class students.

The extraordinary institutional development of Opus Dei between the low point of 1940 and 1960 owed a considerable debt to the determination, organizational ability, and personality of its founder. But its appeal also lay in the perception that it represented something new and dynamic within Spanish Catholicism.[68] Whatever one's opinion of the organization, declared a critic of its development, "One cannot ignore the profound originality of the Work [of God]."[69] Opus Dei shared with Catholic Action the same confidence in an elitist strategy as the best means of assuring the survival of the Catholic Spain that had emerged from the Civil War. But Opus Dei combined the historic conservatism, elitism, and highly traditional view of religion common to other Catholic groups, with a modernizing emphasis on hard work, almost Calvinist in intensity, and professional success on the American business model.[70] This eclectic combination of the traditional with the modern produced an "athletic Christianity" that appealed to highly educated university graduates seeking new answers to the old problem of the survival of Catholic Spain in a changing world.[71] The "politicized clan" holding government office pushed this purpose to its outer limits by advocating economic changes on the Western European model as essential to securing the regime's survival through "the Hispanization of ends, [and] the Europeanization of means."[72]

The influential role of ministers who belonged to Opus Dei provoked intense controversy. The regime's other clans saw their rise as an Opus Dei power grab. The Falange and the "Catholic family" had long nourished resentments following the cutting attacks launched against them by a leading Opus Dei intellectual, Rafael Calvo Serer, in 1953.[73] The ascendancy of the "politicized clan" that began in 1957 intensified this hostility. Fears that Opus Dei would control the State and tailor it to its designs proved exaggerated. Franco was no more disposed to deliver all

68. Escrivá de Balaguer wished to avoid a "Catholicism of facade," emphasizing external ceremony and what he perceived to be the gap between the public profession of faith and an often relaxed application of the Church's moral and religious teaching at the personal level. Artigues, *L'Opus Dei en Espagne*, p. 76.

69. Ibid., p. 117.

70. Escrivá de Balaguer emphasized the importance of the work ethic in *Camino*. According to Hermet, "the Calvinist ethic" entered fully into "the spirit of Opus Dei." *Les catholiques*, vol. 1, pp. 114–15.

71. Ibid.

72. Ibid., p. 142.

73. During the early 1950s, controversy raged among the intellectuals of the clans about the ideology and future of the regime. Although confined to a limited group, the dispute took on a sharper edge as the result of a series of articles published by Rafael Calvo Serer, editor of the journal *Arbor*, controlled by Opus Dei and financed by the CSIC. "The *Arbor* circle strongly supported an authoritarian Catholic monarchist succession to the regime, combatting Falangism, liberalism, and narrowly bureaucratic loyalism to the system." Payne, *The Franco Regime*, p. 438. Calvo Serer singled out Ruiz Giménez, then minister of education, and certain Falangist writers for attack because they advocated a limited opening up of the regime's intellectual life. They were, he said, nothing less than "revolutionary opportunists" who would bring the regime to disaster if allowed to go unchecked. Quoted in Tusell, *Franco y los católicos*, p. 330.

power into its hands than he was to elevate the regime's other factions. Nor did the Opus Dei ministers possess a constituency capable of removing its opponents from a crowded field of jostling competitors.[74] Moreover, although its economic plans were precise, its political projects for remaking the regime were more diffuse. If the larger Catholic Action, strongly supported by the hierarchy, failed to realize its schemes to transform institutions, there was no prospect that Opus Dei would be more successful. In many respects, the political objectives of Opus Dei government officials were as ill defined and impractical as those promoted by the "Catholic family." In the end, Franco used members of the organization as he had used all the clans and coteries supporting his rule. When, by the early 1970s, the accelerated growth of the preceding decade faltered and Opus ministers became embroiled in financial scandals, the era of Opus Dei prominence in government drew to a close.

For the Church, the spectacular rise of Opus Dei accentuated the internal fragmentation of Spanish Catholicism in its political dimension. Catholic Action, particularly the ACNP, viewed Opus Dei as an unwelcome competitor that threatened its plans for the regime's institutional evolution. The commitment to an authoritarian government within the framework of economic liberalism clashed even more directly with the purposes of the HOAC and the JOC. Further, the emergence of clandestine Christian Democratic parties, the Unión Demócrata Cristiana, founded in 1956 by the progressive ex–CEDA minister of the 1930s, Manuel Giménez Fernández, and the Democracia Social Cristiana, established in 1960 by the party's former leader, José María Gil Robles, now an outspoken opponent of the regime, showed that the prospect of achieving political unity among Catholics was more remote than ever. The clerical leadership continued to proclaim its loyalty to Franco, but by 1960 it was evident that the fiction of unanimous Catholic support for the regime on which National Catholicism was based could no longer be sustained.

The Challenge from the Regions

The facade of a National Catholicism was further shaken by the reemergence of support among clergy and laity for autonomous aspirations in the Basque Provinces and Catalonia. Following the Civil War's end, the regime used every means at its command to repress movements that it regarded as separatist. The authorities followed the strategy employed by the Restoration and the Primo de Rivera dictatorship by using the government's patronage rights over episcopal appointments to appoint to the Basque dioceses bishops who could be relied upon to keep the local clergy under control. "I have a bishop for Guipúzcoa. He is a man

74. López Rodó noted that he and his fellow Opus ministers held only a small minority of cabinet positions, "a half dozen among more than a hundred ministers." *Memorias*, vol. 1, p. 98.

who will speak of God by speaking of Spain," Franco is said to have remarked upon the appointment in 1937 of Javier Lauzurica as apostolic administrator of the Vitoria diocese.[75]

Lauzurica did not disappoint the general. The bishop purged the faculty of the Vitoria seminary, long regarded by the regime as a hotbed of Basque nationalism, and eliminated courses in Basque culture from the curriculum. Seminarians were instructed to avoid all political entanglements. Priests in rural districts with a Basque-speaking population found themselves subject to harassment by the ecclesiastical authorities for preaching in Basque.[76] Nor was the government enthusiastic about a project to create new dioceses in the region, although from a pastoral perspective such a reorganization was long overdue.[77]

In 1950, the government finally yielded to Vatican pressure and established the dioceses of Bilbao and San Sebastián. But it was determined to frustrate a historic demand of the local clergy for the creation of a Basque ecclesiastical province with an archdiocese in Vitoria. Fearing that such a reorganization would encourage Basque separatism, the regime followed a divide-and-rule strategy by placing Vitoria and Bilbao in the Burgos ecclesiastical province, while San Sebastián was assigned to Pamplona.[78] The authorities saw to it that native Basques were not appointed to head the region's new dioceses.[79]

These tactics proved counterproductive. The historic identification of the clergy, first with Carlism and later with the Partido Nacionalista Vasco, was too entrenched to be dislodged by the measures employed by the civil and ecclesiastical authorities.[80] Even during the darkest period of repression, between 1940 and 1945, Basque priests received moral encouragement from a clergy in exile, a per-

75. Quoted in Ignacio Villota Elejalde, *La Iglesia en la sociedad española y vasca contemporáneas* (Bilbao, 1985), p. 466.

76. Ibid., pp. 463–64, 466–67. Initially, Lauzurica, a fluent Basque speaker, permitted the use of the language in areas where the population knew no other language. This initiative was cut short by the civil authorities, who threatened legal action against priests using Basque in religious services. Thereafter, Lauzurica only employed the language on his pastoral visits. Javier Sánchez Erauskin, *Por Dios hacia el imperio: nacional catolicismo en las Vascongadas del primer franquismo* (San Sebastián, 1994), p. 162.

77. The decision to divide the Vitoria diocese was not universally welcomed within the Church. Seminarians in the Vitoria seminary were troubled by the change, which meant the end of a single educational institution for the Basque clergy. "Why break that splendid reality!" they declared. José Ignacio Tellechea Idigoras, *Tapices de la memoria: historia clínica 279.952* (San Sebastián, 1991), pp. 128–29.

78. Many Basque clergy saw the diocesan reorganization as the result of the regime's Machiavellian strategy. Ibid., p. 471. This was a correct assessment of the situation. Giving the Basque Provinces "ecclesiastical unity . . . could not be admitted politically by the Government of Franco." Tusell, *Franco y los católicos*, pp. 235–36.

79. The appointment of Casimiro Morcillo to Bilbao and Jaime Font y Andreu to San Sebastián provoked some protests from the clergy, who demanded the appointment of native Basques to the region's bishoprics. Anabella Barroso, *Sacerdotes bajo la atenta mirada del régimen franquista: los conflictos sociopolíticos de la Iglesia en el País Vasco desde 1960 a 1975* (Bilbao, 1995), pp. 48–49.

80. In 1951, Bernard Malley assessed the Basque situation in these terms: "It is safe to say that a plebiscite today would show an overwhelming rejection of General Franco. Socialists, Communists and Republicans would vote, to a man with the [Basque] Nationalists. Nor would the separatist clergy hesitate to join the general clamour for the removal of the common oppressor." "Survey of the Church in

sistent thorn in the regime's side through its propaganda and lobbying activities abroad.

In 1945, Bishop Múgica minced no words in a spirited defense of his clergy's conduct during the Civil War. Because "many of my faithful and priests" were "persecuted, accused and condemned unjustly," the bishop declared that he was compelled "to protest as the judge of . . . the flock entrusted to my care." The bishop reproached the government for the executions of Basque priests during the autumn of 1936, for the "calumnies" it directed against the region's clergy, and for its continuing reprisals against the priests of his diocese.[81] In 1944, a group of Basque clerical exiles asked the Holy See to persuade the hierarchy to reject "all interference on the part of the Spanish State in the affairs of the Church." The petitioners also appealed for the restoration of Basque to religious services as a pastoral necessity and as a means of ending the "great scandal" caused by the Church's "anti-Basque policy."[82]

By the early 1950s, as the regime became less heavy-handed in the use of the repressive tools at its disposal, the focus of resistance shifted from the clergy in exile to a group of younger priests at home. The appearance of the review *Egiz* in 1950 marked the beginning of a resurgent Basque nationalism among the clergy. Ecclesiastical contributors directed their attention primarily to renewing historic pleas for the appointment of native Basques to the region's bishoprics and the use of the Basque language in religious services. Basque was "ferociously persecuted at both the civil and ecclesiastical levels"; Basque names could not be given to children at baptism, while the catechism was taught exclusively in Castilian.[83] An editorial noted the irony of a seminary curriculum that provided instruction in Latin, Hebrew, Greek, French, and English but not in Basque, the language of daily life in many rural parishes.

Egiz also ventured boldly onto dangerous ground by calling for respect for civil rights, social justice, and the independence of the Church from the State. Contributors attacked the monopoly of the vertical syndicates and the harsh repression di-

---

Spain and of Its Attitude towards the Regime," ms. December 12, 1951, p. 23, Public Record Office, Foreign Office/371/102059.

81. "Mi protesta," April 1945, in E. A. Talde, *Historia general de la guerra civil en Euskadi* (6 vols., San Sebastián, 1978–1981), vol. 5, pp. 76, 81. Múgica declared that he had not protested publicly until this date for two reasons. First, he had received a request "that I could not ignore" to remain silent. The bishop did not identify the source of this request, but it is likely that it came from either Pius XII or high Vatican officials. Second, Múgica feared that a public protest would have provoked reprisals against the innocent on the part of the regime through the "ominous proceedings" that it employed under a repressive Law of Political Responsibilities. Ibid., p. 77. Canon Alberto de Onaindia, a strong defender of the Basque Republic during the Civil War, gently reproached Múgica for remaining silent for so long, but recognized that the bishop's stream of reports to the Vatican over the regime's persecution of clergy in his diocese since 1936 made him an effective "ambassador of the Basques" before the papacy. *Hombre de paz en la guerra: capítulos de mi vida* (Buenos Aires, 1973), pp. 116–17.

82. Quoted in Paulo Iztueta Armendariz, *Sociología del fenómeno contestatario del clero vasco, 1940–1975* (Zarauz, 1981), p. 143.

83. Quoted in ibid., p. 144.

rected against members of the clandestine Solidaridad de Trabajadores Vascos (STV), one of the few pre–Civil War Catholic trade unions untarred by the brush of employer influence. They also reproached the hierarchy for tolerating the regime's abuse of authority. The Basque clergy, *Egiz* declared, did not wish to be "servants of the State because they are servants of the Church."[84]

The pastoral and political message delivered by *Egiz* provoked a hostile reaction from the civil and ecclesiastical authorities. The region's bishops, none of them Basques, closed the journal in 1952 on the grounds that it was "politically partisan" and had attacked the hierarchy.[85] Although the review survived for only two years, its long-term significance was great. The opinions appearing on its pages represented the first public expression by the clergy anywhere in Spain of views that challenged the underlying assumptions of National Catholicism. Moreover, the Basque hierarchy's condemnation of the opinions expressed in *Egiz* proved unable to halt the spread of its ideas among the local clergy. A historic sense of discrimination at the hands of the civil and ecclesiastical authorities combined with a keen pastoral awareness of the threat posed to the Church's religious mission by the regime's social and economic policies in one of the country's most industrialized regions to provide fertile ground for the dissemination of the ideas promoted by *Egiz* in the years that followed.

Dissatisfaction among the Basque clergy with the regime and the hierarchy became stronger after 1956, especially among younger priests.[86] In 1960, it exploded into the open. Three hundred thirty-nine priests from the dioceses of Vitoria, San Sebastián, Bilbao, and Pamplona addressed an open letter to their bishops that was nothing less than an explicit denunciation of National Catholicism and the regime with which it was identified.[87] Arguing from the premises of Catholic natural law teaching, the 339 reproached the government for violating the right to personal liberty and freedom of conscience to which every citizen was entitled. They attacked the use of systematic torture by the police, the employment of military courts as a means of repressing dissent, the lack of syndical freedom, and the manipulation of public opinion by the officially controlled media. The open letter declared boldly, "In Spain, an authentic Parliament does not exist, nor is there political liberty."[88] In a final shot over the bow of National Catholicism, the 339 called attention to "the contradiction existing between Catholic doctrine with respect to

84. Ibid., p. 146. *Egiz* also protested against the State's episcopal patronage rights as posing a serious danger to the Church's independence. Barroso, *Sacerdotes bajo la atenta mirada del régimen franquista*, p. 50.

85. Iztueta Armendariz, *Sociología del fenómeno contestatario*, p. 144, note 14.

86. Barroso, *Sacerdotes bajo la atenta mirada del régimen franquista*, p. 56.

87. The majority of the clergy signing the letter were parish priests or assistants. One-third of them had been ordained during the 1950s, an indication of the emergence of a younger clergy. Ibid., pp. 66, 68.

88. "Carta de 339 curas vascos a sus obispos," May 30, 1960, in *Organizaciones obreras cristianas en la oposición al franquismo, 1951–1975*, ed. Javier Domínguez (Bilbao, 1985), p. 62.

the human person and its lack of fulfillment by a regime which officially calls itself Catholic and to which the Spanish Catholic hierarchy has lent its resolute support."[89]

The bishops of the Basque dioceses, backed by the papal nuncio, Hildebrando Antoniutti, an outspoken admirer of Franco, rejected the open letter, alleging that it was the work of a small minority of priests intent upon "promoting a great propaganda scandal of murky origin and with purposes no less murky and with grave repercussions for the Church itself."[90] On this last point, the bishops were correct. The letter of the 339 revealed a powerful current of opposition to National Catholicism. It also marked the beginning of a progressive version of the prophetic denunciation that had been used by the clergy against the Church's perceived enemies since the days of the French Revolution. The object of these modern imitators of the Old Testament prophets was not, as it had been for earlier clerical generations, a succession of ideological evils propagated by the French Revolution—liberalism, socialism, communism, and republicanism—but the principles of National Catholicism itself.

Reaction to the open letter foreshadowed the deep divisions that would soon develop within the Church and between large numbers of clergy and the regime. The 339 received expressions of support from priests and laypeople throughout the country.[91] Although *Ecclesia*, still under the influence of Cardinal Pla y Deniel, approached the controversy with discretion, it reflected the cardinal's spirit of cautious independence with respect to the regime when in June 1960 it called attention to the "contradiction existing between Catholic doctrine with respect to the human person and its lack of fulfillment by the Regime."[92] The authorities promptly ordered confiscation of the offending issue.

That the Basque clergy first threw down the gauntlet before the regime developed from the historic identification of the region's clergy with opposition to centralizing governments in Madrid. In 1931, the future bishop Antonio Pildain remarked with some justification of the Basque Provinces, "We are the Ireland of the West," a reference to the region's persistent quest for autonomy from distant authority.[93] As in Ireland, the clergy of the Basque Provinces played a leading role in the nineteenth and twentieth centuries in the formation of a cultural and political identity based on Catholicism. Successive regimes and episcopal generations had

89. Ibid., p. 63.

90. Quoted in Iztueta Armendariz, *Sociología del fenómeno contestatario*, p. 149.

91. Mimeographed copies of the open letter were widely distributed among the clergy elsewhere in Spain to the consternation of the papal nuncio, who orchestrated a determined counteroffensive through the bishops of the Basque dioceses. Rafael Gómez Pérez, *El franquismo y la Iglesia* (Madrid, 1986), pp. 82–83.

92. Quoted in Blázquez, *La traición de los clérigos*, p. 142.

93. Quoted in Fernando García de Cortázar, "La Iglesia vasca: del carlismo al nacionalismo, 1870–1936," in *Estudios de historia contemporánea del País Vasco*, ed. J. C. Jiménez de Aberasturi (San Sebastián, 1982), p. 261.

done their best to eliminate these ties between religion, clergy, and nationalism. The letter of the 339 provided eloquent testimony to the extent of their failure.

A second focus of resistance began to develop during the late 1950s in Catalonia. Although the clergy in the region had been deeply involved in the first manifestations of autonomist sentiment in the region during the late nineteenth and early twentieth centuries, its initial enthusiasm, though it never disappeared, was tempered by the openly secularist orientation of the regional government, the Generalitat, established during the Republic, and by widespread fear of social revolution. The Franco regime's repressive strategy towards any expression of Catalan cultural or political identity proved as counterproductive over the long term as its policy towards the Basque Provinces.

In Catalonia after the Civil War, ecclesiastical authorities cooperated with the regime's antiseparatist policy by discouraging the use of Catalan in religious services. In 1939, the vicar general of the Barcelona diocese, "acceding with pleasure to the indications which have been given to us by most distinguished authorities," ordered parish priests to use no other "vernacular language than Spanish in the acts of the public cult celebrated in their respective churches." In the Lérida diocese, the ecclesiastical authorities even insisted that the clergy should use the Castilian pronunciation of Latin in the liturgy rather than the traditional Roman historically used in Catalonia.[94] But over time the region's bishops came to defend the use of Catalan in religious services and to oppose "the restrictions which [the authorities] attempted to impose from Madrid."[95]

Resistance to the regime by clergy and laity in Catalonia developed more slowly than it had in the Basque country during the 1940s and 1950s.[96] In 1959, it made its first public appearance. The crude attacks by the pro-Franco editor of Barcelona's largest newspaper on a parish priest who had dared preach in Catalan incited widespread protests. In 1960, events took a more serious turn during the general's visit to the city. Franco's outrage, moved by the singing of the Catalan anthem at a concert he was attending, led to a police crackdown on supporters of autonomy. The authorities arrested hundreds, including the young leader of a

94. Quoted in Josep Massot i Muntaner, *Aproximació a la història religiosa de Catalunya* (Barcelona, 1973), p. 138, note 2; Jaume Barallat i Barés, *L'Església sota el franquisme: una mostra local: Lleida, 1938–1968* (Lérida, 1994), pp. 118–19.

95. Vicente Enrique y Tarancón, *Confesiones* (Madrid, 1996), p. 77.

96. Catholic university students were prominent in the activities of the Joventut Catalana Democràtica, founded in 1945, as a clandestine opponent of the regime, while the Unió Democràtica de Catalunya also functioned as an underground organization. Clergy committed to the defense of Catalan culture also reemerged. In 1949, the Capuchin friar Basilo de Rubí founded the Franciscalia, primarily a cultural discussion group that organized conferences on a variety of contemporary topics. The group attracted the support of "more radical and non-conformist young Christians" and the hostility of the authorities who viewed some of the topics discussed at its meetings as suspect. For a full discussion of the underground opposition to the regime among the Catalan clergy and laity during the 1940s and 1950s, see Josep M. Piñol, *El nacionalcatolicisme a Catalunya i la resistència, 1926–1966* (Barcelona, 1993), chapter 3.

Catholic autonomist group, Jordi Pujol, who was sentenced to a seven-year jail term.

The arrests and the abuse inflicted on prisoners by the police elicited a prompt response from one of the leading religious figures of the region, Abbot Aureli Escarré, head of the great shrine of Catalan Catholicism and the "redoubt in which the essence of the Catalan people was conserved," the Benedictine monastery of Montserrat.[97] During the 1950s, the abbot promoted the use of Catalan in religious services. In 1959, he defended parish priests against the governor of Barcelona province, who accused them of encouraging separatism by preaching in Catalan.[98] With a hierarchy dominated by non-Catalans and easily pressured by the civil authorities, Escarré was the "spiritual leader of Catalan Catholicism."[99] Indignant over the police repression of 1960, Escarré refused to attend a reception held in Franco's honor and sent a telegram of protest lamenting the arrests and police torture. They were "the sad epilogue of Your Excellency's stay in Barcelona."[100] These events also sent tremors through the Church as a whole. Even *Ecclesia* felt compelled to publish an editorial criticizing police torture as an unjustified attack upon "personal rights."[101]

By 1960, the facade of National Catholicism remained intact, but it had begun to crack. Opposition from within the Church did not emerge from a single source, nor was it in any sense coherent. The hierarchy remained loyal to the regime, but individual bishops began to question certain aspects of the regime's organization, especially with respect to social policy. The hierarchy's attitude was full of contradictions. Bishop Pildain attacked the monopoly of the vertical syndicates but remained attached to a deeply antiliberal political philosophy. Cardinal Pla y Deniel and Bishop Herrera promoted a revived social Catholicism that became innovative and progressive, but they drew back from openly challenging the official labor organization. There were signs that some bishops were growing uneasy about the regime's repressive nature, but, whatever their misgivings, they showed no desire to challenge the existing state of affairs.

By this time the prospect of creating a revived "union of Catholics" for political ends was as remote as ever. Clandestine Christian Democratic parties, the "Catholic family," the politicized clan of Opus Dei, regional movements in the Basque Provinces and Catalonia, and Catholic workers' associations promoted distinct programs on which no agreement was possible. The 1950s saw the inevitable

97. Enrique y Tarancón, *Confesiones*, p. 77. The Benedictines of Montserrat, "lovers of the native language and culture," enjoyed considerable freedom of action in the cultural sphere "despite the absurd centralism of Madrid." Ibid.

98. Cardinal Tarancón notes, however, that the bishops "defended and supported the use of Catalan in religious services and opposed the restrictions that Madrid attempted to impose." Ibid.

99. Hermet, *Les catholiques*, vol. 2, p. 327.

100. Quoted in Blázquez, *La traición de los clérigos*, p. 140.

101. Quoted in ibid.

emergence of the inner contradictions of Spanish Catholicism made dormant for a time by the special circumstances prevailing in the years immediately following the Civil War. In retrospect, the decade of the 1950s formed a prelude to the intense conflicts that developed within the Church during the 1960s, when the contradictions that had already emerged burst into a full-blown internal struggle the like of which was unknown in the Spanish Church's modern history.

CHAPTER XVII

THE CHURCH RESTORED

Within the history of modern Spanish Catholicism, there was no period in which the Church more successfully developed the institutional foundations that it believed necessary for its strategy of religious conquest than the Franco era. Generously assisted by the government, the Church undertook the massive task of rebuilding churches destroyed in the former Republican zone. Ecclesiastical finances flourished as never before. A demographic recovery among the diocesan and regular clergy made up some of the losses suffered during the Civil War, while membership in Catholic lay associations expanded significantly. The Church's role in education grew in comparison with the Restoration and the Primo de Rivera dictatorship. Despite its restlessness over official censorship, the Church profited from its relationship with the regime to develop a network of newspapers, magazines, and radio stations unequaled in its modern history. But this impressive institutional resurgence failed to resolve completely historic pastoral and organizational problems arising from an unbalanced distribution of clergy and resources.

Institutional Recuperation

Following the Civil War's end, the Church faced two immediate tasks. First, it needed to reconstitute diocesan administrations in the former Republican zone and normalize them in Nationalist Spain, where episcopal vacancies reached the unprecedented number of thirty by 1941.[1] The 1941 *convenio* between the regime and the Vatican finally removed this obstacle to the hierarchy's replenishment. Second, the Church required vast amounts of capital to reconstruct the five thousand churches and ecclesiastical buildings ruined or damaged during the war.

1. *Ecclesia*, April 18, 1942; Santiago Petschen, *La Iglesia en la España de Franco* (Madrid, 1977),

In 1939, the regime provided funding to rebuild seventy churches. Twice this number were restored in the following year.[2] In March 1941, the government established a Junta for the Reconstruction of Churches, which in its first year of operation rebuilt a hundred churches. By 1943, the pace of reconstruction quickened as a result of low-interest loans made available to the ecclesiastical authorities. The regime also provided financial assistance to the religious orders for the reconstruction of monasteries, friaries, and convents.[3] By the end of 1943, the rebuilding campaign achieved impressive results. More than three thousand churches had been restored. Reconstruction efforts continued through the decade. In 1947 alone, government grants and loans totaling 200 million pesetas permitted the restoration of 809 churches.[4] Overall, it has been estimated that between 1939 and 1964, the regime provided the vast sum of more than 4 billion pesetas for rebuilding churches and constructing new religious edifices.[5]

The regime also expected the Church to raise funds for reconstruction through private donations, as Franco made plain in a 1942 interview. When asked if had confidence in the faithful's generous instincts, the general replied, "Oh yes! Charity is never exhausted."[6] How much the Church raised on its own is impossible to establish. In the large Barcelona diocese, Catholics contributed 46 million pesetas by 1945 to a campaign to rebuild 246 parish churches. Smaller and poorer dioceses fared less well. In the Toledo archdiocese, for example, only half of its destroyed parish churches had been restored by 1946.[7] But by 1950 the Church had largely recovered from the physical damage inflicted during the Civil War.

Assessing the extent of Church wealth under the Franco regime is no easier a task than it is for earlier periods. Income was derived from several sources—the annual government appropriation for diocesan priests' salaries and the maintenance of Church fabrics, additional subsidies for a variety of other purposes, private donations to the secular and regular clergy for ordinary expenses and construction, subventions, and gifts for a wide range of charitable causes operating under ecclesiastical auspices. The *culto y clero* appropriation in 1939 restored the financing formula originally adopted by liberal governments during the nineteenth century. Although the bishops welcomed its reestablishment, they shared the concerns of earlier episcopal generations about a fiscal mechanism that made the Church dependent on the financial decisions of government. The clerical leadership contin-

---

p. 58; "La historia del episcopado español del 41 al 71," *Vida Nueva* (1972), nos. 821–822, p. 11.

2. Bernard Malley, "Survey of the Church in Spain and Its Attitude towards the Regime," ms. December 12, 1951, Public Record Office, Foreign Office 371/102059, p. 5.

3. Petschen, *La Iglesia en la España de Franco*, pp. 58–59; "España reconstruye sus templos," *Ecclesia*, April 18, 1942, p. 5; "Para la reconstrucción de edificios religiosos," ibid., February 14, 1942, p. 8.

4. Malley, "Survey of the Church in Spain," ms., p. 5.

5. J. Castellà-Gassol, *¿De donde viene y donde va el dinero de la Iglesia española?* (Barcelona, 1975), p. 30.

6. *Ecclesia*, January 14, 1942, p. 7.

7. Petschen, *La Iglesia en la España de Franco*, p. 59.

ued to believe that the clergy deserved a generous and autonomous source of official funding because of the "immense theft" of ecclesiastical property by liberal ministries between 1835 and 1860.[8]

The Franco regime had no intention of creating the massive endowment fund the bishops had in mind. In fact, as far as the *culto y clero* budget was concerned, the government proved less generous than had the dictatorship of the 1920s. Estimates of the proportion of the national budget assigned to this appropriation for the Franco period vary from 1.25 percent to 2 percent, both below the 2.65 percent of the Primo de Rivera era.[9] But this parsimony was more apparent than real. The amount provided by the Ministry of Justice through *culto y clero* increased steadily during the regime's history. Even taking inflation into account, the 655,748,000 pesetas provided in 1966 represented substantially more in real terms than the 54,648,400 provided in the monarchy's previous 1931 budget. This appropriation supplied, moreover, only a portion of the subsidies received from the government. A detailed analysis of expenditures (1970) from other ministries and government agencies shows that they furnished significant additional funds, raising the total received annually by the Church either directly or indirectly to the impressive sum of 2,592,568,656 pesetas.[10]

As before 1931, the *culto y clero* appropriation was distributed unevenly among diocesan priests. An elite of bishops, cathedral canons, and diocesan administrators continued to receive higher salaries than did the parochial clergy. But the financial gap separating the elite and the rank and file narrowed compared with the situation prevailing at the turn of the century. In 1900, the archbishop of Toledo received an annual salary of 40,000 pesetas, or approximately twenty times that of the archdiocese's best-paid parish priests. In 1968, the archbishop received 61,920 pesetas. Average salaries for the parochial clergy ranged between 15,000 and 17,000 pesetas.[11] The proportion of *culto y clero* assigned to the clerical elite declined from 15 percent in 1900 to around 10 percent by the late 1960s.

The narrowing of income differences between the clerical elite and parish priests was long overdue. It did not mean that the financial situation of the rural clergy standing at the bottom of the income scale changed significantly. Priests of country parishes continued to be paid less than any other group within the secular clergy, as they had been since the mid-nineteenth century.[12] Even a severe critic

8. Ibid., p. 62.

9. Ibid., p. 61; Castellà-Gassol, *El dinero de la Iglesia*, p. 20; "Los haberes del clero," *Revista Católica de Cuestiones Sociales* (1928), no. 118, p. 16.

10. Castellà-Gassol, *El dinero de la Iglesia*, pp. 28, 54, 52.

11. Q. Aldea Vaquero, "Patronato eclesiástico: Presupuesto del Ministerio de Gracia y Justicia. Año 1900" and "Presupuesto del Ministerio de Justicia: Bienio Económico, 1968–1969," in *Diccionario de historia eclesiástica de España*, ed. Q. Aldea Vaquero et al. (4 vols., Madrid, 1972–1975), vol. 3, pp. 1918, 1931.

12. In the Salamanca diocese, for example, rural priests received an average income of 65,452 pesetas in 1966; urban parish priests, 83,961. *Curas* of city parishes were also in a better position to secure

of ecclesiastical finances during the Franco years concedes that the incomes of rural priests were inadequate in relation to the cost of living and in comparison with working-class wage earners at the low end of the salary scale.[13]

The hierarchy campaigned for years to raise the salaries of the clerical rank and file. The bishops' ambitions were modest: to raise incomes to the level of primary school teachers through a 1 percent increase in the *culto y clero* budget. Despite years of intense ecclesiastical lobbying, the regime satisfied this demand only in 1957. This modest gain proved short-lived given the accelerated inflation of the 1960s. After another round of episcopal lobbying, the government agreed to the single largest increase in the *culto y clero* budget ever recorded by providing an additional 325 million pesetas in 1969.[14]

The economic situation of the diocesan clergy can be determined in approximate terms. The same cannot be said for the religious orders. Operating as autonomous legal corporations outside the control of local bishops, the regulars proved no more disposed to give a public accounting of their finances than they had in 1900 or 1920, when the issue of their wealth created intense public controversy. In fact, there is less information about the regular clergy's finances for the Franco years than for earlier periods. Allegations of immense wealth surfaced from time to time. The Jesuits were alleged to hold liquid assets in 1975 that reached the staggering amount of 4,200,000,000 pesetas, approximately the gross income of the country's largest hydroelectric company.[15] As always in the uncertain history of the religious orders' financial dealings, this allegation must be approached with caution. What can be said is that the Jesuits and other religious orders in possession of valuable urban real estate took advantage of rising values during the 1960s and 1970s to dispose of choice city properties at substantial profit.[16] Other examples of the regular clergy's financial dealings have come to light as a result of court proceedings. Together with hundreds of other Spaniards, the Augustinians invested 15 million, for example, in an American cosmetics firm, Holiday Magic, which operated through a pyramid scheme that soon came to grief and produced a plethora of lawsuits.[17]

Despite the absence of reliable information about the regulars' finances, it is likely that their economic circumstances represented an expanded version of the situation prevailing before 1931. Some orders possessed valuable urban real estate in a rising market, secured income from the tuition fees paid by students in their

additional income through surplice fees charged for baptisms, funerals, and marriage ceremonies. Castellà-Gassol, *El dinero de la Iglesia*, p. 65.

13. Ibid.

14. Petschen, *La Iglesia en la España de Franco*, p. 62; Castellà-Gassol, *El dinero de la Iglesia*, p. 66.

15. Ibid., p. 86.

16. In 1972, for example, the Jesuits sold a parcel of land in central Zaragoza to a private purchaser and the local savings bank for 475 million pesetas. Ibid., p. 84.

17. Ibid., pp. 101–5.

schools, and engaged in commercial ventures. But it is impossible to estimate the regulars' total income or to establish with any precision which orders were deeply involved in capitalist wheeling and dealing. Before 1931, not all orders prospered economically, especially not the cloistered communities of women. It is likely that this pattern continued. Moreover, there is no indication that the financial imbalance between the regulars and the parish clergy created by resources directed towards the activities and building projects of the religious orders changed to a significant degree during the Franco period.

The Church's leadership never judged the financial support it received from the government as sufficient. It had little cause for complaint. The problems lamented by the hierarchy arose less from the actual amounts provided than from the continuation of historic patterns of distribution. The bishops also failed to take into account the additional resources possessed by the religious orders. When all is said and done, the Church secured levels of financial assistance for its strategy of religious reconquest of which earlier clerical generations had only dreamed.

Since the 1870s, the diocesan clergy had failed to keep pace demographically with the religious orders of men and women. The secular clergy under the Restoration and the Primo de Rivera dictatorship never recovered to mid-nineteenth-century levels. On the eve of the Republic, diocesan priests numbered between 31,000 and 34,000 according to different estimates. Losses suffered during the Civil War and the ordinary toll of deaths and retirements reduced their ranks to 22,913 by 1945 despite a surge in late vocations occurring between 1939 and 1941.[18] For several years after the Civil War's end, dioceses in the former Republican zone struggled to find clergy to staff parishes. In 1941, the Toledo archdiocese lacked priests for 147 of its 364 parishes; as late as 1944, 52 of the Málaga diocese's parishes lacked incumbents.[19] No substantial increase in the secular clergy occurred until the 1950s, when expanded seminary enrollments, already evident by the late 1940s, began to produce an abundant crop of new priests.[20] Despite this increase, in 1959, the year of maximum enrollment during the Franco era, the total number of 8,728 major seminarians was only marginally greater than in 1934 and well short of the 12,831 students recorded in 1930.[21]

The emergence of new priestly cohorts increased the number of diocesan clergy to its highest level under the Franco regime during the mid-1960s. In 1966, there

18. Guy Hermet, *Les catholiques dans l'Espagne franquiste* (2 vols., Paris, 1981), vol. 1, p. 44. Between 1939 and 1941, around a thousand members of Catholic Action entered seminaries. Fernando Urbina, "Formas de vida de la Iglesia en España," in Fernando Urbina et al., *Iglesia y sociedad en España, 1939–1975* (Madrid, 1977), p. 29.

19. *Ecclesia*, July 15, 1941, pp. 13–14; July 15, 1944, pp. 13–14.

20. In his 1951 report for the British embassy, Bernard Malley observed that "the Spanish church is today suffering from an acute shortage of priests. Recuperation after the losses in clerical personnel during the civil war is only now beginning." "Survey of the Church in Spain," ms., p. 15.

21. Hermet, *Les catholiques*, vol. 1, p. 48; Severino Aznar, *La revolución española y las vocaciones eclesiásticas* (Madrid, 1949), p. 32.

were 25,906 diocesan priests, a figure still below that of the period immediately before the Republic. Given periodic campaigns launched to attract vocations and repeated episcopal statements exhorting young men to embrace a priestly career, the Church's inability to replenish fully the diocesan clergy's ranks is surprising. Ecclesiastical demographic trends may have reflected a similar decline evident since 1917 among the secular clergy throughout the Catholic world.[22] It is more likely that historic problems affecting the recruitment of parish priests continued into the Franco era. As they had done for generations, commentators on pastoral matters lamented the resistance of middle-class families to the idea of a clerical career for their sons.[23] Historic recruitment problems remained acute in southern Spain. The existence of a religiously indifferent rural population and the discouraging pastoral circumstances encountered by successive clerical generations in the area were no different in 1960 from the situation in 1900. It is hardly surprising that the prospect of being a parish priest in such conditions limited recruitment, as it had done since the late nineteenth century. Seminary enrollments in the dioceses of the ecclesiastical provinces of Seville and Granada lagged well behind their northern counterparts throughout the Franco period.[24]

The secular clergy competed with the male religious orders for recruits. There was nothing new about this competition, which dated back to the late 1870s, when the Cánovas government removed the restrictions on male religious in place since the mid-1830s. During the Restoration and the Primo de Rivera dictatorship, the regulars proved more successful recruiters than the diocesan clergy. This developed in part from the educational role of certain orders, especially the Jesuits and Piarists, who attracted candidates from their own schools. It also reflected the varied range of activities in which the orders were involved. In some respects, male religious were the Church's specialists, performing specific functional tasks, while parish priests were its generalists. The number of orders and their wide-ranging responsibilities offered more flexible opportunities in career terms than the secular clergy provided.

This pattern continued through the Franco period. The years between 1940 and 1970 formed the golden age of the regular clergy in modern Spanish history, even in comparison with the halcyon days of the Restoration and the Primo de Rivera dictatorship. The number of foundations of the male orders expanded from 958 in 1940 to 1,479 by 1962 and experienced an even more spectacular increase to 1,840 by 1972.[25] The male orders also recovered fully from the losses suffered as a result of the Civil War. Between 1945 and 1971, their ranks swelled from 15,953 to

22. Jesús María Vázquez, Félix Medín, and Luis Méndez, *La Iglesia española contemporánea* (Madrid, 1973), p. 164.

23. José María Escudero, "La eficacia del catolicismo español," in Carlos Santamaría et al., *Catolicismo español: aspectos actuales* (Madrid, 1955), pp. 98–99.

24. Hermet, *Les catholiques*, vol. 1, pp. 52–53.

25. Jesús María Vázquez, *Los religiosos españoles, hoy: estudio sociológico* (Madrid, 1973), p. 19.

31,022 members.[26] If one adds the female orders, which also expanded spectacularly during the Franco period, to 4,485 foundations and 71,918 members by 1962, the regulars in the Church's army of reconquest predominated over the diocesan clergy.[27] Overall, the size of the clerical establishment increased significantly during the Franco regime, from an estimated total of 87,000 in 1945 to 152,514 by 1972, an ecclesiastical presence unmatched since the late eighteenth century.[28]

The number of priests, which reached a high point of 35,089 in 1972, never equaled the approximately 43,000 to 45,000 ordained clergy, secular and regular, of the early 1930s.[29] The historic demographic lag of the diocesan clergy relative to population meant that the ratio of parish priests to inhabitants continued, indeed worsened, in the Franco period. The favorable ratio of 1:419 in 1883 deteriorated to 1:709 by the early 1930s, to 1:1,829 by 1959, and to 1:2,229 by 1970, well beyond the norm thought desirable by the Church of one parish priest for every thousand people, although there were significant regional variations in this pattern.[30]

Southern dioceses, where the parish clergy continued to be demographically weak and parochial boundaries often extended deep into the countryside, failed to develop an effective rural apostolate in a region with large estates. "Living distant from the parish and any urban nucleus," agricultural day laborers remained, as they had been for decades, perhaps centuries, beyond the reach of the parochial clergy. There were places in Andalucía and La Mancha, declared a gloomy assessment in 1958, where "the parish priest is unknown or in which the priest arrives only on the occasion of the last sacraments, and in which from birth to death rural families live without ever perceiving . . . the beneficient action of the Church."[31] There is no evidence that historic differences separating southern and northern dioceses in terms of clerical demography and parish organization diminished to a significant degree during the Franco period. Dioceses in the north with peasant populations living in small village communities continued to be well served by the parish clergy.[32]

In the cities, a significant parish expansion began to address the historic weak-

26. The male orders contained 12,219 priests in 1927, 12,008 in 1971. The larger figure given in the text includes unordained brothers and students as well as priests. Hermet, *Les catholiques*, vol. 1, p. 44; *Anuario estadístico de España, 1927* (Madrid, 1929), pp. 601–5; Vázquez, *Los religiosos*, p. 41.

27. The female orders experienced a doubling of membership, from 48,904 in 1945 to 97,000 in 1971. Hermet, *Les catholiques*, vol. 1, p. 44.

28. Ibid., pp. 43–44.

29. Vázquez, Medin, and Méndez, *La Iglesia española contemporánea*, p. 165; E. Vargas Zúñiga, "El problema religioso de España," *Razón y Fe* (1935), vol. 35, pp. 152, 163.

30. "Estadística comparada del clero y comunidades religiosas en Europa, en relación al número de católicos," *La Cruz* (1883), p. 763; Vargas Zúñiga, "El problema religioso de España," p. 153; Vázquez, *La Iglesia española contemporánea*, p. 164. Rafael Gómez Pérez suggests a lower ratio of 1:1,240 for 1963. *El franquismo y la Iglesia* (Madrid, 1986), p. 231.

31. Martín Brugarola, *Sociología rural católica* (Madrid, 1954), p. 164; Secretariado Nacional de Apostolado Rural de la Acción Católica Española, *El apostolado rural* (Madrid, 1958), p. 48.

32. Of the country's 19,784 parishes in 1952, 9,817 contained a thousand inhabitants or less. Gómez Pérez, *El franquismo y la Iglesia*, p. 230.

nesses of urban parochial organization. The regime loosened the tight purse strings that had prevented the Church from substantially increasing the number of urban parishes since the late nineteenth century. In Madrid, where the number of parishes was fixed at thirty for decades despite the city's expanding population, the Church established thirteen more between 1939 and 1941; in Valencia, where the parochial organization had remained unchanged since 1902, the archbishop created nine new parishes within the city limits in 1944 to provide for "the great masses completely lacking in spiritual assistance."[33] Madrid's thirty parishes in 1936 expanded to eighty-five by 1960, although more than half the city's population lived in "macro" parishes of more than thirty thousand residents and parishes in the city center continued to be better staffed than those in outlying districts where much of the working-class population lived. A full-scale campaign to remedy the historic deficiencies of the capital's parochial organization did not take place until the mid-1960s. Launched by Archbishop Casimiro Morcillo, this extraordinary effort saw the number of parishes expand to 316 by 1966.[34]

Bishops encouraged urban parishes to expand their activities beyond the purely religious to include a variety of social, educational, and medical services.[35] The idea of converting the parish into a social agency was hardly new, but in earlier periods few parish priests possessed either the initiative or the resources to follow this model. By the early 1940s, the Church rediscovered the advantages to be derived from expanding the range of parochial activities by filling the vacuum left by the regime's suppression of trade union centers and the Socialist party's Casas del Pueblo, once widespread in working-class districts.

Belated recognition of the city's importance in the Church's pastoral strategy occurred at an opportune time. The proportion of the active population employed in agriculture declined progressively after 1940 from 50.52 percent to 39.70 percent in 1960. Thereafter, it fell more dramatically to 22.91 percent by 1975.[36] This change was only partially reflected in the social background of the diocesan clergy. Rural families continued to provide a disproportionate number of seminarians relative to the active population, as they had done before the Civil War. Although the percentage of seminarians from the countryside declined from 61.2 percent of enrollment in 1934 to 52.7 percent by 1947 and to 42.4 percent by 1967–1968, the fact remains that the Church entered the period of urbanization, which began modestly during the 1950s and then accelerated rapidly in the following decade,

33. "La vida parroquial antes y después de la guerra," *Ecclesia*, April 1, 1941, p. 12; "Veintiocho nuevas parroquias han sido creadas en Valencia después de la liberación," ibid., September 16, 1944, p. 11.

34. *Madrid-Alcalá, una diócesis en construcción, 1961–1982* (Madrid, 1982), pp. 28–29, 44.

35. The parish of San Miguel was located in one of Madrid's poorer districts. During the early 1940s, it constructed "splendid modern installations, a medical dispensary, parish dining hall, schools and a sewing workshop" for residents. "La vida parroquial," p. 13.

36. Joseph Harrison, *An Economic History of Modern Spain* (New York, 1978), p. 150.

with a parochial clergy recruited from a conservative rural milieu removed from the difficult pastoral circumstances of urban parishes.[37] But, as always within the Spanish Church, there were regional variations in this pattern. In Catalonia, for example, the percentage of seminarians drawn from the urban bourgeoisie increased from 7.6 percent of enrollment in 1934 to 25.5 percent by 1947.[38]

The academic preparation given candidates for the priesthood did little to equip them for work in the pastoral trenches. As in the past, the Church saw the seminary as a protective fortress. "The seminary," candidates for the priesthood in Ávila were told in 1943, "is an oasis in the world; it is the ship that leads us safely through a corrupted and immoral century."[39] In their essentials, seminaries of the 1940s and early 1950s hardly varied from those of the Restoration. Neo-scholasticism dominated a formal curriculum largely untouched by the new theological currents already circulating within Catholicism elsewhere, especially in France and Germany, while traditional ideas of spirituality based on the models of Saint Ignatius and the great masters of sixteenth-century Spain emphasized a heroic, personal asceticism more in accord with a monastic life than with the difficult contemporary world that future priests would face in urban and rural parishes.[40] Insofar as the curriculum provided practical training, it emphasized the traditional role of the priest as a "functionary of the cult," saying Mass, administering the sacraments, and organizing parochial activities and associations.[41]

The quality of seminaries varied from one diocese to another. During the late 1940s, the Vitoria seminary maintained high academic standards and an excellent library and permitted students some contact with the innovating currents of European Catholicism.[42] Despite constant vigilance by the ecclesiastical and civil authorities fearful of any manifestation of Basque nationalism, the seminary managed to take the world outside its walls into account through the appointment in the mid-1940s of Father Gregorio Rodríguez de Yurre to the professorship of ethics and sociology. Although constrained by the limits imposed by the regime, Rodríguez de Yurre and some of his colleagues began to address the problem of the

37. Hermet, *Les catholiques,* vol. 1, p. 54. 38. Ibid., p. 56.

39. Quoted in Feliciano Blázquez, *La traición de los clérigos en la España de Franco* (Madrid, 1991), p. 100.

40. Urbina, "Formas de vida de la Iglesia en España," p. 33.

41. One of the most widely used seminary texts dealing with pastoral work, Alejo Sánchez Tarrazo's *Teología pastoral con práctica parroquial* (2d ed., Valencia, 1954), scarcely varied from similar works published half a century earlier in its emphasis on the role of the priest as parish administrator, dispenser of the services of the cult, and promoter of pious devotions. Urbina, "Formas de vida en la Iglesia de España," pp. 36–38.

42. Father José Ignacio Tellechea Idigoras recalled that although students in the Vitoria seminary during the late 1940s and early 1950s were not allowed to read the original texts of Descartes, Leibnitz, and Kant in class, informally they became acquainted with the work of the leading thinkers of French Catholicism. *Tapices de la memoria: historia clínica 279.952* (San Sebastián, 1992), pp. 106–7, 120.

religious alienation of Basque workers and the need for social justice as early as 1943.[43]

The possibility of sustaining indefinitely the hermetically sealed clerical culture of the 1940s diminished during the following decade as the result of generational change among the clergy. By 1962, 38.1 percent of diocesan priests were between twenty-four and forty-four years of age. In some dioceses, where the loss of clergy had been heavy during the Civil War, clerics in this category formed 70 percent of the total.[44] The change from an old to a young clergy between 1940 and 1960 was significant. Priests ordained during the 1950s neither experienced the Civil War nor absorbed the crusading mentality it produced among their elders. Despite draconian seminary discipline, students began to escape from the narrow confines of the traditional curriculum. Jesuit seminarians at the order's house of studies in Chamartín de la Rosa during the early 1950s surreptitiously read the works of liberal Catholic writers such as François Mauriac, and those of Spanish intellectuals like Unamuno and Ortega y Gasset, whose ideas had been condemned more than once by the hierarchy.[45] Although no significant liberalization of seminary education occurred during the decade, bishops, perhaps unaware of the consequences, began to send seminarians and young priests abroad for study, especially to France and Germany, where they came in contact with progressive theological currents and ideas about social justice.[46] The full impact of this broadening of intellectual horizons would not be felt until the 1960s, but there is evidence that by the mid-1950s a minority of younger seminary professors attempted to introduce their students to wider concerns than those entrenched in the formal curriculum.[47]

Historians concerned with the role of the Church during the Franco era have stressed the generational gap separating the bishops from the clerical rank and file. Although this view of the hierarchy as a "senate of old men" is justified for the early 1960s, it reflected less the continuation of appointment patterns characteristic of the Restoration and the Primo de Rivera dictatorship than the circumstance that forty-two new bishops were named between 1941 and 1947.[48] During the regime's

43. Ignacio Villota Elejalde, *La Iglesia en la sociedad española y vasca contemporáneas* (Bilbao, 1985), p. 467. Beginning in 1949, Rodríguez de Yurre wrote articles for *Ecclesia* critical of the regime's shortcomings with respect to social justice, freedom of the press, and the lack of syndical freedom. He soon was regarded as a *persona non grata* by the authorities, who more than once took away his passport. Jesús Iribarren, *Papeles y memorias: medio siglo de relaciones Iglesia-Estado en España, 1936–1986* (Madrid, 1992), pp. 113–16. A former student in the Vitoria seminary recalled that Rodríguez de Yurre allowed criticism of the "defects" of the Franco regime in his classes. Tellechea Idigoras, *Tapices de la memoria,* p. 106.

44. Hermet, *Les catholiques,* vol. 1, p. 46; Petschen, *La Iglesia en la España de Franco,* p. 99.

45. Javier Domínguez, *Enseñanza católica para una generación, víctima y testigo* (Madrid, 1979), p. 81.

46. Urbina, "Formas de vida de la Iglesia en España," pp. 52–53.

47. Ibid., p. 63.

48. Gómez Pérez, *El franquismo y la Iglesia,* p. 111; "La historia del episcopado español," p. 12.

early history, the complex process of appointment, involving a mix of government patronage and ecclesiastical lobbying, broke, in fact, with the pre-1931 practice of naming or promoting bishops of advanced age.[49]

In other respects, the regime's appointment policies also differed from the past. Although the regime clearly wished to appoint bishops sympathetic to its objectives, it does not appear that Franco intervened personally in the selection process. Cardinal Tarancón recalled that in a conversation with several bishops, one of whom thanked him for his nomination, the general replied, "I do not intervene in these matters, I always name the candidates whom the bishops propose to me."[50] Franco did not attempt to imitate Primo de Rivera or Cánovas del Castillo, for that matter, by using the State's patronage rights to pack the hierarchy for narrowly political motives.[51] The process of selection guaranteed, of course, that no one suspected of liberal views could pass through the State's patronage net. But it did not mean that priests known for their "granite-like" commitment to Franco necessarily received advancement. Three prelates esteemed for their special loyalty to Franco, for example—Bishops Temiño, Castán Lecoma, and Moll—finished their careers in obscure dioceses, while the disfavor with which Bishop Tarancón of Solsona was regarded by the regime's hard-liners did not prevent his ascent to the archbishoprics of Oviedo, Toledo, and Madrid.[52]

In any event, there was little reason during the regime's first two decades for the government to use its powers to manipulate appointments, given the commitment of candidates for bishoprics to the Nationalist cause. With the exception of appointments to the Basque and Catalan dioceses, the regime did not attempt to exclude candidates from the country's historic regions from episcopal office. Even here there were occasional exceptions.[53] In fact, Catalonia and Valencia ranked first and second in the number of bishops appointed, while the Basque Provinces provided nearly as many. Episcopal recruitment during the Franco period broke with the past through the larger proportion of bishops appointed from regions bordering the Mediterranean coast.[54]

49. José Manuel Cuenca Toribio, *Sociología del episcopado español e hispanoamericano, 1789–1985* (Madrid, 1986), pp. 349–51.

50. Vicente Enrique y Tarancón, *Confesiones* (Madrid, 1996), p. 42.

51. Cuenca Toribio, *Sociología del episcopado español e hispanoamericano*, pp. 424–28. Another analysis of episcopal appointments during the Franco period argues that "there was no real correlation between ideology and 'nomination.' . . . The influence of state intervention . . . is not as important as many imagine." "La historia del episcopado español," p. 21.

52. Cuenca Toribio, *Sociología del episcopado español e hispanoamericano*, p. 422.

53. In 1951, Joan Pont i Gol was appointed to the Catalan diocese of Segorbe. According to Cardinal Tarancón, who supported the nomination, "The Government was alarmed when it saw his name on the list of six presented by the nuncio" because "he was Catalan: in Madrid, they looked with suspicion on Catalan priests." The nomination prospered because of the intervention of the minister of foreign affairs, Alberto Martín Artajo, in the cabinet. Enrique y Tarancón, *Confesiones*, p. 134.

54. Catalonia produced 13.51 percent of the bishops; Valencia 12.16 percent; Old Castile 11.48 percent; New Castile 9.45 percent; the Basque Provinces 9.45 percent; Andalucía 8.10 percent; Navarra 6.70

Whatever dynamism the hierarchy possessed came in considerable measure from prelates who were natives of these coastal areas. As a group, they were more urban and middle-class than their colleagues elsewhere in the country.[55] During the 1940s and 1950s, prelates such as Archbishop Olaechea of Valencia, Bishop Tarancón of Solsona, and Cardinal Pla y Deniel followed policies on a number of issues that reflected a greater critical sense of the problems facing the Church than that possessed by many of their colleagues. In other respects, historic patterns continued. Only 16.21 percent of bishops came from major urban centers, while the custom of recruiting prelates with doctorates in theology, canon law, and administrative experience remained as common as it had been for centuries. But unlike earlier periods, most bishops served in parishes, if only briefly, at some point in their careers. Bishops emerged from rural and urban families of modest economic means. Only a handful belonged to the aristocracy or the wealthy classes, while relatively few came from the liberal professions, the military, or the commercial bourgeoisie.[56]

Bishops remained virtually sovereign in their dioceses and were irremovable for all practical purposes. As a result, they enjoyed a degree of autonomy accepted by the regime, albeit grudgingly in some cases, that allowed a Cardinal Segura or Bishop Pildain to adopt an independent posture with respect to official policy. It permitted Cardinal Pla y Deniel to support Catholic workers' associations, while his conservative colleague, Bishop Eijo y Garay, followed the opposite course. Similarly, in 1947 a small number of bishops, including Archbishop Marcelino Olaechea of Valencia, a prelate of vaguely populist views, broke the hierarchy's unanimity by publicly announcing their reservations about the forthcoming referendum reestablishing the monarchy.[57]

Episcopal autonomy and the resulting lack of consistency were enhanced by the hierarchy's lack of an effective national organization. The bishops met on occasion for specific purposes and the Committee of Metropolitans continued in existence. But it was less important during the Franco period than during the Republic and the Civil War. Its president, archbishop of Toledo Pla y Deniel, called the committee into session infrequently. Diocesan bishops "felt themselves totally distant"

---

percent; Aragón 4.72 percent; and so on. Cuenca Toribio, *Sociología del episcopado español e hispanoamericano*, p. 358.

55. Ibid., pp. 359–60.

56. Ibid., pp. 358, 365–72; "La historia del episcopado español," pp. 17–19; Frances Lannon, "An Èlite of Grace: The Spanish Bishops in the Twentieth Century," in *Èlites and Power in Twentieth-Century Spain*, ed. Frances Lannon and Paul Preston (Oxford, 1990), p. 14.

57. Ramiro Reig and Josep Picó, *Feixistes, rojos i capelans: Església i societat al País Valencià, 1940–1970* (Palma de Mallorca, 1978), p. 80. The authors argue that Olaechea administered his diocese inspired by a sincere spirit of compassion towards the people manifested, for example, by his concern for the desperate economic situation of workers, which he addressed in pastoral letters, although like most of his episcopal colleagues he did not lay the blame for this state of affairs on the regime. Ibid., pp. 84, 97–99.

from its proceedings and resented the archbishops' pretension to speak in the name of the entire hierarchy.[58] The first serious attempt to provide institutional coordination for the hierarchy occurred in 1956, when Bishop Tarancón was named to head a new Secretariat of the Episcopacy.[59]

Insofar as the hierarchy received direction between 1941 and 1966, it did so through the cardinal primate. Pla y Deniel provided the Church with effective and flexible leadership, although one of his admirers and collaborators, Jesús Iribarren, admitted that his tendency to work as much as possible behind the scenes as a "prudent jurist" kept him from becoming the kind of dynamic leader the hierarchy required.[60] Despite his antiliberal stance early in the regime's history and his loyalty to the regime for having, in his judgment, saved Christian civilization in Spain, the cardinal developed "a sense of the Church and a vital awareness of its rights" that brought him into conflict on more than one occasion with the authorities.[61] His extensive civil and ecclesiastical connections and his key role in Catholic Action and the Committee of Metropolitans reinforced his commanding position as the first of Spain's bishops, but his ability to provide overall direction to prelates still supreme in their dioceses rested primarily on moral rather than legal authority.

Despite their academic credentials, the bishops of the first two decades of the Franco era displayed little intellectual originality or dynamism. As before the Civil War, they were primarily ecclesiastical bureaucrats recruited from a narrow constituency of diocesan vicars general, chancellors, cathedral canons, seminary professors, and other clerics with administrative experience.[62] Bishops presided over highly centralized diocesan administrations and governed their clergy in a relationship of authority that left little room for dissent.

There was nothing new or different about the persistence of this organizational model, which predominated within the Catholic Church as a whole until the early 1960s. Bishops were less isolated, perhaps, from the clerical rank and file than they had been in earlier periods, but they formed an elite based on status, education,

58. The Committee of Metropolitans did not meet at all between 1939 and 1946. Thereafter, it assembled only twice a year. Hermet, *Les catholiques*, vol. 1, p. 162; Enrique y Tarancón, *Confesiones*, pp. 72, 165.

59. The Secretariat represented the interests of the hierarchy as a whole rather than those of the archbishops forming the Committee of Metropolitans. For this reason, its creation has been regarded as the first institutional step towards the establishment of the Episcopal Conference a decade later. Iribarren, *Papeles y memorias*, pp. 181–82. For the origins of the Secretariat, see Vicente Cárcel Ortí, "Estudio histórico jurídico," in *Actas de las conferencias de metropolitanos españoles, 1921–1965*, ed. Vicente Cárcel Ortí (Madrid, 1994), pp. 111–13.

60. Jesús Iribarren, "Episcopado y Conferencia Episcopal," in *El postconcilio en España*, ed. Juan M. Loboa (Madrid, 1988), p. 226. Cardinal Tarancón, who worked closely with Pla y Deniel between 1956 and 1966 as head of the Secretariat of the hierarchy, recalled the cardinal primate's "fine juridical instinct" and his slow, deliberate process of reaching a decision on important matters. *Confesiones*, p. 167.

61. Ibid.

62. Antonio Duato, "Los obispos en el proceso de cambio en la Iglesia de España," in *Iglesia y sociedad en España*, p. 124.

and administrative experience. The resulting gulf between bishops and parish priests was exacerbated by the emergence of a younger clergy during the 1950s. Throughout the decade, the hierarchy managed to sustain its authority over the diocesan clergy, although clashes with the new generation of priests, especially in the Basque Provinces, proved a harbinger of future clerical turbulence and division.

How well individual bishops fulfilled their responsibilities within this traditional organizational framework is difficult to establish. There is evidence that the pre–Civil War pattern of episcopal careerism, a restless quest for advancement from smaller to larger and richer dioceses, was largely broken during the Franco period, when there was less mobility among the bishops.[63] Prelates remained longer in their dioceses and were in a better position to develop policies in accord with local conditions. Bishops of metropolitan centers, even Eijo y Garay in Madrid, paid more attention to the pastoral problems created by urbanization than had their predecessors. By the mid-1950s, some bishops began to introduce modest reforms into their dioceses. The traditional system of differential surplice fees, which allowed the well-off to pay for extravagant baptism and marriage ceremonies, was reformed in Albacete and some parishes of the Zaragoza archdiocese. In 1957, Archbishop Marcelino Olaechea of Valencia ordered an end to these class-based arrangements in the name of creating "true brotherhood" among parishioners regardless of income.[64] But such tepid reforming currents circulated through few diocesan administrations.

The Second Vatican Council's decision to require the resignation of bishops at the age of seventy-five opened the door to renovation of the hierarchy. Between 1964 and 1974, fifty-three new bishops were appointed.[65] Although Luigi Dadaglio, the papal nuncio responsible for maneuvering forty-two of these nominations through the government's patronage net, promoted the cause of candidates sympathetic to the reforming currents released by the Council, no dramatic or sudden liberalization of the hierarchy took place. Indeed, Casimiro Morcillo, appointed the first archbishop of Madrid in 1966 and elected second president of the new Episcopal Conference in 1969, proved more conservative than the aged Pla y Deniel, whom he replaced as leader of the hierarchy. The nuncio favored candidates who, although flexible before the social and political controversies wracking the country during this period, tended to favor a conservative, evolutionary approach to the acute problem of how the Church would secure its position in the regime's future.[66] What was most significant about the emergence of a new episcopal generation was that its members had not experienced the Civil War and were

63. Cuenca Toribio, *Sociología del episcopado español e hispanoamericano*, pp. 362–65.
64. Petschen, *La Iglesia en la España de Franco*, pp. 122–24.
65. Duato, "Los obispos en el proceso de cambio," pp. 130–32.
66. José Chao Rego, *La Iglesia en el franquismo* (Madrid, 1976), pp. 212–13.

more aware than their older colleagues of the need to adapt the Church to new circumstances, although they were far from agreed on a specific course to be followed.

As a result of the Council, a second important development occurred in 1966, when the Committee of Metropolitans was replaced by the Spanish Episcopal Conference (CEE). Its membership included all the country's bishops, even auxiliary bishops directly appointed by the pope without the government's intervention, a concession secured in the 1953 concordat that the authorities later had cause to regret.[67] Although never recognized by the regime as the juridical representative of the Spanish Church, the CEE provided the hierarchy for the first time with an effective national organization. Its appearance by no means signified an abrupt change of direction by the hierarchy. The Conference's first president, Cardinal Quiroga y Palacios, elderly archbishop of Santiago, and its second, Morcillo, pursued an excessively cautious course. But the CEE's representative character and the gradually changing composition of the hierarchy opened the door to a transformation that was not far off.

The Instruments of Reconquest

The clergy regarded education as a key to the strategy of religious reconquest. The Church imprinted public instruction with a Catholic character as result of the 1938 law on secondary education and similar legislation in 1945 governing primary schools. The latter established that primary education must be inspired by a "Catholic spirit" in accord with "the principles of Catholic Dogma and Morality."[68] The 1945 law also restored to the Church its pre-1931 right of "vigilance and inspection" over all instruction related to faith and morals in public and private schools.[69]

Historically, the Church paid more attention to secondary education than to primary, a pattern continued through the first two decades of the Franco regime. As before the Civil War, the Church failed to develop a coordinated approach to primary education. Although some parish schools were established, there was nothing like the centralized diocesan model of parochial education characteristic of the United States. In 1950, only 241 schools were maintained by dioceses and parishes in contrast to the 1,644 of the religious orders.[70] The decision to establish primary schools rested, as in the past, on individual religious orders continuing the old pattern of creating schools in urban centers where a middle-class clientele could afford to pay tuition fees.

67. The Vatican was able to name auxiliary bishops on its own. Many of these appointments would not have prospered had they moved through the regular patronage process.

68. Quoted in Gregorio Cámara Villar, *Nacional-catolicismo y escuela: la socialización política del franquismo* (Jaén, 1984), pp. 252–53.

69. Ibid., p. 253.

70. Ibid., p. 278, Table 14; p. 273, Table 12.

Despite years of official and ecclesiastical rhetoric stressing the importance of Catholicizing education, the Franco regime provided only marginal financial support to Church schools until 1970.[71] Until this time, the government furnished limited assistance to private schools that agreed to admit a certain number of scholarship pupils, but it remained parsimonious when it came to assuming a larger financial commitment. Curiously, until 1953 the schools of the religious orders were legally regarded as commercial enterprises. As such, they were obliged to pay urban taxes at the local level and certain business taxes at the national.[72] These arrangements reinforced the pre–Civil War pattern of Church schools dependent for their survival on tuition fees and, therefore, on the social classes able to pay them.

The number of students in Church primary schools was far from negligible—507,651 during the academic year 1950–1951—but nearly 2.5 million pupils were enrolled in public schools.[73] For this reason, the Church attached importance to Catholicizing public education. Aided and abetted by the civil authorities, the clergy got what it wanted. Crucifixes were placed in every classroom, the school day was opened and closed with prayer, and pupils were marshaled as a body to attend an array of religious ceremonies. Students received instruction in the catechism, while textbooks exalted Catholicism as the inspiration of Spanish culture and the embodiment of national values. "The Spanish soul," declared one, "is naturally Catholic."[74] History texts praised the reign of Ferdinand and Isabella as marking the high point of the country's grandeur, endorsed the persecution of Protestants during the sixteenth century, and attacked nineteenth-century liberalism in no uncertain terms. Many schools continued to use a version of Ripalda's seventeenth-century catechism, updated to include denunciations of sundry modern political and social movements. To the question "What are the principal errors condemned by the Church?" came the reply that there were exactly thirteen: "materialism, Marxism, atheism, pantheism, deism, rationalism, Protestantism, socialism, communism, trade unionism, liberalism, modernism, and Freemasonry." In fact, other "nefarious" errors came under attack in the pages of the new Ripalda, among them the freedoms of education, the press, and association.[75]

In secondary education, the Church retained its predominance until the expansion of public high schools that occurred during the regime's last decade and a half. With sour memories of political ferment among secondary school students during the Republic, the government displayed little enthusiasm for significant ex-

71. The Education Law of 1970 established that private schools could receive subventions for teachers' salaries, administration, and building maintenance in return for entering into formal agreements (*conciertos*), according to which schools were expected to meet educational and social conditions stipulated by the government. Petschen, *La Iglesia en la España de Franco*, p. 173.

72. Ibid., p. 111.

73. Cámara Villar, *Nacional-catolicismo y escuela*, p. 255.

74. Quoted in ibid., p. 324.

75. Quoted in Domínguez, *Enseñanza católica*, p. 36.

pansion in this area. By 1950, there were only 119 State high schools, in contrast to the 625 secondary institutions of the religious orders.[76] There was nothing new about the imbalance between the public and private educational sectors, which was similar to the situation prevailing before 1931. The class-oriented recruitment characteristic of Church high schools during the 1920s scarcely changed through the 1940s and 1950s. "The prestige of the College dependent on fees," asserted a former student of that era, "was beyond discussion. Every person . . . who could, sent his children to a fee paying College. And a fee paying College was synonymous with a College of the religious orders."[77]

These secondary schools catered to a middle-class clientele and often occupied choice locations in prosperous urban districts.[78] Some religious orders, notably the Salesians, made an effort to attract students from other social groups, but the Jesuits continued their tradition of maintaining elite schools.[79] In Madrid, for example, their prestigious Colegio de Areneros existed alongside its vocational school. Working-class students in the latter were forbidden to enter the premises through its main door. A former student of the college during the early 1940s recalled that after seven years he did not know a single student from the adjoining vocational school. "We lived in two distinct worlds," he remembered.[80]

The quasi-monopoly enjoyed by the secondary schools of the religious orders began to erode during the 1960s. Ironically, the economic concerns of ministers affiliated with Opus Dei led to a new emphasis on expanding public secondary education as indispensable for the regime's development plans. As a result, enrollment in public high schools began to grow more rapidly than that of Church schools. These modernizing concerns also lay behind a comprehensive reorganization of education carried out in 1970. The General Law on Education proposed a massive restructuring of the entire educational system designed to raise standards and revise curricula to bring the quality of instruction to the level of Spain's economic competitors in Western Europe. Although the Church extracted an important concession from the regime, namely, a promise to increase official funding for its schools, the hierarchy viewed the new legislation with misgivings because of its overall curricular direction and the increased level of government supervision proposed for all schools.[81]

76. Cámara Villar, *Nacional-catolicismo y escuela*, p. 268.

77. Domínguez, *Enseñanza católica*, p. 14.

78. Hermet provides a detailed analysis of the social recruitment of public, private, and the schools of the religious orders. *Les catholiques*, vol. 1, p. 172.

79. Ibid., p. 173; Petschen, *La Iglesia en la España de Franco*, p. 111. Workers were not entirely excluded from the schools of the orders, although much depended on the recruitment policy of individual congregations. Overall, according to Hermet, 11 percent of male students and 7 percent of female students came from the working class. *Les catholiques*, vol. 1, p. 172.

80. Domínguez, *Enseñanza católica*, p. 38.

81. In 1965, for example, public secondary schools increased enrollment by twenty-eight thousand students, Church schools by only six thousand. Petschen, *La Iglesia en la España de Franco*, p.

During the 1940s and 1950s, the Church recovered the educational ground lost during the Republic and began a significant expansion of its schools. But it did not take advantage of the opportunity to reorganize Church schools at either the primary or secondary level with a view to creating a coherent educational system. In many respects, the Church re-created in expanded form the fragmented organizational structure existing before 1931, just as it reproduced the class orientation characteristic of its schools since the late nineteenth century.

On a broader front, the Church strengthened its strategy of reconquest through a massive presence in publishing, the press, and radio. Catholic publications fell into three principal categories. First were periodicals produced directly by the clergy and organizations linked directly to the hierarchy, particularly through Catholic Action. The 805 weekly or monthly reviews and journals published from this group in 1957 promoted a wide variety of causes. Some were religious in emphasis, such as the *Mensajero del Corazón de Jesús* (106,000 copies), which encouraged devotion to the Sacred Heart. Others served specific organizational ends, whether *Ecclesia* (25,000 copies) for Catholic Action, or *Signo* (6,000 copies) and *Juventud Obrera* (35,000 copies), published by the movement's "apostolic" associations of workers. Still others were primarily cultural in purpose, such as *Serra d'Or*, produced by the Benedictine monastery of Montserrat to promote Catalan language and literature.[82] Given the disparate nature of these publications, it is difficult to assess their impact on the reading public. What can be said is that few Catholic groups missed the opportunity to advance their respective causes in print.

Of greater importance was the role played by the press. In 1956, 34 of the country's 109 daily newspapers were identified with the Church. The publishing house Editorial Católica continued its pre–Civil War predominance as publisher of five dailies, including the most important, *Ya*, although the newspaper never achieved the journalistic reputation of *El Debate*. Opus Dei also entered the field. For all practical purposes, its members controlled the Madrid dailies *El Alcázar* and *Madrid* for brief periods during the 1960s. Conservative Christian Democrats tied to the regime played an influential role in another Madrid newspaper, *Informaciones*, while a number of regional dailies, such as the *Gaceta del Norte* in Bilbao, can also be regarded as Catholic in orientation. But the flourishing of the Catholic press did mean that the Church could count on editorial unanimity. On the contrary, the factional divisions of Spanish Catholicism translated themselves directly to the pages of newspapers identified with specific groups. At times, rivalries reached intense proportions, as during the early 1970s, when the Editorial

112; José María Totosaus, "Presencia de la Iglesia en el sector escolar," in *Iglesia y sociedad en España*, pp. 248–60.

82. Hermet, *Les catholiques*, vol. 1, pp. 179–80; Gómez Pérez, *El franquismo y la Iglesia*, pp. 233–34.

Católica, linked to Catholic Action, engaged in a struggle with followers of Opus Dei for control of the Seville newspaper *El Correo de Andalucía*.[83]

In the third category, general publishing, the Church was also well served. The series Biblioteca de Autores Cristianos, published by the Editorial Católica, sold 4 million books between 1944 and 1963. But the divisions characteristic of the Catholic press were equally evident in the publishing sector. Opus Dei established Ediciones Rialp, while a group of progressive priests launched the Propaganda Popular Católica (PPC) during the mid-1950s. The PPC offered a different vision of the future of Spanish Catholicism from that promoted by Opus Dei.

The Church also took advantage of the regime's willingness to permit private commercial radio stations. Between 1959 and 1964, a radio network controlled by the hierarchy, España Ondas Populares (EOC), increased the number of stations under its control from twenty-five to thirty-nine. Figures connected to Opus Dei were influential in the commercial network, Sociedad Española de Radiodifusión (SER), during the 1960s. The Church was less successful, however, in television. The regime's insistence on developing the new communications medium as a public monopoly left no room for private initiatives, although the authorities permitted extensive religious programming.[84]

The Church's organizational weight was also evident through the prominent role played by the female religious orders in public assistance. As they had done before 1931, they staffed government hospitals, orphanages, and asylums and administered many of the approximately fifteen hundred charitable institutions operating under religious and government auspices.[85] Catholic Action entered a period of expansion beginning in 1940 that brought the organization to the high point of its history before a crisis of the mid-1960s undermined its foundations. In 1950, Catholic Action's 522,470 members operated through 12,349 local chapters, specialized branches, and affiliated associations.[86]

Catholic Action was directly responsible to the hierarchy through the Committee of Metropolitans. Historically, the movement functioned as an umbrella organization embracing a heterogeneous body of associations engaged in a variety of religious, educational, professional, and propaganda activities under a loose federal structure and operating according to their respective purposes at the national, diocesan, and parish levels. In 1939, Cardinal Gomá, believing that this organizational model had failed to provide coherent direction, carried out a centralizing reform through a new secretariat (Dirección General) and a revamped structure of national committees. Another reorganization in 1959 developed this model fur-

83. A. Sáez Alba, *La Asociación Católica de Propagandistas: reproducción y métodos de la derecha permanente* (Paris, 1974), pp. 178–84.

84. Hermet, *Les catholiques*, vol. 1, pp. 185–88.

85. Gómez Pérez, *El franquismo y la Iglesia*, p. 233.

86. Ibid., p. 231.

ther. Whether increased centralization contributed to the resurgence that occurred between 1940 and 1960 is debatable. The new structure represented another attempt to forge a "united front" among the laity acting under the direction of the hierarchy, a religious version of the "union of Catholics" sought by successive episcopal generations.[87]

Catholic Action by no means lost its former character as an umbrella organization covering a variety of Catholic associations. "The list of its functions," asserted a foreign observer during the mid-1940s, "seems endless."[88] In addition to the four core branches organized according to sex and age at the national, diocesan, and parish levels, Catholic Action included as affiliated groups the ACNP, the Saint Vincent de Paul charitable organization, the Confederación Nacional de Padres de Familia (a Catholic lobby concerned with education), the devotional Marian Congregations, and associations of teachers and pharmacists, among others. The central office ran a publishing house, promoted propaganda activities, and administered a secretariat concerned with charitable assistance. This key function expanded massively after 1953 in the form of Caritas, which was given responsibility by the regime for distributing aid received from the United States.[89]

The flexible structure of Catholic Action was its greatest strength. It allowed the Church to develop a multifaceted response to the often differing needs of specific groups within Spanish Catholicism. The development of Catholic workers' associations would have been difficult had it not taken place within the supple framework of Catholic Action. The movement's overall purpose remained what it had been for decades, to contribute to the Church's objective of re-Christianizing the nation. The hierarchy and Catholic Action repeatedly affirmed its apolitical character, but this theoretical neutrality frequently broke down, although in contradictory fashion. On the one hand, prominent members supported by the hierarchy participated in the ongoing struggle for political influence among the regime's factions. On the other, the HOAC and the JOC promoted a program far in advance of the views of Catholic Action's largely middle-class constituencies.

Catholic Action also managed to adapt to changing circumstances. The triumphalist rhetoric and tactics of the 1940s, based on the idea of a victorious Catholicism intent on imposing religion in every nook and cranny of society, yielded to a more spiritual and personal "pastorate of testimony," especially after Alberto Bonet became secretary-general of the central office in 1956. The idea of Spanish Catholicism as a "defensive block" gave way to a concept of re-Christianizing society through personal example rather than through compulsion. Although this new focus anticipated in some measure the reforming currents of the

87. Zacarías de Vizcarra, "El 'frente único' del apostolado católico en la Acción Católica Española," *Ecclesia*, April 11, 1953, p. 13.

88. Emmet John Hughes, *Report from Spain* (New York, 1947), p. 59.

89. Alberto Bonet, "Acción Católica," in *Diccionario de historia eclesiástica*, vol. 1, pp. 3–4.

Second Vatican Council, it was not entirely welcomed by the rank and file, many of whom remained attached to the "heroic, combative and polemical spirit" associated with Catholic Action during the immediate post–Civil War years. They regretted, indeed, the organization's decision to abandon the use of the Spanish flag and other external signs of the old militancy in mass meetings.[90]

Whether Catholic Action was "for Franco, the most dangerous organization in Spain today," as one of its leaders maintained in 1944, is debatable, although there is no doubt that it proved useful to the hierarchy as a means blocking the Falange's ascendancy in politics and education.[91] Catholic Action's most significant contribution lay in its ability to evade the compartmentalization of function imposed by the regime in important areas of activity. In the name of the "apostolic" work that the government tolerated as legitimate expressions of Catholic Action's religious purpose, the organization succeeded in putting its finger in many pies sitting on the exclusionary shelf. Catholic workers' associations reintroduced the Church into social action despite the monopoly enjoyed by the official labor syndicates. Similarly, associations of students and teachers, formed ostensibly for a purely religious purpose, allowed the Church to offer competition to the regime's compulsory syndicates embracing both groups. More than any other institution under the Church's control, Catholic Action contributed to enlarging the "liberty of the Church" within the give-and-take of civil-ecclesiastical relations characteristic of the Franco era.

Emmet Hughes, an American diplomat familiar with Catholic Action during the mid-1940s, perceived it as exceptionally well organized, well financed, and effective.[92] There is little doubt that through the 1950s the organization reached a point of development unequaled in the history of modern Spanish Catholicism. But it was not without its weaknesses. The social background of its members remained what it always had been, largely middle-class and urban. In 1946, 40 percent of the membership came from the ranks of the liberal professions, business, and other middle-class occupations, while 28 to 30 percent emerged from a student constituency reflecting the class orientation of the educational system. Nor was Catholic Action especially successful at establishing itself at the local level, despite constant efforts to do so. In 1960, only one parish in ten had managed to found a chapter. Like so much else within Spanish Catholicism, regional differences were important. Catholic Action was strongly entrenched in the areas that formed Nationalist Spain during the Civil War. It penetrated Catalonia, the Basque Provinces, and the Levante less successfully, although this pattern began to change during the early 1960s. The massive membership expansion of the 1940s and

90. Miguel Benzo Mestre, "Tres etapas de la Acción Católica Española," *Ecclesia* (1964), no. 1, p. 185.

91. Quoted in Hughes, *Report from Spain*, p. 54.

92. Ibid., p. 61.

1950s also tended to water down the organization's highly elitist character, at least as far as the rank and file were concerned. How many participated actively in the movement's activities is difficult to establish, although it has been estimated that only about 15 percent fell into the category of activists.[93]

The Church failed to secure all it wanted from the Franco regime, but it built an institutional presence of which earlier clerical generations had only dreamed. Clerics were correct to see the privileges it enjoyed as offering a unique opportunity to implement a strategy of religious reconquest. Realizing this historic objective was another matter.

93. Hermet, *Les catholiques*, vol. 1, pp. 203–6. Cardinal Tarancón recalled that during his tenure as bishop of Solsona, he attempted to promote Catholic Action throughout the diocese but with disappointing results. *Confesiones*, p. 147.

CHAPTER XVIII

RELIGIOUS RECONQUEST

Following the Civil War's end, reports of processions, pilgrimages, mass communions, confirmations, and devotions filled the pages of a Catholic press consumed by admiration for signs of an "affirmation of faith."[1] The impressive numbers attending these ceremonies, such as the three hundred thousand who attended services held throughout the day and evening in the Madrid shrine of Jesus the Nazarene on March 1, 1940, seemed to the clergy eloquent testimony of a religious revival.[2] The causes of the devotional resurgence were several. For the first time since 1931, the Church was free to organize massive public expressions of religiosity over the entire country.[3] In areas once controlled by the Republic, Catholics felt a deep sense of psychological relief, freed from the emotional terror many had felt during the recent conflict. On Good Friday 1940, thousands lining Madrid's streets for the traditional procession of that day "wept copiously with a very deep sense of consolation" at having survived "the suffering of the past."[4] Religious ceremonies also served a triumphalist purpose by glorifying victory over the enemies of Church and State. Celebrations held in honor of the Virgin of Fuencisla in Segovia (1942) attracted civil and ecclesiastical notables and thousands of laity in a service of thanksgiving to the Virgin Mary for having delivered the city from "Marxist hordes" during the war.[5]

1. *Ya*, March 2, 1940.

2. The massive affluence of the faithful attending this particular service was far greater than had been the case before the Civil War according to *Ya*, which also believed that those who visited the shrine, including many who approached it on their knees, displayed a "fervent spirit of the believer" deeper than in the past. *Ya*, March 2, 1940.

3. In 1942, the minister of the interior (Gobernación) declared that the authorities, "far from interfering with the exterior expression of religious sentiments," would now "facilitate, assure and guarantee the free exercise of these manifestations, . . . deeply rooted in tradition." *Ya*, August 8, 1942.

4. *Ya*, March 23, 1940.

5. *Ecclesia*, June 6, 1942, p. 8.

The euphoria produced as "liberated Spain bursts forth in an explosion of grace" could not disguise the reality facing the Church in its enterprise of religious reconquest.[6] Despite ecclesiastical rhetoric proclaiming a religious revival, a realistic perception of the pastoral difficulties ahead was not entirely lacking among the clergy. Statistics published in *Ecclesia* in 1941 called attention to the massive de-Christianization of the parish of San Ramón (Vallecas) studied by Father Peiró before the Civil War. The parish's religious condition was as bleak as ever from a clerical perspective; only 5,000 of its 90,000 residents attended Sunday Mass, while 10,000 children remained unbaptized. The situation in Andalucía appeared equally grim. In the city of Jaén, only 6,671 of the 44,000 inhabitants observed Church law requiring attendance at Sunday Mass; levels of practice were even lower in the region's smaller towns.[7]

Priests imbued with some sense of realism understood that the Church's project of religious reconquest would require "immense labor."[8] They also approached the formidable pastoral task ahead with a sense of urgency, believing that history had delivered into the their hands a "providential opportunity . . . [that] cannot and must not be lost."[9] The civil-ecclesiastical alliance forged during the Civil War appeared to offer an extraordinary opportunity to carry out the massive spiritual transformation of an entire population. The Church proposed a religious experiment of vast proportions to realize the vision cherished by successive clerical generations of a Spain permeated by Catholic values in every aspect of its life. Government support and the disappearance of the Church's perceived enemies from the field stacked the deck in the clergy's favor. Whether religious reconquest could be achieved within an increasingly secularized world in the middle of the twentieth century by a Church historically deficient in its pastoral strategy was another matter.

Reconquest, 1940–1944

Attaining the goal of religious reconquest through the creation of a "regime of Christianity," or "total religiosity" capable of penetrating society at every level proved more difficult than the clergy imagined in the euphoria of the immediate postwar years.[10] To achieve its objectives, the Church relied primarily on a pastoral strategy from the past. The clergy emphasized religious practice, devotions associated with ultramontane piety, the folkloric customs of popular religion, instruction

6. Félix García, "La Iglesia recobrada," *Ya*, March 31, 1940.

7. *Ecclesia*, April 15, 1941, pp. 7–8.

8. "La recristianización de España," ibid., April 1, 1941, pp. 2–3.

9. Pedro Cantero, *La hora católica de España* (Madrid, 1942), p. 6.

10. Eduardo Obregón, *Santander, 1937–1941: planteamientos para la historia de una diócesis* (Santander, 1971), pp. 11–13; Aurelio L. Orensanz, *Religiosidad popular española, 1940–1965* (Madrid, 1974), p. 9.

in the catechism, missions, spiritual exercises, and rigorous insistence on the observance of Catholic moral standards as the keys to religious restoration.[11]

Clerical efforts were supplemented by the activities of Catholic Action. In 1939, the hierarchy reorganized the movement, which increased its membership by 1941 to approximately one hundred thousand, a significant expansion over the forty-one thousand enrolled on the eve of the Civil War.[12] The revived and militant Catholic Action of the immediate postwar period saw itself as a "model army" called no longer to combat hostile forces with arms, as many of its members had done during the war, but to struggle against an "enemy who applies new tactical principles and even more powerful arms" against religion.[13] The organization contributed to the re-Christianizing efforts of the clergy in a variety of ways. It launched campaigns on behalf of priestly vocations and increased attendance at Sunday Mass, and against indecency in films and theatrical performances. Members participated in catechetical campaigns held throughout the country. In 1943, more than a thousand women members fanned out through the remote villages of the Seville archdiocese to provide religious education to a population that "does not know the name of God."[14]

Convinced that fulfillment of Church law requiring attendance at Sunday Mass formed the cornerstone of faith, a concrete indication of the presence of belief, bishops, parish priests, and their lay associates indefatigably promoted efforts to increase religious practice. In Barcelona during 1942, Jesuits, Dominicans, and Catholic Action joined in an "intense campaign" to this effect. Employers were warned that they must observe an old law from the Restoration requiring them to give workers time off on Sunday to attend Mass. Thousands of posters and leaflets were distributed throughout the city, while the press and radio were urged to call the public's attention to the necessity of fulfilling this religious obligation. Even the organizers of Sunday trips to the country or seaside were admonished to ensure that excursionists attended services before embarking on their journeys of relaxation. In Madrid, the clergy provided Sunday Masses in railroad stations, even devising an elaborate scheme that allowed those packing the overcrowded trains of the time to attend services without losing their places.[15]

The Church also encouraged pious devotions to the Sacred Heart, the Blessed

11. "El Doctor Modrego expone el programa de su actuación en la diócesis barcelonesa," *Ecclesia*, June 19, 1943, p. 21.

12. On the eve of the Civil War, there were 4 diocesan councils and 821 local chapters of Catholic Action. By 1941, there were 58 and 1,600 respectively. In Zaragoza, the organization admitted, on average, 2,000 new members annually until 1936. More than 6,000 entrants were received in 1940 alone. Ibid., November 21, 1941, p. 11; May 1, 1941, p. 11.

13. Ibid., January 23, 1943.

14. Ibid., November 1, 1941, p. 11; November 17, 1943, p. 21.

15. Ibid., February 7, 1942, p. 4; March 7, 1942, p. 5.

Virgin, and the saints that had long formed part of ultramontane piety's arsenal.[16] Although the Church had always entertained doubts about manifestations of popular religion that the clergy could not control, it now promoted pilgrimages and devotions as examples of the underlying religiosity of the population. Even Cardinal Segura, rigorist though he was, authorized the resumption of the traditional gypsy pilgrimage to the shrine of the Virgin at El Rocío, once he had taken measures to eliminate the carousing that had accompanied it in the past.[17]

Insofar as there was anything novel about the Church's strategy, it took the form of a reorganization of certain religious activities. In this respect, the example of the vast campaign of popular missions launched in 1941 and 1942 is revealing. The Church departed from the customary method of conducting missions based exclusively on the parish in favor of massive evangelizing campaigns embracing entire cities. Over five hundred priests recruited from the religious orders preached in 203 churches, rented halls, and factories during the Barcelona mission of 1941, an example followed in Seville during the same year. Organizers left few stones unturned as they sought to create the atmosphere of total religious immersion believed essential to the missionary enterprise. At Vigo, using funds donated by banks, business firms, and municipal and provincial governments, they placed announcements of the mission in store windows and persuaded the local transit company to put large illuminated crosses on streetcars. In La Coruña, thirty cyclists moved in waves through the city distributing leaflets announcing the mission, while in Salamanca, young Catholics distributed thirty thousand leaflets stressing the "eternal truths" to be preached in upcoming services.[18]

Unlike those of the pre–Civil War period, missions were organized to serve functional constituencies. At Vigo, more than 20,000 attended services in parish churches. Separate centers served school children (12,000), secondary school students (3,000), military personnel (2,700), municipal employees (150), dressmakers and female servants (1,700), factory workers (4,000), transport workers (1,000) and newspaper employees (200). Even the 400 inmates in the city's jail received their own missionary service. Public ceremonies held in the course of missions were designed to impress and inspire. The Vigo mission opened with a pro-

16. The hierarchy exhorted the faithful to observe the traditional custom of "enthroning" statues and pictures of the Sacred Heart in their homes. The cult received further encouragement in 1944 when 150,000 pilgrims, including Franco and the entire cabinet, gathered in the evening around the illuminated ruins of the statue of the Sacred Heart upon the twenty-fifth anniversary of its dedication. "Para que el Sagrado Corazón de Jesús reine efectivamente en España," ibid., June 20, 1942, p. 19; "España renueve su consagración al Corazón de Jesús," ibid., June 3, 1944, pp. 7–8.

17. "Normas del Cardenal Segura sobre las devociones tradicionales marianas," ibid., May 27, 1944, p. 21.

18. "Santas misiones en Barcelona y Sevilla," *Ecclesia,* April 1, 1941, pp. 8–9; "Santa misión de Vigo por padres de la Compañía de Jesús," *Sal Terrae* (1942), vol. 30, p. 402; "Santa misión de La Coruña," ibid., p. 302; "Misiones generales en Salamanca," *Boletín Oficial del Obispado de Salamanca* (1940), p. 125.

cession of 45,000 led through the streets by priests carrying crosses and representatives of Catholic associations bearing their respective standards. Later, a "rosary of the sea" attracted a crowd of 80,000 to watch a flotilla of twenty-four boats escorting a statue of the Virgin. Priests using loudspeakers then recited the rosary for the crowd gathered on the shore.[19]

The missions of 1941 and 1942 were impressive for their scale and organization. Indeed, they were unique in the history of modern Spanish Catholicism. But the methods used, the sacralization of space and time aimed at submerging entire cities and towns in a religious atmosphere, and the message delivered, with its emphasis on sin, death, and repentance, varied little from those employed at the turn of the century.[20] Although the clergy expressed satisfaction at the numerous confessions and communions recorded during the missions, it is far from certain that the long-term results were any more successful from a pastoral perspective than in the past, especially in urban areas. Missions had always suffered from the weakness of arousing religious sentiment that was short-lived, like "a ship leaving behind it a star of light and fire which necessarily disappears after a short time."[21] Moreover, a strong dose of compulsion accompanied the missions. Factory workers in Vigo received permission from their employers to attend. Few would have dared absent themselves from the services given the climate of the times.

Religion by compulsion formed an essential part of the strategy of reconquest. The Church expected the civil authorities to lend muscle to its re-Christianizing campaign through legislation and cooperation with the clergy by government officials at every administrative level. "The Catholic State," declared Father Joaquín Azpiazu in 1939, "must cooperate to do whatever is necessary to see that the Church's legislation is perfectly fulfilled."[22] Another clerical commentator, writing in 1941, was more frank. To achieve a religious restoration, the Church required the intervention of "the civil authority through the application of the law and force. The work of the Church which relies upon exhortation will not be sufficient. It is necessary that the sword of the public power, which threatens with temporal punishments, should be seen behind the preacher who indicates those that are eternal."[23]

The authorities were more than willing to provide the support demanded by the clergy. "It is the function of the government," asserted the governor of Guadalajara in 1942, "to care for the spiritual formation of Spaniards in the same way that it attends to [their] material necessities."[24] The regime cooperated with the clergy in numerous ways. Its officials remained vigilant before the perceived dangers of the

19. "Santa misión de Vigo," pp. 403–5.
20. Orensanz, *Religiosidad popular española*, pp. 9–21.
21. Ibid., p. 21.
22. Joaquín Azpiazu, *El estado católico* (Burgos, 1939), p. 31.
23. P. Crisógono, *Grandeza, ruina y resurgimiento de España* (San Sebastián, 1941), p. 207.
24. *Ecclesia*, January 24, 1942, p. 18.

country's minuscule Protestant minority.[25] They also censored works judged dangerous to faith and morals and ensured that legislation dealing with morality, especially with respect to the family, reflected Catholic values.[26] From a clerical perspective, there were occasional lapses in official policy. The regime did not declare houses of prostitution illegal, for example, until 1956. But in general the government imprinted legislation affecting public and private behavior with a strongly Catholic character.

The Church retained its traditional gloomy view of the country's moral condition. Spain stood on the verge of being inundated by a sea of corruption, particularly after the period of the Republic, which appeared as a time of unbridled license. Returning Spaniards to the straight and narrow path of Catholic morality occupied a prominent place in the strategy of reconquest. Although the sporadic moralizing campaigns conducted by the civil authorities in cooperation with the clergy during the Restoration and the Primo de Rivera dictatorship had failed to convert the country into a bastion of virtue, Church and State returned to this frayed model with enthusiasm. Provincial governors saw themselves as implacable moral guardians of society as they campaigned incessantly against bars, dances, and indecent theatrical performances. The offense of blasphemy, public statements injurious to "God or the saints," reentered the criminal code according to a 1938 decree ordering the authorities to exercise vigilance in the matter. This exhortation was taken seriously. In 1942, the governor of Palencia asked members of Catholic Action "to denounce to the authorities all those who, refusing to hear the voice of the apostolate, commit so repugnant a fault." One Catholic magazine even published a standard form for denunciations of blasphemy to allow readers to file formal charges against offenders more easily.[27]

Bishops and priests also acted on their own to protect Spaniards from dangers to faith and morals. Bishops censured as a matter of course the works of prominent writers such as Unamuno and Ortega y Gasset. Bishop Pla y Deniel informed the faithful of his Salamanca diocese that no Catholic could sell, read, or keep Una-

25. In 1939, the regime authorized Protestant churches in Madrid to continue holding services under strict limitations. Elsewhere in the country, the authorities were not as generous. Scarcely a month after the war had ended, they closed a "heretical" chapel in Puertollano. Protestant schools suffered the same fate. The smallest sign of proselytism provoked rapid official response, as in 1940 when the government ordered the confiscation of the entire stock of Bibles found in the Sociedad Bíblica of the capital. Manuel López Rodríguez, *La España protestante: crónica de una minoría marginada, 1937–1975* (Madrid, 1976), pp. 23–26; Guy Hermet, *Les catholiques dans l'Espagne franquiste* (2 vols., Paris, 1981), vol. 2, pp. 133–34.

26. In praise of a recent decree establishing the abandonment of a family by either or both parents as a criminal offense, *Ecclesia* declared, "A truly Catholic State has an inexcusable duty, the mission of safeguarding the institution of the family from the dangers that beset it." *Ecclesia*, March 21, 1942, p. 11.

27. In 1943, for example, the civil governor of Lugo issued elaborate instructions regulating public dances because of their influence "over the moral development of youth." Even the musicians playing at these events were required to obtain a certificate of authorization from his office. Ibid., February 6, 1943, p. 18. Quoted in Hermet, *Les catholiques*, vol. 2, p. 129; *Resurrexit* (1943), vol. 3, no. 7, p. 11.

muno's *The Tragic Sense of Life in Men and Nations* on the grounds that it attempted "to destroy the very foundations of religion."[28] The "unbelieving intellectual," declared *Ecclesia* in 1942, "must adore what he has burned and burn what he adored" before being "incorporated into Christian Spain."[29] The Catholic press also routinely published lists of books regarded as unsuitable for reading by the faithful.[30]

Despite stringent official censorship, the clergy regarded films as a source of special danger. The Church, said the bishop of León in 1943, must exercise vigilance against "bad" movies depicting "voluptuous, sensual, ardent scenes of sentimentalism" or mocking "authority and holy things." Such films endangered public morality and produced an "over-excitement of the nervous system" among viewers.[31] The hierarchy pressed the regime to appoint a priest to the official film censoring agency, an objective finally achieved in 1943. A negative vote cast by the Church's single representative was sufficient to deny permission for projection.[32] The bishops left few stones unturned as they searched for causes of immoral behavior. Eijo y Garay of Madrid found a "grave danger to youth . . . in the exaltation of physical vigor" manifested in "sporting exercises and gymnastics," which led "to the corruption of morality and lewd licentiousness."[33]

A religious strategy based on observance, devotionalism, and moral puritanism appealed primarily to those already practicing their religion. Although the clergy placed excessive confidence in this program of old wine in old bottles, it was not unaware of the need to attempt something different if the Church expected to win the allegiance of industrial workers. When all is said and done, the Church did little more than resort to the shopworn formula of exhorting the rich to Christian charity and organizing, with enormous fanfare, campaigns such as that held in Madrid in December 1941 seeking donations to purchase food and medicine for the poor. This emphasis on charity as a means of solving social problems sometimes displayed astonishing naiveté, as in Barcelona, where Bishop Modrego urged the rich to adopt a poor family as a means of securing "social peace and creating the great Christian family."[34]

Insofar as a working-class apostolate existed, it followed the traditional model of spiritual exercises or retreats for workers. An ambitious example of this approach took place between 1941 and 1943 in Asturias. Five thousand workers received time off from their employers and a financial subsidy to attend the services. Jesuit preachers engaged in a "holy adventure" paid lip service to papal social

28. *Ecclesia*, April 19, 1942, p. 19.
29. Rafael García y García, "La heterodoxia encubierta," ibid., July 4, 1942, p. 23.
30. "Semana literaria," ibid., August 12, 1944, p. 23.
31. "Hacia la completa moralización del cine," ibid., April 3, 1943, p. 19.
32. "Reorganización de los organismos de censura cinematográfica," ibid., January 9, 1943, p. 19.
33. Ibid., December 16, 1941, pp. 3–4.
34. "La 'Campaña de Caridad' se orientará en Madrid principalmente en favor de los suburbios," ibid., December 15, 1941, p. 7; "El Doctor Modrego expone su actuacion," p. 21.

teaching in their homilies but avoided the dangerous terrain of social justice. Although the clergy involved claimed that the results of the Asturian exercises provided a model deserving of imitation, the fact remains that the retreats failed to reach the vast majority of the region's workers.[35]

To what extent the Church's religious strategy produced results is a question not easily answered. Patterns of belief and practice do not change overnight. There is no reason to believe that a dramatic religious transformation took place in the years immediately following the Civil War. The special circumstances prevailing after the conflict's end developed further the militancy of middle-class Catholicism already evident during the Republic, although this "victorious Christianity" introduced little that was innovative. In the southern *latifundio* lands, the Church failed to develop an effective rural apostolate. Twenty years after the war's end, the clergy were still lamenting low levels of observance and the "tremendous religious ignorance" existing in Andalucía, where there were still "villages without a priest . . . [and] where a mission has not been given for years or has never been held."[36]

In urban areas, there is fragmentary evidence that the Church made limited progress at the level of formal observance. The clergy saw the thousands who sought canonical marriage, forty-five thousand couples in Seville alone during 1941, as an indication of "sincere repentance" on the part of those who had married in civil ceremonies during the Republic. Statistics for the Catalan industrial city of Mataró show that reception of the last sacraments (an indicator of religiosity according to sociologists concerned with religious practice), fell from 53.1 percent of the dying in 1900 to 32.3 percent by 1940 but then rose to 57.5 percent by 1945. Missionary preachers in Barcelona reported that they had encountered "surprising cases of conversion" in the city's poor districts during the 1941 mission, while the parish priest of Chamartín de la Rosa in Madrid expressed satisfaction at an increase from 16.6 percent to 41 percent in the proportion of residents fulfilling the Easter communion obligation. By 1942–1943, attendance at Sunday Mass in working-class districts of Madrid increased from an average of 6 percent in 1939 to 18 percent by 1945. But there were differences from one parish to another. The situation in the parish of San Ramón, where only 5.4 percent of the population met the religious test of Sunday observance, was far less promising.[37]

These mixed signals and the lack of reliable statistical evidence for the country as a whole are insufficient to confirm the clergy's optimistic assessment of the results of its re-Christianizing efforts among urban workers. Moreover, an increase

35. By 1943, only five thousand of the region's estimated forty-five thousand workers had participated in the program. "La recristianización de las masas obreras en Asturias," ibid., August 14, 1943, p. 9.

36. *Segundo Congreso de Misiones Parroquiales* (Madrid, 1961), pp. 199, 201.

37. "Santas misiones en Barcelona y Sevilla," p. 8; Rogelio Duocastella, *Mataró 1955: estudio de sociología religiosa sobre una ciudad industrial española* (Barcelona, 1961), p. 291; "La parroquia de Chamartín en los suburbios madrileños," *Ecclesia*, January 31, 1942, p. 9; "Por las afueras de Madrid," ibid., April 15, 1941, p. 8; Hermet, *Les catholiques*, vol. 1, p. 78.

in observance did not necessarily represent a change in attitude. Statistics on practice say little about the degree of religious commitment among a population, whether observant or not. Within a regime attaching importance to Catholicism as a badge of civic identity, it behooved anyone wishing to secure a government position, pension, or other official benefits to possess proper religious credentials. Individuals who were not married in the Church or who did not have their children baptized ran the risk of being regarded as second-class citizens.

The strategy of reconquest pursued by the Church during the immediate postwar period developed further after 1945. Whatever its successes or failures, it did not re-create that Catholic Spain of a distant golden age so enthusiastically evoked by the clergy in the atmosphere of euphoric triumphalism produced after the end of the Civil War. By the 1950s, there were signs that confidence in National Catholicism in its religious aspects was beginning to ebb within the Church. Slowly and imperfectly, a new spirit of self-criticism developed among some laity and, increasingly, among a young clergy untouched by the crusading militancy of an older clerical generation deeply influenced by the experience of the Civil War.

Stability, Recovery, or Reconquest?

In 1952, Father Ramón Sarabia returned to the question posed on the title page of his 1939 book: *Was Spain Catholic?* Nearing the end of his long missionary career, the Redemptorist observed that the question needed to be asked again after more than a decade of intense evangelizing activity by the Church within a confessional State. Sarabia's conclusion was as pessimistic as the one he had reached earlier: "In numerous regions of our Spain churches are seen sad and deserted, and millions of Spaniards can be counted who live nearly entirely on the margin of the religious life." In 1966, a progressive Catholic inspired by the reforming spirit of the Second Vatican Council, Alfredo C. Comín, asked a similar question in a book with an equally provocative title, *Spain: Is It a Mission Country?*[38] Although the conservative Sarabia and the progressive Comín considered the question from different perspectives, each saw the country's religious situation primarily in terms of crisis.

Others offered a different assessment. F. Martín-Sánchez Juliá, Angel Herrera's successor as president of the ACNP, argued in 1959 that although there were problems in certain areas, especially among the industrial working class, the two decades since 1939 had produced "a more vigorous spiritual life" and "more pious

38. Ramón Sarabia, *La España de hoy y la España de mañana* (Madrid, 1952), pp. 277–78; Alfredo C. Comín, *España, ¿país de misión?* (Barcelona, 1966).

generations" than had existed before the war. "In Spain," wrote another believer in a religious revival, "the last twenty years have witnessed a profound renovation of spiritual life. Very ample sectors of the population practice spiritual exercises regularly, frequent the sacraments, live the liturgical spirit and . . . an integral Christian existence in proportions unknown in other times."[39] These favorable judgments on the country's religious condition were written by conservative Catholics satisfied with the benefits secured by the Church from the regime. But some clerical critics of National Catholicism reached a similar conclusion. They wrote in 1967, "In Spain, during the last thirty years, a rich and deep spirituality has developed, Christian life has been 'renovated' among ample sectors of society."[40]

To what extent the privileges and resources enjoyed by the Church in Franco's Spain produced a significant religious revival in comparison with the decades before the Civil War is difficult to determine. The idea of a Catholicism uniform in doctrine and practice as accepted by an entire population irrespective of region, occupation, social class, education, sex, and age lay behind clerical rhetoric of religious reconquest during the immediate postwar years. This idea rested on a simplistic formula that perceptive members of the clergy soon realized was impractical within the complexities of a modern society.

During the 1950s and 1960s, the emergence of a new school of religious sociology employing the techniques associated with Gabriel Le Bras and Fernand Boulard in France led to the publication of numerous diocesan and local studies of religious practice and belief.[41] Based on the study of certain key indicators of religiosity established by its practitioners, such as attendance at Sunday Mass, fulfillment of the Easter communion obligation, the frequency of communion, reception of the last sacraments by the dying, the length of time between birth and baptism, and the effects of educational levels on observance, as well as on questionnaires seeking information about the respondents' perception of Catholic doctrine, this new sociology has not lacked critics who have objected to its narrow pastoral focus and the weaknesses of its methodology.[42] Even its advocates caution against using statistics of observance as a reliable guide to the quality of faith. They readily admit that social and official pressures as well as local customs play a role in determining observance or its absence in the dioceses, towns, and parishes subject to scholarly investigation.

They also acknowledge that until the mid-1960s there were no reliable statis-

39. F. Martín-Sánchez Juliá, *Ideas claras: reflexiones de un español actual* (Madrid, 1959), p. 649; José Orlandis, *El catolicismo en la España de hoy* (Pamplona, 1960), p. 64.

40. Carlos Escartín Núñez et al., *Postconcilio en España* (Madrid, 1967), p. 16.

41. For a discussion of the theory and methodology behind this religious sociology in the Spanish case, see Jesús Marcos Alonso, "Études socio-religieuses espagnoles/Socio-religious Studies in Spain," *Social Compass* (1965), vol. 12, no. 2, pp. 217–24.

42. Jesús Jiménez Blanco, *La secularización en España* (Bilbao, 1972), pp. 146–49.

tics on religious practice gathered for the country as a whole.[43] The absence of national figures for much of the Franco era and for earlier periods makes it impossible to make definitive comparisons even at the limited level of observance between past levels of practice and those established by religious sociologists for the specific localities surveyed from the 1950s onward, although some fragmentary statistics dating back to the turn of the century have been found. Whatever the methodological limitations of the sociology of religious observance, for the first time it has provided an X ray of religion at the grassroots level, which, if nothing else, has established that Spanish Catholicism as practiced and believed was a complex phenomenon embracing widely different patterns of observance and even of belief. What is to be made of the astonishing fact uncovered in a 1960s survey of the Salamanca diocese, one of the country's most observant regions according to all indicators of practice, which showed that 43 percent of regular churchgoers entertained doubts about the existence of life in the hereafter?[44]

At one level, the new studies of observance confirm that a significant majority of Spaniards during the Franco period had their children baptized, married in the Church, and received Christian burial. As late as 1983, when religious choice could be exercised freely without the old constraints imposed by State and Church, 82.76 percent of newborns were baptized, while 94 percent of marriages were carried out in church.[45] When asked to state their religious affiliation, Spaniards during the Franco era identified themselves as Catholics whether or not they participated in religious activities. As late as 1985, 87 percent continued to do so.

Whether increased participation in what religious sociologists call community "rites of passage," such as baptism, marriage in church, and the reception of the last sacraments, provides evidence of a religious revival is a matter of discussion. For the Franco period, the signals are mixed. Some suggest a religious recovery, others the contrary. There is fragmentary evidence that the pre–Civil War pattern prevailing in urban working-class parishes such as San Ramón (Vallecas) in Madrid, where 25 percent of children were unbaptized before 1936, had become a thing of the past by the 1960s.[46] But statistics on the reception of the last rites show a marked contrast between areas traditionally known for high levels of obser-

43. Jesús María Vázquez, *Realidades socio-religiosas de España* (Madrid, 1967), p. 90. In 1966, the Oficina de Estadística y Sociología Religiosa, established by the hierarchy during the 1950s, attempted to gather reliable data on observance from all dioceses. Only half of them, however, were able to provide such information.

44. Rogelio Duocastella et al., *Sociología religiosa y pastoral de conjunto. diócesis de Salamanca* (Barcelona, 1967–1968), chapter 14, p. 32.

45. José Andrés-Gallego, "La religiosidad: las cuatro religiones de tres cuartos de siglo," *XX Siglos* (1990), vol. 1, no. 1, p. 8.

46. Although he does not provide statistical evidence to support the assertion, the well-known religious sociologist José María Díaz Mozaz claimed in 1973 that there were no longer parishes in urban, industrialized areas in which a significant number of children were unbaptized. *La Iglesia de España en la encrucijada* (Madrid, 1973), p. 156.

vance—Salamanca and the Tierra de Campos in the Catholic heartland of Old Castile, for example—and urban, industrialized areas. In 1958, approximately 50 percent of the dying in the Madrid district of El Pacífico, with a population drawn largely from the lower-middle and working classes, and in the city of Barcelona in 1963, departed the world without having received the last sacraments. This contrasted with the results for Salamanca (15 percent) and the Tierra de Campos (5.2 percent) during the same period.[47]

Religious sociologists have approached the near universality of baptism and church marriage with caution.[48] Local custom in village communities and the pressure for religious conformity exerted by the clergy and civil authorities worked to discourage any overt disassociation from the established Church in this respect. Civil marriage was possible during the Franco period, but baptized Catholics wishing to evade a church marriage had to take the audacious and potentially damaging step in personal and career terms of formally abjuring the Catholic faith.[49]

As a result, researchers concerned with the condition of Catholicism have concentrated less on baptism and church marriage than on studying other aspects of religious practice as a means of assessing not the depth or quality of faith but external conformity with the Church's expectations. By the end of the regime, scholars working within the Le Bras tradition had produced an impressive body of literature dealing with observance in cities, towns, the countryside, and individual dioceses.[50] These studies have provided a wealth of information about religious practice in specific areas, particularly with respect to different levels of observance among age groups, social classes, occupations, and between the sexes. They also have made it possible for the first time to draw local maps of observance. A study of the Málaga diocese has shown, for example, that practice was highest in the interior agricultural districts of Ronda and Alora, somewhat lower in the area around Antequera, and lowest along the Mediterranean littoral from Estepona through the

47. Jesús María Vázquez, *Así viven y mueren: problemas religosos de un sector de Madrid* (Madrid, 1958), pp. 260–61; *Realidades socio-religiosas*, pp. 141–42; Duocastella et al., *Sociología religiosa . . . Salamanca*, chapter 9, p. 34; Duocastella et al., *Religiosidad y subdesarrollo: estudio sociológico sobre Tierra de Campos* (Madrid and Barcelona, 1971), chapter 6, p. 21.

48. Marcos Alonso, following the methodology of Le Bras, has argued that these "solemn rites" of passage "seem to have no other purpose to those who undergo them than to provide a highlight in the life of the individual, the family or the community, or, they are simply cultural norms, accepted by the majority, to which they therefore conform. . . . G. Le Bras has already put forward the hypothesis that religious 'conformism' was obedience to the norms and customs of antecedents rather than submission to the commandments of the Church. In the case of Spain the possibility of this theory being correct is strengthened by the fact that these rites are really important cultural norms of society, the validity of which is supported by strong elements of social control." "Études socio-religieuses espagnoles/Socio-religious Studies in Spain," pp. 226–27.

49. Ibid.

50. See the bibliography of Paulina Almerich, "Bibliografía de autores españoles sobre sociología de religión," in Paulina Almerich et al., *Cambio social y religión en España* (Barcelona, 1975), pp. 243–77.

city of Málaga to Nerja.[51] This close analysis has also been applied to the study of practice in some cities. In Salamanca, for instance, levels of observance ranged from 30 percent of those obliged to attend Sunday Mass, according to ecclesiastical precept (*misalizantes*), in some areas of the city, to a high of 74 percent in others.[52]

Sociological studies in the Le Bras tradition have provided a more refined view of religious practice in terms of regional and social analysis than was previously available. On the whole, they have produced few startling revelations about Spanish Catholicism. They have confirmed the regional character of observance, long known in a general way since the mid-nineteenth century, although the simple north-south formula of earlier times has given way to a more complex geographical breakdown. Jesús María Vázquez established eight distinct zones of religious practice in a study of 1967, while Rogelio Duocastella's ambitious attempt to draw a national map of observance in 1975 divided the country into six zones. Levels of practice were highest—more than 60 percent of *misalizantes*—in a contiguous swath running from the dioceses of Astorga, Zamora, and Salamanca to the northeast across León, Old Castile, to the Basque Provinces and Navarra. The lowest levels of observance (15–20 percent) were recorded in Madrid and Barcelona, the country's largest cities, where clerical observers had long noted the effects of massive population growth and urbanization on practice. Even in areas of high observance, attendance at Sunday Mass in the cities was lower than in the countryside.[53] In Andalucía, the dioceses of Cádiz and Almería joined Madrid and Barcelona among the areas of lowest practice. The majority of southern dioceses, with the exception of Granada, fell into the second lowest category of observance (20–30 percent).[54] Studies of practice in the region have also revealed a pattern of higher rates of observance in the cities than in the smaller towns and villages of the country-

51. J. Casco et al., *Málaga: el fenómeno religioso y sus condicionamientos socioculturales* (Madrid, 1972), pp. 176–79. Similarly, Rogelio Duocastella and his collaborators found that in the Vitoria diocese the highest levels of practice were to be found in agricultural areas adjacent to Navarra, which recorded very high levels of observance. *Sociología y pastoral de una diócesis: Vitoria* (Madrid and Barcelona, 1965), p. 137. Another study directed by Duocastella of the diocese of Cartagena has established similar differences among nine distinct geographical zones. *Sociología religiosa y pastoral de la diócesis de Cartagena (Murcia)* (Barcelona, 1971), chapter 15, p. 4.

52. Rogelio Duocastella et al., *Sociología religiosa . . . Salamanca,* chapter 14, p. 23. The issue of determining who should be counted as being required to attend Mass according to the Church's requirements has posed certain methodological problems for those engaged in these studies. In general, they have set the figure of *misalizantes* by excluding from their calculations children under the age of seven, that is, those who had not yet received first communion, the elderly, and the infirm in relation to the total population.

53. In the diocese of Salamanca, for example, where the rate of attendance at Sunday Mass reached 72.5 percent of those obliged to attend according to Church law, attendance in the city was 66.8 percent. Ibid., chapter 14, pp. 21, 23.

54. Rogelio Duocastella, "El mapa religioso de España," in *Cambio social y religión en España,* p. 137. In 1965, Duocastella attempted a similar map of observance, but the lack of information from numerous dioceses, especially in the south, left large gaps in the final survey. "Géographie de la pratique religieuse en Espagne," *Social Compass* (1965), vol. 12, no. 2, pp. 253–302.

side in contrast to elsewhere in the country, where the opposite was the case. Levels of observance in Andalucía were lowest in towns of ten to twenty thousand inhabitants, a fact observed years before by the missionary preachers who traversed the region during the early twentieth century.[55]

Sociological scholarship has also confirmed the clergy's historic perception that women attended religious services more frequently than men. As in the case of other aspects of observance, the study of "sexual dimorphism" has noted differences in distinct regional and urban settings. In this respect, differences between the sexes tended to be fewer in areas of high practice, such as Old Castile, León, and the Basque Provinces. In the Vitoria diocese, for example, where 85 percent of *misalizantes* attended Sunday Mass, some rural districts recorded higher rates of observance among men than among women.[56] The gender gap was widest in industrial towns. Studies of the Catalan manufacturing towns of Mataró, Tarrasa, and the Asturian mining region of the Cuenca del Nalón show that on average twice as many women as men attended Sunday services.[57]

Scholars of the Le Bras school have identified high levels of "sexual dimorphism" either as an indicator of de-Christianization or, in pastoral terms, as a sure sign of religious crisis. It was scarcely surprising that they found religious absenteeism to be highest in industrial areas and the southern countryside. Duocastella's pioneering 1955 study of Mataró, where only 30 percent of *misalizantes* attended Sunday Mass regularly, confirmed what the clergy had long perceived about the effects of industrialization and urbanization. Only 14.04 percent of the obliged working-class population fulfilled the Church's requirement, thereby constituting, in his judgment, "one of the greatest religious problems posed in the city."[58] Later studies have confirmed the connection between social class and level of practice, albeit with interesting variants. In the Basque Provinces, workers attended services more often than did their counterparts elsewhere.[59] In Antequera (Málaga), on the other hand, only 10.8 percent of skilled workers practiced regularly in contrast to 98.7 percent of those belonging to the liberal professions.[60] In the southern coun-

55. José Cazorla, *Problemas de estratificación social en España* (Madrid, 1973), pp. 183, 185. Sixty-four percent of the residents of such towns obliged to attend Sunday Mass reported that they did not do so regularly, a higher percentage than in Seville (54 percent). Cazorla notes, however, that the differences between city and country were less marked in Almería, Cádiz, and Huelva than in Seville, Jaén, and Granada, where it was substantial. Ibid., pp. 183–84. Similarly, a study of the diocese of Cartagena showed that observance in its two largest cities, Cartagena and Murcia, was higher in many cases than in rural districts. Duocastella et al., *Sociología religiosa y pastoral de la diócesis de Cartagena (Murcia)*, chapter 15, p. 4.

56. Duocastella et al., *Sociología y pastoral de una diócesis: Vitoria*, p. 140.

57. In Mataró, 37 percent of female and 22 percent of male *misalizantes* attended Sunday Mass; in Tarrasa, the proportions were 23.3 percent and 16.6 percent; in the Cuenca de Nalón, 29.8 percent and 15.4 percent. Duocastella et al., *Sociología religiosa . . . Salamanca*, chapter 9, p. 4.

58. Duocastella, *Mataró 1955*, p. 243.

59. Vázquez, *Realidades socio-religiosas*, p. 123.

60. Casco et al., *Málaga: el fenómeno religioso*, p. 187.

tryside, the connection between practice and class has also been confirmed, with levels of practice descending in lineal fashion from large estate owners, 80 percent of whom counted themselves as *practicantes,* to small agriculturalists who employed laborers (64 percent), to farmers who worked their land personally without assistance (43 percent), to sharecroppers (36 percent) and landless *braceros* who worked for others (26 percent).[61]

The sociology of religious practice has provided useful analysis of observance in specific chronological periods and geographical settings. It also perceived certain trends, especially in studies carried out during the 1960s and early 1970s, that showed a drift away from practice among young people, a reflection, perhaps, of the effects of accelerated urbanization, industrialization, and the beginnings of a consumer-oriented society.[62] Duocastella has also shown that in Mataró the level of practice among immigrants to the city from strongly observant Navarra and the Basque Provinces declined significantly in their new place of residence.[63] Although these conclusions were harbingers of long-term changes, it should be noted that there is insufficient evidence for the country as a whole to conclude that the country's economic transformation and its social effects during the 1960s immediately altered existing patterns of observance to a significant degree.[64]

The question remains whether observance during the Franco period represented what Guy Hermet has called a "return to the altars" in comparison with pre–Civil War Spain.[65] Experienced researchers of the Le Bras school have reached contradictory conclusions. J. M. Díaz Mozaz has suggested that overall religious practice may not have been any higher than before 1936, although he argues that the massive absenteeism characteristic of some social sectors in the past was ameliorated during the Franco period. On the basis of diocesan statistics that he admits are far from reliable, J. M. Vázquez has advanced the thesis that the proportion of *misalizantes* attending Sunday Mass reached the impressive proportion of 40 per-

61. Cazorla, *Problemas de stratificación social,* p. 188.

62. Díaz Mozaz has noted that by the early 1970s "a deep religious trauma" had developed among young people within the highly observant Catholicism of the Basque Provinces, a region that experienced spectacular economic development in the 1960s. Nearly two-thirds of the youth responding to a survey reported that they viewed religion "in a different way than their parents." *La Iglesia de España en la encrucijada,* p. 165.

63. Immigrants from Navarra, a region where 60 percent of *misalizantes* attended Sunday Mass, fulfilled this obligation at a far lower level (24.3 percent) in Mataró. Duocastella, *Mataró 1955,* p. 261.

64. Two surveys of observance among young people carried out in 1960 and 1968 showed only a marginal decline in attendance, 3 percent among males, 1 percent among females, and 7 percent among students of both sexes, although the number of those who declared that they rarely went to Sunday Mass doubled. Hermet, *Les catholiques,* vol. 1, p. 78. A survey comparing the religious attitudes of youths between the ages of eighteen and twenty-five found that during the 1950s, 85 percent of respondents believed that Christ was the Redeemer and the Son of God as the Church taught. During the 1960s, 75 percent expressed similar beliefs, a significant although not spectacular decline. Fernando F. Fernández, "La religiosidad de la juventud española, ayer y hoy," in Francisco Azcona et al., *Catolicismo en España: análisis sociológico* (Madrid, 1985), p. 195.

65. Hermet, *Les catholiques,,* vol. 1, p. 77.

cent by the mid-1960s. In the same vein, Guy Hermet has suggested that the number of those meeting the Sunday Mass obligation placed Spain in the same category as other areas in the Catholic world known for high levels of observance during the 1950s and early 1960s, namely, Québec, Flemish Belgium, and Italy.[66]

Given the absence of consistent and reliable data for the pre–Civil War period, a definitive conclusion cannot be reached. Although the massive religious conquest of clerical dreams was never realized, fragmentary evidence suggests that at least at the level of practice a recuperation took place over the course of the regime's history, even among the rural population of the south and to a lesser extent among industrial workers. Before 1936, clerical reports of the state of religion in southern towns and villages repeatedly noted levels of attendance at Sunday Mass of around 5 percent of *misalizantes* and nearly complete absenteeism among men. By contrast, a 1967 survey of observance in certain areas of rural Andalucía showed that 42 percent of the male population identifying themselves as Catholic (and this represented the vast majority), reported that they attended Sunday Mass regularly and met the Easter communion obligation.[67] There were, to be sure, significant differences, depending on the size of local populations. Levels of practice tended to be higher in smaller villages and substantially lower in larger rural towns, where an agricultural proletariat lived in desperate economic conditions. There is also the problem, noted by sociologists of observance, of whether respondents actually did what they reported. Even if the survey's results are only approximate, they suggest that rates of observance may have improved in the region compared with the situation earlier in the century, despite clerical laments about low levels of practice in the southern countryside.

Given the professional interest of religious sociologists, many of whom were priests, in providing a sophisticated analysis of practice that would allow the Church to develop a more effective response to pastoral problems, it is not surprising that low levels of practice among industrial workers evoked constant expressions of concern. From their perspective, this apprehension was not misplaced. A survey of more than fifteen thousand workers carried out in 1958 revealed that while the vast majority (86.1 percent) were baptized, had married in church, and intended to have a religious funeral, only 7.6 percent attended Sunday Mass regularly.[68] Elevated participation in liturgical rites of passage almost certainly broke with the pattern prevailing before the Civil War, at least on the basis of the limited information available, although its religious significance may not be great. In fact, the survey suggests that the Church had made little pastoral progress

66. Díaz Mozaz, *La Iglesia de España en la encrucijada*, p. 156; Vázquez, *Realidades socio-religiosas*, pp. 109, 299; Hermet, *Les catholiques*, vol. 1, p. 74.

67. Cazorla, *Problemas de estratificación social*, p. 179.

68. Alfredo C. Comín, *España, ¿país de misión?* (Barcelona, 1966), p. 80. A similar survey carried out among workers in Zaragoza two years later showed that 12 percent of workers were practicing Catholics. Ibid., p. 81.

if one considers that the level of observance was approximately the same (7 percent) as that recorded for the Madrid parish of San Ramón (Vallecas) by Peiró during the early 1930s. Hermet maintains, on the other hand, that practice in the "red suburbs" of Madrid moved from a low point of 6 percent in 1939 to 18 percent by 1945.[69] The statistics gathered for other industrial areas—Mataró in the mid-1950s, the Cuenca del Nalón during the early 1960s, and Tarrasa in 1967—also suggest a modest recuperation in practice to a level of 12–20 percent of working-class *misalizantes* if one accepts the observations of prewar commentators concerned with the massive religious absenteeism among workers as a valid basis for comparison. But there were important differences from one place to another. Duocastella's study of the industrial suburbs of Barcelona, for example, found an extremely low rate of observance in these predominantly working-class areas (2.5 percent).[70]

What conclusions can be drawn from the mixed evidence on religious observance amassed by scholars beginning in the 1950s? First, there is nothing to suggest that reconquest, the religious immersion of an entire country and population, ever took place. Even if one accepts J. M. Vázquez's hypothesis that 40 percent of *misalizantes* attended Sunday Mass, the fact remains that 60 percent did not. Second, there is sufficient, although not overwhelming, evidence that practice increased during the Franco period. This was, however, an uneven recovery that by no means overcame historic regional and social imbalances characteristic of observance for generations, except in the area of baptism and marriage. Third, as a result of the accelerated pace of urbanization and industrialization accompanying the economic boom of the 1960s and the emergence of a consumer society, signs of slippage were detected among young people and rapidly expanding city populations, although no dramatic transformation occurred at this stage.

As the clergy conceived Catholic Spain, these results were disappointing given the euphoria that swept the Church immediately after the Civil War. Despite the uneven nature of the recovery in religious observance, the Church did not do badly given the pressures generated by social and economic developments already evident during the 1950s. A tentative argument can be advanced that, at best, the Church achieved modest gains in practice and that, at worst, it managed to hold its own.

The Faces of Catholicism

The new school of religious sociology moved on less sure ground when it grappled with the complex issue of the doctrinal and spiritual quality of Spanish Catholicism. The degree of commitment or lack of it on the part of individuals to

69. Hermet, *Les catholiques*, vol. 1, p. 78.
70. Duocastella, "Géographie de la pratique religieuse," p. 283.

the corpus of doctrine, concepts of spiritual life, and code of moral behavior defined by the Church depended on a variety of motivations. The clergy derived satisfaction from responses to questionnaires requesting information about specific beliefs. Surveys indicated that most Spaniards believed in God whether they attended church or not. Studies carried out in La Rioja in 1970 and the Tierra de Campos in 1971 showed that less than 3 percent of respondents declared atheistic convictions.[71] There were indications of a higher degree of doubt among youth. Of those between the ages of twenty and twenty-four in the Cartagena diocese in 1971, for instance, 6.5 percent expressed reservations about the existence of God.[72] The ambitious national survey of popular attitudes on virtually every aspect of Spanish life conducted by the FOESSA foundation in 1970 revealed an apparently remarkable acceptance of Church doctrine among housewives of every social class and educational level, although the results must be taken with a grain of salt.[73] Ninety-three percent of those interviewed declared their belief in the doctrine of the Trinity; 96 percent in the real presence in the Eucharist.[74] Not all research confirmed this apparently strong commitment to Catholic doctrine. Clerical scholars examining the religious condition of the Málaga diocese in 1972 found that although a substantial majority of respondents expressed belief in God, for 43.8 percent this was not the faith in divinity as defined by theologians but a vague deism covered by a veneer of Christianity.[75]

Religious sociologists in the Le Bras tradition were aware of the complexity of individual motivations. But they assessed the religious condition of Spaniards in the light of clerical expectations. The reservations expressed by the Málaga researchers were echoed in studies conducted in other areas. Even in regions known for high levels of religious practice, the faith as believed raised the scholarly eyebrows of investigators concerned primarily with doctrinal content and spiritual motivation. In the highly observant peasant districts of the Tierra de Campos, they discovered that 75.8 percent of men and 84.2 percent of women believed firmly in God, a substantial majority, but less than what one would have expected in an area identified as one of the country's most Catholic. Moreover, when queried about the relationship between the individual and God, only a minority (28 percent) saw him as a father who loved men and women as his children and to whom they might turn for spiritual consolation. In this region of small peasant villages where life revolved around the vicissitudes of dry farming, 40 percent saw the divinity prima-

71. Angel Díaz Cerio, *El comportamiento religioso-moral en La Rioja: estructuras condicionantes, prácticas y actitudes, evolución y sus causas, 1958 a 1975, aplicaciones pastorales* (Barañáin, 1992), p. 107; Duocastella et al., *Religiosidad . . . estudio sociólogico sobre Tierra de Campos*, chapter 6, p. 85.

72. Duocastella et al., *Sociología religiosa y pastoral de la diócesis de Cartagena*, chapter 17, p. 18.

73. Duocastella complained that the FOESSA survey contained "very singular data in the realm of fantasy" about levels of religious practice in several dioceses. "El mapa religioso," p. 133.

74. Amando de Miguel et al., *Síntesis del informe sociológico sobre la situación social de España 1970* (Madrid, 1972), p. 115.

75. Casco et al., *Málaga: El fenómeno religioso*, p. 238.

rily as the force who could order good or bad weather, health or misfortune. Eleven percent of respondents declared that it was difficult to know who God was, although they admitted that "good Spaniards" had always held this belief and for this reason they did so. Similarly, 23 percent of men and 11.3 percent of women in the region expressed doubts about the existence of hell.[76]

The results of this survey in the heartland of rural Spanish Catholicism led pastoral-minded investigators to conclude that while "undoubtedly faith existed" in the region, it was "an elemental, naturalist faith and for a Christian who should consider . . . the content of his faith, it could not be considered as exemplary."[77] In fact, there was nothing surprising about what was discovered in the Tierra de Campos and elsewhere in the country. Unanimous adherence to the clergy's model of the faith represented an ecclesiastical ideal never attained in practice.

Belief covered a wide spectrum with respect to specific points of Church teaching. Although conservative commentators on pastoral matters after the Second Vatican Council lamented the emergence of a "pick-and-choose" Catholicism among the faithful, there was little new about it. Resistance to frequent communion, long characteristic of the intensely observant rural areas of central and northern Spain, continued into the 1960s despite decades, indeed centuries, of ecclesiastical efforts to break an attitude that had its origins in the distant past. In the mountainous Castilian village of Valdemora, for example, a majority of residents confessed and received communion just once a year, while in the highly observant diocese of Salamanca, only 30 percent of *misalizantes* in town and country received the Eucharist regularly.[78] Pastoral commentators interpreted this resistance either as a residual manifestation of eighteenth-century Jansenism or as a "deficient interpretation of the principal rite of Christianity" among the faithful.[79] Whatever its causes, it showed that the Church could not impose its theological will easily in the face of long-established custom.

Religious sociologists also realized that Spanish Catholicism as applied in daily life did not conform to a monolithic model based on the theological, spiritual, and pastoral principles developed by the Church. "Religious conduct," declared Jesús Marcos Alonso, one of the most perceptive of the new generation of scholars concerned with the religious condition of Spain during the 1960s, "in many cases . . . is observed more as a reaction to cultural standards and the traditions of the immediate natural groups of global society than as a response to the requirements of the Church."[80]

76. Duocastella et al., *Religiosidad . . . estudio sociológico sobre Tierra de Campos*, chapter 5, pp. 85–86, 88.

77. Ibid., p. 87.

78. Susan Tax Freeman, *Neighbors: The Social Contract in a Castilian Hamlet*, p. 97; Duocastella, *Sociología religiosa . . . Salamanca*, chapter 14, p. 28.

79. Duocastella et al., *Sociología religiosa y pastoral de la diócesis de Cartagena*, chapter 15, p. 16.

80. Marcos Alonso, "Études socio-religieuses espagnoles/Socio-religious Studies in Spain," p. 230.

Scholars concerned with Spain's religious condition during the Franco period have divided it into distinct categories based on modern social science.[81] There was nothing new about the idea of Spanish Catholicism as a multilayered phenomenon. Clerical observers had been aware of it in a vague sort of way for generations. The more sophisticated classifications of researchers have made it possible to appreciate Spanish Catholicism's complexities within a more coherent intellectual framework. Although a case can be made for the distinct categories established by different scholars, those developed by Marcos Alonso are particularly useful. He recognized the existence of a "cultural Catholicism" manifested as a civic religion identifying Spain and Spaniards as a providential nation and chosen people in the biblical sense.[82] This identity of the country and its inhabitants with Catholicism, perceived as fundamental to every aspect of national life, reached its height during the first two decades of the Franco period among the clergy and especially among segments of society closely identified with the regime. Although by the late 1960s the changes introduced into the Spanish Church by the Second Vatican Council, and the emergence of a questioning attitude towards the alliance between Church and State, took much of the wind from the sails of this form of Catholicism, it continued to retain the allegiance of a minority of clergy and the regime's hard-liners.

The category defined as "popular" Catholicism included devotions of ultramontane piety in town and country and attached particular significance to the role of religion as a sustaining element of community identity and its practical needs in the villages of rural Spain existing within a world of perceived irrational forces thought capable of visiting sickness, death, and natural misfortunes upon the population. God appeared as "an omnipotent and capricious Lord who distributes favours, health, wealth, security, well-being and eternal salvation, completely at his whim."[83] In these circumstances, the formal doctrines preached by the Church were less important than the elaboration of religious ceremonies and practices designed to placate the divinity, thereby protecting the faithful in their daily lives from human and natural disasters with which they were familiar through experience. Social anthropologists have also stressed the importance of ritual events revolving around the Church's liturgical calendar as essential to sustaining community solidarity, to providing villagers with a cohesive social base necessary for their collective survival.[84]

The relationship of popular Catholicism in rural Spain to the religious model upheld by the Church is by no means clear, however. It has been suggested that in

81. For a summary of the theoretical basis of a sociology of religion as applied to the Spanish Church, see Juan González-Anleo, *Catolicismo nacional: nostalgia y crisis* (Madrid, 1975), pp. 53–98.

82. Marcos Alonso, "Études socio-religieuses espagnoles/Socio-religious Studies in Spain," pp. 233–36.

83. Ibid., p. 231.

84. WilliamChristian, *Person and God in a Spanish Valley* (New York, 1972), p. 11; Freeman, *Neighbors*, p. 90.

Valdemora, the inhabitants' view of what constitutes a good Christian "places little value on general compliance with Church dogma" and that the "institutions of formal Catholicism are hardly the focus of village religion."[85] The prevalence in southern villages of certain religious manifestations provides a dramatic example of a popular Catholicism based on magical qualities far removed from orthodoxy. In the southern village of Alcalá de Sierra, pious women (*sabías*) thought to possess special powers to secure the intervention of God, the Virgin, and the saints were employed by local residents to find lost objects, cure physical ills, protect the faithful from "acts of God," and to make sure that an individual who died without the last rites would not go to hell.[86]

A study of the Aragonese agricultural town of Belmonte de los Caballeros presents a different picture of a popular Catholicism more closely linked to the practices of ultramontane piety encouraged by the Church. Rituals associated with agricultural cycles and the need to seek the intercession of God, the Virgin, and the saints historically associated with rural religious life continued. As in centuries past, the bells of the village church sounded on May 3 each year to summon residents for a procession that moved to a cross located in nearby fields, where the priest blessed the harvest. But other rituals—the placing of plaques to the Sacred Heart outside houses and a multitude of devotions to the Virgin with particular emphasis on the saying of the rosary—represented forms of piety promoted directly by the Church.[87] In this respect, it is striking that a cult long encouraged by the clergy, Our Lady of the Assumption, occupied an especially important place in the village's devotional life. Celebration of the feast of the Assumption on August 15 emerged as one of the town's principal religious festivals. At dawn the faithful moved through the streets with banners while saying the rosary. Later, a solemn Mass and procession took place as the statue of the Virgin was carried through the town. The day's festivities concluded with another procession accompanied by a constant peal of bells.

The variants in popular religious expression described by social anthropologists reflected their distinctly local origins and the different ways in which village populations used ritual to represent community concerns. These studies also attest to the continuing vitality of popular religion through the Franco period, whatever its specific motivations. Through the 1960s, the celebration of the feast days

85. Ibid., pp. 97, 98.

86. J. A. Pitt-Rivers, *The People of the Sierra* (Chicago, 1961), pp. 190–91. The magical qualities attached to certain individuals and customs were by no means confined to the south. Michael Kenny's study of the village of Ramosierra (Soria) noted the still widespread belief in the ability of the "evil eye" to do injury to livestock. *A Spanish Tapestry: Town and Country in Castile* (New York, 1966), p. 50.

87. This link between activities long promoted by the Church and religious life in Belmonte de los Caballeros can also be seen through the existence of Catholic associations of a distinctly modern type, such as a sodality of women dedicated to devotion to the Sacred Heart and a local chapter of Catholic Action. Similar groups were absent from the village of Valdemora. Carmelo Lisón-Tolosana, *Belmonte de los Caballeros: A Sociological Study of a Spanish Town* (Oxford, 1966), pp. 296–97; Freeman, *Neighbors*, p. 97.

of local holy patrons, whether Christ, the Virgin, or the saints, continued in full vigor in villages as diverse as Valdemora, Ramosierra, and Belmonte de los Caballeros. The same was true of the Nansa valley in Santander province, where in 1969, twenty thousand persons attended the annual celebration held in honor of the Virgin at the regional shrine of El Brezo. The atmosphere, recalled an observer of the scene, appeared similar to that of an American football game. A young priest exhorted the crowd at Mass with the enthusiasm shown at a "pep rally." The Virgin received a new mantle and a baton representing the honorary mayorship of nearby towns. This point in the ceremony was accompanied by wild cheering and the mass waving of white handkerchiefs. Three thousand received communion, while the entire congregation heard a sermon predicting the conversion of Protestants through the Virgin's intervention. An exuberant crowd then moved down the hillside to eat picnic lunches and enjoy other festivities before returning home to their villages after a satisfying day that combined piety and diversion.[88]

During the Franco era, popular religion also received encouragement from the civil and ecclesiastical authorities, who viewed it as an indication of the underlying religiosity of Spaniards. Members of town councils, often conservative men of property and influence sympathetic to the regime, always participated in processions. In larger rural towns such as Belmonte de los Caballeros, the resident detachment of the Civil Guard, perhaps the greatest symbol of the regime's authority at the local level, marched along with the clergy and municipal councillors in religious processions.[89] Although always vigilant before manifestations of popular religious expression removed from orthodoxy, the clergy viewed popular devotions, processions, shrines, and pilgrimages in a favorable light as a confirmation, though an imperfect one in clerical eyes, that Spain remained a Christian nation.

As a result of the Second Vatican Council, this condescending nineteenth-century view of popular religious practices yielded to a more positive interpretation.[90] Even in the south, where popular rituals often escaped priestly control, the clergy came to recognize that popular religion possessed a "singular importance" that formed "part of the life and community of the Church," because it showed "the basic and decisive presence of true Christian faith." Like earlier clerical generations, however, the new pastoral theologians continued to believe that these ceremonies required "purification and education in evangelical faith."[91]

Despite encouragement by Church and State, popular Catholicism survived because it was linked to community concerns and took an eclectic form capable of absorbing constantly changing devotional influences, sometimes introduced by

88. Christian, *Person and God*, pp. 56–57.

89. Lisón-Tolosana, *Belmonte de los Caballeros*, pp. 298–99.

90. Luis Maldonado, *Para comprender el catolicismo popular* (Estella, 1990), pp. 19–25.

91. *El catolicismo popular en el sur de España: documento de trabajo para la reflexión práctica pastoral* (Madrid, 1975), pp. 7, 14.

the clergy, sometimes developed autonomously, that appealed to local populations. Specific devotions rose and fell in popularity, always producing, however, a new and successful pious amalgam. But there were signs that the long-term vitality of popular religious expression in the countryside was far from assured. Continuing urbanization, which accelerated during the 1960s, and the advance of agricultural mechanization led to rural depopulation in many areas and altered the balanced social mix based on sex, age, and occupation essential to traditional community piety in the countryside.

The Church's pastoral attitude, whether in its traditional or post–Vatican II versions, towards popular religion was positive in many respects. But the new pastoral theology of the 1960s also contributed to undermining its foundations. In the Nansa valley, younger priests influenced by new theological currents had little use for the idea of sacred intermediaries manifested in shrines and images to which villagers turned collectively and individually to protect themselves in this world and assure salvation in the next. Instead, the clergy promoted an interior religiosity based on the idea of human society as a brotherhood of Christ that depended on the sacrament of the Eucharist. In this theological universe, a popular religion expressed through holy intercessors who were seen to be visibly present in the physical landscape through shrines and images appeared anachronistic. The devotional world of the valley towns slowly began to change as a result of this new approach.[92]

The doctrinal and institutional expectations of the Church were most fully realized, according to Marcos Alonso, through an "ecclesiastical" Catholicism that, unlike its "popular" counterpart, stressed the individual's quest for salvation through the development of an interior spiritual life and the creation of "a personal relationship with God through the Church."[93] The placatory aspects of popular religion, based on exterior, mechanistic, and quasi-magical rituals, yielded to an emphasis on "piety of life, and rectitude of behaviour and reason" as communicated by the clergy through doctrinal and moral teaching.[94]

To what extent the faithful embraced this ecclesiastical ideal is impossible to establish, although it was probably greatest among urban, middle-class, and well-educated Catholics, according to sociological surveys concerned with the reception of the Eucharist as a specific indication of a more spiritual faith.[95] But it should

92. Christian, *Person and God*, p. 182.

93. Marcos Alonso, "Études Socio-religieuses espagnoles/Socio-religious Studies in Spain," p. 236.

94. Ibid.

95. A survey of the reception of the Eucharist by young people during the 1960s found the highest levels of frequent communion among an upper class divided into two categories. For those in the top socioeconomic category it stood at 43 percent and for the group immediately below at 56 percent. About a third of middle-class youth received communion at least once a month. Among working-class young people, however, the percentage slipped to 27 percent. Among a group defined imprecisely as "poor," it declined to 19 percent. González-Anleo, *Catolicismo nacional*, p. 214. Although the Church regarded reception of the Eucharist as a sure sign of religious commitment, it should be noted that family and social pressures played a role here as in other religious practices.

be noted that the lines of division separating "ecclesiastical" from "popular" Catholicism were never hard and fast. Many devotional practices associated with the ultramontane piety encouraged by the Church since the mid-nineteenth century were closer to those of popular religion in motivation than to the spiritual ideal of interior faith promoted by the clergy.

During the Franco period, the Church by no means neglected efforts to inculcate its commitment to a more inward-looking faith, largely through traditional methods based on missions, spiritual exercise, retreats, and exhortation dispensed through the clergy's extensive media network. Although biblical studies in Spain were poorly developed until the 1960s, the Church engaged in a strenuous effort to make Bibles available to the faithful. Seven million copies were distributed by Catholic publishing houses between the end of the Civil War and the mid-1960s as a means of reacquainting the faithful with "their authentic Christian vocation."[96]

Writing after the Second Vatican Council, a legion of commentators considering the "ecclesiastical" Catholicism of the 1940s and 1950s subjected the Church's religious program to withering criticism. Although this reflected the influence of new reforming currents released by the Council and tended to ignore the fact that the religious message communicated by the Spanish Church to the faithful was scarcely unique within the Catholic world of the time, there is no question that the Church in Spain saw itself, even in the favorable circumstances created by the Franco regime, as a religious redoubt surrounded and threatened by a host of external enemies and corrupting forces. There was nothing new about this dark vision of the place of religion in a secular world.

As a result, the positive aspects of the Church's religious message were subordinated to a pastoral strategy of "segregation" designed to erect a "protective barrier" between the faithful and the countless dangers to faith and morals thought to surround them.[97] In many respects, the strongest glue cementing the alliance between Church and State lay in the clerical perception that the instruments of social control possessed by the clergy as a result of its ties to the civil power provided the instruments necessary to protect the religious redoubt and its inhabitants from countless dangers. Censorship, both civil and ecclesiastical, constant harassment of the country's tiny Protestant minority, and the regime's persecution of democratic political and social movements were seen as indispensable tools for saving Spaniards from a sea of perils.

At no time since the eighteenth century did the Church fulfill its ambition to be the supreme moral censor of society more fully than during the Franco period. The Church relied upon the State to ensure conformity to Catholic morality on mar-

96. Escartín Núñez et al., *Postconcilio en España*, p. 16.

97. *Las misiones populares hoy* (Madrid, 1973), pp. 49–51.

riage and the family. Divorce did not exist and, for all practical purposes, every baptized Catholic wishing to marry had to do so in a religious ceremony. The clergy viewed human sexuality as a necessary but uncomfortable aspect of the human personality. "The sexual appetite," declared the clerical author of a widely circulated book on marriage published in 1950, "is an appetite of lust, in the sense that it is not necessary to satisfy it to live, nor even to enjoy good health. It is only necessary for the survival of the species."[98] The married state was perceived as distinctly inferior, from a spiritual point of view, to the celibate existence of priests and religious. As the founder of Opus Dei expressed it, "Marriage is for the foot soldiers, not for the general staff of Christ."[99] A voluminous clerical literature treated marriage less as a relationship based on mutual respect and affection than as a burden borne largely by women expected to subordinate their personalities to those of their spouses. Father Enciso Viana, author of a popular manual of conduct for future wives, told them in no uncertain terms what their relationship with their husbands should be: "When you are married, never come into conflict with him, neither oppose your character to his, nor your intransigence to his. When he becomes angry, keep quiet; when he shouts, lower your head and do not reply." "*Matrimony is a slavery,*" said a Jesuit writer on the subject. Spouses were "*two slaves bound to the same chain.*" There was no question of separation, however difficult the problems affecting a marriage. Marriage was for life, and "to think in any other way is to cast oneself into hell."[100]

The Church's commitment to defending the family in accord with Catholic moral teaching would have been more persuasive had it not been linked so directly to a preoccupation with sexual matters that viewed human nature in the darkest terms as a swamp of corrupt tendencies ever ready to drag Spaniards into eternal perdition. There was nothing new, of course, about this clerical view of the human condition. Since the mid-nineteenth century, bishops and priests had fulminated against dangers of the flesh as a sign of moral dissolution, the fatal and inevitable effect of social changes associated with liberalism. Although liberal governments of the Restoration, particularly during periods of Conservative party rule, occasionally yielded to the Church's persistent efforts to convert the State into a public moralizer, it was not until the Primo de Rivera dictatorship that official policy fully embodied the clergy's view of morality, although with indifferent results.

During the Franco era, at least until the reforming currents of the 1960s introduced a more positive view of marriage and sexuality, the message remained the same. But for the first time, the clergy was in a position to employ the formidable

98. Quoted in Feliciano Blázquez, *La traición de los clérigos en la España de Franco* (Madrid, 1991), p. 79.

99. Quoted in Frances Lannon, *Privilege, Persecution and Prophecy: The Catholic Church in Spain, 1875–1975* (Oxford, 1987), p. 52.

100. Quoted in Bláquez, *La traición de los clérigos*, p. 79.

institutional power of State and Church to impose its moral code on society as a whole. Few topics were treated more extensively in diocesan bulletins and episcopal pastoral letters of the 1940s and 1950s than that of morality, which, for all practical purposes, meant sexual morality. The bishops of the time may have differed from one another on certain points with respect to social justice, government censorship, and, in a limited way, the political character of the regime. On questions of public and private morality, there were no divisions. Bishop Olaechea of Pamplona, who had dared criticize the bloody reprisals of the Nationalists during the Civil War, thus saw movies as destructive of the "virility of peoples" that in the best of worlds should be consigned to the flames. Despite frequent conflicts with the regime, Bishop Pildain of the Canaries instructed his clergy to refuse absolution to the faithful who swam or sunbathed with members of the opposite sex. Priests who refused to do so were liable to immediate suspension from their sacerdotal functions.[101]

Clerical efforts to protect Spaniards from fleshly temptations focused on four areas: dancing, the cinema, beaches, and female dress. Since the mid-nineteenth century, the clergy had viewed dancing, especially in its modern versions, as a powerful occasion for sin. A leading clerical moralist concluded, after studying the question in the works of Saint Thomas Aquinas, Saint Bonaventure, and Saint Alfphonsus Liguori, that "prolonged contacts of the sexes [in dancing] . . . contains enormous capacity for the most serious sexual excitations." His conclusion that "in a Catholic people like Spain, Catholics should not dance" could not be enforced, as the clergy recognized reluctantly, although some bishops tried mightily.[102] Bishop Nájera of Orense prohibited Catholics from belonging to any group or association that organized dances. The only dances that could be tolerated, according to Cardinal Segura, were traditional country ones in which a "breeze could pass" between a couple. All others represented "the satanic work of moral corruption, public scandal and sin, a school of degrading orgies of concupiscence."[103]

These attempts to eliminate or control dancing had little effect among a rural and urban population for whom dancing had long been a source of recreation. The Church's reach was considerably longer in an area that lent itself more readily to clerical control—the cinema. Although rigorous government censorship of films had existed since the Civil War and nothing deemed scandalous or immoral ever reached the screen, the Church wanted more. It viewed movies, in the words of the Jesuit founder of the ACNP, Father Ayala, as "the greatest calamity that has befallen the world since Adam. More a calamity than the universal flood, the European war, the World War and the atomic bomb."[104] For this reason, the Church went well beyond already stringent government censorship. In 1950, it created a special office

101. Ibid., pp. 80, 85.

102. Quoted in ibid., p. 83.

103. Quoted in ibid., p. 84.

104. Quoted in ibid., p. 81.

to grade films according to their moral content based on more stringent standards than those of the official censorship authorities. Special attention was given to movies judged "seriously dangerous" from the perspective of morality. Parish priests posted signs in church vestibules warning the faithful that they could not attend such films under pain of sin, while Catholic newspapers rejected advertisements for them. None created more controversy during the mid-1940s than the American movie "Gilda," starring Rita Hayworth. Although already heavily censored by the civil authorities, its screening provoked pastoral letters and clerical protests, while enraged Catholic militants paraded before theaters and, on occasion, ripped down advertising posters for the film. The uproar revolved around a single scene in which the actress seductively removed a glove![105]

The clergy devoted considerable attention to the kind of bathing suits thought suitable for beaches and to such questions as the appropriate length of women's skirts. Indeed, the bishops published innumerable pastoral letters on these subjects. At a lower clerical level, moral interventions sometimes bordered on the ridiculous. During the 1940s, for example, groups of students belonging to the Jesuit lay congregation of San Luis Gonzaga roamed Madrid's parks in search of embracing couples, who were surrounded and shamed into proper conduct.[106]

Critics of the clerical preoccupation with sexual matters have argued that it represented an obsession predominating over all other moral issues.[107] There is considerable justification for this argument. The Church made its position absolutely clear on anything related to sexuality and it made no bones about its intention to impose its moral standards on society through coercion. Its position on other issues that should interest any institution concerned with morality in the broadest sense—the abuse of civil rights, including police brutality, official corruption, and glaring examples of social injustice—was either muted or nonexistent. It is also likely that the negative view of sex inherent in the Church's message did its share of psychological damage to individuals, either by perpetuating ignorance (a Jesuit seminarian recalled that one of his fellow novices was still unaware of the facts of life at the ripe age of twenty-three!), or by ignoring the positive importance of emotions in the affective life of human beings.[108]

Whether the Church's preoccupation with looming moral dangers conformed to reality within the tightly controlled and still largely traditional society of the 1940s and 1950s is highly doubtful. Clerical determination to protect Spaniards from vice was the most immediate and visible example of the Church's determina-

105. Javier Domínguez, *Enseñanza católica para una generación víctima y testigo* (Madrid, 1979), pp. 41–42.

106. Blázquez, *La traición de los clérigos*, pp. 81–82.

107. Ibid., p. 80; Lannon, *Privilege, Persecution and Prophecy*, pp. 49–51.

108. Domínguez, *Enseñanza católica para una generación*, p. 42; Lannon, *Privilege, Persecution and Prophecy*, p. 50.

tion to create a fortress of faith and virtue isolated from a corrupt secular world. The circumstances of the relationship between Church and State allowed the clergy to impose a moral *cordon sanitaire* on the country, thus fulfilling the fond dreams of earlier clerical generations. But over the long term, the Church was unable to maintain its tight grip over public and private morality. Ironically, developments encouraged by the regime itself, beginning in the late 1950s in the form of mass tourism and the emergence of a consumer society, began to undermine the clergy's recently constructed redoubt of puritanism. Like National Catholicism itself, the attempt to create a "people of God" hermetically sealed against secular influences, whether cultural or moral, could not be sustained.

"Autocrítica" *and Its Effects, 1950–1960*

Commentators concerned with the history of National Catholicism have recognized the appearance of cracks in its apparently monolithic facade during the 1950s. The growth of "apostolic" associations of workers, the appearance of clandestine Christian Democratic parties, and the revival of strong nationalist currents among the clergy and faithful of the Basque Provinces and Catalonia indicated that the amalgam of crusading religiosity with a conservative political ideology was beginning to break down. The decade's significance for the development of Spanish Catholicism in terms of its spiritual and cultural foundations has produced less agreement. There has been a tendency to regard the Second Vatican Council (1962–1965) as a great divide separating the "sleeping city" of a "traditional, conservative Church, entrenched in its privileges" from "the new situations that the Council was about to address." A protagonist of conciliar reform, Cardinal Tarancón, recalled years after the event that prior to the Council's convocation, Spanish Catholics were simply "outside of the game" with respect to the renovating currents that had long circulated within European Catholicism.[109]

The cardinal was correct in his assessment of a Church still gripped by the archaic formula of National Catholicism and a religious strategy often out of touch with the realities of Spanish society. Nor do students of the Church's history during the 1950s disagree with his conclusion that Spanish Catholicism lagged behind its counterparts in Western Europe in the development of ideas designed to redefine the theological and pastoral role of the Church within a secular world. Although the reforming initiatives of the Council caught the Spanish clergy and laity by surprise, some ecclesiastical commentators have suggested that among a minority of priests and laypeople, the Church of the 1950s was less "outside the

109. Joaquín Losada Espinosa, "La Iglesia española que vive el Concilio Vaticano II," in Angel Suquía et al., *Al servicio de la Iglesia y del pueblo: homenaje al Cardenal Tarancón en su 75 aniversario* (Madrid, 1984), pp. 46, 45.

game" than Tarancón suggested.[110] It has been argued that a process of change began around 1950 that represented "an important advance" in the Church's "ideological attitude" towards its religious mission.[111]

The term *autocrítica* has been used to describe the renovating currents of the 1950s. It is misleading to some extent because it suggests that disparate initiatives constituted a coherent movement of change within the Spanish Church. The "self-criticism" of the 1950s never produced a coordinated challenge to either the principles of National Catholicism or the strategy of religious reconquest. Renovating currents arose from different sources and sometimes moved together in temporary combinations. Their swirling eddies helped erode the foundations of National Catholicism, but they never formed a river capable of sweeping away traditional ideas about the place of the Church within a rigidly confessional State.

Any attempt to categorize the initiatives of the decade cannot do justice to the complexity of the diverse forms of self-criticism promoted by a minority of clergy and laity, but four general categories can be suggested: (1) a primarily pastoral concern motivated by the realization that the strategy of reconquest had failed and indeed had raised obstacles to the development of effective evangelizing methods based on a pragmatic assessment of Spanish social reality; (2) the introduction of new theological ideas stressing the Church as a community of faith rather than as a clerically directed institution relying on external conformity with the traditional requirements of ultramontane piety; (3) a broader intellectual and cultural reassessment of the nature of Spanish Catholicism in a secular world; and (4) a movement emphasizing new models of spirituality designed specifically for the laity.

During the immediate post–Civil War period, bishops and priests realized that the Church's campaign of reconquest would not be easy, but in the euphoria of the times they believed that the religious conversion of an entire population was near at hand. By the early 1950s, it became evident that these lofty hopes were falling far short of realization, although clerical rhetoric continued to proclaim that Spain remained Catholic to the core.

The beginnings of a more realistic assessment of the condition of Spanish Catholicism from a pastoral perspective are identified with a figure who would later play a significant role in moving the Church towards acceptance of democracy. Until 1950, the career of Vicente Enrique y Tarancón, young bishop of the obscure diocese of Solsona, provided few signs of either his prominence as the foremost clerical advocate of institutional self-criticism during the decade or as a promoter of fundamental change within the Church during the 1960s and 1970s. Tarancón supported the rising against the Republic in 1936 and the hierarchy's

110. Hermet, *Les catholiques*, vol. 1, pp. 198–99; José María García Escudero, "La autocrítica religiosa," in *Iglesia, Estado y sociedad en España, 1930–1982*, ed. Joaquín Ruiz Giménez (Barcelona, 1984), p. 126.

111. Fernando Urbina, "Formas de vida de la Iglesia de España," in Fernando Urbina et al., *Iglesia y sociedad en España, 1939–1975* (Madrid, 1977), p. 42.

Collective Letter of 1937, expressed sympathy for the Falange's youth wing (FET), and, as a parish priest in the Tortosa diocese immediately after the war, cooperated with the Nationalist authorities.[112] Moderate and pragmatic in temperament, Tarancón never directly challenged the regime in the 1950s. A pastoral letter of 1950 on social conditions irritated the authorities, but on a later occasion the bishop affirmed the legitimacy of the regime's vertical syndicates. But this prudence was combined with a practical, grassroots knowledge of the state of Catholicism derived from his journeys before the Civil War as a clerical counsellor of Catholic Action. His five-year tenure as a parish priest in Vinaroz during the late 1930s and early 1940s, and his administration of a small diocese, brought him into direct contact with religious reality that few of his episcopal contemporaries could match. Even as a parish priest, Tarancón showed an ability to learn from experience and to seek new pastoral approaches to the problems he encountered in a region where anticlerical currents ran deep.

In 1950, Tarancón began to publish a series of pastoral letters that called into question many of the fundamental assumptions of National Catholicism. There was nothing particularly novel about his critique. In many respects, his observations were not so different from those expressed by figures as different as Cardinals Vidal i Barraquer and Gomá before the Civil War. Tarancón also remained as committed to the ideal of a fully Christianized Spain as any of his episcopal colleagues were. The Church, he maintained, must seek "to obtain the fusion of religion and society, the aspiration of every national Catholicism." The bishop also adhered to the prevailing clerical view that the country stood on the verge of being submerged by a wave of moral dissolution. In a statement worthy of Cardinal Segura, he remarked in 1950, "Morality was declining before the war and has fallen terribly since. . . . Today sin is committed more brazenly than before."[113]

Where Tarancón departed from his fellow bishops was less at the level of these traditional clerical objectives than at the level of strategy. He questioned the effectiveness of a program of religious reconquest based on the uncritical assumption that Spain was well and truly Catholic and that traditional methods of evangelization supported by the State were capable of carrying out the religious transformation of an entire society. Tarancón viewed increased religious observance during the immediate postwar period less as an indication of spiritual revival than as an example of religious "inflation" created by extraordinary and temporary circumstances.[114] He believed that the principles inspiring the Church's campaign of re-

112. Vicente Enrique y Tarancón, *Recuerdos de juventud* (Barcelona, 1984), pp. 196, 253; *Confesiones* (Madrid, 1996), pp. 206–7; Blázquez, *La traición de los clérigos*, p. 67.

113. Quoted in Blázquez, *La traición de los clérigos*, p. 114, and Urbina, "Formas de vida de la Iglesia de España," p. 61.

114. Tarancón believed that the phase of religious "inflation" ended in 1945, though he maintained that the signs of crisis were evident even "in the hours of its most apparent splendor." Quoted in José Luis Martín Descalzo, *Tarancón, el cardenal del cambio* (Barcelona, 1982), pp. 116–17.

conquest were incapable of providing an effective long-term religious strategy because the "atmosphere of crusade and the reaction against laicism never took hold among our people."[115] He also echoed the sentiments of clerical commentators of the early 1930s looking back to the Primo de Rivera dictatorship by questioning, albeit discreetly, the religious benefits the Church derived from its ties to the State. "Despite official Catholicism," he argued, Spain is not "authentically Catholic."[116]

In a pastoral letter of 1956, the bishop described the state of Spanish Catholicism in terms that contrasted sharply with the triumphalist rhetoric of National Catholicism. He saw religious routinism and the "inflation" of observance promoted by Church and State, a poorly trained diocesan clergy moved primarily by paternalistic and bureaucratic concerns, and the "negative and 'moralizing' orientation" of spirituality as serious problems requiring urgent attention. Tarancón went further by questioning the Church's lack of charity towards its enemies and its neglect of human problems as it carried out its religious mission. The "backwardness of the Church and its institutions" raised serious obstacles, he believed, to the development of dynamic pastoral action.[117]

The bishop of Solsona's critique of the quality of Spanish Catholicism created a minor sensation, although its immediate effects were not great. Few of his episcopal colleagues imitated his example. Moreover, Tarancón followed the prudent course, perhaps understandable given the times, of avoiding criticism of specific personalities or institutions. Nor was there anything radical about his message, which in many respects represented a revival of an older tradition of ecclesiastical self-criticism. Further, despite the pessimistic nature of his assessment of Spanish Catholicism, the bishop remained convinced that it rested on a solid base, a "sincere Catholicism" more sociological than religious but one open to a "positive and purifying" renovation.[118] The significance of Tarancón's intervention lay primarily in the appeal that his call for renewal exercised over a new generation of young priests increasingly concerned with the contradiction between the reality of the country's religious condition and the triumphalist rhetoric of National Catholicism.

Stirrings of discontent with the theological foundations of National Catholicism, based on the theory of two perfect societies and with an organizational Church controlled rigidly by the hierarchy, began to surface during the early 1950s among a minority of young priests. The journal *Incunable*, published by clerical students of the Pontifical University of Salamanca, became an important vehicle for spreading pastoral and theological ideas emerging from France and Germany

115. Quoted in Urbina, "Formas de vida de la Iglesia en España," pp. 60–61.

116. Quoted in Blázquez, *La traición de los clérigos*, p. 114.

117. Quoted in Urbina, "Formas de vida de la Iglesia de España," p. 62. The pastoral letter "¿Espiritualidad nueva?" appeared in the diocesan bulletin of the Solsona diocese.

118. Quoted in Martín Descalzo, *Tarancón*, p. 117.

among younger clergy. *Incunable* did not directly challenge existing ties between Church and State. But its contributors, including Bishop Tarancón on occasion, showed an openness about renovating movements within European Catholicism that sowed among some clergy the seeds of a new view of the role of the Church in a modern society.[119]

During this period, Spanish clerical students traveled in increasing numbers to study philosophy and theology in Germany, a movement that culminated in the establishment of a Spanish theological faculty at Munich in 1955. The decade also witnessed a dramatic increase in the publication of foreign theological publications. Between 1950 and 1955, the percentage of translations rose from 25 to 62 percent of the total number of theological books published in Spain. The majority of translated works came from European Catholicism's most advanced theological centers, France and Germany.[120]

The new ecclesiology emphasized the idea of the Church as the mystical body of Christ in the form of a community of believers comprised of priests and people engaged in a cooperative spiritual enterprise. This collective emphasis and the prominence assigned to the laity by the new theology stood sharply at odds with the theory, derived from scholastic philosophy, of the Church as a perfect society in which the hierarchy "assumed total representation" of the community.[121] The emphasis of theological renovators on the transcendent importance of the Church's spiritual goals and the need to take the modern world into account from a positive perspective undermined the historic identification of Spanish Catholicism with the idea of a clerically directed fortress isolated from and suspicious of secular society and its cultural values.

How widely these new ideas circulated among the clergy is not easily established. On the whole, the religious orders remained conservative on theological matters, although even among the regulars there were outposts of sympathy for renewal. By the late 1950s, for example, Jesuit students in the order's theological faculty at Oña (Burgos) were able "to study the latest [scholarly] investigations of French and German theology."[122] The secular clergy was more exposed to renovating currents, as students returned from abroad to assume academic positions, although ideas on renewal were spread less through formal instruction, which remained firmly traditional, than through informal study groups and publications such as *Incunable*. Seminaries continued to follow a conservative curriculum. Ever vigilant before "demons of modernity," opponents of the new theology dominated

119. In 1954, for example, *Incunable* introduced its readers to the work of the German theologian Karl Rahner. Losada Espinosa, "La Iglesia española que vive el Concilio Vaticano II," p. 47.

120. Manuel Gesteira Garza, "Evolución de la teología en la España de la transición," in *Al servicio de la Iglesia y del pueblo: homenaje al Cardenal Tarancón en su 75 aniversario* (Madrid, 1984), p. 124, note 63.

121. Ibid., p. 117.

122. Domínguez, *Enseñanza católica para una generación*, p. 90.

seminary faculties and strongly resisted any change in direction, especially after Pius XII's encyclical, *Humani generis* (1950), condemned the works of progressive French theologians.[123] But over the long term, it proved impossible to maintain the historic isolation of the Spanish clergy from the theological revolution already underway elsewhere in Europe.

In Spain, the practical effect of *Humani generis* was to shift emphasis away from French to German theology. But the "great wave raised by French Catholicism," exemplified in the works of François Mauriac, Jacques Maritain, Emmanuel Mounier, Yves Congar, and others, inspired the most coherent of the renovating movements associated with the *autocrítica* of the 1950s.[124] In 1948, a group of lay Catholic intellectuals and clerics concerned with the state of Spanish Catholicism held the first International Catholic Conversations at San Sebastián. These early discussions evolved into the National Catholic Conversations held at Gredos (Ávila) beginning in 1951. Over the course of a brief history, the Conversations encouraged the development of "a Catholicism independent from the official."[125] Although participants in these meetings discussed many topics, they were primarily concerned with revitalizing Spanish Catholicism by disconnecting it from the centuries-old paradigm that identified Spain with Catholicism and Spaniard with Catholic. For one of the Conversations' leading figures, José Luis Aranguren, who was deeply influenced by French Catholic thought and the philosophy of Ortega y Gasset, religion was primarily a question of developing an inner life, a form of religious existentialism, as he expressed it, that bore little relation to a religion of compulsion and external conformity with the Church's demands for observance characteristic of National Catholicism. The "uninterrupted series of solemn, abstract and inoperative proclamations of Spanish Catholicism," Aranguren argued, must change to recognize "real and concrete Spaniards."[126] The Church, declared Carlos Santamaría, another prominent figure in the Conversations, needed to shift emphasis from the "Christianization of structures" towards the "Christianization of souls."[127]

The lay and clerical intellectuals who gathered annually for the Catholic Conversations during the early 1950s came from different ideological backgrounds and included some members of the Falange who had become disenchanted with the frozen cultural life of the regime. Although the meetings were not political in any sense, a strong undercurrent of dissatisfaction with the cultural and religious rigidities of National Catholicism ran through the discussions. Participants never challenged Church doctrine as such. But they advocated a more open cultural

123. Losada Espinosa, "La Iglesia española que vive el Concilio," pp. 51–52.

124. José María Escudero, "La autocrítica religiosa," p. 127; José María Roman Fuentes, *La autocrítica religiosa en el catolicismo contemporáneo* (Madrid, 1968), p. 7.

125. José Luis Aranguren, *Memorias y esperanzas españolas* (Madrid, 1969), p. 77.

126. *Conversaciones con José Luis L. Aranguren*, ed. Feliciano Blázquez (Madrid, 1976), p. 18.

127. Quoted in ibid., p. 27.

Catholicism that recognized the contribution of modern thought to the development of religious sensibility within a pluralistic society. Aranguren's book *Catolicismo y protestantismo como formas de existencia* (1952) provoked a storm of controversy by suggesting that Spanish Catholicism could learn something about the formation of the religious conscience from Protestant example. "False money can deceive a rustic," declared a disgruntled clerical reviewer of the book, but "it does not fool a banker. Protestantism is false money, . . . because it does not contain the truth."[128] Aranguren and other figures involved in the Conversations also provoked the wrath of clerical and lay supporters of National Catholicism by seeking to integrate the thought of Unamuno and Ortega y Gasset into their vision of Spanish Catholicism.[129]

Insofar as the Catholic Conversations produced a specific plan of action beyond the debate over Spanish Catholicism's cultural foundations, it did so through a 1955 collection of essays first presented at the International University "Menéndez y Pelayo" under the patronage of Bishop Morcillo of Bilbao.[130] Carlos Santamaría defended religious toleration and discreetly questioned the historic identification of Church and State by quoting Jaume Balmes, one of the nineteenth-century Church's few original thinkers: "The future of Religion does not depend on Government, the future of Government depends on Religion." The Church, Balmes had also warned, should not place too much confidence "in repressive and preventive measures" to achieve its religious objectives.[131]

Another contributor, the Jesuit José María Llanos, once an enthusiastic supporter of the regime but now launched on a journey of conscience that eventually led him to communism, criticized the highly individualistic character of ultramontane piety. The observer who enters a Spanish church expecting to find there a "community of faithful" was certain to be disappointed. "The Spanish temple," he remarked, is more "a spiritual marketplace than an assembly of brothers." There are "many saints on our altars," but the "faith of the community" has not increased as a result.[132] José María Escudero stressed the mediocrity of Catholic intellectual life, the inadequate preparation of the clergy, and the dependence of Spanish Catholicism on its bourgeois clientele as obstacles to the development of a revitalized Church open to all social classes. The Church was "bourgeois for the proletariat" and only a drastic change in direction could remedy the situation.[133] Manuel Lizcano took businessmen to task for ostentatiously professing their religion while

128. Quoted in ibid., p. 41.

129. The "autocrítica" movement was the object of attacks from more conservative sectors of Spanish Catholicism, especially through a religious journal published in Barcelona, *Cristianidad*, and to a lesser extent the Jesuit review *Razón y Fe*. The movement was also criticized by figures identified with Opus Dei, notably Florentino Pérez Embid. Roman Fuentes, *La autocrítica religiosa*, pp. 12–13.

130. Carlos Santamaria et al., *Catolicismo español: aspectos actuales* (Madrid, 1955).

131. Carlos Santamaría, "El problema de la intolerancia en el catolicismo español," in ibid., p. 39.

132. José María de Llanos, "El sentido individualista del catolicismo español," in ibid., pp. 57, 62.

133. José María García Escudero, "La eficacia del catolicismo español," in ibid., pp. 107, 109, 116.

engaged in tactics designed to use the Church in defense of their interests, while he reproached the clergy for "a radical absence of conscience and compassion for deep human problems."[134] Manuel Alonso García went further by calling into question the entire apparatus of religious reconquest. "It is neither inexact nor unjust to maintain that the apostolate of Catholic-apostles is the great failure of our time."[135]

Some clerics contributed to the critical spirit developed by the Catholic Conversations, but laypeople played a more decisive role. The Conversations represented the first recognition within the clerically directed Church of the Franco period that the laity must assume more direct religious responsibilities by forming a secular apostolate capable of reaching Spaniards untouched by the blanket strategy of reconquest promoted by the clergy since the end of the Civil War. The idea that a layperson was nothing more than "a soldier in the ranks commanded by the clergy" was rejected in favor of a more positive view of the laity as active protagonists on behalf of religion.[136] This emphasis on the importance of the laity was echoed elsewhere in the Church during the early 1950s. The journal *El Ciervo,* founded by restless young members of the Asociación Católica Nacional de Propagandistas, echoed the concerns of the Conversations. *El Ciervo* criticized National Catholicism on the grounds that a pastoral approach based on converting the religiously alienated masses en bloc through traditional evangelizing methods had proven ineffective and even damaging to the cause of religion. What was required, its contributors maintained, was a shift away from this "pastoral [strategy] of the masses" to a "pastoral [strategy] of minorities," one, that is, conducted by members of the specific groups that the Church wished to reach with its religious message.[137]

During the 1950s, older models of clerically directed spirituality in the form of traditional exercises and retreats for the laity were challenged by the emergence, first on Mallorca and later on the mainland, of a movement largely designed by laypeople. The "Little Courses on Christianity" (*Cursillos de Cristianidad*) originated in a series of pilgrimages to Santiago de Compostela and related spiritual exercises organized by the youth wing of Catholic Action during the early 1940s. In 1943, the movement began to depart from its origins through the efforts of Eduardo Bonnín Aguiló. Bonnín's approach was novel in several respects. He proposed organizing spiritual exercises open to all social classes and to anyone who wished to attend, whether a believer or not.[138] The exercises themselves were di-

134. Manuel Lizcano, "Psicología del catolicismo español actual," in ibid., pp. 141, 149.

135. Manuel Alonso García, "El catolicismo español y las organizaciones apostólicas," in ibid., p. 218.

136. García Escudero, "La autocrítica religiosa," p. 128. Bishop Tarancón strongly supported an enhanced role for the laity in a 1958 book, *Los seglares en la Iglesia.* Gesteira Garza, "Evolución de la teología en la España de la transición," p. 123.

137. Losada Espinosa, "La Iglesia que vive el Concilio Vaticano II," p. 50.

138. Francisco Forteza Pujol, *Historia y memoria de cursillos* (Barcelona, 1991), pp. 23–24.

rected by specially prepared lay members of the group rather than by priests. The *cursillos* departed in dramatic fashion from the rigid organization of traditional spiritual exercises by combining religious instruction with a loose, informal approach that included the singing of secular songs, the telling of jokes, even at Franco's expense, and social excursions.[139]

The *cursillos* attempted to create an atmosphere of psychological immersion based on camaraderie among participants and the communication of doctrine in everyday language. Organizers of the *cursillos* were accused at the time and later of using coercive and other tactics similar to those employed by religious cults.[140] Defenders rejected this accusation, arguing, curiously, that the *cursillos'* emphasis on spontaneous religious expression and inner conversion was similar to the atmosphere prevailing at meetings of Alcoholics Anonymous![141] What can be said is that the *cursillos* introduced a new approach to spirituality based on the laity rather than the clergy.

The *cursillos* eventually spread from their base on Mallorca to the mainland, Europe, and the Americas. But from the beginning they were controversial. Although strongly supported by Bishop Joan Hervás i Bonet of Mallorca, older priests on the island as well as the adult leadership of Catholic Action viewed the movement with suspicion. For many, the brash exuberance of participants in public religious acts appeared indecorous. Others viewed religious instruction expressed in popular language by the group's young leaders as a danger to orthodoxy, while some priests resented a movement in which the role of the clergy was marginal. Even Bishop Tarancón, although generally supportive of the *cursillos*, expressed reservations about the state of "exaltation" characteristic of the movement's activities and the tendency of its members to work in isolation from the rest of the Church.[142] In 1956, Hervás i Bonet's successor as bishop of Mallorca, Jesús Enciso i Viana, responded to this criticism by suspending the *cursillos* until a reorganization could be carried out to subject them more closely to clerical control.[143] But by this time, the movement had spread sufficiently on the mainland to assure its survival.

The history of the *cursillos* says a good deal about the fragmented nature of the renovating currents of the 1950s. The *cursillos'* emphasis on personal salvation, a Catholic version of the "born again" phenomenon, had little in common with the concerns of participants in the Catholic Conversations and advocates of the new theology. All desired a revitalization of Catholicism at the level of the individual conscience. But progressive laypeople and theologians emphasized a renovation extending beyond the single-minded preoccupation of personal conversion char-

139. Ibid., pp. 51, 62.
140. Ibid., p. 67; Lannon, *Privilege, Persecution and Prophecy*, p. 231.
141. Forteza Pujol, *Historia y memoria de cursillos*, p. 46.
142. Enrique y Tarancón, *Confesiones*, pp. 124–26.
143. Lannon, *Privilege, Persecution and Prophecy*, pp. 230–31.

acteristic of the *cursillos.* They stressed the need to transform the cultural foundations of Spanish Catholicism and to move away from the individualistic character of ultramontane piety towards the idea of the Church as a community of believers. Within this framework, the *cursillos* represented less renovation than a modern version of an older tradition of spirituality.

Participants in the *autocrítica* of the 1950s have stressed its importance as a Spanish forerunner of the transformation of the Catholic Church carried out by the Second Vatican Council. "During the 1950s in Spain . . . a change of air, of deep renovation in the life of the Church, was breathed, which would find its logical development in conciliar renovation."[144] Aranguren regarded the Catholic Conversations as "enormously important" for Spanish Catholicism's future development.[145] That a minority of clergy and laity began to examine the condition of Catholicism from a critical perspective was significant. It brought forward alternative visions of the Church distinct from the rigid formula of National Catholicism. *Autocrítica* also revealed the impossibility of preserving intact the narrow cultural and religious confines imposed by National Catholicism.

Whether an effective party of change emerged within the Church during this time is another question. The relationship between the distinct currents of renovation was nonexistent in some cases, tangential at best. The Catholic Conversations stressed the need for a new religious strategy that would appeal to specific minorities, particularly with respect to the working class. But the middle-class intellectuals who discussed this question had little or no impact on the development of the grassroots movement represented by Catholic workers' associations.

Contributors to the Catholic Conversations provoked debate about the Church's role in a secular world, but, as one of their leading participants admitted, their approach was "much more timid" than that of the progressive French Catholics whom they attempted to imitate.[146] Despite the criticism directed against National Catholicism, the lay intellectuals involved in the Conversations were unable to abandon their attachment to a confessional State.[147] How widely their ideas circulated beyond a limited circle that evolved, in Aranguren's words, into "a mys-

144. Losada Espinosa, "La Iglesia española que vive el Concilio Vaticano II," p. 50. A participant in the early Conversations, Father Tellechea Idigoras, maintained that the topics discussed anticipated the Second Vatican Council by fifteen years as far as the Spanish Church was concerned. *Tapices de la memoria: historia clínica 279. 952* (San Sebastián, 1991), p. 163.

145. Aranguren, *Memorias y esperanzas,* p. 77.

146. García Escudero, "La autocrítica religiosa," p. 131. After 1957, the movement began to decline, in part because of the negative reaction of the hierarchy and the civil authorities. The bishops adopted an attitude of greater "prudence and caution" towards the new spirit of self-criticism. It has also been argued that the intellectuals involved simply ran out of ideas as the decade progressed. Roman Fuentes, *La autocrítica religiosa,* p. 16.

147. García Escudero observed that participants in the Conversations accepted the idea of a confessional State with reservations, but in the sense that they believed that government "should serve to Christianize society effectively, not to cover it with a veneer [of religion]." García Escudero, "La autocrítica religiosa," p. 31.

tical country club" is also uncertain. New theological ideas began to influence the clergy but did so sporadically and unevenly. Nor is there any evidence that appeals for sweeping changes in pastoral methods were translated into action at the diocesan and parish levels, save in isolated cases. The immediate effects of the *autocrítica* of the 1950s were limited, therefore, but they scattered seeds among a minority of clergy and laity that would come to fruition during the following decade.

CHAPTER XIX

CHANGE AND UNCERTAINTY, 1961–1970

On May 30, 1969, the hierarchy gathered near Madrid for the fiftieth anniversary of the dedication of the national monument to the Sacred Heart by King Alfonso XIII. Dynamited to bits during the early months of the Civil War, the original statue was replaced in 1944 and the nation reconsecrated to one of its holy patrons in a grandiose display of National Catholicism. The blend of religion and nationalism characteristic of the 1944 ceremony lingered still in 1969, as the bishops praised General Franco for participating in "an act agreeable to God and the Church."[1]

The 1969 ceremony was the last of the great public manifestations of National Catholicism that had begun during the Civil War. The hierarchy's statement on this occasion was more religiously oriented than episcopal pronouncements accompanying the 1944 dedication had been, and for good reason. Some bishops and a majority of younger clergy viewed the government's failure to move forward on the front of social justice with increasing hostility, while official repression, sometimes directed against dissident priests and religious, created serious difficulties in civil-ecclesiastical relations. The troublesome issue of the regime's patronage rights over episcopal appointments resurfaced as a result of the Second Vatican Council and the appeal of Pope Paul VI (1963–1978) to Catholic governments possessing such privileges to renounce them. The historic support of some Catalan and Basque clergy for autonomist aspirations grew apace and provoked frequent conflict with the authorities.

1. "Cincuentenario de la Consagración de España al Corazón de Jesús," May 25, 1969, in *Documentos colectivos del episcopado español, 1870–1974*, ed. Jesús Iribarren (Madrid, 1974), pp. 441, 442.

The principles inspiring National Catholicism were called into question by the Second Vatican Council (1962–1965). Conciliar documents called for recognition of religious liberty and respect for human dignity in social and political life. The Council's decisions on a broad range of issues presented a challenge to Church and State for which neither was prepared. Moreover, the accelerated economic development of the decade, although improving the living standards of most Spaniards, albeit unevenly, stimulated social unrest, intensified urbanization, and introduced secularizing currents that created a society more complex than anything the Church had confronted even in the immediate past. Another problem of concern to the ecclesiastical leadership remained. How would the Church protect its interests within a regime dependent on the survival of an aging dictator, in a time when its old dream of forming a "union of Catholics" disappeared forever?

The process of defending ecclesiastical interests had always been conflictive, but the Spanish Church showed an uncanny ability to secure its future by adapting, albeit grudgingly in many cases, to dramatic political change. Although dubious about certain aspects of official policy, the hierarchy remained loyal to Franco during the 1960s. But among a minority of bishops, the Church's historic instinct for survival resurfaced as it became evident that the future of the dictatorship without Franco was far from assured in view of chronic struggles among its partisans, growing political opposition, and the anachronistic character of an authoritarian regime within a democratic Western Europe. In 1965, a group of bishops led by Cardinal Bueno Monreal of Seville personally informed Franco of their preoccupation with the future. They emphasized the necessity for the regime "to give our country a modern political configuration . . . along the lines of the European democracies."[2]

The reemergence of the historic accidentalism with which the clerical leadership had episodically viewed political change in the past was not surprising. It had been discreetly present in the thought of Pla y Deniel and Herrera during the headiest days of National Catholicism. In fact, many of the new episcopal accidentalists of the late 1960s owed their appointments to Herrera's influence.[3] In its previous incarnations, accidentalism took the form of a tactic designed to defend ecclesiastical interests in periods of political change. This pragmatic approach by no means disappeared among the bishops during the regime's last decade and a half. But accidentalism began to take on a more positive character inspired by the Second Vatican Council's affirmation of the need to recognize human dignity in social, economic, and political structures, and by the pressure from laypeople and the clerical rank and file for social justice and the recognition of human rights.

2. Quoted in Abel Hernández, "El viraje de la Iglesia," *Diario 16* (semanal), July 14, 1985, p. 642. Franco replied that while he understood the need to secure the transition to "a stable regime supported by the people," he had a duty in conscience to guarantee that the "tremendous effort made in the Civil War should not be lost by opening the door to those who have been the enemies of Spain."

3. José Chao Rego, *La Iglesia en el franquismo* (Madrid, 1976), pp. 308–9.

This is not to suggest that the Church approached the future with a coherent strategy. The clerical leadership's adaptation to the challenges of the 1960s formed an ambiguous and sometimes contradictory mixture of advance and retreat rather than linear progress towards acceptance of a pluralistic society governed by democratic principles.[4] Until 1969, an elderly hierarchy attempted to respond to the exigencies of the Vatican Council, while seeking to preserve what might be saved in the Church's privileged relationship with the regime.

The prospect of developing a unified clerical strategy was diminished by the restlessness of priests and religious whose commitment to political and social change exceeded that of the hierarchy. A 1970 survey of approximately 80 percent of the country's clergy revealed that 24.8 percent of priests supported the establishment of a new political system based on socialism. Only 3.6 percent saw the monarchy as a desirable option, while a mere 1 percent expressed support for the Falange. The survey also indicated that younger clergy were more committed to change than their elders; 47.2 percent of priests below the age of thirty endorsed the socialist option.[5]

The political divisions of Catholic opinion also intensified during the 1960s. Ministers associated with Opus Dei used their ascendancy to further their schemes for a modernized version of the existing authoritarian order. Members of the "Catholic family" continued to support Franco but became more critical of the regime's shortcomings. Fearful of a repeat performance of the turmoil produced by the collapse of the Primo de Rivera dictatorship, they maintained their traditional commitment to limited political reform, while remaining suspicious of the designs of the Opus clan.[6] Christian Democratic groups opposed to the dictatorship continued to develop, while priests and laypeople involved in the working-class apostolate moved towards more radical solutions of the country's problems.

The Church had confronted dramatic change in earlier periods, but none matched the whirlwind that swept through it during the 1960s. The historic problem of how it would adapt to changing political realities was joined to that of unprecedented internal turmoil over the role of Church and religion within Spanish society.

Social Unrest and the Church, 1961–1965

By 1960, significant groups within the Church, including some bishops, many younger clergy, and the militants of Catholic workers' associations, grew increas-

4. Juan José Ruiz Rico, *El papel político de la Iglesia católica en la España de Franco, 1936–1971* (Madrid, 1977), p. 184.

5. "Iglesia-mundo a la luz de los datos de la encuesta," in Secretariado Nacional del Clero, *Asamblea Conjunta obispos-sacerdotes* (Madrid, 1971), p. 109.

6. *Ya: medio siglo de historia, 1935–1985*, ed. José María García Escudero (Madrid, 1985), pp. 14–15.

ingly restless with the regime's immobility on the question of social justice. Even Bishop Gurpide of Bilbao, a prelate of conservative views, lamented in a 1961 speech to the JOC of his diocese that the country had made no progress towards providing a minimum wage capable of providing workers with the necessities of life, "despite the insistent teachings of the Church."[7] In the same year, Pope John XXIII (1958–1963) issued the encyclical *Mater et Magistra,* a vigorous appeal for social justice that found a receptive audience among clergy and laity. Moreover, few signs appeared in the early phase of the government's 1959 stabilization plan of a significant improvement in the population's living standards.[8]

As a result of this perception of worsening conditions, during the spring of 1962, a wave of strikes moved from the coal mining areas of Asturias to the Basque Provinces and Catalonia. Although the government dealt with this unaccustomed challenge less harshly than it would have done a decade earlier, the strike movement served as a catalyst for clergy and laity already concerned with social justice. The HOAC and the JOC supported the strikers' demands for decent wages and representative working-class labor organizations.[9]

Attitudes towards social justice and the organization of labor had created tension between the regime and the hierarchy for years. Episcopal reaction to the 1962 strike wave followed the bishops' customary path of avoiding a direct challenge to the government, but it sharpened differences between the ecclesiastical and civil authorities. In a letter to the minister of the interior, Cardinal Pla y Deniel defended the right of Catholic associations to function freely according to the concordat. In an editorial of May 12, 1962, *Ecclesia* defended the right to strike as derived from natural law and Christian ethics. The regime was so irritated by this intervention that it refrained from confiscating the offending issue only after intense behind-the-scenes lobbying by Cardinal Pla y Deniel, assisted, uncharacteristically, by the papal nuncio, Hildebrando Antoniutti, long an admirer of Franco.[10] Pla y Deniel urged the government to act with moderation by freeing arrested strikers, while Cardinal Bueno Monreal of Seville issued a Lenten pastoral letter attacking the so-

7. Quoted in José Castaño Colomer, *La JOC en España, 1946–1970* (Salamanca, 1978), p. 88. Despite his conservative views, Gurpide took a stronger stance on labor questions, to the point that even Franco complained of the prelate's criticism of the regime's social and economic policies. Vicente Cárcel Ortí, *Pablo VI y España: fidelidad, renovación y crisis, 1963–1978* (Madrid, 1997), p. 539.

8. Stanley Payne, *The Franco Regime, 1936–1975* (Madison, 1987), p. 476.

9. "Declaración de HOAC y JOC sobre los conflictos surgidos en la huelga minera y general," May 8, 1962, in *Organizaciones obreras cristianas en la oposición al franquismo, 1951–1975,* ed. Javier Domínguez (Bilbao, 1985), pp. 93–95.

10. "Carta del Cardenal Pla y Deniel al ministro de la gobernación, Carmelo Alonso Vega," May 29, 1962, in Cárcel Ortí, *Pablo VI y España,* pp. 872–73. The cardinal and the nuncio met with the minister and Antonio Iturmendi, minister of justice, and Fernando María Castiella, minister of foreign affairs, to avoid a confiscation of the offending issue of *Ecclesia,* a measure that would have provoked a further deterioration in civil-ecclesiastical relations. On May 25, Pla y Deniel visited Franco to discuss the situation. Jesús Iribarren, *Papeles y memorias: medio siglo de relaciones Iglesia-Estado, 1936–1986* (Madrid, 1992), pp. 217–18.

cial ills of Andalucía, including inadequate salaries, the abuses to which the region's numerous day laborers were subject, and industry's extensive use of poorly paid women and children.[11] The cardinal, who controlled the newspaper *El Correo de Andalucía,* even permitted its editor to collaborate in joint publications with labor activists, among them the young Socialist lawyer Felipe González.[12]

Ecclesiastical support for social reform led to a predictable reaction from Franco and the press of the Falange. In the midst of the rising wave of strike action, the general evoked the danger of the communist menace while lamenting the infiltration of its agents into the Church's lay organizations and the actions of "hotheaded" priests identified with Basque separatism and other movements of dissent. Franco expressed the confident expectation that the Church would restore harmony between the civil and ecclesiastical powers by eliminating their "common enemies."[13]

Only Bishop Eijo y Garay of Madrid, long known for his unswerving devotion to the regime, responded after the publication of a collective statement of May 14, 1962, by the workers' associations of Catholic Action expressing solidarity with the Asturian miners and calling for wage increases, price controls, liberty of association, and the legalization of strikes. Although Cardinal Pla y Deniel and Bishop Tarancón, secretary to the hierarchy, endorsed the text before publication, the civil authorities were so angered by its appearance that they ordered provincial governors and diocesan bishops to confiscate all extant copies.[14] In Madrid, the presidents and vice presidents of the HOAC and JOC, as well as the national counsellor of the JOC, Father Ramón Torella i Cascante, were summoned to police headquarters for interrogation, while heavy fines were imposed on the militants of the HOAC and the JOC involved in publishing the offending document. For his part,

11. Ibid.

12. Feliciano Blázquez, *La traición de los clérigos en la España de Franco* (Madrid, 1991), pp. 144–45. *El Correo de Andalucía* made an arrangement with González to publish a regular column on labor issues that "served as a platform of socialist penetration in Andalucía." On at least two occasions, the government tried to persuade Cardinal Bueno Monreal to close the newspaper because of its criticism of the regime's social policy. Hernández, "El viraje de la Iglesia," p. 650.

13. Quoted in Blázquez, *La traición de los clérigos,* p. 145. The Madrid newspaper of the Falange responded immediately to *Ecclesia*'s editorial, which it attacked as an example of "this horrible meddling which has come to be called Catholic progressivism." Quoted in ibid. Skirmishes with the Falange press over the role of Catholic workers' associations became more frequent in the aftermath of the 1962 strike agitation. In 1963, for example, newspapers and magazines published in Catalonia by the Falange attacked a speech given by Father Cardijn, the Belgian founder of the JOC, at a meeting of the organization held in Oviedo. Cardijn's repeated references to the working class ignored the situation in Spain, the Falange press claimed, where young workers were devoid of any sense of "class hatreds." Castaño Colomer, *La JOC en España,* pp. 98–99.

14. Pla y Deniel gave his verbal approval to publication of this document, which stated that it was appearing with ecclesiastical approval. Since the statement was published in the diocese of Madrid, however, it required the authorization of the local bishop, Eijo y Garay. Iribarren, *Papeles y memorias,* p. 217. A detailed account of the controversy is given in Antonio Murcia, *Obreros y obispos en el franquismo* (Madrid, 1995), pp. 273–82.

the bishop of Madrid suspended Father Torella from functioning as a priest in his diocese.[15] Cardinal Herrera's response to the labor agitation of 1962 was strangely muted for a prelate who had long expressed dissatisfaction with the regime's shortcomings in the realm of social policy. But, like Franco, troubled by the fear of communism and the growing militancy of Catholic workers' associations and the clergy supporting them, Herrera chose to remain silent in the face of events that revealed the inadequacy of the regime's response to acute social problems.[16]

On July 13, 1962, the Committee of Metropolitans returned to the question of social justice in a collective statement marking the first anniversary of the publication of *Mater et Magistra*. As usual, the archbishops approached the topic circumspectly. They avoided specific reference to the agitation of recent months and reaffirmed the Church's historic condemnation of communism as "intrinsically perverse." But they moved beyond the timid recognition of workers' rights contained in their 1960 statement on the social question by rejecting, albeit in general language, criticism directed against "the sacred and legitimate rights of workers" and by defending the importance and activities of Catholic workers' associations. The archbishops indirectly took the regime to task by appealing for official action to remedy a series of grave social and economic problems, including regional disparities, the unjust concentration of wealth in a few hands, and the deleterious effects of external and internal migration.[17]

To what extent the Committee of Metropolitans' program of social reform conformed to reality is another question. An appeal for change on the basis of papal social teaching within a climate of mutual cooperation among workers, employers, and the civil authorities in the name of the common good appeared reasonable on paper, but as so often in the history of the Spanish Church, it was an exhortation already outrun by events. Following the strikes of 1962, clandestine labor syndicates—including the Comisiones Obreras (Workers' Commissions), indirectly associated with the Communist party, the Unión General de Trabajadores, identified with the Socialist party, and other groups—entered a period of organizational growth. Catholic labor militants not only cooperated with other trade unions, they also departed from the model of a social apostolate operating exclusively within Catholic Action by participating in the formation of clandestine labor syndicates, particularly the Comisiones Obreras, and by establishing new organizations, in-

15. Blázquez, *La traición de los clérigos*, p. 144; Castaño Colomer, *La JOC en España*, pp. 90–91. In his recollection of these events, Torella i Cascante noted that the bishop of Madrid reconsidered the suspension after six weeks and restored his right to function as a priest within the diocese. Ramón Torella i Cascante, "Al Gobierno le molestó la fuerza de las organizaciones católicas," *Diario 16* (semanal), July 14, 1985, p. 649.

16. José Sánchez Jiménez, *El Cardenal Herrera Oria: pensamiento y acción social* (Madrid, 1986), p. 107.

17. "Sobre la elevación de la conciencia social, según el espíritu de la 'Mater et Magistra,'" in *Documentos colectivos del episcopado español*, pp. 354–55, 356–57.

cluding the Solidaridad de Obreros Catalanes (SOC) and the Federación Sindical de Trabajadores (FST), established by HOAC activists.[18]

The formal organization of workers' associations operating under the umbrella of Catholic Action in the name of its "apostolic" goals continued. But the emergence of clandestine unions founded by members of the HOAC and the JOC and their frequent participation in the activities of other labor syndicates signaled an important change in direction. Although the new syndicalism associated with Catholic labor activists was deeply fragmented, it adopted an aggressive approach that drew closer in some cases to the idea of the class struggle as essential to the resolution of social conflict. Moreover, the "apostolic" purpose of organizations such as the HOAC and JOC virtually disappeared in many of the new syndicates, which admitted recruits who had little or no interest in religious matters.[19]

The changing character of the Catholic labor movement began to alarm some bishops. In 1963, the hierarchy's Committee on the Social Apostolate informed Catholic workers' associations that they remained subject to episcopal supervision and that they could not act either directly or indirectly against "Catholic doctrine, [and] the respect owed to the authorities and legitimately constituted institutions." The committee explicitly warned members against embracing the idea of the class struggle.[20]

The HOAC and the JOC remained committed to the religious purposes of their organizations. But they grew increasingly discontented with the limitations imposed by the bishops, whom they criticized in 1965 for failing to produce a collective statement unequivocally supporting the "advancement of man, the struggle for justice, . . . the defense of liberty and the dignity of persons."[21] By mid-decade, the cautious balancing act of the bishops, who sought to maintain an equilibrium between a regime ever more irritated by the activities of Catholic labor militants and the demands of their workers' associations for greater autonomy, could not be maintained in the face of events.

Parish clergy in industrial areas were often ahead of their episcopal superiors in perceiving that the Church needed to adapt more quickly than its leadership imagined to the rapidity of economic change and social dislocation. In 1965, the parish priests of the manufacturing towns of Sabadell and Tarrasa (Catalonia), where unemployment was high, lamented the Spanish Church's past silence before the "so-

18. *Organizaciones obreras cristianas*, pp. 83–84. In Barcelona, for example, members of the JOC and HOAC were active promoters of the Comisiones Obreras during the 1960s. Angel Alcázar, "Los cristianos en la creación de Comisiones Obreras," *XX Siglos* (1994), vol. 5, no. 22, pp. 118–22.

19. *Organizaciones obreras cristianas*, p. 84.

20. In October 1963, the secretariat of the committee issued *Normas sobre las publicaciones de los Movimientos Sociales de AC*, which contained these and other recommendations designed to prevent the publications of the HOAC and the JOC from going beyond the limits established by the bishops. Castaño Colomer, *La JOC en España*, pp. 101–2.

21. "Intercambio de experiences de militantes de HOAC sobre elecciones sindicales," in *Organizaciones obreras cristianas*, p. 120.

cial injustice endured by our society" and called upon it to seek pardon from God for its failure to match performance with the lofty ideals of papal social teaching so often proclaimed in clerical rhetoric.[22]

On balance, the Church's position on social justice was stronger in 1965 than it had been a decade earlier, but it was not without ambiguity. Impelled by the social documents of Pope John XXIII and the Vatican Council, the hierarchy developed a more realistic perception of social problems and, in some cases, became bolder in its criticism of official policy. This produced inevitable tension with the regime, although the bishops sought to contain the pressure from Catholic activists and clergy for a more aggressive approach.

During the early 1960s, the resistance of some bishops, many clergy, and laity focused largely on social problems, with the exception of the Basque Provinces and Catalonia, where clerical sympathy for regional autonomy intensified. In 1961, a religious in the monastery of Aránzazu, where Basque nationalist currents ran deep, was expelled from the country for preaching a sermon declaring that Catholics would never be true "disciples of Christ" until they recognized separatists, Socialists, and Communists as brothers.[23] The publication in the French newspaper *Le Monde* on November 14, 1963, of an interview with Abbot Aureli Escarré of the Benedictine monastery of Montserrat created a public furor. Long at odds with the dictatorship, Escarré delivered a stinging rebuke to a "regime which calls itself Christian and which, nevertheless, does not obey the basic principles of Christianity."[24] The abbot reproached the government for holding political prisoners and for its hostility to the legitimate expression of Catalan culture. Further, he lamented the deliberate perpetuation of divisions created during the Civil War by Church and State. The country, he declared, faced an uncertain future unless it came to grips with social problems and the absence of liberty and democracy.[25]

This frontal assault provoked a predictable reaction from the regime and its clerical allies. Bishop Moll of Tortosa and Justo Pérez de Ubel, Benedictine abbot of the monastery erected by Franco alongside the grandiose underground basilica built in memory of the Nationalists who perished in the Civil War, protested strongly against Escarré's intervention. In a public statement, Franco accused the abbot of holding "very advanced liberal ideas" and of supporting "extreme regionalism."[26] The regime pressured the Vatican to take action, an objective secured indirectly in 1965 when the Benedictine order removed the abbot from his post.[27]

22. "Nota doctrinal sobre la situación de crisis y paro en Sabadell y Tarrasa, presentada por sacerdotes de parroquias afectadas más directamente por ella," March 1965, in ibid., pp. 146–49.

23. Guy Hermet, *Les catholiques dans l'Espagne franquiste* (2 vols., Paris, 1981), vol. 2, p. 309.

24. Quoted in Blázquez, *La traición de los clérigos*, p. 153.

25. Hermet, *Les catholiques*, vol. 2, pp. 327–28.

26. Quoted in Cárcel Ortí, *Pablo VI y España*, p. 553.

27. Ibid., pp. 553–54.

The Escarré affair also showed an ugly side, an early example of the new anticlericalism already developing among the regime's hard-liners, when a building in Barcelona maintained by Montserrat was set afire. Escarré's disappearance from the scene failed to dampen growing hostility towards the regime among the Catalan clergy. The Capuchins of Pompeya defied the authorities in 1965 by holding an anniversary Mass marking the death by execution of Lluis Companys, president of the Catalan autonomous government during the Republic, and a year later the bishops of Vich and Castellón attended a similar ceremony for Cardinal Vidal y Barraquer, who had died in exile in 1943.[28]

Other points of tension also developed during the early 1960s. In October 1962, Cardinal Montini, archbishop of Milan, the future Pope Paul VI, angered the authorities by pleading for clemency for a group of anarchists condemned to death by a military tribunal. The pro-regime press attacked the cardinal's intervention publicly, while demonstrations took place in Seville, Málaga, Córdoba, Granada, and Zaragoza. In Madrid, the official university syndicate (SEU) paraded through the streets carrying signs declaring, "Sofía Loren, yes! Montini, no!"[29]

Of greater significance was the emergence of a discreet journalistic opposition through the appearance of several new periodicals tolerated grudgingly by the government as part of its attempt to gain respectability in Europe. From a Catholic perspective, the most important of these was the *Cuadernos para el Diálogo*, a monthly journal of opinion founded in 1963 by Joaquín Ruiz Giménez, once a member of the "Catholic family" and former minister of education, now committed to political reform. The review by no means confined itself to expressing the views of Catholic intellectuals, many of whom had been prominent in the *autocrítica* movement of the 1950s, but it contributed to the evolution of a more sophisticated and pluralistic view of the country's future among educated Catholics.

The history of Spanish Catholicism during the early 1960s saw the intensification of conflicts and tensions both within the Church and between it and the government that had begun to surface during the preceding decade. But the Church's internal development and the future of its relations to the regime would not be determined exclusively by events within Spain. The influence of the Second Vatican Council dramatically altered the assumptions on which the Spanish Church had operated since the Civil War.

28. Hermet, *Les catholiques*, vol. 2, p. 328.
29. Blázquez, *La traición de los clérigos*, pp. 151–52.

The Church and the Council

In 1985, the hierarchy marked the twentieth anniversary of the Second Vatican Council's conclusion by emphasizing the Council's "providential value" for the country's religious development.[30] In 1961, the elderly episcopal generation about to represent the Spanish Church in Rome viewed the Council's convocation by Pope John XXIII in a different light. The Committee of Metropolitans drew a picture of conciliar purposes and organization that might have been written a century earlier to describe the First Vatican Council (1869–1870), as it warned against a "rebellion of any kind against the doctrinal, liturgical and moral authority of the hierarchy." The archbishops admitted that "human progress and its rapid development" posed new challenges for the Church. But they left no doubt of their belief that change should take place under the control of the papacy and the hierarchy, especially in view of the spread among some clergy and laity of "a certain, ever more serious and preoccupying spirit of novelty."[31]

The Council's innovative course surprised and disoriented the Spanish bishops, although a minority, including Bishop Tarancón and Cardinal Bueno Monreal, favored change. Bishop Pildain, a perennial thorn in the side of the regime, won applause in the Council by reaffirming his long-standing opposition to government ecclesiastical patronage rights, while Bishop Fidel Martínez García, regarded as *persona non grata* by official circles for his denunciations of Nazism during the early 1940s, spoke vigorously in favor of reforming initiatives.

A majority of the hierarchy approached the Council with a distinctly conservative mentality.[32] But at no point during the three years of conciliar deliberations did the Spanish bishops form a unified group of resolute traditionalists capable of influencing decisions. They received little direction from the eighty-eight-year-old cardinal primate, whose advanced age and poor health kept him from extensive contacts with his fellow prelates. In any event, Pla y Deniel's decision to allow each bishop to vote according to his conscience prevented the formation of a conservative episcopal block.[33] In many respects, the attitude of the elderly bishops domi-

30. "Respuesta del presidente de la Conferencia Episcopal Española para la sesión extraordinaria del sínodo de los obispos de noviembre de 1985," in *El postconcilio en España*, ed. Juan M. Loboa (Madrid, 1988), p. 393.

31. "Metropolitanos a los fieles sobre el próximo Concilio Vaticano II," in *Documentos colectivos del episcopado español*, pp. 342, 344.

32. It has been suggested that the Spanish episcopal delegation divided into three sectors: a minority of 10 to 20 percent committed to conciliar reform; a majority of ultraconservative, elderly bishops; and the remaining bishops, who sought a middle ground between the other two groups. Ruiz Rico, *El papel de la Iglesia católica*, p. 188. Lines of division were not hard and fast, however. Despite his attack on government patronage rights, Bishop Pildain expressed opposition to the draft text on religious liberty, while Bishop Guerra Campos caused a stir by speaking favorably of a dialogue with Marxism. Hermet, *Les catholiques*, vol. 2, p. 289.

33. Iribarren, *Papeles y memorias*, p. 240.

nating the Spanish episcopal delegation resembled the passivity characteristic of the hierarchy during the Restoration. Although apprehensive about the changes being discussed, bishops in the grips of what one experienced observer called "integrist paralysis" possessed neither the intellectual background nor the initiative to do anything other than be swept along by events.[34]

The Council's decisions on a wide range of religious, social, and political questions fell like a ton of bricks on the underlying assumptions that had sustained Spanish Catholicism since the nineteenth century. Scholars concerned with the Council's impact on the Church in Spain have referred to it in terms of "crisis," "an authentic trauma," "turmoil," "a bomb with a retardant fuse," and "violent shock."[35] The changes introduced by the Council fell into two broad categories, the first concerned primarily with issues revolving around theological redefinition of the Church as a community of believers, the second with the Church's role within modern society.

The *Pastoral Constitution on the Church in the Modern World* (1965), known popularly as *Gaudium et Spes*, built upon earlier encyclicals of John XXIII by appealing for the recognition of the dignity of the person in social, political, and economic life. Article 68 supported free and independent labor unions and affirmed that their members should be allowed to conduct their activities without fear of reprisal. Article 75 declared that all citizens should be able "to participate freely and actively in establishing the constitutional bases of a political community, governing the state, determining the scope and purpose of various institutions, and choosing leaders." Article 76 asserted that the Church was not "bound to any political system" and that "She does not lodge her hope in privileges conferred by civil authority. Indeed, she stands ready to renounce the exercise of certain legitimately acquired rights if it becomes clear that their use raises doubt about the sincerity of her witness."[36] Their reservations aside, and moved by inertia and respect for the papacy, Spanish bishops voted in the end for *Gaudium et Spes* and other conciliar

34. Ibid., p. 235. Cárcel Ortí notes that the majority of the Spanish bishops attending the Council had been ordained before the Civil War. In his judgment, they lacked openness, were not "very tolerant," and were "sufficiently integrist," concerned primarily with moral questions, "less preoccupied with a renovating and evangelizing pastoral approach." *Pablo VI y España*, p. 407, note 62. In his recollection of the Council, Cardinal Tarancón offered a more favorable view of the hierarchy's attitude, arguing that "all the Spanish bishops not only accepted the Council sincerely, they also were positively disposed to apply it in all its orientations." The cardinal admitted that differences existed among the bishops on the practical application of conciliar recommendations but maintained that there were no "irreconcilable differences." Vicente Enrique y Tarancón, *Confesiones* (Madrid, 1996), p. 233.

35. Frances Lannon, *Privilege, Persecution and Prophecy: The Catholic Church in Spain, 1875–1975* (Oxford, 1987), p. 248; Blázquez, *La traición de los clérigos*, p. 147; Hermet, *Les catholiques*, vol. 2, p. 287; Ramón Echarren Ystúriz, "Los sacerdotes a los veinte años del concilio," in *El postconcilio en España*, pp. 266, 147. Even Cardinal Tarancón recalled that the "Council was for us a nasty though salutary shock; it was like a hailstorm." "El Concilio fue para nosotros como una pedrada," *Diario 16* (semanal), July 14, 1985, p. 647.

36. *Pastoral Constitution on the Church in the Modern World*, in *The Documents of Vatican II*, ed. Walter M. Abbott (New York, 1966), pp. 277, 285, 288.

declarations despite their glaring incompatibility with the Church's privileged situation under the Franco dictatorship.

As always in the complicated relationship between Church and politics, the regime did not view unfolding developments in Rome from a neutral perspective. Spanish ambassadors to the Vatican lobbied relentlessly and unsuccessfully to secure a vigorous denunciation of communism from the Council. Despite his reputation as a reformist in the cabinet, the minister of information and tourism, Manuel Fraga Iribarne, worked diligently and equally unsuccessfully to control the flow of information to Spain about the Council's work, especially where sensitive issues, such as government patronage rights over episcopal appointments, were involved.[37]

The regime attempted to use the Spanish hierarchy in Rome to defend its concept of National Catholicism, but the backroom intrigue accompanying this lobbying effort proved unsuccessful. The appearance in 1962 of an anonymous pamphlet directed to all bishops attending the Council indicted the Franco dictatorship for its abuse of human rights and called upon the Church to avoid becoming its propaganda instrument. Outraged by this assault on the "honor of the government of Spain," the regime whipped up a propaganda campaign at home and pressured Pla y Deniel to extract a collective statement from the bishops defending its reputation. Many were prepared to support such a course, including Archbishop Casimiro Morcillo of Zaragoza, secretary of the Committee of Metropolitans and an emerging figure of influence within the Spanish Church. Despite age and infirmity, the cardinal primate kept a clear head and refused to sanction the publication of what would have been an embarrassing defense of the dictatorship in the midst of conciliar reform.[38]

Years after the event, Cardinal Tarancón maintained that the roots of a transformation of civil-ecclesiastical relations were to be found in the Second Vatican Council.[39] Given conciliar pronouncements, this was a reasonable conclusion, although only in the sense that principles were established that would take years to develop. Although the Spanish hierarchy did not dissent from the general lines of reform drawn at Vatican II, a majority of the bishops believed that it was still possible to reconcile the Church's privileges under the Franco regime with the spirit of the Council.

Before leaving Rome in 1965, the hierarchy issued a statement warning against extremism and defending the long-cherished idea of "Catholic unity" in Spain as a "treasure that we must conserve with love." The bishops, some reluctantly, accepted the conciliar document, *Dignitatis Humanae* (1965), which called for religious liberty based on human dignity, freedom of conscience, and natural law, but

37. Iribarren, *Papeles y memorias*, pp. 246–48.
38. Ibid., pp. 248–51.
39. José Luis Martín Descalzo, *Tarancón, el cardenal del cambio* (Barcelona, 1982), pp. 144–45.

they interpreted the text as narrowly as possible by emphasizing that its enactment should depend on the specific circumstances prevailing in each country.[40] They maintained that in the Spanish case religious liberty should not be unlimited but rather should be subject to "efficacious tutelage" by the civil authorities in the name of "public peace." Further, they argued that religious liberty could be established without compromising the confessionality of the State.[41]

The ambiguity of this document carried over to the first important statement of the new Episcopal Conference. In a 1966 statement, the eighteen members of the CEE's executive committee discussed the role of Church and faithful in temporal affairs. The bishops made numerous references to conciliar recommendations, but they avoided criticism of the regime apart from a discreet appeal for the creation of "intermediate associations" designed to allow citizens to participate in public life. It was not the business of the Church, said the committee in a flight of historical inaccuracy, to pass moral judgment on "political-social institutions" unless "fundamental rights of the person, family, or the salvation of souls" were endangered. "We do not believe," they continued, "that this is the case in Spain."[42]

This attempt to secure the best of both possible worlds by defending a regime to which the Church was indebted as legitimate within the principles established by the Council was unrealistic.[43] Vatican policy and the support of younger clergy for conciliar reform undermined any prospect that it would win broad acceptance. Moreover, the document did not represent episcopal unanimity, although less on principle than on jurisdictional grounds. At a later plenary session of the Episcopal Conference, the executive committee received strong criticism for having exceeded its authority by appealing without cause to the need for urgent action.[44] That such a statement was made in the Council's aftermath represented the reaction of a soon-to-retire episcopal gerontocracy aided and abetted by a handful of younger prelates, notably Archbishop Morcillo and Bishop José Guerra Campos,

40. Bishop Tarancón estimated in 1964 that twenty-five of the hierarchy's eighty members opposed the Council's document on religious liberty, although most voted for it in the end. Manuel López Rodríguez, *La España protestante: crónica de una minoría marginada, 1937–1975* (Madrid, 1976), p. 123. Conciliar discussion of religious liberty concerned Spanish bishops more than did any other issue. A concerted effort to halt this threat to "Catholic unity" took the form of a letter to Paul VI that opposed religious liberty on doctrinal grounds. "Carta de obispos a Pablo VI," October 17, 1965, in Iribarren, *Papeles y memorias*, pp. 260–64. Although many bishops sympathized with the letter's intent, they possessed enough sense to refuse to sign a statement so directly opposed to conciliar opinion on the question.

41. "Sobre acción en la etapa posconciliar," December 8, 1965, in *Documentos de la Conferencia Episcopal Española, 1965–1983*, ed. Jesús Iribarren (Madrid, 1984), pp. 61, 66.

42. "La Iglesia y el orden temporal a la luz del Concilio," June 29, 1966, in ibid., p. 101.

43. Rafael Gómez Pérez has interpreted this document more positively as representing an intermediate point in the "optic of the process of separation" between Church and State. *El franquismo y la Iglesia* (Madrid, 1986), p. 152. Others have been less charitable. Feliciano Blázquez concluded that the document in question "showed clearly that the Spanish episcopacy had not assimilated the Council and, possibly, that [the statement] was the last effort to maintain links of collaboration with the regime." *La traición de los clérigos*, p. 172.

44. Iribarren, "Episcopado y Conferencia Episcopal," in *El postconcilio en España*, p. 229.

auxiliary bishop of Madrid and national counsellor of Catholic Action. If supporters of this effort to rescue the alliance of Church and State through a new formula of accommodation cast in conciliar terms imagined that such a goal could be achieved, they were mistaken. In retrospect, the 1966 statement proved the swan song of the series of unequivocal episcopal declarations in support of the regime that had begun with the Collective Letter of 1937.[45]

The attempt to reconcile ecclesiastical privileges in a confessional State with conciliar reform found a counterpart in efforts to modify official institutions and legislation with a view to making them more palatable to Western Europe and to laying the foundations for the regime's survival after Franco. The new cabinet appointed in 1962 reflected the general's habitual tactic of balancing the forces supporting his power. But it contained several younger members who, though drawn from different constituencies, promoted the kind of limited reform believed necessary for future political stability and economic progress.[46] Although the reformists never formed a coherent party of change, they managed to secure the approval of a sometimes reluctant Franco for a program of modest liberalization. The enactment of a new press law in 1966 abolishing prior censorship, alterations to labor legislation to make the official syndicates more responsive to workers' needs, and implementation of other measures designed to ameliorate the regime's repressive character failed to transform the regime, but they appeared to soften its harsh edges.

Reformist currents in Church and State came together over the historically contentious issue of religious liberty. Few issues in the past aroused clerical passions more than the perceived danger to the country's fabled "Catholic unity" from the tiny Protestant minority. Indeed, maintaining the monopoly that Franco had restored to the Church by limiting the practice of other religions to private observance formed one of the cornerstones of National Catholicism. The Vatican Council's acceptance of religious liberty, based on the need to recognize human dignity and freedom of conscience in the name of the common good, was a revolution of sorts for the Catholic Church as a whole. For the Spanish Church, it represented an unprecedented challenge to the historic myth identifying Spaniards and Catholicism in an inseparable relationship.

Accepting religious liberty in principle was one thing for the hierarchy. How it would be applied was another. The debate in 1966 and 1967 over a proposed law establishing religious liberty created strange bedfellows. Bishops who had been at odds with the regime over specific issues in the past opposed its introduction. Archbishop Olaechea of Valencia informed his clergy that the Council's support for religious liberty represented a disaster for the Spanish Church, while Bishop Pildain asked for prayers in the parishes of his diocese against the concession of reli-

45. Juan María Laboa, "El marco histórico y recepción del concilio," in ibid., p. 35.
46. For discussion of these reforms, see Payne, *The Franco Regime*, pp. 503–20.

gious freedom.[47] Although Franco regarded the work of the Vatican Council with incomprehension and increasingly saw the course the Catholic Church was taking as a "stab in the back," his uncomplicated personal view of Catholicism, his generally reactive response to circumstances, and the influence of the foreign minister, Fernando María Castiella, moved him to authorize the preparation of the necessary legislation.[48]

The Law on Religious Liberty (1967) broke with tradition by conceding other religions formal recognition that allowed them to conduct their activities within a juridical framework. For the country's long-suffering Protestant minority, the new law brought relief, but it did not introduce complete religious freedom. In many respects, the legislation represented in new form the old constitutional device of a law of associations, applied in this case to the Protestant churches. They were required to register with the government and their activities were subject to certain limitations, especially where religious proselytizing was concerned. Castiella's original draft was modified in a restrictive direction by hard-liners in the regime's handpicked parliament. "Error has no rights," declared one disgruntled member of the Cortes.[49] In its final form, the law embodied as narrow an interpretation as possible of conciliar pronouncements on the question.[50]

This strict constructionist approach was supported by a majority of the hierarchy.[51] In a television address delivered in early 1967 as the draft law entered the final phase of parliamentary approval, Bishop José Guerra Campos, secretary of the

47. Blázquez, *La traición de los clérigos,* p. 183.

48. Javier Tusell, "Los gobernantes españoles y el catolicismo," *XX Siglos* (1990), vol. 1, no. 1, p. 100. As early as 1961, the government sent the Vatican a proposal to grant religious minorities the right to practice their faith publicly. Developed to placate international opinion, the proposal received short shrift from the Committee of Metropolitans in 1963. But a similar proposal made by Castiella in 1964 won the support in principle of Cardinal Pla y Deniel and Archbishop Morcillo. Franco's influential advisor, Admiral Carrero Blanco, strongly opposed any revision of existing legislation on the matter. Cárcel Ortí, *Pablo VI y España,* pp. 412, 414. Castiella's efforts were crucial for winning acceptance of 1967 legislation against the opposition of Carrero Blanco and hard-liners in parliament. Although Castiella belonged to the ACNP and contributed to *El Debate* during the early 1930s, after the Civil War he identified with the Falange rather than the "Catholic family." After serving as ambassador to the Vatican, he became foreign minister in 1957 and displayed "unexpected liberalism" in the post, especially with respect to the question of religious liberty. Manuel López Rodríguez, *La España protestante: crónica de una minoría marginada, 1937–1975* (Madrid, 1976), pp. 75–76, 144; Hermet, *Les catholiques,* vol. 2, pp. 339–40, 346.

49. Quoted in López Rodríguez, *La España protestante,* p. 164.

50. The law provided that the government should exercise "an efficacious tutelage" designed to safeguard "morality, public order and the special recognition . . . attributed to the Catholic religion." Quoted in Jaime Pérez-Llantada y Gutiérrez, *La libertad religiosa en España y el Vaticano II* (Madrid, 1974), p. 374.

51. Jesús Iribarren's contention that the Spanish "bishops were much more generous than the State when it came to applying to Spain the spirit of religious liberty" must be taken with a grain of salt. Indeed, it has been argued that the bishops were not unhappy with the more restrictive character of the law's final text imposed by parliament in opposition to the more liberal draft of Castiella. Iribarren, *Papeles y memorias,* p. 265; López Rodríguez, *La España protestante,* p. 172. Hermet has suggested that the hierarchy played a "double game" based on endorsement of the principle of religious freedom combined with a desire to minimize its practical effects. *Les catholiques,* vol. 2, p. 345.

CEE, made this clear. He affirmed the State's right to exercise "tutelage" against possible abuses arising from attacks on the rights of all citizens and threats to civil concord and public morality. He was not, of course, referring to attacks and threats from the Catholic Church. At the same time, Guerra Campos restated the old idea of "Catholic unity" in relation to the confessionality of the State: The "true religion has the exclusive right to be recognized as such" by the civil authority.[52] The bishop cast his argument in a somewhat different light from historic justifications for official confessionality by maintaining that the Church deserved special treatment because of its important contribution to the country's social development, a novel argumentative twist that began to appear with increasing frequency as the Church sought to justify its position within a changing society. These views were confirmed by the CEE as a whole in 1968. The bishops not only emphasized "Catholic unity" as a "historical and sociological reality," they also held that, for Spain, it represented "a benefit of the highest spiritual quality."[53]

The task of reconciling the religious program of the Second Vatican Council with the desire of the clerical leadership to preserve the gains the Church had made during the Franco era proved impossible over the long term. Although this strategy coincided with the efforts of laymen identified with the "Catholic family," especially those gathered around *Ya*, to transform the regime along the lines of the limited political reform promoted for years by Herrera and his followers, the prospect of establishing a united front among Catholics on the basis of a watered-down, vaguely pluralistic version of National Catholicism stood little chance of succeeding. Significant groups within the Church rejected it outright, while Franco remained suspicious of any attempt to alter the political system, although he was disposed to allow a measure of liberalizing reform.

A Time of Contradictions, 1966–1970

The hierarchy's attempt to adapt to conciliar change while preserving the substance of ecclesiastical privileges produced contradictory policies. There was some movement among the bishops, who by 1971 favored modifications in civil-ecclesiastical relations that would have been unthinkable a decade earlier. In accord with Vatican policy, they supported the end of government patronage rights over ecclesiastical appointments and the special juridical status enjoyed by the clergy. They also favored new arrangements between Church and State to replace

52. Quoted in Pérez-Llantada y Gutiérrez, *La libertad religiosa en España*, p. 276.

53. "Sobre libertad religiosa," January 22, 1968, in *Documentos de la Conferencia Episcopal Española*, p. 124. For several years after the Vatican Council, the hierarchy "continued following the doctrine of [official] confessionality and interpreted the texts of all conciliar documents from this perspective." Nuría García Balart, "Confesionalidad, tolerancia y libertad religiosa en la doctrina del episcopado español," *Ius Canonicum* (1982), vol. 22, no. 43, p. 92.

the 1953 concordat. But nearly all wished government financial support to continue and remained attached to the idea of official confessionality.

The hierarchy's confidence in limited reform of civil-ecclesiastical relations was not shared by much of the lower clergy. According to a survey carried out by the pro-conciliar journal *Vida Nueva,* the clerical rank and file were far in advance of the hierarchy on these questions. More than 60 percent of priests wished to abolish the concordat outright and have civil-ecclesiastical relations governed by general legislation. Nearly 75 percent called for the end of government patronage rights, although only about a third desired the termination of all forms of government financial support.[54]

The divide between bishops and many, though by no means all, priests rested on more than differences of opinion over civil-ecclesiastical relations. Between 1966 and 1969, an explosion of dissent directed towards the regime and the ecclesiastical leadership ripped through once rigidly controlled clerical ranks. The causes of this avalanche of protest and demonstrations varied.[55] Some protests were inspired by concern over abuses of civil rights, others by issues of social justice, and some, in the Basque Provinces and Catalonia, by regionalist sympathies, while still others were moved by demands for a more open ecclesiastical organization. Taken as a whole, the protest wave revealed widespread discontent with both the dictatorship and the hierarchy's ambiguous response to demands for fundamental reform in the way Spain was governed and in the Church's role within a society undergoing rapid social and economic change. In the past, priests had more than once seen themselves as modern exemplars of the Old Testament prophets, as they fulminated against a host of dangers to religion and Church. This historic and deeply conservative prophetism was now turned on its head in the form of vigorous clerical denunciations of the regime and even the hierarchy for tolerating social, economic, and political abuses regarded as incompatible with Christian values.

In 1966, clerical militancy was spectacularly expressed in Catalonia in two separate incidents. The first was motivated by concern with the abuse of civil rights by police who invaded the Capuchin friary of Sarriá to break up a meeting of university students, intellectuals, artists, and priests seeking to establish a democratic student organization in Barcelona. Reacting to the brutal treatment inflicted on some of those present, more than a hundred priests, many dressed in cassocks,

54. Ruiz Rico, *El papel político de la Iglesia católica,* pp. 203–5. The results of this survey differed from those reported by the more ambitious survey of clerical opinion carried out by the CEE and published in 1970. The later survey showed a more nuanced and ambiguous response with respect to the concordat than that indicated by *Vida Nueva.*

55. Cárcel Ortí has called attention to the complicated origins of clerical protests. "The roots of the entire phenomenon were enormously varied and complex. Some were ideological and practical, some promoted from within the Church and others from outside of it. Some originated in the distant past and others in recent events." *Pablo VI y España,* p. 527.

marched silently through the streets of Barcelona in a public demonstration of clerical dissent unprecedented in the regime's history. The police quickly moved to dissolve the march and arrested many participants, including several clergymen.[56]

If the *capuchinada* was inspired by concern for civil rights, another protest was fired by the regime's insistence upon the appointment of a non-Catalan, Marcelo González Martín, to the archbishopric of Barcelona. Under the slogan, "We want Catalan bishops!" a protest march of more than two hundred priests against yet another use of the regime's exclusionary policy with respect to episcopal appointments in Catalonia was promptly dissolved by the police.[57] Such tactics failed to quell the restlessness of the local priests, who became bolder as time passed. In 1970, a ceremony at the monastery of Montserrat attended by the minister of the interior (Gobernación) was thrown into disarray when a cleric managed to tell the congregation before the loudspeakers were turned off, "For a group of Christians, present in this reunion, it is not easy, not to say impossible, [to hold] the celebration of the Eucharist in the presence of the minister . . . responsible for the repression . . . of the basic rights of the human person."[58]

Clerical protest in the Basque Provinces, especially Vizcaya and Guipúzcoa, became endemic during this period.[59] There was no area of the country where the clergy was more deeply involved in protests focusing on human rights, inspired especially by the regime's heavy-handed repression of resurgent Basque nationalist movements.[60] In 1967, eighty priests in Bilbao marched through the streets to present Bishop Gurpide with a document complaining of repression by the authorities and expressing support for strikers in nearby industrial towns. In the following year, sixty priests occupied the seminary at Derio and issued a statement of radical prophetism inspired by the new currents of liberation theology that had reached Spain from Latin America. In their "prophetic denunciation," the Derio protesters attacked the Spanish Church as "capitalist and linked to power." They called for a "poor," "free," "dynamic" Church that would recognize the right of Basque workers to organize freely. They demanded the introduction of civil liberties and respect for Basque culture and language "today denied to the Basque people." Further, the

56. Blázquez, *La traición de los clérigos*, p. 169.

57. Hermet, *Les catholiques*, vol. 2, p. 310. Although the new archbishop introduced administrative and pastoral reforms in accord with conciliar recommendations, an activist minority of clergy continued to campaign against him until his appointment to the archbishopric of Toledo in 1969. José Andrés-Gallego et al., *Los españoles entre la religión y la política: el Franquismo y la democracia* (Madrid, 1996), p. 160. The Vatican, moreover, took local sentiment into account by naming four Catalans as auxiliary bishops to González Martín. Cárcel Ortí, *Pablo VI y España*, pp. 530–31.

58. Quoted in Santiago Petschen, *La Iglesia en la España de Franco* (Madrid, 1977), p. 163.

59. Lannon, *Privilege, Persecution and Prophecy*, pp. 106–13. Cárcel Ortí, *Pablo VI y España*, pp. 538–46. During this period, "the diocese of Bilbao was perhaps the most conflictive diocese of Spain." Ibid., p. 538.

60. Paulo Iztueta Armendariz, *Sociología del fenómeno contestatario del clero vasco, 1940–1975* (Zarauz, 1981), pp. 230–34.

protesters expressed their lack of confidence in the hierarchy, which in their view required a complete transformation of attitudes and personnel, including popular participation in the selection of bishops.[61] The Derio protest received wide support among the diocese's clergy, 516 of whom wrote to the Vatican seeking papal intervention.[62]

Protests were not confined, as they had been before 1966, to the Basque Provinces and Catalonia. Between 1966 and 1969, the "clerical *fronde*" spread throughout the country.[63] The wave of clerical demonstrations quickly led to attacks in the press sympathetic to the regime, as criticism of "nuisance creating bonzes [monks]" became widespread.[64] The reaction of the government was uncertain at first. On one occasion, even Franco warned General Camilo Alonso Vega, the minister of the interior, not to take action against a group of Basque priests. "Camilo, do not eat *curas*, because the meat of a *cura* is indigestible."[65] But the regime began to adopt a tougher line in 1967 through a policy of repression against insubordinate clerics.[66] Police invasions of churches and ecclesiastical buildings being used by dissidents, particularly members of clandestine trade unions, arrests of clergy and fines imposed on priests for preaching sermons regarded as seditious by the authorities, as well as the construction of a special prison at Zamora in 1969 for convicted priests, showed how far the regime was prepared to go to deal with ecclesiastical rebellion.[67]

For the hierarchy, the rising wave of clerical protest created a dilemma. Elderly bishops nurtured on National Catholicism, such as Cardinal Quiroga Palacios of Santiago de Compostela, saw dissent among their clergy as "rebellious and scandalous for the people."[68] Bishop Gurpide of Bilbao limited homilies in his diocese to specific topics unlikely to provoke the authorities, while in 1968 the bishop of San Sebastián forbade sermons altogether for the same reason.[69] For a clerical leadership long preoccupied with defending the "liberty of the Church," ecclesiastical insubordination was one thing; open government repression directed against a segment of the clergy was another. In general, the bishops were unhappy about the growing and sometimes extreme examples of clerical restlessness occurring almost daily throughout the country. Some remained silent before official harassment of

61. "Resumen oficial del documento presentado al Papa por los sesenta sacerdotes que esperan respuesta en el seminario," November 11, 1968, in Domínguez, *Organizaciones obreras cristianas*, pp. 304–7.

62. Lannon, *Privilege, Persecution and Prophecy*, p. 113.

63. Hermet, *Les catholiques*, vol. 2, p. 310.

64. Quoted in Blázquez, *La traición de los clérigos*, p. 169.

65. Quoted in Laureano López Rodó, *Memorias* (4 vols., Barcelona, 1990–1993), vol. 2, p. 396.

66. Hermet, *Les catholiques*, vol. 2, p. 323.

67. The most detailed account of the regime's repression of dissident clerics during the later Franco regime is given by Cárcel Ortí, *Pablo VI y España*, chapter 6.

68. Quoted in Hermet, *Les catholiques*, vol. 2, p. 189.

69. Ibid., pp. 314–15.

their priests less out of conviction than because of their uncertainty about how to proceed.[70] They were caught, recalled Cardinal Tarancón, "between a rock and a hard place." "They could not justly defend priests who . . . deserved punishment. Nor could they admit that the civil power . . . should take action against priests."[71] But over time, the developing anticlericalism of the regime created powerful tensions between the Church and the dictatorship. In 1968, even the hitherto silent bishops of the three Basque dioceses felt compelled to protest against the harsh treatment inflicted on political prisoners in the region, while in 1969, Archbishop Marcelo González Martín of Barcelona, who was generally sympathetic to the regime, protested against a police invasion of parish buildings as a violation of the concordat.[72] Younger bishops took a tougher line. Although Bishop José María Cirarda, Gurpide's successor in Bilbao as apostolic administrator of the diocese, responded ambiguously at first to an ongoing campaign of arrests and fines imposed on local priests accused of separatist sympathies, he rapidly became aware of the seriousness of the situation and protested vehemently to the authorities, thereby earning official enmity that eventually led to his transfer to another diocese.[73]

Between 1966 and 1969, the contradictions in the hierarchy's policies were especially evident in entirely different responses to the demands of Catholic workers' associations for greater autonomy and to a proposed new law reorganizing the vertical syndicate system. A segment of the hierarchy had long expressed concern about the growing militancy of the HOAC, the JOC, and similar groups operating as "apostolic" associations within Catholic Action.[74] A growing number of bishops feared that these organizations were escaping from episcopal control in the name of political and social causes unrelated to Catholic Action's ostensibly religious purpose. As long as Cardinal Pla y Deniel remained the primate of the Spanish

70. With respect to the seminary occupation at Derio, the executive committee of the CEE issued a statement of public disapproval that criticized the priests in question for forming "a disturbing pressure group" whose activities had left the faithful "consternated by these events." "Nota sobre el encierro de sacerdotes en Bilbao," November 12, 1968, in *Documentos de la Conferencia Episcopal Española*, pp. 138–39.

71. Enrique y Tarancón, *Confesiones*, pp. 272–73.

72. Hermet, *Les catholiques*, vol. 2, p. 324.

73. Cirarda served simultaneously as bishop of Santander and apostolic administrator of Bilbao until his transfer to Córdoba in 1971. Although he remained silent before the arrest of several priests of his diocese accused of providing refuge to ETA militants involved in terrorism, the imprisonment of the Bilbao diocese's vicar general for pastoral affairs, Mikel Etxeberria, on the same charge moved him to action. The bishop succeeded in winning his release, although the other accused remained in jail. Iztueta Armendariz, *Sociología del fenómeno contestatario del clero vasco*, pp. 234–35. Cirarda's relations with the regime deteriorated further as a result of several conflicts involving repressive action against priests of the diocese against which the prelate protested. By 1970, the regime wanted him out of Bilbao "as soon as possible." Cárcel Ortí, *Pablo VI y España*, p. 542.

74. In July 1965, for example, a gathering of bishops at Santiago de Compostela saw several bishops attack Catholic Action for its "temporalism" and call for "energetic measures" to deal with the situation. Castaño Colomer, *La JOC en España*, p. 136. Antonio Murcia has described the increasing concerns of some bishops with the militancy of Catholic workers' associations between 1959 and 1965. *Obreros y obispos en el franquismo*, chapter 6. He argues that the roots of the crisis of Catholic Action during the mid-1960s can be found as early as 1958. Ibid., p. 251.

Church and president of the Committee of Metropolitans, however, no concerted attempt to rein in workers' associations was possible.[75]

The cardinal's resignation from the primatial see in 1966 and the establishment of the Episcopal Conference changed the rules of the game. Dominated in its early history by elderly bishops uneasy about the activities of Catholic workers' associations, the Conference, relying on its Committee on the Social Apostolate (CEAS), announced a reorganization of Catholic Action in a highly centralized direction designed to reassert complete episcopal control over every aspect of the movement's activities.[76] "Apostolic" associations of workers were singled out for special criticism for having abandoned "spirituality" in favor of "temporal compromise" incompatible with their religious mission. Members were warned that they must carry on their work "within legality" and were forbidden to join clandestine labor syndicates. They were bluntly told that they had no right to issue moral condemnations of "structures," a responsibility that the committee claimed for the hierarchy alone.[77]

The impetus to curb Catholic workers' associations came, surprisingly, from two younger bishops rather than from the elderly prelates who predominated in the CEE. There was little in the background of Archbishop Casimiro Morcillo of Madrid, Pla y Deniel's replacement as director general of Catholic Action and president of the CEAS, or of his auxiliary bishop and national counsellor of Catholic Action, José Guerra Campos, to suggest that they would become the protagonists in a bruising conflict that virtually destroyed the working-class apostolate. The attitude of Morcillo, regarded by Catholic labor militants as the principal culprit in the undermining of workers' associations and the Catholic Action movement of which it formed an important part, is not easy to explain.[78] Until

75. Angel Vegas Pérez, "La crisis del apostolado seglar en España," in *Iglesia, Estado y sociedad en España, 1930–1982*, ed. Joaquín Ruiz Giménez (Barcelona, 1984), p. 254. The increasing preoccupation of a majority of the hierarchy with what they saw as the politicization and radicalization of Catholic workers' associations prevented even the cardinal primate from opposing the suppression of the principal journal of the HOAC by the regime. Enrique y Tarancón, *Confesiones*, p. 278.

76. Bishops who had once served as counsellors of Catholic Action, or who sympathized with a reorganization designed to make the organization more flexible in view of the Second Vatican Council and less narrowly dependent on the hierarchy, were deliberately kept off the membership of the CEAS. Vegas Pérez, "La crisis del apostolado seglar en España," p. 254.

77. *Organizaciones obreras cristianas*, pp. 311–12.

78. A Catholic labor activist of the time placed the blame on "the great majority of our bishops, and above all Don Casimiro Morcillo." E. Miret Magdalena, "¿Por qué fracasó el movimiento apostólico?," *El País* (semanal), October 10, 1976. Guerra Campos, a former seminary professor and canon of Santiago cathedral before becoming auxiliary bishop of Madrid in 1964, was regarded as "one of the most advanced Spanish bishops" at the Vatican Council. Why he evolved to become "one of the most severe critics of the excesses committed in its application" remains unclear. Cárcel Ortí, *Pablo VI y España*, p. 1036. Antonio Murcia suggests that Guerra Campos's conservative theological principles, his complete lack of previous experience with Catholic workers' associations, and his view of his position as national counsellor of Catholic Action as a "mission of vigilance . . . so that it does not stray from the path," lay behind his "catastrophic pastoral approach" to the activities of workers' associations. *Obreros y obispos en el franquismo*, pp. 348, 353.

the 1960s, Morcillo's career resembled that of his friend and former colleague in Catholic Action, Bishop Tarancón. Both displayed a limited independence of action uncommon among the bishops of the time. As bishop of Bilbao, Morcillo clashed with the regime over social policy, showed concern for the Basque clergy's cultural preoccupations, and lent his support to the *autocrítica* movement of the early 1950s.

During the 1960s, the paths of Tarancón and Morcillo began to diverge, one moving in a more flexible direction, the other taking a cautious road with respect to the important issues facing the Spanish Church.[79] Although Morcillo's attitude towards Catholic Action and the necessity of introducing fundamental change into the country's ecclesiastical and civil institutions was ambiguous, he did not represent a throwback to the integrist bishop of National Catholicism's early days. In 1969, he strongly opposed the regime's proposed syndical law and resigned his appointed seat in parliament. Why he chose to promote a reorganization of Catholic Action that "shook . . . [its] foundations and undermined the confidence of great activist sectors in the social and political field" remains unclear to this day, although it is likely that he was moved by a desire to defend episcopal authority and avoid confrontations with the regime.[80]

Whatever Morcillo's motives, the reorganization of Catholic Action provoked a storm of controversy among clerical and lay activists who saw it as an attempt to curb their autonomy and remove workers' associations entirely from contact with the world of rapidly expanding clandestine labor unions.[81] The Spanish Church was no stranger to internal disputes carried on with the ferocity of an undeclared civil war. Between 1966 and 1968, a "pitched battle" over the proposed

79. Morcillo's conservative direction during the 1960s appeared "inexplicable and mysterious" to Cardinal Tarancón in view of his earlier record as an "open and realistic" bishop in Bilbao and Zaragoza. *Confesiones*, p. 376.

80. Iribarren, *Papeles y memorias*, p. 273. According to an article in *Vida Nueva* (June 24, 1967), a majority of the bishops supporting reorganization were moved by "an excessive nostalgia for a Catholic Action which they lived in other times that are not ours." Quoted in Castaño Colomer, *La JOC en España*, p. 162. Archbishop Tarancón recalled that in a November 1967 meeting of the CEE, Morcillo argued that "the centers and organizations of Catholic Action were being converted, in fact, into a platform for all those opposed to the actual regime." *Confesiones*, p. 243. During the 1960s, the bishops were subject to intense pressure from the regime for the direction taken by Catholic workers' associations. Murcia, *Obreros y obispos en el franquismo*, p. 342. In a letter to Cardinal Amleto Cicognani with respect to the hierarchy's suspension of a national meeting of Catholic Action, Morcillo stressed the "acute antihierarchical spirit" of its deliberations and the "open resistance with which episcopal directives were received." "Carta de Mons. Morcillo al Cardenal Cicognani," July 14, 1966, in Cárcel Ortí, *Pablo VI y España*, p. 885. The CEAS also sent a confidential report to the Vatican noting that eight hundred priests had come to Madrid to participate in the Catholic Action meeting with a view to imposing "their attitude of opposition and rebellion" on the hierarchy. "Informe confidencial de la CEAS a la Santa Sede," September 1966, in ibid., p. 887.

81. The most detailed account of the crisis in Catholic Action, one strongly critical of the hierarchy, is Murcia, *Obreros y obispos en el franquismo*, chapters 5–7. The crisis is also discussed extensively by Castaño Colomer, *La JOC en España*, chapters 3–4; *Organizaciones obreras cristianas*, pp. 309–48; and Cárcel Ortí, *Pablo VI y España*, pp. 603–26. Cardinal Tarancón recalled the debates within the hierarchy in

new statutes of Catholic Action raged in the form of an angry reaction from the HOAC, the JOC, and related organizations, protests that soon led the hierarchy to suspend militants occupying leadership positions in their respective associations.[82] "In these moments—tragic for us," the HOAC told the bishops in 1967, the "attitude of the majority of the hierarchy . . . will confirm even more the conviction of the working class that the Spanish Church does not have a pastoral strategy . . . of service towards the world of the poor." The bishops' action would be interpreted as an "expression of the alliance with established economic and political powers." If the hierarchy failed to change its policy, the HOAC declared, "We will be obliged . . . to seek other channels of apostolate . . . for the better service of the poor."[83]

This was not an idle threat. Although thirteen bishops voted against the proposed new statutes at the hierarchy's plenary meeting on November 25, 1967, a decisive majority voted in favor, thereby provoking mass resignations among the leaders of the HOAC, the JOC, and other workers' associations, and demoralizing Catholic Action as a whole.[84] By 1969, the hierarchy's "destructive work" had completely undermined Catholic Action and the work of generations of clergy and laity.[85] Although Archbishop Tarancón of Oviedo recognized that the problem of the politicization of Catholic workers' associations created problems for the Church, he believed that the hierarchy's decision was a serious error that closed the "door to all sincere dialogue with priests and laity."[86] Catholic Action survived, subject as the bishops wished to rigorous episcopal control, but remained as a hollow shell abandoned by its most committed members.

The gutting of Catholic Action marked the effective end of an organization that had been identified for decades with the Church's attempt to build a solid foundation of lay support. Whether its decline represented a catastrophe for the Church of the 1960s is less clear. A Catholic Action dominated by middle-class elites may have outlived its usefulness within a Church experiencing a grassroots proliferation of clerical and lay groups, some primarily religious in character, others concerned with social and economic issues, that functioned as a "parallel Church" over which bishops exercised little control. The belief that the laity

Confesiones, pp. 239–48. Bishop Guerra Campos defended his stance during the crisis in a volume of documents interspersed with his commentary. He accused militants in Catholic workers' associations of pretending to represent the entire Church, neglecting "primordial" Christian values, being influenced by the Marxist contagion, and embracing an "apostolate without faith." *Crisis y conflicto en la Acción Católica Española y otros órganos nacionales de apostolado seglar desde 1964* (Madrid, 1989), pp. 25–30.

82. *Organizaciones obreras cristianas*, p. 239.

83. "La HOAC se dirige a la Conferencia Episcopal," April 22–23, 1967, in Castaño Colomer, *La JOC en España*, pp. 152–53.

84. Enrique y Tarancón, *Confesiones*, p. 245. Between June 1967 and May 1968, 112 of Catholic Action's leading figures resigned from the organization, while the HOAC and the JOC rejected the new statutes outright. Hermet, *Les catholiques*, vol. 2, pp. 306–7.

85. Ibid.

86. Enrique y Tarancón, *Confesiones*, pp. 246–47.

could be organized and rigidly controlled by an authoritarian hierarchy in the cause of a narrowly defined clerical program was an idea whose time had come and gone.

Even before the crisis of 1966–1967, the old dream of using "apostolic" associations of workers as a bridge to the formation of a mass Catholic labor union had proven illusory, as members of the HOAC and the JOC began to drift away towards the Workers' Commissions, the Socialist UGT, and other clandestine unions that appeared more likely to realize working-class aspirations.[87] Although the HOAC and the JOC survived, they had already enjoyed their moment of glory produced by specific conditions prevailing during the 1950s.

If the hierarchy's reorganization of Catholic Action appeared as a step backward, the bishops' response to the regime's proposal for a new law to reform the vertical syndicate system represented a step forward, albeit a modest and not entirely unambiguous one. Although the draft text presented to parliament in 1969 and the watered-down version finally approved in 1971 introduced important changes into the existing syndical organization, by making it more representative and providing a variety of social welfare benefits, it failed to satisfy large segments of clerical opinion long dissatisfied with the regime's labor monopoly.[88] In 1968, the CEE called for fundamental reform to recognize "the profound evolution of our society" and the necessity of full and free working-class representation in labor associations.[89] Still fearful of provoking the regime, the bishops stopped short of calling for complete abolition of the existing syndicate system.[90] Others were more forceful. A group of theology professors, including Elías Yanes, later archbishop of Zaragoza and president of the CEE, attacked the proposed law as another example of government-inspired paternalism that failed to provide workers with the complete associational autonomy to which they were entitled.[91]

As debate over syndical legislation continued into 1970, the hierarchy's attitude began to harden. The CEAS criticized the draft law being discussed in parliament on the grounds that it failed to embody "important principles and criteria such as those of liberty, autonomy and representativeness."[92] On July 11, the plenary assembly of the CEE published a statement, "The Church and the Poor," that represented a significant advance over earlier social pronouncements, although the bishops still affirmed a commitment to maintaining "respect and loyal collabora-

87. Rafael Díaz-Salazar suggests that although some Catholic labor militants entered the Socialist UGT or the anarcho-syndicalist Confederación Nacional del Trabajo, the majority joined the Workers' Commissions. *Iglesia, dictadura y democracia* (Madrid, 1981), p. 292.

88. For a detailed description of the law, see Payne, *The Franco Regime*, p. 554.

89. "Principios cristianos relativos al sindicalismo," July 28, 1968, in *Documentos de la Conferencia Episcopal Española*, pp. 133, 136.

90. Rafael Belda, "La Iglesia y el sindicalismo vertical," in Fernando Urbina et al., *Iglesia y sociedad en España, 1939–1975* (Madrid, 1977), p. 233.

91. Blázquez, *La traición de los clérigos*, pp. 193–94.

92. Quoted in ibid., p. 194.

tion" with the authorities.[93] But the hierarchy made no reference, as it had done in previous statements, to the legitimacy of a State-organized syndical system as an acceptable, if far from ideal, method of social organization. On the contrary, the bishops challenged the existing labor system and its political foundations in general terms by affirming "the right of every person to associate and meet freely for licit ends, such as the advance of their professional interests within authentic representative syndicates, and a contribution to public affairs through efficacious channels of political participation."[94]

"The Church and the Poor" contained ideas long in circulation among clerical critics of the official syndical monopoly, although they were now expressed more explicitly. The statement has been correctly regarded, however, as a significant divide between the ambiguous course of the hierarchy after the Second Vatican Council and the emergence of a more critical and independent attitude among the bishops.[95] The bishops indicated as much by repeating the words of Pius VI on the necessity for the Church "to free itself from historic practices which now can be seen as incompatible with its evangelical purpose and its apostolic mission."[96]

Changing attitudes were also evident in the CEE's response to the regime's ever more harsh repression of Basque nationalist movements before a wave of terrorist violence initiated during the late 1960s by the ETA organization (Euzkadi ta Azkatasuna). In 1969 alone, nearly two thousand persons, including thirty-two priests, were arrested as the regime attempted to break the back of this new and radical expression of Basque nationalism. The regime also imposed a two-month State of Exception involving the suspension of civil rights, such as they were, over the country as a whole. The executive committee of the CEE defended the government's action as necessary to defend the "peace and public order . . . upset by unjustifiable violences," although an episcopal delegation visited the minister of justice, Antonio María Oriol, to appeal for a prompt return to normality. Moreover, at least ten bishops, including Archbishop Tarancón, now installed in the primatial see of Toledo, refused to endorse the executive committee's statement.[97]

93. "Comunicado al término de la XII Asamblea Plenaria sobre la 'Iglesia y los pobres,'" in *Documentos de la Conferencia Episcopal Española*, p. 174.

94. Ibid., p. 178.

95. Cardinal Tarancón maintained years after the event that "The Church and the Poor" was the document that "marked a new road" in the development of the hierarchy's response to the changes being experienced by the country. José Luis Martín Descalzo, *Tarancón, el cardenal del cambio* (Barcelona, 1982), pp. 144–45. Audrey Brassloff has called attention, however, to the vagueness of the bishops' views in terms of specific remedies and their continuing commitment to the capitalist system. She argues that they "seemed to be advocating . . . a model of neo-capitalist society which recognized *formal* liberties and social rights, but without demanding a transformation of socio-economic structures as the *sine qua non* of real (social) democracy." *Religion and Politics in Spain: The Spanish Church in Transition, 1962–96* (London and New York, 1998), p. 37.

96. "Comunicado al término de la XII Asamblea Plenaria sobre 'La Iglesia de los pobres,'" p. 173.

97. Hermet, *Les catholiques*, vol. 2, pp. 318–19.

Despite the hierarchy's acceptance of the State of Exception, the government seized the occasion to warn the bishops of the dangers to harmonious civil-ecclesiastical relations created by the activities of priests who were making "political judgments, which are not within their area of competence."[98] Some, the government alleged, provided parish buildings to groups committed "to organizing clandestine and anti-Christian propaganda on behalf of communism or the promotion of the dismemberment of the nation's unity." Others were accused of scandalizing the faithful by participating in street demonstrations and engaging in terrorist conspiracies. The authorities bluntly told the bishops that it was their duty to see that the oath which they took upon taking office was completely fulfilled: "I swear . . . not to take part in any agreement, nor to assist at any meeting which could prejudice the Spanish State and public order, and that I will make my clergy observe similar conduct."

Despite this warning and the hierarchy's endorsement of the State of Exception, the regime failed to win episcopal support for the show trial of Basque nationalists, who included two priests accused of complicity in terrorist acts. Although the government hoped that exposure of ETA's violent methods would gain it popular support, the Burgos trials of December 1970 became a public relations disaster as the accused seized every opportunity to attack the arbitrary and repressive nature of the court martial proceedings.[99] In the face of these events, the bishops issued a public statement appealing for "maximum clemency" for those standing trial, although, as cautious as ever, they declared that the CEE had no intention of interfering in the "actions of justice."[100] Bishop Cirarda of Bilbao, mindful of the turmoil created in his diocese by the trial, went further by calling for the proceedings' transfer to the civil courts and for the commutation of any death sentences.[101]

By 1969–1970, there were definite signs that the hierarchy's immediate post–Vatican II attempt to adapt the Church and its official privileges into the new ecclesiastical framework elaborated by the Council was over. But the waters were still far from clear. Despite growing tension with the regime, the bishops repeatedly reaffirmed their loyalty to the "constituted authorities" and remained attached to the idea of a confessional State and the financial benefits derived from ties to the government. Indeed, they lobbied mightily in 1970, during discussions over a proposed new education law, to insure that the teaching of religion would be protected

98. This and the following quotations in this paragraph are quoted from a *nota verbal* of the government partially republished in Chao Rego, *La Iglesia en el franquismo*, pp. 182–87.

99. Payne, *The Franco Regime*, pp. 558–59.

100. "Tres comunicados sobre las delicadas circunstancias de las diócesis vascas," December 1, 1970, in *Documentos de la Conferencia Episcopal Española*, p. 182. The hierarchy's caution may have reflected the opposition of a significant minority of twenty-three bishops to any episcopal involvement in the question. Hermet, *Les catholiques*, vol. 2, p. 380.

101. Ruiz Rico, *El papel político de la Iglesia católica*, pp. 249–50.

and that Church schools would be subsidized on the same basis as public schools. Although the Church did not receive everything it wanted in the final version of the legislation, it managed to extract from the government an enormous concession through a commitment to finance Church schools for the first time in the long history of the dictatorship.[102] The hierarchy was beginning to distance itself from a regime to which it owed so much, but it was far from ready to abandon the benefits enjoyed by the established Church of a confessional State.

102. José M. Totosaus, "Presencia de la Iglesia en el sector escolar," in *Iglesia y sociedad en España*, pp. 251, 260. Despite ecclesiastical lobbying for unrestricted financial support for Church schools, the government agreed to provide assistance only through a system of formal contracts (*conciertos*), with individual institutions agreeing to certain conditions, especially with respect to educational standards and accessibility. Petschen, *La Iglesia en la España de Franco*, pp. 173–74.

CHAPTER XX

FROM AMBIGUITY TO *RUPTURA*, 1971–1976

The growing distance between the Church and the regime has been interpreted as marking a definitive break or *ruptura* in civil-ecclesiastical relations.[1] This interpretation is justified in the sense that by 1975 a majority of bishops and clergy believed that the country required political reform. But a commitment to change did not entirely clear the muddy waters swirling around the question of the Church's official privileges. Despite rising tension between the hierarchy, the clergy, and the regime over many issues, the Church remained the established Church in full possession of benefits received from the dictatorship over three decades.

No single explanation can account for the Church's gradual shift in direction. It did not require much political savvy for the hierarchy to grasp what millions of Spaniards realized, namely, that the regime's objective of guaranteeing its survival by recasting its political foundations through limited reform was far from assured.[2] It was also obvious that the options promoted by Opus Dei and the "Catholic family" for modernizing the country's political organization stood no chance of succeeding. As a result of financial scandals implicating members of Opus Dei during the early 1970s, the Opus clan began to lose influence within the regime until it

1. Guy Hermet, *Les catholiques dans l'Espagne franquiste* (2 vols., Paris, 1981), vol. 2, p. 367.

2. In 1966, the government adopted a new Organic Law of the State designed to place the regime on a more solid constitutional base, although the legislation introduced only limited changes in the existing system. There was also considerable discussion within the National Movement of converting it into a more pluralistic organization by permitting certain political associations to function within it. The proposal came to nothing, however, because of infighting among the regime's different interest groups. In 1969, Franco formally designated Prince Juan Carlos, son of the pretender Don Juan de Borbón, as his successor according to the terms of the 1947 Law of Succession.

lost cabinet representation entirely in 1974. Although advocates of change along the lines first drawn by Martín Artajo during the 1950s updated their schemes for limited reform during the 1960s, the crisis in Catholic Action and the decline of the ACNP reduced the "Catholic family" to a rump of government officials, professors, and intellectuals without any real constituency.[3] By this time, opposition Christian Democratic groups were cooperating with other clandestine parties, while members of Catholic workers' associations were deserting en masse to underground labor unions. By the early 1970s, the historic objective of forming a "union of Catholics," either to transform the regime from within or to lay the foundation for a mass Catholic party in the future, expired once and for all.[4] For the Church, the time had come to consider new options.

Clergy, Bishops, and Political Change, 1971–1973

Episcopal attitudes began to move closer to those of the lower clergy. In 1967, the CEE undertook an ambitious survey of clerical opinion that, upon its completion in 1970, provided the hierarchy with unmistakable evidence of how far the rank and file were moving on key issues. Of the 15,156 respondents, 61 percent expressed disagreement with the Church's policy on social and political questions, a proportion that rose to 85 percent among younger clergy. Priests supported proposals calling for the Church to renounce "the privileges that it enjoys today" and for an end to "all visible signs of an excessive, dangerous, and confusing union" between Church and State.[5] The clergy also expected bishops to resign from official positions and to curb the participation of government representatives in religious ceremonies. But on the specific question of civil-ecclesiastical relations, responses were mixed. Almost 32 percent regarded existing ties to the regime as damaging to the Church's religious mission; 13.7 percent saw them as an evil difficult to avoid; 19.5 percent believed them positive; and 21 percent maintained that although far from ideal, the current situation was preferable to outright separation.[6] This ambiguous response was countered by strong affirmation of the clergy's prophetic mission. Fully 64 percent of all clergy and 84 percent of younger priests declared

3. Hermet, *Les catholiques*, vol. 2, p. 371.

4. For a brief period, it appeared that a unified Christian Democratic party might be formed. But all efforts to unite the four parties into which Christian Democrats opposed to the regime were divided, the Unió Democràtica de Catalunya, the Izquierda Democrática Cristiana of Joaquín Giménez Fernández, the Democracia Social Cristiana of José María Gil Robles, and the Partido Nacionalista Vasco, failed. Hermet, *Les catholiques*, vol. 2, pp. 423–24. Moreover, more conservative Christian Democrats in the Herrera tradition gathered around *Ya* continued to hope for a substantial change in the regime from within. During the mid-1960s, for example, the newspaper supported the idea of authorizing the formation of political associations within the existing system. *Ya: medio siglo de historia, 1935–1985*, ed. José María Escudero (Madrid, 1985), pp. 16–17.

5. "Iglesia y mundo en la España de hoy," in *Asamblea Conjunta obispos-sacerdotes* (Madrid, 1971), p. 75.

6. "Anexo II: Iglesia-mundo a la luz de los datos de la encuesta," in ibid., pp. 107–8.

that "the Church in Spain cannot evangelize de-Christianized sectors [of the population] without involving itself in social or political judgments."[7]

The 1970 survey formed the first stage in a process of institutional self-examination unmatched before or since in the history of the modern Spanish Church. A second stage involved the distribution of thirty thousand documents for discussion in 1,359 study groups organized by the diocesan clergy in preparation for a joint assembly (Asamblea Conjunta) of bishops and priests. Although the elderly prelates who dominated the CEE when the idea of the assembly was proposed entertained doubts about convoking a body "very distant from the traditions of the Spanish bishops," they accepted it in the end despite their reservations.[8] Some clergy also viewed the hierarchy's commitment to mutual discussion with skepticism. But the Asamblea Conjunta that began on September 13, 1971, in Madrid's seminary opened the door to frank dialogue about the problems and opportunities facing the Spanish Church at a difficult moment in its history. The 171 priests elected by their peers in the country's sixty-four dioceses represented a cross section of the nation's diocesan clergy, although younger priests were more heavily represented.[9]

In his inaugural address, Cardinal Tarancón emphasized that the assembly should focus discussion on means of improving the Church's pastoral effectiveness in a time of rapid social and economic change.[10] But given the concerns of younger priests, it was scarcely surprising that political considerations made their way into the debates, although there was no direct challenge to the regime. Indeed, the assembly took care to affirm that "there is not an a priori plan of hostility towards the State among Spanish priests."[11]

Despite this affirmation of neutrality, the assembly stripped away the ideologi-

7. "Iglesia y mundo en la España de hoy," p. 65.

8. José Andrés-Gallego et al., *Los españoles entre la religión y la política: el franquismo y la democracia* (Madrid, 1996), p. 188. The bishops went along with the idea of the Asamblea Conjunta because it was proposed by the president of the CEE between 1966 and 1969, Cardinal Quiroga Palacios, a prelate who enjoyed great prestige. They also feared that failure to do something might provoke open confrontations with the clergy similar to those experienced with the lay members of Catholic Action. To some extent, their decision also reflected the growing influence of episcopal reformers, although they did not yet form a majority in the CEE. Ibid., pp. 188–89. The hierarchy's acceptance of the principle "one delegate, one vote," whether the individual was a bishop or parish priest, was revolutionary in the Catholic world of the time. Vicente Cárcel Ortí, *Pablo VI y España: fidelidad, renovación y crisis, 1963–1978* (Madrid, 1997), p. 562. The complex background to the organization of the Assembly is described in ibid., pp. 566–76.

9. Priests under the age of forty-six comprised 58 percent of the delegates, although they made up a smaller proportion, 34 percent, of the total number of clergy. "Nota sociológica sobre los presbíteros asistentes a la Asamblea con voto," in ibid., p. 715. To what extent the clerical delegates were representative of the clergy as a whole caused some controversy, especially among conservative prelates and priests. In the third session, eleven bishops "expressed their doubts about the capacity of the Assembly to reach representative conclusions." Andrés-Gallego et al., *Los españoles entre la religión y la política,* p. 196. Others alleged that the proposals formulated at the diocesan level on which the recommendations were based were the work of only 10 percent of the clergy. Ibid., p. 197.

10. "Discurso inaugural pronunciado por El Emmo. y Revmo. Sr. Cardenal Vicente Enrique y Tarancón, presidente de la Conferencia Episcopal," in *Asamblea Conjunta obispos-sacerdotes,* p. 3.

11. "Iglesia y mundo en la España de hoy," in ibid., p. 74.

cal and religious remnants of National Catholicism. The idea that Spain formed "a small island saved from 'contagion,' maintained at the margins of the secularist wave, last reserve of a world rescued from [rising] waters" was rejected in favor of a recognition that the Church had no choice but to accept the cultural and social complexities of the modern world or face an uncertain, perhaps threatening, future.[12] The strategy of religious reconquest characteristic of triumphant National Catholicism was also repudiated because it failed to take into account the pluralistic nature of modern society and its concern with personal liberty.[13]

Further, the delegates opposed a key element of the regime's ideology, the deliberate maintenance of divisions among Spaniards arising from the Civil War. The clergy affirmed that the "Spanish Church has a very concrete duty [to promote] reconciliation of all Spaniards" with a view to establishing civil concord and eliminating "hatred, discord and confrontation."[14] These recommendations constituted "an authentic bomb" for the regime's politicians, according to Cardinal Tarancón, who maintained that the "Asamblea Conjunta was the first public act of the Spanish Church which questioned . . . the intimate connection between the Church and the Regime."[15] The delegates also took a strong stand on the clergy's right to speak out against human rights abuses: "It is necessary that the Spanish Church, especially the hierarchy, . . . should not keep silent . . . before those situations and events which affect the human rights of the community and some of its groups."[16]

The rejection of National Catholicism and the criticism of the regime contained in such resolutions did not translate into a call for the end of all the Church's institutional privileges. To be sure, the assembly expressed disapproval of government patronage rights over episcopal appointments. But by a substantial majority, delegates rejected abandoning the 1953 concordat, although they recognized that its terms were out of date and a source of conflict between the civil and ecclesiastical authorities. They called instead for new arrangements based on partial agreements between the government and the papacy that would rest on the mutual recognition of the independence of Church and State.[17] The conclusions of the Asamblea Conjunta represented a giant leap forward, unimaginable a decade earlier. But this advance should be kept in perspective. Although firm in its rejection of the course the Church had followed since the Civil War, not even the clergy dared to take the final step of calling for separation of Church and State and the ter-

12. "Situación de la sociedad española," in ibid., p. 33.

13. "Situación del mundo actual," in ibid., p. 21.

14. "Iglesia y mundo en la España de hoy," in ibid., p. 72. A proposal calling upon the Church to seek pardon for promoting a "war of brothers" during and after the Civil War passed by a vote of 137 to 78, but it failed to win the two-thirds majority needed for formal approval. "Ponencia primera: conclusiones," in *Asamblea Conjunta obispos-sacerdotes*, p. 170.

15. Vicente Enrique y Tarancón, *Confesiones* (Madrid, 1996), pp. 469, 489.

16. "Ponencia primera: conclusiones," in *Asamblea Conjunta obispos-sacerdotes*, pp. 172–73.

17. Ibid., pp. 171–72.

mination of those practical benefits, especially in the realm of finances, that continued to sustain bishops, priests, and a wide range of Church activities.

To what extent the conclusions of the Asamblea Conjunta were translated into action is a matter of discussion.[18] Although fulsome in his praise for its work, even Cardinal Tarancón observed that the assembly lacked the authority to implement its recommendations, though he promised that the CEE would consider them carefully.[19] The assembly's significance, the cardinal concluded with some justification, lay in its adoption of a position in accord with conciliar reform based on "the massive adherence of thousands of priests in Spain."[20] But the Asamblea's conclusions were severely criticized by the canons of the Madrid cathedral, while a conservative clerical minority organized in the pro-regime Hermandad Sacerdotal del Clero objected vehemently to the spirit and recommendations of the Asamblea Conjunta. Its six thousand members took the CEE and even Pope Paul VI to task, arguing that "Spain was being de-Christianized because the Spanish hierarchy had distanced itself from the regime and Franco, the providential *Caudillo.*"[21]

Some members of Opus Dei intent on assuring the regime's survival also viewed its proceedings with suspicion. Prominent figures in the organization and Bishop Guerra Campos were alleged to have launched a murky plot in the Vatican to blacken the assembly's reputation. The resulting uproar revolved around the publication by a Spanish news agency, Europa-Press, under the influence of Opus Dei, of what became known as the "Document of Rome," a letter of the Vatican's Sacred Congregation of the Clergy to the Spanish hierarchy accusing the Asamblea Conjunta of doctrinal errors. Guerra Campos possessed a copy of the letter, which, his critics in the hierarchy alleged, he intended to use to subvert the work of Asamblea Conjunta and the bishops supporting it.[22] An indignant Cardinal Tarancón, although president of the CEE, never received the letter, which he saw as an attempt

18. José Chao Rego maintains that delegates left the assembly "with more hopes than realities" and that differences between the clergy and the bishops were far from resolved. *La Iglesia en el franquismo* (Madrid, 1976), p. 212.

19. "Discurso pronunciado por el Eminentísimo y Rvdmo. Sr. Cardenal D. Vicente Enrique y Tarancón, presidente de la Conferencia Episcopal Española," in *Asamblea Conjunta obispos-sacerdotes,* pp. 633–34. After the assembly's conclusion, a plenary meeting of the CEE declared its intention to implement the recommendations. "Comunicado sobre las conclusiones de la Asamblea Conjunta de obispos y sacerdotes," March 11, 1972, *Documentos de la Conferencia Episcopal Española 1965–1983,* ed. Jesús Iribarren (Madrid, 1984), pp. 214–15. A minority of bishops demanded, however, substantial revisions to the assembly's recommendations, which, they argued, were ambiguous, inexact, and, in some cases, erroneous. Juan José Ruiz Rico, *El papel político de la Iglesia católica en la España de Franco, 1936–1971* (Madrid, 1977), p. 222.

20. "Discurso pronunciado por el Eminentísimo y Rvdmo. Sr. Cardenal D. Vicente Enrique y Tarancón, presidente de la Conferencia Episcopal Española," in *Asamblea Conjunta obispos-sacerdotes,* p. 634.

21. Cárcel Ortí, *Pablo VI y España,* p. 577; Enrique y Tarancón, *Confesiones,* p. 280.

22. In the meeting of the hierarchy, Bishop Antonio Palenzuela of Segovia accused Guerra Campos of leaking the document to the press. Andrés-Gallego et al., *Los españoles entre la religión y la política,* p. 202.

to undermine the authority of the Episcopal Conference.[23] The cardinal accused Guerra Campos of "falsehood" in a tense meeting of the CEE.[24] Tarancón, fearing that he and the CEE had lost the confidence of the Vatican, even considered resignation. The cardinal journeyed to Rome, where he won the unqualified support of Paul VI and Cardinal Villot, the papal secretary of state.[25] The CEE in turn took the unusual step of publicly reaffirming its "confidence in Spanish clergy and laity," while condemning the propaganda campaign directed against the assembly in the official press.[26] Despite this rearguard action against the assembly, a majority of priests communicated an unequivocal message to the bishops that there could be no return to the model of National Catholicism.

The hierarchy's 1973 statement, "On the Church and the Political Community," reflected the assembly's recommendations and conciliar documents on social and political questions. It also extended further the idea of the "liberty of the Church" promoted by Pla y Deniel and other bishops during the 1940s and 1950s. The statement differed radically from the bishops' 1966 document dealing with the Church and temporal affairs by emphasizing that the rapidity of social and economic change required both Church and State to recognize the pluralistic nature of society. Rejecting criticism that bishops and priests were exceeding their religious mis-

23. Enrique y Tarancón, *Confesiones*, p. 501. A close associate of Cardinal Tarancón, Bishop Ramón Echarren, recalled that during the controversy he had never seen him "so visibly preoccupied, so upset. . . . I saw the Sr. Cardinal suffer." "El Cardenal Tarancón, presidente de la Conferencia Episcopal," in S. Grisolía et al., *Homenaje al Cardenal Enrique y Tarancón* (Valencia, 1997), p. 170. Even the nuncio, Msgr. Dadaglio, and the secretary of the nunciature, Msgr. Pasquinelli, "were astonished and surprised" by the "Document of Rome." Their inquiries in Rome failed to clarify the situation. Ibid. Echarren asserts that certain sections of the statement were taken directly from a denunciation of the Asamblea Conjunta written by the Hermandad Sacerdotal del Clero. Ibid.

24. Richard Eder, "Spanish Cardinal Strikes Back at Conservatives," *New York Times*, March 7, 1972; Chao Rego, *La Iglesia en el franquismo*, pp. 220–21; Ruiz Rico, *El papel político de la Iglesia católica*, pp. 223–26; José Luis Martín Descalzo, *Tarancón, el cardenal del cambio* (Barcelona, 1982), pp. 179–83. In his extensive discussion of the machinations behind this attack on the Asamblea, Tarancón identified Bishop Guerra Campos and Opus Dei as the principal culprits in the plot. *Confesiones*, p. 510. Who actually wrote the "Document of Rome" remains unclear to this day. Some accused Alvaro del Portillo, a member of the Congregation and secretary-general of Opus Dei, although he denied the charge. Andrés-Gallego et al., *Los españoles entre la religión y la política*, p. 202. Andrés-Gallego and his coauthors have questioned certain aspects of the prevailing interpretation of the controversy, especially with respect to the circulation of the text. But Cardinal Tarancón has provided a convincing and detailed account of what he knew and when he knew it. *Confesiones*, pp. 489–98. At the time of the controversy, Opus Dei denied any connection to the plot, although "virtually all other church sources here affirm its involvement." Richard Eder, "Liberal Clerics' Victory in Spain Is Endorsed by the Papal Nuncio," *New York Times*, March 11, 1972.

25. Enrique y Tarancón, *Confesiones*, pp. 506–9. The attitude of Paul VI towards the controversy remains unclear despite his strong support of Cardinal Tarancón. Cárcel Ortí suggests that the pope was perfectly aware of the document prepared by the Congregation of the Clergy and that he did not disagree with its purpose, which was to point out "defects and faults" in the Asamblea's conclusions from a doctrinal perspective. But the pontiff believed that the Congregation's controversial document was a private, confidential communication to the Spanish bishops. Cárcel Ortí maintains that the pope would never have approved publication of the document in the way that it appeared "in abusive form and not [published] by ecclesiastical organs." Cárcel Ortí, *Pablo VI y España*, p. 583.

26. "Comunicado sobre las conclusiones de la Asamblea Conjunta de obispos y sacerdotes," pp. 214–15.

sion by commenting on social and political questions, the hierarchy affirmed the Church's right to engage in the "prophetic denunciation" of abuses, especially in the realm of human rights and social justice: "By promoting social justice and the effective recognition of human rights, the Church aids the dynamism of a society in its evolution towards unity and the progress of healthy civil and economic socialization."[27] The bishops also endorsed in general terms the right of the "political community to determine its own constitutional system."[28]

The 1973 statement angered the regime and its supporters, although the bishops took care to avoid specifics in their comments dealing with the political future. Despite the general tenor of the bishops' statement, there is no question that "it marked in definitive form" the "distancing" of the Church from the regime.[29] As far as civil-ecclesiastical relations were concerned, the hierarchy explicitly recognized that the 1953 concordat no longer corresponded "to the true necessities of the moment or to the doctrine established by the Second Vatican Council," although it had once provided "notable benefits to the people and the Church."[30] The bishops called for new arrangements based on the mutual recognition of the independence of Church and State, a recognition that required the end of government patronage rights over episcopal appointments. For its part, the hierarchy declared that it was willing to renounce certain privileges, such as ecclesiastical representation in official bodies and the special juridical rights enjoyed by the clergy.[31]

The bishops' disposition to abandon certain privileges did not extend to the separation of Church and State. The hierarchy was not yet ready to abandon official confessionality, which, it argued, could still be maintained without injuring the right of Spaniards to full religious liberty. The bishops also made it plain that they did not regard the key areas of government financial support and the Church's extensive subsidized educational system as falling within the framework of privileges at all. They argued the new line that subsidies were fully justified in

27. "Sobre la Iglesia y la comunidad política," January 23, 1973, in *Documentos de la Conferencia Episcopal Española*, p. 256. The debate within the plenary assembly of the CEE took place, however, in "a climate of tension and preoccupation." Some bishops argued that more time was required to draft a document of such importance, particularly in view of the hostility expressed in the pro-regime press, which had come into possession of the draft despite the assembly's efforts to keep the text confidential until publication. In December 1972, for example, Admiral Luis Carrero Blanco, the vice prime minister, commented unfavorably on the bishops' intentions. Cárcel Ortí, *Pablo VI y España*, pp. 462, 464.

28. "Sobre la Iglesia y la comunidad política," p. 265.

29. Cardinal Tarancón later observed that many saw the 1973 statement as an attack on the government. Martín Descalzo, *Tarancón, el cardenal del cambio*, pp. 152–54. García Escudero also remarked that many saw the declaration as a "stab in the back" of the dictatorship but that other defenders of the existing political system saw it as a sign of necessary progress in the Church that did not compromise "their loyalty to the regime." José María Escudero, "Presencia de la Iglesia en la política," in Angel Suquía et al., *Al servicio de la Iglesia y del pueblo: homenaje al Cardenal Tarancón en su 75 aniversario* (Madrid, 1984), p. 248. Cárcel Ortí, *Pablo VI y España*, p. 471.

30. "Sobre la Iglesia y la comunidad política," p. 267.

31. Ibid., p. 265.

recognition of the "service to citizens destined to develop their religious dimension."[32]

The Vatican and a New Hierarchy

The combination of reforming ideas with a desire to preserve the practical benefits derived from ties to the government showed that the hierarchy was still moving cautiously towards redefining its position. But the 1973 declaration represented definite movement towards establishing distance between Church and State. The bishops' emerging commitment to change arose in part from a reaction to a long series of confrontations between the clergy and the regime that saw civil-ecclesiastical relations reach a level of tension unprecedented in the dictatorship's history. It also recognized that the hierarchy's changing composition, promoted by the Vatican through the papal nuncio Luigi Dadaglio, gradually introduced a sufficient number of bishops committed to conciliar reform to tilt the balance of forces in favor of prelates who viewed the prospect of political change with greater flexibility than did the elderly episcopal generation they replaced.

Pope Paul VI's succession to the papacy in 1963 came as a disagreeable surprise to the regime and its supporters.[33] His appeal in 1962, while archbishop of Milan, for clemency for condemned anarchists left a legacy of suspicion in official circles towards the new pontiff, although the pro-government press engaged in spectacular rhetorical somersaults after the papal election to express its loyalty to the Holy See. The Vatican followed a diplomatically correct policy towards the regime, but the pope irritated the civil authorities during protracted negotiations over a new concordat by refusing to yield in his opposition to the State's patronage rights over episcopal appointments.

In 1968, Paul VI wrote a personal letter to Franco requesting the end of this historic regalist privilege. The general had no intention of yielding without extracting substantial concessions. In 1969, the regime proposed to renounce its appointment rights in return for Vatican acceptance of an updated version of the 1953 concordat. These negotiations came to nothing in the end because of the opposition of Cardinal Tarancón and other bishops committed to conciliar reform, who protested to the Vatican that it was not in the Church's best interests to sign a con-

32. Ibid., pp. 269–71, 274. Audrey Brassloff has rendered a harsher judgment of the ideas contained in this document with respect to the bishops' insistent demand that the Church's financial and educational privileges should be retained. "The Church was reluctant to go into society naked of power, influence, and economic backing, with the gospel as its only source of credibility." The hierarchy's repeated sallies in defense of these privileges even as its political views changed was an indication, she argues, of a "bad conscience" that "led to constant self-justification." *Religion and Politics in Spain: The Spanish Church in Transition, 1962–1996* (London and New York, 1998), pp. 57, 55.

33. Juan María Laboa, "España por el Papa," *XX Siglos* (1990), vol. 1, no. 1, p. 60.

cordat in the light of the country's uncertain political future.[34] Negotiations sputtered on until 1972, when they stalled because of the regime's insistence on a settlement through a concordat rather than through the partial agreements favored by Rome and the bishops.[35] Although willing to renounce its patronage rights, the government continued to insist, as it had since negotiations began in the late 1960s, on obtaining the right of "pre-notification," that is, that the pope should submit the names of episcopal nominees to determine whether there were political objections to their appointment. The regime demanded that this provision should apply to all nominees, even auxiliary bishops previously appointed freely by the Vatican.

The Vatican had irritated the regime by circumventing the nomination process established in the 1953 concordat as far as auxiliary bishops were concerned. Between 1968 and 1971, the pope named seventeen auxiliary bishops whose appointments did not require government approval. The dictatorship's hard-line supporters saw this as nothing less than a Vatican Trojan horse designed to undermine the regime from within through the appointment of prelates hostile to the existing order.[36] There is no evidence to support this conspiratorial thesis, although the motives behind the new appointments have generated considerable discussion.[37] It has been argued that the pope followed a strategy of naming regular and auxiliary bishops committed to an evolutionist strategy designed to produce a hierarchy sympathetic to the eventual emergence of a right-wing Christian Democratic government.[38] Others have maintained that neither the Vatican nor the nuncio ever developed a plan "for the intellectual or spiritual reorientation of the Spanish episcopacy, even less for the organization of a political fifth column."[39]

34. Enrique y Tarancón, *Confesiones*, pp. 290–93. Announcement of negotiations between Rome and Madrid on the basis of a text that differed little from the 1953 concordat "created an extraordinary uproar" among bishops and clergy. The bishops resented the Vatican's failure to consult them fully until late in the day. "It appeared evident to all that a postconciliar concordat must be based on completely distinct principles; the religious, social and political reality was very different from that of 1953." Ibid., p. 291. Tarancón remarked that Vatican policy at this time was "difficult to understand." Quoted in Martín Descalzo, *Tarancón, el cardenal del cambio*, p. 162. In his reply to Paul VI's request that the State renounce its patronage rights, Franco made clear that he would not consider a unilateral renunciation unless the Vatican was disposed to make concessions in other areas of ecclesiastical privilege. María Elena Bugueras Segura, "Posición del episcopado español ante la revisión del concordato de 1953," *Ius Canonicum* (1983), vol. 23, no. 45, p. 369. A detailed account of the negotiations between the Vatican and the government is found in Cárcel Ortí, *Pablo VI y España*, chapter 1.

35. Cárcel Ortí, *Pablo VI y España*, pp. 216–17.

36. Feliciano Blázquez, *La traición de los clérigos en la España de Franco* (Madrid, 1991), p. 172.

37. Cardinal Tarancón rejected the widespread view that the auxiliary bishops appointed under this procedure were hostile to the regime. An examination of the CEE's voting records, he argued, shows that some voted in favor of measures sympathetic to the regime, while some bishops who passed through the regular patronage process voted against. Martín Descalzo, *Tarancón, el cardenal del cambio*, p. 147.

38. Chao Rego, *La Iglesia en el franquismo*, p. 213.

39. Jesús Iribarren, "Episcopado y Conferencia Episcopal," in *El postconcilio en España*, ed. Juan M. Loboa (Madrid, 1988), p. 231.

A study of the hierarchy during the early 1970s has established that attitudes towards change covered a wide range. There were bishops who cherished the Church's ties to the regime, such as González Martín and Guerra Campos, a broad though fragmented group of *aperturistas* in the center, and an ecclesiastical Left, including recently named auxiliary bishops Ramón Echarren, Alberto Iniesta, and José María Setién, all of whom were regarded with hostility by the regime for their social activism.[40] Nor did the Vatican always send a clear message through its appointment policies. It was not averse to wheeling and dealing with the regime, hence the appointment of González Martín to the primatial see of Toledo in 1971 to replace Tarancón, named to head the Madrid archdiocese after the death of Morcillo, and the appointment of one of the dictatorship's staunchest defenders, Guerra Campos, to the diocese of Cuenca in 1973.

Insofar as it is possible to discern a Vatican appointment strategy, it consisted of naming bishops committed to conciliar reform, papal social teaching, and a flexible though cautious approach to the political future. This approach matched the concerns of the new generation of episcopal accidentalists formed in the Herrera tradition. Many of the prelates appointed or promoted to larger dioceses between 1967 and 1973 were identified with the "Santa Casa," a popular designation of the ACNP so long identified with Angel Herrera and his followers. Although some of the bishops in this group, notably Bishop Cirarda of Bilbao, clashed with the government, the majority holding regular episcopal appointments managed to pass through the official patronage net because they were not seen as ecclesiastical extremists committed to an open break with the regime.

Despite rising tension with the Church and often difficult negotiations conducted by the nuncio with the authorities over appointments, the regime, at least until 1974–1975, grudgingly accepted the changing character of the hierarchy, although it was unhappy with the papal tactic of directly naming auxiliary bishops.[41]

40. Chao Rego divided the bishops into seven categories: a small group of "arbitrators" not linked to a specific episcopal faction (3); Cardinals Bueno Monreal, Jubany, and Tarancón; the "bunker," comprising committed supporters of the regime, among them Archbishops Cantero Cuadrado of Zaragoza, González Martín of Toledo, and Bishop Guerra Campos (12); integrists, who were conservative and extremely cautious with respect to political and ecclesiastical reform (11); a "civilized" Right, prudent but flexible up to a point before change (12); the *Santa Casa*, made up of prelates in the Herrera accidentalist tradition, including Archbishops Suquía Goicoechea of Santiago, Delicado Baeza of Valladolid, and Bishop Elías Yanes, auxiliary bishop of Oviedo (15); an independent center more open to change (12); and a Left center more disposed to challenge the regime on social and human rights issues, which included Archbishop Díaz Merchán of Oviedo, although auxiliary bishops, including Iniesta and Setién, were more prominently represented in this group than any other (11). *La Iglesia en el franquismo*, pp. 314–15. Hermet used the broader categories of conservatives, progressives, and centrists to describe differences among the bishops. *Les catholiques*, vol. 2, p. 381.

41. Between 1965 and 1968, however, the regime so dug in its heels over the patronage issue raised at the Vatican Council that it refused to approve new appointments, with the result that twenty dioceses lacked bishops. The opening of negotiations over a new concordat removed this roadblock and the normal process of appointment was resumed in 1969.

In 1971, moreover, the government abandoned its policy of seeking to impose non-Catalans on the dioceses of Catalonia by allowing the appointments of Narcis Jubany and Joan Pont i Gol to the archbishoprics of Barcelona and Tarragona respectively.

As a result of the appointment of new bishops, both regular and auxiliary, the balance of power within the CEE shifted in favor of prelates who supported a flexible approach to ecclesiastical reform and the Church's response to the political future. The 1972 election of Cardinal Tarancón to the presidency of the CEE and of Bishop Elías Yanes, identified with the Herrera tradition, as secretary, replacing the Morcillo/Guerra Campos team, marked the definitive end of the dominance of pro-regime prelates in the conference. The triumph of the moderates did not mean that the bishops favoring change formed a single bloc or that they agreed upon a specific policy with respect to the regime.[42] They formed, rather, a loose coalition disposed to respond to circumstances, but not too hastily. This "wait-and-see" strategy left many clergy and laity dissatisfied with the hierarchy's slow response to demands for a fundamental reworking of the Church's relations with the civil power.

The election of Tarancón to the CEE's presidency and his appointment as archbishop of Madrid in the same year brought to the leadership of the Spanish Church an exceptional figure who would make a significant contribution towards adapting the Church to the dramatic political changes that followed Franco's death. Tarancón's rise to influence occurred late in his career. Appointed bishop of Solsona in 1946, the prelate languished in this obscure diocese for nearly two decades before being promoted at the age of fifty-seven to the archbishopric of Oviedo (1964), the primatial see of Toledo (1969), and finally the archbishopric of Madrid. Tarancón's pastoral letters of the 1950s on social injustice and the need for reform within the Church were hardly earthshaking, but they showed a degree of independence unusual among bishops of the time that long retarded his advancement.[43]

42. It was not clear to observers at the time of the CEE elections whether the liberal-moderate coalition was strong enough to survive future challenges. "The coalition could weaken or shift or even fall apart as new issues or new strains arise." Richard Eder, "Liberal Clerics' Victory in Spain Is Endorsed by Papal Nuncio," *New York Times*, March 11, 1972.

43. Tarancón recalled that his 1950 pastoral letter on social issues so irritated the authorities that the "men of government did not pardon me" and vetoed his promotion later to the bishoprics of San Sebastián and Bilbao. Quoted in Martín Descalzo, *Tarancón, el cardenal del cambio*, pp. 84–85. In his memoirs, the cardinal offered two different explanations of why the regime approved his promotion to the sees of Oviedo, Toledo, and Madrid during the 1960s. In the first, he maintained that he had no adequate explanation for his advancement given his reservations about the regime. In the second, he was more specific and attributed his appointment to Oviedo to the efforts of the papal nuncio, Antonio Riberi. He believed that his reputation in the diocese as a moderate who calmed the tension created by some clergy and Catholic workers' groups in their hostility towards the regime earned him the respect of General Camilo Alonso Vega, minister of the interior, who later supported his transfer to Toledo, as did Franco. "By all appearances, no serious difficulty existed" to prevent his nomination by the government to head the primatial see. Enrique y Tarancón, *Confesiones*, pp. 40, 378–79.

From the Vatican's perspective, this background, and his strong support for conciliar reform, made Tarancón an attractive candidate for promotion.[44] His commitment to defending the "liberty of the Church," already evident during the 1950s and significantly greater as a result of the Council, enhanced his reputation in Rome as an agent of change within a hierarchy dominated by elderly bishops dubious about conciliar reform and alterations to the Church's ties to the regime. In many respects, Tarancón proved an effective heir to Pla y Deniel as a defender of the Church's claims to greater independence. Like his predecessor in the primatial see, Tarancón was a shrewd ecclesiastical politician who knew how far the regime could be pressed without provoking a crisis in civil-ecclesiastical relations. Although by 1973 the regime's hard-liners regarded him with open hostility, the fact remains that his ecclesiastical career could not have progressed as rapidly as it did during the 1960s without the regime's permission. Even as many younger clergy were calling upon bishops to resign from official bodies and as Archbishop Morcillo renounced his government positions upon becoming president of the CEE in 1969, Tarancón accepted appointment to the Council of State when he became archbishop of Toledo. On this occasion, he defended the regime's legal legitimacy, while reaffirming the hierarchy's historic view that Spain was a confessional State "comprised by an immense, nearly absolute, majority of Catholics."[45]

Tarancón represented a blend of older traditions concerned with defending the "liberty of the Church" and implementing papal social teaching within the new currents of conciliar reform directed to adapting the Church to the modern world. Moreover, for a hierarchy seeking to find its way through the political maze of the regime's last years while grappling with unprecedented turmoil within the Spanish Church, Tarancón possessed the qualities of leadership suitable for the times. Although definitely within the *aperturista* camp, he did not identify with any of the hierarchy's several factions. Like Pla y Deniel, he enjoyed a reputation for disinterested commitment to defending the Church's interests vis-à-vis the regime that endowed him with the moral authority indispensable for effective leadership.

44. Rafael Gómez Pérez, *El franquismo y la Iglesia* (Madrid, 1986), p. 155. The intention of Paul VI to use the cardinal as the key figure in the evolution of the Spanish Church emerged in spectacular form when the pope appointed him apostolic administrator of the Madrid archdiocese within hours of Archbishop Morcillo's death in 1971. The appointment, a short time later, of the cardinal to the Madrid archdiocese was a personal decision of Paul VI, who informed him that "this is a very difficult moment for the Spanish Church. You are going to be president of the Episcopal Conference. And we need in Madrid and the Conference a person of confidence." Quoted in Cárcel Ortí, *Pablo VI y España*, p. 450. The unexpected and sudden appointment of Tarancón as apostolic administrator of Madrid frustrated a scheme to install Bishop Guerra Campos, whom the regime favored as Madrid's next archbishop, as administrator of the diocese through election to the position of vicar capitular by the cathedral chapter. Ceferino de Blas, *Tarancón, el cardenal que coronó el rey* (Madrid, 1995), pp. 60–64. Although Tarancón initially doubted the existence of this scheme, he concluded that in "certain sectors of the diocesan Church and in some political circles," there was strong opposition to his appointment. "It made me think that something had been prepared." Enrique y Tarancón, *Confesiones*, p. 400.

45. Quoted in Gómez Pérez, *El franquismo y la Iglesia*, p. 156.

This prestige was enhanced by a fact sometimes forgotten in the hagiography that has surrounded his contribution to the transition to democracy. Although he recognized the need for the Church to adapt to changing social and cultural values, Tarancón by no means represented a radical break with the past. He remained committed to the Church's tradition of regarding Spanish society as essentially Catholic, especially with regard to moral standards; he defended the authority of the hierarchy, albeit within a framework of consultation with the clergy; and he viewed the participation of priests in political activities as inappropriate.[46] Although flexible on the question of the country's political future, he saw change not in terms of a complete break with the past but as an evolutionary process. "Spain," he remarked, "cannot break totally with its history and its tradition without the danger of losing its own personality."[47]

Tarancón's leadership proved essential to moving the Church towards greater dissociation from the regime, although the cardinal followed a cautious strategy that attempted to avoid a head-on confrontation. Given the disparate attitudes of bishops favoring change, this was as effective a strategy as possible in the circumstances. For clergy demanding a more aggressive posture, however, it was not good enough. Tarancón was seen as too "centrist," too unwilling to push the hierarchy to the point already reached by many priests in their opposition to the regime.[48] But on balance, Tarancón proved the Church's man of the hour as it faced a series of conflicts with the regime between 1972 and 1975 that took place in an atmosphere of growing uncertainty about the political future.

Impasse and Confrontation

During its final years, the regime was harassed by bolder political opposition, the growing militancy of clandestine labor unions, and the persistence of ETA terrorism. In June 1973, Franco's increasing age and infirmity led him to appoint a prime minister for the first time in the dictatorship's history. Although Admiral Luis Carrero Blanco had often used his influence in the past to frustrate substantive changes in the regime's political structure, even he recognized by this time that something had to be done to satisfy growing pressure within Spain and Western Europe for reform. Knowing that Franco would reject the reintroduction of political parties in any form, the new prime minister endorsed an idea in circulation

46. Tarancón later recalled that the activities of priests during this period who "wished to use political ideologies in their evangelizing work" caused him "true uneasiness." This kind of involvement, he maintained, "is not the mission of the Church either directly or indirectly." "50 años de sacerdocio en España," in *Iglesia, Estado y sociedad en España, 1930–1982*, ed. Joaquín Ruiz Giménez (Barcelona, 1984), p. 391.

47. Quoted in Rafael Díaz-Salazar, *El capital símbolico: estructura social, política y religión en España* (Madrid, 1988), p. 56.

48. Chao Rego, *La Iglesia en el franquismo*, pp. 245–47.

since the mid-1960s, when several of the regime's clans, including the "Catholic family," began to discuss proposals for limited change through the formation of officially approved political associations.[49] This ambiguous constitutional device was designed to attract the support of moderate opposition groups while keeping the door firmly closed to those regarded as extremists, particularly Socialists and Communists.

Whether the new prime minister would have successfully employed his proverbial loyalty to the general and his long years of experience as a skilled behind-the-scenes manipulator to implement constricted reform is uncertain. In any event, after leaving Mass at Madrid's Jesuit church, the prime minister was assassinated by ETA terrorists on December 20, 1973. His successor, a former minister of the interior and mayor of Madrid, Carlos Arias Navarro, attempted a policy of *apertura* based on government authorization of political associations functioning under the umbrella of the virtually moribund National Movement. This policy failed to satisfy either the democratic opposition or a group of intransigent defenders of authoritarianism known as the "bunker."

Despite the problems besetting the regime, there was no danger that it would oblige the opposition by collapsing of its own accord. The army remained steadfastly loyal to the general. But no one concerned with the country's political future could ignore that the regime had failed to reform itself sufficiently to guarantee its survival. In these circumstances, there was no possibility of reworking civil-ecclesiastical relations in a manner acceptable to either Church or State. The Vatican dragged out negotiations over a new concordat but showed little disposition to reach agreement with a "power in bankruptcy," even though the regime's final proposals in 1973 offered terms similar to those adopted later between the papacy and a democratically elected government.[50] Uncertainty about the political future also reinforced the more positive accidentalism of bishops concerned with protecting the Church's interests. Whatever the precise form a new political order would take, the hierarchy recognized that it would be pluralistic and democratic.

49. During the fall of 1973, the cabinet discussed a variety of proposals for the creation of political associations. Stanley Payne, *The Franco Regime: 1936–1975* (Madison, 1987), pp. 587–88.

50. José Manuel Cuenca Toribio, *Relaciones Iglesia-Estado en la España contemporánea, 1833–1985* (Madrid, 1985), p. 127. The government offered to abandon the confessionality of the State, renounce its patronage rights, recognize the Episcopal Conference as the juridical representative of the Church, grant Catholic associations and publications complete liberty, and seek reasonable means of financial support for the clergy. Hermet, *Les catholiques*, vol. 2, p. 397. It should be noted, however, that Vatican policy was not always straightforward with respect to negotiations for a new concordat. Cardinal Tarancón believed that some officials in the papal curia, notably Archbishop Agostino Casaroli, took advantage of the "weakness" of Paul VI in 1974 to reopen talks for a concordat with the Arias Navarro government, which wished to conclude an agreement. This initiative was strongly opposed by the cardinal, who believed it misguided given the uncertainty of the political situation. Enrique y Tarancón, *Confesiones*, pp. 695–98. Private conversations between Casaroli and López Rodó in November 1973 aroused apprehensions that the participants "had stitched up a deal about a new Concordat behind the backs of the CEE, the Nuncio in Madrid, and the rest of the Spanish government." Rumors to this effect upset the

In remarks to the cabinet on the occasion of Franco's eightieth birthday (December 7, 1972), Carrero Blanco expressed bitterness towards a Church that in 1936 had rallied to "a war of Liberation and a Crusade" against atheistic communism. Franco had saved the Church from destruction. The assassinations of thousands of clergy during the Civil War was only an indication of worse to come had the Republic triumphed. After the war, the government granted millions for the construction of churches, seminaries, schools, and charitable centers. "No government in any era," he declared, "has done more for the Catholic Church than Your Excellency." It was "lamentable" that priests, who should recall better than most Spaniards what the regime had done for them, should have forgotten Franco's immense contribution to the salvation of Spain and the Church.[51]

Carrero Blanco's reproach reflected official anger over continuing clerical participation in ever more intense protests against abuses of human rights and social injustice that the bishops seemed unwilling or unable to control. The government's response to the rising wave of demonstrations, protest statements, and sit-ins during the regime's final years took the usual form of arrests, jail terms, and heavy fines imposed on the priests involved. Official anticlericalism was matched by the appearance of virulent hostility towards the hierarchy, the Vatican, and protesting clergy by extreme right-wing groups, of which the provocatively named Guerrillas of Christ the King was the most important. Its members attacked the Church's direction with inflammatory rhetoric that sometimes took violent form through acts of thuggery and even the issuance of death threats against priests and bishops.[52] The hostility of the regime's hard-line supporters was spectacularly expressed at Carrero Blanco's funeral, when Cardinal Tarancón heard repeated calls for his execution from an angry crowd gathered along the procession route.[53] The government also displayed undisguised irritation towards Luigi Dadaglio when the papal nuncio temporized before official pressure aimed at securing explicit Vatican condemnation of the assassination.[54]

Within clerical ranks, opposition centered on the Hermandad Sacerdotal del

---

hierarchy and led progressive Catholics to occupy the nunciature itself for a brief period. Brassloff, *Religion and Politics in Spain*, pp. 62–63.

51. Quoted in Chao Rego, *La Iglesia en el franquismo*, pp. 217–18.

52. On April 28, 1973, the Guerrillas disrupted a workers' meeting being held in the Madrid seminary. A member of the JOC was physically attacked when he left the meeting; two days later, Auxiliary Bishop Oliver of Madrid was insulted and threatened by members of the same group. Blázquez, *La traición de los clérigos*, p. 209.

53. Tarancón not only heard the famous call given prominence in the press, "Tarancón al paredón!" Some in the crowd shouted, "Long live the Bishop of Spain!" in reference to Bishop Guerra Campos and "Long live the cardinal primate!" in reference to Cardinal González Martín of Toledo, who, though less extreme than the bishop of Cuenca, was regarded as a principal opponent of change within the hierarchy. Martín Descalzo, *Tarancón, el cardenal del cambio*, pp. 195–97. Tarancón felt "an immense sadness" over these hostile displays, which the police did nothing to curb, but kept his composure. Enrique y Tarancón, *Confesiones*, p. 611.

54. Hermet, *Les catholiques*, vol. 2, pp. 390–91.

Clero and Bishop Guerra Campos. A 1972 meeting of the Hermandad at Zaragoza attended by two thousand priests declared that conciliar recommendations were being applied too hastily in an atmosphere of theological anarchy. In 1973, Guerra Campos created a minor sensation by publishing a statement rejecting the CEE's recent document dealing with the Church and the political community and denying the Conference's authority over individual bishops. Later he went further, as he praised Franco publicly for having scrupulously respected the "liberty of the Church."[55] The prelate's unequivocal support for the regime won him the sobriquet "bishop of Spain" among clergy and laity opposed to conciliar and political reform. Evidence suggests that the regime encouraged this campaign of opposition. Cardinal Tarancón maintained that Carrero Blanco financed publications of post-conciliar integrists, publications that "insulted the nuncio, me, the [Vatican] Secretariat of State, the Episcopal Conference, even Paul VI."[56]

The opposition of the six thousand priests belonging to the Hermandad Sacerdotal intensified the climate of internal division endemic to the Spanish Church during this period. But the new intregrism stood no more chance of succeeding during the early 1970s than the Carlist version of a century earlier, and for similar reasons. Although a few bishops sympathized with its program, the majority did not. Guerra Campos provided moral support, but his decision to cease attending CEE meetings left the intransigent clerical Right without significant influence in a Church still dominated by the hierarchy.

The new anticlericalism of the regime and its supporters, as well as clerical opposition to conciliar and political change, strengthened the determination of the hierarchy's accidentalist majority. Bishops became bolder in their denunciations of government repression that in any event failed to break the back of clerical protests. As a result, tension between the Church and the regime continued to grow until a serious crisis in 1974 threatened the unimaginable in the regime's history, a unilateral break in relations with the Vatican imposed by the government of an officially Catholic State.

The crisis arose in an expected quarter through a homily given on February 24, 1974, by Bishop Antonio Añoveros of Bilbao, who challenged the regime's repressive policy towards the Basque Provinces. A disciple of Angel Herrera, whom he once served as auxiliary bishop, Añoveros was known as a cautious prelate within his mentor's accidentalist tradition, although his pastoral letters on social justice while bishop of Cádiz-Ceuta (1964–1971) were highly critical of the regime's shortcomings. Paul VI decided to name him bishop of Bilbao directly, without using the appointment procedures of the concordat, a tactic accepted by the government, which was delighted to see a prelate whom it regarded as troublesome,

55. Cárcel Ortí, *Pablo VI y España*, p. 601; Blázquez, *La traición de los clérigos*, pp. 205–8.
56. Quoted in Martín Descalzo, *Tarancón, el cardenal de cambio*, p. 191.

Bishop Cirarda, transferred to Córdoba. Añoveros's appointment was not entirely welcomed by local priests committed to Basque nationalism, however. Although a native of neighboring Navarra, the new bishop did not know the Basque language and, in their judgment, lacked sufficient knowledge and experience of the region to take a leading role in its historic quest for juridical and cultural identity.[57]

Añoveros assumed the administration of a diocese torn by severe conflicts, with powerful political overtones among clergy and laity over this issue. He recognized that the Church needed to deal with the question of Basque aspirations in a straightforward manner if it hoped to devise an effective pastoral strategy in a heavily industrialized diocese beset by the social dislocation created by economic conditions. Material development promoted by the government not only created social problems, he believed, it was incapable of producing peace unless a major effort was undertaken to resolve the problem of Basque cultural and political identity. In his controversial homily, he defended the right of any people "to conserve its identity" through "a socio-political organization that promotes its just liberty and its collective personality." The Basques possessed "a specific identity within the group of peoples constituting the Spanish State" and, like them, required institutions that recognized their legitimate claims to liberty.[58]

This challenge to the regime's implacable opposition to Basque autonomy in any form, made even stronger by reaction to ETA terrorism, fell like a bombshell on official circles. Even his fellow bishops were taken aback and unhappy with Añoveros's intervention, since it occurred at a time when the Arias Navarro government had indicated to the hierarchy that it was prepared to be more conciliatory in resolving civil-ecclesiastical problems. "I did not like the homily either in form or substance," declared Cardinal Tarancón, an opinion shared by other bishops identified with conciliar reform, notably Bishop Cirarda and Cardinal Jubany.[59]

Harsh criticism from the official press rained down on Añoveros, who, among other things, was accused unjustifiably of supporting terrorism. The government's reaction soon transformed the controversy into a full-blown crisis. The cabinet viewed the homily as nothing less than "a very grave attack upon national unity."[60] The police chief of Bilbao placed Añoveros under house arrest, while the government prepared plans to send the bishop to Lisbon by airplane and for a break in relations with the Vatican, which was certain to object strenuously to the kind of action contemplated by the authorities. In these circumstances, the hierarchy rallied behind Añoveros. The government's action appeared intolerable to Cardinal

57. Ignacio Villota Elejalde, *La Iglesia en la sociedad española y vasca contemporáneas* (Bilbao, 1985), pp. 507–8.

58. "Texto de la homilía leída en la diócesis de Bilbao el 24 de febrero de 1974," in Enrique y Tarancón, *Confesiones*, pp. 633, 634.

59. Ibid., p. 629. Jubany believed that the homily was "frankly imprudent, unacceptable for various reasons" (p. 628).

60. Quoted in Chao Rego, *La Iglesia en el franquismo*, p. 237.

Tarancón, who drafted a document excommunicating anyone involved in action against the bishop. To implement its plans for a break in relations with the Vatican, the cabinet required the approval of Franco.[61] But the general drew back from a confrontation with Rome. When the proposal was presented in cabinet, he reacted angrily, reportedly asking, "Have you lost your heads?"[62] The general vetoed their scheme because, according to Tarancón, he was obsessed with the idea that "A Government that clashes with the Church is a Government that falls."[63]

Franco's intervention averted what would have been the most explosive crisis in civil-ecclesiastical relations since the days of the Republic. But the Añoveros affair marked another significant divide in the Church's history under the dictatorship. Led by Cardinal Tarancón, most of the bishops now recognized that little could be expected from the regime as they prepared for an inevitable transition to a democratic system upon the general's disappearance. Significant opposition among the laity to the regime's record on human rights also became more vocal during this period. The National Commission of Justice and Peace, under the presidency of Franco's former minister, ambassador to the Vatican and member of the "Catholic family" Joaquín Ruiz Giménez, organized, for example, a country-wide petition campaign in 1974 calling for the amnesty of political prisoners, an initiative strongly supported by Cardinal Tarancón.[64]

Such appeals went unheeded. Between the spring of 1974 and Franco's death in November 1975, the government returned with a vengeance to the anticlerical tactics it had employed since the late 1960s. It showed displeasure with the Vatican by refusing to approve new episcopal appointments. In October 1974, the police invaded the parish of the Dulce Nombre de María in Madrid, dissolved a meeting taking place, arrested two hundred persons, and imposed heavy fines on some of

61. Why Franco permitted events to escalate is not entirely clear. Cardinal Tarancón believed that the aged and infirm dictator was easily subject to pressure from hard-liners who played on his apprehension that the Añoveros affair was the work of a subversive group of priests gathered around the bishop. Tarancón also believed that the general reacted with "military psychology" against the pressure of public opinion and even some ministers for a peaceful resolution of the conflict. Tarancón saw the origins of the Añoveros conflict in the attempt of certain officials of the Ministry of Foreign Affairs to force the Vatican into a new concordat by making "life impossible for the Church." Enrique y Tarancón, *Confesiones*, pp. 659, 693. Cárcel Ortí places the blame directly on Arias Navarro, maintaining that "it is not believable that the means of intimidation against Mons. Añoveros came from Franco, because long experience had shown that . . . he was always opposed to taking drastic measures against the Church." He argues that the measures against Añoveros were not the work of the full cabinet but of a group of hard-liners who saw the case as an opportunity either to pressure the Church into silence in its attitude towards the regime or to force it back into its old dependence on the State. He also suggests that the prime minister wished to foment dissension within the Church as a means of weakening its growing hostility to the dictatorship. Cárcel Ortí, *Pablo VI y España*, pp. 715–16.

62. Quoted in Blázquez, *La traición de los clérigos*, p. 224.

63. Quoted in Martín Descalzo, *Tarancón, el cardenal del cambio*, p. 217. The Añoveros crisis effectively ended the prospect of successful negotiations for a new concordat between the government and the Vatican, although perfunctory discussions continued. "The damage done to Church-State relations by the Añoveros affair—seen by many as finally marking the end of the Church-State alliance in Spain—was never to be repaired in Franco's lifetime." Brassloff, *Religion and Politics in Spain*, p. 68.

64. Echarren, "El Cardenal Tarancón, presidente de la Conferencia Episcopal," pp. 179–80.

those in attendance. The CEE protested energetically on the grounds that the participants' right of association had been violated. The authorities singled out for special attention gatherings of workers held under ecclesiastical auspices. In April 1975, they forbade such a meeting in Vallecas at which Bishop Alberto Iniesta, labeled the "red bishop" by the official press, was scheduled to speak. Even pastorally oriented activities fell under suspicion.[65] In May, the government prohibited a pastoral assembly in Las Palmas about to be held under the patronage of Bishop Infantes Florido, who responded by calling for the end of official confessionality, "the secularization of politics and the depoliticization of the faith."[66]

By September 1975, the Arias Navarro government abandoned even the pretense of *apertura* when it ordered the execution of five men accused of subversion and the assassination of police officers. The executions created an international uproar as world leaders, including the pope, protested. In Spain, bishops and priests joined the fray. Bishop Iniesta preached a homily affirming that Christian values made it unacceptable to take the life of another human being. As a result, the bishop received numerous death threats that he took seriously enough to remove himself from Madrid for a brief "vacation" in Rome.[67] During this difficult and tense period, the regime was not abandoned by the minority of clergy gathered in the Hermandad Sacerdotal del Clero. Its members called upon the hierarchy to investigate the Commission of Justice and Peace. In September 1974, they gathered in Cuenca to denounce reforming currents within the Church. "In the Spanish Church," declared one of the participants, "parachutists of the devil abound."[68]

The years 1974 and 1975 marked the definitive transition from a strategy through which the hierarchy sought to distance itself from the regime to one in which many, though not all, bridges to the past were burned. The public statements issued in 1974 by the CEE and its committees blended old concerns with a strong affirmation of human rights. The bishops strengthened their traditional commitment to the "liberty of the Church" by declaring, in reference to the Añoveros case, that every bishop possessed the right "to the free and full exercise of his spiritual power and jurisdiction, as well as to project the light of Christian principles with respect to a concrete temporal problem which affects the Catholics of his diocese."[69] They also returned to the historic theme of social justice in a strongly worded statement highly critical of the inequities that had developed as a result of the regime's economic policies.[70]

On the question of civil rights and its political implications, the bishops went

65. Blázquez, *La traición de los clérigos*, pp. 226, 228.

66. Quoted in ibid., p. 228.

67. Ibid., p. 230.

68. Quoted in ibid., p. 226.

69. This unequivocal support of Añoveros was made by the CEE's executive committee. "Comunicado sobre el 'caso Añoveros,'" March 9, 1974, in *Documentos de la Conferencia Episcopal Española*, p. 289.

70. "Actitudes cristianas ante la situación social," September 14, 1972, in ibid., pp. 322–32.

further than ever before. Recalling John XXIII's encyclical *Pacem in Terris* (1963), they declared that they were compelled "to support an evolution in depth of our institutions" that would guarantee the "fundamental rights of citizens, such as those of association, reunion and expression."[71] This statement, elaborated more fully in the following year, showed that a majority of bishops had definitively cast their lot with the many groups in Spanish society clamoring for change. The hierarchy called for national reconciliation designed to leave behind "the harmful effects of the civil conflict that divided . . . citizens into conquerors and conquered" on the basis of "more effective recognition of all the rights of persons and social groups." Although the bishops echoed the customary appeal for Spaniards "to respect the exercise of public authority," they left no doubt of their belief that the regime had failed to establish "the legal norms" sufficient to attain this objective, thereby creating "a permanent factor of imbalance, incompatible with a sincere desire for political reconciliation."[72]

But as apprehensive as their predecessors of 1931 had been about abrupt or violent upheaval, the bishops saw change arriving through an evolutionary process. They did not want "radical changes in socio-economic or political structures" but a middle course in which "neither terrorism nor revolutionary subversion, nor the repression of the human person's rights" played any role.[73] They wished a "change of regime, not of the system."[74] For this reason, the bishops viewed with apprehension the possible triumph of the Socialist and Communist parties through free elections, fearing a Marxist-inspired attack on the existing socioeconomic order. However vigorously they criticized the shortcomings of capitalism and the society it produced, the bishops remained true to the Spanish Church's tradition in this respect, even though a minority of clergy and laity saw no contradiction between Catholicism and Marxism. As early as 1974, the bishops of Catalonia warned the faithful that they must exercise "lucid prudence and discernment" before committing themselves to groups "with ideologies incompatible with the faith." Even Cardinal Tarancón remarked in his opening address to the CEE's 1974 plenary assembly that the faithful must oppose systems that were "intrinsically inseparable from their atheistic doctrine and contradict Christian principles."[75]

Commitment to change did not mean that the hierarchy abandoned its historic claims to influence over public and private morality. If anything, the bishops became more apprehensive about the moral effects produced by the emergence of a consumption-driven and increasingly secularized society, the result of economic development. In 1974, they lamented the "evident deterioration of public moral-

71. "Comunicado final: la violencia, la tutela de los derechos humanos," November 30, 1974, in ibid., p. 341.
72. "La reconciliación de la Iglesia y en la sociedad," April 17, 1975, in ibid., p. 357.
73. "Comunicado final: la violencia, la tutela de los derechos humanos," p. 341.
74. Ruiz Rico, *El papel político de la Iglesia católica*, p. 234.
75. Quoted in ibid., p. 231; quoted in Brassloff, *Religion and Politics in Spain*, p. 73.

ity in magazines, films, theaters, radio and television programs, with great damage to the common moral and religious welfare of our people."[76] Although the regime had loosened controls over the media, it did not abandon them completely. The bishops' statement showed that the hierarchy's endorsement of human rights and political pluralism did not extend to all forms of expression. The bishops used more temperate language than had their predecessors in their critique of the country's moral condition. But they made clear that unrestrained freedom of expression as it affected moral standards should not be regarded as "liberalizing achievements."[77]

By the time of Franco's death on November 20, 1975, the Church had elaborated a strategy based on the end of official confessionality, the protection of ecclesiastical finances and rights in education, the recognition of the Church's influence on moral questions, and openness to evolutionary political reform that would guide it through the difficult period of transition to democracy soon to follow.[78] It was no easier for the Church to perceive how this process would unfold than it was for most Spaniards. The succession of King Juan Carlos I raised expectations, but his decision to confirm Arias Navarro as prime minister caused doubts about the extent of the monarch's commitment to change. In fact, the king was forced to work within a constricted field of action. Much of the democratic opposition doubted his intentions; the regime's hard-liners were opposed to political reform, however limited, while the institutions of the dictatorship remained firmly in place.

In these circumstances, Arias Navarro undertook a final attempt to recast the regime's foundations by resorting to the threadbare idea of creating political associations. Although a law to this effect was finally passed, the prime minister failed to appreciate that the country expected far more. The cabinet, divided between ministers favoring substantial change and those committed to a go-slow strategy, could not agree on a comprehensive package of reforms, while the "bunker" did everything in its power to frustrate any dilution of the regime's authoritarian character. Opposition groups, although in frequent contact with another, were also divided between the option of pressing for a *ruptura democrática,* a complete break with the institutions of the past, or a *ruptura pactada,* a negotiated end to the existing system. This confusing situation was complicated by a wave of strike action and protest demonstrations in the country as a whole. By the spring of 1976, it was evident that the government's attempt at *apertura* was a failure and that its moral authority was eroding rapidly. Vilified by the opposition and the "bunker," a weary Arias Navarro finally threw in the towel, resigning on July 1.

76. "Comunicado final: dificultad con la administración pública: confusionismo y ambiente," May 9, 1974, in *Documentos de la Conferencia Episcopal Española,* p. 290. This document was published by the executive committee of the CEE.

77. Ibid.

78. Ruiz Rico, *El papel político de la Iglesia católica,* p. 229.

Initiative now passed to the king, still in possession of all of Franco's powers. Aware of popular demands for substantive change and in contact with reformists within the regime and some leaders of the democratic opposition, the monarch appeared to be proceeding cautiously when he appointed as prime minister a former minister of the National Movement, Adolfo Suárez. The appointment surprised political pundits, who had expected the king to name a leading reformist, José María de Areilza, and it disappointed the opposition, which viewed the new prime minister's association with the regime's one and only authorized political organization as something less than a ringing endorsement of comprehensive reform. But the king and the prime minister agreed on the model of *ruptura pactada* as the only possible means of resolving the country's political impasse.

The process of negotiating the transition to democratic institutions opened a new era for the Spanish Church. It was one thing for the Church to endorse political change at the level of principle and protest, another to come to terms with a democratic government, to negotiate an ecclesiastical version of the *ruptura pactada* similar to that about to take place in the political sphere.

CHAPTER XXI

THE CHURCH AND THE NEW DEMOCRACY, 1976–1979

Initial doubts about the reforming intentions of the Suárez government soon began to dissipate. Supported by King Juan Carlos I, the prime minister persuaded Franco's last parliament to vote itself out of existence, while seeking to build consensus among the political parties for a transformation of institutions. The national referendum of December 15, 1976, approved the government's reform plans by a substantial majority. Although extremist supporters of the old authoritarian order sought to turn the clock back through acts of thuggery and terrorism, they could not halt the powerful momentum towards a *ruptura pactada* with the past, which inspired a broad coalition of forces ranging from moderate supporters of the Franco regime to the Socialist (PSOE) and Communist (PCE) parties. On June 15, 1977, the first free elections since February 1936 returned a representative parliament that wrote the democratic constitution of 1978.

For the Church, the political changes that occurred between 1976 and 1978 presented both challenge and opportunity. The Suárez government and the prime minister's hastily formed party, the Unión del Centro Democrático (UCD), a coalition of center right groups, included prominent members identified with the "Catholic family" of the Franco era. The cabinet favored an amicable resolution of key problems in civil-ecclesiastical relations. But it was by no means clear as the period of transition opened in 1976 how the nuts and bolts of a new ecclesiastical settlement would fall into place in view of the government's recognition that achieving political consensus required the cooperation of the Socialist and Communist parties.

The PSOE and the PCE viewed the question of the Church from a more open perspective than they had in the past, while remaining suspicious of the hierarchy's ambitions to retain the advantages acquired during the dictatorship in the fields of education, ecclesiastical finances, and the control of public morality. The formation of a UCD cabinet following the June 1977 elections meant that the Church would not have to deal with a government committed to a policy of stringent laicization similar to that of the Second Republic. But the strong representation of the Socialist party in parliament and the government's recognition of the need for broad agreement among the country's political groups introduced an element of give-and-take in the political process that indicated, from the Vatican's and the hierarchy's point of view, that a satisfactory resolution of civil-ecclesiastical issues was far from assured.

The period of transition from dictatorship to democracy occurred at an opportune moment for the Church. The bishops' commitment in principle to political change, the lower clergy's sympathy for a fundamental reworking of Church-State relations, the participation of some Catholic associations in protest movements during the last decade and a half of the Franco regime, and the militant activism of a minority of priests and laypeople belonging to trade unions and new grassroots religious groups failed to produce a unified response on the part of clergy and laity to the problem of redefining the Church's position within the new political order. But taken as a whole, they provided the Church with credibility as a legitimate participant in the democratization of the country.

The Church also benefited from a consensus-driven reform process. As the period of change opened during the summer of 1976, old fears resurfaced about a resurgence of the strong anticlericalism among the parties of the Left that had made the issue of the Church and its privileges a source of divisive controversy during the Second Republic.[1] Despite bouts of rhetorical skirmishing, the passions generated by the so-called "religious question" during the 1930s did not reemerge to undermine the development of the new democracy. Politicians of the major parties knew their history well enough to wish to avoid a recurrence of ancient and destructive conflicts. The principal players in the complex business of redefining the Church's position—the Vatican, the hierarchy, the government, and the opposition—agreed that the confessional State identified with the Franco regime was an unsustainable anachronism within a democratic Western Europe.

The impetus towards consensus also arose from the perception among the major parties that the Church remained a powerful institution capable of upsetting an orderly transition to democracy if an accommodation were not reached with ecclesiastical interests. The UCD took the line that a negotiated agreement was the only way to proceed. Marcelino Oreja, minister of foreign affairs in the Suárez

1. J. M. González Ruiz, "El anticlericalismo como riesgo para la democracia," *El País*, August 15, 1976.

cabinet, defended this strategy because of "the actual sociological fact that the majority of the Spanish people are Catholic."[2] Socialists and Communists rejected the so-called sociological argument. They saw the resolution of the historically contentious issue of civil-ecclesiastical relations as a pragmatic necessity required to stabilize the country's nascent and still fragile democracy. The religious question, declared the PCE, had been a source of "hurricanes and cyclones" in the past. It was now necessary to calm these "winds and storms . . . once and for all."[3] Skepticism about an ecclesiastical settlement compatible with democratic principles was greatest among the Socialists, although in the end they accepted the move towards a consensus solution. The PSOE, asserted one of its parliamentary leaders, Gregorio Peces-Barba, wished "to close the religious quarrel definitively in our country."[4]

Failure to produce a compromise acceptable to the Church would have complicated the process of political reform. Whether in these circumstances the clerical leadership and its supporters were capable of the mass resistance they had displayed towards the Republic between 1931 and 1933 is debatable. The Church's internal cohesion as it confronted the new political situation was far weaker than it had been during the early 1930s. A vocal minority of priests and laypeople representing a variety of popular movements within the Church endorsed a radical break with the past on issues such as the separation of Church and State, particularly with respect to government financing and education, which clashed with the Vatican's and the hierarchy's intentions. Despite the bishops' repeated warnings about the dangers of Marxism, some Catholic clerical and lay social activists joined the Socialist and Communist parties. There was little possibility that the hierarchy could resurrect the negative and deeply conservative "union of Catholics" of the early 1930s even had it wished to do so. From a tactical point of view, it was in the Church's interests to join with reformers to develop a political consensus acceptable to the government, opposition, and public opinion.

On November 27, 1975, a week after the death of Franco, Cardinal Tarancón preached a historic sermon marking the accession of King Juan Carlos I to the throne. In the presence of the monarch and representatives of the regime, the cardinal expressed the Church's support for political changes that would allow "all citizens to participate freely and actively in the life of the country." Within a new society governed by concern with social justice, Tarancón declared that the Church

2. *Ya*, January 4, 1979.

3. Quoted in Matías García, "Valoración política," in *Los acuerdos entre la Iglesia y España*, ed. Carlos Corral and Lamberto de Echeverría (Madrid, 1980), p. 767, note 24. During the 1977 electoral campaign, the leader of the Communist party, Santiago Carrillo, "sought to minimize the differences between the PCE and the Church." In its response to episcopal statements dealing with the elections, the PCE's response "was carefully worded so as to criticize the intervention of the bishops, but to avoid attacks on the Church per se." Richard Gunther, Giacomo Sani, and Goldi Shabad, *Spain after Franco: The Making of a Competitive Party System* (Berkeley and Los Angeles, 1988), p. 225.

4. Quoted in García, "Valoración política," p. 766.

would seek no privilege other than the right to preach its religious message freely.[5] The cardinal's restatement of the opinion of episcopal moderates before the prospect of political change was a lofty affirmation of principle. The practical problem of applying principle to practice was another matter. Repeated statements from the bishops affirming the clergy's willingness to abandon old privileges did not, by any stretch of the imagination, constitute an endorsement of a rigorous separation of Church and State on the French or American models.

Redefining the Church's legal position during the period of transition took two forms. First, the Vatican and the hierarchy sought to avoid the unilateral settlement imposed on the Church by the Republic in favor of bilateral negotiations between the papacy and the Suárez government. For the Church, the cabinet's decision in 1976 to accept this historic mechanism for resolving civil-ecclesiastical questions before parliamentary institutions were in place represented a tactical triumph. It meant that agreements reached between Madrid and the Vatican would enjoy the status of international treaties binding upon future governments, whatever their political composition. Second, the Church faced the more difficult and complex task of participating in the process of political debate and resolution, especially with respect to a new constitution, in such a way as to secure arrangements as favorable as possible to ecclesiastical interests.

Diplomatic Settlement, 1976–1979

On July 15, 1976, the marqués de Mondéjar, head of the royal household, journeyed secretly to the Vatican, where he was received immediately by Pope Paul VI. The monarch's representative carried a letter in which the king informed the pontiff that he would refrain from using his patronage rights over episcopal appointments as a means of reaching a comprehensive agreement within the framework of "the new relations of the Spanish State with the Holy See."[6] Given the glacial pace of negotiations with the Franco regime over a new concordat, Spanish opinion was surprised to hear a few days later of the royal concession and the announcement on July 28 that both parties had accepted an agreement (*acuerdo*) through which the government formally renounced its ecclesiastical patronage rights, while the Church reaffirmed its commitment to religious liberty and renounced certain juridical privileges enjoyed by bishops and clergy under the 1953 concordat. Both

5. "Homilía del Cardenal Enrique y Tarancón," in *Los obispos ante la nueva etapa política* (Madrid, 1976), pp. 11, 12. The homily did not escape criticism, however. The progressive Catholic intellectual José Luis Aranguren criticized it as yet another theocratic intervention of the Spanish Church in civil affairs. He questioned the sincerity of Tarancón and his fellow bishops on the principle of Church-State separation. Ramón Echarren, "El Cardenal Tarancón, presidente de la Conferencia Episcopal," in S. Grisolía et al., *Homenaje al Cardenal Enrique y Tarancón* (Valencia, 1997), pp. 208–9.

6. Quoted in Tomás García Berberena, "Nombramiento de obispos," in *Los acuerdos entre la Iglesia y España*, p. 133.

parties recognized that the "profound transformation" of Spanish society in recent years, particularly with respect to "relations between the political community and religious confessions," required new arrangements to replace those contained in the concordat.[7]

Announcement of the 1976 *acuerdo* startled the public, although negotiations had begun in January during the tenure of Arias Navarro as prime minister through the initiative of the minister of foreign affairs, José María de Areilza, and the minister of justice, Antonio Garrigues. At a meeting held on January 30 in the residence of the papal nuncio, Luigi Dadaglio, the government's representatives proposed a "rapid negotiation" based on redefining the general principles of civil-ecclesiastical relations and abrogation of the 1953 concordat, which in their judgment had been overwhelmed by events. They also offered the carrot of improving the clergy's financial situation should negotiations proceed quickly. The nuncio and his advisors appeared surprised by the proposal. Although recognizing that the concordat was out of date, the nuncio wished to base negotiations on its terms and to move slowly. Areilza believed that the Vatican fell back on the concordat as the basis for negotiations as a means of conserving all "possible advantages" from the existing arrangements, while securing new ones during the negotiating process.[8]

Vatican caution and growing tension between the Church and the Arias Navarro government over other issues prevented the rapid negotiations requested by Areilza. The king's decision to allow his ecclesiastical patronage rights to fall into disuse broke the diplomatic logjam and produced the agreement of July 28.[9] The *acuerdo* did not provide the general statement of principles originally envisaged, except in a limited way. It was a brief document, shorter in length than four subsequent agreements signed in 1979. Nor were its terms dramatic or comprehensive. Renunciation of the government's patronage rights was bound to occur sooner or later. Even Franco had considered such a possibility. Moreover, the regalist ghosts of the past did not entirely disappear in the new agreement, which required the Holy See to notify the government of episcopal appointments before they were announced to ascertain if there were "possible concrete objections of a general political character" to any nominee.[10] The significance of the *acuerdo* was that it initiated long and complicated negotiations designed, according to an offi-

7. "Acuerdo entre la Santa Sede y el Estado Español de 28 de julio de 1976," in ibid., pp. 778–81. Even Cardinal Tarancón was surprised by the news of the king's letter to Paul VI. Vicente Enrique y Tarancón, *Confesiones* (Madrid, 1996), p. 892.

8. Quoted in José Manuel Cuenca Toribio, *Relaciones Iglesia-Estado en la España contemporánea, 1833–1985* (Madrid, 1985), p. 137, note 28.

9. Marcelino Oreja declared that the role of the king as the "motor" driving the decision on patronage rights was decisive. *El País*, July 29, 1976.

10. "Acuerdo . . . de 28 de julio de 1976," pp. 779–80. This clause did not bind the Vatican, however, to any specific course of action should there be such objections other than to exercise "prudent consideration" in reaching a decision.

cial spokesman, to move "from a system of privilege to one of rights" by defining the juridical status of the Church, its place in education, and its financial arrangements with the government.[11]

Marcelino Oreja declared after the conclusion of the 1976 negotiations that all key issues involving civil-ecclesiastical relations would be resolved within two years.[12] This prediction proved optimistic. The issues involved were complex and, at times, difficult to resolve. In 1979, Oreja recalled that the negotiations had been cordial but "long and not easy."[13] The negotiating process, based on the work of nine technical commissions, four representing the Vatican, five the government, proved slow and cumbersome.[14] Political considerations also delayed rapid action, as the energies of the Suárez cabinet and parliament were directed towards political reform, especially during 1978, when the new constitution was being debated. The negotiations themselves created political difficulties. In 1977, Socialist deputies raised the legitimate question of the relationship between the government's negotiations with the Vatican and their compatibility with an as yet unwritten democratic constitution. They demanded that the government should inform parliament fully of the negotiations and called for their suspension until the constitution pronounced on the principles that would govern relations between Church and State.[15]

This objection receded to a degree before the consensus politics that lay behind the drafting of the 1978 constitution and the referral of a final package of four *acuerdos* in 1979 to the appropriate legislative commission and parliament for approval. Marcelino Oreja declared that the agreements rested on "the tacit consensus of the principal parties of the country" with which he had maintained contacts "until the last moment."[16] This assessment was correct up to a point. Three of the four agreements were approved by substantial majorities. But the *acuerdo* dealing with education was opposed by the PSOE and the PCE, which also voted against the financial agreement.[17] In parliamentary debate, the PSOE echoed its earlier objections to negotiating with the Vatican over questions of an internal and constitutional character. Although the Socialists voted in the end for three of the 1979 agreements, they accepted the *acuerdos* at arm's length as a recognition of political reality demanded by the circumstances.[18]

For all practical purposes, the package of five *acuerdos* signed between Madrid

11. *Diario 16*, November 2, 1976.
12. *El País*, July 29, 1976.
13. *Ya*, January 4, 1979.
14. "Nudos de muchos años," *Opinión*, October 16–22, 1976, p. 26.
15. Carlos Corral, "El sistema constitucional y el régimen de acuerdos específicos," in *Los acuerdos entre la Iglesia y España*, p. 100.
16. *Ya*, January 3, 1979.
17. One hundred seventy-eight legislators in the congress of deputies voted in favor of the education agreement; 125 voted against. *Los Acuerdos entre la Iglesia y España*, p. 782.
18. García, "Valoración política," p. 752.

and the Vatican in 1976 and 1979 constituted a new concordat, although neither party wished to use a term that had fallen from favor in the post–Vatican II world. Although the 1978 constitution established the principle that all religious confessions would be treated equally, the fact that the agreements possessed the status of diplomatic treaties meant that the Spanish Church received special treatment that was not available to other religious groups.

The terms of the *acuerdos* have received extensive study, largely by ecclesiastical scholars concerned with their future juridical implications for the Church and its institutions.[19] Although the *acuerdos* provided a new legal framework for the Church within a democratic State, the arrangements established for the future must be understood in the light of historic problems in civil-ecclesiastical relations. No problem had been more persistent than the perennial question of the extent of direct government involvement in ecclesiastical affairs. Although this historic regalism or official interventionism changed over time and regime, it survived in one form or another through the Restoration, the dictatorship of Primo de Rivera, the Second Republic, and the rule of Francisco Franco. Successive regimes, albeit for different reasons and to different degrees, believed it necessary for the State to exercise a significant measure of control over the Church.

The exercise of government patronage rights over episcopal appointments had long been resented by the Vatican and the hierarchy. The 1976 agreement was significant not only because it ended this most spectacular of the State's historic regalist rights. It also represented the first step towards abandoning, for the first time in modern Spanish history save for the period of the First Republic, the idea that the State should exercise a degree of control over ecclesiastical administration as a means of protecting official interests.

The goal of securing the "liberty of the Church," long a goal of the hierarchy even during the Franco era, was secured in the first of the 1979 *acuerdos* dealing with the Church's juridical status. Its initial clauses effectively ended an ancient regalist tradition. The State recognized the "right of the Catholic Church to exercise its apostolic mission" and guaranteed "the free and public exercise of activities which are proper to it." The State abandoned privileges contained in the 1851 and 1953 concordats that gave the government a role in the determination of diocesan and parish boundaries. The long and conflictive history of attempts to regulate the religious orders also fell by the wayside. The State "recognized the civil-juridical personality of orders, religious congregations and other institutes," and their "full capacity to work" in their areas of chosen activity, although a tinge of the old regalism remained. Religious orders were obliged to register formally as legal associations with the government. But, as in the case of Sagasta's controversial *modus*

19. See the essays in *Los acuerdos entre la Iglesia y España* and *Constitución y acuerdos Iglesia-Estado: actas del II Simposio Hispano-Alemán*, ed. Carlos Corral and Joseph Listl (Madrid, 1988).

vivendi with the Vatican in 1902, registration was to be automatic upon presentation of the necessary documentation. The Vatican also received a guarantee that it could freely publish any papal document dealing with the Church's administration and that the pope could communicate with the bishops without government interference.[20]

That the Vatican desired the insertion of such a clause says a good deal about the purposes of the juridical agreement from an ecclesiastical perspective. More than a century had passed since a Spanish government had resorted to a legal device, originally called the *exequatur* when first used during the eighteenth century by King Carlos III, to forbid the publication of papal bulls and briefs judged incompatible with official policy. The presence of this archaic clause in the juridical *acuerdo*, as well as other terms, such as those dealing with the religious orders, reflected less a concern with real and present dangers to ecclesiastical interests than a determination to protect the Church from a revival of regalist or anticlerical measures similar to those imposed by successive regimes from the 1830s onward. The Church was determined that history should not be repeated, although there was no evidence that either the government or the opposition ever contemplated resurrecting the regalist and, in some cases, anticlerical tactics of the past. Such a policy appeared outmoded and counterproductive to politicians committed to the creation of democratic institutions and recognition of the civil rights of individuals and organizations.

Apart from recognition of the Spanish Episcopal Conference as the official representative of the hierarchy before the government, a body that the Franco regime always refused to acknowledge, the articles of the juridical agreement were concerned more with the past than with the future.[21] The *acuerdos* on education and ecclesiastical finances concerned issues of immediate importance for the Church. As a result of its close ties to the regime over forty years, it had ensured that religious instruction in public schools was obligatory for all Catholics. The Church took advantage of favorable legislation to construct an extensive network of schools receiving substantial government financial support, particularly after passage of the 1970 education law. During the Republic, the most optimistic estimates of enrollment in Church schools never exceeded six hundred thousand. By 1976, nearly 2 million students were registered in the Church's primary and secondary schools.[22] The UCD government continued the generous funding arrangements adopted by the Franco regime in its later years. By 1981, the government provided Church schools with an impressive subsidy of 30 billion pesetas, although the hi-

20. "Acuerdo entre el Estado Español y la Santa Sede sobre asuntos jurídicos," in *Los acuerdos entre la Iglesia y España*, pp. 785, 786, 787.

21. Recognition of the Episcopal Conference as "the voice of the Church before the State" was hailed in ecclesiastical circles as a significant concession. *Ya*, January 11, 1979.

22. "El momento actual de la enseñanza," *Misión Abierta* (1978), vol. 2, supplement, p. 115.

erarchy believed that this support was insufficient in comparison with the financial assistance provided to public schools.[23]

The Vatican and the hierarchy were determined to protect the Church's solid gains in education as a matter of vital interest. Memories of fierce battles over Church schools during the Republic also lurked beneath the surface of ecclesiastical strategy. Bishops and Catholic commentators on educational matters feared that a future Socialist government would implement the party's historic commitment to a State monopoly in education, although later events would prove this concern unfounded. In any event, the terms of the educational *acuerdo* satisfied many of the Church's demands. The agreement established, to be sure, the principle of liberty of conscience for students in public schools, who could no longer be obligated to attend religion classes. But religious instruction given by teachers chosen by the bishops was to continue in the public system. The agreement also explicitly recognized the "fundamental right" of parents to exercise influence over the moral and religious education that their children received in public schools, although how this "right" was to be applied was not spelled out. Instruction in the public system was also obliged to respect "the values of Christian ethic[s]." The Church also secured recognition of its legal ability to found universities and other postgraduate institutions, thereby fulfilling one of its historic ambitions in the field of higher education.[24]

However favorable to the Church, these arrangements would have meant little without assurances that its schools would continue to receive government financial support. The Church accepted the commitment contained in the 1978 constitution to free and obligatory education for all Spaniards at the primary and secondary levels. In return, the hierarchy expected that Church schools would receive the same level of funding as the public system. In 1976, the bishops declared that Church and public schools were not "parallel academic systems." In their judgment, both constituted integral parts of "a national system of education" that should be financed accordingly.[25] The educational *acuerdo* of 1979 did not deal with the thorny question of levels of funding for Church schools, but it affirmed the general principle that Church schools and their students "will have the right to receive subsidies, scholarships, fiscal benefits and other forms of assistance that the State grants to nonofficial teaching centers in accord with the regime of equality of opportunities" established by the constitution.[26] The specific conditions and

23. Carlos Corral, "De la dotación estatal para la Iglesia a la asignación tributaria para fines religiosos," in Carlos Corral et al., *La asignación tributaria para fines religiosos* (Madrid, 1989), p. 121; *Cambio 16*, January 12, 1981, no. 476, pp. 43–44.

24. "Acuerdo entre el Estado Español y la Santa Sede sobre enseñanza y asuntos culturales," in *Los acuerdos entre la Iglesia y España*, pp. 791–95.

25. *Los planteamientos actuales de la enseñanza: declaración de la comisión permanente de la Conferencia Episcopal Española*, ed. Promoción Popular Cristiana (Madrid, 1976), p. 13.

26. "Acuerdo entre el Estado Español y la Santa Sede sobre enseñanza y asuntos culturales," p. 795.

funding formula under which government assistance would be provided was left to enabling legislation, a circumstance that later provoked strident controversy over how the principle affirmed in the educational agreement should be applied.

The 1979 agreement dealing with the fate of official subsidies for clerical salaries attempted to resolve a difficult constitutional problem. The 1978 constitution established the equality of all religious groups before the civil authority. Yet the clergy continued to receive officially subsidized salaries. Indeed, between 1969 and 1981, the budgetary appropriation for this purpose rose steadily.[27] Although even the UCD government recognized that this situation was untenable within a democratic society, the historic stinginess of Spanish Catholics towards supporting the diocesan clergy meant that bishops and priests were as dependent on the government for their livelihoods as ever. There was no prospect that the Church could raise enough on its own to replace official financial support.

The solution reached in the financial *acuerdo* resembled a judgment of Solomon. To satisfy constitutional exigencies, the Church agreed that any new financial arrangements must be compatible "with absolute respect" for the equality of all religious groups and that it would undertake to raise the "resources sufficient for . . . its necessities."[28] In return, the State promised that it would collaborate with the Church to ensure that the clergy were adequately supported. Both parties agreed on a model, already being used in the Federal Republic of Germany, that allowed Catholics to assign a small portion of their income taxes to the Church. This device satisfied the constitutional provision on equality since it would also be available to Protestant churches and other religious groups.

But some were more equal than others. The agreement specified neither the exact percentage involved nor provided details about how the new system would work. These issues were left for later negotiations to conclude within three years. In the meantime, the government agreed to continue paying clerical salaries. In fact, negotiations dragged on until 1988, when the Socialist government, first elected in 1982, and the hierarchy agreed on a percentage of .0052.[29] Until this time and despite severe conflicts between the Church and the government over education and abortion, the authorities punctually paid the total subsidy as stipulated in the 1979 *acuerdo*. Indeed, in its first full year in office, the PSOE government increased the appropriation for the Church by a generous 12 percent.[30] Moreover,

27. The official subsidy for clerical salaries rose from 6,075,355,000 pesetas in 1968–1969 to 8,543,000,000 by 1981. Corral, "De la dotación estatal para la Iglesia a la asignación tributaria para fines religiosos," p. 121; *Cambio 16*, January 12, 1981, no. 476, pp. 43–44.

28. "Acuerdo entre el Estado español y la Santa Sede sobre asuntos económicos," in *Los acuerdos entre la Iglesia y España*, pp. 798–99.

29. Corral, "De la dotación estatal para la Iglesia a la asignación tributaria para fines religiosos," pp. 124–28.

30. *Ya*, April 26, 1983. Between 1984 and 1988 the amount provided by the Socialist government increased steadily from 11,051,686,000 pesetas in 1984 to 13,842,985,000 by 1988. Oficina de Estadística y Sociología de la Iglesia, *Estadísticas de la Iglesia Católica, 1989* (Madrid, 1989), p. 95, Table 53.

the authorities promised to make up the difference between the amount assigned to the Church by taxpayers and the total sum previously provided for clerical salaries in the national budget. This proved a generous concession. Catholics did not rush to support the Church financially. In 1989, only 38.34 percent of taxpayers indicated that they wished a minuscule proportion of their taxes to go to the Church, thereby obliging the government to make up the difference by providing 7,584,888,718 pesetas from the national budget.[31] Although the Church has managed to raise significant funds on its own, to this day it remains heavily dependent on government for financial support.[32]

Through the agreements of 1976 and 1979, the Church secured an invaluable binding commitment from the State on key issues deemed essential by the Vatican and the hierarchy, although Pope John Paul II believed that the agreements did not go far enough, as far as the ecclesiastical interests were concerned.[33] But the *acuerdos* by no means resolved all problems affecting civil-ecclesiastical relations. The 1979 agreements recognized as much by leaving the resolution of certain questions, such as arrangements dealing with clerical salaries, to further negotiations. The educational agreement was vague about the extent of funding for Church schools. Further, the *acuerdos* said little about another question to which the hierarchy attached importance. How would a democratic and pluralistic political system deal with important questions of public morality on which the Church had definite views? During the period of transition, bishops repeatedly expressed their concerns about the impact of political change on moral standards. In a 1977 address to the CEE, Cardinal Tarancón, however supportive of the country's move towards democracy, insisted that the new political order should reflect the views of a citizenry that still identified itself as Catholic on issues such as marriage, divorce, education, and respect for human life.[34]

31. Rafael Díaz-Salazar, "La institución eclesial en la sociedad civil española," in *Religión y sociedad en España,* ed. Rafael Díaz-Salazar and Salvador Giner (Madrid, 1993), p. 309, Table 3. The proportion of Catholics indicating that they wished to assign .0052 percent of their taxes to the Church varied according to region. It was not surprising that Castile-León (53.03 percent) and Murcia (50.9 percent), areas long known for their support of the Church, had an impressive rate of response, while Catalonia (30.44 percent), where abstention from religious practice was historically significant, contributed less than any other region. Yet other areas not previously regarded as bastions of support for the Church also responded favorably, particularly Andalucía (47.8 percent) and Extremadura (54.15 percent). Luis Gutiérrez Martínez Conde, "Participación de la Iglesia católica en el IRPF de 1990," *XX Siglos* (1993), vol. 4, no. 13, p. 117.

32. In spite of the low participation rate of Catalonia in the income tax scheme, Catalan Catholics proved especially generous with their private donations. In 1987, the eight dioceses of the region raised enough to meet the cost of approximately 72 percent of their financial needs. *El País,* November 10, 1988.

33. Father Martín Patino, a close associate of Cardinal Tarancón, believed that the "new accords did not suit John Paul II." The pope felt that the cardinal and the papal nuncio, Luigi Dadaglio, had not secured enough for the Church in matters dealing with marriage legislation, the jurisdiction of ecclesiastical courts, and education. Audrey Brassloff, *Religion and Politics in Spain: The Spanish Church in Transition, 1962–1996* (London and New York, 1998), p. 100.

34. Rafael Díaz-Salazar, *El capital simbólico: estructura social, política y religión en España* (Madrid, 1988), pp. 115–16.

However advantageous to the Church, the *acuerdos* left unresolved important issues directly linked to the political process and the elaboration of a new constitution. As the transition from dictatorship to democracy quickened in 1977 and 1978, the Church's place in a new civil order was more precisely defined.

Politics and the Church, 1976–1977

As momentum for political reform gathered force during the summer and autumn of 1976, the bishops published numerous statements expressing support for democratic change. Like the episcopal declarations of the late Franco period, these affirmed general principles of liberty and justice. The hierarchy appealed for full public participation in the electoral process and urged the electorate and political parties to act in accord with the common good within civilized "rules of the game" based on fairness and tolerance.[35] The bishops called for reform to develop within a "climate of serenity" that would open the way to a "stable and peaceful *convivencia.*"[36] But episcopal commentaries were short on specifics because of divisions about the strategy the Church should follow during the period of transition.[37] The hierarchy was more precise in expressing its views on the kind of regime it did not want. Episcopal statements reflected the bishops' long-held view that change should take place within an evolutionary framework structured around democratic institutions designed to prevent the "unlimited increase of state power which threatens . . . the liberty of society and citizens."[38] The hierarchy left no doubt of its opposition to a radical solution to the country's political problems.

The public-spirited tone of the bishops' public statements on reform contributed to the democratic process. But with the prospect of general elections in June 1977, the hierarchy faced some hard questions in the rough-and-tumble world of politics. Here the clerical leadership's response was sometimes confusing, ambiguous, and a source of controversy within the Church.[39] The ecclesiastical leadership had to confront a fundamental question. How would the Church secure its interests within the emerging party system of the new democracy? Although divisions among Christian Democratic groups made the formation of a united party on the Italian model doubtful, the old dream of constituting a political "union of Catholics" had not disappeared. According to Cardinal Tarancón, the office of the

35. "Orientaciones cristianas sobre participación política y social," July 9, 1976, in *Documentos de la Conferencia Episcopal Española, 1965–1983*, ed. Jesús Iribarren (Madrid, 1984), p. 385. This document was produced by the CEE's Commission on the Social Apostolate.

36. "Comunicado final: Satisfacción y esperanza por el acuerdo Iglesia-Estado. Próximo referéndum," September 24, 1976, in ibid., p. 398. This document was produced by the executive committee of the CEE.

37. "Conferencia Episcopal: En columna de a tres," *Cambio 16*, December 6–12, 1976, no. 261, p. 31.

38. "Orientaciones cristianas sobre participación política y social," p. 385.

39. Díaz-Salazar, *El capital simbólico*, pp. 55–56.

Vatican's secretary of state maintained contacts through Archbishop Benelli with leading Christian Democrats with a view to laying the foundations of a party organized on Christian Democratic lines.[40]

The cardinal opposed any attempt to resurrect a confessional party. He bluntly told Benelli that whatever the experience of the Italian Church with Christian Democracy, "I do not believe that it is suitable for us in Spain."[41] Tarancón's hostility arose from his conviction that a confessional party threatened the revival of the rancorous political divisions that had beset the Second Republic. He also believed that the opportunistic and often self-serving character of the Italian party had done more harm than good to the Church. The cardinal feared that the appearance of a confessional party would be counterproductive, for "Spaniards, in their immense majority, are allergic . . . to the intervention of the Church in the political field." Relying on the teachings of the Second Vatican Council, which affirmed that "the political community and the Church are *independent and autonomous*," Tarancón maintained that the "Church cannot give the impression that it is linked to a specific party."[42]

Divided Christian Democrats were in no position to launch an effective organizing initiative, whatever support they received from the Vatican.[43] Nor was there much sympathy among the bishops for what appeared a risky political undertaking.[44] It was also obvious that in contrast to the situation prevailing during the early 1930s, a "very new phenomenon" had appeared, namely, "the political militancy of Catholics within the ample range of parties," including some that the Church regarded with disfavor.[45] The hierarchy's decision to avoid identifying the Church with Christian Democracy meant the abandonment of one of Spanish Catholicism's oldest dreams, the formation of a great political party based on the so-called Catholic masses. But it represented prudent recognition of political reality.

40. José Luis Martín Descalzo, *Tarancón, el cardenal del cambio* (Barcelona, 1982), pp. 252–53.

41. Quoted in ibid.

42. Vicente Enrique y Tarancón, *¿Partidos políticos cristianos?* (1977), in Juan Luis Recio et al., *La transición española: religión y política* (Estella, 1990), pp. 93, 94. The cardinal's position was publicly supported by his influential vicar-general, Father José María Martín Patino, who expressed similar views in a widely cited newspaper article. "Los partidos políticos, reductos de poder político de una Iglesia preconciliar," *El País*, November 25, 1976.

43. Ceferino Santos Escudero, "El democatolicismo hispánico," *El País*, December 14, 1976. Attempts to forge unity among disparate Christian Democratic groups in 1976 are described by Javier Tusell, "The Democratic Center and Christian Democracy in the Elections of 1977 and 1979," in *Spain at the Polls, 1977, 1979, and 1982*, ed. Howard R. Penniman and Eusebio M. Mujal-León (Durham, 1985), pp. 90–94, 95–97. The newspaper *Ya*, linked to the more conservative elements of Christian Democracy, still believed in 1976 that "a great party" of the Catholic masses was possible, although it recognized the danger posed by the movement's political divisions. "Gil Robles y la democracia cristiana," July 24, 1976, in *Ya: medio siglo de historia, 1935–1985*, ed. José María García Escudero (Madrid, 1985), p. 265.

44. Cardinal Tarancón believed that only twelve bishops were committed to the idea of forming a Christian Democratic party; "the immense majority supported and approved my posture as the ideal." Quoted in Martín Descalzo, *Tarancón, el cardenal del cambio*, p. 248.

45. José A. González Casanova, "Los partidos catalanes y las iglesias," *El País*, November 25, 1976.

Tarancón's view of the necessity of neutrality on the part of the Church as the country moved towards its first free elections prevailed among his fellow bishops. Whether the hierarchy's strategy was as apolitical as the cardinal and his supporters maintained is a matter of debate. Although the bishops were far from unanimous in their opinions about specific tactics, there was a high degree of agreement on an essential point. The commitment to neutrality did not mean that they viewed all parties equally. The hierarchy's theoretical political neutrality was "a delicate sleight of hand" that allowed the bishops to question the legitimacy of parties believed hostile to Catholic values.[46] During the late summer and early autumn of 1976, Cardinal González Martín of Toledo, the leading conservative voice among the bishops, vigorously attacked Marxism, as did his more moderate colleague, Cardinal Bueno Monreal of Seville. In May 1977, another ecclesiastical moderate, Archbishop Elías Yanes, secretary of the CEE, put the question directly when he remarked, in clear allusion to the Socialist and Communist parties, "The Christian ought to exclude parties [and] programs . . . inspired by a materialist conception that carries within it denial of God and the human person."[47] Cardinal Tarancón reaffirmed his view that confessional parties were not an option for the Church, but, he argued, "the constitution of parties of Christian inspiration" was "licit, convenient," and could even be considered "necessary."[48]

The archbishop of Madrid did not indicate what parties he had in mind, but as a practical matter there was only one that fit Tarancón's prescription, the UCD of Prime Minister Suárez, a party in which many refugees from the ACNP and Catholic Action had taken refuge. Suárez took advantage of the cardinal's cue towards the end of the campaign by declaring that Spaniards had a choice between "the perspective of Christian humanism which inspires the UCD [and] . . . the materialism of the Marxist, Socialist, or Communist parties."[49] Having abandoned hopes for a unified Christian Democratic party, the country's largest Catholic daily, *Ya*, made no bones about its support for the UCD as the only option available to prevent a Socialist electoral victory.[50] Despite the disparate elements composing the UCD and organizational problems arising from its recent formation, the party rapidly acquired popularity, thanks to the prime minister's deft political talents. Given the hierarchy's fear of a Socialist party victory in the June 1977 elections and the UCD's commitment to a negotiated ecclesiastical settlement, there was no

46. Brassloff, *Religion and Politics in Spain*, p. 94.

47. *Ya*, May 7, 1977.

48. The only bishop who dissented from the official line was Alberto Iniesta, auxiliary bishop of Madrid, who defended "those Christians who believe that a certain Marxism is compatible with Christianity." Quoted in "Cuatro obispos contra el marxismo y uno a favor del socialismo," *Diario 16*, May 16, 1977.

49. Quoted in Gunther, Sani, and Shabad, *Spain after Franco*, p. 225.

50. Ibid., p. 229.

other choice for a clerical leadership concerned with protecting the Church's interests as it perceived them.

Neither Tarancón nor the bishops specifically endorsed the UCD. During the electoral campaign, they were careful to avoid a repetition of events of the early 1930s by forbidding the use of Church buildings for political meetings. A few incidents at the grass roots recalled that earlier time when a disgruntled Franciscan disrupted a Socialist meeting in a town near Ciudad Real by firing shots in the air, or when the nuns of Orense were gathered from across the city to attend a meeting of a regional Christian Democratic party.[51] But there were few such echoes of the past. Moreover, the numerous episcopal statements published during the campaign formed a confusing mix of exhortations combining appeals to Spaniards to participate in the elections as a matter of civic duty with sundry attacks on communism, socialism, capitalism, and liberalism.[52] During the campaign, a small number of bishops in the old integrist tradition even expressed distaste for political reform itself or, like the bishop of Orense, informed the faithful that "no Catholic can support candidates of the Left, because they are opposed to the Catholic creed."[53] The mixed and contradictory signals coming from the hierarchy, declared a progressive theologian and former Jesuit, José María Díez-Alegría, seemed to indicate that Catholics should vote for no party at all, despite repeated episcopal statements urging them to exercise their franchise.[54]

Given the clerical leadership's concern with defending what it perceived as the Church's vital interests, the election of a UCD government was the only option available. Progressive groups and individuals within the Church accused the hierarchy of endorsing a policy of *taranconismo* based on the cardinal's strategy of abandoning Christian Democracy in favor of an insincere political neutrality. José Luis Aranguren, a leading Catholic intellectual active in the self-criticism movement of the 1950s, criticized Tarancón for choosing to support the UCD option to the detriment of Catholics committed to the parties of the Left. This strategy, he argued, represented nothing less than a return to the Church's historic method of supporting the party that could best defend its "rights."[55] The group Christians for Social-

51. "Normas del Obispado de Tortosa," *El País*, May 4, 1977; "El obispo de Zamora prohibe la utilización de templos por los partidos," ibid., May 6, 1977; "Agresiones y coacciones contra partidos de izquierda," ibid., May 29, 1977; "Mitin del Partido Popular Gallego para monjas, en Orense," ibid., June 2, 1977.

52. "Obispos contra capitalismo, marxismo y liberalismo," *Diario 16*, May 21, 1977.

53. Bishops Guerra Campos (Cuenca), Barrachina Estevan (Orihuela-Alicante), Temiño Sáinz (Orense), and Doroteo Fernández (Badajoz) composed this group. "Los obispos tocan a rebato," *Diario 16*, May 27, 1977; quoted in Gunther, Sani, and Shabad, *Spain after Franco*, p. 228.

54. José María Díez-Alegría, "Las 'orientaciones' electorales del episcopado," *El País*, May 18, 1977.

55. José Luis Aranguren, "La Iglesia y el poder" (1977), in *La transición española*, pp. 108–10. Another critic attacked an "ecclesiastical strategy" aimed at curbing any movement within the Church "which tended toward the Left, [and] escaped from the control of 'sure doctrine.'" Santiago Sánchez Torrado, "La Iglesia, entre el ridículo y el silencio," *Diario 16*, May 16, 1977. In his memoirs, the cardinal explicitly rejected the accusation of *taranconismo*. Enrique y Tarancón, *Confesiones*, p. 10.

ism (CpS) was so irritated by the hierarchy's tactics that it urged Spaniards not to vote in the forthcoming elections.[56]

Tarancón's rejection of Christian Democracy also won him the enmity of some of its partisans, especially on the Right of the movement, who regarded him as nothing less than its "assassin."[57] Indeed, during the spring of 1977 rumors circulated in Madrid of a plot to carry out the cardinal's "defenestration" from the archbishopric of Madrid and the presidency of the CEE through a murky scheme launched, it was alleged, by disgruntled Christian Democrats, some officials of the papal curia, members of Opus Dei, and the right-wing party Alianza Popular, all of whom had reasons to oppose Tarancón's centrist policy.[58]

When bluntly asked whether his policy of political neutrality served to buttress the UCD, "a party which more or less unites a majority of Catholics and defends the Church's interests" without the confessional label possibly damaging to the Church, Tarancón replied somewhat disingenuously that he had nothing to do with the origins or development of the UCD.[59] In fact, the cardinal admired Suárez as a shrewd politician who was willing to cooperate with the hierarchy and who could get things done. Tarancón and the country's other cardinals left a meeting with Suárez early in his tenure of office impressed by the prime minister's sincerity and capacity for effective action. This is a "man who is worth more than we thought," they concluded at the end of their discussions.[60]

More than once in the past, the Spanish Church had shown its ability to accommodate itself to changing political circumstances to its advantage. Cardinal Tarancón's commitment to the creation of a democratic system was sincere. His influence as president of the CEE kept a far from united hierarchy within the limits of moderation during a critical period. But when all is said and done, he proved as shrewd an ecclesiastical politician as any in the history of modern Spanish Catholicism. He assessed the political situation correctly from a tactical point of view, identified the Church's vital interests as the hierarchy saw them, and devised a brilliant strategy for protecting those interests within the new democracy.

Tarancón's centrist policy came at a price, however. The success of the UCD in the June 1977 elections indicated that the party had won the support of Catholic

56. "Iglesia: cuestiones terrenales," *Opinión*, December 4–10, 1976, no. 9, p. 17.

57. Martín Descalzo, *Tarancón, el cardenal del cambio*, p. 252. The cardinal recalled later that he had forcefully told Christian Democratic figures who came to him to urge support for the formation of a party that he would never support such an initiative. Some of those given this blunt message received it angrily. Ibid., p. 256.

58. Ricardo de la Cierva, "La conspiración contra el cardenal," *Opinión*, March 5–11, 1977, no. 22, pp. 6–7.

59. Quoted in Martín Descalzo, *Tarancón, el cardenal del cambio*, pp. 257–58.

60. Quoted in ibid., p. 260. A recent laudatory biography of the cardinal declared, "He held Suárez in great esteem." Tarancón supported the prime minister's initiatives and supported the formation of the UCD "from the shadows." Ceferino de Blas, *Tarancón, el cardenal que coronó el rey* (Madrid, 1995), p. 24.

voters.[61] But diverse political groups such as the conservative Alianza Popular party, led by Manuel Fraga Iribarne, some frustrated Christian Democrats, and the political clan of Opus Dei viewed the ascendancy of Suárez and the tacit support it received from Tarancón and his episcopal allies as directly opposed to their interests.[62] Within the Church, a thousand priests gathered in the intransigent Sociedad Cultural Covadonga attacked the "omissions of the Spanish episcopate," which they accused of failing to halt the infiltration of leftist elements into the clergy and laity. At the other end of the spectrum, some of the Church's leading clerical intellectuals warned Tarancón against a policy that promised to "mortgage" the Church to a neo-capitalist economic system and a conservative political structure just as the bishops had done with the Franco regime in 1937.[63]

The tacit support of the UCD implied by Tarancón's policy brought a handsome return when the party formed the government that would have as its primary task the drafting of a new constitution. The terms of that fundamental document would be as important for the Church's future as the diplomatic agreements negotiated with the Holy See.

The Constitution of 1978

In the autumn of 1977, a legislative committee representing all major parties began to draft a constitutional text. The committee met behind closed doors with a view to producing a document capable of winning ready acceptance upon its presentation to parliament. The consensus strategy pursued by the Suárez cabinet and supported by the opposition parties posed another challenge for the ecclesiastical leadership. The hierarchy lacked any direct means of exerting influence over the terms of the new constitution as it was being discussed at the drafting stage in an atmosphere of near secrecy. Rumors that the committee's initial text resembled the constitution of 1931 by affirming that "the Spanish State is not confessional" alarmed the bishops, who feared the creation of a lay State on the model of the Second Republic.[64]

61. An opinion survey indicated that those who regarded themselves as "good" or "practicing" Catholics preferred the UCD (61.9 percent); those who had "positive feelings" towards the Church supported the UCD even more strongly (69.8 percent). Gunther, Sani, and Shabad, *Spain after Franco,* p. 238, Table 21.

62. Although recognizing that Fraga Iribarne was a "good Christian," Cardinal Tarancón resisted his attempts to win clerical support for Alianza Popular. Fraga "wished the support of the Church," the cardinal recalled, "because he could not ignore that with it he would have been able to acquire more force and more votes." Quoted in Martín Descalzo, *El cardenal del cambio,* p. 270. The leaders of AP were unhappy with the editorial line of *Ya,* which, following the Tarancón strategy, "was inexplicably belligerent in favor of the UCD." Quoted in Gunther, Sani, and Shabad, *Spain after Franco,* p. 229.

63. *1.000 sacerdotes españoles rompen el silencio contra las omisiones y complicidades en el campo católico* (Madrid, 1976), pp. 3–4; "Iglesia: cuestiones terrenales," p. 17.

64. Dionisio Llamazares, "Actitud de la España democrática ante la Iglesia," in *Iglesia católica y regímenes autoritarios y democráticos: experiencia española e italiana,* ed. Iván C. Ibán (Madrid, 1987), p. 188.

The Episcopal Conference's plenary assembly attempted to influence parliamentary discussions through publication of a collective statement on November 26. Although segments of the press alleged that the bishops took action because they had improperly secured a copy of the drafting committee's text, in fact the hierarchy had shown concern with the content of a new constitution as early as September.[65] At that time, the CEE's executive committee warned that "without religious and ethical orientations . . . democratic societies run the grave risk of decadence and perversion." The bishops called upon Catholic deputies to use their influence "to secure a text that favors the integral rights of the person," including "the defense of human life, the family, and the right of parents over the education of their children."[66]

In its November statement, the hierarchy developed the case more fully for including recognition of Catholic moral values in the constitution. The bishops asserted that a "Christian concept" of life deserved formal recognition because of the country's religious traditions, which, they maintained, enjoyed considerable popular support. Although endorsing the inclusion of individual and collective rights in the fundamental charter, the hierarchy declared that such rights were neither "absolute nor unlimited." The right to free expression could not be used "to justify offenses against the moral and religious . . . values of citizens." The bishops appealed for a constitution capable of providing an effective "tutelage of public morality" on the grounds that a "free people cannot be confused with what is today called . . . 'the permissive society.'" The hierarchy turned again to the so-called sociological argument to justify its demands. It warned that if the new constitution contained "equivocal formulations" capable of secularist interpretations, it would not provide "sufficient response to the religious reality of Spaniards" given the "unquestionable weight of Catholicism" in the country.[67]

The episcopal statement of November 26 attempted to balance the hierarchy's commitment to a pluralistic, democratic society with its desire to retain as much control as possible over public morality. This attempt to secure the best of all possible worlds proved ineffective and controversial. Journalistic opinion ranging from the *Cuadernos para el Diálogo*, to which progressive Catholic intellectuals frequently contributed, through left-wing magazines such as *Triunfo* reproached the

65. The draft text was completed on November 17. Four days later, Cardinal Tarancón addressed the CEE's plenary assembly. Whether the cardinal possessed a copy of the text is unclear, but his remarks on the constitution indicated that he was fully aware of what it contained. Antonio Trabajo, "El tema religioso en la constitución española de 1978," *XX Siglos* (1995), vol. 6, no. 24, p. 88.

66. "Ante la actual situación española," September 22, 1977, in *Documentos de la Conferencia Episcopal Española*, pp. 437, 438. The accusation that the bishops had improperly come into possession of the drafting committee's text has been firmly denied, however. Jesús Iribarren, *Papeles y memorias: medio siglo de relaciones Iglesia-Estado en España, 1936–1986* (Madrid, 1992), p. 374.

67. "Los valores morales y religiosos ante la Constitución," November 26, 1977, in *Documentos de la Conferencia Episcopal Española*, pp. 441, 442, 443, 445.

bishops for interfering in a constitutional process entrusted to the elected representatives of the people.[68] Allegations surfaced that machinations on the part of Cardinal Tarancón and the Vatican had inspired the bishops' statement. The bishops, declared one commentator, were seeking "a Constitution for the Catholic majority, not a Constitution for all Spaniards."[69] Episcopal intervention also had political repercussions. Felipe González, leader of the substantial Socialist minority in parliament, declared, "We do not want to participate in the synod of bishops . . . and we would wish that the bishops likewise do not participate in the writing of the constitution."[70] But there is no evidence that the hierarchy was attempting anything more than a lobbying effort to bring the pressure of Catholic opinion to bear on the constitutional discussions.

In any event, the elaboration of a final constitutional text owed more to the consensus-driven nature of the political process than to ecclesiastical intervention. The clauses dealing with religion and the Church attempted to strike a compromise between the idea of a religiously neutral lay State on the model of the French Republic and the concept of a State that regarded religion more positively, by affirming its contribution to society and according all religious confessions a constitutionally recognized juridical status beyond simple recognition of the right to association available to all Spaniards. This model was based on the constitutional arrangements of the Federal Republic of Germany, which granted religious confessions the special status of "corporations of public law."[71] Indeed, the final version of the 1978 constitutional text replaced the wording of the first draft that had so distressed the bishops—"The Spanish State is not confessional"—with a more flexible formula taken almost literally from the earlier constitution of the Weimar Republic: "No confession will have a State character" (Article 16).[72]

The Spanish constitution did not go as far as the German model by granting the churches special juridical status. But it departed from the Second Republic's constitution by affirming that "The public powers will take into account the religious beliefs of Spanish society and as a result will maintain relations of cooperation with the Catholic Church and other confessions" (Article 16, clause 3).[73] The Church

68. Iribarren, *Papeles y memorias*, pp. 374–76; Trabajo, "El tema religioso en la constitución española de 1978," pp. 90–92.

69. Quoted in Iribarren, *Papeles y memorias*, p. 375.

70. Quoted in James M. Markham, "Dispute Erupts in Spain over Move to Separate Church and State," *New York Times*, December 1, 1977.

71. Llamazares, "Actitud de la España democrática ante la Iglesia," pp. 187–88.

72. Ibid., p. 189; Laura and Ramón Tamames, *Introducción a la constitución española* (5th ed., Madrid, 1991), p. 36. The UCD abandoned its position on the wording of the original draft in favor of the formula eventually adopted because it feared that it would lose right-wing votes to the Alianza Popular party. Brassloff, *Religion and Politics in Spain*, pp. 96–97.

73. Tamames, *Introducción a la constitución española*, p. 36. The specific mention of the Catholic Church in the revised text was due to the intervention of the UCD, supported by the Alianza Popular. Trabajo, "El tema religioso en la constitución española de 1978," pp. 97–98.

welcomed this specific constitutional acknowledgment and implied acceptance of the so-called sociological argument often advanced by the hierarchy.[74] No other religious group was mentioned by name. Socialist representatives on the drafting committee saw clause 3 as a vehicle for introducing "covert confessionality" into the constitution and voted against it. Communist deputies supported it as a means of avoiding a revival of divisive conflict damaging to the stability of democratic institutions.[75] In fact, the vague wording of Article 16 left it open to different interpretations that later would generate controversy between the hierarchy and the Socialist government that took power in 1982.

Article 27 dealt with the sensitive issue of education. It satisfied one of the Church's demands by recognizing the right of parents to secure the "religious and moral education" of their children, although there were no specific details about how this objective would be realized. It also recognized the right of individuals and groups to maintain and establish schools. The article allowed that private schools could receive official subsidies but only if they met certain conditions, including the participation of parents, students, and teachers in their administration, a condition unpalatable to the religious orders, who were the legal proprietors of the vast majority of Church schools. On the crucial question of the level of government financial support for private schools, Article 27 said little beyond ambiguously indicating that some form of assistance would be available, subject to later enabling legislation.[76]

The final text failed to meet the hierarchy's demands for the incorporation of Catholic moral values into the Constitution. Article 32 on marriage did not end the prohibition on divorce in effect since the beginning of the Franco era, but it left the door open to its introduction by declaring that the State possessed the legislative right to regulate "forms of matrimony," including the legal instruments necessary to deal with cases of separation and marriage dissolution. Although Article 39, dealing with the protection of the family, recognized the family unit as the foundation of society, the article's terms focused primarily on defending the right of minors to adequate support from their parents. There was no ringing endorsement of the family as the embodiment of Catholic moral values.[77]

On balance, the ecclesiastical leadership fared less well in its efforts to enshrine constitutionally what it perceived as the Church's vital interests than the Vatican achieved through diplomatic negotiations. The 1978 constitution rested on compromise between the country's political parties. As a result, its terms on matters af-

74. Archbishop Yanes of Zaragoza observed that the constitution mentioned political parties, labor unions, and professional associations. To have ignored the Church given its importance in the country, he argued, would make no sense. Juan María Laboa, *Iglesia y religión en las constituciones españolas* (Madrid, 1981), p. 102.

75. Ibid., pp. 101, 102–3.

76. Tamames, *Introducción a la constitución española*, p. 51.

77. Ibid., pp. 62, 71–72.

fecting religion and the Church were rarely specific save on the question of religious liberty. The Church received constitutional acknowledgment, a general and vague promise of future cooperation from the State, and recognition of the legitimacy of its school system. The question of how much financial support Church schools would receive remained unresolved. Nor did the constitution meet clerical expectations as far as public morality was concerned.

When all is said and done, the constitution followed an ambiguous model in which Church and State were "not quite separate," as a journalist of the time shrewdly observed.[78] Progressive theologians took a similar line, arguing that the constitution's "hybrid formula" gave the Church a privileged status through a legal back door.[79] Given the consensus nature of the constitutional process, the Church probably did as well as political reality allowed. But the hierarchy was divided about the public stance the bishops should take with respect to the constitution and the national referendum called to approve it. Although Cardinal Tarancón entertained reservations because of the presence of "many ambiguous and confused formulas" in the final text, he showed his usual keen political sense by urging his episcopal colleagues to view the constitution positively.[80] His efforts to secure a strong episcopal endorsement of the constitution were opposed by a minority of bishops led by Cardinal Marcelo González Martín.

As a result, the Episcopal Conference's executive committee watered down a first draft of a public statement in favor of a weaker declaration that balanced criticism of the "ambiguities, omissions, or dangerous formulas" of certain articles with recognition of the "undeniable intrinsic values" contained in the constitution as a whole. The statement suggested indirectly that Catholics should vote for the constitution as a vehicle for civic peace and "to avoid more grave alternatives."[81] But the bishops were unwilling to give an explicit endorsement on the grounds that the Church could not tell citizens how to vote. It is more likely that divisions within the hierarchy lay behind this tepid approach.

Tarancón and his episcopal allies modified their position because they wished the hierarchy to present a united front to the country. We were willing to accept a "less vibrant" statement, he later recalled, rather than risk "a very enthusiastic text" opposed by a minority of bishops.[82] Tarancón also hoped that the weaker statement finally published would restrain dissenting bishops from publicly ex-

78. James F. Markham, "Spanish Church, State: Not Quite Separate," *New York Times*, November 12, 1978.

79. They also argued that the hierarchy's acceptance of this model of civil-ecclesiastical relations indicated that the bishops did not fully accept the essential characteristics of a modern, non-confessional State. Fernando Urbina and Antonio Duato, "Cristianos en una sociedad pluralista," *Iglesia Viva* (1979), vol. 80–81, p. 154.

80. Quoted in Martín Descalzo, *Tarancón, el cardenal del cambio*, p. 251.

81. "Nota sobre el referéndum constitucional," September 28, 1978, in *Documentos de la Conferencia Episcopal Española*, pp. 17, 18.

82. Quoted in Martín Descalzo, *Tarancón, el cardenal del cambio*, p. 251.

pressing their views. This assumption proved mistaken. On November 28, 1978, Cardinal González Martín published a controversial pastoral letter dealing with the constitution. Reaction to the cardinal's intervention generated a heated debate similar in some respects to that unleashed in the spring of 1931 by Cardinal Segura at the time of the Second Republic's proclamation.

The situation in 1978 was, of course, different from that of 1931. A majority of bishops favored Tarancón's moderate strategy. Sixty of the eighty prelates attending the autumn plenary assembly of the CEE opposed González Martín's attempt to draft a more conservative statement on the constitution. The archbishop of Toledo enjoyed the support of only eight of his fellow bishops.[83] But the cardinal's pastoral letter generated controversy for two reasons. First, although the archbishopric of Toledo had lost its traditional leadership of the Spanish Church upon creation of the Episcopal Conference in 1966, the archdiocese's incumbent remained in possession of the honorific title of primate. His pronouncements enjoyed, therefore, a measure of prestige. Second, González Martín was generally recognized as the leader of the conservative faction within the hierarchy.

The cardinal brought certain strengths to this role. An able polemicist, he possessed sufficient flexibility to avoid identifying himself as an intransigent opponent of political change in the style of Bishop Guerra Campos. But he disagreed with the moderate compromise strategy pursued by Tarancón and his supporters. The Church, he believed, must take a tougher line to secure its interests within a democratic Spain. He was less concerned with the form and content of political institutions than with assuring the incorporation of Catholic moral values into the constitution. He was not prepared to follow the example of the majority of his fellow bishops, who were willing to subordinate their reservations to the larger objective of securing a new civil order within which the Church could function effectively.

The cardinal's pastoral letter fired a broadside at the constitution and, by implication, at clergy and politicians who supported it. The constitution failed to mention the name of God and was, therefore, "agnostic." In a "nation of the baptized," it took a position of neutrality on Christian values. There was no reference to divine and natural law. The "moral orientation of the law" was left to the mercy of whatever government was in power. In a veiled attack on the Socialist party, the cardinal foresaw "legal aggressions against the inalienable rights of man" on the part of certain "parliamentary forces" if they came to power. The constitution failed to guarantee "the moral values of the family" or to provide the means to combat divorce, the use of contraceptives, sexual promiscuity, and abortion. For a Christian

83. "Enfrentamiento entre el Episcopado," *El País*, November 30, 1978. The dissenting bishops were Archbishop García de Sierra (Burgos), Bishops Peralta (Vitoria), Castán (Sigüenza), Guerra Campos (Cuenca), Franco (Tenerife), Temiño (Orense), Mansilla (Ciudad Rodrigo), and Barrachina (Orihuela-Alicante).

people, the constitution would produce "disastrous consequences." González Martín refrained from directly telling Catholics to vote against the constitution in the forthcoming referendum, but taken as a whole, his statement left no doubt as to how those inspired by a "Christian conscience" should act.[84]

The cardinal's statement threw a bombshell into the delicate process of consensus building to which the political parties and a majority of the hierarchy were committed. Angry press editorials accused González Martín of imitating Cardinal Gomá, author of the hierarchy's controversial 1937 Collective Letter in support of Franco, while representatives of the UCD and the Socialist party rejected the pastoral letter as an unwarranted and dangerous interference in politics.[85] The cardinal's intervention, declared the Madrid newspaper *El País*, would spread division in the country and revive old passions about clerical meddling in politics.[86] González Martín received expressions of support indirectly from Manuel Fraga Iribarne, leader of the rightist Alianza Popular party, and directly from Franco's former minister and prominent member of Opus Dei Laureano López Rodó, who praised the "judicious points" made by the pastoral letter.[87]

Within the Church, progressive groups and theologians objected strongly to the pastoral letter. The faithful's freedom to vote as they chose, the association of Popular Christian Communities of Madrid declared bluntly, did not arise from "a concession of the bishops." Theologians at the pontifical universities of Salamanca and Comillas accused the cardinal of a "*political act*" that ignored the positive aspects of the constitution and promoted "serious equivocation" by using religion as a pretext to inspire opposition to the nation's charter.[88]

Members of the hierarchy also entered the fray, though Cardinal Tarancón remained curiously silent. Archbishop Gabino Díaz Merchán of Oviedo asserted that the constitution contained "very estimable values from a Christian perspective," while Bishop Ramón Echarren of Las Palmas declared, "In no way can an affirmative vote [for the constitution] be interpreted as opposed to Christian morality."[89] Catholic right-wing extremists viewed these statements with outright hostility. In Barcelona, they moved through the city's parish churches and seized ten thousand

84. "Pastoral del primado sobre el referéndum," November 28, 1978. *ABC*, November 29, 1978.

85. "Los escrúpulos del cardenal," *Diario 16*, November 30, 1978; "Preocupación entre las fuerzas democráticas por la postura del primado," *El País*, November 30, 1978. The minister of the interior in the UCD government, Rodolfo Martín Villa, declared in a press conference, "as a practicing Catholic that this is a constitution that can be voted for affirmatively." "La Iglesia progresista, contra el primado," *Diario 16*, November 30, 1978; "El Gobierno, disgustado por la pastoral de González Martín," *Diario 16*, November 30, 1978.

86. "La política del cardenal primado," *El País*, November 30, 1978.

87. "La Iglesia progresista, contra el primado," *Diario 16*, November 30, 1978.

88. "El cardenal de Toledo matiza su oposición a la Constitución," *El País*, December 1, 1978. A well-known progressive theologian, Olegario González de Cardenal, declared that the constitution did not contradict any of the "essential principles" of Christianity. "La Iglesia progresista, contra el primado," *Diario 16*, November 30, 1978.

89. Ibid.

copies of a diocesan newsletter supporting the constitution. In a sign of protest, they piled them on the archbishop's doorstep. Blas Piñar, leader of the extreme right-wing Fuerza Nueva party, minced no words when he attacked members of the Episcopal Conference as "traitors" for their stance on the constitution.[90]

Controversy over the archbishop of Toledo's pastoral letter raged for a brief period. But the statement produced no serious political repercussions, despite some exaggerated commentary suggesting that the country faced a return to the bitter civil-ecclesiastical conflicts characteristic of the Second Republic. Even the opposition press and political parties recognized that González Martín represented a small minority of bishops.[91] It was equally clear that the day was long past when an episcopal pronouncement could influence the Catholic electorate one way or the other. Indeed, on December 6, Catholic voters overwhelmingly approved the new constitution.

The dispute over González Martín's statement was, however, something more than the proverbial tempest in a teapot. The bishops opposed to the cardinal primate realized that they had few cards to play in the constitutional game and could only trust the UCD government's influence to produce a moderate text as far as the Church's interests were concerned. Their differences with the archbishop of Toledo over the constitution's failure to incorporate Catholic moral standards were differences more of degree than of substance. The hierarchy still held to the sociological argument that because Spaniards in their vast majority still identified themselves as Catholics, the constitution should reflect their values.

These concerns took on greater urgency from the ecclesiastical leadership's perspective in view of what it saw as the dissolving moral effects of secularization, which it associated with economic development and the social dislocation that accompanied it.[92] The cardinal primate stressed the danger to Catholic moral values more spectacularly than other bishops. But others were equally apprehensive about the survival of Catholic Spain based on a highly idealized image of what it had been in the past. However exaggerated its apocalyptic rhetoric, the cardinal's pastoral letter threw into sharp relief the tension, perhaps even contradiction, between the Church's commitment to a pluralistic society and its desire to enforce Catholic morality through democratic institutions. At one level, the hierarchy

90. "El cardenal Jubany reafirmará el 'sí,'" *Diario 16*, November 30, 1978; *Diario 16*, November 26, 1978.

91. In its editorial on the question, *El País*, generally sympathetic to the Socialist party, took pains to point out that the status of primate of the Spanish Church was purely honorific and that the archbishop of Toledo no longer possessed the leadership of the hierarchy. The bishops supporting him formed a "small" minority, many of whom "cooperated willingly with the old regime." "La política del cardenal primado," *El País*, November 30, 1978.

92. Even while the Arias Navarro government was in office and official controls over public morality were still in place, the plenary assembly of the CEE lamented "a systematic invasion of pure eroticism or degrading pornography" into the country. "Nota sobre la invasión erotizante y pornográfica," February 28, 1976. *Documentos de la Conferencia Episcopal Española*, p. 382.

managed to defend the Church's interests within the new political order remarkably well, but there remained even among moderate bishops a strong undercurrent of frustration over the constitution's shortcomings in the area of public morality. The controversy provoked by González Martín foreshadowed a series of conflicts that would trouble civil-ecclesiastical relations, particularly after the Socialist party began to govern the country.

The national referendum approving the constitution brought to an end the constituent phase of the period of transition. The diplomatic agreements with the Vatican and those clauses in the constitution affecting the Church redefined its place within a pluralistic democracy. But they left a gray area on a number of issues, such as funding for Church schools and the government's role in the control of public morality, that were certain to produce future conflict. These struggles would be fought out in the arena of public opinion and the normal legislative process of a democratic system.

CHAPTER XXII

DEFENSE OF CATHOLIC SPAIN, 1979–1998

As the constituent period drew to a close, Cardinal Tarancón observed with characteristic realism that the Church's "disengagement from the political power has not been easy." Believing that the process was far from over, the cardinal foresaw difficulties if clergy and laity failed to remove "the weight of the past" exemplified by the Church's reliance on "the political arm to preach the gospel."[1] The president of the Episcopal Conference correctly assessed the difficulties faced by the Church as it sought balance between its commitment to democracy and its historic inclination to defend ecclesiastical interests with the civil power's support. Despite reservations about the constitution, the hierarchy remained comfortable with a UCD government that was doing its best to meet the Church's concerns, especially in education and clerical finances, although conflict developed over the legalization of divorce and the attitude of the Basque bishops towards the region's resurgent nationalism.

The PSOE's electoral victory in October 1982 changed the rules of the game. Civil-ecclesiastical relations became conflictive, although early in its mandate, the government announced its intention to observe the five *acuerdos* signed by its predecessor with the Vatican and to seek the "definitive pacification" of historic disputes between Church and State.[2] This optimism was premature. Legislation decriminalizing abortion, the imposition of stricter controls over Church schools and their financing, and protracted negotiations over subsidies for clerical salaries

1. *Ya*, January 18, 1979.

2. Interview with Gustavo Suárez Pertierra, director-general of religious affairs, "Relaciones Iglesia-Estado," *Ya*, February 15, 1983.

created difficulties that for a time evoked memories of conflicts during the Second Republic.

In the midst of periodic battles, the Church's defenders compared the government's legislative program to the Republic's between 1931 and 1933. As debate raged over a proposal to decriminalize abortion in early 1983, *Ya*, the country's leading Catholic newspaper, accused the PSOE of seeking "to bother, aggravate, [and] insult from power, like an ill wind carrying an echo of the spirit of revenge that has always been its sin."[3] But neither the government nor the ecclesiastical leadership wished a return to the politics of extreme confrontation that had brought the Church into conflict with the Republic. The Socialists pursued a more openly secularist policy and took a tougher line on concessions towards the Church than did the UCD. But the PSOE's commitment to a purely lay State on the model of the Republic fell by the wayside when the party accepted the 1970s *acuerdos* and the 1978 constitution.

The government accepted the terms of the ecclesiastical settlement arranged by its predecessor, though it interpreted those terms more narrowly. Nor did the cabinet have any stomach for reviving the intense divisions over religious matters characteristic of the Republic. The hierarchy knew that it had few cards to play in view of the PSOE's parliamentary majority and the prospect that the party would remain in power for years. As a result, relations between Church and State followed a rocky road of conflict over specific issues, but most were resolved through negotiations after periods of rhetorical outburst by both sides.

The policy of wary accommodation between the civil and ecclesiastical authorities did not extend to moral standards. The concerns expressed by the hierarchy during the period of transition about incorporating Catholic values into the constitution and general legislation developed into a powerful source of friction between the Church and the PSOE government. The tensions generated by conflicts over morality were not new, but they became stronger because of changes within the Catholic Church after the succession of John Paul II to the papacy in 1978. Using the powers of free episcopal appointment established by the *acuerdo* of 1976, the pope named, on the whole, bishops of distinctly conservative views, who blamed official policies for the development of a morally loose society. For the hierarchy of the 1980s and early 1990s, evident slippage in religious practice and the advance of sexual permissiveness signified a national moral crisis of disturbing proportions.

The resolution of civil-ecclesiastical conflicts envisioned by the government failed to occur, beyond a pragmatic recognition by Church and State that neither would profit from a break in relations. The hierarchy adopted a defensive strategy to secure its interests within the political process as best it could. At the same time,

3. "Manchado de sangre," *Ya*, February 3, 1983.

it promoted its historic claim to be the nation's moral guide in a time when the emergence of a consumer society and secular values emphasizing the autonomy of the individual undermined ecclesiastical authority over moral questions. The expectations of the 1970s that the Church would develop new and dynamic methods to re-evangelize the country within a framework of cooperation with the civil power proved illusory. The hierarchy returned to a modified version of an older tradition present since the first conflicts with liberalism, the idea of a defensive bastion surrounded by social, political, and cultural forces opposed to the realization of its religious mission.

A Period of Respite, 1979–1982

After the constitution's approval, the UCD government continued its benign policies towards the Church. In early 1979, the minister of justice rejected a proposal from an official legal commission recommending the limited decriminalization of abortion.[4] The prospect of changes to legislation concerning abortion had long troubled a hierarchy fearful of a future Socialist government. As the general elections of March 1979 approached, the bishops again expressed indirect support for the UCD by warning Catholic voters against supporting parties with programs opposed to "religious values" and "fundamental human rights." The hierarchy cited proposals to legalize abortion contained in some political platforms, an allusion to the PSOE, although the party was not mentioned by name. The bishops informed the faithful that they were obliged in conscience to cast their votes in a way compatible "with their faith."[5] During the campaign, Prime Minister Suárez used the abortion issue effectively in a strategy designed to persuade voters that the PSOE was committed to an extremist program.[6]

The electoral success of the UCD calmed the hierarchy's apprehensions. With its hold on power confirmed, the government dealt with an immediate concern of the Church by passing enabling legislation on education. The education law of 1980 (LOECE) did not interfere with the continuation of generous subsidies to Church schools with few fiscal controls.[7] But the law provoked strong Socialist criticism for subordinating the academic freedom of teachers and students to the *ideario* of the legal proprietors of educational establishments, in the case of Church

4. The proposal called for the removal of criminal penalties for doctors and for women having abortions during the first twelve weeks of pregnancy where there was danger to the life of the mother or the pregnancy resulted from rape. *Ya*, January 23, 1979.

5. "La responsabilidad moral del voto," February 8, 1979, in *Documentos de la Conferencia Episcopal Española, 1965–1983*, ed. Jesús Iribarren (Madrid, 1984), p. 519. This was a document of the CEE's executive committee.

6. Javier Tusell, "The Democratic Center and Christian Democracy in the Elections of 1977 and 1979," in *Spain at the Polls, 1977, 1979, and 1982*, ed. Howard R. Penniman and Eusebio M. Mujal-León (Durham, 1985), p. 124.

7. The law's full title was Ley Orgánica del Estatuto de Centros Escolares.

schools, the religious orders, and by failing to allow parents, teachers, and students a significant administrative role in institutions financed by public funds.[8] The LOECE required schools receiving subsidies to meet government standards, particularly on accessibility, through a system of contracts with the Ministry of Education. Although irritated by this provision, the Church had little cause for complaint. Church schools retained a high degree of administrative, financial, and ideological autonomy in a religious educational system funded largely by the public treasury.

Relations between the Church and the UCD government followed a generally smooth course. But they were not free of controversy, especially during 1981, when conflict arose over the hierarchy's tardy response to an attempted coup d'état on February 23, the introduction of divorce legislation, and the increasingly nationalistic attitude of the bishops of the Basque dioceses.

As internal strains began to undermine the fragile unity of the UCD in 1981, Prime Minister Suárez announced his resignation. On February 23, parliament assembled to approve the appointment of Leopoldo Calvo Sotelo as his successor. The sitting was disrupted by an invasion of Civil Guards, who held the cabinet and deputies prisoner for nearly twenty-four hours. As later investigation proved, this spectacular intervention sought to provoke a general military rising against the democratic system. At the very moment that armed men rushed into the congress of deputies, the plenary assembly of the Episcopal Conference was in session. The bishops knew no more of what was happening than their fellow citizens did. The hierarchy's immediate reaction was to issue a statement on the evening of the 23rd that simply urged Spaniards to pray.[9] Whether they were being asked to pray for the failure or success of the coup was unclear in what was at best an ambiguous declaration. But on the following day, the assembly communicated its support for the established order to King Juan Carlos I and expressed solidarity with the ministers and deputies held prisoner in the congress of deputies.[10] On February 28, the bishops published a longer statement defending "constitutional normality" and censuring the "grave and reprobate events" that had threatened civil peace.[11]

The hierarchy went beyond a simple declaration of support for democracy and the constitution, however. The bishops muddied the waters by suggesting that while the coup attempt deserved condemnation, it arose as a response to "diffuse disenchantment" with the failures of the political system and "systematic disinterest" in the public good that demanded measures to revive "confidence in institu-

8. *Ley Orgánica del Derecho a la Educación y disposiciones reglamentarias* (Madrid, 1987), preamble; p. 13.

9. José Luis Martín Descalzo, *Tarancón, el cardenal del cambio* (Barcelona, 1982), p. 249.

10. "Comunicado sobre el intento de golpe militar y telegrama al Rey," February 24, 1981, in *Documentos de la Conferencia Episcopal Española*, pp. 615–16.

11. "Amenaza a la normalidad constitucional. Llamada a la esperanza," February 28, 1981, in ibid., p. 616.

tions."[12] The implication that politicians had brought this unfortunate turn of events upon themselves bore little relation to sordid reality. The coup attempt was the work of a minority of disgruntled military men. Their intervention had nothing to do with the kind of general crisis in civic institutions and morale described by the bishops.

Episcopal reaction to the events of "23-F" produced criticism of the ambiguous initial statement and of the five-day delay between the coup attempt and the full declaration of the 28th. Did these events suggest that in a critical moment the bishops entertained doubts about the democratic system sufficient to prevent a quick and decisive statement in its defense? Given the hierarchy's aversion to political adventurism and the dominance of ecclesiastical moderates in its ranks, there is no reason to doubt Cardinal Tarancón's interpretation that the confusing circumstances of the night of February 23 accounted for the initial declaration, which even he admitted was not "a very happy" one. The cardinal believed that the "immense majority" of his colleagues would have rejected the coup had it been successful, although he also admitted that some bishops were, if not "hostile" towards democracy, at least "troubled" by it.[13] The statement of the 28th suggests that these concerns were strong enough to prevent the kind of vigorous and unequivocal defense of the democratic system demanded by the circumstances.

Since 1976, the hierarchy had viewed with concern the possibility of legislation allowing divorce. In twentieth-century Spain, divorce had been permitted only during the Second Republic. The Franco regime abolished divorce, but by the time of the general's death, public opinion had shifted dramatically in its favor.[14] Support for a divorce law figured in the Socialist program and enjoyed support among liberal and social democratic groups, who saw it as necessary for the development of a pluralistic society on the Western European model. The issue also generated tension within the UCD. Although refugees from the "Catholic family" of the Franco era and Christian Democracy exercised significant influence within the party, the UCD formed a disparate ideological coalition that included some liberals and Social Democrats who viewed the introduction of divorce as desirable and inevitable.[15]

12. Ibid., p. 617.

13. Quoted in Martín Descalzo, *Tarancón, el cardenal del cambio,* p. 250. Bishop Ramón Echarren provides a somewhat different interpretation. He maintains that on the evening of the attempted coup d'état and during the following days, "no bishop spoke against democracy and in favor of the coup." "El Cardenal Tarancón, presidente de la Conferencia Episcopal," in S. Grisolía et al., *Homenaje al Cardenal Enrique y Tarancón* (Valencia, 1997), p. 212. Archbishop Díaz Merchán, the newly elected president of the CEE, observed that on the night of the attempted coup d'état, the bishops did not believe that democracy was endangered. They assumed that a madman had entered the congress of deputies. Brassloff has correctly observed that the bishops' attitude "has never been fully clarified." Audrey Brassloff, *Religion and Politics in Spain: The Spanish Church in Transition, 1962–1996* (London and New York, 1998), p. 107.

14. A survey of 1975 indicated that 71.8 percent of Spaniards favored legislation allowing divorce. *Diario 16,* December 1, 1976.

15. Rafael Díaz-Salazar, *El capital simbólico: estructura social, política y religion en España* (Madrid, 1988), p. 75.

In 1976, the strong support for a divorce law expressed by the public led to predictions that it would be introduced within the year.[16] Faced with the prospect of provoking controversy with the hierarchy, the Suárez government preferred to put the question aside and avoided its inclusion in the 1978 constitution.[17] The appointment of Francisco Fernández Ordóñez, a respected politician of pronounced Social Democratic views, to the Ministry of Justice in 1980 accelerated preparation of the necessary legislation despite the dissatisfaction of the UCD's more conservative members. They were unable to prevent Prime Minister Calvo Sotelo from proceeding with legislation that the government now regarded as necessary.[18]

During the spring of 1981, presentation of the divorce law to parliament provoked a storm of public debate. The legislation proposed to grant Spaniards a right enjoyed by citizens in every Western European country save the Republic of Ireland and end the social ills created by thousands of separated couples living in legally ambiguous relationships because of the prohibition on divorce. Although progressive clerical critics of the damaging effects of this situation, which had existed even in the days of National Catholicism, argued that divorce was necessary to avoid worse social evils, the hierarchy and the Catholic press surged to the attack.[19]

That the bishops objected to the legislation was understandable, given the Church's historic opposition to divorce. Their firm and sometimes extreme opposition to the divorce law suggests that when push came to shove, the Church fell back on its historic strategy of insisting that legislation should reflect Catholic moral values, despite constitutional recognition of Spanish society's pluralistic character. In a campaign against the legislation, the hierarchy attempted to thread an ideological needle by maintaining that within a democratic and nonconfessional State its opposition was based on the needs of the common good and respect for human rights.[20] The bishops refrained from resorting to the sociologi-

16. "El divorcio podría ser una realidad dentro de un año," *Diario 16*, December 1, 1976.

17. During 1977, the bishops and the Catholic press commented incessantly on the evil of divorce as a threat to family stability. See, for example, a survey of episcopal statements on the question, "El matrimonio es indisoluble," *Ya*, May 5, 1977.

18. José Manuel Cuenca Toribio, *Relaciones Iglesia-Estado en la España contemporánea, 1833–1985* (Madrid, 1985), pp. 143–47.

19. In 1976, a clerical authority on marriage questions, Father Antonio Aradillas, argued that the right to divorce was a civil right found in civilized societies. The Church, he believed, should not oppose its introduction for this reason and should concentrate its energies on educating Catholic couples on the value of a lifelong commitment to their marriages. "Antonio Aradillas: 'el divorcio no es politizable,'" *El País*, November 27, 1976. The hierarchy had modified its position, however, to the extent that it was willing to tolerate, albeit reluctantly, the original draft of the divorce legislation, which allowed a judge to refuse a divorce if it could harm either the children or one of the parties. Fernández Ordóñez dropped this clause in the legislation's final version, which for all practical purposes permitted divorce by mutual consent, thereby provoking intense ecclesiastical opposition. Brassloff, *Religion and Politics in Spain*, p. 107, note 31, p. 161.

20. "Sobre regulación del matrimonio en el Código Civil," February 3, 1981, in *Documentos de la Conferencia Episcopal Española*, p. 613. This document was the work of the CEE's executive committee.

cal argument that they had often used to justify the Church's claims during the period of transition. The thesis that Spaniards identified themselves as Catholics and that, as a result, legislation should reflect their values lacked credibility in view of opinion surveys showing massive public support for the divorce law. The hierarchy's lobbying campaign bore no fruit, as parliament approved the legislation, although a minority of UCD deputies opposed it in the final vote.

During the spring of 1981, tensions between the civil and ecclesiastical authorities also developed over the persistent question of Basque nationalism. The UCD government inherited the problem of revolutionary terrorism promoted by the ETA organization. The pattern of assassinations followed by indiscriminate police repression characteristic of the Franco era continued into the new regime, though the 1978 constitution provided a mechanism for creating limited autonomy in the Basque Provinces and other regions. This concession failed to satisfy ETA militants committed to complete independence and social revolution. It also proved difficult for the government to moderate the repressive tactics of police and military forces still dominated by personnel of the Franco regime.

The dictatorship had failed to undermine the historic support of the Basque clergy for autonomist aspirations other than through the device of securing the appointment of local bishops, who were expected to restrain nationalist zeal among their priests. This tactic did not always work, as the Añoveros case revealed in 1974. After 1976, the pope used his newly acquired power of free appointment to name native Basques to head the dioceses of Vitoria, Bilbao, and San Sebastián. The attitude of these prelates towards Basque aspirations was by no means uniform. Bishop Luis María Larrea Legarreta, named to succeed Añoveros in 1979, was viewed as too moderate by the Partido Nacionalista Vasco (PNV), the historic party of Basque nationalists. José María Larrauri Lafuente, appointed to Vitoria in the same year, fell into the same category. José María Setién Alberro, who succeeded to the bishopric of San Sebastián in 1980, was more closely identified with support for Basque nationalism. The Franco regime objected strongly to the Vatican upon his appointment as auxiliary bishop of the diocese in 1972 on precisely these grounds. Auxiliary Bishop José María Uriarte Goiricelaya of Bilbao, a theological conservative who refused to support the controversial occupation of the Derio seminary during the 1960s, maintained close contacts with the PNV, to the point that his critics accused him of being a member in all but name.[21]

The remaking of the Basque hierarchy during the late 1970s represented a revolution of sorts for the region's Church. Appointment of native Basques bridged the historic chasm between bishops and priests that had existed since the creation of the Vitoria diocese in 1861, except for the example of Bishop Múgica during the 1930s. The new bishops encouraged the widespread use of the Basque language in

21. "Los cuatro pastores," *Cambio 16,* April 13, 1981, no. 489, pp. 23–26.

liturgical ceremonies and campaigns of religious propaganda. The existence of a native hierarchy also made possible a more coherent response to the political malaise gripping a region where civil peace was constantly disrupted by terrorism and repression.

After 1976, the Basque Church faced a more complex political situation than had its predecessor of the 1930s, when the lower clergy gave powerful support to the PNV, the party historically associated with the quest for autonomy by a Catholic people for whom religion and a distinctive political identity appeared one and the same. During the Franco era, industrialization and waves of immigration from elsewhere in the country undermined the PNV's old monopoly. In the June 1977 elections, the party came in second to the PSOE in the popular vote.[22] Although the region's principal parties, including the UCD, agreed on the general necessity for autonomy, political fragmentation made a consensus resolution difficult to achieve. Finally, over this unstable mix, there loomed the unsettling effects of terrorist violence and police repression.

On more than one occasion, the bishops of the Basque dioceses condemned ETA terrorism. By the late 1970s, the new Basque hierarchy began to raise the question of repression by the police and the Civil Guard as a contributing factor to the cycle of violence. After serious disturbances in San Sebastián in March 1977 in which two ETA militants were killed by the Civil Guard, Bishop Jacinto Argaya and Auxiliary Bishop Setién demanded a judicial inquiry and criticized the "Forces of Order" for engaging in actions that went beyond "legitimate defense" to include the "elimination of human persons" by those responsible for assuring "the integrity of citizens."[23] This statement was read at the funeral of the ETA members in a ceremony that took on the character of a political demonstration by the organization's supporters. The episcopal intervention angered the minister of the interior (Gobernación), Rodolfo Martín Villa, who wrote immediately to Argaya rejecting the accusations against the government and the Civil Guard as unwarranted.[24]

The conflict between the prelates of San Sebastián and the government was the first in a series of disputes between the Basque bishops and the government that continued long after the UCD lost power. If the 1977 controversy was limited to a single diocese, the 1981 pastoral letter of the region's four bishops, following another round of ETA violence and police repression, attempted to identify the Basque hierarchy more fully with the nationalist cause. The bishops condemned terrorist violence and the ETA's revolutionary program, but they resurrected the old ideal of a Catholic Basque people who could realize their just aspirations of faith and identity only through the achievement of an autonomy far more extensive than

22. John Coverdale, "The Elections in the Basque Country," in *Spain at the Polls, 1977, 1979, and 1982*, p. 236.

23. The full text of the statement was published in *El País*, March 12, 1977.

24. "Martín Villa rechaza las veladas acusaciones de los obispos," *Diario 16*, March 12, 1977.

that granted by the 1978 constitution. They echoed the line of an earlier generation of priests by arguing that the national political system fell far short of satisfying Basque aspirations. They ventured on even more controversial ground by questioning the use of the police and army to repress violence as "a serious danger more than an authentic defense of the people."[25]

The government reacted quickly to the pastoral letter. The prime minister summoned the papal nuncio to express the cabinet's displeasure and ordered the Spanish ambassador at the Vatican to lodge a similar protest with the papal secretariat of state. The Socialist opposition in parliament was no less vociferous. The party's second in command, Alfonso Guerra, declared that the bishops' reference to repression by the central government appeared unseemly in a hierarchy that had kept silent for decades about the excesses of the Franco regime. The PSOE leader, Felipe González, saw the pastoral letter as irrelevant to the facts and wondered why a statement of similar vigor had not been issued following the events of "23-F."[26] The pastoral letter also received widespread criticism from a broad segment of the press. For its part, the hierarchy viewed the negative reaction to the Basque bishops' statement as excessive. Tarancón's successor as president of the CEE, Archbishop Gabino Díaz Merchán of Oviedo, defended his Basque colleagues, arguing that their intervention was moved by ethical and not political considerations. He declared that the Episcopal Conference had no intention of contesting the authority of local prelates to provide pastoral direction to the faithful of their dioceses.[27] But the CEE was sufficiently aware of the possibly damaging effects of its stance to issue a general statement condemning terrorism.[28]

The tensions generated by the Basque bishops' pastoral letter far exceeded those produced by controversy over the divorce law and the hierarchy's reaction to the coup attempt. The issue of the degree of autonomy that should be granted to the country's regions remained a question of intense, persistent controversy. Linked in the Basque Provinces to powerful, historic nationalist currents exacerbated by terrorism and repression, the issue had deep roots that could not be easily removed.

The intervention of the bishops of Vitoria, Bilbao, and San Sebastián represented something new, as far as the role of the region's hierarchy was concerned. Whether the Basque bishops acted because of ethical and evangelical considerations, as Díaz Merchán maintained, is a matter of controversy. A critic of the bishops' pastoral letter and an authority on modern Basque history, Father Fernando García de Cortázar, maintained that the letter was directly political. He argued that the region's hierarchy now identified itself fully with the nationalist cause so widely

25. Quoted in "Una pastoral polémica," *Cambio 16*, April 13, 1981, p. 21.

26. "La lectura de Madrid," ibid., p. 24.

27. "Díaz Merchán: La clave religiosa," ibid., p. 26.

28. "Ante el terrorismo y la crisis del país," May 12, 1981, in *Documentos de la Conferencia Episcopal Española*, pp. 618–20. This document was the work of the CEE's executive committee.

supported by their lower clergy for generations and that the "Basque Church, which is an important institutional and ideological power, is making a pact with . . . another power called nationalism."[29] Whatever the motives of the Basque bishops, the 1981 controversy, following upon that of 1977, indicated that the question of the Basque Church's response to the complex relationship of the region to the nation's political organization was certain to arise again.

The difficulties between the civil and ecclesiastical authorities during the winter and spring of 1981 showed that even under a government well disposed towards the Church, problems could arise. But on balance the Church derived substantial advantages from the UCD government. This generally favorable situation changed dramatically with the Socialist electoral victory in the October 1982 elections.

First Conflicts, 1982–1985

As the general elections of October 28, 1982, approached, the hierarchy pursued the strategy followed in 1977 and 1979. Appeals for civic responsibility mingled with exhortations urging Catholic voters to cast their ballots for parties that would advance the common good identified with "religious life" and "moral conduct."[30] But the Church faced a different political situation from the one it encountered in 1977 and 1979. The comforting prospect of another UCD electoral success receded as the party's fragile unity splintered. Former Prime Minister Suárez broke with his old political allies to establish a new party of his own.[31] The UCD's disintegration and the image of moderation and competence projected by the PSOE during the campaign gave the Socialists an absolute majority in parliament. The UCD won eleven seats in the congress of deputies; the new Centro Democrático y Social party (CDS) of Suárez only four. The principal beneficiary of the UCD's collapse was the Alianza Popular party (AP), led by Manuel Fraga Iribarne. Considerably more conservative than the UCD, the AP won 26.5 percent of the popular vote and became the main opposition party by winning 107 seats.[32]

The extent of the PSOE's triumph caught the Church by surprise despite the UCD's progressive disintegration after 1979. The Church, declared a close associate of Cardinal Tarancón, "did not perceive the likelihood of the Socialist Party coming to power as soon or as solidly as it did."[33] Since 1976, many bishops and

29. Quoted in "ETA te absolvo," *Cambio 16,* April 13, 1981, p. 20.

30. "La conciencia cristiana ante las próximas elecciones," September 23, 1982, in *Documentos de la Conferencia Episcopal Española,* p. 705.

31. The reasons behind the fragmentation and eventual collapse of the UCD are discussed by Rafael López-Pintor, "The October 1982 Elections and the Evolution of the Spanish Party System," in *Spain at the Polls, 1977, 1979, and 1982,* pp. 303–5.

32. Ibid., pp. 294–95.

33. José María Martín Patino, "Spain and the Future," *National Catholic Register,* July 20, 1986.

the Catholic press had viewed the prospect of a Socialist government with apprehension, recalling the party's commitment to the "complete and imperial laicization of the State" during the Second Republic.[34] These fears by no means disappeared following the elections, but the initial reaction of the hierarchy and the Catholic media to the PSOE victory proved moderate, though cautious. They recognized that times had changed and that the new government was unlikely to pursue an intransigent policy capable of alienating a significant part of the population. In a January 1983 radio address, Cardinal Tarancón expressed the hope that despite the party's historic "anticlerical tendencies," "Spanish Socialists will do everything possible not to confront the Church" because of its contribution to the transition to democracy.[35]

For the Church, coming to terms with the government was a necessity. The PSOE won a massive victory and appeared to possess the popularity and organization sufficient to remain in power for years. The narrow electoral base of Alianza Popular and the former association of its controversial leader with the Franco regime made it unlikely that the one major party disposed to cooperate with the Church stood a chance of winning an election in the near future.

The PSOE's attitude towards the Church had evolved since the 1930s. Generational change in its leadership and recognition of the role played by militant Catholic workers' associations during the labor struggles of the 1950s and 1960s moved the party to declare as early as 1967, "There cannot nor ought there to be conflicts between democratic socialism . . . and the Church, above all the Church of the post-conciliar era."[36] During the period of transition, the PSOE followed a flexible policy on civil-ecclesiastical relations, although it criticized what it saw as unjustified concessions to the Church.

Early in its term of office, the government showed its conciliatory intentions in an interview given to the Catholic press by the director-general of religious affairs, Gustavo Suárez Pertierra, a respected former professor of canon law. The government, he declared, would observe the terms of the constitution, including the articles requiring the State to recognize the "religious beliefs of Spanish society" and would maintain "collaborative relations" with the churches. He went further by recognizing that the Catholic Church "is the most important religious collectivity" in the country with "a tradition within the Spanish State." Suárez Pertierra also

34. Quoted in Victor M. Arbeloa, *La semana trágica de la Iglesia en España* (Barcelona, 1976), p. 76.

35. *Ya*, January 6, 1983.

36. Quoted in Díaz-Salazar, *El capital simbólico*, p. 114. In 1989, a PSOE document dealing with relations with the Church expressed more nuanced views. It distinguished between bishops following the flexible Tarancón line and those committed to the Vatican's more rigid approach. Opinion within the party also covered a wide range between those who regarded the role of the Church positively and those who saw it negatively but recognized that it could not be ignored. Others saw the Church as "an obstacle to Spain's development which should not be allowed to interfere with 'the monopoly of the civil power in the legal ordering of society,' since religion was a private matter and must be kept 'privatised.'" Brassloff, *Religion and Politics in Spain*, p. 121.

praised the Church's attitude of "openness" and "dialogue." He gave substance to these generous words by announcing that the government accepted all the agreements with the Vatican negotiated by the UCD because of their status as international treaties, including the *acuerdo* on education that Socialist deputies had opposed in 1979. In a final burst of optimism, the director-general expressed the conviction that the "definitive pacification" of historic civil-ecclesiastical conflicts was near at hand.[37]

Suárez Pertierra's statement indicated that the government had no intention of seeking to overturn the ecclesiastical settlement arranged by its predecessor. The statement went further by implicitly accepting the idea advanced by clerical apologists that the Church deserved special treatment vis-à-vis other religious groups in a pluralistic democracy because of tradition and sociological reality. In May 1983, the government announced, for example, negotiations with the Church to resolve issues raised by the diplomatic agreements of 1979 through a technical commission composed of representatives of Church and State. Protestants, Jews, and Muslims waited for nearly a decade for their concerns to be addressed in a similar way. Agreements in 1990 and 1992 finally granted them most, though not all, of the rights already conceded to the Church through the *acuerdos* of the 1970s and later negotiated arrangements.[38]

The government's conciliatory approach and the optimism of Cardinal Tarancón about the possibility of cordial dialogue between Church and State proved unrealistic. The cardinal's confident assessment that there were "no great difficulties" between the civil and ecclesiastical authorities over key issues ignored the existence of problems arising from the ambiguous nature of the Church's constitutional position established during the period of transition.[39] Major questions affecting official financial support for church schools, the teaching of religion in the public educational system, and the complex issue of government subsidies for clerical salaries remained unresolved. Controversy over the stance of the Basque hierarchy and clergy towards the region's quest for greater autonomy was also certain to resurface as a troubling concern for the national government.

The possibility of smooth relations between Church and State was further di-

37. "Relaciones Iglesia-Estado," *Ya*, February 15, 1983.

38. *Ya*, May 20, 1993; "El Gobierno firma acuerdos con confesiones no católicas," *El País* (edición internacional), February 26, 1990; "El Estado español reconoce derechos a otras religiones sin equipararlas con la católica," ibid., April 6, 1992. Protestants, Jews, and Muslims did not receive, for example, the fiscal exemption from the Value Added Tax (IVA) granted to the Catholic Church for the construction of churches. Nor did they receive the same recognition of their religious holidays as did the Catholic Church, which negotiated with the government over the number of such days, on which employees did not have to work. All citizens were obliged to observe these religious/civic holidays irrespective of their religious beliefs.

39. The cardinal declared in a press conference with respect to relations with the government, "Normal. They wish to dialogue and we do too." Although admitting that there were points of conflict between Church and State, he believed that these were not "any more difficult than in other circumstances." *Ya*, January 14, 1983.

minished by political reality. The PSOE won an impressive electoral victory and possessed the votes in parliament to pursue its legislative program. The government neither intended nor desired a bare-knuckles confrontation with the Church. But insofar as it is possible to perceive an overall Socialist strategy, it rested on an effort to interpret constitutional and treaty obligations as narrowly as possible, while extending the reach of ordinary legislation as far as possible without causing irreparable damage to civil-ecclesiastical relations. Although government leaders avoided inflammatory rhetoric in their dealings with the Church, anticlerical currents still ran high among the PSOE's rank and file. During the spring of 1983, Socialist and Communist municipal councillors in Ávila voted to dismiss the chaplain of the city's cemetery in the midst of an exchange of "shouts and insults" with the conservative opposition, on the grounds that Spain was "a lay State" that could not favor "the interests of one religion to the prejudice of others."[40] This echo of the 1930s was not widely imitated, although it provided a reminder to the political leadership that old fires could still burn at the local level. The emergence of the Alianza Popular party meant that Socialist initiatives affecting the Church's interests would be challenged aggressively in parliament. The honeymoon between Church and State during the months immediately following the October elections would prove short-lived.

While Suárez Pertierra was expressing the government's conciliatory intent towards the Church, controversy began over a legislative proposal for the limited decriminalization of abortion.[41] The issue quickly developed into a crisis between Church and State. Except for a minority of progressive grassroots movements, Catholic opinion condemned the proposed law.[42] The confessional press attacked it with virulence. The government, declared *Ya*, would be stained "with blood" if it proceeded to enact the legislation.[43] Archbishop Díaz Merchán, president of the CEE, criticized the government for acting so soon in its mandate, arguing that many Catholics voted for the PSOE on the assumption that it would introduce social reforms "to protect the dignity of life, but not suppress it."[44] The bishops condemned the proposal as "totally unacceptable," but prelates of pronounced conservative views saw it as part of a broader official conspiracy to undermine Catholic

40. *Ya*, July 3, 1983. Similarly, the municipality of Lugo voted to remove religious statues from the chapel in the public cemetery on the ground that "since the corporation is aconfessional," the chapel was open to "all religious communities existing within municipal boundaries." *Ya*, March 23, 1983.

41. The proposal was essentially the same as that submitted in 1979 to the UCD government by an official legal commission.

42. Thirty of Madrid's approximately three hundred "Christian communities" provoked the wrath of the bishops by opposing the hierarchy's stance on the proposed abortion law. *Ya*, May 17, 1983. The secretariat of the CEE issued a statement criticizing "some groups or communities" for advocating views that "cannot be accepted by anyone as an expression of Catholic doctrine." "Opiniones contrarias a las del Episcopado," May 16, 1983, *Documentos de la Conferencia Episcopal Española*, p. 736.

43. "Manchado de sangre," *Ya*, February 3, 1983.

44. *Ya*, January 27, 1983.

moral values. Bishop Guerra Campos saw the law as nothing less than "a brutal attack against the family, of a systematic and officially encouraged erosion of the Christian sense of life," while Bishop Carles of Tortosa attributed the proposal to "a very well-orchestrated effort to persuade us to accept moral and social degeneration under the pretext of making us Europeans."[45]

Archbishop Díaz Merchán did not believe that the hand of the government lay behind a conspiracy to destroy moral standards, although he shared a widespread belief among the bishops that an offensive was being launched "against traditional values."[46] Controversy over the proposed abortion law threw into sharp relief tensions between the Church's belief that Catholic morality should influence legislation in a country where most of the population still identified itself as Catholic and a by now diverse social reality that weakened the apparently monolithic values of the past. "We Catholics have the duty to respect others," declared *Ya* in a concise summary of the Church's position, but "we have the right to exact that others should respect our beliefs."[47]

Even ecclesiastical moderates shared the view that the government was encouraging, at least indirectly, the erosion of moral values through what Cardinal Tarancón called "a kind of 'revenge' that pretends to deprive this people of what has been its firmest support over the centuries."[48] Such an approach, he argued in veiled criticism of the government, could never be justified in the name of serving the people. Controversy over abortion during the winter and spring of 1983 soon expanded to the broader question of a national moral crisis for which the government was blamed at least in part.[49]

That Spanish society and its values had changed since the 1950s was as evident to the bishops as it was to ordinary Spaniards and to sociologists engaged in surveys of public opinion. As a result of industrialization, massive urbanization uprooted rural populations and placed them in settings where traditional religious and moral values could not be easily sustained. Economic development produced a consumer society and materialist culture emphasizing the well-being of the individual in a pattern of social development similar to that which prevailed elsewhere in Western Europe. The behavioral revolution sweeping through youth during the 1960s and 1970s in Western Europe and North America appeared also in Spain in

45. *Ya*, February 6, 27, 1983.

46. *Ya*, January 27, 1983.

47. *Ya*, January 6, 1983. Similarly, Bishop Fernando Sebastián of León, secretary of the CEE, attacked the "aggressive treatment against the religious and moral conscience of millions of Spaniards." *Ya*, May 8, 1983.

48. "Carta cristiana," *Ya*, May 7, 1983.

49. The CEE's executive committee issued a public statement lamenting the "collapse of moral values" in the country. "Quiebra de valores morales," May 13, 1983, in *Documentos de la Conferencia Episcopal Española*, p. 734. Archbishop José Delicado Baeza of Valladolid told the faithful of his diocese that a "great historical responsibility" rested on those in power if the "demolition" of the family, "the height of perversion," was part of their program. "Carta semanal," *Ya*, July 8, 1983.

the form of styles of dress, musical tastes, and sexual permissiveness that clergy and parents alike found shocking.

To what extent a government can be held responsible for behaviors caused by complex social, cultural, and economic developments is debatable. Catholic critics of national moral decline forgot that some of the conditions they lamented arose directly from the economic policies of the Franco regime. The advance of sexual permissiveness often lamented by the clergy, for example, was long underway by the time the Socialists assumed power in 1982. An opinion survey conducted in 1977, when the UCD controlled the government, showed that Spanish youths were no different from their European counterparts in their views on abortion, divorce, and birth control.[50] Critics also ignored that the moral fortress of National Catholicism rested on repressive social controls that could not be justified in a democracy. This is not to suggest that the development of Spanish society after the end of the Franco regime lacked problems. The rapidity of the changes transforming the country economically, socially, and politically between 1960 and the 1980s produced dislocation that magnified the social problems common to Western societies.

The Church had every right to present its moral vision and to criticize the evils produced by the excesses of a consumer society. But it proved more difficult for the hierarchy to reconcile its commitment to pluralistic democracy with the exercise of a "pastoral magisterium" aimed at forming the "conscience of Catholics" within the workings of the political system.[51] The clerical leadership and the confessional press expressed frustration over the failure of an elected government to embody Catholic moral values through legislation. Some figures within the Church appreciated the complex nature of the changes affecting Spanish society and the place of religion within it, the shift, as Cardinal Jubany of Barcelona expressed it, from a Catholicism of the majority to one of a "minority that struggles to live its personal faith within a world that is being secularized."[52] But the old idea of Spain as a nation and a people identified still with Catholicism by no means disappeared. "Spain," wrote a prominent journalist, "is Catholic more than any other thing. The . . . real identity of Spain . . . is its Catholicism."[53] The substitution of Catholic values in favor of the "moral vacuum" promoted by a single party, argued the secretary of the CEE in a broad indictment of the Socialist government, was unacceptable. The country required "an ethical patrimony that corresponds to our historic identity."[54]

50. Raymond Carr and Juan Pablo Fusi, *Spain: Dictatorship to Democracy* (2d ed., London, 1981), p. 98.

51. Gabino Díaz Merchán, "Discurso de apertura de la XL asamblea plenaria de la Conferencia Episcopal Española" (1984), in Juan Luis Recio et al., *La transición española: religion y política* (Estella, 1990), p. 189.

52. *Ya*, March 11, 1983.

53. *Ya*, February 23, 1983.

54. Fernando Sebastián made these remarks in a public lecture. *Ya*, December 6, 1983.

Controversy over the abortion law and the hierarchy's grim view of a society caught in the grips of moral crisis soured civil-ecclesiastical relations just as the government announced its intention in February 1983 to replace the UCD's educational law of 1980 (LOECE). Until final passage in December, the proposed Ley Orgánica del Derecho a la Educacción (LODE) provoked passionate parliamentary debate, street demonstrations, and heated public exchanges between defenders and opponents of the legislation reminiscent of confrontations between the Church and the Second Republic.

Debate over the LODE brought to the surface memories of distant wrongs. A Catholic editorialist saw the law as another stage in a long campaign against church schools that had originated in the conde de Romanones's education legislation of 1901. *Ya* evoked bitter memories of the Republic by alleging that Socialists at that time had sought to destroy Catholic education "by fire and blood." They had learned something, the newspaper suggested, because now they were attempting to achieve the same goal through "starvation and asphyxiation" of the religious school system.[55] Politicians of the Alianza Popular and a recently formed Christian Democratic party, the Partido Democrático Popular, seized upon the issue to launch a full-scale parliamentary offensive against the government.[56] In June, the papal nuncio, Antonio Innocenti, ruffled official sensibilities by suggesting that the government was violating the educational *acuerdo* of 1979 with the Vatican.[57]

Even the usually optimistic Cardinal Tarancón believed that relations between Church and government had so deteriorated by October that he feared the country was returning to historic patterns of civil-ecclesiastical confrontation. He saw "a bloodless civil war" as inevitable.[58] As the LODE began to move through the parliamentary process, protest demonstrations organized by Catholic teachers, students, and parents multiplied. On December 17, more than 250,000 demonstrators, many of whom had arrived by bus and train from across the country, marched through Madrid on the eve of the final vote in the congress of deputies. They shouted slogans against the minister of education and sang "LODE no! LODE no!" to the tune of "Jingle Bells" as they moved along the streets.[59]

The confrontational situation produced by the LODE debate was exacerbated by lesser controversies. In August, a "war of the catechisms" broke out when the Ministry of Education refused to authorize the use of texts approved by the CEE for use

55. *Ya*, December 27, 1983; "No se mata; se afixia," *Ya*, April 19, 1983.

56. Fraga Iribarne attacked the government for beginning a "war of the schools" designed "to nationalize private education." *Ya*, April 26, 1983.

57. The nuncio's statement was reproduced in *Ya*, June 21, 1983. The government's director-general of religious affairs quickly riposted that the "government considers that [the agreements] are compromises of international law and wishes their fulfillment." *Ya*, June 22, 1983.

58. Tarancón made these remarks in a radio interview reproduced in *Ya*, October 11, 1983.

59. *Ya*, December 14, 1983.

in public schools. In October, the Vatican's decision to resume beatification proceedings for priests assassinated during the Civil War was viewed by government supporters as an overtly political act. An ongoing struggle was also conducted over government attempts to limit extensive religious broadcasts on the State-controlled television network. The running battles waged in parliament and the press over these issues added more fuel to the fires of controversy produced by the LODE.

The passions generated by the LODE reflected the importance of the issue at stake. The Church regarded defense of its extensive educational system, heavily subsidized by the State since the education law of 1970, as vital to its interests. The bishops believed that Church schools, functioning on the basis of the guarantee of free education established in the constitution, deserved the same level of funding as the public system. They also wished to retain the high degree of administrative, financial, and ideological autonomy enjoyed by Church schools under the Franco regime and the UCD government.

Debate over the LODE revolved around the fundamental questions of money and control. The government refused to accept the blank-check approach of its predecessor. But it did not intend to deprive Church schools of subsidies. The minister of education, José Maravall, declared in the early stages of the controversy, "We Socialists are not going to end them because they provide the only formula that can be applied to establish a true pluralism in teaching."[60] But the government refused to guarantee equal funding to Church schools.

The LODE was a complex piece of legislation, but it provoked the Church by requiring schools accepting government funds to accept contractual arrangements with the government. This provision was also part of the LOECE, but the LODE expanded its scope. Schools accepting public monies (*centros concertados*) were ordered to entrust virtually all aspects of administration to elected councils representing the institution's legal proprietors, teachers, parents, students, and the nonacademic staff.[61] Schools were also obliged to recognize the academic freedom of teachers and liberty of conscience for teachers and students. They were forbidden to require attendance at religious services.

The law allowed the legal proprietors of the *centros concertados* "to define the particular character" of their institutions, but it required them to submit such definitions to the authorities for approval. This provision was more restrictive than the terms of the LOECE, which established academic freedom for teachers but with the significant limitation that it was subject to the *ideario* of the school's proprietors, the religious orders in the case of church schools. Opponents of the LODE

60. *Ya*, April 28, 1983.

61. These *consejos escolares* were to be composed of the school's principal, three representatives of the corporation holding its legal title, four teachers, four parents, two students (in secondary schools), and one representative of the ranks of the nonacademic staff. *Ley Orgánica del Derecho a la Educación y disposiciones reglamentarias* (Madrid, 1987), p. 36.

believed that its reference to "the particular character" of a school watered down an institution's right to expect teachers to conform to its religious orientation.[62]

The bishops and the religious orders, including the twenty-five thousand of their members belonging to the Federación Española de Religiosos de Enseñanza (FERE), saw the creation of school councils as a direct attack on the autonomy of the regular clergy's educational institutions, while they perceived the LODE's amplification of academic freedom as a device for introducing an "ideological pluralism" designed to compromise "Christian ideals."[63] The hierarchy saw the powers assigned to the new councils (*consejos escolares*) responsible for administering the *centros concertados* as failing to provide sufficient guarantees to maintain the "Catholic identity" of Church schools.[64]

The LODE imposed other restrictions. Schools accepting government funds could no longer accept students only on the basis of their own admissions criteria. The law required them to give priority to students in the neighborhood where a school was located. The LODE also restricted the financial autonomy of the *centros concertados*. Teachers received their salaries directly from the government, which distributed operating funds to Church schools. The law also prohibited schools operating under these arrangements from charging additional fees, which were regarded as a violation of the constitutional guarantee to a free education.[65]

Were the apocalyptic predictions of impending disaster for the Catholic school system justified? The Church saw the ideological and financial autonomy of its schools restricted, although the Constitutional Tribunal struck down on appeal the LODE's requirement that proprietors of the *centros concertados* must submit a definition of their "character" to the authorities as a violation of "the liberty of teaching" established in the constitution.[66] But the Church received guaranteed financing for its extensive network of schools. If nothing else, the LODE showed that the old Socialist dream of a public monopoly in education had been abandoned once and for all. In the final parliamentary vote, Communist deputies abstained on the grounds that the LODE made too many concessions to the Church.[67]

The law's accessibility requirements wrote the final chapter of Spanish Catholicism's historic identification of its schools with the country's social elite, except for institutions choosing to remain private schools funded only by tuition fees.[68]

62. Francisco Riu, *La comunidad eclesial ante el reto de la LODE* (Madrid, 1986), p. 25.

63. *Ya*, June 10, 1983.

64. Note of the CEE, reproduced in *Ya*, June 12, 1983.

65. Riu, *La comunidad eclesial ante el reto de la LODE*, p. 27.

66. "La sentencia sobre la ley de Educación," *El País*, June 28, 1985.

67. Ibid., December 21, 1983. The labor union, Workers Commissions (CC. OO.), identified with the Communist party, objected to the final draft of the LODE on the grounds that it "has suffered erosions [at the hands] of the Right." Ibid., November 29, 1983.

68. Seventy percent of Church schools accepted the status of *centros concertados*. "Balance 1992," *XX Siglos* (1993), vol. 1, p. 27. It should be noted that as a result of the terms of the 1970 education law and the LOECE many Church schools were already providing free education to most of their students.

Schools accepting the status of *centros concertados* were forced to alter traditional recruitment practices. The elite college of El Pilar in Madrid opened its doors to a more socially diverse student body drawn from the neighborhood where it was located, although it retained some of its former constituency.[69] Nor is there any evidence that implementation of the LODE's terms on academic freedom for teachers and students affected the religious character of church schools in a significant way.

Few years in the history of the country's new democracy generated more conflicts between Church and State than did 1983. But neither side wished to burn bridges. In the midst of the LODE controversy, Prime Minister Felipe González visited Pope John Paul II and announced that he hoped for continuing good relations with the Spanish Church.[70] By the end of the year, Cardinal Tarancón believed that his earlier prediction of a "bloodless civil war" between Church and government had been "absurd," as he recognized that "desires for collaboration based on sincerity" were present on both sides.[71] In the midst of heated public debate, the civil and ecclesiastical authorities maintained contacts. However angry the bishops' reaction to the introduction of abortion legislation early in the year, by April they were ready to enter discussions with the government over the LODE.[72] The government remained firm in its commitment to preserve the integrity of the proposed law. But because of representations from the CEE, the FERE, and other Catholic groups, it modified the law's initial draft to establish with greater clarity the right of the legal proprietors of the *centros concertados* to define their character (Article 22). The LODE also reaffirmed earlier legislation establishing that in all schools parents were guaranteed the right to have their children receive "religious and moral formation in accord with their own convictions" (Article 4).[73]

After the dust settled from the LODE controversy, the Church emerged with its school system substantially intact. On the part of the government, there was no return to the Socialist party's historic commitment to a state educational monopoly. Nor did the government use widespread and intense opposition to its educational policies by the Church, Catholic politicians, and the press to launch an anticlerical campaign. Indeed, it beat a hasty and embarrassing retreat in its dispute with the hierarchy over the authorization of catechisms for use in public schools.[74] Even

69. Lola Galán, "Colegios 'bien' para chicos del barrio," *El País*, October 24, 1988.

70. *Ya*, October 16, 1983.

71. Tarancón made these remarks in an address given to the clergy of Córdoba, reproduced in *Ya*, December 2, 1983.

72. In April, representatives of the CEE's committee on teaching, including its president, Archbishop Yanes, met with high level officials, among them the vice president of the government, Alfonso Guerra. *Ya*, April 19, 1983.

73. *Ley Organica del Derecho a la Educación*, pp. 23, 18.

74. The government announced that, although unauthorized by the Ministry of Education, the catechisms could be used "without sanctions or difficulties of any kind" in public schools. The CEE agreed to consider the "suggestions" of the ministry but declared that it had no intention of altering the texts in question. *Ya*, September 29, 1983.

as the polemical fires burned in 1983, the government authorized a generous increase of 12 percent in the budgetary appropriation for clerical salaries.[75]

When all is said and done, relations between the Church and the Socialist government conformed to the pattern of conflictive accommodation that had emerged more than once in the past to produce tension between the civil and ecclesiastical authorities. The Church had always found it difficult to accept that governments were unwilling to write a blank check on which every clerical demand could be written. The struggles of 1983–1985 continued a conflictive tradition that had prevailed since the Church's first conflicts with liberalism. Reflecting the normal give-and-take of the country's new democratic politics, the battles of the early 1980s were far from the worst in this ongoing saga.

The pattern of wary accommodation established during the first two years of Socialist rule would continue. But there was little indication that in the future problems would be resolved in the climate of amicable cooperation once imagined by Cardinal Tarancón. A chasm separated the Church and the government on moral values. As the moderate Díaz Merchán finished his first term as president of the CEE, he lamented, "We live in difficult times for the Church" within a world of accelerating change characterized by "neo-pagan and materialist ways of living, that our ancestors abandoned centuries ago."[76] More struggles lay ahead as the Socialist party consolidated its hold on power in the elections of 1986.

An Uneasy Balance, 1986–1998

Through the late 1980s and early 1990s, relations between the Church and the government followed a roller-coaster track of occasional cooperation and periodic conflict. From an ecclesiastical perspective, the political situation remained more or less what it had been since 1982. The PSOE retained its political dominance in the 1986 and 1989 elections. It fared less well in those of 1993 as a result of deteriorating economic conditions. Although it lost its absolute majority in the congress of deputies, the PSOE remained the largest party in parliament and continued in power with the support of the Catalan nationalist party, Convergència i Unió.

As far as the Church was concerned, a significant political development occurred that revived hopes for an alternative to Socialist hegemony. In 1989, the conservative Alianza Popular party broadened its base by incorporating some Christian Democratic groups into its ranks and by renaming itself the Partido Popular (PP). Although the hierarchy during the period, when Cardinal Tarancón and Archbishop Díaz Merchán served as presidents of the CEE, kept its distance from

75. *Ya*, April 26, 1983.

76. From the text of an address to the CEE's plenary assembly reproduced in *Ya*, June 21, 1983.

the AP, this attitude changed during the tenure of Cardinal Angel Suquía of Madrid, elected to head the Episcopal Conference in 1987. Suquía, Bishop Fernando Sebastián, the CEE's secretary, and the papal nuncio, Mario Tagliaferri, worked behind the scenes to encourage the transformation of the AP into a more centrist organization on the model of European Christian Democratic parties.[77]

The decision of the PP's flamboyant leader, Manuel Fraga Iribarne, to abandon national politics, and the eventual appointment of José María Aznar to the leadership enhanced the party's standing with influential members of the hierarchy. Shortly after becoming party leader in 1989, Aznar entered discussions with Suquía and Bishop Agustín García-Gasco, the CEE's new secretary, to promote "mutual respect and cooperation" between the PP and the bishops.[78] Widespread disenchantment with the government's economic policies allowed the PP to enlarge its share of parliamentary seats and the popular vote significantly in the 1993 elections, thereby raising the possibility, for the first time since the PSOE came to power, of a future electoral victory by a party disposed to heed clerical demands.[79]

The hierarchy avoided explicit endorsement of the PP, although for a time it resumed the tactics followed in earlier elections. As municipal and regional elections approached in 1991 in the midst of acrimonious controversy over a government proposal to liberalize abortion legislation further, the bishops refrained from direct support for the PP and avoided specific attacks on the PSOE but called upon the faithful to vote for political "alternatives that inspire more confidence."[80] Before the 1993 elections, the hierarchy reaffirmed the Tarancón strategy that the Church would not support a specific party, although Bishop José Gea Escolano of Mondoñedo-Ferrol published a pastoral letter urging Catholics to vote against the PSOE, whose government appeared "like a dictatorship."[81] His episcopal colleagues quickly distanced themselves from this public attack on the government.

The Spanish bishops appointed by Pope John Paul II reflected the pontiff's traditional theological views and his aggressive defense of Catholic moral values. The appointments of Angel Suquía to succeed Cardinal Tarancón as archbishop of Madrid (1983) and of Ricard Carles as archbishop of Barcelona (1990) to succeed Cardinal Jubany placed the country's two most important dioceses in the hands of prelates reflecting the Vatican's orientation. Carles enjoyed the support of the nun-

77. J. G. Ibáñez and F. Valls, "La Iglesia propició el giro democristiano del PP," *El País* (edición internacional), February 13, 1989.

78. Juan G. Ibáñez, "Aznar abre un cauce de diálogo permanente con el episcopado," ibid., March 12, 1990.

79. The PP increased its seats in the congress of deputies from 107 to 141 and its share of the popular vote from 25.9 percent to 34.81 percent. The PSOE fell from 175 seats to 159, although its proportion of the popular vote declined less drastically from 39.8 percent to 38.68 percent. Ibid., June 7, 1993.

80. Quoted in F. Valls, "Permitir el aborto abre las puertas al totalitarismo, según los obispos," ibid., April 15, 1991.

81. A. Rodríguez, "Los obispos dejan a los creyentes votar con libertad y en conciencia"; "Críticas del Gobierno a los obispos que piden no votar socialista," ibid., April 26, January 18, 1993.

cio, Tagliaferri, who, after taking up his post in 1985, promoted candidates of a distinctly conservative bent for episcopal office. The powerful role assumed by the nuncio in the affairs of the Spanish Church caused the now retired Cardinal Tarancón to complain, to the Vatican's irritation, that "In Latin America, nuncios command a lot; in Europe, little; nevertheless, he believes that he is still there."[82] At the same time, bishops of progressive theological views found themselves in an "uncomfortable and difficult" situation within the CEE, so much so that two prelates resigned their bishoprics in 1991.[83] The nuncio also used his influence to bring about a significant change in the leadership of the Episcopal Conference. In 1987, Archbishop Diáz Merchán of Oviedo lost the presidency to Suquía, the candidate of the nuncio, the Vatican, and conservative bishops.[84]

The hierarchy's changing composition should be kept in perspective. Although a majority of bishops named by the pope were theological traditionalists, John Paul II's concern with social justice led to the occasional appointment of prelates identified with Catholic social activism. In 1983, the pope named Ramón Torella i Cascante, expelled from the Madrid diocese during the mid-1960s for his activities in Catholic workers' associations, to the archbishopric of Tarragona.[85] Nor did the new conservatives represent a throwback to the intregrist bishops of the Franco era. Although harshly criticized by progressive groups within the Church, Suquía formed part of the moderate bloc of bishops backing Cardinal Tarancón during the 1970s and supported the implementation of conciliar reforms during his tenure as archbishop of Santiago. But by the time he succeeded Tarancón in the archbishopric of Madrid, he was regarded as a "herald of dogmatism and authoritarianism" that contrasted with the "prudence" of his predecessor.[86]

In any event, the transformation of the hierarchy into a monolithic body docile to every directive of the Vatican could not be accomplished overnight. As late as 1989, only twenty-one of the eighty members of the CEE owed their appointments to John Paul II, although by the end of Mario Tagliaferri's tenure as nuncio (1985–1995), half of the bishops had been replaced.[87] The bishops retained a strong sense of autonomy, especially in relation to the role of the CEE. Its margin-

82. Quoted in F. Valls, "'Tagliaferri manda mucho en la Iglesia y cree que aún está en Latinoamérica,' dice Tarancón," ibid., July 11, 1988; "Malestar en el Vaticano por las declaraciones de Tarancón sobre el poder del nuncio," ibid., July 25, 1988.

83. F. Valls, "Momentos difíciles para los obispos progresistas," ibid., September 16, 1991. The two bishops were Nicolás Castellanos (Palencia) and Ramón Buxarráis (Málaga).

84. F. Valls, "Los obispos conservadores aspiran a que Suquía ocupe la presidencia del episcopado español," ibid., January 19, 1987.

85. *El País*, April 13, 1983.

86. "Tarancón y el final de una era," *El País*, April 13, 1983. After reaching the age of seventy-five in the autumn of 1982, the cardinal submitted his resignation to the pope in accord with Vatican policy. It was up to John Paul II to decide when to accept the resignation. In Tarancón's case, he did so "with unaccustomed rapidity," an indication of the pontiff's conservative direction. Ceferino de Blas, *Tarancón, el cardenal que coronó el rey* (Madrid, 1995), p. 94.

87. A. Rodríguez, "El nuncio del cambio," *El País*, July 14, 1995.

alization by Suquía, who preferred to operate on his own in close cooperation with the nuncio and the Vatican, led finally to a rebellion of sorts. In 1993, the bishops rebuffed the nuncio and the Vatican by rejecting the candidacy of Archbishop Carles to succeed Suquía in the presidency in favor of Archbishop Elías Yanes of Zaragoza, an ecclesiastical centrist.[88]

The thirty votes cast for Carles suggest that prelates following the Tagliaferri-Vatican line were still far from supreme in the CEE, despite allegations that a conservative episcopal axis including Cardinal Suquía, Archbishops Carles, and Rouco (Santiago) dominated the Spanish Church with the support of the Vatican and Opus Dei. Perhaps fifteen of the forty-five ballots cast for Yanes came from episcopal moderates unhappy with an ongoing purge of progressive theologians from ecclesiastical faculties. The remaining thirty represented a diverse center moved primarily by frustration with the diminished role of the CEE and dissatisfied with the confrontational approach identified with Suquía.[89] But these were divisions of tactics rather than substance. A majority of bishops shared the belief that the country was sinking deeper into moral crisis and remained committed to defending the Church's vital interests vis-à-vis the Socialist government. But the election of Yanes suggests that the hierarchy wanted a more restrained approach to achieving common goals.

Controversy over education and the extent of official support for clerical salaries continued through the late 1980s and early 1990s, while episcopal preoccupation with the nation's moral condition deepened and produced sharper attacks on official policy. During this period, civil-ecclesiastical relations ebbed and flowed. They were relatively stable between 1986 and most of 1988, though they developed in a climate of tension produced by controversy over issues of no real substance. In 1986, the hierarchy fired a "torpedo" against the government by following the AP line urging voters to abstain in the referendum called to approve Spain's entry into NATO.[90] Some bishops, reflecting the pope's concern with social justice, criticized the government's neo-liberal economic policies as widening the gap between rich and poor in the country.[91] In 1987 and 1988, John Paul II's deci-

88. A. Rodríguez, "Los obispos españoles votan por Yanes como presidente y se 'rebelan' contra Roma," *El País* (edición internacional), February 22, 1993.

89. Ibid. In 1991, it was estimated that about a fifth of the seventy members of the CEE were progressives. "Momentos difíciles para los obispos progresistas," ibid., September 16, 1991.

90. "Orientaciones eclesiales," ibid., February 17, 1986.

91. In 1994, the Social Pastoral Commission of the CEE published a document, "The Church and the Poor," which took the government to task for following a capitalist development model that had contributed to widening the gap between rich and poor. Brasloff, *Religion and Politics in Spain,* p. 130. Brassloff traces the origins of the hierarchy's critique of the excesses of capitalism to John Paul II's 1981 social encyclical *Laborem Exercens,* which stressed "the role of the person as being more important than economic systems. . . . The Pope appeared to be advocating a 'third way' between capitalism and socialism." The historic obsession of the bishops with communism by no means disappeared, but "it no longer figured so prominently in their documents: *Laborem Exercens* seems to mark a point from which the excesses of capitalism took precedence over marxism in their denunciations." Ibid., p. 110.

sion to advance the beatification of priests and religious assassinated during the Civil War irritated the government, which saw the papal initiative as an unfortunate decision that could reopen old wounds.[92] In 1988, another storm of controversy broke when the government attempted to eliminate the feast of the Immaculate Conception (December 8) as a national holiday. An avalanche of pastoral letters, editorials in the Catholic press, and demonstrations stimulated a national debate of extraordinary proportions that ranged far beyond the importance of the issue in question. Surprised by the reaction not only of the Church but also of professional and employers' associations, the government abandoned an initiative that promised to do more political harm than good.[93]

These controversies were significant not because of the issues involved but because they created a climate of confrontation that contributed to a serious deterioration in civil-ecclesiastical relations in 1989 and 1990. In 1989, the question of the moral condition of the nation resurfaced in more virulent form when Cardinal Suquía criticized "the gaps and defects" of the constitution with respect to marriage, family, and abortion.[94] In 1990, the bishops issued a collective statement on the same topic that unleashed another whirlwind of controversy. The hierarchy saw Spanish society as "morally infirm" and left little doubt about who was to blame. The bishops complained of the "open introduction . . . of 'official' ideological propaganda from the dominant culture, which was frequently antireligious and devoted to silencing or ridiculing 'what is Catholic.'"[95] The PSOE attacked the statement as anti-democratic, while the government rejected it as mistaken and denied that it intended to de-Christianize Spain. "This is not an anticlerical government," declared the minister of education.[96] As polemic swirled, the Church refused to send a delegation to the twelfth anniversary celebration of the constitution; the government riposted by postponing negotiations dealing with ecclesiastical finances.[97]

The deterioration of civil-ecclesiastical relations corresponded to another round of controversy caused by the government's proposal in 1990 for a law reorganizing the school curriculum. The Ley de Ordenación General del Sistema Educativo (LOGSE) aroused the hierarchy's anger because it relegated religion courses in the schools to an inferior academic status. The bishops also objected to the new curriculum's scientific and pragmatic orientation as threatening a "rupture

92. M. Bango, "La beatificación de muertos en la guerra enfría las relaciones entre la Iglesia y el Estado español," *El País* (edición internacional), April 6, 1987.

93. *Ya; El País*, November 12, 1988.

94. Angel Suquía, *La Iglesia de España: tradición y futuro* (Madrid, 1989), p. 47.

95. *La verdad os hará libres: instrucción pastoral de la Conferencia Episcopal Española sobre la conciencia cristiana ante la actual situación moral de nuestra sociedad*, ed. Promoción Popular Cristiana (Madrid, 1990), pp. 13, 19.

96. S. Martín, "El PSOE acusa a los obispos de intentar desestablizar la democracia," *ABC*, November 24, 1990.

97. *El Sol*, December 8, 1990; *El País*, January 14, 1991.

between culture and the faith."[98] On this occasion, the hierarchy proved more cautious in its criticism than in the case of the LODE, although some priests in Madrid publicly attacked the proposed legislation from the pulpit, while the PP attacked it at every turn in parliament.[99] In 1991, the government's proposal to disqualify religious courses in secondary schools as one of the subjects acceptable for university admission provoked further controversy. The pope also entered the fray by complaining that "legal restrictions" on Catholic education threatened its very existence.[100]

Relations between Church and State were complicated further by the increasingly strong identification of the Basque bishops with the region's quest for autonomy. Following another round of ETA terrorism, they published a pastoral letter in December 1987 that stirred passionate debate and led King Juan Carlos I to depart from his usual neutrality on political questions. In his annual Christmas message to the nation, the king condemned terrorist violence and criticized those seeking to excuse or justify it, "whatever their political, social or religious positions."[101] The royal comments were directed in part against the pastoral letter, although the Basque bishops had denounced terrorism in their statement. But their affirmation that every people had the right to self-determination and that negotiations should be opened between the government and ETA on the basis of mutual concessions unleashed a firestorm of controversy. The hierarchy itself was caught by surprise. Conservative bishops favoring the excommunication of ETA militants were aghast at their colleagues' intervention. In response to the public uproar produced by the pastoral letter, the CEE issued a communiqué discreetly criticizing its colleagues but reaffirming the traditional line that bishops possessed the right to provide pastoral direction to the faithful of their dioceses.[102]

Tense relations between the hierarchy and the government slowly began to ease. In the midst of the crisis of 1990, the minister of foreign affairs, Francisco Fernández Ordóñez, visited John Paul II and reassured the pontiff that as far as education and clerical finances were concerned, the government wished to show its "good will" by cooperating with the Holy See "within the framework of the Spanish Constitution and the agreements of 1979."[103] In 1992, the Vatican dispatched the secretary of state, Cardinal Angelo Sodano, to conduct extensive conversations with

98. "Los obispos critican la LOGSE ante el nuevo curso," *El País* (edición internacional), September 8, 1990.

99. "Púlpitos contra la LOSE," ibid., April 2, 1990; E. S. Barcia, "El Pleno del Senado rechaza el veto que presentó el Grupo Popular a la LOGSE," ibid., September 6, 1990.

100. P. Egurbide, "El Papa critica las 'restricciones' a la enseñanza católica en España," ibid. (edición internacional), December 23, 1991.

101. Ibid., December 28, 1987.

102. F. Valls, "Malestar en el episcopado por la pastoral de los obispos vascos," ibid., December 21, 1987.

103. M. Castellvi, "Ordóñez promete al Papa mantener la ayuda para la Iglesia y la enseñanza religiosa," *ABC*, September 14, 1990.

Prime Minister González to ease tension between the hierarchy and the government.[104] In June 1993, John Paul II visited the country and calmed an uneasy government aware of the pope's 1991 indictment of the "neo-pagan" character of Spanish society. On this occasion, the pontiff praised the "appreciable progress" of democratic Spain and avoided the harsh language employed by some members of the hierarchy in their critique of the nation's moral failings.[105]

The pope's visit and the succession of Elías Yanes to the presidency of the CEE quickly produced results through the conclusion of a series of agreements between Church and government. The authorities agreed to normalize the employment status of teachers of religion in public schools and to raise their salaries to the level of regular teachers, at considerable cost to the public treasury.[106] But the easing of civil-ecclesiastical tensions was far from complete. The government's decision to press forward with the further liberalization of abortion legislation following the 1993 elections led to a renewed barrage of criticism from the hierarchy, while a papal statement of November 21, 1994, identifying the Second Republic with the totalitarian regimes of Nazi Germany and Soviet Russia in terms of their impact on the Church, set off another controversy, as a press sympathetic to the government berated the pope for his remarks.[107]

The "definitive pacification" of conflicts between Church and State so confidently predicted by the Socialist government in 1982 has proven elusive. Yet when all is said and done, the rocky road of periodic crises and compromises characteristic of civil-ecclesiastical relations was inevitable, given the ambiguities of the Church's legal position as established during the period of transition and political reality. The idealized vision of harmonious relations, promoted by ecclesiastics and politicians alike during the heady days following Franco's death, ignored the fact that even in countries with a long tradition of Church-State separation, conflicts were bound to arise. The controversy in France during the 1980s over Catholic education and the ongoing battles in the United States over prayer in public schools suggest that there is no ideal model of civil-ecclesiastical relations capable of resolving all points at issue without conflict.

Despite moments of extreme tension, neither the Church nor the government wished to push events too far. Even as public debate over the new education law of 1990 raged and civil-ecclesiastical relations reached their lowest point in years, representatives of the CEE and the government met in secret to discuss the legis-

104. A. Rodríguez, "El cardenal Sodano reconoce el papel mediador del Vaticano entre el Gobierno y la Iglesia española," *El País* (edición internacional), June 1, 1992.

105. A. Rodríguez, "El Gobierno, satisfecho del tono utilizado por Juan Pablo II en sus discursos," ibid., June 18, 1993.

106. A. Rodríguez, "Gobierno e Iglesia firman los estatutos de los profesores religiosos y los curas de prisiones," ibid., May 24, 1993.

107. P. Egurbide, "El Papa compara a la España republicana con la Alemania nazi o la Rusia soviética," ibid., November 21, 1994.

lation and official subsidies for the clergy.[108] There were points of conflict about moral values where a mutually acceptable resolution was impossible. Questions of a more practical nature were resolved, perhaps not to the entire satisfaction of either party, through the process of give-and-take shown in legislation such as the LODE, the agreement over official subsidies for clerical salaries, and increased funding for religion teachers in public schools.

As long as the Socialist government remained in power, periodic crises were resolved through the kind of rough-edged compromise characteristic of civil-ecclesiastical relations. The long tenure of the PSOE in office ended with the general elections of March 3, 1996. The Partido Popular won the largest number of seats, although it required the support of the Catalan autonomist party, Convergència i Unió, and the Basque nationalists of the PNV to form a government. The hierarchy followed the strategy employed in previous elections. It did not endorse any party, although its exhortation to the faithful to vote for parties opposed to abortion worked to the benefit of the PP.[109] The PP's electoral success raised questions about the role of the Church in relation to a government more disposed to heed its demands. Would the Church, as it had often done in the past, seize the moment to try to use government to strengthen its position? Still a thorn in the side of his increasingly conservative colleagues, Cardinal Tarancón agreed in 1991 with a statement of Prime Minister González that "it was not sure that . . . the Spanish Church will continue the line of non-intervention in politics followed during the [period of] transition." Fearing that this policy was beginning to erode, the cardinal warned, "the Church should not involve itself in politics."[110] But despite dire predictions of excessive clerical influence over the PP, the new government did not rush to make concessions. It refused to re-negotiate the terms of the financial agreement with the Church made by its predecessor, while it expressed irritation over a campaign by Bishops Ricardo Blázquez of Bilbao and José María Setién of San Sebastián for negotiations with the ETA organization.[111]

On moral questions, however, the PP has supported the Church's position. A controversial legislative proposal advanced in 1998 by the PSOE and other left-wing parties to liberalize existing abortion law provoked strident public debate.

108. F. Valls, "Gobierno y obispos dialogan en secreto sobre la nueva ley de educación y las cuentas de la Iglesia," ibid., March 19, 1990.

109. "La Iglesia española aconseja votar a partidos 'antiaborto,'" *El País* (edición internacional), January 22, 1996. In November 1994, a statement of Elías Yanes calling for the restoration of ethical values to a political system beset by corruption and for a limited term of office for elected officials, a reform demanded by the PP, led to charges from the PSOE that the president of the CEE was advocating a change in government and promoting the PP's interest. Ibid., November 21, 1994.

110. Francesc Valls, "Tarancón, sorprendido por la rápida beatificación," ibid., July 15, 1991.

111. In reference to the initiative of Setién, the secretary of the PP in the Basque Provinces declared that the bishop's intervention was "unhelpful rhetoric" in view of continuing terrorist attacks by ETA. "La Conferencia Episcopal respalda el derecho del arzobispo Setién a ser mediador ante ETA," ibid., October 21, 1996. "El obispo Setién cree que la negociación con ETA es el camino para la paz," ibid., December 9, 1996.

The hierarchy organized a massive public relations campaign in the country's twenty thousand parishes against the legislative project. The proposal lost by a single vote in parliament because of the unanimous opposition of PP deputies and the pressure exerted by its leadership on Basque and Catalan nationalist deputies, who were all too aware of the substantial benefits they had secured for their regions as a result of their alliance with the governing party.[112]

Relations between the PP and the Church have followed a smoother course than was the case with the PSOE. But it is unlikely, in view of its tenuous hold on power and the existence of a powerful Socialist minority in parliament, that the PP government will embark on a policy of wholesale concessions to the Church save in exceptional circumstances involving issues such as abortion. The historic pattern of conflictive accommodation between Church and State will continue, albeit within an amicable framework of relations.

112. The PP warned deputies of the Basque and Catalan nationalist parties, on which it depended for its survival in office, that passage of the Socialist proposal might endanger the political alliance with the PP. The prospect of a political crisis arising from a favorable vote produced the desired effect among nationalist deputies. "La Iglesia movilizó ayer a las paroquias de todo el país en su campaña contra el aborto," *El País*, September 21, 1998; "Rechazada por un voto la ampliación del aborto en España," ibid. (edición internacional), September 29, 1998.

CHAPTER XXIII

THE CHURCH AFTER THE COUNCIL

The remaking of civil-ecclesiastical relations in democratic Spain appears at first glance as another act in a long-running play. Official financial support for clerical salaries, the Church's place in education, and the role of government as moral censor resurfaced in public debate, as so often in the past. Although the hierarchy gradually abandoned historic theories of civil-ecclesiastical relations by accepting political pluralism, the bishops continued to believe that the Church's future depended on maintaining some of the bulwarks raised to protect clerical interests prior to 1931 and during the Franco era.

These historic residues existed in uneasy combination with a process of internal change affecting important aspects of the Church's organization and religious activity. During the 1950s, a diffuse movement of institutional self-criticism spread among a minority of priests and laypeople. These fragmented reforming tendencies prepared some clergy and laity for the changes introduced by the Second Vatican Council but had little impact on a powerful hierarchical organization still confident in the religious strategy developed during and after the Civil War.

The effects of the Council on the Spanish Church proved "complicated and traumatic" not only because conciliar decisions affected civil-ecclesiastical relations.[1] They also challenged long-held assumptions about how the Church should convey its religious message within a pluralistic, secular society. The Council's call for liturgical reform, new pastoral methods adapted to contemporary cultural and social conditions, and a greater role for the laity and the lower clergy as members of a community of believers provided general direction rather than a detailed master plan capable of being applied uniformly throughout the Catholic world.

To what extent the application of conciliar principles transformed Spanish

1. "Presentación," *El postconcilio en España*, ed. Juan M. Loboa (Madrid, 1988), p. 9.

Catholicism is a matter of debate. Even Cardinal Tarancón admitted years after the Council's close that realizing its objectives created a "trauma" for the Spanish Church and that many of the faithful found conciliar teachings "indigestible," at least for a time.[2] In 1985, the hierarchy concluded that the Council's influence was "so great, and on the whole so positive," that it had transformed Spanish Catholicism.[3] Reflecting on the effects of the Council over nearly three decades, progressive Catholics have rendered a harsher judgment. The Council initially produced euphoria among clergy and laity ready to embark on pastoral innovation based on "true pluralism" within the Church. The expectation that it would strike out on "new roads, break old forms, [and] begin to think that [the Church] is more than certain rites" proved illusory in their judgment.[4]

Differing interpretations of the application of conciliar principles inevitably produced conflict. Following the Council, the Spanish Church entered a period of turmoil marked by debate about how it could best fulfill its religious mission. The proliferation of popular religious movements and new theological currents produced alternative models that in the eyes of some clerical observers converted Spanish Catholicism into a "mosaic of sects," as a once "monolithic Church" experienced "a process of fragmentation."[5] The bishops tried to impose order over clergy and laity, but enforcing unity from above, as far as moral and religious questions were concerned, met with indifferent success. By the early 1990s, more than one-third of the clergy opposed the hierarchy's and the Vatican's position on birth control.[6] Nor is there much evidence that the numerous documents published by the CEE for the religious and moral guidance of the faithful exercised significant influence over Catholic opinion.[7]

Reworking civil-ecclesiastical relations in democratic Spain proved straightforward compared with the Church's quest for new approaches to replace the strategy of religious conquest that had dominated clerical thinking from the nineteenth century through the first three decades of the Franco period. The search was immeasurably more complicated because it took place within a society undergoing

2. *Ya*, January 14, 28, 1983.

3. "Memoria-informe de la Conferencia Episcopal Española enviada a la secretaría del sínodo de obispos como contribución a la asamblea extraordinaria del sínodo, celebrada en noviembre–diciembre de 1985," *El postconcilio en España*, p. 424.

4. Ramón Echarren, "Veinticinco años en la vida de la Iglesia española," in Juan Martín Velasco et al., *La Iglesia en la sociedad española* (Estella, 1990), pp. 38, 39.

5. Víctor Codina, Miguel Angel de Prada, and Carlos Pereda, *Analizar la Iglesia* (Madrid, 1981), p. 234.

6. Thirty-seven percent of 2,097 priests surveyed differed with the Church's official position on birth control, while 27 percent expressed indifference to the question. Only 39 percent of the clergy supported the official policy without reservations. F. Valls, "Un tercio de los curas de España difiere de la Iglesia sobre el control de la natalidad," *El País* (edición internacional), July 16, 1990.

7. Casiano Floristán, "Presencia pastoral de la Iglesia en la sociedad actual," in *La Iglesia en la sociedad española*, p. 142. In 1983, Bishop Fernando Sebastián, secretary of the CEE, complained that even the religious press paid insufficient attention to the Episcopal Conference's declarations on pastoral matters. *Ya*, September 21, 1983.

accelerated social and economic change that produced powerful secularizing effects. Declining religious practice, the rejection of Catholic moral teachings, especially in sexual matters, by segments of the population, and an emphasis on individual well-being and autonomy associated with the development of a consumer society encouraged either religious indifference or a do-it-yourself Catholicism, a kind of "spiritual *bricolage*," according to some pastoral commentators.[8] Confronted with this situation, concerned clergy and laity asked: "Where are we going? Where do we wish to go? Where should we be going?"[9]

There were no clear answers. Inspired by the Vatican Council, many clergy and laity believed that Spanish Catholicism was on the eve of a profound movement of renovation that would allow it to flourish within a changing society. By the early 1970s, however, optimism yielded to pessimism before a "bubbling broth . . . of personal and institutional crises" characterized by a decline in vocations, the departure of a significant number of priests from clerical ranks, a crisis of identity among clergy and laity, disorientation among Catholic lay associations, and signs of declining religious practice.[10] As the optimism of the immediate post-conciliar period receded, conservative and progressive commentators on the state of religion shared the belief that the Church faced a crisis in the "historic forms of Catholicism" and in the "essence of [its] institutions."[11] But they offered different opinions of how the crisis could be resolved. Advocates of "renovation" believed that the Church had not gone far enough to transform pastoral methods and organization to meet the challenges posed by a complex modern society. After 1978, supporters of "restoration," encouraged by the Vatican and a more conservative hierarchy, sought to recreate an updated version of a unified Church committed to the traditional goal of converting the population to historic patterns of belief, practice, and respect for ecclesiastical authority.[12]

Internal debate provoked by the search for a new strategy of religious action and the conclusions of sociologists of religion about Spanish Catholicism's complex patterns of belief and practice have overshadowed the significance of changes that altered the Church's organizational and religious framework in comparison with the past. The road to change developed an abundant supply of potholes, sometimes jarring in effect, while its direction has wandered over difficult and often contested terrain.

8. Luis González-Carvajal, "Retos de la sociedad española a la Iglesia," in *La Iglesia en la sociedad española*, p. 85.

9. Echarren, "Veinticinco años en la vida de la Iglesia española," p. 51.

10. Ibid.

11. Juan María Laboa, "Marco histórico y recepción del Concilio," in *El postconcilio en España*, p. 87.

12. For these differing interpretations, see ibid.; Vicente Cárcel Ortí, *¿España neopagana?: Análisis de la situación y discursos del papa en las visitas "ad limina"* (Valencia, 1991).

Organizational Change

On the surface, the ecclesiastical map of late-twentieth-century Spain differed little from the past. The diocese remained the basic unit of the Church's organization. Since 1975, the number of dioceses has increased from sixty-three to sixty-seven with the addition of Ciudad Real and Jerez de la Frontera, created in 1980, and Alcalá de Henares and Getafe, established in 1991. The number of ecclesiastical provinces expanded from twelve to thirteen with the elevation of Madrid to the status of a metropolitan see. Barcelona remained a freestanding archbishopric. Although changes to ecclesiastical cartography were slight, the conversion of Madrid into a metropolitan see, with Alcalá de Henares and Getafe as suffragan dioceses, completed a reorganization begun by Cardinal Tarancón during the 1970s.

Recognizing the administrative and pastoral problems of the country's largest diocese, the cardinal established six episcopal vicarates in a decentralized model that was also adopted in Barcelona and elsewhere, although some dioceses were subdivided into pastoral vicarates that enjoyed less autonomy than their episcopal counterparts.[13] Plans for a decentralized model of diocesan organization sometimes encountered difficulties. A few ecclesiastical administrators appointed by Archbishop Morcillo opposed Tarancón's administrative reform in Madrid. But the cardinal persisted in believing that a restructuring of the diocese was "necessary and urgent."[14]

The creation of episcopal vicarates in the country's largest dioceses was a major attempt to adapt diocesan organization to the administrative and pastoral complexities of massive urban agglomerations. Vicarates created a new framework designed to address local needs more directly and promptly through consultation between clergy and laity. During the 1970s, the Vallecas vicarate of Madrid established a pastoral council composed of the episcopal vicar, clerical deans representing pastoral districts, one lay member, and other delegates elected by deanery councils. The council was concerned less with administrative affairs than with planning and coordinating overall pastoral policy in an area long known for high levels of religious alienation among working-class immigrants from Andalucía and Extremadura.[15]

13. "The Diocese of Madrid: Pastoral Care in Large Cities," *Pro Mundi Vita: Dossiers* (1983), no. 1, p. 14; *¿Qué es la diócesis de Barcelona?* (Barcelona, 1985), p. 25. By 1984, 249 pastoral vicarates had been created among the country's sixty-five dioceses. Oficina de Estadística y Sociología de la Iglesia, *Estadísticas de la Iglesia católica, 1989* (Madrid, 1989), p. 67, Table 40. Episcopal vicars, as the name suggests, enjoyed more ample powers than did pastoral vicars. The Vatican Council called for the creation of episcopal vicarates but left responsibility for creating them to individual bishops.

14. Vicente Enrique y Tarancón, "50 años de sacerdocio en España," in *Iglesia, Estado, y sociedad en España, 1930–1982,* ed. Joaquín Ruiz Giménez (Barcelona, 1984), p. 399.

15. "The Diocese of Madrid," pp. 15–16.

In 1972, Cardinal Tarancón entrusted the Vallecas vicarate to Bishop Alberto Iniesta. He soon aroused the hostility of the Franco regime and clerical conservatives by promoting a program based on "concentration on the grass roots and on communities, on realistic analysis, support for democracy, arousing awareness in the social and political fields; an option for the poor; and the prophetic teaching of the Gospel." In 1974, Iniesta convoked the Christian Vallecas Assembly comprised of 180 elected representatives of clergy and laity to elaborate a long-term strategy of pastoral action. Before being prohibited by the Franco regime, the Assembly intended to discuss a program based on the need "to foster a church of the people, prophetic and free, to create small communities, to reform the parish radically" by making it a "community of communities, to give priority to evangelization that sets people free, to review the sacraments from the viewpoint of faith and religious liberty, to recover the social and political dimension of the faith."[16] Although the organization behind this pastoral approach functioned unevenly, especially at the level of deanery and parish councils, and although Iniesta's bold initiatives provoked a torrent of criticism from conservative clergy and laity, the operation of the Vallecas vicarate showed adaptation to the grass roots unimaginable in the highly centralized diocesan administrations of the past. The success of vicarates over the country as a whole is less certain. Critics have alleged that in many cases diocesan curias retained their preponderant role, often reducing vicarates to an "uncomfortable and not very effective situation."[17]

The flexible and open character of the Vallecas vicarate owed a considerable debt to Cardinal Tarancón. Although few bishops were so strongly committed to organizational initiatives, the historic model of supreme episcopal authority dictating pastoral policy through the diocesan curia gave way throughout the country to the creation of consultative bodies. In response to the Vatican Council's directives, diocesan administrations became more collective through the creation of episcopal councils composed of representatives of the curia and local ecclesiastical administrators. Bishops established Councils of Priests to discuss issues of common concern, while diocesan pastoral councils with lay and clerical representatives appeared in many sees. At the national level, a Council of the Laity was established to reflect the Church's recognition of the importance of laypersons in the community of believers promoted by the Vatican Council. The consultative surge sometimes took on spectacular proportions. In 1979, Cardinal Jubany of Barcelona called a Diocesan Assembly attended by twenty-five thousand priests, religious,

16. Ibid., pp. 18–19. The controversy provoked by the government's prohibition has been discussed in detail by Cardinal Tarancón, *Confesiones* (Madrid, 1996), pp. 751–801. Although the cardinal entertained some doubts about the direction of the Assembly, he agreed to preside over its proceedings and publicly defended it when the government ordered its suspension.

17. Fernando Urbina, "Formas de vida de la Iglesia de España, 1939–1975," in Fernando Urbina et al., *Iglesia y sociedad en España, 1939–1975* (Madrid, 1977), p. 70.

laypersons, and representatives of religious associations of every description "to engender a new dynamism" reflecting conciliar principles.[18]

The proliferation of consultative bodies represented a break with the past. How effectively these arrangements bridged the historic gap between bishops and priests and between laity and clergy is more difficult to establish. In the immediate post-conciliar period, consultative organs were established in individual dioceses more through trial and error than through application of a consistent organizational plan. As in the past, success or failure depended on the attitude of individual bishops. Even conservative bishops went through the motions of creating consultative bodies, but, as in the case of Bishop Gurpide of Bilbao in the years immediately after the Council, they often paid little attention to them.[19] But Cardinals Tarancón and Jubany enthusiastically promoted the consultative process in their dioceses.

In the immediate aftermath of the Council, acute tensions sometimes developed between diocesan authorities and the new Councils of Priests. In 1971, for example, six members of the Valencia council resigned their posts because of "deceptions and frustrations" arising from the conduct of diocesan administrators.[20] By the early 1980s, such conflicts began to subside, although the president of the CEE at the time recognized that priests wanted "more representative" councils to play a decisive role in diocesan life.[21] There is evidence in some dioceses, notably Bilbao, that beginning in 1969 during the administration of Bishop Cirarda, a genuine dialogue between bishops and priests was created that eventually provided for the election of episcopal vicars by the clergy.[22]

Whatever their limitations, diocesan Councils of Priests created a climate of dialogue previously lacking in the Church's organization. At the same time, the traditional figure of the bishop bedecked in official decorations and set off from his clergy by marked differences in income and style of life vanished from the scene. By the early 1990s, the ten to one salary ratio between prelates and parish priests prevailing in 1900 had narrowed to less than two to one.[23] Although bishops appeared from time to time in official ceremonies, they did not do so, as before 1931 and during the Franco regime, as ecclesiastical notables of a Catholic State. In dem-

18. *¿Qué es la diócesis de Barcelona?*, p. 15.

19. In 1966, Gurpide created a Diocesan Pastoral Council but "ignored its proposals with respect to the most burning questions." Angel María Unzueta, *Vaticano II e Iglesia local* (Bilbao, 1994), p. 273.

20. Josep M. Soriano i Bessó, "Crisi i desorientació a l'Església de València," *Serra d'Or* (1971), no. 141, p. 11.

21. Gabino Díaz Merchán, "Respuesta del presidente de la Conferencia Episcopal Española para la sesión extraordinaria del sínodo de los obispos de noviembre de 1985," in *El postconcilio en España*, p. 399.

22. Unzueta, *Vaticano II e Iglesia local*, pp. 277, 287–88.

23. In 1990, the salary of Gabino Díaz Merchán as archbishop of Oviedo and president of the CEE was 77,000 pesetas a year. The minimum salary guaranteed to the parochial clergy of his diocese was 55,000. Gabino Díaz Merchán, "La Iglesia no puede mantener su mensaje y su vitalidad sin el apoyo decidido de los laicos," in *España 2000 ¿cristiana?*, ed. María José Francés (Madrid, 1990), pp. 70–71.

ocratic Spain, they occupied no ex-officio seats in parliament and held no official positions. The removal of these secular encumbrances allowed bishops to direct their energies primarily to pastoral concerns for the first time in the Spanish Church's modern history.

In one important area, the influence of some bishops increased substantially following the end of the government's ecclesiastical patronage rights. The papal nuncio, whose influence over episcopal appointments increased dramatically after 1976, solicited the names of possible candidates for bishoprics from members of the hierarchy who, to a greater or lesser degree (depending on their personal stature before the nunciature and the Vatican), provided the personnel filter necessary for those aspiring to episcopal office.[24] Although simpler in form than the civil-ecclesiastical filter of the Franco era, the selection process rested on behind-the-scenes maneuvering within a narrow episcopal circle that contrasted with the consultative procedures adopted in other ecclesiastical activities. In response, progressive Catholic groups often called for the participation of priests and faithful in the selection of bishops. There was also strong sentiment in the CEE for a more collegial approach to episcopal nominations to replace a system based on the recommendations of the nuncio and a select few of their colleagues.[25]

The Vatican refused to change appointment procedures. Having waited for so long to secure the right of free appointment, it was not about to give away a benefit so recently acquired. Nor was it prepared to abandon the opportunity to create a hierarchy in accord with papal objectives. Whether the appointments of Suquía to replace Tarancón (1983), of Antonio María Rouco to succeed Suquía (1994), or of Ricard Carles to replace Jubany (1990) would also have resulted from a broader consultative process is problematical. But John Paul II did recognize the concerns of clergy and laity in those regions with a strong sense of cultural and linguistic identity. The historic practice, episodic during the Restoration and more consistent during the Primo de Rivera and Franco dictatorships, of appointing nonnative bishops in the Basque Provinces and Catalonia gave way to the nomination of prelates who were either native to their regions and/or, in the case of Catalonia, were fluent in the Catalan language. There was no repeat performance of the 1966 appointment of the non-Catalan speaking González Martín to the archdiocese of Barcelona, a nomination that evoked widespread lay and clerical protests, although, inexplicably, the pope appointed a non-Basque to the

24. During the tenure of Luigi Dadaglio as nuncio, for example, Cardinal Bueno Monreal of Seville secured the appointment of six priests of his diocese to episcopal office. José Manuel Cuenca Toribio, *Sociología del episcopado español e hispanoamericano, 1789–1985* (Madrid, 1986), p. 429. The archbishops of Madrid, Tarancón and Suquía, Barcelona, Jubany, among others, were "decisive agents" in the nomination of "a good number of prelates" (pp. 429–30). From 1985, the papal nuncio, Mario Tagliaferri, played a key role in the selection of new bishops. Emilio Zuñeda, "1993: año santo, año de crisis, año de diálogo," *Siglo XX* (1994), vol. 5, no. 18, p. 11.

25. "Memoria-informe de la Conferencia Episcopal Española," p. 431.

bishopric of Bilbao in 1995, despite the intense lobbying efforts of the regional government.[26]

Demands for the appointment of native bishops also surfaced in other autonomous regions created by the 1978 constitution, although the pressure from below was less intense than in Catalonia and the Basque Provinces. The partial regionalization of the hierarchy stirred an undercurrent of resistance from conservative clergy, who believed that it compromised the national, historical character of the hierarchy that had allowed two Catalans, Cardinals Gomá and Pla y Deniel, to occupy the primatial see of Toledo between 1933 and 1966. Critics also objected that for all practical purposes nonnative clergy were excluded from the possibility of securing episcopal positions in the Basque Provinces and Catalan-speaking regions. Such protests received little support from the Episcopal Conference. In 1983, Archbishop Díaz Merchán, then president of the CEE, argued that an individual's place of birth should not be a determining factor in episcopal nominations, but he defended the new appointment policy by stressing that a candidate's "capacity of assimilation of the culture [and] knowledge of the language" of his diocese were necessary qualifications for high ecclesiastical office.[27]

Criticism directed against the balkanization of the hierarchy along regional lines proved ineffective because the creation of the Episcopal Conference in 1966 endowed the hierarchy for the first time in its history with an effective national organization. In the past, occasional meetings of the bishops dealt with *ad hoc* questions of importance. After 1923, the Committee of Metropolitans met regularly, but it represented only the archbishops heading the ecclesiastical provinces.[28] In contrast, the CEE included all active bishops, including auxiliary bishops. It also developed a sophisticated internal organization with a plenary assembly meeting twice a year, a permanent executive committee of twenty members that met more frequently to advise the president, and fifteen technical commissions, each headed by a bishop, responsible for specific areas of the Church's activity, including the

26. The transfer of the bishop of Palencia, Ricardo Bláquez Pérez, to Bilbao provoked the strong opposition of the regional government, dominated by the PNV. It alleged that the Vatican's decision to appoint a non-Basque was a "stratagem of the papal nuncio in Madrid, Mario Tagliaferri, and the most conservative sectors of the Church" to counter the influence of the more strongly nationalist Bishop Setién of San Sebastián. A. Guenaga, "El PNV rechaza el nombramiento de un obispo no vasco para Bilbao," *El País* (edición internacional), September 11, 1995. Nor did the Vatican yield to continuing pressure from the Basque clergy for the creation of an ecclesiastical province in the region based in Vitoria. In 1983, Bishop Uriarte of Bilbao appealed for the establishment of a Basque metropolitan see to no avail. *Ya*, February 15, 1983.

27. The president of the CEE discussed the controversy over episcopal appointments in an extensive statement published in *Ya*, February 20, 1983.

28. The establishment of the CEE arose from the recommendation of the Second Vatican Council, which called the creation of episcopal conferences "a form of assembly in which the bishops of a certain country or region exercise their pastoral office jointly in order to enhance the Church's beneficial influence on all men." Quoted in Frances Lannon, "An Élite of Grace: The Spanish Bishops in the Twentieth Century," in *Élites and Power in Twentieth-Century Spain: Essays in Honour of Sir Raymond Carr*, ed. Frances Lannon and Paul Preston (Oxford, 1990), p. 17.

clergy, seminaries, the lay apostolate, the liturgy, and pastoral strategy. The agreements of the late 1970s between the UCD government and the Vatican enhanced the CEE's importance by recognizing it as the official negotiating body of the Spanish Church with the government dealing with matters such as ecclesiastical finances and education included in the diplomatic *acuerdos* of the 1970s. Recognition of this official role, of the "bishops together . . . as the voice of the Church before the State," an objective never attained during the Franco era, was seen as an achievement of historic dimensions.[29]

The CEE's official standing brought the Church important benefits, especially in the realm of ecclesiastical finances. As a result of the 1970s *acuerdos*, the Episcopal Conference received the global sum appropriated in the national budget for clerical salaries. The new arrangements replaced the system in place since the mid-nineteenth century, which provided each diocese with funding calculated on the number and parochial status of its clergy. Although the historic method of ecclesiastical finances was equitable in the sense that it rested on a uniform base for all dioceses, it failed to take into account that the population and wealth of some sees, particularly in large urban areas, gave their bishops more resources than those available to prelates in smaller, largely rural dioceses. During the Republic, Cardinal Vidal i Barraquer attempted to remedy these severe imbalances in diocesan income but with indifferent success. As the recipient of government funds for ecclesiastical purposes, the CEE was able to create a Common Interdiocesan Fund that included the official subsidy and contributions assessed on individual dioceses according to their wealth.[30] As a result, the Church was able to eliminate, for the most part, the uneven distribution of resources among dioceses present since the earliest days of its history.

Adequately financed and staffed by an ecclesiastical version of a civil service, the CEE provided the hierarchy with an effective organization that allowed the bishops to engage in constant dialogue and address measures of common concern in a collegial setting. From a canonical point of view, the Episcopal Conference's decisions did not supersede the authority of individual bishops in their dioceses, and the precise extent of the CEE's authority "remains unclear."[31] But policies approved by the plenary assembly enjoyed a moral authority that few prelates dared ignore. Only Franco's old admirer, Bishop Guerra Campos of Cuenca, had the temerity to declare his autonomy from the Conference during the mid-1970s.

The CEE's autonomy was also limited by dependence on the Vatican. During the pontificate of Pope John Paul II, the Vatican has kept a close check on the activi-

29. *Ya*, January 11, 1979.

30. Until the new financial arrangements negotiated with the Socialist government came into force in 1989, government funds provided the lion's share of the interdiocesan fund. In 1988, for example, the *dotación estatal* furnished 13,842,985,000 pesetas, diocesan assessments only 1,139,017,314. *Estadísticas de la Iglesia católica*, p. 95, Table 53.

31. Lannon, "An Élite of Grace," p. 18.

ties of episcopal conferences to prevent serious differences from papal policy.[32] In 1988, a Vatican proposal to limit the role of episcopal conferences met with little sympathy from Spanish bishops despite their increasingly conservative inclinations.[33] On occasion, the Vatican has also acted unilaterally. Pope John Paul II's decision to raise the status of Opus Dei to the equivalent of a supra-national diocese with its own bishop was taken, for example, against the advice of many members of the Spanish hierarchy.[34] The Conference also had to contend with the influence exercised by the papal nuncio, who remains a key and independent link between the Spanish Church and Rome.

The Conference's creation and development provided a forum for episcopal debate designed to produce consensus decisions capable of furnishing the faithful with unified direction.[35] From the beginning of the CEE's history, the desire to project an image of unity created a closed, behind-the-scenes approach to transacting business that contrasted with the emergence of consultative bodies elsewhere in the Church. Although reports of debates and dissension filtered into the press, members of the hierarchy have revealed little about either the substance of the discussions or the divisions of opinion within the CEE's plenary assemblies and episcopal commissions.[36] Although defenders of the closed-door approach argue that confidentiality is an essential guarantee of free debate, critics have maintained that the CEE's decision-making procedures were out of step with openness in the conduct of ecclesiastical affairs and the evolving nature of Spanish society.[37] The Conference's failure to respond in a systematic way to the 1971 recommendations of the Asamblea Conjunta of bishops and priests produced, for example, a sense of disillusionment and frustration among clergy who believed that a new day of dialogue and renovation had arrived as the assembly began its deliberations.[38]

32. Pedro González Blasco and Juan González-Anleo, *Religión y sociedad en la España de los 90* (Madrid, 1992), pp. 135–36.

33. Francesc Valls, "Divergencias entre los obispos españoles por el documento vaticano sobre conferencias episcopales," *El País*, November 19, 1988. The proposal emerged from the Congregation for the Doctrine of the Faith headed by the conservative Cardinal Joseph Ratzinger. Only four Spanish bishops, among them Cardinal Suquía of Madrid and Antonio Rouco of Santiago de Compostela, supported the proposal without reservations. Ibid., November 20, 1988.

34. Lannon, "An Élite of Grace," p. 19.

35. José Luis Martín Descalzo observed that "it is an historic fact that all the decisions of the Spanish Episcopal Conference are taken either by very ample majorities or by moral unanimity among its members." On occasion, individual bishops set aside their opinions for the "good of the Church's pastoral unity." Quoted in González Blasco and González-Anleo, *Religión y sociedad*, p. 136.

36. The one important exception is the recently published work of Cardinal Tarancón, *Confesiones* (Madrid, 1996).

37. For a defense of the CEE's procedures, see José Delicado, "La Conferencia Episcopal Española," in Ruiz Giménez, *Iglesia, Estado y sociedad*, pp. 277–88.

38. It has been argued that the Assembly marked the "passing of the equator" for the Spanish Church, a high point of renovation that soon began to weaken before conservative attacks on its work and the spread of a spirit of "uncertainty" among clergy previously inspired by the reforming principles of the Council. Echarren, "Veinticinco años en la vida de la Iglesia española," pp. 46–48.

Progressive critics within the Church perceived the CEE as a centralized, technical bureaucracy, a national version of the powerful diocesan *curias* of the past. Even commentators who assess the Conference's work positively believe that the search for consensus has produced a "false unanimity," as dissenting bishops kept quiet rather than challenge their colleagues in open debate.[39] Whatever the merit of these criticisms, they reflected the existence of ongoing tensions between a hierarchy committed to consultation up to a point but concerned with defending episcopal authority and providing unified direction to the faithful in a time of extraordinary and not easily controlled effervescence among clergy and laity.

On balance, the organizational changes introduced at the highest levels of the Spanish Church represented a definite though limited break with the past. Bishops remained supreme in their dioceses, but they operated on the whole within a framework of advice and consultation. Although they debated the future of the Spanish Church behind closed doors, the CEE's technical commissions operated more openly. Free of the secular role in the State played by earlier episcopal generations, the bishops were able to concentrate more fully on pastoral activity than they had been in the past. Nowhere was this more evident than in Madrid during the tenure of Cardinal Tarancón. Although known primarily for his contribution to the country's transition to democracy, the cardinal built an extraordinary record of pastoral work. He introduced episcopal vicarates, reorganized the diocesan seminary, promoted the involvement of the laity, and recognized the need for grassroots religious action through support for small "Christian communities." The cardinal oversaw the construction of one hundred parish churches, rejecting pressure to spend a fortune on completion of the city's ugly neo-Gothic cathedral until the religious needs of the "poorest districts" were met, a decision set aside by his successor.[40]

Parishes and Their Clergy

The parish remained the local unit of ecclesiastical organization despite the appearance following the Vatican Council of religious groups and movements operating either independently or semi-autonomously from the traditional parochial structure. Between 1960 and 1987, the Church reversed a long and progressive decline in the number of parishes. The 20,250 recorded in 1927 fell to 18,869 by 1960 but rose to 22,488 by 1987.[41] Expansion was concentrated in the cities, a clear recognition by the bishops of the increasingly urban character of Spanish society.

39. Codina, Prado, and Pereda, *Analizar la Iglesia*, pp. 234–35; Jesús Iribarren, "Episcopado y Conferencia Episcopal," *El postconcilio en España*, p. 246.

40. *ABC*, September 5, 1976.

41. *Anuario estadístico de España*, 1927 (Madrid, 1929), p. 602; González Blasco and González-Anleo, *Religión y sociedad*, p. 130, Table 7:5.

In 1900, for example, the Madrid diocese contained 240 parishes. This figure remained stable for decades until the massive construction program carried out by Archbishop Morcillo and Cardinal Tarancón increased the number of parishes in the diocese to 652 by 1983.[42] For the first time since the mid-nineteenth century, the Church succeeded in establishing a workable balance between its parochial infrastructure and population in the country's largest diocese.

There was a less favorable side to the parochial ledger. The Church gave priority to increasing the number of city parishes in a period of urban growth. But it continued to sustain an ecclesiastical organization in which 53 percent of the country's parishes, concentrated in rural districts of central and northern Spain, contained five hundred persons or less.[43] Since the turn of the century, advocates of parochial reform had called for a sweeping reorganization to reduce the number of small parishes. Such appeals went unheeded for six decades and stood no more chance of being realized following the Vatican Council. Parochial amalgamation was considered, for example, in Galicia, where "microparishes" predominated in the countryside. But diocesan authorities were reluctant to close rural parishes, recognizing that they remained a focus of community identity for villagers.[44] But maintaining this parochial organization exacted a price once clerical ranks began to thin. By 1986, 10,433 parishes, nearly half of the total in the country, lacked resident priests.[45] The dioceses with the most vacancies, Astorga, Burgos, León, Lugo, Oviedo, Urgel, and Vitoria, were for the most part dioceses with a rural population identified historically with high rates of religious observance. Addressing the pastoral needs of peasant villages that have long formed an important base of Spanish Catholicism remains an unresolved problem for the Church.

The growing number of parishes lacking a resident priest also reflected a massive decline in vocations. The number of major seminarians declined from 6,995 to 1,684 between 1968 and 1982.[46] Between 1970 and 1982, the number of diocesan priests fell from 25,105 to 22,592.[47] New ordinations were insufficient to replace priests who either died or abandoned the priesthood. Over a twenty-year period, approximately 3,000 priests left the ministry, a rate of departure consistently

42. J. C. Grey, "Madrid-Alcalá, Diocese of," in *The Catholic Encyclopedia*, ed. Charles G. Herbermann (16 vols., New York, 1907–1914), vol. 9, p. 518; *Estadísticas de la Iglesia católica*, p. 63, Table 36. Parochial expansion in Barcelona followed a similar course, although it was less spectacular than in the case of Madrid. The Barcelona diocese contained 231 parishes in 1900, 443 in 1985. Tirso López, "Barcelona, Diocese of," *The Catholic Encyclopedia*, vol. 2, p. 290.

43. *Ya*, January 13, 1983.

44. Xosé M. R. Pampín, *Nova concencia na Igrexa galega* (Pontevedra, 1976), p. 149.

45. *Estadísticas de la Iglesia católica*, p. 66, Table 39.

46. Juan González-Anleo, "La identidad de los católicos españoles," in Fernando Azcona et al., *Catolicismo en España: análisis sociológico* (Madrid, 1985), p. 93.

47. Bernardo G. Cendán, "El clero español, ayer y hoy," in Azcona et al., *Catolicismo en España*, p. 294, Table 1.

higher in Spain than in France.[48] But during the 1980s and early 1990s, the number of priests leaving the ministry began to level off, while seminary enrollments grew modestly. This has not prevented further decline, as an increasingly elderly clergy passes from the scene.[49] But there is evidence that dire predictions of a plunge in the size of the secular clergy to 17,000 by the year 2000 are excessive. If current trends continue, a figure of approximately 19,000 by the end of the decade appears more likely.[50]

A seminary recruitment leaflet published in 1960 drew a traditional picture of the parish priest as primarily an agent of the cult who "upbraided vices, proclaimed the Kingdom of God among the humble," and "directed the good progress of his village," while living in isolation to avoid "backbiting" gossip should he mingle too closely with his congregation.[51] Within a decade, this time-honored image was questioned by restless younger clergy inspired by the Vatican Council. They called upon priests to live "closer to the actual world and secular culture," to avoid using their positions to impose their "temporal" views on the laity, and to break with the idea that clerics formed a "closed group" isolated from their congregations.[52]

The effect of the religious changes flowing from the Council, the secularizing influence of socioeconomic change on the traditional role of the priest, and debates over the obligation to celibacy produced a widespread perception of a clergy suffering from a crisis of identity.[53] This was not by any means an exclusively Spanish phenomenon; but were there specifically Spanish causes for the massive decline in vocations? The Church emphasized the priesthood as spiritual calling, but the ideal in Spain often fell short of reality. In the past, the position of the parish priest as an ecclesiastical civil servant with a modest education, local prestige, job security, and limited financial rewards had represented a way out for the sons of the peasantry within a society that provided few other opportunities. Since the turn of the century, clerical commentators had criticized the damaging effects on pastoral work caused by priests inspired less by spiritual than by careerist motives. Beginning in the 1960s, economic change, including a massive expansion of public ed-

48. The number of "defections" from the priesthood reached a peak in 1977 when 263 left the clergy. Compare the situation in France, where 129 did so. Ibid.; "Memoria-informe de la Conferencia Episcopal Española," p. 435.

49. By 1989, only 18.57 percent of diocesan priests were under forty-four years of age. González Blasco and González-Anleo, *Religión y sociedad,* p. 128. By the academic year 1987–1988, the number of major seminarians increased to 2,119. The archdiocese of Madrid-Alcalá, for example, saw the number of seminarians increase from a low of 75 in the late 1970s to 180 during this period. *Estadísticas de la Iglesia católica,* p. 163, Table 98.

50. González Blasco and González-Anleo, *Religión y sociedad,* p. 128. The number of diocesan priests declined by 513 between 1989 and 1992, suggesting that the rate of loss has become less dramatic. Ricardo Coarasa, "Más vocaciones y menos secularización logran estabilizar el número de sacerdotes en España," *ABC,* February 21, 1995.

51. *El cura de cualquier pueblo* (Astorga, 1960). No page numbers given.

52. José Puente Egido, "El nacional-catolicismo como desviación del catolicismo," *Iglesia Viva* (1970), no. 30, pp. 512–13.

53. Cendán, "El clero español, ayer y hoy," p. 296.

ucation, provided more employment choices in a range of professions paying decent incomes, while the salaries of diocesan priests lagged behind those of the more attractive occupational competition.[54] The diminished social and economic appeal of a priestly career within a rapidly modernizing society corresponded to a similar decline in status observed for military officers.[55]

The Church lamented the severe decline in seminary enrollments, but recognized that the situation brought some benefits. Seminarians embraced a clerical life as a result of personal decision rather than because of societal pressures. On average, they were older and more mature than earlier student generations. Many entered the seminary after completing university or working in a profession, in contrast to the historic pattern of recruiting major seminarians from minor seminaries in which students enrolled at the age of twelve or thirteen. In 1968, one in four seminarians expressed doubts about his vocation but by 1988 only one in twenty held such reservations.[56] At the same time, clerical education broke with the long-cherished idea of the seminary as a fortress isolating impressionable students from the dangers of the secular world. During the 1970s, Cardinal Tarancón transformed the Madrid seminary that his predecessor had sought to keep within a traditional framework. Students formed small groups working with a team of carefully chosen instructors and left the seminary for extensive periods of pastoral activity in the archdiocese's poorest parishes.[57] To a limited extent, the emergence of new generations of highly motivated parish priests trained in direct contact with the conditions they were to face in the field compensated for declining clerical numbers. An important shift also occurred in the geographical and social origins of seminarians. In 1969, 60 percent of seminarians came from towns of less than five thousand inhabitants, a proportion that declined to 37 percent by 1988, while recruitment from the urban working class doubled from 20 percent to 40 percent.[58]

In the years immediately following the Vatican Council, the Spanish Church possessed a large, young clergy committed to a program of change. Priests attending the Asamblea Conjunta of 1971 demanded an end to what they saw as the traditional caste status of the clergy within the Church. They called upon the bishops to abandon the honors and offices bestowed by the State. They asked the hierarchy to abandon its authoritarian style in favor of dialogue and to give clergy and faith-

54. During the early 1990s, 27.8 percent of the clergy received a monthly income of 80,000 pesetas, while 54 percent of the general population did so. At the lower end of the salary scale, monthly income of 65,000 and below, the proportion was reversed. Almost two-thirds of the clergy, or 62.5 percent, fell into this salary category, versus 28.3 percent of the population as a whole. González Blasco and González-Anleo, *Religión y sociedad*, p. 147, Table 8:6.

55. Julio Busquets, *El militar de carrera en España* (2d ed., Barcelona, 1971), pp. 196–97.

56. *Ya*, February 26, 1983; Alberto Iniesta, "Los curas del siglo XXI," *El País* (edición internacional), March 21, 1988.

57. Vicente Enrique y Tarancón, "50 años de sacerdocio en España," in Ruiz Giménez, *Iglesia, Estado y sociedad*, pp. 400–401; *Ya*, March 17, 1983.

58. Iniesta, "Los curas del siglo XXI."

ful a role in administering ecclesiastical finances. They also sought open debate over the obligation to celibacy. They appealed for a pluralistic pastoral strategy designed to reach every segment of society, especially workers, in innovative ways. They stressed the need for new methods to reinvigorate the parish and promote the formation of smaller "Christian communities." The Church, they maintained, must move from the "obscure night" of the past to a "more purified image" of Christ's kingdom.[59]

The impulse to renovation and institutional reform that lay behind these appeals surged ahead of the still cautious attitude of the hierarchy. But it would have been difficult in the best of circumstances to sustain such clerical effervescence indefinitely. It became more difficult to do so as the young clergy of the early 1970s became older, its ranks depleted with every passing year. By the early 1980s, criticism of priests submerged in a "pastoral and existential routine" began to appear.[60] There was nothing unusual about a situation often noted by pastoral commentators in the past. In the normal course of events, an aging clergy lacks the energy of a younger generation that in the case of Spain failed to appear in significant numbers. By 1990, priests over the age of fifty formed 67 percent of clerical ranks, while clergy under forty were only marginally greater in number than those over seventy.[61]

In these circumstances, it was not surprising that the most dynamic phase of parochial renovation occurred in the decade following the end of the Vatican Council. However imperfectly developed, the new spirit of consultation between bishops and clergy opened the door to a parochial reorganization based on a team approach to the ministry, in place of the traditional hierarchical structure of pastoral work moving upward from the parish priest to his immediate superior, the archpriest, and then to the bishop and his curia. During the late 1960s in the diocese of Solsona, for example, a recently formed Pastoral Council divided the diocese into five zones, each headed by a coordinator elected by the clergy. At a lower level, teams of priests experienced in pastoral work replaced the single archpriest of the past and worked closely with the parochial clergy of their districts.[62]

The parochial clergy of several small towns in the Vallès Oriental of Catalonia came together to provide collective services as a group to the entire area, an arrangement that in their judgment was more effective than the traditional system based on priests working only in their own parishes.[63] Similar arrangements based on a collective but still largely conventional ministry appeared elsewhere, especially in rural districts, where they appear to have functioned with some success.

59. "Exigencias evangélicas de la misión del presbítero," *Asamblea-Conjunta obispos-sacerdotes*, ed. Secretariado Nacional del Clero (Madrid, 1971), p. 490.

60. Ramón Echarren Ysturiz, "Los nuevos curas," in *Iglesia, Estado y sociedad*, p. 285.

61. Rafael López Pintor, "La Iglesia española en cifras," *XX Siglos* (1993), vol. 4, no. 13, p. 23.

62. "Situació pastoral del bisbat de Solsona," *Presbyterium* (1970), no. 8, pp. 45–46.

63. "Sis pobles, un sol objectivu pastoral: una tarda amb l'equip de l'Ametella," in ibid., no. 9, pp. 20–23.

Applying this model to urban, working-class parishes proved more difficult, in part because attempts at pastoral innovation were often associated with social activism that the ecclesiastical authorities viewed with either suspicion or uncertainty.[64] The parish of San Lorenzo in the Egara district of the Catalan industrial town of Tarrasa was one of the more successful and controversial because it gave priority to social action as essential to effective pastoral work in a "working-class, conciliar parish."[65] The three priests forming its team ministry converted the rectory from the "house of the *cura*" to a "house of the people" in which all were welcome. The clergy supported the district's workers during a series of confrontations with the Franco regime during the late 1960s and early 1970s. During a 1970 strike against the AEG factory, several priests were arrested and the rectory raided by the police. Such actions aroused the hostility of the local police chief, who declared, "I shall finish with these *curas* in four months."[66]

The priests of the Vallès Oriental and San Lorenzo worked in pastoral teams, but the first adopted an expanded and more efficient version of traditional parochial activity, while the second pursued a more radical approach closely linked to the social, economic, and political concerns of the local population. In fact, there was no single model of team ministry applied to the country as a whole. As always in the Spanish Church, the attitude of individual bishops and diocesan administrators was important. During the 1960s, Bishop Eduardo Martínez González of Zamora readily agreed to a request of the team ministry in the rural district of Aliste to suppress surplice fees. But Archbishop González Martín had no scruples about removing priests in Tarrasa whose parishes were alleged to contain "rebellious people."[67]

Inspired by the example of the worker-priest movement in France, a small number of clergy combined their pastoral ministry with industrial employment as a means of identifying more closely with the people living within their parishes. If the Church wishes "to incorporate itself into the people, into the working class," declared an advocate of worker-priests, it must create "new *curas*" formed on the model of evangelical poverty associated with Saint Joseph.[68] During the early 1970s, ten priests of the Logroño diocese worked either full- or part-time for several hours a day as mechanics, day laborers, sawyers, and plasterers. In Santa Coloma, an industrial suburb of Barcelona, a group of priests rejected the traditional idea of the parish as a vehicle for filling the church for services and administering the sacraments. They believed it necessary to accept manual labor as an in-

64. Jorge Bertrán, *Los difíciles caminos de la misión obrera* (Barcelona, 1968), p. 15.

65. Josep Ricart Oller, *Egara: una parroquia obrera bajo el franquismo, 1963–1977* (Tarrasa, 1979), p. 28.

66. Quoted in ibid., p. 183.

67. "Testimonio misionero en una zona rural," *Pastoral Misionera* (1967), p. 124; Ricart Oller, *Egara: una parroquia obrera*, p. 83.

68. José Luis Martín Vigil, *Los curas "comunistas"* (2d ed., Oviedo, 1965), pp. 246, 83.

tegral part of their ministry if they were to stand any chance of reaching the "heart" of working-class life.[69]

The worker-priest movement experienced some successes, especially in industrial Catalonia, but it never developed as fully as its counterpart in France, in part because it arose from the clerical grass roots rather than from any national initiative. By the early 1980s, only two hundred clerics were functioning as worker-priests.[70] During the later Franco regime, such experiments were viewed with deep suspicion by the authorities and conservative Catholics, who viewed worker-priests as "red" *curas*. Nor did the hierarchy in general provide unqualified support to an experiment through which worker-priests often embraced the more radical views of the people with whom they lived and worked. The worker-priests of Logroño believed that they were at best simply tolerated by the local bishop and that their work was marginal to the diocese's pastoral strategy.[71]

Collective parochial ministries also encountered their share of problems. The Aliste team lost one of its members, who became depressed by the "tension and pressure" to which he was subjected by older parish priests who were unsympathetic to the idea of a collective ministry.[72] A member of the San Lorenzo group, discouraged by what in his judgment was the official Church's failure to recognize an evangelical commitment to social justice, concluded after years of work, "I see no future for the Church, none."[73] Team members, often influenced by new theological currents, sometimes abandoned traditional practices that aroused popular opposition. The priests of San Lorenzo announced that they were giving up the custom of giving a church burial to everyone "without distinction." They argued that there was no reason to provide Christian burial to individuals who never attended religious services. In view of their record of social activism, they were puzzled by popular reaction to this theologically correct policy. The people of the parish did not like it. "These *curas* do not even wish to bury," some declared.[74]

An overall assessment of the effectiveness of team ministries is not possible. It is not known how many of the country's parishes adopted it as a model, although it is likely that only a minority did so. On the positive side, the appearance of group ministries showed that the Church recognized the need for more flexible parochial arrangements at the grass roots in accord with conciliar exhortations for renovation of the parish. The team approach also provided a practical means for ministering to rural populations in areas where many small parishes lacked a priest. On

69. Ricardo Gil González, "Reflexión de los sacerdotes en el trabajo," *Pastoral Misionera* (1973), no. 6, p. 431; Jaime-P. Sayrach, "La evangelización desde la parroquia," in ibid., pp. 450, 455.

70. Fernando Urbina, "La evangelización del mundo industrial y rural en España," in Angel Suquía et al., *Al servicio de la Iglesia y del pueblo: homenaje al Cardenal Tarancón en su 75 aniversario* (Madrid, 1984), p. 203.

71. "Reflexión de los sacerdotes en el trabajo," pp. 434–35.

72. "Testimonio misionero en una zona rural," p. 121.

73. Ricart Oller, *Egara: una parroquia obrera*, p. 235.

74. Ibid., pp. 164–65.

the negative side, in spite of innumerable discussions, conferences, and studies on how to reinvigorate the parish, carried out by diocesan bishops and the CEE through its Commission on the Clergy, a clearly focused and comprehensive organizational plan never emerged. In 1983, the CEE's secretary appealed for greater coordination of pastoral work among dioceses to replace prevailing methods of "improvisation and dispersion," while a later national conference concerned with making the parish central to evangelizing activity admitted that the parish, "such as it exists and is conceived today is insufficient to realize this mission."[75]

Whether this state of affairs developed from vestiges of the Church's historic disorganization as far as pastoral work was concerned or, as progressive clerics maintained, from the hierarchy's excessive caution before "any creative pastoral activity" is not clear.[76] In any event, success or failure depended on the energy and commitment of the parochial clergy. Once the enthusiasm and euphoria of the immediate post-Council years passed and the clergy grew older, the possibility receded of converting the country's parishes into the "22,000 vital centers of [evangelizing] irradiation" called for by advocates of parochial renovation.[77]

The Religious Orders

Male and female regulars, who had outnumbered the diocesan clergy by a substantial margin since the late nineteenth century, continued to form a varied and significant force in ecclesiastical ranks. But religious orders experienced a significant decline in membership, which fell from a high point of 117,556 during the 1960s to 90,323 by 1986–1987.[78] During this period, male religious declined from 27,810 to 18,557, nuns from 89,778 to 71,766. But there was an interesting difference in the chronology of decline between the male and female orders. The male regulars' demographic crisis occurred between 1968 and 1972, a period corresponding to a similar pattern of losses among diocesan priests. The female orders held their own until the mid-1970s, when the number of nuns began to decrease significantly.

As far as recruitment was concerned, the male orders managed better than did either the secular clergy or the orders of nuns. The number of candidates for full admission (novices) fell from 2,879 in 1963 to 1,053 in 1972, a figure that has since remained relatively stable. This was a significantly lower rate of decline than that among diocesan seminarians and stands in sharp contrast to a catastrophic reduction of novices in the female orders, which fell from 6,595 in 1966 to 751 by 1980.

75. *Ya*, September 21, 1983; "Congreso Parroquia Evangelizadora," *Ya*, November 13, 1988.

76. Floristan, "Presencia pastoral de la Iglesia," p. 125.

77. José María Javierre, "Mirando a la torre parroquial," *Ya*, November 13, 1988.

78. The statistics on the religious orders are compiled from Jesús María Vázquez, "Los religiosos españoles," *Catolicismo en España*, pp. 308–24; *Estadísticas de la Iglesia católica*, p. 146, Table 88, p. 154, Table 92.

Between 1980 and 1987, membership in the male orders declined modestly, while the female orders saw their numbers continue to fall in a severe downward spiral. There was also a significant difference in the age profile of male and female regulars. In 1984, nearly one-fourth of male religious were below the age of forty, in contrast to one-tenth of nuns.

The parish clergy benefited from a significant change of emphasis on the part of the male religious, who became more extensively involved in parish work. In the past, the masculine orders had contributed to pastoral activity through religious services in their own churches, supplementary assistance to parish priests, and a variety of evangelizing activities, of which missions were the most spectacular example. But there was little effective coordination with diocesan priests, who often saw the regulars as unwelcome competitors drawing the faithful away from parish churches. Submissions to the Asamblea Conjunta from the secular clergy appealed for the full integration of the male religious orders into diocesan pastoral activity.[79]

Circumstances favored a redirection of the orders' priorities in a pastoral direction within a framework of coordination with the parochial clergy. In response to the Vatican Council's call for the religious orders to redefine their mission in the light of conciliar principles, the regulars, both male and female, engaged in a process of self-criticism that was in many ways more intense and far-reaching than that of the secular clergy.[80] Despite debate and conflict, there was general recognition that "Spanish religious must go to the people" wherever they were to be found "with adequate initiatives."[81]

It also became evident that some of the traditional religious activities of the masculine orders revolving around the promotion of pious devotions and mass evangelization were losing their appeal in a changing and increasingly urban society. The institution of the popular mission, an important activity of the male orders for centuries, made a final spectacular appearance in 1965. The Seville mission assembled 387 priests who preached to 330,000 people gathered in 170 locations.[82] But as a result of the Council's emphasis on the idea of clergy and faithful forming a community, a "people of God," the traditional missionary formula of an "evangelization of the masses" directed towards individual "moral conversion based on fear, threats, a 'save your soul'" approach gave way to more specialized "evangelization of groups" designed to inspire "more solid motivations" among the faithful.[83] For all practical purposes, the traditional mission vanished from the Church's religious arsenal by the early 1970s.

As the mission declined, the male regulars began to enter parish work more ex-

79. "Relaciones de los obispos y presbíteros con los religosos y seglares," in *Asamblea Conjunta obispos-sacerdotes*, p. 391.

80. Jesús Álvarez Gómez, "Los religiosos/as," *El postconcilio en España*, pp. 285, 288–89.

81. "XII Semana Nacional para religiosos," *Ya*, April 5, 1983.

82. *Sevilla: misión 1965* (Madrid, 1965), p. 9.

83. B. Caballero, "La nueva evangelización," *Las misiones populares, hoy* (Madrid, 1973).

tensively than in the past. Between 1971 and 1986, the number of parishes staffed by the orders increased from 382 to 917, while nearly two-thirds of their priests performed pastoral duties in dioceses.[84] The increase in parishes directed by the orders was concentrated in urban areas, especially in Madrid, where the regulars administered nearly a sixth of the diocese's parishes by the mid-1980s.

The male orders also possessed sufficient internal flexibility to allow for pastoral experiments that would have been unimaginable in the past. None was more spectacular than the initiative taken by Father José María Llanos. Until the mid-1950s, his career was identified with National Catholicism as flamboyantly as that of any cleric of the time. The son of a military officer, Llanos was a convinced monarchist who entered the Jesuits before the Civil War. His confidence in the Nationalist cause deepened upon the assassination of a brother in the Republican zone. Ordained in 1939, Llanos wished to become a chaplain with the Blue Division sent by Franco to fight with the Germans on the Russian front. This ambition went unrealized, but through the 1940s he built a formidable reputation as a preacher and director of spiritual exercises to the Falange, military officers, and, on one occasion, to General Franco. In this phase of what he later called his "poetic militarism," he believed it possible to unite "militarism, spirituality, and *falangismo*" into a powerful religious force, a "Spanish Militia for Christ," in the "New Spain" that had emerged from the Civil War.[85]

Possessed of a strong independence of spirit, Llanos slowly began to move away from his conservative ideological origins during the early 1950s, when he showed sympathy for the self-criticism movement that spread among a minority of Spanish Catholics. In 1955, he received permission from his religious superiors to embark on an apostolate among the poor, working-class population of the Pozo del Tío Raimundo *barrio* in the Vallecas district of Madrid. There he remained for nearly four decades, increasingly convinced that social justice must form the cornerstone of effective pastoral work. Years of contact with the enormous economic and social disadvantages faced by the poor finally moved him towards greater sympathy with the Communist party, of which he became an official member after its legalization in 1977. Along with a fellow Jesuit, the progressive theologian José María Díez Alegría, he was welcomed with enormous enthusiasm to a PCE meeting in Vallecas, known as "Little Russia" by detractors. A widely circulated photo of Llanos raising a clenched fist in Communist salute provoked a torrent of criticism in the Church, especially in view of a statement issued by the hierarchy a week earlier calling upon Catholics to reject Marxist candidates in the upcoming June elections.[86]

84. Jesús María Vázquez, *Los religiosos españoles, hoy* (Madrid, 1973), pp. 100–101, Table 1; *Estadísticas de la Iglesia católica*, p. 65, Table 38. In 1984, for example, 9,304 of the country's 16,564 ordained regular clergy were involved in pastoral work, p. 137, Table 81; pp. 145–46, Table 88.

85. Quoted in José Luis González-Balado, *Padre Llanos: un jesuita en el suburbio* (Madrid, 1991), p. 183.

86. Ibid., pp. 302–4.

The response of Jesuit superiors to Llanos's activism says a good deal about the changes that had occurred in what had once been Spain's most elitist order, long identified with the social exclusivism of the Catholic bourgeoisie. In view of the uproar produced by the Vallecas meeting, the Jesuits' local superior published a statement disapproving of Llanos's intervention but recognizing that "his ideas are not in contradiction with his Christian faith and priestly ministry."[87] Llanos remained a Jesuit in good standing until his death in 1993, always using the initials S. J. after his name.

Llanos's personal odyssey was spectacular among members of the regular clergy, but it was by no means an isolated example. Another Jesuit, Joan García-Nieto, the son of a prominent banking family, cofounded the local unit of the Workers' Commission in the Baix Llobregat industrial area of Barcelona, participated in the establishment of the Christians for Socialism (CpS) movement during the early 1970s, and joined the Communist party of Catalonia.[88] Other Jesuits, inspired by the liberation theology that had developed in Latin America during the 1960s, advocated a radical approach to social justice with Marxist overtones that provoked intense criticism from conservative clergy and laity.[89]

But for the most part, religious orders have continued in their traditional role as educators and dispensers of charitable assistance. During the late 1980s, they staffed 1,545 hospitals, orphanages, and old age homes under direct ecclesiastical administration and provided 20,510 teachers to the Catholic school system. They also supplied personnel to 127 public health institutions managed by autonomous regional governments.[90] During the 1980s, the Socialist government removed a small number of religious (334) from some public health and social assistance institutions. This may have reflected a residual anticlericalism in official circles, but it is unlikely that any government can afford to dispense with the cost-effective services provided by religious in the future.[91] The greatest threat to the regulars' traditional educational and charitable activities has and will come from their declining numbers. Since 1977, the number of priests, brothers, and nuns teaching in Catholic schools has fallen significantly, while the proportion of lay instructors has increased.[92]

87. Quoted in ibid., pp. 305–6. This quotation is reproduced from the full text of the superior's statement.

88. "Joan García-Nieto," *El País*, July 25, 1994.

89. See, for example, the sustained attack of the historian Ricardo de la Cierva on members of the regular and secular clergy who were accused of introducing Marxist ideas into the Church under the cover of liberation theology. *Oscura rebelión en la Iglesia: jesuitas, teología de liberación, carmelitas, marianistas y socialistas* (Esplugues de Llobregat, 1987).

90. *Estadísticas de la Iglesia católica*, pp. 245–48, Tables 154–157.

91. In 1983, nearly half of the country's homes for the elderly were administered by the female orders. Two male orders, the Brothers of St. John of God and the Hospital Brothers of the Sacred Heart, ran 45 percent of institutions for the mentally ill. *Ya*, January 13, 1983.

92. In 1977, 27,136 religious taught in Church schools versus 20,510 a decade later. *Estadísticas de la Iglesia católica*, pp. 296–97, Tables 195–196.

From the 1830s until the recent past, the educational and charitable work of the religious orders was often the object of anticlerical criticism and periodic outbursts of violence. It is ironic that in democratic Spain the regulars face an uncertain future at a time when the powerful anticlerical currents of the past have virtually disappeared. Opinion surveys of the 1980s have indicated that only 12 percent of Spaniards consider themselves anticlerical, while 21 percent assess the Church's influence on Spanish society as negative, as opposed to 66 percent who perceive it as a defender of the poor and oppressed.[93]

The Laity

Conciliar recommendations for a new role for the laity in accord with the definition of the Church as a community of believers appeared to challenge historic clerical supremacy over lay associations. In twentieth-century Spain, the administrative history of Catholic Action took the form of successive internal reforms directed towards establishing complete episcopal control over the organization, a process that culminated in the controversial preemptive strike launched by the bishops in 1966. Cardinal Tarancón's observation years later that "we are too accustomed in Spain to demand that the hierarchy support, direct and even promote Christian movements" suggests that old habits died hard.[94] Expanding the laity's role within a Church long directed from the top down posed a daunting challenge that in the end was imperfectly met.

In some areas of activity, especially the liturgy and catechetical instruction, the Spanish Church managed to enlarge the laity's contribution without much difficulty. Laypeople served as readers of scriptural texts at Mass and as eucharistic ministers distributing communion to the faithful. Creating institutions for meaningful lay participation at the level of policy and decision making posed greater difficulties in view of the preponderance assumed by the Episcopal Conference after 1966. The bishops had no intention of abdicating what they saw as their responsibility for the direction of the Church to either clergy or laity, a tendency that became more pronounced following the succession of John Paul II to the papacy in 1978. To be sure, the CEE's technical commissions, and even a synod of bishops organized by the Episcopal Conference in 1987, invited lay participation. The attendance of forty lay assessors at the synod could scarcely have been imagined two decades earlier.[95] But lay representatives attended as advisors and remained excluded from the closed-door deliberations of the CEE itself.

Despite interminable discussion about the necessity of expanding the laity's

93. Rafael Díaz-Salazar, "La transición religiosa de los españoles," in *Religión y sociedad en España*, p. 116; "La institución eclesial en la sociedad española," in ibid., p. 297.

94. Pastoral letter reproduced in *Ya*, January 13, 1979.

95. Pedro Escartín Celaya, "Las instituciones intermedias," *XX Siglos* (1993), vol. 4, no. 13, p. 74.

contribution to the Church's life, the range of action open to increased lay participation was limited for all practical purposes to pastoral activity broadly conceived. Laypersons attended a variety of ecclesiastical assemblies, including diocesan pastoral councils and special meetings such as that organized by Cardinal Jubany of Barcelona in 1979, which sought to develop new evangelizing strategies. They also served on parochial councils, although by the mid-1980s many parishes still lacked them despite repeated episcopal exhortations urging their creation.[96] A significant innovation took the form of diocesan councils of laity founded in many dioceses during the 1970s. In 1971, Bishop Cirarda, administrator of the Bilbao diocese, established such a council to join ecclesiastical administrators and clergy in a broad effort to devise effective pastoral techniques adapted to changing social and economic conditions.[97] The CEE promoted the formation of a national Council of the Laity representing fifty lay associations in an attempt to pick up the pieces left in the wake of the crisis in Catholic Action.[98]

Lay participation in these diverse organizations, particularly at the parochial and diocesan levels, represented a breakthrough of sorts by recognizing that laypersons could contribute in a positive way to the development of pastoral policy, developed on the basis of cooperation between clergy and laity. But when all is said and done, the laity's role remained primarily consultative in character.

Despite the new role assigned to the laity in the development of pastoral policy, lay participation in the life of the Church continued to follow a traditional course for the most part. The 3,951,538 Catholics who belonged to seventy-three recognized secular associations in 1993 engaged in activities that would have been familiar to earlier generations.[99] Although the number of individuals involved was large, it was less impressive than first appears. Three million individuals belonged to the Confederación Católica de Padres de Familia y Padres de Alumnos (CONCAPA), an organization committed to defending the interests of the Church in education. How many of its members participated actively in its affairs or simply paid their membership fees as dutiful parents with children in Catholic schools is unclear.[100] Like its predecessor, formed after the turn of the century to combat the educational reforms of Liberal party governments and used later to oppose the education legislation of the Second Republic, the CONCAPA functioned primarily as a specialized lobby in support of the hierarchy's efforts on behalf of Catholic schools rather than as a movement of religious innovation. The organization stood

96. "Memoria-informe de la Conferencia Episcopal Española," p. 445.

97. Anzueta, *Vaticano II e Iglesia local*, pp. 285–87.

98. Ibid.; Pedro Escartín Celaya, "Veinte años de apostolado seglar asociado," in *El postconcilio en España*, pp. 323–24.

99. Students of Catholic lay associations agree that accurate statistics are hard to come by, largely because of the extraordinary variety of these organizations' activities and the absence of many from a larger organizational framework. González Blasco and González-Anleo, *Religión y sociedad*, p. 104; López Pintor, "La Iglesia española en cifras," pp. 24–25.

100. González Blasco and González-Anleo, *Religión y sociedad*, p. 104.

in the front line of the Church's campaign against the LODE during the intense battles of 1983 with the PSOE government.

Other organizations included devotional associations, specialized groups like the Catholic Boy Scouts, and charitable foundations. Caritas, the country's largest charity, depended on the work of 26,600 volunteers. Following the crisis of 1966, Catholic Action finally reemerged as a functioning organization, but on a reduced scale. By 1988, it contained 30,000 militants with an additional 60,000 involved in affiliated groups, in contrast to a membership of 533,000 in 1956.[101] That the organization was by this time headed by a woman, Eva Gómez Pina, provides an indication of change in an association long dominated by men. Although Catholic Action declared that it had a "clear vision of the future" and avoided the political entanglements characteristic of its past in favor of a commitment to "evangelization," it was no longer the central institution that for so long had been the Church's principal channel for enlisting the laity in defense of its interests.[102]

The sheer variety of Catholic lay associations functioning in the 1990s indicates that the Church has managed to sustain a reasonable level of associational activity among the laity. But how effectively these numerous organizations, so diverse in purpose, function within an effective framework of coordination is open to discussion. The Spanish Church has always found it difficult to create an institutional model capable of providing coherent direction to its multitude of lay associations. Even ardent supporters of such groups during the 1990s have admitted that collaboration among them is still "not easy."[103] Nor is it clear how many practicing Catholics participated actively in the work of lay organizations. If one discounts a significant portion of the CONCAPA membership as nominal, a not unreasonable assumption, the participation of approximately five hundred thousand in associations that could recruit from the millions of faithful who regard themselves as Catholics in good standing is scarcely earth-shattering.

The Church has also continued to project its message to the laity and the public through the media. But a significant change occurred in 1988, when the holding company controlled by the CEE decided to sell the country's largest Catholic daily, *Ya*, and other newspapers. Financial losses created by intense competition for circulation among an ever-larger number of newspapers in democratic Spain lay behind the decision to abandon a field to which the Church had attached enormous importance since the nineteenth century. The end of a long journalistic tradition, with its best example in *El Debate* (1911–1936), created regrets, but the ecclesiastical leadership did not long dwell in the realm of nostalgia. The CEE shifted

101. Ibid., pp. 104–5; Pintor, "La Iglesia española en cifras," p. 25.

102. Javier Fernández, "Eva Gómez Pina: 'La Acción Católica está viva y trabaja con una clara visión de futuro,'" *Ya*, November 27, 1988.

103. Luis G.-Fierro, "Movimientos laicales en la Iglesia: punta de lanza para la nueva evangelización," *ABC*, June 26, 1993.

its attention and money to strengthening its network (COPE) of 104 radio stations. The second largest radio network in the country, the COPE has generally prospered since 1988. In 1995, it returned handsome profits to its principal shareholders, notably the CEE and diocesan bishops, while providing the Church with an effective means of reaching a mass audience.[104]

How deeply the organizational changes introduced in the decades following the Council contributed to transforming the Church remains a matter of debate. But a process of uneven and sometimes ambiguous change occurred that made the Church of 1990 a different institution from its predecessor of 1960. Despite ongoing tension over the nature and pace of reform, bishops, clergy, and the laity were affected in one way or another by the application of conciliar principles to an institution that had remained organizationally immobile through much of its modern history. The purpose of change was primarily religious. The Church sought to adapt its organization to the demands of the modern world with a view to fulfilling its traditional objective of spreading religion and deepening the quality of faith among Spaniards. Realizing this objective, even during the heady days of the Franco dictatorship, had never been easy. In a secular, democratic Spain swept by social and economic changes, achieving this historic goal has proved no less difficult and complicated.

104. "La Iglesia potencia su cadena de emisoras de radio después de abandonar la prensa diaria," *El País*, June 12, 1989; "La COPE dice haber obtenido 535 millones de beneficio en 1994," in ibid., June 1, 1995.

CHAPTER XXIV

PAST AND FUTURE

Organizational change formed one side of the campaign for renewal urged upon Catholics everywhere by the Vatican Council. Even the elderly, conservative Spanish bishops of the conciliar period recognized that clergy and laity needed "to reinvigorate our religious life within the renovating spirit of the Council." The bishops admitted that debate would form part of the process. But they left no doubt that change must rest on the "unity of all in fully accepting what the Council has taught and a common effort to put it in practice."[1]

This expectation of a unified response, a religious version of the old idea of a "union of Catholics," proved unrealistic. In the years immediately following the Council, debate about renewal spread among some theologians and lay activists and led to the emergence of groups often at odds with the hierarchy. The bishops responded in an episodic and far from uniform way to these groups until the mid-1980s. Then the hierarchy's more conservative composition and the influence of the Vatican caused the ecclesiastical authorities to take a hard line towards dissent as the "creative insecurity" of the immediate post-conciliar period yielded to the search for "order."[2]

To what extent the measures advocated either by the bishops or by those who disagreed with their approach were capable of allowing the Church to realize its religious objectives within a society experiencing accelerated social, economic, and political change is another matter. When asked, most Spaniards identified themselves as Catholic and observed traditional liturgical rites of passage in the form of baptism, canonical marriage, and Christian burial. But sociological studies have

1. "Sobre acción en la etapa postconciliar," December 8, 1965, in *Documentos de la Conferencia Espicopal Española, 1965–1983*, ed. Jesús Iribarren (Madrid, 1984), p. 69.

2. Francesc Valls, "Diez años del papado de Juan Pablo II en España," *El País*, October 17, 1988.

shown a decline in religious observance and the development of greater independence on questions of doctrine and morality even among practicing Catholics. Spanish Catholicism in the nineteenth and early twentieth centuries was always more complex than apologists for a monolithic Church maintained. That complexity increased in the decades following the Vatican Council. There also remains the question of Spanish Catholicism's future. Is the pattern of declining religious commitment among the population as a whole likely to continue within a highly secularized and economically advanced society?

Fragmented Responses

National Catholicism's strategy of religious reconquest failed. But it rested on a simple idea, that the mass evangelization of an entire population was possible through the use of time-honored methods supplemented by a dose of compulsion. The Second Vatican Council's recognition of the pluralistic nature of modern society and its cultural impact on belief forced the Church to seek new methods to attain an old objective.

This was easier said than done. Reports of the Council's proceedings and published documents received wide circulation among clergy and laity. Extensive discussion took place throughout the Spanish Church about how the conciliar goal of renewal could be achieved. Conciliar documentation was abundant, but it focused on general objectives and the theological ideas that lay behind them. The application of conciliar recommendations was left to episcopal conferences, diocesan bishops, and, to a limited extent, the secular and regular clergy. Few Spanish bishops and priests rejected the Council's program outright, although clerical supporters of National Catholicism, especially those organized in the Hermandad Sacerdotal del Clero during the early 1970s, remained deeply suspicious of change. Critics have suggested that many bishops and priests accepted the Council in a spirit more of obedience than of personal conviction, although they also have admitted that clergy and laity were willing to undertake an "honest effort to reconstruct the Church in the light of the Council."[3] It is impossible to assess the Council's religious impact on a national scale given the Church's decentralized diocesan and parochial organization. In general, bishops and priests followed conciliar directives by emphasizing the Church as a community of believers. They paid greater attention to the Scriptures in pastoral and catechetical instruction and stressed the need for developing a more spiritual faith.

There was nothing extreme about this attempt to translate conciliar recom-

3. Ramón Echarren, "Los sacerdotes a los veinte años del Concilio," in *El postconcilio en España*, ed. Juan M. Loboa (Madrid, 1988), pp. 270–71.

mendations into reality. The religious innovations introduced following the Council represented less radical reform than a change in emphasis aimed at purifying the "ecclesiastical Catholicism" of the Franco era. Efforts to deepen the spiritual content of Spanish Catholicism altered some traditional patterns of religious activity. The importance attached to the Mass and the Eucharist as central to the spiritual life of the community of believers affected the popularity of devotions associated with ultramontane piety despite episcopal efforts to infuse them with deeper spiritual meaning.[4] Once one of Church's great religious-patriotic cults and the cause of many a street battle between Catholics and anticlericals, devotion to the Sacred Heart virtually disappeared by the early 1990s.[5] The once popular devotions of the rosary and the Stations of the Cross survived but largely among the elderly and the residents of certain regions, notably Castile and León.[6] But the decline of ultramontane piety was not uniform. Some devotional practices, visits to shrines, attendance at religious processions, and celebrations held in honor of patron saints continued to attract a significant number of practicing Catholics through the early 1990s.[7]

At the same time, the world of shrines, vows, pilgrimages, and devotions to saintly patrons characteristic of rural popular Catholicism suffered under the influence of new theological thinking unsympathetic to an approach that appeared far removed from spiritual concerns focusing on the Mass and the Eucharist.[8] The hierarchy was less disposed to abandon these forms of religious expression, although, like earlier episcopal generations, the bishops believed it necessary to purify them of abuses they judged incompatible with their spiritual purpose.[9]

Despite rural depopulation and the reach of modern means of communication, popular rituals survived in village communities where they had existed for centuries. During the month of September 1989, for example, processions in honor of Christ were held in a multitude of small towns throughout the country. Some were conventional in character, as in Bargas, where the village women, clad in traditional dress, moved through the streets carrying candles. Others were more bizarre. At Hontenar in the Toledo hills, villagers carrying money in their lips climbed upon the backs of others to form "human towers" in front of the image of the Cristo del Buen Camino before releasing the sacred gift to flutter downward

4. Secretariado Nacional de Liturgia, *Liturgia y piedad popular: directorio litúrgico-pastoral* (Madrid, 1989), pp. 23–24.

5. Luis Maldonado, *Para comprender el catolicismo popular* (Estella, 1990), p. 126.

6. Pedro González Blasco and Juan González-Anleo, *Religión y sociedad en la España de los años 90* (Madrid, 1992), pp. 83–84.

7. Ibid., p. 84. Approximately one-half of practicing Catholics indicated that they participated in one or all of these activities.

8. William Christian, *Person and God in a Spanish Valley* (New York, 1972), p. 182.

9. *El catolicismo popular: carta pastoral de los obispos de las provincias eclesiásticas de Granada y Sevilla*, ed. Promoción Popular Cristiana (Madrid, 1985), p. 25.

into a basket. In Galicia, where a cult of the dead antedated Christianity, villagers of Puebla del Caramiñal, who had escaped death in the preceding year, dressed in shrouds as they moved through the town accompanied by relatives carrying coffins.[10] In many respects, these popular rituals were incompatible with the spirit of conciliar reform, although, as the episcopal generation at the turn of the century had done when faced with a rising wave of anticlericalism and secularization, the bishops saw these manifestations as a sign of faith, albeit an imperfect one, in a time that appeared no less dangerous.

The role of Catholicism as a civic religion, so prominent until 1931 and during the Franco period, declined significantly in democratic Spain. But it by no means disappeared. King Juan Carlos I imitated his grandfather, Alfonso XIII, his great-grandfather, Alfonso XII, and General Franco by journeying to Santiago de Compostela on July 25, 1983, to make the traditional dedication of the nation to Saint James. The celebration of this religious-patriotic cult by the head of State, who was accompanied by the Socialist ministers of justice, foreign affairs, defense, and culture shows that the lines separating religion and government in a constitutionally aconfessional State were still far from clear.[11]

Nor were Socialist ministers averse to participating in religious processions that would have been anathema to their predecessors of the Second Republic. In 1983, the minister of justice requested the archbishop of Toledo's permission to lead an official delegation in the city's celebrated Corpus Christi procession. Cardinal González Martín, who had participated in many a civic-religious manifestation during the Franco era, rejected the request. Irritated by the government's initiatives on abortion and education, the cardinal used an old republican argument, that in a constitutionally aconfessional State it was unsuitable for government representatives to participate in a purely religious event. But this did not prevent Socialist municipal councillors from taking their place in the line of march, although, in a nod to their political origins, they were dressed in business suits, while the councillors of the conservative Coalición Popular party trudged along in formal dress.[12]

To what extent changes introduced as a result of the Council deepened the faith among practicing Catholics and purified the "ecclesiastical Catholicism" of the past is difficult to determine. Surveys have shown that the Church has held its own among those observing their faith on a regular basis. During the early 1990s, more than half of those identifying themselves as "very good Catholics" received communion, long regarded as a sign of religious commitment, with some frequency, while more than a third of those who saw themselves as "practicing Catholics" did

10. César Justel, "Los Cristos de septiembre," *El País* (edición internacional), September 18, 1989.

11. *Ya*, July 24, 1983.

12. *Ya*, June 1, 3, 1983.

so several times a year.[13] On the whole, both groups also accepted traditional Catholic doctrine.

This hopeful situation, from the Church's perspective, was not without its complexities. Frequent reception of communion varied considerably among the observant. Older Catholics who stood higher on the social scale received communion more often than young adults and those further down the socioeconomic ladder. The observant also went to confession far less frequently than they received communion and showed less unanimity on certain points of doctrine. For example, only 64.6 percent of "very good Catholics" believed firmly in the existence of hell and 71.1 percent in the certainty of life in the hereafter.[14]

Despite these ambiguities, the Church has retained a high level of religious commitment among a core constituency of practicing Catholics. In the decades following the Council, the Church became an institution more committed to a faith based on spiritual motivations. Whatever its limitations and inadequacies, conciliar renewal worked to a point, but only to a point. In the heady days of the immediate post-Council period, many bishops and clergy expected that renewal would initiate a new age of spiritual renovation that would deepen faith among practicing Catholics and provide a new and dynamic framework for evangelizing Spaniards who had abandoned religious observance.[15]

The question of how a renewed Church should communicate its message to the growing number of Spaniards who were not practicing their religion had no clear answer. By the early 1990s, nearly a third of the laity and half of the diocesan clergy believed that the historic objective of building a "Church of the masses" should be abandoned in favor of a Church comprised of "exemplary minorities" strongly committed to the faith and inspired by Christian principles.[16]

Most bishops remained attached to the idea of a renewed Catholicism capable of realizing the old dream of a Catholic Spain. Even before the episcopal backlash of the 1980s, they rejected the idea of Catholicism as a privatized faith of believers. For Cardinal Jubany of Barcelona, a faith focused on the "personal, private" development of the individual's conscience threatened "to marginalize" Christianity within society. Spanish Catholicism must assume a public role "in accord with the most profound identity of our people," the cardinal maintained.[17] As the hierarchy

13. During the early 1990s, 54.8 percent of "very good Catholics" received communion several times a month, as did 39.4 percent of "practicing Catholics." González Blasco and González-Anleo, *Religión y sociedad*, p. 79.

14. Ibid., pp. 75, 60–63.

15. Laboa, "Marco y recepción del Concilio," in *El postconcilio en España*, p. 49.

16. González Blasco and González-Anleo, *Religión y sociedad*, pp. 88–89.

17. *Ya*, August 24, 1983. The hierarchy affirmed similar views in 1983. The bishops declared that the Church had no intention of being pushed by a secular, pluralistic society to a situation in which "the religious and the moral were relegated to the narrow sphere of the private." "Exhortación colectiva del Episcopado Español," *Ya*, July 30, 1983.

became more conservative during the 1980s, some progressive ecclesiastical critics accused the bishops of abandoning the Council's spirit in favor of a new version of National Catholicism, devoid of political content but inspired by the same catastrophic vision of pervasive moral decay that could be remedied only by the conversion of all Spaniards.[18]

Following the Council, clergy and laity appeared who saw the Church's future in a different light. An unprecedented wave of theological discussion and religious experimentation swept through the Spanish Church. Young clerics educated abroad formed the vanguard of a movement of theological renovation. Their admirers saw them as nothing less than the "providential instrument that God granted to Spain . . . to apply . . . the texts of the Second Vatican Council."[19]

The theological effervescence of the late 1960s and 1970s lacked coherence. But virtually all progressive theological currents swirled through the Spanish Church, including liberation theology from Latin America, the "theology of hope" associated with the Protestant scholar J. Moltman, the theology of Hans Küng, with its emphasis on the authority of the community of believers in ecclesiastical governance, and a theology that saw no incompatibility between Christianity and Marxism.[20] Theologians made their views known through a growing number of theological faculties and postgraduate institutions, thirty-nine in number by 1980, and a flood of books and periodicals. At no time in the Spanish Church's modern history had theology received such widespread attention.

The connection between new theological currents and the emergence of specific groups was sometimes direct, sometimes diffuse. Liberation theology, with its harsh critique of capitalist excess, the selfishness of the bourgeoisie, and the Church's historic support for a class-based society and its neglect of the poor inspired the foundation of Christians for Socialism (CpS) in 1973, at a time when the bishops rejected outright any suggestion that Christianity and Marxism were compatible. Two hundred priests and laypeople gathered in Ávila to proclaim their faith in "Jesus Christ liberator," criticize the hierarchy for condemning Catholics who embraced Marxism, and announce that they intended to wage an "ideological struggle whose objective is the construction of a Church free of all feudal ties."[21] Establishment of Christians for Socialism provoked extensive discussion in ecclesiastical publications. The bishops were not impressed. Archbishop Roca of Valencia attacked the group's members because "they affirmed the primacy of revolutionary praxis over the faith," although Cardinal Tarancón

18. Echarren, "Los sacerdotes a los veinte años del Concilio," in *El postconcilio en España*, p. 261.

19. Olegario González de Cardenal, "Teología en España, 1965–1987," in *El postconcilio en España*, p. 68.

20. Ibid., pp. 103–20; Feliciano Blázquez, *La traición de los clérigos en la España de Franco* (Madrid, 1991), pp. 209–20.

21. Quoted in Alfredo Fierro Bardaji and Reyes Mate Rupérez, *Cristianos por el socialismo* (Estella, 1977), pp. 29–30.

worked behind the scenes to avoid a complete rupture between the hierarchy and the CpS.[22]

In some respects, Christians for Socialism resembled the Christian Democracy movement of the early twentieth century. The CpS did not seek to organize the Catholic masses. It was made up of a small group of clerical and lay activists who acted as a gadfly within a Church unsympathetic to its objectives. But other groups emerged to attract a larger following. Although sometimes described as forming a "parallel Church," they were inspired by different motives.

The Popular Christian Communities (Comunidades Cristianas Populares), which first appeared during the 1960s, were influenced by liberation theology and its commitment to "the struggle for a society without classes."[23] Members aspired "to a liberating and popular Church as opposed to a hierarchical and powerful institution."[24] The Neocatechumens (Neocatecumenales), founded in 1966, worked among the poor but emphasized the religious formation of members through "a neocatechumenate similar to that of the early Church."[25] The Communities of Charismatic Renovation (Comunidades de Renovación Carismática), established in 1973 on the model of similar groups in the United States, provided a Spanish Catholic version of pentecostalism free of social activism.[26]

Many groups took the institutional form of "base communities" (*comunidades de base*) that had developed in Latin America during the 1960s, that is, small groups of Christians who sought new ways to deepen their faith within a community setting often standing outside the Church's traditional parochial organization. Following the crisis in Catholic Action during the mid-1960s, many members of base communities committed to social activism came from the ranks of the HOAC, the JOC, and other associations victimized by the hierarchy's preemptive strike.[27]

The disparate origins and organizational fluidity of individual communities, comprised for the most part of fifty members or less, make accurate statistics on their number and membership difficult to establish. In 1982, the CEE estimated that five thousand communities with two hundred thousand members were in existence.[28] The hierarchy's attitude towards these associations varied, depending, as always in the Spanish Church, on the reaction of individual bishops. In Madrid, Archbishop Morcillo initially encouraged the Neocatechumens but his enthusiasm had cooled by 1970. But Cardinal Tarancón viewed them positively when he assumed direction of the archdiocese.

22. Quoted in Blázquez, *La traición de los clérigos*, p. 220.
23. "Comunidades cristianas," *Ya*, July 20, 1983.
24. "Spain: The Socio-Religious Situation," *Pro Mundi Vita Dossiers* (1979), nos. 7–8, p. 30.
25. Ibid., p. 29.
26. "Comunidades cristianas," *Ya*, July 20, 1983.
27. Blázquez, *La traición de los clérigos*, pp. 186–88.
28. *Ya*, July 20, 1983.

By the early 1980s, the bishops had developed a policy towards the Christian communities that testified to their still uncertain place within the Church. Bishops searching for new religious strategies appreciated their dynamism, religious commitment, and critical spirit. But they expressed serious reservations about the communities' tendency towards "hypercriticism and narcissism," and their disconnection from diocesan administrations that led in episcopal eyes to "impatience and inconstancy" among community members.[29]

Tension between individual bishops and base communities began almost from the moment of their appearance. Some groups, notably the Neocatechumens, were viewed more favorably by the hierarchy, largely because they were disposed to work with the ecclesiastical authorities and avoid what was seen as the extreme program of the Popular Christian Communities, with their demand for the creation of a "popular Church" based on the participation of the faithful in ecclesiastical governance.[30] But the decentralized organization of communities made it impossible, even in the case of the Neocatechumens, for the bishops to exercise effective control over these diverse groups. The episodic skirmishing of the late 1960s and 1970s between individual bishops and communities gave way during the following decade to more serious conflict.

As the hierarchy became more conservative during the 1980s, it reaffirmed its commitment to conciliar teachings but stressed the necessity of strengthening episcopal authority to provide unified direction to a Church that in their judgment had produced fragmented and contradictory responses to the Council. In the hierarchy's view, groups and individuals had developed "conceptions of the faith" that were difficult to reconcile "with healthy Catholic doctrine." The bishops also charged that these groups were contributing to the "fragmentation of the Catholic community" by ignoring the unifying mission entrusted to the hierarchy and the papacy.[31] That some base communities expressed dissent from the CEE's policies on Socialist legislation on education and abortion added a political dimension to an increasingly tense atmosphere.

At the same time, some groups, especially the Comunidades Cristianas Populares (CCP), developed a stronger organizational framework, expressed primarily through regular meetings, that allowed them to respond more effectively to the bishops. At the national meeting of the CCP in 1988, speakers criticized what they

29. "Servicio pastoral a las pequeñas comunidades cristianas," March 15, 1982. *Documentos de la Conferencia Episcopal Española*, pp. 680–83, 684–85.

30. *Ya*, July 20, 1983. Kiko Argüello, a young painter living and working among the poor of the Madrid district of Palomeras Altas, founded the Neocatechumens in 1966. Conflicts with the hierarchy occurred from time to time, as in Almería in 1983, when the bishop ordered the dissolution of the Neocatechumens in his diocese. But Argüello was sufficiently well regarded by the Vatican that in 1983 Pope John Paul II invited him to attend a forthcoming synod of bishops in Rome. *Ya*, November 5, September 24, 1983.

31. "Exhortación colectiva del Episcopado Español," *Ya*, July 30, 1983.

saw as the hierarchy's growing tendency to resolve contentious issues unilaterally in defiance of the spirit of the Council.[32]

Earlier in the year, a coalition of groups including the CCP and CpS had declared the papal nuncio, Mario Tagliaferri, *persona non grata* for seeking to make the Spanish Church a "closed" institution through behind-the-scenes manipulation.[33] Although the 1988 assembly recognized the necessity of ecclesiastical authority, the CEE responded within the week. The bishops admitted that there was room for different approaches to living the "same faith," but they warned against what they saw as erroneous interpretations of conciliar documents by groups that had fallen "into the temptation of enclosing themselves within their own position justified by the *model* of the Church that they have chosen."[34]

The hierarchy took action against theologians and editors of ecclesiastical publications whose views were regarded as detracting from doctrinal unity. In 1988, two Jesuit professors on the theological faculty of Granada lost their positions because of their progressive views. The clerical editors of the journal *Misión Abierta* were also dismissed on the grounds that they presented a negative view of the Church, encouraged the idea of a popular Church, and criticized the hierarchy excessively. For good measure, the editors were expelled from the Claretian order that published the journal, a measure that was approved by the Vatican.[35] It was alleged that the nuncio, Mario Tagliaferri, and conservative bishops lay behind the dismissal of the editor of the country's largest religious journal, *Vida Nueva,* a strongly pro-conciliar publication that was moderate in approach and respectful of the hierarchy but committed to open debate about the problems facing the Spanish Church. The hierarchy also began to develop stricter "means of control" over seminaries, theologians, and religious publications.[36]

In earlier times, such episcopal action would have consigned dissenting clergy to ecclesiastical oblivion. In democratic Spain, the bishops had no effective means of suppressing the expression of ideas of which they disapproved. On the contrary, the purges of 1987–1988 generated a storm of controversy amply reported in the

32. Francesc Valls, "Críticas a la jerarquía eclesiástica en el octavo encuentro de cristianos de base," *El País,* October 31, 1988.

33. *El País* (edición internacional), January 4, 1988.

34. "El episcopado advierte sobra la otrodoxia de algunos modelos de Iglesia," in ibid., November 5, 1988.

35. One of the country's leading progressive clerics, the biblical scholar and canon of Málaga cathedral José María González Ruiz, saw the attack on *Misión Abierta* as an effort orchestrated in the Vatican by Cardinal Ratzinger. The canon believed that this and other measures taken by Rome and the Spanish hierarchy against organizations on the "frontier" of conciliar change formed part of a campaign to reconstruct "old walls" within the Church. José María González Ruiz, *Memorias de un cura: antes de Franco, con Franco y después de Franco* (Málaga, 1995), pp. 282–83.

36. Francesc Valls, "La jerarquía destituyé a tres teólogos progresistas," *El País* (edición internacional), May 16, 1988; A. Rodríguez, "El Vaticano expulsa a Benjamín Forcano y a otros cinco claretianos españoles progresistas," in ibid., May 3, 1988; Francesc Valls, "Destituido el director de 'Vida Nueva' por presiones de la jerarquía conservadora," in ibid., November 23, 1987; "El episcopado propone medidas de control para seminarios, publicaciones y teólogos," in ibid., June 6, 1988.

secular press. The Jesuit professors of Granada responded publicly that their dismissal was the result of a "neoconservative offensive" designed to return the Spanish Church to "a uniform model that does not conform to social reality."[37] Fifteen hundred delegates to a congress of progressive theologians raised the question of civil rights within the Church and accused the Vatican of functioning as a "totalitarian system."[38] The Popular Christian Communities, Christians for Socialism, and other groups singled out the papacy's Congregation for the Doctrine of the Faith and its prefect, Cardinal Ratzinger, as the authors of a "new Inquisition" that still held the power "to condemn [the Church's] prophets." "If once they were burned at the stake, today . . . they are condemned little by little, one after the other, . . . without the possibility of defending themselves, without concrete accusations, without the most minimum respect for human dignity."[39] The actions taken by the hierarchy in 1987–1988 and later against progressive theologians and associations failed to achieve their objective. Advocates of an alternative vision of Spanish Catholicism continued to publish their views, albeit within an increasingly conflictive atmosphere.

Residues of the Catholic working-class movements of the 1950s and 1960s also survived in various associations, including the HOAC, JOC, and diverse youth groups committed primarily to work in the countryside. The development of free trade unions, however, diminished the appeal of these once vital organizations. In many respects, they never recovered fully from the crisis of Catholic Action during the mid-1960s. "What was lost in the time of that crisis has not been retrieved right up to the present day."[40]

More traditional groups also remained on the scene, the largest of which was Opus Dei, with twenty-eight thousand members. Long absent from the political arena, the organization remained the subject of intense interest and scrutiny, although its public role was largely confined to education, especially through the University of Navarra, a well-financed private university regarded as one of the country's best institutions of higher learning.[41]

The 1992 beatification of Opus Dei's founder, Father Escrivá de Balaguer, attracted enormous public interest in Spain. It also created controversy, especially

37. Alejandro V. García, "Los teólogos destituidos creen que hay una 'ofensiva neoconservadora,'" in ibid., May 23, 1988.

38. Francesc Valls, "Los procesos del Vaticano son propios de un sistema totalitario, según el IX Congreso de Teología," in ibid., September 25, 1989.

39. Francesc Valls, "La destitución de tres teólogos es obra de la 'nueva Inquisición,' según colectivos cristianos," in ibid., May 30, 1988.

40. "Spain: The Socio-Religious Situation," p. 30.

41. Juan Arias, "Una fuerza que reside en las aulas," *El País* (edición internacional), June 28, 1994. A highly critical article in a widely circulated magazine alleged that Opus Dei "controls dozens of businesses and organizations of every description," including the Banco Popular, a press agency, Europa Press, and a periodical devoted to economic matters. Javier Arce and Julio Algañaraz, "El Opus se hace con el control de las finanzas católicas," *Cambio 16*, March 21, 1989, pp. 14–19.

among priests and laypeople who saw the organization as an ascendant conservative force in the Church, in league with the Vatican and some members of the hierarchy.[42] The rapidity with which Escrivá de Balaguer passed from death to beatification was seen as confirmation of Opus Dei's growing influence within the Spanish Church, especially since in the same year Pope John Paul II derailed an attempt to beatify Queen Isabel the Catholic, who had been waiting for nearly five hundred years for similar recognition.[43] Cardinal Tarancón expressed surprise at the "unaccustomed rapidity" with which the cause of Escrivá de Balaguer progressed in Rome and regret that Pope John XXIII, "adored by the whole world, including non-believers," had not yet been beatified.[44] Whatever the merits of the arguments for or against sainthood for the founder of Opus Dei, the beatification controversy brought out the latent tensions between the organization and its clerical and lay critics.

The emergence of progressive groups added another layer to what had always been a complex religious institution based on a mix of civic religion, "ecclesiastical Catholicism," ultramontane piety, and rural popular religion. Put another way, members of the so-called parallel Church formed a new lobby that jostled with other groups, including Opus Dei and an amorphous center of clergy and laity committed to moderate conciliar reform over the course Spanish Catholicism should follow in the future. Spanish Catholicism has become more, not less, complex since the Second Vatican Council. This growing complexity suggests that the hopes of advocates of a Church united around a single religious strategy directed by episcopal and papal authority will not be easily realized.

Debate within the post–Vatican II Church took place in a society experiencing rapid socioeconomic change. As the country became more urban and industrialized, more open to a range of social and cultural influences, it was inevitable that religion and Church would be affected by what an apprehensive Cardinal Suquía called the "secularizing hurricane."[45] The greatest threat to the Church emerged not from the virulent anticlericalism of the past but from a changing society.

Religion and Society

In 1991, three young professionals appeared on a popular television quiz show. When asked the name of a large city located near the mouth of the Mississippi River, one answered without hesitation. When asked the name of the dog sent into

42. José Luis Barbería, "Barruntando los altares," *El País*, August 19, 1991.

43. Marifé Moreno, "El comité pro canonización de Isabel la Católica culpa al Papa de paralizar el proceso," in ibid., June 28, 1992.

44. Francesc Valls, "Tarancón, sorpendido por la rápida beatificación," in ibid. (edición internacional), July 15, 1991.

45. Francesc Valls, "'El vendaval secularizador' aleja a los jóvenes de la Iglesia, según Suquía," *El País*, November 15, 1988.

space by the Soviet Union, another responded promptly. When asked what the forty days before Easter were called, brows furrowed. None of the contestants knew the answer.[46] That three well-educated individuals failed to identify Lent in a country where the external signs of Catholicism still abounded confirms on a small scale that "'emigration' from religiosity to indifference" formed the most significant aspect of religious life in democratic Spain.[47] Surveys indicate that between 1970 and 1989 one-fifth of Spaniards, whether they practiced their faith or not, journeyed from Catholicism to religious indifference or atheism. The 3 percent of Spaniards who identified themselves as indifferent to religion in 1970 had increased to 26 percent by 1989. The percentage of those committed to atheism moved from virtually zero to 5 percent during the same period, while the percentage of those who declared that they were non-practicing Catholics doubled.[48]

From the Church's perspective, the most alarming aspect of this shift was its generational character. Young people, especially those in their twenties, became the "principal protagonists of the great change in the religious self-identification of Spaniards."[49] The percentage of youth who saw themselves as practicing Catholics fell by 50 percent between 1960 and 1975 to a reach a low of 15 percent in 1989. Of the young people interviewed, 38 percent declared that they were either indifferent or atheist, while 47 percent said that they were non-practicing Catholics.[50] In contrast, 36.4 percent of Spaniards born before 1944, the generation of National Catholicism, maintained that they practiced their faith on a regular basis.[51]

Sociological studies of contemporary Spanish Catholicism have also noted a decline in religious practice. Between 1973 and 1990, the percentage of Spaniards who declared that they attended Sunday Mass regularly declined from 68 percent to 43 percent. Sociologists have established, however, that surveys based on the responses of individuals to questionnaires about observance exaggerate participation rates.[52] A 1985 survey based on actual attendance at Sunday Mass showed participation in the range of 29–33 percent by those obliged to assist according to ecclesiastical law (*misalizantes*).[53]

46. "El Gordo," June 16, 1991.

47. González Blasco and González-Anleo, *Religión y sociedad*, p. 23.

48. Ibid. In democratic Spain, Protestant churches were allowed to function free of government restrictions. Although some fundamentalist churches, notably the Jehovah's Witnesses, have won converts, the massive desertion of Catholics to Protestantism predicted by clerical opponents of religious toleration since the mid-nineteenth century has not occurred. According to a survey of 1990, only 3 percent of Spaniards declared that they belonged to other Christian denominations. *El Sol*, December 9, 1990.

49. Rafael Díaz-Salazar, "La transición religiosa de los españoles," in *Religión y sociedad en España*, ed. Rafael Díaz-Salazar and Salvador Giner (Madrid, 1993), p. 95.

50. Ibid.

51. González Blasco and González-Anleo, *Religión y sociedad*, p. 27.

52. Francisco Azcona, "La práctica religiosa ayer y hoy," in Francisco Azcona et al., *Catolicismo en España: análisis sociológico* (Madrid, 1985), p. 39.

53. Secretariado Nacional de Liturgia, *Asistencia a la misa dominical* (Madrid, 1985), p. 18. It should be noted that this survey covered forty-five dioceses and did not include the Basque Provinces or Catalonia, with the exception of the diocese of Lérida.

The literature concerned with observance has tended to interpret declining religious practice in democratic Spain as marking a radical turning point in Spanish Catholicism's development. There is no question that the social changes produced by economic development, the country's increasing conformity to European secularizing trends, and the establishment of a pluralistic democracy contributed to declining observance. But patterns of religiosity rarely change suddenly. They develop over long periods. The religious changes occurring in Spain after 1975 did not appear overnight. At most, National Catholicism formed a parenthesis in a long process of secularization that began during the nineteenth century and accelerated in the twentieth until the establishment of the Franco dictatorship temporarily interrupted its advance.

The results of sociological surveys indicate that religious trends evident since the 1970s will continue. The significant increase in the number of Spaniards who declared that they were non-practicing Catholics, the 55 percent between the ages of eighteen and thirty-four who said during the early 1990s that they did not consider themselves "religious persons," and the high proportion of young people who asserted that they were either indifferent to religion or nonobservant suggests that the Church will find it difficult to halt a further decline in practice.[54] At what point levels of observance will stabilize is difficult to predict. The Church is likely to emerge with a core constituency of regular observants forming perhaps one-fifth or one-fourth of *misalizantes*. Although such a result will afford scant comfort to bishops and priests still committed to the idea of a "Catholic Spain," it is by no means catastrophic in comparison with Western Europe. As late as 1982, only Ireland surpassed Spain in religious practice. By the end of the decade, according to a study of religiosity in the European Union, the percentage of individuals identifying themselves as "religious persons" ranged from a low of 48 percent in Denmark to 72 percent in the Irish Republic. The Spanish percentage of 68 percent exceeded all other countries except Ireland, Portugal, and Greece.[55]

In the face of a process of secularization that is likely to continue, the Church possesses some advantages. The fierce anticlericalism of the past has receded, while Spaniards have expressed a more positive than negative opinion of the Church's role in society. According to a 1982 survey, 52 percent viewed the Church's influence positively and only 21 percent negatively, while a similar study in 1990 noted that young people placed more confidence in the Church than in government institutions.[56] The Church also retains a significant place in educa-

54. Díaz-Salazar, "La transición religiosa de los españoles," p. 127.

55. Azcona, "La práctica religiosa ayer y hoy," p. 45; González Blasco and González-Anleo, *Religión y sociedad*, p. 36.

56. Díaz-Salazar, "La institución eclesial en la sociedad civil española," in *Religión y sociedad en España*, p. 296; *El País* (edición internacional), January 22, 1990. Seventy-four percent of the young people interviewed indicated that "respect for religion" was either "very important" or "sufficiently important" to them. *El Sol*, December 9, 1990.

tion, although how effectively religious instruction in Catholic schools translates into commitment is far from certain.

Even some practicing Catholics disagree with aspects of the Church's moral teachings, especially in matters of sexual morality, but the values of Spanish society still reflect a Catholic emphasis on the family.[57] In 1990, 93 percent of respondents to a survey indicated that they regarded the family as important to their values, an opinion confirmed by the fact that during the early 1990s Spain possessed the lowest divorce rate of any country in the European Union.[58] At the same time, a substantial majority of the population continues to identify itself as Catholic. During the mid-1980s, 87 percent did so; 83 percent of newborns were baptized, while 94 percent of marriages were performed in church.[59] Participation in liturgical rites of passage does not say much about the depth of religious commitment, but it testifies to a limited degree of acceptance of Catholicism as part of the country's social and cultural fabric. These circumstances do not diminish the extent or gravity of the challenge facing the Spanish Church as it approaches the next century. It remains to be seen whether it can build on conditions favorable to its religious interests to recover lost ground.

Historic patterns of religiosity linked to social class have also changed since 1970. A 1989 survey indicates that the extreme class differences related to high or low levels of practice have ameliorated considerably. Although individuals belonging to the upper and upper middle classes identified themselves as "very good Catholics" or "practicing Catholics" to a greater degree than did the lower middle and working classes (37.1 percent versus 26.2 percent), the difference is less substantial than one would have expected given the marked class orientation of Spanish Catholicism in earlier periods, at least outside those peasant regions long identified with high levels of observance. It is even more striking that, in terms of occupation, the differences separating those who saw themselves as "good Catholics," "practicing Catholics," "infrequent practicing Catholics," "nonpracticing Catholics," "religiously indifferent," or "atheist" were roughly similar for all occupational categories, with the exception of businessmen, who reported a higher degree of religious commitment.[60] The results suggest that a "religious homogeneity" has developed to break the traditional class-religion connection of the past.[61]

57. According to a survey of 1990, one in four practicing Catholics resorted to contraception. Ibid.

58. Ibid.; *El País*, June 22, 1993. In Spain, the ratio of divorces to marriages was 1:9.6, in the United Kingdom, 1:2.3.

59. José Andrés-Gallego, "La religiosidad: las cuatro religiones de tres cuartos de siglo," *XX Siglos* (1990), vol. 1, no. 1, p. 8. The number of canonical marriages declined, however, between 1981, when 201,113 were celebrated, and 1985, when 160,014 were performed. By the end of the decade, this number began to increase moderately. Belén Gopegui, "Aumentan las parejas que prefieren casarse dentro de la Iglesia," *Tribunal de Actualidad* (1988), vol. 1, no. 5, p. 86.

60. González-Blasco and González-Anleo, *Religión y sociedad*, pp. 30–31.

61. Ibid., p. 30.

To what extent the map of religious observance has changed over the past two decades is uncertain. Some studies indicate that with the exception of regions recording the highest percentage of self-declared practicing Catholics—León-Castile (44 percent), Galicia (37 percent), and La Rioja (41 percent)—and those with the lowest—Catalonia (15 percent), the Balearic Islands (20 percent), Madrid (21 percent), and Aragón (22 percent)—there was relatively little difference among the others. Andalucía, Extremadura, Castile–La Mancha, Asturias, Santander, the Basque Provinces and Navarra, Murcia, and Valencia all fell within the range of 27 to 33 percent. That Andalucía, long regarded as a virtual mission field by the Church, and the Basque Provinces, historically known for extremely high levels of observance, contained the same percentage of individuals declaring themselves practicing Catholics (28 percent) suggests that the traditional north-south division of Spanish Catholicism has diminished considerably.[62]

The 1985 survey of actual attendance at Sunday Mass by *misalizantes* confirms some of these observations but contradicts others. In Madrid, only 22 percent of those obliged to attend Mass did so, while in Lérida, the only Catalan diocese surveyed, a similar percentage was reported. But the study also suggests that north-south differences in observance remained stronger than has been assumed. With the exception of Córdoba (32 percent), the dioceses of Andalucía reported uniformly low attendance levels: Almería (18 percent), Cádiz-Ceuta (16 percent), Jaén (25 percent), and Seville (17 percent). The archdiocese of Valencia (20 percent) conformed to the southern pattern. By contrast, dioceses of the Catholic heartland of Old Castile and León recorded a high level of attendance: Ávila (49 percent), Burgos (52 percent), Ciudad Rodrigo (57 percent), León (50 percent), Palencia (55 percent), Zamora (48 percent), Osma-Soria (52 percent). Only Salamanca (38 percent) and Valladolid (36 percent) fell below the regional norm.[63]

These results raise the question of whether or not the geographical distribution of religious practice has changed dramatically over the past two decades. There is no convincing evidence that this has occurred. The historic pattern of higher observance in peasant areas of central and northern Spain, lower in the south, along the Mediterranean coast, in large cities, and industrial zones continues, albeit within a framework of declining practice everywhere.

The case of the Basque Provinces departs significantly from this pattern. In 1967, the region was included among the country's most observant. Duocastella estimated a participation rate of 75 percent at Sunday Mass, except for the industrial city of Bilbao, where it fell to 53.6 percent.[64] The historic connection between religion and Basque autonomist aspirations, whether in the form of Carlism in the

62. Ibid., p. 41.

63. *Asistencia a la misa dominical,* pp. 45–46, Table 4.

64. Cited by Alfonso Pérez-Agote et al., "Religión, política y sociedad en el País Vasco," in *Religión y sociedad en España,* p. 262.

nineteenth century or the new nationalism of the twentieth, reinforced popular identification with the Church and the already strong commitment of the region's rural population to Catholicism. The resistance of the lower clergy against the Franco regime's repression of Basque nationalism strengthened these links further.

But circumstances during the 1960s altered the situation. The regime's economic policies promoted intense industrial development, which brought in its wake rural depopulation and greater urbanization that altered the old balance between city and countryside. Acute social tensions between the industrial working class, employers, and the dictatorship also constantly troubled the region. Finally, to this unstable mix was added the radical, violent nationalism of the ETA organization. Its members represented only a small minority of Basques, but the vicious circle of terrorism and official repression begun during the 1960s deeply unsettled Basque society. As early as 1973, a clerical observer noted that a "profound religious trauma" was already developing in the region.[65] By 1987, the percentage of those identifying themselves as "practicing Catholics" (43 percent) stood only marginally above the national average of 42 percent.[66] The actual rate of observance was undoubtedly lower given the tendency of respondents to exaggerate the extent of their practice.

The cartography of practice between the late Franco period and 1990 shows a combination of relative stability in some regions, change in others. But, as a pioneer in the sociology of Spanish Catholicism noted in 1973, regional differences in observance were less important than in earlier periods, although they have by no means disappeared.[67] A significant decline in the rural population and a corresponding demographic expansion in cities experiencing rapid economic development diminished the religious weight of those areas of "traditional and honest Christianity" identified by Father Sarabia before the Civil War.[68] The Church could take some satisfaction from continuing high levels of observance in Old Castile and León. But a massive population shift from countryside to urban areas threw into sharp relief a fundamental problem for the Church. How could it effectively conduct its religious mission within an urbanized society in which, historically, its evangelizing efforts had produced indifferent results? Since the mid-nineteenth century, the Church has struggled to devise a pastoral strategy capable of meeting the religious challenge posed by the emergence of urban centers, where secularizing currents swept more freely than in a more easily controlled Catholic countryside. The challenge itself is not new. In the highly urbanized Spain of the late twen-

65. José María Díaz Mozaz, *La Iglesia de España en la encrucijada* (Madrid, 1973), p. 165.

66. Pérez-Agote et al., "Religión, política y sociedad en el País Vasco," pp. 262–63.

67. Díaz Mozaz, *La Iglesia de España en la encrucijada*, p. 146.

68. Quoted in Pedro R. Santidrián, *El Padre Sarabia escribe su historia: medio siglo de misiones en España* (Madrid, 1963), p. 162.

tieth century, however, that challenge has become vastly more complex and difficult.

Whether, in these circumstances, the lingering dream of a Catholic Spain can become a reality is highly questionable, if indeed it was ever possible in the modern era. The Church remains an impressive organization. It can count upon a core constituency committed to the faith. Its charitable and educational activities give it a substantial presence within society. In a diffuse way, it still touches much of the population as an institution linked to Spanish history and culture. But the period of what has been aptly called "religious transition" characteristic of the past three decades is likely to continue.[69] In the nineteenth and early twentieth centuries, the Spanish Church faced a series of challenges, some met successfully, others not. It now faces challenges fully as serious as those that it encountered in the past.

69. Díaz-Salazar, "La transición religosa de los españoles," p. 127.

SELECT BIBLIOGRAPHY

Primary Sources

Documentary Collections and Archival Sources[1]

Actas de las conferencias de metropolitanos españoles, 1921–1965. Ed. Vicente Cárcel Ortí. Madrid, 1994.

Los acuerdos entre la Iglesia y España. Ed. Carlos Corral and Lamberto de Echeverría. Madrid, 1980.

Arxiu Vidal i Barraquer: Església y Estat durant la Segona República Espanyola, 1931–1936. Ed. M. Batllori and V. M. Arbeloa. 4 vols. Montserrat, 1971–1991.

Asamblea Conjunta obispos-sacerdotes. Ed. Secretariado Nacional del Clero. Madrid, 1971.

Constituciones sinodales de la diócesis de Málaga que hizo y ordenó su obispo Excmo. e Ilmo. Señor Dr. D. Juan Muñoz Herrera en el sínodo que celebró el XXVI de diciembre de MCMIX. Málaga, 1910.

Constituciones sinodales promulgadas por el Exmo. e Ilmo. Señor Dr. D. Eustaquio Ilundain y Esteban. Orense, 1908.

Crónica oficial del Primer Congreso Catequístico Nacional Español. 2 vols. Valladolid, 1913.

Crónica del Segundo Congreso Católico Nacional Español celebrado en Zaragoza. Madrid, 1890.

Crónica del Segundo Congreso Nacional de Música Sagrada. Seville, 1909.

Crónica del Sínodo Diocesano celebrado en Jaca los días 23, 24 y 25 de agosto de 1899. Madrid, 1899.

Department of State. *Foreign Relations of the United States, 1950.* Vol. 3, *Western Europe.* Washington, 1977.

Documentos colectivos del episcopado español, 1870–1974. Ed. Jesús Iribarren. Madrid, 1974.

Documentos de la Conferencia Episcopal Española, 1965–1983. Ed. Jesús Iribarren. Madrid, 1984.

Documentos inéditos para la historia del Generalísimo Franco. Ed. Fundación Nacional Francisco Franco. 4 vols. Madrid, 1992–1994.

The Documents of Vatican II. Ed. Walter M. Abbott. New York, 1966.

Iglesia y sociedad en la España del siglo XX: catolicismo social. Ed. Quintín Aldea Vaquero, Joaquín García Granda, and Jesús Martín Tejedor. 4 vols. Madrid and Valladolid, 1987–1991.

Instrucciones secretas a los nuncios de España en el siglo XIX, 1847–1907. Ed. F. Díaz de Cerio and M. F. Núñez Muñoz. Rome, 1989.

1. A number of the books cited in the bibliography also include important documents. Such works are indicated by an asterisk (*).

Ley Orgánica del Derecho a la Educación y disposiciones reglamentarias. Madrid, 1987.

Malley, Bernard. "Survey of the Church in Spain and of Its Attitude towards the Regime." December 12, 1951. Ms., Public Record Office, Foreign Office 371/102059.

Relaciones sobre el estado de las diócesis valencianas. Ed. María Milagros Cárcel Ortí. 3 vols. Valencia, 1989.

Episcopal Documents

Bertrán, Felipe. *Colección de las cartas pastorales del Exmo. Señor Don Felipe Bertrán.* 2 vols. Madrid, 1783.

Casas y Souto, Pedro. *Carta pastoral sobre la situación de España.* Madrid, 1899.

El catolicismo popular: carta pastoral de los obispos de las provincias eclesiásticas de Granada y Sevilla. Madrid, 1985.

Guerra Campos, José. *Crisis y conflicto en la Acción Católica Española y otros órganos nacionales de apostolado seglar desde 1964.* Madrid, 1989. *

Guisasola, Victoriano. *La acción del clero.* Valencia, 1910.

———. *Justicia y caridad en la organización cristiana del trabajo.* Madrid, 1916.

López Peláez, Antolín. *Por la Iglesia española: discursos parlamentarios durante el Gobierno del Señor Canalejas.* Madrid, 1913.

Los obispos ante la nueva etapa política. Madrid, 1976.

Los planteamientos actuales de la enseñanza: declaración de la comisión permanente de la Conferencia Episcopal Española. Madrid, 1976.

Reig y Casanova, Enrique. *Carta pastoral: la Acción Católica en España.* Madrid, 1924.

Sancha, C. M. *Carta pastoral sobre la obediencia debida a los prelados.* Toledo, 1899.

Suquía, Angel. *La Iglesia de España: tradición y futuro.* Madrid, 1989.

Torras y Bages, J. *Obres completes.* Barcelona, 1948.

La verdad os hará libres: instrucción pastoral de la Conferencia Episcopal Española sobre la conciencia cristiana ante la actual situación moral de nuestra sociedad. Madrid, 1990.

Newspapers and Periodicals

ABC (1976–1993).

Acción Española (1931–1932).

Boletín de la Obra de la Defensa de la Fe en España (1935).

Boletín Oficial Eclesiástico del Obispado de Málaga (1887).

Boletín Oficial del Obispado de Salamanca (1940).

Boletín Oficial del Obispado de Segovia (1936–1938).

Boletín de la Provincia Española: publicación privada para exclusivo uso de las comunidades de Padres Redentoristas (1979).

Cambio 16 (1976–1981).

El Católico (1841–1851).

El Consultor de los Párrocos (1872–1876).

La Cruz (1842, 1868–1909).

El Defensor de los Párrocos (1898).

Diario 16 (1976–1985).

La Ciencia Tomista (1917–1933).

La Cruzada Católica (1933).

El Debate (1913–1934).

Ecclesia (1941–1953, 1964).

La Enseñanza Católica (1913, 1926).

España y América (1914–1920).

La España Católica (1875).

Estudios Franciscanos (1909).

Espino (1957).

Iglesia Viva (1970, 1979).

Ilustración del Clero (1918–1936).

Misión Abierta (1978).

El Movimiento Católico (1896).

El Motín (1882).

National Catholic Register (1986).

The New York Times (1960, 1972, 1977–1978).

El Obrero Católico (1895).

Opinión (1976–1977).

El País (1976–1995).

El País (Edición Internacional) (1987–1998).

La Paraula Cristiana (1931).

La Parroquia (1894–1895).

Pastoral Misionera (1967, 1973).

La Paz Social (1909).

Presbyterium (1970).

Razón y Fe (1935–1939).

Religión y Cultura (1933).

Resurrexit (1943).
La Revista Católica (1842, 1858).
Revista Católica de Cuestiones Sociales (1895, 1917–1928).
Revista Eclesiástica (1899–1934).
Revista de Ciencas Eclesiásticas (1915).
Revista del Clero Español (1914).
Sal Terrae (1912–1923, 1942).
La Semana Católica (1873, 1907, 1929–1931).
La Semana Católica de Salamanca (1923).
Serra d'Or (1971).
El Sol (1990).
Tribunal de Actualidad (1988).
Unión y Caridad (1925–1928).
La Unión Católica (1887).
El Universo (1909).
Vida Eclesiástica (1931).
Vida Nueva (1972).
La Voz Católica de Madrid (1899).
Ya (1939–1942, 1977–1988).

Collections of Editorials

El pensamiento de "El Debate": un diario católico en la crisis de España, 1911–1936. Ed. José María García Escudero. Madrid, 1983.
Ya: medio siglo de historia, 1935–1985. Ed. José María García Escudero. Madrid, 1985.

Statistical Surveys

Anuario estadístico de España, 1927. Madrid, 1929.
Asistencia a la misa dominical. Ed. Secretariado Nacional de Liturgia. Madrid, 1985.
Censo de la población de España, 1860. Madrid, 1863.
Estadística de las comunidades religiosas existentes en España en 1 de abril de 1923. Ed. Dirección General de Estadística. Madrid, 1923.
Estadísticas de la Iglesia Católica, 1989. Ed. Oficina de Estadística y Sociología de la Iglesia. Madrid, 1989.
Reseña geográfica y estadística de España. Madrid, 1888.

Books and Articles

Aberrigoyen, Inak de. *Sept mois et sept jours dans l'Espagne de Franco*. Paris, 1938.
Alcalá-Zamora, Niceto. *Memorias*. Barcelona, 1977.
———. *Los defectos de la constitución de 1931*. Madrid, 1981.
Almanaque popular de cultura religiosa. Madrid, 1931.
Amo, León del. *Las dos espadas o la Iglesia y el Estado*. Valladolid, 1938.
Andrade y Uribe, Benito. *La Iglesia y la política: católicos y liberales*. Burgos, 1911.
El apostolado rural. Ed. Secretariado Nacional de Apostolado Rural de la Acción Católica Española. Madrid, 1958.
Aranguren, José Luis. *Memorias y esperanzas españolas*. Madrid, 1969.
Arbiol, Antonio. *La familia regulada con doctrina de la sagrada escritura y santos padres de la Iglesia*. Barcelona, 1746.
Arboleya-Martínez, Maximiliano. *Sermón perdido: los católicos de "Acción" bajo la dictadura española*. Madrid, 1930.
Azaña, Manuel. *Obras completas*. Ed. Juan Marichal. 4 vols. Mexico City, 1966–1968.
Aznar, Severino. *Problemas sociales de la actualidad*. Barcelona, 1914.
———. *La revolución española y las vocaciones eclesiásticas*. Madrid, 1949.
———. *Estudios religiosos-sociales*. Madrid, 1949.
Azpiazu, Joaquín. *El Estado católico*. Burgos, 1939.
Bahamonde, Antonio. *Memoirs of a Spanish Nationalist*. London, 1939.
Balmes, Jaume. *La sociedad*. 4th ed. Barcelona, 1873.
Basaldu, Pedro de. *En España sale el sol*. Buenos Aires, 1946.
Bensusan, Samuel L. *Home Life in Spain*. 2d ed. London, 1910.
Bergamín, José. *Detrás de la cruz: terrorismo y persecución religiosa en España*. Mexico, 1941.
Bertrán, Jorge. *Los difíciles caminos de la misión obrera*. Barcelona, 1968.
Blázquez, Feliciano, ed. *Conversaciones con José Luis L. Aranguren*. Madrid, 1976.

Brugarola, Martín. *Sociología rural católica*. Madrid, 1954.
Cadenas, Manuel, and Enrique del Portillo. *La provincia de Toledo de la Compañía de Jesús, 1880–1914*. Madrid, 1916.
Cantero, Pedro. *La hora católica de España*. Madrid, 1942.
Carreras, Luis. *Grandeza cristiana de España: notas sobre la persecución religiosa*. Toulouse, 1938.
Casanovas, Ignaci. *Estudios sociales*. Barcelona, 1952.
Castro Albarrán, Aniceto de. *Guerra santa: el sentido católico del movimiento nacional español*. Burgos, 1938.
El catolicismo popular en el sur de España: documento de trabajo para la reflexión práctica pastoral. Madrid, 1975.
Chica, José María de la. *Las luchas políticas: cómo se incendian los conventos de Madrid*. Madrid, 1931.
El clero y los católicos vasco-separatistas y el Movimiento Nacional. Madrid, 1940.
Comín, Alfredo C. *España, ¿país de misión?* Barcelona, 1966.
Cortacero y Velasco, Miguel. *Cuestiones eclesiásticas*. Madrid, 1915.
Cortés Cavanillas, J. *Gil Robles ¿monárquico? Misterios de una política*. Madrid, 1935.
Crisógono, P. *Grandeza, ruina y resurgimiento de España*. San Sebastián, 1941.
El cura de cualquier pueblo. Astorga, 1960.
Domínguez, Javier. *Enseñanza católica para una generación, víctima y testigo*. Madrid, 1979.
Ellis, Havelock. *The Soul of Spain*. Boston and New York, 1914.
Enrique y Tarancón, Vicente. *Recuerdos de juventud*. Barcelona, 1984.
———. *Confesiones*. Madrid, 1996. *
Episodios de la revolución en Asturias: los Pasionistas de Mieres y la revolución de octubre de 1934: episodios narrados por los mismos protagonistas. Santander, 1935.
Fernández Almuzara, Eugenio. *Evangelio de la Nueva España*. Valladolid, 1937.
Fernández Santana, Ezequiel. *Nuestra escuela*. Los Santos, 1919.
Field, Henry M. *Old Spain and New Spain*. New York, 1888.
Fierro Bardaji, Alfredo, and Reyes Mate Rupérez. *Cristianos por el socialismo*. Estella, 1977.
Franquesa i Alberch, Josep. *Reports biografies d'en Pere de la Pipa*. Vich, 1972.
García y García de Castro, Rafael. *¿El catolicismo en crisis?* Madrid, 1935.
———. *La tragedia espiritual de los vascos*. Granada, 1938.
García Gallego, Jerónimo. *Miscelánea política y religiosa*. Madrid, 1927.
Genovés Olmo, Eduardo. *Práctica parroquial*. Valencia, 1914.
Gil Robles, José María. *La fe a través de mi vida*. Bilbao, 1975.
González Alonso Getino, Luis. *Incendios de conventos de España y supresión de misiones y colegios españoles de ultramar*. Madrid, 1932.
González García, Manuel. *Lo que puede un cura hoy*. Seville, 1910.
———. *El decrecimiento de las vocaciones sacerdotales y sus causas*. Palencia, 1936.
González Ruiz, José María. *Memorias de un cura: antes de Franco, con Franco y después de Franco*. Málaga, 1995.
Grito de alarma dirigido a los católicos de nuestros días por el presbítero N. S. Valladolid, 1922.
Guerra Díaz, Juan. *Manual del católico campesino o sea correspondencia entre un cura de aldea y un feligrés en que se dan armas a los débiles para defender sus creencias contra los errores y calumnia de los impíos*. Valladolid, 1919.
———. *El amigo del católico campesino o sea cartas entre un cura de aldea y un feligrés*. Valladolid, 1919.
Gutiérrez-Ravé, José. *España en 1931*. Madrid, 1932.
———. *Yo fui un joven maurista*. Madrid, 1946.
Herranz Establés, Hilario. *El párroco y la parroquia en los tiempos presentes*. Barcelona, 1923.
Herrera, Angel. *El pensamiento de Angel Herrera: antología política y social*. Ed. José María García Escudero. Madrid, 1987.
Hughes, Emmet John. *Report from Spain*. New York, 1947.

Iribarren, Jesús. *Papeles y memorias: medio siglo de relaciones Iglesia-Estado en España, 1936–1986*. Madrid, 1992. *

Irurzún Muru, Luis. *El catolicismo social y el socialismo al desnudo*. Tafalla, 1918.

Isern, Damián. *Del desastre nacional y sus causas*. Madrid, 1900.

Kodasver [pseud.]. *Medio siglo de vida diocesana matritense, 1913–1963*. Madrid, 1967.

Liturgia y piedad popular: directorio litúrgico-pastoral. Ed. Secretariado Nacional de Liturgia. Madrid, 1989.

Llovera, José M. *Tratado elemental de sociología cristiana*. Barcelona, 1909.

López Galvá, Enrique. *Futura grandeza de España según notables profecías*. 2d ed. La Coruña, 1941.

López Peláez, Antolín. *El derecho español en sus relaciones con la Iglesia*. Madrid, 1902.

López Rodó, Laureano. *Memorias*. 4 vols. Barcelona, 1990–1993.

Macías Picavea, Ricardo. *El problema nacional: hechos, causas, remedios*. Madrid, 1899.

Manjón, Andrés. *El problema social y de la acción del clero*. Madrid, 1908.

Martín, Luis. *Memorias del P. Luis Martín, General de la Compañia de Jesús*. 2 vols. Ed. J. R. Equillor, M. Revuelta González, and R. M. Sanz de Diego. Rome, 1988.

Martín-Sánchez Juliá, F. *Ideas claras: reflexiones de un español actual*. Madrid, 1959.

Los mártires de Turón: notas biográficas y reseña del martirio. Madrid, 1935.

Maura, Miguel. *Así cayó Alfonso XIII*. 5th ed. Barcelona, 1968.

Menéndez-Reigada, Ignacio. *Acerca de la guerra santa*. Salamanca, 1937.

Merino Movilla, Eugenio. *Manual de táctica político-social*. Valladolid, 1917.

1.000 sacerdotes españoles rompen el silencio contra las omisiones y complicidades en el campo católico. Madrid, 1976.

Las misiones populares, hoy. Madrid, 1973.

Monescillo, Antolín. *Manual de seminarista*. Madrid, 1848.

Montero y Gutiérrez, Eloy. *El porvenir de la Iglesia de España*. Madrid, 1933.

Morote, Luis. *Los frailes en España*. Madrid, 1904.

Noguer, Narciso. *Las cajas rurales en España y en el extranjero*. Madrid, 1912.

Olalla, Sabino. *El servicio militar de los eclesiásticos*. Burgos, 1916.

Onaindia, Alberto de. *Hombre de paz en la guerra: cápitulos de mi vida*. Buenos Aires, 1973.

Orlandís, José. *El catolicismo en la España de hoy*. Pamplona, 1960.

Ossorio y Gallardo, Angel. *La España de mi vida: autobiografía*. Barcelona and Buenos Aires, 1977.

"Où va l'Espagne?" *Les Dossiers de l'Action Populaire*, no. 234 (1930), pp. 1077–86.

Palau, Gabriel. *Diario íntimo de un cura español*. Buenos Aires, 1932.

Peiró, Francisco. *El problema religioso-social en España*. 2d ed. Madrid, 1936.

Perales y Gutiérrez, José de los. *El problema religioso en España*. Madrid, 1909.

Pérez-Arnal, Manuel. *Compendio de la urbanidad sacerdotal*. Valencia, 1921.

Planas, Juan. *Arte pastoral o método para gobernar bien una parroquia*. 2d ed. 3 vols. Barcelona, 1860.

Plenn, Abel. *Wind in the Olive Trees: Spain from Inside*. New York, 1946.

Polo Benito, José. *Del periodismo católico*. Madrid, 1908.

———. *De la España católica: las crónicas de un año de acción*. Madrid, 1917.

¿Qué es la diócesis de Barcelona? Barcelona, 1985.

Reig y Casanova, Enrique. *Presente y porvenir económico de la Iglesia en España*. Madrid, 1908.

Rodríguez, Teodoro. *El problema social y las derechas: nuevas orientaciones*. El Escorial, 1935.

———. *Nueva reconquista de España*. Valladolid, 1938.

———. *Así es España y así la anti-España*. Madrid, 1942.

Rodríguez Ancieto, Nicolás. *Necesidad de la vigorización espiritual de España*. Salamanca, 1938.

Roldán, Federico. *El vicario de Écija*. Seville, 1920.

Romanones, conde de. *Notas de una vida, 1868–1912*. 2 vols. Madrid, n.d.

Romero Flores, H. R. *Perfil moral de nuestra hora*. Madrid, 1935.
Ruíz-Castillo, J., ed. *Antonio Maura: treinta y cinco años de vida pública*. 2 vols. Madrid, 1917. *
Santamaría, Carlos, et al. *Catolicismo español: aspectos actuales*. Madrid, 1955.
Santamaría Peña, Federico. *El apóstol social: D. José María Roquero y Vera*. Madrid, 1912.
———. *Provisión de las parroquias en concurso y fuera de él*. Madrid, 1920.
Sarabia, Ramón. *¿España . . . es católica? Charlas de un misionero*. Madrid, 1939.
———. *La España de hoy y la España de mañana*. Madrid, 1952.
———. *Experiencias misionales: testamento misionero del P. Ramón Sarabia*. Ed. Pedro R. Santidrián. Madrid, 1959.
Sardá y Salvany, Félix. *¿El liberalismo es pecado?* 2d ed. Barcelona, 1884.
Segundo Congreso de Misiones Parroquiales. Madrid, 1961.
Seisdados Sanz, Jerónimo. *El sacerdote y el párroco*. Barcelona, 1918.
Serrano Suñer, Ramón. *Entre el silencio y la propaganda: la historia cómo fue. Memorias*. Madrid, 1977.
Sevilla: misión 1965. Madrid, 1965.
Shaw, Rafael. *Spain from Within*. London, 1910.
Taboada, José María. *Los caballeros del ideal*. Madrid, 1928.
———. *La Acción Católica en España*. Barcelona, 1934.
Tellechea Idigoras, José Ignacio. *Tapices de la memoria: historia clínica 279.952*. San Sebastián, 1991.
Torrubiano Ripoll, Jaime. *Política religiosa de la democracia española*. Madrid, 1933.
Townsend, Joseph. *A Journey through Spain in the years 1786 and 1787*. 3 vols. London, 1791.
La Unión Católica: datos para su historia. Madrid, 1881.
Vegas Latapié, Eugenio. *Memorias políticas: el suicidio de la Monarquía y la Segunda República*. Barcelona, 1983.
Vilaplana Jové, José. *Teología pastoral y práctica parroquial*. Pamplona, 1918.
Villada, Juan. *El matrimonio del clero*. Valladolid, 1896.
Viñas Dausá, Narciso. *Agenda parroquial y de sus feligresías*. Madrid, 1922.
Yaben, Hilario. *¿Monarquía o república?* Madrid, 1931.

Secondary Sources

Alberdi, Ramón. *Una ciudad para un santo: los orígenes de la obra salesiana en Barcelona*. Barcelona, 1966.
Alcázar, Angel. "Los cristianos en la creación de Comisiones Obreras." *XX Siglos*, vol. 5, no. 22 (1994), pp. 118–26.
Almerich, Paulina, et al. *Cambio social y religión en España*. Barcelona, 1975.
Alted Vigil, Alicia. *Política del nuevo Estado sobre el patrimonio cultural y la educación durante la guerra civil española*. Madrid, 1984.
Álvarez Bolado, Alfonso. *El experimento del nacional-catolicismo*. Madrid, 1976.
Álvarez Bolado, Alfonso, and José F. Alemany Briz. "Gabriel Palau. S. J. y la Acción Social Popular." *Miscelánea Comillas*, vol. 38, no. 72 (1980), pp. 123–78.
———. *Para ganar la guerra, para ganar la paz: Iglesia y guerra civil*. Madrid, 1995.
Álvarez Junco, José. *La ideología política del anarquismo español, 1868–1910*. 2d ed. Madrid, 1991.
Alzaga Villaamil, Oscar. *La primera democracia cristiana en España*. Barcelona, 1973.
Amoveri, Francesco. *Stato cattolico e chiesa fascista in Spagna*. Milan, 1973.
Andrés, Melquiades, et al. *Aproximación a la historia social de la Iglesia española contemporánea*. El Escorial, 1978.
Andrés-Gallego, José. "Génesis de la Acción Católica Española, 1868–1936." *Ius Canonicum*, vol. 12 (1973), pp. 369–402.

———. *La política religiosa en España, 1889–1913*. Madrid, 1975.

———. *Pensamiento y acción social de la Iglesia en España*. Madrid, 1984.

———. "Sobre las formas de pensar y de ser: la Iglesia." In *Historia general de España y América*. Ediciones Rialp. 19 vols. Vol. 16, pt. 1, pp. 283–382. Madrid, 1985–1992.

———. "La religiosidad: las cuatro religiones de tres cuartos de siglo." *XX Siglos*, vol. 1, no. 1 (1990), pp. 2–6.

———. "La crítica falangista del catolicismo político." *Hispania Sacra*, vol. 43, no. 87 (1991), pp. 105–20.

———. *¿Fascismo o Estado católico? Ideología, religión y censura en la España de Franco, 1937–1941*. Madrid, 1997.

Andrés-Gallego, José, et al. *Estudios históricos sobre la Iglesia española contemporánea*. El Escorial, 1979.

Andrés-Gallego, José, Antón M. Pazos, and Luis de Llera. *Los españoles entre la religión y la política: el franquismo y la democracia*. Madrid, 1996.

Anes, Gonzalo. *Las crisis agrarias en la España moderna*. Madrid, 1970.

Arbeloa, Víctor M. "La expulsión de Monseñor Mateo Múgica y la captura de documentos al Vicario General de Vitoria en 1931." *Scriptorium Victoriense*, vol. 18 (1971), pp. 155–95. *

———. *Socialismo y anti-clericalismo*. Madrid, 1973.

———. *Aquella España católica*. Salamanca, 1975.

———. *La semana trágica de la Iglesia en España*. Barcelona, 1976.

———. "La separación de la Iglesia y el Estado en la constitución de 1931." *Revista Española de Derecho Canónico*, vol. 34, no. 98 (1978), pp. 342–74.

———. "La masonería y la legislación de la República." *Revista Española de Derecho Canónico*, vol. 37, no. 108 (1981), pp. 363–88.

Artigues, Daniel. *L'Opus Dei en Espagne: son évolution idéologique et politique, 1928–1957*. Paris, 1968.

Avilés, Juan, and Javier Tusell. *La derecha española contemporánea: sus orígenes: el maurismo*. Madrid, 1986.

Ayala, Pedro María de. *Vida documentada del Siervo de Dios P. Francisco Paula Tarín de la Compañía de Jesús*. Seville, 1951.

Azcona, Francisco, et al. *Catolicismo en España: analisis sociológico*. Madrid, 1985.

Balfour, Sebastian. *The End of the Spanish Empire, 1898–1923*. Oxford, 1997.

Barallat i Barés, Jaume. *L'Església sota el franquisme: una mostra local, Lleida, 1938–1968*. Lérida, 1994.

Barberini, G. "El artículo 11 de la constitución de 1876: la controversia diplomática entre España y la Santa Sede." *Anthologica Annua*, vol. 9 (1961), pp. 279–412. *

Barraquer y Roviralta, Cayetano. *Los religiosos en Cataluña durante la primera mitad del siglo XIX*. 4 vols. Barcelona, 1915–1917.

Barroso, Anabella. *Sacerdotes bajo la atenta mirada del régimen franquista: los conflictos sociopolíticos de la Iglesia en el País Vasco desde 1960 a 1975*. Bilbao, 1995.

Bayle, Constantino. *El segundo marqués de Comillas, Don Claudio López Bru*. Madrid, 1928.

Beck, Earl R. *A Time of Triumph and Sorrow: Spanish Politics during the Reign of Alfonso XII, 1874–1885*. Carbondale, 1979.

Ben-Ami, Shlomo. *The Origins of the Second Republic in Spain*. Oxford, 1978.

———. *Fascism from Above: The Dictatorship of Primo de Rivera in Spain, 1923–1930*. Oxford, 1983.

Benavides Gómez, Domingo. *El fracaso social del catolicismo español, Arboleya-Martínez, 1870–1951*. Barcelona, 1973.

———. *Democracia y cristianismo en la España de la Restauración, 1875–1931*. Madrid, 1978.

———. "Maximiliano Arboleya y su interpretación de la revolución de octubre." In *Octubre 1934: cincuenta años para la reflexión*, ed. G. Jackson et al., pp. 253–67. Madrid, 1985.

Benet, Josep, and Casimir Martí. *Barcelona a mitjan segle XIX: el moviment obrer durant el Bienni Progressista, 1854–1856*. 2 vols. Barcelona, 1976.

Blas, Ceferino de. *Tarancón, el cardenal que coronó el rey*. Madrid, 1995.

Blázquez, Feliciano. *La traición de los clérigos en la España de Franco*. Madrid, 1991.

Botti, Alfonso. *La Spagna e la crisi modernista: cultura, società civile e religiosa tra otto e novecento*. Brescia, 1987.

———. *Cielo y dinero: el nacionalcatolicismo en España, 1881–1975*. Madrid, 1992.

Boulard, Fernand. *Matériaux pour l'histoire religieuse du peuple français, XIXe–XXe siècles*. Paris, 1982.

Boyd, Carolyn. *Praetorian Politics in Liberal Spain*. Chapel Hill, 1979.

Brandes, Stanley. *Metaphors of Masculinity: Sex and Status in Andalusian Folklore*. Philadelphia, 1980.

Brassloff, Audrey. *Religion and Politics in Spain: The Spanish Church in Transition, 1962–96*. London and New York, 1998.

Bravo Morata, Federico. *El golpe de estado de Primo de Rivera*. Madrid, 1973.

Brenan, Gerald. *The Spanish Labyrinth*. Cambridge, 1943.

Busquets, Julio. *El militar de carrera en España*. Barcelona, 1971.

Callahan, William J. "The Problem of Confinement: An Aspect of Poor Relief in Eighteenth-Century Spain." *Hispanic American Historical Review*, vol. 51, no. 1 (1971), pp. 1–24.

———. *Church, Politics and Society in Spain, 1750–1874*. Cambridge, Mass., 1984.

———. "Was Spain Catholic?" *Revista Canadiense de Estudios Hispánicos*, vol. 8, no. 2 (1984), pp. 159–82.

———. "The Spanish Church and the Restoration State, 1874–1900." *Journal of Church and State*, vol. 26, no. 2 (1984), pp. 313–22.

———. "The Evangelization of Franco's 'New Spain.'" *Church History*, vol. 56, no. 4 (1987), pp. 491–503.

———. "The Spanish Parish Clergy, 1874–1930." *Catholic Historical Review*, vol. 75, no. 3 (1989), pp. 405–22.

———. "Un clero liberal." In *La voluntad de humanismo: homenaje a Juan Marichal*, ed. B. Ciplijauskaité and C. Maurer, pp. 45–56. Barcelona, 1990.

———. "Church and State in Spain, 1976–1991." *Journal of Church and State*, vol. 34, no. 3 (1992), pp. 503–19.

———. "Regalism, Liberalism and General Franco." *Catholic Historical Review*, vol. 83, no. 2 (1997), pp. 201–16.

Calvo, José, and Javier Tusell. *Giménez Fernández: precursor de la democracia española*. Seville, 1990.

Cámara Villar, Gregorio. *Nacional-catolicismo y escuela: la socialización política del franquismo*. Jaén, 1984.

Campomar Fornieles, Marta M. *La cuestión religiosa en la Restauración: historia de los heterodoxos españoles*. Santander, 1984.

Camps i Arboix, J. *Durán i Bas*. Barcelona, 1961.

Carasa Soto, Pedro. *Historia de la beneficencia en Castilla y León: poder y pobreza en la sociedad castellana*. Valladolid, 1991.

Carballo, Francisco, and Alfonso Magariños. *La Iglesia en la Galicia contemporánea: análisis histórico y teológico del periodo 1931–1939, II República*. Madrid, 1978.

Cárcel Ortí, Vicente. *Tercera época del seminario conciliar de Valencia*. Castellón de la Plana, 1970.

———. *Historia de la Iglesia de Valencia*. 2 vols. Valencia, 1987.

———. *León XIII y los católicos españoles*. Pamplona, 1988. *

———. "Iglesia y Estado durante la dictadura de Primo de Rivera, 1923–1930." *Revista Española de Derecho Canónico*, vol. 45, no. 134 (1988), pp. 209–48.

———. *La persecución religiosa en España durante la Segunda República, 1931–1939*. Madrid, 1990.

———. *¿España neopagana? Análisis de la situación y discursos del papa en las visitas "ad limina."* Valencia, 1991.
———. *Pablo VI y España: fidelidad, renovación y crisis, 1963–1978.* Madrid, 1997. *
Cárcel Ortí, Vicente, et al. *Historia de la Iglesia en España. La Iglesia en la España contemporánea, 1808–1975.* Madrid, 1979.
Caro Baroja, Julio. *Introducción a una historia contemporánea del anticlericalismo español.* Madrid, 1980.
Carr, Raymond. *Spain, 1808–1939.* Oxford, 1966.
Carr, Raymond, and Juan Pablo Fusi. *Spain: Dictatorship to Democracy.* 2d ed. London, 1981.
Carrasco Calvo, Salvador. "Pensamiento social y acción sindical en el catolicismo innovador español." *Escritos de Vedat,* vol. 14 (1984), pp. 209–52.
———. "El paso del 'catolicismo social catalán' al pluralismo de los católicos de Cataluña." *Perspectiva Social,* vol. 21 (1985), pp. 111–32.
———. "Teoría y práctica del sindicalismo católico, libre y profesional, 1911–1936." In *La crisis de la Restauración: España entre la primera guerra mundial y la Segunda República,* ed. José Luis García Delgado, pp. 315–36. Madrid, 1986.
———. "Control social y religión: el caso del catolicismo social innovador." In *Historia ideológica del control social (España-Argentina, siglos XIX y XX),* ed. R. Bergalli and E. E. Mari, pp. 31–58. Barcelona, 1989.
Casanova, Julián. *Anarquismo y revolución en la sociedad rural aragonesa, 1936–1938.* Madrid, 1985.
Casco, J., et al. *Málaga: el fenómeno religioso y sus condicionamientos socioculturales.* Madrid, 1972.
Castaño Colomer, José. *La JOC en España, 1946–1970.* Salamanca, 1978. *
Castellà-Gassol, J. *¿De dónde viene y donde va el dinero de la Iglesia española?* Barcelona, 1975.
Castillo, Juan José. *El sindicalismo amarillo en España.* Madrid, 1977.
———. *Propietarios muy pobres: sobre la subordinación política del pequeño campesino.* Madrid, 1979.
The Catholic Encyclopedia. Ed. Charles G. Herbermann. 16 vols. New York, 1907–1914.
Cazorla, José. *Problemas de estratificación social en España.* Madrid, 1973.
Cervera, Angel. *Angel Ayala.* Madrid, 1975.
Chao Rego, José. *La Iglesia en el franquismo.* Madrid, 1976.
Chatellier, Louis. *L'Europe des dévots.* Paris, 1987.
Cholvy, Gérard, and Yves-Marie Hilaire. *Histoire religieuse de la France contemporaine.* 2 vols. Toulouse, 1985.
Christian, William. *Person and God in a Spanish Valley.* New York, 1972.
———. *Local Religion in Sixteenth-Century Spain.* Princeton, 1981.
———. *Moving Crucifixes in Modern Spain.* Princeton, 1992.
———. *Visionaries: The Spanish Republic and the Reign of Christ.* Berkeley and Los Angeles, 1996.
Cierva, Ricardo de la. *Oscura rebelión en la Iglesia: jesuitas, teología de liberación, carmelitas, marianistas y socialistas.* Esplugues de Llobregat, 1987.
Codina, Víctor, Miguel Angel de Prada, and Carlos Pereda. *Analizar la Iglesia.* Madrid, 1981.
Codinachs i Verdaguer, P. *La Federació de Joves Cristians de Catalunya, 1931–1936.* Barcelona, 1990.
Corcuera Atienza, Javier. *Orígenes, ideología y organización del nacionalismo vasco, 1876–1904.* Madrid, 1979.
Corral, Carlos, and Joseph Listl, eds., *Constitución y acuerdos Iglesia-Estado: actas del II Simposio Hispano-Alemán.* Madrid, 1988.
Corral, Carlos, et al. *La asignación tributaria para fines religiosos.* Madrid, 1989.
Crespo Redondo, Jesús. *Purga de maestros en la guerra civil.* Valladolid, 1987.
Cuenca Toribio, José Manuel. *Notas para el estudio de los seminarios españoles en el pontificado de Pío IX.* Valencia, 1973.

———. *Sociología de una elite de poder de España e Hispanoamérica contemporáneas: la jerarquía eclesiástica, 1789–1965*. Córdoba, 1976.
———. *Iglesia y burguesía en la España liberal*. Jaén, 1979.
———. *Relaciones Iglesia-Estado en la España contemporánea, 1833–1985*. Madrid, 1985.
———. *Sociología del episcopado español e hispanoamericano, 1789–1985*. Madrid, 1986.
———. "Un posible punto de partida para el análisis de una cuestión clave de la historia española contemporánea: el anticlericalismo." In *Masonería, política y sociedad*, 2 vols., vol. 2., ed. J. A. Ferrer Benimeli, pp. 709–30. Castellón (Zaragoza), 1989.
Cuesta Bustillo, Josefina. *Sindicalismo católico agrario en España, 1917–1919*. Madrid, 1978.
———. "Una perspectiva ante le crisis de 1917–1920: hubo respuesta católica." In Manuel Tuñon de Lara et al., *VIII Coloquio de Pau: la crisis del Estado español, 1898–1936*. Madrid, 1978.
———. "Estudios sobre el catolicismo social español, 1915–1930." *Studia Historica*, vol. 2 (1984), pp. 193–244.
Cueva Merino, Julio de la. *Clericales y anticlericales: el conflicto entre confesionalidad y secularización en Cantabria, 1875–1923*. Santander, 1994.
———. "The Stick and the Candle: Clericals and Anticlericals in Northern Spain, 1898–1913." *European History Quarterly*, vol. 26, no. 2 (1996), pp. 241–65.
———. "Religious Persecution, Anticlerical Tradition and Revolution: On Atrocities against the Clergy during the Spanish Civil War." *Journal of Contemporary History*, vol. 33, no. 3 (1998), pp. 355–69.
Dedieu, Jean Pierre. "'Christianisation' en Nouvelle Castille: catéchisme, communion et confirmation dans l'archevêché de Tolede, 1540–1640." *Mélanges de la Casa de Velázquez*, vol. 15 (1979), pp. 261–94.
Delumeau, Jean. *Le catholicisme entre Luther et Voltaire*. Paris, 1971.
Díaz Cerio, Angel. *El comportamiento religioso-moral en La Rioja: estructuras condicionantes, prácticas y actitudes, evolución y sus causas, 1958 a 1975*. Barañáin, 1992.
Díaz de Cerio, Franco. *Un cardenal filósofo de la historia, Fr. Zeferino González O. P., 1831–1894*. Rome, 1969.
Díaz del Moral, Juan. *Historia de las agitaciones campesinas andaluzas*. 2d ed. Madrid, 1967.
Díaz Mozaz, José María. *La Iglesia de España en la encrucijada*. Madrid, 1973.
Díaz-Salazar, Rafael. *Iglesia, dictadura y democracia*. Madrid, 1981.
———. *El capital simbolico: estructura social, política y religión en España*. Madrid, 1988.
Díaz-Salazar, Rafael, and Salvador Giner, eds., *Religión y sociedad en España*. Madrid, 1993.
Diccionario de historia eclesiástica de España. 4 vols. Ed. Q. Aldea Vaquero, T. Marín, and J. Vives Gatell. Madrid, 1972–1975.
Díez Llama, Santiago. *La situación socio-religiosa de Santander y el Obispo Sánchez de Castro, 1884–1920*. Santander, 1971.
"The Diocese of Madrid: Pastoral Care in Large Cities." *Pro Mundi Vita: Dossiers*, no. 1 (1983), pp. 2–23.
"Discussion du rapport de M. Rémond sur la déchristianisation au XIXe siècle." *Cahiers d'Histoire*, vol. 9 (1964), pp. 89–119.
Domínguez, Javier, ed. *Organizaciones obreras cristianas en la oposición al franquismo, 1951–1975*. Bilbao, 1985. *
Duncan, Martha Grace. "Spanish Anarchism Refracted: Theme and Image in the Millenarian Revisionist Literature." *Journal of Contemporary History*, vol. 23, no. 3 (1988), pp. 323–46.
Duocastella, Rogelio. *Mataró 1955: estudio de sociología religiosa sobre una ciudad industrial española*. Barcelona, 1961.
———. "Géographie de la pratique religieuse en Espagne." *Social Compass*, vol. 12, no. 2 (1965), pp. 253–302.
Duocastella, Rogelio, et al. *Sociología y pastoral de una diócesis: Vitoria*. Madrid and Barcelona, 1965.

Duocastella, Rogelio, et al. *Sociología religiosa y pastoral de conjunto: diócesis de Salamanca.* Barcelona, 1967–1968.

Duocastella, Rogelio, et al. *Religiosidad y subdesarrollo: estudio sociológico sobre Tierra de Campos.* Madrid and Barcelona, 1971.

Duocastella, Rogelio, et al. *Sociología religiosa y pastoral de la diócesis de Cartagena (Murcia).* Barcelona, 1971.

Duocastella, Rogelio, et al. *El fenómeno religioso y sus condicionamientos socio-culturales: estudio socio-religioso de la diócesis de Málaga.* Málaga, 1972.

Echarren, Ramón. "Veinticinco años en la vida de la Iglesia española." In Juan Martín Velasco et al., *La Iglesia en la sociedad española,* pp. 27–78. Estella, 1990.

———. "El Cardenal Tarancón, presidente de la Conferencia Episcopal." In S. Grisolía et al., *Homenaje al Cardenal Enrique y Tarancón,* pp. 128–217. Valencia, 1997.

Elorza, Antonio. "La Confederación Española de Sindicatos Obreros, 1935–1938." *Revista de Trabajo,* no. 33 (1971), pp. 172–412. *

Escartín Celaya, Pedro. "Las instituciones intermedias." *XX Siglos,* vol. 4, no. 13 (1993), pp. 72–80.

Escartín Núñez, Carlos, et al. *Postconcilio en España.* Madrid, 1967.

Espadas Burgos, Manuel et al. *Iglesia, sociedad y política en la España contemporánea.* El Escorial, 1983.

Felipe, Dionisio de. *Fundación de los Redentoristas en España.* Madrid, 1965.

Fernández Almagro, Melchor. *Historia política de la España contemporánea.* Alianza Editorial edition. 3 vols. Madrid, 1968.

———. *Historia del reinado de Don Alfonso XIII.* Barcelona, 1933.

Fernández Areal, M. *La política católica española.* Barcelona, 1971.

Fernández Conde, Javier. "Pensamiento político del Cardenal Guisasola, 1852–1920." *Studium Ovetense,* vol. 2 (1974), pp. 143–78.

Flynn, Maureen. *Sacred Charity: Confraternities and Social Welfare in Spain, 1400–1700.* Ithaca, 1989.

Forner Muñoz, Salvador. *Canalejas y el Partido Liberal Democrático, 1900–1910.* Madrid, 1993.

Forteza Pujol, Francisco. *Historia y memoria de cursillos.* Barcelona, 1991.

Francés, María José, ed. *España 2000 ¿cristiana?* Madrid, 1990.

Freeman, Susan Tax. *Neighbors: The Social Contract in a Castilian Hamlet.* Chicago, 1990.

———. "Faith and Fashion in Spanish Religion: Notes on the Observation of Observance." *Peasant Studies,* vol. 7, no. 2 (1978), pp. 101–22.

Fuenmayor, Amadeo, Valentín Gómez-Iglesias, and José Luis Illanes. *El itinerario jurídico del Opus Dei.* Pamplona, 1988.

Fusi, Juan Pablo, and Fernando García de Cortázar. *Política, nacionalidad e Iglesia en el País Vasco.* San Sebastián, 1988.

García Balart, Nuria. "Confesionalidad, tolerancia y libertad religiosa en la doctrina del episcopado español." *Ius Canonicum,* vol. 22, no. 43 (1982), pp. 87–113.

García de Cortázar, Fernando. "Análisis sociológico del episcopado español de la Restauración." *Revista Internacional de Sociología,* vol. 34 (1976), pp. 63–90.

———. "La Iglesia española de la Restauración: definición de objetivos y práctica religiosa." *Letras de Deusto,* vol. 10, no. 6 (1978), pp. 5–34.

———. "La Iglesia en la crisis del Estado español, 1898–1923." In Manuel Tuñón de Lara et al., *VIII Coloquio de Pau: la crisis del Estado español, 1898–1936,* pp. 343–77. Madrid, 1978.

———. "La nueva historia de la Iglesia contemporánea en España." In *Historiografía española contemporánea: X Coloquio del Centro de Investigaciones Hispánicas de la Universidad de Pau: balance y resumen,* ed. Manuel Tuñón de Lara, pp. 207–30. Madrid, 1980.

———. "La Iglesia vasca: del carlismo al nacionalismo, 1870–1936." In *Estudios de historia contemporánea del País Vasco,* ed. J. C. Jiménez Aberasturi, pp. 203–78. San Sebastián, 1982.

———. "Mateo Múgica, la Iglesia y la guerra civil en el País Vasco." *Letras de Deusto,* vol. 16, no. 35 (1986), pp. 5–32.
García Escudero, José María. *Vista a la derecha.* Madrid, 1988.
García i Jordan, Pilar. *Els catòlics catalans i la Segona República, 1931–1936.* Barcelona, 1986.
García Nieto, Juan N. *El sindicalismo cristiano en España.* Bilbao, 1960.
García Prous, Concha. *Relaciones Iglesia-Estado en la Segunda República española.* Córdoba, 1996.
García Regidor, Teódulo. *La polémica sobre la secularización de la enseñanza en España, 1902–1914.* Madrid, 1985.
García Sánchez, Antonio. *La Segunda República en Málaga: la cuestión religiosa, 1931–1933.* Málaga, 1984.
García Valverde, María Luisa. *Los problemas económicos de la Iglesia en el siglo XIX: el clero parroquial de Granada, 1840–1900.* Granada, 1983.
García Venero, M. *Santiago Alba: monárquico de razón.* Madrid, 1963.
Garralda García, Angel. *La persecución religiosa del clero en Asturias (1934 y 1936–1937).* 2d ed. 2 vols. Avilés, 1983.
Garrido, Samuel. *Los trabajadores de las derechas.* Segorbe and Castellón de la Plana, 1986.
Garriga, Ramón. *El Cardenal Segura y el Nacional-Catolicismo.* Barcelona, 1977.
Gervilla Castillo, Enrique. *La escuela del nacional-catolicismo: ideología e educación religiosa.* Granada, 1990.
Gómez Molleda, Dolores. *La masonería en la crisis española del siglo XX.* Madrid, 1986.
Gómez Pérez, Rafael. *Política y religión en el régimen de Franco.* Barcelona, 1976.
———. *El franquismo y la Iglesia.* Madrid, 1986.
Goñi Galarraga, Joseba M. *La Guerra Civil en el País Vasco: una guerra entre católicos.* Vitoria, 1989.
González-Anleo, Juan. *Catolicismo nacional: nostalgia y crisis.* Madrid, 1975.
González Armendia, José Ramón. *Dotación del Estado a la Iglesia española (siglos XIX–XX).* Salamanca, 1990.
González-Balado, José Luis. *Padre Llanos: un jesuita en el suburbio.* Madrid, 1991.
González Blasco, Pedro, and Juan González-Anleo. *Religión y sociedad en la España de los 90.* Madrid, 1992.
González Calbet, Teresa. *La dictadura de Primo de Rivera: el Directorio Militar.* Madrid, 1987.
———. "La destrucción del sistema político de la Restauración: el golpe de septiembre de 1923." In *La crisis de la Restauración: España, entre la primera guerra mundial y la Segunda República,* ed. José Luis García Delgado, pp. 101–20. Madrid, 1986.
González Moralejo, Rafael. "Las Semanas Sociales de España." *Revista de Trabajo,* no. 16 (1966), pp. 219–39.
González Novalin, José Luis et al. *Estudios, seminarios y pastoral en un siglo de la historia de la Iglesia en España, 1892–1992.* Rome, 1992.
González Ruiz, Nicolás, and Isidoro Martín Martínez. *Seglares en la historia del catolicismo español.* Madrid, 1968.
Granados, Anastasio. *El Cardenal Gomá, Primado de España.* Madrid, 1969. *
Granados, Mariano. *La cuestión religiosa en España.* Mexico City, 1959.
Guasch Borrat, Juan María. *"El Debate" y la crisis de la Restauración, 1910–1923.* Pamplona, 1986.
Gunter, Richard, Giacomo Sani, and Goldi Shabad. *Spain after Franco: The Making of a Competitive Party System.* Berkeley and Los Angeles, 1988.
Gutiérrez Martínez Conde, Luis. "Participación de la Iglesia católica en el IRPF de 1990." *XX Siglos,* vol. 4, no. 13 (1993), pp. 115–17.
Haliczer, Stephen. *Sexuality in the Confessional: A Sacrament Profaned.* New York and Oxford, 1996.
Harrison, Joseph. *An Economic History of Modern Spain.* New York, 1978.

———. "The Regenerationist Movement in Spain after the Disaster of 1898." *European Studies Review*, vol. 9, no. 1 (1979), pp. 1–28.

———. *The Spanish Economy in the Twentieth Century*. London, Sydney, 1985.

Hermet, Guy. *Les catholiques dans l'Espagne franquiste*. 2 vols. Paris, 1981.

Herr, Richard. *Rural Change and Royal Finances in Spain at the End of the Old Regime*. Berkeley and Los Angeles, 1989.

Hibbs-Lissorgues, Solange. *Iglesia, prensa y sociedad en España, 1868–1904*. Alicante, 1995.

Hilaire, Yves-Marie. *Une chrétienté au XIX siècle: la vie religieuse des populations du diòcese d'Arras, 1840–1914*. 2 vols. Villeneuve d'Asoq, 1977.

"La historia del episcopado español del 41 al 72." *Vida Nueva*, nos. 821–822 (1972), pp. 10–21.

Ibán, Iván C., ed. *Iglesia católica y regímenes autoritarios y democráticos: experiencia española e italiana*. Madrid, 1987.

Iribarren, Jesús. "La Iglesia y el franquismo en la postguerra: 'Ecclesia' y el Cardenal Pla y Deniel." *Revista de Fomento Social*, no. 128 (1977), pp. 426–37.

Iturralde, Juan de. *El catolicismo y la cruzada de Franco*. 3 vols. Vienne and Toulouse, 1965.

Iztueta Armendariz, Paulo. *Sociología del fenómeno contestatario del clero vasco, 1940–1975*. Zarauz, 1981.

Jackson, Gabriel. *The Spanish Republic and the Civil War, 1931–1939*. Princeton, 1965.

Jiménez Blanco, Jesús. *La secularización en España*. Bilbao, 1972.

Jiménez Duque, Baldomero. *La espiritualidad en el siglo XIX español*. Madrid, 1974.

Jiménez Lozano, José. *Los cementerios civiles y la heterodoxia española*. Madrid, 1978.

Kaplan, Temma. *Anarchists of Andalusia, 1868–1903*. Princeton, 1977.

Kenny, Michael. *A Spanish Tapestry: Town and Country in Castile*. New York, 1966.

Laboa, Juan María. *Iglesia y religión en las constituciones españolas*. Madrid, 1981.

———. *Iglesia e intolerancias: la guerra civil: una historia que habla de dos Españas*. Madrid, 1987.

———. "España por el Papa!" *XX Siglos*, vol. 1, no. 1 (1990), pp. 47–64.

Lacomba, Juan Antonio. *La crisis española de 1917*. Madrid, 1970.

Lannon, Frances. "A Basque Challenge to the pre–Civil War Spanish Church." *European Studies Review*, vol. 9, no. 1 (1979), pp. 29–48.

———. "The Church's Crusade against the Republic." In *Revolution and War in Spain, 1931–1939*, ed. Paul Preston, pp. 35–58. London, 1984.

———. *Privilege, Persecution and Prophecy: The Catholic Church in Spain, 1875–1975*. Oxford, 1987.

———. "An Élite of Grace: The Spanish Bishops in the Twentieth Century." In *Élites and Power in Twentieth-Century Spain: Essays in Honour of Sir Raymond Carr*, ed. Frances Lannon and Paul Preston, pp. 11–31. Oxford, 1990.

La Parra López, Emilio, and Jesús Pradells, eds., *Iglesia, sociedad y Estado en España, Francia e Italia (ss. XVIII al XX)*. Alicante, 1991.

Lazo, Alfonso. *La Iglesia, la Falange y el fascismo: un estudio sobre la prensa española de posguerra*. Seville, 1995.

Lincoln, Bruce. "Revolutionary Exhumations in Spain, July 1936." *Comparative Studies in Society and History*, vol. 17, no. 2 (1985), pp. 241–60.

Lisón-Tolosana, Carmelo. *Belmonte de los Caballeros: A Sociological Study of a Spanish Town*. Oxford, 1966.

Llorca, Carmen. *Emilio Castelar: precursor de la democracia cristiana*. Madrid, 1966.

Llorens, Montserrat. "El P. Antonio Vicent, S. I. (1837–1912): notas sobre el desarrollo de la acción social católica en España." *Estudios de Historia Moderna*. Vol. 4 (1954), pp. 395–495.

Loboa, Juan M., ed. *El postconcilio en España*. Madrid, 1988.

Longares Alonso, Jesús. *Política y religión en Barcelona, 1833–1843*. Madrid, 1976.

López García, Basilisa. *Aproximación a la historia de la HOAC, 1946–1981*. Madrid, 1995.
López Pintor, Rafael. "La Iglesia española en cifras." *XX Siglos*, vol. 4, no. 13 (1993), pp. 20–30.
López Rodríguez, Manuel. *La España protestante: crónica de una minoría marginada, 1937–1975*. Madrid, 1976.
Lucchini, Ricardo. *Sociologie du fascisme*. Fribourg, 1976.
Madrid-Alcalá, una diócesis en construcción, 1961–1982. Madrid, 1982.
Maldonado, Luis. *Para comprender el catolicismo popular.* Estella, 1990.
Malefakis, Edward. *Agrarian Reform and Peasant Revolution in Spain: Origins of the Civil War.* New Haven and London, 1970.
Manent i Segimon, Albert, et al. *Contribució a la història de l'Església catalana*. Montserrat, 1983.
Manent i Segimon, Albert, and Josep Raventós i Giralt. *L'Església a Catalunya durant la guerra civil, 1936–1939*. Montserrat, 1984.
Marcos Alonso, Jesús. "Études socio-religieuses espagnoles/Socio-religious studies in Spain." *Social Compass*, vol. 12, no. 2 (1965), pp. 217–43.
Marichal, Juan. *La vocación de Manuel Azaña*. Madrid, 1968.
Marquina Barrio, Antonio. *La diplomacia vaticana y la España de Franco*. Madrid, 1983.
———. "El Vaticano y la guerra civil española." In Aldo Albónico et al., *Italia y la guerra civil española*, pp. 83–102. Madrid, 1986.
Martí, Casimir. *L'Església de Barcelona, 1850–1857*. 2 vols. Barcelona, 1984.
Martin, Benjamin. *The Agony of Modernization: Labor and Industrialization in Spain*. Ithaca, 1990.
Martín, Isidro. "En el segundo centenario del concordato español de 1753." *Revista Española de Derecho Canónico*, vol. 8, no. 24 (1953), pp. 745–59.
Martín Descalzo, José Luis. *Tarancón, el cardenal del cambio*. Barcelona, 1982.
Martín Vigil, José. *Los curas "comunistas."* 2d ed. Oviedo, 1965.
Martínez, Mateo. *Tierra de Campos: cooperativismo y sindicalismo agrario*. Valladolid, 1982.
Martínez López, Alberte. *O cooperativismo católico no proceso de modernización da agricultura galega, 1900–1943*. Vigo, 1989.
Massot i Muntaner, Josep. *Aproximació a la història religiosa de la Catalunya contemporánea*. Barcelona, 1973.
———. *L'Església catalana al segle XIX*. Barcelona, 1975.
———. *Església i societat a la Mallorca del segle XX*. Barcelona, 1977.
Mateo Avilés, Elías de. *Paternalismo burgués y beneficencia religiosa en la Málaga de la segunda mitad del siglo XIX*. Málaga, 1985.
———. *Piedades e impiedades de los malagueños en el siglo XIX: una aproximación a la religiosidad española contemporánea*. Málaga, 1987.
———. *El anticlericalismo en Málaga, 1874–1923*. Málaga, 1990.
Matilla Tascón, Antonio. *La única contribución y el catastro de Ensenada*. Madrid, 1947.
Maza Zorilla, Elena. *Pobreza y asistencia social en España, siglos XVI al XX*. Valladolid, 1987.
———. "Asociacionismo confesional en Valladolid: la Asociación Católica de Escuelas y Círculo de Obreros." In *Investigaciones históricas: época moderna y contemporánea*, ed. C. J. Hernando Sánchez, pp. 169–202. Valladolid, 1988.
McDonough, Gary Wray. *Good Families of Barcelona: A Social History of Power in the Industrial Era*. Princeton, 1986.
Meaker, Gerald H. "A Civil War of Words: The Ideological Impact of the First World War on Spain, 1914–1918." In *Neutral Europe between War and Revolution, 1917–1923*, ed. H. A. Schmitt, pp. 1–65. Charlottesville, 1988.
Meer, Fernando de. *La cuestión religiosa en las Cortes Constituyentes de la II República*. Pamplona, 1975.
Miguel, Amando de. *Sociología del franquismo*. 5th ed. Madrid, 1975.

Miguel, Amando de, et al. *Síntesis del informe sociológico sobre la situación social de España 1970*. Madrid, 1972.

Mintz, Jerome. *The Anarchists of Casas Viejas*. Chicago, 1982.

Mitchell, Timothy J. *Violence and Piety in Spanish Folklore*. Philadelphia, 1988.

Moncada, Alberto. *El Opus Dei: una interpretación*. Madrid, 1974.

Montero, José R. *La CEDA: el catolicismo social y político de la II República*. 2 vols. Madrid, 1977.

Montero, Mercedes. *Historia de la Asociación Católica Nacional de Propagandistas: la construcción del Estado confesional, 1936–1945*. Pamplona, 1993.

Montero García, Feliciano. *El primer catolicismo social y la "Rerum Novarum" en España, 1889–1902*. Madrid, 1983.

———. "Juventud y política: los movimientos juveniles de inspiración católica, 1920–1970." *Studia Historica*, vol. 5, no. 4 (1987), pp. 105–21.

———. "Catolicismo social en España: una revisión histórica." *Historia Social*, no. 2 (1988), pp. 157–64.

———. *El movimiento católico en España*. Madrid, 1993.

Montero Moreno, Antonio. *Historia de la persecución religiosa en España, 1936–1939*. Madrid, 1961. *

Moreno Fernández, Luis Miguel. *Acción Popular Murciana: la derecha confesional en Murcia durante la Segunda República*. Murcia, 1987.

Morodo, Raúl. *Los orígenes ideológicos del franquismo: Acción Española*. Madrid, 1985.

Muntanyola, Ramón. *Vidal y Barraquer: el cardenal de la paz*. Barcelona, 1974.

Murcia, Antonio. *Obreros y obispos en el franquismo*. Madrid, 1995.

Nalle, Sara T. *God in La Mancha: Religious Reform and the People of Cuenca, 1500–1650*. Princeton, 1992.

Núñez Múñoz, María F. *La Iglesia y la Restauración, 1875–1881*. Santa Cruz de Tenerife, 1976.

Obieta Villalonga, María. *Los integristas guipuzcoanos, 1888–1898*. Zarauz, 1996.

Obregón, Eduardo. *Santander, 1937–1941: planteamientos para la historia de una diócesis*. Santander, 1971.

O'Connell, James R. "The Spanish Republic: Further Reflections on Its Anticlerical Policies." *Catholic Historical Review*, vol. 57, no. 2 (1971), pp. 275–89.

Ordóñez Marquéz, Juan. *La apostasía de las masas y la persecución religiosa en la provincia de Huelva, 1931–1936*. Madrid, 1968.

Ordovas, José Manuel. *Historia de la Asociación Católica Nacional de Propagandistas: de la dictadura a la Segunda República, 1923–1936*. Pamplona, 1993.

Orensanz, Aurelio L. *Religiosidad popular española, 1940–1965*. Madrid, 1974.

Oyarzun, Román. *Historia de Carlismo*. Madrid, 1969.

Palacios Bañuelos, Luis. *Círculos de obreros y sindicatos agrarios en Córdoba, 1877–1923*. 2d ed. Córdoba, 1985.

Pampín, Xosé M. R. *Nova concencia na Igrexa galega*. Pontevedra, 1976.

Pascual, Carlos. *Guía sobrenatural de España*. Madrid, 1976.

Payne, Stanley G. *Falange: A History of Spanish Fascism*. Stanford, 1961.

———. *Politics and Society in Twentieth-Century Spain*. New York, 1976.

———. "Spanish Conservatism, 1834–1923." *Journal of Contemporary History*, vol. 13 (1978), pp. 765–89.

———. *Spanish Catholicism*. Madison, 1984.

———. *The Franco Regime, 1936–1975*. Madison, 1987.

Pazos, Antón M. *El clero navarro, 1900–1936*. Pamplona, 1990.

———, ed. *Un siglo de catolicismo social en Europa, 1891–1991*. Pamplona, 1993.

Penniman, Howard R., and Eusebio M. Mujal-León. *Spain at the Polls, 1977, 1979 and 1982*. Durham, 1985.

Perea, Joaquín. *El modelo de Iglesia subyacente en la pastoral del clero vasco.* 4 vols. Bilbao, 1991.

Pérez Delgado, Rafael. *Antonio Maura.* Madrid, 1974.

Pérez-Llantada y Gutiérrez, Jaime. *La libertad religiosa en España y el Vaticano II.* Madrid, 1974.

Pérez de Olaguer, Antonio. *El canónigo Collell.* Barcelona, 1933.

Perfecto García, Miguel Angel. "Cooperativismo y catolicismo social en la dictadura de Primo de Rivera." *Studia Historica,* vol. 2, no. 4 (1984), pp. 123–47.

Petschen, Santiago. "Año 1904: primer gobierno Maura: el arzobispo Nozaleda es rechazado en Valencia." *Historia Internacional,* no. 10 (1976), pp. 39–43.

———. "Maura y los obispos se ganan a las derechas." *Historia Internacional,* no. 15 (1976), pp. 59–64.

———. *La Iglesia en la España de Franco.* Madrid, 1977.

Piñol, Josep M. *El nacionalcatolicisme a Catalunya i la resistència, 1926–1966.* Barcelona, 1993.

Pitt-Rivers, J. A. *The People of the Sierra.* Chicago, 1961.

Plongeron, Bernard. *La religion populaire.* 2 vols. Paris, 1976.

Preston, Paul. *The Coming of the Spanish Civil War: Reform, Reaction and Revolution in the Second Republic.* London and New York, 1978.

———. *Franco: A Biography.* London, 1993.

Puelles Benítez, Manuel de. *Educación e ideología en la España contemporánea.* Barcelona, 1980.

———. "Secularización y enseñanza en España. " In *España entre dos siglos, 1875–1931: continuidad y cambio,* ed. José Luis García Delgado, pp. 191–250. Madrid, 1991.

Puerto y Reyna, Juan A. *Biografía del R. P. Francisco Tarín.* Seville, 1911.

Raguer, Hilari. "Antonio Montero, 'Historia de la persecución religiosa en España, 1936–1939.'" *Revue d'Histoire Ecclésiastique,* vol. 57 (1962), pp. 618–30.

———. *La Unió Democràtica de Catalunya i el seu temps, 1931–1939.* Montserrat, 1976.

———. *La espada y la cruz: la Iglesia, 1936–1939.* Barcelona, 1977.

———. "La Iglesia española en la Segunda República." *Arbor,* vol. 109, nos. 426–437 (1981), pp. 51–66.

———. "Los obispos españoles y la guerra civil." *Arbor,* vol. 112, nos. 439–440 (1982), pp. 295–320.

———. "El Cardenal Gomá y la guerra de España." *Arbor,* vol. 111, no. 436 (1982), pp. 43–82.

Real Cuesta, Javier. *El carlismo vasco.* Madrid, 1985.

Recio, Juan Luis, Octavio Uña, and Rafael Díaz-Salazar. *La transición española: religión y política.* Estella, 1990.

Redondo, Gonzalo. *Historia de la Iglesia en España, 1931–1939.* 2 vols. Madrid, 1993.

Reig, Ramiro. *Blasquistas y clericales: la lucha por la ciudad en la València de 1900.* Valencia, 1986.

Reig, Ramiro, and Josep Picó. *Feixistes, rojos i capelans: Església i societat al País Valencià, 1940–1970.* Palma de Mallorca, 1978.

"La repercusión de la encíclica 'Rerum Novarum.'" *Revista de Trabajo,* no. 16 (1966), pp. 257–89.

Requejo San Román, Jesús. *El Cardenal Segura.* Toledo, 1931.

Revuelta González, Manuel. *La exclaustración, 1833–1843.* Madrid, 1976.

———. *La Compañía de Jesús en la España contemporánea.* 2 vols. Madrid, 1984–1991.

———. "La recuperación eclesiástica y el rechazo anticlerical en el cambio del siglo." In *España entre dos siglos, 1875–1931: continuidad y cambio,* ed. José Luis García Delgado, pp. 213–34. Madrid, 1991.

Rial, James H. *Revolution from Above.* Fairfax, London, and Toronto, 1986.

Ricart Oller, Josep. *Egara: una parroquia obrera bajo el franquismo, 1963–1977.* Tarrasa, 1979.

Risco, Alberto. *El Padre Francisco de Paula Tarín*. Madrid, 1921.

Riu, Francisco. *La comunidad eclesial ante el reto de la LODE*. Madrid, 1986.

Robinson, Richard. *The Origins of Franco's Spain: The Right, the Republic and Revolution, 1931–1936*. Pittsburgh, 1970.

Robles Múñoz, Cristóbal. *Insurrección o legalidad: los católicos y la Restauración*. Madrid, 1988.

———. "Frente a la supremacía del Estado: la Santa Sede y los católicos de la Restauración." *Anthologica Annua*, vol. 34 (1987), pp. 189–306; vol. 36 (1989), pp. 317–490; vol. 37 (1990), pp. 131–252.

———. *Antonio Maura, un político liberal*. Madrid, 1995.

Rodríguez de Aisa, María Luisa. *El Cardenal Gomá y la guerra de España: aspectos de la gestión pública del primado, 1936–1939*. Madrid, 1981. *

Rodríguez de Coro, Francisco. *Colonización política del catolicismo*. San Sebastián, 1979.

Roman Fuentes, José María. *La autocrítica religiosa en el catolicismo español contemporáneo*. Madrid, 1968.

Romero Maura, Joaquín. *La rosa de fuego: republicanos y anarquistas: la política de los obreros barceloneses entre el desastre colonial y la Semana Trágica*. Barcelona, Buenos Aires, and Mexico City, 1975.

———. "Terrorism in Barcelona and Its Impact on Spanish Politics, 1904–1909." *Past and Present*, no. 41 (1968), pp. 130–83.

Rueda, Germán, ed. *La desamortización en la Península Ibérica*. Madrid, 1993.

Ruiz, David. *Insurrección y revolución obrera: el octubre español de 1934*. Barcelona, 1988.

Ruiz Giménez, Joaquín, ed. *Iglesia, Estado y sociedad en España, 1930–1982*. Barcelona, 1984.

Ruiz Manjón, Octavio. *El Partido Republicano Radical, 1908–1936*. Madrid, 1976.

Ruiz Rico, Juan José. *El papel político de la Iglesia católica en la España de Franco, 1936–1971*. Madrid, 1977.

Ruiz Rodrigo, Cándido. *Catolicismo social y educación: la formación del proletariado en Valencia, 1891–1917*. Valencia, 1982.

Ruiz Sánchez, José-Leonardo. *Política e Iglesia durante la Restauración: la Liga Católica de Sevilla, 1901–1923*. Seville, 1994.

Sacerdote según el corazón de Dios: Don Avelino González López, cura párroco de San Pedro de Lugo, 1871–1924. Vitoria, 1964.

Sáez Alba, A. *La Asociación Católica de Propagandistas: reproducción y métodos de la derecha permanente*. Paris, 1974.

Sáez de Ocariz y Ruiz de Azúa, M. "El cumplimiento pascual en la ciudad de Logroño a lo largo del siglo XIX." *Berceo*, no. 76 (1965), pp. 269–87.

Sáez Marín, Juan. *Datos sobre la Iglesia española contemporánea, 1768–1868*. Madrid, 1975.

Sáinz Ripa, Eliseo. "La religiosidad en La Rioja durante el siglo XIX." *Berceo*, no. 83 (1972), pp. 159–83.

Sanabre Sanromá, José María. *Martirologio de la Iglesia en la diócesis de Barcelona durante la persecución religiosa*. Barcelona, 1943.

Sánchez, José M. *Reform and Reaction: The Politico-Religious Background of the Spanish Civil War*. Chapel Hill, 1962.

———. *The Spanish Civil War as a Religious Tragedy*. Notre Dame, 1987.

Sánchez Andrés, Amparo. "El patronato de la Juventud Obrera de Valencia." *Saitabi*, vol. 19 (1969), pp. 185–200.

Sánchez Erauskin, Javier. *Por Dios hacia el imperio: nacionalcatolicismo en las Vascongadas del primer franquismo, 1936–1945*. San Sebastián, 1994.

Sánchez Jiménez, José. *El Cardenal Herrera Oria: pensamiento y acción social*. Madrid, 1986. *

Santamaría, Carlos et al. *Catolicismo español: aspectos actuales*. Madrid, 1955.

Santidrián, Pedro R. *El Padre Sarabia escribe su historia, 1875–1958: medio siglo de misiones en España*. Madrid, 1963.

Sanz de Diego, Rafael María. "La actitud de Roma ante el artículo 11 de la constitución de 1876." *Hispania Sacra*, vol. 28 (1975), pp. 167–96.

———. "La vertiente social de los Congresos Católicos Españoles, 1889–1902." *Revista de Fomento Social*, no. 128 (1977), pp. 177–87.

———. "El P. Vicent: 25 años de catolicismo social en España, 1886–1912." *Hispania Sacra*, vol. 33 (1981), pp. 323–72.

Scholl, S. H., ed. *Historia del movimiento obrero cristiano*. Barcelona, 1964.

Seco Serrano, C., et al. *La cuestión social en la Iglesia española contemporánea*. El Escorial, 1981.

Shubert, Adrian. "The Social Origins of Labour Militancy in Asturias, 1860–1914." *European Studies Review*, vol. 12 (1982), pp. 167–85.

———. "The Epic Failure: The Asturian Revolution of October 1934." In *Revolution and War in Spain, 1931–1939*, ed. Paul Preston, pp. 113–36. London and New York, 1984.

———. "Entre Arboleya y Comillas: el fracaso del sindicalismo católico de Asturias." In *Octubre 1934: cincuenta años para la reflexión*, ed. G. Jackson et al., pp. 243–52. Madrid, 1985.

Simon Segura, Francisco. *La desamortización española del siglo XIX*. Madrid, 1973.

Sobrino, José A. de. *El Venerable Spínola: perfil y espíritu*. Madrid, 1984.

Southworth, Herbert R. *Guernica! Guernica! A Study of Journalism, Propaganda and History*. Berkeley, Los Angeles, and London, 1977.

"Spain: The Socio-Religious Situation." *Pro Mundi Vita Dossiers*, nos. 7–8 (1979), pp. 2–55.

Suárez, Federico. "Génesis del concordato de 1851." *Ius Canonicum*, vol. 3 (1963), pp. 215–418.

Suárez Fernández, Luis. *Francisco Franco y su tiempo*. 8 vols. Madrid, 1984. *

Suquía, Angel et al. *Al servicio de la Iglesia y del pueblo: homenaje al Cardenal Tarancón en su 75 aniversario*. Madrid, 1984.

Talde, E. A. *Historia general de la guerra civil en Euskadi*. 6 vols. San Sebastián and Bilbao, 1978–1981.

Tamames, Ramón, and Laura Tamames. *Introducción a la constitución española*. 5th ed. Madrid, 1991.

Tellería, Raimundo. *Un instituto misionero: la Congregación del Santísimo Redentor en el segundo centenario de su fundación, 1732–1932*. Madrid, 1932.

Tello, José Angel. *Ideología y política: la Iglesia católica española, 1936–1959*. Zaragoza, 1984.

Trabajo, Antonio. "El tema religioso en la constitución española de 1978." *XX Siglos*, vol. 6, no. 24 (1995), pp. 88–106.

Turin, Yvonne. *La educación y la escuela en España de 1874 a 1902*. Trans. J. Hernández. Madrid, 1967.

Tusell, Javier. *Historia de la democracia cristiana en España*. 2 vols. Madrid, 1974.

———. "The Functioning of the Cacique System in Andalusia, 1890–1931." In *Politics and Society in Twentieth-Century Spain*, ed. Stanley Payne, pp. 1–28. New York, 1976.

———. *Franco y los católicos: la política interior española entre 1945 y 1957*. Madrid, 1984.

———. *La dictadura de Franco*. Madrid, 1988.

———. "Los gobernantes españoles y el catolicismo." *XX Siglos*, vol. 1, no. 1 (1990), pp. 93–101.

Ullman, Joan Connelly. *The Tragic Week: A Study of Anticlericalism in Spain*. Cambridge, Mass., 1968.

———. "The Warp and Woof of Parliamentary Politics in Spain, 1808–1939: Anticlericalism versus 'Neo-Catholicism.'" *European Studies Review*, vol. 13, no. 2 (1983), pp. 145–76.

Unzueta, Angel María. *Vaticano II e Iglesia local*. Bilbao, 1994.

Urbina, Fernando et al. *Iglesia y sociedad en España, 1939–1975*. Madrid, 1977.

Urigüen, Begoña. *Orígenes y evolución de la derecha española: el neo-catolicismo*. Madrid, 1986.

Valle, Florentino del. *El P. Antonio Vicent, S. J. y la acción social católica española*. Madrid, 1947.

Valls, Rafael. *La derecha regional valenciana: el catolicismo político valenciano, 1930–1936*. Valencia, 1992.

Varela Ortega, José. *Los amigos políticos: elecciones y caciquismo en la Restauración, 1875–1900*. Madrid, 1977.

Vázquez, Jesús María. *Así viven y mueren: problemas religiosos de un sector de Madrid*. Madrid, 1958.

———. *Realidades socio-religiosas de España*. Madrid, 1967.

———. *Los religiosos españoles hoy: estudio sociológico*. Madrid, 1973.

Vázquez, Jesús María, Félix Medín, and Luis Méndez. *La Iglesia española contemporánea*. Madrid, 1973.

Vázquez Prado, Andrés. *El fundador del Opus Dei: Mons. Josémaría Escrivá de Balaguer, 1902–1975*. Madrid, 1983.

Velasco, Juan Martín et al. *La Iglesia en la sociedad española*. Estella, 1990.

Verdera, Francisco. *Conflictos entre la Iglesia y el Estado en España: la revista "Ecclesia" entre 1941 y 1945*. Pamplona, 1995.

Vernoy, Alfredo. *Los bienes de los jesuitas. Disolución e incautación de la Compañía de Jesús durante la Segunda República*. Madrid, 1995.

Vicens Vives, J., et al. *Historia de España y América*. 5 vols. Barcelona, 1961.

Vigil y Vázquez, Manuel. *El drama de la Acción Católica y el "Nacional Catolicismo."* Barcelona, 1990.

Vilar, Sergio. *La naturaleza del franquismo*. Madrid, 1977.

Villota Elejalde, Ignacio. *La Iglesia en la sociedad española y vasca contemporáneas*. Bilbao, 1985.

Vincent, Mary. "The Spanish Church and the Popular Front: The Experience of Salamanca Province." In *The French and Spanish Popular Fronts: Comparative Perspectives*, ed. Martin S. Alexander and Helen Graham, pp. 79–92. Cambridge, 1989.

———. *Catholicism in the Second Spanish Republic: Religion and Politics in Salamanca, 1931–1936*. Oxford, 1996.

Williams, Michael E. *St. Alban's College, Valladolid*. London and New York, 1986.

Winston, Colin M. *Workers and the Right in Spain, 1900–1936*. Princeton, 1985.

Yetano, Ana. *La enseñanza religiosa en la España de la Restauración, 1900–1920*. Barcelona, 1988.

Yllán Calderón, Esperanza. *Cánovas del Castillo: entre la historia y la política*. Madrid, 1985.

Ynfante, Jesús. *La prodigiosa aventura del Opus Dei: génesis y desarrollo de la Santa Mafia*. Paris, 1970.

Zuñeda, Emilio. "1993: año santo, año de crisis, año de diálogo." *XX Siglos*, vol. 5, no. 18 (1994), pp. 3–15.

INDEX

The Catholic Church in Spain, 1875–1998 was composed in Berkeley
by Graphic Composition, Athens, Georgia; and designed by
Kachergis Book Design, Pittsboro, North Carolina.

CPSIA information can be obtained at www.ICGtesting.com
Printed in the USA
BVOW01s2052210414

350907BV00004BA/11/P

9 780813 219813